Introduction to Python Network Automation

The First Journey

Brendan Choi

Apress®

Introduction to Python Network Automation: The First Journey

Brendan Choi
Sydney, NSW, Australia

ISBN-13 (pbk): 978-1-4842-6805-6 ISBN-13 (electronic): 978-1-4842-6806-3
https://doi.org/10.1007/978-1-4842-6806-3

Managing Director, Apress Media LLC: Welmoed Spahr
Acquisitions Editor: Celestin Suresh John
Development Editor: James Markham
Coordinating Editor: Aditee Mirashi

Cover designed by eStudioCalamar

Cover image designed by Freepik (www.freepik.com)

Distributed to the book trade worldwide by Springer Science+Business Media New York, 1 New York Plaza, Suite 4600, New York, NY 10004-1562, USA. Phone 1-800-SPRINGER, fax (201) 348-4505, email orders-ny@springer-sbm.com, or visit www.springeronline.com. Apress Media, LLC is a California LLC, and the sole member (owner) is Springer Science + Business Media Finance Inc (SSBM Finance Inc). SSBM Finance Inc is a **Delaware** corporation.

For information on translations, please e-mail booktranslations@springernature.com; for reprint, paperback, or audio rights, please e-mail bookpermissions@springernature.com.

Apress titles may be purchased in bulk for academic, corporate, or promotional use. eBook versions and licenses are also available for most titles. For more information, reference our Print and eBook Bulk Sales web page at www.apress.com/bulk-sales.

Any source code or other supplementary material referenced by the author in this book is available to readers on GitHub via the book's product page, located at www.apress.com/978-1-4842-6805-6. For more detailed information, please visit www.apress.com/source-code.

Printed on acid-free paper

For my wife Sue and children, Hugh, Leah, and Caitlin.

Table of Contents

About the Author

Brendan Choi currently works as a senior technical consultant for Australia's leading IT integrator and Internet service provider, Telstra. He is a Certified Cisco Network Engineer and a Certified VMware Data Center Engineer, working on enterprise networking, data center, unified communications, security, and virtualization technologies for more than 17 years and now using Python automation to manage enterprise devices. He began his IT career with Cisco Systems and then moved on to networking and systems integrator roles with several reputable enterprise IT integrators. He previously worked for Dimension Data for seven years as a senior network engineer focusing on trending technologies to streamline processes, increase work efficiency, and develop technical training to improve team productivity through various open source software. He started exploring Python and network automation about seven years ago but got serious about its potential in the last five years. He prepared *Python 3 Network Automation Lab Guide for Network & System Engineers* for his colleagues and trained more than 100 network and systems engineers in his last company. Based on blog content and the lab guide, he authored and published *Python Network Automation: By Building an Integrated Virtual Lab* in Korean. He is interested in all aspects of IT technologies but most interested in enterprise networking, security, and virtualization technologies. He writes to share his love for general IT. His learning experience is shared through his blog (`https://italchemy.wordpress.com/`) and YouTube channel (Python Automation).

About the Technical Reviewer

Giuseppe Citerna, CCIE No. 10503, was the first CCIE Academy Instructor in Europe, the Middle East, and Africa. Passionate about technologies and learning systems, he is obsessed with the constant research of systems to allow everyone to leverage the Internet as a tool for both human and professional growth. He is currently working as a learning director at IeXa Academy (`www.iexa.it`), a startup founded with his longtime friend and partner Aldo Menichelli. It is active in the education technology field, and it is radically changing the vocational training system. He is also working as a learning and development consultant for Dimira, a Cisco Gold Partner system integrator. He started his career at Telecom Italia's TAC in 1999. Then he moved to NextiraOne, where he worked on enterprise networking, data center virtualization, unified communications, and knowledge management projects. Alongside his technical career, in 1999 he started working in education at the ELIS Center in Rome at the Italian Cisco Academy Training Center. Throughout his 20-year career, he has trained thousands of network engineers at several major companies. His core areas of interest are data center virtualization, network automation and programmability, and anything related to technologies applied to learning.

Acknowledgments

This book's content is based on various resources, including my study notes, work instructions, cheat sheets, content shared on personal blogs, and training guides used for internal network automation training (2018). The original version was published in Korean on July 25, 2019, but more than half of the content had to be rewritten to make this book suitable for its new audience. So, technically, this is my second published book, and I have spent many hours locked up in my study authoring this book.

I am very thankful to both my English publisher (Apress) and my Korean publisher (Acorn) for allowing me to write and publish the Python network automation learning techniques I have compiled over the years from the enterprise networking field. I am also grateful to my family, who stood by me while completing this book. My wife Sue is the biggest supporter of my work, and publication of my work has been only possible with her support. I had dreamed of writing a book and dedicating it to our three lovely children, Hugh, Leah, and Caitlin, so they can grow into strong and healthy adolescents who will live up to their dreams and also learn to share any valuable knowledge or unique experiences with others around them. Hugh, you will be a kind young man playing piano; Leah, you will continue to set the standard for everyone and strive for excellence; and Caitlin, one day, you will learn coding to become an outstanding data scientist/white hacker to help others.

I also would like to give special thanks to Giuseppe Citerna for his excellent technical review; this book has been made twice as good for our readers because of his experience. I also thank all the Apress staff who helped me to polish this book. Finally, I sincerely thank all the readers who have purchased this book to begin their Python network automation journey.

Brendan Choi (2021)

Introduction

A decade ago, network engineer roles consisted of installing, configuring, maintaining, and troubleshooting LANs, WANs, and any other IP connectivity technologies. Practical working knowledge of networking concepts and strong networking protocol knowledge were must-have skills for network engineers. Some of these protocols included OSPF, EIGRP, BGP, MPLS, VRF, IPsec, QoS, DNS, VTP, VPN, Broadcast, Multicast, and GRE. Even then, the job requirements for a network engineer demanded real-world experience; broad application of the advanced principles, theories, concepts, and techniques of networking; and the ability to troubleshoot, report, and resolve a networking problem.

Roughly five years ago, network engineers were forced to take on more administrative responsibilities based on ITIL's IT Service Management and ISO 9001's designated quality management standards. Middle management found a way to push down their administration work onto their subordinates. During this period, new buzzwords were invented by some tech geniuses and sold to the enterprise network market as the silver bullet to solve all of the IT industry's problems; these hot keywords were *software-defined network* and *network automation*. The introduction of these words hinted that the enterprise networking market was about to rapidly change. In fact, the industry started to demand more hybrid engineers with network programming skills on top of their existing responsibilities. In short, the market wanted more network engineers who could think and code like real application developers using one or more programming languages and open source programs. In line with the current market trend, Python has become one of the most popular programming languages among network engineers for networking task automation because of its ease of use and shorter development cycle. Python is not the only programming language used in network automation; other programming or scripting languages currently used include Shell, Bash, Perl, Java, API, Ansible, JSON, SOAP, Ruby, and REST.

Interestingly, a few years ago, not many organizations or engineers thought network engineers needed to know how to write code and develop automation scripts or applications. At that time, the network engineer role was clearly defined, with different groups of engineers divided based on the technology domain groups. Back then, the term *network automation* only meant creating ad hoc and simple Tcl scripts based on the Cisco IOS built-in feature. Network engineers, especially those who studied and worked mainly on Cisco technologies, were hesitant to dive into any programming language to make their work more efficient. Although network automation skills could become a real weapon for many network engineers, it would be a bumpy road to network programmability.

Traditional network engineers only had to deal with OSI layer problems between layers 1 through 4; they were happy in their bubble, and there was no hurry for any innovation. They had an excellent working knowledge of networking concepts and protocols that kept them on the job for many years with decent salaries. But the concept of a software-defined network had been taking the enterprise networking industry by storm. Cisco was the world leader and a household name for enterprise networking in routing and switching, security, voice services, and, more recently, server equipment–related data center solutions. Cisco had been the trusted vendor and partner to larger enterprise customers as well as to smaller, SMB customers all around the world. Remarkably, it had been a "one-stop shop" enterprise IT solutions vendor for more than 40 years. This meant you bought complete IT solutions from a single IT vendor, and Cisco's famous SmartNet Support, the best post-sales technical assistant center (TAC) support at any time of the day around the world, was available to all paid customers. Think of Cisco Systems as the world's largest supermarket for enterprise equipment and solutions. Unfortunately, ever since Cisco's lawsuit against a Chinese networking equipment manufacturing vendor, Huawei in 2003, Cisco has not been the same. Its technologies and intellectual properties were stolen, copied, and used by the Chinese vendor, undercutting Cisco's business model and eating up Cisco's market shares.

A few years ago, to have a successful career as a network engineer, you only had to focus on learning Cisco-specific technologies to keep your job. Many enterprise networks were predominantly designed and deployed with IP devices manufactured and supported by Cisco until ten years ago. It probably was the Golden Age of Cisco, where Cisco led the enterprise networking and infrastructure solutions market based on its robust hardware-based solutions. Even today, when many IT companies hire a new network engineer, the first qualification they look at is what level of Cisco certification the candidate holds. During the initial job application process, having a current Cisco certification or not could be a single deciding factor to make it through the next round of the job interview process. Of course, practical experience is more important than the actual certification. Still, specific Cisco certifications have been an important measure of networking and technical proficiency.

No doubt, Cisco Systems has been the dominant vendor in the enterprise networking equipment and solutions market since the early 1990s and still is in the current market. Still, with the introduction of disruptive virtualization and software-defined networking (SDN) concepts and the recent onset of open source tools, network automation technologies have been threatening to disrupt Cisco's existing business models. The concept of automation has been around for many years; its roots can be found in the modern industrialization of the 1900s, and about 20 years ago, the automation phenomena swiped out many industries relying on electronic terminals (older computer types with specific functions). So, why has automation become the hot topic in today's IT industry in general, which includes networking, security, data center, unified communications, storage, systems, and the cloud?

When you examine the main driver for the latest automation craze in enterprise networking, you will see there has been a rapid development in high-performance computing based on faster and more efficient hardware. The hardware components have shrunk in size, providing smaller but more powerful hardware platforms for software to run in an optimized environment. The existing hardware-centric infrastructure architecture that required tens to hundreds of servers can now run on a handful of powerful yet energy-efficient servers running on a virtualized environment. What used to run on hardware-based servers became virtual machines, happily running on bare-metal hypervisors. Software-centric solutions based on high-performance hardware, faster intranet speed, and faster LAN and SAN network connectivity are now dominating our IT industry. The realization of the software-based solution over the traditional hardware-based solutions empowers organizations to be more flexible and economical, using more robust and reliable IT services throughout the whole life of the infrastructure devices and applications. For example, one of the most popular virtualization technology examples is cloud computing. There is very little client-owned, on-premise hardware in such an environment, and many of the IT services are on-demand services. Today these new technologies are already replacing more traditional IT infrastructures.

Engineers with passive learning strategies under the current enterprise networking market trend will have only a grim future waiting ahead. As history repeats itself, the market will leave those engineers behind and move on quickly. In the last decade, virtualization solutions have become the new norm of server and storage platforms. Now, even the networking devices are gradually moving away from hardware-based platforms and moving into the virtual environment, where everything can be controlled by application programming interfaces (APIs). Two such solutions making their mark are VMware's NSX and Cisco's ACI. Virtualized networking devices are just a handful of files running on hypervisors, making the administration of control, data, and management planes extremely easy with software. Soon, more and more engineers' work will be replaced by automated applications that talk to each other through APIs and programming languages such as Python and Go. Also, the fine lines between specific technologists based on different technology domains are getting blurred. Simultaneously, what traditional IT engineers have been doing will be replaced slowly with lines of code or intelligent applications.

As seen in many industries, there is no doubt that software and automation technologies will be taking over our lives. The enterprise network automation is part of this unstoppable movement. Software removes the traditional barriers that stood between systems, software, and network engineers, and all engineers are now encouraged to learn and write code. As a network engineer, once you learn to code and apply your new skills in your own company's network, there is a good chance that you will remain well-footed in the industry. This is my argument for why all network engineers must learn to code in a programming language. You must keep learning and apply your newly acquired coding skills to your work to take advantage of software-defined networks.

Target Audience

Before writing any documentation, you have to think about the context and consider who your target audience is. The same goes when writing a book of this magnitude. As the book's title suggests, this book is about introducing Python network automation and is written for people with little or no Python network automation experience. In other words, this book is not just about Python, nor an introduction to networking basics; it is a guide to help networking students and engineers pick up Python to start on their network automation journey.

Topics Covered

This book covers a wide range of IT topics to expose you to a selection of technologies in three different IT domains: networking, systems, and programming. This book focuses on IT technologies that will provide a strong foundation to extend your knowledge to the next level. Readers are recommended to read each chapter sequentially, from Chapter 1 to Chapter 19. Even if you are a seasoned network professional, you are recommended to read each chapter in sequence to get the most out of this book. Your success in reaching and completing the last lab in this book depends on building your lab environment in the first half of the book.

On the first page of each chapter, this book provides recommended difficulty scales based on the intricacies of tasks involved in each chapter; this is to set the right mindset and expectation of the readers. You start with a casual reading in Chapter 1, and as you progress through the book, each chapter's difficulty increases compared to the previous chapter. Each chapter was designed to equip you with different IT skills and by the time you reach the end of this book, you will reach at least an intermediate IT and Python skill level where you can build a fully functional proof-of-concept networking lab and start writing Python code for Network Automation. The difficulty levels are only there as a guideline, and the actual difficulty of tasks in each chapter will be dependent on your own experience and prior knowledge of the covered contents.

Figure I-1 shows the difficulty levels of each chapter, and Figure I-2 displays the topics covered in each chapter.

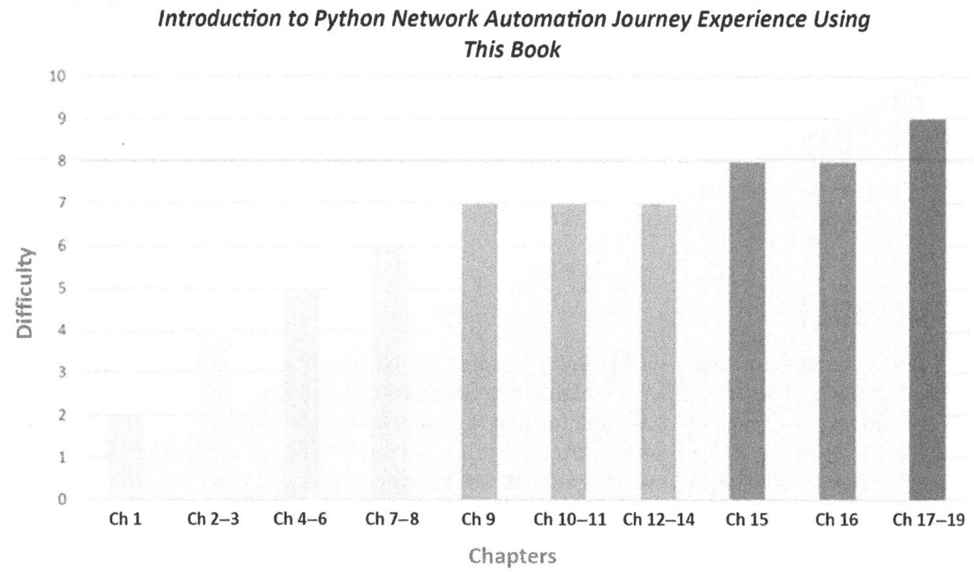

Figure I-1. Chapter difficulty increments

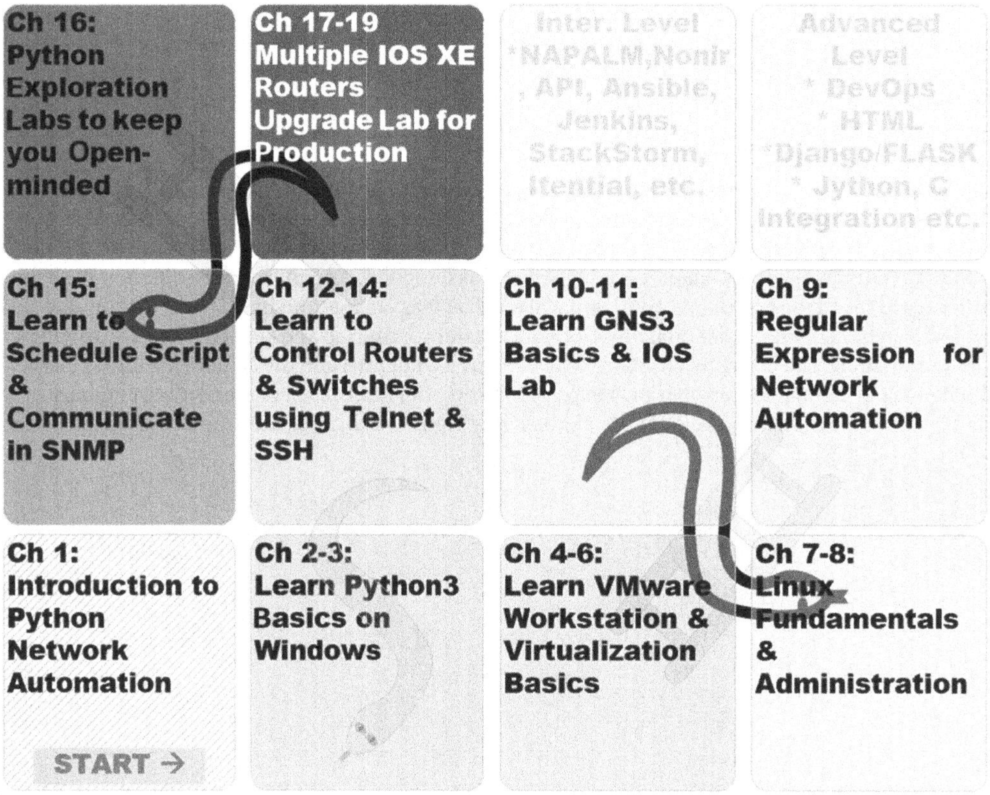

Figure I-2. Chapter topics covered in this book

Chapter 1: Introduction to Python Network Automation

The first chapter talks about why you want to study Python as the de facto network automation programming language for your work. It discusses the available skill sets of three IT domain groups: systems, DevOps, and network. You will study a network engineering group's weaknesses in network programmability and strategize how to embark on network automation studies using Python. Also, the chapter outlines the system and software requirements for a successful journey using this book.

Chapters 2–3: Learn and Practice Python Basics on Windows

You have to master Python basics to write working network automation code in Python. In Chapters 2 and 3, you are taken through a series of basic Python syntax and concepts on Windows 10. As the most commonly used end-user operating system is Windows, the entry to Python becomes easier while learning Python on Windows. These two chapters contain hands-on Python exercises connecting some Python concepts to networking concepts.

Chapters 4–6: Learn VMware Workstation Basics and Build Virtual Machines

VMware's desktop virtualization will be the gel holding together all our development integration. The chosen desktop virtualization software for this book is VMware Workstation 15 Pro, and you will be provided with a step-by-step user guide on how to use VMware Workstation 15 Pro on Windows 10. You will download Linux bootable and GNS3 VM ova images to start building virtual machines as part of initial lab preparation. You will get familiar with all the VMware Workstation basics and some virtualization basics while installing and creating virtual machines.

Chapters 7–8: Linux Fundamentals

Linux administration knowledge is a key to your Python network automation success as around 30 percent of enterprise systems are based on Linux operating systems (OSs). Using the two Linux virtual machines from Chapters 5 and 6, you will briefly learn the fundamentals of Linux. You will use Ubuntu 20 LTS (Debian derivative) and CentOS 8.1 (Red Hat derivative) servers to get exposure to two different Linux distros. In Chapter 7, you will learn to manage files and directories and use vi and nano text editors. In Chapter 8, you will learn the basic Linux system administration, Linux kernel validation, and networking commands to build TFTP, FTP, SFTP, and NTP servers.

Chapter 9: Regular Expression for Network Automation

If you want to write an intermediate to advanced Python script, you are going to need a tool called a *regular expression*, aka the `re` module in Python. In this chapter, you will experience the wonderful world of regular expressions. The chapter teaches you how to use various regular expressions and use Python's `re` module in certain networking-related scenarios. To move up to the intermediate level, you have to know how to handle or massage various data using regular expressions. This topic will make you so much stronger in your programming skills.

Chapters 10–11: GNS3 Basics and Cisco IOS Lab

GNS3 VM is a Linux (Ubuntu) virtual server hosting all our networking devices such as routers, switches, and firewalls. You will learn to install GNS3 on your Windows Host PC and then integrate the GNS3 VM to run on VMware Workstation as a VM. In Chapter 11, you will learn how to install an old Cisco IOS router image and then learn and master how to drive basic networking lab on GNS3 with ease. You will learn the GNS3 tips and tricks learned over the years working on the GNS3 lab building. At the end of these chapters, you will build various networking labs with flexibility and speed.

Chapters 12–14: GNS3 Cisco CML-PE integration and CML-PE labs

GNS3 is compatible with the later Cisco Modeling Lab (CML) layer 2 and layer 3 images; here, you will learn to integrate CML switch (L2) and router (L3) images with GNS3. For your network automation labs, you need both later model switches and routers; CML image integration with GNS3 replaces the hardware-based switches and routers and allows us to configure many routers and switches as virtual networking devices on GNS3. You will learn to build a test network topology and learn the basics to control routers and switches using Python's Telnet and SSH (paramiko) libraries. Your commands will be written into Python networking codes, and you will see the configuration changes on your routers and switches right in front of your eyes.

Chapter 15: Python Network Automation Exploration Labs: Cron and SNMPv3

Full automation does not involve human interaction; if you want to run your script at 2 a.m. while you are asleep, then cron is the right tool for this job. In this chapter, you will learn how to use Linux's task scheduler, cron. You will learn to use this tool on both Ubuntu and CentOS. You will trigger scripts to run at a specified time using the cron scheduler. You will also be introduced to Python and SNMPv3 to get you started with Python's SNMP network monitoring. You will get exposure to a set of tools that are very different, but you will be better equipped with two more tools under your belt.

Chapter 16: Python Network Automation Development Labs

This chapter will help you to think outside of the box for Python network automation use cases. You will learn how to use virtualenv in Python to avoid library incompatibilities and save time for new library testing. You will then get exposure to Docker images by downloading a Python network automation Docker image and running the Docker container using a tiny portion of the Linux host's resources. Using Docker, you will learn how to send an email notification to your email using Sendmail. You will also write a CPU utilization monitoring application and integrate a simple Twilio API script to send SMS to your mobile device when your testing router experiences high CPU utilization.

Chapter 17-19: Practical Python Network Automation Lab: IOS XE Upgrade Lab

You are now moving up to the next level! These final chapters are the highlight of this book. First, you will learn object-oriented programming (OOP) in Python in the context of networking devices. Then the chapter will briefly discuss the application flow control, followed by ten mini tools development for a Cisco CRS 1000v IOS XE router upgrade. By putting together smaller tools, you will build a fully functional and interactive IOS XE upgrade application to upgrade one or more Cisco Cloud Service Routers. Imagine upgrading 20 or 200 networking devices in one change window using Python's loop statements. You will begin to realize the real power of Python in enterprise network automation.

Configuring the Lab Environment

A significant part of software installations and lab building will be outlined in this book. Some chapters will require you to download essential software installation guides and complete a supplementary software installation before beginning the chapters. You can download the supplementary pre-installation guides from my GitHub page. There you will also find all the source code used in this book.

- *GitHub*: `https://github.com/pynetauto/apress_pynetauto`

CHAPTER 1

Introduction to Python Network Automation

This chapter serves as a primer to this book and discusses what it feels like to be an IT professional in today's IT industry. We will also discuss the different enterprise IT engineering domain groups and their responsibilities. The chapter then compares each domain group's weaknesses and strengths and draws up a working study plan that serves as the book's foundation. This chapter will also discuss why you might want to learn a programming language, in our case, Python, since this is your primary reason for purchasing this book and get started on your network automation journey. Finally, we will discuss the minimum PC/laptop requirements to build a fully working Python/Linux/network automation lab on a single PC. All lab machines, Linux servers, routers, and switches will be installed on a single PC/laptop using a recommended software set.

**Suggested difficulty level only.*
**This level may vary based on the reader's experience.*

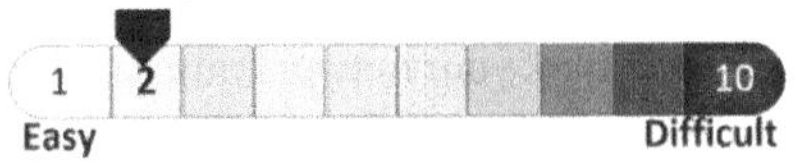

Laying the Foundation

In recent years, network programmability concepts have been taking the enterprise networking industry by storm, and network automation has been at the eye of the storm for a few years. Enterprise businesses and organizations that are spending millions of dollars on traditional IT lifecycle management based on traditional IT frameworks have been searching for a new IT framework that will provide more stable and predictable network operations without interruption to their IP service and end-user applications. Quite a few network engineers have already started exploring network automation, and the remaining engineers are still trying to make a start. Still, many are encountering various challenges. Looking back on my own networking automation journey, I know it can be a slow, painful, and daunting experience.

Whether you have never touched a programming language in your career or are new to software-defined networks, starting on the network automation journey feels like you are trying to climb up a big mountain. Once you reach the first peak, you may realize that even bigger mountains await. You may even want to give up.

You probably have been living a comfortable life as a network engineer for the past few decades. Now your bosses expect you to upskill your nonexistent programming skills so you can replace manual tasks with lines of code so that you can add more value to your company. If you say no, your bosses have a Plan B: somebody else will write the code for your team to automate your work, and you will start losing credibility (and maybe even your job). You need to step outside of your comfort zone to start on our network programmability journey. Network programmability still is uncharted ground for most traditional network engineers.

B. Choi, *Introduction to Python Network Automation*, https://doi.org/10.1007/978-1-4842-6806-3_1

In this chapter, we will identify three main IT domain groups in a typical IT environment today. Then, we will define the common IT skill sets that each IT domain group possesses to determine each group's relational strengths and weaknesses. This book was written by a network engineer for network engineers and reviewed by a Cisco Network Academy instructor. The strengths and weakness discussions will be from an enterprise network industry perspective. The point is to learn how the Network group can use realistic learning strategies to get closer to the other two groups (DevOps and systems groups) and grow into cross-functional engineers who have strong networking skills as well as the skill sets to manage Linux operating systems and write code to develop business applications. This chapter also introduces a cross-functional "hybrid engineer" concept, which will soon be in enormous demand in the IT job market. The career knowledge growth for such hybrid engineers will take the shape of a *T*, as they have a firm foothold in their main IT domain and extend out to other domain skill sets as the top of the letter *T*.

In almost every chapter of this book, except this one, you will install, configure, practice, code, and learn from your PC or laptop, so your system's minimum requirements are the success of your Python network automation study with this book. Hence, we will review the minimum system requirements for your system and introduce you to the software used to gauge the size of crucial tasks outlined in this book. We will also briefly touch on an integrated development environment (IDE) for Python network automation development and provide all the download links for the software, source code, and files used in this book. At the end of this chapter, you will better understand a current network engineer's strengths and weaknesses. Hence, you will know the gaps (target study areas) you have to focus on to start writing Python code to develop your own network automation applications.

Exploring Your Skills and Prerequisites

The section discusses the three main IT domain groups' skill sets at work today. You will learn each group's strengths and weaknesses. From the network group's perspective, we will discuss and dissect the weaknesses in your skill set and develop workable study strategies to work on the weaknesses and turn them into your strengths. Studying Python syntax and concepts will help you reach 25 percent of your network automation goals. What about the other 75 percent? To write Python network automation code, you have to become strong in many other areas besides networking, and this chapter will help you become better in these areas. Of course, we will also cover Python basics from a networking perspective. Together, we will work on a study plan to address the common network engineer's weaknesses and guide you in the right direction for network automation using Python.

If you are currently working in the IT industry, especially on enterprise-level routing, switching, and security technologies, you should take pride in your job. You probably can relate to the image presented in Figure 1-1. Although the image might make you laugh, you have probably seen an IT engineer who walks and talks like he knows it all. We have all been in that situation where our clients expect us to know everything as the technical expert.

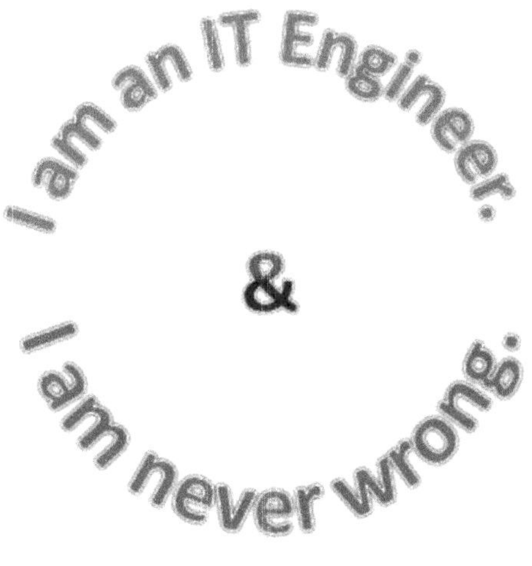

Figure 1-1. *IT engineers*

Sadly, the image in Figure 1-1 holds some truth to how some IT engineers think and behave at work. Since the first personal computer was invented in 1971, many IT jobs have come and gone as different technologies have emerged and disappeared. Most enterprise IT ecosystems continuously evolve as new technologies are introduced into the IT market. Unfortunately, some IT engineers are too stubborn to move with the times and often get caught out during technology transitional periods, which results in early termination from their IT careers. Currently, the age of artificial intelligence (AI) and IT automation has arrived in the enterprise network IT industry. If you refuse to skill up, your position might not be as secure as you think.

In fact, for many years, the IT industry has been trying to drive the operational costs down by offloading less-skilled jobs to developing countries where the IT operational cost is relatively cheaper than on the home turf. For many years, driving the operational costs down and reducing the overheads spent on human resources were trends for many organizations. We live in an era where human resources are an overhead cost in a business model, and many clients these days want to pay less but still demand quality IT delivery services. Contrary to many organizations' claims, many local IT jobs are considered overhead rather than valuable human resources for an organization in advanced countries. That is, many IT organizations claim they value their staff, and their priority is the well-being of these human resources in the organization's IT operation. Still, when the crunch time comes, almost every organization succumbs to the financial pressure and cuts IT operational costs to maximize the organization's profit. In the last 20 years, IT outsourcing and offshoring efforts have had great success to some extent. Still, each IT department is driven harder than before to drive the operational cost down, which has been the catalyst in speeding up the adoption of IT automations such as software-defined networks and infrastructure as code.

General Competencies of Three Main IT Domain Group

Bangalore, India, is commonly known as the Silicon Valley of India, and there is a common saying there: "There are two types of people in IT profession; one, IT professionals, and two, professionals who manage these people." In this book, to help your understanding, we are dividing IT domain groups into three different groups based on each group's competencies and characteristics. Then we'll compare their general technical competencies to each other to forecast what the near-future IT industry may look like for one particular group of engineers, that is, the network engineering (connectivity) group. Who will be at the forefront of the networking field in the next five years and beyond? Let's review the gaps and requirements to look ahead and develop a plan to study Python, network automation, and any other requirements to build your confidence to skill up in IT.

At the enterprise level, many organizations have three main domain groups that look after IT infrastructure.

- *Network*: The network group, sometimes known as connectivity group, looks after all infrastructures and end-user connectivity.
- *Systems*: The systems group looks after servers and applications to provide service to other infrastructure or end users as service; these will include corporate emails, shared storage, and various business applications critical to the success of the company.
- *DevOps*: Last is the group of software engineers or programmers who test, develop, and implement various business applications to cater for a company's business requirement. Recently these group of engineers have become known as DevOps engineers.

We will refer to these three main domain groups as *network group, systems group*, and *DevOps groups* for the simplicity of this book. The network group works on IP connectivity and services, including technology subdomains such as RS, security, data center, cloud, and unified collaboration engineers. A network connection is the foundation of any enterprise business connectivity, and we consider both applications and services as the tenants of connected networks. Hence, the entire business comes to a halt if there is a major network outage on the corporate network.

The systems group is responsible for critical business applications and operating systems running on both Windows and Linux OS.

The DevOps group comprises software developers and programmers who specialize in developing software and applications using various programming languages and software development tools. By comparing and analyzing each group's current capabilities, we will better understand each group's strengths and weaknesses. Hence, we identify several weaknesses in the network group so that you can work on these weaknesses. Although the networking vendor technology used in this book is from Cisco, note that the network automation concepts shown in this book will apply to any vendor networking and security technologies including Cisco, Arista, Juniper, Check Point, Palo Alto, and HP.

First, let's compare what technical capability differences exist among these three domain groups. To analyze each group's competencies, we will use a spiderweb graph to plot and illustrate different technical capabilities. After this simple comparison, we will recommend on ways to embark upon network automation using Python as the preferred programming language.

To easily compare and help your understanding of the three IT domain groups' capabilities, let's first plot each group's competencies on a graph, as shown in Figure 1-2. The graph uses ten scores for all competencies plotted on the graph. For example, a competent level in an area would be eight out of ten, and a less capable person would get a score of two out of ten.

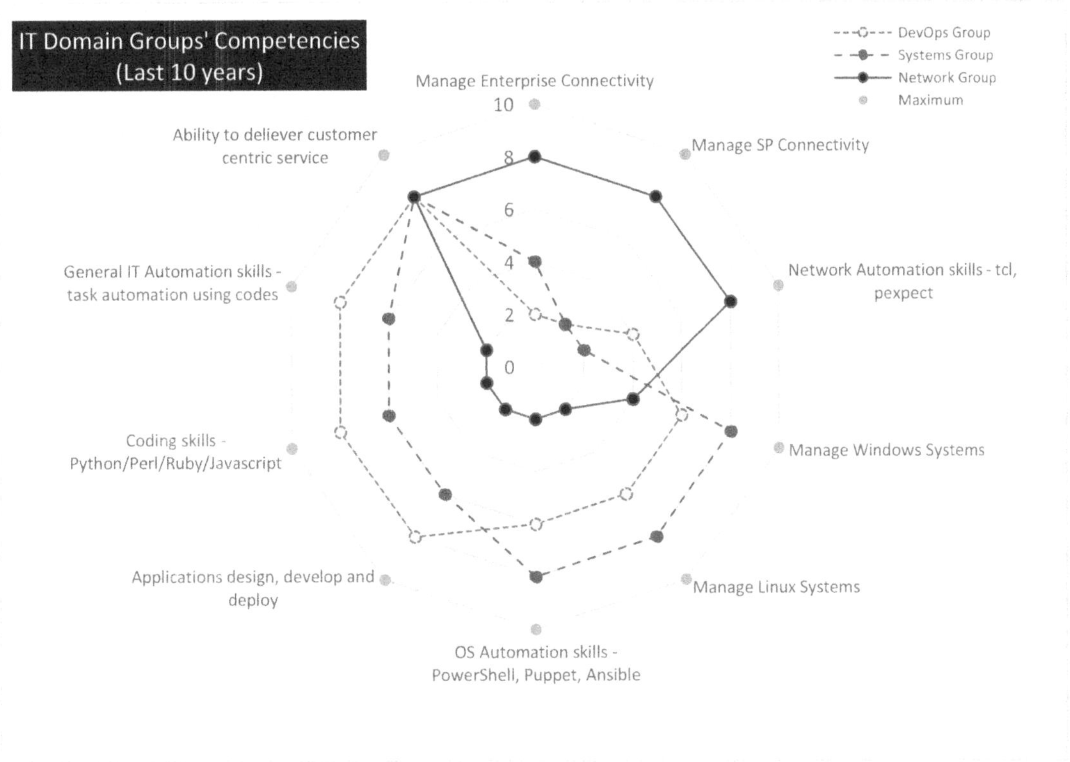

Figure 1-2. *IT domain groups' general competencies comparison*

The graph represents the common competencies required by each engineering group in the past ten years. Plotting the common competencies on such a graph already gives us an eagle-eye view of where each group's strengths and weaknesses exist. Traditionally, network engineers did not have a strict requirement to learn software engineering or write code as the work pace was a lot slower than today's networks need. As discussed, most of the work has been done by conventional network engineers sitting in front of their computer, through command lines. The system group has been exposed more to system automation tools and languages because of the work as they have to perform most tasks in batches (bulk). From a network group's perspective, writing code to automate the enterprise network was a new concept until five years ago. Hence, network engineers had no urgency to expand their skill sets toward the systems or DevOps domain. For someone to automate an enterprise network, one must possess a combination of all three groups. None of the three groups has all the competencies to achieve enterprise network automation from the graph. And it would be safe to guess that you would have minimal exposure to managing enterprise systems or be involved in enterprise tools (application) development projects at work if you are coming from a conventional network engineering background. In recent times, everyone is expected to deliver more bang for the customer's buck and with a good customer (end-user) experience.

This same mentality has caught up to the work of network group. Still, you cannot throw in more bodies to deliver the service levels as in the offshoring method or cut corners to make up the numbers, as many sales operations promise more but deliver the bare minimum. Also, as the graph suggests, most companies now realize that there is no single group with all the competencies to deliver an enterprise network automation solution for the company. The company does not want to pay for the overhead of running all three IT domain groups; hence, the current focus is to upskill the existing employees to achieve IT automation for the company. IT business insiders have been saying, "The walls of different IT domains are crumbling." Now, network engineers must know how to administer a Linux operating system, have the skills to manage a programming language, and must know how to develop a specific application to automate the enterprise network they manage. On the flip side, any engineers from the systems or DevOps groups can learn networking technologies and automate the network group's work.

Of course, the graph contains the generalized capabilities of each IT domain group, and the competencies of each engineer in each group will vary from one person to the next. Still, this graph provides us with accurate pointers on where and how a network group approach should approach Python network automation studies.

Comparative Analysis of IT Engineers' Responsibilities

In Figure 1-2, you saw the competencies of the three IT domain groups. In this section, we will look at the typical responsibilities of engineers from each group to pinpoint the areas a network engineer has to improve to embark on enterprise network automation using Python. Spend about five minutes studying the responsibilities of each group, and you can easily see where a conventional network engineer must focus to gain the required skills to write a scripted application to automate their work. As the shaded area shows, the first requirement is mastering operating systems such as Linux and Windows; this is on top of strong networking skills.

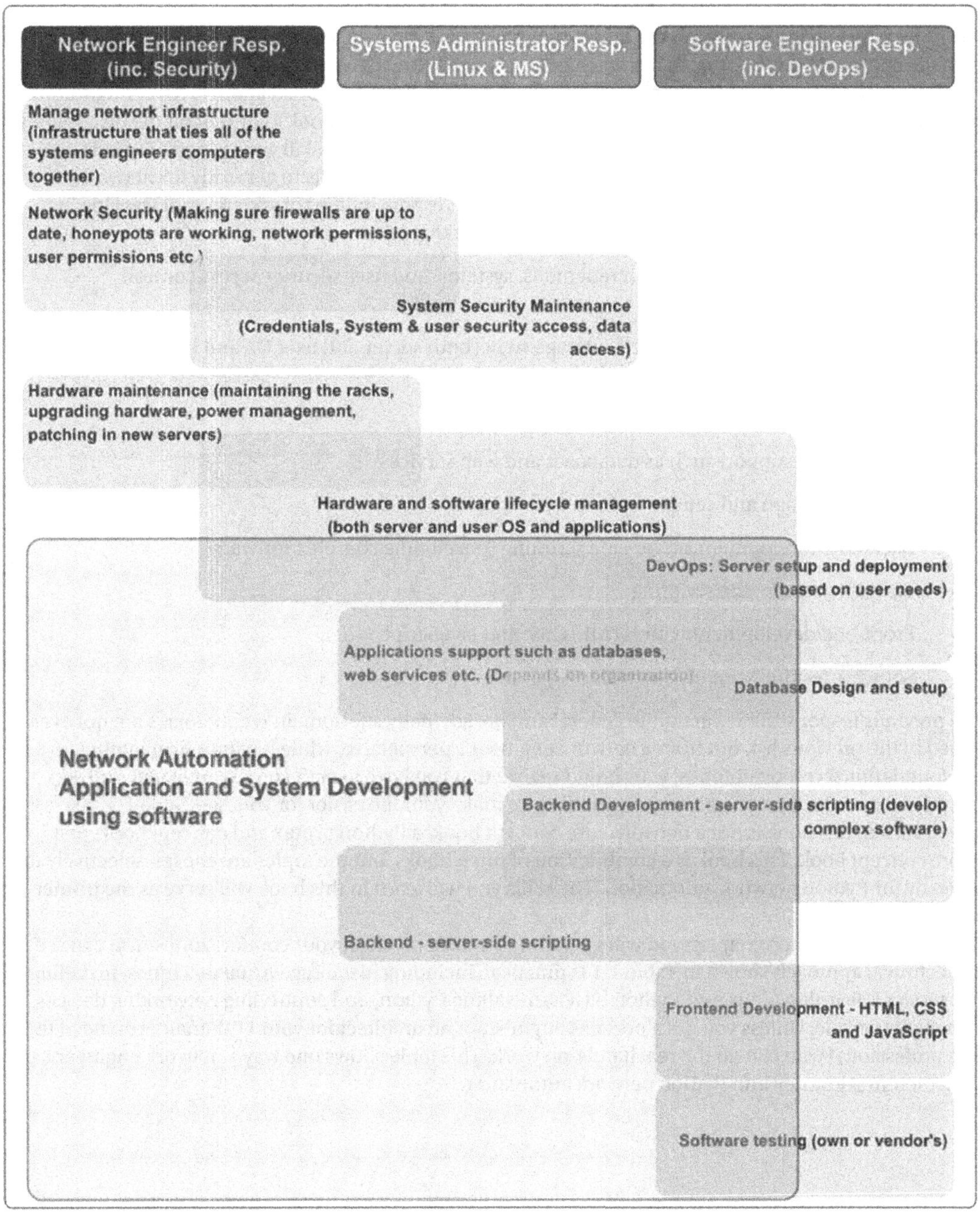

Figure 1-3. *IT engineers' general responsibilities*

For enterprise automation, the default operating system used is Linux. After getting familiar with basic to intermediate Linux administration, you can start with basic Python syntax and slowly discover how DevOps work. At the same time, you need exposure to Linux grep or, even better, general regular expressions, as data processing is the key to any programming language. From this point on, you can gradually expand to other areas of interest.

As mentioned, you are expected to have a working knowledge of Cisco CCNA to get the most out of this book, so if you are studying for or have already completed CCNA, you will get a lot more from this book. Although the content of this book does not teach general networking concepts from Cisco Systems, much of the book is very hands-on, and the labs in later chapters are based on Cisco's IOS and IOS XE configurations. Even if you are not a certified Cisco Certified network engineer, I base this book's content on the discussions in Figures 1-2 and 1-3, so the topics are broad with many helpful parts to upskill your general IT skills.

Based on Figure 1-3, let's draw on the skill sets a network engineer needs to get ready for network automation using Python. The following are derived from the responsibilities of systems and DevOps engineers, but not the core responsibilities of a typical networking job:

- System security maintenance (credentials, systems, and user security access control, data access control)
- Hardware and software lifecycle management (both server and user OS and OS-specific applications)
- DevOps, server setup, and deployment
- Applications support such as databases and web services
- Database design and setup
- Back-end development server-side scripting (developing complex software)
- Back-end server-side scripting
- Front-end development with HTML, CSS, and JavaScript
- Software testing (your own or vendors')

The previous responsibilities are quite general and broad. Many subdomain technologies are not even mentioned in the previous list. But from a network engineer's perspective, while having a firm footing in network foundational responsibilities, you should realize that you have to shift your interest and skill sets toward systems and DevOps groups' responsibilities. To make your life easier for you, see Table 1-1. As mentioned earlier, this book is not a network core concept book, a Python syntax and concept book, or a Linux core concept book. This book is a combination of three books, but the topics are chosen selectively to get you ready for Python network automation. The skills you will learn in this book will serve as the primer for your knowledge.

As you go through each chapter, you will gain new IT skills outside of your comfort zones. You can see that the technical approach shown in Table 1-1 is practical, including installing virtual machines, installing network services, learning Linux and Python basics, installing Python, and controlling networking devices by writing Python code. Unless you are a presales engineer or an architect for your IT domain, you need to be a true professional who can do the real hands-on work. This table shows one way a network engineer can approach their first journey into Python network automation.

Table 1-1. Skill Recommendations for Network Engineers Embarking on Python Network Automation

Required Skills	Recommended Topics to Study
Python basics	Install Python on your computer Learn basic Python syntax Relate and apply basic Python syntax to a Python network context
VMware and virtualization basics	Install the latest VMware Workstation Pro version Learn virtualization basics Learn to build virtual machines
Operating system management, patching, upgrading, troubleshooting, and configuration skills	Install two different flavors of Linux, Ubuntu 20.04 LTS and CentOS 8.1 Use a VMware template to install a prestaged server; import GNS3 VM Server Read the Python installation guide and troubleshoot any installation problems
Learn Linux basics	Understand the Linux directory Understand Linux file management and practices Learn how to use the vi and nano text editors without a GUI desktop app GUI Desktop Linux remote connection concepts, SSH, Telnet, basic APIs Install the FTP, SFTP, TFTP, and NTP servers
Regular expressions	Learn regular expression basics Learn how regular expressions are used in Python Learn to relate and apply regular expressions to networking ideas and concepts
Network emulator (GNS3) skills	Learn to install and integrate GNS3 Learn to configure basic to complex network topology Learn to integrate GNS3 with VMware Workstation
Cisco IOS and IOS XE command lines	Learn to integrate Cisco IOS, IOS-XE, and CML-Personal L2 and L3 images into GNS3 Learn basic router and switch commands for the network automation lab setup Write Python code to control emulated Cisco network devices via SSH, Telnet, FTP, and SNMP Practice Python scripting in a virtual lab Install and set up virtual routers and switches with Python scripts
Application development and establishment	Install Python 3 Install Python Telnet and SSH modules Understand application development for network automation with Python code Understand basic DevOps development concepts
Specific engineer's task automation	Understand the task flow to automate specific tasks

The recommended topics to study from Table 1-1 form the basis for this book. At various points of this book, you will be introduced to different technologies and exercise-based tasks, which require you to follow the book's content in front of your PC (or laptop). To complete this book in full, you must complete all exercises in each chapter to get enough practice and build various skills required for network automation using Python. I want you to learn the basics in one place and learn them well.

Python and Network Automation Studies

Why do you want to study Python for network automation? This question might be tricky to answer. The answer may vary from one person to the next person. Still, perhaps the common goal in studying Python for network automation is to convert physically repetitive tasks into code lines so that you can focus on more valuable and important tasks at work. The process of network automation using Python could be very different from the process of network automation using Ansible or other device management tools. You have the freedom to structure your thought and task processes while trying to automate actual physical tasks and thinking processes targeted for automation. So, what does it mean to streamline the thought process? Perhaps you are talking about performing your work more effectively, systematically, and quickly using Python code.

Are you hinting that what you and your team have been doing all these years has been inefficient, slow, and unstructured? Maybe that is why you are here and reading this book. If so, first review the currently inefficient work your team is performing and break each logical thinking process and physical task performed into steps. It can be extremely handy to determine what you are trying to automate with lines of Python code. This will give you a great foundation to start your first network automation project and approach your current automation challenges.

Rather than embarking on your Python studies, look around and identify the manually intensive tasks at work that you want to automate and then document current processes. Now, you can start learning Python syntax. This simple process will keep your motivation high and also keep you focused on your first Python studies because you are not studying Python for the sake of learning one of the most popular programming languages at the moment. You are learning it for a purpose.

Why Do People Want to Learn Python?

Python is used by leading IT service vendors and enterprises such as Google, YouTube, Instagram, Netflix, Dropbox, and NASA. There are many areas where Python programming can be developed in a short time and applied to solve actual problems. The barrier to learning it is one of the lowest out of all the major programming languages in use today.

According to RedMonk.com , in June 2020, Python is the second most popular programming languages globally, overtaking Java and gaining momentum. There are pros and cons of each programming language, and Python is not immune to various cons, but why is it becoming so popular? In October 2019, Python even overtook JavaScript as the most asked for languages on Stack Overflow.

So, how do you begin? You must master the basic Python syntax and concepts well. There are many books on Python basics and concepts, some of which are outstanding, but I still could not make the connection between Python concepts and network automation concepts when I was learning. Strangely, there were also intermediate to advanced Python networking automation books, but they did not explain where to start and what drills to do to reach the intermediate to advanced level. Everyone tells you that Python is such an easy language to learn and the barrier to entry is low, but they do not tell you that if you want to become great at any programming language, you need to put your head down and be persistent and passionate about the language you have chosen. Be ready to give up your social nights and weekends to learn some silly Python library features and watch hundreds of hours of so-called Python gurus' YouTube videos and online training videos.

That is correct; a low barrier to entry does not mean that Python is the most straightforward language to study. It means that anyone can start learning Python as a programming language, but how many people are persistent and passionate enough to make writing Python code their life? The most challenging part of learning Python often is to be persistently pushing yourself to learn different ways of doing things using Python and keeping your passion alive as long as you can. To do this, you have to find practical use cases and small projects that are personal and that matter to you and your work. Remember that automation is a slow and steady process as everything you want to automate must be written into lines of code. Somebody or something (in the case of AI) has to write the code. There is no AI good enough to imitate an experienced and logical network engineer. Hence, the network engineer has to automate tasks until the artificial intelligence (AI) can imitate and automate the network engineer's actions.

In summary, Figure 1-4 is from a 2019 Stack Overflow survey. Python is the fastest-growing programming language and the most wanted language for the third year in a row, meaning that developers who have not yet used it say they want to learn Python to develop applications.

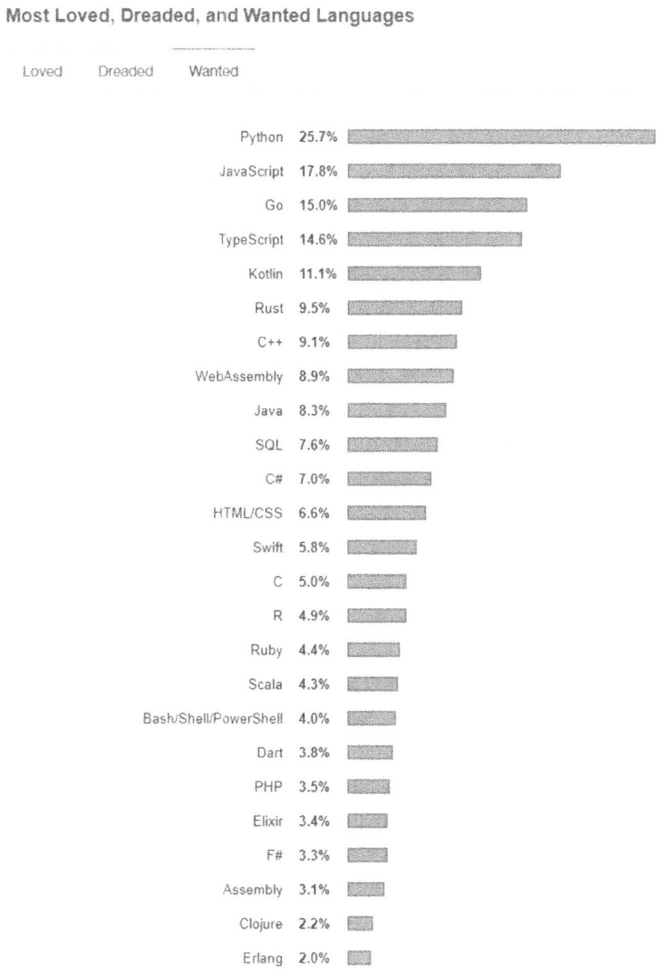

Figure 1-4. *Most wanted programming language for developers in 2019*
Source: `https://insights.stackoverflow.com/survey/2019#most-loved-dreaded-and-wanted`

Figure 1-5 shows the growth of major programming languages in 2017.

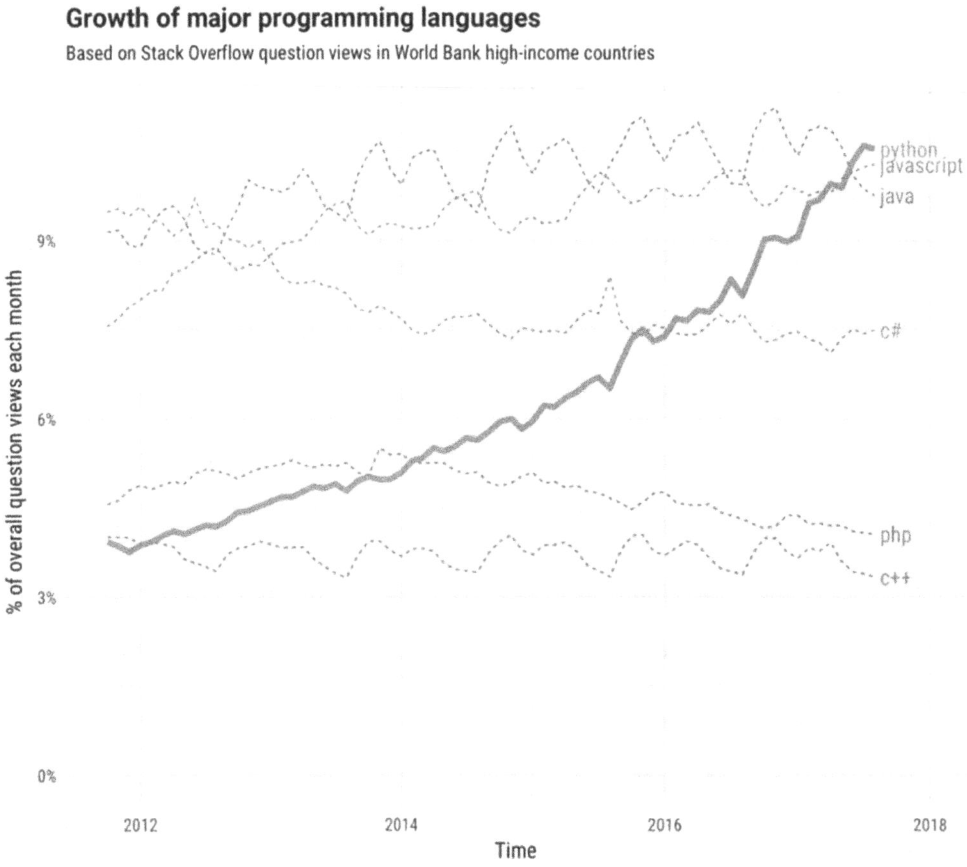

Figure 1-5. *Growth of major programming languages based on Stack Overflow questions, 2017*
Source: `https://stackoverflow.blog/2017/09/06/incredible-growth-python/`

What Do I Need to Study Network Automation Using Python?

Most network engineers who have been studying network automation will agree that having a flexible integrated development environment (IDE) will help engineers develop applications. There are many ways you can study basic Python syntax, but not everyone has the comfort of the company's provided network automation development lab environment, although Cisco dCloud or similar online sandboxes offer timed lab environments. Still, it is not exactly available to you on-demand around the clock. So, I recommend you use your own equipment to control your lab. Such a lab environment can be configured in several forms. First, it can be configured with 100 percent hardware using routers, switches, and servers. Second, it can be part hardware and part virtualized, a hybrid development environment, or third, it can be 100 percent of equipment virtualized and live inside a server or a PC. The first method will require a large initial investment to purchase second-hand equipment and incur ongoing electricity bills to keep the physical devices operational. A hybrid development environment will become cumbersome to have some devices run on physical devices, and some run on a virtualized environment. The last environment would be an ideal lab environment for anyone studying Python for network automation. This has been made possible by integrating several systems and network operating systems running on a virtualization solution. It is almost impossible to practice and experience everything that occurs in the real network environment, but building the integrated development lab will be the closest thing you can get to. If you are learning everything through books or passively learning Python network automation by binge-watching YouTube videos, that is not good enough. Build your IDE and type your code to learn and master Python.

To study Python network automation through this book, all you need is a reasonably powerful desktop or laptop computer that has enough central processing unit (CPU) power and enough random access memory (RAM). Next, let's discuss the minimum hardware specifications to follow this book.

Hardware: Minimum Specifications for Laptop or PC

To install, configure, and practice all the exercises and Python network automation labs in this book, your computer must meet or exceed the minimum specifications listed in Table 1-2. Since most network engineers at work use Windows 10, we will also use this OS as the base operating system for building our IDE lab environment. Unfortunately, if you are using macOS or Linux, then you are on your own with finding the right software and compatibility. If you have a powerful laptop or PC with Windows 10 freshly pre-installed, you are in a perfect place to read this book, but if your system is still running Windows 8.1 or 7, it is highly recommended that you upgrade to the latest Windows 10. If you have a reasonably powerful desktop PC with optimized CPU and system cooling, it will run much better than a laptop. However, if your laptop is the latest and greatest, I would recommend using your laptop for mobility and a lower electricity bill.

Since a large part of this book focuses on installing software, creating a practical lab, and running network automation labs on a single Windows 10 system, make sure your system meets the minimum requirements specified in Table 1-2. Otherwise, you will encounter system performance issues such as slow system response time in your lab.

Table 1-2. *Laptop or PC: Minimum Specifications*

PC Components	Minimum Specification
CPU	Intel: CPU i7 Gen3 (64-bit) or above AMD: Ryzen 3600 or above
RAM	16GB or more for DDR4 (or 24GB for DDR3)
SSD	240GB or more (with 15 percent or free space for system paging)
OS	Microsoft Windows 10 (64-bit) or newer

Figure 1-6 shows the desktop system I have used to write this book.

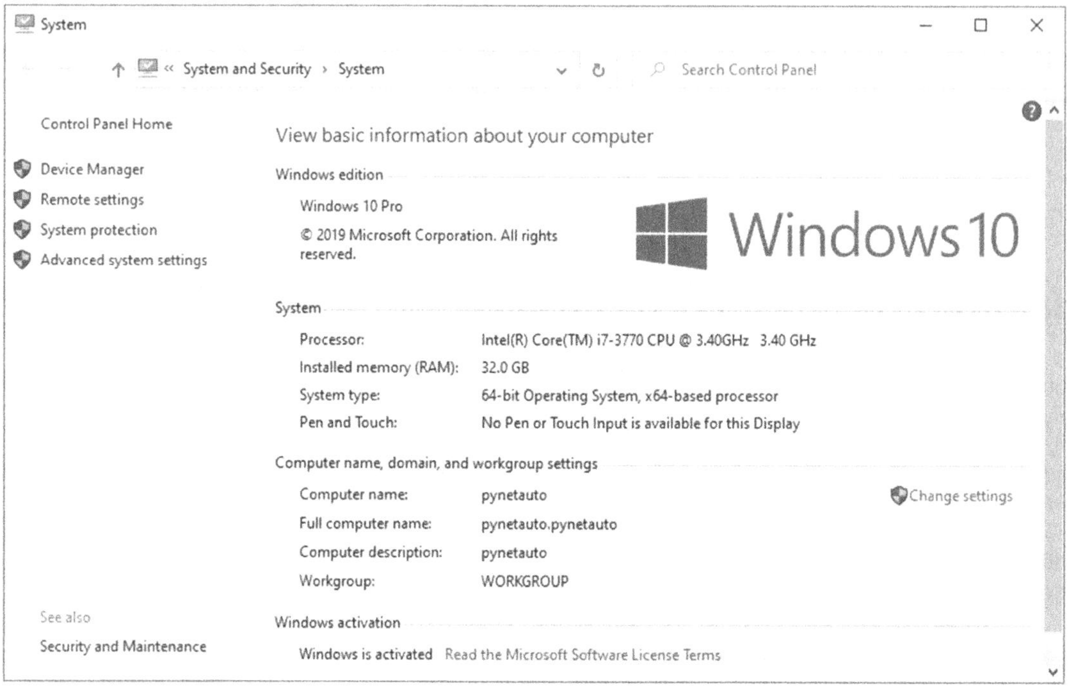

Figure 1-6. *My system specs*

If your CPU is on par or better than Intel i7-3770, as shown in Figure 1-6, and has more than 16GB DDR4 (or 24GB DDR3) RAM, all labs should run smoothly. Also, SSD is recommended over HDD because the mechanical hardware is one component that can become the system bottleneck. This book aims to enable you to create a hands-on lab where you can study Python, virtualization, Linux, networking, and network automation, all from a single PC/laptop. As we will explain later, the labs in this book are useful for Python network automation study and those studying for various certifications such as Cisco CCNA/CCNP/CCIE, Checkpoint, Palo Alto, and Juniper Junos, as GNS3 supports various vendor OSs.

Software Requirements

You will learn how to install and integrate various technologies while building a highly flexible and integrated lab on a single PC/laptop. Table 1-3 contains all the software and provides the download links. You can download all software before beginning Chapter 2 or follow along with the book and download different software as instructed at the beginning of each chapter.

Please note that not all software used here is freeware or open source software, and you may have to use demo software or paid software. For example, VMware's Workstation 15/16 Pro will run in demo mode for the initial 30 days, and then you will have to purchase a valid key. Another example is Cisco Modeling Labs-Personal Edition (CML-PE), which has a subscription of $199 yearly. For our lab, you are only going to require the three files outlined in Table 1-3. All other software used here is either freeware or open source software.

Table 1-3. *Software and Download Links*

Required Software	Usage	Download links

VMware Workstation Pro 15 or 16 (demo/paid)	Desktop Virtualization	`https://my.vmware.com/web/vmware/downloads/info/slug/desktop_end_user_computing/vmware_workstation_pro/15_0`
		or
		`https://my.vmware.com/web/vmware/downloads/info/slug/desktop_end_user_computing/vmware_workstation_pro/16_0`

GNS3-2-2-14-all-in-one or later (for Windows)	Network device emulator	`https://github.com/GNS3/gns3-gui/releases`
		or
		`https://www.gns3.com/software/download`

GNS3.VM.Vmware.Workstation.2.2.14.zip	VMware Workstation GNS3 VM ova image	`https://github.com/GNS3/gns3-gui/releases`
IOSv-L3-15.6(2)T.qcow2 or newer (paid)	Cisco CML L3 image	`https://learningnetworkstore.cisco.com/cisco-modeling-labs-personal/cisco-cml-personal`
IOSv_startup_config.img (paid)	Cisco CML L3 booting image	`https://learningnetworkstore.cisco.com/cisco-modeling-labs-personal/cisco-cml-personal`
IOSvL215.2.4055.qcow2 or newer (paid)	Cisco CML L2 image	`https://learningnetworkstore.cisco.com/cisco-modeling-labs-personal/cisco-cml-personal`
python-3.8.5.amd64.exe or newer (for Windows)	Python 3.8.5 or higher	`https://www.python.org/ftp/python/`
Notepad++ v.7.8.5 (64-bit)	Text editor for Windows	`https://notepad-plus-plus.org/downloads/`

Putty.exe (64-bit) (for Windows)	SSH/Telnet client	`https://www.putty.org/`
		or
		`https://the.earth.li/~sgtatham/putty/0.74/w64/`

Ubuntu-20.04-live-server-amd64.iso (952.1MB)	Ubuntu Server image - Bootable	`https://linuxclub.cs.byu.edu/downloads/isos/ubuntu/`
		or
		`https://www.ubuntu.com/download/server`

CentOS-7-x86_64-DVD-1804.iso (4.16GB)	CentOS Server image, bootable	`https://www.centos.org/download/`
		or
		`http://centos.mirror.omnilance.com/`

c3725-adventerprisek9-mz.124-15.T14.bin or c3745-adventerprisek9-mz.124-15.T14d.bin	Cisco IOS image for GNS3 integration	From old used Cisco devices or Through Google search
Unpack.exe	Cisco image unpacker 0.1 binary for Windows	`http://downloads.sourceforge.net/gns-3/Unpack-0.1_win.zip?download`

(continued)

Table 1-3. (*continued*)

Required Software	Usage	Download links
WinMD5Free	Windows MD5 Checker	`https://www.winmd5.com/`
WinSCP	Secure File Transfer for Windows-Linux	`https://winscp.net/eng/download.php`
FileZilla client (64-bit, for Windows)	Secure File Transfer for Windows-Linux	`https://filezilla-project.org/`

Building a Network Automation Development Environment Using GNS3

A network automation development environment is an IDE lab for network application development. For our convenience in this book, we will call this environment the *lab* or the *network lab* instead of an *integrated development environment* or *network automation development environment*. As discussed earlier, there are different ways to create a learning lab for your Python network automation. About 15 years ago, while networking students studied Cisco routing and switching, many students used a mix of hardware-based labs, a networking OS simulator from Cisco called Packet Tracer, and an open source emulator called Dynamips. This was followed by the introduction of GNS3, which is Dynamips with a GUI interface for ease of use. Dynamips was a good networking device emulator used for study, but it lacked the GUI and made it a little challenging for beginners. GNS3 was a program that provided a graphical user interface (GUI) to manage emulated lab devices with ease.

In the early days, GNS3 had a lot of bugs and did not always work well. With the development of more advanced CPU architecture, increased RAM capacity, and the introduction of the solid-state drive (SSD), emulating vendor network devices from an application on your laptop or PC has become more comfortable and more accessible. The price reduction of PC hardware components and more open source network emulators made studying networking extremely accessible. The latest versions of GNS3 are free from many pre-existing bugs and can run a very stable lab environment. GNS3 has evolved to support older Cisco IOS and integrate Cisco IOU and CML's (VIRL) L2 and L3 IOS. You can run both L2 switches, and L3 routers can be emulated and run in a virtualized lab environment. Although the best way to study any technology is to use the proper equipment or the same virtual infrastructure, this option might not be available to everyone. If both the money and time are available, it is best to study with proper equipment. It is always better to study with an emulator than with a simulator and is even better if you can afford to run the real lab using the proper equipment. Table 1-4 provides a tabulated list of applications used for network labs to help you with some history of network simulators and emulators for networking studies.

Table 1-4. *Network Emulation/Simulation Program for Networking Studies*

Application	Simulator / Emulator	Free/Open Source/ Proprietary	Pros and Cons
Cisco Packet Tracer	Simulator	Proprietary	**Pros:** Free to Network Academy students Very easy to use (suits beginners) Useful for learning the basic concept Readily available on torrent sites or free file share sites (download and use at your own risk) OK study tool for Cisco Certification **Cons:** Nothing close to real Cisco IOS Nothing close to real Cisco hardware
Dynamips	Emulator	Open source (still requires extracted Cisco IOS image(s))	**Pros:** Free Reasonably easy to use (suits intermediate users) Useful for learning the basic concept Support for older router platforms Very versatile Easy integration with virtual machines Easy integration with other hardware Fewer bugs than GNS3 Support for both Windows OS and Linux OS Excellent study/work tool for Cisco certification **Cons:** You'll have to find your own IOS copies Only support older IOS routers (except for 7200 routers) Limited switching capabilities Support through open source forums only

(*continued*)

Table 1-4. *(continued)*

Application	Simulator / Emulator	Free/Open Source/ Proprietary	Pros and Cons
GNS3	Emulator	Open source (still requires extracted Cisco IOS image(s))	**Pros:** Free Very easy to use (suits beginners) Useful for learning the basic concept Support for older router platforms Very versatile Easy integration with Virtual Machines Easy integration with other hardware Support for both Windows OS and Linux OS Perfect study/work tool for Cisco certification **Cons:** Locate your own IOS copies Only support older IOS routers (except for 7200 routers) Limited switching capabilities Lots of bugs Lots of performance issues Support through open source forums only
Cisco IOU	Emulator	Proprietary	**Pros:** Reasonably easy to use (suits intermediate users) Support for later or latest IOS Excellent L2/L3 switch emulation Can run on most WIN/Linux hosts Readily available on torrent sites or free file share sites Excellent study/work tool for Cisco certification **Cons:** Proprietary Requires a relatively powerful host machine No support from Cisco. Find your copy and use at your own risk

(continued)

Table 1-4. (*continued*)

Application	Simulator / Emulator	Free/Open Source/ Proprietary	Pros and Cons
Cisco CML (VIRL)	Emulator	Proprietary	**Pros:** Fairly easy to use Support for later or latest IOS Excellent L2/L3 switch emulation Can run on most WIN/Linux host Excellent study/work tool for Cisco certification Support from Cisco if paid for subscription Readily available on torrent sites or free file share sites **Cons:** Proprietary Requires a relatively powerful host machine
UNL Lite (EVE-NG)	Emulator	Proprietary	**Pros:** Support for later or latest IOS Excellent L2/L3 switch emulation Can run on most WIN/Linux host Excellent study/work tool for Cisco Certification **Cons:** Requires a relatively powerful host machine
Vagrant		Open source	**Pros:** Free Tool for building and managing virtual machine environments in a single workflow Easy-to-use workflow Focus on automation Lowers development environment setup time Increases production parity **Cons:** Requires a relatively powerful host machine

Other emulators introduced in the last decade include Unified Networking Lab's UNL Lite (renamed EVE-NG), Cisco's IOU (IOS On Unix), and Cisco's CML (Cisco Modeling Lab, old VIRL). Cisco Packet Trace can be used while studying Cisco certifications using Cisco Network Academy account. The software was used for experimentation only within the Cisco Technical Assistance Center (TAC) with Cisco IOU. It cannot be used by companies or individuals other than Cisco TAC. There have been many books and free guides on the Web on how to use the previous software, but in this book, GNS3 VM running on VMware Workstation Pro, integrated with Cisco IOS and CML images, will provide us with the emulated network infrastructure for Python network automation labs.

For this book, the ideal lab is the one that is optimized for less power consumption, which can be operated conveniently at any time and anywhere. So, this book has carefully laid out the topics in sequence, from easy to intermediate. Also, as long as you use the same or newer versions of software used in this book, most of the lab setup should work without software compatibility issues, and all labs should be reproducible.

Suppose you want to use this book's content for group training and only want to teach students in Python labs. In that case, you could install Windows 10 as a virtual machine on ESXi 6.5 (Figure 1-7), install all software, complete the integration, and then make clones of the original virtual machine and provide RDP accesses to designated virtual machines.

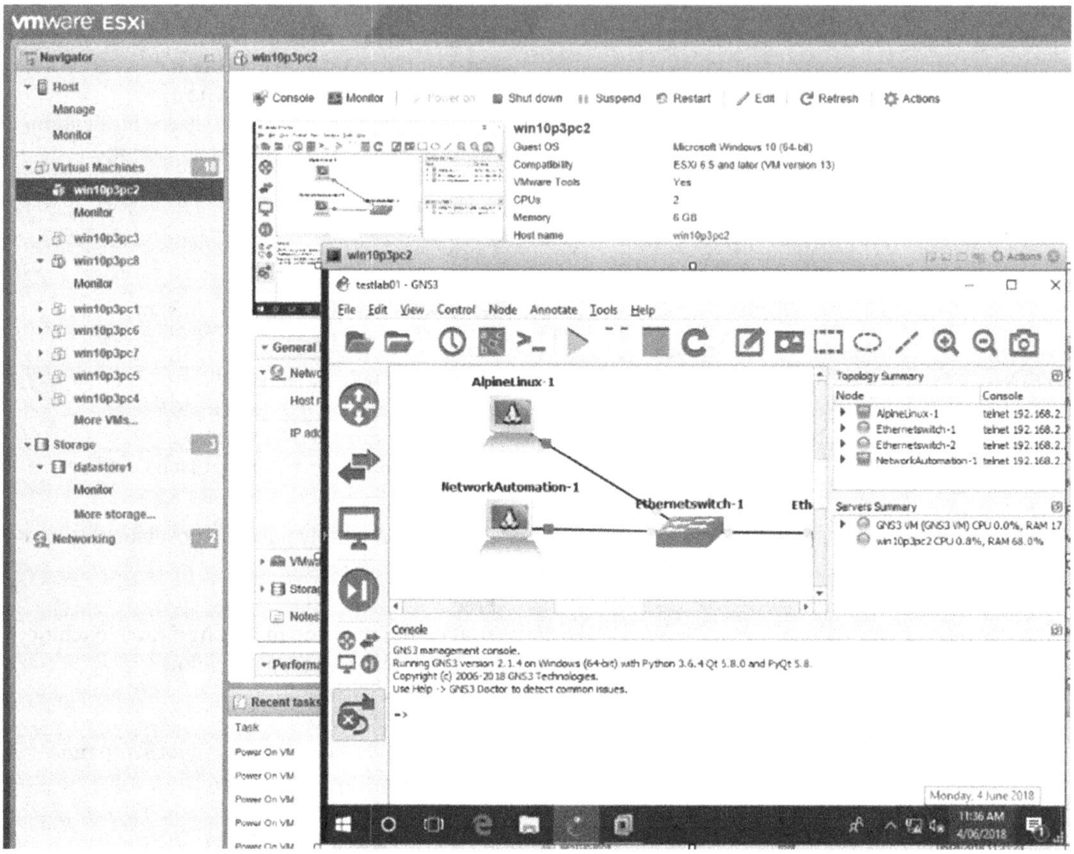

Figure 1-7. Example of running a network automation lab on ESXi 6.5 for group training

Downloading Supplementary Guides and Source Code

Download all pre-installation guides and source code before reading Chapter 2.

Supplementary pre-installation guides download:

- Author's URL: `https://github.com/pynetauto/apress_pynetauto`

Source code download:

- Author's URL: `https://github.com/pynetauto/apress_pynetauto`

Summary

We discussed IT network automation in general and did a quick comparative analysis of three main IT domain groups. We identified areas that the network engineer group must focus on to start writing Python code for network automation application development. Finally, we discussed the minimum hardware and software requirements to embark on your network automation journey. You probably noticed no networking hardware requirement is mentioned as part of the hardware requirement; everything will be software-based, even the routers and switches.

Storytime 1: Mega Speed Shoe Factory

In 2016, there was a great hype around robotics and automation replacing human labor in the shoe manufacturing industry. A famous shoe and sports apparel manufacturer, Adidas of Germany, announced a new robotic shoe factory; during the announcement, there was a prediction that up to 90 percent of 9 million workers in Southeast Asia could face unemployment because of this type of factory. However, in 2020, Adidas announced it would halt production at its two robotic "speed factories" in Germany, Ansbach, and the U.S. factories. The robotic shoe manufacturing line could only produce a limited number of models that mainly consisted of running shoes with a knit upper sole; the robots could not produce leather shoes with rubber soles. The old pieces of machinery have been moved and are currently used by Adidas suppliers in Vietnam and China.

Some people say machines will take over the world and take all our jobs sooner than later, but this example amplifies the need for more careful planning and the introduction of workplace automation. Each industry is learning the power of automation through trial and error.

This failure also takes us back to the early 1990s when automated teller machines (ATMs) were introduced. In that case, some studies in the United States have found that the economic forecasts made by many prominent economists and scholars were as accurate as your local taro fortune teller. So, if we are well prepared and embrace the changes, we should not fear automation or AI in the IT industry. While supporting your company's IT ecosystem and having pride in what you do at work is extremely important to all IT engineers, we have to be truthful about what we can do and what we know. An IT engineer does not know every aspect of all the IT technologies they support. Hence, they should not attempt to cover up their inability to perform specific tasks. We should always be ready to discover new things and gain additional skill sets to advance our careers.

CHAPTER 2

Learn Python Basics on Windows

Windows is the most commonly used end-user operating system for both private and enterprise users. More people will start their Python journey on a Windows PC rather than Linux or macOS, and the barrier to Python is lower when you begin to code in Python on Windows operating systems. This chapter contains hands-on Python exercises connecting selective Python concepts to general programming concepts, and some exercises will refer to real-world scenarios. The chapter will serve as a primer to the Python network automation scripting labs in the later chapters. Following the coding tradition, you will start your Python learning with the obligatory "Hello World!" program. Before starting the exercises, you will be guided to set up a simple Windows Python environment and will be introduced to some foundational Python coding etiquette. You will learn the most basic Python syntax and concepts, build stronger foundational blocks, and gain the essential Python skills required for Python network automation labs.

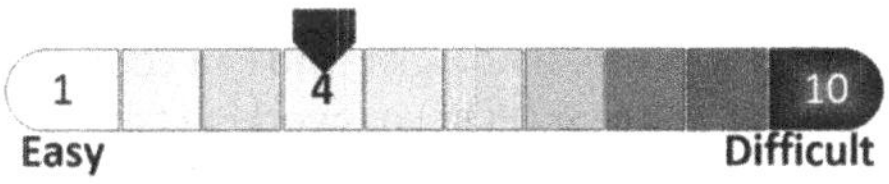

To learn and revisit basic Python concepts on the Windows operating system (OS), install Python 3 on your laptop or PC to follow along with exercises in this chapter. Download `CH02_Pre_Task_Install_Python3_on_WIN10_NotepadPP.pdf` from GitHub.

URL: `https://github.com/pynetauto/installation_guide`

Here I will share my own experience. I first started learning Python in 2013 with the hope to apply it to my work. In this first attempt, just trying to learn simple Python syntax took too long, and it felt tedious and pointless, so I gave up after two months. In 2015, I took another stab at Python syntax and concepts. I went through the basic Python syntax and concepts in three months but could not relate Python syntax and concepts to my work, so I gave up again. Fast-forward to 2017, when I endlessly searched for what I was missing. I finally realized that learning and mastering a programming language on its own is a useless exercise unless you have a set of objectives and a clear road map to get there.

In simple terms, my objective was to learn and use Python to automate repetitive tasks as a network engineer. The conclusion was that learning Python is only part of the journey. I had to cover a lot more parts, for example, improve on Linux system admin skills, master regular expressions, and learn to use various Python modules for both built-in and external modules and anything ad hoc to make quick adjustments to my code.

Getting started on the first programming language learning journey requires strong motivation and personal dedication from most of us. Continual learning takes patience and strong will power. With any

B. Choi, *Introduction to Python Network Automation*, https://doi.org/10.1007/978-1-4842-6806-3_2

learning, once you complete the first part of your journey, the second part awaits, and after you complete the second part, the third part is waiting for you. The learning continues with no definite end, and you will get caught in this vicious cycle as you will have to go back and forward in different parts of the journey. To make your Python learning curve more comfortable, first spend some time thinking about your motivation, why you want to learn Python, and where you want to use it; when you slack off, use it as a reminder to put you back on the course. Also, set the right expectations with plenty of time to absorb Python syntax and concepts in-depth and also explore various Python modules for your use case. Writing code in Python is no different from writing code in other programming languages. Also, learning Python syntax is like learning a non-native language, and it will take a long time to complete the basics and move to the next level. Like any other study, it is a constant struggle within you, but a well-planned study strategy can get you there with less pain.

Now let's examine different ways you can interact with your computer; there are three primary ways you can interact and instruct the computer to carry out a task. First, you sit in front of the physical computer or a remote console machine directly connected to a system and give real-time instructions in a one-to-one or one-to-n manner. Second, you can write a piece of code using a text editor or IDE and manually execute the code. This method is known as *semi-automation*. Third, you can write the code and schedule it to run at a specific time, and the system (computer) automatically executes your code with no human interaction. This method is known as *full automation* or *fully automated*. As you know, Python is an interactive programming language that does not require precompiling. An interactive programming language interprets the source code on the spot and gives the computer instructions when code needs to execute.

As mentioned in Chapter 1, although this is a book about Python network automation, this book considers Python knowledge and skills as part of many skill sets required to realize Python network automation. So, this book does not solely focus on Python syntax and concepts but aims to broaden your perspective on various IT technologies required on your network automation journey. The book will attempt to expose you to several technologies that will enable you to be a well-rounded technologist who can code in Python, administrate Linux, develop applications, and build a proof-of-concept (POC) networking lab for work. Suppose you only want to study basic Python syntax. In that case, it will be more appropriate to purchase a good Python basics book that is readily available on Amazon or in your local bookstore.

Your Python knowledge and experience will vary by mileage. But in this chapter, I will assume that you are a first-time or novice Python coder, so this chapter will cover a selection of essential Python syntax and concepts to grasp in order to perform all the tasks required in this book. This book builds your Python network automation skill set gradually and linearly. As a reader, we encourage you to follow along with each exercise presented in this chapter on your keyboard. You must type the code and complete all exercises in this chapter before moving onto the next chapters.

Unlike other books, this book will present you with various exercises to perform first, and then explanations will follow in this chapter and throughout the book. There are way too many books explaining the concepts in excessive detail. This book is for the doers, not for the conceptual thinkers. Some exercises will contain explanations as embedded comments, but in most cases, the explanation will follow each exercise to further aid to your understanding. At the end of each Python concept milestone, you will find a brief concept summary as a reminder of what you have learned. Finally, this book does *not* present you with trivial quizzes, irrational questions, or absurd challenges to put you into brain blackouts.

"Hello, World!" and print() Function in Interactive Mode

Learn to print the obligatory "Hello, World!" and understand the difference between interactive versus scripting modes.

■ **Hint** >>> with a space is the Python prompt, indicating that you are working in interactive mode.

If you want to learn Python interactively on Windows 10, there are few methods, but the three principal methods are in the Python shell, at the command prompt, and in Windows PowerShell (Figure 2-1). In interactive mode, when you open a Python shell, it welcomes you with >>> (three right-pointing brackets and a space) and a blinking cursor. Python is telling you it is ready for your interactive input. When you write code in this mode, you are writing code in interactive mode, and it saves your code in the computer's random memory and then is interpreted instantaneously by Python. In the examples shown in this chapter, you will use a simple `print()` function to print out an obligatory "Hello World!" statement on the screen to start your Python journey. Write some strings enclosed in a set of round brackets with a set of single or double quotes and then press the Enter key on your keyboard. The Python interpreter immediately interprets the code and prints the output to your computer screen. Python, like Ruby and Perl, is an interpreted programming language.

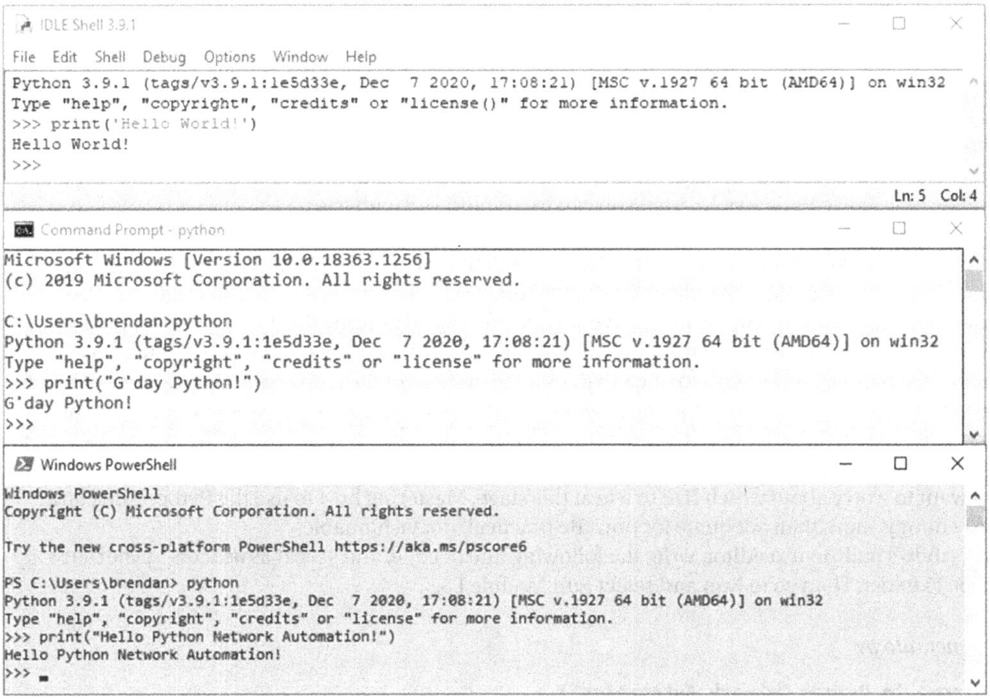

Figure 2-1. *Python interactive coding on Windows 10*

Open one of the prompt methods to type in the obligatory `print('Hello World!')` or `print("Hello World!")` statement. You have learned three things. First, you have learned how to use the `print()` function; second, you have learned that Python uses a set of single quotes (' ') or a set of double quotes (" ") to wrap strings. The `print()` function and the use of quotation marks will be discussed throughout various examples in this chapter. Third, this exercise has introduced you to the obligatory `print('Hello World')` statement as a verification tool.

Whether you are new or old to Python programming language, it is worthwhile to read about the origin of "Hello World!" and its use cases. The following are two URLs for you to visit and learn about the famous "Hello World!" program. For our use in this book, you will use it to validate that Python, as a program, is functioning correctly and can print the strings on the console screen when you run the `print()` function.

For more information about the "Hello, World!" program, see the following:

URL: `https://en.wikipedia.org/wiki/%22Hello,_World!%22_program`

URL: `https://www.youtube.com/watch?v=ycl1VL0q1rs`

In Python 3, `print()` is a built-in function and a standard function used to display processed data on the user's computer screen. As the Python 2.7.18 version marks the end of version 2.x support and reached the end of life on January 1, 2020, all the Python code in this book is written in Python 3.6.4. Do not bother with Python 2.x as once you get a firm grasp of Python 3.x, you will realize there are not many differences between the two. A fair analogical comparison would be the differences between Windows 8 and Windows 10; if you know how to use Windows 10, then you can use Windows 8 with ease.

You can also write Python code in a text editor and save it in the `.py` file format before running the script on Windows 10. When you write code in a text editor, we call this *writing a script* or working in *scripting mode*. When you install Python on Windows 10 PC, Python provides a built-in text editor (Figure 2-2), or you can use a text editor of your choice to write your code and save it as a `.py` file. Python code is platform-independent, so code written on the Windows operating system (OS) can run on macOS or Linux OS and vice versa. In this chapter, I expect you to open Python IDLE and the built-in text editor to practice each line of code on your keyboard so you can experience what it feels like to write code in Python. Coding in a more feature-rich integrated development environment (IDE) is also possible, but we will briefly discuss this later in this chapter. For now, try to write code using the Python interpreter and a simple text editor environment. You do not want to worry about which IDE to use at this stage. Mastering how to use the Python shell and built-in text editor is more than adequate for now. Be practical, not fashionable!

Open Python's built-in text editor, write the following line of code, and save it as `welcome_pynetauto.py` in the `Python39` folder. Then go to Run and select Run Module F5.

welcome_pynetauto.py

```
print("Welcome to Python Network Automation")
```

```
print("Welcome to Python Network Automation")
```

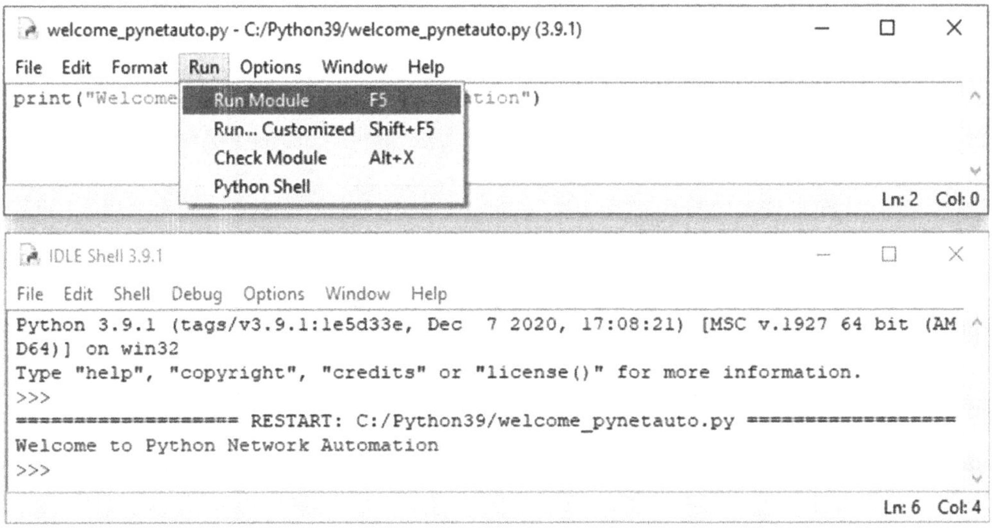

Figure 2-2. *Coding in Python's built-in text editor in Windows*

After completing all the exercises in this chapter, you will become more familiar with basic but core Python concepts; this understanding is mandatory before moving on to the following chapters in the second half of this book. If you are using Linux or macOS, you can open a terminal window and type in `python` or `python3` to start interactive mode. We will talk about coding in Linux OS later in this book.

Preparing for the Python Exercises

The vast majority of this book's target audience consists of Windows users. To begin the exercises in this chapter, you should have followed the installation guide at `CH02_Pre_Task_Install_Python3_on_WIN10_NotepadPP.pdf` to install the latest version of Python 3 on your Windows 10 host machine. According to 2019 statistics, Windows users still outnumber Linux users by a 20-to-1 ratio. So, beginning your Python journey on the Windows environment is ideal, and then you can transition to Linux. Since most enterprise servers supporting Python run on one of the many Linux OS flavors, this is enough reason for enterprise engineers to skill up in Linux. In the later chapters, you will learn Linux basics, and you will perform tasks in a Linux environment, so we will start with Python on Windows and then learn to use Python on Linux. If you have been a Windows user all your life, you must start working on Linux OS to get ahead of the rest of the pack in most IT technician jobs. If you are already familiar with Linux, then you will fly in business class while going on your Python network automation journey.

Throughout this chapter, you will go through various exercises and use the explanations and concept summaries to review what you have learned from these exercises. To get you started with Python coding, you will first learn about four obligatory Python concepts, see some examples, and then you will try the exercises.

- Python data types
- Indentation and code blocks
- Commenting
- Basic Python naming conventions

You can practice all the exercises presented in this chapter on either Linux or macOS with minor directory location slash modifications. When you open Python in Python's built-in IDLE or Windows command prompt or Windows PowerShell and type in `python`, Python will run and greet you with a friendly interactive Python prompt. Please pay close attention; you will see it has three greater-than symbols followed by a single space.

```
>>>
```

When you see the three greater-than signs and a space, Python is telling you that you can type in the next code line. Get comfortable with this symbol, as you will spend many hours staring at it.

Understanding Data Types

In this section, you will learn about the different data types used in Python: numbers, sequences, mapping, sets, and `None`.

> **Hint** Try to wrap your head around Python data types to save time in the future.

A Python data type is a set/group of values with similar characteristics. Data types can belong to one of the groups shown in Figure 2-3. We will study each data type using Python's built-in function `type()`.

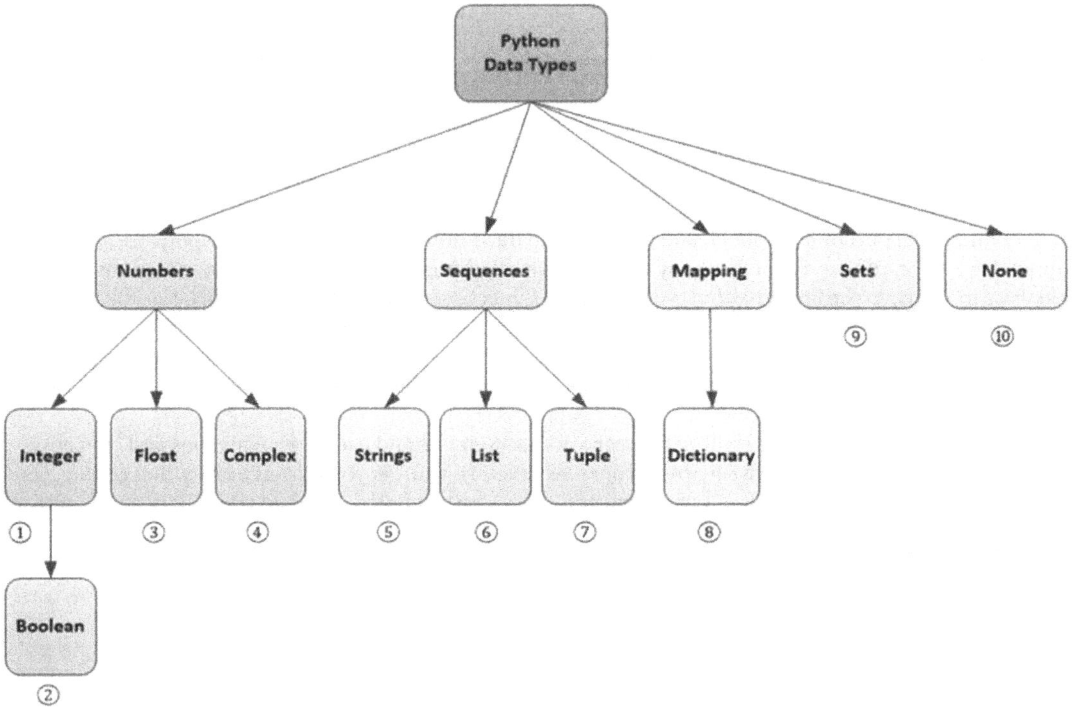

Figure 2-3. Python data types

Everything is treated as an object in Python and classified into different data or data types depending on the object's characteristics. First, let's take a quick look at Python's data types. This book attempts to build on your knowledge of basic to intermediate Python code while developing various network automation applications. So, you do not have to know all the data types in-depth, but you have to know the most commonly used data types; we will only cover the basics required to get through this book.

You will use Python's built-in function type() to find out how Python classifies different data objects. Open your Python shell and type in the text after >>> and the space; then press the Enter key.

#	Exercise	Explanation
①	>>> type (3) <class 'int'>	An integer is a subclass of numbers. 1 is an example of an integer. Whole numbers with + or - signs like -3, 0, 5 are integers. They are used in numeric data for calculation.

②	>>> type (True)
	<class 'bool'>
	>>> type (False)
	<class 'bool'>
		A Boolean (True or False) is a subclass of an integer. A Boolean operation tests some conditions for True or False. The constant 1 represents True, and 0 represents False.

③	>>> type (1.0) <class 'float'>	A float is a subclass of numbers, also known as *floating point*. In this example, 1.0 is an example of a float. Floats are numbers with fractions or decimal points.
④	>>> type (1 + 2j) <class 'complex'>	A complex number is a combination of real and imaginary numbers. You can think of it as numerical data used to make calculations convenient and used often in science calculations.

⑤	>>> type ('123')
	<class 'str'>
	>>> type('word')
	<class 'str'>
		A string is a subclass of sequence, mutable, and an ordered sequence of letters or characters. A sequence is an ordered collection of items indexed by integers from 0 to n. Any data type enclosed in double or single quotation marks, for example, '123' or "word", is a string in Python.

⑥	>>> type ([1, 2, 3]) <class 'list'>	A list is a subclass of the sequence of values of any data type. Values in the list are items, and they are mutable, indexed by integers from 0 to n, and ordered. The list uses a set of square brackets, [ ], to carry items in the order.
⑦	>>> type ((3, 2, 1)) <class 'tuple'>	A tuple is a sequence of values of any data type and is indexed by integers. It's an immutable data type that lists elements in round brackets, ( ), separated by commas. The difference between a list and a tuple is their immutability.
⑧	>>> type ({1: 'apple', 2: 'banana'}) <class 'dict'>	A dictionary is an unordered mapping data type created by constructing key: value pairs, separating them by comma, and wrapping them in braces, { }. For example, a in 'a':'apple' is called a *key*, and apple that follows the colon is called a *value*. In the dictionary, the order of elements is ignored, and the value is paged by calling a key.

#	Exercise	Explanation

⑨	>>> type ({1, 2, 3, 3, 2, 1})
	<class 'set'>
	>>> {1, 2, 3, 3, 2, 1}
	{1, 2, 3}
		Sets are an unordered collection of values of any data type without duplicate entry. The set data type is also immutable. As shown in the example, the set only allows a single entry of the same value.

⑩	>>> type (None) <class 'NoneType'>	None is a special data type with a single value. It's a constant that represents the absence of a value. If you assign None to a variable, it means the variable is empty.

⑪	>>> int(7.24)
	7
	>>> float(3.00)
	3.0
	>>> str("365")
	'365'
	>>> bool(1)
	True
		Explicit typecasting can specify a precise data type. Python does an outstanding job of automatically detecting the data type, but sometimes, some data needs to be fixed to avoid confusion. The data type constructors such as int(), float(), str(), and bool() are often used while handling different data types in Python code.

We can reference more detailed explanations of each data type on the Python.org documentation site.
URL: https://docs.python.org/3/library/stdtypes.html

Indentation and Code Blocks

Most programming languages such as C, C++, and Java use braces, { }, to structure code. Python uses indentation to define a code block to give its unique code structure; a block of code is a group of statements in a program or script consisting of at least one statement and declarations for the programming block. In Python, a code block starts with indentation and ends with the first unindented line; examples include the body of a function, loop, and class. In this section, you'll learn to use indentation or whitespaces as code blocks.

■ **Hint** Python uses four spaces to differentiate between code blocks.

①
```
with open("C:\\Python39\\ip_adds.txt", "r") as f:
□□□□for line in f:
□□□□□□□□print(line)

# Output: 10.20.30.1

172.168.1.254

192.168.0.2

10.20.34.25
```

②
```
with open("C:\\Python39\\ip_adds.txt", "r") as f:
□□for line in f:
□□□□print(line, end="")

# Output: 10.20.30.1
172.168.1.254
192.168.0.2
10.20.34.25
```

Explanation

① Python uses spaces to group statements; this is also known as *indentation*. The first line of code usually starts with no spacing; when the statement ends with a colon (:), the next line needs to be indented to show that it is part of the group. Example ① is code that opens a file with IP addresses and reads the IP addresses. Four indentations are the PEP80 recommendation and the most widely used indentation convention when coding in Python. The example shows the second line with four spaces, followed by eight spaces on the third line.
The output is shown for demonstration only, but you can create a text file called `ip_adds.txt` under `C:\Python39\`, enter a few IP addresses, and test the code shown in your Python interpreter.

② The same code still works with two spaces for indentation. As long as your spacing is consistent, you can use any spacing for your code blocks; however, four spacing is the norm. At Google, the Python coding standard uses two spaces.
In the last line of code, I have added `end=""` to eliminate the whitespaces created while reading the information from the file. Using `end="`, `end=" "`, `end = "/"`, `end=":"`, and more, you can manipulate how unwanted whitespaces are handled in the output.

Commenting

Comments are part of the code that does not affect the program's flow and that provide descriptions of your application's important sections. Comments can explain the purpose of certain functions or explain complex code snippets to assist readers. Python uses a # sign when processing comments, and subsequent characters are commented out and have no effect on the program. To add multiple-line comments, you can use either triple-single quotations (`'''  '''`) or triple-double quotation marks (`"""  """`) across multiple lines. Another use of Python commenting is to make some part of the code inactive while still developing an application.

In this section, you'll learn how to add comments to your code.

Hint Code is read more times than written. Good commenting habits can save time when decoding.

---

①
```
# This code can SSH into multiple devices & download IOS from a TFTP server
# and upgrades old IOS to the latest version.
# Please... [skip]
```

②
```
# Ask new driver's age.
age = 17
if age > = 18:
   print('You are old enough to drive a car.')
#elif age > 80:
# print('You are too old to drive a car!') else:
   print('You are too young to drive a car.')
```

③
```
"""
This code can SSH into multiple devices and download IOS from a TFTP server
And upgrades old IOS to the latest version. Please check MD5 values of the new
IOS image before uploading it to the router flash.
"""
```

Explanation

① Add comments by entering the # hash (sharp) symbol at the beginning of each line. Python ignores everything after #. Comments are used to explain and clarify the meaning of source code or give guidance to source code used as in example ①.

② Or temporarily disable parts of code during application development, as shown in example ②.

③ For multiple lines (the recommendation is three or more lines), use the triple quotation marks.

Python Naming Convention

In this section, you'll learn the standard Python-related object naming conventions.

Hint To write consistent and high-quality Python code, you have to adopt standardized naming conventions.

As in every other programming language, Python also has some naming conventions to follow. If your Python code will be read by others, then it is a best practice to follow these conventions to avoid confusion and misunderstanding at later times. When you name variables, functions, modules, classes, and so forth, give meaningful, sensible, and descriptive names to avoid ambiguity for others. Use the # or triple quotation marks to add additional comments in your code. Table 2-1 outlines the recommended naming conventions for new Python coders.

Table 2-1. *Python Naming Conventions*

Type	Examples	Conventions	Description
Variable	x, y, z, var, tmp, f_name, s_name	No capitalization A letter, word, or words with underscore(s)	Use a lowercase letter (for augments), words, or words with underscore separator(s).
Function	function my_function	No capitalization word or words with underscore(s)	Use lowercase words or words, or words with underscore separator(s).
Method	method class_method	Same as function	Use a lowercase word or words with underscore separator(s).
Module	module.py network_tools.py	Same as function + module saved as .py file	When saving a module as a .py file, use a short, lowercase word or words with underscore separator(s).
Package	package firstpackage	All lowercase word or words with no underscore(s)	Use a short, lowercase word or words without underscore separator(s).
Class	Class FirstClass	First letter capitalization with no underscore(s)	Use camel casing; start each word with a capital letter without underscore separator(s).
Constant	CONSTANT FIRST_CONSTANT FIRST_TIME_CONSTANT	Capitalized with underscore(s)	Use an uppercase single letter, word, or words with underscore separator(s).

Take your time to study each type, example, and convention before moving onto the next section. You can also come back to this table as a reference point later as needed.

Doing the Python Exercises

Complete all exercises to master the basic Python syntax and concepts required for network automation coding.

■ **Hint** All the exercises in this chapter will help you better understand the network automation code presented later in the book. You have to understand the Python basics to continue your Python network automation journey.

You are encouraged to open Python IDLE and perform all the exercises given in this book. You type in the syntax in the Python IDLE first, and then the explanation follows the exercises to aid your understanding of the practiced topics. The selective exercises provided in this chapter are the same as what I used while learning Python for the first time. This will make you familiar with Python syntax and concepts. If you are a novice Python learner, you will get enough exposure to start network automation coding using Python. You will learn the necessary Python skills required to understand the Python code to prepare you for later chapters in this book. I would like to teach you more about Python syntax, but this book's focus is on network automation, virtualization, Linux, and Cisco networking. Hence, relevant exercises have been chosen selectively to cover Python basics so that when you get to the final lab chapters, you will feel comfortable following the exercises.

In this chapter, when you type the first character in the exercise, try to get to the last line in the exercise in one session. Even if you don't understand the code on your first attempt, repeat the whole exercise for a second time. Many of the examples used in this chapter are self-explanatory, or follow-up explanations will clarify each code. There are plenty of Python introduction books for sale on Amazon and an abundance of free and paid online lessons. So, after attempting the exercises in this chapter, if you feel you would like to improve by doing more Python concepts and syntax, please find a book or website of your choice and spend more time practicing Python basics.

We will use Python 3 instead of Python 2 for a simple reason; Python 2 versions reached the end of life on January 1, 2020.

Also, I encourage you to complete all exercises from a Windows-based computer so you can learn the minor syntax differences between the Windows and Linux operating systems, mainly dealing with file handling and how directory structures are different between the two operating systems. I have not mentioned macOS as it is a derivative of a BSD UNIX, which is the same as many of the Linux distributions (distros). In Chapters 5 and 6, you will build virtual machines from the most popular Linux distros, CentOS (Red Hat derivative), and Ubuntu (Debian derivative). For a smoother transition, you will need to get familiar with the Linux OS and then use Python 3 on Linux.

When you launch Python IDLE, it will welcome you with three greater-than symbols (>>>) and a cursor (|). If you see the three greater-than symbols in the exercises, you must type in the content into your Python IDLE. If you must save your code and run it as a Python file, which has a file extension ending with `.py`, you will have to follow the instructions and write the code in either Python's built-in text editor or Notepad. Although I could introduce you to various text editors and IDEs, our focus in this chapter is purely on Python syntax and concepts, so a fancy IDE or text editor is an obstruction.

It's time to launch your Python IDLE. When you see the prompt, start typing the code in the first exercise.

Variables and Strings

We'll start with variables and strings.

Exercise 2-1: Create Variables and Assign Various Data Types

①
```
>>> x = 1
>>> y = 2
>>> x + y
3
>>> type(x + y)
<class 'int'>
```

②
```
>>> x = '1'
>>> y = '2'
>>> x + y
'12'
>>> type(x + y)
<class 'str'>
```

③
```
>>> fruit = 'apple'
>>> applause = 'bravo'
>>> dec1 = 1.0
>>> bool_one = True
>>> bool_0 = False
>>> _nada = None
```

Explanation

① You created variables x and y and assigned two integers. Perform a simple addition to check the sum of two numbers. Python supports other arithmetic operations; the equal sign (=) in Python is an assignment operator. So, you must read `x = 1` as "x is assigned to 1" or "x is pointing to 1" or "tag x is assigned to object 1." Unlike other programming languages, in Python, there is no need to declare the variable up front; the value assigned to the variable determines the variable type, and in this example, they are all integers.

② We created variables x and y; then they got assigned to two different strings. Although 1 and 2 are integer data types, we wrapped these numbers in single quotation marks, and this automatically converted them into strings. So, performing concatenations with two strings will return a string, 12, and not the sum of the two numbers, which is 3.

③ You should give variables with brief and intuitive names. Variable names usually start with a-z or _. Also, avoid capitalization of the first variable letter. The variable names must be continuous without whitespacing or breaks. If you try to name a variable with a number, arithmetic operator, or special characters, you will receive various syntax errors. Also, Python is case sensitive, and a string is immutable. You cannot overwrite an immutable object's values, but there is a trick to changing characters in a string. You will learn this trick in Exercise 2-22.

Exercise 2-2: Create Variables and Use the print() Function to Print Output

①
```
>>> x = 100
>>> y = 200
>>> z = 300
>>> total = x + y + z
>>> print(total) 600
```

Explanation

① We have created and assigned the x, y, and z variables to different values and created another variable called *total*, the sum of the three variables. We used print(total) to print the result on the screen. You usually use the `print()` function to display the output on the screen. The `print()` statement has no impact on the existing variable values from the computer's or Python's perspective.

Exercise 2-3: Use Abbreviated Variable Assignment

①
```
>>> x, y, z = 10, 20, 30
>>> x
10
>>> y
20
>>> z
30
>>> type(x)
<class 'int'>
>>> x, y, z
(10, 20, 30)
```

②
```
>>> a, b, c = "apple", "banana", "coconut"
>>> a, b, c
('apple', 'banana', 'coconut')
```

Explanation

① You can assign multiple variables to multiple values on a single line using a comma (,) as the separator. When you page an individual variable, it returns as an integer object, but when paged as a group using commas, it returns a tuple.

② The same applies to the objects with a string data type. Did you notice that double quotation marks are used instead of single quotation marks? You can use both as long as you are consistent through the whole code.

Exercise 2-4: Enter a String, Escape Character Backslash (\), and type() Function

①
```
>>> 'He said, "You are one of a kind."'
'He said, "You are one of a kind."'
```

②
```
>>> said = "He said, \" You are one of a kind.\""
>>> print(said)
He said, "You are one of a kind."
>>> type(said)
<class 'str'>
```

Explanation

① You can express a string of text in a set of single or double quotation marks. This example uses single quotation marks on Python IDLE.

② This example uses double quotation marks and two backslashes (\) just before inner double quotation marks ("). A backslash escapes (removes) the functional meaning of double quotation marks and marks them as normal characters only. It is common practice to use one style of quotation marks to stay consistent and improve your code's readability. Use the `type()` function to check the data type.

Table 2-2 provides examples of backslash use cases. Review the table before moving on to the next exercise. You can also type the examples into your Python interpreter to learn the subtle differences between the unique examples.

Table 2-2. *Backslash Examples*

\ Use	Example	Explanation
\\	`>>> print('\\represents backslash\\')` `\represents backslash\`	The backslash is used to escape the leading backslash. We also know this process as negating the meaning of a metacharacter and taking a character as a literal character.
\'	`>>> print('\'Single quotes in single quotes\'')` `'Single quotes in single quotes'`	The backslash is used to escape a single quote.
\"	`>>> print("\"double quotation marks inside double quotation marks\"")` `"double quotation marks inside double quotation marks"`	The backslash is used to escape a double quote.

\n	`>>> print('Line 1\nLine 2\nLine 3')`
	`Line 1`
	`Line 2`
	`Line 3`
		Combining \ with n takes another meaning and becomes a newline character, \n.

\r (for Linux)
\r\n
(for Windows)
	`>>> print('Line 1\r\nLine 2\r\nLine 3')`
	`Line 1`
	`Line 2`
	`Line 3`
		On a Linux machine, to emulate pressing the Enter key, `\r` is used but, you have to use `\r\n` on a Windows machine.

\t	`>>> print('No tab\tTab\tTab')` `No tab Tab Tab`	Tab has the same effect as pressing the Tab key on a physical keyboard.

Exercise 2-5: Determine If a Variable Is a Container, a Tag, or a Pointer

①
```
>>> x = "apple"
>>> y = "apple"
>>> id(x)
2590130366512
>>> id(y)
2590130366512
>>> x == y
True
```

Explanation

① Many Python books teach novice Python learners about variables using a variables-as-containers analogy. In this analogy, variable containers temporarily store objects. To some extent, this seems to be a correct analogy, but not exactly 100 percent correct. Variables are more like tags or pointers pointing at an object (see Figure 2-4). The container analogy does not work. As seen in the previous exercise, x and y have been assigned to the same string (an object), "apple" (pointing to the same object). You can use the id() function to check the object IDs for validation; x and y have the same ID. Using the comparison operator, you can confirm that x is equal to y, and hence they are both pointing to the same object, "apple".

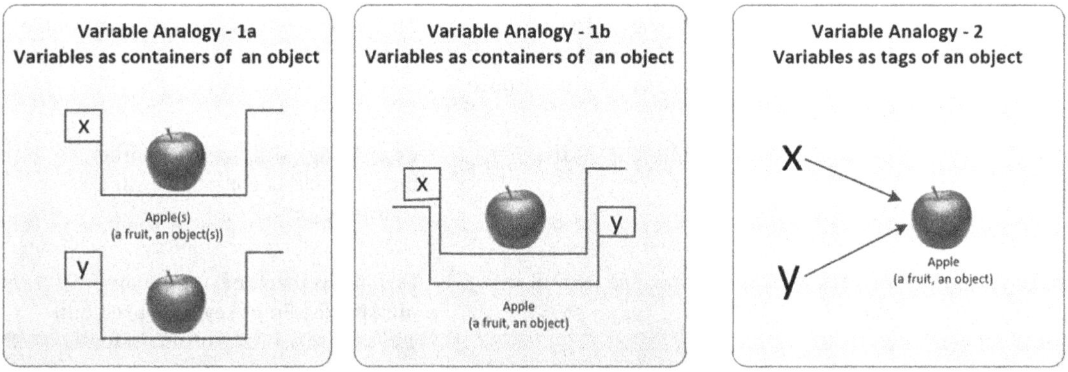

Figure 2-4. *Variables: container versus tag/pointer analogy*

Here are some Python variable naming conventions recommendations:

1. Use a lowercase single letter, word, or words.
2. If more than two words are used, separate words with an underscore (_) for readability. Use numbers to differentiate the same variables with similar object characteristics, for example, `fruit_1= "apple"` and `fruit_2 = "orange"`.

3. Variable names are case sensitive. `fruit_1` and `Fruit_1` are two separate variables.
4. Avoid using Python reserved words; this will be discussed in the later exercise.

You can practice a character or sentence that you define by putting it in double or single quotation marks in the following example. Also, check for string errors.

Exercise 2-6: Use String Indexing

①
```
>>> bread = 'bagel'
>>> bread [0]
'b'
>>> bread [1]
'a'
>>> bread [4]
'l'
```

Explanation

① Python indexing starts at 0. For the word *bagel* used in the example, the letter `b` is the 0 index, and the letter `l` is the index 4.

String: b a g e l
Index : 0 1 2 3 4

While writing Python code, you will encounter various Python error messages. If you get familiar with commonly encountered errors in advance, you will resolve these errors quickly and enjoy Python coding much more. In the following examples, you will intentionally trigger several Python errors to learn more about them.

Exercise 2-7: Understand Variable Assignment Errors

①
```
>>> +lucky7 = 777
SyntaxError: can't assign to operator
>>> 7lucky= 777
SyntaxError: invalid syntax
>>> 7_lucky = 777
SyntaxError: invalid decimal literal
>>> lucky7 = 777
>>> lucky7
777
```

Explanation

① The previous syntax errors display the errors triggered by incorrect variable naming conventions. If you use an arithmetic operator symbol at the beginning, Python will raise an error. If you place a number at the beginning of the variable name, Python will return an invalid syntax error. If you assign variables correctly, you will not encounter error messages, as shown in the previous example. Errors are a crucial part of any coding, as they are there to help you correct your coding mistakes.

Exercise 2-8: Avoid "SyntaxError: EOL While Scanning String Literal"

①
```
# On Python Shell:
>>> q1 = 'Did you have a wonderful day at work?"
SyntaxError: EOL while scanning string literal

# On Window Command-Line or PowerShell:
>>> q1 = 'Did you have a wonderful day at work?"
File "<stdin>", line 1
q1 = 'Did you have a wonderful day at work? "
^

SyntaxError: EOL while scanning string literal

>>> q1 = 'Did you have a wonderful day at work?' # Use correct quotation marks, no
error prompted.
>>>
```

Explanation

① You cannot mix single and double quotes when assigning a string to a variable. You will get a scanning string literal error as shown. This exercise shows the same error output from the Python shell and Windows PowerShell. To correct this error, make sure you type incorrect quotation marks at the beginning and the end of the string.

Exercise 2-9: Avoid "NameError: name 'variable_name' is not defined"

①
```
>>> print(a1)
Traceback (most recent call last):
   File "<pyshell#1>", line 1, in <module>
      print(a1)
NameError: name 'a1' is not defined
>>> a1 = 'Yes, I had a lovely day.'
>>> print(a1)
Yes, I had a lovely day.
```

Explanation

① `NameError` occurs when your variable is not predefined. To avoid this error, define your variable first and use it in a function like `print(a1)`.

Exercise 2-10: Avoid "SyntaxError: invalid syntax"

①
```
#On Python 3.9Shell:
>>> for = 'I drove my car for 4 hours before taking the first break.'
SyntaxError: invalid syntax
```

②
```
#On Window Command-Line or PowerShell
>>> for = 'I drove my car for 4 hours before taking the first break.'
File "<stdin>", line 1
for = 'I drove my car for 4 hours before taking the first break.'
^
SyntaxError: invalid syntax

>>> first_break = 'I drove my car for 4 hours before taking the first break.'
>>>
```

Explanation

① Python returns this error when you use words that are in Python's reserved words list. To avoid this error, avoid using reserved words as variable names.

② It triggered the same error in the Windows command line, and it gives a little more information. The ^ (caret) symbol is used to indicate a potential problem area. Python tells you to make corrections roughly around where ^ is pointing.
Give a more descriptive or meaningful name to your variable. I renamed the variable name to `first_break`, so the variable name is in context with the string assigned to this variable.

Exercise 2-11: Avoid "TypeError: 'str' object is not callable"

①
```
>>> help = 'Please help me reach my goal.'
>>> print(help)
Please help me reach my goal.
>>> help (print)
Traceback (most recent call last):
File "<pyshell#77>", line 1, in <module> help (print)
TypeError: 'str' object is not callable
```

Explanation

① When you assign a built-in function name as a variable name, you disable the function name, and it immediately becomes unusable. Avoid using keywords and built-in function names as your variable names. You can check all built-in function names using the `dir(__builtins__)` command, which will be discussed in a later example.

:

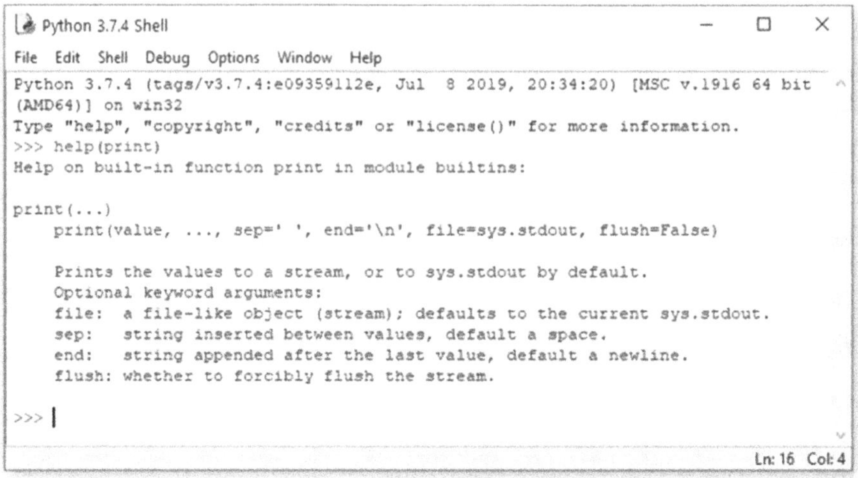
Python 3.7.4 Shell
File Edit Shell Debug Options Window Help
Python 3.7.4 (tags/v3.7.4:e09359112e, Jul 8 2019, 20:34:20) [MSC v.1916 64 bit (AMD64)] on win32
Type "help", "copyright", "credits" or "license()" for more information.
>>> help(print)
Help on built-in function print in module builtins:
print(...)
print(value, ..., sep=' ', end='\n', file=sys.stdout, flush=False)
Prints the values to a stream, or to sys.stdout by default.
Optional keyword arguments:
file: a file-like object (stream); defaults to the current sys.stdout.
sep: string inserted between values, default a space.
end: string appended after the last value, default a newline.
flush: whether to forcibly flush the stream.
>>>
Ln: 16 Col: 4

When help() works normally, the help information appears as shown here:

```
----------------------------------------------------------------------

Python 3.9.1 (tags/v3.9.1:1e5d33e, Dec  7 2020, 17:08:21) [MSC v.1927 64 bit (AMD64)] on win32

Type "help", "copyright", "credits" or "license()" for more information.

>>> help(print)

Help on built-in function print in module builtins:

print(...)
    print(value, ..., sep=' ', end='\n', file=sys.stdout, flush=False)

    Prints the values to a stream, or to sys.stdout by default.
    Optional keyword arguments:
    file:  a file-like object (stream); defaults to the current sys.stdout.
    sep:   string inserted between values, default a space.
    end:   string appended after the last value, default a newline.
    flush: whether to forcibly flush the stream.

>>>
----------------------------------------------------------------------
```

You have reviewed a few common syntaxes related to Python errors. As you write and run your code, you will be encountering various error codes. Some error codes are easy to troubleshoot, but some error codes are stubborn to troubleshoot, and you will have to search on the Stack Overflow website (`https://stackoverflow.com/questions`) for answers.

Exercise 2-12: Add Multiline Comments with Triple Quotation Marks

①
```
>>> """You're one of a kind. You're my best friend.
I've never met someone like you before. It's been wonderful getting to know you. """
"You're one of a kind.\nYou're my best friend.\nI've never met someone like you
before.\nIt's been wonderful getting to know you.\n"
```

②
```
>>> cook_noodles = '''How to cook a bowl of instant noodles? Pour 2.5 cups of water in
a saucepan,
boil it first, and then
put dried vegetables, powder soup, and noodles. Then boil it for another 5 minutes.
Now you can eat delicious instant noodles.'''
>>> print(cook_noodles)
How to cook a bowl of instant noodles? Pour 2.5 cups of water in a saucepan, boil it
first and then
put dried vegetables, powder soup, and noodles. Then boil it for another 5 minutes.
Now you can eat delicious instant noodles.
```

③
```
# Use PEP-8 to keep per line of code less than 80 characters
>>> cook_noodles = '''How to cook a bowl of instant noodles? \
Pour 2.5 cups of water in a saucepan, boil it first, and then put dried \
vegetables, powder soup, and noodles. Then boil it for another 5 minutes.\
Now you can eat delicious instant noodles.'''
>>> print(cook_noodles)
'How to cook a bowl of instant noodles? Pour 2.5 cups of water in a saucepan, boil
it first and then put dried vegetables, powder soup, and noodles. Then boil it for
another 5 minutes. Now you can eat delicious instant noodles.'
```

Explanation

① If you wrap a long string with triple quotation marks (three single or double quotation marks), you can enter multiple lines of comments. This is a valid commenting method when entering long descriptions.

② You can also use triple quotation marks when you assign a long string to a variable.

③ If your code line gets too long, use the backslash (\) at the end of the line to continue writing comments or strings, as shown in this example. PEP-8 recommends that a line of code should be less than 80 characters long.
Go to the following Python.org site to read more about the PEP-8 writing style and more: `https://www.python.org/dev/peps/pep-0008/`.

Exercise 2-13: Use \ as an Escape Character to Remove Special Character Meanings

①
```
>>> single_quote_string = 'He said, "arn\'t, can\'t shouldn\'t woundn\'t."'
>>> print(single_quote_string)
He said, "arn't, can't shouldn't wouldn't."
```

②
```
>>> double_quote_string = "He said, \"arn't can't shouldn't wouldn't.\""
>>> print(double_quote_string)
He said, "arn't can't shouldn't wouldn't."
```

Explanation

① Using the backslash symbol as an escape character inside single quotation marks removes the special character meaning and makes the next character regular plain text. So, Python recognizes \' as a plaintext '. The escape character (or the backslash) plays an essential role in Python coding.

② You can use the escape character in a string marked with double quotation marks. Since ' (single quote) is different from the outer " (double quote), there's no need to use backslash escape characters as many times as in example ①.

Exercise 2-14: Enter (Inject) Values/Strings in a String Using %s

①
```
>>> exam_result = 95
>>> text_message = 'Congratulations! You have scored %s in your exam!'
>>> print(text_message% exam_result)
Congratulations! You have scored 95 in your exam!
```

②
```
>>> wish = 'You need %s to make your wish come true.'
>>> genie = 'a Genie in the bottle'
>>> print(wish% genie)
You need a Genie in the bottle to make your wish come true.
```

③
```
>>> fast_car = 'Fast cars have %s & %s to make the car go faster.'
>>> part1 = 'a supercharger'
>>> part2 = 'a turbocharger'

>>> print(fast_car% (part1, part2))
Fast cars have a supercharger & a turbocharger to make the car go faster.
```

④
```
>>> ccnp_score = 'My exam scores are %s forENCOR, %s for ENARSI and %s forENAUTO.'
>>> ccnp_score% (95, 92, 90)
'My exam scores are 95 for ENCOR, 92 for ENARSI and 90 for ENAUTO.'
>>> print(ccnp_score% (95, 92, 90))
My exam scores are 95 for ENCOR, 92 for ENARSI and 90 for ENAUTO.
```

Explanation

① You can enter a digit variable into a string message using `%s`.

② You can enter a string variable into a string message using `%s`.

③ You can enter two or more variables into a string using multiple `%s` characters and wrap them as a tuple sequence.

④ You do not have to define values as variables; first, you can add the expected augments directly, as shown in this example. The `ccnp_score` variable expects three strings (arguments), so we provided three arguments (95, 92, 90).

Printing, Concatenating, and Converting Strings

Exercise 2-15: Use the print() and len() Functions to Create a Simple Function

①
```
>>> print('Paris baguette')
Paris baguette

>>> bread = 'NY bagel'
>>> print(bread)
NY bagel
```

②
```
>>> aussie = 'meat pie'
>>> print(len(aussie))
8

>>> print(type(aussie[4]))
<class 'str'>
```

③
```
>>> bread = 'naan'
>>> def bread_len():
□□□□length = len(bread)
□□□□print(length)

>>> bread_len()
4
```

Explanation

① Use the `print()` function to print output to your display.

② Use the `len()` function to check the length of a string. The `len()` function even counts the whitespace as a string.

③ Define a variable and then create a simple function that reads your bread choice length and prints the character count. To create a function, always start the line with `def` and finish the header line with a semicolon (:). The next line then places four spaces, as shown. (You have already learned about indentation.) To call the function, simply type in the function name and `()`, in this example, `bread_len()`. You have just created your first function.

Exercise 2-16: Use the lower() and upper() String Methods

①
```
>>> "Bagel Is My Favorite Bread!".lower()
'bagel is my favorite bread!'
>>> bread = 'BAGEL'
>>> print(bread.lower())
bagel
```

②
```
>>> "baguette is also my favorite bread.".upper()
'BAGUETTE IS ALSO MY FAVORITE BREAD.'
>>> bread = 'baguette'
>>> print(bread.upper())
BAGUETTE
```

Explanation

① Both `lower()` and `upper()` are built-in methods used for string handling. The `lower()` string method converts all uppercase characters to lowercase. If lowercase characters exist, it returns the original string.

② The `upper()` string method works precisely opposite to the `lower()` string methods.

Exercise 2-17: Perform String Concatenation and Use the str() Method

①
```
>>> print('Best' + 'friends' + 'last' + 'forever.')
Bestfriendslastforever.
>>> print('Best ' + 'friends ' + 'last ' + 'forever.')
Best friends last forever.
>>> print('Best' + ' ' + 'friends' + ' ' + 'last' + ' ' + 'forever.')
Best friends last forever.
>>> print('Best', 'friends', 'last', 'forever.')
Best friends last forever.
>>> print('~'*50)
~~~~~~~~~~~~~~~~~~~~~~~~~~~~~~~~~~~~~~~~~~~~~~~~~~
>>> love = ('like' * 10)
>>> print(love)
likelikelikelikelikelikelikelikelikelike
```

②
```
>>> time = 30
>>> print('You have' + time + 'minutes left.')
Traceback (most recent call last):
File "<stdin>", line 1, in <module>
TypeError: can only concatenate str (not "int") to str
>>>print('You have ' + str (time) + ' minutes left.')
You have 30 minutes left.
```

Explanation

① You have just practiced string concatenation using +, whitespaces, commas, and * to manipulate the output. String concatenation is an essential skill in coding.

② The variable was assigned with an integer, 30. You cannot concatenate an integer with strings, first, convert the integer into a string using the `str()` method, which converts an integer data type into a string data type. This conversion is also known as *casting*.

Exercise 2-18: Learn to Change a String Using Curly Brackets and .format()

①
```
>>> 'She is {} years old.'.format(25)
'She is 25 years old.'
>>> 'She is {{}} years old.'.format()
'She is {} years old.'
>>> 'She is {{}} years old.'.format(25)
'She is {} years old.'
>>> 'She is {{{}}} years old.'.format(25)
'She is {25} years old.'
```

②
```
>>> 'Learning Python 101 is {}.'.format('important')
'Learning Python 101 is important.'
>>> '{} {} {} {} {}'.format ('Learning', 'Python', 101, 'is', 'important.')
'Learning Python 101 is important.'
```

③
```
>>> '{} | {} | {}'.format ('bread', 'quantity', 'date')
bread | quantity | date
>>> '{} | {} | {}'.format ('bagel', '100', '01/12/2020')
'bagel | 100 | 01/12/2020'
```

Explanation

① Change the string using {} (curly brackets) and the `.format()` method. To show {} within a string, you must use double curly brackets. To show {`value`} within a string, you must use triple curly brackets.

② Use multiple curly brackets with the `.format()` method to form a string.

③ You can also create a table-like format using curly brackets and the pipe (|) symbol.

Exercise 2-19: Adjust the Text Position with Curly Brackets and .format()

①
```
>>> '{}|{}'.format ('bagel', '10')
'bagel|10'
>>> '{} | {}'.format ('bagel', '10')
'bagel | 10'
>>> '{0:1} | {1:1}'.format ('bagel', '10')
'bagel | 10'
```

②
```
>>> '{0:1} | {0:1}'.format ('bagel', '10')
bagel | bagel
>>> ('{0:1} | {0:1} | {1:1} | {1:1}'.format ('bagel', '10'))
'bagel | bagel | 10 | 10'
```

③
```
>>> '{0:>1} | {1:1}'.format ('bagel', '10')
'bagel | 10'
>>> '{0:>10} | {1:1}'.format ('bagel', '10')
bagel | 10'
>>> '{0:>20} | {1:1}'.format ('bagel', '10')
bagel | 10'
```

④
```
>>> '{0:^10} | {1:^10}'.format ('bagel', '10') ' bagel | 10 '
>>> '{0:^20} | {1:^20}'.format ('bagel', '10')
Bagel    |    10    '
>>> '{0:^30} | {1:^30}'.format ('bagel', '10')
Bagel   |    10    '
```

Explanation

① You can adjust text positions using options within curly brackets and `format()` methods. The string positioning special characters include < (adjust to left), ^ (adjust to center), or > (adjust to right). The examples here show you the default indexing and positioning of items if you leave curly brackets blank or filled in.

② You can page the items as you like at any place in the string.

③ The greater-than symbol (>) is used to move the string x spaces. `{0:>10}` means that the first indexed item will end at position 10 and so forth. The first integer, 0, in `{0:>1}` refers to the first item in tuple, `('bagel', '10')`, so it refers to bagel. Similarly, the first integer 1 in `{1:1}` refers to the second item, 10.

④ These examples showcase what happens when you adjust both strings using different positioning values and center them.

Exercise 2-20: Adjust the Number of Decimal Places

①
```
>>> '{0:^10} | {1:10}'.format('pizza', 27.333333)
' pizza | 27.333333'
>>> '{0:^10} | {1:10.2f}'.format('pizza', 27.333333)
'  pizza   |    27.33'
```

②
```
>>> '{0:^10} | {1:10}'.format('Cisco IOS XE 4351', 16.1203)
'Cisco IOS XE 4351 | 16.1203'
>>> '{0:1} | {1:10.2f}'.format('Cisco IOS XE 4351', 16.1203)
'Cisco IOS XE 4351 |    16.12'
```

③
```
>>> '{0:1} | {1:1.2f}'.format('Cisco IOS XE 4351', 16.1203)
'Cisco IOS XE 4351 | 16.12'

>>> router = ('Cisco IOS XE 4351', 16.1203)
>>> router[0] + ' | ' + str( round(router[1], 2))
'Cisco IOS XE 4351 | 16.12'
```

Explanation

① Using `nf`, you can format the number of decimal places. Here, `n` is the number of decimal places, and `f` represents the format specifier. Hence, `2f` means to reduce the float to two decimal places. To better understand the format specifier or any other content in this book, you must enter the lines and learn from your keyboard and screen.

② Apply formatting to a network example.

③ Another way to achieve the same result is to use the concatenation and round method in your code. First, use the indexing method to call out the router name with `'router[0]`. Second, index the second item, `float` (Cisco IOS XE version number). Third, use the round method with decimal reference of 2. Fourth, convert the shortened float as a string. Finally, use the + method to concatenate the values as a string.

Exercise 2-21: Ask for and Receive User Input with input()

①
```
>>> fav_bread = input('Name of your favorite bread: ')
Name of your favorite bread: pita
>>> print(fav_bread)
Pita

>>> num_bread = input("How many " + fav_bread + " would you like? ")
How many pita would you like? 5
>>> print(num_bread)
5

>>> 'So, you wanted {} {} bread.'.format(num_bread, fav_bread)
'So, you wanted 5 pita bread.'
```

Explanation

① You can use input() to receive the user's input through the keyboard. The previous example shows that the input() function takes user input and can store the returned information as variables. You can recall the stored information from your computer's random memory.

Exercise 2-22: Change a Word or Characters in a String

①
```
>>> your_phone = 'iPhone 12 Pro'
>>> your_phone.split()
['iPhone', '12', 'Pro']
>>> your_phone = your_phone.split()
>>> your_phone
['iPhone', '12', 'Pro']
>>> your_phone[2] = 'ProMax'
>>> your_phone
['iPhone', '12', 'ProMax']
>>> " ".join(your_phone) # " " has a whitespace
'iPhone 12 ProMax'
```

②
```
>>> my_phone = 'Galaxy S10 +'
>>> len(my_phone)
12
>>> my_phone = list(my_phone)
>>> my_phone
['G', 'a', 'l', 'a', 'x', 'y', ' ', 'S', '1', '0', ' ', '+']
>>> my_phone[8], my_phone[11] = '2', 'Ultra'
>>> my_phone
['G', 'a', 'l', 'a', 'x', 'y', ' ', 'S', '2', '0', ' ', 'Ultra']
>>> "".join(my_phone) # "" has no whitespace
'Galaxy S20 Ultra'
```

Explanation

① The first example teaches you how to split a string and replace a word. Your aim here is to replace the word Pro with ProMax. So, you have used the split() method and then indexed the third item pro and replaced it with ProMax; then we used the " ".join method with spacing to put the strings back together. Your phone is now iPhone 12 ProMax.

② In this exercise, you aim to convert the string Galaxy S10 + into Galaxy S20 Ultra. Because of a Python string's immutable nature, to replace characters in a string, you must use a workaround. So, the 9th character, 1, must be replaced with 2, and the 12th character, + must be replaced with the word Ultra. Remember, in Python, the index starts from 0, so index 8 is the 9th character, and index 11 is the 12th character.

First, use the list () method to split the string into individual characters in a list. Then use indexing to replace 1 and + with 2 and Ultra. Finally, use the .join method with no spacing separator "" to join all the elements.

You may think that the previous exercise is rather anal. If you enjoyed the previous exercises, you will probably enjoy writing code as you have excellent attention to detail.

Recap: Variables and Strings

Here's a recap of variables and strings:

- A string is an immutable sequence data type.
- You can express strings in either single or double quotation marks.
- Variables are labels for a location in memory.
- A variable can hold a value.
- Python uses basic variable naming conventions to make code more readable and usable.
- A Python variable must start with a letter, word, or words with underscore separator(s). It cannot start with an integer, special characters, or space, and if more than two words are used, you cannot place whitespace between two words.
- As a best practice, avoid using Python reserved words or function names as variable names.
- A function is a reusable piece of code written to do a specific task.
- You have learned about using the built-in functions, `print()`, `len()`, `str()`, and `list()`, to work with string data types.

Table 2-3 contains the reserved keywords in Python 3.8; avoid using these words as your variable names.

Table 2-3. *Python 3 Reserved Keywords*

and	del	from	not	while
as	elif	global	or	with
assert	else	if	pass	yield
break	except	import	~~print~~	FALSE
class	exec	in	raise	TRUE
continue	finally	is	return	None
def	for	lambda	try	nonlocal

* print is a keyword in Python 2 but it is a function in Python 3.

Unlike in Python 2.7, in Python 3.x, the `print` statement is a built-in function, not a reserved keyword.

To view reserved keywords, type `help("keywords")` in your Python interpreter.

To view the full list of built-ins, type **dir(__builtins__)** in your Python interpreter.

Numbers and Arithmetic Operators

Next, you will continue learning about the numbers, operators, and functions using simple examples. Arithmetic is all about numbers, and mathematics is all about theory; here, we are dealing only with numbers.

Exercise 2-23: Use Arithmetic Operators

①
```
>>> 1 + 2
3
>>> 1 - 2
-1
>>> 1 * 2
2
>>> 1 / 2
0.5
```

②
```
>>> 1 + 2.0
3.0
```

③
```
>>> 2 ** 3
8
```

④
```
>>> 7 // 3
2
```

⑤
```
>>> 7 % 3
1
>>> 4 % 2
0
```

Explanation

① Addition, subtraction, multiplication, and division operators can carry out the calculation of numbers.

② When Python calculates an integer and a float, the result takes a form of a float.

③ Python expresses 2 to the power of 3 as 2**3.

④ // performs a floor division. 7 contains two lots of 3, so the correct answer is 2 and the remaining 1 is discarded.

⑤ To find a remainder, you can use the % symbol.

Exercise 2-24: Understand Integers vs. Strings

①
```
>>> int_3 = 3
>>> str_3 = '3'
>>> total = int_3 + str_3
raceback (most recent call last):
File "<pyshell#304>", line 1, in <module> total = int_3 + str_3
TypeError: unsupported operand type(s) for +: 'int' and 'str'
```

②
```
>>> total = int_3 + int(str_3)
>>> print(total)
6
```

Explanation

① Assign an integer to a variable, and assign a string to another variable. Use an operator to add the two. Python will return a `TypeError`. You can only perform additions of the same object types.

② Now use the `int()` method to convert the string into an integer, and it will perform standard calculation and return 6.

Recap: Arithmetic Operators

Here's a recap of arithmetic operators:

- Python uses arithmetic operators to perform calculations with integers. When used with strings, the plus sign (+) can concatenate a series of strings, and the multiplier sign (*) can multiply a string n number of times. Table 2-4 shows Python arithmetic operators.

Table 2-4. *Python Arithmetic Operators*

Operator	Meaning
+	Addition
-	Subtraction
*	Multiplication
/	Division
**	Power of
//	Floor division
%	Remainder

- When entering numbers, do not use quotation marks.
- If a number is in quotation marks, Python recognizes the object as a string.
- To convert a string into an integer, use the `int()` function.
- To convert a string to decimal, use the `float()` function.

Booleans and Relational Operators

We'll now look at Booleans and relational operators.

Exercise 2-25: Use Booleans

①
```
>>> a = True
>>> b = False

>>> print(a)
True
>>> print(b)
False
>>> type (a)
<class 'bool'>
>>> type (b)
<class 'bool'>
```

②
```
>>> type (True)
<class 'bool'>
>>> print((1).__bool__())
True
>>> type (False)
<class 'bool'>
>>> print((0).__bool__())
False
```

Explanation

① A Boolean can have a value of either `True` or `False`. Boolean tests the `True` or `False` value of some conditions.

② In a Boolean operation, the constant 1 represents `True`, and 0 represents `False`. You can use the `bool` method to test the value 1 or 0 in a Boolean operation. The constants defined to be false include `None` and `False`. Zero of any numeric type—0, 0.0, 0j, decimal(0), integer(0.1)—are all `False`. Also, empty sequences and collections—' ', (), [], {}, set(), range(0)—are also `False`.

Exercise 2-26: Use Relational Operators

The following is a Boolean table put together as an exercise. Do not waste your time staring at a Boolean table to understand Boolean operators. Instead, do the following exercise to wrap your head around Boolean operators.

①
```
>>> 1 == 2                    # Equal to
False
>>> 1 > 2                     # Greater than
False
>>> 1 >= 2                    # Greater or equal to
False
>>> 1 < 2                     # Less than
True
>>> 1 <= 2                    # Less or equal to
True
>>> 1 != 2                    # Not equal to
True
```

Explanation

① The relational operators are self-explanatory, so the more you practice, the better you will get with their usage.

Exercise 2-27: Use Boolean Expressions to Test True or False

①
```
>>> True and True is True
True
>>> True and False is False
True
>>> False and True is False
False
>>> False and False is False
False
>>> not True is False
True
>>> not False is True
True
```

Explanation

① In the previous examples, Python tests the `True` and `False` of each statement to understand Booleans better. Staring at the book may not make any sense; type in the Boolean statements into your Python interpreter window.

Exercise 2-28: Use Logical (Membership) Operators

①
```
>>> True and False or not False
True
>>> True and False or True
True
>>> False or True
True
>>> True or False
True
```

Explanation

① The previous conditionals always return the result as `True`. The logical operators `and`, `or`, and `not` are also known as *membership operators* in Python.

Exercise 2-29: Change the Order of Operation with ()

①
```
>>> True and False or not False
True
```

②
```
>>> (True and False) or (not False)
True
```

③
```
>>> ((True and False) or (not False))
True
```

Explanation

① This example is simple conditional testing from left to right.

② Using parentheses, you can alter the order of operation, although, in this example, the expected output is the same, `True`.

③ Using parentheses, you can change the flow of evaluation.

Control Statements: if, elif, and else

Let's talk about control statements.

Exercise 2-30: Use if and else

①
```
>>> if 1 < 2:
...     print('One is less than two.')
...
One is less than two.
```

②
```
>>> if 1 > 2:
...     print('One is bigger than two.')
...
>>>
```

③
```
>>> if 1 > 2:
...     print('One is bigger than two.')
... else:
...     print('One is NOT bigger than two.')
...
One is NOT bigger than two.
```

Explanation

① The `if` statement can be a single statement. If the condition is `True`, it will run the next statement, which is the `print` statement.

② If the `if` statement is `False`, it will exit from the `if` loop. As you can see, the conditional statement ends with a semicolon (:).

③ This is an if and else example; the first condition is not met so that the else statement will catch all other conditions.

Exercise 2-31: Use if, elif, and else

①
```
>>> age = 21
>>> if age >= 18:
...     print('You are old enough to get your driver\'s license.')
...
You are old enough to get your driver's license.
```

②
```
>>> age = 17
>>> if age >= 18:
...     print('You are old enough to drive a car.')
else:
...     print('You are too young to drive a car.')
...
You are too young to drive a car.
```

③
```
>>> age = 100
>>> if age <18:
...     print('You are too young to drive a car.') elif age> 99:
...     print('You are too old to drive a car.')
else:
...     print('You are in an eligible age group, so you can drive a car.')
...
You are too old to drive a car.
```

Explanation

① In this exercise, you have used only a single `if` statement.

② In this exercise, you have used the `if` and `else` statements.

③ In this last exercise, you used the `if`, `elif`, and `else` statements. If there are more conditions, you can use as many `elif` statements as required.

Exercise 2-32: Write Code with if, elif, and else

Step 1. For this exercise, in your Python shell, go to File ➤ New File. Type the source code into Python's built-in text editor.

①
```
# Enter the following code and save it as a .py file format. # ex2_32.py

q1 = input ('What is your legal age?') age = int(q1)

if age < 16:
...     print('You are too young to take a driving test.')
elif age > 99:
...     print('You are too old to take a driving test.')
else:
...     print('You\'re in the right age group to take a driving test.')
...
```

Step 2. From the text editor's menu, go to File ➤ Save and save the file as `ex2_32.py`. Afterward, save your code as `driverage.py` under the Python root folder `C:\Python39`. In the Python text editor, go to Run ➤ Run module or press the F5 key to run your script. Then your Python shell will prompt you to enter your age as follows:

②
```
What is your legal age? 15
You are too young to take a driving test.
```

③
```
What is your legal age? 18
You're in the right age group to take a driving test.
```

④
```
What is your legal age? 100
You are too old to take a driving test.
```

Explanation

① This source code uses the Python basics we have learned so far and uses `if`, `elif`, and `else` statements for flow control. Also, user input is required to test the conditions and run the next line of code accordingly.

② Example 1 of the ex2_32.py script runs.

③ Example 2 of the ex2_32.py script runs.

④ Example 3 of the ex2_32.py script runs.
If you are running this script on Linux/macOS, you can run the code by typing `python3 ex2_32.py` from where you saved your Python source file.

Recap: Boolean and Conditionals

Here's a recap:

- Boolean data types deal with a condition's truthiness, which is if something is `True` or `False`.
- The relational operators compare one number with another to answer as a Boolean.
- In Boolean, you can change the order of operations using round brackets, ( ).
- Express more complex conditionals using Boolean logical operators such as `and` and `not`.
- The logical operators `and`, `or`, and `not` in Boolean are also known as *membership operators*.
- `and` is True if both or more conditions are true.
- `or` is True even if only one of several conditions is true.
- `not` calculates the inverse condition of the used operator.
- In Boolean, operations are executed in the order of `not`, `and`, then `or`.
- Control statements such as `if`, `elif`, and `else` are used with the Boolean operators in Python code.

Functions

Let's talk about functions.

Exercise 2-33: Defining a Function

①
```
>>> def say_hello():
...     print('Hello')
...
>>> say_hello()
Hello
```

②
```
>>> say_goodbye()
Traceback (most recent call last): File "<stdin>", line 1, in <module>
NameError: name 'say_goodbye' is not defined
```

Explanation

① In Python, you define functions using the word `def` and always end with a colon. You can create a new function in the following format:
`def function_name(): # Code block`

② If you use a function without defining it, a `NameError` will be encountered.

Exercise 2-34: Assign Default Values to a Function

①
```
>>> def say_hello(name):
...     print('Hello {}.'.format (name))
...
>>> say_hello('Hugh')
Hello Hugh.
```

②
```
>>> say_hello()
Traceback (most recent call last):
File "<stdin>", line 1, in <module>
TypeError: say_hello() missing 1 required positional argument: 'name'
```

③
```
>>> def say_hello(name = 'son'):
...     print('Hi {}.'. format (name))
...
>>> say_hello()
Hi son.
>>> say_hello('Hugh')
Hi Hugh.
```

Explanation

① This is a function that returns a `Hello` when you enter a name.

② If you forget to enter a name, `TypeError` will be returned.

③ In this example, you have assigned a default name to make the code run without `TypeError`. You can consider it as an error handling mechanism. We will learn about error handling in the later exercises.

Exercise 2-35: Define Hello and Goodbye Functions

①
```
>>> def say_hello(f_name, s_name):
...     print('Hello {} {}!'. format (f_name, s_name))
...
>>> say_hello ('Michael', 'Shoesmith')
Hello Michael Shoesmith!

>>> say_hello ('Michael')
Traceback (most recent call last):
File "<stdin>", line 1, in <module>
TypeError: say_hello() missing 1 required positional argument: 's_name'
```

②
```
>>> >>> say_hello(f_name='Leah', s_name='Taylor')
Hello Leah Taylor!

>>> say_hello(s_name = 'Johnson', f_name = 'Caitlin')
Hello Caitlin Johnson!
```

③
```
>>> def say_goodbye(f_name, s_name = 'Doe'):
...    print('Goodbye {} {}!'. format (f_name, s_name))
...
>>> say_goodbye('John')

Goodbye John Doe!
>>> say_goodbye('John', 'Citizen')
Goodbye John Citizen!
```

Explanation

① In this example, you have defined the `say_hello` function with two variables. This means when the function runs, it would expect two positional arguments. If you give only a single argument, you will encounter `TypeError` with a missing argument.

② If variable names are used to call the function, the order of variables does not matter as the function uses the named variables.

③ You can also assign a default variable value to the function to accept even the single positional argument's responses. In this example, one or two arguments are accepted and processed without the `TypeError`. This could be an acceptable error avoidance strategy to continue your code to run.

Exercise 2-36: Use the Odd or Even Function

①
```
>>> def odd_or_even(number):
...     if number%2 == 0:
...         return 'even'
...     else:
...         return 'odd'
...

>>> odd_or_even(3)
'odd'
>>> odd_or_even(4)
'even'
```

②
```
>>> def even_num(number):
...     if number%2 == 0:
...         return True
...     else:
...         return False
...

>>> even_num(1)
False
>>> even_num(2)
True
```

Explanation

① You have just made a simple application returning whether a number is even or odd. Do not look at the function's simplicity; think about how you can apply it at work.

② You can tweak example ① and make it into a `True` or `False` function. Try to learn the basics of Python each day and think about scenarios or applications to use such functions.

Exercise 2-37: Nest a Function Within a Function

①
```
>>> def name():
...     n = input('Enter your name: ')
...         return n
...
>>> def say_name(n):
...     print('Your name is {}.'.format(n))
...
>>> def say_the_name():
...     n = name()
...         say_name(n) #The first function is nested here.
...
>>> say_the_name()
Enter your name: Michael Shoesmith Your name is Michael Shoesmith.
```

Explanation

① You have created two functions, and then on the third function, you have nested (reused) them. This is a straightforward exercise, but if a function is lengthy and complicated, you can save the code lines as a separate file and import a specific function as a customized module. You will learn about modules in the later chapters, so in this section, try to focus on the Python syntax.

Recap: Functions

Here's a recap:

- Define a function before use. The basic function syntax begins with `def function_name(parameter_name):`.
- A function can perform any action with small code in the reusable main code and return data.
- Functions can take parameters, or you can set default parameter values to use arbitrary parameters.
- Functions can be used to control the flow of your script.
- You can get more help by using the built-in function `help()` and then type in `def`.

Lists

Let's talk about lists.

Exercise 2-38: Create a List and Index Items

①
```
>>> vehicles = ['car', 'bus', 'truck']
>>> print(vehicles[0])
car
>>> print(vehicles[1])
bus
>>> print(vehicles[2])
Truck
```

②
```
>>> vehicles = ['car', 'bus', 'truck']
>>> vehicles[0] = 'motorbike'
>>> vehicles

['motorbike', 'bus', 'truck']
```

③
```
>>> print(vehicles[-1])
truck
>>> print(vehicles[-2])
bus
>>> print(vehicles[-3])
Motorbike
```

④
```
>>> vehicles
['motorbike', 'bus', 'truck']
>>> vehicles[0] = ['sedan', 'wagon', 'convertible', 'SUV']
>>> vehicles
[['sedan', 'wagon', 'convertible', 'SUV'], 'bus', 'truck']
```

⑤
```
>>> cars = ['sedan', 'wagon', 'SUV', 'hatchback']
>>> for car in range(len(cars)):
...     print('{} is at position {}. '.format(cars[car], car))
...
sedan is at position 0. wagon is at position 1. SUV is at position 2. hatchback is at
position 3.
```

Explanation

① In Python, lists are written with square brackets. In this example, only strings items are used, but the list supports all other data types. The indexing starts from 0 and increases by one, so to page `truck`, which is the third item in the list, index [2].

② A list is a collection that is ordered and mutable. So you can replace an item using the indexing method. In this exercise, `car` has been replaced with `motorbike`.

③ You can use minus signs to index items backward. More slicing examples will follow soon.

④ The list can also contain most of the other data types. This example shows a list of cars as part of the parent list, `vehicle`.

⑤ In example ①, you have seen that the indexing starts at 0. Quickly write a function to check the item positions and see if it starts at 0.

Exercise 2-39: Use append, extend, and insert in a List

①
```
>>> cars = ['sedan', 'SUV', 'hatchback']
>>> cars.append('convertible')
>>> cars
['sedan', 'SUV', 'hatchback', 'convertible']
```

②
```
>>> cars.extend(['crossover', '4WD'])
>>> cars
['sedan', 'SUV', 'hatchback', 'convertible', 'crossover', '4WD']
```

③
```
>>> cars.insert(1, 'wagon')
>>> cars
['sedan', 'wagon', 'SUV', 'hatchback', 'convertible', 'crossover', '4WD']
```

Explanation

① append adds an item at the end of a list.

② To add multiple items to the end of a list, use the `extend()` function.

③ To insert an item in a specific location, use an index number to insert the new item. In this example, wagon was inserted in index 1 and pushed the other items to the right index.

Slicing

Let's talk about slicing.

Exercise 2-40: Slice a List

①
```
>>> bread = ['bagels', 'baguette', 'ciabatta', 'crumpet', 'naan', 'pita', 'tortilla']
>>> some_bread = bread[1:3]
>>> some_bread
['baguette', 'ciabatta']
>>> print('Some Bread: {}'.format (some_bread))
Some Bread: ['baguette', 'ciabatta']
```

②
```
>>> first_two = bread[0:2]
>>> first_two
['bagels', 'baguette']
```

③
```
>>> first_three_bread = bread[:3]
>>> print(first_three_bread)
['bagels', 'baguette', 'ciabatta']
```

④
```
>>> last_two_bread = bread[-2:]
>>> print('Last two bread: {}'.format (last_two_bread))
Last two bread: ['pita', 'tortilla']
```

⑤
```
>>> bread = ['bagels', 'baguette', 'ciabatta']
>>> ciabatta_index = bread.index('ciabatta')
>>> print(ciabatta_index)
2
```

Explanation

① You can use the slicing method to call the items in a list. In this example, we want to index items 1 and 2, so we have to use [1:3]. The first indexed item is included but not the last indexed item.
You can also use the `print()` function to prettify your output.

② If you want the first two items, use [0:2] as the slicing index.

③ If you do not specify the start index number, Python will page from index 0.

④ You can also page backward using minus indexing.

⑤ You can also create a variable and check the index number of an item from the list.

Exceptions and Error Handling

Let's talk about exceptions and error handling.

Exercise 2-41: Avoid a ValueError Error

①
```
>>> bread = ['bagels', 'baguette', 'ciabatta']
>>> crumpet_index = bread.index('crumpet')
Traceback (most recent call last): File "<stdin>", line 1, in <module> ValueError:
'crumpet' is not in list
```

Explanation

① You will encounter `ValueError` if you page an item that does not exist in a list.

Exercise 2-42: Handle Errors with try and except in a List

Learn the concept of error handling.

■ **Hint** When an error occurs, your program will suddenly stop. When Python runs into an error, it detects it as a sign to stop and exit the application. If you know what errors are expected, in most of the scenarios, you want to be in control of how errors are handled. Do not let Python decide what to do with the errors.

■ **Note** You have to save the following code in a file and save it as `ex2_42.py`.

---

①
```
>>> bread = ['bagels', 'baguette', 'ciabatta']
>>> try:
...     crumpet_index = bread.index('crumpet')
... except:
...     crumpet_index = 'No crumpet bread found.'
...     print(crumpet_index)
...
No crumpet bread found.
```

② Open Notepad++ and enter the following lines of code as shown in Figure 2-5. Then save the file as ex2_42.py under the C:\Python39\ folder.

```
# ex2_42.py
bread = ['bagels', 'baguette', 'ciabatta']
try:
    crumpet_index = bread.index('crumpet')
except:
    crumpet_index = 'No crumpet bread found.'
print(crumpet_index)
```

After saving the file, press Ctrl+F6 combo keys to run the script.

```
#Output:
C:\Python39\python.exe "C:\Python39\ex2_42.py"
Process started (PID=6916) >>>
No crumpet bread found.
<<< Process finished (PID=6916). (Exit code 0)
================ READY ================
```

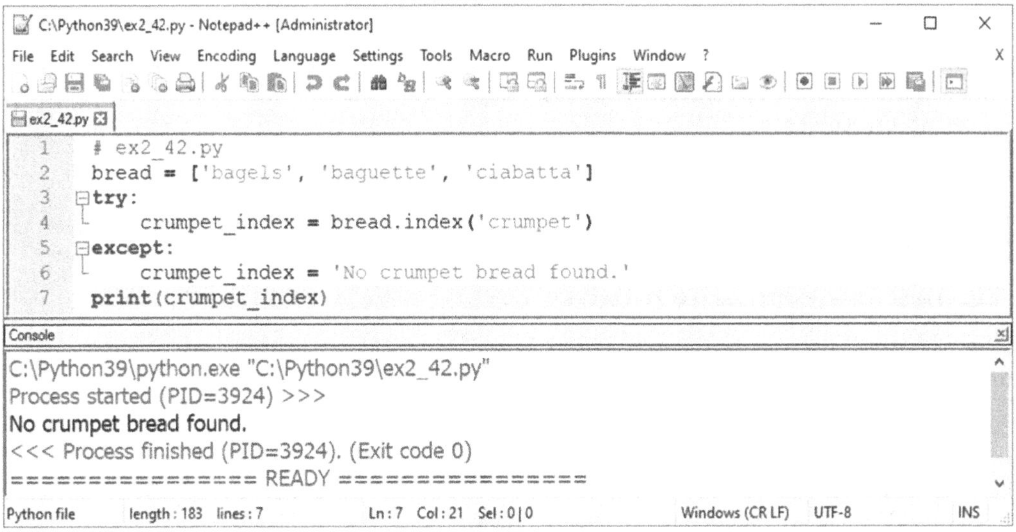

Figure 2-5. *Python coding on Notepad++ example*

Explanation

① When you encounter errors in an application, the program must continue running the rest of the application, or it will stop to prevent more significant problems. Errors are a constructive part of the script, and they help your application stop, so it does not cause more problems. So, as a programmer, you want to know which errors are expected and how you want to handle them when they occur. If you know how to handle errors like `ValueError` in the previous example in this exercise, you will have cleaner Python code. You can customize and process the error message as you want to express it. In the previous example, the error message tells explicitly that the paged bread type, crumpet, does not exist.

② It is much easier to use a text editor than coding it directly in Python IDLE in this example. The figure showed you the source code ex2_42.py in Notepad++ and ran the code by pressing Ctrl+F6 keys.

Exercise 2-43: Find an Index of an Item in a List with the Customized Exception

---

Note Save the code with the exercise name given and run it from the Python prompt. All the code is available for download from the GitHub site. The file names are ex2_43_1.py for Exercise 2-43 ① and ex2_43_2.py for Exercise 2-43 ②.

---

①
```
# ex2_43_1.py
bread = ['bagels', 'baguette', 'ciabatta', 'crumpet']

try:
    crumpet_index = bread.index ('crumpet')
except:
    crumpet_index = 'No crumpet bread was found.'
    print(crumpet_index)

# Output from Notepad++
C:\Python39\python.exe "C:\Python39\ex2_43_1.py"
Process started (PID=5852) >>>
<<< Process finished (PID=5852). (Exit code 0)
================ READY ================
```

②
```
# ex2_43_2.py
bread = ['bagels', 'baguette', 'ciabatta', 'naan']

try:
    crumpet_index = bread.index ('crumpet')
except:
    crumpet_index = 'No crumpet bread was found.'
    print(crumpet_index)

# Output from Notepad++
C:\Python39\python.exe "C:\Python39\ex2_43_2"
Process started (PID=4580) >>>
No crumpet bread was found.
<<< Process finished (PID=4580). (Exit code 0)
================ READY ================
```

Explanation

① In this example, we are trying to find the index number of `crumpet`. `bread.index('crumpet')` will look for the index number of the item. In the output, index 3 is returned.

② If we replace `crumpet` with naan bread and run the script, then it will return a customized exception error as shown in the output.

Practicing Lists

Practice the list concepts you have learned so far. I encourage you to type in every single word and character shown. While you are typing, try to guess what the exercise is trying to teach you. You might be getting tired, but nobody will practice these exercises for you; you have to do everything yourself.

Exercise 2-44: Practice a List

①
```
>>> shopping_list1 = 'baseball hat, baseball shoes, sunglasses, baseball bat, sunscreen lotion, baseball meat'
>>> print(shopping_list1)
baseball hat, baseball shoes, sunglasses, baseball bat, sunscreen lotion, baseball meat
>>> type(shopping_list1)
<class 'str'>
```

②
```
shopping_list2 = ['baseball hat', 'baseball shoes', 'sunglasses', 'baseball bat',
'sunscreen lotion', 'baseball meat']
>>> print(shopping_list2 [2])
sunglasses
>>> type(shopping_list2)
<class 'list'>
```

③
```
>>> shopping_list2 = ['baseball hat', 'baseball shoes', 'sunglasses', 'baseball bat',
'sunscreen lotion', 'baseball meat']
>>> shopping_list2.pop(5)
'baseball meat'
>>> shopping_list2
['baseball hat', 'baseball shoes', 'sunglasses', 'baseball bat', 'sunscreen lotion']
```

④
```
>>> print(shopping_list2 [2])
sunglasses
>>> print(shopping_list2 [2: 5])
['sunglasses', 'baseball bat', 'sunscreen lotion']
```

⑤
```
>>> shopping_list2 [2] = 'ball'
>>> print(shopping_list2)
['baseball hat', 'baseball shoes', 'ball', 'baseball bat', 'sunscreen lotion']
```

⑥
```
>>> some_numbers = [1, 3, 5]
>>> some_strings = ['which', 'Olympic', 'sports']
>>> numbers_and_strings = ['which', 1, 'Olympic', 3, 'sports', 5]
```

⑦
```
>>> numbers = [3, 6, 9, 12]
>>> strings = ['soccer', 'baseball', 'basketball', 'swimming']
>>> new_list = [numbers, strings]
>>> print(new_list)
[[3, 6, 9, 12], ['soccer', 'baseball', 'basketball', 'swimming']]
```

⑧
```
>>> summer_sports = ['swimming', 'diving', 'baseball', 'basketball', 'cricket']
>>> summer_sports.append ('beach volleyball')
>>> print(summer_sports)
['swimming', 'diving', 'baseball', 'basketball', 'cricket', 'beach volleyball']
```

⑨
```
>>> print(summer_sports)
['swimming', 'diving', 'baseball', 'basketball', 'cricket', 'beach volleyball']
>>> del summer_sports [1]
>>> print(summer_sports)
['swimming', 'baseball', 'basketball', 'cricket', 'beach volleyball']
```

⑩
```
>>> summer_sports = ['swimming', 'baseball', 'basketball', 'cricket', 'beach volleyball']
>>> winter_sports = ['skiing', 'ice skating', 'ice hockey', 'snowboarding']
>>> print(summer_sports + winter_sports)
['swimming', 'baseball', 'basketball', 'cricket', 'beach volleyball', 'skiing', 'ice
skating', 'ice hockey', 'snowboarding']
```

Explanation

① You have just created `shopping_list1` as a string.

② `Shopping_list2` is a list as the items are wrapped around [ ] (square brackets), a square bracket set. Use indexing to return sunglasses.

③ Indexing does not change the list, but if you use the `pop()` method, it will take the called item out permanently.

④ Using a single index or a range of indexes, you can call out the items from a list.

⑤ You can insert a new item into the list using the indexing as a mutable object.

⑥ The list can contain numbers or strings or a combination of unique items.

⑦ A list can store another list.

⑧ You can use the `append()` method to join two lists and make them into one list.

⑨ Use del and indexing to delete items you want to delete from your list.

⑩ You can concatenate lists using the + operator.

Using for Loops and while Loops

Let's talk about loops.

Exercise 2-45: Use the for Loop's upper() and capitalize() Methods

①
```
>>> bread_type = ['bagels', 'baguette', 'ciabatta']
>>> for bread in bread_type:
...     print(bread.upper())
...
BAGELS
BAGUETTE
CIABATTA
```

②
```
>>> bread_type = ['bagels', 'baguette', 'ciabatta']
>>> for bread in bread_type:
...     print(bread.capitalize())
...
Bagels
Baguette
Ciabatta
```

Explanation

① As the name suggests, the `for` loop loops through the list until the last item is paged from the list. This example calls out the index 0 item first and then goes back to the loop and calls the index 1 item and then the last item, which has index 2. Also, appending `upper()` will convert the returned values into uppercase.

② You can also use Python's `capitalize()` method to change each bread's first letter into capital letters.

Exercise 2-46: Use the while Loop and len() Function

①
```
>>> basket = ['bagels', 'baguette', 'ciabatta', 'crumpet', 'naan', 'pita', 'tortilla']
>>> bread = 0
>>> while bread < len(basket):
...     print(basket[bread], end=" ") # " " contains a whitespace
...     bread += 1
...
bagels baguette ciabatta crumpet naan pita tortilla >>>
```

Explanation

① The while loop and len() function are used to call out and print each bread. This `while` loop uses indexing and loops until the list is empty. Although the `len()` function returns the number of items in an object; in this example, it is used with the `for` loop to return each item until the list is empty. Notice that `end=" "` is used to print the output on a single line.

Sorting and Ranges

Let's talk about sorting and ranges.

Exercise 2-47: Use sort() vs. sorted() in a List

①
```
>>> bread = ['naan', 'baguette', 'tortilla', 'ciabatta', 'pita']
>>> bread.sort()
>>> bread
['baguette', 'ciabatta', 'naan', 'pita', 'tortilla']
```

②
```
>>> bread = ['naan', 'baguette', 'tortilla', 'ciabatta', 'pita']
>>> bread_in_order = sorted(bread)
>>> bread_in_order
['baguette', 'ciabatta', 'naan', 'pita', 'tortilla']
>>> bread
['naan', 'baguette', 'tortilla', 'ciabatta', 'pita']
```

Explanation

① When you use the `sort()` function on a list, it sorts the items from A to Z permanently.

② The `sorted()` function only sorts A to Z temporarily. It does not change the order of the original data. The different effects of the `sort()` and `sorted()` seem to be insignificant and unnoticed to novice Python programmers, but in programming fundamentals, `sorted()` would be the recommended method over the `sort()` method as it does not permanently alter the original item; you can reuse the original item as well as the newly created item as objects.

Exercise 2-48: Link Two Lists

①
```
>>> bread = ['naan', 'baguette', 'tortilla', 'ciabatta', 'pita']
>>> more_bread = ['bagels', 'crumpet']
>>> all_bread = bread + more_bread
>>> print(all_bread)
['naan', 'baguette', 'tortilla', 'ciabatta', 'pita', 'bagels', 'crumpet']
>>> all_bread.sort()
>>> print(all_bread)
['bagels', 'baguette', 'ciabatta', 'crumpet', 'naan', 'pita', 'tortilla']
>> all_bread.reverse()
>>> all_bread
['tortilla', 'pita', 'naan', 'crumpet', 'ciabatta', 'baguette', 'bagels']
```

Explanation

① In this example, we created two lists and then merged them into one list. Then we used the `sort()` function to organize the items in the list from A to Z. Finally, we used the `reverse()` method to reverse the list's order to Z to A.

Exercise 2-49: Find the List Length Using the len() Function

①
```
>>> bread = ['bagels', 'baguette', 'ciabatta']
>>> print(len(bread))
3
>>> bread.append('naan')
>>> print(len(bread))
4
```

Explanation

① Use the `len()` function to check how many bread types are in a list. Next, add another bread type using the append method, and then recheck the number of bread types with the `len()` function. It has increased by 1.

Exercise 2-50: Use range() and the for Loop

①
```
>>> for number in range (3):
...     print(number)
...
0
1
2
```

②
```
>>> for number in range (2, 5):
...     print(number, end=" ")
...
2 3 4
```

③
```
>>> for number in range (1, 8, 2):
...         print(number, end=" ")
...
1 3 5 7
```

④
```
>>> for bread in ['bagels', 'baguette', 'crumpet', 'naan']:
...         print(bread, end=" ")
...
bagels baguette crumpet naan
```

⑤
```
>>> for bread in ('bagels', 'baguette', 'crumpet', 'naan'):
...         print(bread, end=" ")
...
bagels baguette crumpet naan
```

Explanation

① If you use a `for` loop with the `range()` function, you can call out the list items with ease. `range(3)` means up to but not including 3, so this example loops through 0, 1, and 2.

② Using commas, you can specify where to begin and where to finish. In this `for` loop example, the first argument (digit) represents the first number, and the second argument (digit) represents the ceiling number of finishing the loop, so the last number is always going to be n-1, which is 4 in this example.

③ In the previous example, you are using three arguments to loop through a range of numbers. The first and last numbers carry the same meaning as explained in example ② previously, but the last digit, 2, represents the interval or frequency. Starting from 1, it will loop through to odd numbers only until it reaches the ceiling number, 8. So, as expected, Python only prints the odd numbers 1, 3, 5, 7.
You must master the `for` loop well to make your Python scripts work harder for you.

④ You are applying the `for` loop to a list. Instead of a `range()` function, you have used a list with items inside the list.

⑤ You are applying the `for` loop to a tuple. So, what is the difference between this and the previous example? You cannot feel it in these examples, but the difference is in the speed. Since tuples are immutable and have fewer indexing pointers than lists, they can process the data faster while looping through each item in a tuple. If you need to process a million data lines, then speed will matter, so use tuples over lists.

Exercise 2-51: Use the String List for loop() and range() with Arguments

①
```
>>> bread = ['bagels', 'baguette', 'ciabatta', 'crumpet', 'naan', 'pita', 'tortilla']
>>> for number in range (0, len (bread), 2):
...     print(bread [number] , end=" ")
...
bagels ciabatta naan tortilla
```

②
```
>>> bread = ['bagels', 'baguette', 'ciabatta', 'crumpet', 'naan', 'pita', 'tortilla']
>>> for number in range (0, len (bread), 3):
...     print(bread [number] , end=" ")
...
bagels crumpet tortilla
```

③
```
>>> bread = ['bagels', 'baguette', 'ciabatta', 'crumpet', 'naan', 'pita', 'tortilla']
>>> for number in range (0, len (bread), 5):
...      print(bread [number] , end=" ")
...
bagels pita
```

Explanation

① In this example, you have a nested `len()` function inside a `range()` function to loop through a bread list with three arguments similar to Exercise 2-50's example ③. Since the last argument is 2, it will step through the bread list, index items 1, 3, 5, and 7.

② This is the same example as the previous example, but with a stepping value of 3, the indexed items are bagels, crumpet, and tortilla.

③ This is the same example with a stepping value of 5, so this example prints out the first value and sixth values, bagels and pita bread.

Recap: Lists and Loops

Here's a recap:

- When creating and assigning a variable to a list, enclose the elements in square brackets, [ ], and separate each item in the list with a comma. A typical list syntax looks like this:

  ```
  List_name = [element_1, element_2, ..., element_n]
  ```

- List items can be indexed by the index number starting from 0 to n. To index the first item in a list, use index number 0. To index an item from the last item, use an index number of -1.
- Use slicing to index part of a list. For example, use List_Name [3, 6].
- Use a for `loop()` to index a range of numbers in a list.
- A while loop will continue to run as long as the condition is `True` and only stops when the condition becomes `False`.
- You can sort a list using the `sort()` and `sorted()` list methods.
- If you use built-in functions like `range()`, you can index sequential numbers.
- Handle Python exception errors using `try` and `except` code blocks.

Tuples

Let's talk about tuples.

Exercise 2-52: See Some Basic Tuple Examples

①
```
>>> tuple1 = (0, 1, 3, 6, 9)
>>> tuple2 = ('w', 'x', 'y', 'z')
>>> tuple3 = (0, 1, 'x', 2, 'y', 3, 'z')
```

②
```
>>> tuple1 = (0, 1, 3, 6, 9)
>>> tuple [1] = 12
Traceback (most recent call last):
File "<stdin>", line 1, in <module>
TypeError: 'type' object does not support item assignment
```

③
```
>>> tuple1 = (0, 1, 3, 6, 9)
>>> tuple2 = ('w', 'x', 'y', 'z')
>>> print(tuple1 + tuple2)
(0, 1, 3, 6, 9, 'w', 'x', 'y', 'z')
```

Explanation

① These are examples of tuples. Notice that tuples are almost identical to lists, except the items are wrapped around a set of the round brackets, ( ). Notice that they are aesthetically different.

② You have tried to change 1 to 12, and tuple will spit the dummy back at you with a `TypeError`. Therefore, tuples are known as *immutable sequential objects* in Python.

③ But you can still conjoin two tuples together by using the + sign.

Exercise 2-53: Convert a Tuple to a List

①
```
>>> tuple3 = (0, 1, 'x', 2, 'y', 3, 'z')
>>> list (tuple3)
[0, 1, 'x', 2, 'y', 3, 'z']
```

②
```
>>> tuple1 = (0, 1, 3, 6, 9)
>>> tuple2 = ('w', 'x', 'y', 'z')
>>> list (tuple1 + tuple2)
[0, 1, 3, 6, 9, 'w', 'x', 'y', 'z']
```

Explanation

① To change a tuple into a list, use `list(tuple_name)`.

② You can conjoin two or more tuples and still convert them using the `list()` conversion technique.

Exercise 2-54: Determine Whether a Tuple Immutable

①
```
>>> days_of_the_week = ('Monday', 'Tuesday', 'Wednesday', 'Thursday', 'Friday',
'Saturday', 'Sunday')>>> for day in days_of_the_week:
...     print(day, end=" ")
...
Monday Tuesday Wednesday Thursday Friday Saturday Sunday
```

②
```
>>> days_of_the_week = ('Monday', 'Tuesday', 'Wednesday', 'Thursday', 'Friday',
'Saturday', 'Sunday')
>>> days_of_the_week [0] = 'Funday'
Traceback (most recent call last):
File "<stdin>", line 1, in <module>
TypeError: 'tuple' object does not support item assignment
```

③
```
>>> days_of_the_week = ('Monday', 'Tuesday', 'Wednesday', 'Thursday', 'Friday',
'Saturday', 'Sunday')
>>> print(days_of_the_week)
('Monday', 'Tuesday', 'Wednesday', 'Thursday', 'Friday', 'Saturday', 'Sunday')
>>> del days_of_the_week
>>> print(days_of_the_week)
Traceback (most recent call last):
File "<stdin>", line 1, in <module>
NameError: name 'days_of_the_week' is not defined
```

Explanation

① This is a simple tuple example containing the days of a week.

② When you try to update an item with another, Python will return a `TypeError` to remind you that a tuple is an immutable object in Python.

③ Although tuples are immutable, it does not mean you cannot delete the whole tuple. Use `del tuple_name` to delete a tuple.

Exercise 2-55: Convert a Tuple to a List and a List to a Tuple

①
```
>>> weekend_tuple = ('Saturday', 'Sunday')
>>> weekend_list = list (weekend_tuple)
>>> print('weekend_tuple is {}.'. format (type (weekend_tuple)))
weekend_tuple is <class 'tuple'>.
>>> print('weekend_list is {}.'. format (type (weekend_list)))
weekend_list is <class 'list'>.
```

②
```
>>> country_list = ['US', 'England', 'Germany', 'France']
>>> country_tuple = tuple (country_list)
>>> type (country_list)
<class 'list'>
>>> type (country_tuple)
<class 'tuple'>
```

Explanation

① This is a simple example of converting a tuple to a list. You can check the data type using the `type ()` function.

② Similarly, this is an example of converting a list to a tuple.

Exercise 2-56: Use a for Loop in a Tuple

①
```
>>> countries = ('US', 'England', 'Germany', 'France')
>>> for country in countries:
...     print(country, end=" ")
...
US England Germany France
```

Explanation

① Like a list, you can index items in a tuple by using a for loop. Tuples and lists have a lot of common properties. The differences are that one is immutable (tuple) and the other is mutable (list), and that one is faster (tuple) and the other is slower (list) during indexing.

Exercise 2-57: Assign Multiple Variables to a Tuple

①
```
>>> weekend = ('Saturday', 'Sunday')
>>> (saturn, sun) = weekend
>>> print(saturn)
Saturday

>>> weekdays = ('Monday', 'Tuesday', 'Wednesday', 'Thursday', 'Friday')
>>> (moon, tiu, woden, thor, freya) = weekdays
>>> print(thor)
Thursday
```

②
```
>>> country_info = ['England', '+44']
>>> (country, code) = country_info
>>> print(country)
England
>>> print(code)
+44
```

Explanation

① You can assign multiple variables to items in a tuple. This example uses the seven-day week and the meanings of the names of the days. Sunday and Monday were named after Sun and Moon, and other days were named after mythological gods.

② You can also use a list as items in a tuple.

Exercise 2-58: Create a Simple Tuple Function

①
```
>>> def high_and_low (numbers):
...     highest = max (numbers)
...     lowest = min (numbers)
...     return (highest, lowest)
...
>>> lotto_numbers = [1, 37, 25, 48, 15, 23]
>>> (highest, lowest) = high_and_low (lotto_numbers)
>>> print(highest)
48
>>> print(lowest)
1
```

Explanation

① You can make a simple function and use a tuple to page the highest number or the lowest number. Spend a few minutes to understand how this function works and then move to the next exercise.

Exercise 2-59: Use Tuples as List Elements

①
```
>>> country_code = [('England', '+44'), ('France', '+33')]

>>> for (country, code) in country_code:
...     print(country, code)
...
England +44
France +33

>>> for (country, code) in country_code:
...     print(country, end=" ")
...
England France

>>> for (country, code) in country_code:
...     print(code, end=" ")
...
+44 +33
```

Explanation

① You can use tuples as elements in a list. You can choose to call out single items in each tuple. Enter something meaningful to you to get more practice on this.

Recap: Tuples

Here's a recap of tuples:

- Tuples are sometimes called *immutable lists*, and once created, they cannot be changed in the same tuple form. You need to convert tuples back into a list first, and then the elements can be changed. The general tuple syntax is as follows:

```
Tuple_name = (element_1, element_2, ..., element_n)
```

- However, you can delete the entire tuple in Python.
- You can convert a tuple to a list using the built-in function `list()`.
- You can convert a list to a tuple using the built-in function `tuple()`.
- You can find the maximum and minimum values of a tuple using the `max()` and `min()` methods.

Dictionaries

Let's talk about dictionaries.

Exercise 2-60: Understand Dictionary Basics

①
```
>>> fav_activity = {'hugh': 'computer games', 'leah': 'ballet', 'caitlin': 'ice
skating'}
>>> print(fav_activity)
{'hugh': 'computer games', 'leah': 'ballet', 'caitlin': 'ice skating'}
```

②
```
>>> fav_activity = {'hugh': 'computer games', 'leah': 'ballet', 'caitlin': 'ice
skating'}
>>> print(fav_activity ['caitlin'])
ice skating
```

③
```
>>> fav_activity = {'hugh': 'computer games', 'leah': 'ballet', 'caitlin': 'ice
skating'}
>>> del fav_activity ['hugh']
>>> print(fav_activity)
{'leah': 'ballet', 'caitlin': 'ice skating'}
```

④
```
>>> print(fav_activity)
{'leah': 'ballet', 'caitlin': 'ice skating'}
>>> fav_activity ['leah'] = 'swimming'
>>> print(fav_activity)
{'leah': 'swimming', 'caitlin': 'ice skating'}
```

Explanation

① Create a dictionary called `fav_activity`. Make your family member's favorite hobbies into a dictionary. A dictionary usually has key and value elements as in a real dictionary. A Python dictionary key:value elements are wrapped in a curly bracket set, { }, with comma separators.

② You can use a key called `caitlin` to call out the value of the key.

③ Delete the key hugh using the `del` statement. When you delete a key, its value also gets deleted. Now you know a dictionary in Python is a mutable object.

④ Change the value of the key `leah` in the dictionary to `swimming`.

Exercise 2-61: Avoid a Dictionary TypeError and Convert Two Lists to a Single Dictionary

①
```
>>> fav_activity = {'leah': 'swimming', 'caitlin': 'ice skating'}
>>> fav_subject = {'leah': 'math', 'caitlin': 'english'}
>>> print(fav_activity + fav_subject)
Traceback (most recent call last):
File "<stdin>", line 1, in <module>
TypeError: unsupported operand type (s) for +: 'dict' and 'dict'
```

②
```
>>> keys = ['a', 'b', 'c', 'm', 'p']
>>> values = ['apple', 'banana', 'coconut', 'melon', 'pear']
>>> fruits = dict (zip (keys, values))
>>> fruits
{'a': 'apple', 'b': 'banana', 'c': 'coconut', 'm': 'melon', 'p': 'pear'}
```

Explanation

① In Python, you cannot link two or more dictionaries into a single dictionary. Trying to conjoin two dictionaries into one will return `TypeError: unsupported operand`.

② However, if one list contains only keys and the other list contains the same number of corresponding values, the two lists can be conjoined to form a dictionary. In this example, you have just created a dictionary called fruits using one list of letters (keys) and another list with corresponding fruit names (values).

Exercise 2-62: Use Keys to Print Values from a Dictionary

①
```
>>> dialing_code = {'France': '+ 33', 'Italy': '+ 39', 'Spain': '+ 34', 'England': '+ 
44'}
>>> France_code = dialing_code ['France']
>>> Italy_code = dialing_code ['Italy']
>>> Spain_code = dialing_code ['Spain']
>>> England_code = dialing_code ['England']
>>> print('Press {} first to call France.'. format (France_code))
Press +33 first to call France.
>>> print('Press {} first to call Italy.'. format (Italy_code))
Press +39 first to call Italy.
>>> print('Press {} first to call Spain.'. format (Spain_code))
Press +34 first to call Spain.
>>> print('Press {} first to call England.'. format (England_code))
Press +44 first to call England.
```

Explanation

① In the previous dictionary example, you used the keys to call corresponding values and printed them on your computer monitor. Try to practice all the examples. Many newbie programmers ask the same question on how to get better in coding; there is no substitute for practice.

Exercise 2-63: Change a Dictionary Value

①
```
>>> dialing_code = {'France': '+ 33', 'Italy': '+ 39', 'Spain': '+ 34', 'England': '+ 44'}
>>> dialing_code ['England'] = '+ 44-20'
>>> England_London = dialing_code ['England']
>>> print('Dial {} to call London, England.'. format (England_London))
Dial + 44-20 to call London, England.
```

Explanation

① As with other mutable objects in Python, you can also change dictionaries. In this exercise, you have updated the value of the key `England`. You have just included the area code of 20 for London behind the country code +44. Then you printed out a simple statement using the `format()` function.

Exercise 2-64: Add a New Set of Keys and Values to a Dictionary

①
```
>>> dialing_code = {'France': '+ 33', 'Italy': '+ 39', 'Spain': '+ 34',
'England': '+ 44'}
>>> dialing_code ['Greece'] = '+30'
>>> dialing_code
{'England': '+44', 'Greece': '+30', 'Italy': '+39', 'Spain': '+34', 'France': '+33'}
```

Explanation

① You can add other keys and value pairs as you like. Dictionaries, like lists, are mutable containers. Notice the unordered manner of the dictionary in this example. There is no need for number indexing in Python dictionaries, as the keys are used to call the values.

Exercise 2-65: Find the Number of Dictionary Elements

①
```
>>> dialing_code = {'England': '+44', 'Greece': '+30', 'Italy': '+39', 'Spain': '+34',
'France': '+ 33 '}
>>> print(len (dialing_code))
5
```

Explanation

① Use `len()` to find the number of `key:value` pairs in a dictionary.

Exercise 2-66: Delete Dictionary Keys and Values

①
```
>>> dialing_code = {'England': '+44', 'Greece': '+30', 'Italy': '+39', 'Spain': '+34',
'France': '+ 33 '}
>>> del dialing_code ['Italy']
>>> print(dialing_code)
{'England': '+44', 'Greece': '+30', 'Spain': '+34', 'France': '+33'}
```

Explanation

① To delete a key, use a value pair in a dictionary; use "`del`" with a key. The value will be removed along with the key automatically.

Exercise 2-67: Write a Python Script with a Dictionary

①
```
# ex2_67.py
dialing_code = {'England': '+44', 'Greece': '+30', 'Italy': '+39', 'Spain': '+34',
'France': '+33'}
for code in dialing_code:
    print('The country code for {0} is {1}.'. format (code, dialing_code [code]))
# Output:
The country code for England is +44.
The country code for Greece is +30.
The country code for Italy is +39.
The country code for Spain is +34.
The country code for France is +33.
```

■ **Note** Try to save the `ex2_67.py` script on Notepad++, save the file with the same name, and run the code using the Ctrl+F6 keys as shown in Figure 2-6.

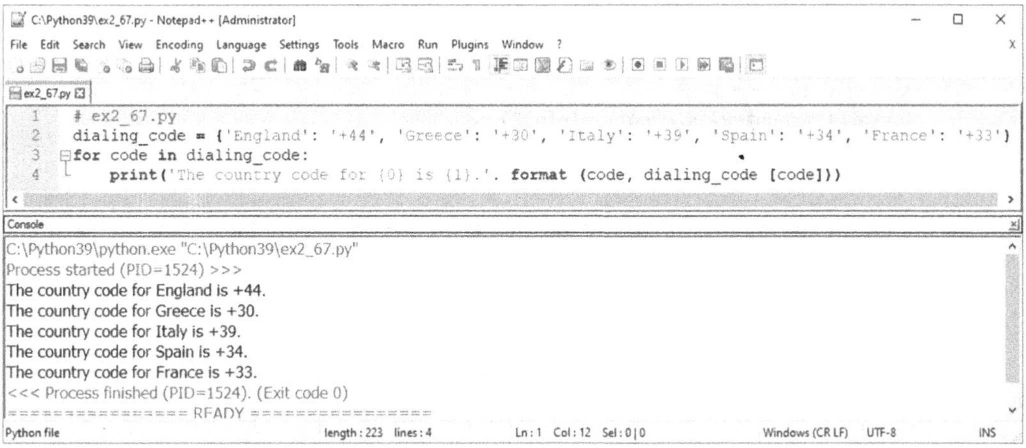

Figure 2-6. *Notepad++ dictionary example*

Explanation

① Now let's get familiar with making simple scripts like this and run it on IDLE or Notepad++. In this example, you have used the format function to call both key and value pairs and put them through a for loop to print out each country's international dialing codes.

Exercise 2-68: Use a Dictionary for a Loop and Formatting

①
```
>>> countries = {'England': {'code':'+ 44', 'capital_city':'London'}, 'France':
{'code':'+ 33', 'capital_city':'Paris'}}
>>> for country in countries:
...     print("{} 's country info:" .format (country))
...     print(countries [country] ['code'])
...     print(countries [country] ['capital_city'])
...
England 's country info:
+ 44
London
France 's country info:
+ 33
Paris
```

②
```
>> countries = {'England': {'code':'+ 44', 'capital_city':'London'}, 'France':
{'code':'+ 33', 'capital_city':'Paris'}}
>>> for country in countries:
...     print(f"{country}'s country info:")
...     print(countries [country] ['code'])
...     print(countries [country] ['capital_city'])
...
England's country info:
+ 44
London
France's country info:
+ 33
Paris
```

Explanation

① You can nest dictionaries within a dictionary. Use a `for` loop to print elements of the dictionary, `countries`.

② `print("{} 's country info:" .format (country))` in example ① is the same as `print(f"{country}'s country info:")` in example ②. The second version is the simplified version and helps us to write shorter code.

Recap: Dictionaries

Here's a recap:

- A dictionary comprises `key:value` pair collections, which are separated by a commas separator wrapped around braces, `{ }`. The general dictionary syntax is as follows:

  ```
  dictionary_Name = ['Key_1': 'Value_1', 'Key_2': 'Value_2', 'Key_n': 'Value_n']
  ```

- To call a value stored in a dictionary, you must use a key rather than indexing. The dictionary doesn't use number indexing, so it is an unordered sequence collection.
- You can change the value of a key using the key as an index. Here's an example: `dictionary_name ['key_1'] = 'new_value_1'`.
- Deleting a key using `del` deletes both key and value. Here's an example: del dictionary_name ['key_1'].
- `value_x` in `dictionary_name.values()` will tell you if a key is part of a dictionary or not.
- `dictionary_name.keys()` returns only the keys of the dictionary.
- `dictionary_name.values()` returns only the value of the dictionary.

- You can use a `for` loop on a dictionary, as in lists and tuples.
- Dictionaries can have any data types as elements as long as they have the correct `key: value` pairings.

Handling Files

File handling skills in Python are fundamental, as business-critical data must be processed using various file handling modules and methods. The simplest form of file handling is reading and writing a text file. As you become familiar with more complex file handling, you can learn more advanced file handling methods using Python modules such as Pandas and NumPy for data processing or xlrd and openpyxl for Excel files. However, even before becoming familiar with such modules, master how to do basic data processing using indexing or slicing or using regex to process your data. There is a 500-page book written on how to use the Python Pandas module, so it is an unenviable task to cover all the topics of data processing and file handling in one section.

However, this book aims to expose you to various basic data processing exercises and file handling methods. You will become familiar with how Python processes data, and then the processed data can be processed through a basic file handling method.

Exercise 2-69: Read and Display Hosts File from Your PC

Run this from the Microsoft Windows Python interactive shell.

①
```
>>> hosts = open('c://windows//system32//drivers//etc//hosts')
>>> hosts_file = hosts.read()
>>> print(hosts_file)
# Copyright (c) 1993-2009 Microsoft Corp. #
# This is a sample HOSTS file used by Microsoft TCP/IP for Windows. #
# This file contains the mappings of IP addresses to host names. Each # entry should
be kept on an individual line. The IP address should
# be placed in the first column followed by the corresponding host name. # The IP
address and the host name should be separated by at least one # space.
#
# Additionally, comments (such as these) may be inserted on individual # lines or
following the machine name denoted by a '#' symbol.
#
# For example:
#
#   102.54.94.97 rhino.acme.com # source server #    38.25.63.10  x.acme.com
# x client host
# localhost name resolution is handled within DNS itself. #   127.0.0.1   localhost
#   ::1   localhost
```

Optionally, run this from the Linux or macOS Python interactive shell:

②
```
>>> hosts = open ('/etc/hosts')
>>> hosts_file = hosts.read()
>>> print(hosts_file)
127.0.0.1 localhost.localdomain localhost
:: 1 localhost6.localdomain6 localhost6

The following lines are desirable for IPv6 capable hosts
:: 1 localhost ip6-localhost ip6-loopback fe00 :: 0 ip6-localnet
ff02 :: 1 ip6-allnodes ff02 :: 2 ip6-allrouters
ff02 :: 3 ip6-allhosts
```

Explanation

① You have just read the hosts file from your Windows machine and printed it out on your computer screen.
Reading a file is this easy, and if you do not specify the reading method, it usually opens in `r` (reading) mode.
Notice while opening the hosts file how each \ in the Windows OS file system has been replaced with `//`. If you insist on running Python on Windows and must handle files, then this is a significant point to take away from this example.

② You can use the same code on a Linux or macOS system to read the hosts file (object), but this time the hosts file exists under `/etc/hosts` instead. In Python, it takes only three lines of code to open, read, and print a file's content.

Exercise 2-70: Open and Close Hosts Files

①
```
>>> hosts = open('c://windows//system32//drivers//etc//hosts')
>>> hosts_file = hosts.read()
>>> print(hosts_file)
# Copyright (c) 1993-2009 Microsoft Corp.
.
[... omitted for brevity]
.
# localhost name resolution is handled within DNS itself.
# 127.0.0.1 localhost
# ::1 localhost
>>> hosts.close ()
```

Explanation

① After opening a file with the `open('file_path')` method, you must close the file after use. This process is the same as you would open a text or word file on your computer, and after use, you must close the file. You can close the file using the `file_variable.close()` method. In our example, close the open file using `hosts.close()`.

Exercise 2-71: Create Code to Close a File in Two Ways

①
```
>>> hosts = open ('c://windows//system32//drivers//etc//hosts', 'r')
>>> hosts_file_contents = hosts.read()
>>> print('File closed? {}'.format(hosts.closed))
File closed? False
>>>
>>> if not hosts.closed:
...     hosts.close()
...
>>>
>>> print('File closed? {}'.format(hosts.closed))
File closed? True
>>>
```

②
```
>>> with open ('c://windows//system32//drivers//etc//hosts', 'r') as hosts:
...     print('File closed? {}'.format (hosts.closed))
...     print(hosts.read())
...     print('Finished reading the file.')
...
File closed? False
# Copyright (c) 1993-2009 Microsoft Corp.

[... omitted for brevity]

# localhost name resolution is handled within DNS itself.
# 127.0.0.1 localhost
# ::1 localhost
Finished reading the file.
>>>
>>> print('File closed? {}'. format (hosts.closed))
File closed? True
>>>
```

③
```
try:
    f = open('c://windows//system32//drivers//etc//hosts', encoding = 'utf-8')
    f_read = f.read()
    print(f_read)
finally:
    f.close()
```

Explanation

① Type in simple Python scripts to open the hosts file and then close it. Then check if the file has been properly closed. True means the file has closed correctly. Sometimes this file open option comes in handy.

② When you use the `open()` option, this removes the need to add a `close()` line. The `with open` statement opens the file and closes the file automatically with no `close()` statement. Try to open files using this option over the `file.open()` method.

③ If you insist on using the file `open()` method, open the file in a `try-finally` block, so if some file operation fails and suddenly closes, it closes the file correctly. Also, notice that encoding has been specified as UTF-8. On Python 3.4+, this is already the default encoding method but specified for demonstration purposes only in this example.

Exercise 2-72: Create a Text File, and Read, Write, and Print

①
```
>>> f = open('C://Users//brendan//Documents//file1.txt', 'w+') # Replace my name with yours
>>> for i in range(3):
...     f.write('This is line %d.\r' %(i + 1))
...
16
16
16
>>> f.close() #Always close file. Data gets written as file closes.
>>>
>>> f = open('C://Users//brendan//Documents//file1.txt')
>>> f_read = f.read()
>>> print(f_read)
This is line 1. This is line 2. This is line 3.
□# whitespace
>>>
>>> print(f_read.strip())#Removes undesired whitespaces.
This is line 1. This is line 2. This is line 3.
>>>
>>> print(f_read, end='') # Removes undesired whitespaces.
This is line 1. This is line 2. This is line 3.
>>>
>>> f.close() # Always close file.
>>>
```

②
```
>>> with open('C://Users//brendan//Documents//file1.txt', 'w+') as f:
...     for i in range(3):
...     f.write('This is line %d.\n' %(i + 1))
...
16
16
16
>>> with open('C://Users//brendan//Documents//file1.txt', 'r') as f:
...     for line in f:
...     print(line)
...
This is line 1.
□# whitespace
This is line 2.
□# whitespace
This is line 3.
□# whitespace
```

③
```
>>> with open('C://Users//brendan//Documents//file1.txt', 'r') as f:
...     for line in f:
...     print(line, end=' ')
...
This is line 1. This is line 2. This is line 3.
```

④
```
>>> with open('C://Users//brendan//Documents//file1.txt', 'r') as f:
...     for line in f:
...     print(line.strip())
...
This is line 1. This is line 2. This is line 3.
```

⑤
```
>>> with open('C://Users//brendan//Documents//file1.txt', 'r') as f:
...     skip_header = next(f) #Removes the header or the first line.
...     for line in f:
...         print(line.strip())
...
This is line 2. This is line 3.
```

⑥
```
>>> with open('C://Users//brendan//Documents//file1.txt', 'w+') as f:
...     for i in range(3):
...         f.write('This is line %d.\r\n' %(i + 1))
...
17
17
17
>>> with open('C://Users//brendan//Documents//file1.txt', 'r') as f:
...     for line in f:
...         print(line)
...
This is line 1.
# whitespaces


This is line 2.
# whitespaces


This is line 3.
# whitespaces


```

Explanation

① This is a basic example of opening (creating) a file in write mode (`w+`) and writing to the file. The file is closed after the information is written. Then the file is opened again in reading (`r`) mode, and the content of the file is printed out on the screen. The file has to be closed after each use. Use `strip()` or `end=''` to remove any whitespace created during file writing. You can remove the unwanted whitespaces if you want.

② In this second example, you have used the `open with` method to create and read the file, so there is no need to close the file. Also, while you created the file, you used `\n` (newline) rather than `\r` (return carriage), and when the content was read, you can see that the new lines have been added. Whitespaces include `\t` (tab), `\n` (newline), and `\r` (return carriage).

③ Once again, you have used `end='` to remove the undesired whitespaces.

④ Similarly, use `strip()` to remove any whitespaces.

⑤ `skip_header = next(f)` can remove the header or the first line of your file to print from the second line.

⑥ Be careful using `\r` and `\n` together as the end product will behave differently depending on your operating system. If you are handling files in Linux or macOS, the use of `\r` and `\n` will differ.

Exercise 2-73: Use rstrip() or lstrip() to Remove Whitespace

①

```
>>> with open('C://Users//brendan//Documents//file1.txt', 'w+') as f:
...     for i in range(3):
...     f.write('□□□□This line contains whitespaces %d.□□□□\n' %(i + 1))
...
42
42
42
>>> with open('C://Users//brendan//Documents//file1.txt', 'r') as f:
...     for line in f:
...     print(line)
...
□□□□This line contains whitespaces 1.□□□□# whitespaces
□# whitespace
□□□□This line contains whitespaces 2.□□□□
□
□□□□This line contains whitespaces 3.□□□□
□
```

②

```
>>> with open('C://Users//brendan//Documents//file1.txt', 'r') as f:
...     for line in f:
...     print(line.lstrip())
...
This line contains whitespaces 1.□□□□
□
This line contains whitespaces 2.□□□□
□
This line contains whitespaces 3.□□□□
□
```

③

```
>>> with open('C://Users//brendan//Documents//file1.txt', 'r') as f:
...     for line in f:
...         print(line.rstrip())
...
□□□□This line contains whitespaces 1.
□□□□This line contains whitespaces 2.
□□□□This line contains whitespaces 3.
```

④

```
>>> with open('C://Users//brendan//Documents//file1.txt', 'r') as f:
...     for line in f:
...         print(line.strip())
...
This line contains whitespaces 1. This line contains whitespaces 2. This line contains
whitespaces 3.
```

Explanation

① Create a file with four spaces on the left and four spaces on the right.

② Use `lstrip()` to remove whitespaces on the left side.

③ Use `rstrip()` to remove whitespaces on the right side, including \n, the newline character.

④ Use `strip()` to remove all whitespaces.

Exercise 2-74: Python File Mode Exercise: Use r Mode

When you open a file in reading (r) mode, the file pointer is placed at the beginning of the file, which is the default mode.

---

①

```
#1  >>> with open('C://Users//brendan//Documents//file2.txt', 'r') as f:
    ...     print('Created file2.txt')
    ...
    Traceback (most recent call last):
    File "<stdin>", line 1, in <module>
    FileNotFoundError: [Errno 2] No such file or directory: 'C://Users//brendan//
    Documents//file2.txt'
    >>> import os
#2  >>> os.path.isfile('C://Users//brendan//Documents//file2.txt')
    False
#3  >>> with open('C://Users//brendan//Documents//file2.txt', 'w') as f:
    ...     print('Created file2.txt')
    ...
#4  Created file2.txt
    >>> import glob
    >>> print(glob.glob('C://Users//brendan//Documents//*.txt'))
#5  ['C://Users//brendan//Documents\\file1.txt', 'C://Users//brendan//Documents\\file2.txt']
    >>> import os
    >>> os.path.isfile('C://Users//brendan//Documents//file2.txt')
#6  True

    >>> with open('C://Users//brendan//Documents//file2.txt') as f:
    ...     print(f.mode)
    ...
#7  r # If file mode is not specified, the file opens in default reading only.
    >>> with open('C://Users//brendan//Documents//file2.txt') as f:
    ...     f.write ('Writing to a file is fun.')
    ...
    Traceback (most recent call last):
    File "<stdin>", line 2, in <module>
    io.UnsupportedOperation: not writable
```

Explanation

① #1. You tried to create a file in default reading mode, but Python does not allow file creation in only read (r) mode.
#2. You imported the os module and used the `os.path.isfile()` method to check if a file has been created, but as expected, no file has been created.
#3. Now you have opened and created `file2.txt` in write (w) mode.
#4. Then you imported the globe module to confirm that the file exists in your Document folder.
#5. Using the `os.path.isfile()` method, you double-checked the file created and exists in the folder (the directory in Linux).
#6. You have used `.mode` to validate file mode.
#7. You have opened `file2.txt` in reading mode and attempted to write to the file, and Python reminded you that you could not write to the file in this case.

Exercise 2-75: Python File Mode Exercise: Use r+ Mode

Open a file for both reading and writing. The file pointer will be at the beginning of the file.

①

```
#1  >>> import os
    >>> os.remove('C://Users//brendan//Documents//file2.txt')
    >>> os.path.isfile('C://Users//brendan//Documents//file2.txt')
#2  False
    >>> with open('C://Users//brendan//Documents//file2.txt', 'r+') as f:
    ...     f.write('* Test Line 1')
    ...     print('Trying to write the first line.')
    ...
    Traceback (most recent call last):
    File "<stdin>", line 1, in <module>
#3  FileNotFoundError: [Errno 2] No such file or directory: 'C://Users//brendan//
    Documents//file2.txt'
    >>> with open('C://Users//brendan//Documents//file2.txt', 'w+') as f:
    ...     f.write('* Test Line 1')
    ...     print('Just created file2.txt with line 1')
    ...
    13
    Just created file2.txt with line 1
    >>> with open('C://Users//brendan//Documents//file2.txt', 'r+') as f:
```

```
#4  ...     print(f.mode)
    ...
    r+ # Opens a file for both reading and writing.
#5  >>> with open('C://Users//brendan//Documents//file2.txt', 'r+') as f:
    ...     f_read = f.read()
    ...     print(f_read)
    ...
#6  * Test Line 1
    >>> with open('C://Users//brendan//Documents//file2.txt', 'r+') as f:
    ...     f.write('# This will overwrite Line 1')
    ...
    28
    >>> with open('C://Users//brendan//Documents//file2.txt', 'r+') as f:
    ...     f_read = f.read()
    ...     print(f_read)
    ...
    # This will overwrite Line 1
```

Explanation

① #1. Use the `os.remove()` method to remove an existing file, file2.txt. This file was created in Exercise 2-74. You can also check if the file has been deleted successfully using the `os.path.isfile()` method.
#2. Try to open and create a file in `r+` mode; just as in r mode, Python will return `FileNotFoundError`. You cannot create a new file using r+ mode.
#3. This time use the `w+` mode to re-create the file2.txt file and write the first line for testing. As in Exercise 2-74, `w+` allows you to open and create a new file; you will find more on this on the following `w` and `w+` exercises.
#4. Use the `.mode` method to check your file handling mode.
#5. Now reopen `text2.txt` in `r+` mode and write to the file.
#6. When you read the file, you can see that the last action has overwritten the old information.

Exercise 2-76: Python File Mode Exercise: Use a Mode

Open a file for an appending exercise. The file pointer is at the end of the file if the file exists. The file is in the append mode. If the file does not exist, it creates a new file for writing.

①

```
#1   >>> import os
     >>> os.remove('C://Users//brendan//Documents//file2.txt')
     >>> os.path.isfile('C://Users//brendan//Documents//file2.txt')
     False
     >>> with open('C://Users//brendan//Documents//file2.txt', 'a') as f:
     ...     f.write('This is line 1.')
     ...
#2   15
     >>> with open('C://Users//brendan//Documents//file2.txt', 'a') as f:
     ...     f_read = f.read()
     ...     print(f_read)
     ...
     Traceback (most recent call last):
#3   File "<stdin>", line 2, in <module>
     io.UnsupportedOperation: not readable
     >>> with open('C://Users//brendan//Documents//file2.txt', 'r') as f:
#4   ...     f_read = f.read()
     ...     print(f_read)
     ...
#5   This is line 1.
     >>> with open('C://Users//brendan//Documents//file2.txt', 'a') as f:
     ...     f.write('This is line 2.')
     ...
#6   15
     >>> with open('C://Users//brendan//Documents//file2.txt', 'r') as f:
     ...     f_read = f.read()
     ...     print(f_read)
     ...
     This is line 1.This is line 2.

     >>> with open('C://Users//brendan//Documents//file2.txt', 'a') as f:
     ...     f.write('\rThis is line 3.')
#7   ...
     16
     >>> with open('C://Users//brendan//Documents//file2.txt', 'r') as f:
     ...     f_read = f.read()
     ...     print(f_read)
#8   ...
     This is line 1.This is line 2. This is line 3.
     >>> with open('C://Users//brendan//Documents//file2.txt', 'a') as f:
#9   ...     f.write('\nThis is line 4.')
     ...
     16
     >> with open('C://Users//brendan//Documents//file2.txt', 'r') as f:
     ...     for line in f.readlines():
#10  ...         print(line.strip())
     ...
```

```
     This is line 1.This is line 2. This is line 3.
#11  This is line 4.
     >>> with open('C://Users//brendan//Documents//file2.txt', 'r') as f:
     ...      f.readline()
     ...
#12  'This is line 1.This is line 2.\n'
     >>> with open('C://Users//brendan//Documents//file2.txt', 'r') as f:
     ...     f.readlines()
     ...
     ['This is line 1.This is line 2.\n', 'This is line 3.\n', 'This is line 4.']
     >>> with open('C://Users//brendan//Documents//file2.txt', 'r') as f:
     ...     f.tell()
     ...
     0
     >> with open('C://Users//brendan//Documents//file2.txt', 'a') as f:
     ...     f.tell()
     ...
     63
```

Explanation

① #1. Remove `file2.txt` and re-create a file with the same name in an (append) mode. As you have already noticed, append mode will also allow you to create a new file if it does not exist already.
#2. Open `file2.txt` in append mode to read the file. Python will tell you that in this mode, you cannot read the file.
#3. Open the file in reading mode and print out the content to the screen.
#4. This time open the file in append mode and add some more information.
#5. Open the file in reading mode again and print the file content. As you have noticed, the second sentence you have written to the file has been appended immediately after the first sentence, without proper spacing or newline entry. In append mode, the pointer starts at the end of the last sentence to append any additional information at the end of the last character entry.
#6. Open `file2.txt` in append mode and add a new line. This time, add `\r` to add the line to the next line.
#7. Confirm the entry in reading mode.
#8. This time, use `\n` to add another line.
#9. When you use the `strip()` method, whitespaces such as `\r` or `\n` get deleted.
#10. When you use the `read()` method, Python reads the whole file content and dumps out the information. Sometimes this is not the desired method as you only want to read per line. Use `readline()` to read one line at a time.
#11. If you use the `readlines()` method, Python will read each line and return them as a string item list.
#12. Python's file method `tell()` returns the file's current position read/write pointer within the file. As you can observe, when a file is opened in r/r+ mode, the pointer starts from index 0. Whereas if you open the file in a/a+ mode, the pointer will begin at the end of the index.

Exercise 2-77: Python File Mode Exercise: Use a+ Mode

Open a file for an appending and reading exercise. The file pointer is at the end of the file if the file exists. The file opens in the append mode. If the file does not exist, it creates a new file for reading and writing.

```
①  >>> import os
#1  >>> os.remove('C://Users//brendan//Documents//file2.txt') # Removes old file2.txt
    >>> with open('C://Users//brendan//Documents//file2.txt', 'a+') as f:
    ...     print(f.mode)
    ...     f.write('This is line 1.\rThis is line 2.\rThis is line 3.\r')
    ...
    a+
    48
#2  >>> with open('C://Users//brendan//Documents//file2.txt', 'a+') as f:
    ...     f_read = f.read()
    ...     print(f_read, end='')
#3  ...
    >>> with open('C://Users//brendan//Documents//file2.txt', 'r') as f:
    ...     f_read = f.read()
    ...     print(f_read, end='')
    ...
    This is line 1. This is line 2. This is line3.
```

Explanation

① #1. Remove `file2.txt` once again and open and re-create the `file2.txt` file in a+ mode with three lines.
#2. Open the file in a+ mode, read, and print the file. But since the pointer is at the end of the file in a+ mode, no information is printed.
#3. When you open the file in the default r mode again, the pointer starts at the beginning of the file and prints out the file content on the screen. Although a+ supports file reading mode, because of its pointer location when the file is opened in this mode, really there is no fair use case to open a file in this mode over the normal a mode.

Exercise 2-78: Python File Mode Exercise: Use w Mode

Open a file for writing only. This overwrites the file if the file exists. If the file does not exist, create a new file for writing.

①

```
#1  >>> with open('C://Users//brendan//Documents//file2.txt', 'w') as f:
    ...     f.tell()
    ...     print(f.mode)
    ...     f.write('This is line 1.')
    ...
    0
    w
    15
#2  >>> with open('C://Users//brendan//Documents//file2.txt', 'r') as f:
    ...     f_read = f.read()
    ...     print(f_read)
    ...
#3  This is line 1.
    >>> with open('C://Users//brendan//Documents//file2.txt', 'w') as f:
    ...     f_read = f.read()
    ...     print(f_read)
    ...
    Traceback (most recent call last): File "<stdin>", line 2, in <module>
    io.UnsupportedOperation: not readable
```

Explanation

① #1. There's no need to remove the old file. Opening a file in w mode will overwrite the old file and create a new file. If there is no file with the same name, Python will create a new file.
#2. You opened `file2.txt` in read mode and printed the file content in r mode.
#3. If you try to read the file content in `w` mode, you will encounter an IO-related error, as shown in this example.

Exercise 2-79: Python File Mode Exercise: Use w+ Mode

Open a file for both writing and reading. This overwrites the existing file if the file exists. If the file does not exist, create a new file for reading and writing.

①

```
#1   >>> with open('C://Users//brendan//Documents//file2.txt', 'w+') as f:
     ...     f.tell()
     ...     f.write('This is line 1.')
     ...     f.tell()
     ...     print(f.read())
     ...
     0
     15
     15
#2   >>> with open('C://Users//brendan//Documents//file2.txt', 'w+') as f:
     ...     print(f.mode)
     ...     f.write('This is line 1.')
     ...     f.seek(0)
     ...     print(f.read())
     ...
     w+
     15
     0
     This is line 1.
```

Explanation

① #1. When you open in w+ mode, the pointer begins at index 0, after writing to the file. It moves to the end of the content. When you try to print information while the pointer is at the end of the line, Python will return a blank.
#2. To write in w+ mode and then read and print out the file content, then you have to move the pointer to position zero using the seek(0) method. In this example, you have reset the pointer position to 0, or the beginning of the file, and Python printed the lines correctly.

Exercise 2-80: Python File Mode Exercise: Use x Mode

x is like w. But for x, if the file exists, raise FileExistsError.

①

```
#1   >>> with open('C://Users//brendan//Documents//file2.txt', 'x') as f:
     ...     print(f.mode)
     ...
     Traceback (most recent call last):
     File "<stdin>", line 1, in <module>
     FileExistsError: [Errno 17] File exists: 'C://Users//brendan//Documents//file2.txt'
     >>> with open('C://Users//brendan//Documents//file4.txt', 'x') as f:
#2   ...     print(f.mode)
     ...
     x
```

Explanation

① #1. `file2.txt` already exists from the previous exercise. When you try to open `file2.txt` in `x` mode, it will raise `FileExistsError`. This new file handling mode can come in handy if you do not want to overwrite the existing file mistakenly using `w/w+` mode.
#2. Now create a new file in x mode, and Python is happy with this operation.

Exercise 2-81: Python File Mode Exercise: Use x Mode

`x` is writeable only. `x+` can write and read.

①
```
>>> with open('C://Users//brendan//Documents//file5.txt', 'x+') as f:
...     print(f.mode)
...
x+
```

Explanation

① This is a write and read mode of x mode. It's almost identical to w+ mode, but it will not overwrite the existing file. It will require exclusivity to create a new file. Look at Table 2-5 for all file modes; you do not have to memorize all modes now, but you will get familiar with each modes as you write more Python code.

Table 2-5. *File Processing Modes*

Mode	Descriptions
`r`	Opens a file for reading only. This mode places the file pointer at the beginning of the file. This is the default mode.
`rb`	Opens a file for reading only in binary format. This mode places the file pointer at the beginning of the file.
`r+`	Opens a file for both reading and writing. The file pointer will be at the beginning of the file.
`rb+`	Opens a file for both reading and writing in binary format. The file pointer will be at the beginning of the file.
`a`	Opens a file for appending. The file pointer is at the end of the file if the file exists. The file is in the append mode. If the file does not exist, it creates a new file for writing.
`ab`	Opens a file for appending in binary format. The file pointer is at the end of the file if the file exists. The file is in the append mode. If the file does not exist, it creates a new file for writing.
`a+`	Opens a file for both appending and reading. The file pointer is at the end of the file if the file exists. The file opens in the append mode. If the file does not exist, it creates a new file for reading and writing.

(continued)

Table 2-5. *(continued)*

Mode	Descriptions
ab+	Opens a file for both appending and reading in binary format. The file pointer is at the end of the file if the file exists. The file opens in the append mode. If the file does not exist, it creates a new file for reading and writing.
w	Opens a file for writing only. Overwrites the file if the file exists. If the file does not exist, creates a new file for writing.
wb	Opens a file for writing only in binary format. Overwrites the file if the file exists. If the file does not exist, create a new file for writing.
w+	Opens a file for both writing and reading. Overwrites the existing file if the file exists. If the file does not exist, creates a new file for reading and writing.
wb+	Opens a file for both writing and reading in binary format. Overwrites the existing file if the file exists. If the file does not exist, create a new file for reading and writing.
x	x mode is like w mode. But for x, if the file exists, raise FileExistsError.
x+	x is only writable. "x+" can write and read.

Exercise 2-82: Open a Byte File in Python

①
```
>>> with open('C://Users//brendan//Pictures//ex82_horse.jpg', 'rb') as horse_pic:
...     horse_pic.seek(2)
...     horse_pic.seek(4)
...     print(horse_pic.tell())
...     print(horse_pic.mode)
...
2
4
4
Rb
```

Explanation

① Python can also open and read byte files such as images and other files. This example shows you how to open and uses the seek method to read byte files. When you open in byte mode, you add b behind the normal r/r+, a/a+, and w/w+ modes.

You can download the ex82_horse.jpg file from the pynetauto GitHub site as part of the Chapter 2 code. This JPEG file is included in the chapter2_codes.zip file. This is my photo, so there is no copyright on this photo.

URL: https://github.com/pynetauto/apress_pynetauto

Exercise 2-83: Handle Errors with try and except

Optionally, you can download the source code files called ex2_83_countries.py and ex2_83_countries.txt and then run the code from Notepad++.

①
```
>>> try:
...     countries = open('C://Users//brendan//Documents//ex2_83_countries.txt', 'r')
... except FileNotFoundError as e:
...     print(str(e))
... else:
...     nations = countries.read()
...     print(nations)
...     countries.close()
...
[Errno 2] No such file or directory: 'C://Users//brendan//Documents//ex2_83_countries.
txt'
```

②
```
>>> try:
...     countries = open('C://Users//brendan//Documents//ex2_83_countries.txt', 'r')
... except FileNotFoundError as e:
...     print(str(e))
... else:
...     nations = countries.read()
...     print(nations)
...     countries.close()
...
United States England Germany France
Japan Italy Spain Australia
```

Explanation

① You can use try and except, try, except and else, or try and finally to handle errors that occur during file handling. This first exercise shows you an example of an error where there was no file in the directory. Download and drop the ex83_countries.txt file in your Documents folder and perform the next task.

② If you have the correct file in the directory, the Python code will reach the else statement and print out the names of the countries in the file. try and except error handling becomes handy while working with errors, especially while working with files.

Recap: Python file Handling Concept

Here's a recap:

- Use the `open()` built-in function to open a file. The general syntax is as follows:
    - `open(file_location, mode)`
- If the file mode is not specified, the file opens in default `r` (read) mode.
- In `read()` file mode, the entire content of the file is read.
- When a file is opened with the `open()` function, the best practice is to close the file with the `close()` function.
- If you open a file using `open ~`, you do not have to use the `close()` function to close the opened file.
- The for loop reads the file content line by line.
- Whitespaces created during handling of a file can be deleted using the `strip()`, `rstrip()`, `lsetrip()`, and `end='` methods.
- You can write data to a file using the **write()** function.
- The file opens in text mode unless specified to be opened in byte mode using `b` mode. Computers prefer to handle data in binary format.
- English alphabets or numbers are recognized as 1 byte in size, but some characters in UTF-8 format, such as Korean, Chinese, and Japanese, can be larger than 1 byte in size.
- `try` and `except` error handling can help you write more robust Python scripts.

Using Python Modules

The words *modules* and *packages* could be used interchangeably in Python, but how are they different? Yes, they are closely related, and often new Python learners get confused. They both serve the same purpose in organizing code, but there are some subtle differences between the two as they each provide slightly different ways of organizing code. Usually, a module is a single `.py` Python file with some function. A package is a directory that contains multiple Python modules. So, a package is a collection of modules. A module can be considered a self-contained package, and a package is a collection of various modules that are separated across multiple files. Usually, you start with a module, and as the requirements grow, you turn the multiple modules into a package to serve some purpose in your work.

As you work more with Python code, you will use many built-in modules and packages, adopt and use someone else's modules and packages, or create your custom modules and packages to use in your Python applications. Let's learn some basics using the modules.

Time Module

Let's talk about the time module.

Exercise 2-84: Import the time Module

①
```
>>> import time
>>> print(time.asctime())
Sun Apr 12 00:48:07 2020
```

②
```
>> print(time.timezone)
-36000
```

③
```
>>> from time import asctime
>>> print(asctime())
Sun Apr 12 00:49:44 2020
```

Explanation

① Import the time module and print the time from your computer.

② Find your time zone using the `time.timezone` method.
-36000 is the time zone value for Sydney, Australia.

③ Use from ~ import ~ to only import required functions from the time module. You can import multiple functions on the same line.
For example, from time, import gmtime and strftime.

Sleep Method

Let's talk about the sleep method.

Exercise 2-85: Use the time.sleep() Function

①
```
#Ex2_85.py (optional)
>>> from time import asctime, sleep
>>> print(asctime())
Sun Apr 12 01:00:01 2020
>>> sleep(10)
>>> print(asctime())
Sun Apr 12 01:00:11 2020

# Output:
Sun Apr 12 01:02:05 2020
Sun Apr 12 01:02:15 2020
```

Explanation

① `time.sleep()` is used to put your script into sleep for a designated period. Whenever you can, avoid using `import *` (import all) when importing modules; only import the explicit function you are going to use. The * wildcard means load all modules and functions, so it will add slowness to your code as it takes more time to load all modules than loading only a single module.

For example, try to avoid using this:

```
from time import * #Avoid *, as * is too greedy
```

This is preferred:

```
from time import asctime, sleep #importing two modules here
```

If you don't remember the name of the function from the module, you can import the module first and use `dir(module_name)` to find the name of all the methods you can choose from.

```
>>> import time
>>> dir(time)
['CLOCK_MONOTONIC', 'CLOCK_MONOTONIC_RAW', 'CLOCK_PROCESS_CPUTIME_ID', 'CLOCK_
REALTIME',
'CLOCK_THREAD_CPUTIME_ID', '_STRUCT_TM_ITEMS', ' doc ', ' loader ', ' name ', ' '
asctime ',' clock ',' clock_getres', 'clock_gettime', 'clock_settime', 'ctime',
'daylight', 'get_clock_info', 'gmtime', 'localtime', 'mktime', 'monotonic', 'perf_
counter' , 'process_time', 'sleep', 'strftime', 'strptime', 'struct_time', 'time',
'timezone', 'tzname', 'tzset']
```

Exercise 2-86: Browse a Path Using the sys Module

①
```
# For Windows
>>> import sys
>>> sys.path
['', 'C:\\Python39\\python39.zip', 'C:\\Python39\\DLLs', 'C:\\Python39\\lib', 'C:\\
Python39', 'C:\\Python39\\lib\\site-packages']

# For Linux
>>> import sys
>>> sys.path
['', '/usr/lib/python36.zip', '/usr/lib/python3.6', '/usr/lib/python3.6/lib-dynload',
'/ usr/local/lib/python3.6/dist-packages', '/usr/lib/python3/dist-packages']
```

②
```
# For Windows
>>> import sys
>>> for path in sys.path:
...     print(path)
...

C:\Python39\python39.zip
C:\Python39\DLLs
C:\Python39\lib
C:\Python39
C:\Python39\lib\site-packages

# For Linux
>>> import sys
>>> for path in sys.path:
...     print(path)
...

/usr/lib/python36.zip
/usr/lib/python3.6
/usr/lib/python3.6/lib-dynload
/usr/local/lib/python3.6/dist-packages
/usr/lib/python3/dist-packages
```

Explanation

① First, import the target module and then use `sys.path` to find where Python files exist on your system.

② To prettify the output, use the `for` loop method to give you the system directory path line by line. In this example, you can compare where `PYTHONPATH` and related packages are installed in Windows vs. Linux. `PYTHONPATH` is an environment variable to add additional directories where Python will look for modules and packages.

Exercise 2-87: Add a New Filepath Using the sys Module

①
```
# For Windows
>>> import sys
>>> sys.path.append('C:\Python39\my-packages')
>>> for path in sys.path:
...     print(path)
...

C:\Python39\python39.zip
C:\Python39\DLLs
C:\Python39\lib
C:\Python39
C:\Python39\lib\site-packages
C:\Python38Python39\my-packages # Newly added FILEPATH
```

```
# For Linux
>>> import sys
>>> sys.path.append('/Users/root/my-packages')

>>> for path in sys.path:
...     print(path)
...

/usr/lib/python36.zip
/usr/lib/python3.6
/usr/lib/python3.6/lib-dynload
/usr/local/lib/python3.6/dist-packages
/usr/lib/python3/dist-packages
/Users/root/my-packages # Newly added FILEPATH
```

Explanation

① If you want to create and add new modules/packages to a FILEPATH, Python will also look at the customized modules/packages under the new directory. You can add the new FILEPATH using the sys module.

Exercise 2-88: Check Built-ins and sys.builtin_module

①
```
>>> dir(__builtins__)
['ArithmeticError', 'AssertionError', 'AttributeError',
[... omitted for brevity]
'staticmethod', 'str', 'sum', 'super', 'tuple', 'type', 'vars', 'zip']

>>> import sys
>>> for name in sys.builtin_module_names:
...     print (name, end=' ')
...
_abc _ast _bisect _blake2 _codecs _codecs_cn _codecs_hk
[... omitted for brevity]
faulthandler gc itertools marshal math mmap msvcrt nt parser sys time winreg xxsubtype
zlib
```

Explanation

① In the Python interpreted session, you can use the `dir()` function to view built-in modules. You can also use the `for` loop method to view what's inside built-in modules. There are other ways to view this information, and this is just a way to check built-ins and modules.

Exercise 2-89: Use a Simple import sys Module in a try and except Exercise

①
```
# ex2_89.py
import sys
file = 'C://Users//brendan//Documents//test.txt'
try:
    with open (file) as test_file:
      for line in test_file:
        print(line.strip())
except:
    print('Could not open {}'. format(file))
    sys.exit(1)
```

②
```
C:\Users\brendan> python C://Users//brendan//Documents/ex2_89.py
Could not open C://Users//brendan//Documents//test.txt # output
```

③
```
>>> with open('C://Users//brendan//Documents//test.txt', 'w') as f:
...     f.write('This is a test file only.')
...     f.write('Study Python, Network, Linux and Automation all from a single book.')
...
26 67
```

④
```
>>> with open('C://Users//brendan//Documents//test.txt', 'r') as f:
...     print(f.read())
...
This is a test file only. # output
Study Python, Network, Linux, and Automation all from a single book. # output
```

⑤
```
C:\Users\brendan> python C://Users//brendan//Documents/ex2_89.py
This is a test file only. # output
Study Python, Network, Linux, and Automation all from a single book. # output
```

Explanation

① First, create a script called ex2_89.py and copy the code. This example script was created and saved in the C://Users//brendan//Documents folder.

② From the Windows command-line prompt or Windows PowerShell, run the ex2_89.py script. Optionally, if you have set up Notepad++ for Python, run the code. Since there is no text.txt file in the designated folder, Python will trigger the customized exception error. The script had an import sys module statement, and it triggered an exit action after printing the exception error.

③ Now create a test.txt file and add a couple of lines.

④ To check the content, open and read the file, and then print the lines.

⑤ Now run the Python script (ex2_89.py) to print the content. This was a small exercise, but I hope you are taking away something from this exercise. If you haven't, then let's go back and review what we have learned here.

Exercise 2-90: Understand Lambdas by Making a Calculator

①
```
>>> def sum(x, y):
...     return x +y
...
>>> sum(3, 2)
5
```

②
```
>>> sum = lambda x, y: x + y
>>> sum(3, 2)
5
```

③
```
>>> lamb_cal = [lambda x,y:x+y, lambda x,y:x-y, lambda x,y:x*y, lambda x,y:x/y]

>>> lamb_cal[0]
<function <lambda> at 0x000001BF34AFC3A0>
>>> lamb_cal[0](3, 2)
5

>>> lamb_cal[1]
<function <lambda> at 0x000001BF34AFC670>
>>> lamb_cal[1](3, 2)
1

>>> lamb_cal[2]
<function <lambda> at 0x000001BF34AFC700>
>>> lamb_cal[2](3, 2)
6

>>> lamb_cal[3]
<function <lambda> at 0x000001BF34AFC790>
>>> lamb_cal[3](3, 2)
1.5
```

Explanation

① This is a simple function that adds and returns the sum of x and y.

② You can use lambda on a single line of code to achieve the same result. This is the re-creation of the function in ① but with fewer lines.

③ You have just created a simple calculator on a single line using a lambda. The calculator is self-explanatory; `lamb_cal` can perform the basic arithmetic.
As we become more familiar with Python coding, there are certain situations we can apply lambdas. You do not have to use a lambda, but you can see the real value of lambdas in this exercise.

Recap: Module Concepts

Here's a recap:

- Modules are Python code that can use a set of variables, functions, and classes in the `.py` file format.
- You can import a module by issuing `import module_name`.
- The default location of the module is set during Python installation.
- The Python built-in library is a set of reusable Python programs that contain a variety of codes.
- The `dir()` built-in function allows you to view the modules in a package.
- If you do not have the required module, you can create one, add `FILEPATH`, and add your packages.

If you want to go over what you have learned in this chapter or repeat the exercises for the second or third time, download `ex2_1_to_2_90.txt` and use it for your practice; this file contains all the exercises from Exercise 2-1 to Exercise 2-90. If you are totally new to Python, I am recommending you repeat the previous exercise at least three times.

URL: `https://github.com/pynetauto/apress_pynetauto/tree/master`

Summary

I hope you have been busy on your keyboard throughout this chapter and tried some basic Python exercises. An interpreted programming language such as Python was designed to mimic a human language. Many years ago, I studied the pragmatics of language at university. According to Cambridge Dictionary, *pragmatics* is "the study of how language is affected by the situation in which it is used, of how language is used to get things or perform actions, and of how words can express things that are different from what they appear to mean." As we become more comfortable with Python as a programming language or a tool, we have to continue to learn to communicate with computers (machines), give a set of instructions to the computers, and interpret Python's feedback or errors. We have covered the most basic Python concepts through practical examples and exercises. The best way to learn a programming language is through more exercises that are relatable to real scenarios. Now that we have learned the basics, let's get some more practice to link the concepts to real scenarios in Chapter 3. The next chapter contains general Python exercises as well as work-related exercises.

CHAPTER 3

More Python Exercises

The Romans borrowed an old Athenian concept and turned it into a proverb: "Repetito master sturdiorum," which means "Repetition is the mother of all learning." In the previous chapter, you practiced basic Python concepts, but you will get more practice with more relatable subjects and scenarios in this chapter. Some parts of the exercises will contain content that will be directly relatable to the scripts you will be writing in the second half of this book. When we do each exercise in this chapter, let your fingers do the typing, but let your brain think about how a certain exercise can help you automate parts of your work.

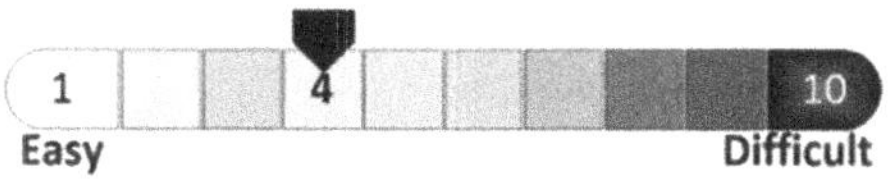

Getting Ready for the Exercises

This book works on the assumption that you are new to network automation using Python. When we look at the day-to-day tasks of a typical IT engineer, systems engineers and network engineers do not have to type as much as DevOps engineers. This is just the nature of the job because DevOps engineers are always on the move, writing code and creating applications as part of various projects. In other words, for most of the non-DevOps IT staff who are reading this book, your time will be spent on installing, configuring, and troubleshooting various issues in your field. It will be challenging to find the time during work hours to practice as you are not paid to learn to code and develop automation applications. Yet, almost all enterprise IT teams are trying to push their IT engineers to start learning a programming language and automating repetitive tasks. Being a good employee and exemplary IT engineer, you have probably been using time outside of work hours to learn Python. Not all of us will understand programmability concepts or learn the Python basics on our first attempt; just be consistent and keep trying until you do. The only way to overcome the challenges is through more exercises. If you have specific Python challenges, please get into the habit of searching for that topic on Google and reading further about it. Now, let's get some more Python practices using relatable examples.

In Chapter 2, you learned the basics of Python. This chapter will help you practice even more to prepare you for network automation using Python. The more you practice, the better you will get.

B. Choi, *Introduction to Python Network Automation*, https://doi.org/10.1007/978-1-4842-6806-3_3

Exercise 3-1: Concatenate a List and a Tuple into a Single List

①
```
>>> fruits = ['apple', 'orange', 'mango']
>>> vegetables = ('broccoli', 'potato', 'spinach')
>>> favorites = fruits + list(vegetables)
>>> print(favorites)
['apple', 'orange', 'mango', 'broccoli', 'potato', 'spinach']
```

Explanation

① Create one variable in the list and create one variable in a tuple. Convert the tuple to a list using the `list()` method. Concatenate and merge one list and one tuple into a single list.

Exercise 3-2: Use Python as a Calculator

①
```
>>> eigrp, ospf, rip = 90, 110, 120
>>> path1, path2, path3 = 3, 6, 9
>>> admin_distance = (eigrp * path1) + (ospf * path2) + (rip * path3)
>>> print(admin_distance)
2010
```

Explanation

① Use Python as a calculator and calculate an administrative distance.

Exercise 3-3: Do Some Basic String format() Exercises

①
```
>>> name = 'Hugh'
>>> age = 15
>>> detail = 'His name is %s and he is %d.'
>>> print(detail %(name, age))
His name is Hugh and he is 15.
```

```
② >>> Name, age, height = 'Hugh', 15, 174.5
#1 >>> detail = ('His name is {}, he is {} and {} cm tall.'.format(name, age, height))
   >>> print(detail)
#2 His name is Hugh, he is 15 and 174.5 cm tall.

#3 >>> detail = ('His name is {0}, he is {1} and {2} cm tall.'.format(name, age, height))
   >>> print(detail)
#4 His name is Hugh, he is 15 and 174.5 cm tall.

   >>> detail = ('His name is {name}, he is {age} and {height} cm
   tall.'.format(name='Joshua', age=16, height=178))
   >>> print(detail)
   His name is Joshua, he is 16 and 178 cm tall.

   >>> detail = ('His name is {0}, he is {age} and {height} cm tall.'.format('Michael',
   age=12, height=170))
   >>> print(detail)
   His name is Michael, he is 12 and 170 cm tall.
③ >>> person = {'height':174.5, 'name':'Hugh', 'age':15}
   >>> print('{name} is {age} years old and {height} cm tall.'.format(**person))
   Hugh is 15 years old and 174.5 cm tall.
```

Explanation

① This is a basic string (%s) and digit (%d) formatting example.

② #1. format() example: Default arguments
#2. format() example: Positional arguments
#3. format() example: Keyword arguments
#4. format() example: Mixed arguments

③ This is an str.format(**mapping) example. This is an example of the argument parsing used in Python, so make a special note of the two asterisks used in the example.

Exercise 3-4: Ask for a Username

Write the code in Notepad++ as shown in Figure 3-1.

```
① # ex3_4.py
print('Please enter your name: ')
name = input()
print('Thank you, ', name)
```

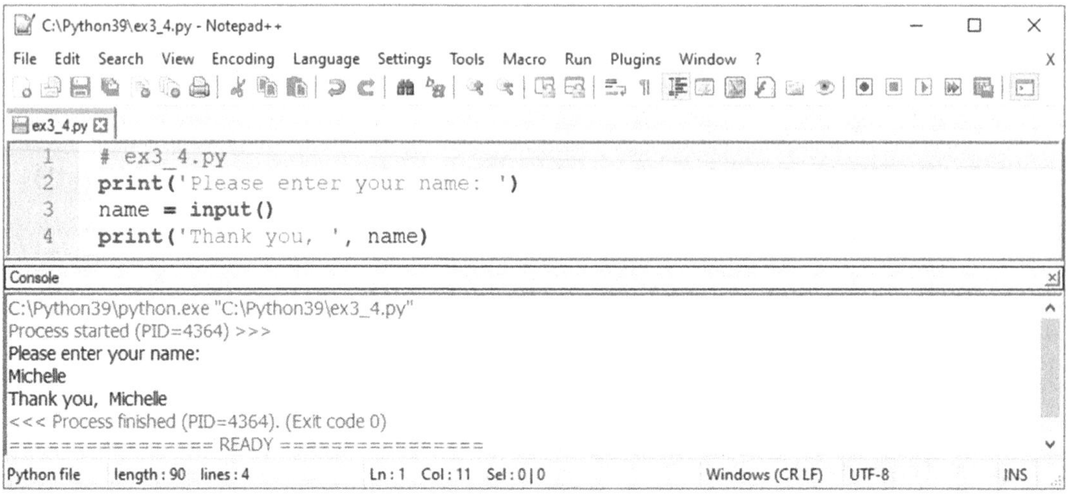

Figure 3-1. *User input, thanking the user*

Explanation

① Create some Python code that will ask for the user's name. You are going to use this as the basis of username and password tool development. You will have some fun while asking for someone's name.

Exercise 3-5: Get a Username: Version 1

Write the code and save it as ex3_5.py and run the code in Notepad++. (see Figure 3-2)

①
```
#ex3_5.py
name = input('Please enter your name: ')

print(f'Hi, {name}.')
```

Figure 3-2. *User input, saying "hi"*

Explanation

① Reiterate ex3_4.py and write some simplified code in ex3_5.py. The number of code lines has shrunk. In this exercise, you are learning how to reduce two code lines into a single line of code and also use an abbreviated formatting method.

Exercise 3-6: Get a Username: Version 2

On Notepad++, enter the following code, save the file as ex3_6.py and run the code. (see Figure 3-3).

①
```
#Ex3_6.py
import re

name = input("Enter your name: ")
while True:
    while not re.match("^[a-zA-Z]+$", name):
      name = input("Enter your name: ")
else:
    print(name)
    exit()
```

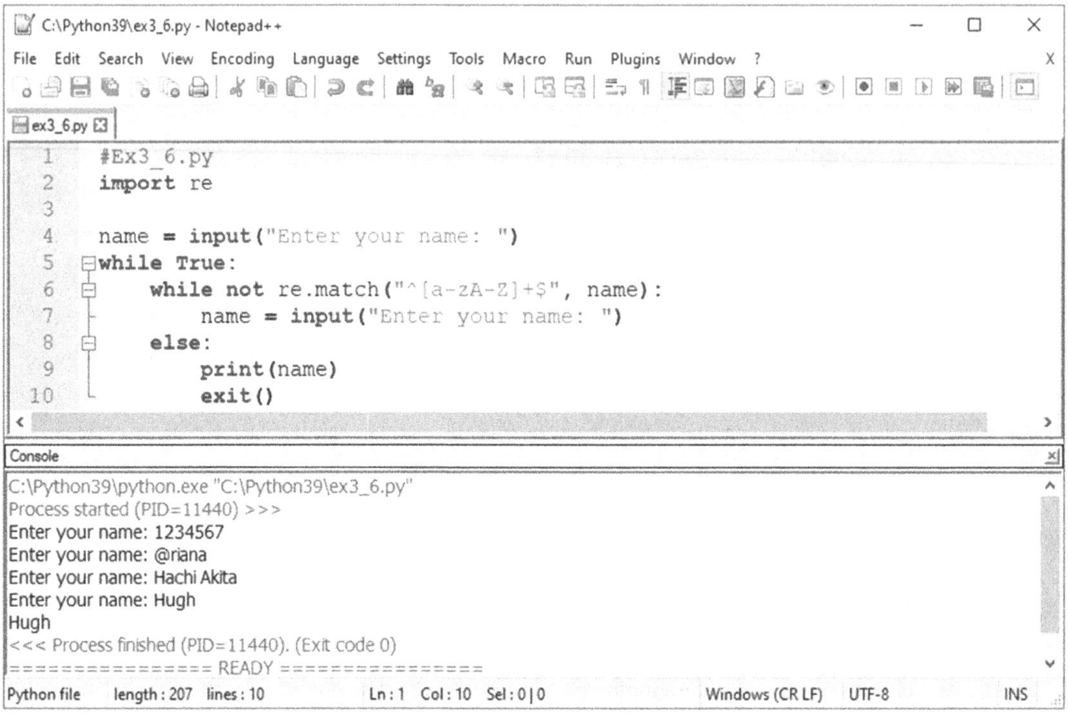

Figure 3-3. *User input, getting correctly formatted input*

Explanation

① Using ex3_5.py as the basis, you have just created a simple Python application asking for someone's name with some requirements. You have imported the re (regular expression) built-in Python module to force the user to provide a name starting with an alphabetical letter that accepts letters only.

^[a-zA-Z]+$ means any character starting with a letter with one or more characters and ending with a letter. So, yomu cannot enter a number or a special character as a name. If the user cannot adhere to this rule, the script asks until the user provides an expected response. Once the correct response is received, the name is printed and exits the application.

You will learn more about regular expressions in Chapter 9. An entire chapter will be dedicated to learning regular expressions and how to use the re module. Scripting is all about data handling and how we process them. We must master regular expressions and conquer our fear of regular expressions to become confident programming engineers.

Exercise 3-7: Get a Username: Version 3

Enter the code and save the file as ex3_7.py on Notepad++. Run the code as shown in Figure 3-4.

①
```
# ex3_7.py
import re

def get_name():
   name = input("Enter your name: ")
   while True:
     while not re.match("^[a-zA-Z]+$", name):
       name = input("Enter your name: ")
     else:
       print(name)
       exit()
get_name()
```

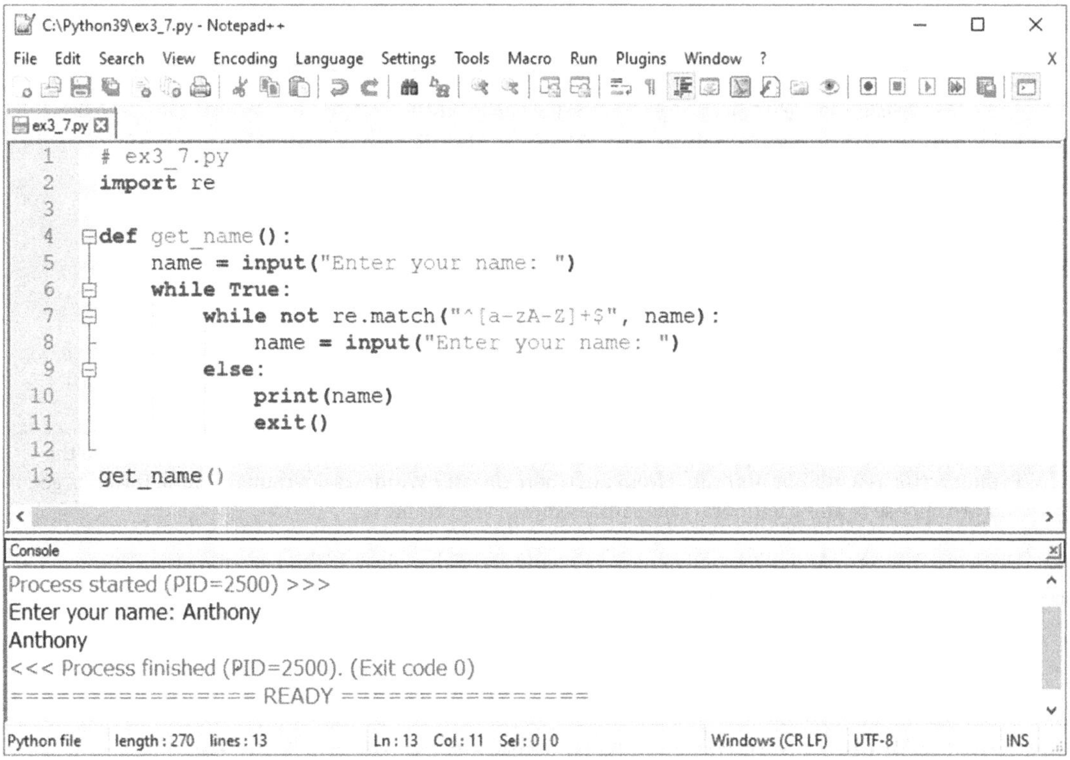

***Figure 3-4.** User input, getting the username script into a function*

Explanation

① Create the ex3_7.py script and run it to learn how you can create a function based on ex3_6.py and convert it into a function. The last statement, get_name(), will trigger the script to run. This is the same script as ex3_6.py, but we have converted it into a function so you can understand the reiteration process.

Exercise 3-8: Add a Temporary Filepath, Import ex3_7.py as a Module, and Run the Script

①
```
C:\Users\brendan>python
Python 3.9.1 (tags/v3.9.1:1e5d33e, Dec  7 2020, 17:08:21) [MSC v.1927 64 bit (AMD64)]
on win32
Type "help", "copyright", "credits" or "license" for more information.
>>> import ex3_7.py
Enter your name: Brendan
Brendan

C:\Users\brendan>
```

②
```
# If your script is under a different folder, for example, under 'C:\Users\brendan\
Documents\'. You have to manually add the Filepath using append.
>>> import sys
>>> sys.path.append('C:\\Users\\brendan\\Documents\\') # Add temporary filepath
>>> print(sys.path)
['', 'C:\\Python39\\python39.zip', 'C:\\Python39\\DLLs', 'C:\\Python39\\lib', 'C:\\
Python39', 'C:\\Python39\\lib\\site-packages', 'C:\\Users\\brendan\\Documents\\']

>>> import ex3_7.py
9
Enter your name: Ryan
Ryan
```

Explanation

① If you selected Add Python 3.9 to PATH during the Python installation, you should be able to call the Python script as a module and run it from anywhere on your Windows operating system. If you forget, you can choose to add a temporary filepath, as shown in example ②.

② Open the Python command prompt and add a temporary filepath so Python can read the Python module created in Exercise 3-7. Here you are adding a new (temporary) filepath and importing a custom module to run from your interpreter session to learn how importing and customizing modules work.

Exercise 3-9: Use Commas to Add Spaces Between Strings

①
```
>> print('Around' + 'the' + 'World' + 'in' + '100' + 'days.')
AoundtheWorldin100days. # by default, no spaces are added when '+' is used

>>> print('Around ' + 'the ' + 'World ' + 'in ' + '100 ' + 'days.') # manually enter
spaces between words
Around the World in 100 days.

>>> print('Around', 'the', 'World', 'in', '100', 'days.')
Around the World in 100 days. # adds spaces automatically
```

Explanation

① Practice the previous exercises and compare the output. Notice that commas are used in the previous exercise, and the output adds spaces between the strings.

Exercise 3-10: Practice if; if and else; and if, elif, and else

①
```
>>> y = 5
>>> if x > y:
...     print('x is greater than y.')
...
>>> # No output as if the statement was False

>>> x = 3
>>> y = 5
>>> if x < y:
...   print('x is less than y.')
...
x is less than y. # prints output as if the statement was True

>>> y = 5
>>> if x >= y:
...     print('x is greater or equal to y.')
... else:
...   print('x is smaller than y.')
...
x is smaller than y. #  prints output of else statement

>>> x = 3
>>> y = 5
>>> z = 3
>>> if x < y > z:
...   print('y is greater than x and greater than z.')
...
y is greater than x and greater than z. # all conditions met

>>> x = 5
>>> y = 10
>>> if x < y:
...   print('x is smaller than y.')
... elif x > y:
...   print('x is greater than y.')
... else:
...   print('x is equal to y.')
...
x is smaller than y. # if the statement was satisfied
```

Explanation

① You have just practiced if; if and else; and if, elif, and else. These exercises are self-explanatory; this is one beauty of Python.

Exercise 3-11: Practice for ~ in range with end=' '

①
```
>>> for n in range (1, 11):
...     print(n)
...
1
2
3
[omitted for brevity]
9
10

>>> for n in range (1, 11):
...   print(n, end='')
...
12345678910
>>>
>>> for n in range (1, 11):
...   print(n, end=' ') # adds spaces and print horizontally
...
1 2 3 4 5 6 7 8 9 10
>>>
>>> for n in range (1, 11):
...   print(n, end=',') # adds commas between output
...
1,2,3,4,5,6,7,8,9,10,
>>>
>>> for n in range (1, 11):
...   print(n, end='/') # adds forward slashes
...
1/2/3/4/5/6/7/8/9/10/
>>>
>>> for n in range (1, 11):
...   print(n, end='|') # adds pipes (vertical bars)
...
1|2|3|4|5|6|7|8|9|10|
>>>
```

Explanation

① Practice each for ~ in range statement with end= and compare the variations in the outcome.

Exercise 3-12: Practice for ~ in range

①
```
>>> for n in range (2, 11):
...   print(("Creating VLAN") + str(n))
...
Creating VLAN2 Creating VLAN3 Creating VLAN4 Creating VLAN5 Creating VLAN6 Creating
VLAN7 Creating VLAN8 Creating VLAN9 Creating VLAN10
```

Explanation

① `for ~ in range()` becomes handy when you have to loop through several lines to add configuration to networking devices. We will apply the previous code in the later Python network automation labs. Try to get familiar with this example.

Exercise 3-13: Practice for line in ~

①
```
>>> txt1 = "Seeya later Alligator"
>>> for line in txt1:
...     print(line)
...
S
e
e
[omitted for brevity]
o
r

>>> txt1 = "Seeya later Alligator"
>>> for line in txt1:
...   print(line, end='')
...
Seeya later Alligator
```

Explanation

① For strings, you can use the `for line in ~` method, and you will get the same effect as the `for n in range()` method for numbers.

Exercise 3-14: Use the split() Method

①
```
>>> txt1 = "Seeya later Alligator"
>>> print(txt1.split())# splits at every white spaces
['Seeya', 'later', 'Alligator']
>>> print(txt1.split( )) # same as above
['Seeya', 'later', 'Alligator']
>>> print(txt1.split('e', 1))
['S', 'eya later Alligator'] #splits at first instance of 'e
>>> txt2 = (txt1.split('e', 1))
>>> print(txt2[0]) #  you only want to extract the letter 'S'
S
>>> txt3 = (txt1.split('a', 3))
>>> print(txt3) # splits at every 'a', three times
['Seey', ' l', 'ter Allig', 'tor']
>>> print(txt3[1]) # you only want to extract the first letter 'l'
L
```

Explanation

① Getting enough practice with string indexing and splicing becomes a powerful tool when used with regular expressions. Unfortunately, to become a good programmer, we have to get familiar with general data handling: data gathering, data processing, and data flow control.

Exercise 3-15: Practice with lstrip(), rstrip(), strip(), upper(), lower(), title(), and capitalize()

①
```
>>> australia = ' terra australis incognita '
>> print(australia.title())# title() method capitalizes first letters
Terra Australis Incognita
>>> print(australia.rstrip().upper())# upper() for capitalization
TERRA AUSTRALIS INCOGNITA
>>> x = (australia.lstrip().lower())# lower() for lower casing
>>> print(x.capitalize())# capitalize() for capitalization of first letter only
Terra australis incognita
>>> print(australia.strip().upper())# strip() remove both left and right white spaces
TERRA AUSTRALIS INCOGNITA
```

Explanation

① You have just completed the uppercasing and lowercasing and strip method practice. Can you think of some interesting and relatable words for you to practice? Add some fun into your exercise by changing the words to have more meaning to you.

Exercise 3-16: Create a file and read it four different ways

①
```
>>> with open('test123.txt', 'w') as f:
...   f.write('This is line 1.\nThis is line 2.\nThis is line 3.\n')
...
48
```

②
```
>>> with open('test123.txt', 'r') as f:
...   lines = f.readlines()
...   print(lines)
...
['This is line 1.\n', 'This is line 2.\n', 'This is line 3.\n']
```

③
```
>>> with open('test123.txt', 'r') as f:
...   lines = list(f)
...   print(lines)
...
['This is line 1.\n', 'This is line 2.\n', 'This is line 3.\n']
```

④
```
>>> f = open('test123.txt', 'r')
>>> lines = f.readlines()
>>> print(lines)
['This is line 1.\n', 'This is line 2.\n', 'This is line 3.\n']
>> f.close()
```

⑤
```
>>> f = open('test123.txt', 'r')
>>> lines = list(f)
>>> print(lines)
['This is line 1.\n', 'This is line 2.\n', 'This is line 3.\n']
f.close()
```

Explanation

① Create `test123.txt` in `w` mode and write something.

② This is with the open method with a `readlines()` example.

③ This is with the open method with a `list()` example.

④ This is a simple `open()` method with a `readlines()` example. Always close the file after use.

⑤ This is a simple `open()` method with a `list()` example. Make sure `f.close()` is issued to close the file.

Exercise 3-17: Read and Output Files for a More Detailed Understanding

①
```
>>> with open('test123.txt', 'w') as f:
...     f.write(' this is a lower casing line.\n')
...
33
>>> with open('test123.txt', 'r') as f:
...     print(f.read())
...
this is a lower casing line.
```

②
```
>>> with open('test123.txt', 'a') as f:
...     f.write('THIS IS AN UPPER CASING LINE. \nThisIsACamelCasingLine.\n')
...
58
```

③
```
>>> with open('test123.txt', 'r') as f:
...     print(f.read())
...
this is a lower casing line. THIS IS AN UPPER CASING LINE.
ThisIsACamelCasingLine.

>>> with open('test123.txt', 'r') as f:
...     print(f.readline())
...
this is a lower casing line.

>>> with open('test123.txt', 'r') as f:
...     print(f.readlines())
...
[' this is a lower casing line. \n', 'THIS IS AN UPPER CASING LINE .\n',
'ThisIsACamelCasingLine.\n']
```

④
```
>> >>> with open('test123.txt', 'r') as f:
...     print(f.read().lower().strip())
...
this is a lower casing line. this is an upper casing line. thisisacamelcasingline.
```

⑤
```
>>> with open('test123.txt', 'r') as f:
...     x = (f.read().lower().strip())
...     y = set(x.split())
...     print(y)
...     print(len(y))
...
{'lower', 'casing', 'a', 'this', 'is', 'upper', 'thisisacamelcasingline.', 'an',
'line.'} 9
```

Explanation

① Create a new `test123.txt` file. Since the file opens in `w` mode, it will overwrite the file created in Exercise 3-17. Write to the file in the same way as shown in this book.

② You can write more content to your file in a mode.

③ Try to read and print in three different modes: `read()`, `readline()`, and `readlines()`. Do you see the difference?

④ Practice using other methods to manipulate your strings and whitespaces.

⑤ You are using the `set()` and `split()` methods together to count the total number of words and characters in your file.

Exercise 3-18: Use the getpass() Module and User Input

For this exercise, open Python IDLE (interpreter) to write the code.

①
```
>>> import getpass
>>> def get_pwd():
...     username = input('Enter username : ')
...     password = getpass.getpass()
...     print(username, password)
...
>>> get_pwd()
Enter username : admin
Password: *********
admin mypassword
```

Explanation

① Use `import` to load the `getpass` library. Use `def` to change your password into a function. Then use the `input()` function to ask for the user's name; then use the `getpass.getpass()` module to ask for the user's password. While the password is entered, the `getpass()` module will hide the entered password. Just for testing, we have printed out the username and password. The `getpass()` module comes in handy when creating a login request for SSH and Telnet to networking devices.

Exercise 3-19: Understand the Difference Between Encoding and Decoding

①
```
>>> text_1 = 'Network Automation'
>>> print(text_1)
Network Automation
>>> byte_1 = text_1.encode()
>>> print(byte_1)
b'Network Automation '
```

②
```
>>> byte_2 = b'Mission completed.'
>>> print(byte_2)
b'Mission completed. '
>>> text_2 = byte_2.decode()
>>> print(text_2)
Mission completed.
```

Explanation

① Computers communicate in bits (0s and 1s), and the computer handles files in bytes. But we humans want to communicate in plaintext to the machines, so encoding and decoding are required. This is a simple exercise to convert a string into bytes. You will see this in action during the Telnet Python lab exercises in Chapter 13. Make a special note of this exercise.

② In Python 3, all strings are recognized as Unicode, and the `decode()` method must be used to convert bytes, which are binary stream data that computers understand. When executing commands on machines such as routers and switches, be wary of bytes to string conversion and string to bytes conversion to avoid code execution errors.

Exercise 3-20: Handle CSV Files in Python with the csv Module

①
```
# Use the following information to create .py called ex3_20.py and save it to your
Documents folder.
# ex3_20.py
import csv

with open ('C://Users//brendan//Documents//2020_router_purchase.csv', 'w', newline=''
) as csvfile:
    filewriter = csv.writer (csvfile, delimiter = ',', quotechar = '|', quoting = csv.
    QUOTE_MINIMAL)
    filewriter.writerow (['Site', 'Router_Type', 'IOS_Image', 'No_of_routers', 'Unit_
    price($)', 'Purchase_Date'])
    filewriter.writerow(['NYNY', 'ISR4351/K9', 'isr4300-universalk9.16.09.05.SPA.bin',
    4, '$ 9100.00', '1-Mar-20'])
    filewriter.writerow(['LACA', 'ISR4331/K9', 'isr4300-universalk9.16.09.05.SPA.bin',
    2, '$ 5162.00', '1-Mar- 20'])
```

```
filewriter.writerow(['LDUK', 'ISR4321/K9', 'isr4300-universalk9.16.09.05.SPA.bin',
1, '$ 2370.00', '3-Apr- 20'])
filewriter.writerow(['HKCN', 'ISR4331/K9', 'isr4300-universalk9.16.09.05.SPA.bin',
2, '$ 5162.00', '17-Apr-20'])
filewriter.writerow(['TKJP', 'ISR4351/K9', 'isr4300-universalk9.16.09.05.SPA.bin',
1, '$ 9100.00', '15-May-20'])
filewriter.writerow(['MHGM', 'ISR4331/K9', 'isr4300-universalk9.16.09.05.SPA.bin',
2, '$ 5162.00', '30-Jun-20'])
```

② Open the Windows command prompt or Windows PowerShell, and run the Python code to create your CSV file (see Figure 3-5).

```
PS C:\Users\brendan> cd Documents # change directory to Documents
PS C:\Users\brendan\Documents> dir ex3_20.py # check ex3_20.py exists under Documents
folder
PS C:\Users\brendan\Documents> python ex3_20.py # run ex3_20.py to create a csv file
PS C:\Users\brendan\Documents> dir 2020_router_* # check 2020_router_purchase.csv file
has been created
```

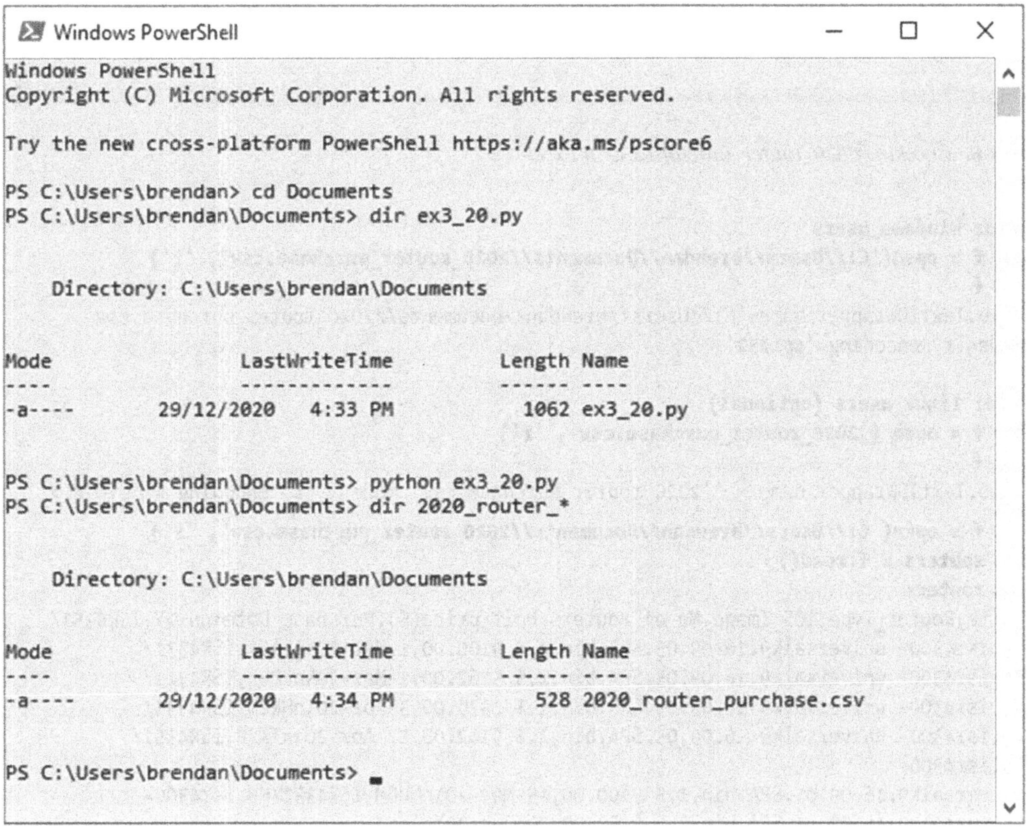

***Figure 3-5.** Running the CSV script to create an Excel file on Windows PowerShell*

③ Use Microsoft Excel to open the file and check the newly created file. It should look similar to Figure 3-6.

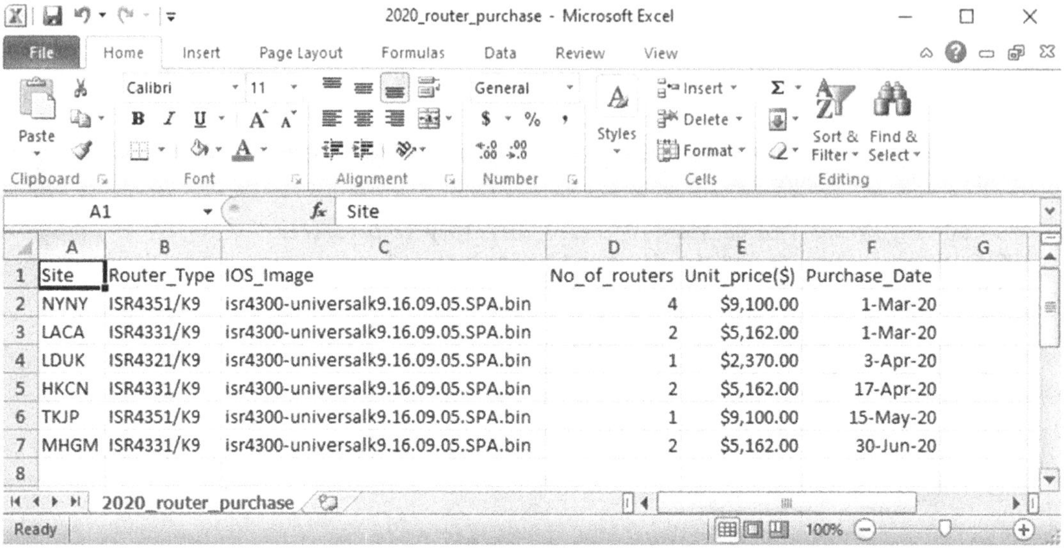

	A	B	C	D	E	F	G
1	Site	Router_Type	IOS_Image	No_of_routers	Unit_price($)	Purchase_Date	
2	NYNY	ISR4351/K9	isr4300-universalk9.16.09.05.SPA.bin	4	$9,100.00	1-Mar-20	
3	LACA	ISR4331/K9	isr4300-universalk9.16.09.05.SPA.bin	2	$5,162.00	1-Mar-20	
4	LDUK	ISR4321/K9	isr4300-universalk9.16.09.05.SPA.bin	1	$2,370.00	3-Apr-20	
5	HKCN	ISR4331/K9	isr4300-universalk9.16.09.05.SPA.bin	2	$5,162.00	17-Apr-20	
6	TKJP	ISR4351/K9	isr4300-universalk9.16.09.05.SPA.bin	1	$9,100.00	15-May-20	
7	MHGM	ISR4331/K9	isr4300-universalk9.16.09.05.SPA.bin	2	$5,162.00	30-Jun-20	
8							

Figure 3-6. *Checking 2020_router_purchase.csv in Excel*

④
```
# For Windows users
>>> f = open('C://Users//brendan//Documents//2020_router_purchase.csv', 'r')
>>> f
<_io.TextIOWrapper name='C://Users//brendan//Documents//2020_router_purchase.csv'
mode='r' encoding='cp1252'>

# For Linux users (optional)
>>> f = open ('2020_router_purchase.csv', 'r')
>>> f
<_io.TextIOWrapper name = ''2020_router_purchase.csv' mode = 'r' encoding = 'UTF-8'>
```

⑤
```
>>> f = open('C://Users//brendan//Documents//2020_router_purchase.csv', 'r')
>>> routers = f.read()
>>> routers
'Site,Router_Type,IOS_Image,No_of_routers,Unit_price($),Purchase_Date\nNYNY,ISR4351/
K9,isr4300- universalk9.16.09.05.SPA.bin,4,$ 9100.00,1-Mar-20\nLACA,ISR4331/
K9,isr4300- universalk9.16.09.05.SPA.bin,2,$ 5162.00,1-Mar-20\nLDUK,ISR4321/
K9,isr4300- universalk9.16.09.05.SPA.bin,1,$ 2370.00,3-Apr-20\nHKCN,ISR4331/
K9,isr4300- universalk9.16.09.05.SPA.bin,2,$ 5162.00,17-Apr-20\nTKJP,ISR4351/
K9,isr4300-
universalk9.16.09.05.SPA.bin,1,$ 9100.00,15-May-20\nMHGM,ISR4331/K9,isr4300-
universalk9.16.09.05.SPA.bin,2,$ 5162.00,30-Jun-20\n'
```

```
>>> print(routers)
Site,Router_Type,IOS_Image,No_of_routers,Unit_price($),Purchase_Date
NYNY,ISR4351/K9,isr4300-universalk9.16.09.05.SPA.bin,4,$ 9100.00,1-Mar-20
LACA,ISR4331/K9,isr4300-universalk9.16.09.05.SPA.bin,2,$ 5162.00,1-Mar- 20
LDUK,ISR4321/K9,isr4300-universalk9.16.09.05.SPA.bin,1,$ 2370.00,3-Apr- 20
HKCN,ISR4331/K9,isr4300-universalk9.16.09.05.SPA.bin,2,$ 5162.00,17-Apr-20
TKJP,ISR4351/K9,isr4300-universalk9.16.09.05.SPA.bin,1,$ 9100.00,15-May-20
MHGM,ISR4331/K9,isr4300-universalk9.16.09.05.SPA.bin,2,$ 5162.00,30-Jun-20

>>> f.close ()
```

⑥
```
>>> with open('C://Users//brendan//Documents//2020_router_purchase.csv', 'r') as f:
...     routers = f.readlines()
...     for router in routers:
...         print(router, end=(" "))
...
Site,Router_Type,IOS_Image,No_of_routers,Unit_price($),Purchase_Date
NYNY,ISR4351/K9,isr4300-universalk9.16.09.05.SPA.bin,4,$ 9100.00,1-Mar-20
LACA,ISR4331/K9,isr4300-universalk9.16.09.05.SPA.bin,2,$ 5162.00,1-Mar- 20
LDUK,ISR4321/K9,isr4300-universalk9.16.09.05.SPA.bin,1,$ 2370.00,3-Apr- 20
HKCN,ISR4331/K9,isr4300-universalk9.16.09.05.SPA.bin,2,$ 5162.00,17-Apr-20
TKJP,ISR4351/K9,isr4300-universalk9.16.09.05.SPA.bin,1,$ 9100.00,15-May-20
MHGM,ISR4331/K9,isr4300-universalk9.16.09.05.SPA.bin,2,$ 5162.00,30-Jun-20
```

Explanation

① Create a new code file called `ex3_20.py` using the information. The file needs to be saved in your `Documents` folder.

② Then open a command prompt of your choice and run the Python command to create a CSV file using the `ex3_20.py` script.

③ Open the newly created `2020_router_purchase.csv` file in Microsoft Excel to check it.

④ If you open and read the file, you can see that the Windows-created file will use the encoding of `cp1252`, whereas on Linux, UTF-8 encoding will be used as the default decoding method.

⑤ Use `read()` to read the file. The content is a long string of data. If you use `print()`, then the new lines will be displayed as individual lines, and it becomes easier to read.

⑥ If you do not want to be bothered with the ending `f.close()` statement, you can also use the `with open` command to open the file and read it. In this example, we are using the `f.readlines()` method to read each line separately and then using the `for` loop to call out each line in the CSV file. Take your time carefully studying the difference between the `read()`, `readlines()`, and `readline()` methods.

Exercise 3-21: Output a CSV File

```
① >>> f = open('C://Users//brendan//Documents//2020_router_purchase.csv', 'r')
  >>> for line in f:
  ...     print(line.strip())
  ...
  Site,Router_Type,IOS_Image,No_of_routers,Unit_price($),Purchase_Date NYNY,ISR4351/
  K9,isr4300-universalk9.16.09.05.SPA.bin,4,$ 9100.00,1-Mar-20 LACA,ISR4331/
  K9,isr4300-universalk9.16.09.05.SPA.bin,2,$ 5162.00,1-Mar-20 LDUK,ISR4321/
  K9,isr4300-universalk9.16.09.05.SPA.bin,1,$ 2370.00,3-Apr-20 HKCN,ISR4331/K9,isr4300-
  universalk9.16.09.05.SPA.bin,2,$ 5162.00,17 -Apr-20
  TKJP,ISR4351/K9,isr4300-universalk9.16.09.05.SPA.bin,1,$ 9100.00,15 -May-20
  MHGM,ISR4331/K9,isr4300-universalk9.16.09.05.SPA.bin,2,$ 5162.00,30 -Jun-20
  >>> f.close()
```

Explanation

① As in a normal text file, you can use the `for` loop method to read each line and print one line at a time. Make sure you use the `strip()` method to remove any leading or trailing whitespaces, newline, or tabs.

Exercise 3-22: Find the Price of a Cisco ISR 4331 Router from a CSV File

```
①  >>> f = open('C://Users//brendan//Documents//2020_router_purchase.csv', 'r')
#1  >>> x = f.read().split('\n')
    >>> x
    ['Site,Router_Type,IOS_Image,No_of_routers,Unit_price($),Purchase_Date',
    'NYNY,ISR4351/K9,isr4300- universalk9.16.09.05.SPA.bin,4,$ 9100.00,1-Mar-20',
    'LACA,ISR4331/K9,isr4300- universalk9.16.09.05.SPA.bin,2,$ 5162.00,1-Mar-20',
    'LDUK,ISR4321/K9,isr4300- universalk9.16.09.05.SPA.bin,1,$ 2370.00,3-Apr-20',
    'HKCN,ISR4331/K9,isr4300- universalk9.16.09.05.SPA.bin,2,$ 5162.00,17 -Apr-20',
    'TKJP,ISR4351/K9,isr4300- universalk9.16.09.05.SPA.bin,1,$ 9100.00,15 -May-20',
    'MHGM,ISR4331/K9,isr4300- universalk9.16.09.05.SPA.bin,2,$ 5162.00,30 -Jun-20', '']
#2  >>> y = x[2]
    >>> y
    'LACA,ISR4331/K9,isr4300-universalk9.16.09.05.SPA.bin,2,$ 5162.00,1-Mar-20'
#3  >>> z = y.split(',')
    >>> z
    ['LACA', 'ISR4331/K9', 'isr4300-universalk9.16.09.05.SPA.bin', '2', '$ 5162.00', '1-
    Mar-20']
#4  >>> price_4331 = z[4]
#5  >>> print(price_4331)
    $ 5162.00
```

Explanation

① In this example, you have just practiced reading data from a CSV file and extracting specific information.

#1. The `read().split()` method reads the file, splits the items, and saves the items in a list for each line.
#2. x's index 2 was assigned to variable y.
#3. Once again, `split()` breaks the string into a list. The list was assigned to a variable z.
#4. z's fifth or index 4 elements were assigned to a variable called `price_4331`.
#5. The price of a Cisco 4331 was printed on the screen.

Exercise 3-23: Calculate the Total Cost of the Router Purchases: No Module

①
```
# ex3_23.py

total = 0.0
with open ('C://Users//brendan//Documents//2020_router_purchase.csv', 'r') as f:
   headers = next (f)
   for line in f:
     line = line.strip ()
     devices = line.split (',')
     devices[4] = devices[4] .strip ('$')
     devices[4] = float (devices[4])
     devices[3] = int (devices[3])
     total += devices[3] * devices[4]
print('Total cost: $', total)
```

②
```
C:\Users\brendan\Documents> python ex3_23.py
Total cost: $ 78842.0
```

Explanation

① Using the method learned in Exercise 3-23, create a program that calculates the total cost of routers called `ex3_23.py`. We set the initial value of the total at 0.0 dollars. Use indexes 3 and 4 in the list to find the sum spent on the router purchase. To avoid errors that can occur during calculations, we use `header=next(f)` to skip the first line's header information. Split, strip, and convert between various data types. Save the script in the `Document` folder, and make sure you change the file path to suit your computer settings.

② Run the Python application to find the total cost of the router purchases. According to our script, the total cost was $78,842. These exercises seem very anal and meaningless but will become useful while processing meaningful data and developing real work applications.

Exercise 3-24: Calculate the Total Cost of the Router Purchases: Using the csv Module

①
```
# ex3_24.py

import csv

total = 0.0
with open ('C://Users//brendan//Documents//2020_router_purchase.csv') as f:
   rows = csv.reader (f)
   headers = next (rows)
   for row in rows:
     row [4] = row [4].strip ('$')
     row [4] = float(row [4])
     row [3] = int(row [3])
     total += row[3] * row[4]
print('Total cost: $', total)
```

②
```
C:\Users\brendan\Documents> python ex3_24.py
Total cost: $ 78842.0
```

Explanation

① We re-created the same application using Python's built-in `csv` module. First, import the `csv` module and follow the same process of striping and converting between data types. There is a famous saying in programming, "There's more than one way to skin a cat."

② Run the new code, but the total cost will be the same.

As we discussed earlier, this chapter only covers basic and specific Python topics. I recommend you pick up other basic Python books and go deeper into the topics discussed in this book. Well done! You have completed the basic Python exercises to get you ready for some Python network automation, but more advanced topics will follow in the later chapters.

Exercise 3-25: Convert dd-mmm-yy and Calculate the Difference in Days and Then in Years

While working in networking, you'll notice that different vendors have different date and time formats in their software. One good example is the date format of Cisco routers and switches. While I was manipulating the data collected from actual Cisco IOS software, I had to spend an hour converting and manipulating the release date of Cisco IOS in a particular format and work out how old the IOS image was since its release date. This exercise is from a real production example script. Here's the format of the IOS release date given: 12-Jul-17.

The objective is to manipulate and convert the date to the correct format so Python can work out how old the IOS is since its release date. Note, your date will differ from the result given in this example as it uses `today()` as the calculation date. Follow along with example ① first and then follow through with the iteration example ②.

```
①   # Follow this exercise in Python IDLE
#1  >>> from datetime import datetime
#2  >>> IOS_rel_date = '12-Jul-17'
#3  >>> x = IOS_rel_date.replace('-', ' ')
#4  >>> y = datetime.strptime(x, '%d %b %y')
#5  >>> y
    datetime.datetime(2017, 7, 12, 0, 0)
#6  >>> y.date() datetime.date(2017, 7, 12)
    >>> y_day = y.date()

#7  >>> datetime.today()
#8  datetime.datetime(2020, 4, 15, 11, 56, 3, 370515)
    >>> datetime.today().date()
#9  datetime.date(2020, 4, 15)
    >>> t_day = datetime.today().date()
#10 >>> delta = t_day - y_day
#11 >>> print(delta.days)
#12 1008
    >>> years = round(((delta.days)/365), 2)
#13 2.76
```

```
②   # Reiterated and reduced version of example 1:
    >>> from datetime import datetime
    >>> x = IOS_rel_date.replace('-', ' ')
    >>> y_day = (datetime.strptime(x, '%d %b %y')).date()
    >>> t_day = datetime.today().date()
    >>> delta = t_day - y_day
    >>> years = round(((delta.days)/365), 2)
    >>> print(years)
    2.76
```

Explanation

① #1. Import the datetime module from the datetime library. We need this library to complete our challenge.

#2. Enter the IOS release date as a string to begin this exercise.

#3. Replace - with blank spaces.

#4. Use the datetime module's `strptime` method to convert x to the correct date format. %d represents days, %b represents abbreviated months such as JAN, Jun, and Jul, and %y represents the abbreviated year without the first two leading digits. Python's datetime module expects the date to be in a specific format, and we are trying to normalize the format to achieve our goal.

#5. Now type y to check the current format. It has two 0s separated by a comma, which is the hour and minute. We have to lose these two zeros.

#6. Now use the `date()` method on y to drop the hour and minute information. Check first before applying this. This is the date format required to solve half of our challenge. We are at 50 percent now.

#7. Now we are happy with the date format, so assign it to the variable y_day.

#8. It is time to work with today's date. To find the number of days since the IOS release, we need to work out what today is and then minus the day of the release date. Use the `datetime()` module again, this time on `today()`.
#9. If the result is acceptable, then append `.date()` at the back to drop the time elements. This will return the date in the correct format.
#10. Now assign the object from #9 to a variable, `t_day`.
#11. The delta or the difference between the two dates is `t_day - y_day`.
#12. Print the result, and it will return the delta in the number of days.
#13. Now divide the delta by 365 days to convert the days to years. Use the `round()` function to give the last two decimals. This single exercise will give you some insight into how to massage specific data, in this case, dates.

② This example is a reiterated version of example 1. I have crunched some functions into one line to shorten the conversion processes. This is just one example of data manipulation, and there are many other ways to do the same conversion. Still, the important thing is to understand the thought process so you can adapt it to your situation. Finally, if you have 10 minutes, please visit the following site to review what *strftime* code formats are available: `https://strftime.org/`.

Exploring the Python IDE Environment

After completing this chapter, you need to start thinking about an integrated development environment (IDE) for Python code development. Working in a text editor is straightforward, but it has its limitations. Working within an IDE is not compulsory, but as you write more complex and longer Python code, your coding efficiency drops when using text editors such as Notepad, EditPlus, or Notepad++ on Windows or vi, Emacs, Gedit, or nano on Linux. IDEs provide many features not available from standard text editors. When you work in collaboration with team members, suddenly the version control of your documents becomes essential. Many organizations use GitHub with cloud storage as their code version control solution. Still, you do not have to worry about GitHub or version control at this stage. You have to learn to crawl before you can walk. Hence, this topic is not discussed beyond this section in this book. You do not have to start using an IDE application in this book, but I encourage you to explore them one at a time and find the perfect match for your coding style. On enterprise Linux systems, you rarely see graphical user interfaces (GUIs), so only Windows-compatible IDEs are discussed here. To help you explore various Python IDEs available for Windows, see Table 3-1. Although Jupyter Notebook (Anaconda) is not an IDE, it is included in Table 3-1 to give you another path to studying Python.

Table 3-1. Python IDEs and Anaconda (Jupyter Notebook)

Recommended IDE	Pros and Cons, Download URL
PyCharm*	**Pros**: Feature-rich, intuitive user interface, supports cross-platform, made for Python, free Community version, friendly for both beginners and experts **Cons**: Paid Professional version **URL**: `https://www.jetbrains.com/pycharm/download/`
Microsoft Visual Studio	**Pros**: Windows-friendly, easy to use (especially if you are a Windows user), feature-rich, Community version free **Cons**: The interface can be slow to start up. **URL**: `https://visualstudio.microsoft.com/vs/features/python/`
Eclipse	**Pros**: Multiple programming language support, familiar user interface, free **Cons**: JRE (JDK) dependency, tricky to set up for beginners, older IDE **URL**: `https://www.eclipse.org/downloads/packages/installer`
Atom	**Pros**: Developed by GitHub's Electron text editor, supports cross-platform and multiple programming languages, feature-rich via extensions and plug-ins, good documentation on application programming interface (API), free, easy to use, light yet still powerful **Cons**: Not as intuitive as PyCharm, closer to a text editor than PyCharm **URL**: `https://atom.io/`
Sublime Text 3	**Pros**: Popular code editor with fast, stable, and mature user interface; many features with modular approach and extendability **Cons**: Not as versatile as other IDEs, still feels more like a text editor than an IDE, have to purchase a license for continued use, no debugging option **URL**: `https://www.sublimetext.com/3`
Anaconda - Jupyter Notebook	**Pros**: Beginner friendly, excellent Python learning tool, web-based, used by scientific communities for data analytics **Cons**: Not an IDE, web-based, system resource-heavy **URL**: `https://jupyter.org/install`

Summary

This chapter was brief but contained a lot more substance than Python's `print()` function and syntax. This chapter served as a test-drive chapter that gives you the feel for what is ahead of us in the next chapter; you learned more Python basics by looking at some new Python modules, handling files, and processing data using simple Python code. Chapters 2 and 3 should serve as a good foundation for the Python network automation labs to be presented later in this book. If you still do not fully comprehend some parts of the exercise, it is OK to go back and repeat the exercises two to three times. If you have the time, you should repeat the exercises in both chapters three times by the time you get to Chapter 11. Chapters 4 to 6 will focus on building the virtually integrated Python network automation labs, starting with VMware Workstation Pro installation. It's time to move on to Chapter 4 to learn VMware Workstation basics and general virtualization technology basics. VMware Workstation and its virtualization technologies will help you to build your complete virtual networking lab and serve as the glue holding together virtual machines in your lab, so I encourage you to read the next chapter in its entirety.

Storytime 2: Machine vs. Human, The First Confrontation

According to Wikipedia, the first machine versus human confrontation took place in the United States of America around the 1870s, when a miner named John Henry challenged an automatic steam drilling machine to make a railway tunnel. The story of John Henry has been passed down to younger generations in American nursery rhymes. In the olden days, to drill a railway tunnel, the railway miners had to use hammers, chisels, and drills to make holes and use dynamite to blow up the landmass to make a tunnel. This human to machine competition became so famous in America that the story of John Henry versus the steam engine became an American folk legend. According to the story, the competition for tunnel boring went on for a day and a half to bore dynamite holes and lay the tracks.

According to the folk story, John Henry beat the steam drill and was victorious while defending his job. Sadly, according to the story, John Henry died of a heart attack due to fatigue and the severe stress after the competition. Of course, the steam drill continued to drill the holes the next day and the following days. What is clear here is that John Henry and his colleagues' jobs were getting automated out, and the U.S. Railroad Corporation did not hesitate to replace the miners with machines. The same thing happened in farming and manufacturing during the first Industrial Revolution, and automation of human tasks continues today and will continue in the future.

According to Wikipedia, "Automation is the technology by which a process or procedure is performed with minimal human assistance." We all agree that automation generally improves human life's quality, but there are always two sides to the automation coin. John Henry was a simple miner, digging holes for a living with little education in machinery or machine operations. It would have been challenging for him to learn how to operate the heavy machinery, the steam drill, which was the latest and greatest technology in the 1870s. So, transitioning from an old job to a new job would have been almost impossible for the poor fellow. Looking at today's automation and IT automation, in particular, the existing engineers are already finding themselves in the same situation as John Henry, and more will face the music in the future as IT technologies are evolving rapidly. The advancement in IT technologies will replace many existing IT jobs. Still, the good news is that new technologies will also create new jobs and opportunities for those who keep learning to survive our cutting-edge IT industry. If your work gets automated and you find yourself out of your job, you will feel miserable for losing your job, but you may also enjoy it if you have been preparing to transition to IT automation.

Source: `https://en.wikipedia.org/wiki/John_Henry_(folklore)`

CHAPTER 4

Introduction to VMware Workstation

VMware Workstation Pro is one of the most popular end-user desktop virtualization solutions used by enterprise IT personnel. It allows IT engineers to build and test real-world-like virtual machines and network devices from their own PC/laptop. Learning to build a fully functioning and integrated virtual lab on a single computer and master Python network automation basics on a single PC is this book's underlying goal. This chapter is designed to teach you the basics of the most popular and versatile VMware product, VMware Workstation 15 Pro, and basic virtualization concepts. After reading this chapter, you will gain the following knowledge: you'll understand the difference between Type-1 and Type-2 hypervisors, understand various IT vendors offering different desktop virtualization solutions, learn how to install VMware Workstation, learn how to perform general administration on VMware Workstation, and understand how VMware Workstation's network adapters operate.

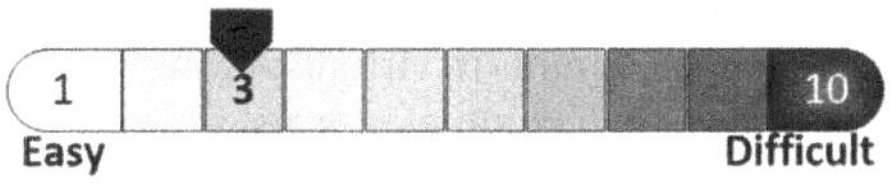

VMware Workstation at a Glance

VMware was created in Palo Alto, California, in 1998, and the company has been growing and leading the enterprise virtualization market for more than two decades. With the exceptions of the first three chapters in this book, this book will rely on VMware's desktop virtualization technology, namely, VMware Workstation 15 Pro. Before embarking on your journey into Python automation, you must approach your studies with an open mind into the various IT technologies. Learning to write Python code does not guarantee you will be successful with your network automation attempts. You will need to learn about regular expressions and Linux administration, which are topics often outside of a network engineer's comfort zone but are essential to writing functional code. That's right; it is a rocky road to Python network automation. For a novice Python learner, learning Python syntax on its own may take months, and it may take years to be able to call yourself an expert in that programming language. Still, the more significant challenge is applying Pythonic concepts and syntax to your work. You need to learn and build Python knowledge on top of your current networking and general IT knowledge. Writing Python code is only the first step of your journey. It requires you to better understand Linux, networking, simple mathematics, regular expressions, interaction with several APIs, and much more.

With limited time and resources, you are trying to learn essential skills required to make the right start in network automation using Python, where all the learning will take place on a single Windows PC (or a laptop). To do this, we must leverage the power of VMware's desktop virtualization solution. The reason for using VMware Workstation 15 is straightforward. It ticks all the boxes for novice Python coders like you to make a practical yet straightforward virtual lab for learning in multiple scenarios.

B. Choi, *Introduction to Python Network Automation*, https://doi.org/10.1007/978-1-4842-6806-3_4

First, we have to get comfortable with the basic virtualization concepts and some basic functions of VMware Workstation 15. Even if you are a longtime user of various virtualization solutions, including VMware products, there will be something new that you will take away from this chapter, so I hope you can read this chapter in its entirety. After reading this chapter, you will have no problem following the rest of the book's content and eventually building a Python network automation lab. In the previous chapter, you installed Python 3 on your host Windows PC and learned Python basics on Windows 10. However, in this chapter and the coming chapters, you will be guided through installing two flavors of Linux distribution servers on the same Windows host using VMware Workstation 15 Pro. Therefore, you can also comfortably learn the Python basics of Linux servers and start picking up Linux basic administration skill sets in Chapters 7 and 8. To run various operating systems, we have to use virtualization technology to help us run multiple machines on the same host platform; VMware Workstation 15 can help us. As part of the pre-tasks for this chapter, you will download and install VMware Workstation 15 on your PC. After that, you will learn the basics of VMware Workstation 15 and then install the latest version of the Ubuntu 20 and CentOS 8 servers in the following two chapters. Throughout the book, these servers will be used to teach you Linux administration, Python installation, and Python module installation, and how to build the CentOS server as an all-in-one IP services server, which can be used as a pocket knife tool in our proof-of-concept (PoC) labs at the end of this book.

The more you know about VMware Workstation 15's features and basic virtualization functions, the more you will become more effective in building this testing lab environment. When designing and building a PoC lab for enterprise IT solutions, often expensive and extremely powerful devices are deployed only to test the most straightforward concept. Sometimes real equipment is required and justified, for example, for stress testing in hardware-related system performance tests. Also, the procurement process to purchase the right equipment can take weeks, if not months. And what about finding the rack space with the sufficient power voltage and cooling to keep your lab running smoothly? Also, physical labs involve the right cables with the correct connector types to suit the vendor's equipment interfaces, which can slow you down while building your company's PoC lab. Too often, thousands of dollars are wasted on a company lab when it is only utilized by a couple of people in your company. This is a total waste of the company's money, and definitely, there is no green IT on this side of the court. Thanks to advancements in virtualization technologies in the past decade, more and more equipment is moving to virtualization platforms, as you have seen with the explosion of cloud-based computing and software-as-a-service IT offerings, and anything IT-as-a-service leverages off the power of virtualization technology in one form or another.

VMware Workstation 15 Pro is VMware's most popular, cross-platform desktop virtualization program that supports both Windows and Linux. For the macOS operating system, VMware Fusion provides the same features. There is a VMware Workstation Player for the free version, but it lacks all the features you need to make your lab a complete lab. For this reason, you will use VMware Workstation 15 Pro. You will install a series of software applications, one at a time, on the Microsoft Windows 10 host system. According to Wikipedia, the 2017 figures suggested that the percentage of desktop/laptop users using the Windows operating system accounts is around 88 percent, macOS users account for roughly 10 percent, and finally, there are only 2 percent of Linux desktop/laptop users in the world. From my own experience, even within the IT industry, similar user percentages are reflected. However, with enterprise-level automation solutions based on Python as the preferred programming language, Linux is the default operating system for added flexibility, higher performance, low cost of ownership, and better security.

You can download Workstation 15 Pro Evaluation for Windows from VMware's official website and take advantage of the 30-day free trial period. After 30 days, you can purchase a 15.5 version license and permanently activate the evaluation software. When writing this book, the latest VMware Workstation for Windows version was 15.5.1, build 15018445, but your downloaded version will be newer (version 15.5 or even version 16.x), but it should still work with most of the software recommended in this book. For your reference, version 13 of VMware Workstation has never been released, and version 14 was released, but it had multiple bugs with GNS3 integration. Strangely enough, GNS3 and Cisco VIRL IOS software will work best on either VMware Workstation 12.5.x or 15.x, but not with the 14.x version. So if you are using VMware 14, you must upgrade to the latest VMware Workstation 15.x version to avoid any problems. It is also recommended that you disable auto-update features to keep your version of software stable at all times. This compatibility recommendation is based on my software compatibility testing. Figure 4-1 shows the product information for VMware Workstation 15 Pro used in this book (filename: `VMware-workstation-full-15.5.1-15018445.exe`).

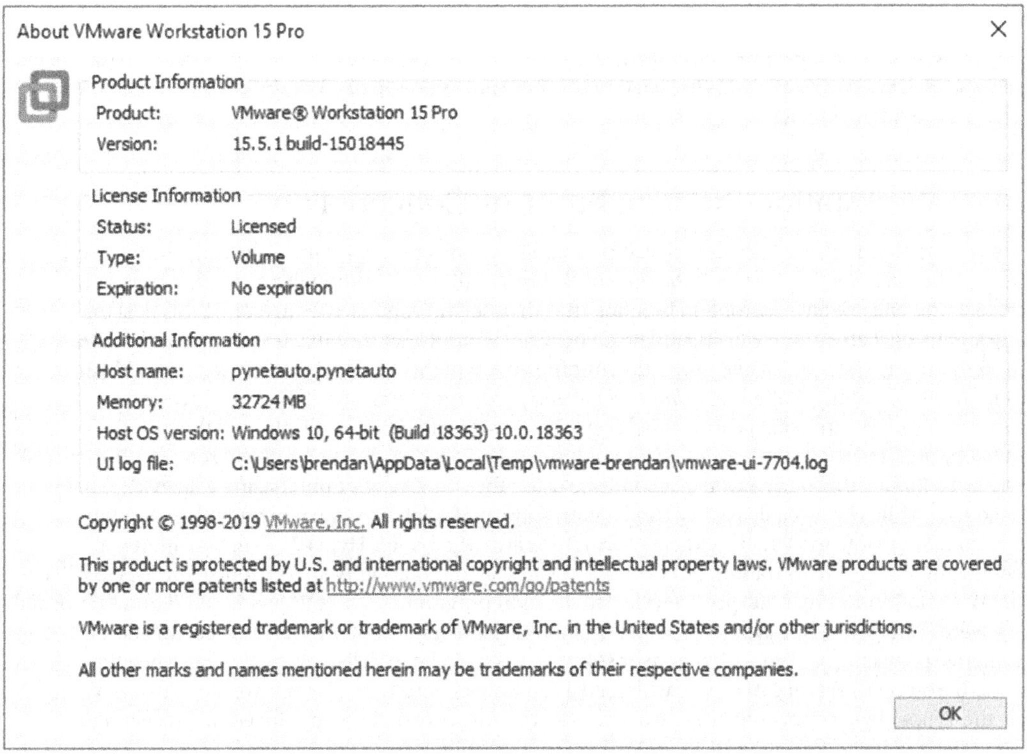

Figure 4-1. *About VMware Workstation 15 Pro*

Even if you are not yet familiar with the concept of virtualization and this software, you will not have any problem following this chapter's content, as this book assumes that you have had no previous experience with this VMware product. Those who are not familiar with a desktop virtualization program such as this still can read through the chapter to get familiar with this software and some basic desktop virtualization concepts. For those who have many years of virtualization experience, please skim through this chapter and jump to the next two chapters, which cover installing Ubuntu 20.04 and CentOS 8 Linux virtual machines (VMs).

Type-1 vs. Type-2 Hypervisors

The first thing to understand about virtualization (hypervisor) software is the difference between Type-1 and Type-2 hypervisors. To explain the difference between Type-1 and Type-2 virtualization software, if the hosting hardware does not require separate operating system software, the virtualization software is executed directly on the hosting hardware. It is classified as a Type-1 hypervisor. If the hosting hardware requires separate operating system software, it is classified as a Type-2 hypervisor. To put it more bluntly, the Type-1 hypervisor is typically used for business use, and the Type-2 hypervisor is designed and used for personal and experimental use. That doesn't mean that Type-2 shouldn't be used for business use. However, there is very little reason to use Type-2 hypervisors over Type-1 in a commercial environment as Type-1 hypervisors provide better stability, high availability, and better scalability features. The Type-1 hypervisor family, also known as *bare metal*, refers to enterprise-level server platforms released without built-in OS software. Typical Type-1 hypervisor products include VMware's ESXi, Microsoft's Hyper-V for Servers, Citrix's XenServer, and Oracle VM.

In contrast, examples of Type-2 hypervisors being developed for desktop applications include VMware's VMware Workstation, Fusion, Player, Oracle's VM VirtualBox (formerly Sun Microsystems), Microsoft's VirtualPC, and Red Hat's Enterprise Virtualization. Type-2 hypervisors are also known as desktop (or hosted) hypervisors. VMware Workstation 15 Pro, used in this book, runs on top of a Windows 10 host machine, making it a Type-2 hypervisor.

VMware Workstation Pro for a Proof-of-Concept Lab

VMware Workstation 15 Pro is VMware's flagship desktop virtualization program. Version 1 was released in 1999, and the latest version was 16 at the time of authoring this book. Although this book is based on version 15.x, you will not have a problem building the lab based on version 16.x. Installing this desktop program and using it are intuitive tasks, and it can be used without user training. It supports both Windows and Linux operating systems. Virtual programs running on top of the operating system, such as VMware Workstation, are sometimes called *experimental virtualization programs*, and the latest software trial versions are available from VMware's official download page. The basic installation is simple, and the installation gets completed by pressing a few buttons. If you do not have a valid license, the program will run on a 30-day trial license. After a 30-day trial period, you can continue using the software after purchasing a license.

Of course, while choosing desktop virtualization software for lab use, you will find other popular software from Microsoft and Oracle. Oracle's VirtualBox and Microsoft's Hyper-V were considered a replacement of VMware Workstation, but because of software compatibility and system stability, we will use VMware Workstation 15 Pro. Enterprise-level virtualization programs such as VMware's ESXi and Microsoft's Hyper-V were considered, but Type-1 hypervisors such as these have higher hardware specification requirements. For example, Type-1 hypervisor software needs to be installed on hypervisor-specific hardware (bare-metal) servers. Also, you will need a separate client PC to remote console to the server to operate the Type-1 hypervisor software. Also, Type-1 hypervisors usually get deployed in data centers or company communication rooms and are not meant to be mobile.

Before Using VMware Workstation

When installing Type-1 hypervisor software such as ESXi 6.5, there are a few stringent hardware requirements during the installation process. The software has a built-in process to check the minimum hardware requirements. Luckily, for VMware Workstation 15 Pro installation on your host's operating system, there are no or minimal hardware prerequisites. If your computer's CPU and motherboard support virtualization technology, then you can start the installation. The BIOS of the newer PCs or laptops come out of the factory with the Virtualization Technology option enabled. If you are using an older type of PC or laptop, this setting needs to be enabled, but this is the only thing you have to change before installing the software on your PC. Until recently, VMware's virtualization solutions tended to favor Intel's CPU architecture slightly more than AMD's CPU architecture. Intel CPUs are far superior to AMD CPUs in terms of performance, compatibility, and efficiency in my own experience. Of course, AMD has invested heavily in CPU development lately, but AMD CPUs are better geared toward individual users who enjoy PC gaming.

Before installing VMware Workstation 15 Pro, ensure that the virtualization support is set to Enabled after entering the BIOS of your laptop/PC motherboard, as shown in Figure 4-2.

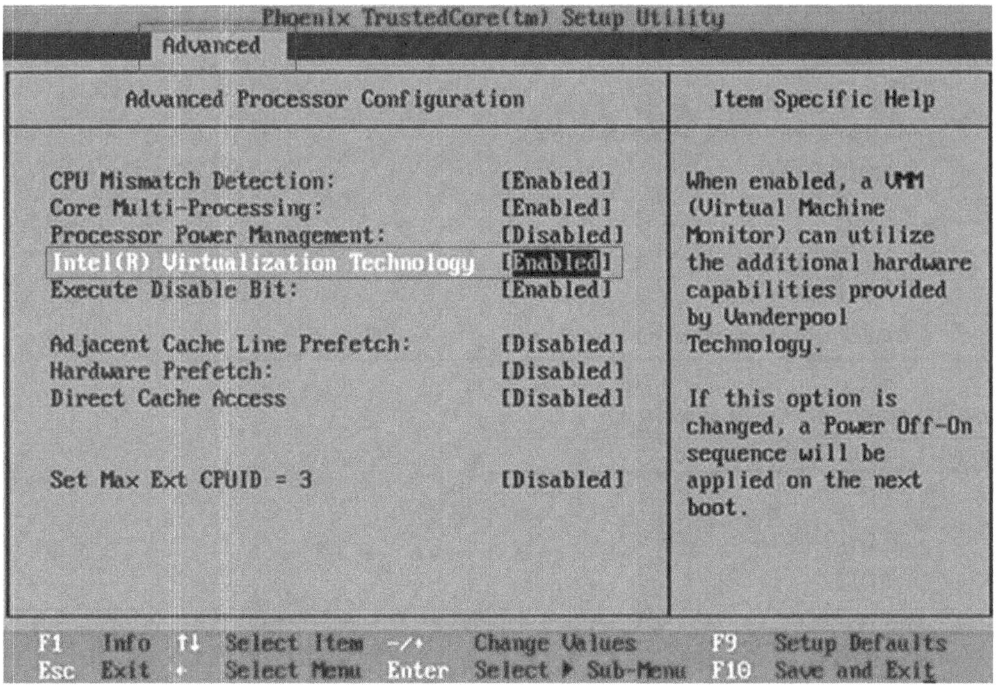

Figure 4-2. *Checking the Intel CPU motherboard virtualization support setting*

If the use of Intel VT (or AMD-V) is set to Disabled in the BIOS, change the setting to Enabled, and then press the F10 key to save the changes and log into Windows 10 normally. Tables 4-1 and 4-2 list the BIOS entry keys for the major motherboard and laptop manufacturers. The function key or key combo to enter the BIOS varies from one manufacturer to another, and the most common manufacturers' keys are provided for your reference. If you can't find your laptop manufacturer in the table, go to the manufacturer's website and locate the BIOS information to change the BIOS settings.

Table 4-1. *BIOS Setup Entry Key by Laptop Manufacturer*

Manufacturer	BIOS Key Combo
Acer	F2/Del (new) F1/Ctrl+Alt+Esc (old)
Asus	F2/F10/Del/Insert/Alt+F10
Compaq	F1/F2/F10/Del
Dell	F1/Del/F12/F3 (new) (press when the Dell logo appears on the screen) Ctrl+Alt+Enter/Fn+Esc or Fn+F1/Ctrl+F11 (old)
eMachines	F2/Del
Fujitsu	F2
Gateway	F1/F2
HP	F1/F2/F6/F9/F10/F11/Esc Tablet PC: F10/F12

(continued)

Table 4-1. *(continued)*

Manufacturer	BIOS Key Combo
Lenovo	F1/F2/F11 (new) Ctrl+Alt+F3/Ctrl+Alt+Ins/Fn+F1 (old)
LG	F10/F11/F12
Samsung	F2/F4
Sony	F1/F2/F3/Assist
Toshiba	F2/F1/ESC/F12
Other	Refer to the respective vendor website

Table 4-2. *BIOS Setup Entry Key by Motherboard*

Manufacturer	BIOS Key/Key Combo
ASROCK	F11
ASUS	F12/F2/F8/F9
BIOSTAR	F7/F9
Compaq	F10
EMTec	F9
Foxconn	F7/Esc
GIGABYTE	F12
HP	F9
Intel	F10
LG	F12
MSI	F11
Pegatron	F11
Samsung	ESC
Other	Refer to the respective vendor website

Here's one more reminder on the VMware Workstation version: the latest version of VMware Workstation 15 Pro at the time of publication was 15.5.1 build-15018445. Also note that version 14 showed compatibility issues with some applications used in this book. The problem was identified as the security file and VIRL integration requirement for the GNS3 Docker program download process. Please use the latest 15.5 version, which is compatible with GNS3. This book uses version 15.5.1, the latest version of 15.5 at the time of writing this chapter. If you do not have a copy of version 15, then use version 12. Version 12 is also compatible and stable with GNS3, VIRL software, and GNS3 Docker images. After the first draft and technical review of this book, VMware released version 16. You should be able to use version 16 or the latest version and still follow the contents of this book. For now, please use VMware Workstation 15.x Pro or 16.x or 12.x but not 14.x.

⚠ Download and install VMware Workstation 15 (or 16) Pro on your Windows PC before reading this chapter. The download and installation is straightforward, but in case you need help, the link to download the installation guide is provided with this book.

Download VMware Workstation 15/16 from the following URL:

URL: `https://www.vmware.com/au/products/workstation-pro/workstation-pro-evaluation.html`

The "Chapter 4 Pre-task – Installing VMware Workstation" guide is available from here:

URL: `https://github.com/pynetauto/apress_pynetauto`

What's Next on VMware Workstation 15 Pro?

As a pre-task to this chapter, you must install VMware Workstation 15 Pro on your host PC. We will quickly review the menu options for those who are new to virtualization technology and this program before installing two Linux virtual servers and importing the GNS3 VM. If you are confident that you know the VMware Workstation feature inside and out, skip to Chapter 5. Anyway, you can think of a virtual machine (VM) as another independent computer running on a host computer's operating system (Type-2). Users can interact with the VM through the Workstation 15 Pro's main user console and use various operating system installation media files to initially create and install VMs and then configure, import, export, control, and manage all aspects of the VMs. You already saw the main user console of VMware Workstation 15 Pro after the pre-task, and you already noticed that the user interface is concise and intuitive. However, the operation and behavior of VMs are much more sophisticated than you might think at first. A VM looks like an application, but it is a computer with many of the native features of a real hardware computer. The best way to get to know Workstation 15 Pro is to use it, but to make your learning a little easier, we will go through some console-related terminology in the next section. Let's look at the user interfaces, menus, and the Virtual Network Editor.

After a quick review, you will be guided to links to download and install a couple of VMs and also download and import a VM using the GNS3 `.ova` file. You must create all three VMs by the end of this chapter as the rest of the book will rely on these VMs to learn Linux, learn regular expressions, install Python and network-related modules, and learn how to write Python network automation scripts in the virtual labs. To emulate the real lab scenarios, you will test various networking concepts and get familiar with the most commonly used file-sharing services. For instance, this book's last few chapters will have lab scenarios involving FTP, SFTP, and TFTP servers based on a CentOS 8 virtual machine.

Optionally, if you want to create new VMs here and then export them to a real production environment, you can do so by using the VMware Converter software. VMs can be prestaged on VMware Workstation and then converted later, converting the VMs to Type-1 VMs running on VMware's vSphere 6.5. For now, let's first look at the main user console and its menus of Workstation 15 Pro.

VMware Workstation 15 Pro User Console

The Workstation 15 Pro user window (or console) lets you install, control, and manage various types of VMs. Figure 4-3 shows the main user interface and default buttons of VMware Workstation 15 Pro. This figure will provide you with information on various features of menus and keys. No special skills are required to use this program, and you can easily create and use a VM after installation. Now, let's learn the menus and key features.

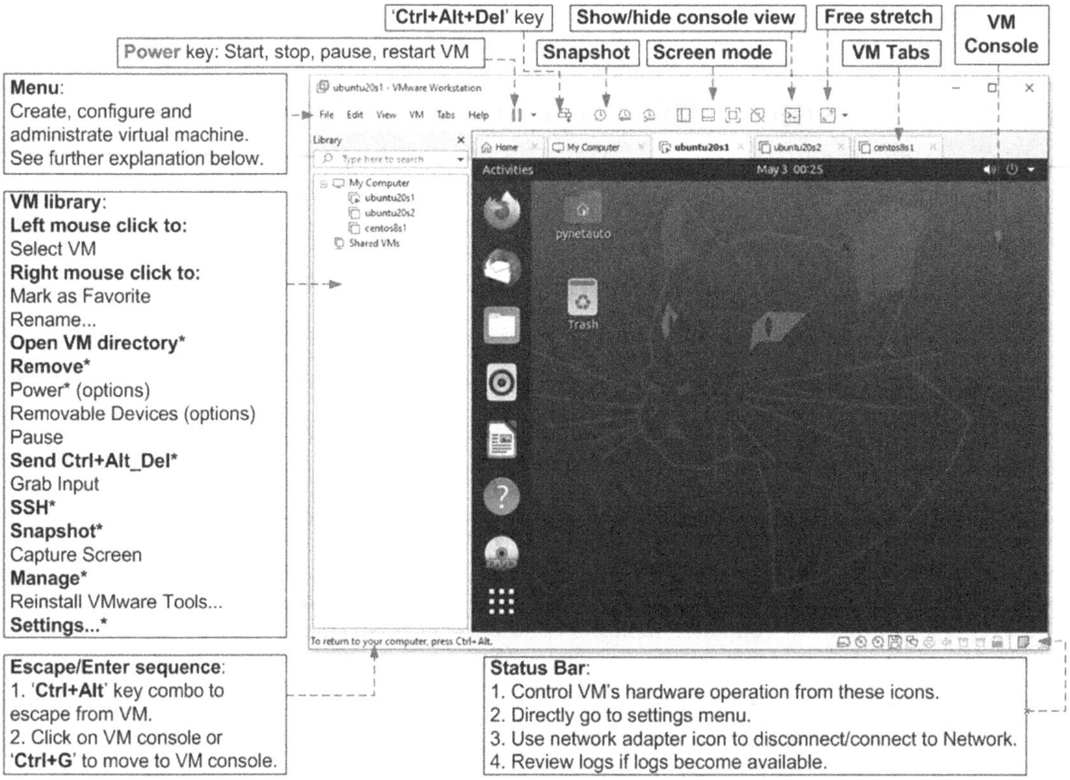

Figure 4-3. *VMware Workstation, user window*

Basic Operations of VMware Workstation 15 Pro

Figure 4-4 depicts the main user interface for VMware Workstation 15 Pro, and this is the primary interface where you will manage your VMs. Compared to Microsoft Hyper-V on Windows 10 and Oracle VirtualBox, VMware Workstation Pro has the most friendly user interface and powerful features at the user's fingertips. Let's quickly learn the most basic functions of this program.

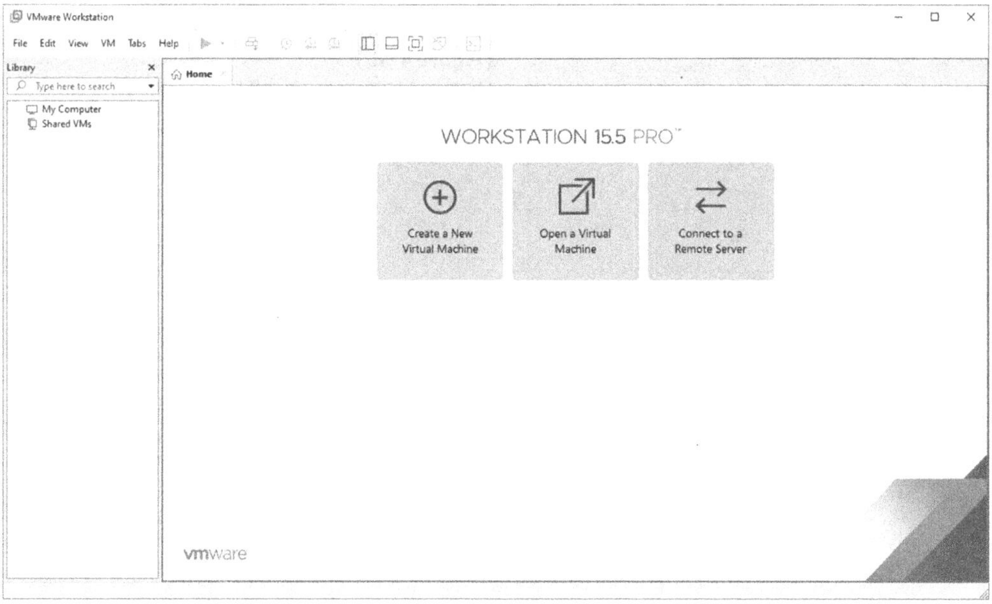

Figure 4-4. *VMware Workstation, main user window*

VMware Workstation Pro: Basic Operations

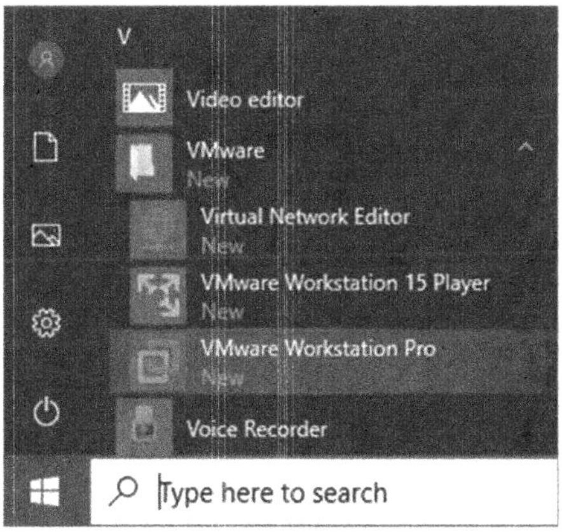

Figure 4-5a. *Starting VMware Workstation Pro*

To start VMware Workstation 15 Pro (Figure 4-5a):
You can start the program by using the VMware shortcut on the Windows desktop or Windows 10's Start menu: Start ➤ Programs ➤ VMware ➤ VMware Workstation.

To power on/off, suspend or reset a VM (Figure 4-5b):
One way to power on/off or pause a VM is to select a VM from the VM menu: VM ➤ Power ➤ Start Up Guest.

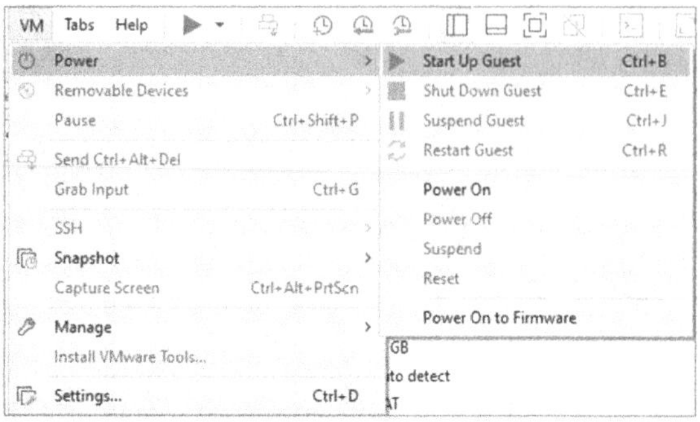

Figure 4-5b. Power Options 1

The second way to power on/off, suspend or reset a VM is to select a VM on VM Library (Figure 4-5c).
Right-click a VM and select Power ➤ Start Up Guest.

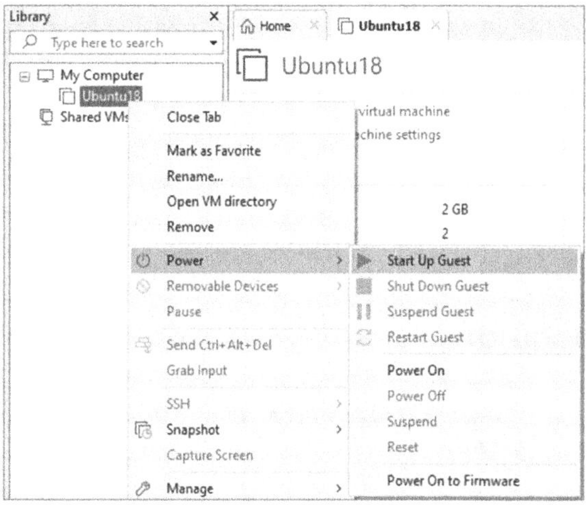

Figure 4-5c. Power Options 2

The third way to power on/off, suspend or reset a VM is to use the power key options on the top of the user window (Figure 4-5d).

Figure 4-5d. Power Options 3

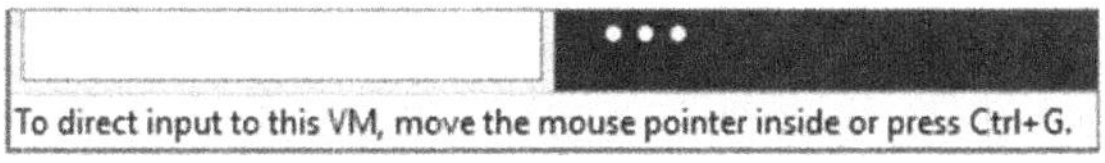

Figure 4-5e. *To move to a VM*

To move to a VM (from the host PC), press Ctrl+G.
To use a running VM, click the VM console using the left mouse or press Ctrl+G on your keyboard (Figure 4-5e).

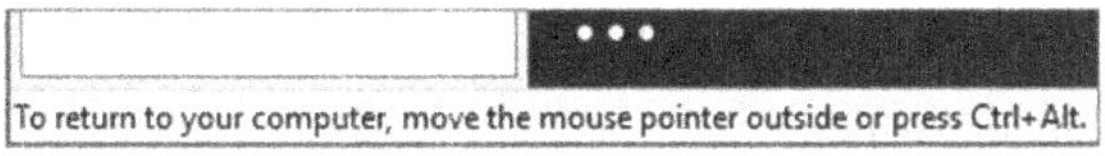

Figure 4-5f. *To exit a VM*

To exit a VM (to move the cursor back to the host PC), press Ctrl+Alt.
To exit the mouse cursor back to the Windows host while using the VM, press the Ctrl+Alt keys to exit the host (Figure 4-5f).

For more detailed user instructions, please refer to `https://docs.vmware.com/en/VMware-Workstation-Pro/15.0/workstation-pro-15-user-guide.pdf`.

VMware Workstation Menu

Table 4-3 shows all the menus at a glance. The most commonly used features are marked with an asterisk (*). You may find it helpful to check the features and skip to creating virtual machines.

Table 4-3. *Menus at a Glance*

Menu Screen Capture	Menu Function
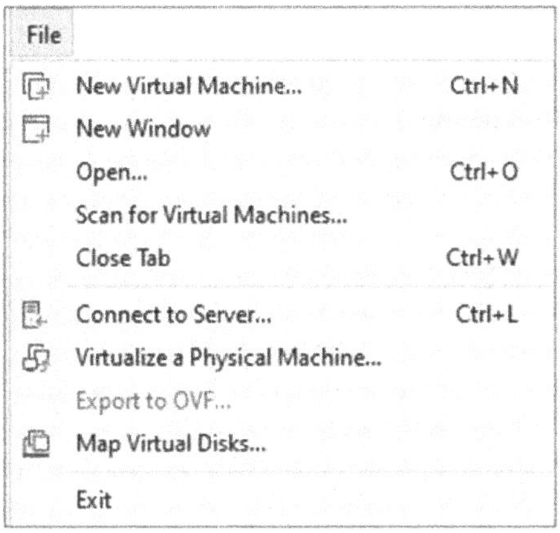 File menu	**File menu:** Create a new VM Open a new window Open a VM* Scan for VMs Close tab Connecting to external servers, vCenter, and vSphere servers Connect to vCloud Air Create p2v (physical to virtual) Export to OVF file* Connecting to a virtual disk Exit*
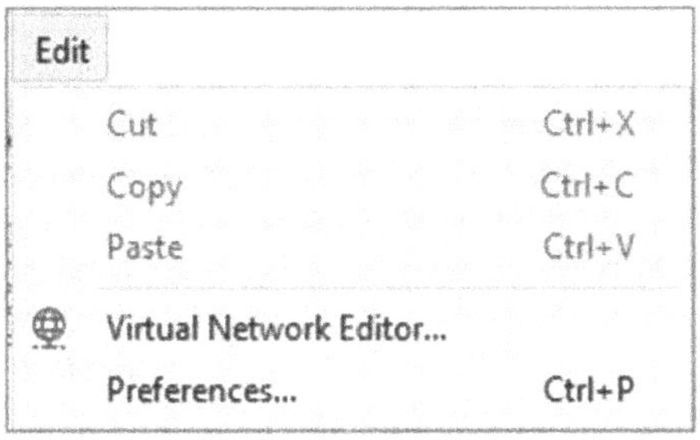 Edit menu	**Edit menu:** Cut Copy Paste Virtual Network Editor* Preferences*

(continued)

Table 4-3. (*continued*)

Menu Screen Capture	Menu Function
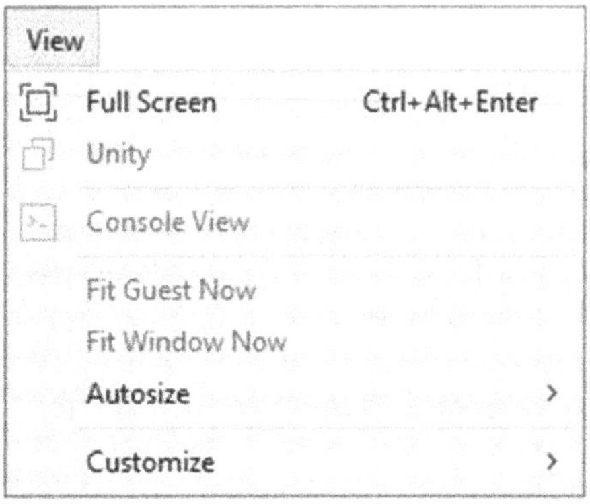 View menu	**View menu:** View in full-screen* Unity mode Console view Fit screen to guest OS Fit screen to window Auto size Custom view
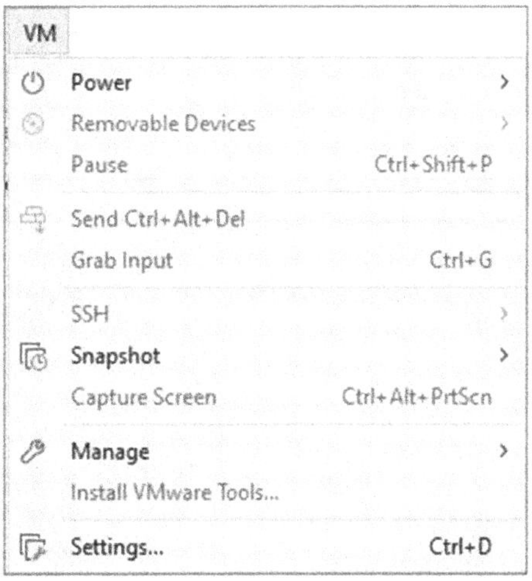 VM menu	**VM (Virtual Machine):** Power* Removable devices Pause Send Ctrl+Alt+Del key* Catch typing Snapshot Management* Screen capture Manage VMware Tools installation Settings*
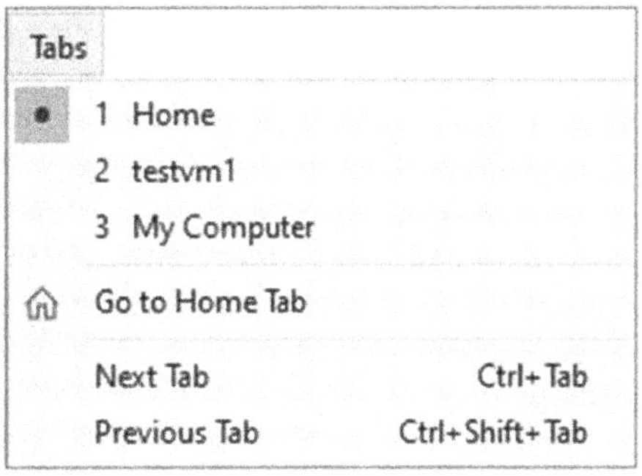 Tabs menu	**Tabs Menu:** Home Go to Home Tap Next tab Previous tab

(*continued*)

Table 4-3. *(continued)*

Menu Screen Capture	Menu Function
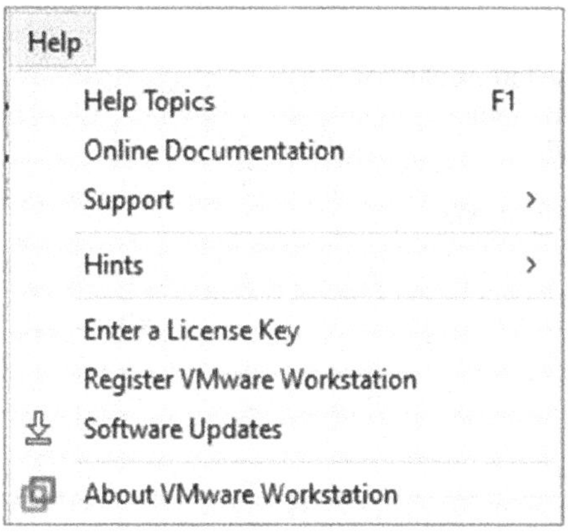 Help menu	**Help:** Help Online documentation support hint Enter License Key* VMware Workstation Registration Software update About VMware Workstation
 VM power icon	**VM power icon:** Guest On* Guest Off* Guest Suspend Resume Guest* Power on Power off Pause reset Enters BIOS when powered on *
 Send Ctrl+Alt+Del icon	Send Ctrl+Alt+Delete to the VM
 Snapshot icons	Take a snapshot of this VM Revert this VM to its parent snapshot Manage snapshots for this VM

(continued)

Table 4-3. (*continued*)

Menu Screen Capture	Menu Function
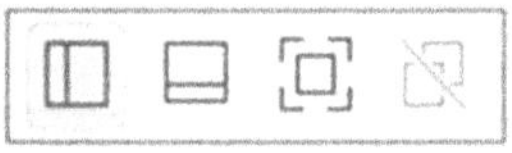 Screen mode option icons	Show or hide the library Show or hide the thumbnail bar Enter full-screen mode Enter Unity mode
 Show or hide Console view icon	Show or hide console view
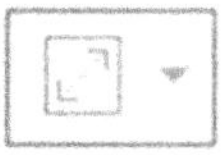 Free stretch icon	Free stretch

Virtual Network Adapters

One of the most common questions beginners ask about VMware Workstation 15 Pro is how to use different virtual network adapter settings. It is difficult to provide an answer in a nutshell; you could read the unnecessarily lengthy documents on the VMware website, but most of us do not have hours to read vendor-provided documentation. Here, we will cover the very basics to get started with the VM network. First-time users need to know how each virtual network adapter differs from one another and how to use each one. The best way to explain this is to review which virtual network adapters are available to a user. Try to understand each network adapter types' definition and then look at different adapter settings in your programs to reveal how each adapter is configured on your PC. First, let's look at the Virtual Network Editor to review out-of-the-box virtual network adapter settings.

Virtual Network Editor Overview

VMware Workstation provides virtual network features in virtual switches, where three virtual switches are mapped to three specific networks and up to 17 virtual switches can be created by the user as needed. The different networking types will be discussed in detail in the next section. So, you can have up to 20 virtual switches (VMnet0 through VMnet19), with each virtual switch representing a single flat network or a subnet. Like in a real production environment, you can connect multiple VMs to the same network (virtual switch). First, open the Virtual Network Editor menu to review which default connection types are available.

#	Task
1a	When starting VMware Workstation Pro, it is a best practice to start the program by right-clicking the desktop icon and selecting the "Run as administrator" option, as shown in Figure 4-6. This way, you are launching the program with a full administrator-level privilege to change any program settings.

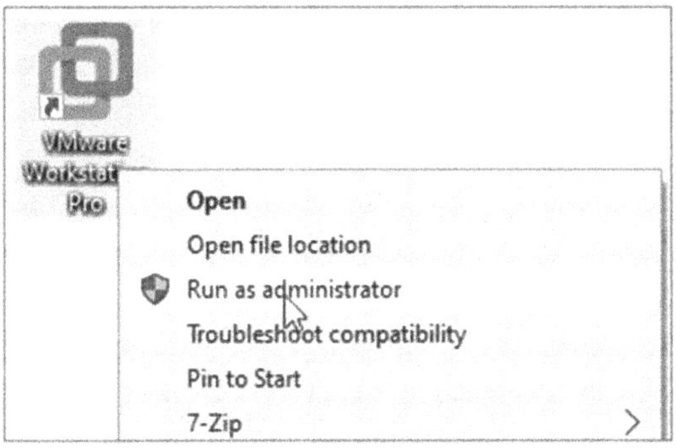

Figure 4-6. *VMware Workstation Pro, running as administrator*

#	Task
1b	If you don't want to click the "Run as administrator" option every time you start the program, you can change the shortcut properties to make the program run in administrator mode. Go to VMware Workstation Pro's Desktop icon and right-click your mouse and select Properties, as shown in Figure 4-7.

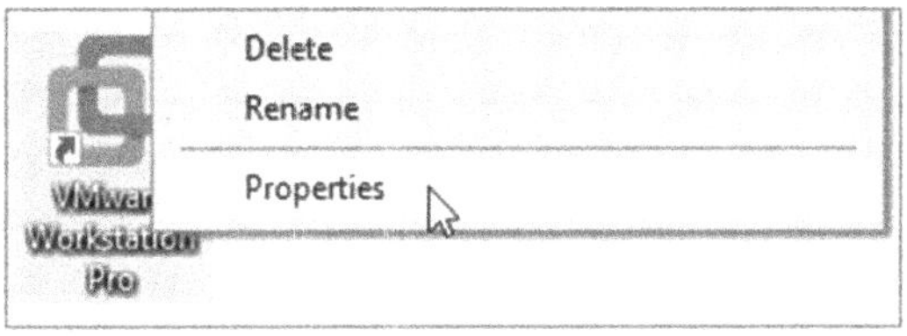

Figure 4-7. *VMware Workstation Pro, shortcut icon Properties*

(*continued*)

#	Task
	In the shortcut properties menu, click Compatibility, and under the Settings option, check "Run this program as an administrator" and then click the Apply and OK buttons. Now your program will always run as an administrator (see Figure 4-8).

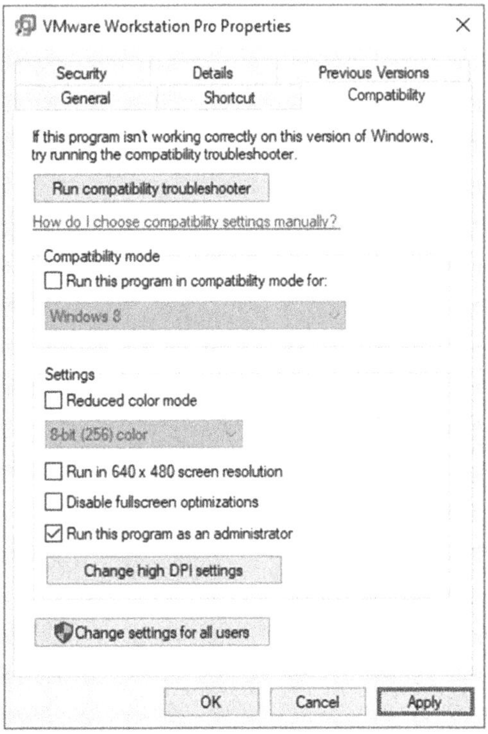

Figure 4-8. *VMware Workstation Pro, changing the properties Compatibility settings*

2	Now, to open and view virtual network adapters from the menu, select Edit ➤ Virtual Network Editor (Figure 4-9).

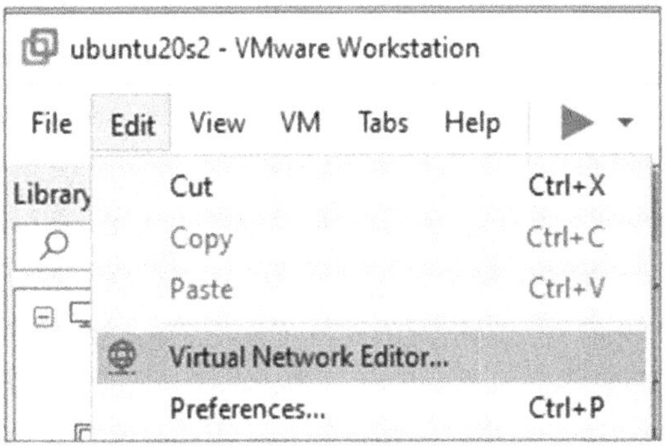

Figure 4-9. *Selecting Virtual Network Editor*

#	Task
3	When the Virtual Network Editor opens for the first time, as expected, there are three virtual switches (VMnets). Like a real network adapter, a virtual adapter can be referred to as a virtual NIC or a virtual network interface. The Virtual Network Editor is the default control tower to manage different virtual networks, such as adding/removing networks, enabling/disable DHCP, and more (Figure 4-10).

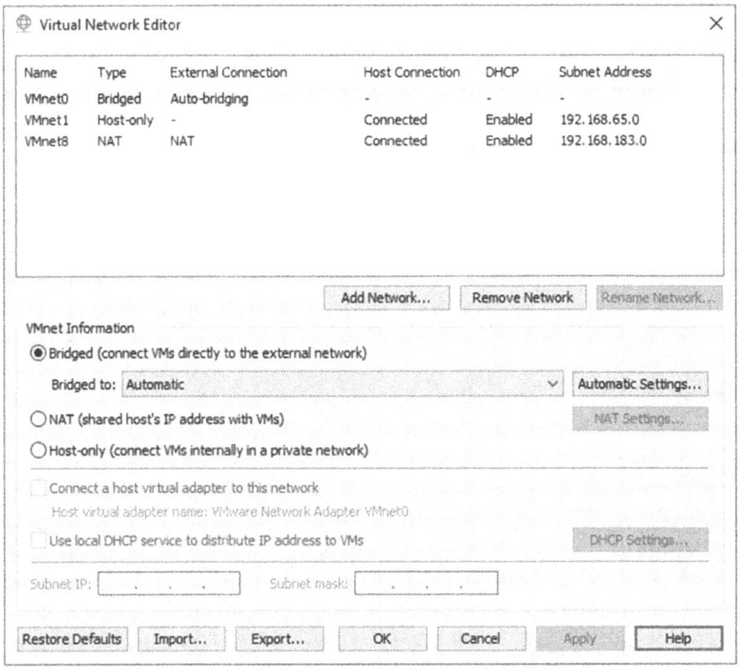

Figure 4-10. *Virtual Network Editor, default adapter types*

In the Virtual Network Editor window shown in Figure 4-10, click the Help button, which will open the documentation on the official VMware site to "Using the Virtual Network Editor."

Virtual Network Interface Description

Here is a quick overview of the different network modes and networking jargon we have been discussing. If you have studied or studied Cisco CCNA, you will be already familiar with these networking terminologies in the network industry. If you are studying for CCNP or completed CCNP studies, you probably will be able to relate these network adapter modes to the real production environment. However, even if you are not familiar with the networking technologies, you will not have any trouble understanding the following explanations. As mentioned earlier, there are three out-of-the-box network adapters, but you can add or remove more adapters as required. Also, the subnets can be specified to your preference as you build your lab. Table 3-4 describes the three virtual network modes and one user (custom) mode.

VIRTUAL NETWORK ADAPTER MODES EXPLAINED

By default, in bridged network adapter mode, all virtual machines share the host machine's network connection. By default, the bridged network uses VMnet0 in VMware Workstation, and all computers use the same gateway and hence the same DHCP and DNS server used by the host PC. Both the host PC and virtual machines acquire the same subnet's IP addresses with the same default gateway address. Figure 4-11 depicts a typical bridged network on VMware Workstation Pro.

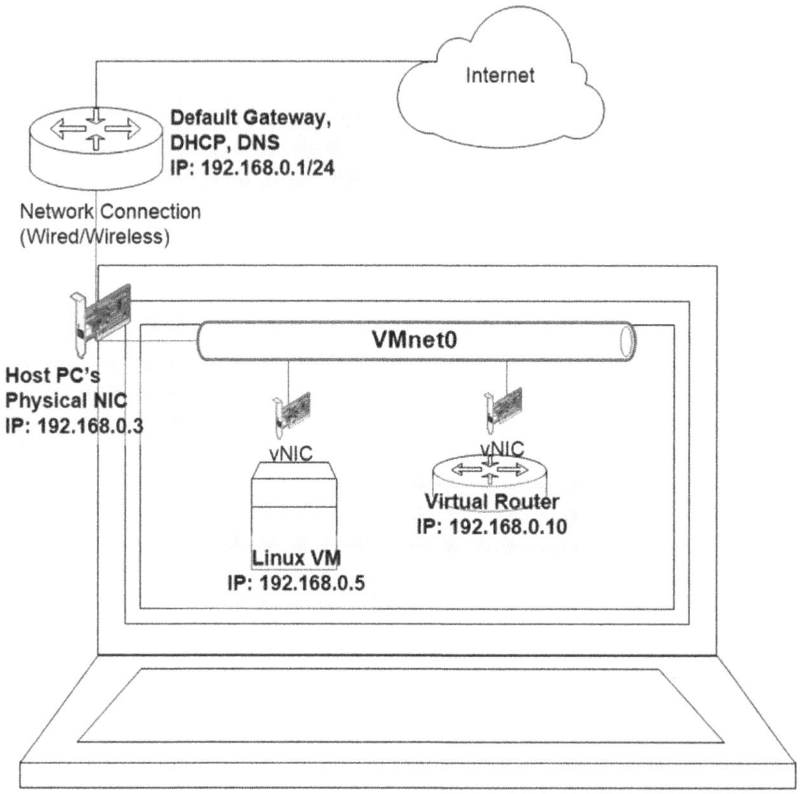

Figure 4-11. *VMware network adapters, bridged mode*

Host-only mode is perfect for testing two or more VMs in an isolated network within the virtual environment. By default, a host-only mode connects to VMnet1, and VMs are connected in the same subnet for experimenting with no interaction outside of the experimental network. Your host PC and VMs can still communicate via VMnet1. In Figure 4-12, notice that the workstation provides the DHCP service.

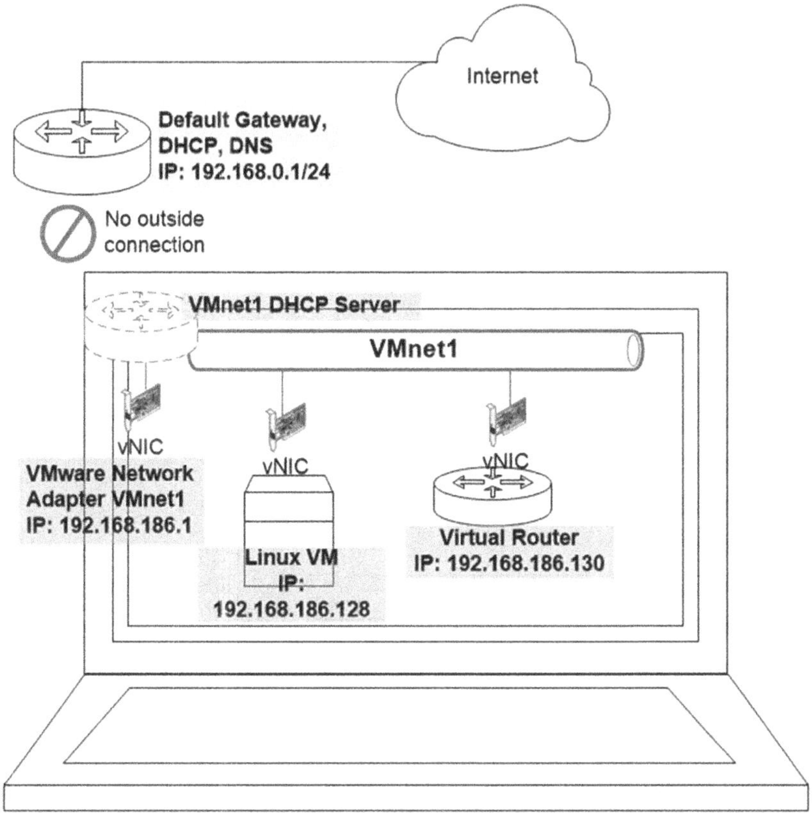

***Figure 4-12.** VMware network adapters, host-only mode*

Network Address Translation (NAT) mode connects via VMnet8 by default. Network address translation means that the VM's internal IP address and the host's external IP address are different. In an external network, you can only see the host's subnet address. If the host can connect to the Internet, it can communicate with the Internet. Figure 4-13 depicts an example of a NAT configuration on VMware Workstation Pro.

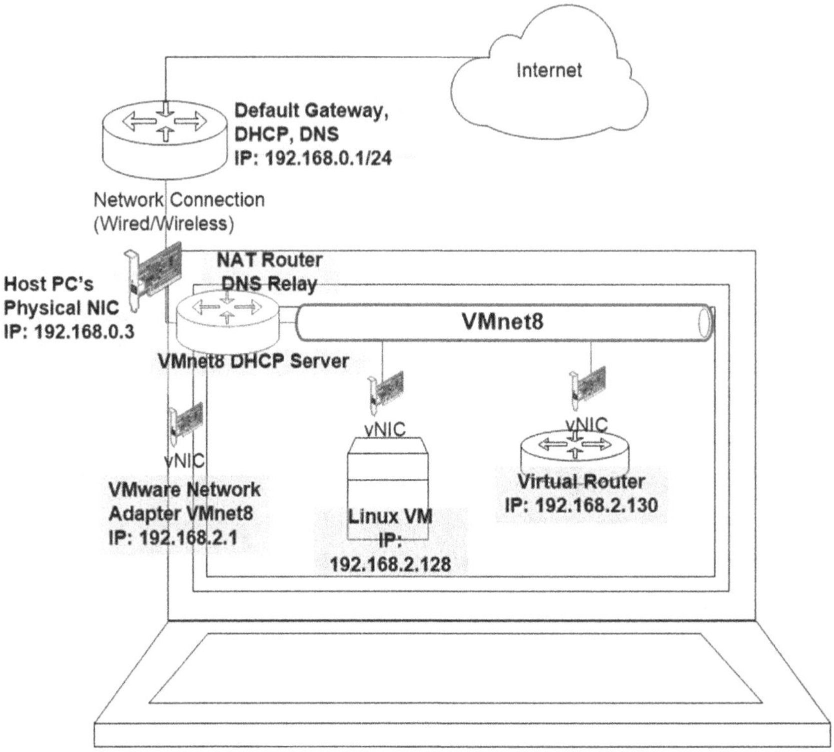

Figure 4-13. *VMware network adapters, NAT mode*

In custom networking, you can select one of the previous modes and customize it to suit your scenarios. It is the same mode as NAT mode but with some changes in the default settings.

You are encouraged to spend enough time understanding different virtual network modes, compared to how they are different from the real physical network, and then visualize how you can use different modes in your PoC labs. Getting familiar with how each network mode interacts with your host machine and other networks will help you build a lab that can test more advanced IT theories. Open the Virtual Network Editor from the menu and spend some time exploring the settings, adding/removing new VMnets, and customizing settings. In the following section, you will review VM settings in more detail.

Tip Why perform a PoC? In the field of IT, the abbreviation PoC stands for *proof of concept*, and it means proving an existing or new IT concept (or a problem) in a given scenario. A PoC experimental lab tests that a certain theory works the same way as the technology was designed for. To better understand and go beyond your colleagues, you must spend many hours in PoC labs because you will gain broader knowledge than a book or real-life scenarios can teach you. You always learn more by studying a theory and testing the theory in a PoC lab as you will not encounter all the theories or problems in the real production environment.

Revealing Each Virtual Network Interface Types

Let's look at each type.

Host-Only Networking

In this mode, your VMs share a private network with the host and other virtual devices in the same subnet. This mode is useful if your VMs do not need communications outside of your host. If you are using the default host-only networking, all VMs will connect to VMnet1, and you can think of VMnet1 as a single virtual network switch. In this mode, a built-in DHCP server provides IP addresses to hosts connecting to this network for convenience. Figures 4-14 to 4-18 display how VMnet1 is configured, and related configuration settings can be found on your host's operating system. Refer to the following tutorial for even more clarification on VMware networking concepts: `https://rednectar.net/2011/07/20/vmware-interfaces-tutorial/`.

Figure 4-14 displays that the out-of-the-box VMnet1 subnet assigned to this network is 192.168.65.0/24. Of course, the subnet and CIDR can be changed as required. Also, there is an option to disable the DHCP service so you can manually assign IP addresses within a VM's OS.

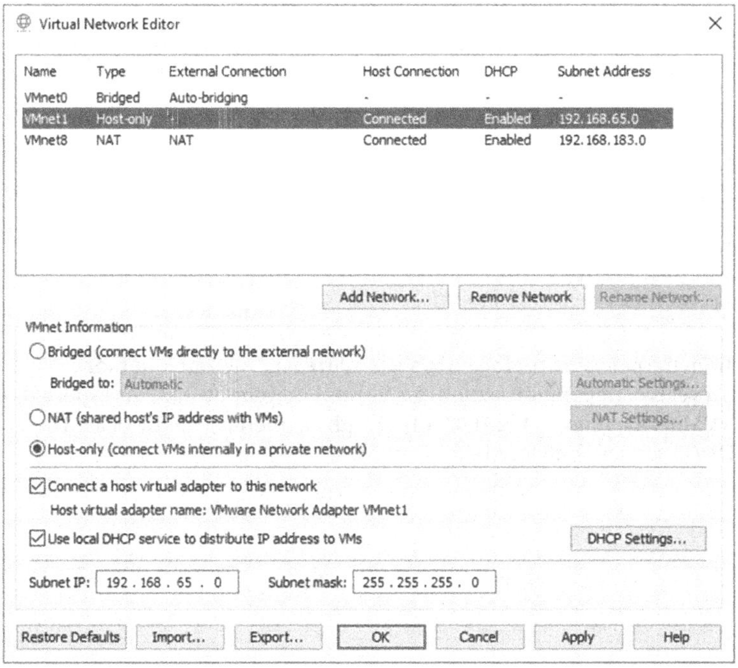

Figure 4-14. *Virtual Network Editor, VMnet1 host-only network*

Figure 4-15 shows you the VM settings where the relevant network connection is configured.

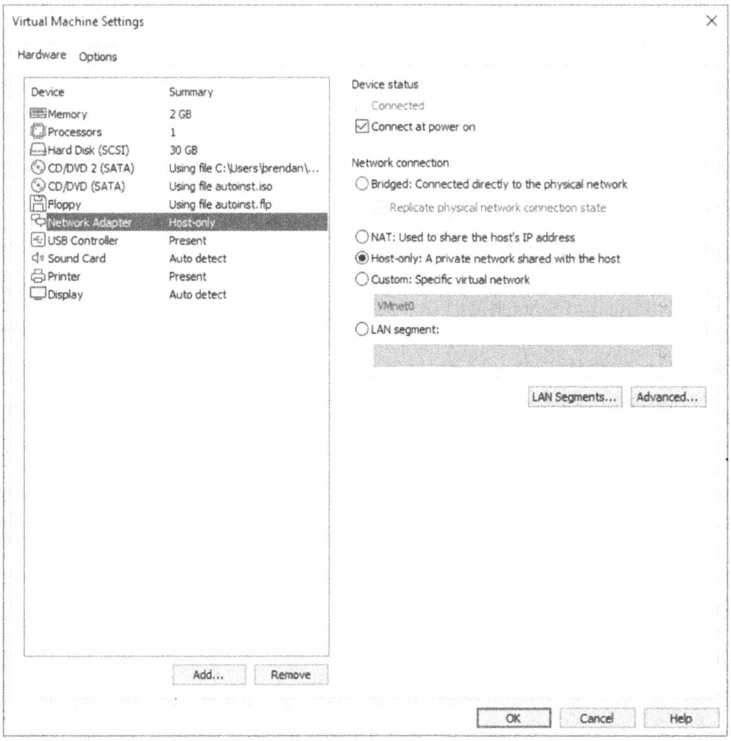

Figure 4-15. *Virtual machine settings, host-only network connection*

Figure 4-16 displays the result from the `netsh interface ip show addresses "VMware Network Adapter VMnet1"` command, which reveals configuration settings for VMnet1 on your host PC. As expected, the IP address assigned to the host's VMnet1 adapter is 192.168.65.1/24 with an interface metric of 35. The interface metric 35 means that the DHCP service configured this IP address.

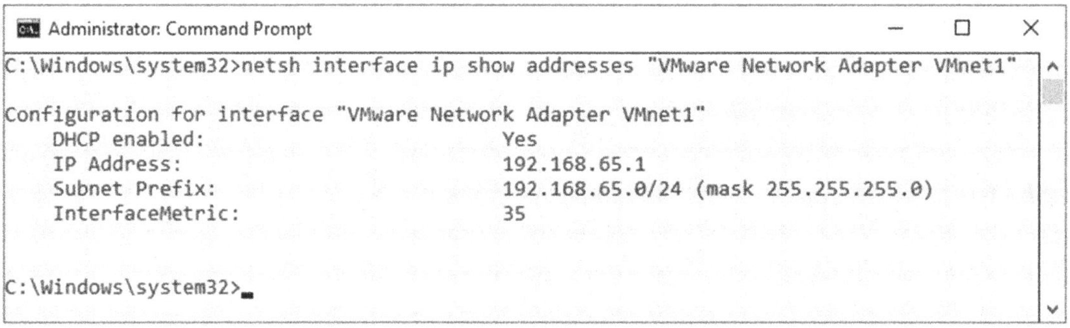

Figure 4-16. *Windows host PC, VMware network adapter VMnet1*

As shown in Figure 4-17, when you start a VM and check the network interface settings, the DHCP server-assigned IP to your VM will be from the same subnet as your VMnet1 network. Since you have not created and installed any VMs, you can check this setting after completing the Linux installation in Chapters 5 and 6. Note that the interface name assigned to the Ubuntu VM is ens33; the network adapter name for Linux machines depends on your Linux OS version and distro type.

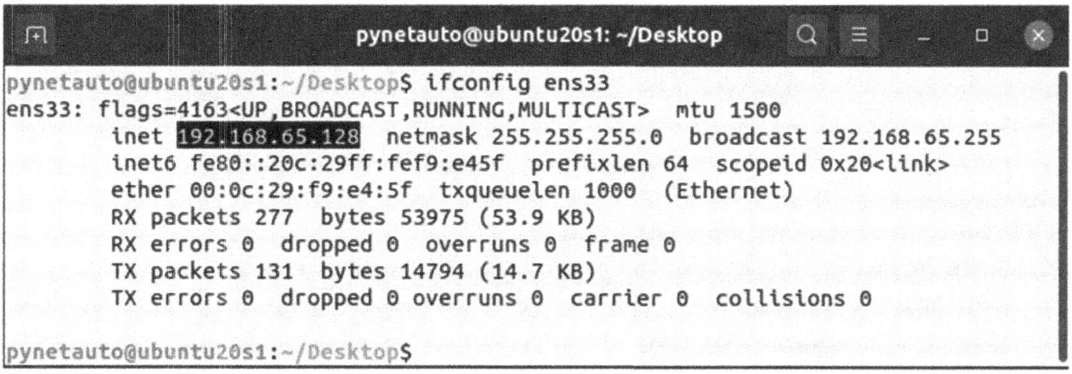

Figure 4-17. *Virtual machine, ens33 network adapter*

Refer to the earlier Figure 4-12 to visualize and help you understand the host-only network mode. Now you know where to find the information on the host-only virtual network for your VMs. Next, let's look at the bridged mode.

Bridged Networking

In bridged mode, a VM will act as if it is another computer on the same network as the host computer, so the VM receives an IP address from the real network. For default bridged mode, the VMnet0 network is assigned. If you are connecting to the Internet using your home network, your home network router usually provides DHCP services. By default, ISP-provided internet modems/routers will have an IP subnet of either 192.168.0.0/24 or 192.168.1.0/24, with the default gateway taking the first IP (.1) and last IP (.254) addresses on the network. In bridged mode, other physical computers can communicate to your VMs, and you can also emulate multiple computers from one computer. In bridged network mode, by default, your VMs can communicate to the Internet physically and VMs on your network.

Figure 4-18 displays the default bridged network in the Virtual Network Editor. The IP address will be assigned from the real network device on the host's physical adapter network, so the DHCP options are grayed out under the settings.

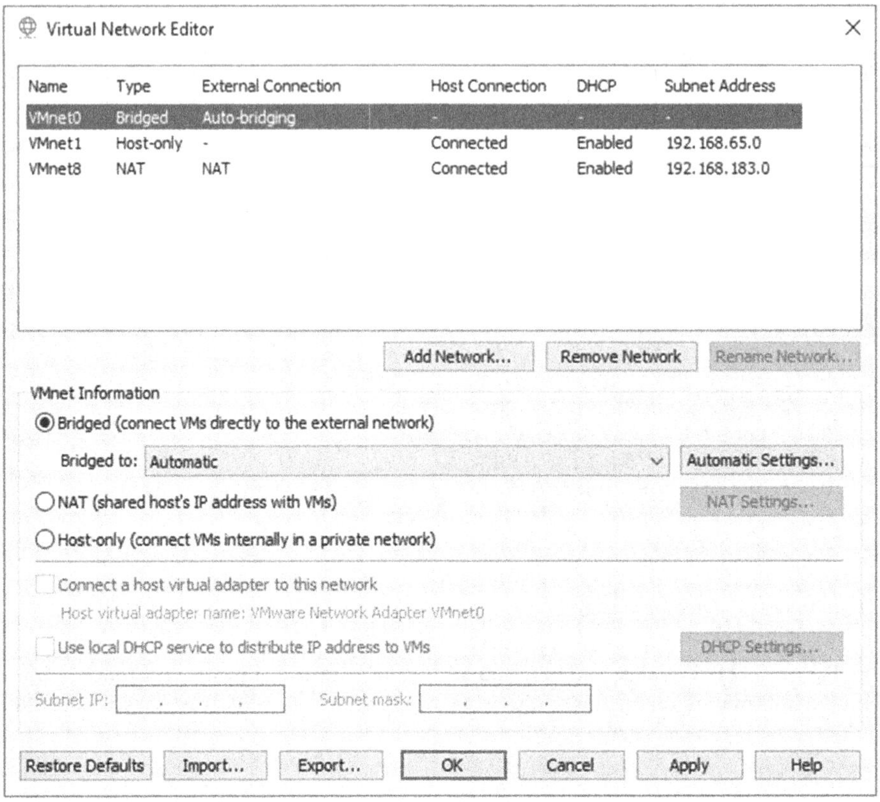

Figure 4-18. *Virtual Network Editor, VMnet0 bridged network*

Figure 4-19 shows the VM settings where the bridged network is configured and used.

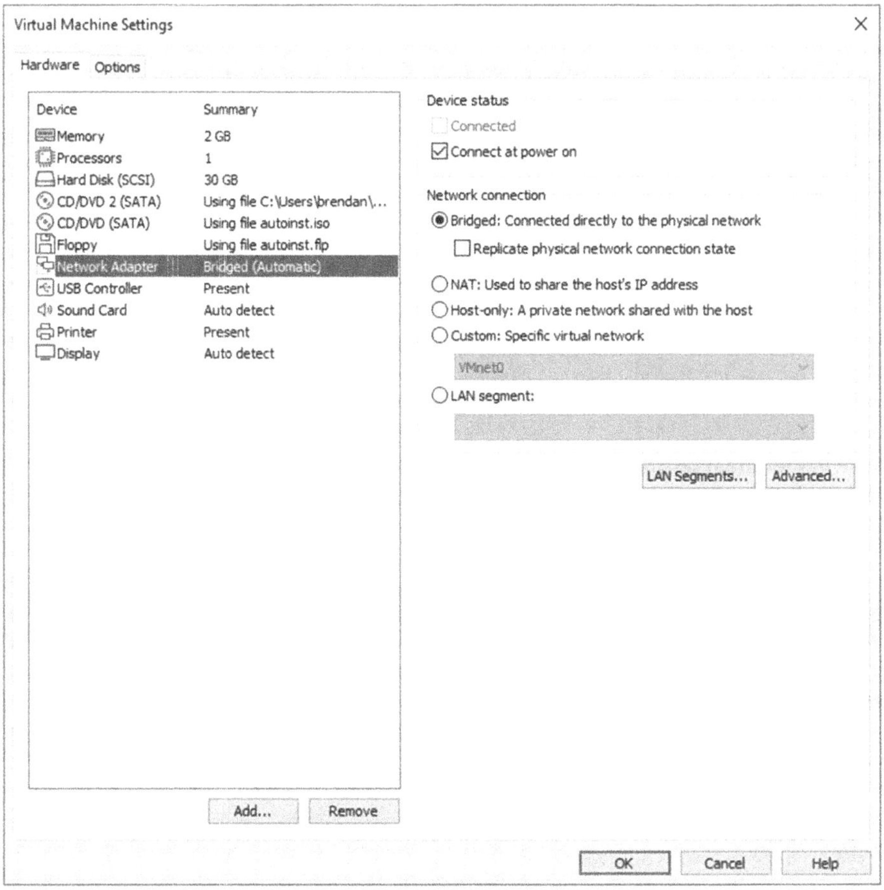

Figure 4-19. *Virtual machine settings, bridged network connection*

Figure 4-20 reveals the host's physical adapter network configuration from the DHCP server at 192.168.0.1; the default gateway doubles as a DHCP server in a typical home network. My host connects to the Internet via wireless, so a Wi-Fi 3 interface is shown as the adapter name, but your settings will differ from Figure 4-20.

Administrator: Command Prompt

```
C:\Windows\system32>netsh interface ip show addresses "Wi-Fi 3"

Configuration for interface "Wi-Fi 3"
    DHCP enabled:                         Yes
    IP Address:                           192.168.0.232
    Subnet Prefix:                        192.168.0.0/24 (mask 255.255.255.0)
    Default Gateway:                      192.168.0.1
    Gateway Metric:                       0
    InterfaceMetric:                      55


C:\Windows\system32>
```

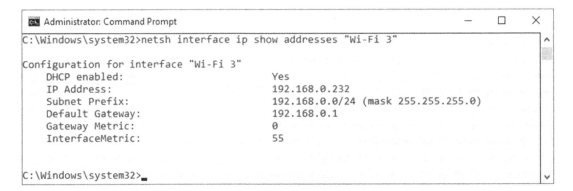

Figure 4-20. *Windows host PC, local PC's internet adapter (Wi-Fi)*

Figure 4-21 shows a VM terminal session revealing the IP address received from the home network's DHCP server. Also, refer to the previous Figure 4-11 to visualize and help you understand the bridged network mode.

pynetauto@ubuntu20s1: ~/Desktop

```
pynetauto@ubuntu20s1:~/Desktop$ ifconfig ens33
ens33: flags=4163<UP,BROADCAST,RUNNING,MULTICAST>  mtu 1500
        inet 192.168.0.244  netmask 255.255.255.0  broadcast 192.168.0.255
        inet6 fe80::20c:29ff:fef9:e45f  prefixlen 64  scopeid 0x20<link>
        inet6 2001:8003:221c:a600:20c:29ff:fef9:e45f  prefixlen 64  scopeid 0x0<global>
        ether 00:0c:29:f9:e4:5f  txqueuelen 1000  (Ethernet)
        RX packets 126  bytes 26224 (26.2 KB)
        RX errors 0  dropped 0  overruns 0  frame 0
        TX packets 80  bytes 8807 (8.8 KB)
        TX errors 0  dropped 0 overruns 0  carrier 0  collisions 0

pynetauto@ubuntu20s1:~/Desktop$
```

Figure 4-21. *Virtual machine, ens33 network adapter*

Network Address Translation Networking

In Network Address Translation (NAT) mode, a VM shares the host's IP and MAC addresses. The outside network (Internet) sees your network as a single network identity, and the internal network is not visible outside the network. Typically and in the traditional sense, NAT is used to hide the internal network from outsiders and extend the number of useful IPv4 IP addresses within your network. If you have already undertaken Cisco CCNA routing and switching studies, understanding NAT or PAT is part of the study curriculum, so understanding this type of networking mode will also make immediate sense. Throughout this book, you will utilize NAT's features for your entire lab configuration to keep the networking configuration to a minimum.

Let's look at Figure 4-22 and review how NAT is configured under VMware Workstation Pro configuration. In NAT mode, VMware Workstation provides the DHCP service, meaning that another subnet is used inside the network; in this case, the subnet assigned to NAT is in the 192.168.183.0/24 range, and this is the primary method in which our lab will connect to the Internet and host.

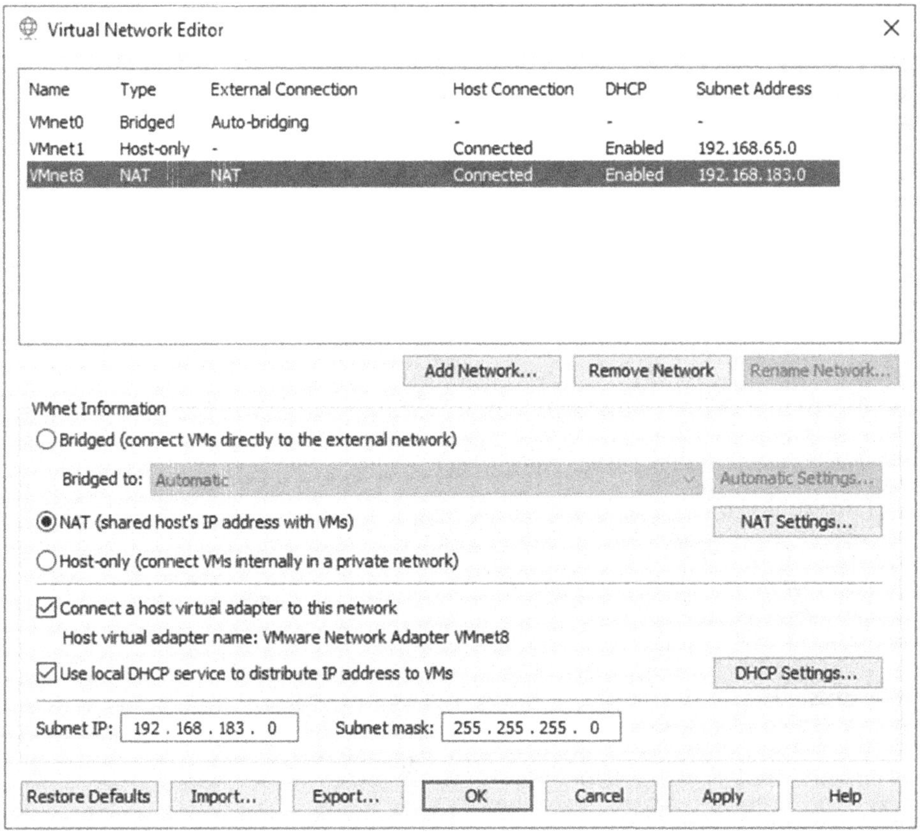

Figure 4-22. *Virtual Network Editor, VMnet8 NAT adapter*

Click the NAT settings button in Figure 4-21; it reveals NAT or VMnet8 settings below. You will notice that the gateway IP address for this subnet is 192.168.183.2, and we can assume that 192.168.183.1 would have been assigned to the VNnet8 adapter on the host PC; this will be verified in Figure 4-23.

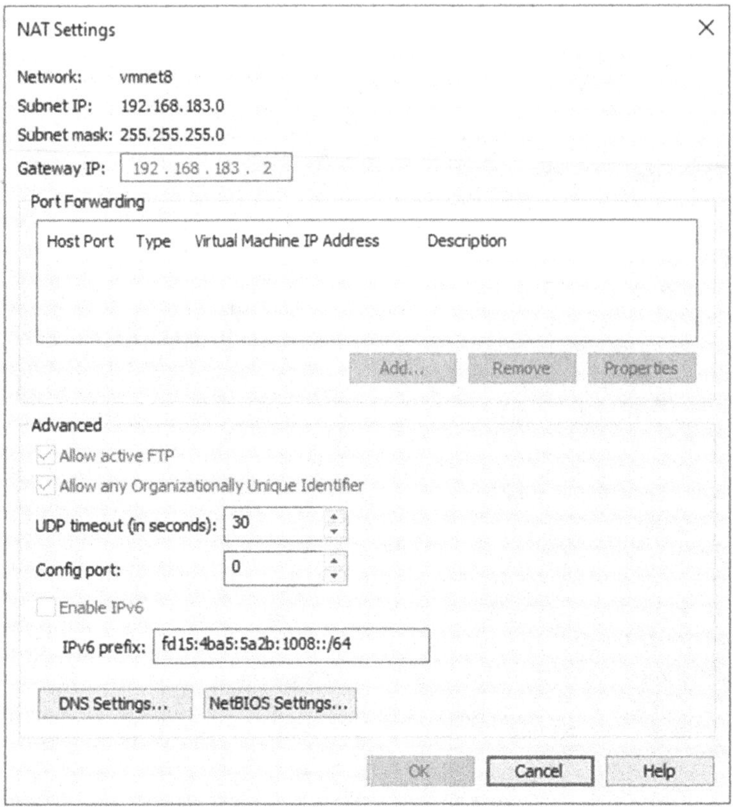

Figure 4-23. *Virtual Network Editor, NAT settings*

Figure 4-24 shows the network connection configuration of a VM.

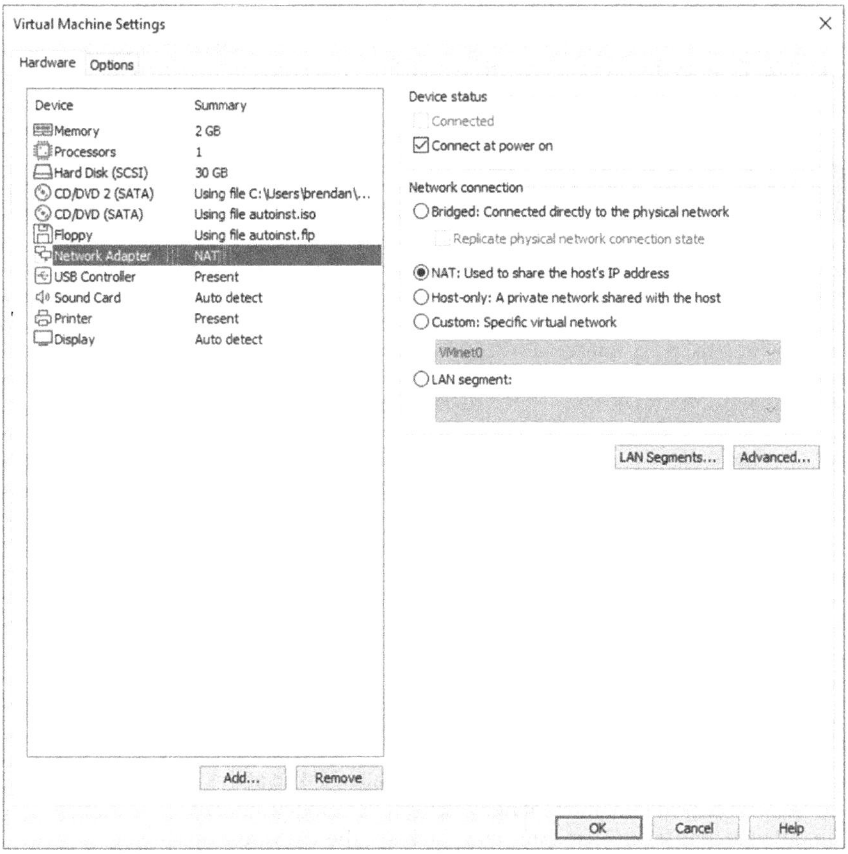

Figure 4-24. *Virtual machine settings, NAT network connection*

Figure 4-25 shows the IP address configuration from the DHCP server; as discussed, 192.168.183.1/24 is assigned to VMnet8 on the host. However, the default gateway for the VMs is 192.168.183.2.

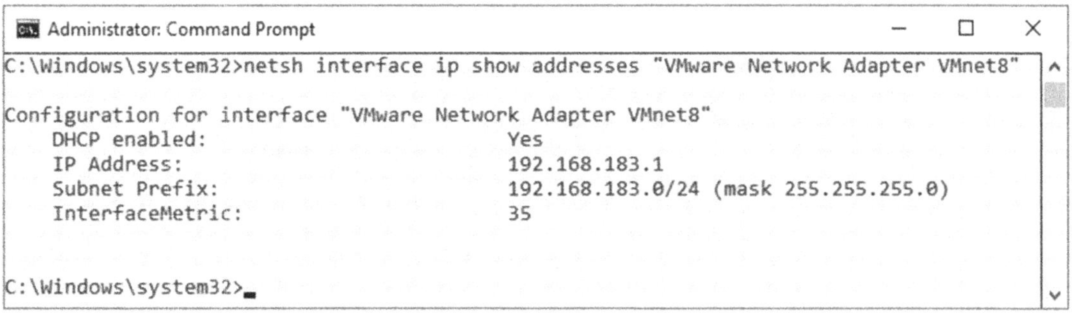

Figure 4-25. *Windows host PC, VMware network adapter VMnet8*

As expected, a VM on the NAT network within VMware Workstation Pro will assign an IP address from the same 192.168.183.0/24 network. In Figure 4-26, 192.168.183.129/24 has been assigned to the Linux server's ens33 network interface. Refer to the previous Figure 4-13 to help you better understand the NAT mode.

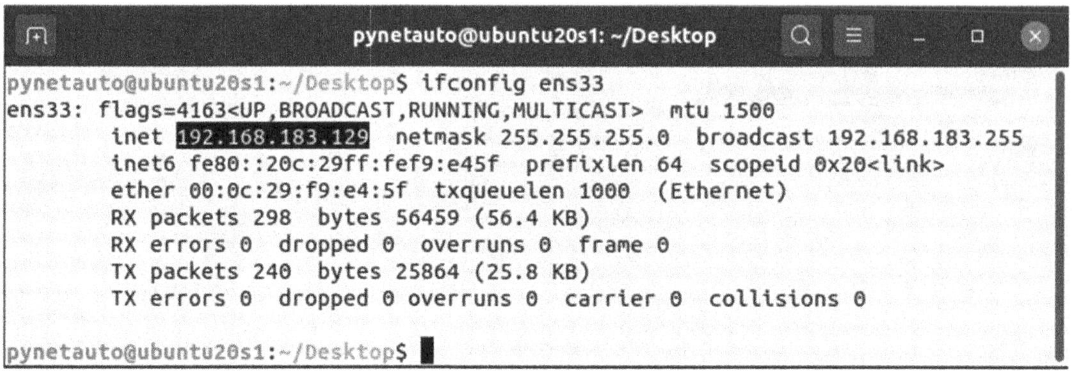

Figure 4-26. *Virtual machine, ens33 network adapter*

Summary

Virtualization technology makes cloud services possible, so we discussed the difference between Type-1 and Type-2 hypervisors of current virtualization technology. This chapter also introduced you to VMware Workstation 15 Pro and why we are using this solution over others. We also looked at this software's basic operations on our Windows PC and delved into different networking modes that users can use to build a virtual lab environment for our work and leisure use. Now that you know the VMware Workstation essential features, it is time to download, install, and create virtual machines, namely, Ubuntu 20.04 LTS (Chapter 5) and CentOS 8.1 servers (Chapter 6).

CHAPTER 5

Creating an Ubuntu Server Virtual Machine

In this chapter, you will be downloading the latest Ubuntu Server 20 bootable image to install and create a virtual machine on your VMware Workstation instance. Ubuntu is a Debian Linux-derivative distro and provides one of the best user experiences on Linux. For most Windows users, Ubuntu Desktop would be the first Linux entry point. However, for this book, we will be using Ubuntu Server 20 instead with a little twist: we will choose to install a UI to add more flexibility to our lab. At the end of this chapter, you will be able to create a Ubuntu Server virtual machine from the ground up, customize selective settings on the operating system, take a snapshot of a virtual machine, and clone a virtual machine

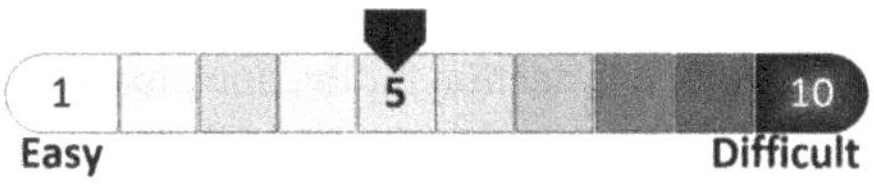

You can create virtual machines (VMs) using bootable image files of different operating systems and load a VM image prepared by others in advance. If you choose the second option and import or convert premade VMs, you will miss out on learning how to build the virtual server from scratch. Anyway, with more powerful desktops and laptops, building and installing a VM from scratch does not take a lot of time, so you will be guided through the entire installation process starting from downloading the image files to doing basic configurations. Although the VMs in this book are simplified versions of more powerful, scalable enterprise and cloud infrastructure and network solutions, the VM provisioning concepts and techniques are much the same.

In the last five years, the buzzword in IT has been *cloud computing*. In its most basic form, cloud computing is squeezing a lot of powerful servers into centralized or decentralized data centers to provide on-demand services via the Internet. Everything is off-premise, and users are connecting via thin client machines or applications running on remote nodes. Underneath the cloud computing machines are the virtualization technologies, and understanding virtualization means you can get a step closer to cloud services.

After installing VMware Workstation 15 Pro on your laptop, you will need to download a bootable image file for your preferred operating system to build a VM. This image can be any flavor of Windows or Linux image. Our intention is clear that we want to move away from the Windows operating system and get comfortable with the Linux operating system, so our choice is evident. We will download Linux-installable images and start the installation. Since we also want to know the difference between two of the most popular Linux distro versions, namely, Ubuntu and CentOS, we will work with them both. Ubuntu is one of the most popular Debian-based Linux distros, and CentOS is the most widely used Red Hat–based free distribution version. To give you more hands-on experience with both Linux distributions, Ubuntu Server will be installed in this chapter, followed by the CentOS server installation in the next chapter. These two servers will be used throughout this book with full flexibility. The basic kernels are almost identical between

B. Choi, *Introduction to Python Network Automation*, https://doi.org/10.1007/978-1-4842-6806-3_5

the two Linux distributions. Still, there are subtle differences that you can learn if you use them side by side, so installing both and trying to learn basic and general administration tasks will add more value to your learning and to your career.

For the remainder of this chapter, you will concentrate on installing the latest Ubuntu, which will be used as the primary Python network automation server. When you are ready, let's create a Ubuntu Server 20.04 LTS virtual machine.

We are using the latest Ubuntu Server 20.04 LTS and CentOS 8.1 in this book, but in production environments, often system administrators choose to use the n–1 version of the latest software. The n–1 software concept is to use the previous software version to avoid bugs and software compatibility issues, aiming for the five 9s (99.999 percent uptime each year). Also, you have the flexibility to go one version up if the n–1 version does not deliver the performance or services you are looking for.

If you are going to run these servers in the production, consider using Ubuntu 18.04 LTS or CentOS 7.5 for better software compatibility. This makes more sense now for CentOS 8 as it will be supported only until the end of 2021, whereas CentOS 7.5 will still enjoy support until 2024. You'll learn more about this in Chapter 6.

Downloading and Installing a Ubuntu Server 20 Image

To install the latest Ubuntu server, you first need to download a bootable Ubuntu Server image (`.iso`) file from Ubuntu's official download site. Make sure you have a reliable Internet connection for the download and follow the directions in the next sections.

Ubuntu Server 20.04 LTS: what's in a name?

Traditionally, Ubuntu Linux server versions are named with a YY.MM format for the release year and month. So, Ubuntu Server 20.04 indicates that it was first released on the market in the fourth month of 2020. LTS stands for Long Term Support and indicates that this software version is supported for five years as opposed to beta versions. It's the same naming convention for Ubuntu 18.04 LTS, which was released in the fourth month of 2018.

Downloading the Ubuntu Server 20.04 LTS Image

#	Task
01	Open your favorite web browser, and then go to the Ubuntu download page. The expected file size is approximately 908MB. `https://www.ubuntu.com/download/server` Download the Ubuntu server version, which is the 64-bit PC (AMD64) server install image; the downloaded installable filename is `ubuntu-20.04-live-server-amd64.iso`. See Figure 5-1.

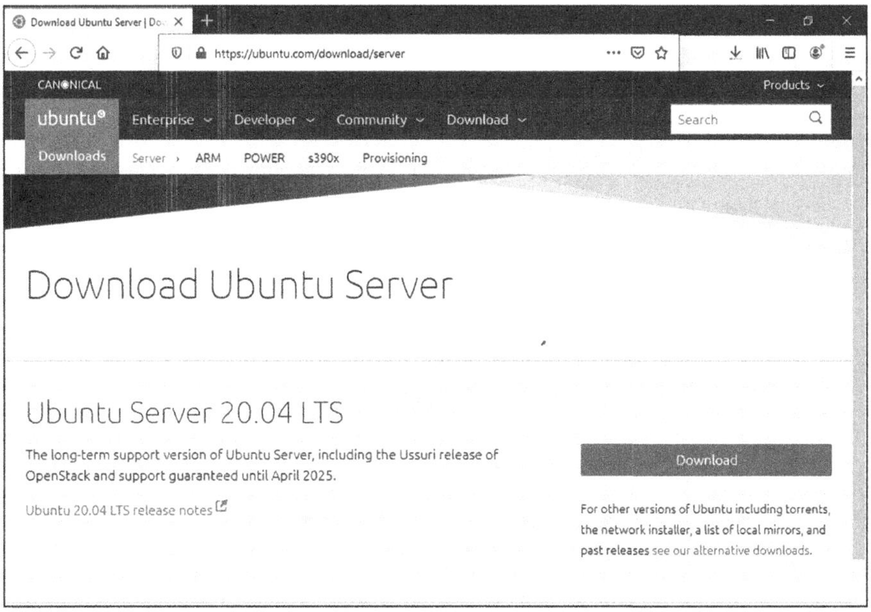

Figure 5-1. *Ubuntu Server 20.04 LTS image download page*

(*continued*)

#	Task
02	To check whether the downloaded ISO file has been correctly downloaded, use WinMD5 or a similar tool to check the MD5 value before your installation. See Figure 5-2.

WinMD5 can be downloaded for free from here:

`www.winmd5.com/` or `www.winmd5.com/download/winmd5free.zip`

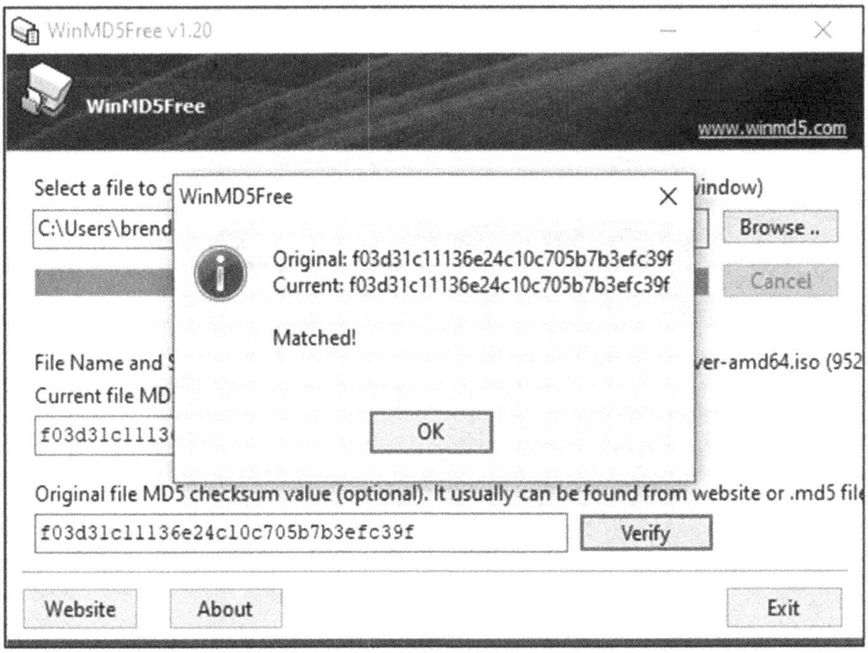

Figure 5-2. *Ubuntu Server 20.04 ISO MD5 checksum verification*

The Ubuntu Server 20 LTS MD5 value can be found at the following link:

`https://releases.ubuntu.com/20.04/MD5SUMS`

You will see something like this:

MD5 value: f03d31c11136e24c10c705b7b3efc39f

Filename: *ubuntu-20.04-live-server-amd64.iso

Installing Ubuntu Server 20.04 LTS

Installing a Linux VM on VMware Workstation is easy, but you have to learn how to create and install various VMs using different bootable ISO images. The Ubuntu Server 20.04 installation process is as follows:

#	Task
01	First, start VMware Workstation 15 Pro using the shortcut icon on the host PC (Windows 10). See Figure 5-3.  ***Figure 5-3.*** *VMware Workstation shortcut icon*
02	Then select the File menu and then choose New Virtual Machine, as shown in Figure 5-4. 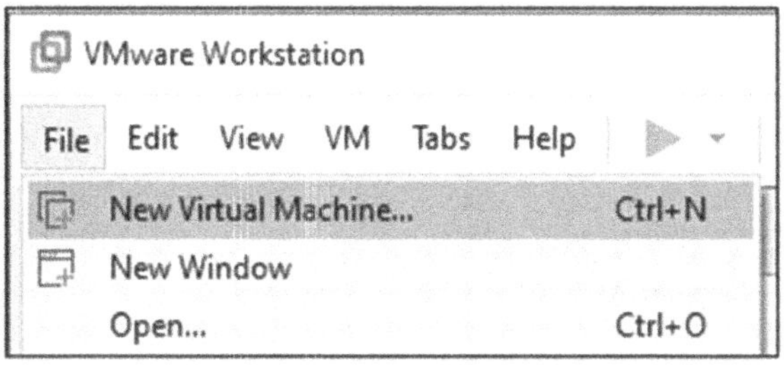 ***Figure 5-4.*** *Creating a new virtual machine*

(*continued*)

#	Task
03	When the New Virtual Machine Wizard window appears, leave "Typical (recommended)" selected and click the Next button at the bottom. See Figure 5-5.

***Figure 5-5.** New Virtual Machine Wizard*

#	Task
04	In the next window, select "Installer disk image file (iso)" and click the Browse button on the right. See Figure 5-6.

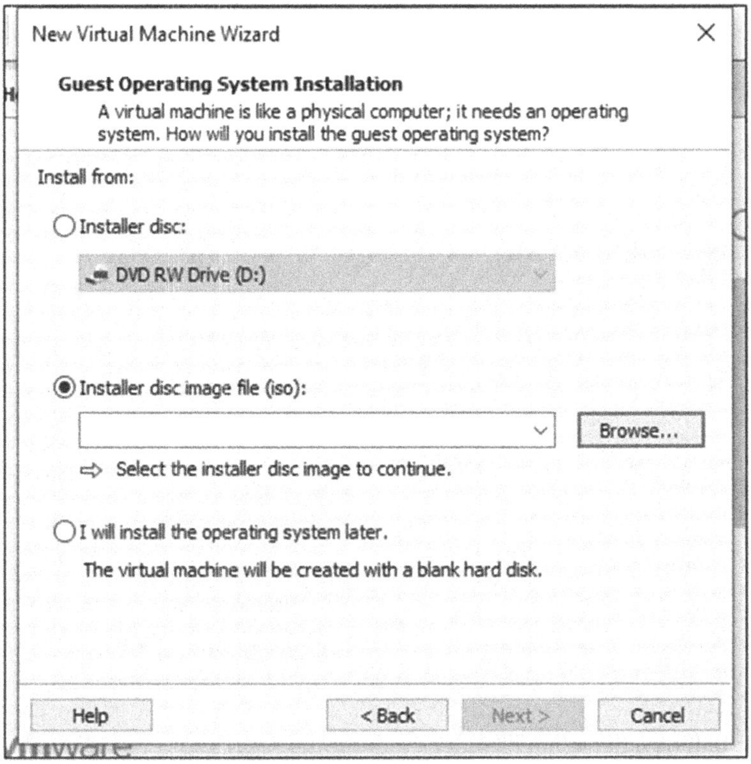

Figure 5-6. *Ubuntu installation, selecting installation media*

(*continued*)

#	Task
05	When the Browse for ISO image window appears, navigate to the `Downloads` folder where you have downloaded and saved the Ubuntu Server 20.04 installable file and select it. Click the Open button at the bottom. See Figure 5-7.

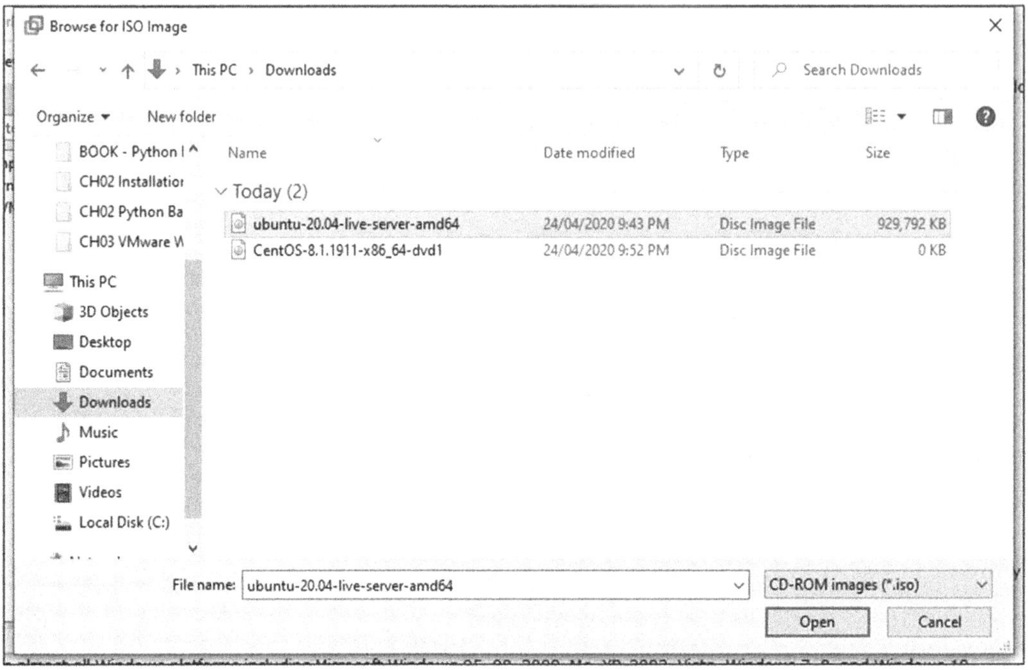

Figure 5-7. *Ubuntu installation, selecting an installable image*

#	Task
06	When you return to the previous screen, click the Next button. See Figure 5-8.

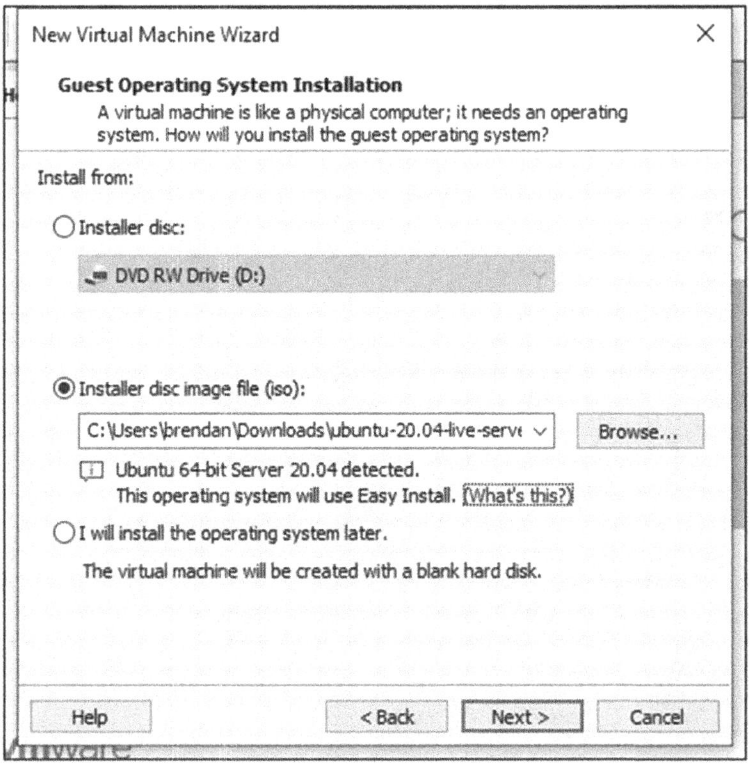

***Figure 5-8.** Ubuntu installation, selected installable image*

(*continued*)

#	Task
07	Enter your name, user ID, and password and click the Next button. See Figure 5-9.

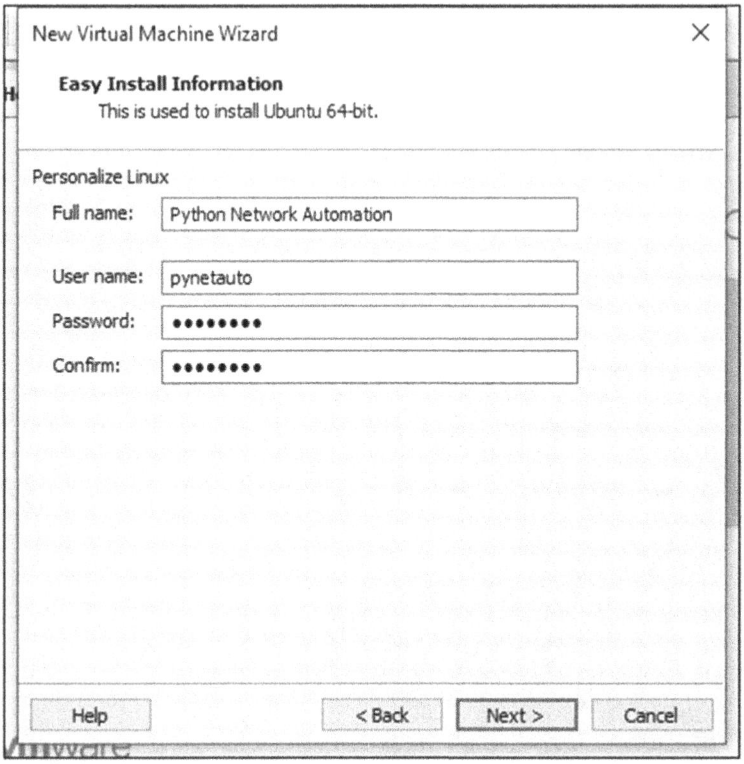

Figure 5-9. *Ubuntu installation, entering user credentialss*

#	Task
08	Choose a meaningful server name for your Ubuntu server. This example is using the default folder, but if you want to store and run your VMs from another folder, you can change the settings now. `ubuntu20s1` is the server name given to my Ubuntu Server 20 server. See Figure 5-10.

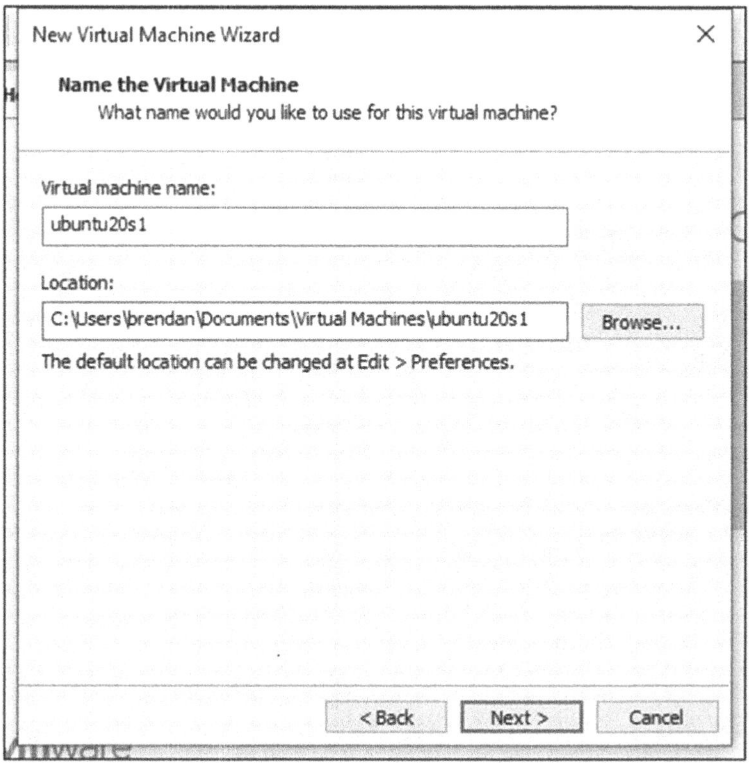

***Figure 5-10.** Ubuntu installation, VM folder selection*

(*continued*)

#	Task
09	By default, 20GB will be allocated to your VM. I have enough disk space on my SSD, so I will increase this to 30GB for future use. Also, I prefer to store the virtual disk file as a single file as this makes migration and VM conversions easier. Click the Next button. Since thin provisioning is used, the entire 30GB of disk space is not used, but the disk size will gradually increase on demand while using up the VM's disk space. See Figure 5-11.

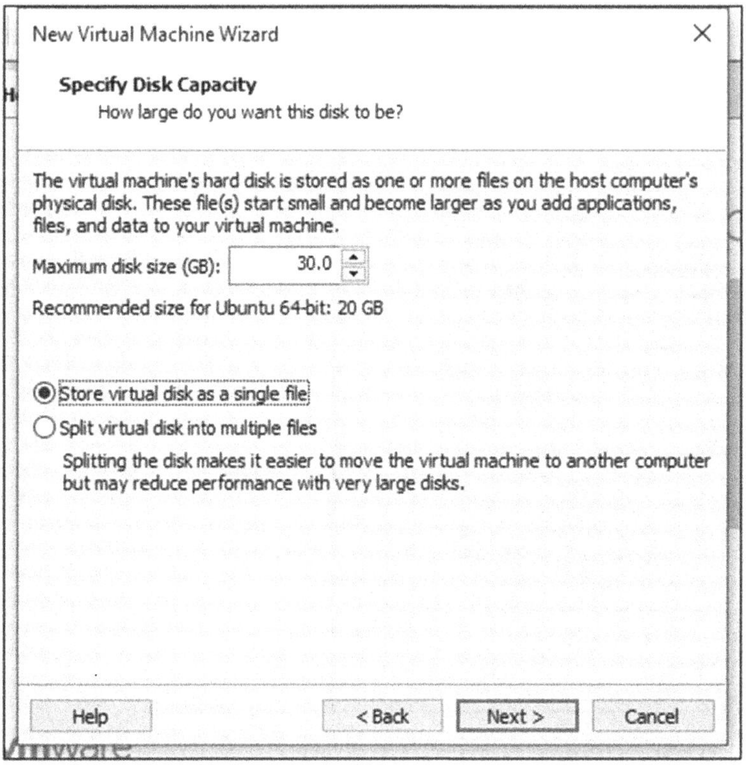

Figure 5-11. *Ubuntu installation, disk size allocation, and single virtual disk file option*

#	Task
10	On the next screen, click the Finish button with the default setting "Power on this virtual machine after creation" selected. See Figure 5-12.

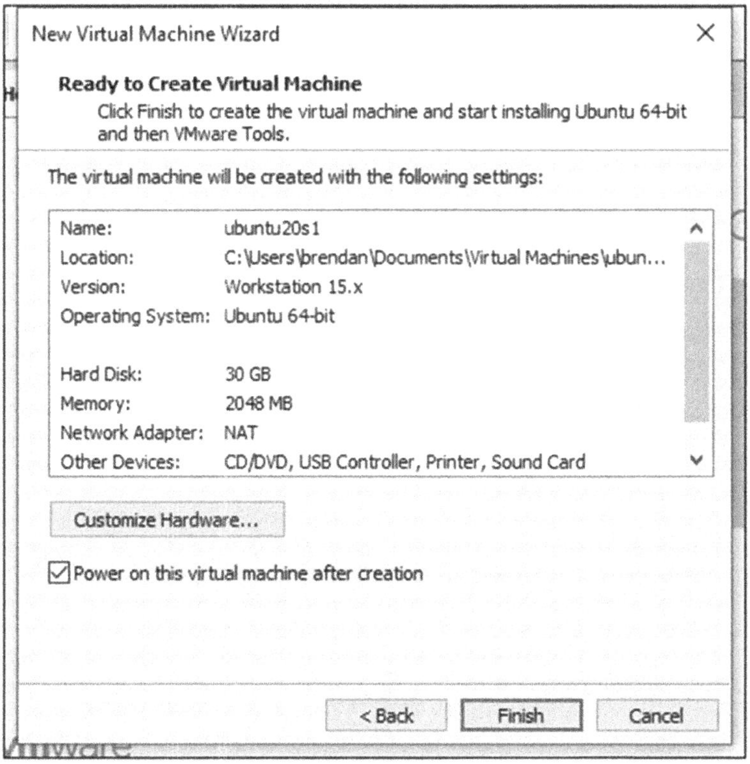

Figure 5-12. *Installing Ubuntu, finishing VM configuration*

(*continued*)

#	Task
11	The new VM will use the Ubuntu boot image to begin the Ubuntu Server installation on the first screen. See Figure 5-13.

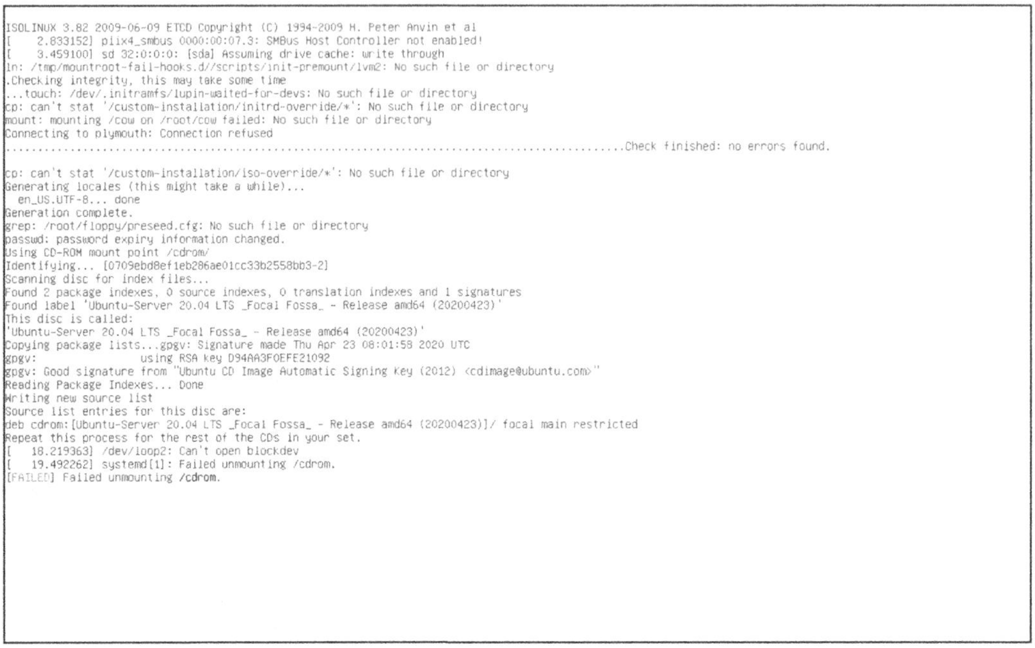

ISOLINUX 3.82 2009-06-09 ETCD Copyright (C) 1994-2009 H. Peter Anvin et al
[2.833152] piix4_smbus 0000:00:07.3: SMBus Host Controller not enabled!
[3.459100] sd 32:0:0:0: [sda] Assuming drive cache: write through
ln: /tmp/mountroot-fail-hooks.d//scripts/init-premount/lvm2: No such file or directory
.Checking integrity, this may take some time
...touch: /dev/.initramfs/lupin-waited-for-devs: No such file or directory
cp: can't stat '/custom-installation/initrd-override/*': No such file or directory
mount: mounting /cow on /root/cow failed: No such file or directory
Connecting to plymouth: Connection refused
....Check finished: no errors found.
cp: can't stat '/custom-installation/iso-override/*': No such file or directory
Generating locales (this might take a while)...
en_US.UTF-8... done
Generation complete.
grep: /root/floppy/preseed.cfg: No such file or directory
passwd: password expiry information changed.
Using CD-ROM mount point /cdrom/
Identifying... [0709ebd8ef1eb286ae01cc33b2558bb3-2]
Scanning disc for index files...
Found 2 package indexes, 0 source indexes, 0 translation indexes and 1 signatures
Found label 'Ubuntu-Server 20.04 LTS _Focal Fossa_ - Release amd64 (20200423)'
This disc is called:
'Ubuntu-Server 20.04 LTS _Focal Fossa_ - Release amd64 (20200423)'
Copying package lists...gpgv: Signature made Thu Apr 23 08:01:58 2020 UTC
gpgv: using RSA key D94AA3F0EFE21092
gpgv: Good signature from "Ubuntu CD Image Automatic Signing Key (2012) <cdimage@ubuntu.com>"
Reading Package Indexes... Done
Writing new source list
Source list entries for this disc are:
deb cdrom:[Ubuntu-Server 20.04 LTS _Focal Fossa_ - Release amd64 (20200423)]/ focal main restricted
Repeat this process for the rest of the CDs in your set.
[18.219363] /dev/loop2: Can't open blockdev
[19.492262] systemd[1]: Failed unmounting /cdrom.
[FAILED] Failed unmounting /cdrom.

Figure 5-13. *Ubuntu installation, server installation's first screen*

#	Task
12	*Language selection*: You are prompted to select a language. English is selected as the default language. If you speak another language, select your native language from the selection. See Figure 5-14.

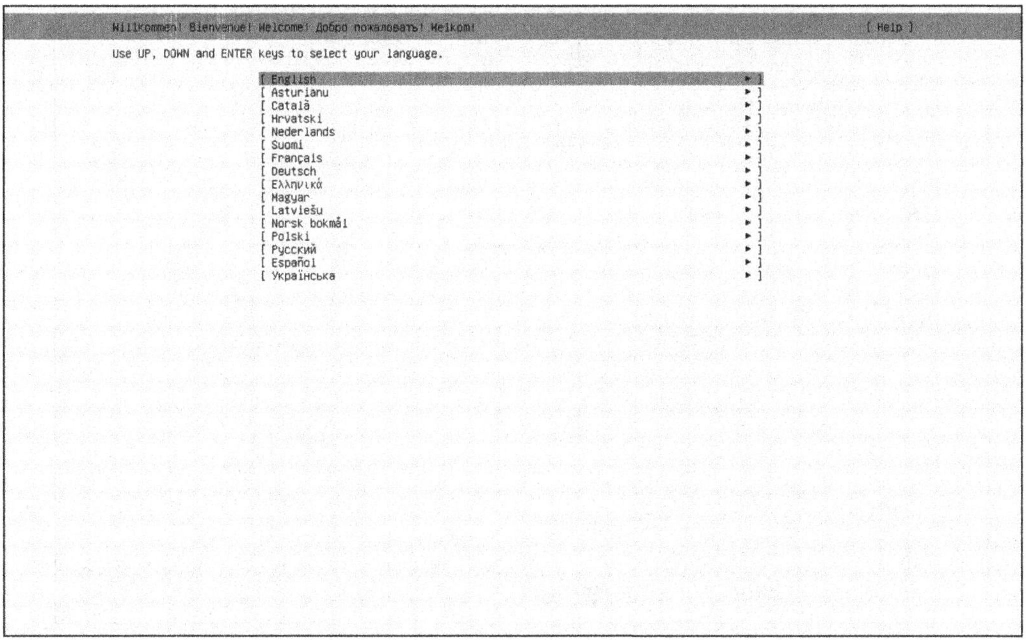

Figure 5-14. *Ubuntu installation, default language selection*

(*continued*)

#	Task
13	*Keyboard configuration*: Leave the keyboard configuration at the default settings, highlight the Done button, and hit the Enter key. See Figure 5-15.

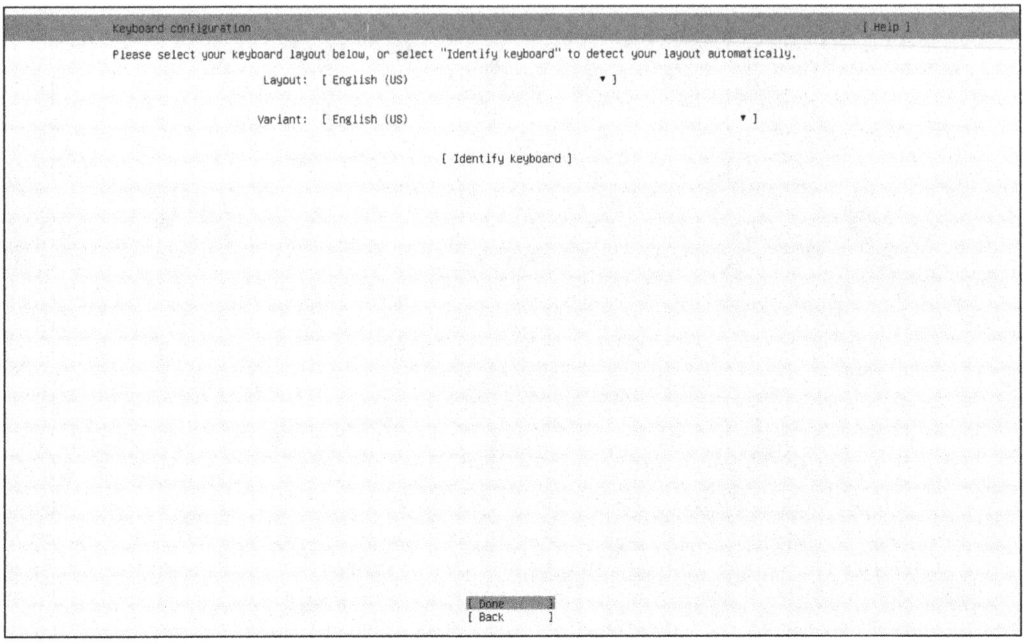

Figure 5-15. *Ubuntu installation, keyboard selection*

#	Task
14	*Network connections*: If you did change the default network settings during VM creation, your VM will use a Network Address Translation (NAT) network. The first available IP address will be assigned to your VM from VMware Workstation's NAT DHCP subnet pool, and the default IP range is from 192.168.183.128 to 192.168.183.254. If you changed the subnet, your IP subnet and IP address range will differ from the example shown in this book. If your NAT network's DHCP service has not been disabled, you will receive a valid IP address similar to Figure 5-16.

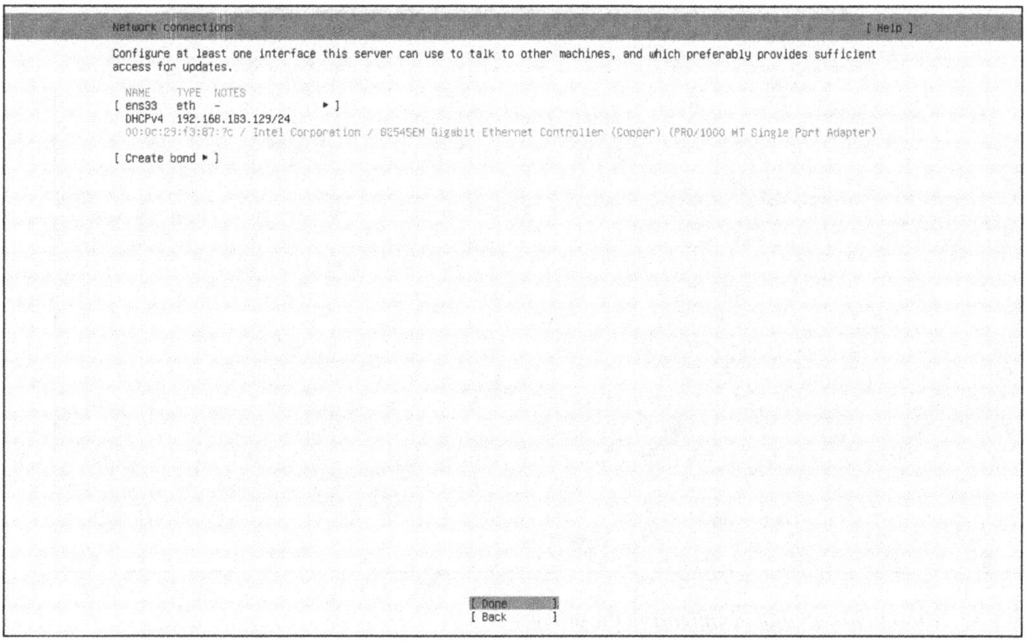

***Figure 5-16.** Ubuntu installation, network connections*

(continued)

#	Task
15	*Configure proxy*: No proxy server is used on the current network, so there is no need to specify a proxy IP address. However, if you connect to the Internet via your company's proxy server at work, then add the proxy information here. Of course, this information can be changed later. Assuming that you are also connecting via your home network, leave this blank, and let's move on. See Figure 5-17.

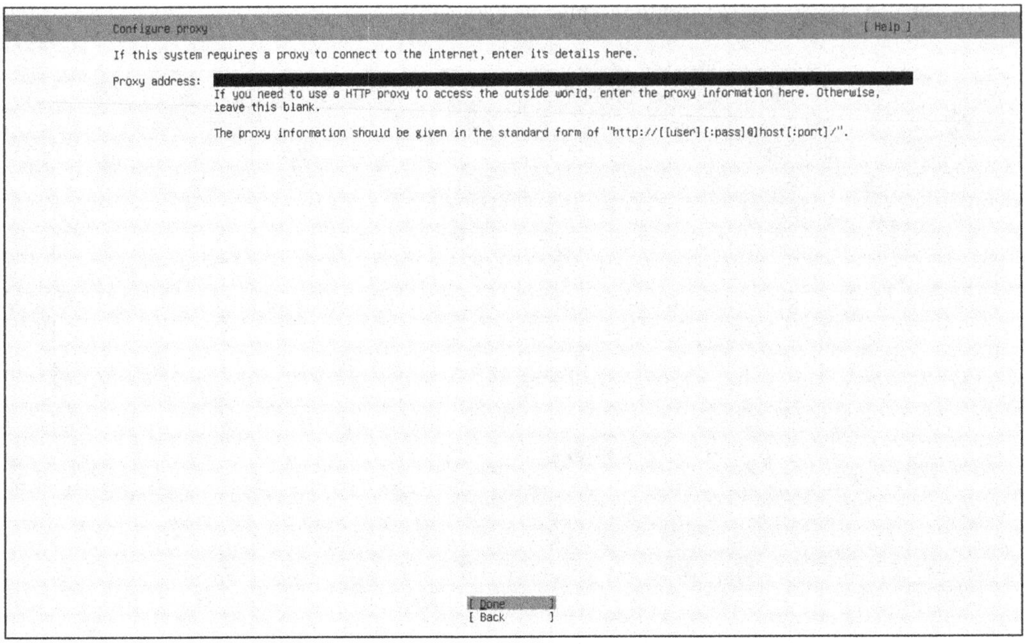

***Figure 5-17.** Ubuntu installation, configuring the proxy*

#	Task
16	*Configure Ubuntu archive mirror*: Leave the default selection for this section, then highlight the Done key, and hit the Enter key. See Figure 5-18.

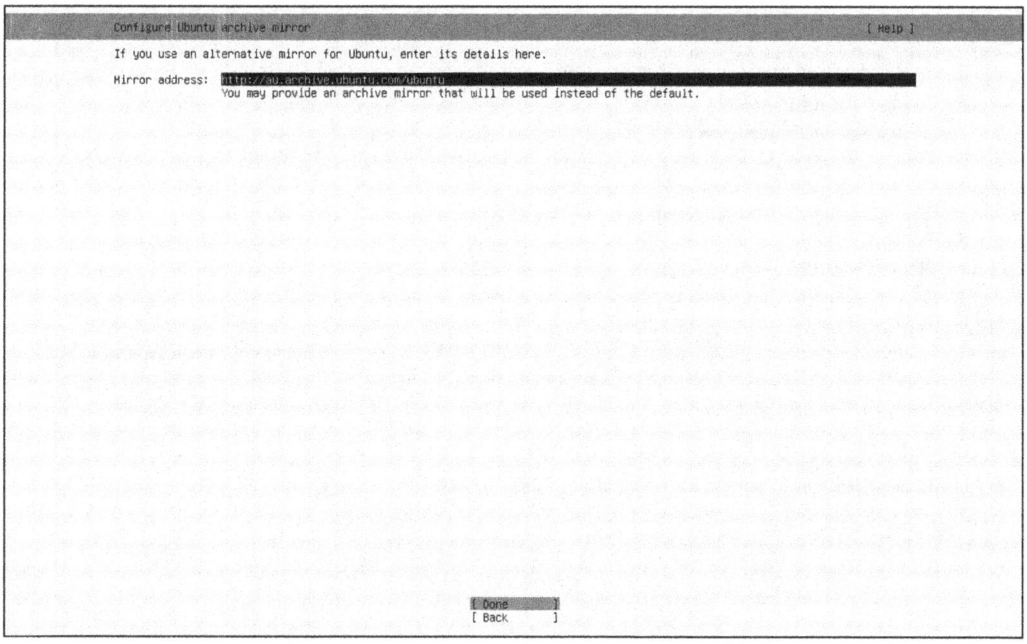

Figure 5-18. *Ubuntu installation, configuring the Ubuntu archive mirror*

(*continued*)

#	Task
17	*Guided storage configuration*: Confirm that the /dev/sda size is the same as what you have allocated, then highlight the Done key, and hit the Enter key again. See Figure 5-19.

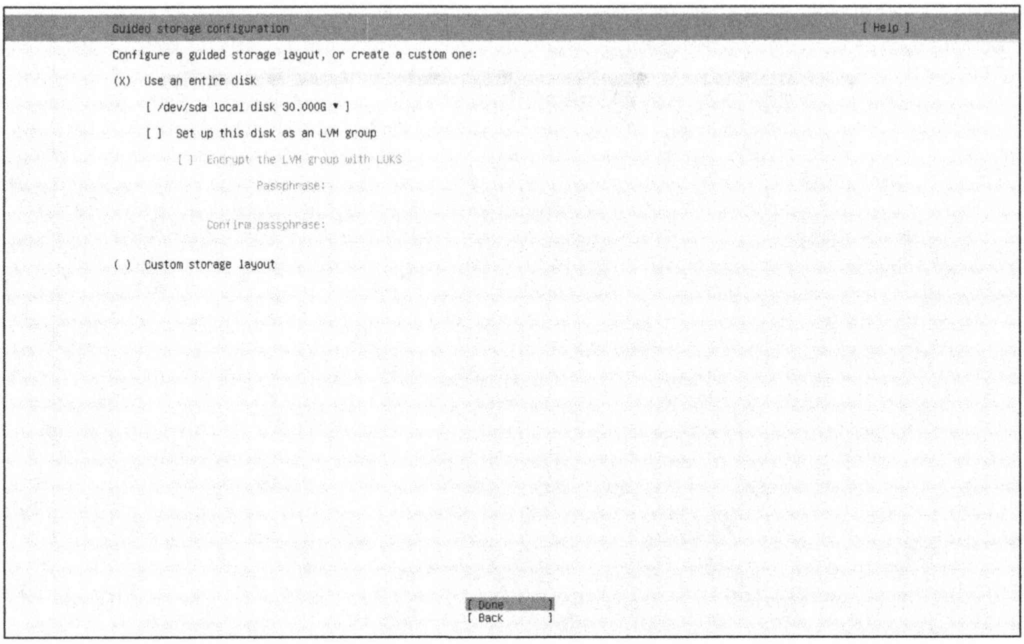

***Figure 5-19.** Ubuntu installation, guided storage configuration*

#	Task
18	*Storage configuration*: Once again, review and confirm the configuration, then highlight Done, and hit the Enter key on your keyboard to move to the next screen. See Figure 5-20.

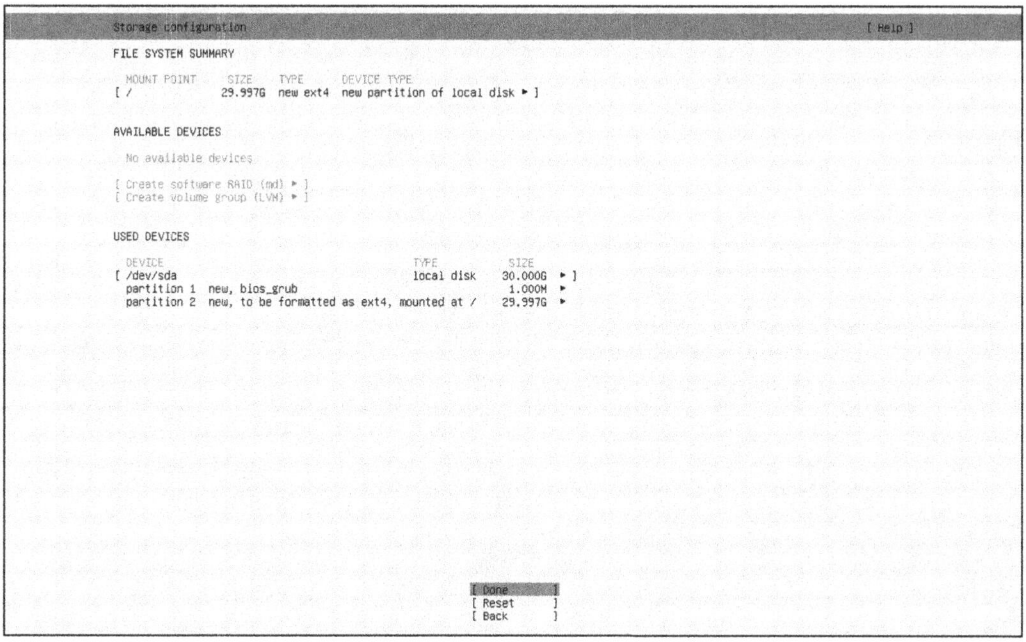

Figure 5-20. *Ubuntu installation, storage configuration*

(*continued*)

#	Task
19	*Storage configuration*: In the "Confirm destructive action" box, highlight the Continue button and hit the Enter key to complete storage configuration. See Figure 5-21.

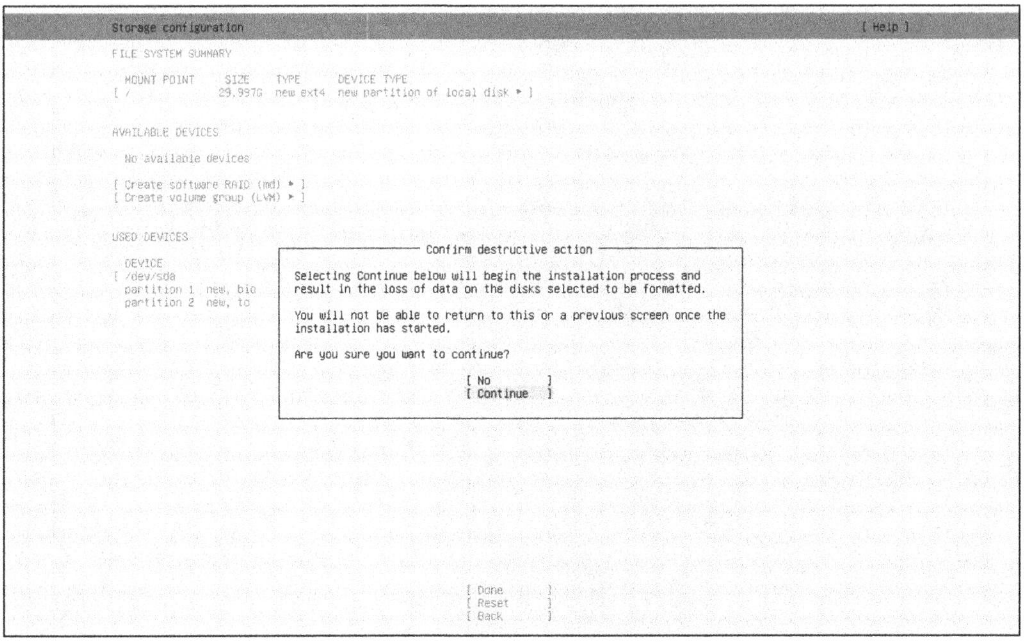

Figure 5-21. *Ubuntu installation, storage configuration (confirm destructive action)*

#	Task
20	*Profile setup*: Fill in your profile with a unique user ID and password. Make the server's name the same as what you have specified during VM creation; in this case, it is ubuntu20s1 for Ubuntu Server 20 1. Highlight the Done key and hit the Enter key again. See Figure 5-22.

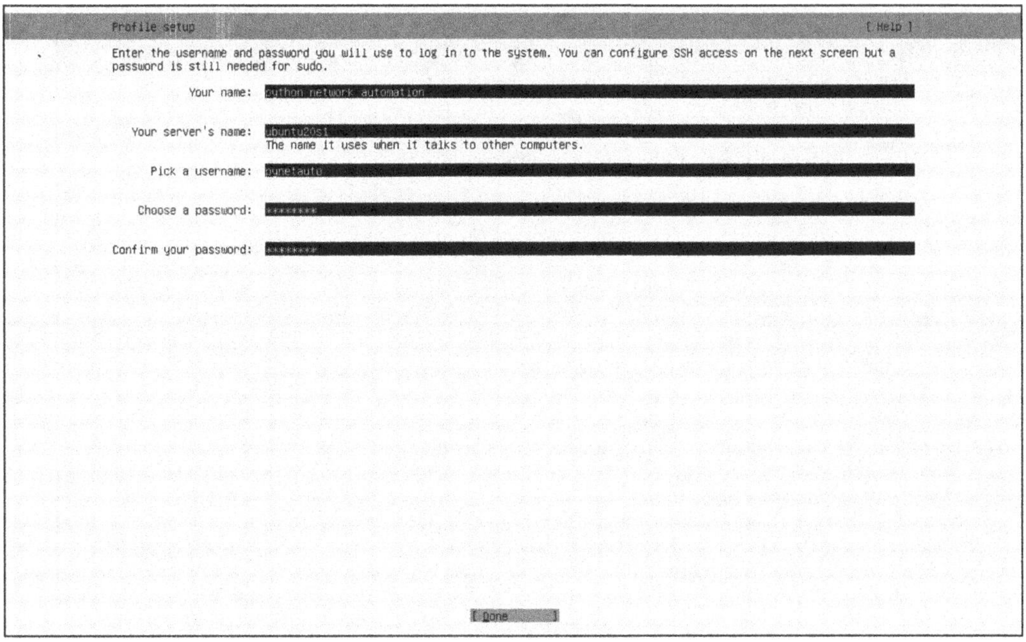

Figure 5-22. *Ubuntu installation, setting up the profile*

(*continued*)

#	Task
21	*SSH Setup*: You will connect to this server via an SSH connection, so installing the OpenSSH server for an SSH connection is recommended. We can install this service after the OS installation, but it makes sense to install the SSH server now rather than later. Use the spacebar to select the "Install OpenSSH server" option, then highlight the Done key, and hit the Enter key again. See Figure 5-23.

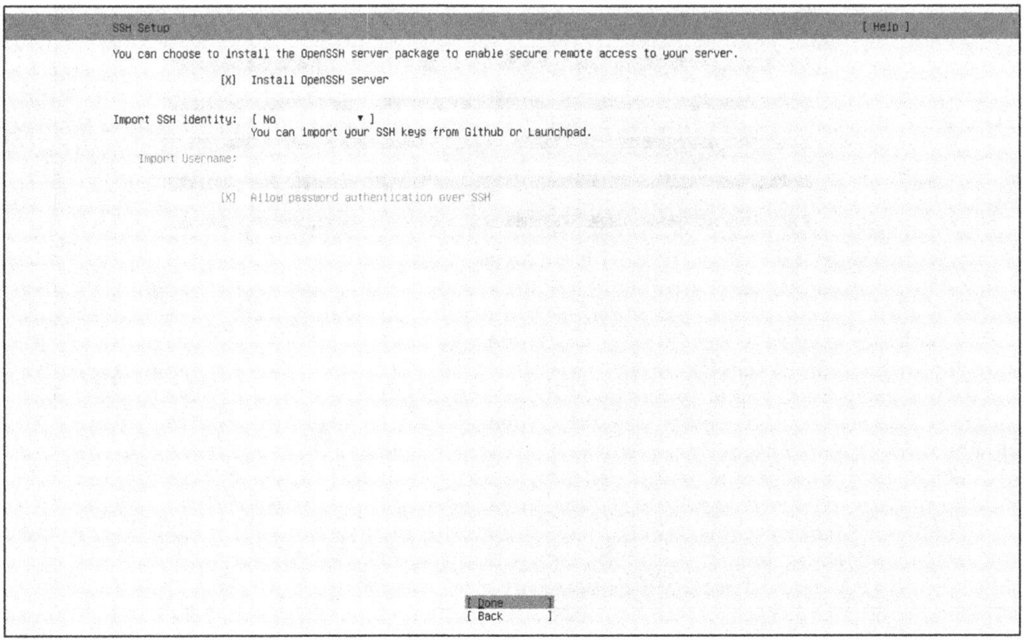

Figure 5-23. *Ubuntu installation, setting up SSH*

#	Task
22	*Featured Server Snaps*: If you plan to use any of the services immediately after the installation, make your selections using the spacebar. Docker and PowerShell have been selected in Figure 5-24, as they are often useful services on any Linux server. Once all the selections are made, then highlight the Done key and hit the Enter key on your keyboard.

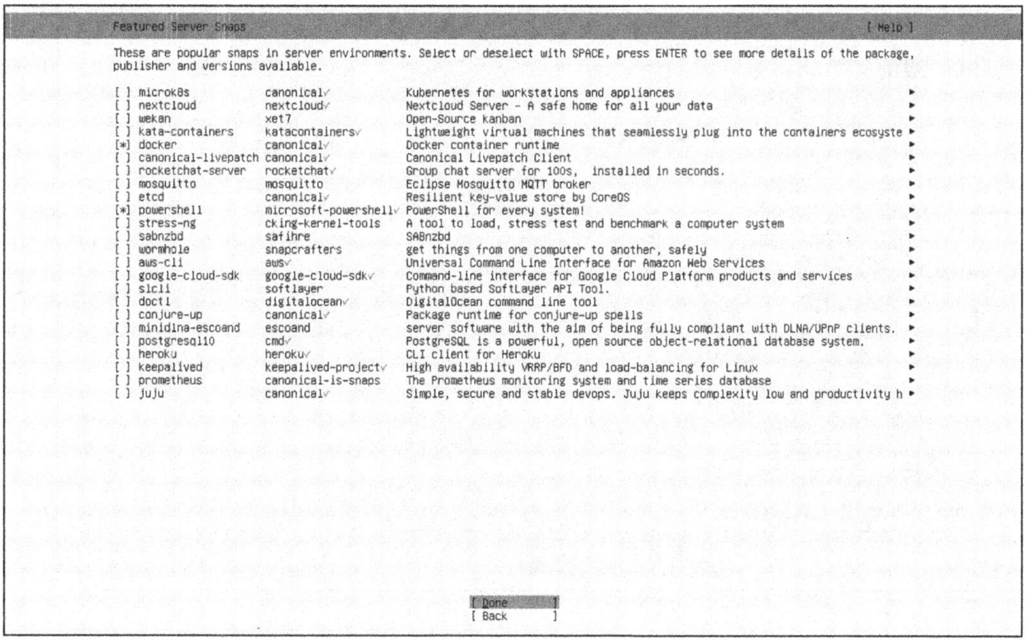

Figure 5-24. *Ubuntu installation, featured server snaps*

(*continued*)

#	Task
23	*Installation complete*: Once you get to the final installation screen, click the Reboot option, and press the Enter key to restart your first VM. See Figure 5-25.

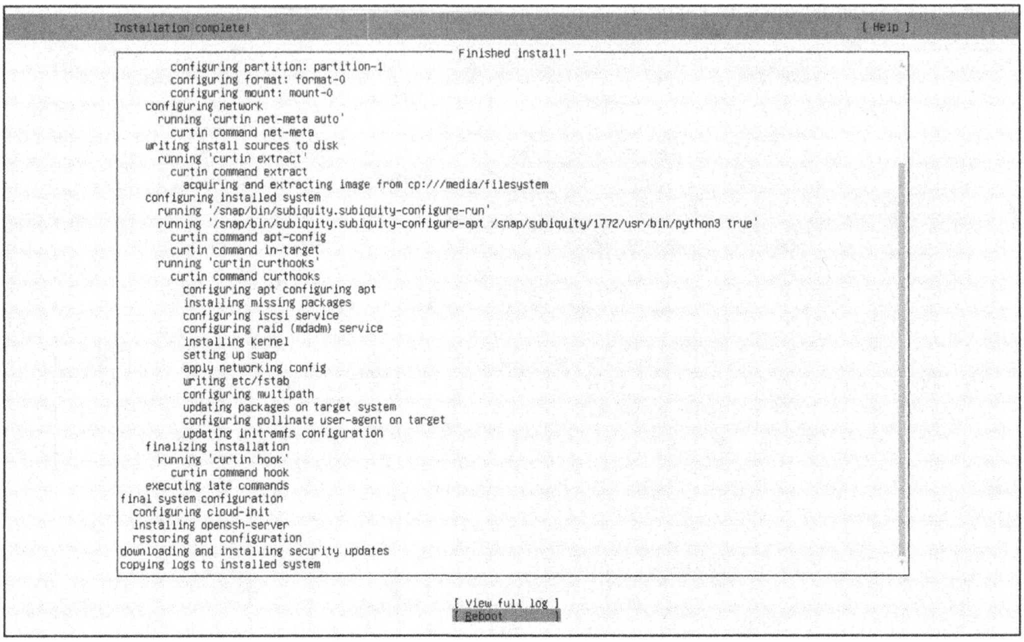

Figure 5-25. *Ubuntu installation, installation completed*

#	Task
24	After the reboot, your screen will look similar to Figure 5-26.

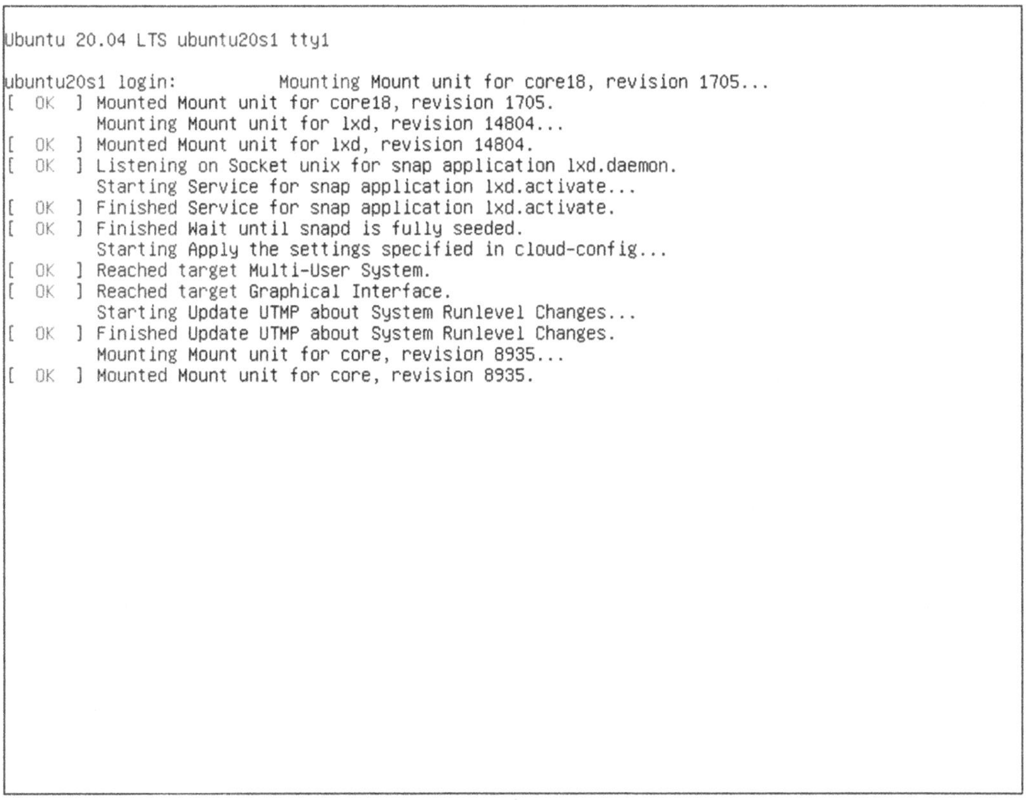
Ubuntu 20.04 LTS ubuntu20s1 tty1
ubuntu20s1 login: Mounting Mount unit for core18, revision 1705...
[OK] Mounted Mount unit for core18, revision 1705.
Mounting Mount unit for lxd, revision 14804...
[OK] Mounted Mount unit for lxd, revision 14804.
[OK] Listening on Socket unix for snap application lxd.daemon.
Starting Service for snap application lxd.activate...
[OK] Finished Service for snap application lxd.activate.
[OK] Finished Wait until snapd is fully seeded.
Starting Apply the settings specified in cloud-config...
[OK] Reached target Multi-User System.
[OK] Reached target Graphical Interface.
Starting Update UTMP about System Runlevel Changes...
[OK] Finished Update UTMP about System Runlevel Changes.
Mounting Mount unit for core, revision 8935...
[OK] Mounted Mount unit for core, revision 8935.

Figure 5-26. *Ubuntu operation rebooted, initial screen*

(*continued*)

#	Task
25	Now use your user ID and password to log into your Ubuntu VM. Now your server is ready to serve you, but how well you will use this server in your study is entirely up to you. See Figure 5-27.

```
ubuntu20s1 login: pynetauto
Password:
Welcome to Ubuntu 20.04 LTS (GNU/Linux 5.4.0-26-generic x86_64)

 * Documentation:  https://help.ubuntu.com
 * Management:     https://landscape.canonical.com
 * Support:        https://ubuntu.com/advantage

  System information as of Fri Apr 24 13:53:13 UTC 2020

  System load:  0.06              Processes:             191
  Usage of /:   14.4% of 29.40GB  Users logged in:       0
  Memory usage: 17%               IPv4 address for ens33: 192.168.183.129
  Swap usage:   0%

0 updates can be installed immediately.
0 of these updates are security updates.



The programs included with the Ubuntu system are free software;
the exact distribution terms for each program are described in the
individual files in /usr/share/doc/*/copyright.

Ubuntu comes with ABSOLUTELY NO WARRANTY, to the extent permitted by
applicable law.

[  OK  ] Created slice User Slice of UID 1000.
         Starting User Runtime Directory /run/user/1000...
[  OK  ] Finished User Runtime Directory /run/user/1000.
         Starting User Manager for UID 1000...
[  OK  ] Started User Manager for UID 1000.
[  OK  ] Started Session 1 of user pynetauto.
To run a command as administrator (user "root"), use "sudo <command>".
See "man sudo_root" for details.

pynetauto@ubuntu20s1:~$
```

Figure 5-27. *Ubuntu installation, first login screen*

Logging In to a New Ubuntu Server 20 via SSH

As you will soon discover, accessing the new VM via VMware Workstation's console screen is cumbersome. An easier way to manage our server is to connect to this server via an SSH connection, using an SSH client software from our Windows host PC. This is like how system administrators manage their systems on their network. Suppose you have already memorized the server's allocated IP address during the Ubuntu server installation process in the "Network connections" section. In that case, you have a sharp mind, but if you have forgotten the assigned IP address, let's find the IP address so we can SSH into the server.

01a The first and most straightforward way to find the IP address on an Ubuntu is to issue an IP address or `IP adds` command. A NATted IP address from the VM NAT network should be assigned to your ens33 network adapter. The server in this example received the 192.168.183.129/24 IP address. Your server's allocated IP address does not have to match, but if you have a valid IP address, that is a good indicator that your VM's network is working correctly. If you received an IP address from a different subnet or have not received a valid IP address, then you must go back and review your VM network editor or VM network settings. See Figure 5-28.

```
pynetauto@ubuntu20s1:~$ ip add
1: lo: <LOOPBACK,UP,LOWER_UP> mtu 65536 qdisc noqueue state UNKNOWN group default qlen 1000
    link/loopback 00:00:00:00:00:00 brd 00:00:00:00:00:00
    inet 127.0.0.1/8 scope host lo
       valid_lft forever preferred_lft forever
    inet6 ::1/128 scope host
       valid_lft forever preferred_lft forever
2: ens33: <BROADCAST,MULTICAST,UP,LOWER_UP> mtu 1500 qdisc fq_codel state UP group default qlen 1000
    link/ether 00:0c:29:f3:87:7c brd ff:ff:ff:ff:ff:ff
    inet 192.168.183.129/24 brd 192.168.183.255 scope global dynamic ens33
       valid_lft 1134sec preferred_lft 1134sec
    inet6 fe80::20c:29ff:fef3:877c/64 scope link
       valid_lft forever preferred_lft forever
```

Figure 5-28. *Ubuntu operation, finding the server IP address using ip add*

01b The second and more traditional way to find the IP address on any Linux server is to issue the `ifconfig` command. If you are only starting to transition to Linux OS from Windows OS, you will immediately notice that this command is like an `ipconfig` command at the Windows command prompt. On Ubuntu Server 20.04, we need to install `net-tools` first to enable this command. Run the `sudo apt install net-tools` command to install `net-tools`; this is also an excellent test for your Internet connectivity from the virtual Ubuntu server. See Figure 5-29.

```
pynetauto@ubuntu20s1:~$ ifconfig

Command 'ifconfig' not found, but can be installed with:

sudo apt install net-tools

pynetauto@ubuntu20s1:~$ sudo apt install net-tools
[sudo] password for pynetauto: _
```

Figure 5-29. *Ubuntu operation, net-tools installation to enable the ifconfig command*

Once the installation has been completed, issue the `ifconfig` command to check the IP address. Because we installed the Docker service during the Ubuntu installation, the tool even picked up the docker0 interface and is displaying it in Figure 5-30. But here, we are only interested in the information from the ens33 network adapter, and as expected, an IP address of 192.168.183.129/24 is given to the ens33 adapter with a broadcast address of 192.168.183.255.

```
pynetauto@ubuntu20s1:~$ ifconfig
docker0: flags=4099<UP,BROADCAST,MULTICAST>  mtu 1500
        inet 172.17.0.1  netmask 255.255.0.0  broadcast 172.17.255.255
        ether 02:42:be:ac:2f:e3  txqueuelen 0  (Ethernet)
        RX packets 0  bytes 0 (0.0 B)
        RX errors 0  dropped 0  overruns 0  frame 0
        TX packets 0  bytes 0 (0.0 B)
        TX errors 0  dropped 0 overruns 0  carrier 0  collisions 0

ens33: flags=4163<UP,BROADCAST,RUNNING,MULTICAST>  mtu 1500
        inet 192.168.183.129  netmask 255.255.255.0  broadcast 192.168.183.255
        inet6 fe80::20c:29ff:fef3:877c  prefixlen 64  scopeid 0x20<link>
        ether 00:0c:29:f3:87:7c  txqueuelen 1000  (Ethernet)
        RX packets 86901  bytes 131309226 (131.3 MB)
        RX errors 0  dropped 0  overruns 0  frame 0
        TX packets 27333  bytes 1657185 (1.6 MB)
        TX errors 0  dropped 0 overruns 0  carrier 0  collisions 0

lo: flags=73<UP,LOOPBACK,RUNNING>  mtu 65536
        inet 127.0.0.1  netmask 255.0.0.0
        inet6 ::1  prefixlen 128  scopeid 0x10<host>
        loop  txqueuelen 1000  (Local Loopback)
        RX packets 106  bytes 8382 (8.3 KB)
        RX errors 0  dropped 0  overruns 0  frame 0
        TX packets 106  bytes 8382 (8.3 KB)
        TX errors 0  dropped 0 overruns 0  carrier 0  collisions 0
```

Figure 5-30. *Ubuntu operation, finding the server IP address using ifconfig*

02 Stop here for one moment and think! The gateway IP for the 192.168.183.0/24 subnet is 192.168.183.2, not 192.168.183.1. 192.168.183.2 is the NAT gateway IP, and 192.168.183.1 is the assigned IP address of the Windows 10 host's VMnet8 (VMware Network Adapter VMnet8) interface. See Figure 5-31.

You can confirm this information from the Ubuntu server console by running `ip route | grep ^default` (or `ip r | grep ^def`). The meaning of this command is to look at the IP route with a general regular expression (`grep`) and find a string that begins with ^ and the word `default`. See Figure 5-32.

```
pynetauto@ubuntu20s1:~$ ip route | grep ^default
default via 192.168.183.2 dev ens33 proto dhcp src 192.168.183.129 metric 100
```

Figure 5-31. *Ubuntu operation, confirming default gateway on Linux*

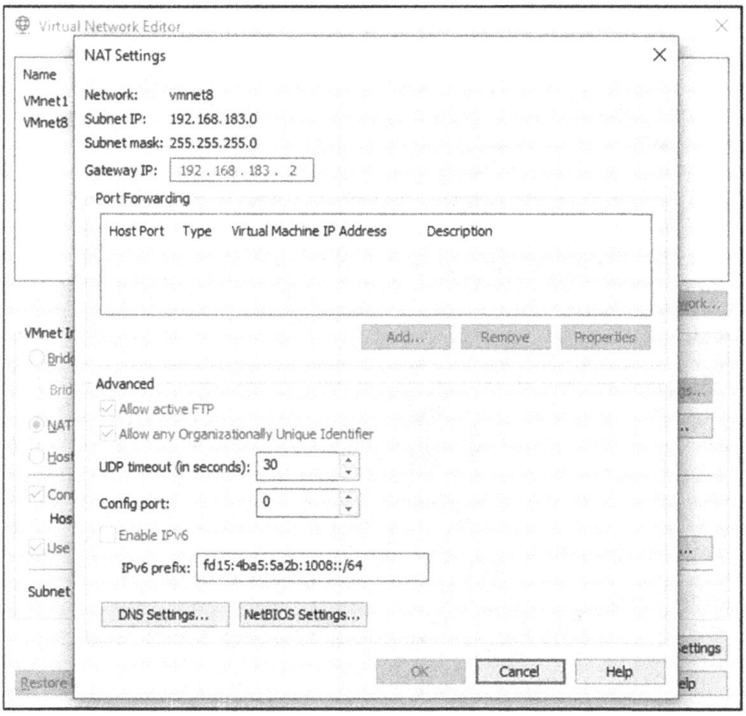

Figure 5-32. *Ubuntu operation, confirming default gateway on VMware Workstation*

Run the `netsh interface ip show addresses "VMware Network Adapter VMnet8"` command from your Windows 10 host PC. See Figure 5-33.

```
C:\Users\brendan>netsh interface ip show addresses "VMware Network Adapter VMnet8"

Configuration for interface "VMware Network Adapter VMnet8"
    DHCP enabled:                         Yes
    IP Address:                           192.168.183.1
    Subnet Prefix:                        192.168.183.0/24 (mask 255.255.255.0)
    InterfaceMetric:                      35
```

Figure 5-33. *Ubuntu operation, VMnet8 host IP address*

03 Now, if you have not yet downloaded PuTTY from the Internet, go to PuTTY's home page (`https://www.putty.org/`) and download a copy of PuTTY. Launch PuTTY from your Windows 10 host and then type in Ubuntu Server's IP address with port 22 for the SSH connection. Click the Open button at the bottom-right corner of the PuTTY Configuration window. See Figure 5-34.

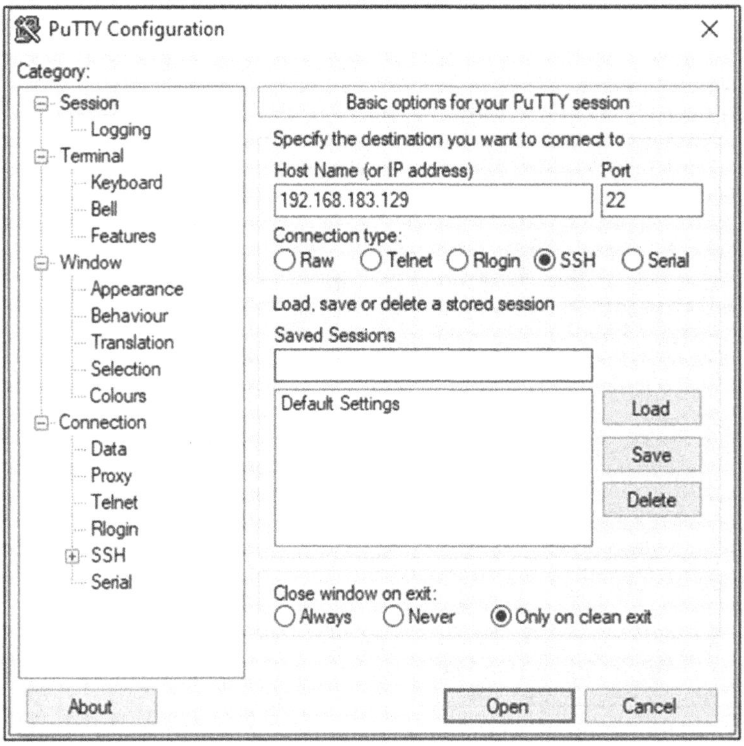

Figure 5-34. *Ubuntu operation, SSH client login from PuTTY*

04 The server will send the server's rsa2 key fingerprint to your PuTTY (SSH) session. Click Yes to proceed to the server's login screen. See Figure 5-35.

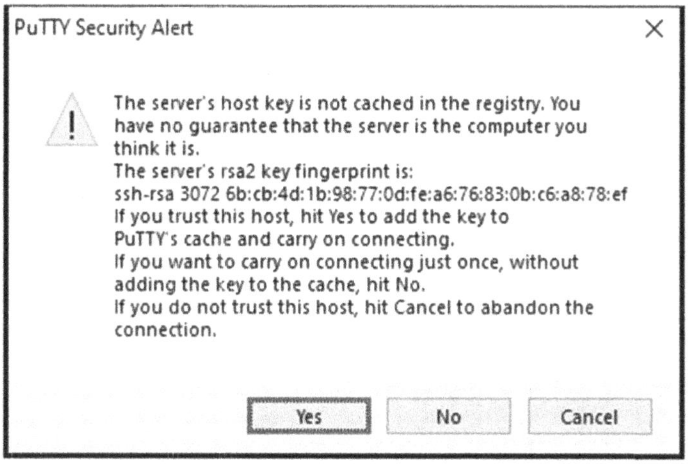

Figure 5-35. *Ubuntu operation, accepting the PuTTY security alert from the server*

05 Enter your username and password and hit the Enter key on your keyboard to log into your Ubuntu server. Now you are connected to your server via SSH. See Figure 5-36.

Figure 5-36. *Ubuntu operation, SSH server login*

06 Customize the PuTTY configuration to suit your preferences. In Figure 5-37, I have changed the font and background color of my PuTTY console session and then saved the settings.

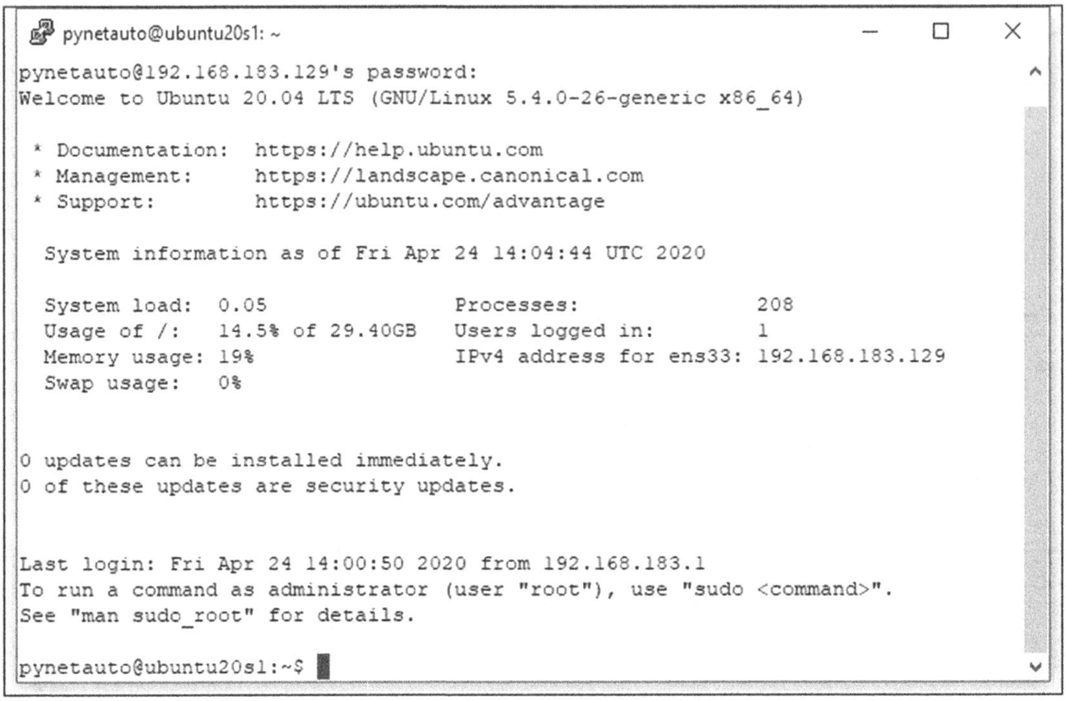
pynetauto@ubuntu20s1: ~
pynetauto@192.168.183.129's password:
Welcome to Ubuntu 20.04 LTS (GNU/Linux 5.4.0-26-generic x86_64)
* Documentation: https://help.ubuntu.com
* Management: https://landscape.canonical.com
* Support: https://ubuntu.com/advantage
System information as of Fri Apr 24 14:04:44 UTC 2020
System load: 0.05 Processes: 208
Usage of /: 14.5% of 29.40GB Users logged in: 1
Memory usage: 19% IPv4 address for ens33: 192.168.183.129
Swap usage: 0%
0 updates can be installed immediately.
0 of these updates are security updates.
Last login: Fri Apr 24 14:00:50 2020 from 192.168.183.1
To run a command as administrator (user "root"), use "sudo <command>".
See "man sudo_root" for details.
pynetauto@ubuntu20s1:~$

Figure 5-37. *Ubuntu operation, PuTTY background and font color change*

Customize Ubuntu Server

After creating your Ubuntu Server 20 LTS virtual machine, it works out of the box; however, Ubuntu has a few critical settings disabled by default. We want to get full access to these settings for our testing lab purposes to add more flexibility. We can tweak a few things to make this server more user-friendly to add more value to your learning. If you are running an Ubuntu server in production, do not enable these settings as they are not the best practice. Since this is our lab VM, we are going to perform some system customizations. First, enable `root user ssh login` from remote clients; this allows you to connect to this server via SSH as the root user, saving time during system administration. Second, install a desktop GUI; this will allow you to log into the desktop settings and then use it as a standard end-user machine and use the available applications via the Linux GUI. Third, enable root user GUI access. This feature is disabled by default too, but root user GUI access to the server may be required for quick troubleshooting.

Ubuntu VM Customization 1: Enable Root User SSH Login on Ubuntu Server 20.04

In general, most recent Ubuntu servers do not allow root users to log into the terminal console or log in via SSH for security reasons. Still, this security feature can often slow you down during your lab scenarios, demanding you to enter sudo in front of every command you type in and deny you permission to work with flexibility in your lab. For this reason, we can allow SSH logins to add a little flexibility to your lab. However, it is best practice to leave the root console and SSH login disabled for security purposes in the real production environment. First, to enable direct root user SSH access, log into your server as yourself, and run the command `sudo passwd`. Type in your password, and you are immediately prompted to enter a new UNIX password. Entering the password twice here will enable the root user password. Asterisks are used for illustration purposes, but the password will be hidden while you are typing it.

#	Task

01	Enable the root user password by performing the following tasks:
	`pynetauto@ubuntu20s1:~$ sudo passwd`
	`sudo password for pynetauto: **********`
	`Enter new UNIX password:********`
	`Retype new UNIX password:********`
	`passwd: password updated successfully`

02	The previous action does not automatically allow SSH login to the server; this needs to be manually enabled by updating the SSH server configuration file. To enable root user SSH login, take the next steps: `pynetauto@ubuntu20s1:~$ sudo nano /etc/ssh/sshd_config`

■ **Note** If you have logged in as a root user at this stage, you do not have to add `sudo` in front of your command.

If you have been using the older Ubuntu version, first you may have to install the nano text editor or use vi as your text editor.

#	Task
03	The line starting with `#PermitRootLogin prohibit-password` prevents root user SSH login, and we have to uncomment this line to allow root user SSH login. For simplicity and best practices, leave the default line unchanged and add a new line as you may have to restore the configuration to the original setting. Add the following line after the original line and save the file: `PermitRootLogin yes` See Figure 5-38.

(continued)

**Task**

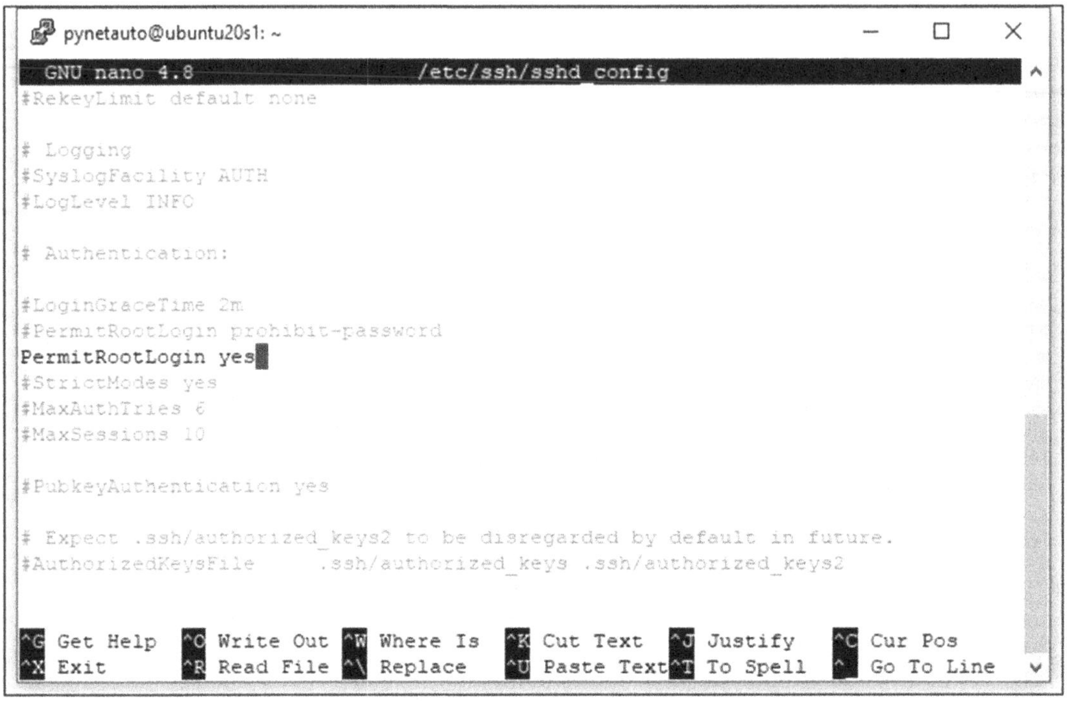

Figure 5-38. *Ubuntu VM customization 1, changing sshd_config*

04 To make the previous change take effect, you must restart the SSH server service.

```
pynetauto@ubuntu20s1:~$ sudo service ssh restart
```

05 Now from your Windows 10 host PC, launch PuTTY, enter the IP address of your server, and SSH in with port 22. Once you successfully logged into your server via an SSH session, you will see a screen similar to Figure 5-39.

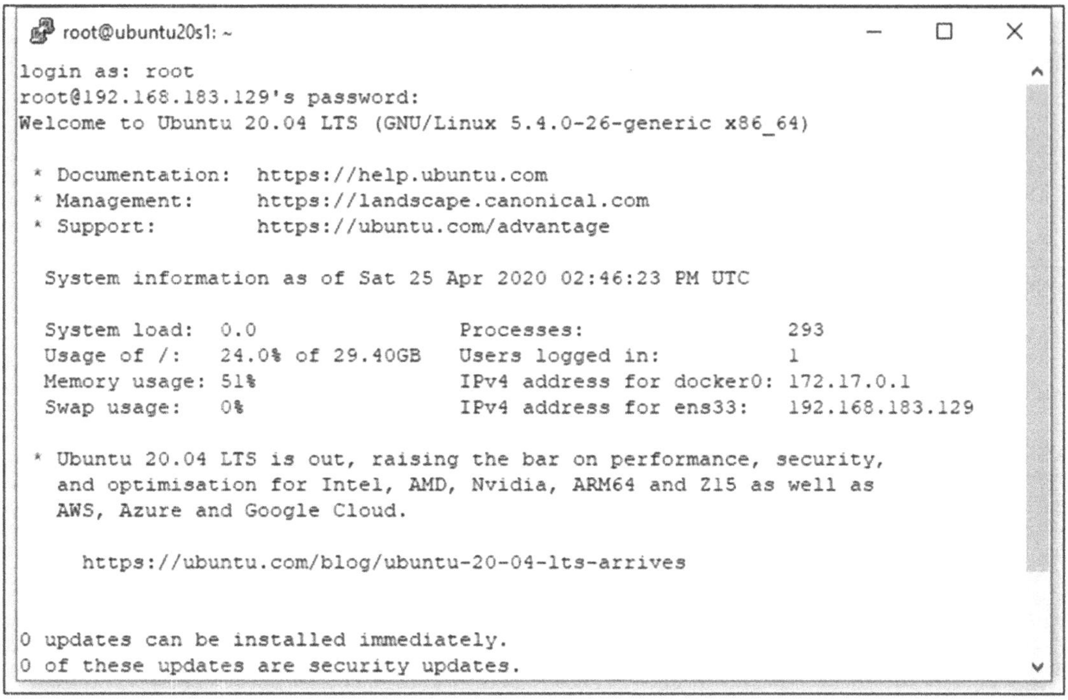
root@ubuntu20s1: ~
login as: root
root@192.168.183.129's password:
Welcome to Ubuntu 20.04 LTS (GNU/Linux 5.4.0-26-generic x86_64)
* Documentation: https://help.ubuntu.com
* Management: https://landscape.canonical.com
* Support: https://ubuntu.com/advantage
System information as of Sat 25 Apr 2020 02:46:23 PM UTC
System load: 0.0 Processes: 293
Usage of /: 24.0% of 29.40GB Users logged in: 1
Memory usage: 51% IPv4 address for docker0: 172.17.0.1
Swap usage: 0% IPv4 address for ens33: 192.168.183.129
* Ubuntu 20.04 LTS is out, raising the bar on performance, security, and optimisation for Intel, AMD, Nvidia, ARM64 and Z15 as well as AWS, Azure and Google Cloud.
https://ubuntu.com/blog/ubuntu-20-04-lts-arrives
0 updates can be installed immediately.
0 of these updates are security updates.

Figure 5-39. *Ubuntu VM customization 1, root user SSH login*

You can use a single-line command to grant the SSH access to the root user. Simply run the command from your terminal session.

```
sudo sed -i 's/#PermitRootLogin prohibit-password/PermitRootLogin yes/' /etc/ssh/sshd_config
[sudo] password for pynetauto: ********
```

Ubuntu VM Customization 2: Install a Desktop GUI and Other Packages

Optionally, you can install a desktop GUI to run on an Ubuntu Server. In a testing lab, GUI can provide the extra features required while testing various IT networking scenarios, for example testing an HTTPS connection via a web browser. In a typical production environment, Linux is usually installed as a headless server without a GUI for increased server performance and security; a GUI for Linux server is not a prerequisite in the production environment. Anyway, you should know how to install a GUI on Ubuntu Server, so let's learn how to install a desktop GUI and other software packages from the initial Ubuntu Server 20 terminal console.

#	Task

01 First, we have to install `tasksel` on the newly installed Ubuntu Server 20.04. Run the following command from the VMware Workstation Console or SSH session:

```
sudo apt install tasksel
```

See Figure 5-40.

```
pynetauto@ubuntu20s1:~$ tasksel

Command 'tasksel' not found, but can be installed with:

sudo apt install tasksel

pynetauto@ubuntu20s1:~$ sudo apt install tasksel
Reading package lists... Done
Building dependency tree
Reading state information... Done
The following additional packages will be installed:
  laptop-detect tasksel-data
The following NEW packages will be installed:
  laptop-detect tasksel tasksel-data
0 upgraded, 3 newly installed, 0 to remove and 2 not upgraded.
Need to get 40.0 kB of archives.
After this operation, 309 kB of additional disk space will be used.
Do you want to continue? [Y/n] _
```

Figure 5-40. *Ubuntu VM customization 2, installing tasksel*

02 After the `tasksel` installation finishes, you can run `tasksel` by issuing the `sudo tasksel` command. This will launch the Ubuntu package configuration application to select and install other useful applications; Ubuntu desktop is one option under this package manager.

Select "Ubuntu desktop" and move to OK to start the desktop installation. See Figure 5-41.

#	Task

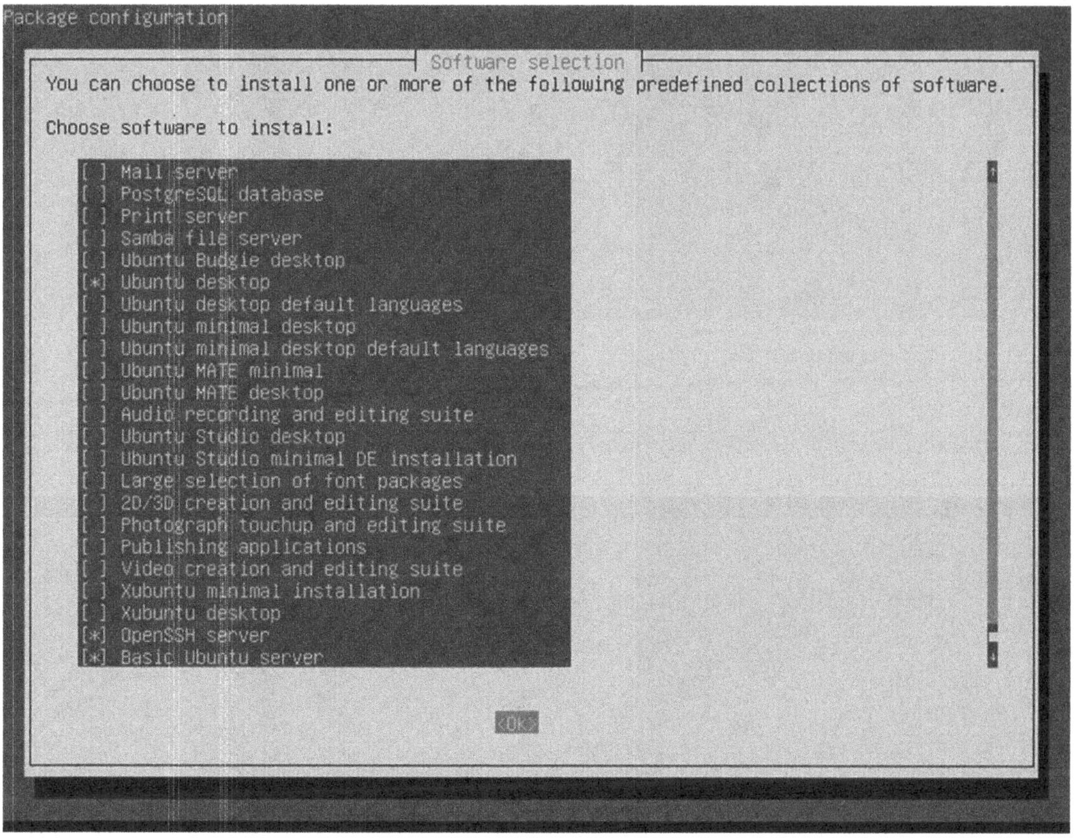

Figure 5-41. *Ubuntu VM customization 2, selecting "Ubuntu desktop" (GUI)*

03 Wait until the desktop installation is 100 percent complete, and then issue the `sudo reboot` command to restart your server. See Figure 5-42.

(*continued*)

#	Task

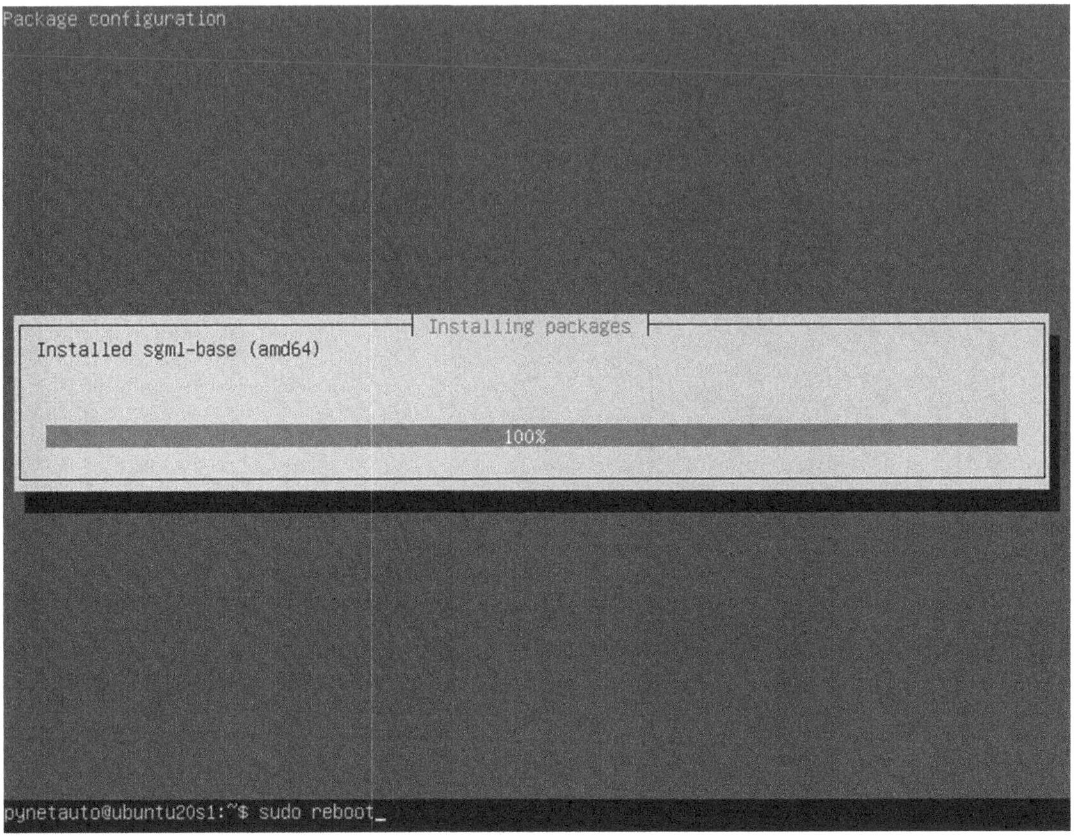

Figure 5-42. *Ubuntu VM customization 2, Ubuntu desktop installation*

04	After the reboot, you will be prompted with the Ubuntu GUI login interface. Enter your login credentials and log into your server. See Figure 5-43.

#	Task
	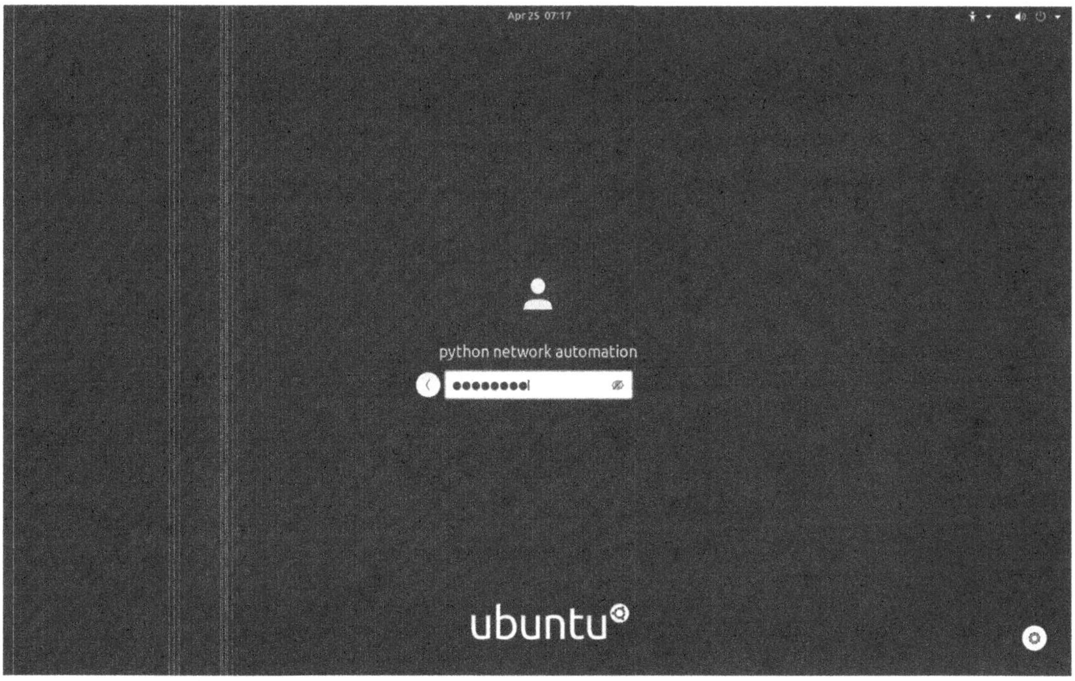 *Figure 5-43. Ubuntu VM customization 2, Ubuntu desktop login*
05	You have successfully installed Ubuntu desktop on an Ubuntu Server. See Figure 5-44.

#	Task

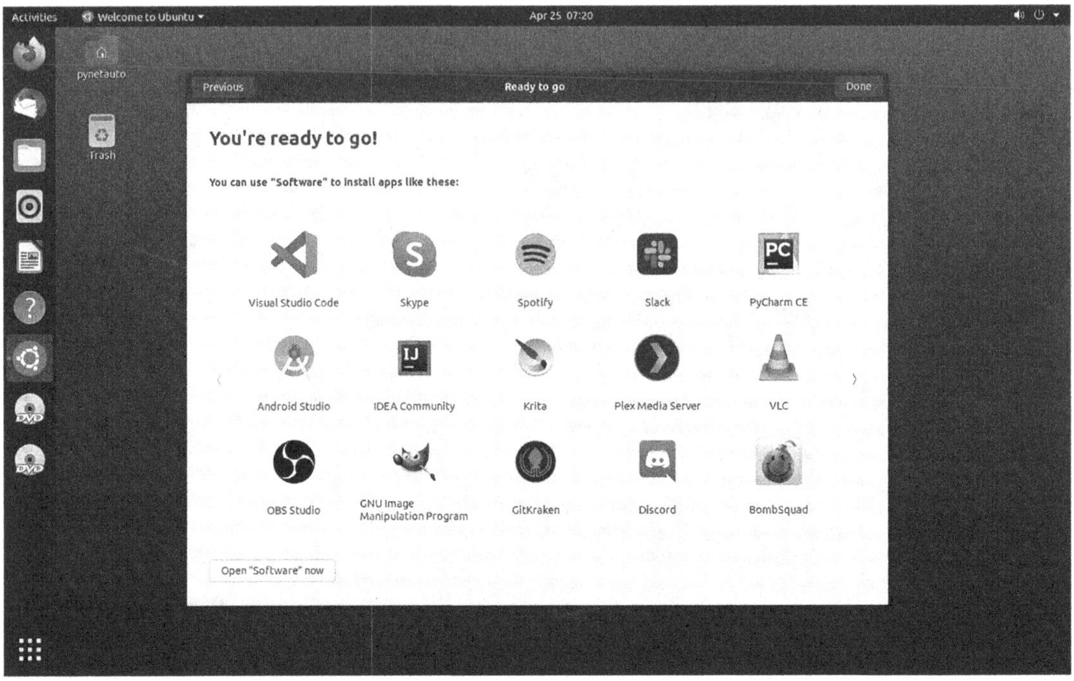

Figure 5-44. *Ubuntu VM customization 2, Ubuntu desktop GUI*

Ubuntu VM Customization 3: Enable Root User GUI Access

If you have sharp eyes, you probably noticed that root user GUI login does not work, and you are questioning, how can I enable root user GUI login? Since this is our lab server and we can explore and customize as much as we want, let's enable the root user GUI login. First, you have to be logged into the server as a normal user (yourself) to complete this task or, optionally, SSH into the server from PuTTY.

**Task**

01 Open and edit `/etc/gdm3/custom.conf`, which is the GDM configuration file, using the nano text editor to allow root login. Add `AllowRoot=true`, as shown in Figure 5-45, and save the file.

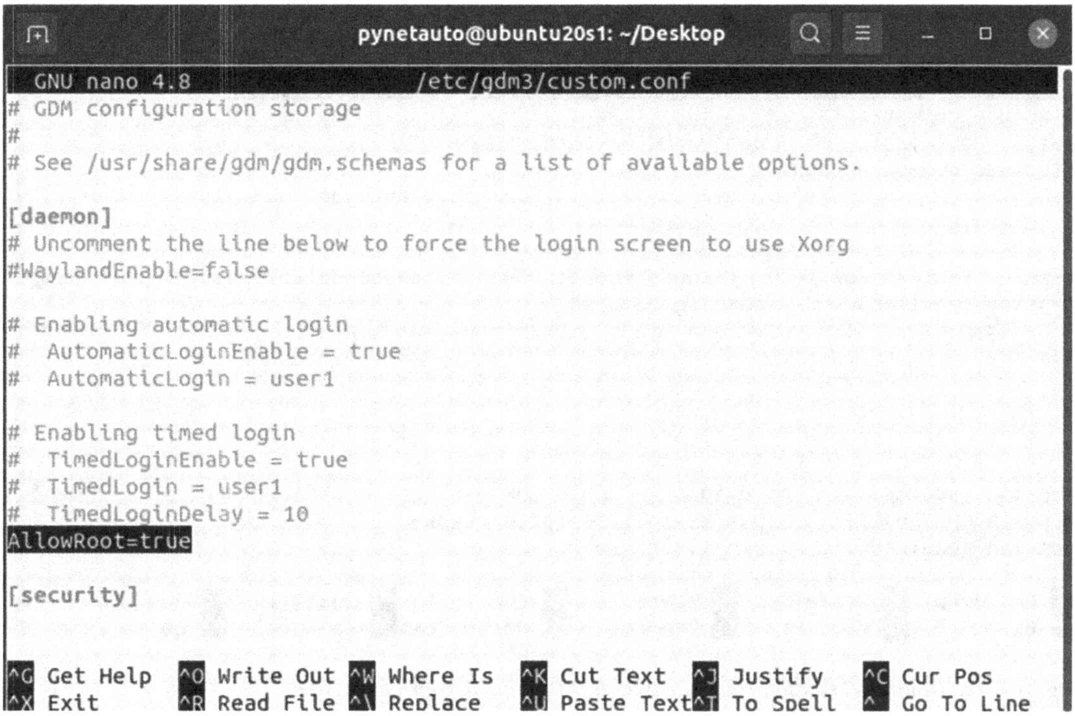

Figure 5-45. *Ubuntu VM customization 3, updating the gdm3/custom.conf file*

02 Next, edit the PAM authentication daemon configuration file at `/etc/pam.d/gdm-password` and comment on the specific line that denies root access to the graphical user interface. Use the nano or vi editor and open the `/etc/pam.d/gdm-password` file. Put # at the beginning of the line, which starts with `auth required  pam_succeed_if.so user!= root quiet_success`, that you are commenting out, which means you are disabling the feature. See Figure 5-46.

(*continued*)

#	Task

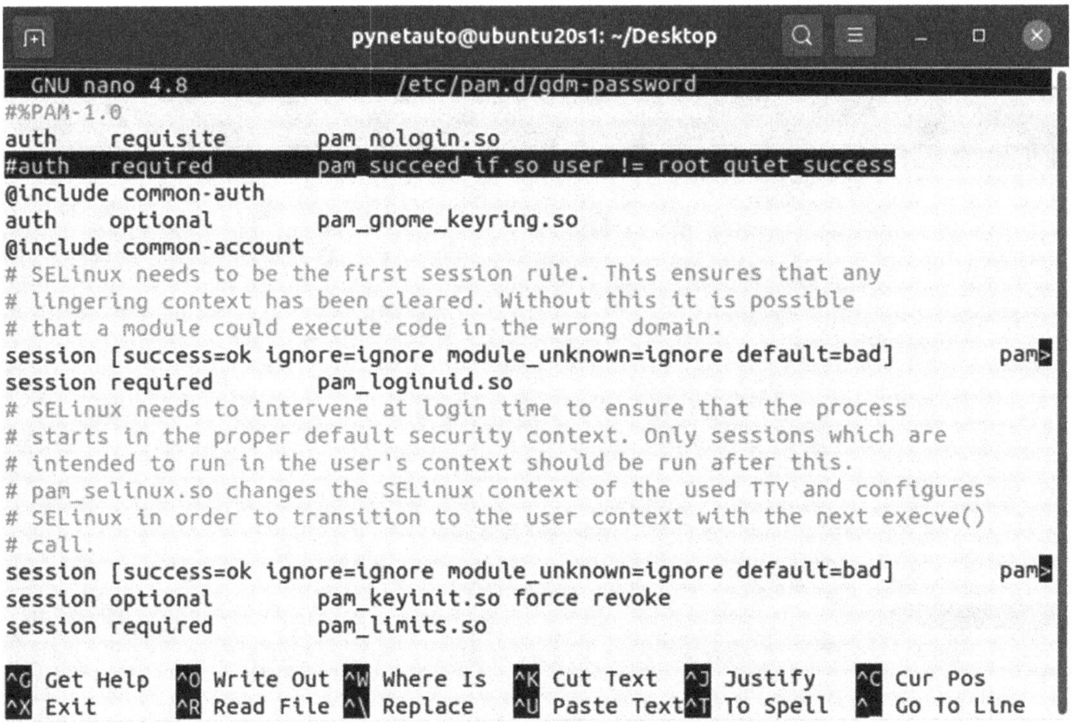

Figure 5-46. *Ubuntu VM customization 3, updating the pam.d/gdm-password file*

03 A mandatory reboot is required here once again. Reboot your Ubuntu server using the `sudo reboot` command or using the power button on the top-right corner of your Ubuntu desktop. Once the server has been restarted, log in as another user and enter **root** as the username and enter the root user's password. See Figure 5-47.

#	Task
	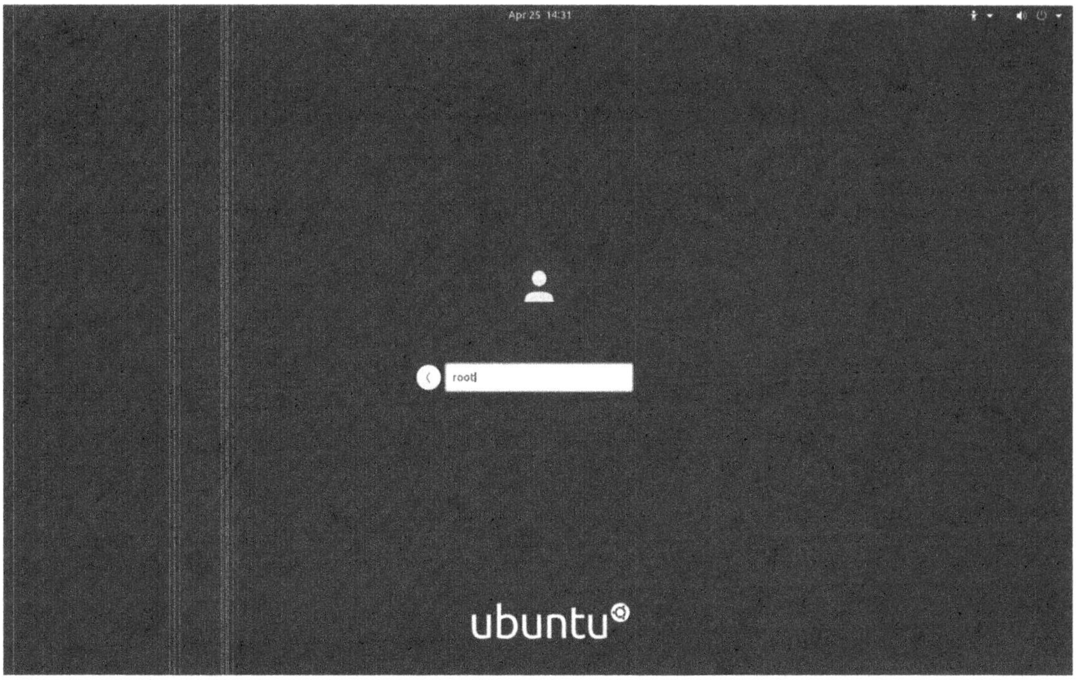 *Figure 5-47. Ubuntu VM customization 3, root user GUI login*
04	Congratulations! You can log into Ubuntu desktop as a root user. See Figure 5-48.

#	Task
	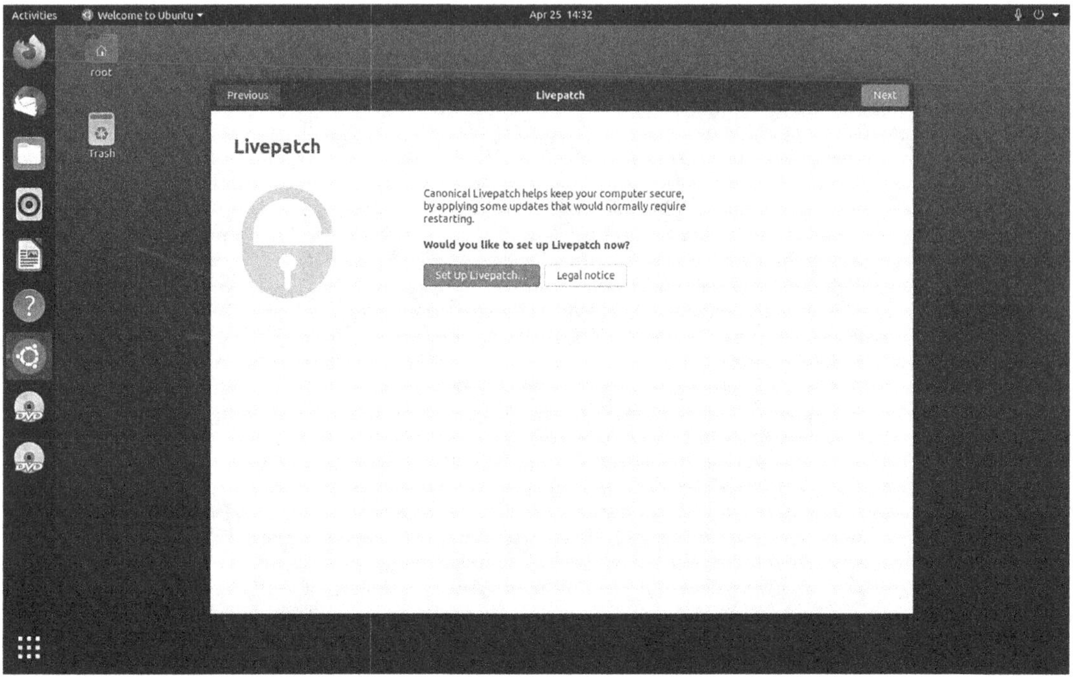 *Figure 5-48. Ubuntu VM customization 3, Ubuntu desktop root user login*

Taking a Snapshot of a Virtual Machine

One of the most powerful features of running an operating system as a VM is the power of snapshots. In a real production environment with ESXi and vCenter-based solutions, taking snapshots and cloning are potent ways to prevent system failure and recover from failures. In the VMware technology world, other system recovery features include high availability, vMotion, and DRS. But on the VMware Workstation Pro solution, we have snapshots and clones to preserve the current state of our VMs. A snapshot is like taking a photo of your system, so you can reverse unintended or failed system changes back to the prime system state of a VM. The cloning feature allows you to make a partial or full backup of your VMs to preserve the system state in the case of system failure.

For Python network automation labs, you can choose to use a snapshot or full cloning as a fail-safe recovery feature. Snapshots will allow us to move in time to various points during our lab. Follow the next tasks to make a snapshot of your Ubuntu server before installing other software on the server.

#	Task
01	To take a snapshot of your current server state, from your VMware Workstation menu, select VM ➤ Snapshot ➤ Take Snapshot. See Figure 5-49.

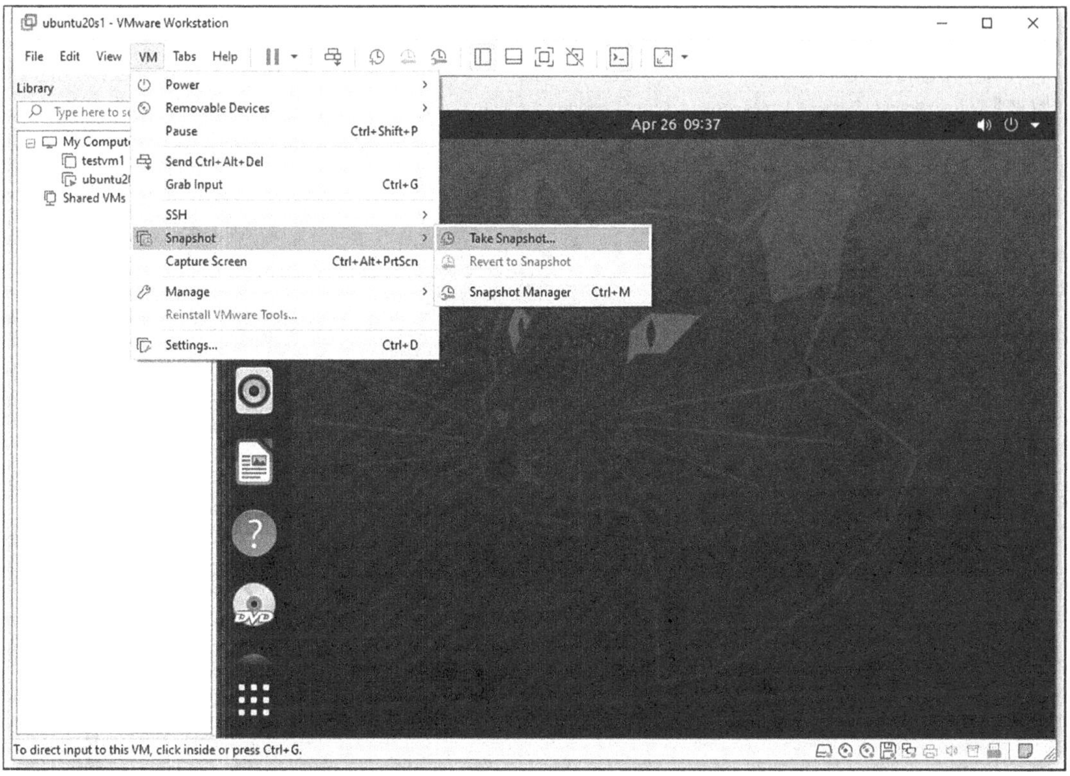

Figure 5-49. *VMware snapshot, navigating to the Snapshot menu*

#	Task
02	Enter the name and tasks performed as a description, and click the Take Snapshot button to create a snapshot, as shown in Figure 5-50.

(*continued*)

#	Task
	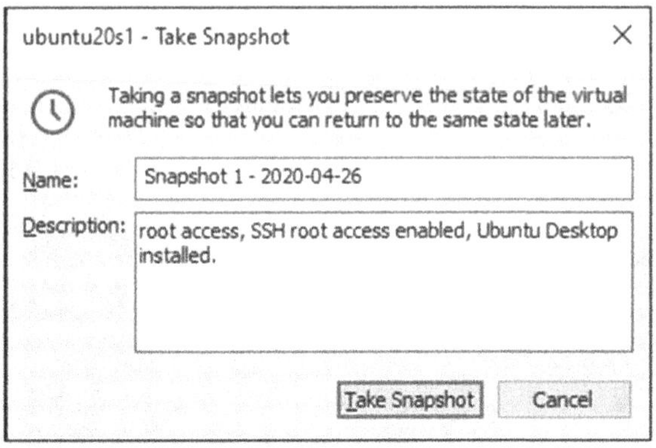

Figure 5-50. *VMware snapshot, creating a VM snapshot*

03 At the bottom-left corner of the window, the percentage of snapshot progress will be displayed. Once it reaches 100 percent, navigate to the Snapshot Manager from the menu, and confirm the snapshot. See Figure 5-51.

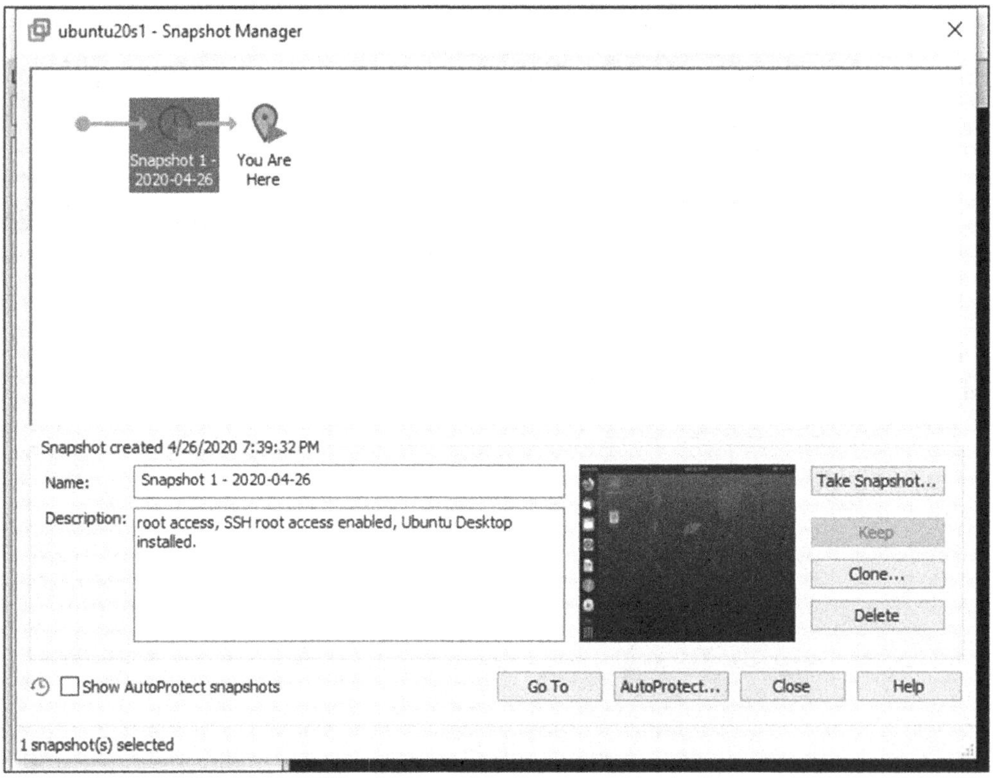

Figure 5-51. *VMware snapshot, confirming snapshot*

Cloning a Virtual Machine

Now you have a customized Ubuntu virtual server; if you want to make another VM, you can do so by cloning the same VM. Cloning allows you to re-create the same machine at the speed of lightning compared to how much time you spent installing a new VM from scratch. Cloning also can make a full backup of the current VM state and preserve the server state. Now let's take a look at this process.

#	Task
01	To clone a VM, navigate to VM ➤ Manage ➤ Clone. (See Figure 5-52) Alternatively, you can also start the cloning process within the Snapshot Manager.

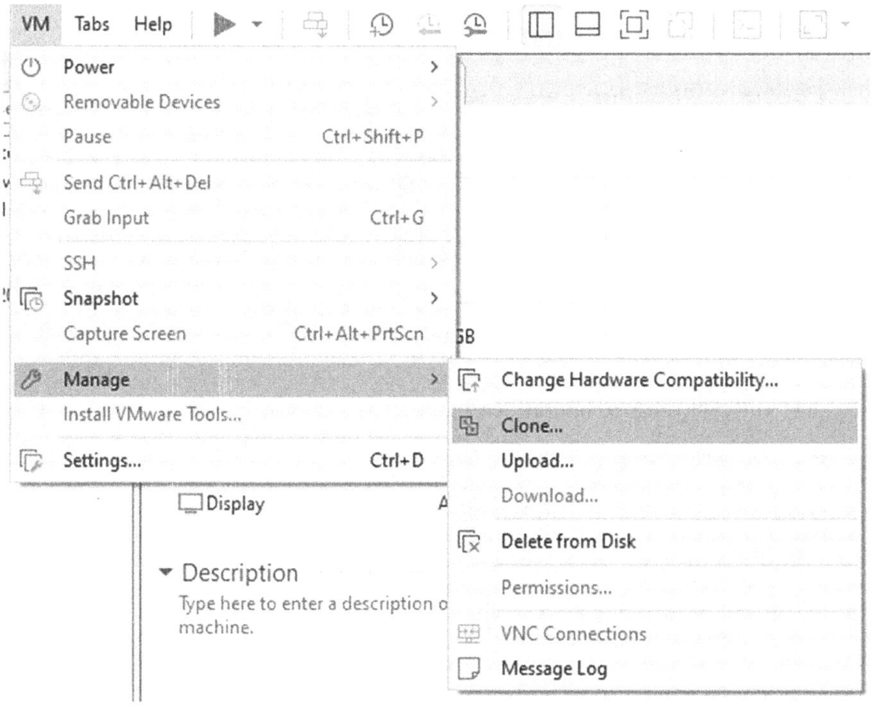

Figure 5-52. *VMware cloning 1, making a clone*

02	Leave the default settings and click the Next button. See Figure 5-53.

#	Task
	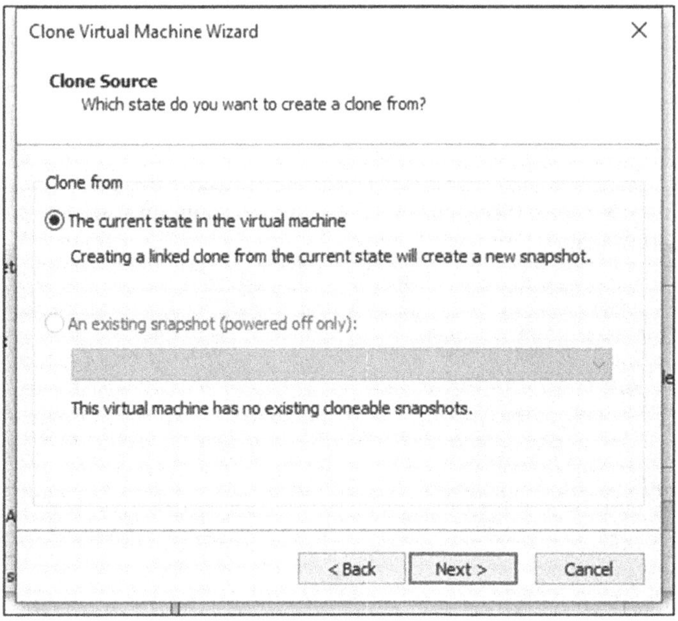 ***Figure 5-53.*** *VMware cloning 1, clone source*
03	Select "Create a full clone" and click the Next button. See Figure 5-54.
	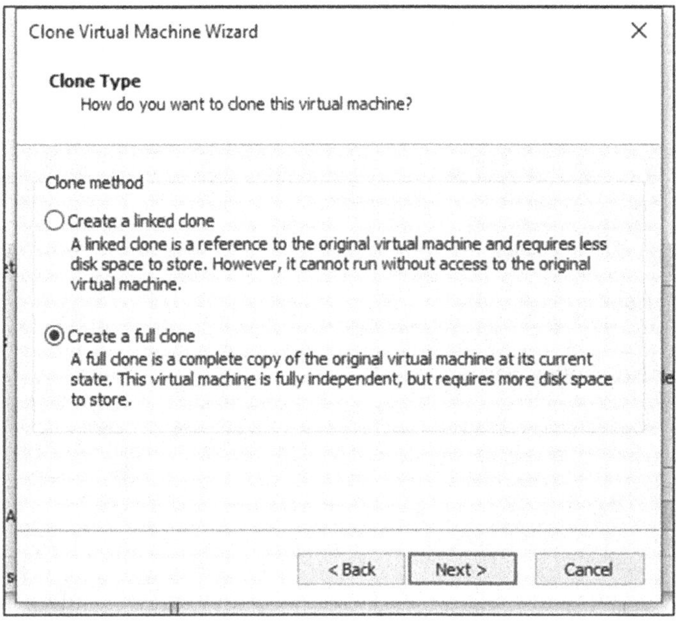 ***Figure 5-54.*** *VMware cloning 1, clone type, a full clone*

#	Task
04	Rename the cloned VM and click the Finish button. See Figure 5-55.

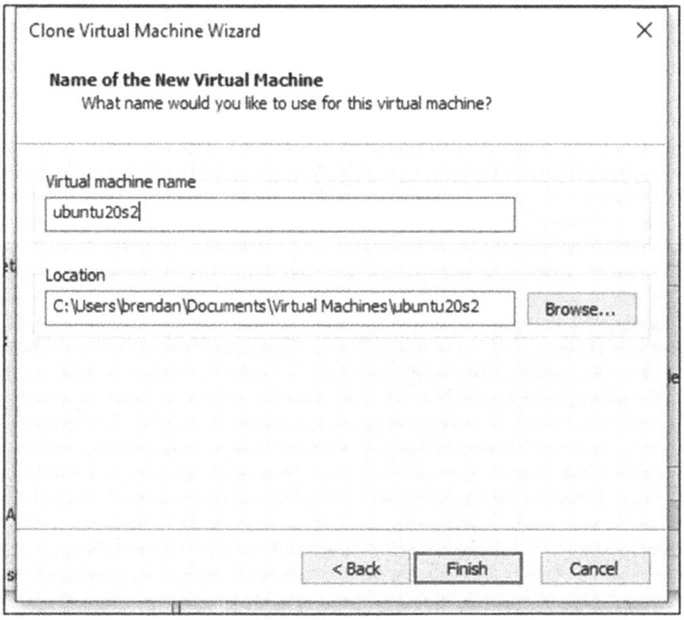

Figure 5-55. *VMware cloning 1, renaming the cloned VM*

#	Task
05	Now click the Close button. See Figure 5-56.

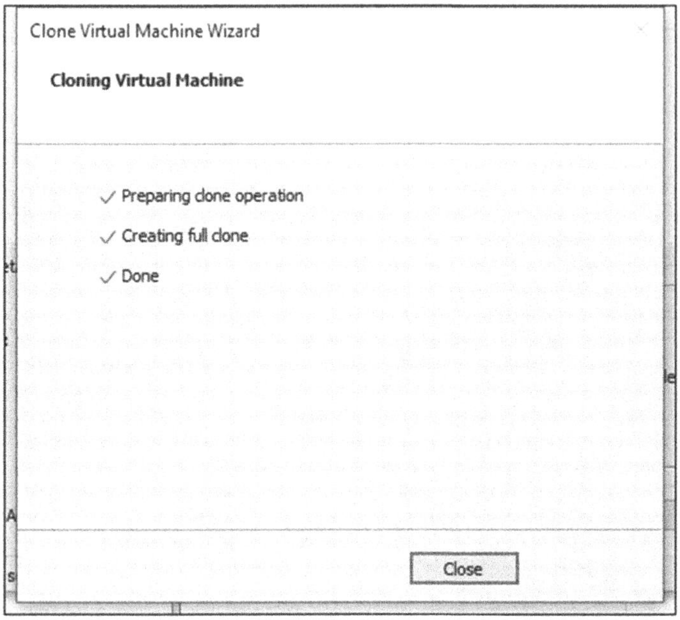

Figure 5-56. *VMware cloning 1, closing the VM cloning wizard*

#	Task
06	You will see another Ubuntu server added to your VM library. See Figure 5-57.

#	Task

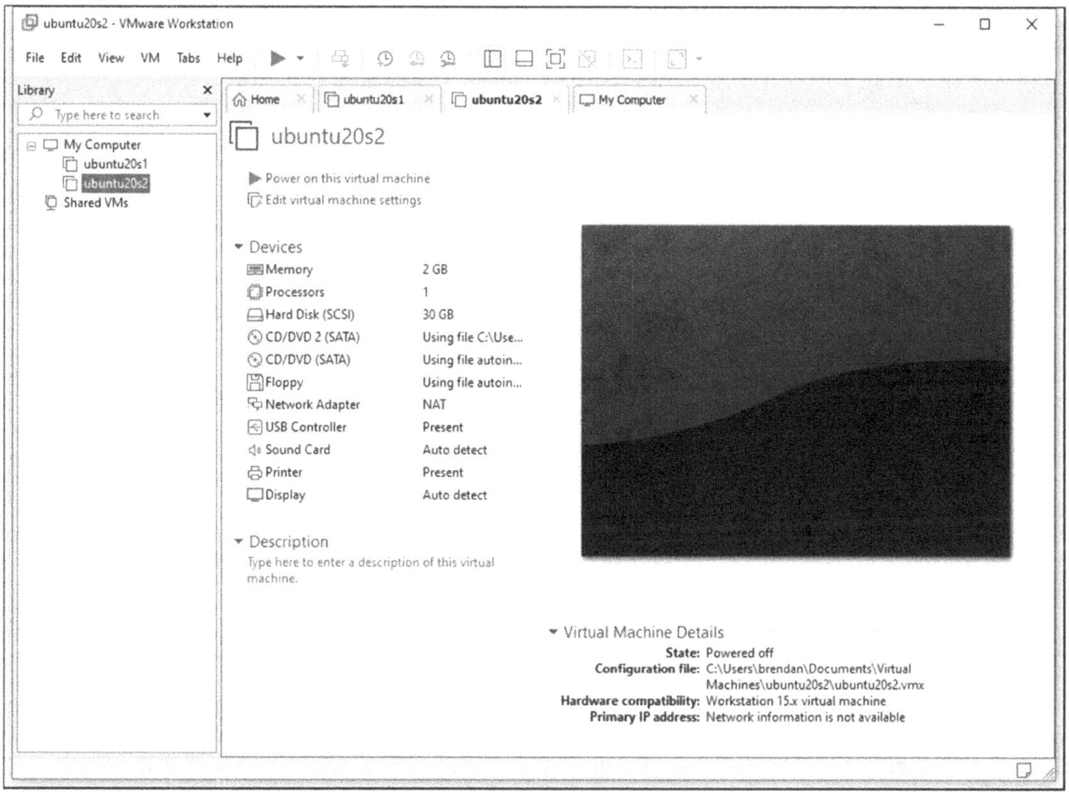

Figure 5-57. *VMware cloning 1, cloned VM added to the library*

07	Optionally, if you want to copy and duplicate your VM simply, simply copy the folder containing all the VM files to other storage. This method will take up a lot of hard disk space, so if you are using a smaller SSD, then a snapshot is a better option than fully cloning a VM. See Figure 5-58.

#	Task

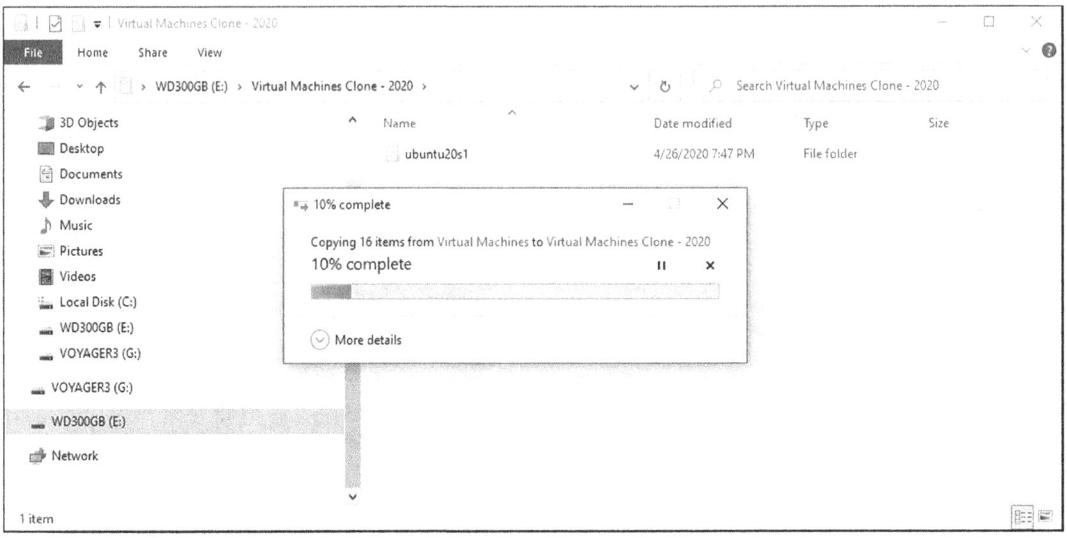

Figure 5-58. *VMware cloning 2, copying the VM folder to an external drive*

Summary

Installing an Ubuntu Server as a virtual machine is a straightforward process, but installing a graphical user interface is an option. Now you have successfully installed, customized, backed up, and cloned a newly created Ubuntu server VM, and it is time to create another Linux server as our second server. In the next chapter, you will follow similar steps to create a virtual machine for CentOS 8.1, which will serve as an all-in-one IP services server for our network automation labs.

CHAPTER 6

Creating a CentOS 8 Server Virtual Machine

In this chapter, you will download a CentOS 8 bootable image to install and create a second virtual machine on your VMware Workstation. The CentOS 8 server is based on a community version of Red Hat Enterprise Linux 8 (RHEL8), one of the most popular enterprise Linux OSs among the Linux community users because of its stability and security. By the end of this chapter, you will be able to create a CentOS 8 Server VM from scratch and customize the network settings using the `nmtui` package to add flexibility to your network automation lab. In preparation, you will download the GNS3 `.ova` template file and import and create a GNS3 VM for Cisco IOS and IOSv image integrations later.

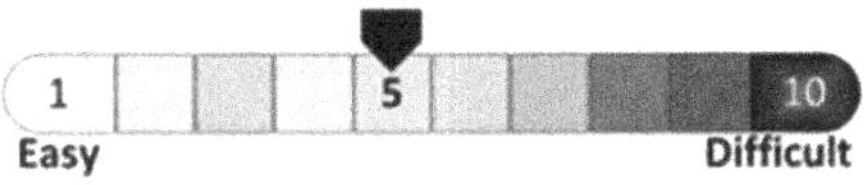

In the previous chapter, you created an Ubuntu server machine and learned how to customize its settings to make it more usable for our lab. This chapter is one of the shorter chapters in this book, and in it you will create another Linux virtual machine using a CentOS 8 bootable image. Although we could simply clone the existing Linux VM to create more virtual machines, this prevents us from learning the basic operations of other Linux distributions. Therefore, we will download and install a second and different Linux distribution. You will learn how to turn this server into a server with multiple IP services for lab testing purposes in Chapter 8. As in the previous process, you will search for and download the bootable image and then install the image and create a virtual machine. After creating the CentOS 8 virtual machine, you will test the server's connection via SSH and learn an easy way to manage the network adapter on a Linux server. To prepare for GNS3 integration, we will need to download the correct copy of GNS3 VM for VMware Workstation, so using the downloaded GNS3 VM `.ova` file, the GNS3 VM will be created ahead of time for smoother integration. Let's quickly create your second virtual machine.

Downloading and Installing a CentOS 8 Server Image

The actual process of downloading and installing a CentOS VM is identical to the Ubuntu 20.04 server installation. As in the Ubuntu 20.04 LTS VM installation, you must first download a bootable CentOS 8 installation image (`.iso`) file. First, check your Internet connection and follow the steps in this chapter to create and install your new CentOS 8 VM on VMware Workstation 15 Pro. At the time of writing this book, the latest CentOS version was 8.1.1804. By the time you read this book, newer versions will be available, but as long as you stick with the main 8.x (or 7.x) version, you will be able to follow along and successfully install

B. Choi, *Introduction to Python Network Automation*, https://doi.org/10.1007/978-1-4842-6806-3_6

your CentOS server illustrated in this book. If you opt to download and install another CentOS version, the installation steps will still be almost identical. In Chapter 8, you will be installing different software to turn this server into a multipurpose lab server, so you may have to follow the software installation procedures suggested for your version of CentOS system because one version of software compatible on this CentOS version may not be compatible on previous or newer software versions. This CentOS VM also can be used as a multipurpose lab server running several IP services for any future IT certification preparations.

As IBM has purchased Red Hat, there have been some changes for future developments and support for CentOS servers. The community support for CentOS 8 servers will cease on December 31, 2021, and only CentOS 8 Stream or a newer Stream versions of CentOS will be available to community users. CentOS Stream is positioned between Fedora (the beta version of Red Hat Enterprise Linux) and Red Hat Enterprise Linux, so we can say it is the early release version of Red Hat Enterprise Linux. If you use Stream in production, there will be issues getting support from Red Hat (IBM), as this removes Red Hat's obligation to support a bug or problems in no longer supported CentOS server versions. However, using a Stream version in a lab environment is still acceptable as most functions will meet our testing needs.

First, let's download the latest CentOS 8 installation ISO file from the official CentOS site.

Downloading the CentOS 8 Server Image

#	Task
01	From your favorite web browser, go to the CentOS's official site suggested and click the x86_64 link on the web page. Optionally, you can choose to download the CentOS Stream version. See Figure 6-1. URL: `https://www.centos.org/download/`

#	Task

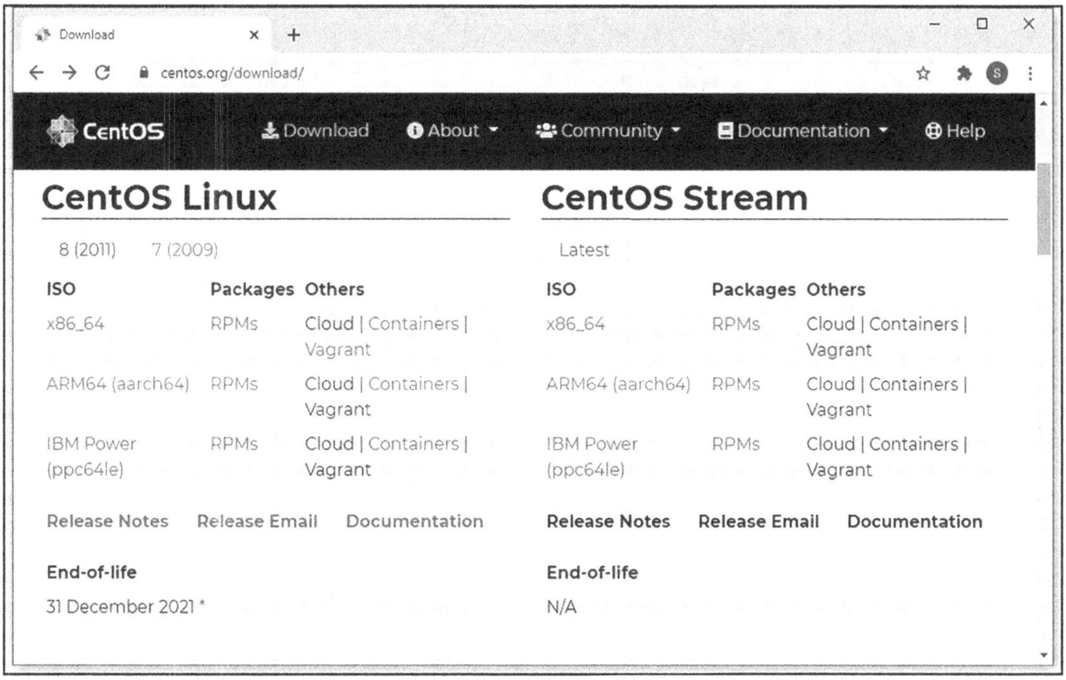

Figure 6-1. CentOS official download page

02	Next, locate the closest CentOS image download server to your location and download the latest CentOS 8 ISO from the FTP server. The estimated file size will vary depending on which file you download, but here you will download the file ending with `-x86-64-dvd1.iso`, which is more than 7GB in size. At the time of writing this book, the latest CentOS 8 file available was `CentOS-8.1.1911-x86_64-dvd1.iso`. See Figure 6-2. URL: `http://isoredirect.centos.org/centos/8/isos/x86_64/`

(continued)

#	Task

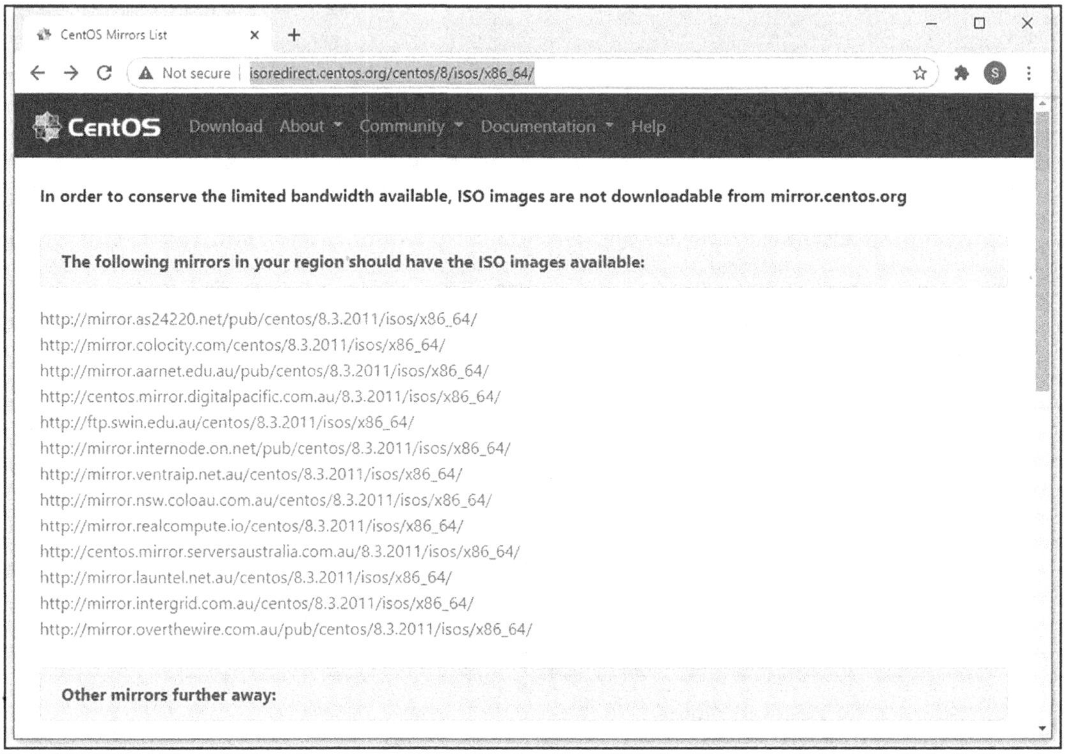

Figure 6-2. *CentOS 8, official download page mirror example*

After the software download completes and is saved to your Downloads folder, you are ready to create a CentOS VM from VMware Workstation 15 Pro.

Installing CentOS 8 Server

The CentOS 8 server VM installation process is like the Ubuntu server installation process, so let's quickly go through this process and create a new server VM.

#	Task
01	In your VMware Workstation menu, select File ➤ New Virtual Machine. See Figure 6-3.

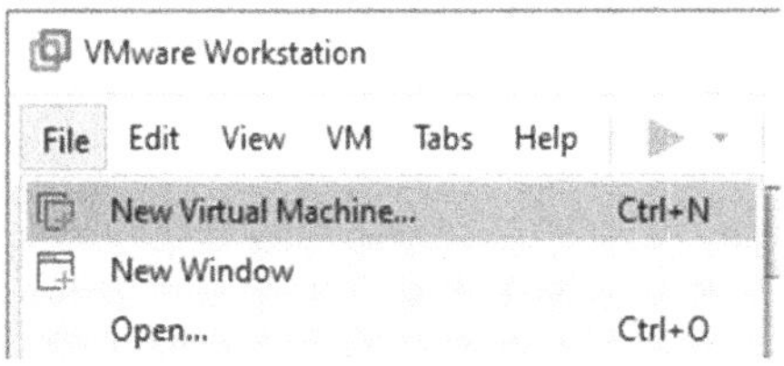

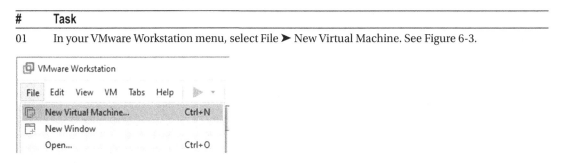

Figure 6-3. *CentOS 8 installation, creating a new VM*

#	Task
02	When the New Virtual Machine Wizard appears, click the "Typical (recommended)" option and click the Next button. See Figure 6-4.

Figure 6-4. *CentOS 8 installation, New Virtual Machine Wizard start page*

03	When you come back to the New Virtual Machine Wizard window shown in Figure 6-5, choose the "I will install the operating system later" option. If you choose the "Installer disc image file (iso)" option here, the CentOS 8 image will return `Pane is a dead error`, and you won't be able to install the operating system. See Figure 6-5.

■ **Note** Make sure you select "I will install the operating system later" here.

(continued)

#	Task

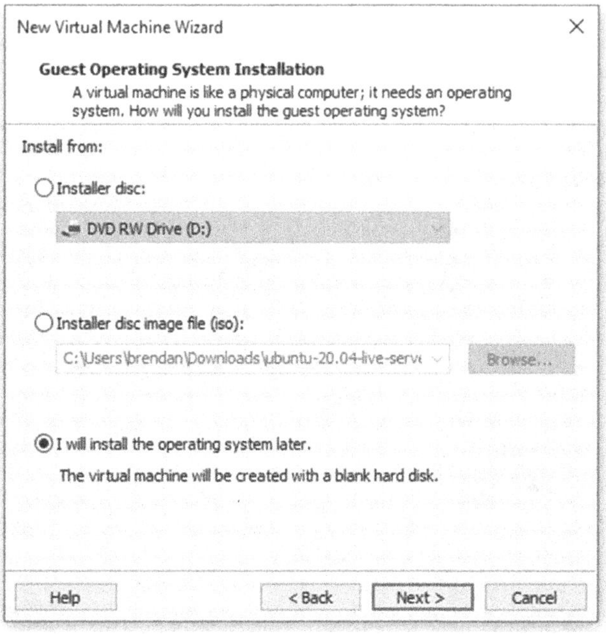

Figure 6-5. *CentOS 8 installation, selecting the "I will install the operating system later" option*

04	Depending on the version of VMware Workstation 15 you have installed on your host PC, the CentOS 8.x version may not be available. If you encounter this problem, you can always choose the Red Hat Enterprise Linux (REHL) 8 64-bit version of your choice as CentOS 8 is the same version as RHEL 8 without the logo and proprietary contract. See Figure 6-6.

■ **Note** Note that IBM acquired Red Hat in July 2019. CentOS has been the community version of the current production Red Hat Enterprise Linux; when RHEL runs into a bug, Red Hat provided a fix for CentOS within three days. This made CentOS dependable as the RHEL Linux, but the users could still use CentOS in production. By contrast, CentOS Stream is a development preview or experimental version of RHEL's pre-release, and Fedora is ahead of CentOS Stream and even more experimental. On December 9, 2020, Red Hat (IBM) announced that CentOS Linux 8 will be unsupported at the end of 2021. This does not affect your lab environment; however, avoid deploying CentOS 8 in production. For your lab build, we can use CentOS Stream or Fedora to replace CentOS 8 after 2021.

#	Task

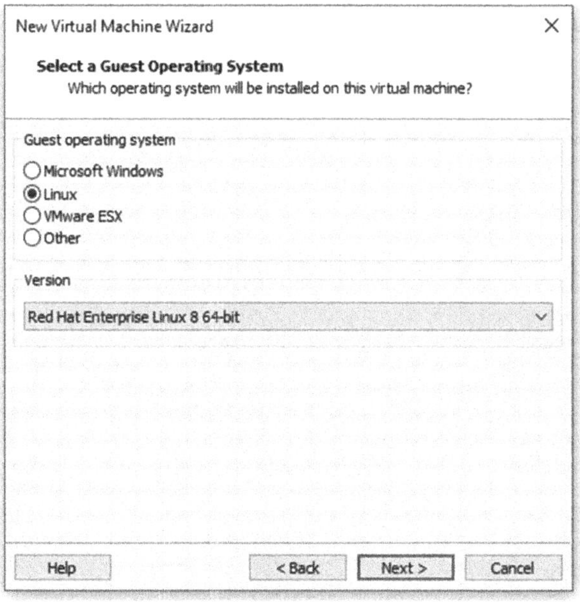

Figure 6-6. *CentOS 8 installation, OS selection*

05 In the next window, enter the user credentials as requested and click Next. See Figure 6-7.

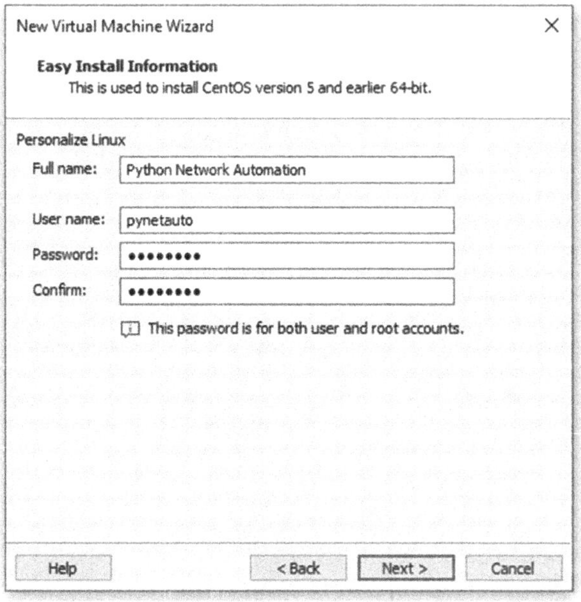

Figure 6-7. *CentOS 8 installation, entering user credentials*

(continued)

#	Task
06	Use some imagination to give your server a meaningful name that is easy to recognize. The server was named CentOS8s1, referring to CentOS8 Server 1. Click the Next button. See Figure 6-8.

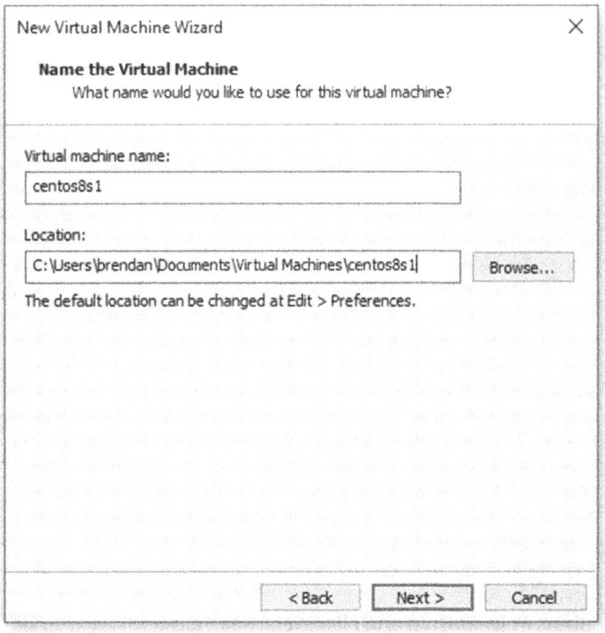

Figure 6-8. *CentOS 8 installation, server name and folder configuration*

#	Task
07	Allocate the desired free disk space; in the following example, 30GB disk space was allocated to the GUI, and other software will be installed. By default, the disk is set to thin provisioning, increasing disk size incrementally until it reaches 30GB so that the initial disk space will be a lot less. Also, click "Store virtual disk as a single file" for easier file management later. Then click Next. See Figure 6-9.

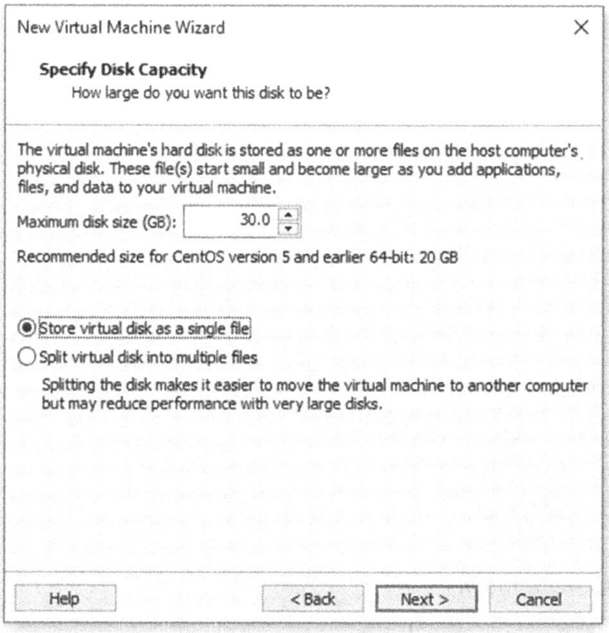

Figure 6-9. *CentOS 8 installation, allocating disk capacity for use*

(*continued*)

#	Task
08	Click the Finish button to finish the VM configuration. See Figure 6-10.

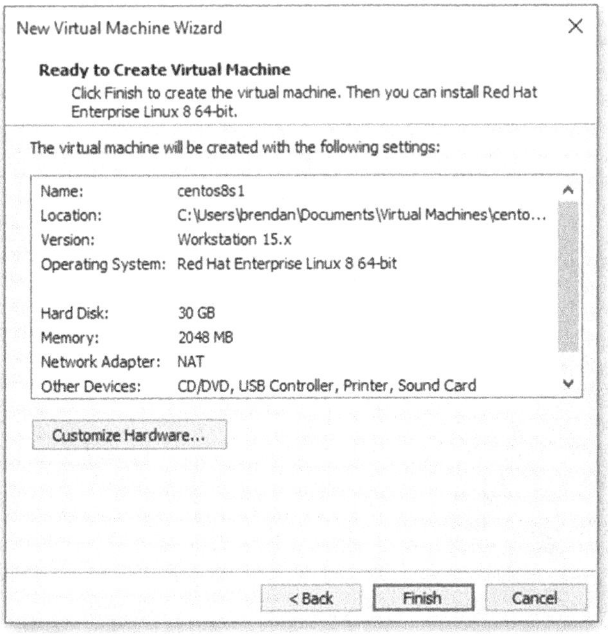

Figure 6-10. *CentOS 8 installation, finishing the configuration*

#	Task
09	Now click "Edit virtual machine settings" to change the CD/DVD selection. See Figure 6-11.

Figure 6-11. *CentOS 8 installation, selecting "Edit virtual machine settings"*

#	Task
10	Click CD/DVD (SATA) in the left pane, click "Use ISO image file," and then click the Browse button. See Figure 6-12.

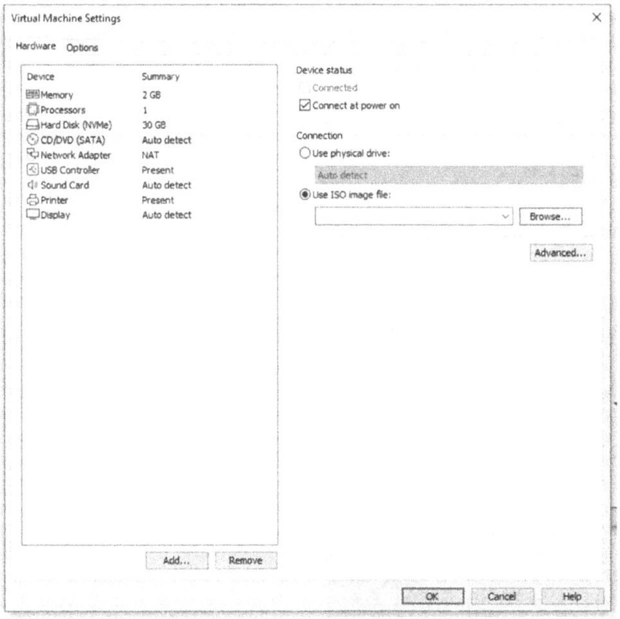

Figure 6-12. *CentOS 8 installation, selecting virtual machine settings*

#	Task
11	Select the CentOS installation file already downloaded in your `Downloads` folder, and then click Open. See Figure 6-13.

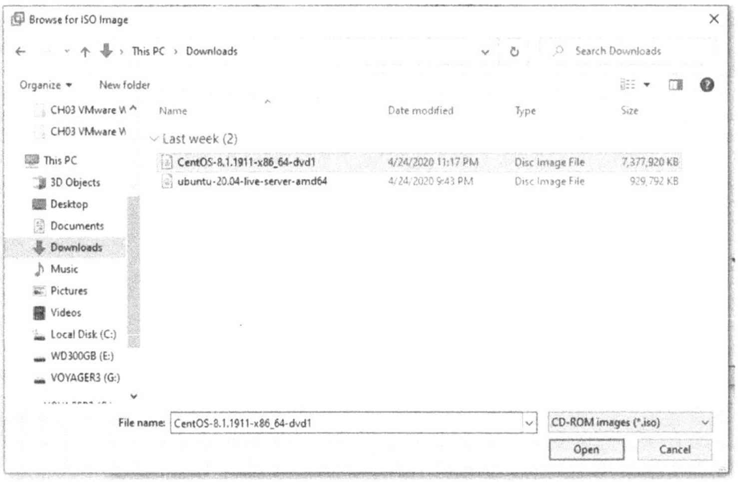

Figure 6-13. *CentOS 8 installation, selecting the CentOS ISO file*

(continued)

#	Task
12	Now click "Power on this virtual machine" to start the CentOS installation. See Figure 6-14.

Figure 6-14. *CentOS 8 installation, powering on hte VM*

13 Click Install CentOS Linux 8 to begin the installation. See Figure 6-15.

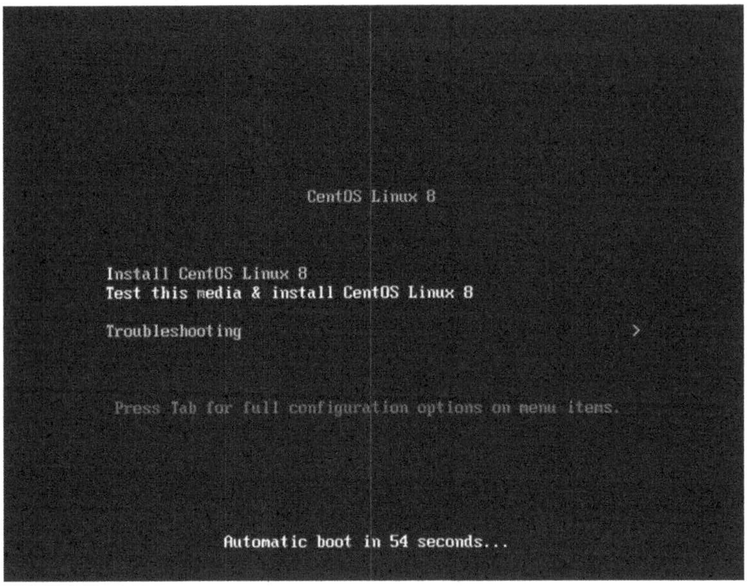

Figure 6-15. *CentOS 8 installation, selecting installation options*

#	Task
14	Leave the default language as English (United States) and click Continue to move to the next page. See Figure 6-16.

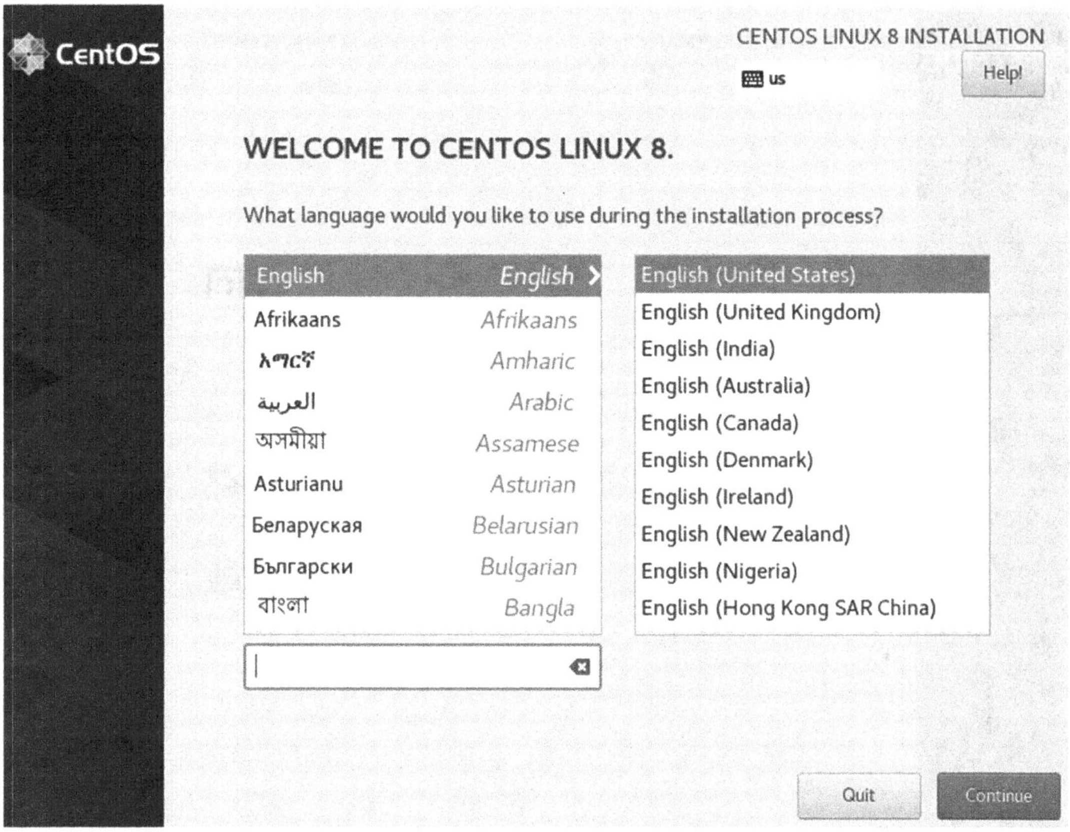

Figure 6-16. *CentOS 8 installation, language selection*

(*continued*)

#	Task
15	In the Installation Summary window, select Installation Destination under System to enter and select the operating system installation disk. See Figure 6-17.

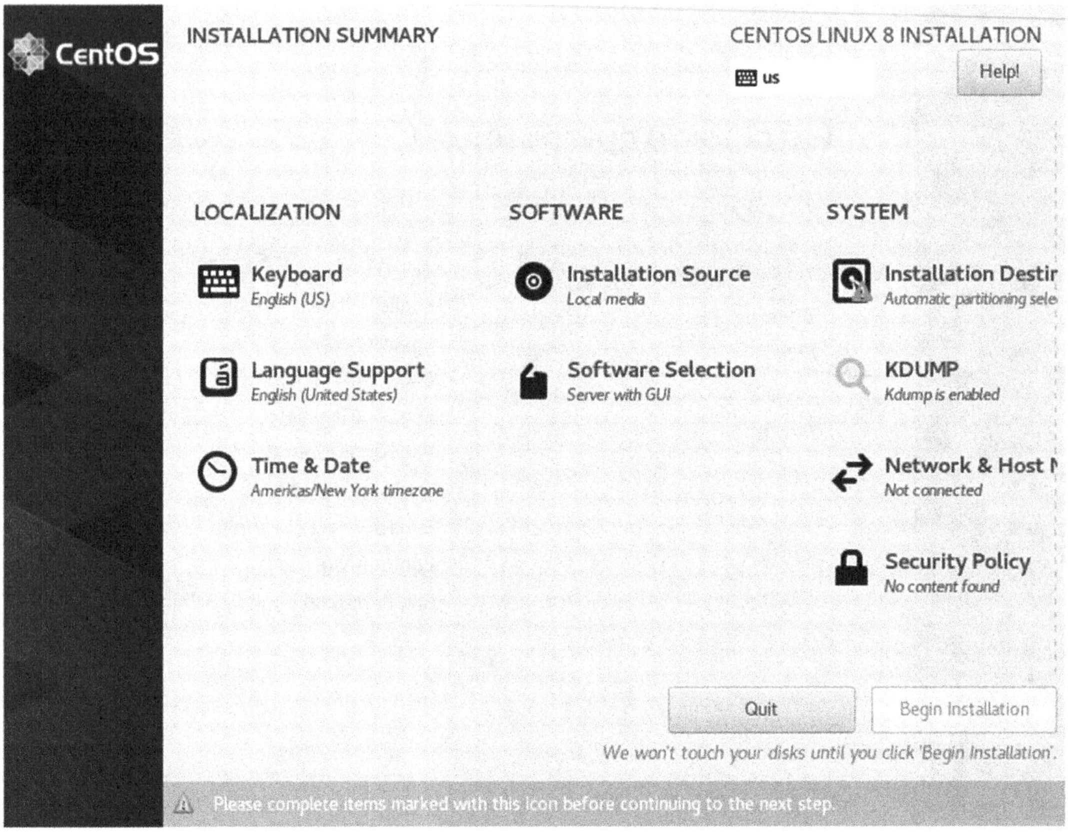

Figure 6-17. *CentOS 8 installation, installation summary*

#	Task
16	Highlight VMware Virtual NVMe Disk 30 GiB and click the Done button to return to the previous installation window. See Figure 6-18.

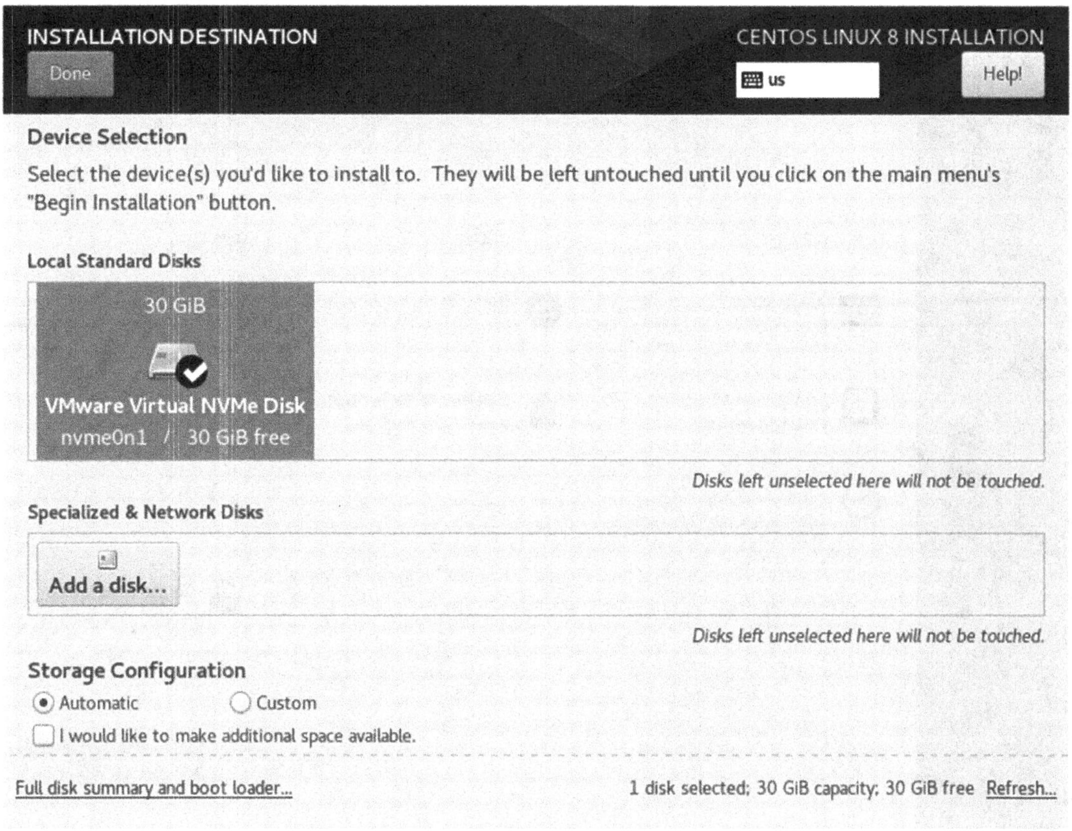

Figure 6-18. *CentOS 8 installation, installation destination selection*

(continued)

#	Task
17	Next, click on "Software Selection Server with GUI" to install extra software during the installation. See Figure 6-19.

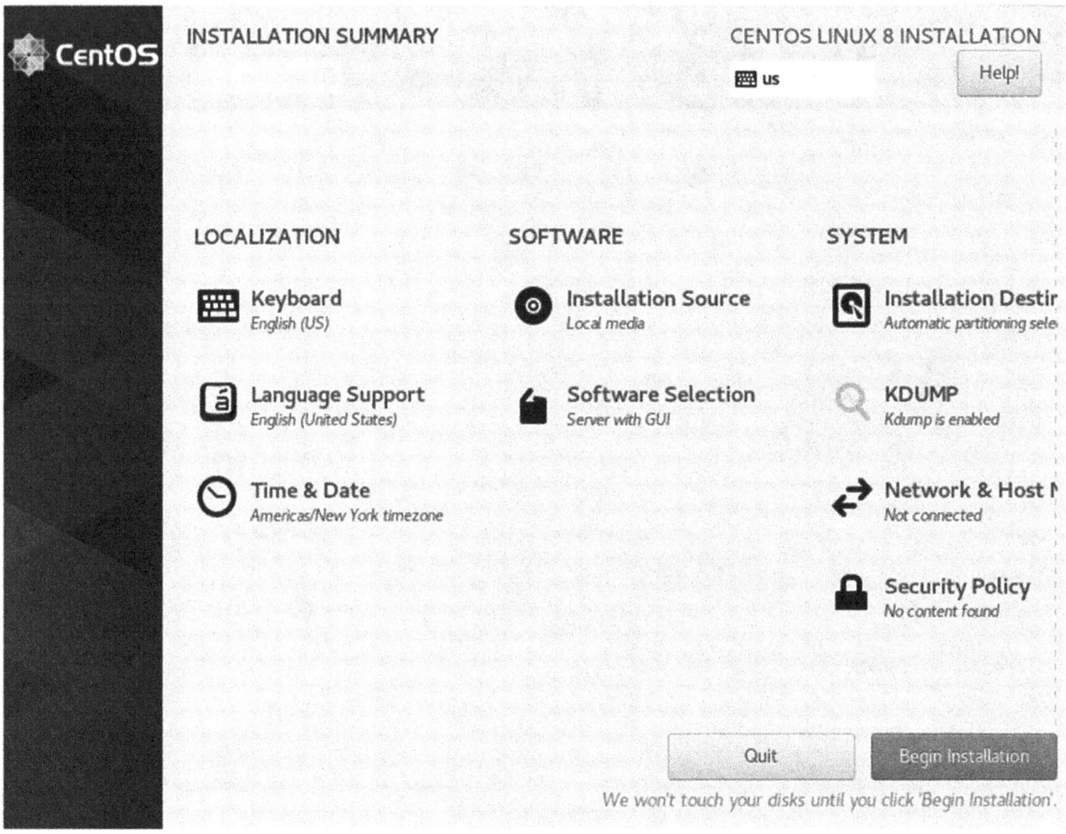

Figure 6-19. *CentOS 8 installation, software selection*

#	Task
18	In the Software Selection window, select Server with GUI and select other software such as FTP Server, Mail Server, and more. Here, install at least FTP Server to save time for later. Other IP services will be installed manually in the next chapter. Once you are happy with your selection, click the Done button. Figure 6-20, Figure 6-21, and Figure 6-22 show the additional software you can select under Software Selection.

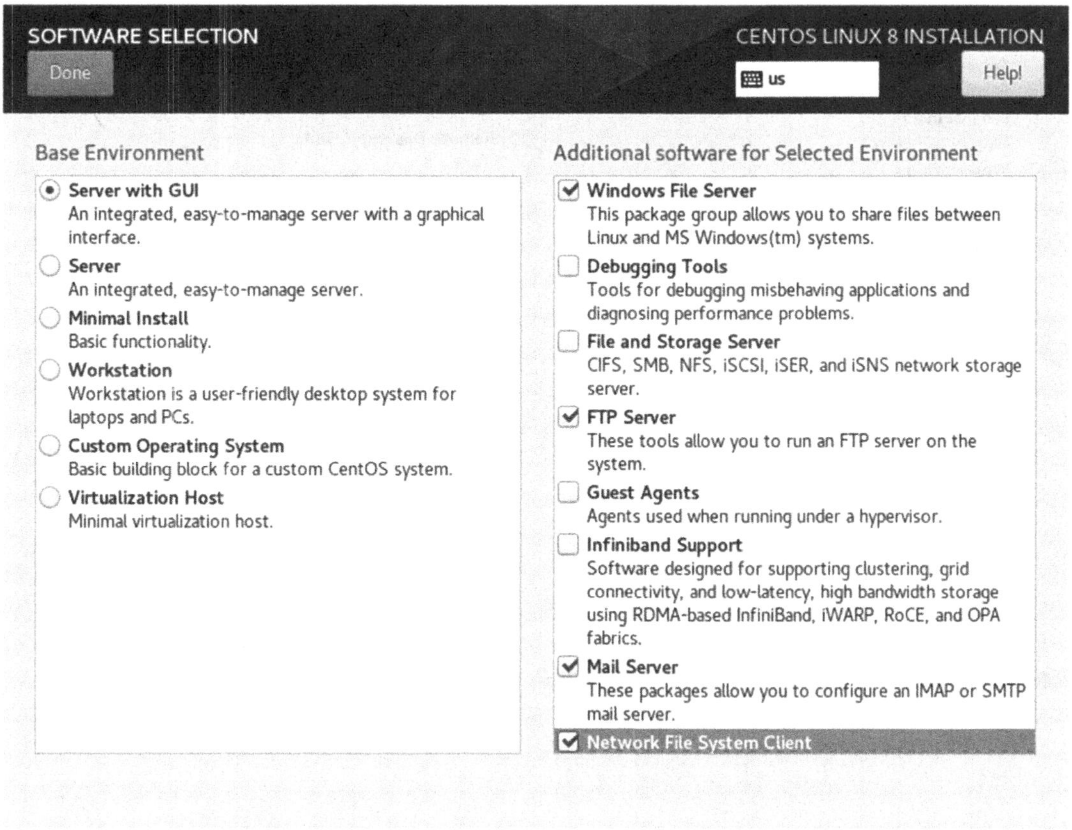

Figure 6-20. *CentOS 8 installation, software selection 1*

(continued)

#	Task

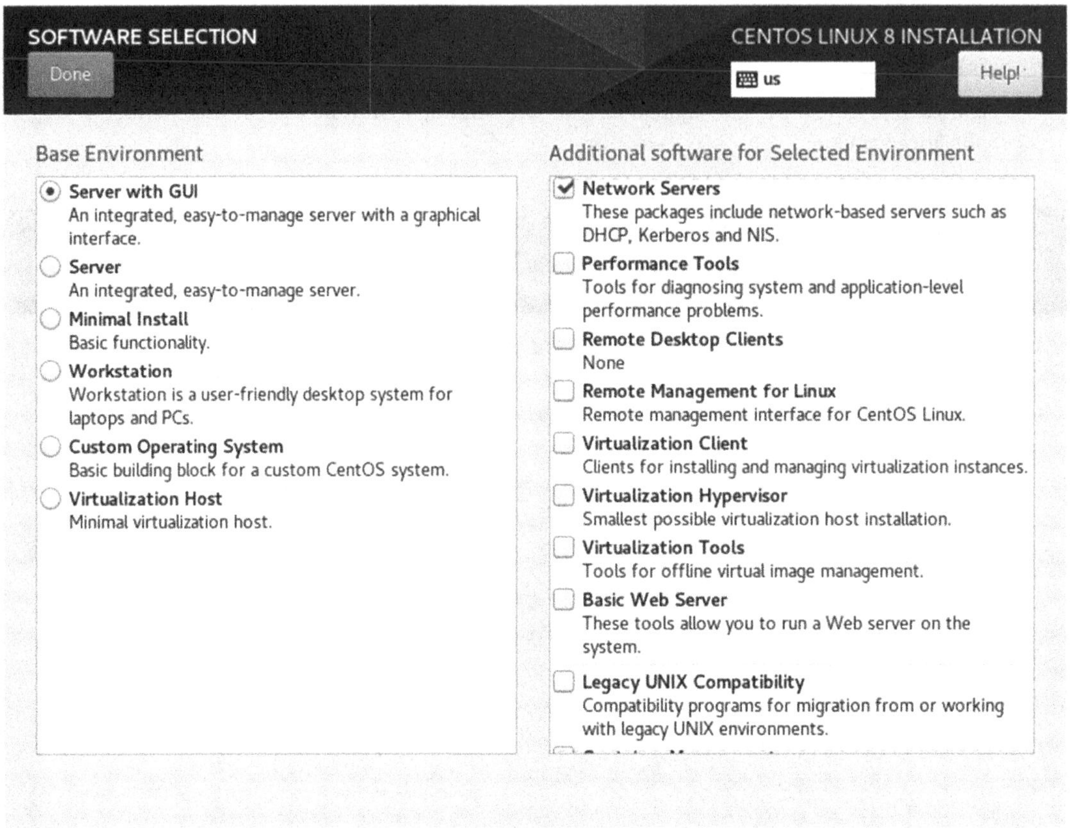

Figure 6-21. *CentOS 8 installation, software selection 2*

#	Task

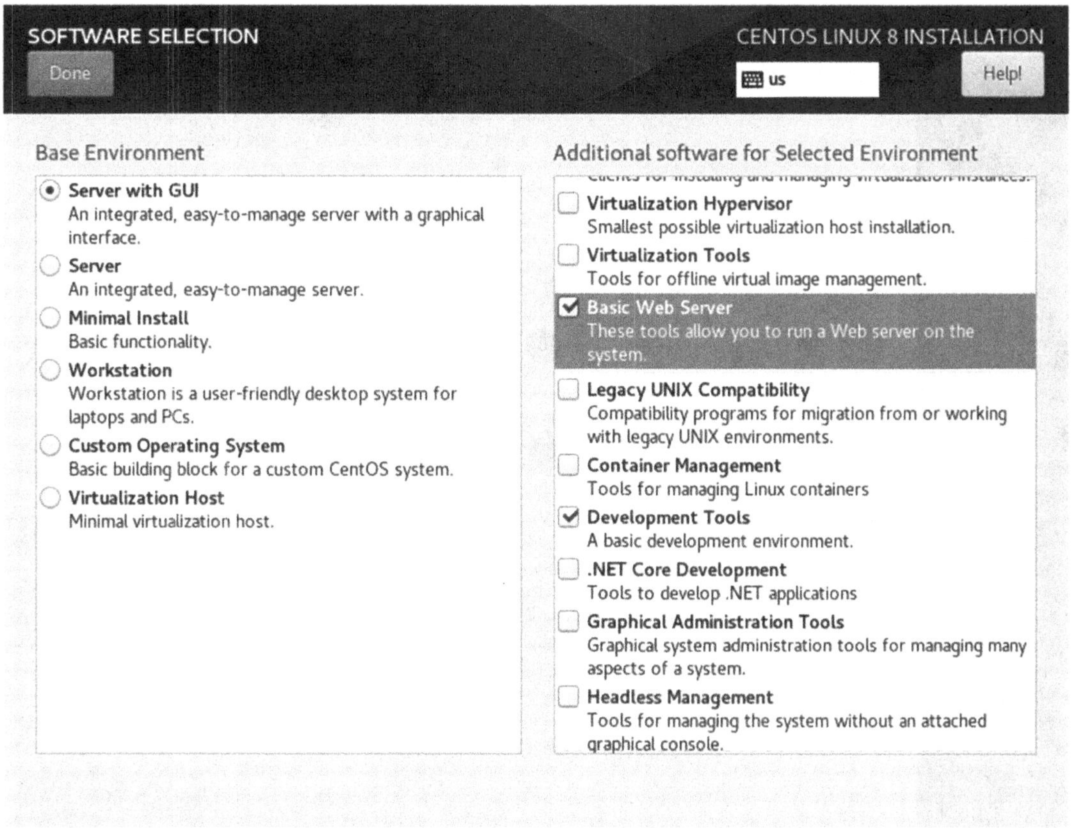

Figure 6-22. *CentOS 8 installation, software selection 3*

(*continued*)

#	Task
19	Next click Network & Hostname. See Figure 6-23.

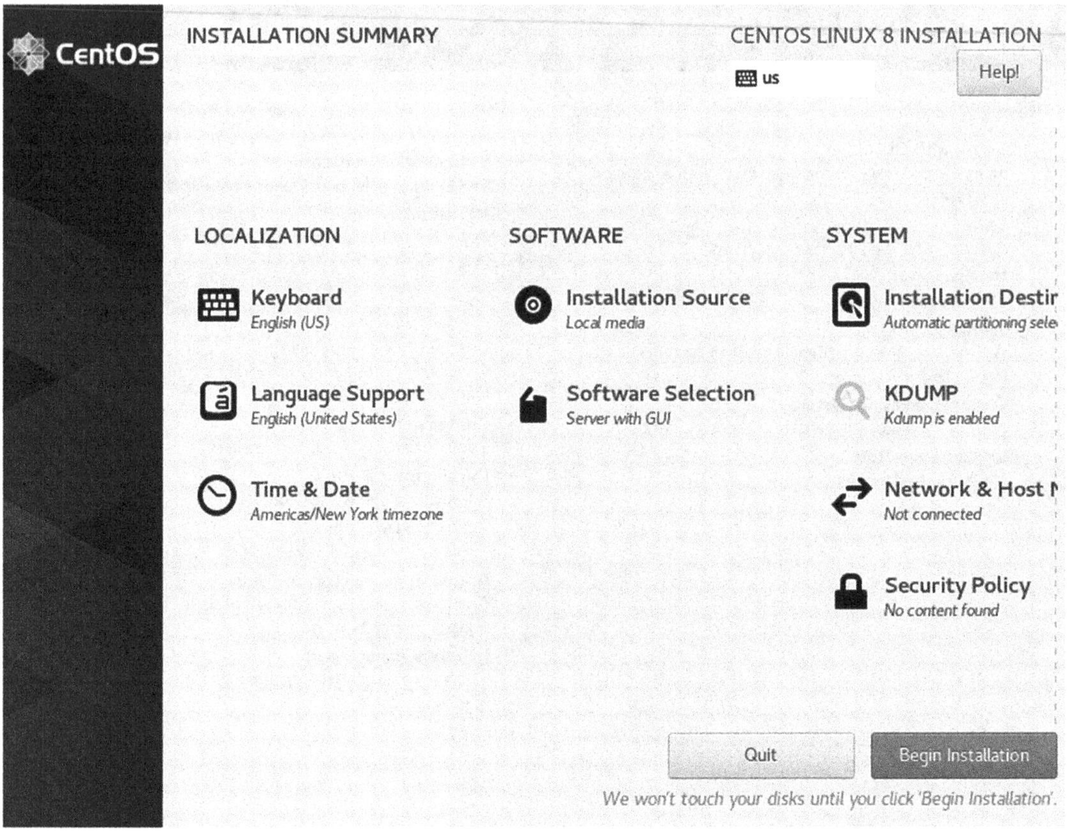

Figure 6-23. *CentOS 8 installation, installation summary*

#	Task
20	The network adapter of the CentOS server is turned off by default. Click the ON button to switch on the network adapter. Once the switch is powered on, an IP address will be automatically assigned from the NAT's DHCP subnet. Figure 6-24 received an IP address of 192.168.183.130/24. Once you have confirmed the DHCP allocates the IP assignment, click Done to exit. See Figure 6-24.

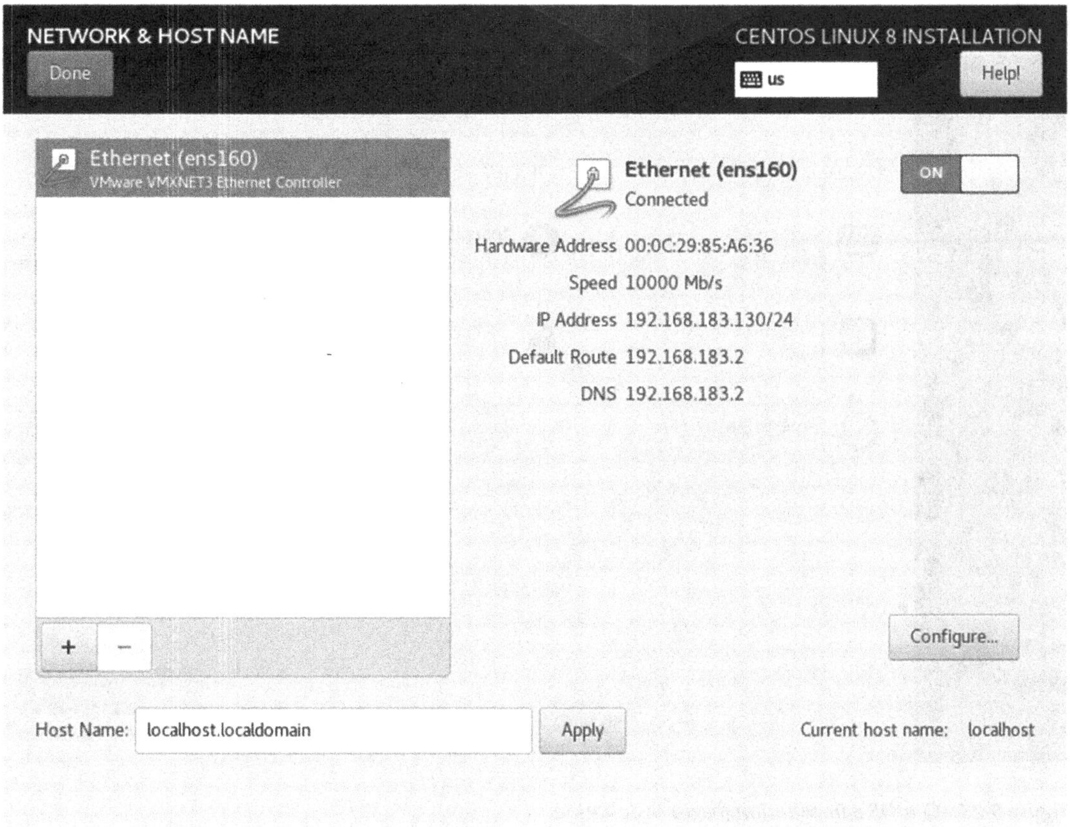

Figure 6-24. *CentOS 8 installation, connecting to a network*

(continued)

#	Task
21	Once you return to the Installation Summary window, click the Begin Installation button to begin the OS installation. See Figure 6-25.

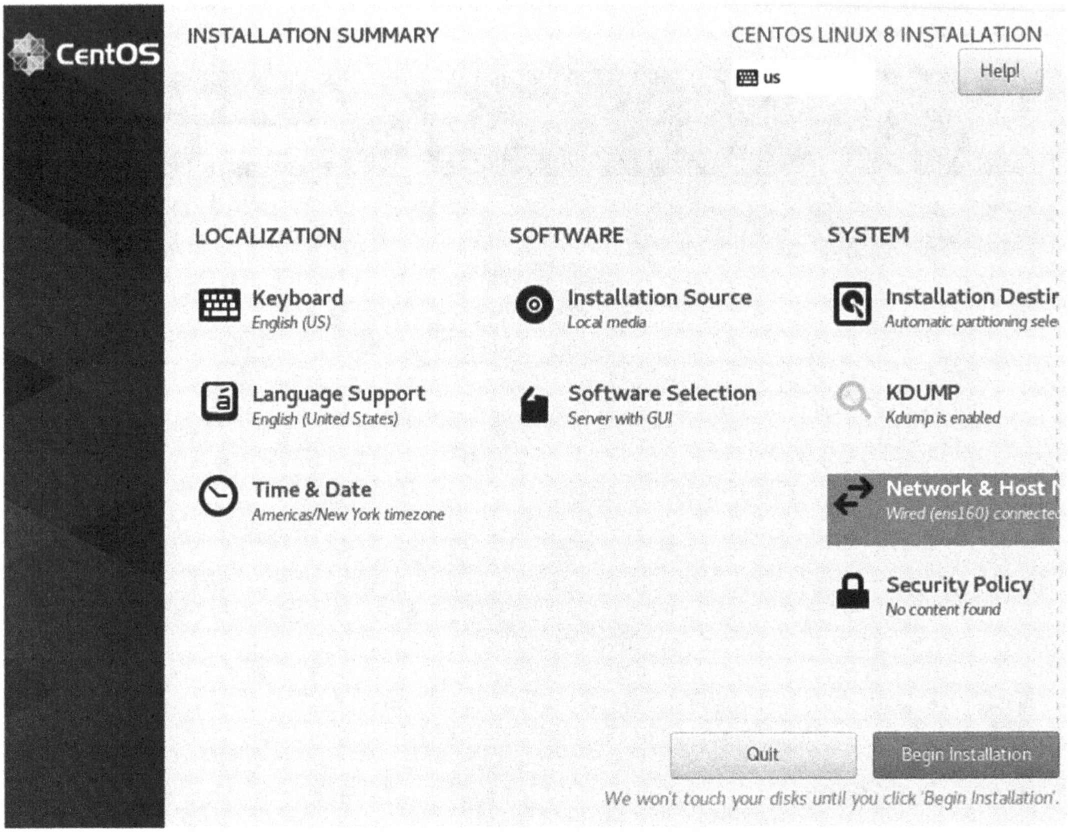

***Figure 6-25.** CentOS 8 installation, begin installation*

#	Task
22	While downloading packages, you can try to set the root user's password before entering the installation mode. Click Root Password. See Figure 6-26.

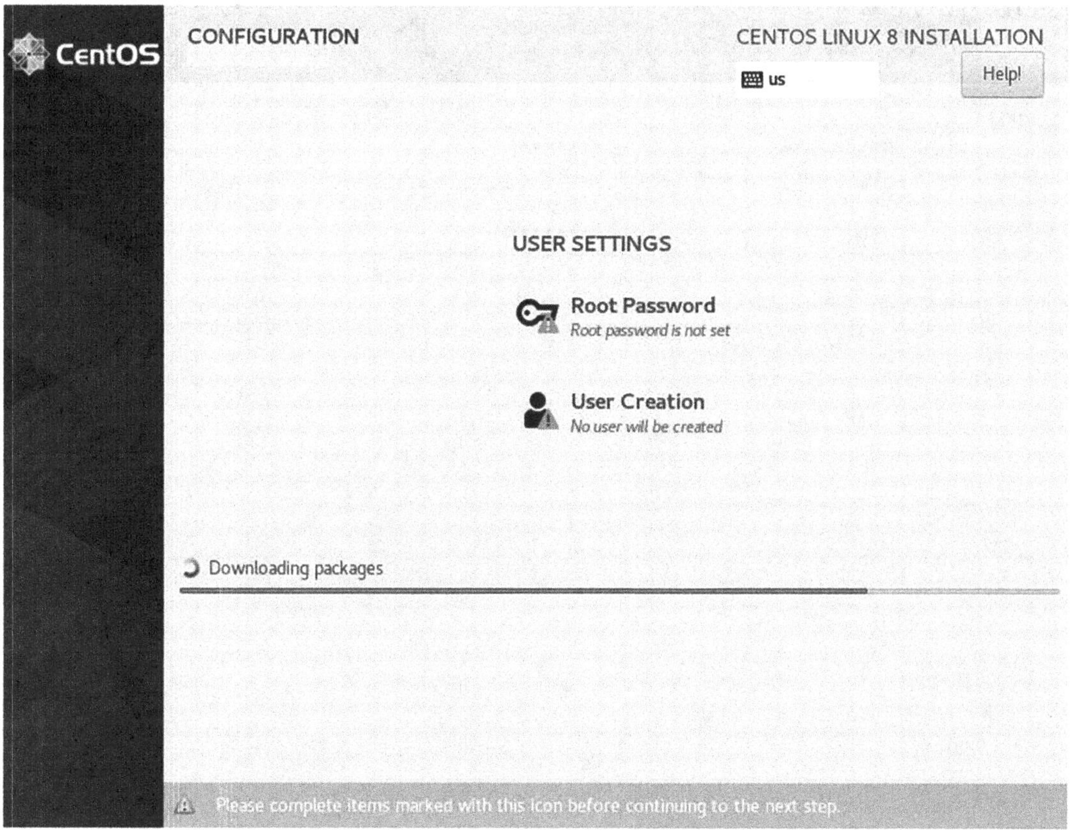

Figure 6-26. *CentOS 8 installation, setting up the root user password*

(continued)

#	Task
23	Enter a root user password twice and click the Done button to exit. See Figure 6-27.

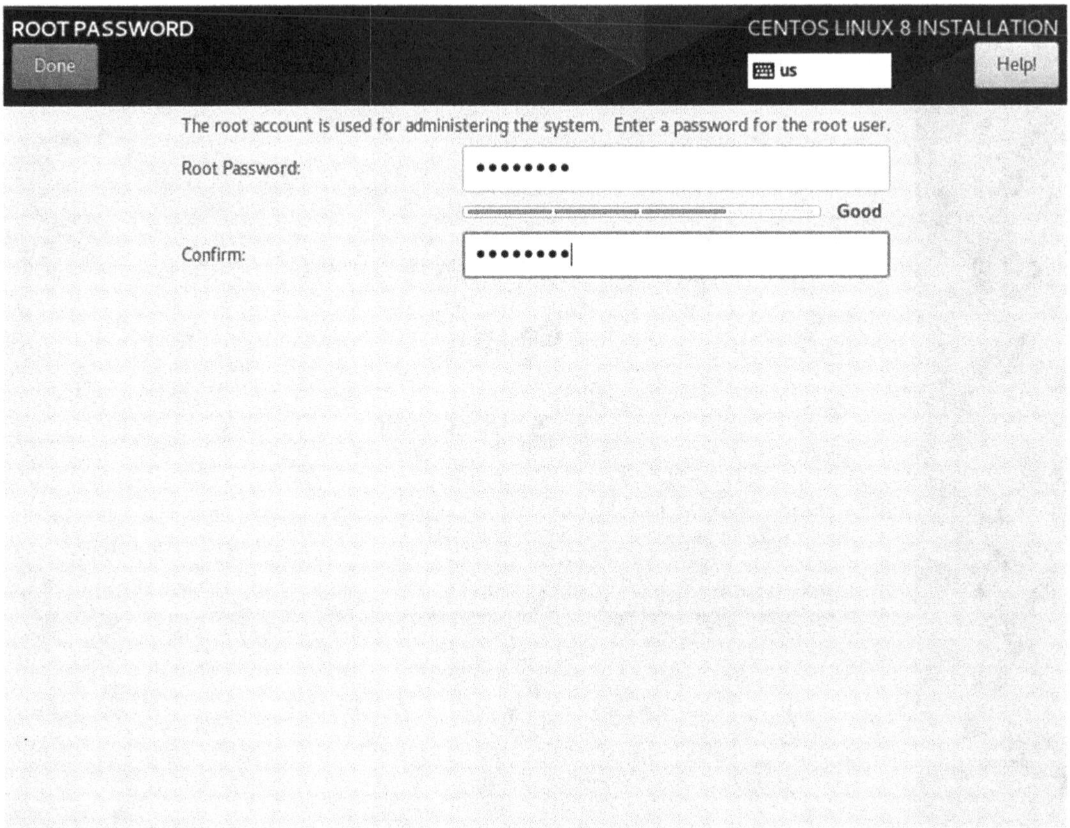

***Figure 6-27.** CentOS 8 installation, entering the root user password*

#	Task
24	As soon as you return to the previous screen, the CentOS8 server installation will begin. Now, wait for about five minutes for the installation to complete. See Figure 6-28.

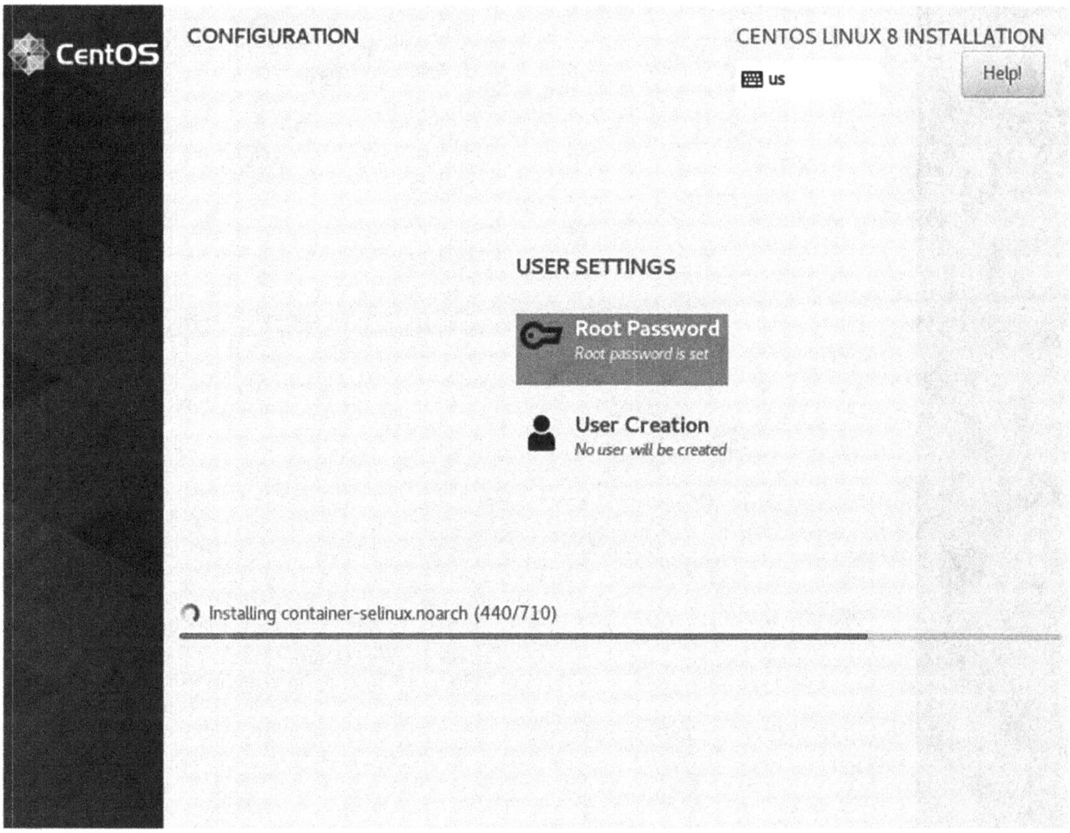

Figure 6-28. *CentOS 8 installation, server installation in progress*

(*continued*)

#	Task
25	Once the CentOS 8 installation completes, you will be prompted for a reboot. Click Reboot to restart your new Linux server. See Figure 6-29.

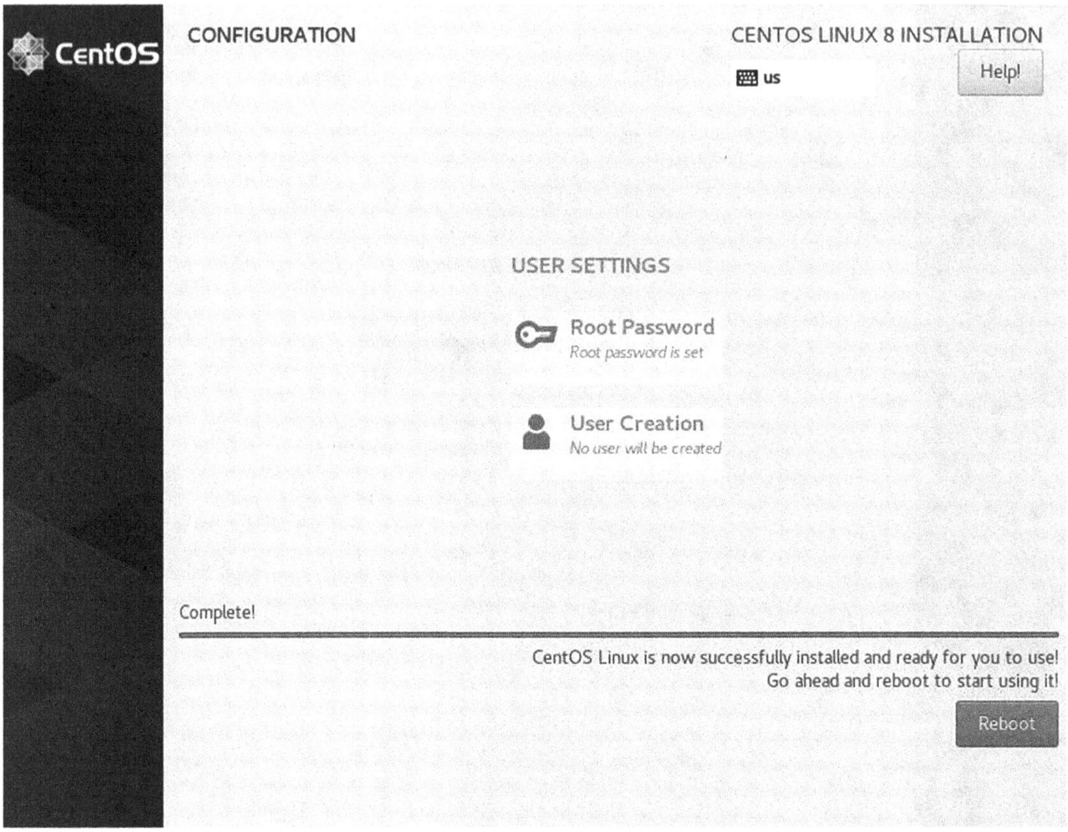

Figure 6-29. *CentOS 8 installation, installation completed and reboot*

#	Task
26	After rebooting the server, you will see an initial configuration screen. Click License Information to agree to the end-user license agreement to use CentOS for free. See Figure 6-30.

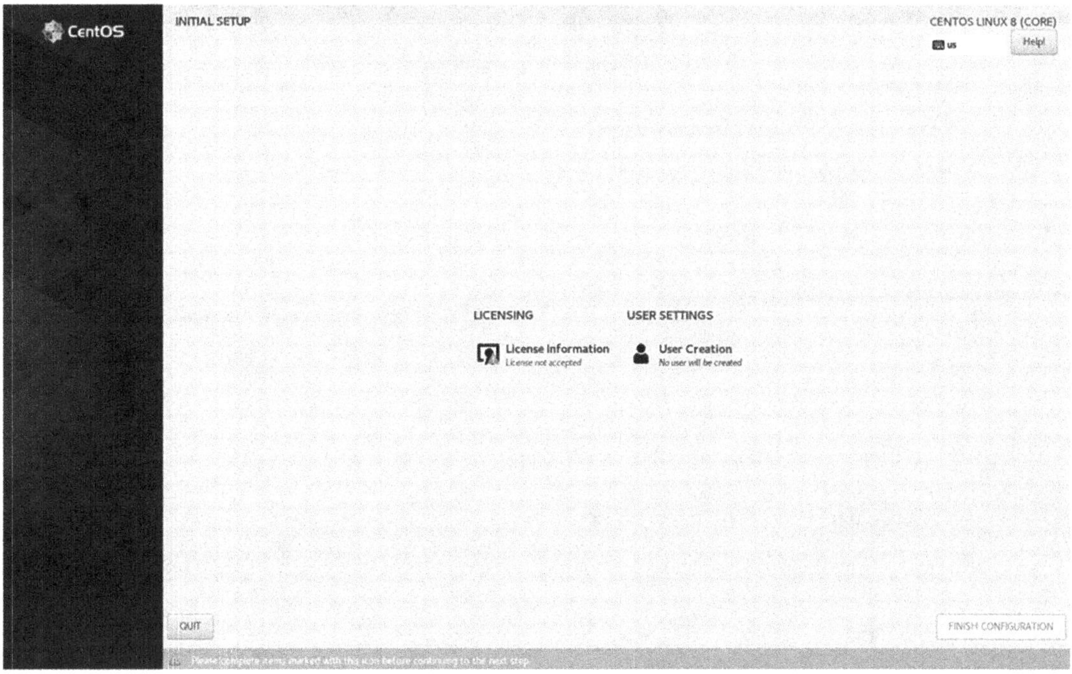

Figure 6-30. *CentOS 8 installation, initial configuration window*

(*continued*)

#	Task
27	Click the "I accept the license agreement" checkbox and click Done. See Figure 6-31.

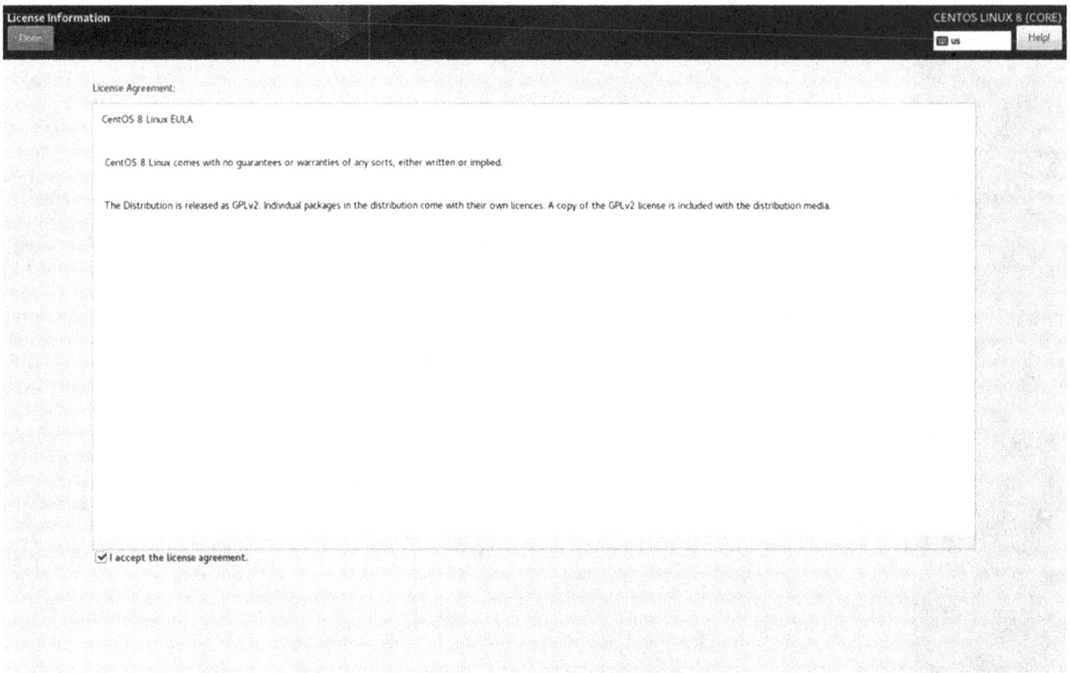

Figure 6-31. *CentOS 8 installation, accepting the end-user license agreement*

#	Task
28	When you return to the initial setup window, you notice that the warning sign has disappeared in the License Information field. Now click the Finish Configuration button to log into CentOS for the first time. See Figure 6-32.

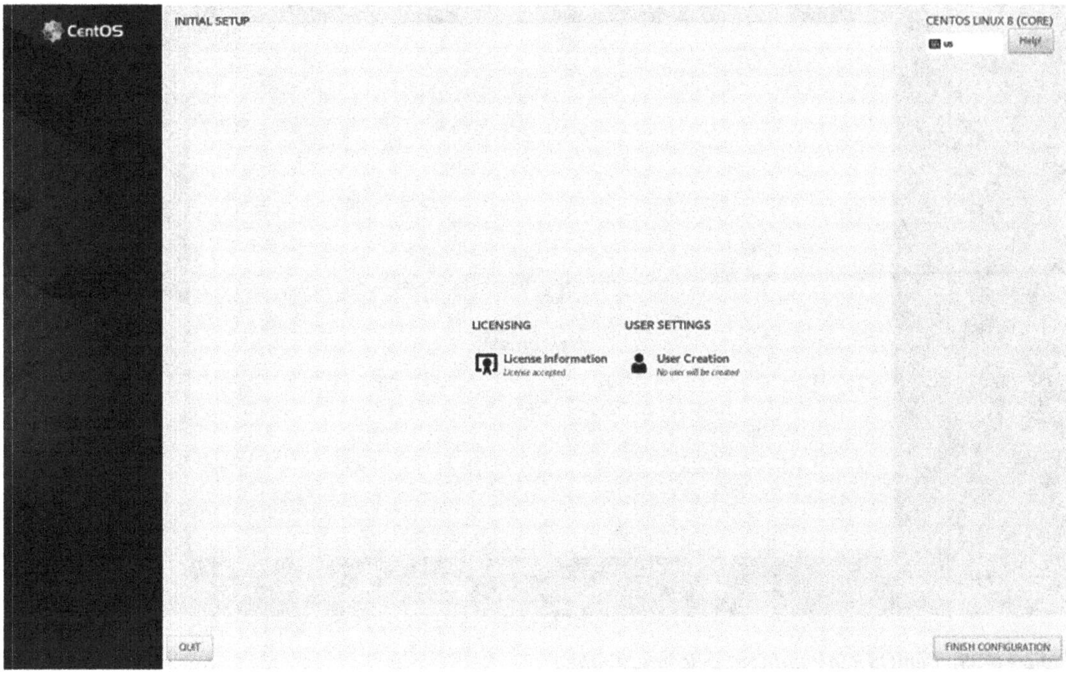

Figure 6-32. *CentOS 8 installation, initial setup completed*

(*continued*)

#	Task
29	Click Next. See Figure 6-33.

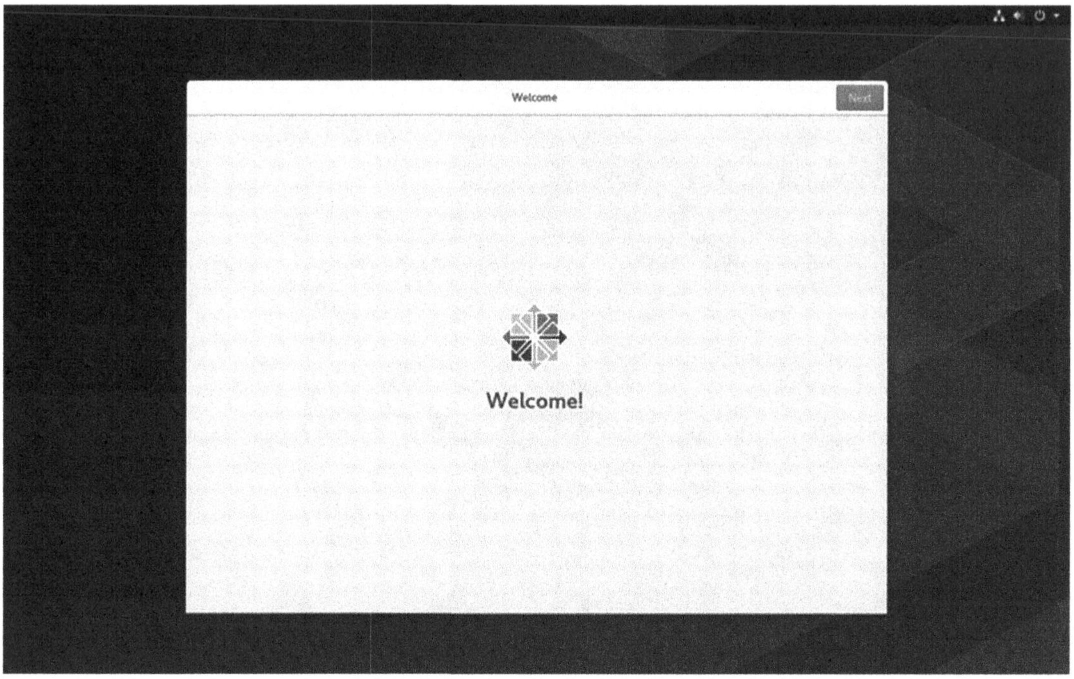

Figure 6-33. *CentOS 8 installation, welcome window*

#	Task
30	Click the Next button. See Figure 6-34.

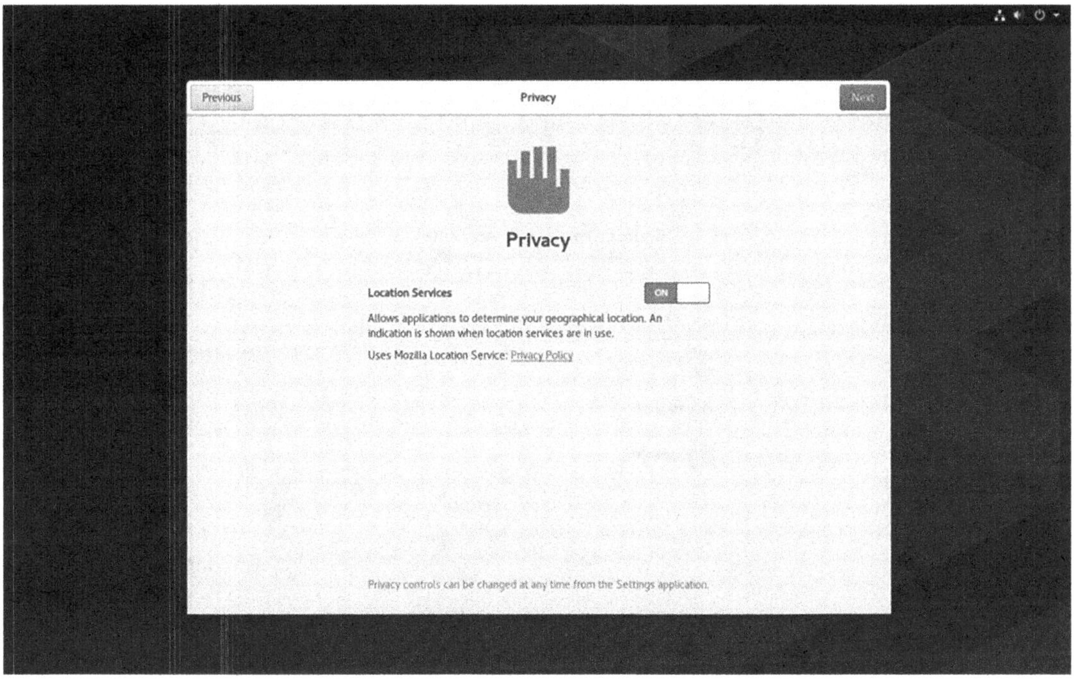

Figure 6-34. *CentOS 8 installation, privacy location services*

(*continued*)

#	Task
31	Click the Skip button to skip the online accounts configuration. See Figure 6-35.

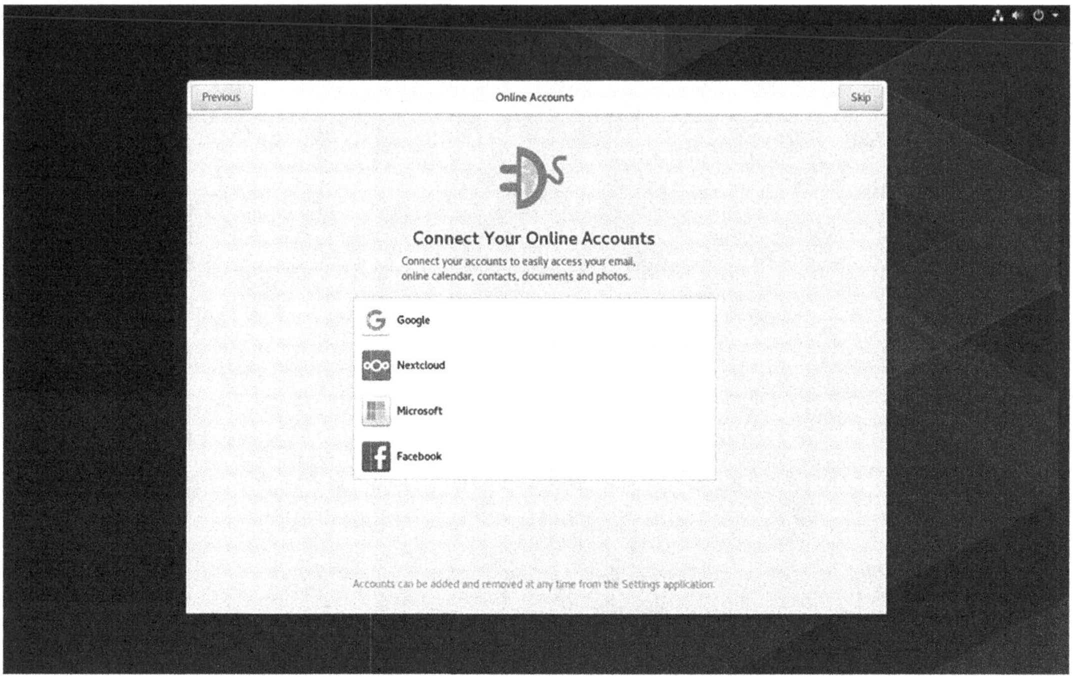

Figure 6-35. *CentOS 8 installation, online accounts*

#	Task
32	Enter your details and click Next. See Figure 6-36.

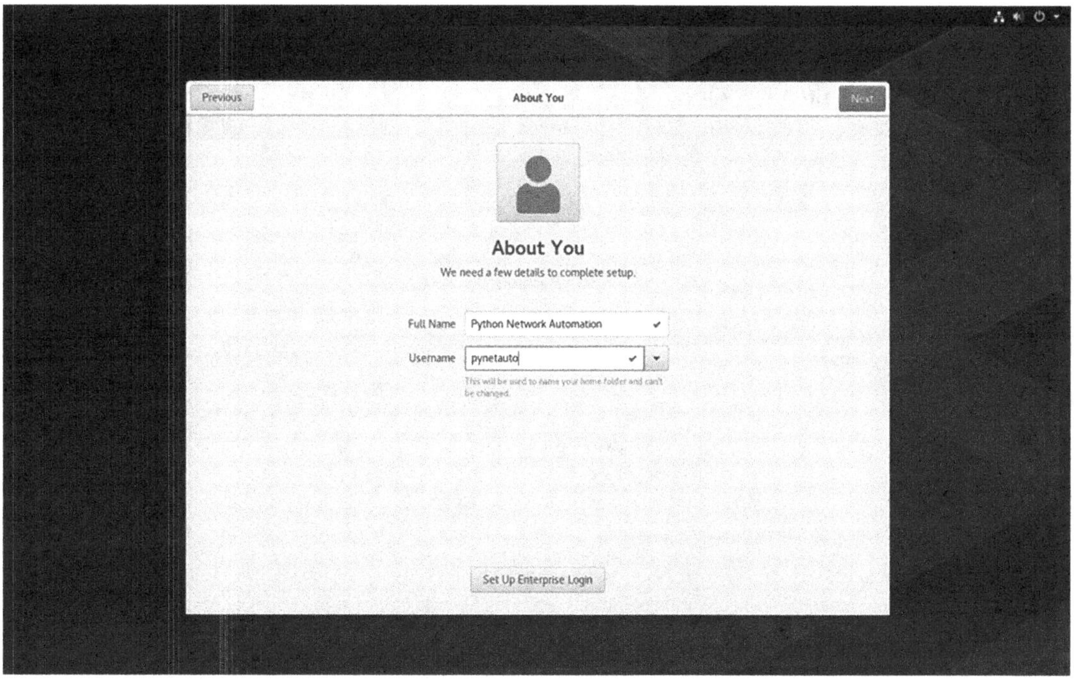

***Figure 6-36.** CentOS 8 installation, About You screen*

(continued)

#	Task
33	You will be taken to the Password screen next. Enter your password twice and click the Next button. See Figure 6-37.

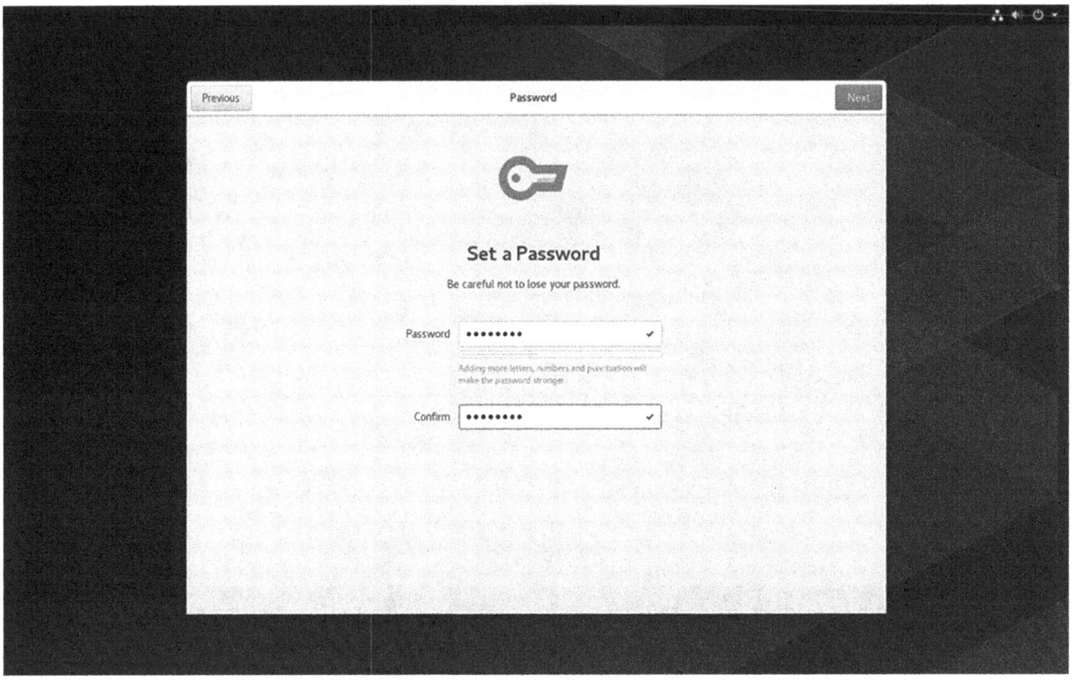

***Figure 6-37.** CentOS 8 installation, setting a password*

#	Task
34	On the Ready to Go screen, click Start Using CentOS Linux to complete the configuration. See Figure 6-38.

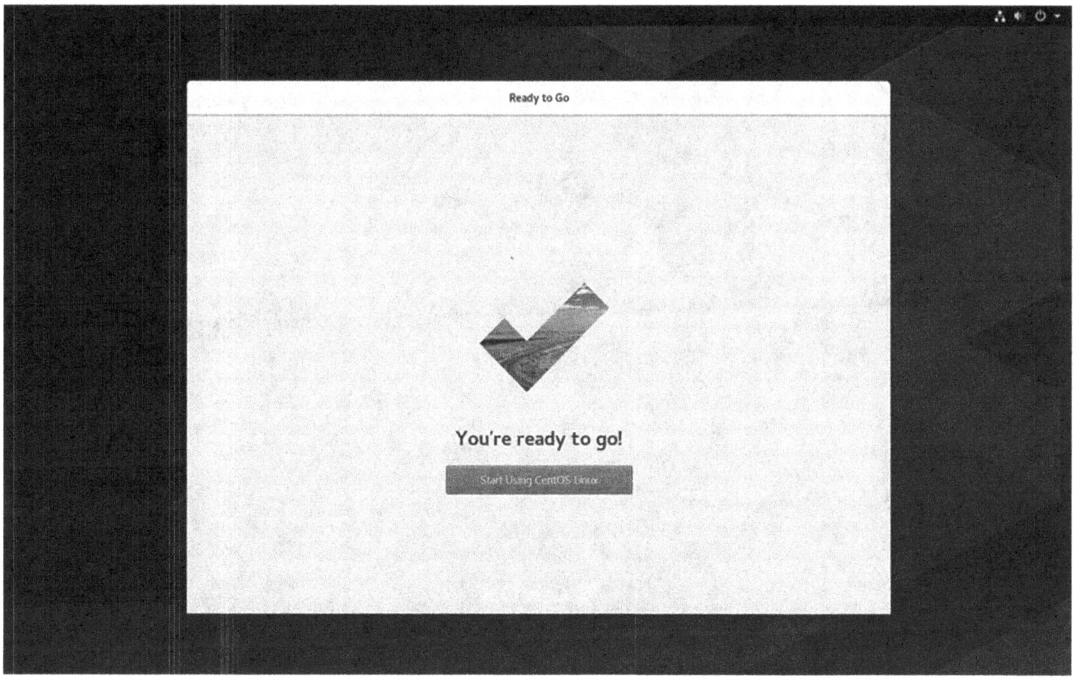

Figure 6-38. *CentOS 8 installation, Ready to Go screen*

(*continued*)

#	Task
35	Enter your password and click the Sign In button. See Figure 6-39.

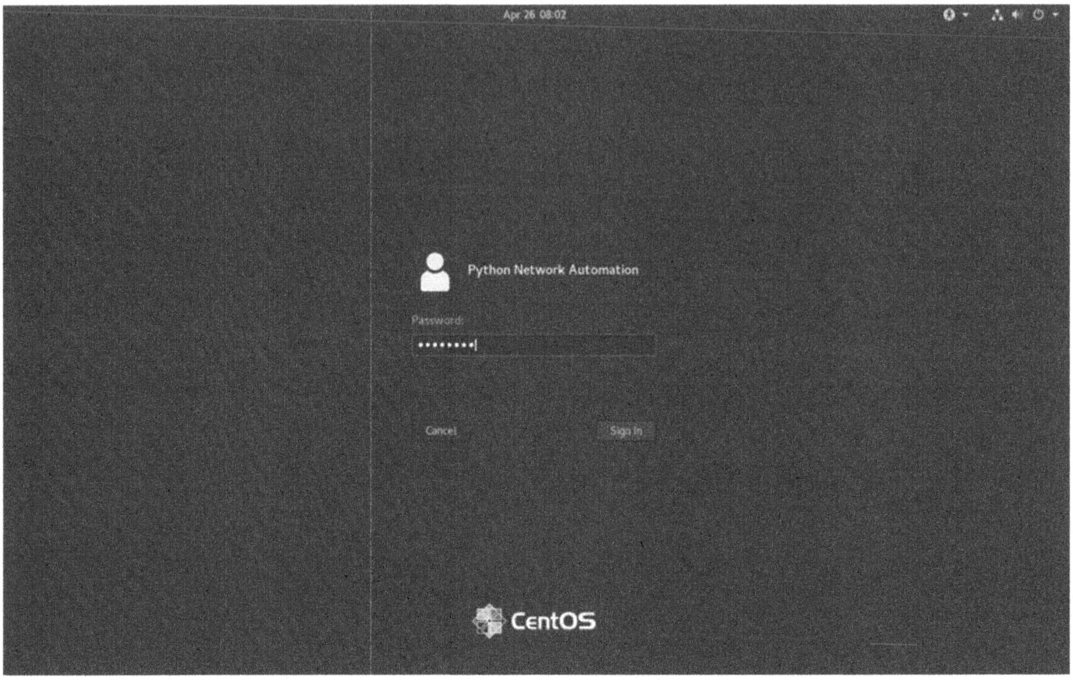

Figure 6-39. *CentOS 8 installation, first sign-in*

#	Task
36	You will now see the Getting Started screen. It is safe to close the window and begin using your CentOS server now. See Figure 6-40.

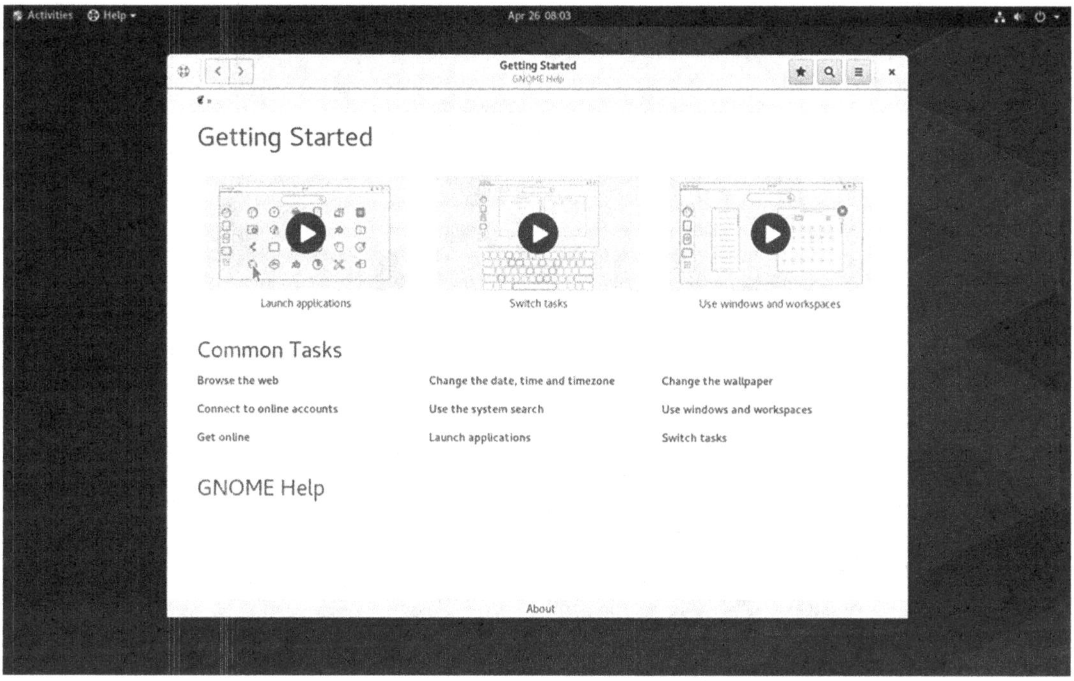

Figure 6-40. *CentOS 8 installation, password configuration*

(continued)

#	Task
37	Launch an application such as the Terminal Console to use the server. See Figure 6-41.

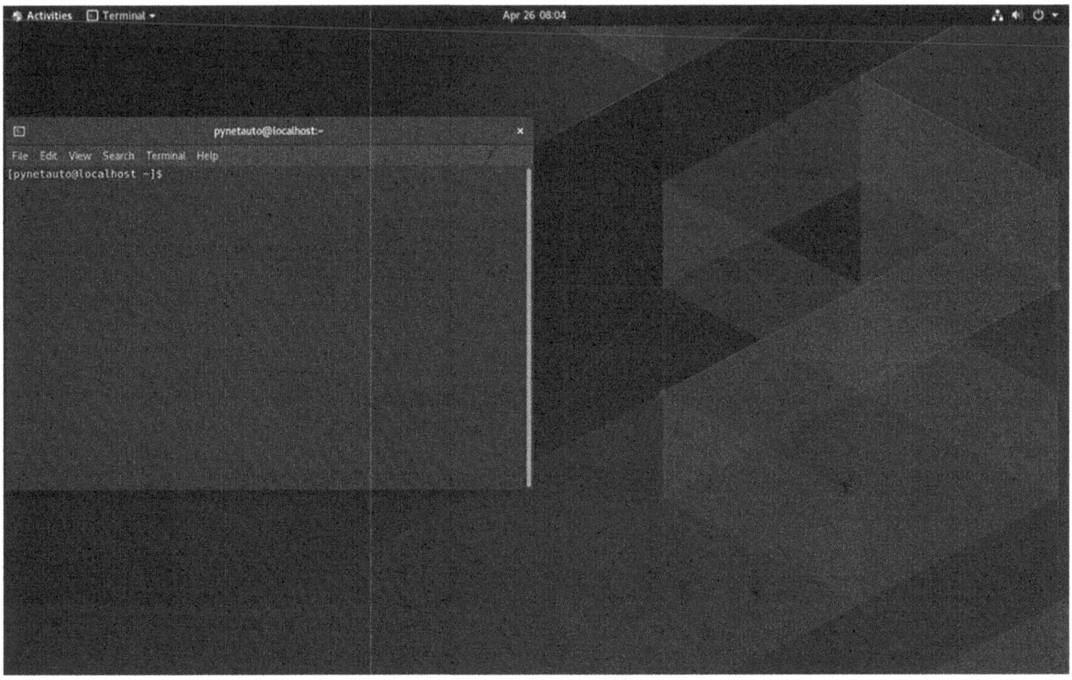

Figure 6-41. *CentOS 8 installation, first-time use*

Logging In to a New CentOS 8 Server via SSH

On CentOS 8, you do not have to change any settings to connect to the server remotely using an SSH connection; both the user and root user will be allowed to connect to the server using the SSH protocol by default. Do not take my word for this. Let's quickly validate this by opening up PuTTY on your host Windows 10 and connecting via SSH into the host Windows 10 desktop server.

#	Task
1	First, from your host's Windows desktop, open PuTTY and enter the IP address of your CentOS 8 VM. The example shown here uses an IP address of 192.168.183.130, but your IP address may be different, and that is still OK. Click the Open button. See Figure 6-42.

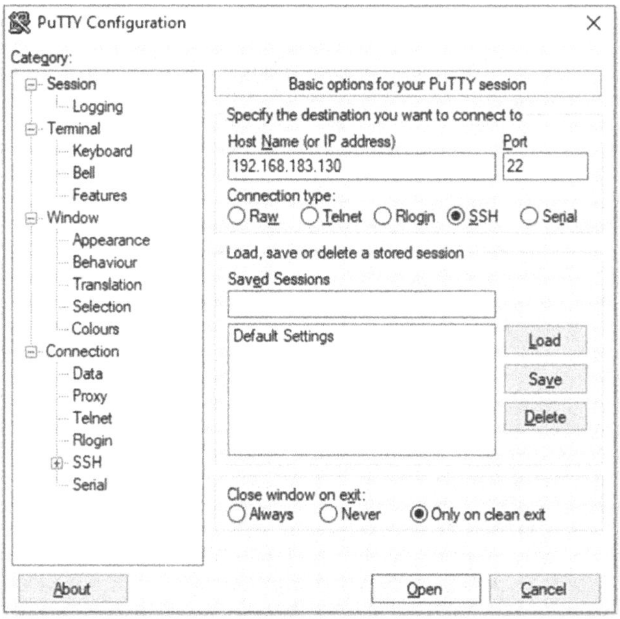

Figure 6-42. *CentOS 8 SSH login, PuTTY SSH login to CentOS 8*

2	When the PuTTY security alert is prompted, accept the rsa2 key, and click the Yes button. See Figure 6-43.

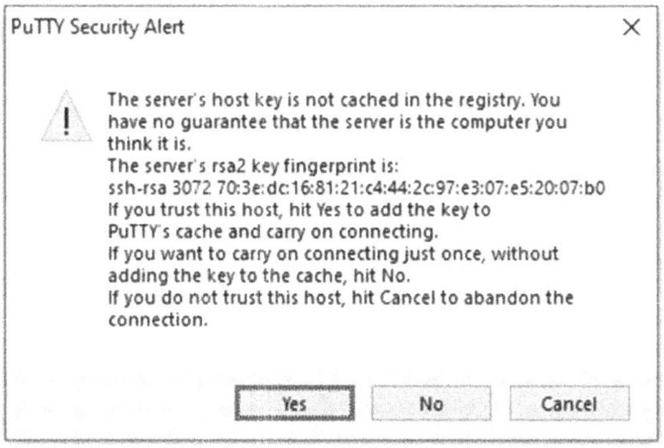

Figure 6-43. *CentOS 8 SSH login, accepting the rsa2 server key*

3	Now use your user ID and password to confirm that the SSH login works. See Figure 6-44.

#	Task

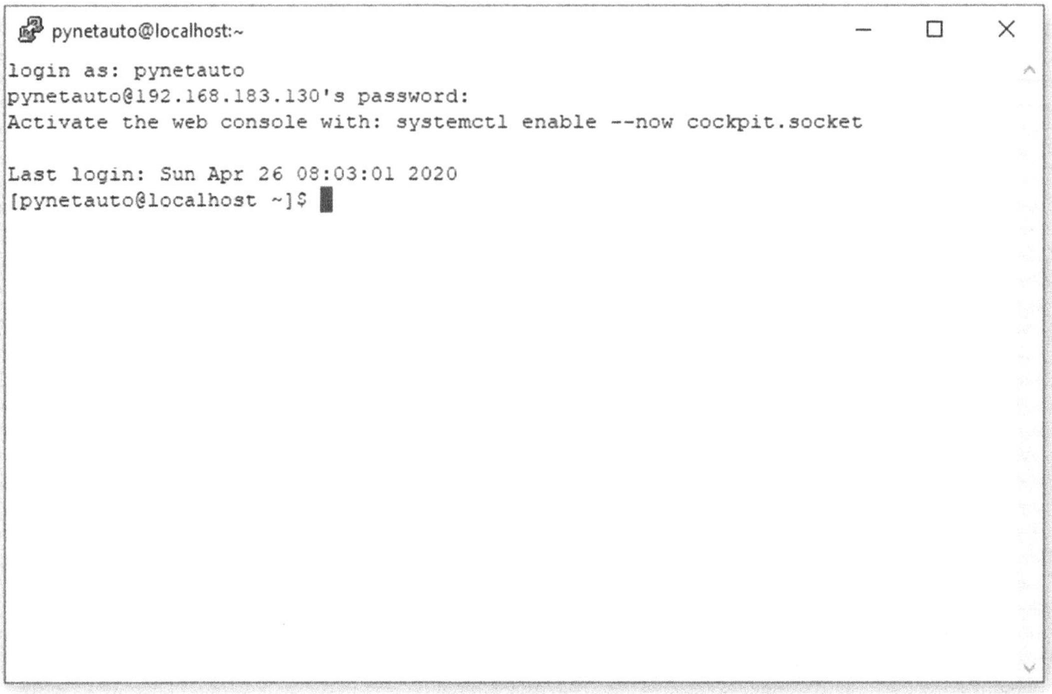
pynetauto@localhost:~
login as: pynetauto
pynetauto@192.168.183.130's password:
Activate the web console with: systemctl enable --now cockpit.socket
Last login: Sun Apr 26 08:03:01 2020
[pynetauto@localhost ~]$

Figure 6-44. *CentOS 8 SSH login, user login*

#	Task
4	Optionally, start another PuTTY session and, this time, log in as the root user. You have made no system changes, but CentOS 8 will allow you to connect to the server using the SSH protocol. As you will discover, just like Ubuntu, CentOS has real potential to become one of your favorite Linux distro systems. See Figure 6-45.

#	Task

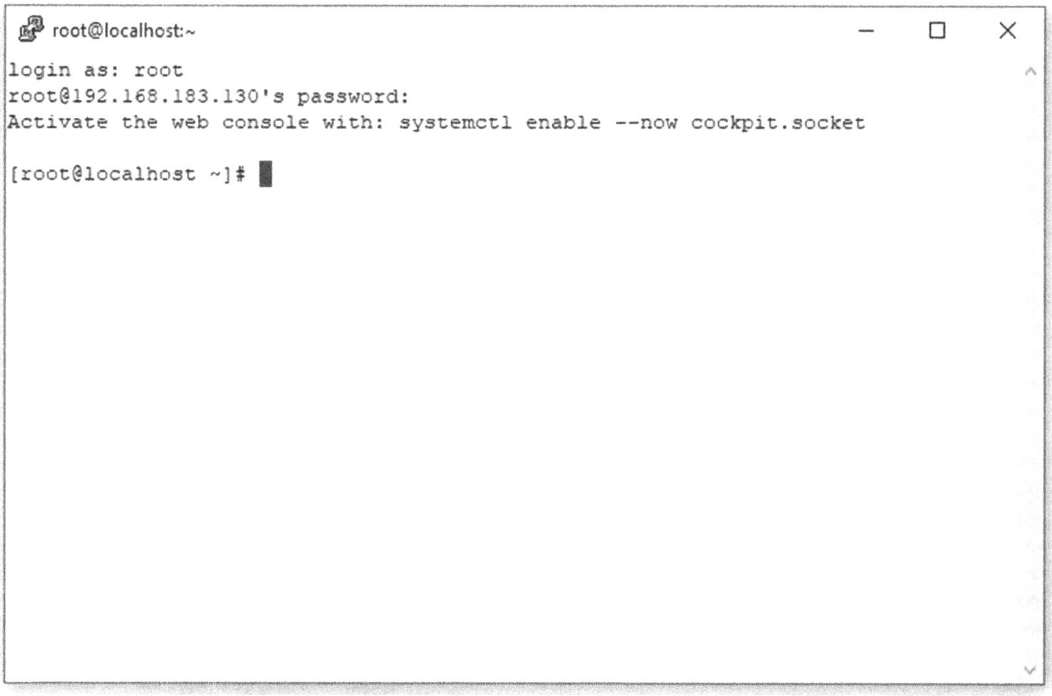
root@localhost:~
login as: root
root@192.168.183.130's password:
Activate the web console with: systemctl enable --now cockpit.socket
[root@localhost ~]#

Figure 6-45. *CentOS 8 SSH login, root user login*

This completes the CentOS 8 installation and initial setup. Before moving onto the next topic, here are some of my thoughts on the Linux operating system.

Quick Internet research reveals that the total percentage of PC users preferring the Linux operating system over Windows OS is only a minor percentage; however, at the enterprise level of IT services, the percentage of Linux OS used is almost equal to Microsoft Windows OS, and the popularity of the Linux system is gaining momentum. If you are a new IT technician entering the IT industry, this is actually important news as more opportunities are offered to those who can tame and master Linux as their preferred OS at the enterprise level.

I have been a network engineer for many years now. I admit I have gotten too cozy with my Windows desktop and server operating systems; I have also been guilty of refusing to open my mind and start learning Linux. This changed as soon as I started teaching myself Python as I was getting frustrated and struggling to do more using Windows OS. After studying Python, I think network automation using Python is easier on Linux OS than Windows OS; hence, if you are serious about making Python your profession, start learning Linux. For network automation using Python, Linux knowledge is a prerequisite, not an option. Learn Python and Linux at the same time based on your substantial networking knowledge and experience.

Managing a Network Adapter on Linux

If you want to change the network settings on your Linux machine, for example, give your CentOS server a static IP address, so the IP address does not change after the DHCP lease expires. You can easily change this setting using the `nmtui` tool. If you forgot to power on the network adapter during Linux installation, you could change the settings using this tool. Quickly run the `sudo nmtui` command from your CentOS. If you are logged in as a `sudo` user, you can omit `sudo` in front of your command.

#	Task
01	You can run the `nmtui` command from the VMware Workstation Console or PuTTY SSH session. Type in `sudo nmtui` and hit the Enter key on your keyboard. See Figure 6-46.

Figure 6-46. *CentOS 8 configuration, sudo nmtui command*

02	When CentOS's NetworkManager TUI appears, select "Edit a connection." See Figure 6-47.

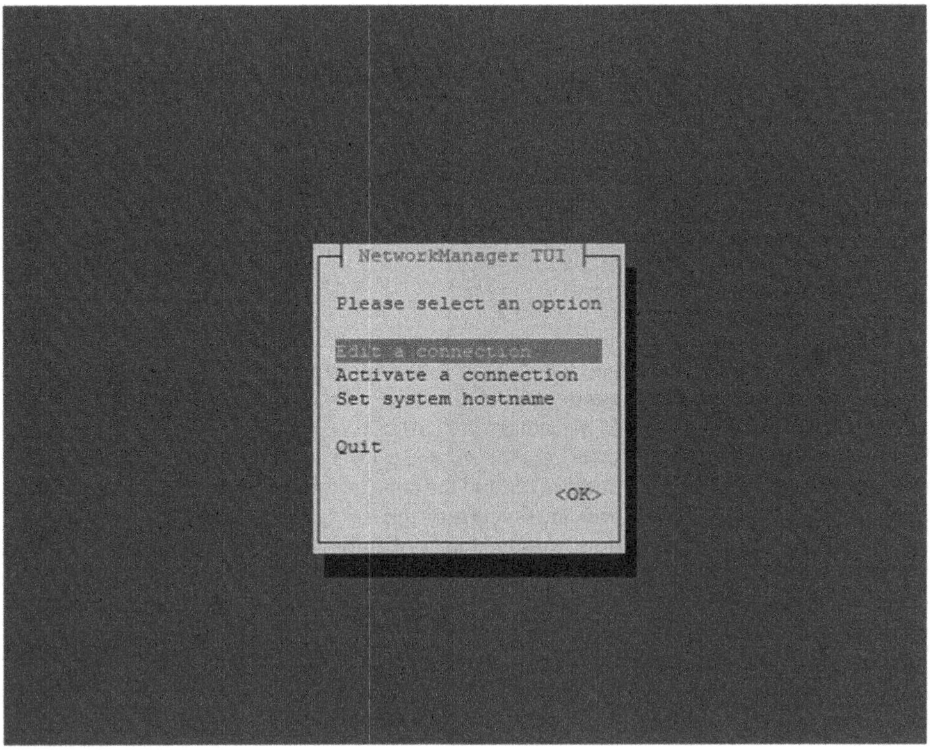

Figure 6-47. *CentOS 8 configuration, NetworkManager TUI*

#	Task
03	Select ens160 and click Edit. See Figure 6-48.

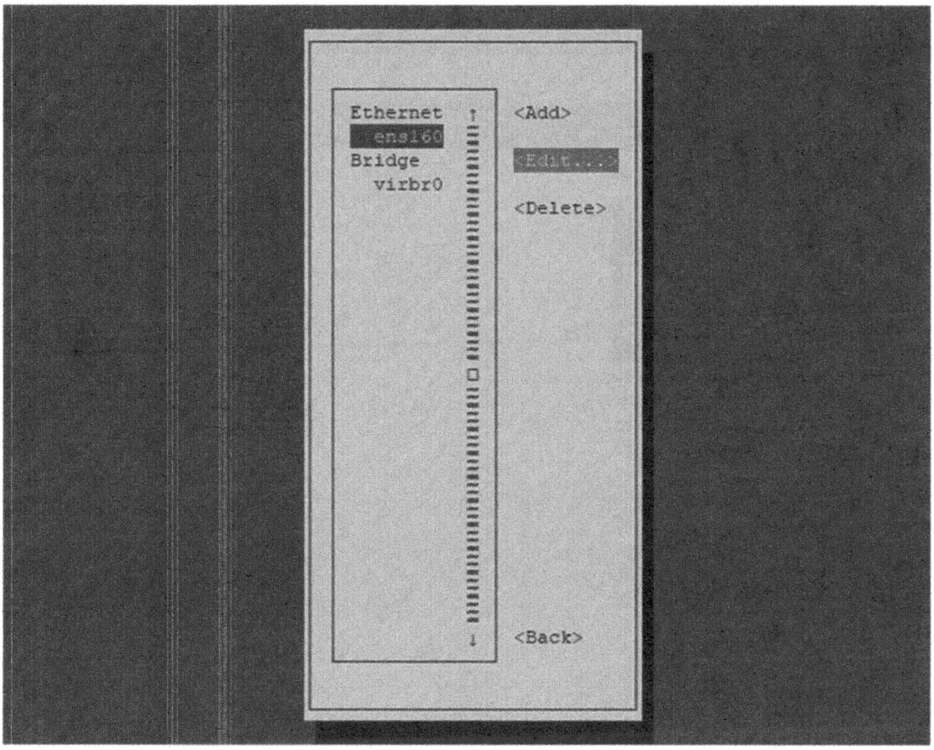

Figure 6-48. *CentOS 8 configuration, selecting a network adapter*

(*continued*)

#	Task
04	Click the Automatic option on the right side of IPv4 Configuration and change it to Manual. Click the Show option on the right. See Figure 6-49.

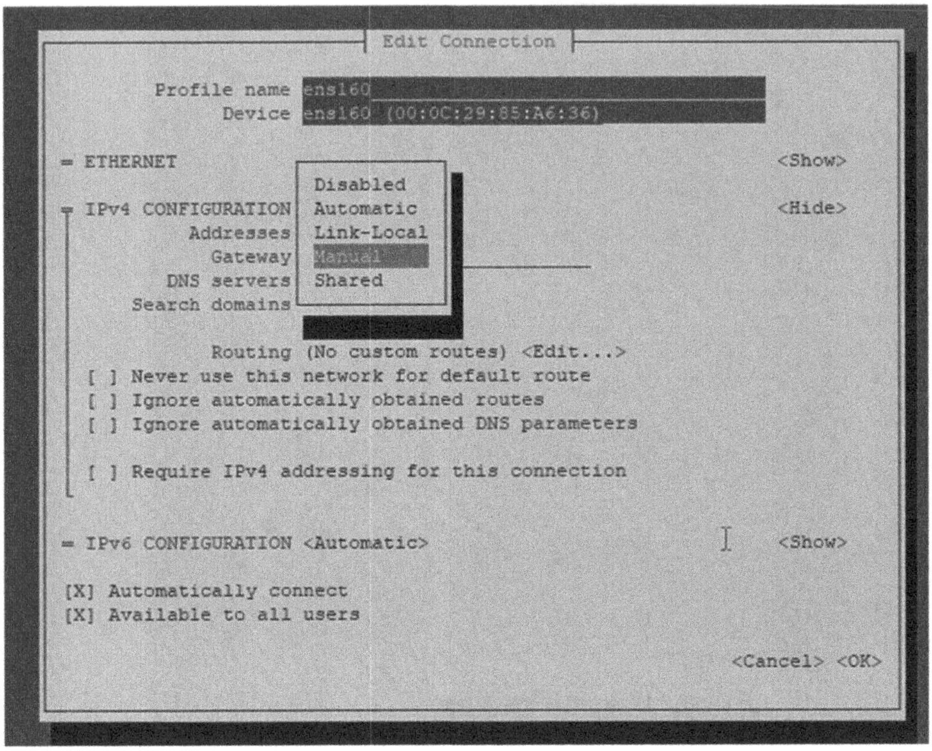

Figure 6-49. *CentOS 8 configuration, selecting a manual configuration*

#	Task
05	Now enter your server IP address and the NAT gateway's IP address. Move down and click OK. See Figure 6-50.

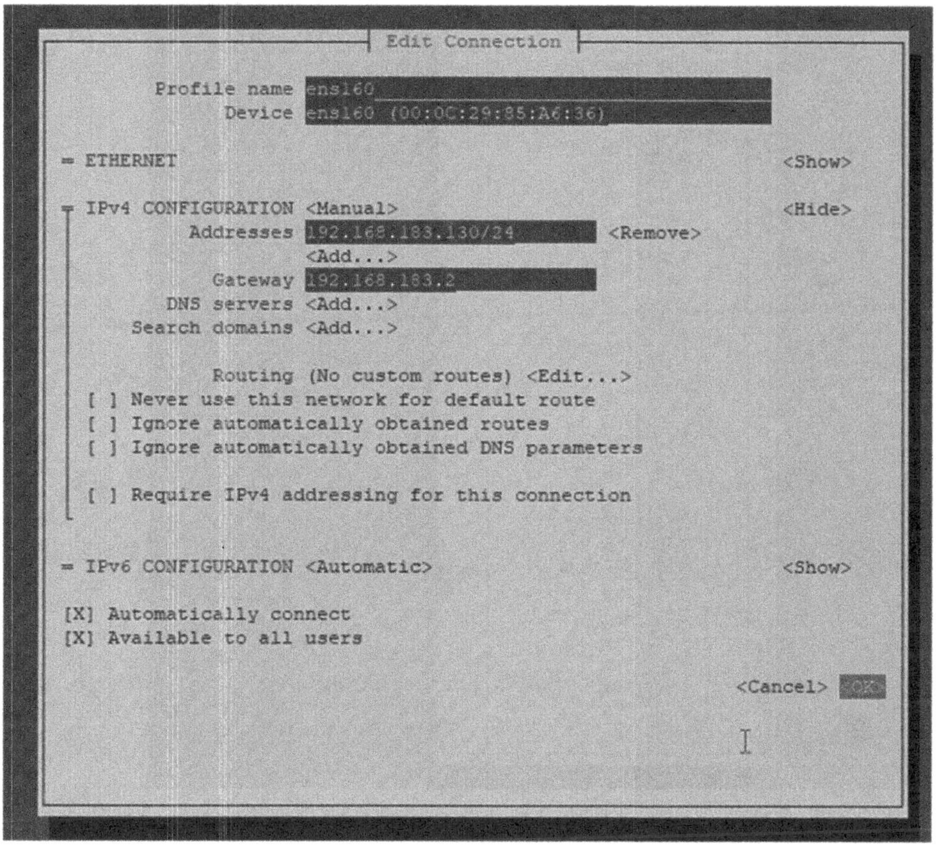

Figure 6-50. *CentOS 8 configuration, saving manual changes*

(*continued*)

#	Task
06	Press the Tab key to move down and select Back to return to the first TUI interface. See Figure 6-51.

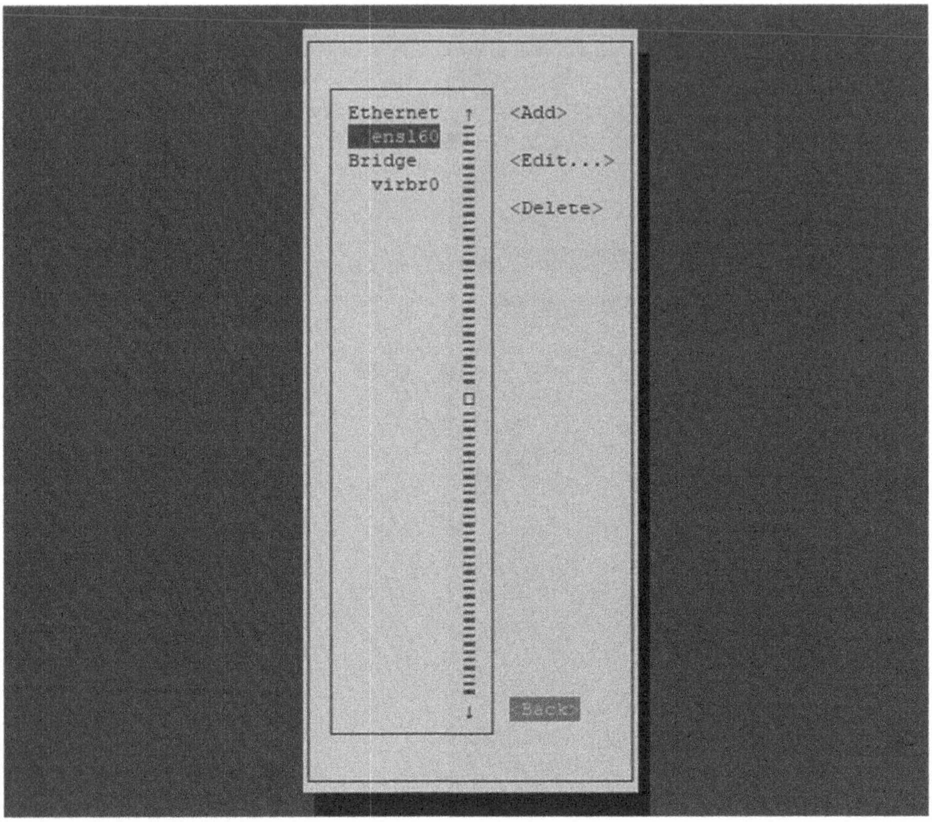

Figure 6-51. *CentOS 8 configuration, Back option*

#	Task
06	Click Quit to save your changes and exit the application. See Figure 6-52.

Figure 6-52. *CentOS 8 configuration, saving and exiting TUI*

At this stage, consider how you are going to use this server in your lab and install any software. Once you are satisfied with the current state of your CentOS 8.1, Linux VM customization takes a snapshot of the VM while running or makes a full clone of powered-off VM files. Taking a snapshot or cloning is the same as in the previous Ubuntu 20 process. Later in this chapter, you will create a third VM from an ova file, which is another way to create your VMs. An ova file is a virtual appliance used by VMware Workstation and Oracle VM VirtualBox. An ova file is a packaged file that contains files used to describe a VM, which includes an ova descriptor file, optional manifest (.MF) and certificate files, and other related files. In other words, an ova file is a predefined VM template that another VM administrator has prepared in advance to deploy a specific server instantly. You will download a GNS3 VM ova file from the GNS3 GitHub site and create a GNS3 VM by importing the file; this is a preparation step for GNS3 installation and integration, which will take place in Chapter 10. So, do not skip the GNS3 VM creation process here.

Creating a GNS3 VM by Importing an .ova File

A GNS3 VM `.ova` file is maintained by community developers at `www.gns3.org` and is used to create a VM that hosts network, security, and system images running on the GNS3 application. This server is a Linux server purposefully built to offload the workload of the physical host of GNS3, so the emulated GNS3 devices run smoothly without affecting the underlying physical host. You will soon find out that the GNS3 VM offers a lot more than running routers and switches. It can also host containerized Linux servers and more. GNS3 and the GNS3 VM are open source and free to everyone. In this book, we are using VMware Workstation on Windows 10, so we need to download the GNS3 VM files that work on Windows. When writing this chapter, the latest GNS3 version was v2.2.8, and this version will be used here, but try to download the latest version of GNS3 files as the newer versions always offer performance improvements, and many of the bugs have been ironed out. Here we will use GNS3 v2.2.8 so that we will download the corresponding `GNS3.VM.VMware.Workstation.2.2.8.zip` file. You will be reminded to download the `GNS3-2.2.8-all-in-one.exe` file again, but you can also download it now to save time.

Downloading and Installing the GNS3 VM from an .ova File

The process for downloading the GNS3 VM file and creating a GNS3 VM is as follows:

#	Task
01	First, go to GNS3's GitHub site specified here to download the GNS3 VM file. Download the latest version of the GNS3 VM file. The latest version is `GNS3.VM.VMware.Workstation.2.2.8.zip` at the time of writing this book. At the time of writing this book, the latest GNS VM release version is 2.2.8. See Figure 6-53. `https://github.com/GNS3/gns3-gui/releases`

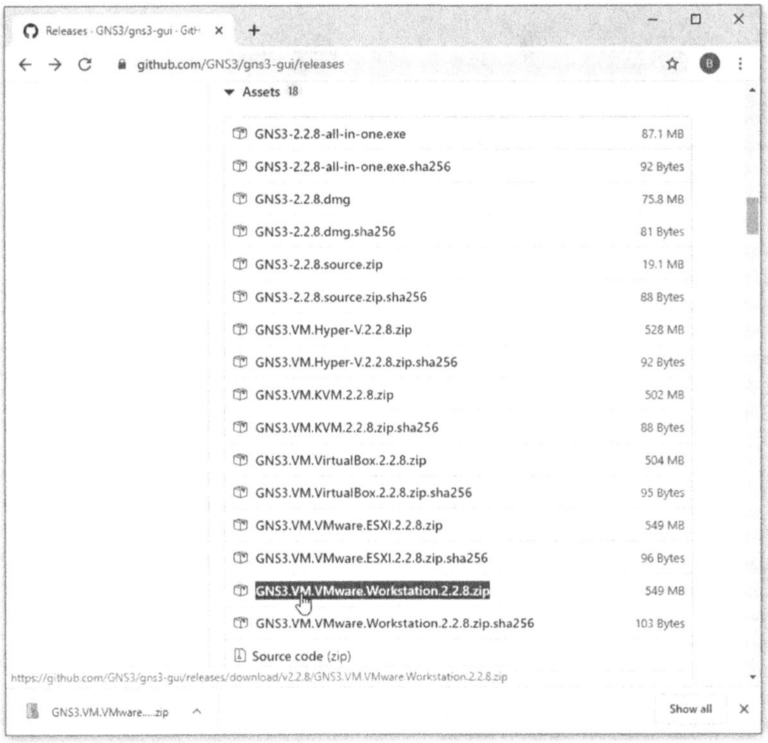

Figure 6-53. *GNS3 and GNS3 VM, downloading the .ova file from GitHub*

#	Task
02	Now go to your `Downloads` folder and unzip the downloaded file in the same location. See Figure 6-54.

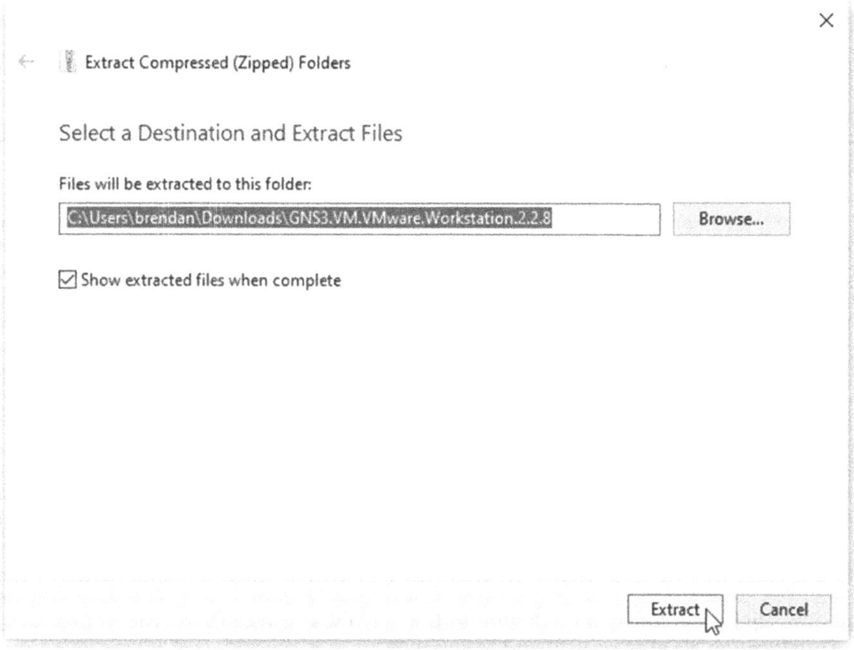

Figure 6-54. *Unzipping the GNS3 VM .ova file to a folder*

#	Task
03	Now go back to your VMware Workstation 15 Pro and select the File ➤ Open menu. See Figure 6-55.

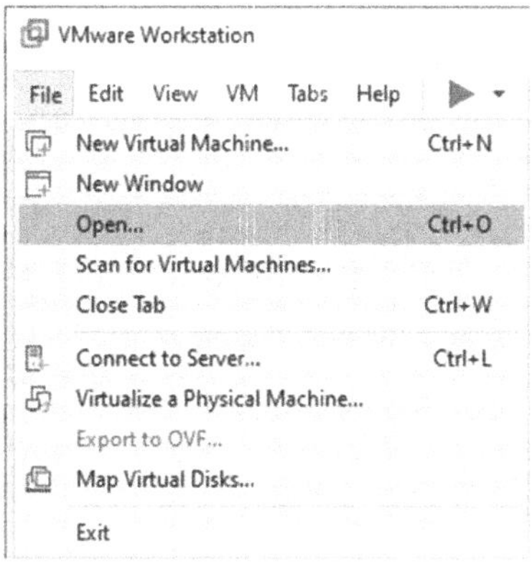

Figure 6-55. *VMware Workstation menu, File ➤ Open*

(continued)

#	Task
04	Locate the extracted GNS3 VM `.ova` file, select the file, and then click Open. See Figure 6-56.

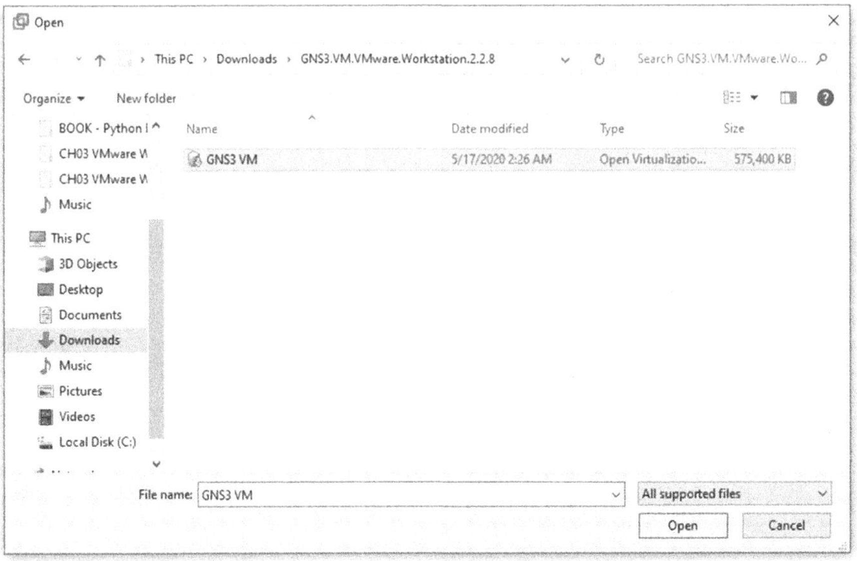

Figure 6-56. *VMware Workstation, GNS3 VM .ova file open*

#	Task
05	In the next window, click the Import button to import the GNS3 VM. You can leave the storage path as the default location. See Figure 6-57 and Figure 6-58.

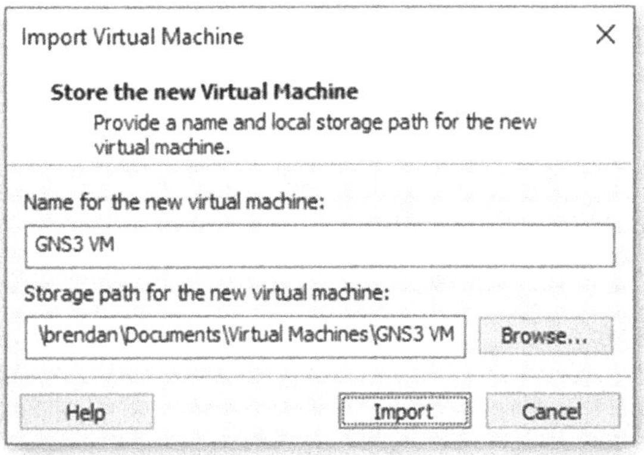

Figure 6-57. *VMware Workstation, GNS3 VM import*

#	Task

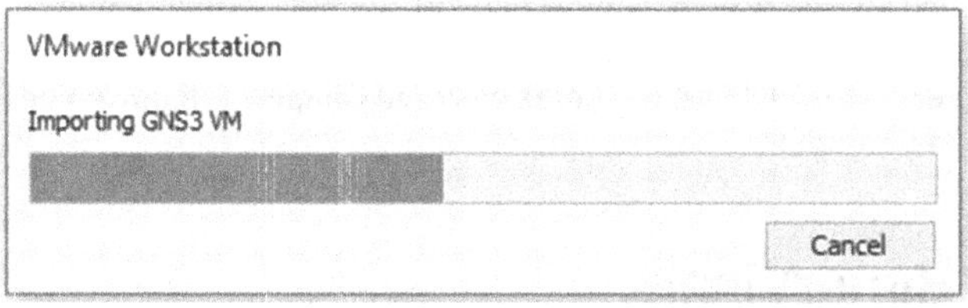

Figure 6-58. *VMware Workstation, GNS3 VM import in progress*

06 Now, GNS3 VM has been created on your VMware Workstation 15 Pro and ready for use. You do not have to do anything with this VM at this stage as GNS3 software installation and integration are required for this VM to become useful. See Figure 6-59.

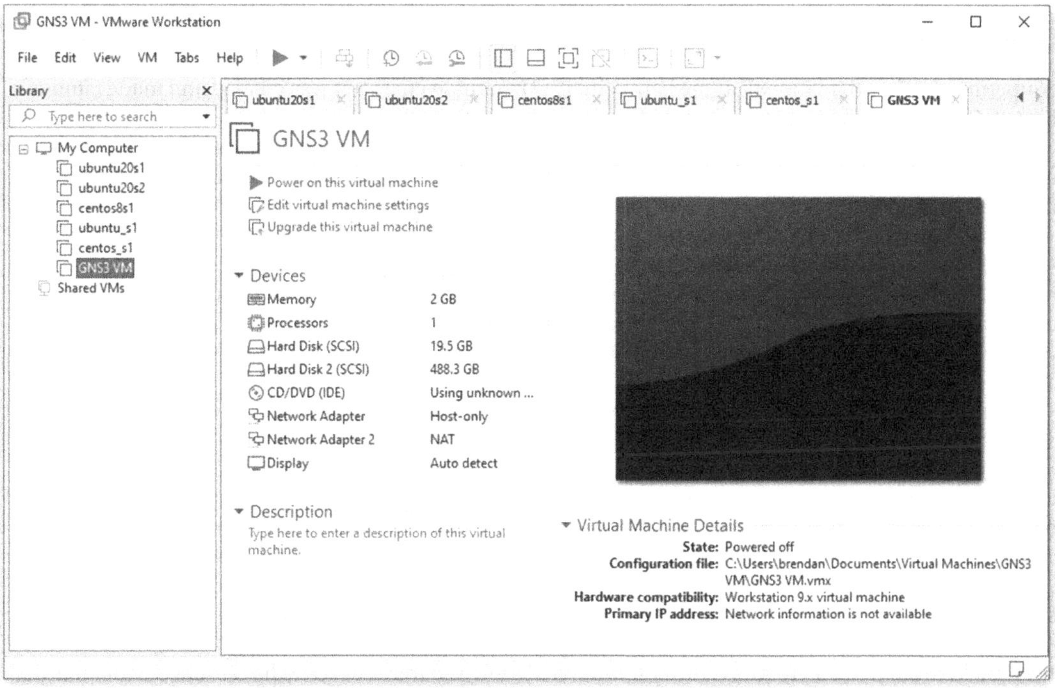

Figure 6-59. *VMware Workstation, GNS3 VM installed*

This completes downloading, importing, and installing the GNS3 VM for GNS3 integration later. Now that we have all the required VMs, we can learn about Linux basics, Python on Linux, GNS3, and Python network automation. Now the learning platform is almost complete.

Summary

You downloaded, installed, and created a CentOS 8 virtual machine in this chapter. You tested the SSH login to the newly created CentOS VM and learned an easy way to manage network adapter settings using the `nmtui` package method. Finally, you added the GNS3 VM in preparation for Cisco IOS integration later. Now you have two different flavors of Linux servers; you will learn the Linux basics in Chapter 7, followed by Linux software installation and administration in Chapter 8.

Storytime 3: The Origin of Hypervisors

Earlier, you studied two different virtualization programs, and they are classified into either a Type-1 or Type-2 hypervisors. The hype around the cloud and cloud computing and on-demand IT concepts has been made because of the rapid development in hardware and software, specifically the virtualization technologies. If you look up the dictionary definition of *hypervisor*, you will soon discover that this word is a compound word made up of two words: *hyper* and *visor*. You can trace the origin to the Greek word *hyper*, meaning above, and the word *visor* is derived from the Old Anglo-French word *visor*, meaning to hide. Wikipedia.com suggests that *hypervisor* is a variant of the word *supervisor*. According to Wikipedia, the word *hypervisor* is the supervisor of supervisors. The word *hyper* carries a stronger synonymic meaning, at least linguistically, than the word *super*.

If you are also interested in DC Comics superhero characters, you know the most powerful character is Superman (although many will argue here). But if a Hyperman character was created and made famous through DC Comics, the Hyperman would be even stronger than Superman.

To understand the concept of virtualization more realistically, think of a hypervisor as the lubricant used in your car engine. A typical combustion engine car has larger components such as an engine and transmission. And inside a larger component, there are many smaller moving parts. Consider the hypervisor as the car engine's lubricant to prevent friction and wear on several smaller parts that reside inside the larger part. VM can run smoothly on its hosting server with very little or no compatibility issues. The hypervisor hides (or fabricates) the real hardware from the VM, thinking it is a real computer, but the VM is a handful of files running on hypervisors. The hypervisor is associated with the word *fabrication* in this sense, and the word *fabrication* means false. VMs think they are running on real hardware based servers, but all hardware are files, so the VMs are bunch of files running on a software.

Some of my clients' environments that I support still use the Cisco 6500/4500 Series of enterprise switches and Cisco 9000 Series switches with supervisor modules inserted into a large-framed switch body. If you are studying CCNA, you probably have heard of these enterprise-level switches. These switches can become a router, a switch, or both based on the OS and feature sets switched on. Some older engineers refer to these devices as SRouters because they can support multiple OSI layers. A supervisor in these devices is a modular hardware version of virtualization technology, running as a separate OS with its CPU and RAMs. Cisco had already begun hardware-based virtualization using various modules even before virtualization technologies took off years ago. For reference, the Nexus 3K/ 5K/6K/7K and Enterprise 9K switches offered on the current networking market support the Python APIs and come with Python 2.7.2 or newer by default. However, like many Cisco products, the Python version built into these switches has several restrictions and is limited to what you can do with it. For more information on these switches, visit Cisco.com (`https://www.cisco.com/c/en/us/products/switches/catalyst-9400-series-switches/index.html`).

CHAPTER 7

Linux Fundamentals

In this chapter, you will learn Linux basics to get you up to speed with the essential Linux administration skills that you will learn in Chapter 8. Since you probably already work in network automation, you do not have to become a full-time Linux administrator. However, you must know what you are doing on these systems so that you do not bring down the critical services running on enterprise Linux systems. Other Python network automation books often forget to mention the importance of general Linux administration skills for network automation purposes. In fact, Linux and Python network automation go hand in hand.

In this chapter, you will learn how to get started with Linux and about directories and the file structure. Then you will learn to use vi and nano for basic file and directory management. By the end of this chapter, you will be able to use the Linux terminal and text editors to manage directories and files.

⚠ There are no pre-installation tasks for this chapter, but this chapter assumes you have read and completed Chapters 1–3. You will be using both the Ubuntu Server 20 LTS and CentOS 8.1 virtual servers installed in the previous chapters. If you have not completed those installations, please go back to the previous chapters and create your virtual machines. You can download additional installation guides from the following GitHub website:

URL: `https://github.com/pynetauto/apress_pynetauto`

In this chapter, you will learn Linux basics using the CentOS 8.1 and Ubuntu Server 20 LTS virtual machines. Figure 7-1 shows the logical lab topology required for this chapter. You will need both Linux servers up and running, connected via the VMnet8 (NAT) network, and your Windows host connected to the Internet. The third octet of your VMnet8 network subnet could be different from the one shown in the figure. If so, you will work within your given subnet, or you can update the VMnet8 subnet from VMware Workstation's Virtual Network Editor so the subnet is also sitting on the 192.168.183.0/24 subnet.

B. Choi, *Introduction to Python Network Automation*, https://doi.org/10.1007/978-1-4842-6806-3_7

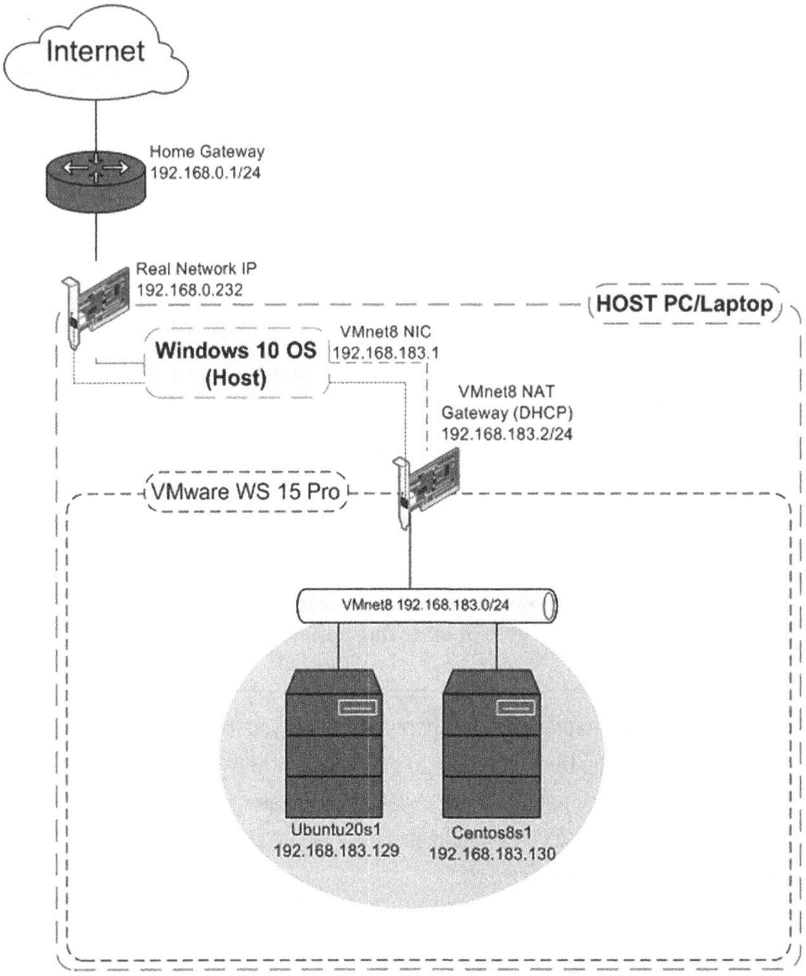

***Figure 7-1.** Logical network topology*

Why Learn Linux?

This chapter is dedicated to learning Linux basics. You will learn about the history of Linux, different types of Linux distributions, basic file and directory management, and how to use the vi/nano text editors for fundamental Linux administration. You might be a content Windows user or asking, "Why should an IT technician learn Linux?" or "Why should anyone learn Linux?" My simple answer to this question is that there is nothing to lose by learning Linux as an IT technician; this includes network, security, systems, and software engineers alike. The current IT industry lacks IT engineers who possess good Linux administration skills, which indicates that there could be significant job opportunities for you if you know both Linux and Windows administration.

To be direct, from a Microsoft Windows user's perspective, it is a rocky road ahead trying to tame and master the Linux operating system (OS) and make a smooth transition to Linux. The thought of losing Windows or the graphical user interface (GUI) is a big deal for many people. If you are already savvy with Linux, that is fantastic; you got a head-start and a well-deserved one indeed. Almost 20 years ago, when I got my first IT support job, I met a mentor, and he suggested that I take more interest in Linux and then pursue a career as a Linux administrator. Back then, I was more interested in Cisco networks, unified communications, and Windows, so I did not find a convincing reason to take up Linux seriously. It wasn't until 2015 that I began taking an interest in Python coding. I realized how sorry I was for not taking my old mentor's advice to study Linux. A lot of IT engineers, especially network engineers, make this same mistake in our industry. I am sharing my story with other Windows users now so they keep their minds open to Linux. Do not miss out on this opportunity.

At least at the enterprise (business) level, a high percentage of application servers are running on some sort of Linux-based operating system. It could be Amazon Web Services (AWS) or Facebook or Google in the cloud; an application server requires a secure and reliable operating system to run day in, day out. In the past 15 years, the usage of Linux servers has dramatically increased at the same rate as the cloud, and Big Data businesses have gained momentum. Over the years, more and more enterprise systems have migrated to Linux from Windows in enterprise IT and data center environments. There are many reasons behind this trend, but to name a few, Linux offers more performance for the buck; it has better reliability, security, scalability, and high availability with flexibility that is not seen in the Windows server environment. Linux is now the new norm for how we live our lives. In 2020, Microsoft released a Windows 10 patch that has built-in Linux kernel support and supports Windows Subsystem for Linux (WSL). So, now you can even run a Linux VM on Windows.

Visit the Microsoft Windows documentation site to read more about WSL.

URL: `https://docs.microsoft.com/en-us/windows/wsl/install-win10`

If you have been in enterprise networking industry for some time, you will be most familiar with Cisco technologies. Just looking at Cisco as an example, about 20 years ago, most of Cisco's network, security, and voice services applications were based on Windows 2000 and 2003. An excellent example of this is Cisco's IP PABX servers, known as Cisco CallManager (version 3 and 4.1), which were built on Windows 2000 servers. Other examples include the old UCCX, UCCE, and CiscoWorks servers; they all used Windows servers as their base platforms. However, in 2010, Cisco decided to ditch Windows servers and go with the appliance model; it migrated many of its application servers to a Red Hat–based Linux operating system (OS). Cisco's decision to drop Windows servers and replace them with Linux was in line with the IT trend even before 2010. In addition, an adaptation of the Linux OS can be found in Juniper's core operating system, such as Junos and Palo Alto's PAN products; they both use Linux as their base operating systems.

As mentioned earlier, some benefits of Linux over Windows include stability, high security, and lower ownership cost. Linux is an effective enterprise operating system that all IT engineers must learn and apply to their work. Not all of us indeed want to make a living as Linux system administrators, but we have to know enough to keep our jobs as IT technicians. In this book, you want to learn enough Linux fundamentals to be comfortable performing the basic lab tasks. If you're going to study Linux professionally to become a Linux system administrator, you can study Red Hat 8 certification systematically. In this book, we will learn selective Linux materials to get started with Python networking automation.

To get to know a technology, it is always good to start with a little history, or where it all began. Let's get started with some Linux history, learn the different types of Linux distributions available to us, study Linux file and directory structures, and master both the vi and nano text editors to do things without the aid of a graphical user interface (GUI). But just in case you may need a GUI for some reason, we already have the optional GUI-based Linux desktop on our servers. You are expected to perform some basic administration on both Ubuntu and CentOS Linux servers at the end of this chapter.

The Beginning of Linux

To understand Linux, let's quickly examine the early history of Linux and then review what kinds of Linux distributions are most popular today. For your reference, the timeline in Table 7-1 shows only the initial development highlights until 1991, when the first Linux distribution was released. If you would like to find other timelines, please refer to `https://en.wikipedia.org/wiki/Linux`.

Table 7-1. *Early Linux Development Timeline*

Year	Linux Development Highlights
1969	First developed UNIX at AT&T Labs, with Ken Thompson, Dennis Ritchie, Douglas Mcilroy, and Joe Ossanna.
1971	Unix was first written in assembly language.
1973	Dennis Richie first wrote UNIX using the C language.
1983	Richard Stallman introduced the GNU Project.
1984	Complete UNIX-compatible software system. Free software development begins.
1985	Richard Stallman establishes the Free Software Foundation.
1989	General Public License (GNU) is introduced.
1990	Many programs are developed for the operating system.
August 25, 1991	Linus Benedict Torvalds, then a 21-year-old Finnish student, publicly announces the free version of the Linux kernel. The 1991 Linux kernel is released under the GNU GPL license.

Source: *`https://en.wikipedia.org/wiki/Linux`*

As you can see from Table 7-1, Linux has its roots in UNIX. We can guess that Linux syntax and operations will be similar to UNIX. Since Linus Torvalds released the free Linux kernel in 1991, many Linux distributions have been developed and distributed under GNU. Some Linux types are commercially driven for business use, and some are created for community or personal use. Most Linux distributions can run business applications, but some also offer great desktop versions such as Ubuntu desktop.

Table 7-2 lists the ten most popular Linux distributions since 2017 and some characteristics of each Linux type. If you need a Linux OS in your enterprise infrastructure, the most recommended Linux system is Red Hat Enterprise Server. If you have to use it for work and study, Ubuntu, CentOS, and Debian are incredibly flexible and user-friendly Linux distributions. Out of these three very popular Linux distributions, Ubuntu has the most user-friendly features, has a great GUI if required, and is an excellent choice for beginners. Note that Ubuntu is a Debian derivative. CentOS uses the same Linux kernels and software as Red Hat and Fedora. The three Linux mentioned here, Red Hat, CentOS, and Fedora, are the same Linux distros with a minor aesthetical difference. Fedora is a development version of Red Hat. Red Hat is the enterprise-level commercialized Linux for large enterprises, and CentOS is the open source version of Red Hat. Fedora offers the latest beta software but lacks the stability of CentOS and Red Hat Linux. Hence, when learning Linux, any version of the CentOS server or CentOS Stream should be your preferred Linux distribution for Red Hat-derived Linux versions. The main difference between the open source versus commercial versions of Linux is whether you will get full technical support from a vendor support team or get best-effort support from a Linux developer community. Now quickly review Table 7-2 and find the Linux distribution you want to use. Most of the Linux software is free for personal use with no commercial restrictions.

Table 7-2. Top 10 Linux Server Distributions for 2017

Rank	Linux Distro	OS Derivative	User Skill Level	Advantages
1	Ubuntu Server	Debian-based	Intermediate	Performance, stable, flexibility, DC support, secure
2	Red Hat Enterprise Linux (RHEL)	Fedora-based	Advanced	Vendor support, performance, secure, cloud and IoT support, data and virtualization support
3	SUSE Linux Enterprise Server	RPM-based	Intermediate	Open source, stable, secure, cloud service support
4	CentOS	RHEL-based	Intermediate	Free community support; same as RHEL without the logo
5	Debian	Debian-based	Intermediate to advanced	Free, open source, stable, educational, commercial, government and NGO can use
6	Oracle Linux (Oracle Enterprise Linux)	RHEL-based	Advanced	Free, open source, off-cloud, SMB and enterprise use, cloud and data center support
7	Mageia	Mandriva-based	Intermediate	Free, stable, secure, community support, range of software, MariaDB support
8	ClearOS	RHEL/CentOS-based	Intermediate to Advanced	Open source, SMB support, commercial use, network gateway and server support, web server support
9	Arch Linux	Other	Advanced	Open source, simplicity, optimized performance, stable, flexibility
10	Slackware Linux	Slackware-based	Advanced	Free, open source, closest UNIX system, simplicity, stable

Source: `https://www.tecmint.com/10-best-linux-server-distributions/`

Understanding the Linux Environment

Linux is an operating system (OS) installed on a physical or virtual machine for personal or commercial use. The significant difference between Linux Desktop and Linux Server is the graphical user interface. Linux servers are usually installed to provide a specific service to users or business and usually managed by Linux administrators, who are well versed in Linux commands. Linux usually gets installed with the minimum software for better performance, stability, and higher security. This difference aside, the Linux desktop and server versions use the same base kernel for each release version of a Linux OS. As shown in the previous chapters, you can optionally install the GUI on Linux servers. Earlier in this book, you installed a desktop on a Linux server for learning and convenience. As you get familiar with Linux and its command line, you will slowly move away from the GUI and will be able to run all of the basic Linux administration tasks using the command line only. As you will discover, in Linux, everything is made up of files and directories; it is a free and very flexible operating system. Once again, if you are used to administrating Cisco devices through a command-line interface (CLI), then you will feel right at home. Even you do not have a Cisco networking background or have zero Linux experience, you will be able to follow along; we will only cover the very basics of Linux so you can run the labs to reach the end of your first Python network automation journey.

Understanding Linux Directories and File Formats

Earlier, we briefly looked at the Linux development timeline and learned about popular Linux distribution types. Next, let's take a quick look at the Linux directory structure. In Linux, everything is written in text and saved in various directories. Since the Windows operating system can also trace its roots to *nix, the Windows file and folder structure is similar. But Linux does not have a `C:` drive like Windows; instead, it has the root folder, or `/`. Figure 7-2 depicts a general Linux directory structure and what kinds of files usually reside in each directory. Of course, you can create your custom directories and files just like in Windows OS. Review the figure and use it as a point of reference if you forget the purpose of each directory. You don't have to memorize it all at this stage, but take a look and see if you can find anything interesting.

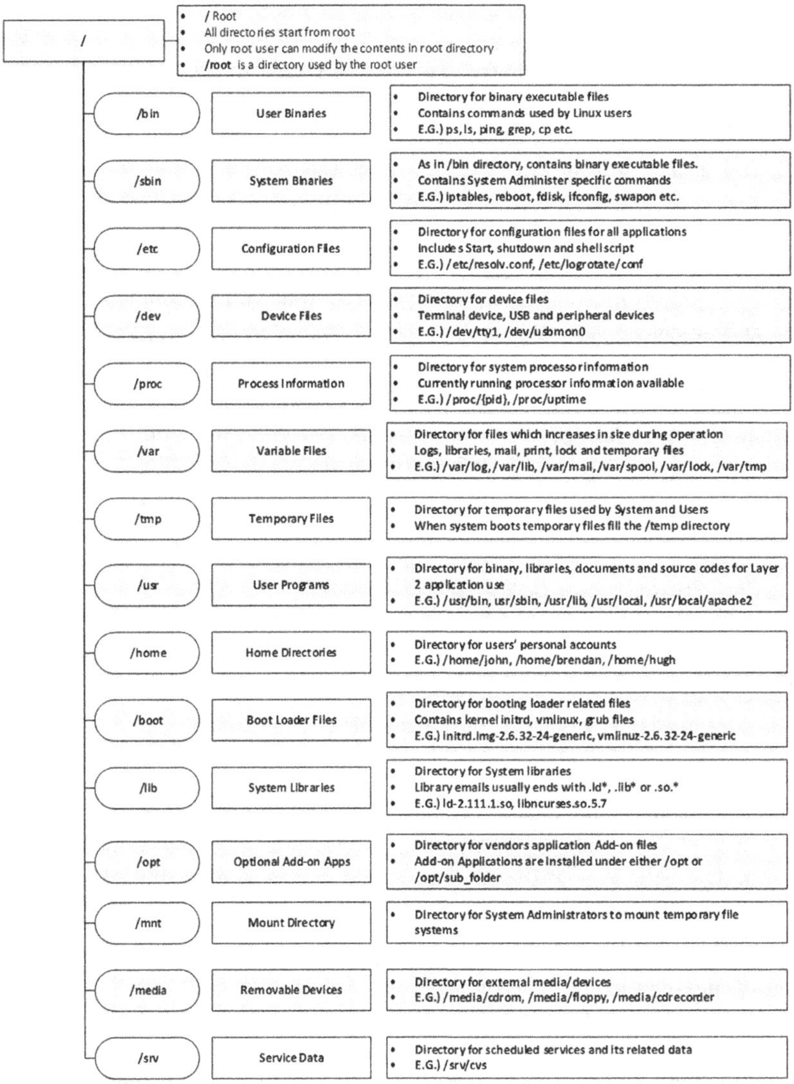

Figure 7-2. *Typical Linux directory and file structure*

Figure 7-2 shows a typical Linux directory structure. Different Linux types will have slightly different directory and file structures but are generally identical to one another.

Figure 7-3 shows the CentOS 8 server's root directory. Carefully look and compare the listed directories; you will see the similarities to Figure 7-2.

```
[root@localhost ~]# cd /
[root@localhost /]# pwd
/
[root@localhost /]# ls -l
total 24
lrwxrwxrwx.   1 root root    7 May 10  2019      -> usr/bin
dr-xr-xr-x.   6 root root 4096 Apr 26 07:58 boot
drwxr-xr-x.  20 root root 3260 May 25 10:05 dev
drwxr-xr-x. 150 root root 8192 May 25 10:05 etc
drwxr-xr-x.   3 root root   23 Apr 26 08:02 home
lrwxrwxrwx.   1 root root    7 May 10  2019      -> usr/lib
lrwxrwxrwx.   1 root root    9 May 10  2019        -> usr/lib64
drwxr-xr-x.   2 root root    6 May 10  2019 media
drwxr-xr-x.   3 root root   18 Apr 26 07:52 mnt
drwxr-xr-x.   2 root root    6 May 10  2019 opt
dr-xr-xr-x. 331 root root    0 May 25 10:05 proc
dr-xr-x---.   5 root root  242 May 25 05:49 root
drwxr-xr-x.  45 root root 1300 May 28 07:07 run
lrwxrwxrwx.   1 root root    8 May 10  2019       -> usr/sbin
drwxr-xr-x.   2 root root    6 May 10  2019 srv
dr-xr-xr-x.  13 root root    0 May 25 10:05 sys
drwxrwxrwt.  20 root root 4096 May 28 07:06 tmp
drwxr-xr-x.  12 root root  144 Apr 26 07:48 usr
drwxr-xr-x.  23 root root 4096 Apr 26 07:58 var
[root@localhost /]# 
```

***Figure 7-3.** CentOS 8 Linux directory example*

vi vs. nano

You've briefly learned about the typical Linux directory and file structures. Now let's think about Linux file and directory management. Readers who already have good Linux knowledge will ask, "Why do you teach how to use the vi text editor here?" If you are an experienced Linux user, you can skip most of this chapter, but make sure you read Chapter 8 to install the various IP services on the CentOS 8.1 server before moving on to Chapter 9. If you have little exposure to Linux, you must learn vi (visual editor) and nano before jumping to the next chapter. You need to get comfortable with a Linux text editor and perform most of the tasks through the terminal console or command lines. On Linux servers, pretty much everything is made up of text files, and you are expected to use the terminal console to manage your day-to-day tasks. In other words, you have to become familiar with the Linux file structure, file, and directory management through the command line. Usually, when you perform a task on Linux servers, your intention must be clear, and you exactly know what you want to achieve from your actions. Learning to use Linux's text editors is essential to learning Python, as script-based coding will involve many hours in your favorite text editor.

Of course, there are various text editors for Linux, but the standard text editor on most of the modern Linux systems is vi. Learning how to use it is not optional but mandatory to become good at Linux. Yes, vi lacks user controls on a black background and may be awkward for first-time Linux users. Let's learn how to use the vi editor once and for all so you don't have to worry about learning this dreadful text editor again (initially dreadful anyway).

In this chapter, you are encouraged to explore file and directory management using vi and a secondary text editor called nano. This is another Linux text editor that is best suited for beginners because it uses pseudo-graphic layouts. Unlike vi, it is not pre-installed on all Linux distributions, but it is good to know both. As stated, learning how to use vi is not optional. It might be the only text available to you while managing your enterprise servers and networking devices in the client's production environment.

First, let's learn how to use the vi text editor, which will become the primary Linux text editor of your choice, and then you'll learn how to use the nano text editor as the second text editor of your choice.

Introduction to vi

We can say that vi in Linux has its roots in vi in UNIX. vi in Linux is almost identical to vi in the UNIX operating system, so it is clear where Linux OS and its applications have their origins. First, vi ("visual editor") uses two modes to prevent unintentional edits by keeping the command and insert modes separate. There are two modes of operation in vi.

- *Command mode*: This is the starting point when a file is first opened. In this mode, every character typed is a command to change the text file being opened.
- *Insert mode*: This is editing mode. In this mode, every character typed is added to the text in the file; pressing the Esc key turns off Insert mode and gets you back to Command mode.

Second, in Command mode, vi has many useful commands, but you are going to need only a handful of commands to get you started. Table 7-3 contains basic but the most useful vi commands. With some practice, your fingers will remember these commands before your brain can.

Table 7-3. *vi Text Editor Basic Commands*

Vi Commands		Description
BASIC	`vi`	Open the vi text editor
	`i`	Enter Insert mode
	Esc	Exit Insert mode
	`:x`	Quit vi without saving changes
	`:q` or `:q!`	Quit or quit forcefully
	`:w`	Write
	`:wq` or `:wq!`	Save and quit

(*continued*)

Table 7-3. (*continued*)

Vi Commands		Description
MOVE	`j`	Move cursor down one line
	8 key	
	$ key	
	`k`	Move cursor up one line
	# key	
	`h`	Move cursor left one character
	Backspace key	
	! key	
	`l` (lowercase L)	Move cursor right one character
	Spacebar	
	" key	
	0 (zero)	Move the cursor to the start of the current line (cursor line)
	`$`	Move the cursor to the end of the current line
	`w`	Move the cursor to the beginning of the next word
	`b`	Move the the cursor back to the beginning of the preceding word
	`:0`	Move the the cursor to the first line in the file
	`:n`	Move the cursor to line n
	`:$`	Move the cursor to the last line in the file
COPY/ PASTE	`dd`	Copy (cut)
	`p`	Paste under the cursor
	`P`	Paste on top of the cursor
UNDO	`u`	Undo the last change, a simple toggle
SEARCH TEXT	`/string`	Search forward for the occurrence of a string in text
	`?string`	Search backward for the occurrence of a string in text
	`n`	Move to the next occurrence of the search string
	`N`	Move to the next occurrence of the search string in the opposite direction

If you have browsed through Table 7-3 about five times and memorized some of vi's key commands, you can now open VMware Workstation and SSH into either Ubuntu or the CentOS server to prepare for the first exercise in this chapter (Figure 7-4). In the real production environment, system administrators usually remotely connect to Linux servers and networking devices using SSH clients such as Putty, Tera Term, or SecureCRT. It does not matter which Linux server you prefer to use. Although we are working on a single computer, think of your server as a remote Linux server and your host's Windows OS as the remote client. Let's practice some essential vi and Linux commands.

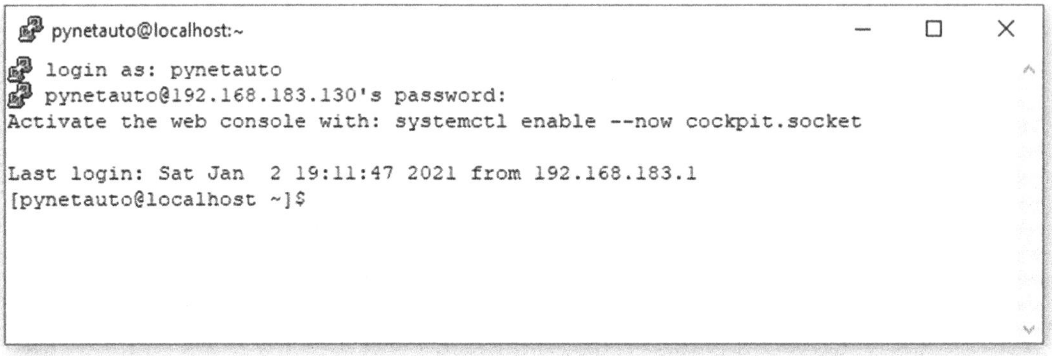
pynetauto@localhost:~
login as: pynetauto
pynetauto@192.168.183.130's password:
Activate the web console with: systemctl enable --now cockpit.socket
Last login: Sat Jan 2 19:11:47 2021 from 192.168.183.1
[pynetauto@localhost ~]$

Figure 7-4. *Logging in to CentOS 8.1 via SSH using PuTTY*

Basics of vi

For some people, learning how to use vi could be the first hurdle to Linux, but for others, vi is just another tool they have to acquire so they proudly can hang it on their belt. As you practice, you will get familiar with vi and a step closer to developing good Linux administration skills.

After typing in each Linux command, you have to press the Enter key on your keyboard. In some parts of the exercises where you have to press the Enter key, you may see the left arrow (↵) symbol.

Here's an example: `:wq` (↵).

The previous example means after you type in `:wq`, you have to press the Enter key.

For the following exercise, the user is logged into the CentOS 8.1 server with the username pynetauto via an SSH connection.

① Check the present working directory (pwd), make a working directory (mkdir) called ex_vi, list (ls) files and directories in the current working folder, and change the directory (cd) to the ex_vi directory. Finally, check the present working directory (pwd) again.

Objective: Learn how to check, create, and navigate to a new directory.

```
---------------------------------------------------------------------
[pynetauto@localhost ~]$ pwd
/home/pynetauto
[pynetauto@ localhost ~]$ ls
Desktop  Documents  Downloads  Music  Pictures  Public  Templates  Videos
[pynetauto@ localhost ~]$ mkdir ex_vi
[pynetauto@ localhost ~]$ ls
Desktop    Downloads  Music     Public     Videos
Documents  ex_vi      Pictures  Templates
[pynetauto@ localhost ~]$ cd ex_vi
[pynetauto@ localhost ex_vi]$ pwd
/home/pynetauto/ex_vi
---------------------------------------------------------------------
```

② As soon as the text file opens in vi, you will notice that this is a proper minimalistic text editor. The most exciting thing about vi is the information shown at the base of the application about the filename and line number. Try to type something on the keyboard; you cannot type anything in Command mode. Go to the next exercise to add data (text) to this file.

You may create a new file by typing vi filename and then pressing the Enter key.

Objective: Learn how to create/open a file.

```
---------------------------------------------------------------------
[pynetauto@localhost ex_vi]$ vi myfile01.txt
---------------------------------------------------------------------
```

When the new file opens, you will see blank lines, each line with a tilde (~) and a line at the bottom with the filename and status of the new file.

```
---------------------------------------------------------------------
~

~

~

"myfile01.txt" [New File]                         0,0-1         All
---------------------------------------------------------------------
```

③ If you want to enter text to your text file, you must first enter Insert mode. First, press the I key on your keyboard to enter `-- INSERT --` mode. If you see `--INSERT--` in the lower-left corner, vi is now ready for your input.

Objective: Learn how to get into Insert mode in vi.

Press the I key on your keyboard.

```
-------------------------------------------------------------------
~
~
~
-- INSERT --                                   0,1          All
-------------------------------------------------------------------
```

④ Now type some text into this file and press the Esc key on your keyboard to exit Insert mode and move back into Command mode. As soon as you press the Esc key, look at the lower-left corner. `-- INSERT --` disappears from the screen, and you are in Ex mode. Now enter `:wq` or `:wq!` and press the Enter ↵ key to save the changes and exit vi.

Objective: Learn how to write, save, and exit a file in vi by pressing `:wq` ↵.

```
Python lives in the jungle.
Also, python lives on my computer.
Have a Pythonic day!
~
:wq ↵
```

⑤ Like the previous example, after making changes to your file, you usually want to save the modified file while exiting vi. Another way to exit vi is by typing `:x` in Command mode.

Objective: Learn another way to save and exit a file in vi.

```
Python lives in the jungle.
Also, python lives on my computer.
Have a Pythonic day!
~
:x ↵
```

⑥ Once you have exited vi and are back in the Linux terminal console, issue `ls` (`list`) and then `cat myfile01.txt` to verify the changes.

Objective: Learn to list (`ls`) files under the current directory and view the file content in vi.

```
[pynetauto@localhost ex_vi]$ ls
myfile01.txt
[pynetauto@localhost ex_vi]$ cat myfile01.txt
Python lives in the jungle.
Also, python lives on my computer.
Have a Pythonic day!
```

⑦ Now you will be introduced to a few new Linux commands here to perform the following tasks. You will learn how to log in as a sudo user, check the current working directory, find your text file, copy the file to the root directory, and then return to normal user mode. You have just seen a glimpse of what will follow in this chapter.

Objective: Learn to log in as the root user, check that a file exists, search for the file, and copy a file to the root user folder.

```
[pynetauto@localhost ex_vi]$ pwd
/home/pynetauto/ex_vi
[pynetauto@localhost ex_vi]$ su -
Password: **********
[root@localhost ~]# pwd
/root
[root@localhost ~]# ls myfile*
ls: cannot access 'myfile*': No such file or directory
[root@localhost ~]# find / -name myfile*
/home/pynetauto/ex_vi/myfile01.txt
[root@localhost ~]# cp /home/pynetauto/ex_vi/myfile01.txt ~/
[root@localhost ~]# ls myfile*
myfile01.txt
[root@localhost ~]# find / -name myfile*
/root/myfile01.txt
/home/pynetauto/ex_vi/myfile01.txt
```

Reopening a File in vi

Here you will practice reopening and closing a file in vi.

① If you are continuing from the previous exercise, you should still be in root user mode. Now let's go back to user mode using `su - username`. Check the current working directory and then move to the original ex_vi directory.

Replace the username with your own. Now you should be back to the user's home directory and in the ex_vi directory.

Objective: Learn to log back in as a standard user.

```
[root@localhost ~]# su - pynetauto
[pynetauto@localhost ~]$ pwd
/home/pynetauto
[pynetauto@localhost ~]$ ls
Desktop    Downloads  Music     Public     Videos
Documents  ex_vi      Pictures  Templates
[pynetauto@localhost ~]$ cd ex_vi
[pynetauto@localhost ex_vi]$ pwd
/home/pynetauto/ex_vi
```

② To reopen an existing file, simply type in vi followed by the filename. If you opened a file by mistake and did not want to make any changes, simply type in :q and hit the Enter key.

Objective: Learn to reopen existing file and exit (quit) without modifying the file from vi.

```
[pynetauto@localhost ex_vi]$ ls
myfile01.txt
[pynetauto@localhost ex_vi]$ vi myfile01.txt
```

```
Python lives in the jungle.
Also, python lives on my computer.
Have a Pythonic day!
~
:q ↵
```

③ If you opened the file, entered into Insert mode, and started editing the file but decided to quit without saving your changes, you can use :q!. In this example, "Goodbye." was added to the fourth line, but we want to discard it and exit without saving the change.

Objective: Learn to quit after modifying the file.

```
Python lives in the jungle.
Also, python lives on my computer.
Have a Pythonic day!
Goodbye.
~
:q! ↵
```

If you modified the file and only use :q and press Enter, vi will ask you to add ! after :q.

```
Python lives in the jungle.
Also, python lives on my computer.
Have a Pythonic day!
Goodbye.
~
E37: No write since last change (add ! to override)
4,8           All
```

④ To view a file's content without opening it in vi, you can use the cat, more, and less commands. Try all three commands, but you can exit by using Ctrl+Z keys when you use the less command.

Objective: Learn to view file content using the cat, more, and less commands.

```
[pynetauto@localhost ex_vi]$ cat myfile01.txt
Python lives in the jungle.
Also, python lives on my computer.
Have a Pythonic day!
[pynetauto@localhost ex_vi]$ more myfile01.txt
Python lives in the jungle.
Also, python lives on my computer.
Have a Pythonic day!
[pynetauto@localhost ex_vi]$ less myfile01.txt
```

```
[2]+  Stopped                 less myfile01.txt
```

Copying and Pasting a Line in vi

You can use dd to copy a line in vi and use the P key to paste a line below the cursor position. Or use the P key to paste a line above the cursor position. You can easily remember this operation. Try to use the P key to paste below the cursor position and use the P key to paste above the cursor position.

① Open myfile01.txt in vi again. Move the cursor to the third line as you are going to cut the third line.

Objective: Move the cursor in vi Command mode.

```
Python lives in the jungle.
Also, python lives on my computer.
|Have a Pythonic day!                                      # cursor line
~
"myfile01.txt" 3L, 84C                                    3,1         All
```

② Press the D key twice in a row. This operation will cut the line where the cursor was positioned.

Objective: Cut strings on the active line using dd.

```
dd
Python lives in the jungle.
|Also, python lives on my computer.                        # cursor line
~
~
"myfile01.txt" 3L, 84C                                    3,1         All
```

③ Now press the P key to paste "Have a Pythonic day!" before "Also, python lives on my computer." You have successfully swapped the second and third lines.

Objective: Paste the copied line to the line above the cursor position.

```
P
Python lives in the jungle.
|Have a Pythonic day!                                      # cursor line
Also, python lives on my computer.
~
"myfile01.txt" 3L, 84C                                    2,1         All
```

④ Now you want to add the same sentence in the fourth line. Move the cursor to the third line position.

Objective: Move the cursor down.

```
Python lives in the jungle.
Have a Pythonic day!                                       # cursor line
|Also, python lives on my computer.
~
"myfile01.txt" 3L, 84C                                    3,1         All
```

⑤ This time press the P key to paste "This is my file 01." above the first line.

Objective: Paste the copied line to the line below the cursor position.

```
p
Python lives in the jungle.
Have a Pythonic day!
Also, python lives on my computer.
|Have a Pythonic day!                                      # cursor line
~
4,1         All
```

⑥ Now press the Esc key once and then use :wq to save the changes and exit vi.

Objective: Save changes and exit vi.

```
:wq ↵
Python lives in the jungle.
Have a Pythonic day!
Also, python lives on my computer.
Have a Pythonic day!
~
:wq ↵
```

Undo Last in vi

If you make a mistake, you can undo the last action using :u in Command mode.

① :u (undo) is one of the essential commands as it allows you to undo your last action. In vi, this acts as a toggle, undoing and redoing your most recent action. First, reopen myfile01.txt and type something in line 5 while you are in -INSERT-- mode, as shown here.

Objective: Learn to undo the last action in vi.

```
Python lives in the jungle.
Have a Pythonic day!
Also, python lives on my computer.
Have a Pythonic day!
You can do it!|                                    # cursor line
~
-- INSERT --                                                 All
```

Press the Esc key to exit Insert mode and move back to Command mode. Type in :u and press the Enter key on your keyboard to undo your last action.

```
Python lives in the jungle.
Have a Pythonic day!
Also, python lives on my computer.
Have a Pythonic day!
You can do it!
~
:u ↵
```

As soon as you hit the Enter key, the fifth line you have just added will be removed (undone).

```
Python lives in the jungle.
Have a Pythonic day!
Also, python lives on my computer.
Have a Pythonic day!
~
1 line less; before #1  23:18:48              4,20          All
```

Some people like the vi editor so much they will install a Windows version of vi called gvim on Windows and use it as their preferred Windows text editor. For most new users, it may take some time for vi to grow on you.

URL: `https://www.vim.org/download.php`

Searching for Text in vi

The vi editor also offers a string search. You can use `/string` in Command mode to search for the string you are looking for. This feature is also available with the Cisco IOS `show` commands. For example, while running the `show run` command, on your Cisco router, you can use `/line vty` to jump across to the end of the line.

① Again, open the `myfile01.txt` file in vi. You can use a string to search through the text. Place the cursor at the beginning of the file and type `/Python` in Command mode. The search words will be highlighted. Remember that the P in Python is in capital letters, so this search is case-sensitive. Notice that the word `python` on the third line is not highlighted.

Objective: Learn to search a string and navigate through a text file in vi.

```
Python lives in the jungle.
Have a Pythonic day!
Also, python lives on my computer.
Have a Pythonic day!
~
/Python                  # cursor line
```

Press the Enter key once to move to the first occurrence of the string `Python`. The cursor moves to the first letter of the searched word.

Type in `/Python` one more time and press the Enter key to locate the next occurrence of the string.

```
Python lives in the jungle.
Have a Pythonic day!
Also, python lives on my computer.
Have a Pythonic day!
~

/Python ↵
```

Press the Enter key and then the N key once to move to the last occurrence of the string `Python`.

```
Python lives in the jungle.
Have a Pythonic day!
Also, python lives on my computer.
Have a |Pythonic day!                # cursor line
~
/Python                             4,8          All
```

Press Shift+N to move backward. Notice that the / sign changes to ? at the bottom-left corner.

```
Python lives in the jungle.
Have a |Pythonic day!                # cursor line
Also, python lives on my computer.
Have a Pythonic day!
~
?Python                             2,8          All
```

If you want to make vim into an IDE, refer to the following article for a reference.

URL: `https://realpython.com/vim-and-python-a-match-made-in-heaven/`

Display the Line Number in vi

While working in the vi text editor, a few text lines or code is manageable, but as the lines of text/codes increase, you can easily get lost in the lines of text/code. To keep track of the current working position, vi has a numbering feature. You can turn on the line numbering by typing `:set number` in Command mode.

① Reopen `myfile01.txt` in vi, type in `:set number`, and press the Enter key.

Objective: Enable and disable the line number.

```
1 Python lives in the jungle.
2 Have a Pythonic day!
3 Also, python lives on my computer.
4 Have a Pythonic day!
~
:set number ↵
4,1          All
```

■ **Note** If you want to turn off the numbering, type `:set nonumber` in Command mode.

```
Python lives in the jungle.
Have a Pythonic day!
Also, python lives on my computer.
Have a Pythonic day!
~
:set nononumber ↵
4,1          All
```

There are many more commands in vi, but the exercise you have completed contains the very basics you will need to get started in Linux OS. Next, you will learn about the nano text editor. For most Windows PC users, nano could be a better text editor while working with files in a Linux OS environment.

If you want to learn more about vi, visit these URLs for more details:

URL: `https://www.tecmint.com/vi-editor-usage/`

URL: `https://www.washington.edu/computing/unix/vi.html`

Introduction to nano

Unlike vi, nano has almost no learning curve on Linux; it is an easy-to-use text editor with a versatile and straightforward user interface. The nano text editor is installed by default on most newer Linux distributions but probably not on older distributions. It also works well in conjunction with the `sudo` command. On the latest CentOS 8.1, nano 2.9.8 or newer version should be pre-installed and available for immediate use. If you are using Ubuntu Server 20 for the Linux exercises, you should have nano 4.8 or newer pre-installed already. If it is not pre-installed, then it takes only a single `yum` command to install the program on your Linux machine. Before installing the nano text editor, let's look at some key commands used in nano. These commands are available from the nano interface, so you do not have to memorize them. Review the available commands in Table 7-4 and read the descriptions at least once before moving to the next section.

Table 7-4. *nano Text Editor Primary Keys*

Command	Description
`nano[filename]`	Open editor command.
Ctrl+X	Exit edit mode key combo.
Y	Press Ctrl+X and choose Y to save the file.
N	Press Ctrl+X and choose N to ignore edit.
Cancel	Press Ctrl+X and select Cancel to return to the nano editor.
Ctrl+K	Copy (Cut).
Ctrl+U	Paste.

Installing nano

Let's quickly see how we can check if your Linux OS already has nano pre-installed. In the following example, the username pynetauto was used for logging into Linux. If you used another username during the Linux installation section, your username will be different.

① From your Linux terminal console, run nano -V or nano --version. The following example shows the output of the nano -V command on CentOS 8.

Objective: Lean how to check the nano version or the availability of nano on Linux.

```
nano -V or nano --version

# On CentOS 8.1 server
[pynetauto@localhost ~]$ nano -V
GNU nano, version 2.9.8
(C) 1999-2011, 2013-2018 Free Software Foundation, Inc.
(C) 2014-2018 the contributors to nano
Email: nano@nano-editor.org    Web: https://nano-editor.org/
Compiled options: --enable-utf8

# On Ubuntu 20.04 LTS server
pynetauto@ubuntu20s1:~$ nano --version
GNU nano, version 4.8
(C) 1999-2011, 2013-2020 Free Software Foundation, Inc.
(C) 2014-2020 the contributors to nano
Email: nano@nano-editor.org    Web: https://nano-editor.org/
Compiled options: --disable-libmagic --enable-utf8
```

② Another way to check if nano is installed on your Linux system is to create and open a new file using the nano [filename] command. If the nano text editor is not installed on your Linux system, Linux will return a "No such file or directory" -bash error. Also, when we studied the Linux directory structure earlier, we saw that the executable program files typically reside in /usr/bin/; quickly check if nano exists under this directory to reconfirm.

Objective: Check if nano is available on your Linux system by looking at the /usr/bin directory.

```
[pynetauto@localhost ~]$ nano -V
bash: nano: command not found...
Install package 'nano' to provide command 'nano'? [N/y] N
[pynetauto@localhost ~]$ nano myfile02.txt
bash: nano: command not found...
Install package 'nano' to provide command 'nano'? [N/y] N
[pynetauto@localhost ~]$ ls /usr/bin/nano
ls: cannot access '/usr/bin/nano': No such file or directory
```

② If you encountered a similar error as earlier, then it is time to install nano on your Linux OS. You can install nano with a single line with a -y handle for yes. If you log in as a standard user like the following example, run the sudo yum install -y nano command and enter the sudo password. If you log in as a root user, you can drop sudo before the yum command. Replace the word install with remove to uninstall nano.

Objective: Install and uninstall nano on your Linux server.

```
# To install nano on CentOS/Red Hat/Fedora Linux
[pynetauto@localhost ~]$ sudo yum install nano
[sudo] password for pynetauto: **********

# To uninstall nano
[pynetauto@localhost ~]$ sudo yum remove -y nano

# To install nano on Ubuntu/Debian/Mint Linux
pynetauto@ubuntu20s1:~$ sudo apt-get install -y nano
[sudo] password for pynetauto: **********

# To uninstall nano
pynetauto@ubuntu20s1:~$ sudo apt-get remove -y nano
```

If you are using Ubuntu Server 20 and are missing the nano editor, install nano using the apt-get install nano command. The subtle syntax differences between CentOS and Ubuntu are usually from the use of different installer programs. On Red Hat-based distributions such as CentOS, Red Hat, and Fedora, you have to run the yum (*Yellowdog Updater Modified*) command. And the new kid on the block slowly replacing yum is dnf, which is using RPM Package Manager. Debian-based distributions such as Ubuntu, Debian, and Mint Linux use apt (Advanced Package Tool) as an installer program.

④ Now quickly run the ls /usr/bin/nano command to confirm the installation success.

Objective: Check for nano installation success.

```
# On CentOS 8.1 server
[pynetauto@localhost ~]$ ls /usr/bin/nano
/usr/bin/nano

# On Ubuntu 20.04 LTS server
pynetauto@ubuntu20s1:~$ ls /usr/bin/nano
/usr/bin/nano
```

Create/Open a File with nano

You have confirmed that nano has been installed successfully, and you are ready to edit files using the new application. As mentioned, you can use either your Ubuntu or CentOS virtual server for this exercise.

Let's log back in as a standard user and create a new directory to begin the nano exercises.

① First, make a new directory called ex_nano by typing mkdir ex_nano. You will use this directory to store exercise files created during your exercises. Change the working directory to ex_nano by typing cd ex_nano.

Objective: Create a new directory to practice using the nano text editor.

```
[pynetauto@localhost ~]$ mkdir ex_nano
[pynetauto@localhost ~]$ cd ex_nano
[pynetauto@localhost ex_nano]$ ls
[pynetauto@localhost ex_nano]$ pwd
/home/pynetauto/ex_nano
```

② If you execute the command `nano myfile02.txt` as shown next, if a file with the same name does not exist, a new file will open. If a file with the same name exists, then it will reopen the existing file.

Nano has a pseudographical user interface, and as soon as you open a file, you feel at home with the help menu displaying at the base; you want to jump right in and use it. If you are used to Notepad on Windows, you will have no problem using this user-friendly tool.

Objective: Create a new file using the `nano` command.

```
nano filename ↵

[pynetauto@localhost ex_nano]$ nano myfile02.txt

GNU nano 2.9.8                    myfile02.txt
|

^G Get Help  ^O Write Out   ^W Where Is  ^K Cut Text    ^J Justify    ^C Cur Pos
^X Exit      ^R Read File   ^\ Replace   ^U Uncut Text  ^T To Spell   ^_ Go To Line
```

③ After opening a new file and immediately deciding to exit nano without editing the file, the file will be discarded. To exit nano, use ^X (the Ctrl+X keys). If you want to create a new file first, use `touch myfile02.txt` and then open it with the nano `myfile02.txt` command. In nano, if you see the ^ symbol, that means the Ctrl key.

Objective: Use the `touch` command to create a new file.

```
[pynetauto@localhost ex_nano]$ nano myfile02.txt
[pynetauto@localhost ex_nano]$ ls
[pynetauto@localhost ex_nano]$ touch myfile02.txt
[pynetauto@localhost ex_nano]$ ls
myfile02.txt
```

④ Now rerun the `nano myfile02.txt` command and enter a few text lines. As you have discovered, the nano editor does not require you to press the I key to move you into `-- INSERT --` mode as in the vi editor. After you have finished, to exit nano, you have to press Ctrl+X (^X).

Objective: Write to a new file and exit.

```
GNU nano 2.9.8                    myfile02.txt                      Modified

List of tasks to be automated this year.
1. IOS upgrade
2. Network monitoring
3. Configuration backup
4. Life-cycle management

Save modified buffer?  (Answering "No" will DISCARD changes.)
Y Yes
N No           ^C Cancel
```

⑤ To save the file, press Y (Yes) and then press the Enter key. Or to ignore change, press N (No). To go back to the file for further editing, press ^C (Ctrl+C). On the Linux operating system, most of the programs are case sensitive, but the nano menu is an exception; it is not case sensitive, so you can use y for Y and n for N interchangeably.

Objective: Save a changed file.

```
Y ↵

GNU nano 2.9.8                    myfile02.txt                       Modified

List of tasks to be automated this year.
1. IOS upgrade
2. Network monitoring
3. Configuration backup
4. Life-cycle management

File Name to Write: myfile02.txt
^G Get Help          M-D DOS Format      M-A Append          M-B Backup File
^C Cancel            M-M Mac Format      M-P Prepend         ^T To Files
```

⑥ Use the `more`, `less`, or `cat` command followed by the saved filename, `myfile02.txt`. If you used the `less myfile02.txt` command, you could use the Q key to exit `less`.

Objective: View content of the file using `cat`, `more`, or `less`.

```
[pynetauto@localhost ex_nano]$ ls -l
total 4
-rw-rw-r--. 1 pynetauto pynetauto 127 Jan  3 01:27 myfile02.txt
[pynetauto@localhost ex_nano]$ more myfile02.txt

List of tasks to be automated this year.
1. IOS upgrade
2. Network monitoring
3. Configuration backup
4. Life-cycle management
```

You have just learned how to create/open, save, and close a file in nano. Many great text editors are available in Linux, such as emacs, gedit, leafpad, and Komodo, but these text editors will not be discussed in this chapter or this book. When you have some spare time, you should explore other Linux-based text editing tools from a Google search.

Reopen a File with nano

① To reopen an existing text file in nano, you use `nano [filename]`, just like in the previous exercise. So, type `nano myfile02.txt` to open an existing file.

Objective: Reopen an existing file.

```
[pynetauto@localhost ex_nano]$ nano myfile02.txt
GNU nano 2.9.8                    myfile02.txt

List of tasks to be automated this year.
1. IOS upgrade
2. Network monitoring
3. Configuration backup
4. Life-cycle management

[ Read 5 lines ]
^G Get Help  ^O Write Out   ^W Where Is  ^K Cut Text    ^J Justify   ^C Cur Pos
^X Exit      ^R Read File   ^\ Replace   ^U Uncut Text  ^T To Spell  ^_ Go To Line
```

Cut (Delete) and Paste with nano

① While working in nano, to cut a line, first move to the line you want to cut (or copy) and then use the Ctrl+K key combination to paste (UnCut) using Ctrl+U key combination. If you do not paste the cut information, the information in the computer's memory will be discarded and works like delete.

Reopen `myfile02.txt` and place the cursor on line 4.

Objective: Cut (delete) a line in nano.

```
[pynetauto@localhost ex_nano]$ nano myfile02.txt

GNU nano 2.9.8                    myfile02.txt

List of tasks to be automated this year.
1. IOS upgrade
2. Network monitoring
3. Configuration backup
4. Life-cycle management

[ Read 5 lines ]
^G Get Help  ^O Write Out ^W Where Is  ^K Cut Text    ^J Justify    ^C Cur Pos
^X Exit      ^R Read File ^\ Replace   ^U Uncut Text  ^T To Spell   ^_ Go To Line
```

To delete line 4, press Ctrl+K. Line 4 appears to have been deleted to us, but nano cuts and puts the line 4 in your server's memory.

```
GNU nano 2.9.8                    myfile02.txt

List of tasks to be automated this year.
1. IOS upgrade
2. Network monitoring
|4. Life-cycle management                # cursor line
```

```
[ Read 5 lines ]
^G Get Help  ^O Write Out   ^W Where Is  ^K Cut Text    ^J Justify   ^C Cur Pos
^X Exit      ^R Read File   ^\ Replace   ^U Uncut Text  ^T To Spell  ^_ Go To Line
```

② If you want to copy and paste specific strings, first move your cursor to the first position where you want to begin your copy. In this example, we want to cut the word `Life-cycle` from line 4.

Objective: Learn how to copy and past a specific string.

```
GNU nano 2.9.8                     myfile02.txt

List of tasks to be automated this year.
1. IOS upgrade
2. Network monitoring
4. |Life-cycle management                  # cursor line

[ Read 5 lines ]
^G Get Help  ^O Write Out  ^W Where Is  ^K Cut Text    ^J Justify   ^C Cur Pos
^X Exit      ^R Read File  ^\ Replace   ^U Uncut Text  ^T To Spell  ^_ Go To Line
```

Then press Ctrl+6 and use the right arrow [→] to a highlight word or string.

```
GNU nano 2.9.8                     myfile02.txt

List of tasks to be automated this year.
1. IOS upgrade
2. Network monitoring
4. Life-cycle| management                  # cursor line

[ Read 5 lines ]
^G Get Help  ^O Write Out  ^W Where Is  ^K Cut Text    ^J Justify   ^C Cur Pos
^X Exit      ^R Read File  ^\ Replace   ^U Uncut Text  ^T To Spell  ^_ Go To Line
```

Then press Ctrl+K to cut the string.

```
GNU nano 2.9.8                     myfile02.txt

List of tasks to be automated this year.
1. IOS upgrade
2. Network monitoring
4. | management                  # cursor line

[ Read 5 lines ]
^G Get Help  ^O Write Out  ^W Where Is  ^K Cut Text    ^J Justify   ^C Cur Pos
^X Exit      ^R Read File  ^\ Replace   ^U Uncut Text  ^T To Spell  ^_ Go To Line
```

③ Now move the cursor to line 3 using the arrow keys and cut line 3. We want to move line 3 to line 2. Press Ctrl+K to copy the line.

Objective: Use the cut-and-paste function in nano.

```
GNU nano 2.9.8                     myfile02.txt

List of tasks to be automated this year.
1. IOS upgrade
|2. Network monitoring          # cursor line
4. management

[ Read 5 lines ]
^G Get Help  ^O Write Out  ^W Where Is  ^K Cut Text    ^J Justify   ^C Cur Pos
^X Exit      ^R Read File  ^\ Replac    ^U Uncut Text  ^T To Spell  ^_ Go To Line
```

Now move the cursor to line 2.

```
GNU nano 2.9.8                     myfile02.txt

List of tasks to be automated this year.
|1. IOS upgrade                 # cursor line
4. management

[ Read 5 lines ]
^G Get Help  ^O Write Out  ^W Where Is  ^K Cut Text    ^J Justify   ^C Cur Pos
^X Exit      ^R Read File  ^\ Replace   ^U Uncut Text  ^T To Spell  ^_ Go To Line
```

Press Ctrl+U to paste (insert) the copied line.

```
GNU nano 2.9.8                     myfile02.txt

List of tasks to be automated this year.
2. Network monitoring
|1. IOS upgrade                 # cursor line
4. management

^G Get Help  ^O Write Out  ^W Where Is  ^K Cut Text    ^J Justify   ^C Cur Pos
^X Exit      ^R Read File  ^\ Replace   ^U Uncut Text  ^T To Spell  ^_ Go To Line
```

④ If you want to cut multiple lines, place the cursor in the first position, and press the Ctrl+K keys multiple times. The copied multiple lines will be stored in computer memory. I have put the cursor at the beginning of line 2 and then pressed Ctrl + K ↵ three times consecutively.

Objective: Cut and paste multiple lines in nano.

```
Position the cursor in the first line to cut.
GNU nano 2.9.8                    myfile02.txt

List of tasks to be automated this year.
|2. Network monitoring
1. IOS upgrade                 # cursor line
4. management

^G Get Help  ^O Write Out  ^W Where Is  ^K Cut Text   ^J Justify   ^C Cur Pos
^X Exit      ^R Read File  ^\ Replace   ^U Uncut Text ^T To Spell  ^_ Go To Line
```

Use Ctrl+K multiple times to cut three lines.

```
GNU nano 2.9.8                    myfile02.txt

List of tasks to be automated this year.
|

^G Get Help  ^O Write Out  ^W Where Is  ^K Cut Text   ^J Justify   ^C Cur Pos
^X Exit      ^R Read File  ^\ Replace   ^U Uncut Text ^T To Spell  ^_ Go To Line
```

Now the cursor should be positioned on the second line; press the Ctrl+U keys twice to paste the three lines copied twice.

```
GNU nano 2.9.8                    myfile02.txt

List of tasks to be automated this year.
2. Network monitoring
1. IOS upgrade
4. management
2. Network monitoring
1. IOS upgrade
4. management
|                 # cursor line

^G Get Help  ^O Write Out  ^W Where Is  ^K Cut Text   ^J Justify   ^C Cur Pos
^X Exit      ^R Read File  ^\ Replace   ^U Uncut Text ^T To Spell  ^_ Go To Line
```

Use Ctrl+X and press N to discard changes and exit nano. When you open the file again, the content of the file should remain as it was in the original file.

```
GNU nano 2.9.8                    myfile02.txt

List of tasks to be automated this year.
1. IOS upgrade
2. Network monitoring
3. Configuration backup
4. Life-cycle management

^G Get Help  ^O Write Out  ^W Where Is  ^K Cut Text   ^J Justif    ^C Cur Pos
^X Exit      ^R Read File  ^\ Replace   ^U Uncut Text ^T To Spell  ^_ Go To Line
```

String Search and Replacing String(s)

① In nano, you can use Ctrl+W to search for a string, and the search is case insensitive. In the following example, you will search for the word *backup*.

Objective: Search for a specific word or string in nano.

Press Ctrl+W, and then type in the word backup ↵.

```
GNU nano 2.9.8                     myfile02.txt

List of tasks to be automated this year.
1. IOS upgrade
2. Network monitoring
3. Configuration backup
4. Life-cycle management

Search: backup| # cursor line
^G Get Help  ^O Write Out  ^W Where Is  ^K Cut Text    ^J Justify   ^C Cur Pos
^X Exit      ^R Read File  ^\ Replace   ^U Uncut Text  ^T To Spell  ^_ Go To Line
```

As soon as you hit the Enter key, the cursor moves to the word *backup*.

```
GNU nano 2.9.8                     myfile02.txt

List of tasks to be automated this year.
1. IOS upgrade
2. Network monitoring
3. Configuration |backup                # cursor line
4. Life-cycle management

^G Get Help  ^O Write Out  ^W Where Is  ^K Cut Text    ^J Justif    ^C Cur Pos
^X Exit      ^R Read File  ^\ Replace   ^U Uncut Text  ^T To Spell  ^_ Go To Line
```

② To search for a string and replace matched string(s), you can use ^\ (Ctrl+\).
Objective: Search and replace words in nano.

```
Ctrl+\
```

First, let's append the fifth item, "5. Device database management," in our list as follows:

```
GNU nano 2.9.8                     myfile02.txt

List of tasks to be automated this year.
1. IOS upgrade
2. Network monitoring
3. Configuration backup
4. Life-cycle management
5. Device database management|                # cursor line

^G Get Help  ^O Write Out  ^W Where Is  ^K Cut Text    ^J Justify   ^C Cur Pos
^X Exit      ^R Read File  ^\ Replace   ^U Uncut Text  ^T To Spell  ^_ Go To Line
```

Use Ctrl+\ to search for a string, a word in this case: *management.* We want to replace this word with *administration.*

```
GNU nano 2.9.8                    myfile02.txt

List of tasks to be automated this year.
1. IOS upgrade
2. Network monitoring
3. Configuration backup
4. Life-cycle management
5. Device database management

Search (to replace): management|                                          # cursor line
^G Get Help  ^O Write Out  ^W Where Is  ^K Cut Text    ^J Justify   ^C Cur Pos
^X Exit      ^R Read File  ^\ Replace   ^U Uncut Text  ^T To Spell  ^_ Go To Line
```

Enter the replacement word, *administration,* and press the Enter key on your keyboard.

```
GNU nano 2.9.8                    myfile02.txt

List of tasks to be automated this year.
1. IOS upgrade
2. Network monitoring
3. Configuration backup
4. Life-cycle management
5. Device database management
Replace with: administration

^G Get Help                 ^Y First Line               ^P PrevHstory
^C Cancel                   ^V Last Line                ^N NextHstory
```

nano will highlight the first instance of the search word *management.* We want to replace all matches with *administration,* so select A.

```
GNU nano 2.9.8                    myfile02.txt

List of tasks to be automated this year.
1. IOS upgrade
2. Network monitoring
3. Configuration backup
4. Life-cycle management
5. Device database management

Replace this instance?
Y Yes          A All
N No          ^C Cancel
```

All instances will be replaced as highlighted here:

```
GNU nano 2.9.8                    myfile02.txt
```

```
List of tasks to be automated this year.
1. IOS upgrade
2. Network monitoring
3. Configuration backup
4. Life-cycle administration
5. Device database administration

[ Replaced 2 occurrences ]

^G Get Help  ^O Write Out  ^W Where Is  ^K Cut Text    ^J Justify  ^C Cur Pos
^X Exit      ^R Read File  ^\ Replace   ^U Uncut Text  ^T To Spell ^_ Go To Line
```

③ You can use ^O (Ctrl+O) and then the Enter key to save the changes without closing the nano editor. This command works like a Save button.

Objective: Save the file using the Ctrl+O option.

```
Ctrl+O ↵
GNU nano 2.9.8                   myfile02.txt

List of tasks to be automated this year.
1. IOS upgrade
2. Network monitoring
3. Configuration backup
4. Life-cycle administration
5. Device database administration

File Name to Write: myfile02.txt
^G Get Help  ^O Write Out  ^W Where Is  ^K Cut Text    ^J Justify   ^C Cur Pos
^X Exit      ^R Read File  ^\ Replace   ^U Uncut Text  ^T To Spell  ^_ Go To Line
```

Customize nano for Python Coding

While coding in Python using nano, you will notice some missing features such as a four-space tab to avoid pressing the spacebar four times and line numbering options to quickly tell the current working position. To customize these settings, you have to change a couple of settings in the `/etc/nanorc` file.

① To make a tab character four spaces instead of eight spaces in nano, perform these steps:
Use `sudo nano /etc/nanorc` to open a `nanorc` file. Enter the `sudoer` password if it prompts for the password.

Objective: Enable four-space tabbing in nano for Python coding.

Search the nanorc file using the `^W` (Ctrl+W) command with key `set tabsize`.

```
GNU nano 2.9.8                   /etc/nanorc
## Allow nano to be suspended.
# set suspend

## Use this tab size instead of the default; it must be greater than 0.
# |set tabsize 8

## Convert typed tabs to spaces.
# set tabstospaces
Search: set tabsize
^G Get Help  ^O Write Out  ^W Where Is  ^K Cut Text    ^J Justify   ^C Cur Pos
^X Exit      ^R Read File  ^\ Replace   ^U Uncut Text  ^T To Spell  ^_ Go To Line
```

Remove the # (hash) to activate this configuration setting; change 8 to 4. Then add the next line, set tabstospaces, as shown next. Make sure you save the updated nanorc configuration file.

```
GNU nano 2.9.8                    /etc/nanorc
## Allow nano to be suspended.
# set suspend

## Use this tab size instead of the default; it must be greater than 0.
set tabsize 4
set tabstospaces|

## Convert typed tabs to spaces.
# set tabstospaces

[ line 172/279 (61%), col 3/16 (18%), char 5826/9448 (61%) ]
^G Get Help  ^O Write Out ^W Where Is  ^K Cut Text    ^J Justify     ^C Cur Pos
^X Exit      ^R Read File ^\ Replace   ^U Uncut Text  ^T To Spell    ^_ Go To Line
```

Now it is time to check the changes, reopen myfile02.txt, and use the Tab key to add four spaces to lines 3–6 to confirm. Every time you use the Tab key, you are adding four spaces to working Python code. Four spaces to the second line, eight spaces to the third line, and twelve spaces to the fourth line have been added.

```
GNU nano 2.9.8                    myfile02.txt

List of tasks to be automated this year.
1. IOS upgrade
2. Network monitoring
3. Configuration backup
4. Life-cycle administration
|5. Device database administration

^G Get Help  ^O Write Out ^W Where Is  ^K Cut Text    ^J Justify     ^C Cur Pos
^X Exit      ^R Read File ^\ Replace   ^U Uncut Text  ^T To Spell    ^_ Go To Line
```

If you want to reverse the previous change, you can open the /etc/nanorc file and add the # to the two lines and save.

② Use sudo nano /etc/nanorc to reopen the nanorc file one more time. Search for set linenumbers and remove the # sign at the beginning of this line and save the changes.

Objective: Enable line numbering in nano.

```
[pynetauto@localhost ex_nano]$ sudo nano /etc/nanorc
[sudo] password for pynetauto: **********
```

Remove the # in front of set linenumbers; this will enable line numbering in nano.

```
GNU nano 2.9.8                    /etc/nanorc                        Modified

## Remember the used search/replace strings for the next session.
# set historylog

## Display line numbers to the left of the text.
set linenumbers

## Enable vim-style lock-files.  This is just to let a vim user know you
## are editing a file [s]he is trying to edit and vice versa.  There are

^G Get Help  ^O Write Out ^W Where Is  ^K Cut Text    ^J Justify     ^C Cur Pos
^X Exit      ^R Read File ^\ Replace   ^U Uncut Text  ^T To Spell    ^_ Go To Line
```

Open `myfile02.txt` in nano and check if the line numbers are visible.

```
GNU nano 2.9.8                    myfile02.txt

1 List of tasks to be automated this year.
2 1. IOS upgrade
3     2. Network monitoring
4         3. Configuration backup
5             4. Life-cycle administration
6                 5. Device database administration
7

[ Read 6 lines ]
^G Get Help  ^O Write Out ^W Where Is  ^K Cut Text    ^J Justify      ^C Cur Pos
^X Exit      ^R Read File ^\ Replace   ^U Uncut Text  ^T To Spell     ^_ Go To Line
```

If you want to reverse the changes, you can open the `/etc/nanorc` file and add the # back to the same line and save.

At first, the vi and nano text editors are challenging to use for Windows users, but this is because you are not familiar with these programs. As you spend more time using these applications, you will become more comfortable. So, take it slow, but never give up on these applications. If you know how to use the vi text editor properly, you have mastered a significant part of Linux administration. This is my dad joke, but it's so true: "Learning the first half of Linux administration is learning how to use vi." Of course, the nano text editor supports lots more features. If you want to learn more about other commands, please refer to this link: `https://www.cheatography.com/pepe/cheat-sheets/nano/`.

Many readers will not like the Linux chapters as this involves users distancing themselves from the GUI and being stuck in the terminal console for hours, but this is an extremely important process to get comfortable with in Linux and, later, when writing code in Python on Linux.

Linux Basic Administration

Now that you are getting familiar with vi and nano text editors, let's learn some fundamental Linux administrations to get you started.

Changing the Hostname

In Chapters 5 and 6, you installed the Ubuntu 20 and CentOS 8.1 servers with the desktop options, but the server name (`hostname`) on the CentOS 8.1 server was left as `localhost`. In contrast, on Ubuntu Server 20, the server name (`hostname`) was configured during the installation of the OS. In this section, let's change the hostname of the CentOS server to `centos8s1`, which gives more meaning to what the server is. Although the desktop is available, we will update the hostname via terminal console. The following hostname-changing process will work on both Red Hat (CentOS) and Debian (Ubuntu) Linux servers:

① First, let's learn how to check the hostname. There are a few ways to check the hostname currently assigned to your server, and here are some of the Linux commands. The `hostnamectl` command provides the most useful information if you are checking more than the hostname itself. Also, the file that contains the name is under the `/etc/hostname` file. All these commands are Linux commands, so they are case sensitive.

Objective: Learn how to change the hostname on Linux using the command line.

```
[pynetauto@localhost ~]$ hostname
localhost
[pynetauto@localhost ~]$ echo "$HOSTNAME"
localhost
[pynetauto@localhost ~]$ printf "%s\n" $HOSTNAME
localhost
[pynetauto@localhost ~]$ hostnamectl
  Static hostname: localhost
        Icon name: computer-vm
          Chassis: vm
       Machine ID: e53c131bb54c4fb1a835f3aa435024e2
          Boot ID: 9acca137c1f04ca0ae0db3b6b28db63e
    Virtualization: vmware
  Operating System: CentOS Linux 8 (Core)
       CPE OS Name: cpe:/o:centos:centos:8
            Kernel: Linux 4.18.0-193.14.2.el8_2.x86_64
      Architecture: x86-64
[pynetauto@localhost ~]$ cat /etc/hostname
localhost
```

② Use `sudo hostnamectl set-hostname [new_name]` to update the server hostname.

Objective:

```
[pynetauto@localhost ~]$ sudo hostnamectl set-hostname centos8s1
[sudo] password for pynetauto:
[pynetauto@localhost ~]$
```

If you use a text editor such as nano, you can open the `/etc/hosts` file and update the current hostname (`localhost`) to the new server name using the Ctrl+\ method. In this example, the new hostname is `centos8s1`.

```
GNU nano 2.9.8                    /etc/hosts

1 127.0.0.1   localhost localhost.localdomain localhost4 localhost4.localdomain4
2 ::1         localhost localhost.localdomain localhost6 localhost6.localdomain6

[ Read 2 lines ]
^G Get Help  ^O Write Out ^W Where Is  ^K Cut Text    ^J Justify     ^C Cur Pos
^X Exit      ^R Read File ^\ Replace   ^U Uncut Text  ^T To Spell    ^_ Go To Line
```

Use nano's Ctrl+\ to change all localhost instances to centos8s1.

```
GNU nano 2.9.8                    /etc/hosts

1 127.0.0.1   localhost localhost.localdomain localhost4 localhost4.localdomain4
2 ::1         localhost localhost.localdomain localhost6 localhost6.localdomain6

Search (to replace) : localhost
^G Get Help  ^O Write Out ^W Where Is  ^K Cut Text    ^J Justify     ^C Cur Pos
^X Exit      ^R Read File ^\ Replace   ^U Uncut Text  ^T To Spell    ^_ Go To Line

GNU nano 2.9.8                    /etc/hosts

1 127.0.0.1   localhost localhost.localdomain localhost4 localhost4.localdomain4
2 ::1         localhost localhost.localdomain localhost6 localhost6.localdomain6

Replace with: centos8s1
^G Get Help                ^Y First Line             ^P PrevHstory
^C Cancel                  ^V Last Line              ^N NextHstory

GNU nano 2.9.8                    /etc/hosts
1 127.0.0.1   localhost localhost.localdomain localhost4 localhost4.localdomain4
2 ::1         localhost localhost.localdomain localhost6 localhost6.localdomain6

Replace this instance? A
Y Yes            A All
N No            ^C Cancel
```

After modifying the hosts file, it should look similar to this:

```
GNU nano 2.9.8               /etc/hosts                              Modified

1 127.0.0.1   centos8s1 centos8s1.localdomain centos8s14 centos8s14.localdomain4

2 ::1         centos8s1 centos8s1.localdomain centos8s16 centos8s16.localdomain6

[ Replaced 8 occurences ]

^G Get Help  ^O Write Out ^W Where Is  ^K Cut Text    ^J Justify     ^C Cur Pos

^X Exit         ^R Read File   ^\ Replace      ^U Uncut Text^T To Spell  ^_ Go To Line
```

Now use the sudo reboot command to restart your server for the new hostname to take effect.

```
[pynetauto@localhost ~]$ sudo reboot

[sudo] password for pynetauto: **********
```

When your CentOS server reboots, SSH into the server using PuTTY, and you should see the hostname changed to centos8s1.

```
login as: pynetauto

pynetauto@192.168.183.130's password: **********

Activate the web console with: systemctl enable --now cockpit.socket

Last login: Mon Jan  4 11:23:12 2021 from 192.168.183.1

[pynetauto@centos8s1 ~]$
```

③ Note, Ubuntu's hostname is already set during the installation process, and you do not have to perform any other actions here.

```
pynetauto@ubuntu20s1:~$ hostname
ubuntu20s1
pynetauto@ubuntu20s1:~$ echo "$HOSTNAME"
ubuntu20s1
pynetauto@ubuntu20s1:~$ printf "%s\n" $HOSTNAME
ubuntu20s1
pynetauto@ubuntu20s1:~$ hostnamectl
  Static hostname: ubuntu20s1
        Icon name: computer-vm
          Chassis: vm
       Machine ID: ea202235f9834d979436db10d89b1347
          Boot ID: 6a4035617bf348cba128be8e9d29d6a9
   Virtualization: vmware
 Operating System: Ubuntu 20.04.1 LTS
           Kernel: Linux 5.4.0-47-generic
     Architecture: x86-64
pynetauto@ubuntu20s1:~$ cat /etc/hostname
ubuntu20s1
```

Linux Basic File and Directory Commands

We will first learn the necessary commands to manage basic files and directories of the Linux operating system. It usually takes a lot of time to get a deeper understanding of the Linux commands. This book was not written for a general Linux administration, so this chapter aims to help you build up the Linux administration basics, so you can comfortably perform the basic tasks on Linux systems. Only the most basic commands are covered here. Please take the time to review each command in Table 7-5 before starting the exercises. You do not have to memorize all of the commands right now, but try to get familiar with some command syntax.

Table 7-5. *Linux File and Directory Basic Commands*

Command	Description and Example
`pwd`	Present working directory `$pwd`
`ls`	List segment: Lists files and directories in the present working directory `$ ls`
`ls [directory]`	`$ ls /home/pynetauto/Documents`
`ls -a`	List all files, including hidden directories and files `$ ls -a .bashrc`
`dir`	Directory `$dir`

(*continued*)

Table 7-5. *(continued)*

Command	Description and Example
`mkdir`	Make directory `$ mkdir myapps`

`cd`	Change directory
	`$ cd myapps`
	`$ cd /usr/local`

`cd ..`	Change current directory to parent directory. `/myapps$ cd ..`

`cd ~`	Move to user's home directory from anywhere.
	`$ cd /usr/sbin`
	`:/usr/sbin$ cd ~`
	`$ pwd`
	`/home/pynetauto`

`cd -`	Switch back to previous directory where you were working earlier.
	`$ cd /usr/local`
	`:/usr/local$ cd -`
	`/home/pynetauto`

`rm OR rm -r`	Remove file(s). `/myapps$ rm router_app.py`
`rmdir`	Remove directory `$ rmdir myapps`
`mv`	Rename a filename. `$ mv file01.py myfile01.py`
`mv file directory`	Move file to another directory. `$ mv file01.py ./Documents`
`mv directory_A directory_B`	Rename one directory to another directory. `$ mv myapps myscripts`

`touch filename`	Create a file(s).
	`$ touch myfile04.txt`
	`$ touch myfile05.txt myfile06.txt`

`cp`	Copy a file to another directory or copy and paste with another filename. `$ cp myfile01.py /home/pynetauto/Documents`
`cp -a directory_A directory_B`	Copy one directory to another directory. `$ cp -a Documents Mydocs`
`find`	Find a file. `$ find /home/pynetauto -name "myfile*"`

`grep`	Search for a string from a file.
	`$ grep pynetauto /etc/passwd`
	`$ grep 'Python' /home/pynetauto/myfile10.py`

Linux File and Directory Exercises

Now let's learn Linux basic file and directory management with some exercises.

Up until this point, the previous exercises were completed on the CentOS server. In the following exercises, the Ubuntu Server 20 LTS server will be used. Please log into your Ubuntu virtual machine as a root user this time and complete the exercises. If you are an experienced Linux administrator, you can jump to the next chapter and start installing IP network applications on CentOS 8.1. For any commands highlighted in bold, you must type them in to your Linux console terminal.

```
login as: root
root@192.168.183.132's password: **********
Welcome to Ubuntu 20.04.1 LTS (GNU/Linux 5.4.0-47-generic x86_64)

[omitted for brevity]

Last login: Sun Jun  7 08:37:49 2020 from 192.168.183.1
root@ubuntu20s1:~#
```

Exercise 7-1

① Use the pwd command to check the current working directory. As you learned in the previous section, pwd stands for present working directory. Think of this as your compass to navigate around the Linux system.

```
root@ubuntu20s1:~# pwd
/root
```

② ls is a Unix/Linux-specific command to view files and directories. You will learn about the ls command options in detail later. Make a directory with the mkdir command and use ls to list the new directory.

```
root@ubuntu20s1:~# mkdir directory1
root@ubuntu20s1:~# ls
Desktop     Documents  Music     Pictures  snap       Videos
directory1  Downloads  myscript  Public    Templates
```

③ Use the ls directory_name command to see the files and child directories in your directory. Continuing from the previous exercise, create a file under directory1 using the touch command and then use the ls command to see the newly created file under directory1.

```
root@ubuntu20s1:~# touch directory1/myfile01.txt
root@ubuntu20s1:~# ls directory1/
myfile01.txt
```

④ The ls -d command instructs ls to simply list directory entries rather than the contents. You can use the ls -l command to see details of files and directories. l stands for long listing. Now compare the three outputs: ls, ls -d, and ls -l.

```
root@ubuntu20s1:~# ls directory1
myfile01.txt
root@ubuntu20s1:~# ls -d directory1
directory1
root@ubuntu20s1:~# ls -l directory1
total 0
-rw-r--r-- 1 root root 0 Jan  4 01:39 myfile01.txt
```

⑤ Use the `ls -a` command to show hidden files and folders together. a stands for all and reveals even the hidden directories and files.

```
root@ubuntu20s1:~# ls -a
.              .cache      Documents  Music     Public  Templates
..             .config     Downloads  myscript  .rpmdb  Videos
.bash_history  Desktop     .gnupg     Pictures  snap
.bashrc        directory1  .local     .profile  .ssh
```

⑥ You have already used this command a couple of times; you can use the `mkdir` command to create a new directory. A directory is similar to the folders in Windows OS; it can contain child directories and files. Make another directory to get more practice.

```
root@ubuntu20s1:~# mkdir directory2
oot@ubuntu20s1:~# ls -d directory*
directory1  directory2
```

⑦ The `cp -a` command allows you to copy an entire directory, including the files and child directories inside the original directory. In this exercise, you are copying `directory1` to make another directory containing the same `myfile01.txt`.

```
root@ubuntu20s1:~# cp -a directory1 directory3
root@ubuntu20s1:~# ls -d directory*
directory1  directory2  directory3
root@ubuntu20s1:~# ls directory*
directory1:
myfile01.txt

directory2:

directory3:
myfile01.txt
```

⑧ `rmdir` will allow you to remove an empty directory; this command will delete the entire directory. `directory2` is empty, so go ahead and delete it using the `rmdir` command.

```
root@ubuntu20s1:~# ls directory2/
root@ubuntu20s1:~# rmdir directory2
root@ubuntu20s1:~# ls -d directory*
directory1  directory3
```

⑨ If you want to delete a directory that contains other files and directories, you can use `rm -rf directory_name`. The `rm -rf` command should be used with caution as this option will not prompt user confirmation and delete items instantly.

```
root@ubuntu20s1:~# ls directory3
myfile01.txt
root@ubuntu20s1:~# rm directory3
rm: cannot remove 'directory3': Is a directory
root@ubuntu20s1:~# rm -rf directory3
root@ubuntu20s1:~# ls -d directory*
directory1
```

⑩ The mv command can be used to move or rename both files and directories. You can also use this command to move a file or directory to another directory; let's learn this through the following exercise:

```
# Renaming a directory
root@ubuntu20s1:~# ls -d directory*
directory1
root@ubuntu20s1:~# mv directory1 directory5
root@ubuntu20s1:~# ls -d directory*
directory5

# Moving a directory to another directory
root@ubuntu20s1:~# mkdir directory3
root@ubuntu20s1:~# ls -d directory*
directory3  directory5
root@ubuntu20s1:~# mv directory3 directory5
root@ubuntu20s1:~# ls -d directory*
directory5
root@ubuntu20s1:~# ls directory5
directory3  myfile01.txt
```

Is there a better way to see directories and files in Linux at a glance?

Yes, there is a handy directories tool called `tree` in Linux. After installing `tree`, type the command `tree` in the current working directory to display directories and files listed in tree format. Use the `apt install tree` command to install the software.

```
root@ubuntu20s1:~# apt-get install tree
Reading package lists... Done
Building dependency tree
Reading state information... Done
The following NEW packages will be installed:
tree
0 upgraded, 1 newly installed, 0 to remove and 125 not upgraded.
[...omitted for brevity]
Preparing to unpack .../tree_1.8.0-1_amd64.deb ...
Unpacking tree (1.8.0-1) ...
Setting up tree (1.8.0-1) ...
Processing triggers for man-db (2.9.1-1) ...
root@ubuntu20s1:~# tree
.
```

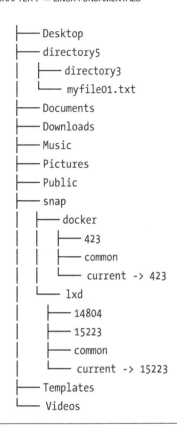

```
├── Desktop
├── directory5
│   ├── directory3
│   └── myfile01.txt
├── Documents
├── Downloads
├── Music
├── Pictures
├── Public
├── snap
│   ├── docker
│   │   ├── 423
│   │   ├── common
│   │   └── current -> 423
│   └── lxd
│       ├── 14804
│       ├── 15223
│       ├── common
│       └── current -> 15223
├── Templates
└── Videos
```

■ **Note** If you cannot install `tree` on Ubuntu, you may have to enable the universe repository. Run the following commands on your Ubuntu before installing `tree`:

```
root@ubuntu20s1:~# sudo add-apt-repository "deb http://archive.ubuntu.com/ubuntu $(lsb_release -sc) main universe restricted multiverse"
root@ubuntu20s1:~# apt update
root@ubuntu20s1:~# apt-get install tree
```

Exercise 7-2

① Use the `ls -d $PWD/*` command to display the path of working directories.

```
root@ubuntu20s1:~# ls -d $PWD/*
/root/Desktop      /root/Downloads  /root/Pictures  /root/Templates
/root/directory5   /root/Music      /root/Public    /root/Videos
/root/Documents    /root/myscript   /root/snap
```

② The cd, cd .., and cd ~ change directory commands can be used to move the user's working directory location. Get some practice, and you will save a lot of time while working with files and directories. Let's look at some examples and follow through.

Let's make multiple directories using the mkdir command.

```
root@ubuntu20s1:~# mkdir directory1 directory2 directory4
root@ubuntu20s1:~# ls -d directory*
directory1  directory2  directory4  directory5
root@ubuntu20s1:~# mv directory2 directory4
root@ubuntu20s1:~# ls -d directory*
directory1  directory4  directory5
root@ubuntu20s1:~# tree directory*
directory1
directory4
└── directory2
directory5
├── directory3
└── myfile01.txt

2 directories, 1 file
```

Type cd (change directory) and press Enter key, and you always return to the user's home directory. Move to root/directory4/directory2 and use cd to return to root's working folder. Notice the use of the shortcut ./ to specify the current working directory. ./directory4/directory2 is short for /root/directory4/directory2.

```
root@ubuntu20s1:~# pwd
/root
root@ubuntu20s1:~# cd ./directory4/directory2
root@ubuntu20s1:~/directory4/directory2# pwd
/root/directory4/directory2
root@ubuntu20s1:~/directory4/directory2# cd
root@ubuntu20s1:~# pwd
/root
```

③ The cd .. command moves the working directory up one level from the child directory. This time let's move down to /root/directory5/directory3 and use the cd .. command to move up to the parent directories. Notice that you can also use cd ../../ to jump up multiple levels.

```
root@ubuntu20s1:~# cd /root/directory5/directory3
root@ubuntu20s1:~/directory5/directory3# pwd
/root/directory5/directory3
root@ubuntu20s1:~/directory5/directory3# cd ..
root@ubuntu20s1:~/directory5# pwd
/root/directory5
root@ubuntu20s1:~/directory5# cd ..
root@ubuntu20s1:~# pwd
/root
root@ubuntu20s1:~# cd ./directory5/directory3
root@ubuntu20s1:~/directory5/directory3# pwd
/root/directory5/directory3
root@ubuntu20s1:~/directory5/directory3# cd ../../
root@ubuntu20s1:~# pwd
/root
```

④ If you know the exact directory path, you can jump from one working directory to the next directory by typing cd followed by a specific directory path. The following exercise shows jumping from directory3 under parent directory5 to directory2 under parent directory4:

```
root@ubuntu20s1:~# cd ./directory5/directory3
root@ubuntu20s1:~/directory5/directory3# pwd
/root/directory5/directory3
root@ubuntu20s1:~/directory5/directory3# cd
/root/directory4/directory2
root@ubuntu20s1:~/directory4/directory2# pwd
/root/directory4/directory2
```

⑤ cd ~ can also be used to return to the user's home directory.

```
root@ubuntu20s1:~# cd /root/directory4/directory2
root@ubuntu20s1:~/directory4/directory2# pwd
/root/directory4/directory2
root@ubuntu20s1:~/directory4/directory2# cd ~
root@ubuntu20s1:~# pwd
/root
```

⑥ Unlike the ./ command, cd ~ also allows you to jump between directories that are not dependent on the present working directory.

```
root@ubuntu20s1:~# cd /root/directory4/directory2
root@ubuntu20s1:~/directory4/directory2# pwd
/root/directory4/directory2
root@ubuntu20s1:~/directory4/directory2# cd ~/directory5/directory3
root@ubuntu20s1:~/directory5/directory3# pwd
/root/directory5/directory3
```

⑦ The dir (directory) command is the same as the ls -C -b command and said to have been included for both Linux and Windows users. The difference is that when you use dir, the directory names are black, but using ls -C -b returns colored directory names.

```
root@ubuntu20s1:~# dir
Desktop     directory4  Documents  Music     Public  Templates
directory1  directory5  Downloads  Pictures  snap    Videos

root@ubuntu20s1:~# ls -C -b
Desktop     directory4  Documents  Music     Public  Templates
directory1  directory5  Downloads  Pictures  snap    Videos
```

⑧ The touch command is used to create a file. If you enter touch file_name as shown here, a file will be created. You can also create multiple files using a single touch command.

```
root@ubuntu20s1:~# touch myfile02.txt
root@ubuntu20s1:~# ls myfile*
myfile02.txt
root@ubuntu20s1:~# touch myfile03.txt myfile04.txt
root@ubuntu20s1:~# ls myfile*
myfile02.txt  myfile03.txt  myfile04.txt
```

⑨ The cp (copy) command allows you to copy files or directories. Don't forget to use the -r (recursive) option when copying a directory.

```
root@ubuntu20s1:~# ls myfile*
myfile02.txt  myfile03.txt  myfile04.txt
root@ubuntu20s1:~# cp myfile03.txt myfile05.txt
root@ubuntu20s1:~# ls myfile*
myfile02.txt  myfile03.txt  myfile04.txt  myfile05.txt
```

```
root@ubuntu20s1:~# ls -d directory*
directory1  directory4  directory5
root@ubuntu20s1:~# cp -r directory1 directory2
root@ubuntu20s1:~# ls -d directory*
directory1  directory2  directory4  directory5
```

⑩ rm (remove) can be used to delete a file(s) or delete directories. In the following example, directory4 will be deleted using the -r option.

```
root@ubuntu20s1:~# ls myfile*
myfile02.txt  myfile03.txt  myfile04.txt  myfile05.txt
root@ubuntu20s1:~# rm myfile02.txt
root@ubuntu20s1:~# ls myfile*
myfile03.txt  myfile04.txt  myfile05.txt
root@ubuntu20s1:~# rm myfile*
root@ubuntu20s1:~# ls myfile*
ls: cannot access 'myfile*': No such file or directory
```

```
root@ubuntu20s1:~# tree directory*
directory1
directory2
directory4
└── directory2
directory5
├── directory3
└── myfile01.txt

2 directories, 1 file
```

```
root@ubuntu20s1:~# rm -r directory4
root@ubuntu20s1:~# tree directory*
directory1
directory2
directory5
├── directory3
└── myfile01.txt

1 directory, 1 file
```

Exercise 7-3

① The mv (move) command allows you to change the filename or move files and directories to another directory. Let's learn this through some examples.

```
# Rename myfile01.txt in root/directory5 to yourfile01.txt.
root@ubuntu20s1:~# ls ./directory5/
directory3  myfile01.txt
root@ubuntu20s1:~# mv ./directory5/myfile01.txt ./directory5/yourfile01.txt
root@ubuntu20s1:~# ls ./directory5/
directory3  yourfile01.txt

# Move yourfile01.txt to /root directory.
root@ubuntu20s1:~# mv ./directory5/yourfile01.txt ./
root@ubuntu20s1:~# ls ./directory5/
directory3
root@ubuntu20s1:~# pwd
/root
root@ubuntu20s1:~# ls your*
yourfile01.txt
```

② Now let's rename directory5 to directory4. Then nest directory2 inside directory3 and then directory1 into directory2.

```
root@ubuntu20s1:~# mv directory5 directory4
root@ubuntu20s1:~# tree directory*
directory1
directory2
directory4
└── directory3

1 directory, 0 files
root@ubuntu20s1:~# mv directory2 ./directory4/directory3/
root@ubuntu20s1:~# mv directory1 ./directory4/directory3/directory2/
root@ubuntu20s1:~# tree directory*
directory4
└── directory3
└── directory2
└── directory1

3 directories, 0 files
```

③ Now using the . (dot) method, let's move directory1, directory2, and directory3 to the root user's folder, at the same level as the parent directory, directory4.

```
root@ubuntu20s1:~# tree directory*
directory4
└── directory3
└── directory2
└── directory1

3 directories, 0 files
root@ubuntu20s1:~# mv ./directory4/directory3/directory2/directory1 .
root@ubuntu20s1:~# mv ./directory4/directory3/directory2 .
root@ubuntu20s1:~# mv ./directory4/directory3 .
root@ubuntu20s1:~# tree directory*
directory1
directory2
directory3
directory4
```

④ Now let's use the rm and rm -r commands to clean the file and directories to reset the clock. We have one text file and four directories to delete in this exercise.

```
root@ubuntu20s1:~# rm yourfile01.txt
oot@ubuntu20s1:~# ls -d directory*
directory1  directory2  directory3  directory4
root@ubuntu20s1:~# rm -r directory*
root@ubuntu20s1:~# ls -d directory*
ls: cannot access 'directory*': No such file or directory
```

⑤ Create the mysecrete file with your name and a secrete password. Create a hidden directory hideme using the . (dot) method and move the secrete file into the .hideme directory. To see the hidden files, use the -a option with the ls command.

```
root@ubuntu20s1:~# nano mysecrete
root@ubuntu20s1:~# cat mysecrete
pynetauto
fairdinkum
root@ubuntu20s1:~# ls my*
mysecrete
root@ubuntu20s1:~# mkdir .hideme
root@ubuntu20s1:~# ls
Desktop  Documents  Downloads  Music  Pictures  Public  snap  Templates  Videos
root@ubuntu20s1:~# ls -a
.              .bashrc  Desktop    .gnupg   Music     Public  Templates
..             .cache   Documents  .hideme  Pictures  snap    Videos
.bash_history  .config  Downloads  .local   .profile  .ssh

root@ubuntu20s1:~# mv mysecrete .hideme
root@ubuntu20s1:~# ls .hideme
mysecrete
root@ubuntu20s1:~# ls
Desktop  Documents  Downloads  Music  Pictures  Public  snap  Templates  Videos
root@ubuntu20s1:~# tree .hideme
.hideme
└── mysecrete

0 directories, 1 file
```

How do I view command options?

You can use the `--help` or `man` command. The following example shows the `ls --help` and `man ls` commands:

```
root@ubuntu20s1:~# ls --help
```

```
root@ubuntu20s1:~# man ls
```

Also, quickly search the words *Linux command cheat sheet*, and Google will return hundreds of searched results. One such site is listed here for your reference:

https://cheatography.com/davechild/cheat-sheets/linux-command-line/

Linux File and Directory Exercise 7-2

You have just completed an essential Linux file and directory exercise in Exercise 7-1. Next, let's learn some more commands. The user-friendly GUI is often a missing feature on enterprise Linux systems, and much of the administrator's tasks are carried out via a command-line or console interface.

Your Linux study success depends on how well you can handle files and directories using the basic file and directory commands.

Echo, Cat, More, and Less Command Exercise

① Create a new file called greet01 and use the echo command to write a question, "Can you say Hello in different languages?" into the greet01 file.

```
root@ubuntu20s1:~# touch greet01
root@ubuntu20s1:~# ls greet*
greet01
root@ubuntu20s1:~# echo "Can you say Hello in different languages?" > greet01
root@ubuntu20s1:~# more greet01
Can you say Hello in different languages?
```

② Create another file called greet02. This time write Hello in various languages and write to the file using the echo command again. You are going to learn how to say "Hi" in ten different languages in this exercise.

```
root@ubuntu20s1:~# touch greet02
root@ubuntu20s1:~# echo "Hi Bonjour Nihao Konichiwa Shalom Merhaba Ola Namaste Ciao
Anyoung" > greet02
root@ubuntu20s1:~# cat greet02
Hi Bonjour Nihao Konichiwa Shalom Merhaba Ola Namaste Ciao Anyoung
```

③ In the previous exercise, the cat command was used to display the content of greet02. Another use of the cat command is to merge multiple files into a single file. Here you will merge greet01 and greet02 and create the greet03 file.

```
root@ubuntu20s1:~# cat greet01 greet02 > greet03
root@ubuntu20s1:~# ls -d greet*
greet01  greet02  greet03
root@ubuntu20s1:~# more greet03
Can you say Hello in different languages?
Hi Bonjour Nihao Konichiwa Shalom Merhaba Ola Namaste Ciao Anyoung
```

④ If you want to add more content to the same file, use the cat >> command.

```
root@ubuntu20s1:~# cat >> greet03
How do you say "Love" in different languages?
Love Amour Ai Ai Ahaba Ask Amor Amore Mohabbat Sarang

#To exit, press Ctrl+D keys.

root@ubuntu20s1:~# more greet03
Can you say Hello in different languages?
Hi Bonjour Nihao Konichiwa Shalom Merhaba Ola Namaste Anyoung
How do you say "Love" in different languages?
Love Amour Ai Ai Ahaba Ask Amor Amore Mohabbat Sarang
```

⑤ You can also create a new file using the cat > command.

```
root@ubuntu20s1:~# cat > greet04
This is a test file created with the "cat >" command.
You can write something meaningful or anything you like.
#To exit, press Ctrl+D keys.
root@ubuntu20s1:~# cat greet04
This is a test file created with "cat >" command.
```

You can write something meaningful or anything you like.

⑥ You can also use more commands to view the content of your file. If the file is long, use the spacebar to scroll down the page or use the Enter key to scroll down by line. If you want to exit in the middle of reading, use the Ctrl+C or Ctrl+Z key.

```
root@ubuntu20s1:~# more greet03
Can you say Hello in different languages?
Hi Bonjour Nihao Konichiwa Shalom Merhaba Ola Namaste Anyoung
How do you say "Love" in different languages?
Love Amour Ai Ai Ahaba Ask Amor Amore Mohabbat Sarang
```

⑦ You can also use the less command to view your file's content, but the less command will not print the content on the terminal. To scroll down the page, use the spacebar, and to scroll down by line, use the Enter key. To exit, use Ctrl+Z (or Ctrl+C and then :q).

```
root@ubuntu20s1:~# less greet03
Can you say Hello in different languages?
Hi Bonjour Nihao Konichiwa Shalom Merhaba Ola Namaste Anyoung
How do you say "Love" in different languages?
Love Amour Ai Ai Ahaba Ask Amor Amore Mohabbat Sarang
greet03 (END)
```

Where can I find the best Linux study material?

Often, the best things in life are free. Thanks to Paul Cobbaut sharing his book *Linux Fundamentals* on the Linuxfun website, more people can have fun with Linux. I highly recommend you download this free PDF file and use it to your advantage.

UR: `https://linux-training.be/linuxfun.pdf`

---

ls Command with Options

You may be thinking that drilling into these exercises seems to be so far away from the goal of where you want to take your Python network automation. But you must do the drills and lay down one brick at a time to build a strong foundation. So, this is the process of building a strong foundation. Try to get as much practice from the chapter exercises and use other external Linux command study materials online and offline.

`ls` enumerates files and directories.

`ls -l` shows file and directory details.

`ls -a` lists all files in the current working directory.

`ls -al` shows details of files and directories in the current working directory.

---

① Use the `ls` command with the `search` keyword and the all-inclusive or greedy `*`. The following example lists all files or folders starting with the word `greet` in the current working directory.

```
root@ubuntu20s1:~# ls greet*
```

```
greet01  greet02  greet03  greet04
```

② Create a new directory called `greetings` and run the `ls` command with the `-d` and `-l` (list) options to compare the difference between files and directories. At the beginning of the directory greetings, notice the letter d. This indicates that this is a directory.

```
root@ubuntu20s1:~# mkdir greetings
root@ubuntu20s1:~# ls -d -l greet*
-rw-r--r-- 1 root root   42 Jun  3 11:45 greet01
-rw-r--r-- 1 root root   62 Jun  3 11:51 greet02
-rw-r--r-- 1 root root  204 Jun  3 12:10 greet03
-rw-r--r-- 1 root root  106 Jun  3 12:15 greet04
drwxr-xr-x 2 root root 4096 Jun  3 12:35 greetings
```

③ This -a command lists all files, including hidden files. Hidden files start with . (dot).

```
root@ubuntu20s1:~# ls -a
.                .cache      Downloads  greet03    .local    Public     test01
..               .config     .gnupg     greet04    Music     snap       Videos
.bash_history    Desktop     greet01    greetings  Pictures  .ssh
.bashrc          Documents   greet02    .hideme    .profile  Templates
```

④ You can combine various ls options to list the files and directories as you like. Other options are -R, -o, -g, -i, -s, -t, -S, -r. If you have an hour to explore these options, please go to the Internet and spend an hour or two to find each one of them and mix and match. The following is the combined use of -l (list) and -h (human-readable) commands:

```
root@ubuntu20s1:~# ls -lh greet*
-rw-r--r-- 1 root root  42 Jun  3 11:45 greet01
-rw-r--r-- 1 root root  62 Jun  3 11:51 greet02
-rw-r--r-- 1 root root 204 Jun  3 12:10 greet03
-rw-r--r-- 1 root root 106 Jun  3 12:15 greet04

greetings:
total 0
```

Delete files and directories at once

① If you want to delete all files starting with the same name in a directory, you can use rm filename *. If you want to delete all files in a directory, use *. Continuing from the previous exercise, let's move all files starting with the word greet into the greetings directory.

```
roroot@ubuntu20s1:~# pwd
/root
root@ubuntu20s1:~# ls
Desktop    Downloads  greet02  greet04    Music     Public  Templates  Videos
Documents  greet01    greet03  greetings  Pictures  snap    test01
root@ubuntu20s1:~# ls -lh greet*
-rw-r--r-- 1 root root  42 Jun  3 11:45 greet01
-rw-r--r-- 1 root root  62 Jun  3 11:51 greet02
-rw-r--r-- 1 root root 204 Jun  3 12:10 greet03
-rw-r--r-- 1 root root 106 Jun  3 12:15 greet04

greetings:
total 0

root@ubuntu20s1:~# mv ./greet0* ./greetings
root@ubuntu20s1:~# ls
Desktop    Downloads  Music     Public  Templates  Videos
Documents  greetings  Pictures  snap    test01
root@ubuntu20s1:~# ls ./greetings
greet01  greet02  greet03  greet04
```

Let's create another four files called bye01 – by04.

```
root@ubuntu20s1:~# cd greetings
root@ubuntu20s1:~/greetings# touch bye01 bye02 bye03 bye04
root@ubuntu20s1:~/greetings# ls
bye01  bye02  bye03  bye04  greet01  greet02  greet03  greet04
```

Now let's check the files in the greetings directory one more time and delete files containing specific strings; our targets are the files ending with 04. * is a wildcard replacing all characters.

```
root@ubuntu20s1:~/greetings# ls
bye01  bye02  bye03  bye04  greet01  greet02  greet03  greet04
root@ubuntu20s1:~/greetings# find . -name "*04"
./bye04
./greet04
root@ubuntu20s1:~/greetings# rm *04
root@ubuntu20s1:~/greetings# ls
bye01  bye02  bye03  greet01  greet02  greet03
```

Next, let's delete all the files containing greet using the rm greet* handle.

```
root@ubuntu20s1:~/greetings# rm greet*
root@ubuntu20s1:~/greetings# ls
bye01  bye02  bye03
```

Then let's clean all files in the folder by using the rm * option. After this command, the directory should be empty.

```
root@ubuntu20s1:~/greetings# rm *
root@ubuntu20s1:~/greetings# ls
root@ubuntu20s1:~/greetings#
```

② If you want to delete the directory in the same way, you have to use rm -r. -r stands for recursive; if you do not use the -r option, Linux does not allow you to delete directories, but you have to use it with care. Working from the same directory, let's make two directories below it and use the * wildcard character to remove the directories containing specific strings. To delete directories containing hi, you will be using a double wildcard, one at the front and one at the end. At the end of this exercise, your directory should be empty.

```
root@ubuntu20s1:~/greetings# mkdir sayhi01 sayhi02 saybye01 saybye02
root@ubuntu20s1:~/greetings# ls
saybye01  saybye02  sayhi01  sayhi02
root@ubuntu20s1:~/greetings# rm *hi*
rm: cannot remove 'sayhi01': Is a directory
rm: cannot remove 'sayhi02': Is a directory
root@ubuntu20s1:~/greetings# rm -r *hi*
root@ubuntu20s1:~/greetings# ls
saybye01  saybye02
root@ubuntu20s1:~/greetings# rm -r saybye*
root@ubuntu20s1:~/greetings# ls
root@ubuntu20s1:~/greetings#
```

Create a Python Application, Make Your File Executable, Add a Shebang, and Run the Application

You can change the file's permissions with the chmod command. This Linux command is handy when changing a Python script file's properties to make it executable. There are currently no Python files in the root user directory. Let's quickly create a simple Python script and see how this works with a Python script:

① To create a Python script on Linux, add a .py file extension to the end of the filename. To create your Python script, follow the echo and cat commands we have learned in section 4.4.2.1 or simply use the vi or nano text editor, which you have learned in this chapter. The \n after the word *Automation* denotes the newline and adds/changes the line. Create this file and run the application using python3 print5times.py to verify that your script runs smoothly.

```
root@ubuntu20s1:~/myscript# echo "x = 'Python Network Automation\n'" > print5times.py
root@ubuntu20s1:~/myscript# more print5times.py
x = 'Python Network Automation\n'
root@ubuntu20s1:~/myscript# cat >> print5times.py
print(x*5)

#To exit, press Ctrl+D keys.

root@ubuntu20s1:~/myscript# more print5times.py
x = 'Python Network Automation\n'
print(x*5)
root@ubuntu20s1:~/myscript# python3 print5times.py
Python Network Automation
Python Network Automation
Python Network Automation
Python Network Automation
Python Network Automation
```

② Now we have created a working Python script (or application) and reviewed the file mode. Yes, this file can also be referred to as an *application* as it is an application that prints x five times each time you run the application.

Run ls -l print5times.py to review the access. You have to look at the result starting with -rw-r--r--. As you can see, it is missing the x, or executable-level access. You need to modify this file's property to include x to make this file an executable, so we can run the application without specifying Python 3 as the application.

```
root@ubuntu20s1:~/myscript# ls -l print5times.py
-rw-r--r-- 1 root root 43 Jun  6 10:42 print5times.py
root@ubuntu20s1:~/myscript# ./print5times.py
-bash: ./print5times.py: Permission denied
```

Use chmod +x print5times.py to make the script executable. The file color should change to green automatically, indicating that this is now an executable file.

```
root@ubuntu20s1:~/myscript# chmod +x print5times.py
root@ubuntu20s1:~/myscript# ls -l print5times.py
-rwxr-xr-x 1 root root 45 Jun  6 10:46 print5times.py
```

Try to run the application without the python3 command. But when you run the script, you will encounter an unexpected token error as follows because we forgot to add the infamous shebang (#!/usr/bin/python3) line on the top; a shebang line defines where the interpreter is located.

```
root@ubuntu20s1:~/myscript# ./print5times.py
./print5times.py: line 1: x: command not found
./print5times.py: line 2: syntax error near unexpected token `x*5'
./print5times.py: line 2: `print(x*5)'
```

③ Let's add #!/usr/bin/python3 (shebang) at the beginning of our script. This time, we'll use the sed command with the -I and -e options. Sed or Stream Editor is also a powerful Linux/Unix tool for text manipulation. You do not have to be 100 percent familiar with this tool yet, but it will come in handy one day just knowing how it works.

```
root@ubuntu20s1:~/myscript# cat print5times.py
x = "Python Network Automation\n"
print(x*5)
root@ubuntu20s1:~/myscript# sed -i -e '1i#!/usr/bin/python3\' print5times.py
root@ubuntu20s1:~/myscript# cat print5times.py
#!/usr/bin/python3
x = "Python Network Automation\n"
print(x*5)
```

Now we checked that the shebang line is on the first line, let's run the Python script from the working directory. It should print x five times, as shown here:

```
root@ubuntu20s1:~/myscript# ./print5times.py
Python Network Automation
Python Network Automation
Python Network Automation
Python Network Automation
Python Network Automation
```

④ What if you wanted to run the application even without ./?. You can use a Linux command PATH="$(pwd):$PATH", but as soon as your Linux terminal session ends, the added PATH disappears.

```
root@ubuntu20s1:~/myscript# ls -lh print5times.py
-rwxr-xr-x 1 root root 64 Jun  6 11:23 print5times.py
root@ubuntu20s1:~/myscript# PATH="$(pwd):$PATH"
root@ubuntu20s1:~/myscript# print5times.py
Python Network Automation
Python Network Automation
Python Network Automation
Python Network Automation
Python Network Automation
```

⑤ To permanently add the /root/myscript directory or the current directory you are working into the PATH variable, you can use the following command. Now even after you have exited the session and come back, you should still be able to run the script without ./. After adding the path, make sure you restart the bash by executing the source ~/.bashrc or exec bash command to make the change take effect.

```
root@ubuntu20s1:~/myscript# echo "export PATH=\$PATH:$(pwd)" >> ~/.bashrc
root@ubuntu20s1:~/myscript# exec bash  #(source ~/.bashrc)  restarts bash
root@ubuntu20s1:~/myscript# print5times.py
Python Network Automation
Python Network Automation
Python Network Automation
Python Network Automation
Python Network Automation
```

You want to study more Linux and get certified?

If you want to study Linux further, you will need to study Linux Profession Institute 101 and Red Hat's RHCSA/RHCE. For those of you who have spare time and money, there are plenty of free and paid training programs available both online and offline. If you are interested in the LPI and RHCE certification track, please refer to the following link.

Linux Professional institute URL:

`https://www.lpi.org/our-certifications/exam-101-objectives`

Red Hat Certified System Administrator (RHCSA) URL: https://www.redhat.com/en/services/certification/rhcsa

Red Hat Certified Engineer:

`https://www.redhat.com/en/services/certification/rhce`

Summary

Now, this completes the file and directory exercises. We have covered only the tip of an iceberg here, but it's enough for you to perform your tasks in later Python network automation labs. You have to practice Linux file and directory navigation regularly, if not each day, to become accustomed to it. This is where all the magic begins with your Python network automation.

In the following chapter, we will quickly cover some basic Linux commands to locate important Linux system information. In the real production environment, you will not be fortunate enough to choose the flavor of Linux you like or always have root access to the servers. You must know how to find your new Linux system information and find compatible software for your Linux tools, Python, and related modules.

CHAPTER 8

Linux Basic Administration

There are plenty of books on Linux topics, and some of these books focus on only one Linux distribution while being hundreds of pages long. Continuing from the previous chapter, we will be covering the most fundamental Linux subjects in this chapter so that you can get through this book. If you are a newcomer to Linux and want to understand more about the Linux operating system (OS), it is a good idea to use a dedicated Linux book. You will learn to locate Linux system information, use Linux network commands, and then install TFTP, FTP, SFTP, and NTP services on your CentOS 8.1 server.

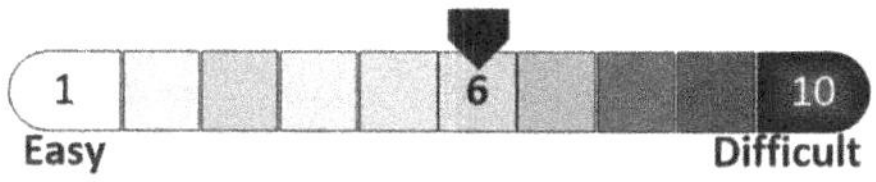

Information on Linux: Kernel and Distribution Version

Most of the new Linux users come up with this first question, "How can I check the exact Linux distribution version and kernel?" The Linux kernel is the main component of a Linux OS and is the core interface between a computer's hardware and processes. How do you check the Linux kernel and distribution versions on your OS? The exercises in this chapter are based on CentOS (a Red Hat-based OS), and due to the command syntax of different Linux distributions, some commands used might not work on Debian-based OSs (Ubuntu). If this is the case, then you will be reminded of such differences. However, most of the Linux commands across different Linux distributions are similar.

B. Choi, *Introduction to Python Network Automation*, https://doi.org/10.1007/978-1-4842-6806-3_8

① How do you check the Linux kernel version? Use the uname command with different options; the commands used on CentOS and Ubuntu are the same for uname commands.

```
For CentOS 8.1
[root@centos8s1 ~]# uname
Linux
[root@centos8s1 ~]# uname -o
GNU/Linux
[root@centos8s1 ~]# uname -r
4.18.0-193.14.2.el8_2.x86_64
[root@centos8s1 ~]# uname -or
4.18.0-193.14.2.el8_2.x86_64 GNU/Linux

For Ubuntu 20.04 LTS
root@ubuntu20s1:~# uname
Linux
root@ubuntu20s1:~# uname -o
GNU/Linux
root@ubuntu20s1:~# uname -r
5.4.0-47-generic
root@ubuntu20s1:~# uname -or
5.4.0-47-generic GNU/Linux
```

② The following exercise is an additional uname command exercise that stores null-terminated operating system information strings into structured references by name. Run the uname commands with different options. Note, the same commands can be used on a Ubuntu 20.04 LTS server.

```
[root@centos8s1 ~]# uname -a          # -a option for all
Linux centos8s1 4.18.0-193.14.2.el8_2.x86_64 #1 SMP Sun Jul 26 03:54:29 UTC 2020
x86_64 x86_64 x86_64 GNU/Linux
[root@centos8s1 ~]# uname -n          # -n for name or hostname
centos8s1
[root@centos8s1 ~]# uname -r          # -r for Linux kernel version
4.18.0-193.14.2.el8_2.x86_64
[root@centos8s1 ~]# uname -m          # -m for system architecture
x86_64
[root@centos8s1 ~]# uname -v          # -v for system time and timezone
#1 SMP Sun Jul 26 03:54:29 UTC 2020
[root@centos8s1 ~]# uname -rnmv          # combined options
centos8s1 4.18.0-193.14.2.el8_2.x86_64 #1 SMP Sun Jul 26 03:54:29 UTC 2020 x86_64
```

③ On CentOS and Red Hat-based Linux OSs, you can also use the grep command to check the Grub Environment Block. Use the grep saved_entry /boot/grub2/grubenv command. This command does not work on Debian-based Linux distributions.

```
For CentOS 8.1
[root@centos8s1 ~]# grep saved_entry /boot/grub2/grubenv
saved_entry=e53c131bb54c4fb1a835f3aa435024e2-4.18.0-193.14.2.el8_2.x86_64
```

④ Use hostnamectl to check the hostname, OS, kernel version, architecture, and more.

```
For CentOS 8.1
[root@centos8s1 ~]# hostnamectl
   Static hostname: centos8s1
      Icon name: computer-vm
         Chassis: vm
      Machine ID: e53c131bb54c4fb1a835f3aa435024e2
         Boot ID: 648950d070634d3e856b015f4a7cf7cd
   Virtualization: vmware
Operating System: CentOS Linux 8 (Core)
   CPE OS Name: cpe:/o:centos:centos:8
      Kernel: Linux 4.18.0-193.14.2.el8_2.x86_64
   Architecture: x86-64

For Ubuntu 20.04 LTS
root@ubuntu20s1:~# hostnamectl
   Static hostname: ubuntu20s1
      Icon name: computer-vm
         Chassis: vm
      Machine ID: ea202235f9834d979436db10d89b1347
         Boot ID: 9bcbe4f6d00e407a81634dd61d74ff39
   Virtualization: vmware
Operating System: Ubuntu 20.04.1 LTS
      Kernel: Linux 5.4.0-47-generic
   Architecture: x86-64
```

⑤ You can also use the lsb_release -d command to check your OS. Unlike Ubuntu OS, CentOS does not have lsb pre-installed. You can install it by using the yum install -y redhat-lsb command or just running lsb_release -d and, when prompted, say Y to install.

```
For CentOS 8.1
[root@centos8s1 ~]# lsb_release -d
[root@centos8s1 ~]# yum install -y redhat-lsb
[root@centos8s1 ~]# lsb_release -d
Description:    CentOS Linux release 8.2.2004 (Core)
```

You can also use the -sc and -a options to view even more information about your Linux operating system.

```
For Ubuntu 20.04 LTS
root@ubuntu20s1:~# lsb_release -d
Description:    Ubuntu 20.04.1 LTS
root@ubuntu20s1:~# lsb_release -sc
focal
root@ubuntu20s1:~# lsb_release -a
No LSB modules are available.
Distributor ID: Ubuntu
Description:    Ubuntu 20.04.1 LTS
Release:        20.04
Codename:       focal
```

⑥ You can also use the `cat` command to output information under the `/etc/` directory. Notice that this works on CentOS, but *not* on Ubuntu, so the better way to view the system information is to use `cat` with a wildcard *. See the next exercise.

```
For CentOS 8.1
[root@centos8s1 ~]# cat /etc/centos-release
CentOS Linux release 8.2.2004 (Core)
[root@centos8s1 ~]# cat /etc/system-release
CentOS Linux release 8.2.2004 (Core)
```

⑦ To check your Linux's distro release version information, use the `cat /etc/*release` command. This `cat` command is a good Linux command to remember as it provides an abundance of information on your Linux operating system. This command works on both CentOS and Ubuntu Linux OS.

```
[root@centos8s1 ~]# cat /etc/*release
CentOS Linux release 8.2.2004 (Core)
NAME="CentOS Linux"
VERSION="8 (Core)"
ID="centos"
ID_LIKE="rhel fedora"
VERSION_ID="8"
PLATFORM_ID="platform:el8"
PRETTY_NAME="CentOS Linux 8 (Core)"
ANSI_COLOR="0;31"
CPE_NAME="cpe:/o:centos:centos:8"
HOME_URL="https://www.centos.org/"
BUG_REPORT_URL="https://bugs.centos.org/"

CENTOS_MANTISBT_PROJECT="CentOS-8"
CENTOS_MANTISBT_PROJECT_VERSION="8"
REDHAT_SUPPORT_PRODUCT="centos"
REDHAT_SUPPORT_PRODUCT_VERSION="8"

CentOS Linux release 8.2.2004 (Core)
CentOS Linux release 8.2.2004 (Core)
```

Also, try to run the `cat /etc/os-release` command and check the difference.

Information on Linux: Use the netstat Command to Validate TCP/UDP Ports

To get you ready for IP services installation, make your Linux servers useful for our lab, and apply what you have learned in the production, you first have to know how to use some Linux network tools. All devices are running on some network segment and are connected on the network; hence, we have to be aware of which ports are opened or closed. In other words, which IP services are running and available to your users are part of server network security, which can be part of network access control. Let's see how we can check network configurations on Linux systems.

① First, to get the list of all network interfaces on your Linux server, use `netstat -i`.

```
[root@centos8s1 ~]# netstat -i
Kernel Interface table
```

Iface	MTU	RX-OK	RX-ERR	RX-DRP	RX-OVR	TX-OK	TX-ERR	TX-DRP	TX-OVR	Flg
ens160	1500	5601	0	0	0	2587	0	0	0	BMRU
lo	65536	0	0	0	0	0	0	0	0	LRU
virbr0	1500	0	0	0	0	0	0	0	0	BMU

② To practice our `netstat` commands, let's install the nginx web services server on your CentOS server and start web services. After starting the Nginx web services, run the `netstat -tulpn : grep :80` command to confirm that your CentOS server is listening on port 80 on the local interface.

For CentOS 8.1, install and start the nginx web server.

```
[root@centos8s1 ~]# yum install -y nginx
[root@centos8s1 ~]# whatis nginx
nginx (3pm)          - Perl interface to the nginx HTTP server API
nginx (8)            - "HTTP and reverse proxy server, mail proxy server"
[root@centos8s1 ~]# whereis nginx
nginx: /usr/sbin/nginx /usr/lib64/nginx /etc/nginx /usr/share/nginx /usr/share/man/
man3/nginx.3pm.gz /usr/share/man/man8/nginx.8.gz
[root@centos8s1 ~]# systemctl start nginx
[root@centos8s1 ~]# netstat -tulpn | grep :80
tcp      0      0 0.0.0.0:80        0.0.0.0:*         LISTEN      6046/nginx: master
tcp6     0      0 :::80                  :::*         LISTEN      6046/nginx: master
```

At this point, if you log into your CentOS desktop through VMware's main console, you will be able to open the Nginx home page in the Firefox web browser using `http://localhost` or `http://192.168.183.130`. See Figure 8-1.

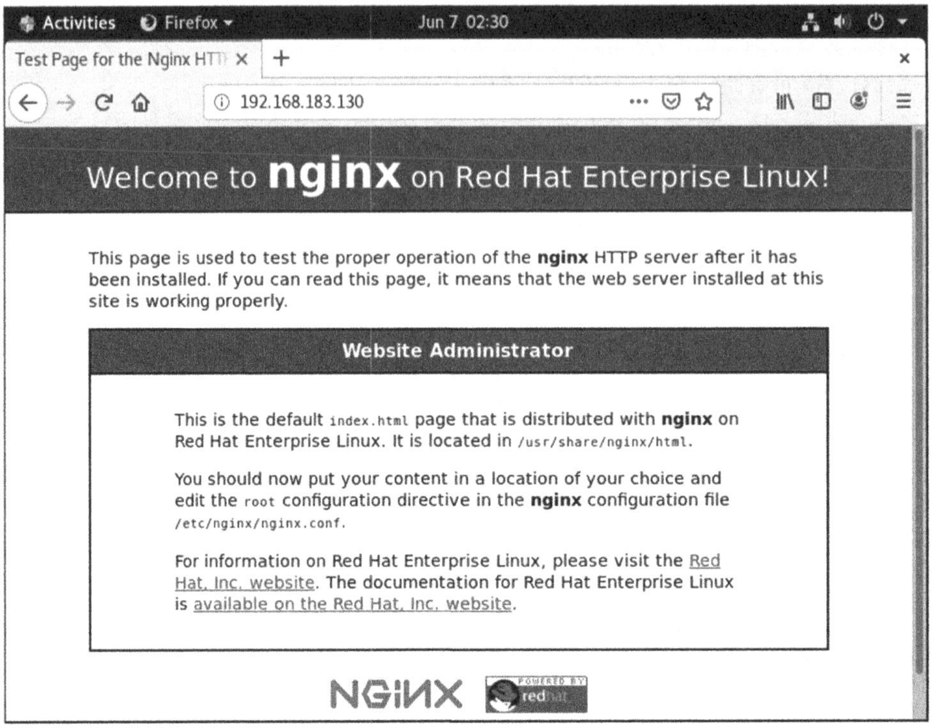

Figure 8-1. *CenOS desktop, opening http://192.168.183.130*

③ To permanently enable HTTP connections on port 80 and allow other machines to connect via HTTP, add the HTTP service into the CentOS firewall's services list. Then verify that the HTTP firewall service is running correctly. To apply the changes, you must reload the firewall service using the `firewall-cmd --reload` command. The full commands are listed here:

```
[root@centos8s1 ~]# firewall-cmd --permanent --add-service=http
success
[root@centos8s1 ~]# firewall-cmd --permanent --list-all
public
target: default
icmp-block-inversion: no
interfaces:
sources:
services: cockpit dhcpv6-client ftp http ntp ssh tftp
ports: 40000-41000/tcp
protocols:
masquerade: no
forward-ports:
source-ports:
icmp-blocks:
rich rules:

[root@centos8s1 ~]# firewall-cmd --reload
success
```

There is no DNS server in our network, so we have to use our CentOS server's IP address. We already know that our server IP is 192.168.183.130, but to verify this information, let's run the following command. Optionally, you can use the `ip add` command and browse through the information.

```
[root@centos8s1 ~]# ip addr show ens160 | grep inet | awk '{ print $2; }' | sed
's/\/.*$//'
192.168.183.130
fe80::f49c:7ff4:fb3f:bf32

[root@centos8s1 ~]# ip add
[...omitted for brevity]
2: ens160: <BROADCAST,MULTICAST,UP,LOWER_UP> mtu 1500 qdisc fq_codel state UP group
default qlen 1000
    link/ether 00:0c:29:85:a6:36 brd ff:ff:ff:ff:ff:ff
    inet 192.168.183.130/24 brd 192.168.183.255 scope global noprefixroute ens160
    valid_lft forever preferred_lft forever
    inet6 fe80::f49c:7ff4:fb3f:bf32/64 scope link noprefixroute
    valid_lft forever preferred_lft forever
[...omitted for brevity]
```

At this point, you can open a web browser from your Windows 10 host PC/laptop and open the Nginx home page using `http://192.168.183.130`. Now you have successfully installed Nginx and opened port 80 on your server. See Figure 8-2.

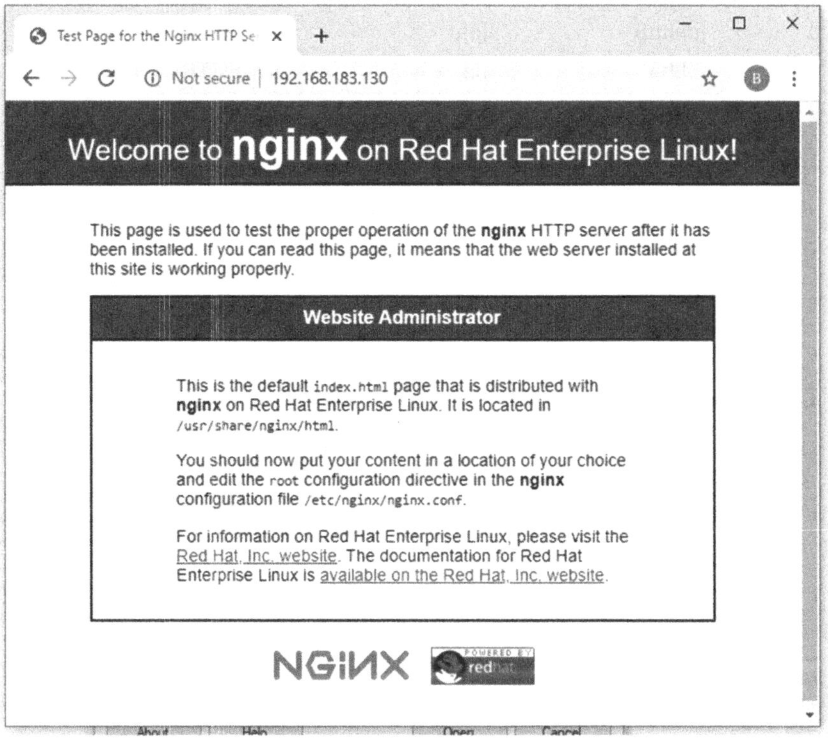

Figure 8-2. *Windows host, opening http://192.168.183.130*

④ To list all the TCP or UDP ports on your Linux server, you can use the `netstat -a` command; the `-a` option stands for `all`. You can specify the `-t` option for TCP ports only or the `-u` option for UDP ports in use.

For TCP:

```
[root@centos8s1 ~]# netstat -at
```

Active Internet connections (servers and established)

Proto	Recv-Q	Send-Q	Local Address	Foreign Address	State
tcp	0	0	centos8s1:smux	0.0.0.0:*	LISTEN
tcp	0	0	0.0.0.0:hostmon	0.0.0.0:*	LISTEN
tcp	0	0	0.0.0.0:sunrpc	0.0.0.0:*	LISTEN
tcp	0	0	0.0.0.0:http	0.0.0.0:*	LISTEN
tcp	0	0	centos8s1:domain	0.0.0.0:*	LISTEN
tcp	0	0	0.0.0.0:ssh	0.0.0.0:*	LISTEN
tcp	0	0	centos8s1:ipp	0.0.0.0:*	LISTEN
tcp	0	64	centos8s1:ssh	192.168.183.1:54572	ESTABLISHED
tcp6	0	0	[::]:hostmon	[::]:*	LISTEN
tcp6	0	0	[::]:sunrpc	[::]:*	LISTEN
tcp6	0	0	[::]:http	[::]:*	LISTEN
tcp6	0	0	[::]:ftp	[::]:*	LISTEN
tcp6	0	0	[::]:ssh	[::]:*	LISTEN
tcp6	0	0	centos8s1:ipp	[::]:*	LISTEN

For UDP

```
[root@centos8s1 ~]# netstat -au
```

Active Internet connections (servers and established)

Proto	Recv-Q	Send-Q	Local Address	Foreign Address	State
udp	0	0	0.0.0.0:48026	0.0.0.0:*	
udp	0	0	centos8s1:58365	_gateway:domain	ESTABLISHED
udp	0	0	centos8s1:domain	0.0.0.0:*	
udp	0	0	127.0.0.53:domain	0.0.0.0:*	
udp	0	0	0.0.0.0:bootps	0.0.0.0:*	
udp	0	0	centos8s1:bootpc	192.168.183.254:bootps	ESTABLISHED
udp	0	0	0.0.0.0:tftp	0.0.0.0:*	
udp	0	0	0.0.0.0:sunrpc	0.0.0.0:*	
udp	0	0	0.0.0.0:ntp	0.0.0.0:*	
udp	0	0	0.0.0.0:snmp	0.0.0.0:*	
udp	0	0	0.0.0.0:mdns	0.0.0.0:*	
udp	0	0	0.0.0.0:hostmon	0.0.0.0:*	
udp	0	0	centos8s1:323	0.0.0.0:*	
udp6	0	0	[::]:tftp	[::]:*	
udp6	0	0	[::]:sunrpc	[::]:*	
udp6	0	0	[::]:mdns	[::]:*	
udp6	0	0	[::]:hostmon	[::]:*	
udp6	0	0	centos8s1:323	[::]:*	
udp6	0	0	[::]:53619	[::]:*	

⑤ If you want to list only the listening ports, then `netstat -l` can be used. The list was too long, so the following output only shows the top of the listening port information, but perhaps you can run this command on your CentOS VM and study the returned result.

```
[root@centos8s1 ~]# netstat -l
```

Active Internet connections (only servers)

Proto	Recv-Q	Send-Q	Local Address	Foreign Address	State
tcp	0	0	centos8s1:smux	0.0.0.0:*	LISTEN
tcp	0	0	0.0.0.0:hostmon	0.0.0.0:*	LISTEN
tcp	0	0	0.0.0.0:sunrpc	0.0.0.0:*	LISTEN
tcp	0	0	0.0.0.0:http	0.0.0.0:*	LISTEN
tcp	0	0	centos8s1:domain	0.0.0.0:*	LISTEN

[...omitted for brevity]

⑥ Like the `netstat -a` command, `netstat -l` also can be used with the `-t` or `-u` option for TCP- and UDP-only information. `netstat -lt` will only list TCP listening ports, whereas `netstat -lu` lists only UDP listening ports.

```
netstat -lt
netstat -lu
```

Run the previous commands on your Linux concole and see what output you receive from your CentOS server.

⑦ If you want to check which process uses a specific port, you can check it by typing `netstat -an` combined with a pipe (|) and `grep ':port_number'`. So if you want to check who is using SSH (port 22), you would issue the `netstat -an | grep ':22'` command.

```
netstat -an | grep ':22' <<< for SSH service
[root@centos8s1 ~]# netstat -an | grep ':22'
tcp        0      0 0.0.0.0:22              0.0.0.0:*               LISTEN
tcp        0     64 192.168.183.130:22      192.168.183.1:54572     ESTABLISHED
tcp6       0      0 :::22

netstat -an | grep ':80'  <<< for http service
[root@centos8s1 ~]# netstat -an | grep ':80'
tcp        0      0 0.0.0.0:80              0.0.0.0:*           LISTEN
tcp6       0      0 :::80                   :::*                LISTEN
```

⑧ To check which IP network services are running on your server, you can issue the `netstat -ap` command. Here is an example of the `netstat -ap | grep ssh` command:

```
[root@centos8s1 ~]# netstat -ap | grep ssh
tcp   0      0 0.0.0.0:ssh     0.0.0.0:*             LISTEN       1257/sshd
tcp   0     64 centos8s1:ssh   192.168.183.1:54572   ESTABLISHED  1609/sshd: root [pr
tcp6  0      0 [::]:ssh        [::]:*                LISTEN       1257/sshd
unix  2      [ ]         STREAM     CONNECTED     42663     1609/sshd: root [pr
unix  2      [ ]         STREAM     CONNECTED     35797     1609/sshd: root [pr
unix  2      [ ]         STREAM     CONNECTED     43450     2204/sshd: root@pts
unix  2      [ ]         DGRAM                    43437     1609/sshd: root [pr
unix  3      [ ]         STREAM     CONNECTED     43441     1609/sshd: root [pr
unix  3      [ ]         STREAM     CONNECTED     43440     2204/sshd: root@pts
unix  3      [ ]         STREAM     CONNECTED     32383     1257/sshd
unix  2      [ ]         STREAM     CONNECTED     32584     1257/sshd
```

⑨ Display the process ID (PID) and program names in your output; you can use the `netstat -pt` command. It will display the protocol, IP service, and IP address information for your reference. The following command displays the `netstat -pt` output of an active SSH connection:

```
[root@centos8s1 ~]# netstat -pt
Active Internet connections (w/o servers)
Proto Recv-Q Send-Q Local Address  Foreign Address     State       PID/Program name
tcp    0    64 centos8s1:ssh    192.168.183.1:54572     ESTABLISHED 1609/sshd: root [pr
```

⑩ The last set of commands consists of statistics commands; since the output is quite long, you can run the following commands from your CentOS VM console. Your clue to the -s handle is the word *statistics*.

Please run the following commands from your CentOS Linux server to study the output at your own pace:

```
[root@centos8s1 ~]# netstat -s
[root@centos8s1 ~]# netstat -st
[root@centos8s1 ~]# netstat -su
```

Installing TFTP, FTP, SFTP, and NTP Servers

Here is a quick vocabulary lesson for non-CCNA readers:

FTP: File Transfer Protocol

SFTP: Secure File Transfer Protocol

TFTP: Trivial File Transfer Protocol

NTP: Network Time Protocol

In the world of business, PC end users and IT engineers alike use all kinds of network services supported within their network. Among the many IP services, the most popular network services used and supported by network and system engineers today include FTP, SFTP, TFTP, and NTP services. Each service can be installed on multiple distributed servers or even on networking platforms if the installation and configuration are supported. But in the lab, there is no reason to distribute network services across four separate virtual servers to support four different network services. Since we already have installed Nginx services, this makes five IP services on a single server. You can install all services on a single Linux server for testing purposes, but these services could be distributed across multiple servers in a real production environment.

In the production environment, FTP, SFTP, and TFTP are file services that require a large amount of storage space. The mass storage requirement means that these services are usually almost always installed on enterprise Linux or Windows servers, but not on networking devices such as routers and switches. NTP is a time service, so this service can run from Cisco routers. In NTP's case, the time synchronization service is provided so that both servers and network devices can run on standard time. All four of these IP services can be bundled into a single server and used as the IP services server in our lab for convenience. If you are coming from a pure networking background, you probably do not have a lot of experience building and supporting the Linux servers' enterprise IP services. Wouldn't it be great to have a better understanding of both the network and systems administration skill sets? Knowing more is freedom. Let's install FTP, SFTP, TFTP, and NTP servers on the CentOS 8 server for lab purposes. Remember, we are reserving the Ubuntu server as a Python + Docker server for later labs.

FTP Server Installation

File Transfer Protocol (FTP) is a secure and stable network service designed to send and receive many files between the server and clients. In other words, the simple advantage is that you can quickly send and receive files simultaneously compared to slower TFTP. FTP uses TCP port 21 by default and is less secure than its secure version, SFTP. There are several open source FTP servers available for Linux, for example, PureFTPd, ProFTPD, and vsftpd. In our example, we will install and use Very Secure FTP daemon (`vsftpd`) as it is secure, stable, and fast. First, let's check if the FTP service is running on our CentOS 8 server.

The FTP server installation and verification in CentOS 8 are as follows:

① While installing the CentOS 8 virtual machine, we have selected to install the FTP server, but we do not know exactly which software version is installed. By default, CentOS will install `vsftpd` when you choose to install the FTP server from the installation media. Run the `vsftpd -version` command to check the current version of `vsftpd` on your CentOS server.

```
As expected, vsftpd version 3.0.3 is available.
[root@centos8s1 ~]# vsftpd -version
vsftpd: version 3.0.3
```

If you do not have the FTP software installed on your CentOS server, use the following two commands to complete your installation:

```
[root@centos8s1 ~]# sudo yum makecache
[root@centos8s1 ~]# yum install -y vsftpd
```

② Check if `vsftpd` is running on your server by typing `systemctl status vsftpd`.

```
[root@centos8s1 ~]# systemctl status vsftpd
● vsftpd.service - Vsftpd ftp daemon
   Loaded: loaded (/usr/lib/systemd/system/vsftpd.service; enabled; vendor preset:
   disabled)
   Active: active (running) since Mon 2021-01-04 19:15:34 AEDT; 1h 43min ago
   Process: 1238 ExecStart=/usr/sbin/vsftpd /etc/vsftpd/vsftpd.conf (code=exited,
   status=0/SUCCESS)
   Main PID: 1248 (vsftpd)
Tasks: 1 (limit: 11166)
Memory: 932.0K
CGroup: /system.slice/vsftpd.service
      ice248 /usr/sbin/vsftpd /etc/vsftpd/vsftpd.conf

Jan 04 19:15:33 centos8s1 systemd[1]: Starting Vsftpd ftp daemon...
Jan 04 19:15:34 centos8s1 systemd[1]: Started Vsftpd ftp daemon.
```

Use `Ctrl+C` to exit from the `vsftpd` status file.

③ You want the `vsftpd` daemon to start automatically during OS startup, so you must enable this service with the `systemctl enable` command. Once you have enabled the `vsftpd` service, use the same status command used previously to check the running status. When Active is `active (running)`, then the `vsftpd` service is active and working correctly.

```
[root@centos8s1 ~]# systemctl enable vsftpd --now
[root@centos8s1 ~]# systemctl status vsftpd
```

④ To use FTP for the lab, a few lines of the `vsftpd.conf` file need to be updated. Open the `vsftpd.conf` file in nano, check the existing configuration, and add a few configuration lines.

```
[root@centos8s1 ~]# nano /etc/vsftpd/vsftpd.conf
```

The following configuration should be ready out of the box, but configure the settings as follows if they are different:

```
anonymous_enable=NO
local_enable=YES
write_enable=YES
```

To control the access to the FTP server using `user_list`, add the following lines after `userlist_enable=YES`:

```
userlist_file=/etc/vsftpd/user_list
userlist_deny=NO
```

To grant writable access to your user to its home directory, use this:

```
allow_writeable_chroot=YES
```

Also, `vsftpd` can use any port range for passive FTP connections. It is best practice to specify the port range for this use. Append the following configuration at the end of the `vsftpd.conf` file and save the file:

```
pasv_enable=YES
pasv_min_port=40000
pasv_max_port=41000
```

To change where the files are uploaded and downloaded, update the `local_root` configuration. In this example, `$USER` will take your user's ID and open FTP sessions from the `/home/pynetauto/ftp` directory.

```
user_sub_token=$USER
local_root=/home/$USER/ftp
```

After checking and updating the previous settings, append the following lines at the end of the `/etc/vsftpd/vsftpd.conf` file:

```
### ADDED by Admin ###
# Use user_list
userlist_file=/etc/vsftpd/user_list
userlist_deny=NO
# Allow writeable_chroot to the user
allow_writeable_chroot=YES
# Control passive port range to use between 40000-41000
pasv_enable=YES
pasv_min_port=40000
pasv_max_port=41000
# Use ftp directory under /home/user/
user_sub_token=$USER
local_root=/home/$USER/ftp
```

Remember the last line: `local_root = /home/$USER/ftp`. Make sure you create a local folder called `ftp` for the FTP access. We will be using the standard user to log into the FTP server, in my example, the `/home/pynetauto/ftp` directory.

```
[pynetauto@centos8s1 ~]$ mkdir ftp
```

⑤ Use the vi editor to change the FTP server configuration file so that all users can access it. Now add your user ID to the `user_list` file under `/etc/vsftpd`.

```
[root@centos8s1 ~]# vi /etc/vsftpd/user_list
# vsftpd userlist
# If userlist_deny=NO, only allow users in this file
# If userlist_deny=YES (default), never allow users in this file, and
# do not even prompt for a password.
# Note that the default vsftpd pam config also checks /etc/vsftpd/ftpusers
# for users that are denied.
root
bin
[...omitted for brivety]
nobody
pynetauto
~
"/etc/vsftpd/user_list" 21L, 371C
```

⑥ Once the changes have been saved to the file, open FTP and passive ports using the `firewall-cmd` commands. To allow firewall access to the FTP ports 20 and 21, run the following command:

```
firewall-cmd --add-service=ftp --permanent
(OR firewall-cmd --permanent --add-port=20-21/tcp)
firewall-cmd --permanent --add-port=40000-41000/tcp
setsebool -P ftpd_full_access on
firewall-cmd --reload
```

⑦ Make sure that `systemctl enable vsftpd` is issued to make `vsftpd` start automatically at the system startup. Also, here are the FTP troubleshooting commands for you to use. Use these commands as required to keep the service up and running.

```
systemctl enable vsftpd.service
systemctl start vsftpd.service
systemctl restart vsftpd.service
systemctl stop vsftpd.service
systemctl status vsftpd.service
```

We have learned `netstat` commands in the previous section, and you can use `netstat` commands to check that the FTP services are running smoothly.

```
netstat -ap | grep ftp
netstat -tupan | grep 21
netstat -na | grep tcp6
```

⑧ If the FTP service is working correctly, you should open your favorite web browser and open the FTP page using `ftp://SERVER_IP_ADDRESS` for your server. If you are prompted with the user ID and password, enter your details. See Figure 8-3.

```
ftp://192.168.183.130/
```

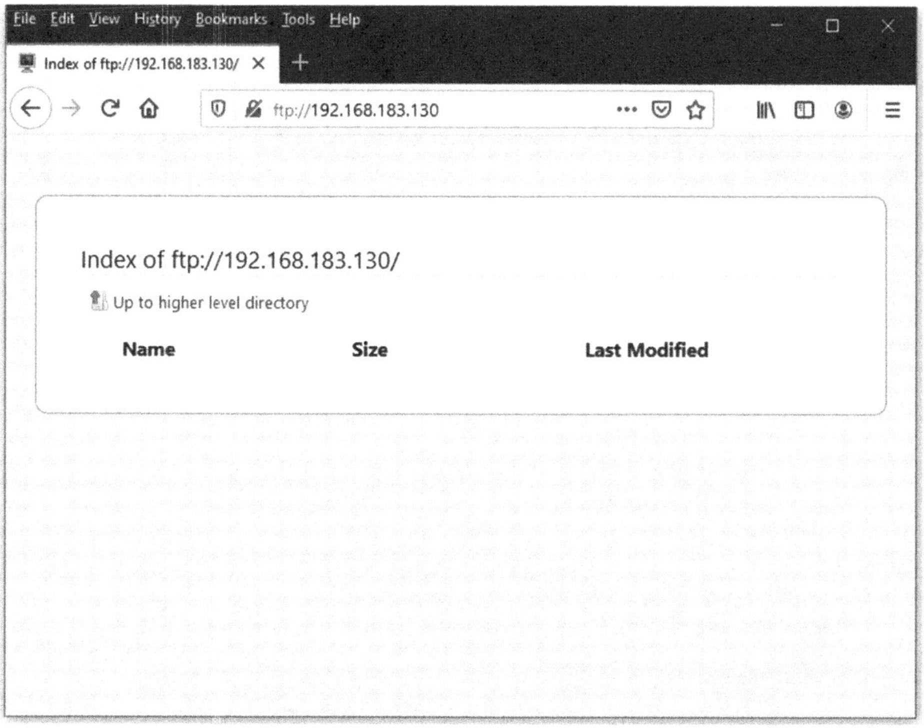

Figure 8-3. CentOS FTP server, FTP opened in Firefox web browser

⑨ You can also download the FileZilla client from your Windows host PC or Linux desktop and connect to your new FTP server using port 21.

URL: `https://filezilla-project.org/download.php?platform=win64`

■ **Tip** Enter `ftp://192.168.183.130` in the Host field. See Figure 8-4.

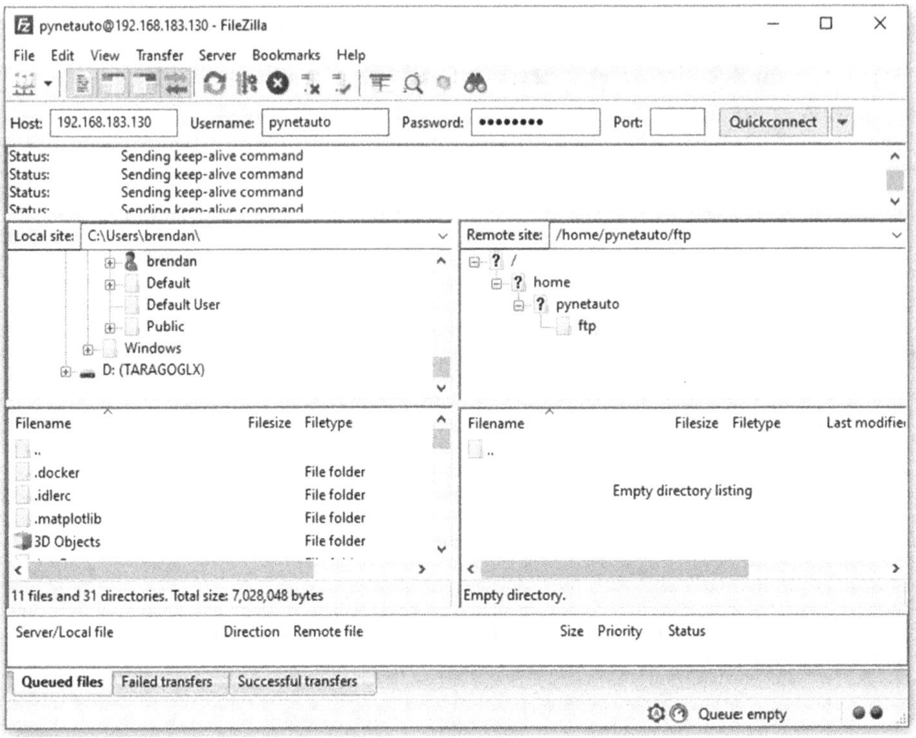

Figure 8-4. *FileZilla client connected to FTP server*

⑩ WinSCP is also another Windows application that comes in handy when connecting to your FTP server for file management. Upload or download between your host's Windows OS and CentOS 8 Linux server. See Figure 8-5 and Figure 8-6.

You can download WinSCP for free from the following URL:

URL: `https://winscp.net/eng/download.php`

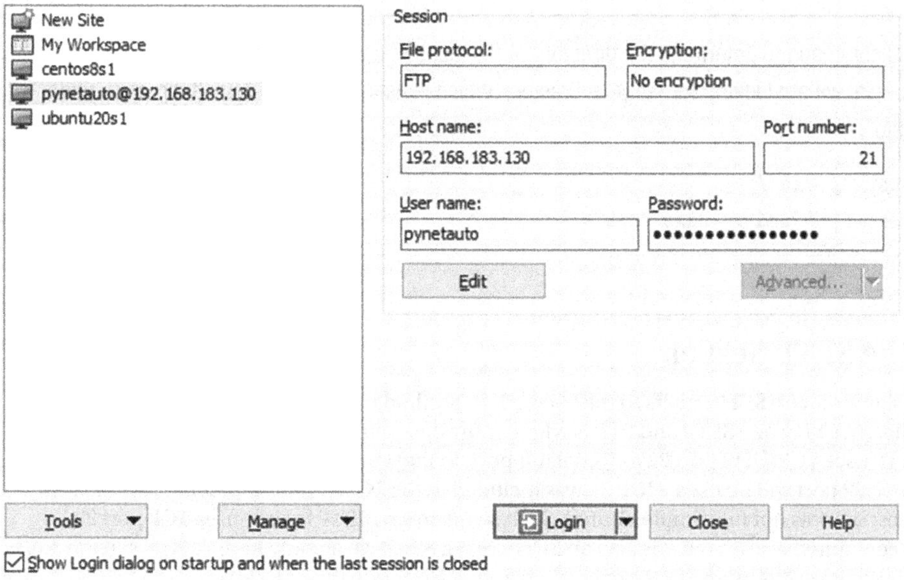

Figure 8-5. *WinSCP, connecting to CentOS FTP server*

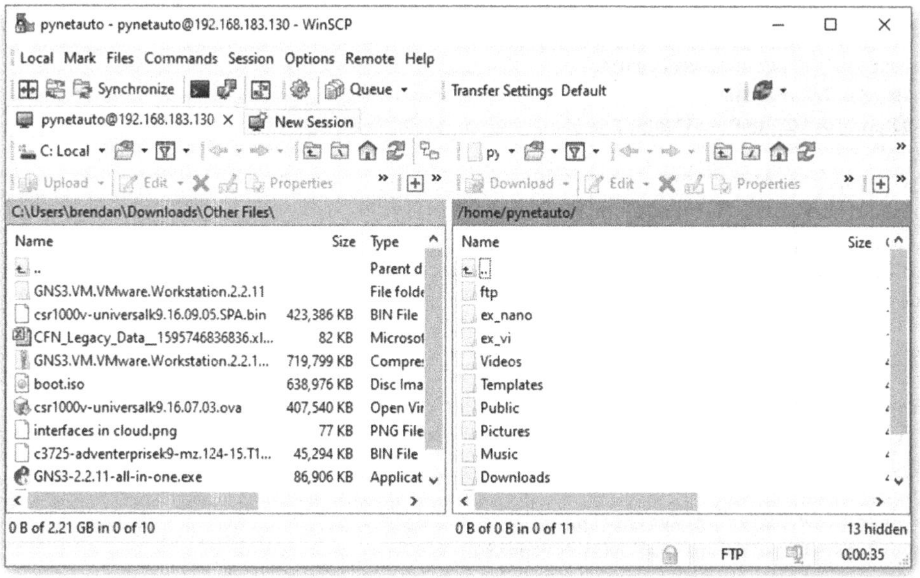

Figure 8-6. *WinSCP, Connected to CentOS FTP server*

You have completed the setup and FTP server login testing. You can now use the FTP server to share various files, such as IOS and configuration files, between the server and other network devices. Of course, you can also use FTP to back up router and switch configurations.

Use the `find` command to determine the directory or file location containing a file or directory name. In the following example, we are looking for the `pub` directory, which is usually the `ftp` default directory under the `./var/ftp/` directory.

```
[root @ localhost ~] # cd /
[root @ localhost /] # find . -name "pub"
```

Installing the SFTP Server

Secure File Transfer Protocol (SFTP) refers to the Secure FTP method to share files securely over the network. The difference between SFTP and FTP is whether the data sent across the network is encrypted or unencrypted. SFTP uses TCP/UDP port 22 as its default port. In most of the file transfer scenarios over the SFTP protocol, TCP 22 port will be used. UDP 22 was included in the TCP/IP development process at the developer's request but was not fully implemented. So, it is safe to say, SFTP mainly uses TCP port 22.

`vsftpd` was configured as FTP, but it is also an SFTP server. Since we already have `vsftpd` version 3.0.3 installed, we will configure this as an SFTP server too, running alongside the FTP server.

① First, log into CentOS 8 VM as the root user via the SSH client, PuTTY. You do not need to install new software for SFTP, but to begin, you need to create an SFTP-specific user account. Use `adduser` and `passwd` to create a new user for SFTP file transfer; the username created here is `sftpuser`.

```
[root@centos8s1 ~]# adduser sftpuser
[root@centos8s1 ~]# passwd sftpuser
Changing password for user sftpuser.
New password: **********
Retype new password: **********
passwd: all authentication tokens updated successfully.
```

A quick tip: if you want to remove and re-create a user, you can use `userdel` command. To delete the user's home directory and mail pool, add `-r`.

```
[root@centos8s1 ~]# userdel -r sftpuser
```

② Create a directory `sftp` under the `/var/` directory and then create another child directory `sftpdata` under the `/var/sftp/` directory, where you will store and share your files. The directory name given here is `sftpdata`.

```
[root@centos8s1 ~]# mkdir -p /var/sftp/
[root@centos8s1 ~]# mkdir -p /var/sftp/sftpdata
```

③ Change the ownership of the `sftp` directory so that `sftpuser` can change the contents of `/var/sftp`. Make the root user become the owner of the `/var/sftp/` directory. Change the permissions to 75 5 so that `sftpuser` can modify directories and files. Make the `sftpuser` user the owner of the `/var/sftp/sftpdata` directory.

```
[root@centos8s1 ~]# chown root:root /var/sftp
[root@centos8s1 ~]# chmod 755 /var/sftp
[root@centos8s1 ~]# chown sftpuser:sftpuser /var/sftp/sftpdata
```

④ To restrict SSH access to the `/var/sftp/sftpdata` directory, you have to modify the `sshd_config` file in the `/etc/ssh/` directory. Open the `sshd_config` file to add/modify the following configuration. Copy the contents specified here to the bottom of the configuration file and save it.

```
[root@centos8s1 ~]# vi /etc/ssh/sshd_config

# Add the following to the end of the file.

### ADDED by Admin ###
Match User sftpuser
ForceCommand internal-sftp
PasswordAuthentication yes
ChrootDirectory /var/sftp
PermitTunnel no
AllowAgentForwarding no
AllowTcpForwarding no
X11Forwarding no
```

⑤ Restart the `sshd` service for the previous change to take effect.

```
[root@centos8s1 ~]# systemctl restart sshd
```

⑥ If you try to SSH into the CentOS server using the `sftpuser` account, the connection will be refused and disconnected. Even though SSH and SFTP use the same connection port, the `sftpuser` account can only be used for SFTP connections but not SSH connections. Give it a try.

```
[root@centos8s1 ~]# ssh sftpuser@192.168.183.130
The authenticity of host '192.168.183.130 (192.168.183.130)' can't be established.
ECDSA key fingerprint is SHA256:b17PV5polHEKIcl+cFUCGA1KHGcl7xJkw/jhTfOkfZY.
Are you sure you want to continue connecting (yes/no/[fingerprint])? yes
Warning: Permanently added '192.168.183.130' (ECDSA) to the list of known hosts.
sftpuser@192.168.183.130's password: ********
This service allows sftp connections only.
Connection to 192.168.183.130 closed.
```

⑦ This time, try to connect to the SFTP server using the sftp command. Enter the password to login, then use Ctrl+Z to disconnect from the SFTP server.

```
[root@centos8s1 ~]# sftp sftpuser@192.168.183.130
sftpuser@192.168.183.130's password: ********
Connected to sftpuser@192.168.183.130.
sftp>
```

Press Ctrl+Z to disconnect from the sftp server.

```
[1]+  Stopped                 sftp sftpuser@192.168.183.130
```

⑧ Use the following commands to check if port 22 and sshd are working correctly (see Figure 8-7):

```
[root@centos8s1 ~]# netstat -ap | grep sshd
[root@centos8s1 ~]# netstat -tupan | grep 22
[root@centos8s1 ~]# netstat -na | grep tcp6
```

```
[root@centos8s1 ~]# netstat -tupan | grep 22
tcp        0      0 192.168.122.1:53        0.0.0.0:*               LISTEN
2083/dnsmasq
tcp        0      0 0.0.0.0:22              0.0.0.0:*               LISTEN
7681/sshd
tcp        0      0 192.168.183.130:48476   192.168.183.130:22      ESTABLISHED
7811/ssh
tcp        0      0 192.168.183.130:22      192.168.183.1:54798     ESTABLISHED
3215/sshd: root [pr
tcp        0     64 192.168.183.130:22      192.168.183.1:56444     ESTABLISHED
7417/sshd: root [pr
tcp        0      0 192.168.183.130:22      192.168.183.130:48476   ESTABLISHED
7812/sshd: sftpuser
tcp6       0      0 :::22                   :::*                    LISTEN
7681/sshd
udp        0      0 192.168.122.1:53        0.0.0.0:*
2083/dnsmasq
[root@centos8s1 ~]#
```

Figure 8-7. *CentOS, netstat -tupan | grep 22 example*

⑨ Finally, verify that your SFTP server is working correctly. You can use Windows applications such as FileZilla or WinSCP with user ID sftpuser, your password, and connecting port 22. See Figure 8-8 and Figure 8-9.

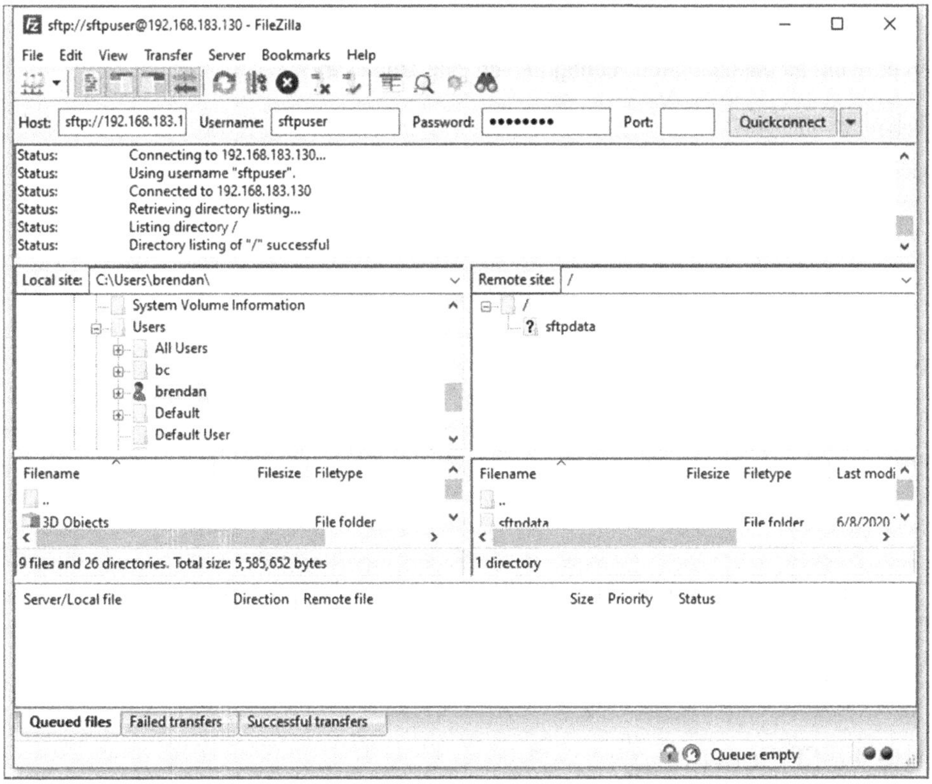

Figure 8-8. *FileZilla client, SFTP connection example*

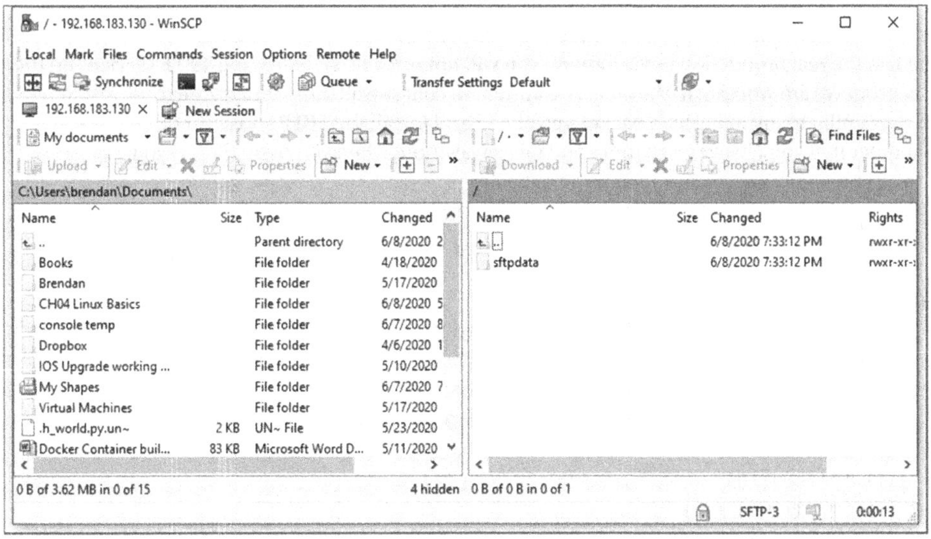

Figure 8-9. *WinSCP, SFTP connection example*

How do you print out all the usernames configured on your Linux server?

Just run the following command:

```
[root@centos8s1 ~]# awk -F ':' '{print $ 1}' /etc/passwd
root
bin
daemon
adm
[... omitted for brevity]
tcpdump
pynetauto
nginx
sftpuser
tftpuser
```

Now your CentOS server is running SFTP services for secure file sharing over the network. Whenever possible, SFTP must be used over FTP or TFTP for secure file transfers between two nodes (devices). Next is the installation of TFTP and its configuration.

Installing the TFTP Server

Trivial File Transfer Protocol (TFTP) uses UDP 69 as its default communication port. Because TFTP uses UDP, it has a much lighter operation than FTP or SFTP for file transfers. TFTP has been one of the most common file-sharing methods used to send and receive Cisco IOS or NX-OS images or configuration files across an internal network. It is still in use in many networks, but it still uses plain text for communication, and file transfer over UDP does not always guarantee the complete file transfer or security.

As mentioned, in the real production environment, you will not run all FTP, SFTP, and TFTP services on the same server at once, but we are working in the lab environment to collapse all three servers into one. Installing TFTP on CentOS 8 is similar to installing `vsftpd`. Let's go ahead and install the TFTP server for our lab use. It is important to remember that you always learn more and take away more when you build the lab yourself.

① First, log in to CentOS 8.1 using the root user account and SSH into the server using PuTTY. As soon as you have logged in, check the firewall status by running the `systemctl status firewalld` command.

```
[root@centos8s1 ~]# systemctl status firewalld
●ifirewalld.service - firewalld - dynamic firewall daemon
  Loaded: loaded (/usr/lib/systemd/system/firewalld.service; enabled; vendor preset:
  enabled)
  Active: active (running) since Mon 2021-01-04 19:15:30 AEDT; 3h 18min ago
    Docs: man:firewalld(1)
Main PID: 1111 (firewalld)
  Tasks: 3 (limit: 11166)
  Memory: 33.8M
  CGroup: /system.slice/firewalld.service
       ervicewausr/libexec/platform-python -s /usr/sbin/firewalld --nofork --nopid
```

② Change the server firewall setting using the following command to enable TFTP traffic to communicate with your server:

```
[root@centos8s1 ~]# firewall-cmd --permanent --zone=public --add-service=tftp
[root@centos8s1 ~]# firewall-cmd --reload
```

③ Use yum install command to install tftp-server, xinetd service daemon and tftp client package. Run the following set of commands to complete your installation on your CentOS server:

```
[root@centos8s1 ~]# yum install xinetd tftp-server tftp
[root@centos8s1 ~]# systemctl enable xinetd tftp
[root@centos8s1 ~]# systemctl start xinetd tftp

[root@centos8s1 ~]# systemctl status xinetd
●ixinetd.service - Xinetd A Powerful Replacement For Inetd
  Loaded: loaded (/usr/lib/systemd/system/xinetd.service; enabled; vendor preset:
enabled)
  Active: active (running) since Mon 2021-01-04 19:15:34 AEDT; 3h 20min ago
    Docs: man:xinetd
        man:xinetd.conf
        man:xinetd.log
  Process: 1245 ExecStart=/usr/sbin/xinetd -stayalive -pidfile /var/run/xinetd.pid
(code=exited, status=0/SUCCESS)
  Main PID: 1281 (xinetd)
    Tasks: 1 (limit: 11166)
  Memory: 1.3M
  CGroup: /system.slice/xinetd.service
        ice281 /usr/sbin/xinetd -stayalive -pidfile /var/run/xinetd.pid
```

④ Now that we know the TFTP server service is running correctly, we want to create a user account named `tftpuser` to assign just enough privileges to do its job, which is file transfer over UDP port 69. The `tftp` account created here is for system use only, so you cannot use it as a user account.

```
[root@centos8s1 ~]# useradd -s /bin/false -r tftpuser
```

⑤ Create a directory called `tftpdir` under the `/var` directory. All future TFTP file-sharing will be through this directory.

```
[root@centos8s1 ~]# mkdir /var/tftpdir
```

⑥ Change the permissions of the `tftpdir` directory so the `tftp` system account has permissions to this directory. To allow some freedom, we'll modify the directory with `chmod 777`.

```
[root@centos8s1 ~]# chown tftpuser:tftpuser /var/tftpdir
[root@centos8s1 ~]# chmod 777 /var/tftpdir
```

⑦ Next, create a service file called tftp in /etc/xinetd.d/, copy the following content, and save the file:

```
[root@centos8s1 ~]# nano /etc/xinetd.d/tftp

service tftp
{
    socket_type = dgram
    protocol = udp
    wait = yes
    user = root
    server = /usr/sbin/in.tftpd
    server_args = -c -s /var/tftpdir -v -v -v -u tftpuser -p
    disable = no
    per_source = 11
    cps = 100 2
    flags = IPv4
}
```

⑧ For TFTP to work well within SELinux, we must update the change context (chcon) of our tftp directory file tftpdir.

```
[root@centos8s1 ~]# chcon -t tftpdir_rw_t /var/tftpdir
```

Let's restart the tftp and xinetd services once more.

```
[root@centos8s1 ~]# systemctl restart xinetd tftp
```

⑨ Before performing the verification task for the TFTP server, let's check two configurations, which are important for the TFTP operation on the CentOS server. First, make sure that the /etc/selinux/config configuration is adjusted, and second, check the setsebool settings to allow tftp write and directory access.

First, save the file after changing SELINUX = enforcing to SELINUX = permissive. See Figure 8-10.

```
[root@centos8s1 ~]# nano /etc/selinux/config
```

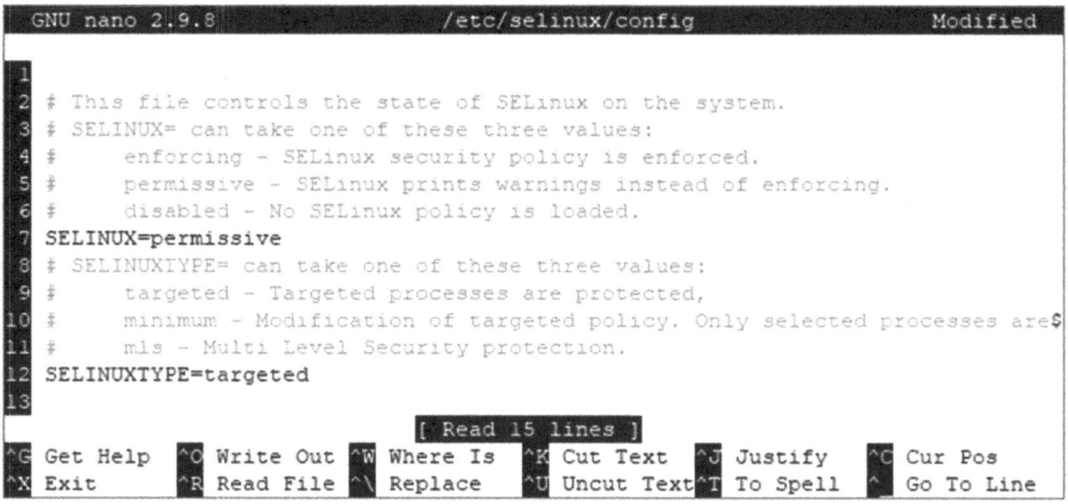

Figure 8-10. *CentOS, /etc/selinux/config update*

Second, we have to check the SELinux Boolean values of `tftp_anon_write` and `tftp_home_dir`, so SELinux allows TFTP file transfers. Check the `tftp` permissions using the following `getsebool` command if both `tftp_anon_write` and `tftp_home_dir` are showing as `off`. You must enable them using the subsequent commands.

```
[root@centos8s1 ~]# getsebool -a | grep tftp
tftp_anon_write --> off
tftp_home_dir --> off
```

Update the SELinux Boolean values of `tftp_anon_write` and `tftp_home_dir`.

```
[root@centos8s1 ~]# setsebool -P tftp_anon_write 1
[root@centos8s1 ~]# setsebool -P tftp_home_dir 1
[root@centos8s1 ~]# getsebool -a | grep tftp
tftp_anon_write --> on
tftp_home_dir --> on
```

Finally, give the last restart of the `xinetd` and `tftp` services on the CentOS server.

```
[root@centos8s1 ~]# systemctl restart xinetd tftp
```

⑩ On another Linux machine, the `ubuntu20s1` (192.168.183.129) server, install the `tftp` client using the `apt install -y tftp` command and perform the following verification tasks.

First, install the `tftp` client on the `ubuntu20s1` server.

```
root@ubuntu20s1:~# apt install tftp
```

Second, create `transfer_file01` and add some text as shown here:

```
root@ubuntu20s1:~# nano transfer_file01
This is a file transfer test file only.
Please contact the administrator if you have any issues.

root@ubuntu20s1:~# cat transfer_file01
This is a file transfer test file only.
Please contact the administrator if you have any issues.
```

Third, to test the `tftp` login to the CentOS `tftp` server, run `tftp 192.168.183.130`. Once connected, use the put command to upload `transfer_file01` to the TFTP server (192.168.183.130).

```
root@ubuntu20s1:~# tftp 192.168.183.130
tftp> put transfer_file01
Sent 99 bytes in 0.0 seconds
tftp>
```

Now go back to the `centos8s1` server and use the `ls /var/tftpdir` command to check that the file has been uploaded correctly.

```
[root@centos8s1 ~]# ls -lh /var/tftpdir
total 4.0K
-rw-rw-r--. 1 tftpuser  tftpuser    97 Jan  4 22:54 transfer_file01
```

Fourth, now the other way around, let's download a file from the TFTP server (`cenos8s1: 192.168.183.130`) to the file client (`ubuntu20s1: 192.168.183.132`) with the filename `transfer_file77`.

On the CentOS server, let's copy the `transfer_file01` file as `transfer_file77`.

```
[root@centos8s1 ~]# cp /var/tftpdir/transfer_file01 /var/tftpdir/transfer_file77
[root@centos8s1 ~]# ls /var/tftpdir
transfer_file01  transfer_file77
```

On the Ubuntu server, issue the `get file_name` command to download the `transfer_file05` file from the CentOS TFTP server.

```
root@ubuntu20s1:~# tftp 192.168.183.130
tftp> get transfer_file77
Received 99 bytes in 0.0 seconds

tftp> ^Z # Use Ctrl+Z to exit tftp mode
[1]+  Stopped                  tftp 192.168.183.130
root@ubuntu20s1:~# ls transfer*
transfer_file01  transfer_file77
```

You have successfully installed TFTP software on the CentOS 8 server and verified the TFTP operations between the server and a client. So far, FTP, SFTP, and TFTP are all up and running on the CentOS server, and next, you will quickly install the time services (NTP server) software on CentOS. When we test various scenarios in our lab or study or work, these servers will come in handy.

You can check if TFTP is working properly by using `net-tool`. If your CentOS VM does not recognize the `netstat` command, you can use `yum install -y net-tool` to install it and run the following set of commands to check the TFTP-related port operation:

```
netstat -na | grep udp6
netstat -lu
netstat -ap | grep tftp
netstat -tupan
netstat -tupan | grep 69
```

Installing the NTP Server

Network Time Protocol (NTP) is used to synchronize the time for enterprise devices such as servers, firewalls, routers, and switches. The NTP services use UDP port 123 and an IP network service that must be present in the corporate network to keep the time correct. The devices running in the same network segment or time zone need to have a consistent time, and the NTP server can provide this service to other devices. If hundreds or thousands of networked devices on a network all run on their hardware clock time, there will be no consistent timestamps for log and system files. NTP servers serve as a time aid to help the network equipment agree on a single referenced time. Let's go ahead and install the NTP server on the CentOS 8 server and perform a quick test run for our confirmation. On the previous version of CentOS, CentOS 7.5, NTP was available for installation, but on CentOS 8, the `chrony` daemon provides both NTP server and NTP client services.

① First, use the SSH client to log into the CentOS 8 VM using the root user credentials. After you have logged in, check whether the server time and time zone are correct. If any of this information is incorrect, follow these directions to set your clock and time zone correctly:

1a. Check the time on the server.

```
[root@centos8s1 ~]# clock
2021-01-05 09:09:56.710758+11:00
```

1b. Check the time zone, NTP status, and other time details.
[root@centos8s1 ~]# `timedatectl1c`. If your timezone is not correct, search the time zones list and find your country/city. Press Ctrl+Z to exit the list.

```
[root@centos8s1 ~]# timedatectl list-timezones
```

1d. Now set the correct time zone. If you are in another city and country, your time zone will be different mine, so adjust the time according to your geolocation.

```
[root@centos8s1 ~]# timedatectl set-timezone Australia/Sydney
```

1e. Confirm that your server is running at the correct local time.

```
[root@centos8s1 ~]# clock
2021-01-05 09:16:05.039324+11:00
[root@centos8s1 ~]# date
Tue Jan  5 09:16:13 AEDT 2021
```

② Next, if chrony is not yet installed, install the NTP server and client using the dnf command, dnf install chrony.

```
[root@centos8s1 ~]# dnf install chrony
```

③ To make chronyd run at startup, enable the chrony services by typing systemctl enable chronyd.

```
[root@centos8s1 ~]# systemctl enable chronyd
```

④ Open the chrony.conf file under /etc/chrony.conf and allow your server and lab network. chrony will work as an NTP server for a local network after the subnet is allowed under the configuration file. Make sure you update the subnet to reflect your VM NAT subnet. Also, to make this time server more believable, we will change the local stratum to 3. Most of the network devices and server will be happy to sync time with the NTP server with equal or less than stratum 5.

```
[root@centos8s1 ~]# vi /etc/chrony.conf
```

Update the following lines in bold in vi's --INSERT-- mode and then save the change with the :wq command:

```
[...omitted for brevity]

# Allow NTP client access from local network.
#allow 192.168.0.0/16
# ADDED by pynetauto
allow 192.168.183.0/24    # Add this line to allow local communication

# Serve time even if not synchronized to a time source.
# local stratum 10
# ADDED by pynetauto
local stratum 5           # Add this line to make this as a stratum 3 server

[...omitted for brevity]

:wq
```

Restart the chronyd service to make the changes take effect.

```
[root@centos8s1 ~]# systemctl stop chronyd
[root@centos8s1 ~]# systemctl start chronyd
[root@centos8s1 ~]# systemctl status chronyd
```

⑤ Open the firewall port to allow for incoming NTP requests on the network and reload the firewall.

```
[root@centos8s1 ~]# firewall-cmd --permanent --add-service=ntp
success
[root@centos8s1 ~]# firewall-cmd --reload
Success
```

⑥ Finally, to apply the change, restart the chronyd daemon.

```
[root@centos8s1 ~]# systemctl restart chronyd
```

⑦ Go to your `Ubuntu 20 LTS` server, set the time zone, install `ntpdate`, and use `ntpdate 192.168.183.130` to synchronize time with this server. If your NTP server IP is different, do not forget to update the IP address to reflect your NTP server IP.

7a. Update the time zone using the `timedatectl` commands.

Check the current time and date on your Ubuntu server.

```
root@ubuntu20s1:~# timedatectl
        Local time: Mon 2021-01-04 22:32:42 UTC
    Universal time: Mon 2021-01-04 22:32:42 UTC
          RTC time: Mon 2021-01-04 22:32:42
         Time zone: Etc/UTC (UTC, +0000)
System clock synchronized: yes
       NTP service: active
    RTC in local TZ: no
```

Update the time zone and check the time and date one more time.

```
root@ubuntu20s1:~# timedatectl set-timezone Australia/Sydney
root@ubuntu20s1:~# timedatectl
        Local time: Tue 2021-01-05 09:33:29 AEDT
    Universal time: Mon 2021-01-04 22:33:29 UTC
          RTC time: Mon 2021-01-04 22:33:29
         Time zone: Australia/Sydney (AEDT, +1100)
System clock synchronized: yes
       NTP service: active
    RTC in local TZ: no
```

7b. Check the date, hardware clock, and time zone.

```
root@ubuntu20s1:~# date
Tue 05 Jan 2021 09:35:23 AM AEDT
root@ubuntu20s1:~# hwclock --show
2021-01-05 09:35:33.118208+11:00
root@ubuntu20s1:~# cat /etc/timezone
Australia/Sydney
```

7c. Install `ntpdate` on your Ubuntu server.

```
root@ubuntu20s1:~# apt-get install ntpdate
```

Notice the use of `apt-get` here. apt (Advanced Package Tool) merges the functionalities of `apt-get` and `apt-cache`, but for some packages, you still have to run `apt-get` to install certain packages. The `apt` command should work in most of the situations, but not always. There are plenty of articles on this difference on Google; you can do a quick lookup on this difference on Google.

URL: `https://askubuntu.com/questions/445384/what-is-the-difference-between-apt-and-apt-get`

URL: `https://phoenixnap.com/kb/apt-vs-apt-get`

7d. Synchronize the Ubuntu server time with the CentOS 8 NTP server time. If the NTP service is running correctly, the Ubuntu server will synchronize its clock and start referencing the NTP server for time requests.

```
root@ubuntu20s1:~# ntpdate -d 192.168.183.130
5 Jan 10:26:42 ntpdate[5667]: ntpdate 4.2.8p12@1.3728-o (1)
Looking for host 192.168.183.130 and service ntp
host found : 192.168.183.130
transmit(192.168.183.130)
receive(192.168.183.130)
[...omitted for brevity]

server 192.168.183.130, port 123
stratum 5, precision -26, leap 00, trust 000

[...omitted for brevity]
    0.000000 0.000000 0.000000 0.000000
delay 0.02592, dispersion 0.00006
offset 5.987462

5 Jan 10:26:58 ntpdate[5667]: step time server 192.168.183.130 offset 5.987462 sec

root@ubuntu20s1:~# date
Tue 05 Jan 2021 10:27:04 AM AEDT
```

Check the time on the NTP server (`centos8s1`). If time synchronization took place correctly as shown earlier, your NTP client's time will be synced to the NTP server's time.

```
[root@centos8s1 ~]# date
Tue Jan  5 10:27:10 AEDT 2021
```

Optionally, you can use the `ntpdate 192.168.183.130` or `ntpdate -u 192.168.183.130` command to update and resynchronize the time.

⑧ If you break this IP services server, now is the perfect time to take a snapshot of your CentOS server to preserve the server's working state. See Figure 8-11.

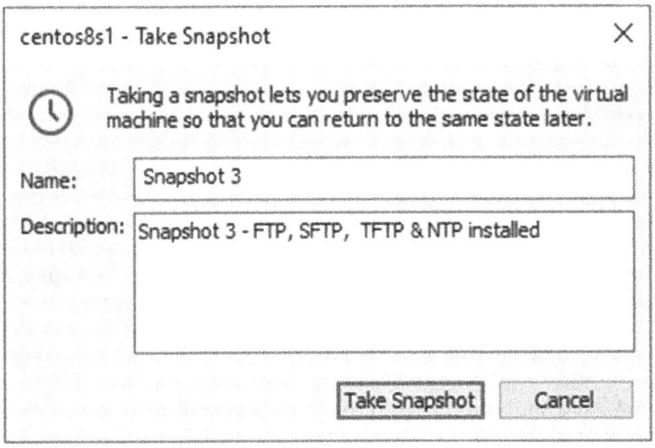

Figure 8-11. *CentOS, taking a snapshot*

You have successfully installed the NTP server, and this completes NTP, FTP, SFTP, and TFTP installation and verification. These servers will make your lab scenarios a lot more interesting, and also, you will be able to study, break, and rebuild your labs like your childhood favorite toys.

Linux TCP/IP Troubleshooting Exercise

This is the last exercise of this chapter. You will learn some Linux networking basic troubleshooting tips to test the TCP- and IP-related issues. When you encounter server networking issues, you can troubleshoot them yourself rather than palm them off to a Linux administrator.

① The first exercise is to check if your server allows ping (ICMP). Using `cat /proc/sys/net/ipv4/icmp_echo_ignore_all`, you can check if your server will respond to ICMP requests. The output is either 0 or 1. 0 indicates that ICMP is enabled and can respond; 1 indicates that ICMP is disabled, which means ICMP requests will be ignored.

For a CentOS server:

```
[root@centos8s1 ~]# cat /proc/sys/net/ipv4/icmp_echo_ignore_all
0
```

For a Ubuntu server:

```
root@ubuntu20s1:~# cat /proc/sys/net/ipv4/icmp_echo_ignore_all
0
```

For our testing purpose, let's update the Ubuntu server's value to 1 (from 0) so the ICMP response is disabled on the Ubuntu server. Then ping between two servers. After the testing, make sure you update this value back to 0.

```
root@ubuntu20s1:~# nano /proc/sys/net/ipv4/icmp_echo_ignore_all
root@ubuntu20s1:~# cat /proc/sys/net/ipv4/icmp_echo_ignore_all
1
[root@centos8s1 ~]# ping 192.168.183.130
root@ubuntu20s1:~# ping 192.168.183.130 -c 4
PING 192.168.183.130 (192.168.183.130) 56(84) bytes of data.
64 bytes from 192.168.183.130: icmp_seq=1 ttl=64 time=0.386 ms
64 bytes from 192.168.183.130: icmp_seq=2 ttl=64 time=0.602 ms
64 bytes from 192.168.183.130: icmp_seq=3 ttl=64 time=0.576 ms
64 bytes from 192.168.183.130: icmp_seq=4 ttl=64 time=0.607 ms

--- 192.168.183.130 ping statistics ---
4 packets transmitted, 4 received, 0% packet loss, time 3053ms
rtt min/avg/max/mdev = 0.386/0.542/0.607/0.091 ms
```

As expected, there is no response from the Ubuntu server as ICMP requests from the CentOS server are ignored. If you ping the Ubuntu server from the CentOS server, 100 percent packet loss will result, as shown here:

```
[root@centos8s1 ~]# ping 192.168.183.132 -c 4
PING 192.168.183.132 (192.168.183.132) 56(84) bytes of data.

--- 192.168.183.132 ping statistics ---
4 packets transmitted, 0 received, 100% packet loss, time 79ms
```

② To test a server's open ports from a remote machine, you can use `telnet` + the IP address of remote server + the TCP port number. Telnet can be used for testing simple network socket connectivity but will only work on TCP ports (it does not work with UDP ports). For example, if you want to test the FTP (21) and SFTP (22) TCP connections from the Ubuntu server to the CentOS FTP/SFTP server, you can perform the following `telnet` test and confirm the end-to-end connection. After connected, to quit, type in `QUIT` and press Enter.

2a. Here is the FTP connection test:

```
root@ubuntu20s1:~# telnet 192.168.183.130 21
Trying 192.168.183.130...
Connected to 192.168.183.130.
Escape character is '^]'.
220 (vsFTPd 3.0.3)
QUIT
221 Goodbye.
Connection closed by foreign host.
```

2b. Here is the SSH/SFTP connection test:

```
root@ubuntu20s1:~# telnet 192.168.183.130 22
Trying 192.168.183.130...
Connected to 192.168.183.130.
Escape character is '^]'.
SSH-2.0-OpenSSH_8.0
QUIT
Invalid SSH identification string.
Connection closed by foreign host.
```

③ To see if a program or process is listening on a port, ready to accept a packet, use the `netstat` command. `netstat` arguments (options) are listed here, so mix and match and try to run them on your Ubuntu server:

- `t`—show TCP port
- `u`—show UDP port
- `a`—show all
- `l`—show only listening processes
- `n`—do not resolve network IP address names or port numbers
- `p`—show process names listening on different ports

3a. Run the `netstat -tulnp` command from your Ubuntu server.

```
root@ubuntu20s1:~# netstat -tulnp
```

Here are the active Internet connections (only servers):

Proto	Recv-Q	Send-Q	Local Address	Foreign Address	state	PID/Program name
tcp	0	0	127.0.0.1:45715	0.0.0.0:*	LISTEN	939/containerd
tcp	0	0	127.0.0.53:53	0.0.0.0:*	LISTEN	843/systemd-resolve
tcp	0	0	0.0.0.0:22	0.0.0.0:*	LISTEN	1015/sshd: /usr/sbi
tcp	0	0	127.0.0.1:631	0.0.0.0:*	LISTEN	3251/cupsd
tcp6	0	0	:::22	:::*	LISTEN	1015/sshd: /usr/sbi
tcp6	0	0	::1:631	:::*	LISTEN	3251/cupsd
udp	0	0	127.0.0.53:53	0.0.0.0:*		843/systemd-resolve
udp	0	0	0.0.0.0:5353	0.0.0.0:*		859/avahi-daemon: r
udp	0	0	0.0.0.0:43413	0.0.0.0:*		859/avahi-daemon: r
udp	0	0	0.0.0.0:631	0.0.0.0:*		3252/cups-browsed
udp6	0	0	:::51143	:::*		859/avahi-daemon: r
udp6	0	0	:::5353	:::*		859/avahi-daemon: r

3b. Run the `netstat -tuna` command from your Ubuntu server.

```
root@ubuntu20s1:~# netstat -tuna
```

Here are the active Internet connections (servers and established):

Proto	Recv-Q	Send-Q	Local Address	Foreign Address	State
tcp	0	0	127.0.0.1:45715	0.0.0.0:*	LISTEN
tcp	0	0	127.0.0.53:53	0.0.0.0:*	LISTEN
tcp	0	0	0.0.0.0:22	0.0.0.0:*	LISTEN
tcp	0	0	127.0.0.1:631	0.0.0.0:*	LISTEN
tcp	0	0	192.168.183.132:22	192.168.183.1:56036	ESTABLISHED
tcp6	0	0	:::22	:::*	LISTEN
tcp6	0	0	::1:631	:::*	LISTEN
udp	0	0	127.0.0.53:53	0.0.0.0:*	
udp	0	0	0.0.0.0:5353	0.0.0.0:*	
udp	0	0	0.0.0.0:43413	0.0.0.0:*	
udp	0	0	0.0.0.0:631	0.0.0.0:*	
udp6	0	0	:::51143	:::*	
udp6	0	0	:::5353	:::*	

④ You can also use `ss` command with arguments to see the listening ports or the port readiness. To see if a program or process is listening on a port, ready to accept a packet, use `ss`. The `ss` commands work on both Ubuntu and CentOS servers. See Figure 8-12.

`t`—display TCP sockets
`u`—display UDP sockets
`l`—display listening sockets
`n`—do not resolve names
`p`—display process using socket

```
[root@centos8s1 ~]# ss -nutlp
```

OR

```
root@ubuntu20s1:~# ss -nutlp
```

```
root@ubuntu20s1:~# ss -nutlp
Netid State  Recv-Q Send-Q          Local Address:Port  Peer Address:PortProcess
udp   UNCONN 0      0                     0.0.0.0:631        0.0.0.0:*    users:(("cups-browsed",pid=4980,fd=7))
udp   UNCONN 0      0                     0.0.0.0:35619      0.0.0.0:*    users:(("avahi-daemon",pid=932,fd=14))
udp   UNCONN 0      0               127.0.0.53%lo:53         0.0.0.0:*    users:(("systemd-resolve",pid=914,fd=12))
udp   UNCONN 0      0        192.168.183.129%ens33:68        0.0.0.0:*    users:(("systemd-network",pid=912,fd=19))
udp   UNCONN 0      0                     0.0.0.0:5353       0.0.0.0:*    users:(("avahi-daemon",pid=932,fd=12))
udp   UNCONN 0      0                        [::]:56859         [::]:*    users:(("avahi-daemon",pid=932,fd=15))
udp   UNCONN 0      0                        [::]:5353          [::]:*    users:(("avahi-daemon",pid=932,fd=13))
tcp   LISTEN 0      4096            127.0.0.53%lo:53         0.0.0.0:*    users:(("systemd-resolve",pid=914,fd=13))
tcp   LISTEN 0      128                   0.0.0.0:22         0.0.0.0:*    users:(("sshd",pid=1123,fd=3))
tcp   LISTEN 0      5                   127.0.0.1:631        0.0.0.0:*    users:(("cupsd",pid=4976,fd=7))
tcp   LISTEN 0      128                      [::]:22            [::]:*    users:(("sshd",pid=1123,fd=4))
tcp   LISTEN 0      5                       [::1]:631           [::]:*    users:(("cupsd",pid=4976,fd=6))
root@ubuntu20s1:~#
```

Figure 8-12. *Ubuntu – ss –nutlp example*

⑤ Use `lsof` to list the open ports on a Linux OS. To list the process name and PID numbers and open ports, type in `lsof -i`. You can use this command on most Linux OSs. See Figure 8-13.

```
[root@centos8s1 ~]# lsof -i
```

OR

```
root@ubuntu20s1:~# lsof -i
```

```
ESTABLISHED)
root@ubuntu20s1:~# lsof -i
COMMAND    PID             USER   FD   TYPE DEVICE SIZE/OFF NODE NAME
systemd-n  912 systemd-network   19u  IPv4 142598      0t0  UDP ubuntu20s1:bootpc
systemd-r  914 systemd-resolve   12u  IPv4  36876      0t0  UDP localhost:domain
systemd-r  914 systemd-resolve   13u  IPv4  36877      0t0  TCP localhost:domain (LISTEN)
avahi-dae  932            avahi   12u  IPv4  40739      0t0  UDP *:mdns
avahi-dae  932            avahi   13u  IPv6  40740      0t0  UDP *:mdns
avahi-dae  932            avahi   14u  IPv4  40741      0t0  UDP *:35619
avahi-dae  932            avahi   15u  IPv6  40742      0t0  UDP *:56859
sshd      1123             root    3u  IPv4  44022      0t0  TCP *:ssh (LISTEN)
sshd      1123             root    4u  IPv6  44033      0t0  TCP *:ssh (LISTEN)
cupsd     4976             root    6u  IPv6  75194      0t0  TCP ip6-localhost:ipp (LISTEN)
cupsd     4976             root    7u  IPv4  75195      0t0  TCP localhost:ipp (LISTEN)
cups-brow 4980             root    7u  IPv4  75381      0t0  UDP *:631
sshd      5913             root    4u  IPv4  85072      0t0  TCP ubuntu20s1:ssh->192.168.183.1:58984 (ESTABLISHED)
root@ubuntu20s1:~#
```

Figure 8-13. *Ubuntu - lsof -i example*

⑥ Use the `iptables` command to list more TCP IP communication information. Run `iptables -xvn -L` to display packets, interfaces, source and destination IP addresses, and ports in use. See Figure 8-14.

```
root@ubuntu20s1:~# iptables -xvn -L
```

OR

```
[root@centos8s1 ~]# iptables -xvn -L
```

```
[root@centos8s1 ~]# iptables -xvn -L
Chain INPUT (policy ACCEPT 1895 packets, 244220 bytes)
    pkts      bytes target     prot opt in     out     source               destination
       0        0 ACCEPT     udp  --  virbr0 *       0.0.0.0/0            0.0.0.0/0            udp dpt:53
       0        0 ACCEPT     tcp  --  virbr0 *       0.0.0.0/0            0.0.0.0/0            tcp dpt:53
       0        0 ACCEPT     udp  --  virbr0 *       0.0.0.0/0            0.0.0.0/0            udp dpt:67
       0        0 ACCEPT     tcp  --  virbr0 *       0.0.0.0/0            0.0.0.0/0            tcp dpt:67

Chain FORWARD (policy ACCEPT 0 packets, 0 bytes)
    pkts      bytes target     prot opt in     out     source               destination
       0        0 ACCEPT     all  --  *      virbr0  0.0.0.0/0            192.168.122.0/24     ctstate RELATED,ESTABLISHED
       0        0 ACCEPT     all  --  virbr0 *       192.168.122.0/24     0.0.0.0/0
       0        0 ACCEPT     all  --  virbr0 virbr0  0.0.0.0/0            0.0.0.0/0
       0        0 REJECT     all  --  *      virbr0  0.0.0.0/0            0.0.0.0/0            reject-with icmp-port-unreachable
       0        0 REJECT     all  --  virbr0 *       0.0.0.0/0            0.0.0.0/0            reject-with icmp-port-unreachable

Chain OUTPUT (policy ACCEPT 1563 packets, 221252 bytes)
    pkts      bytes target     prot opt in     out     source               destination
       0        0 ACCEPT     udp  --  *      virbr0  0.0.0.0/0            0.0.0.0/0            udp dpt:68
[root@centos8s1 ~]#
```

Figure 8-14. *CentOS, iptables -xvn -L example*

⑦ Perhaps you are connecting to your FTP server from a Windows client. Then how do you make an FTP connection to your FTP server from your Windows PC? You can use the Windows command-line prompt or Windows PowerShell. `Test-NetConnection` is a native PowerShell command and can be used to test simple connectivity such as FTP port 21.

Let's start PowerShell from your Windows 10 host PC/laptop and quickly test if the FTP connection to the CentOS FTP server works correctly. See Figure 8-15.

PS C:\Users\brendan> `test-NetConnection -ComputerName 192.168.183.130 -Port 21`

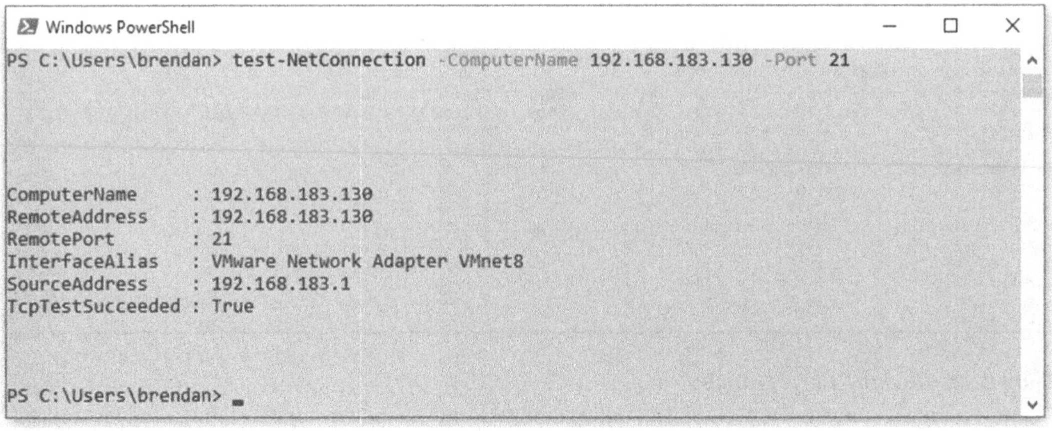

Figure 8-15. *Windows 10 host PC, PowerShell test-NetConnection example*

Summary

In this chapter, you learned some more Linux administration, starting with how to check system information and how to check TCP and UDP ports on the Linux systems. Then you were guided through IP services installation on a CentOS server to make an all-in-one lab server for TFTP, FTP, SFTP, and NTP services. This server will be used later for Python network automation labs in the second half of this book. Finally, you learned some basic TCP/IP and connection troubleshooting on Linux, so you can troubleshoot the connectivity issues on the move. I hope this was an interesting chapter for everyone. In the next chapter, Chapter 9, you will be tackling another challenging topic, regular expressions (a.k.a. regex). Understanding the inner workings of regex can boost your Python coding ability. You have to stay on course and complete the next chapter.

Storytime 4: Becoming a Savvy Linux Administrator, Perhaps Every IT Engineer's Dream?

Everyone in IT will agree that investing time and resources studying enterprise Linux is a worthwhile future investment while working in the IT industry. Becoming a savvy Linux administrator is many IT engineers' dream, if not every engineer. At least it has been my dream for some time. Can you remember your first Linux experience? Here are some common experiences Linux users may go through while trying to learn Linux, especially if you have been a Windows user all your life.

- Everyone said Ubuntu Desktop is the best Linux for beginners, so you downloaded the latest Linux `.iso` file and installed it on your PC. Within a few days, you wiped it with Windows 10, and you are back on the Windows OS like nothing ever happened.
- Dual-booting sounded like a cool thing to do, so you installed both Windows and Linux on the same host and tried the multibooting option on your laptop. A few weeks later, you noticed a sizable unused partition on your Windows Partition Manager and thought, what a waste of storage space. Then you remembered: it was the partition for your Linux operating system.

- As time went by, you were logging into Windows more and more, even though your PC had a multibooting option.
- Ubuntu or Gnome Desktop experience seemed like an OK user interface connected to the Internet, but you were still craving the Windows graphical user interface. You are hooked to the Windows GUI.
- Everyone said you have to study Linux commands, but no one told you how to study Linux commands. All the websites and videos said you have to learn them by heart, so you tried your best to memorize as much as you can, squeezing every command into your tiny brain, and the next day, you could not even remember a single command from the previous day's study.
- There is always some Linux guru at your work, and he is putting pressure on you to make sure you take on Linux again even though you left it for a few years. Never give up!

Perhaps you liked Linux from the get-go and enjoyed the experience of learning Linux. For some people, the Linux chapters could pose the first barrier in your Python network automation journey, but we must continue. Based on some quick Internet research, there is still only a small percentage of true Linux administrators in the IT industry. There were three Linux engineers out of 80 IT engineers at my last workplace, and on my current team, there are only two members (out of 20) who are well-versed in Linux. Almost every engineer who can write programming code will agree that it is impossible to develop code and run it as a service only on Windows servers. If you are a Microsoft guru, it is possible that the blue screen of death appears a couple of times a year, and your best fix for Windows Server is to press the Reboot button. In other words, as a novice network automation engineer, we have to become familiar with Linux systems and start using Python on Linux. After all, Python and Linux go hand in hand. If you want to become good at Python or any coding, you must cover the Linux basics well. I agree, it is challenging to learn and master Linux administration, but we can always take one step at a time, and over time, we will get there slowly but surely. Still, I hope the contents in this chapter and the previous chapter will be enough to get you through this book and keep your interest in Linux alive. Since studying Python, I improved my game with Linux, and Linux has made me rethink my career and take a different IT career path. I highly recommend everyone take another crack at Linux. Let's keep trying!

CHAPTER 9

Regular Expressions for Network Automation

This chapter is dedicated to learning regular expressions basics. Python provides native ways to process and dissect strings of text but requires many lines of code to locate the exact string. Although Python provides powerful string indexing methods, in real life you will face challenges each time you need to handle a large string. I find it fascinating that no other Python network automation books genuinely emphasize the importance of data wrangling (or massaging) with regular expressions. Many books sweep regular expressions under the rug as it is not the most exciting topic to discuss. I realized that I must master regular expressions to get anywhere with any programming language. Still, I also did not dare tackle it seriously at first. Only when I started working on real projects did I realize my ignorance over regular expressions. I understand that this chapter's content will be painful to digest for many readers, but you should stick with it and focus on completing this chapter; you will thank me later.

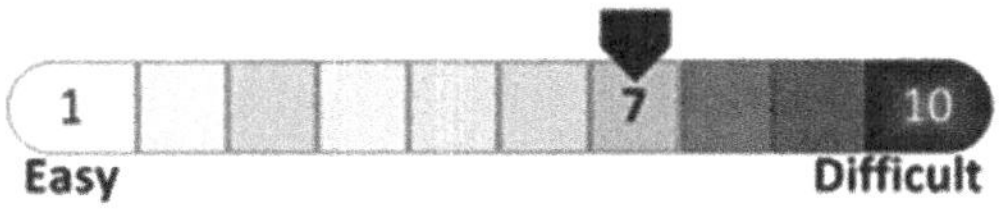

Regular expressions universally apply to all computer programming languages and are not unique to Python. Once you have mastered them, you can apply them to all programming languages such as Java, C++, JavaScript, Ruby, and Perl. In Python, the `re` module provides you with the passageway to regular expressions. By having a deep understanding of regular expressions and applying this knowledge to your Python programs via `re` modules, you will become a better Python coder. What you learn here will be applied to network automation application development in the labs. Mastering regular expressions is one topic no Python coder should skip. Although this is one of the shorter chapters in the book, you will gain valuable skills that will last for a lifetime.

After learning basic Python syntax and concepts, you will want to write Python applications fluently. As I will be mentioning throughout the book, writing code in Python is not all about the syntax and concepts; as with all things in computing, writing code has everything to do with proper data handling. This data could come from the user and application variables, reading files, scraping the Web, or logs between two computers. Writing code in any programming language almost always involves handling data. After some time writing Python code, I soon realized that it is impossible to develop any network automation application without understanding regular expressions in full.

B. Choi, *Introduction to Python Network Automation*, https://doi.org/10.1007/978-1-4842-6806-3_9

If you are serious about Python coding, you must master the art of regular expressions and the `re` module. You will learn the basics of regex and apply regular expressions on real Cisco router and switch text files so you can relate the information to the real production examples.

For the chapter requirements, you will need access to your Windows 10 host PC and Ubuntu Server virtual machine running on VMware Workstation 15 Pro, as depicted in Figure 9-1.

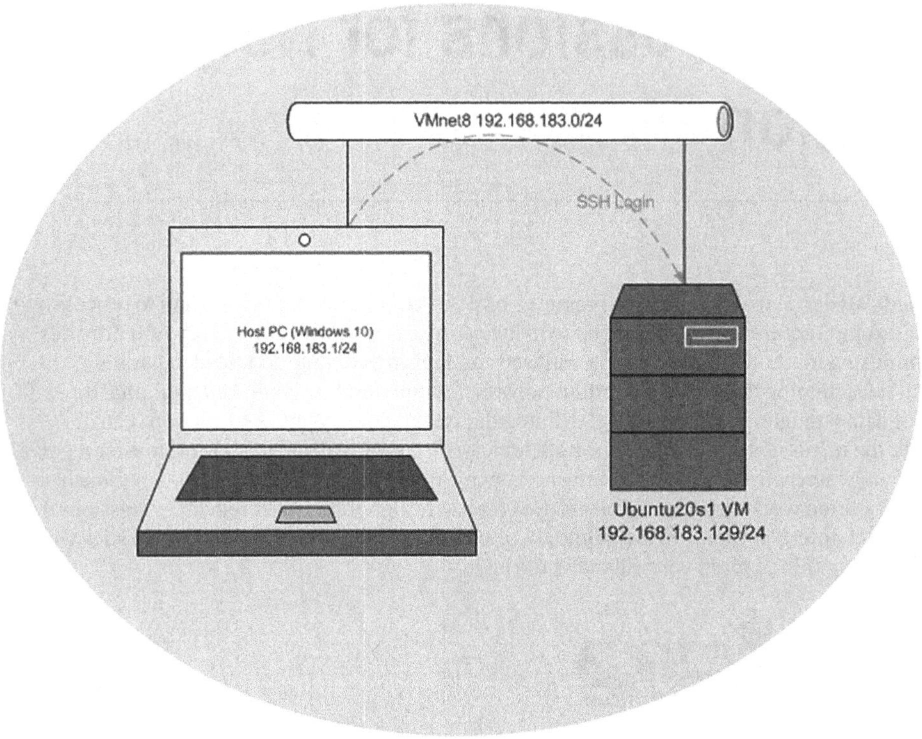

Figure 9-1. *Devices required in Chapter 9*

Why Regex?

text. A regular expression (*regex*) is a standard method used in computing to process complicated strings of text and is not exclusive to Python; it is used everywhere while performing data processing. At first glance, learning regular expressions can be seen as a distant subject to learning Python. Still, as you move to the intermediate level, the real power of regular expressions will come to light. In Python, the regular expression is also supported through a built-in Python module called the `re` module. Some readers may argue that learning regular expressions is not an essential part of learning Python, but as you work on real problems to solve automation problems, you will need to extract specific strings (data) from a source file or large strings. In coding, every comma, full stop, and whitespace matters while handling data to create variables and run your applications to avoid data handling errors. If anyone asks me what programming languages such as C, C++, Java, Perl, Ruby, R, and Python do, without hesitation, my straightforward answer would be data processing. Every program written in a computer programming language must handle and process data to serve their purpose. In other words, we need a tool to improve our data handling and processing. As you have learned in Chapter 2, there are built-in methods to slice, concatenate, and index data in strings.

When dealing with a more extensive set of data, you will run into many inconveniences as you might have to come up with your functions to handle big data better. The re module comes to the rescue as it is seen as a super-charged data handling method based on old regular expressions from the 1970s. Knowing when and where to use different Python modules can save you time from reinventing the wheel. First, you need to handle your data using the Python native methods. Second, explore data handling using the built-in re module. Third, explore even more advanced data handling methods using widely used Python libraries such as NumPy and Pandas. The NumPy library provides objects for multidimensional arrays, whereas Pandas provides an in-memory 2D table object called a *dataframe*. Every Python coder must learn regular expressions well and use them to their advantage to handle the data to extract a specific piece of string.

Another reason for including the topic of regex as a fully dedicated chapter was based on my recent experience while working on network automation. Regular expressions play a crucial role in coding, and I cannot emphasize enough their usefulness while working with Python code on various network automation projects. Once you reach an intermediate level in Python coding, inevitably you will confront data handling challenges, and if you refuse to learn how to use a regex, you will not progress. After following all exercises in this chapter, you will be well equipped with one of the most useful coding tools invented. The examples shown in this chapter may not be comprehensive enough for some, but enough scenarios are covered to help you get a grip on data handling through Python's re module. Every string match requirements are unique, so I urge you to go beyond this book and spend time researching more regex tutorials. There are plenty of free online training materials to practice use cases that apply to your data handling situations.

To re or Not to re

For starters, let's consider a straightforward example. You have applied for a job as a Python developer with a networking background. After you passed the first technical interview, the hiring manager has given you a take-home task to analyze a string of texts to be analyzed and transformed. Your task is to extract switch names and their MAC addresses to present the information in a specific format.

You have been given the following string. Your task is to print the switch name followed by the MAC address in 12 hexadecimal characters, where the first six digits (OUI) must be preserved to identify the manufacturer's ID. But the last six digits are masked with * to hide the real MAC address.

Here's a given string:

```
sw_mac = '''pynetauto-sw01 84:3d:c6:05:09:11
pynetauto-sw17 80:7f:f8:80:71:1b
pynetauto-sw05 f0:62:81:5a:53:cd'''
```

Also, any letters, including the hexadecimal a-f, must be capitalized, so the result must match the expected output shown here:

```
PYNETAUTO-SW01 843DC6******
PYNETAUTO-SW17 807FF8******
PYNETAUTO-SW05 F06281******
```

If you have not studied regular expressions, you may take the following steps to write your program:

1. Remove colons and convert the string to capital letters.
2. Split the strings at the whitespace and add them to a list.
3. Remove whitespaces using the strip() method and make an updated list.
4. Use the len() method to identify names and MAC addresses based on the list's length of items. If the item has 14 characters, then it is a switch name; add to the sw list. If the item has 12 characters, then it is a MAC address; add it to the MAC list. During MAC appending, add ****** to replace the second half of the MAC address.

5. Use Python dictionary's zip method to convert two lists into one dictionary.
6. Use the for loop to print the key and value from the dictionary's key-value pair.

In programming languages, they say, "There's more than one way to skin a cat" but one of the ways (through code) that will achieve the desired result without using the re module will look similar to Listing 9-1.

Here's a code and example string download tip: all the code presented in this book is available for download from pynetauto on GitHub. For the code used in this chapter, look for a zip file called chapter9_codes.zip.

URL: https://github.com/pynetauto/apress_pynetauto

Listing 9-1. Native Python Methods

```
>>> sw_mac = '''pynetauto-sw01 84:3d:c6:05:09:11
... pynetauto-sw17 80:7f:f8:80:71:1b
... pynetauto-sw05 f0:62:81:5a:53:cd'''
>>>
>>> sw_mac = sw_mac.replace(":", "").upper()          # 1
>>> sw_mac
'\nPYNETAUTO-SW01 843DC6050911 \nPYNETAUTO-SW17 807FF880711B \nPYNETAUTO-SW05
F062815A53CD\n'
>>> list1 = sw_mac.split(" ")          # 2
>>> list1
['\nPYNETAUTO-SW01', '843DC6050911', '\nPYNETAUTO-SW17', '807FF880711B', '\nPYNETAUTO-SW05',
'F062815A53CD\n']
>>> list2 =          # 3
>>> for i in list1:          # 4
...     list2.append(i.strip())          # 5
...
>>> list2
['PYNETAUTO-SW01', '843DC6050911', 'PYNETAUTO-SW17', '807FF880711B', 'PYNETAUTO-SW05',
'F062815A53CD']
>>>
>>> sw_list =          # 6
>>> mac_list =          # 7
>>> for i in list2:          # 8
...     if len(i) == 14:          # 9
...         sw_list.append(i)          # 10
...     if len(i) == 12:          # 11
...         i = i[:6] + "******"          # 12
...         mac_list.append(i)          # 13
...
>>> sw_list
['PYNETAUTO-SW01', 'PYNETAUTO-SW17', 'PYNETAUTO-SW05']
>>> mac_list
['843DC6******', '807FF8******', 'F06281******']
>>> sw_mac_dict = dict(zip(sw_list, mac_list))          # 14
>>> for k,v in sw_mac_dict.items():          # 15
```

```
...     print(k, v)          # 16 lines
...
PYNETAUTO-SW01 843DC6******
PYNETAUTO-SW17 807FF8******
PYNETAUTO-SW05 F06281******
```

You do not need to worry about or understand how to read the previous code. What is important is that you can count the number of code lines needed to achieve the expected result. Not counting the newline and data lines, exactly 16 code lines were required to print the result using only Python methods (without using any modules). Yes, it works, but it takes many lines of code to achieve the goal.

After you have learned how to use a regular expression, you can use Python's `re` module to do the same task, and the data manipulation becomes a breeze. The number of code lines drops, and it is easier to write and read. Count the number of code lines in Listing 9-2; exactly four code lines were needed to print out the expected result (not counting the newline and data lines). So, when you compare the number of code lines between the two listings, you can see significant savings in the number of code lines used. This was a simple example, but think about more complex tasks working with big data. It will take a lot of time and elbow grease to write lengthy custom code to achieve the end goal. Using the regular expression module in Python code, your application code will become more concise, easier to write, and easier to read.

Listing 9-2. re Example

```
>>> sw_mac = '''pynetauto-sw01 84:3d:c6:05:09:11
... pynetauto-sw17 80:7f:f8:80:71:1b
... pynetauto-sw05 f0:62:81:5a:53:cd'''
>>> import re          # 1
>>> sw_mac = sw_mac.replace(":", "").upper()          # 2
>>> pattern = re.compile("([0-9A-F]{6})" "([0-9A-F]{6})")          # 3
>>> print(pattern.sub("\g<1>******", sw_mac))          # 4
PYNETAUTO-SW01 843DC6******
PYNETAUTO-SW17 807FF8******
PYNETAUTO-SW05 F06281******
>>>
```

There is no need to write the code yourself at this stage. To download and run the code, you can go to my `pynetauto` GitHub site and download the code in Listings 9-1 and 9-2.

Studying Regular Expressions Using Python

There are many ways you can study regular expressions with Python, and here we will discuss how you can study in a few different ways. Try a study method that suits you the best and stick to it until you complete the exercises in this chapter.

If you want to follow along with Listings 9-3 and 9-4, you can download the `sh_ver.txt` file from my GitHub site and save it as `sh_ver.txt` in your Linux directory.

URL: `https://github.com/pynetauto/apress_pynetauto`

Method 1: Using Notepad++

You already installed Notepad++ in Chapter 2, and it is a great tool to use to explore regular expressions. With Notepad++, there are two ways to study regular expressions, and depending on the size of the data or text, you can choose either approach. You can use a single Python file for a short string, as shown in Figure 9-2, and execute the script by using Ctrl+F6 or Ctrl+F5 from Notepad++.

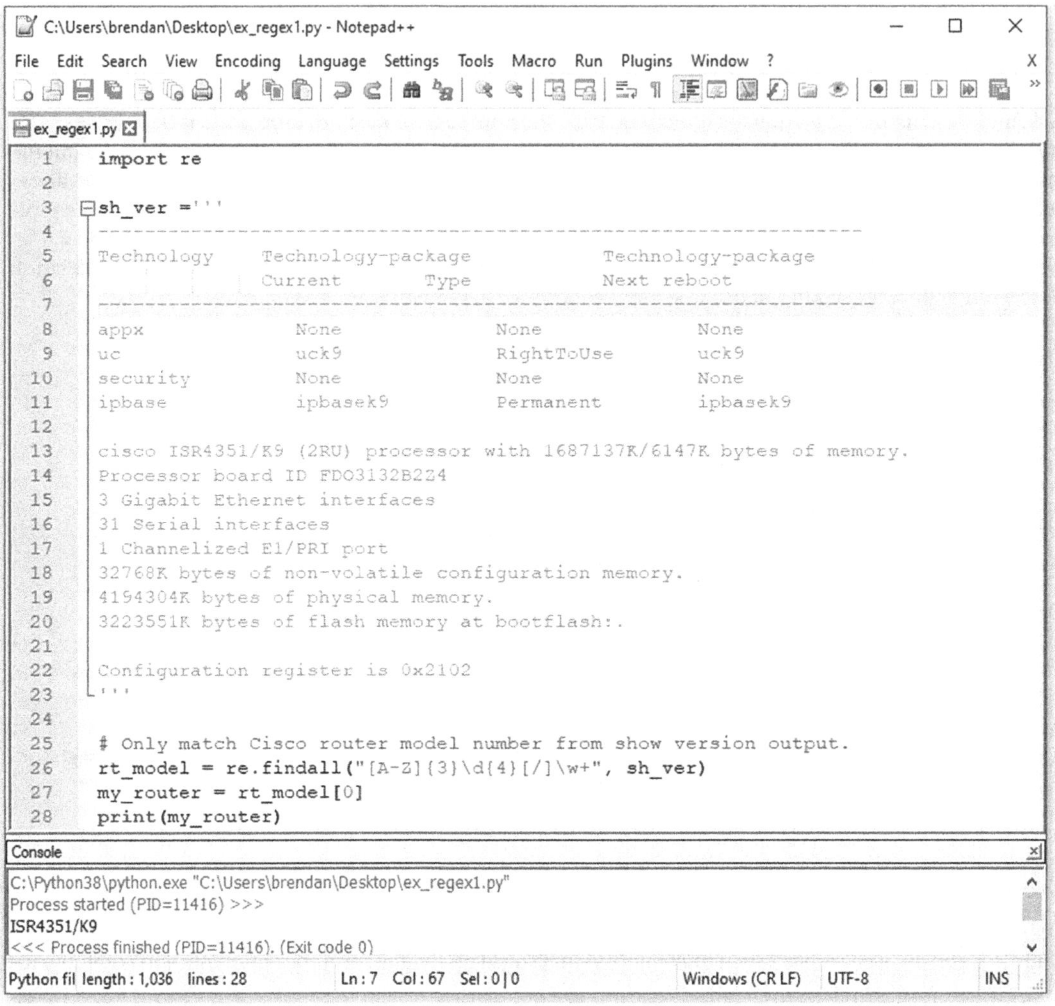

Figure 9-2. *Studying regular expressions using Notepad++ with a single script*

If the text data is lengthy or you have multiple files to read, you can use the file read method to read the files into your Python script and run the Python code you have written. This example is shown in Figures 9-3 and 9-4.

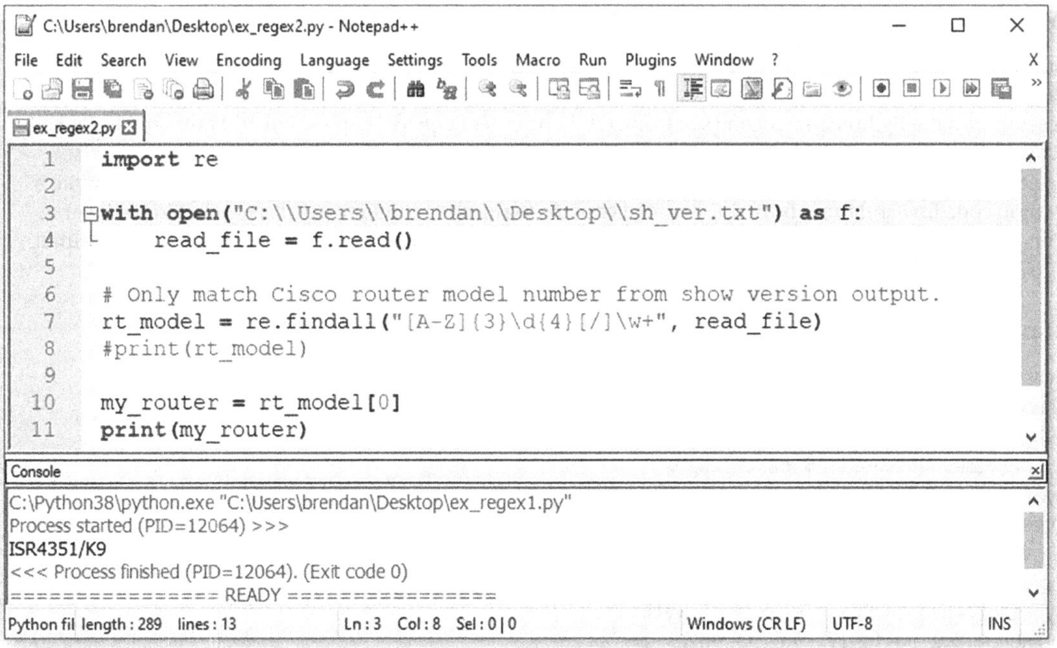

Figure 9-3. *Regular expression using Notepad++, read file method re script*

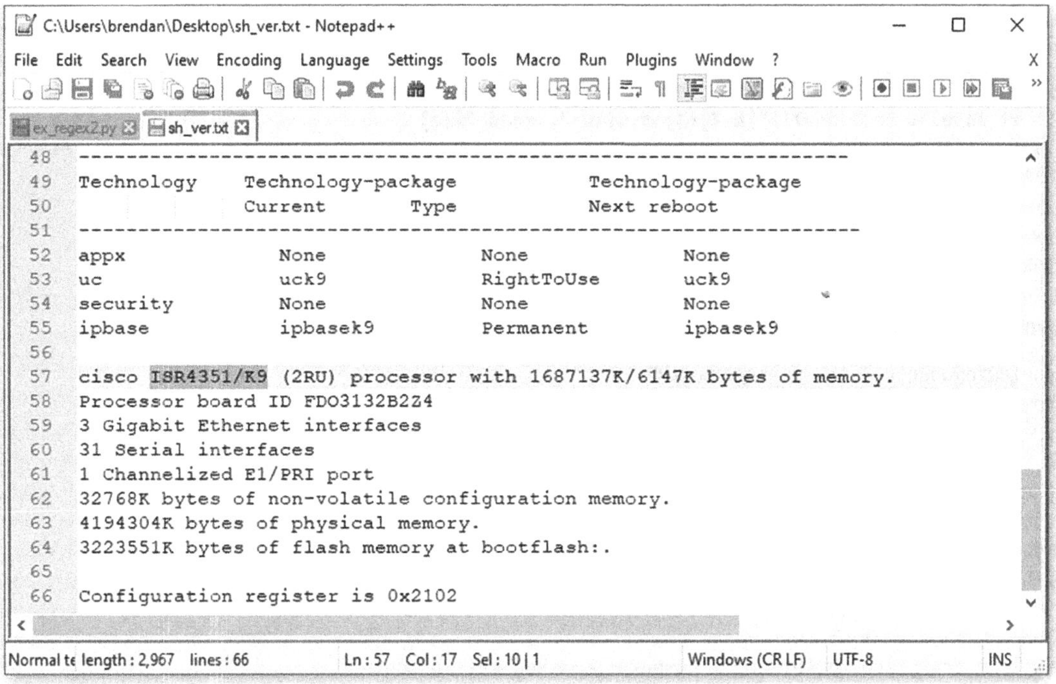

Figure 9-4. *Regular expression using Notepad++, read file method data file*

Method 2: Using the Linux Shell

Like the Notepad++ method, you can run one of your Linux VM servers and SSH into the server to practice regular expressions on Python. If you want to test a simple regular expression, you can start an interactive session with the Python interpreter (see Listing 9-3). After you type the expression and press the Enter key, it immediately returns the result, or no result if your expression did not match any strings. You can also use this method using Python 3 on your Windows 10 host machine. As in Notepad++, you can also write a Python code first and run it from the terminal console to run the re match script, as shown in Listing 9-4. This method may sound difficult, but when you practice a couple of examples, you will get familiar with it, and using regular expressions with Python becomes easier.

Listing 9-3. Regular Expression on Python Interpreter

```
pynetauto@ubuntu20s1:~$ pwd
/home/pynetauto
pynetauto@ubuntu20s1:~$ mkdir ex_regex
pynetauto@ubuntu20s1:~$ cd ex_regex
pynetauto@ubuntu20s1:~/ex_regex$ nano sh_ver.txt
pynetauto@ubuntu20s1:~/ex_regex$ ls
sh_ver.txt
pynetauto@ubuntu20s1:~/ex_regex
pynetauto@ubuntu20s1:~/ex_regex$ python3
Python 3.8.2 (default, Jul 16 2020, 14:00:26)
[GCC 9.3.0] on linux
Type "help", "copyright", "credits" or "license" for more information.
>>> import re
>>> with open("/home/pynetauto/ex_regex/sh_ver.txt") as f:
...     read_file = f.read()
...
>>> # Only match Cisco router model number from show version output.
>>> rt_model = re.findall("[A-Z]{3}\d{4}\w+", read_file)
>>> print(rt_model)
['ISR4351/K9']
>>> my_router = rt_model[0]
>>> my_router
'ISR4351/K9'
```

Listing 9-4. Regular Expression Writing Python Code on Linux

```
pynetauto@ubuntu20s1:~/ex_regex$ pwd
/home/pynetauto/ex_regex
pynetauto@ubuntu20s1:~/ex_regex$ ls
sh_ver.txt
pynetauto@ubuntu20s1:~/ex_regex$ nano ex9.4_sh_ver.py
pynetauto@ubuntu20s1:~/ex_regex$ cat ex9.4_sh_ver.py
import re
with open("/home/pynetauto/ex_regex/sh_ver.txt") as f:
    read_file = f.read()

# Only match Cisco router model number from show version output.
rt_model = re.findall("[A-Z]{3}\d{4}\w+", read_file)
print(rt_model)
```

```
my_router = rt_model[0]
print(my_router)
pynetauto@ubuntu20s1:~/ex_regex$ python3 ex9.4_sh_ver.py
['ISR4351/K9']
ISR4351/K9
```

Regular Expression Breakdown: [A-Z]{3}\d{4}[/]\w+

[A-Z]{3}	\d{4}	[/]	\w+
Three capital letters	Four digits	Character /	Any string with at least one occurrence

Method 3: Using the Internet to Study Regular Expressions

One of the most effective ways to study regular expressions is to use a web browser and view content on the Internet. There are plenty of websites providing free regular expression exercises. Some sites are biased toward one programming language over another, but try to find programming language-neutral sites and practice more. Once you build your confidence in regular expressions, you can start using one of the first two Python re methods shown earlier. Practicing the re module in Python is important as that is the way you will be using a regular expression in Python. One of the better regular expression practice sites is regex101 (https://regex101.com). See Figure 9-5.

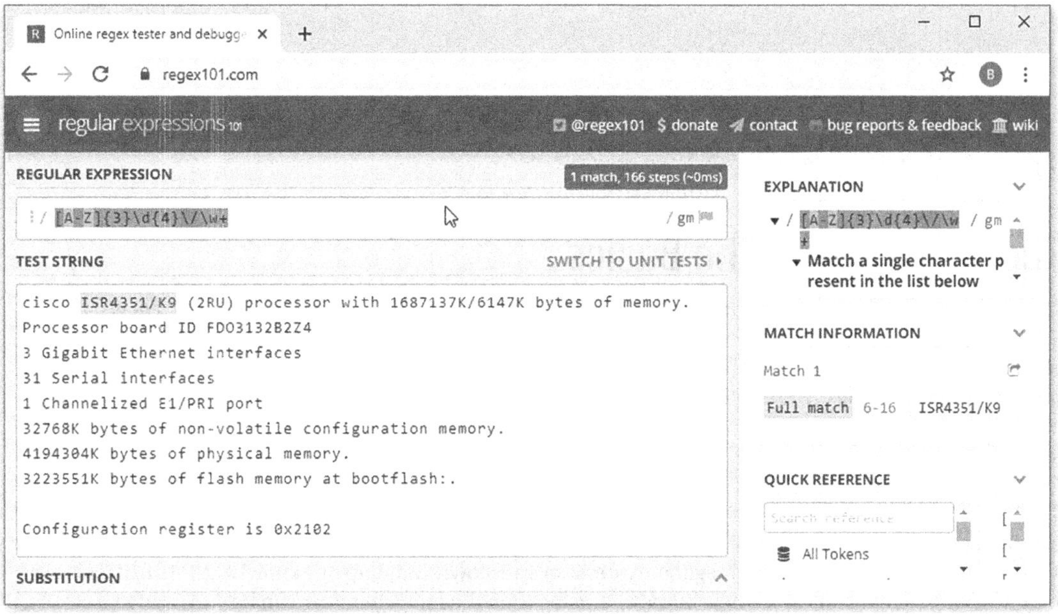

Figure 9-5. Regular expressions practice website

If you are on the go all the time but still want to get regular expression practice, you can practice on Android devices or Apple iOS devices. Download RegexPal (for Android phones) or RegEx Lab (for iOS devices) or similar apps on your mobile device. These applications are useful for on-the-go simple regular expression practice at any time, anywhere. See Figure 9-6.

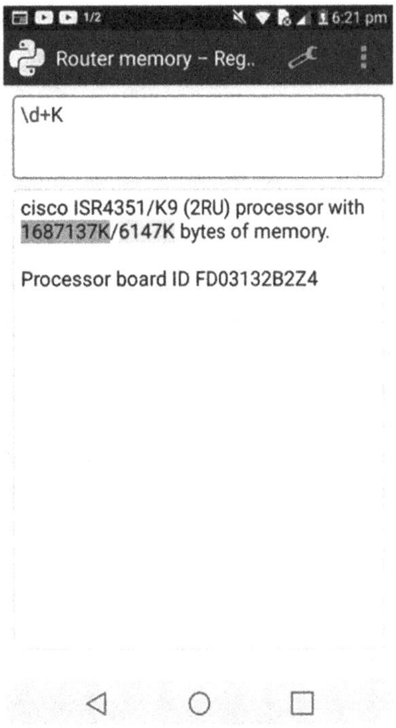

Figure 9-6. *Android regular expression app example*

Regex Operation: The Basics

Regular expressions use metacharacters to match static or dynamic data strings. The word *meta* is a Latin (Greek) word meaning *beyond, after*, or *behind*. When used in a programming language, metacharacters have special meaning from their real representation so that metacharacters can be defined as the characters having hidden meanings. The metacharacters include the following:

```
. ^ $ * + ? \ | ( ) [ ] { }
```

When one of these metacharacters is used in regular expressions, it carries some special meaning. The last six characters are in pairs of two, so the brackets must be used in pairs in the regular expressions. Let's start with the most straightforward regular expression and slowly build up our knowledge. Also, if you want to express these characters as a single literal character, then the metacharacter can be enclosed in a set of a square bracket ([ ]) or escaped using the backslash (\). However, pay special attention to metacharacters ^ and \; these two characters cannot be literally matched using the square bracket method. See Table 9-1.

Table 9-1. Regular Expression Meatacharacters

<table>
<tr><th>Metacharacter</th><th>Terminology</th><th>Escape with \</th><th>Match Literally Using [ ]</th></tr>
<tr><td>.</td><td>Dot</td><td>\.</td><td>[.]</td></tr>
<tr><td>^</td><td>Caret</td><td>\^</td><td>[\^]</td></tr>
<tr><td>$</td><td>Dollar</td><td>\$</td><td>[$]</td></tr>
<tr><td>*</td><td>Star</td><td>*</td><td>[*]</td></tr>
<tr><td>+</td><td>Plus</td><td>\+</td><td>[+]</td></tr>
<tr><td>?</td><td>Question mark</td><td>\?</td><td>[?]</td></tr>
<tr><td>\</td><td>Backslash</td><td>\\</td><td>[\\]</td></tr>
<tr><td>|</td><td>Pipe</td><td>\|</td><td>[|]</td></tr>
<tr><td>( )</td><td>Round brackets</td><td>\(\)</td><td>[(] [)]</td></tr>
<tr><td>[ ]</td><td>Square brackets</td><td>\[\]</td><td>[[] []]</td></tr>
<tr><td>{ }</td><td>Curly brackets</td><td>\{ \}</td><td>[{] [}]</td></tr>
</table>

To get around with the literal matching method with ^ and \, you can add a backslash in front of the ^ and \ inside the square bracket. See Listing 9-5.

As all other chapters, to get a full understanding of regular expression concepts, you are expected to open your Python interpreter and type all the content marked in bold in each exercises. This includes everything after the three greater-than signs (>>>).

Listing 9-5. Matching Metacharacter ^ and \ Using Square Brackets ([ ])

```
>>> import re
>>> expr = " . ^ $ * + ? \ | ( ) [ ] { }"
>>> re.search(r'[\^]', expr)
<re.Match object; span=(3, 4), match='^'>
>>> re.search(r'[\\]', expr)
<re.Match object; span=(13, 14), match='\\'>
```

If ^ or \ is used inside a square bracket set, you are required to add the escape backslash in front of the metacharacters. There are good reasons for this, and when used inside square brackets, ^ is used to negate the character following it. Type in Listing 9-6 into your Python interpreter and study it carefully. `[^a]` would mean match all characters but *a*. In Listing 9-6, all characters are matched except the letter *a*.

Listing 9-6. Meaning of [^a]

```
>>> import re
>>> re.findall('[^a]', 'abracadabra')
['b', 'r', 'c', 'd', 'b', 'r']
```

The backslash inside the brackets, `[\]`, also has a minor problem as the regular expression recognizes the backslash as a negating character for the closing square bracket, `]`. So, we have to negate the backslash by adding another backslash. Look at Listing 9-7, where the backslash had to be used to match backslash and a closing square bracket, `]`.

Listing 9-7. Meaning of [\]]

```
>>> re.search(r'[\\]', 'match \ or ]')
<re.Match object; span=(6, 7), match='\\'>
>>> re.search(r'[\]]', 'match \ or ]')
<re.Match object; span=(11, 12), match=']'>
```

Character Class ([])

The first metacharacter we will learn is the character class metacharacter. Usually, a regular expression made up of character classes is expressed between the left open square bracket (`[`) and the right closed square bracket (`]`). All characters are allowed inside the character class, [ ].

For example, a regular expression of `[aei]` will match any one of the vowel letters *a*, *e*, or *i*. Let's look at the real use of words associated with alarms: *ding, buzz, beep, clang*.

Regular Expression	Words (String)	Matched	Explanation
`[aei]`	`ding`	ding	Matches the character *i* literally (case sensitive)
	`buzz`	buzz	No match; *buzz* does not contain *a*, *e*, or *i*
	`beep`	beep	Matches the character *e* twice
	`clang`	clang	Matches the character *a* literally

When a hyphen (`-`) is used inside the square brackets with letters or numbers, it abbreviates the expressions of a range. For example, `[a-z]` takes a meaning of all lowercase letters. `[A-Z]` takes a meaning of all uppercase letters from *A* to *Z*. You already have guessed it: to express all letters in both lowercase and uppercase, the regular expression to match becomes `[a-zA-Z]`. If you want to express a hexadecimal number, you will use `[0-9a-fA-F]`, meaning all whole numbers and both lower and uppercase letters starting from *a* to *f*. In a regex, capitalization does matter. A common example of `[0-9]` takes the meaning of from 0 to 9, meaning `[0 1 2 3 4 5 6 7 8 9]`.

Almost all characters can be used between the square brackets, [ ], but with a single exception of ^ (caret) symbol (^ metacharacter). When ^ is used inside the square brackets, the expression used takes the opposite meaning or meaning of `NOT`. For example, if you want to use an expression to exclude any whole numbers, you can use `[^0-9]`. If you want not to match any uppercase letters, you can use `[^A-Z]`.

For commonly used regular expressions such as `[0-9]` and `[a-zA-Z]`, there are particular expressions to save time and make the regular expressions more compact and readable. These are tabulated here for your reference:

Regular Expression	Interchangeable Expression	Explanation
\d	[0-9]	Matches whole numbers from 0 to 9.
\D	[^0-9]	Matches all characters except whole numbers.
\s	[\t\n\r\f\v]	Matches all whitespace. A whitespace is included.
\S	[^ \t\n\r\f\v]	Matches all characters except whitespace characters.
\w	[a-zA-Z0-9]	Matches all alphanumeric letters.
\W	[^a-zA-Z0-9]	Does not match alphanumeric letters. Matches all symbols such as % # @.

In the world of programming, the backslash (\) is commonly used to negate the meaning of the expression that comes after the backslash. For example, d is the letter *d* in the alphabet, but if it is combined with the backslash and becomes \d, this takes on a different meaning. Also, the particular expressions with capital letters always take the opposite meaning of the small, lettered expression.

Dot (.): Single Character Match

The regular expression . (dot) matches all characters except for line terminators such as \n. Interestingly, a regular expression provides a method to include \n, as we will see in an example later, but by using the re.DOTALL option, the . (dot) can also include the newline character \n.

Let's consider the following regular expression example.

Regular Expression	Explanation
d.g	Matches any single character between the letters *d* and g

Any character specified must match. For example, the letter *d* must be matched in the first position, and the letter *g* must match in the third position. The middle character can match any character except the new character \n.

Regular Expression	Words (String)	Matched	Explanation
d.g	dog	dog	Matches all characters *d*, *o*, and *g*.
	d%g	d%g	Matches all characters *d*, % sign, and *g*.
	d\ng	None	Not matched, *\n* is ignored and not matched. *d* and *g* are matched, but *\n* is ignored, so *d\ng* is not matched.

What if the dot character is in between the square brackets, [ ]?

Regular Expression	Explanation
d[.]g	The dot character between the brackets takes its literal meaning as a single dot (.). So, it will only match d.g but not dog or d%g.

Asterisk (*): Repetition

Let's zoom through this one and look at the following regular expression.

Regular Expression	Explanation
`zo*m`	Match if the character in front of the star occurs zero, one, or many times. The preceding expression is matched. In this case, the letter *o*.

The metacharacter * has the meaning of repetition, and it matches the preceding expression *o* zero, one, or almost infinite number of times. * becomes handy while trying to match unpredictable occurrences where a character may or may not appear; hence, it may or may not match.

All of the examples are matched by the * metacharacter.

Regular Expression	Words (String)	Matched	Explanation
`zo*m`	zm	zm	Matches *o* zero times. Even without *o*, `zm` is matched.
	zom	zom	Matches *o* once.
	zoom	zoom	Matches *oo* in the middle.

Plus (+): Repetition

A plus sign (+) is another metacharacter associated with the repetition. It is a little bit similar to the star but slightly different because zero times is not considered a match. With the use of the + metacharacter, at least one character must be matched. Let's use the same character again for an explanation.

Regular Expression	Explanation
`zo+m`	Matches if the letter *o* appears one or more times

The + metacharacter matches some words.

Regular Expression	Words (String)	Matched	Explanation
`zo+m`	zm	None	No o in the middle, so not matched
	zom	zom	Matches *z*, *o*, and *m*
	zoom	zoom	Matches *z*, *oo*, and *m*

{m, n}: Repetition

Using the metacharacter `{m, n }`, you can match the number of repetitions. The letter `m` is the start of the match count, and `n` is the end of the match count. For example, `o{1, 3}` takes the meaning of matching the character *o* one to three times. Another example is `o{3, }`, which means that the repetition of the prepending character *o* must match at least three times or more. Another example is `o{, 3}` will match the same character *o* up to three times. So, the regular expression of `{0,}` is equivalent to + and `{1,}` is equivalent to *. Let's study `{m, n}` by looking at some examples first.

{m}

The reference letter or `m` is the exact number of repetitions required to match the prepending character. Look at a simple example and explanation.

Regular Expression	Explanation
`Zo{1}e`	Matches the first letter *Z*, then matches the letter *o* `m` number of times (`m=1`), in this case once only, and then matches the letter *e*. So, the expected match letter is `Zoe`. Note, the regular expressions are case sensitive.

Let's look at more examples to help your understanding. If you can type these on your computer keyboard while following the book, you will learn a lot more.

Regular Expression {m}	Words (String)	Matched	Explanation
`o{2}`	oo	oo	Matches characters *oo*
	zoo	zoo	Matches characters *oo*
	boom	boom	Matches characters *oo*
`zo{2}m`	zm	None	Missing *oo*, so not matched
	zom	None	Missing *oo*, so not matched.
	zoom	zoom	Matches characters *z*, *oo*, and *m*

{m, n}

The first reference number, or `m`, is the minimum repetition number, and the second reference number, or `n`, is the maximum repetition number. First, a simple explanation of how `{m, n}` works.

Regular Expression	Explanation
`o{2, 5}`	Matches characters *oo*, *ooo*, *oooo*, or *ooooo*. Matches from two to five occurrences of the letter *o*.

Now let's look at some simple examples.

Regular Expression {m, n}	Words (String)	Matched	Explanation
`zo{1,3}m`	zm	None	Not matched, *o* matches 0 times
	zoom	zoom	Matches *z*, *oo*, and *m*
	zoooom	None	Not matched, one too many o

? (Question Mark: Repetition)

The metacharacter uses the same meaning as `{0, 1}` and can be used interchangeably. Again using a simple example, here is more explanation of how ? works in a regular expression.

Regular Expression	Explanation
`Zoe?`	Matches *Zo* or *Zoe*. The character before the question mark, which is *e*, becomes optional. So, even the string is Zo. The regular expression will still match the word. This can be written as `Zoe{0, 1}`.

Use the same example as before to better understand the ?.

Regular Expression ?	Words (string)	Matched	Explanation
`zo?m`	zm	zm	Matches `z` and `m`. Letter *o* is optional, so it does not have to match.
	zom	zom	Matches *z*, *o*, and *m*.
	zoom	None	Not matched as only expecting one *o*.

As shown earlier, *, +, and ? metacharacters can be replaced by `{m, n}` methods, but using *, +, and ? makes regular expression easier to read and understand, so whenever possible, try to use *, +, and ? instead of `{m, n}` format.

Python's re Module

As discussed earlier, Python provides the regular expression feature out of the box, and it is supported by a standard module called `re` (regular expression). This module will be pre-installed as part of the standard Python library when Python is installed on your OS.

To begin your journey into the Python `re` module, it is worth mentioning that there is some difference in the ways or styles you can write your Python code using the `re` module. You can choose to keep your script structure simple, standard, or structured. In a simple style, you can write the regular expression statement in a single line of code, as shown in the simple style example in Table 9-2. When you use the standard style, you do not have to use a `re.compiler` statement, but you can still add some style by separating the string and regular expression statement. If you choose to have a little more consistency in your code, you can use the compiler style, using the `re.compiler` statement. Any coding style will work fine, but the advantage of using a `re.compiler` statement in your code is obvious. It gives a little bit more control and structure to your code and hence also adds styling consistency.

Let's compare three styles in questions quickly by looking at each example. All three examples will return the same result but written in two different styles.

Table 9-2. Different Ways to Use re Module in Python

Style	Example

Simple	`import re`
	
	`m = re.findall('\dx\d{4}', "Configuration register is 0x2102")`
	`print(m)`

Standard	`import re`
	
	`expr = "Configuration register is 0x2102"`
	`m = re.findall('\dx\d{4}', expr)`
	`print(m)`

Compiler	`import re`
	`expr = "Configuration register is 0x2102"` ← **expr for expression**
	`p = re.compile('\dx\d{4}')` ← `p for pattern`
	`m = p.findall(expr)` ← `m for match`
	`print(m)`

Result	`['0x2102']`

In the third compiler style, we have given a separate variable p to the compiler statement, which contains the regular expression we want to match. And then the variable m performs the match function using variables expr and p. If the compiled regular expression has to be used more than two times, it would be advantageous to use this method over the simpler methods. You have to note that Python allows you to write shortcodes, but you lose the structure and style, whereas more code lines give you better control and structure, but you have to write more lines of code to achieve the same result. In my honest opinion, there are no right or wrong answers here; this all depends on your style and personal preference.

Python re String Methods

There are four basic types of regular expression search methods we have to master. Let's quickly go over the four methods and then review each by doing some exercises on the Python interpreter. See Table 9-3.

Table 9-3. re String Methods

Method	Explanation
`re.match()`	Search the regular expression pattern on the first line and return the match object. (Only searches the first line.) If a match is not found, returns `None`.
`re.search()`	Search the regular expression pattern and return the first occurrence. Unlike the `re.match()` method, this method will check all lines. If a match is not found, returns `None`.
`re.findall()`	Search the regular expression pattern and match all occurrences. Unlike the `re.match()` or `re.search()` method, this method returns all the nonoverlapping matches of patterns in a string as a list of strings.
`re.finditer()`	Search the regular expression pattern, and this method returns an iterator yielding `MatchObject` instances over all nonoverlapping matches for the string's re pattern.

re.match()

Listing 9-8, Listing 9-9, and Listing 9-10 will return the same matched objective but are written differently. Carefully study how each line is written differently. Again, there is no right or wrong answer here but different ways to write the same code to achieve the same objective.

Listing 9-8. re.match() method 1

```
>>> import re
>>> re.match(r'\d\w\d{4}', '0x2142 Configuration register is 0x2102')
<re.Match object; span=(0, 6), match='0x2142'>
```

Listing 9-9. re.match() method 2

```
>>> import re
>>> expr = '0x2142 Configuration register is 0x2102'
>>> re.match(r'\d\w\d{4}', expr)
<re.Match object; span=(0, 6), match='0x2142'>
```

Listing 9-10. re.match() method 3

```
>>> import re
>>> expr = '0x2142 Configuration register is 0x2102'
>>> p = re.compile(r'\d\w\d{4}')
>>> m = p.match(expr)
>>> print(m)
<re.Match object; span=(0, 6), match='0x2142'>
```

Let's do another match exercise. In Listing 9-11, the `match` object is returned with the span containing the `match` string's start and end positions. By contrast, if there is no matched object in Listing 9-12, the returned value is None. In Python, None serves the same purpose as `null` in other languages, meaning that it did not match anything.

Listing 9-11. re.match()

```
>>> import re
>>> p = re.compile('[a-z]+')
>>> expr = "five regular expression"
>>> m = p.match(expr)
>>> print(m)
<re.Match object; span=(0, 4), match='five'>
```

Listing 9-12. re.match()

```
>>> import re
>>> p = re.compile('[a-z]+')
>>> expr = "5 regular expression"
>>> m = p.match(expr)
>>> print(m)
Result: None
```

The previous exercises are essential in the way we structure our Python regular expression script flow. Looking at the returned values, it could be a best practice to structure our Python re scripts in the following format, so the script continues to run only if a match is found:

Recommended script flow for regular expression for this chapter

```
import re                                   ← import re module

p = re.compile("Enter_re_here")             ← compile a pattern
expr = 'string_to_search_here'              ← data or expression
m = p.match(expr)                           ← matching patterns using pattern
if m:
  print('Match found: ', m.group())         ← execute only if a match is found
else:
  print('Match not found')
```

re.search()

As shown earlier, let's use the `re.search()` method to perform the match function, and in Listing 9-13, the returned result is the same as `re.match()` where the regular expression matched the string and returned the matched object.

Listing 9-13. re.search()

```
>>> import re
>>> p = re.compile('[a-z]+')
>>> expr = "five regular expression"
>>> m = p.search(expr)
>>> print(m)
<re.Match object; span=(0, 4), match='five'
```

On the other hand, in Listing 9-14, unlike the `re.match()` method, the `re.search()` method regular expression did not match digit 5, so it jumped to the next match and returned the word *months*, which matched the regular expression. So, the `match()` method is typically used if searching from the beginning of the string, whereas the `search()` method can be used to match the first instance, searching the whole string.

Listing 9-14. re.search()

```
>>> import re
>>> p = re.compile('[a-z]+')
>>> expr = "5 regular expression"
>>> m = p.search(expr)
>>> print(m)
<re.Match object; span=(2, 9), match='regular'>
```

re.findall()

This time let's get some practice with the `findall()` method using the same regular expression flow. Enter each line into your Python Interpreter console to get more practice. Unlike the previous two methods, the `findall()` method returns the matched objects as a list. In Listing 9-15, each word has been returned as strings in a list.

Listing 9-15. re.findall() exercise 1

```
>>> import re
>>> p = re.compile('[a-z]+')
>>> expr = "five regular expression"
>>> m = p.findall(expr)
>>> print(m)
['five', 'regular', 'expression']
```

In Listing 9-16, `findall()` matches all strings satisfying the regular expression condition but ignores the digit 5. This method will try to match and return all matched objects in a list format.

Listing 9-16. re.findall() exercise 2

```
>>> import re
>>> p = re.compile('[a-z]+')
>>> expr = "5 regular expression"
>>> m = p.findall(expr)
>>> print(m)
['regular', 'expression']
```

re.finditer()

The last exercise is on the `finditer()` method. As before, let's type in the code and learn by doing some exercises (see Listing 9-17 and Listing 9-18). The `finditer()` method returns the same result as the `finditer()` method, but it returns an iterator over all nonoverlapping matches for the string's regular expression pattern. It might be a powerful tool for text processing, but the use cases for the `finditer()` method are very narrow.

Listing 9-17. re.finditer() exercise 1

```
>>> import re
>>> p = re.compile('[a-z]+')
>>> expr = "five regular expression"
>>> m = p.finditer(expr)
>>> print(m)
<callable_iterator object at 0x000001E581F1B5E0>
>>> for r in m:
...     print(r)
...
<re.Match object; span=(0, 4), match='five'>
<re.Match object; span=(5, 12), match='regular'>
<re.Match object; span=(13, 23), match='expression'>
```

Listing 9-18. re.finditer() exercise 2

```
>>> import re
>>> p = re.compile('[a-z]+')
>>> expr = "5 regular expression"
>>> m = p.finditer(expr)
>>> print(m)
<callable_iterator object at 0x000001E581F1B5E0>
```

```
>>> for r in m: print(r)
...
<re.Match object; span=(2, 9), match='regular'>
<re.Match object; span=(10, 20), match='expression'>
```

Match Object Method

Earlier, we saw the returned objects from regular expression matches using match and search methods, but we still had some questions about the matched strings and exactly how they work. To better understand the attributes of these returned objects, after running the match and search methods, we can use match object methods to answer some of our questions. First, let's quickly review Table 9-4.

Table 9-4. *re Match Object Method*

Match Method	Explanation
`group()`	Returns matched string
`start()`	Returns the start position of the matched string
`end()`	Returns the end position of the matched string
`span()`	Returns the start and end position of matched string in tuple format

Now let's learn match object methods through exercises to confirm the returned objects from the matched returned objects. In the first exercise with the match method, we can individually get the `match` object attributes using `group`, `start`, `end`, and `span` match methods. Enter the code in Listing 9-19 into the interpreter and check the result interactively.

Listing 9-19. re.match()

```
>>> import re
>>> p = re.compile('[a-z]+')
>>> expr = "automation"
>>> m = p.match(expr)
>>> print(m)
<re.Match object; span=(0, 10), match='automation'>
>>> m.group()
'automation'
>>> m.start()
0
>>> m.end()
10
>>> m.span()
(0, 10
```

In the search match method shown in Listing 9-20, if we want to find out the exact `match` object location in the memory, we can issue `group`, `start`, `end`, and `span` without the round bracket set at the end. Anyway, we should focus more on the `group()`, `start()`, `end()`, and `span()` result of the `match` object attributes.

Listing 9-20. re.search()

```
>>> import re
>>> p = re.compile('[a-z]+')
>>> expr = "5. regular expression"
>>> m = p.search(expr)
>>> print(m)
<re.Match object; span=(3, 10), match='regular'>
>>> m.group
<built-in method group of re.Match object at 0x000001E581F00C00>
>>> m.group()
'regular'
>>> m.start
<built-in method start of re.Match object at 0x000001E581F00C00>
>>> m.start()
3
>>> m.end
<built-in method end of re.Match object at 0x000001E581F00C00>
>>> m.end()
10
>>> m.span
<built-in method span of re.Match object at 0x000001E581F00C00>
>>> m.span()
(3, 10)
```

Compile Options

When you compile regular expressions, you can also add options to your expressions. First, quickly review the options. When using these regular expression options, you can use the full descriptive option names like `re.DOTALL`, `re.IGNORECASE`, `re.MULTILINE`, and `re.VERBOSE` or use the abbreviated version such as `re.S`, `re.I`, `re.M`, and `re.X`. See Table 9-5.

Table 9-5. *re Compile Options*

Options	Abbreviation	Explanation
DOTALL	S	Matches any character including a newline, \n.
IGNORECASE	I	Makes the regex case-insensitive or ignore case. All major regex engines match in case-sensitive mode; I mode disables case sensitivity.
MULTILINE	M	^ and $ will match the start and end of a line, instead of the whole string. It enables the regular expression engine to handle an input string that consists of multiple lines.
VERBOSE	X	Allows the use of verbose mode. Whitespace is ignored. Spaces, tabs, and carriage returns are not matched as spaces, tabs, and carriage returns.

Once again, no pain, no gain, so let's type the following exercises into the Python Interpreter and learn from the examples.

re.DOTALL (re.S)

The DOTALL option is used to include a newline in the match string, and let's check how the DOTALL option works in real use. See Listing 9-21 and Listing 9-22,

Listing 9-21. Without re.DOTALL()

```
>>> import re
>>> expr = 'a\nb'
>>> p = re.compile('a.b')
>>> m = p.match(expr)
>>> print(m)
None                                    ← No match found due to newline
```

Listing 9-22. re.DOTALL()

```
>>> import re
>>> expr = 'a\nb'
>>> p = re.compile('a.b', re.DOTALL)
>>> m = p.match(expr)
>>> print(m)
<re.Match object; span=(0, 3), match='a\nb'>  ← Matches object
```

In Listing 9-21, \n literally represents a newline, and for this reason, the regular expression a.b alone cannot match a\nb. In Listing 9-22, when we enable the DOTALL option using re.DOTALL, we can confirm that even the \n character is matched as part of the string. Under normal circumstances, you will not be using the DOTALL option to match the newline character. Instead, it will be used to match strings in multiple lines by ignoring the newline characters.

re.IGNORECASE (re.I)

When the IGNORCASE option is enabled, it makes the regular expression case insensitive so both uppercase and lowercase letters are matched, disregarding the casing of alphabet characters. Again, let's do some exercises to see how re.IGNORECASE (re.I) works in action. See Listing 9-23.

Listing 9-23. re.IGNORECASE()

```
>>> import re
>>> expr1 = 'automation'
>>> expr2 = 'Automation'
>>> expr3 = 'AUTOMATION'
>>> p = re.compile('[a-z]+', re.IGNORECASE)
>>> m1 = p.match(expr1)
>>> print(m1)
<re.Match object; span=(0, 10), match='automation'>
>>> m2 = p.match(expr2)
>>> print(m2)
<re.Match object; span=(0, 10), match='Automation'>
>>> m3 = p.match(expr3)
>>> print(m3)
<re.Match object; span=(0, 10), match='AUTOMATION'>
```

Only a single exercise is enough to comprehend the use of `re.IGNORECASE` or `re.I` use. In Listing 9-23, the same pattern has been used three times to match the patterns in three different expressions (strings). Three casing types (all lowercase, first-letter capitalization, and all uppercasing expressions) are used as our target strings. The regular expression will match all three strings as the `re.I` option was enabled in the regular expression pattern.

re.MULTILINE (re.M)

The `re.MULTILINE` or `re.M` option is used with ^ and $ regular expression metacharacters. As explained before, the ^ metacharacter is used to indicate the start of a string, and $ is used to mark the end of a string. In layman's term, a regular expression of `^Network` means the first string must begin with the word *network*, whereas `automation$` means the last string must end with the word automation. Once again, let's learn `MULTILINE` by doing. See Listing 9-24 and Listing 9-25.

Listing 9-24. without re.MULTILINE()

```
>>> import re
>>> expr = '''Regular Engineers
... Regular Network Engineers
... Regular but not so regular Engineers'''
>>> p = re.compile('^R\w+\S')
>>> m = p.findall(expr)
>>> print(m)
['Regular']
```

Listing 9-25. ^ and re.MULTILINE()

```
>>> import re
>>> expr = '''Regular Engineers
... Regular Network Engineers
... Regular but not so Regular Engineers'''
>>> p = re.compile('^R\w+\S', re.MULTILINE)
>>> m = p.findall(expr)
>>> print(m)
['Regular', 'Regular', 'Regular']
```

In both exercises, the data (expression) consists of three lines starting with the common word `Regular`. Each line begins with the same word, and the regular expression `^R\w+\S` matches the first word only, starting with a capital *R* followed by alphanumeric letters to nonwhitespace (`\S`). In Listing 9-24, without re.MULTILINE option, the search only matches the first occurrence of the word, Regular. Whereas in Listing 9-25, with re.MULTILINE option enabled, the search matches the word, Regular at the start of a new line on the multiple lines.

re.VERBOSE (re.X)

Try to type as much as you can and as accurately as you can. If you need to cross-check your typos, you can download the exercises used in this chapter from my download site. You can optionally copy and paste the information for your exercise as required.

URL: `https://github.com/pynetauto/apress_pynetauto/`

Most of the regular expression examples introduced in this chapter have been basic compared to the regular expressions used in real, production-ready scripts.

Now, look at the following two examples (Listing 9-26 and Listing 9-27); nevertheless, they are the same scripts returning the same value. For novice Python coders with limited exposure to regular expressions, the compiled regular expression in the first example (`r'[1-9](?:\d{0,2})(?:,\d{3})*(?:\.\d*[1-9])?|0?\.\d*[1-9]|0'`) will look like nothing more than gibberish. The compiled regular expression seems somewhat over-complicated. It is used to match the digits related to the dates and purposefully matches digits or digits with a comma used in the year. The first example will be what we are familiar with thus far, but the second example takes full advantage of the regular expression `re.VERBOSE` option to add comments and explain how the regular expression works. Although both return the same result, the latter increases the readability, perhaps even for the person who has written this regular expression. With the `re.VERBOSE` or `re.X` option, you can decode and add optional comments to add readability.

Listing 9-26. Without re.VERBOSE

```
import re

expr = 'I was born in 2,009 and I am 15 years old. I started my primary school in 2,010'
p = re.compile(r'[1-9](?:\d{0,2})(?:,\d{3})*(?:\.\d*[1-9])?|0?\.\d*[1-9]|0')

m = p.findall(expr)

print(m)
```

Listing 9-27. With re.VERBOSE

```
import re

expr = 'I was born in 2,009 and I am 15 years old. I started my primary school in 2,010'
p = re.compile(r"""
[1-9]           # Match a single digit between 1-9
(?:\d{0,2})     # Match digit equatl to [0-9] between 0 and 2 times
(?:,\d{3})*     # Match the character ,(Comma) literally, match a digit equal to [0-9] \
                  exactly 3 times) Zero and unlimited times
(?:\.\d*[1-9])? # Match the character. (Dot) literally, match a digit equal to [0-9] \
                  zero and unlimited times, match a single digit between [1-9]) \
                  zero and one time.
|               # OR
```

```
0?\.\d*[1-9]     # Match 0 zero or one time, match . (Dot) literally, match a digit \
                   equal to [0-9] zero or unlimited times, and match a digit between [1-9]
|                # OR
0                # Match one 0
""", re.VERBOSE)

m = p.findall(expr)

print(m)
```

Result: ['2,009', '15', '2,010']

\: Confusing Backslash Character

\ in Python gives special meaning to a metacharacter; it is an escape character in both Python strings and for the regex engine, to which you are eventually passing your patterns. When the slash character is used in the Python re engine, this can cause some confusion around how many escape characters you have to use to match the exact string you want to extract from your data. To remove confusion, when compiling a regular expression in Python, r (raw string notation) is appended immediately before the regular expression. Let's type in the following two examples (Listing 9-28 and Listing 9-29), the first without the use of raw string notation, r, and the second using the raw string notation, r. In the following examples, we are trying to match the string \scored.

Listing 9-28. Backslashes Without Raw String Notation

```
>>> import re
>>> expr = 'Our team \scored three goals\\'
>>> p1 = re.compile('\scored')
>>> p2 = re.compile('\\scored')
>>> p3 = re.compile('\\\scored')
>>> p4 = re.compile('\\\\scored')
>>> p5 = re.compile('\\\\\scored')
>>> print(p1.findall(expr))
[]
>>> print(p2.findall(expr))
[]
>>> print(p3.findall(expr))
['\\scored']
>>> print(p4.findall(expr))
['\\scored']
>>> print(p5.findall(expr))
[]
```

In Listing 9-29, the compiled regular expression with three backslashes and four backslashes matched and returned the same result. This can be confusing as you might be unsure whether you have to use three or four backslashes to match the word with the literal backslash character, \scored.

Listing 9-29. Backslash with Raw String Notation

```
>>> import re
>>> expr = 'Our team \scored three goals\\'
>>> p1 = re.compile(r'\scored')
```

```
>>> p2 = re.compile(r'\\scored')
>>> p3 = re.compile(r'\\\scored')
>>> p4 = re.compile(r'\\\\scored')
>>> print(p1.findall(expr))
[]
>>> print(p2.findall(expr))
['\\scored']
>>> print(p3.findall(expr))
[]
>>> print(p4.findall(expr))
[]
```

In Listing 9-30, we are using the raw string notation, r, and it is clear that the result indicates that you have to use two backslashes to match the target string \scored. Using one, three, and four backslashes with raw string notation will not match the target string.

Listing 9-30. Backslash with Raw String Notation

```
>>> import re
>>> expr = 'Our team \scored three goals\\'
>>> p2 = re.compile(r'\\scored')
>>> m = p2.findall(expr)
>>> print(m)
['\\scored']
>>> n = m[0]
>>> n
'\\scored'
>>> for x in n:
...     print(x, end='')
...
\scored
```

In Listing 9-30, the raw string match method is used, and in this example, the raw string match method matches both \'s (backslashes) and returns the matched string, \\scored in a list. To convert an item in a list, you can use the indexing method.

Regular Expressions: A Little Revision Plus More

In this section, let's quickly review what we have learned so far and cover a few more metacharacters and regular expression methods such as grouping, lookahead search, etc.

More Metacharacters

We have covered the most commonly used metacharacters so far, but we have to cover a few more common metacharacters to move forward. The characteristics of the metacharacters we discuss here are a little different from the ones discussed earlier in this chapter. We have already studied metacharacters such as +, *, [ ], and { }. These metacharacters will only search the strings once as they change their positions in a matching string. Let's now extend our metacharacter vocabulary by introducing a few more new ones, and then we will look at the grouping and lookahead and lookbehind examples.

OR Operator (|)

In a regular expression, the | (pipe) metacharacter has the same meaning as or. The regular expression of a|b has a similar meaning to [ab], but they operate differently. Both | and [ ] are OR operators, and they will try to match specified characters in the string, but the matched and returned results are a little different. Let's look at the following examples and precisely understand the real difference between | and [ ]. See Listing 9-31 and Listing 9-32.

Listing 9-31. a[bc]

```
>>> import re
>>> re.findall('a[bc]', 'a, ab, ac, abc, acb, ad')
['ab', 'ac', 'ab', 'ac']
```

Listing 9-32. a(b|c)

```
>>> re.findall('a(b|c)', 'a, ab, ac, abc, acb, ad')
['b', 'c', 'b', 'c']
```

In Listing 9-31, you have used the [ ] regular expression to match b or c; the regular expression match's returned values also contain the leading a. But in Listing 9-32, you replaced [ ] with |, and the returned values are only the matched values of either b or c but no leading a. So, the difference between [ ] and | is the way it matches the leading character(s), but one returns the leading character(s), and one doesn't.

Now, looking at Listing 9-33 and Listing 9-34, this is illustrated with a regular expression's range option, and it becomes more apparent that one prints the leading character and one doesn't.

Listing 9-33. 3[a-f]

```
>>> re.findall('3[a-f]', '3, 3a, 3c, 3f, 3g')
['3a', '3c', '3f']
```

Listing 9-34. 3(a|b|c|d|e|f)

```
>>> re.findall('3(a|b|c|d|e|f)', '3, 3a, 3c, 3f, 3g')
['a', 'c', 'f']
```

Listing 9-35 and Listing 9-36 are simple examples of | (OR) with the words *apple* and *raspberry*. In Listing 9-36, re.findall match method matches both words, *rasberry* and *apple*. The matched words are returned as a list.

Listing 9-35. apple|rasberry

```
>>> re.match('apple|raspberry', 'raspberry pie')
<re.Match object; span=(0, 8), match='rasberry'>
```

Listing 9-36. apple|rasberry

```
>>> print(re.findall('apple|raspberry', 'raspberry and apple pie'))
['rasberry', 'apple']
```

^ and $ (Anchors)

^ (caret) will look for a match beginning at the first character of a string. When you use it with the re.MULTILINE or re.M option, you enable the regular expression at each newline of your data or strings. Let's quickly do some exercises using your Python interpreter. Listing 9-37 and Listing 9-38.

Listing 9-37. ^Start

```
>>> re.findall('^Start', 'Start to finish')
['Start']
```

In Listing 9-38, ^ instructs the regular expression ^Start to match the word *start* at the start of the string.

Listing 9-38. finish$

```
>>> re.findall('finish$', 'Start to finish')
['finish']
```

In Listing 9-38, $ instructs the regular expression to match the word *finish* at the end of the string.

In Listing 9-39, combining both ^ and $, the regular expression matches the exact string starting with *S* and end with *sh*.

Listing 9-39. ^S.+sh$

```
>>> re.findall('^S.+sh$', 'Start to finish')
['Start to finish']
```

Listing 9-40. ^S.+sh$' and re.M

```
>>> re.findall('^S.+sh$', 'Start to finish\nSpecial fish\nSuper fresh', re.MULTILINE)
['Start to finish', 'Special fish', 'Super fresh']
```

In Listing 9-40, using the re.M module, you have matched three lines of strings starting with *S* and ending with *sh*.

Now let's take a look at a simplified practical example through another exercise. The code is available for download from my GitHub website, and the filename is 5.7.1.2_5.py for this exercise (https://github.com/pynetauto/apress_pynetauto). See Listing 9-41.

Listing 9-41. ^Gig.+up$ and re.M

```
>>> import re

>>> expr = '''SYDCBDPIT-ST01#sh ip int brief
... Interface              IP-Address      OK? Method Status                Protocol
... Vlan1                  unassigned      YES NVRAM  up                    up
... Vlan50                 10.50.50.11     YES NVRAM  up                    up
... FastEthernet0          unassigned      YES NVRAM  down                  down
... GigabitEthernet1/0/1   unassigned      YES unset  down                  down
... GigabitEthernet1/0/2   unassigned      YES unset  up                    up
... GigabitEthernet1/0/3   unassigned      YES unset  up                    up
... '''
```

```
>>> p = re.compile('^Gig.+down$', re.MULTILINE)
>>> m = p.findall(expr)
>>> print(m)
['GigabitEthernet1/0/1    unassigned      YES unset  down                    down']
```

You can easily apply this to the real scenario where you want to extract some interface information from your networking device show commands. In Listing 9-41, we use the first few lines of Cisco switch's show ip interface brief commands to demonstrate this. Using the regular expression ^Gig.+up$, we can quickly match the interfaces that have down status. For demonstration purposes, the example has been oversimplified. Still, in the real environment where you have to manage hundreds and thousands of switchport interfaces, you need the power of regular expression to process the collected data.

\A and \Z

In a single-line string match, ^ and \A work the same way, but the behavior differs while trying to match strings with multiple lines (see Listing 9-42 and Listing 9-43). The same applies to $ and \Z; the matching behaviors change while trying to match strings with multiple lines (see Listing 9-44). When re.M or re.MULTILINE option is enabled, ^ can match at the start of strings and after each line break, but \A only ever matches at the start of the string (see Listing 9-45). Also, $ can match at the end of the string and before each line break (see Listing 9-46), but \Z only ever matches at the end of the string (see Listing 9-47).

Listing 9-42. ^S.+sh

```
>>> re.findall('^S.+sh', 'Start to finish')
['Start to finish']
```

Listing 9-43. \AS.+sh

```
>>> re.findall('\AS.+sh', 'Start to finish')
['Start to finish']
```

Listing 9-44. ^S.+sh with re.MULTILINE

```
>>> re.findall('^S.+sh', 'Start to finish\nSuper special fish\nSuper fresh fish\nSuper
smelly fish', re.M)
['Start to finish', 'Super special fish', 'Super fresh fish', 'Super smelly fish']
```

Listing 9-45. \AS.+sh with re.MULTILINE

```
>>> re.findall('\AS.+sh', 'Start to finish\nSuper special fish\nSuper fresh fish\nSuper
smelly fish', re.M)
['Start to finish']
```

Listing 9-46. S.+sh$ with re.MULTILINE

```
>> re.findall('S.+sh$', 'Start to finish\nSuper special fish\nSuper fresh fish\nSuper smelly
fish', re.M)
['Start to finish', 'Super special fish', 'Super fresh fish', 'Super smelly fish']
```

Listing 9-47. S.+sh\Z with re.MULTILINE

```
>>> re.findall('S.+sh\Z', 'Start to finish\nSuper special fish\nSuper fresh fish\nSuper
smelly fish', re.M)
['Super smelly fish']
```

The following exercises demonstrate how mixed use of ^ or \A and $ or \Z affects the matched return results. We artificially add newlines by separating each line with \n to create the newline effect. Come up with your examples and test these metacharacters to extend your understanding. See Listing 9-48, Listing 9-49, Listing 9-50, and Listing 9-51.

Listing 9-48. ^S.+sh$ with re.M

```
>>> re.findall('^S.+sh$', 'Start to finish\nSuper special fish\nSuper fresh fish\nSuper
smelly fish', re.M)
['Start to finish', 'Super special fish', 'Super fresh fish', 'Super smelly fish']
```

Listing 9-49. \AS.+sh$ with re.M

```
>>> re.findall('\AS.+sh$', 'Start to finish\nSuper special fish\nSuper fresh fish\nSuper
smelly fish', re.M)
['Start to finish']
```

Listing 9-50. ^S.+sh\Z with re.M

```
>>> re.findall('^S.+sh\Z', 'Start to finish\nSuper special fish\nSuper fresh fish\nSuper
smelly fish', re.M)
['Super smelly fish']
```

Listing 9-51. \AS.+sh\Z with re.M

```
>>> re.findall('\AS.+sh\Z', 'Start to finish\nSuper special fish\nSuper fresh fish\nSuper
smelly fish', re.M)
[]
```

\b and \B

In a regular expression, \b represents a word boundary. In a sentence, the whitespacing between the leading word and the following word is represented by the usual word boundaries.

Word Boundary	Description
\b	Represents an anchor like ^ (similar to $ and ^) matching positions where one side is a word character (like \w), and the other side is not a word character; for example, it may be the beginning of the string or a space character.
\B	It comes with its negation, \B. This matches all positions where \b does not match and could be if we want to find a search pattern surrounded by word characters.

According to regular expression literal rules, \b represents a backspace; hence, when you use it in a regular expression, you always have to use the raw string notation r to specify that this is not a backspace character.

In Listing 9-52, you are trying to match the word computers in the expression. In the pattern compiled, we have used the leading \b and ending \b as the word we are trying to match leading whitespace and ending with whitespace, so the word matches and returns the result.

Listing 9-52. \b(word)\b matched

```
>>> import re
>>> expr = "Small computers include smartphones."
>>> p = re.compile(r'\bcomputers\b')
>>> m = p.search(expr)
>>> print(m)
<re.Match object; span=(6, 15), match='computers'>
```

In Listing 9-53, the word *microcomputers* has the word *computers* but starts with *Micro*, so the whitespace cannot match the word computers trailing the word *Micro*. The result is None as expected.

Listing 9-53. \b(word)\b not match

```
>>> import re
>>> expr = "Microcomputers include smartphones."
>>> p = re.compile(r'\bcomputers\b')
>>> m = p.search(expr)
>>> print(m)
None
```

In Listing 9-54, the first \b was dropped in our regular expression compiler, and now the match target word, *computers*, is matched and returns the expected result.

Listing 9-54. (word)\b matched

```
>>> import re
>>> expr = "Microcomputers include smartphones."
>>> p = re.compile(r'computers\b')
>>> m = p.search(expr)
>>> print(m)
<re.Match object; span=(5, 14), match='computers'>
```

\B has an opposite meaning to \b and hence can be used to achieve the reverse of \b. In Listing 9-55, you try to match the word *computer* without the plural *s* at the end. So, use the leading \B and ending \B to match the word with pinpoint accuracy.

Listing 9-55. \B(word)\B matched

```
>>> import re
>>> expr = "Microcomputers include smartphones."
>>> p = re.compile(r'\Bcomputer\B')
>>> m = p.search(expr)
>>> print(m)
<re.Match object; span=(5, 13), match='computer'>
```

Grouping

Say you have a string consisting of up and down status from a flapping link on a router, and you want to perform a match to search for continuous up status. After searching and matching the continuous up status, you can use the `group()` option to print the output (Listing 9-56). To compile a group in a regular expression, you have to use `( )`. This is an impractical example only to introduce you to the concept of regular expression grouping. The next example will be more within the real context.

Listing 9-56. Grouping exercise 1

```
>>> import re
>>> expr = "downupupupdowndownupdowndown"
>>> p = re.compile("(up)+")
>>> m = p.search(expr)
>>> print(m)
<re.Match object; span=(4, 10), match='upupup'>
>>> print(m.group(0))
upupup
```

Now let's consider a technical assistant center's country name and the fully qualified number for the United States. First, we want to compile a regular expression to match the whole string, starting with the country name and then followed by the technical assistant center telephone number. See Listing 9-57.

Listing 9-57. Grouping exercise 2

```
>>> import re
>>> expr = "United States 1 408 526 1234"
>>> p = re.compile(r"\w+\s\w+\s\d\s\d{3}\s\d{3}\s\d+")
>>> m = p.search(expr)
>>> print(m)
<re.Match object; span=(0, 28), match='United States 1 408 526 1234'>
```

In Listing 9-57, you have used a mix of alphanumeric shorthand character `\w`, whitespaces shorthand character `\s`, and digit shorthand character `\d` with repetition `{n}` to match all characters. If we stop the string matching here, the data captured in this example is not well utilized. By using grouping, we can extract specific information from the matched strings. Say we want to extract only the country name (see Listing 9-58).

Listing 9-58. Grouping exercise 3

```
>>> import re
>>> expr = "United States 1 408 526 1234"
>>> p = re.compile(r"(\w+\s\w+)\s\d?\s\d{3}\s\d{3}\s\d+")
>>> m = p.search(expr)
>>> print(m)
<re.Match object; span=(0, 28), match='United States 1 408 526 1234'>
>>> country = m.group(1)
>>> country
'United States'
```

In Listing 9-58, we can use the `group(1)` method to separate the information from the whole matched string, and now we can use this data as a variable or data in our script. Now let's quickly review the group method index to understand how the regular expression groupings are numbered. See Table 9-6.

Table 9-6. Group Method Index Meanings

Group Index	Explanation
group(0)	Whole matched string
group(1)	Matched first group
group(2)	Matched second group
group(3)	Matched third group
group(n)	Matched n^{th} group

The grouping method indexing is better explained using practical examples, as shown in Listing 9-59.

Listing 9-59. Grouping Method Indexing exercise 1

```
>>> import re
>>> expr = "United States 1 408 526 1234"
>>> p = re.compile(r"(\w+\s\w+)\s(\d?\s\d{3}\s\d{3}\s\d+)")
>>> m = p.search(expr)
>>> print(m)
<re.Match object; span=(0, 28), match='United States 1 408 526 1234'>
>>> phone_number = m.group(2)
>>> phone_number
'1 408 526 1234'
```

In Listing 9-60, the group(1) is (\w+\s\w+), which is the same group(1) from Listing 9-59 and (\d?\s\d{3}\s\d{3}\s\d+) becomes the group(2), which captures the telephone number. See Figure 9-7.

Listing 9-60. Grouping Method Indexing exercise 2

```
>>> import re
>>> expr = "United States 1 408 526 1234"
>>> p = re.compile(r"(\w+\s\w+)\s((\d?)\s(\d{3})\s(\d{3}\s\d+))")
>>> m = p.search(expr)
>> m.group(0)
'United States 1 408 526 1234'
>>> m.group(1)
'United States'
>>> m.group(2)
'1 408 526 1234'
>>> m.group(3)
'1'
>>> m.group(4)
'408'
>>> m.group(5)
'526 1234'
```

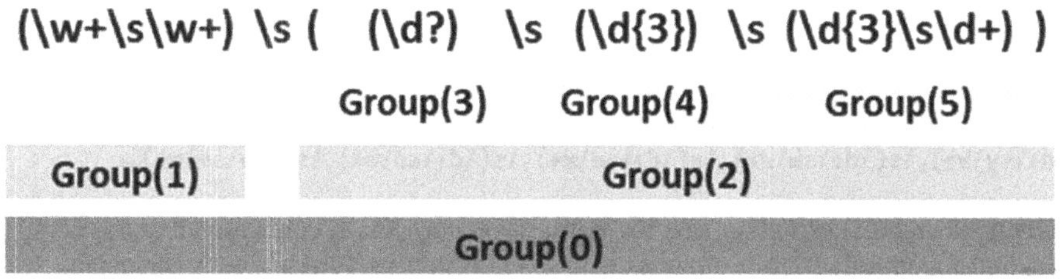

Figure 9-7. *Group index in regular expression example*

In Listing 9-61, the groups have been broken down into even smaller groups, and now we can separate the country code 1, area code 408, and local number 526 1234 from each other. Imagine all the possible things we can do with regular expression groupings in real networking automation scenarios. Imagine what you can do with the captured data from real production routers and switches and control your devices based on the collected and analyzed data.

Listing 9-61. Referencing Grouped String

```
>>> import re
>>> expr = "Did you know that that 'that', that that person used in that sentence, is wrong."
>>> p = re.compile(r'(\bthat)\s+\1')
>>> m = p.search(expr)
>>> print(m)
<re.Match object; span=(13, 22), match='that that'>
>>> m = p.search(expr).group()
>>> print(m)
that that
```

Another advantage of using group indexing is that you can use shorthand like `+\1` to re-reference the first group. In the regular expression of `(\bthat)\s+\1`, the + has the meaning of matching the same strings as the previous group, and `\1` has the meaning of re-referencing group number 1. If there is a second group and you want to reference it, `\2` can be used.

Regular Expression Named Groups

Let's assume that we are working on a project and writing a regular expression to process the data and fully utilizing the `re` grouping methods. This will make your regular expression extremely hard to decode and bring some confusion while trying to understand what the regular expression is trying to match. In networking, we have an access control list (ACL) and a named access control list (NACL); similarly, the regular expression also offers named groups to attach a name to a group for easier data manipulation. Named groups become handy when there are a large number of groups in a regular expression. Naming groups are for more convenience of use when you find and replace in advanced search and replace.

We have to work with a line extracted from a router's `show version` command, and it contains the router name and uptime. We want to use regular expression groups to extract the router name, the precise number of years, weeks, days, hours, and minutes the device has been running.

```
expr = "SYD-GW1 uptime is 1 year, 9 weeks, 2 days, 5 hours, 26 minutes"
```

To match them as each group, one example of the grouping that will work will look similar to the regular expression. Still, since there are multiple groupings and you are reading somebody else's code, you would probably feel overwhelmed with just a single regular expression line.

```
(\w+[-]\w+)\s.+((\d+\sy\w+),\s(\d+\sw\w+),\s(\d+\sd\w+),\s(\d+\sh\w+),\s(\d+\sm\w+))
```

After carefully studying the regular expression for 10 minutes, you have finally concluded that this is how the strings are matched and grouped. Unfortunately, with so many groups, you can easily get lost in translation. See Figure 9-8.

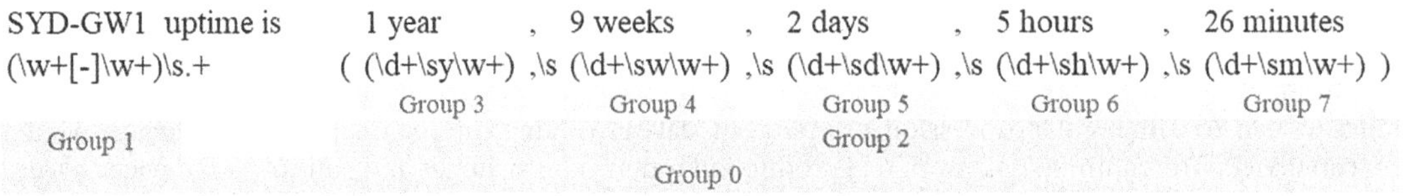

Figure 9-8. *Regular expression multiple numbered groups example*

Now, let's do the exercise to learn how this regular expression works in real Python. Again, you will follow the recommended regular expression flow and compile your regular expression and apply it to the string. As you have expected, you can separate the router name SYD-GW1 as group 1, print the whole uptime by printing out group 2, then followed by smaller groups embedded inside group 2 such as group 3 (year), 4 (weeks), 5 (days), 6 (hours), and 7 (minutes). If you are not confused already, you are really on track and doing well at this stage. See Listing 9-62.

Listing 9-62. Multiple Numbered Groups exercise

```
>>> import re
>>> expr = "SYD-GW1 uptime is 1 year, 9 weeks, 2 days, 5 hours, 26 minutes"
>>> p = re.compile(r'(\w+[-]\w+)\s.+((\d+\sy\w+),\s(\d+\sw\w+),\s(\d+\sd\w+),\s(\d+\sh\w+),
\s(\d+\sm\w+))')
>>> m = p.search(expr)
>>> print(m.group(0))
SYD-GW1 uptime is 1 year, 9 weeks, 2 days, 5 hours, 26 minutes
>>> print(m.group(1))
SYD-GW1
>>> print(m.group(2))
1 year, 9 weeks, 2 days, 5 hours, 26 minutes
>>> print(m.group(3))
1 year
[... omitted for brevity]
>>> print(m.group(7))
26 minutes
```

To make such an over convoluted use of grouping methods in the regular expression and add flexibility, regular expressions have a handy named group. You can simply add ?P<group_name> at the beginning of the group and refer to the group as the group name you have specified. If we have to give group names to the previous example, it will look similar to Listing 9-63. Giving a name to a group gives more meaning to the data it matches, and you do not have to spend much time decoding the regular expression.

Listing 9-63. Named Group exercise

```
>>> import re
>>> expr = "SYD-GW1 uptime is 1 year, 9 weeks, 2 days, 5 hours, 26 minutes"
>>> p_named = re.compile(r'(?P<hostname>\w+[-]\w+)\s.+(?P<uptime>(?P<years>\d+\sy\w+),\
s(?P<weeks>\d+\sw\w+),\s(?P<days>\d+\sd\w+),\s(?P<hours>\d+\sh\w+),\s(?P<minutes>\d+\sm\
w+))')
>>> m = p_named.search(expr)
>>> print(m.group("minutes"))
26 minutes
[... omitted for brevity]
>>> print(m.group("uptime"))
1 year, 9 weeks, 2 days, 5 hours, 26 minutes
>>> print(m.group("hostname"))
SYD-GW1
```

When you analyze the groups named above against the string data, the groupings will look like Figure 9-9.

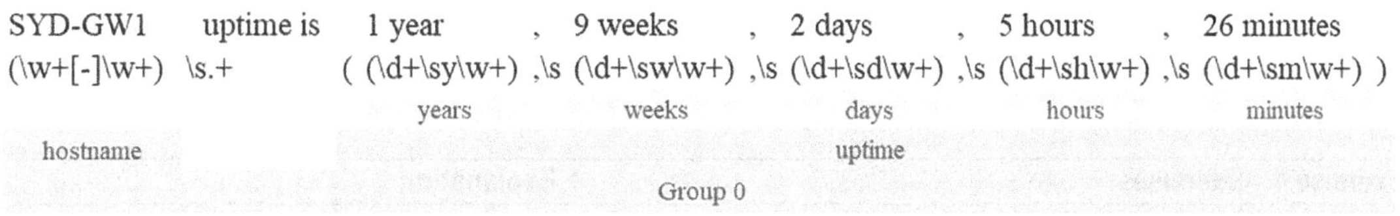

Figure 9-9. *Regular expression named groups example*

As you can see, the names relate to the information you are trying to match, and there is very little confusion coming from the multiple groupings. Rather than trying to decode someone else's cryptic regular expressions, you should be spending the valuable work hours on more mission-critical issues or providing good customer support experiences.

Lookahead and Lookbehind Assertions

Before diving into this section, I have to be up front with you. If you are a first-time regular expression apprentice, you may not understand the lookaheads and lookbehinds immediately. To ease the pain, I have used exercises and examples, but you may have to come back to this topic a few times before getting a full grasp of this concept.

Lookahead, Lookbehind, and Noncapturing group

Lookaaheads and lookbehinds are known as *lookarounds* and often confuse novice regex learners. At first glance, lookaheads and lookbehinds look very confusing as they all start with a ?, and the difference comes from the second and third metacharacter use. But once mastered well, they are handy tools to shorten our regular expressions. You do not need to comprehend this section straightaway; you can take your time to learn the lookarounds. Also, use this section as a reference point for future reference. In lookarounds, there are four lookarounds and a noncapturing group, which all start with the ? mark.

As a quick reminder before getting our hands dirty, Table 9-7 shows quick lookarounds and simple examples.

Table 9-7. *The re Lookahead, Lookbehind, and Noncapturing Groups*

Lookaround	Name	String	Example	Explanation
?=	Lookahead	abc	a(?=b)	Asserts that the regex must be matched
?!	Negative lookahead	abc	a(?!b)	Asserts that it is impossible to match the regex
?<=	Lookbehind	abc	(?<=a)b	Asserts that the regex must be matched
?<!	Negative lookbehind	abc	(?<!a)b	Asserts that it is impossible to match the regex
?:	Noncapturing group	abc	a(?:b)	Regex inside the parentheses must be matched but doesn't create the capturing group

Now go ahead and start typing in the text marked in bold in your Python interpreter and see how the returned objects differ from one another. In the following exercises, you will be using an abbreviated print function with a regular expression and the target string 'abc'. The explanation is included next to each exercise.

Exercise #	Exercises	Explanation

1	>>> **print(re.search('a(?=b)', 'abc'))**
	<re.Match object; span=(0, 1), match='a'>
	
	>>> **print(re.search('a(?=b)', 'xbc'))**
	None
		Matches a as the next letter is b.
		No match as the first letter is not a before letter b.

2	>>> **print(re.search('a(?!b)', 'abc'))**
	None
	
	>>> **print(re.search('a(?!b)', 'acd'))**
	<re.Match object; span=(0, 1), match='a'>
		No match as the next letter is b.
		Matches a as the next letter is not b (it is c).

3	>>> **print(re.search('(?<=a)b', 'abc'))**
	<re.Match object; span=(1, 2), match='b'>
	
	>>> **print(re.search('(?<=a)b', 'xbc'))**
	None
		Matches b as the previous letter is a.
		No match as the previous letter is not a.

4	>>> print(re.search('(?<!a)b', 'abc'))
	None
	
	>>> **print(re.search('(?<!a)b', 'xbc'))**
	<re.Match object; span=(1, 2), match='b'>
		No match as the previous letter is a.
		Matches b as the previous letter is not a.

5	>>> **print(re.search('a(?:b)', 'abc'))**
	<re.Match object; span=(0, 2), match='ab'>
	
	>>> **print(re.search('a(?=b)', 'abc'))**
	<re.Match object; span=(0, 1), match='a'>
		Matches a and b, because b is followed by a. Both ab are matched.
		Matches a as the next letter is b. (This is the same as exercise 1.)

Exercise #	Exercises	Explanation

6	`>>> import re`
	`>>> expr = "+1 408 526 1234"`
	`>>> p = re.compile(r"((?:(\+1)[ -])?\`
	`(?(\d{3})\)?[ -]?\d{3}[ -]?\d{4})")`
	`>>> m = p.search(expr)`
	`>>> print(m)`
	`<re.Match object; span=(0, 15), match='+1 408 526 1234'>`
	`>>> print(m.group(2))`
	`+1`
		?: represents noncapturing group, Without ?:, +1 and the trailing space are captured as a group. With ?:, the regular expression will not make a group by the match inside the parentheses like it would otherwise do (typically, parentheses create a group). In other words, when you use ?:, the group is matched but is not captured for backreferencing, which is why it's called a *noncapturing* group.

Go to the RexEgg regex site for more deep dives and regular expression examples. This is one of my favorite sites to learn about regular expressions.

URL: `www.rexegg.com/regex-lookarounds.html`

Practice More Lookarounds

You need a lot of practice to wrap your head around this topic. This time, let's use the string 'abba' to make the exercise more exciting and use the full compile method to structure our learning.

```
expr = 'abba'
```

Please open the Python interpreter and enter the text marked in bold next to the three greater-than signs. Reading through this section will not help you retain the information, so you must do all exercises, from 1 to 10.

Exercise #	Exercise	Regex	Explanation

1	`>>> import re`
	`>>> expr = 'abba'`
	`>>> p = re.compile('a(?=b)')`
	`>>> m = p.search(expr)`
	`>>> print(m)`
	`<re.Match object; span=(0, 1), match='a'>`
		a(?=b)	Find the a, which has b after it.

2	`>>> import re`
	`>>> expr = 'abba'`
	`>>> p = re.compile('b(?=b)')`
	`>>> m = p.search(expr)`
	`>>> print(m)`
	`<re.Match object; span=(1, 2), match='b'>`
		b(?=b)	Find the first b, which has b after it.

(continued)

Exercise #	Exercise	Regex	Explanation

3	`>>> import re`
	`>>> expr = 'abba'`
	`>>> p = re.compile('a(?!b)')`
	`>>> m = p.search(expr)`
	`>>> print(m)`
	`<re.Match object; span=(3, 4), match='a'>`
		`a(?!b)`	Find the second a, which does not have b after it.

4	`>>> import re`
	`>>> expr = 'abba'`
	`>>> p = re.compile('b(?!b)')`
	`>>> m = p.search(expr)`
	`>>> print(m)`
	`<re.Match object; span=(2, 3), match='b'>`
		`b(?!b)`	Find the second b, which does not have b after it.

5	`>>> import re`
	`>>> expr = 'abba'`
	`>>> p = re.compile('(?<=a)b')`
	`>>> print(m)`
	`<re.Match object; span=(1, 2), match='b'>`
		`(?<=a)b`	Find the first b, which has a before it.

6	`>>> import re`
	`>>> expr = 'abba'`
	`>>> p = re.compile('(?<=b)b')`
	`>>> m = p.search(expr)`
	`>>> print(m)`
	`<re.Match object; span=(2, 3), match='b'>`
		`(?<=b)b`	Find the second b, which has b before it.

7	`>>> import re`
	`>>> expr = 'abba'`
	`>>> p = re.compile('(?<!a)b')`
	`>>> m = p.search(expr)`
	`>>> print(m)`
	`<re.Match object; span=(2, 3), match='b'>`
		`(?<!a)b`	Find the second b, which does not have a before it.

8	`>>> import re`
	`>>> expr = 'abba'`
	`>>> p = re.compile('(?<!b)b')`
	`>>> m = p.search(expr)`
	`>>> print(m)`
	`<re.Match object; span=(1, 2), match='b'>`
		`(?<!b)b`	Find the first b, which does not have b before it.

Exercise #	Exercise	Regex	Explanation

9	`>>> import re`
	`>>> expr = 'abc'`
	`>>> p1 = re.compile('a(?:b)')`
	`>>> m1 = p1.search(expr)`
	`>>> print(m1)`
	`<re.Match object; span=(0, 2), match='ab'>`
		a(?:b)	

10	`>>> p2 = re.compile('a(?=b)')`
	`>>> m2 = p2.search(expr)`
	`>>> print(m2)`
	`<re.Match object; span=(0, 1), match='a'>`
		a(?=b)	

Lookaround Application Examples

For current and future engineers studying the Python programming language, there is a lot of ground to cover. Until you start working on real projects at work, you may not see real value and power of regular expressions. So far, you have been introduced to some basic regular expressions using exercises, and now you are gradually skilling up on regular expressions. However, unless you live and breathe regex every day on your job, it will take a long time to get to the top level. However, you can still learn the basics from this chapter and supplement with other materials found on the Internet and other books to get to the intermediary and advanced levels.

Let's use Cisco TAC's URL `http://www.cisco.com/techsupport` to practice what we have learned. See Listing 9-64.

Listing 9-64. Only Use Lookahed Method to Print http

```
>>> import re
>>> m = (re.search(r"\w{4,5}(?=:)", "http://www.cisco.com/techsupport"))
>>> print(m.group())
http
```

In Listing 9-64, the regular expression `\w{4,5}(?=:)` matches the previous alphanumerics 4 to 5 times which occurs in front (lookahead) of the colon (:).

Listing 9-65. Only Use Lookahead and Lookbehind Method to Print `www.cisco.com`

```
>>> import re
>>> m = (re.search(r"(?<=\/)\w.+[.]\w+[.]\w+(?=/)", "http://www.cisco.com/techsupport"))
>>> print(m.group())
www.cisco.com
```

To match `www.cisco.com` only, we have used a lookbehind method (`?<=`), which starts with the forward slash, `/`, and then matched the `www` format. We then used a lookahead (`?=`) ending with `/`. Using lookrounds, you can match the strings quickly and more precisely.

The following expression can match any filenames that have the format of the `filename.file_extension`, such as `vlan.dat`, `sw1.bak`, `config.text`, and even a Cisco switch IOS name such as `2960x-universalk9-mz.152-2.E6.bin`. In the following example, we will compare the negative lookahead method compared to the ^, the negation method.

```
.*[.].*$
```

In the expr (expression or string), take special care that `\n` has been used between filenames to create a newline effect in a single string. This is to simplify our exercise and save pages. The explanations are followed after the lines of each exercise.

In Listing 9-66, you will be using regular expression `.*[.].*$` to match all files in expr.

Listing 9-66. Match All File Types Using Regular Expression - .*[.].*$

```
>>> import re
>>> expr = "vlan.dat\nsw1.bak\nconfig.text\npynetauto.dat\nsw1_old.bak\n2960x-universalk9-
mz.152-2.E6.bin"
>>> m = re.findall(".*[.].*$", expr, re.M)
>>> m
['vlan.dat', 'sw1.bak', 'config.text', 'pynetauto.dat', 'sw1_old.bak', '2960x-universalk9-
mz.152-2.E6.bin']
```

In Listing 9-67 the ^ (caret) method is used to negate any files ending with the `.dat` extension and returns all the matched file names in a list. Make a special note that we are using the `re.findall` and `re.M` (`MULTILINE`) methods that we have learned earlier in this chapter.

In Listing 9-68 negative lookahead example returns the same result as Listing 9-67. There's more than one way to extract the same data.

Listing 9-67. Filter files with file extensions not starting with the letter d (Not using lookaround method)

```
>>> import re
>>> expr = "vlan.dat\nsw1.bak\nconfig.text\npynetauto.dat\nsw1_old.bak\n2960x-universalk9-
mz.152-2.E6.bin"
>>> m = re.findall(r".*[.][^d].*$", expr, re.M)
>>> m
['sw1.bak', 'config.text', 'sw1_old.bak', '2960x-universalk9-mz.152-2.E6.bin']
```

Listing 9-68. Filter files with file extensions not starting with the letter d (using lookaround method)

```
>>> import re
>>> expr = "vlan.dat\nsw1.bak\nconfig.text\npynetauto.dat\nsw1_old.bak\n2960x-universalk9-
mz.152-2.E6.bin"
>>> m = re.findall(r".*[.](?!dat$).*$", expr, re.M)
>>> m
['sw1.bak', 'config.text', 'sw1_old.bak', '2960x-universalk9-mz.152-2.E6.bin']
```

In Listing 9-69 and Listing 9-6687, you have negated any filenames ending with the `.dat` or `.bak` using both negation methods. Still, the latter method has an advantage if the file extension extensions begin with the same letter or the length of the extension starts to vary.

Listing 9-69. Filter Any Files Ending with .dat and .bak Without Using Lookaround Method

```
>>> import re
>>> expr = "vlan.dat\nsw1.bak\nconfig.text\npynetauto.dat\nsw1_old.bak\n2960x-universalk9-mz.152-2.E6.bin"
>>> m = re.findall(r".*[.][^d|^b].*$", expr, re.M)
>>> m
['config.text', '2960x-universalk9-mz.152-2.E6.bin']
```

Listing 9-70. Filter Any Files Ending with dat and bak Using Lookaround Method

```
>>> import re
>>> expr = "vlan.dat\nsw1.bak\nconfig.text\npynetauto.dat\nsw1_old.bak\n2960x-universalk9-mz.152-2.E6.bin"

> m = re.findall(r".*[.](?!dat$|bak$).*$", expr, re.M)
>>> m
['config.text', '2960x-universalk9-mz.152-2.E6.bin']
```

Let's check this in Listing 9-71.

Listing 9-71. Filter Any Files Ending with dat or bak Using ^ Negation Method

```
>>> import re
>>> expr = "file1.bak\nfile2.dat\nfile3.bakup\nfile4.data"
>>> m = re.findall(r".*[.][^d|^b].*$", expr, re.M)
>>> m
[]
```

In Listing 9-71 and Listing 9-72, the returned result is different as the regular expression used in Listing 9-71 filtered or negated all files, but in Listing 9-72, only the files ending with `.dat` or `.bak` files have been filtered. If we try to write a working regular expression without the negative lookahead method in Listing 9-72, the regular expression will be lengthy and cryptic. In Listing 9-72, using the negative lookahead method, you can simply append the exact extension name with the | (OR) sign in the regular expression.

Listing 9-72. Filter Any Files Ending with dat or bak Using Negative Lookahead Method

```
>>> import re
>>> expr = "file1.bak\nfile2.dat\nfile3.bakup\nfile4.data"
>>> m = re.findall(r".*[.](?!dat$|bak$).*$", expr, re.M)
>>> m
['file3.bakup', 'file4.data']
```

sub Method: Substituting Strings

Using the `sub` method in the regular expression, you can change or swap out matched strings. Let's do the first exercise and review the result.

Substitute Strings Using sub

As always, let's start with an exercise first and then review what you have learned from the exercise. See Listing 9-73.

Listing 9-73. Use sub to substitute multiple matching words

```
>>> import re
>>> p = re.compile('HP|Juniper|Arista')
>>> p.sub('Cisco', 'Juniper router, HP switch, Arista AP and Palo Alto firewall')
'Cisco router, Cisco switch, Cisco AP and Palo Alto firewall'
```

In Listing 9-73, using the sub method, "Juniper router, HP switch, Arista AP and Palo Alto firewall" was changed to "Cisco router, Cisco switch, Cisco AP and Palo Alto firewall." Since Palo Alto was not in the compiled regular expression, only Juniper and HP were substituted with Cisco.

Follow through to Listing 9-74, what if we only want to control the number of replacement?

Listing 9-74. Use sub to substitute a matching word only once

```
>>> p.sub('Cisco', 'Juniper router, HP switch, Arista AP and Palo Alto firewall', count=1)
'Cisco router, HP switch, Arista AP and Palo Alto firewall'
```

You can control the substitutions using the count parameter. In the previous example, count 1 was used, so in Listing 9-74, only Juniper was replaced with Cisco but not HP or Arista.

What if we want to find out the number of replacements in a long string?

Listing 9-75. Use subn to count the number of replacements

```
>>> import re
>>> expr = '''Juniper router, HP switch, Palo Alto firewall, Juniper router, HP switch, Palo
Alto firewall, Juniper router, HP switch, Palo Alto firewall, Juniper router, HP switch,
Palo Alto firewall, Juniper router, HP switch, Palo Alto firewall, Juniper router, HP
switch, Palo Alto firewall, and Arista router'''
>>> p = re.compile('HP|Juniper|Arista')
>>> p.subn('Cisco', expr)
('Cisco router, Cisco switch, Palo Alto firewall, Cisco router, Cisco switch, Palo Alto
firewall, Cisco router, Cisco switch, Palo Alto firewall, Cisco router, Cisco switch, Palo
Alto firewall, Cisco router, Cisco switch, Palo Alto firewall, Cisco router, Cisco switch,
Palo Alto firewall and Cisco router', 13)
```

You can use the subn method to substitute the string and find out the number of replaced strings. In Listing 9-75, 13 strings have been replaced with the word *Cisco*.

Using sub and \g to Swap Positions

When you use the sub method in a regular expression, you can combine it with relative group referencing (\g). Let's say we have a string "Model Number : WS-C3650-48PD", and we want to switch the position of 'WS-C3650-48PD' and 'Model Number'. So, it looks like this:

From		To
Model Number : WS-C3650-48PD	➔	**WS-C3650-48PD : Model Number**

On your Python interpreter, type in the code in each exercise. You will quickly learn how this works.

In Listing 9-76, you have compiled the match regular expression into three groups and, using the sub method, simply reversed the group sequence after matching each group. The group remains in the same place, but groups 1 and 3 have switched places.

Listing 9-76. Use sub and grouping to swap positions

```
>>> import re
>>> expr = "Model Number : WS-C3650-48PD"
>>> p = re.compile(r"(\w+\s\w+)(\s[:]\s)(\w+[-]\w+[-]\w+)") ← (r"(grp1)(grp2)(grp3)")
>>> m = p.sub("\g<3>\g<2>\g<1>", expr)
>>> print(m)
WS-C3650-48PD : Model Number
Listing 9-x >>> p = re.compile(r"(?P<Desc>\w+\s\w+)(\s[:]\s)(?P<Model>(\w+[-]\w+[-]\w+))")
>>> m = p.sub("\g<Model>\g<2>\g<Desc>", expr)
>>> print(m)
WS-C3650-48PD : Model Number
```

In Listing 9-77, you can also apply the named grouping and give meaningful names to each group and achieve our goal. Note that the group was not given a name like (?P<comma>\s[:]\s) to demonstrate that you can mix-and-match the named groups and numbered groups.

Listing 9-77. Use sub and named group method to swap positions

```
>>> p = re.compile(r"(?P<Desc>\w+\s\w+)\s[:]\s(?P<Model>(\w+[-]\w+[-]\w+))")
>>> m = p.sub("\g<Model> : \g<Desc>", expr)
>>> print(m)
WS-C3650-48PD : Model Number
```

In Listing 9-77, you have only used two named groups and left the comma group out, but when you matched using sub method, you added the (:) in your expression to return the desired result.

Insert a Function in sub Method

In network operations, we use binary, decimal, and hexadecimal values. Two examples where we use hexadecimal values are MAC addresses and IPv6 addresses. This becomes most useful in IPv6 addressing scheme; it is instrumental in understanding how you can calculate from hexadecimal to binary and decimal or the other way around.

In the following exercises, we will practice functions with the sub method.

In Listing 9-78, you have used standard Python methods to convert decimal a random IP address to binary numbers. The same conversion result can be achieved by using the sub commands in Listing 9-79.

Listing 9-78. Decimal to Binary Using the join Method

```
>>> ip = '172.168.123.245'
>>> print ('.'.join([bin(int(x)+256)[3:] for x in ip.split('.')]))
10101100.10101000.01111011.11110101
```

Listing 9-79. Decimal to Binary Using the sub Method

```
>>> ip = '172.168.123.245'
>>> def dec2bin(match):
...     value = int(match.group())
...     return bin(value)
...
>>> p = re.compile(r'\d+')
>>> p.sub(dec2bin, ip)
'0b10101100.0b10101000.0b1111011.0b11110101'
```

When the sub method is used, the compiled return result stars with 0b, which indicates that this is a binary number. In Listing 9-80, we have created a function called dec2bin and used it in the sub method to get the decimal IP address into binary numbers.

Listing 9-80. Binary to Decimal Using Join Method

```
>>> ip = "00001010.11010110.10001011.10111101"
>>> ip1 = ip.replace(".", "")
>>> ip1
'00001010110101101000101110111101'
>>> def bin2dec():
...     return ".".join(map(str, int(ip1, 2).to_bytes(4, "big")))
...
>>> bin2dec()
'10.214.139.189'
```

In Listing 9-81, we have selected a random binary IP address and demonstrate binary to decimal number conversion using the Python join method. After converting the binary number into the decimals, we know that the IP address we are trying to find is 10.214.139.189.

Listing 9-81. Hexadecimal to Decimal Numbers

```
>>> mac = "84:3d:c6:f5:c9:ba"
>>> mac1 = mac.replace(":", "")
>>> mac1
'843dc6f5c9ba'
>>> i = int(mac1, 16)
>>> str(i)
'145400865868218'
```

In Listing 9-82, we have captured a MAC address of a switch and want to convert this hexadecimal numbers into decimal numbers. Using the basic Python methods we can easily convert the hexadecimal number into a decimal. This is a good example of how efficient Python could be converting numbers from one form to another.

Listing 9-82. Decimal to Hexadecial

```
>>> def hexrepl(match):
...     value = int(match.group())
...     return hex(value)
...
```

```
>>> p = re.compile(r"\d+")
>>> p.sub(hexrepl, 'MAC address: 145400865868218')
'MAC address: 0x843dc6f5c9ba'
```

Once again, you have written a Python code with the sub method to reverse the decimal MAC address back into a hexadecimal number for demonstration purposes. 0x at the beginning of the number indicates that this number is a hex number.

If you are new to regular expressions, this might have been pretty tough chapter. But as mentioned at the beginning of this chapter, in general programming, mastering the regular expressions is a must, not optional.

To get even more help on the topic, go to the following Regular Expressions Cheat Sheets.

URL: `https://cheatography.com/davechild/cheat-sheets/regular-expressions/`

URL: `http://web.mit.edu/hackl/www/lab/turkshop/slides/regex-cheatsheet.pdf`

Summary

Some people will find this chapter to be the most challenging chapter to digest. I do not expect anyone to understand this chapter in full in a single read. You will have to come back to this chapter over and over again and slowly let the regular expression syntax and concepts soak into your brain. You have just completed all the Chapter 9 exercises, and ideally, you will be able to find some spare time each week to practice regular expressions. As you write Python code, you will have to store and process more and more data. The real power in network programmability is also in the power of data processing. In the next chapter, you will be completing the necessary lab preparation and integration for Python network automation.

CHAPTER 10

GNS3 Basics

If you do not build your lab yourself, then you will not know how everything works in the lab. Building your virtual lab on your own is one of the best ways to master IT skills in a particular technology. In this chapter, you will learn how to install and build a simple networking lab using GNS3 and VMware Workstation Pro. This chapter will guide you through each step of installing and configuring GNS3 correctly to get the most out of your setup. You will also learn various features of GNS3 on Windows. As you are aware by now, there is no need for hardware-based networking equipment. After completing the simple lab topology, you will integrate an old IOS image and test-drive the lab for verification purposes and get you familiar with the lab setup.

In this chapter, you will be learning GNS3 basics by building simple IOS labs. The GNS3 skills learned here will allow you to build various network automation labs on GNS3. You can extend the use of these labs to your work for proof-of-concept (POC) labs or vendor networking certifications.

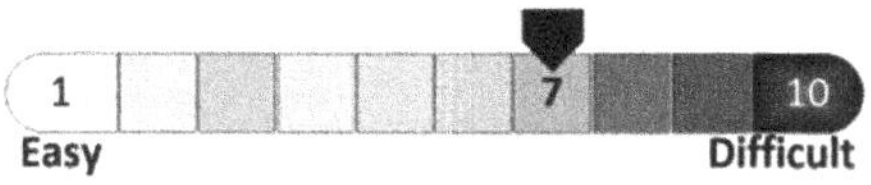

GNS3 at a Glance

At the end of Chapter 6, you downloaded the GNS3 `VM.ova` file for your GNS3 version, and then you imported it as a virtual server to host your networking devices. If you have not completed this task yet, you must go back and complete the task detailed in the section "Downloading and Installing the GNS3 VM from an .ova File." Then come back to this chapter and continue.

In this chapter and throughout this book, the terms Cisco CML and Cisco VIRL (or CML and VIRL) are used interchangeably. They are basically the same software for emulating Cisco networking devices in virtual environments. VIRL stands for Virtual Internet Routing Lab, and CML stands for Cisco Modeling Lab. CML replaced VIRL in 2020.

B. Choi, *Introduction to Python Network Automation*, https://doi.org/10.1007/978-1-4842-6806-3_10

GNS3 is a multivendor network emulator that was introduced in 2008. Supported on Windows, Linux, and macOS, GNS3 is also known as the graphical user interface (GUI) Dynamips. You only need to understand that the GUI-based GNS3 operates on top of Dynamips. GNS3 was developed and is supported on a community basis, and you can download it for free after user registration on the GNS3.org website. For this chapter, you will need the latest version of GNS3 to run GNS3 as a virtual server on VMware Workstation. Running GNS3 on VMware Workstation Pro as a virtual machine is recommended, and this is a best practice for our lab. When running GNS3 as a local server on the host operating system, your Windows performance degrades significantly; it is always better to run GNS3 as a separate VM on VMware Workstation; this will prevent any CPU and memory contention issues between the host PC and GNS3 server. Another reason for using GNS3 is to create a completely integrated lab with the Linux VMs. You can use the Linux servers as the Python servers to control virtual routers and switches in various PoC labs to study and test networking concepts.

When installing GNS3 on a Windows machine, you need only a single installation `.exe` file, but some additional software will be installed automatically during the installation. During the installation, your computer must be directly connected to the Internet. The installation procedures shown in this book include tips that I have learned over the years, and it is recommended that you follow each step closely to replicate all the tasks in this chapter.

To test routers, switches, or firewalls, you will need to locate the software separately and quickly integrate it into GNS3 for various labs. GNS3 does not support all IOS/IOS-XE/IOS-XR versions; it still supports older IOS 12.x trains for testing purposes. Although Cisco's 7200 router IOS version 15.x is supported, two apparent problems exist with the 7200 router IOS 15.x version; it hogs your computer's CPU and memory resources, and there is no support for the layer 2 switching function. Cisco's IOU has been available to internal Cisco TAC engineers, and the spinoff from IOU seems to be the new VIRL L2 and L3 software for networking studies. Cisco recently renamed VIRL to CML Personal Edition (PE). The new CML-PE L2 and L3 images are identical to the preceding VIRL images, so in this book, you can use either image from Cisco.

GNS3 offers more useful features for other software integrations, and it is a great study tool for networking students and engineers alike. CME-PE, VIRL, and IOU images support using Qemu as the key features of the new GNS3. There is support for appliance integration via Docker images as well. That's right—in GNS3, Docker and virtualization programs can run side by side on the GNS3 VM server. Since the introduction of IOU and VIRL, the most significant advantage of configuring such a lab setup has been the layer 2 switching function through L2 IOSv images. GNS3 continues to support both CML-PE's L2 IOSv and L3 IOS images. If you want to study Cisco routing and switching, I highly recommend using either Cisco CML-PE or EVE-GN lab solutions. If you are new to GNS3, you will enjoy the installation procedures in this chapter; most of the installation process is straightforward. If you have been a longtime GNS3 user, then you will learn various installations and configuration tips in this chapter and improve on your existing GNS3 integration skills.

GNS3 was briefly discussed in Chapter 1 while comparing various emulation and simulation tools for networking studies. Also, we looked at the advantages and disadvantages of each tool. At the end of Chapter 6, you learned how to build a virtual machine, namely, a GNS3 VM from an `.ova` file; the `.ova` file is a pre-installed virtual machine for faster deployment. You have already downloaded and created a virtual machine named GNS3 VM as part of the virtual machine creation. You have been slowly gaining the essential IT skills in Python, virtualization, Linux administration, and regular expressions to get ready for Python and network automation. Beginning in this chapter, you will build an environment where you can learn, test, validate, and master various network automation scenarios using Python.

The GNS3 installation in this chapter is a continuation of where we ended in Chapter 6. Let's go ahead and install GNS3 to integrate Cisco IOS in this chapter and later to integrate the CML-PE L2 and L3 IOSv software with the Windows host PC and Linux VMs.

Installing GNS3 for the First Time

Creating a virtual machine GNS3 VM on VMware Workstation 15 Pro in Chapter 6 was in preparation for GNS3 integration with VMware Workstation and Cisco software. Cisco's IOS and VIRL images will be configured and controlled by GNS3 software, but the actual images will be running from the GNS3 VM and running on VMware Workstation. A virtual machine running within another virtual machines is known as a *nested* virtualization environment.

Before downloading the GNS3 installation file for Windows 10, check the installed version of your GNS3 VM machine and make sure that you download the version in line with your GNS3 VM version. If you want the newest and greatest GNS3 version, then you can download the GNS3 install file and GNS3 `VM.ova` file from the GNS3 official site or the GitHub site. For this book, I have downloaded the version 2.2.11 files, which was the latest version at the time of writing this chapter. As newer GNS3 software is released regularly, version 2.2.11 or the newer version of GNS3 will work just fine.

Downloading the GNS3 Installation File

If you have not downloaded the GNS3 installation file yet, then first go to the GNS3 download URL at `https://github.com/GNS3/gns3-gui/releases` and download the correct GNS3 .exe file for your GNS3 VM version (see Figure 10.1). The version downloaded in this book is 2.2.11 (`GNS3-2.2.11-all-in-one.exe`). You can safely assume that the GNS3 VM version used in this book is also version 2.2.11, and this virtual machine has already been pre-installed on VMware Workstation 15. If you want to follow the steps in this book exactly, you can use the same software versions, but if you are using VMware Workstation 16 Pro and the latest GNS3 files, the installation and setup processes will be almost identical, so you should not have major drama setting up your GNS3 environment.

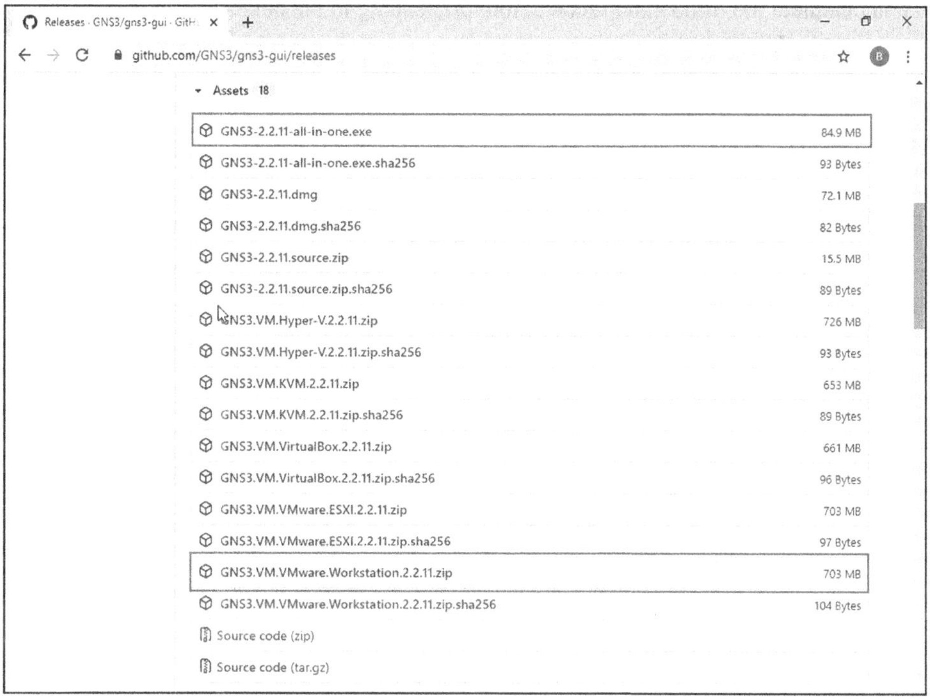

Figure 10-1. *GNS3 installation file download for Windows*

In this example, the software is downloaded via the developer's GitHub website using the Assets button. Alternatively, the same software can be downloaded from the GNS3.org site after registering your user account.

GNS3 Installation and Setup

As part of the installation, GNS3 will install essential software such as Microsoft Visual C++ 2017 Redistributable (x64), Wireshark, WinPcap, and Npcap. Suppose your PC already has the essential software installed. In that case, the GNS3 installation wizard will detect the software automatically, but if no software is installed, it will automatically install the essential software. Under most installation scenarios, the GNS3 installation will go through without a hiccup, but if your installation does not go smoothly, then you can pre-install the correct versions of Wireshark, WinPcap, and Npcap before GNS3 installation. You will also be offered to sign up and install the SolarWinds software; in my opinion, it is bloatware, so if you care about your computer's performance, ensure you decline SolarWinds' free offer.

GNS3 Installation

The most basic installation tasks have been documented in full and provided as an additional installation guide to include more quality content in this book. Installing GNS3 on the Windows host PC is as simple as clicking the Next buttons a few times until the installation completes. Please refer to `Chapter 10 Pre-task - Installing GNS3.pdf` for the initial GNS3 installation steps; the installation guide is available at `https://github.com/pynetauto/apress_pynetauto`.

Download and complete the GNS3 installation before proceeding to the next section!

GNS3 Setup Procedures

Now we have to set up the GNS3 so you can use it to build your networking lab. There are other setup options available, but since we have imported the GNS3 VM on the Windows host PC, this will be our preferred setup method. Follow the instructions and begin the GNS3 setup.

#	Task
1	As soon as GNS3 launches, you will be prompted with the GNS3 server Setup Wizard. Here, we are using the GNS3 VM, so you must choose "Run appliances in a virtual machine." Check the "Don't show this again" box and click the Next button. See Figure 10-2.

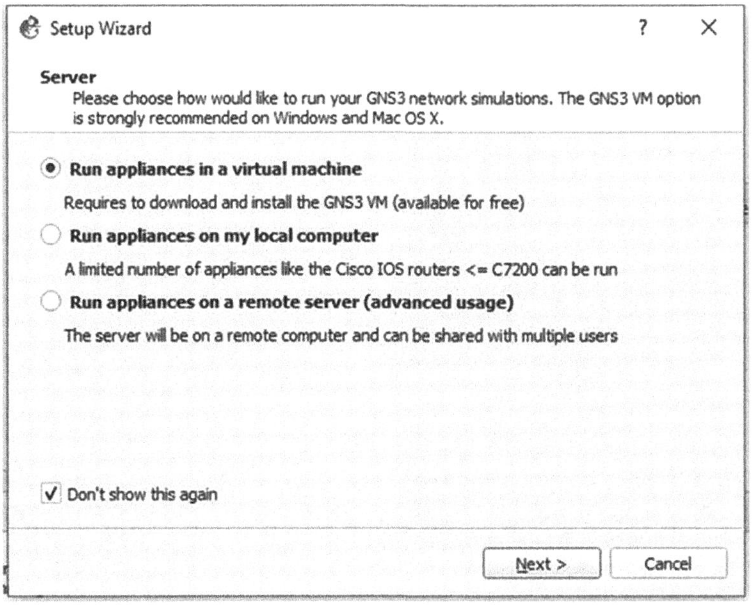

Figure 10-2. *GNS3 setup, GNS3 server Setup Wizard*

(*continued*)

#	Task
2	Under "Local server configuration," leave everything as the default. GNS3 on Windows uses TCP port 3080 for the server to localhost communication. This number is rarely altered unless you have an installation problem or want to configure it differently from out-of-the-box installation. Click the Next button again. See Figure 10-3.

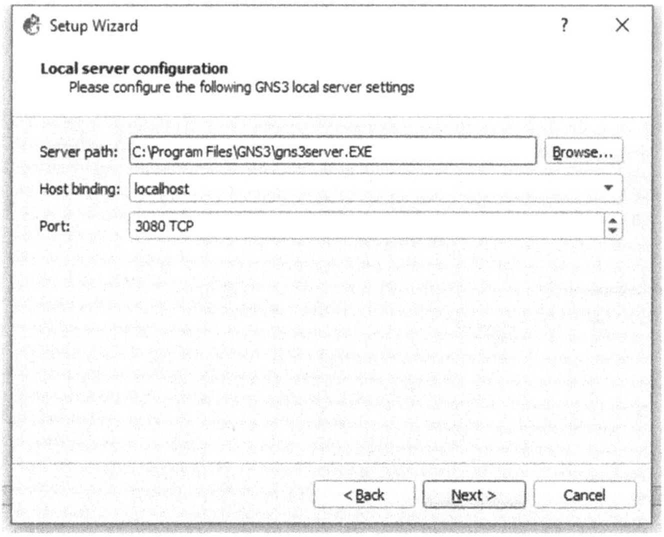

Figure 10-3. *GNS3 setup, local server configuration*

3 There is nothing to select for the local server status, so click the Next button to proceed. See Figure 10-4.

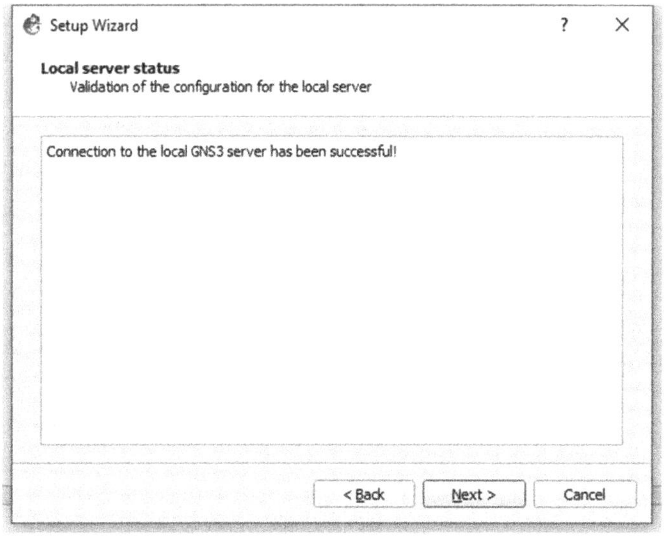

Figure 10-4. *GNS3 setup, local server status*

#	Task
4	The default GNS3 RAM recommendation is 2GB (2048MB); update this to 4GB (4096MB) or more based on your computer specification. My computer has 32GB memory, so my host will still have plenty of memory after allocating 8GB (8192MB) of memory to the GNS3 VM. If you have 16GB of memory, the recommendation is between 4GB and 6GB of memory to this VM. When you reset the memory allocation here, it will be reflected on VMware Workstation's GNS3 VM server. If you are using an older CPU, leave the vCPU cores at 1, but if the CPU is newer, the vCPU cores can be increased to 2 or more. Click Next. See Figure 10-5.

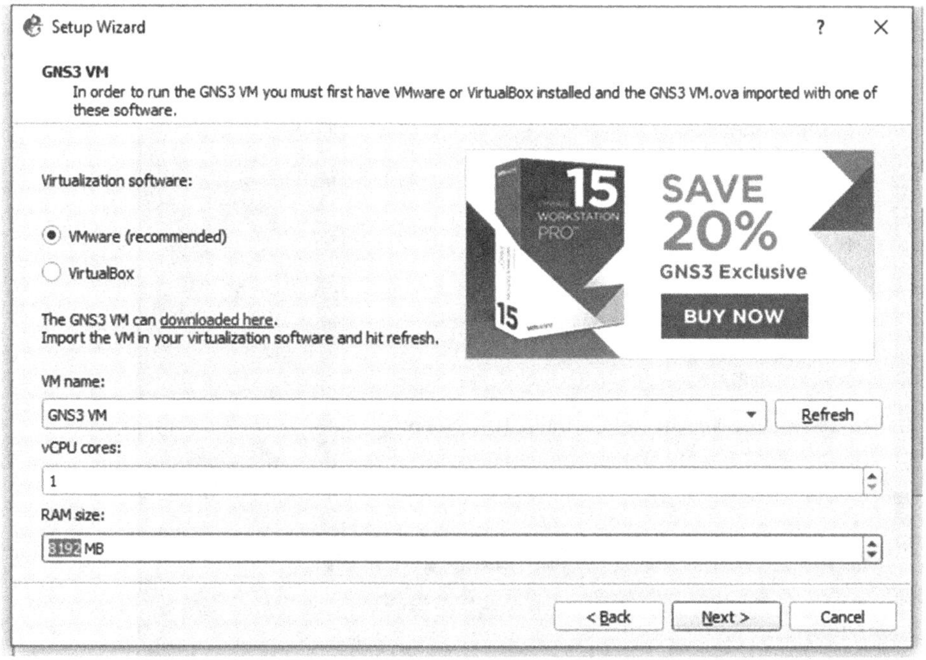

Figure 10-5. *GNS3 setup, GNS3 VM*

(*continued*)

#	Task
5	As soon as you click the Next button, the GNS3 VM on the workstation will boot up. And once it goes through the Power-On Self-Test (POST), you will see a blue welcome screen similar to Figure 10-6 on VMware Workstation 15 Pro. The GNS3 VM is a Linux (Ubuntu) appliance server configured to run various GNS3-compatible appliances from many vendors. GNS3 is a lot more than just a Cisco IOS emulator and has many use cases for studying other vendor products. Your GNS3 VM will be launched automatically; give it enough time to stabilize.

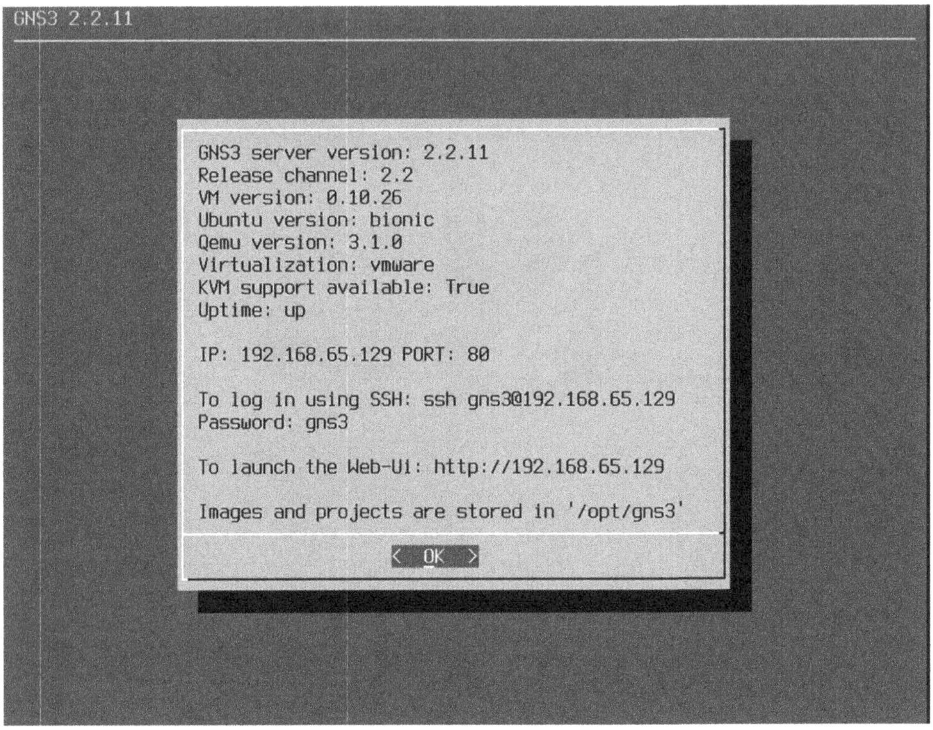

Figure 10-6. *GNS3 setup, GNS3 VM server started on the workstation*

#	Task
6	The GNS3 Setup Wizard summary window appears, and you can review and click the Finish button to complete your setup. See Figure 10-7.

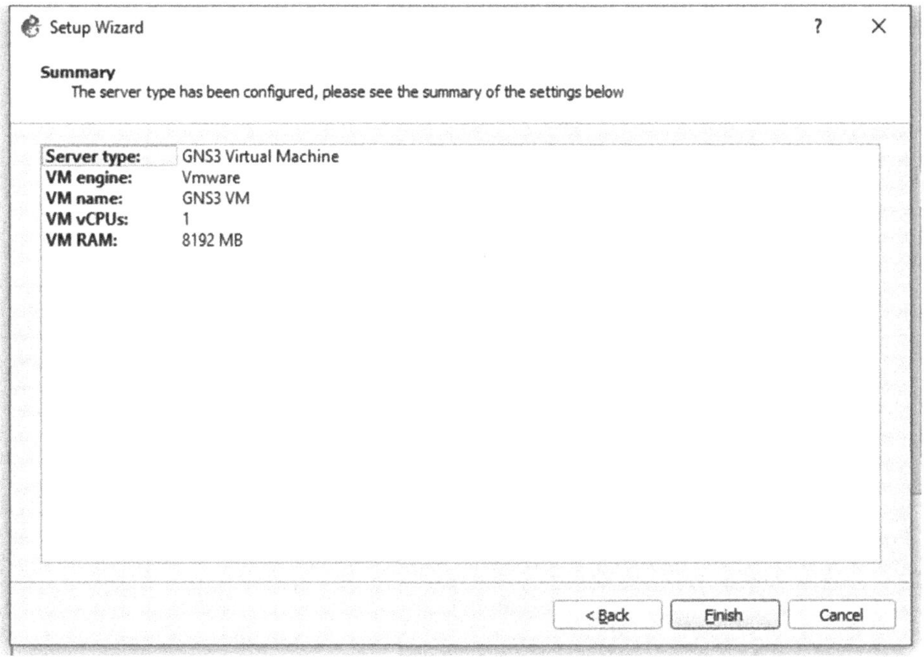

Figure 10-7. *GNS3 setup, setup summary*

(*continued*)

#	Task
7	Now you will see the GNS3 GUI with the GNS3 VM and your hostname (local host) with green status lights. If you see a red or amber light, it is an indication that your GNS3 installation has not been completed cleanly, and you may need to review your installation and setup processes and troubleshoot the issue. See Figure 10-8.

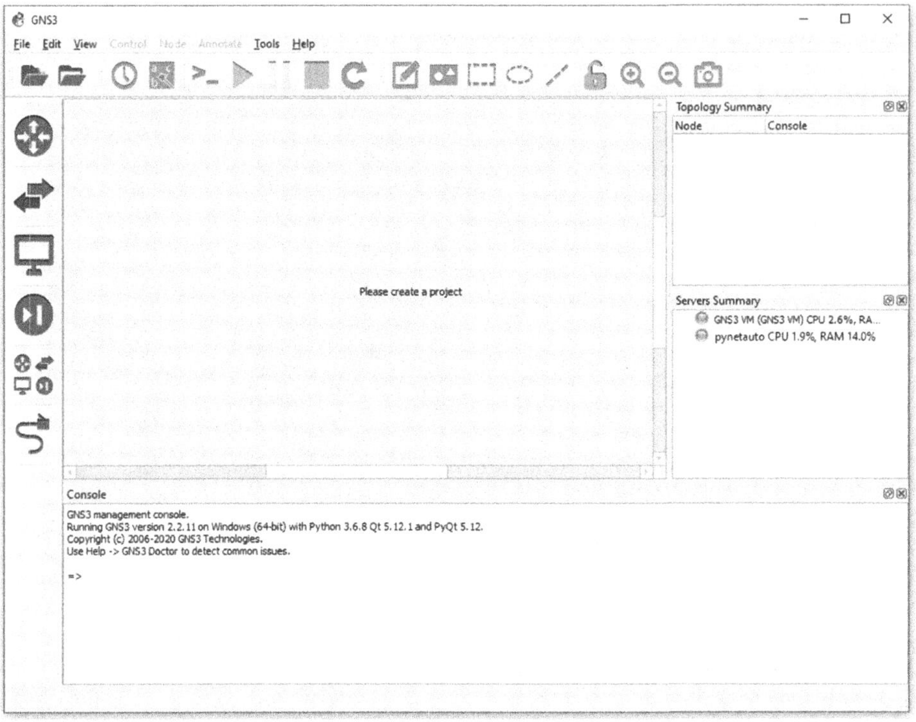

Figure 10-8. *GNS3, first time started and running*

Getting Familiar with GNS3

Now that the GNS3 has been installed and launched, you are ready to use the application. Before jumping into GNS3 and creating test network topologies, let's quickly study the user interface to understand each menu's functionalities and options better. All the icon menus plus more menu options are available from the main drop-down menu options. The following sections are a quick introduction to the GNS3 menu and a couple of tips to help you run networking labs smoothly from GNS3.

GNS3 Menus and GUI

Figure 10-9 shows GNS3's main window, and Table 10-1 describes each option. Getting familiar with where each menu is located and where the most used features are placed as icons on the GNS3 GUI interface will help you save time as you use GNS3 on your host PC.

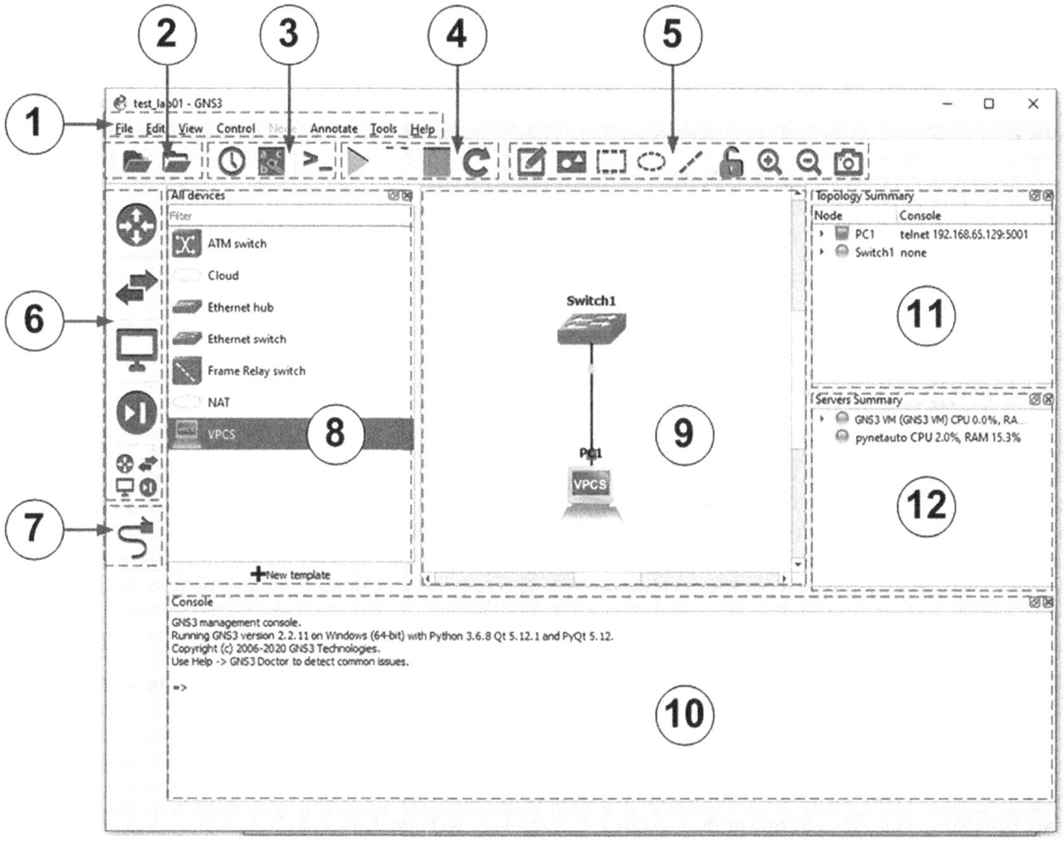

Figure 10-9. *GNS3 GUI*

Table 10-1. *GNS3 GUI Elements*

#	Menu	Explanation
①	Menu option	Use the menu to access all the options from the drop-down menu.
②	File option	Open or save GNS3 projects.
③	Device and Topology option	Manage snapshots, show/hide connectors, and console into devices.
④	Simulation option	Power on/off, pause, and restart devices.
⑤	Drawing tools	Decorate the GNS3 Topology canvas with drawing tools.
⑥	Device Type icons	Show devices based on different device types.
⑦	Add a Link tool	Connect various devices.
⑧	Device List	List installed devices. Use the search menu to filter displayed devices.

(*continued*)

Table 10-1. *(continued)*

#	Menu	Explanation
⑨	Topology canvas	Select and drop devices on a canvas to make a working topology.
⑩	Log window	Displays GNS3 operational status. You can also send some commands using this window.
⑪	Topology/Node Summary	Displays current GNS3 device summary.
⑫	Server Summary	Displays the GNS3 VM and local server status. Also, it displays the CPU and memory utilization of each server.

Gracefully Shutting Down GNS3 and GNS3 VM

This is a friendly reminder before you start plotting icons on GNS3's Topology canvas. Because of the GNS3's sensitivity with Windows installation and how the software tries to emulate the physical hardware, GNS3 running on Windows OS never has been 100 percent reliable. To avoid headaches and time troubleshooting some minor issues, I cannot emphasize enough that you should take a softer approach when starting and shutting down GNS3 on your Windows OS. When you start GNS3, you must give it enough time to start all its background services and also the GNS3 VM if you are using the GNS3 VM for hosting all your virtual network devices. Most importantly, you must follow a stringent set of procedures while shutting down GNS3 to avoid any configuration loss and to avoid deleting the whole project due to file corruption caused by abrupt application closures. GNS3 is one of the best free study tools for studying the basic networking concepts, but unfortunately, it does not come with the enterprise level of reliability.

After you have finished Cisco or any other vendor labs on GNS3, it is crucial that you first save the running configurations. For the case of Cisco IOS devices, run `copy running-config start-config` or `write memory` to save the router's or switch's running configurations to the startup configuration. After that, bring any other devices to shutdown status using the big red stop button or individually selecting each device to shut down each one (see Figure 10-10). Once all configurations have been saved and the devices are properly powered off, then you can gracefully shut down GNS3 using the X in the top-right corner (see Figure 10-11).

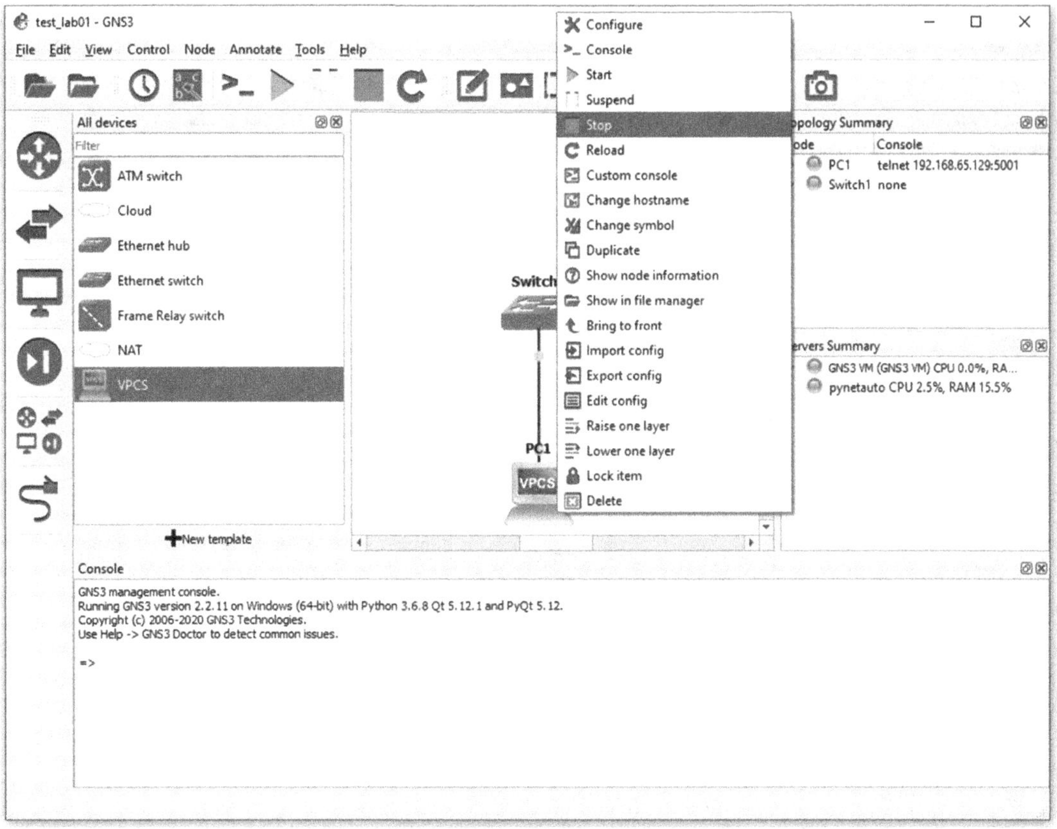

Figure 10-10. *GNS3, stopping a device using the right-click option*

After GNS3 shuts down, the GNS3 VM running on VMware Workstation 15 Pro will also shut down automatically. It would be best if you did not shut down the VM from the workstation; it is recommended that you use the X mark in the top-right corner to close the GNS3 application. As you become familiar with GNS3 and its quirks, this shutdown process becomes a standard procedure. If you are not careful, your working lab configuration and projects may often malfunction due to incorrect shutdown procedures.

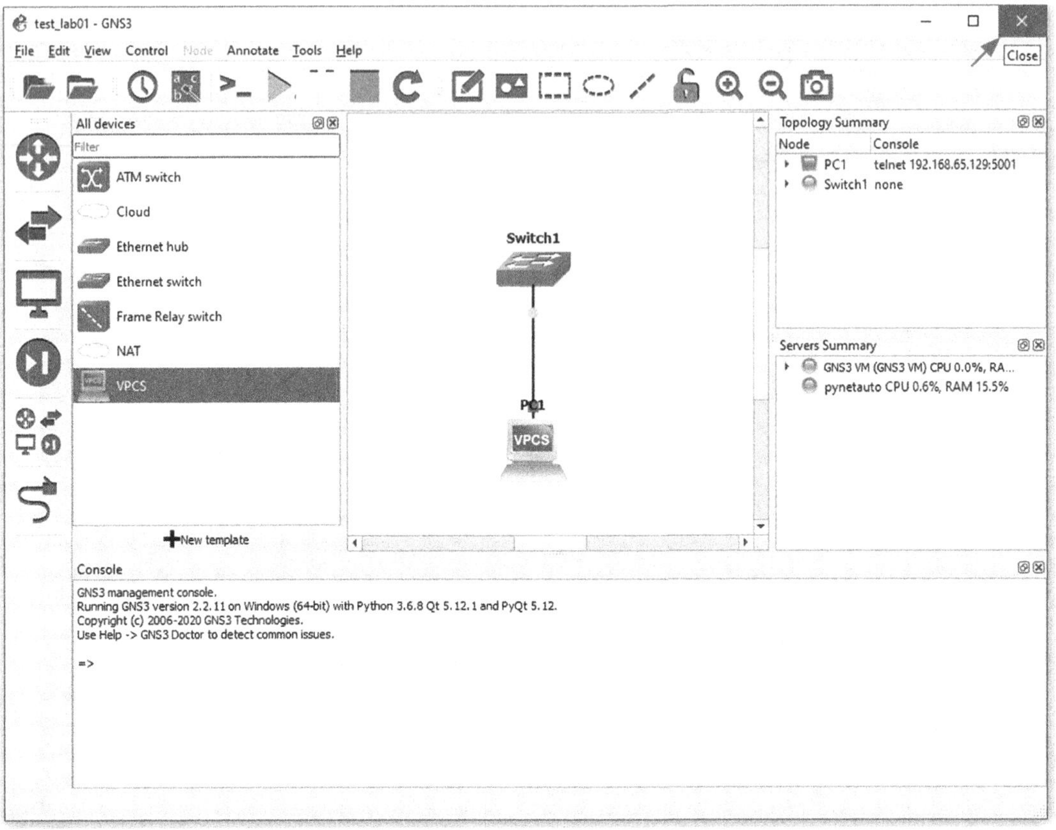

Figure 10-11. *GNS3, graceful shutdown using the X key*

Starting GNS3 as an Administrator

Here is a quick tip while starting GNS3 for the first time on your Windows operating system. When GNS3 gets installed on your Windows PC, if you did not deselect this option, the GNS3 startup icon will be created on your Windows desktop by default. Starting GNS3 using this icon is the quickest way to start the program; however, not starting GNS3 as an administrator can restrict you from making GNS3 configuration changes to network adapter settings and other settings. So, the best practice is to always launch GNS3 as an administrator. One tip to always start as the GNS3 administrator is to change the settings under the GNS3 icon.

#	Task
1	First, go to the desktop of your host PC, locate the GNS3 icon, and right-click it to open Properties. See Figure 10-12.

Figure 10-12. *GNS3, start icon on Windows host desktop*

#	Task
2	Now, go to the Compatibility tab. Under Settings, select the "Run this program as an administrator" option, click the Apply button, and click the OK button to save the settings. See Figure 10-13.

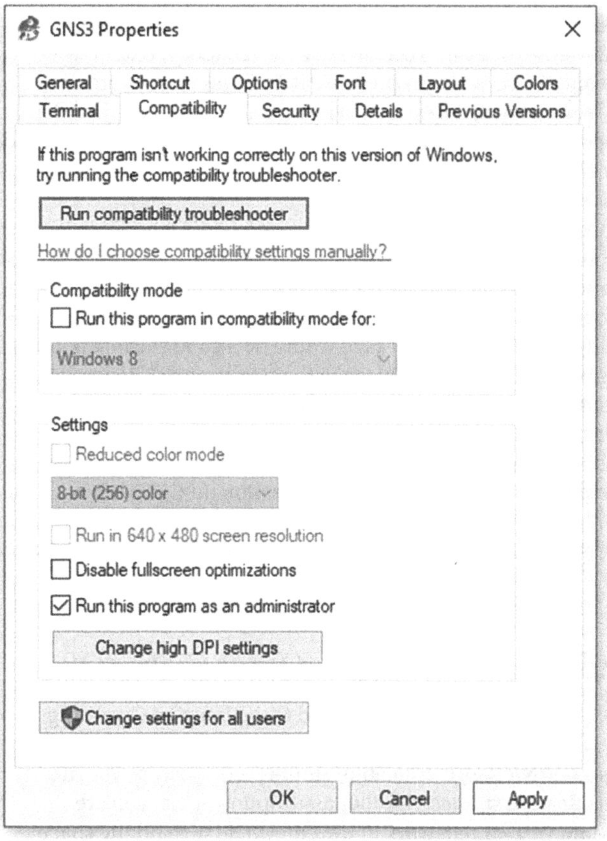

Figure 10-13. *GNS3, changing the program icon startup settings*

Now you are ready to learn some GNS3 tricks to improve your skills. For the rest of this chapter, you will be introduced to some cool GNS3 tricks such as connecting GNS3 devices to the host, connecting GNS3 to the Internet, adding the Microsoft loopback into the lab topology, and cloning a GNS3 project for making your base lab template.

Using GNS3 for the First Time: Cisco IOS and Windows Lab

Initially, the only way to study Cisco technologies and certifications was to use a physical hardware-based lab with a stack of routers and switches. When Dynamips was developed to emulate old Cisco router platforms by Christophe Fillot in August 2005, it permanently changed the way networking students study Cisco technologies. Before Dynamips, there was Cisco's PacketTrace, but it was more of a simulator than an emulator. As mentioned, GNS3 is the GUI version of Dynamips, and GNS3's underlying application is still Dynamips.

More recently, it was a known secret that Cisco was using UNIX-based Cisco IOU for its internal staff training, but IOU was not released as a product on the market. There was a transitional period where Cisco IOU was leaked to Cisco partners, and networking students were using Cisco IOU. Cisco has recently reinterpreted Cisco IOU into Cisco CML (previously VIRL) and developed it into a subscription-based product that is available as a paid product on the market.

Before GNS3 developers integrated VIRL and IOU images, old-school networking students used somewhat outdated Cisco IOS images on GNS3 to study for Cisco certifications. Even today, older Cisco IOS images are supported by GNS3; this is relevant to CCNA studies because it provides ways to emulate more than 90 percent of CCNA routing studies without using any physical equipment. Although there have been some new advancements in networking technologies and the networking education market, many old routing and switching concepts are still relevant to CCNA studies, so when studying the basic networking concepts, the Cisco IOS 12.4.x version will suffice for your learning needs.

There are two main disadvantages of learning networking using old IOS-based GNS3 labs. First, it can only support older IOS 12.4 versions on most router platforms, except for Cisco 7200. Second, layer 2 support for switching is only through the NM-16ESW module installed on router platforms. Using newer VIRL L2 and L3 images, you can build more functional Cisco routing and switching labs on GNS3 with many IOS features.

As part of the GNS3 introduction, integrating old Cisco IOS into a lab would be a good starting point. Actually, in the VIRL integration, the only thing replaced is the IOS image with more recent VIRL images. This chapter will gradually introduce you to a handful of techniques you can use on Cisco IOS running on GNS3. For the most part, all the techniques learned here in this chapter are extendable to the CML labs in Chapters 12, 13, and 14, and they will help you build various GNS3 labs with greater effectiveness and flexibility. Even if you are an old CCNA student familiar with the older IOS integration on GNS3, do not skip this chapter as there are some new skills you will acquire throughout the chapter.

Let's begin with a quick discussion of the Cisco software license model, including Cisco IOS, IOU, and VIRL images.

Cisco IOS Software License and Downloading an Older Cisco IOS

First, to configure your GNS3 lab with Cisco IOS, you must find and download Cisco Internet Operating System (IOS) images for GNS3-supported Cisco router models. As mentioned, this book works on the assumption that either you have completed Cisco CCNA R&S certification studies previously or you are currently completing Cisco's associate-level certification studies. Another assumption is that you are interested in how Cisco carries out its business and you want to work in the enterprise networking space as a network/security/data center engineer for many years to come. Cisco increases its revenue by selling the hardware, software, and service support contract. To understand how Cisco raises revenue with software, you must understand the software proprietorship and licensing agreements for Cisco software. To understand Cisco's software licensing model, you have to approach it from Cisco's business model. You already know that Cisco is a leading vendor selling networking equipment for the enterprise and SMB market; it sells the technical support contract packages on its hardware and software to drive the company's profit margins up. The technical support agreement also includes the right to use Cisco's software. In other words, if you purchased equipment from one of Cisco's partners through a regular channel, you as a customer have the rights to use platform-specific software running on your networking devices and receive 24/7 support from Cisco TAC if you need technical support, which is until the last day of the service contract.

Second, note that if you purchased a device running Cisco IOS version 15, usually you are only allowed to minor patch upgrades within the same software version unless there is a field notice for a security vulnerability or a field notice to upgrade to the latest major software version. Usually, your devices age, and the newer software's minimum hardware requirements are increased. You will be limited to upgrading the device's software to a certain level, and you are forced to upgrade to the latest hardware models. As Cisco devices come to end of life (EoL), Cisco will not support any EoL devices. Most of Cisco's software is regarded as Cisco proprietary and part of Cisco's intellectual property, so Cisco owns all IOS and other software rights; therefore, individuals are not allowed to freely distribute this software. After purchasing

Cisco equipment through a channel partner, the technical support service contract also allows for software downloads and technical support from Cisco TAC. If you are currently working for a Cisco partner, you will be able to download the most up-to-date IOS software with ease, but probably not the older IOS software. Another good way to get an older IOS for your study is to purchase used lab routers from online auction sites such as eBay, Craigslist, or Gumtree, or even from someone you know who no longer has any use for his old CCNA/CCNP lab equipment. You will find a working IOS in your device's flash memory, and the IOS can be copied across to your PC using TFTP file transfer; then it can be used as a GNS3 IOS base image. Even if you have the right to download IOS from the Cisco site, locating an older GNS3-compatible IOS from Cisco's official site can be challenging as most of the older devices already have reached EoL. Suppose you are a full-time student who wants to work in the networking industry as a network or security engineer. In that case, Google searches can lead you to some sites where you might be able to locate older IOS versions. This book uses older versions of IOS from my older Cisco equipment, but ultimately downloading a working copy of an older IOS version is your responsibility to follow this book.

Third, when you visit GNS3's official site, you will first notice that GNS3 supports older Cisco routers, namely, C1700, C2600, C2691, C3600, C3700, and C7200 series routers and older-style Cisco PIX firewalls. For quick demonstration purposes, this chapter uses an old Cisco 3725 router's IOS version 12.4.15 T15, which is compatible with the latest GNS 3.2.11. Although the Cisco 7200 router's IOS version 15.x is supported, the RAM requirement is 512MB, consuming more computer memory than older 3700 series routers. If you have a PC with a relatively strong CPU and memory, you can choose to use Cisco 7200 IOS version 15.x in place of the 3725's IOS. In this chapter, the exact IOS version used is the `c3725-adventerprisek9-mz.124-15.T14.bin` image, and this is the one supported currently by GNS3.2.11.

Here are some older IOS versions you can use for our study purposes:

- `c3725-adventerprisek9-mz.124-15.T14.bin` (old)
- `c3745-adventerprisek9-mz.124-25d.bin` (old)
- `c7200-adventerprisek9-mz.124-24.T5.bin` (old)
- `c7200-adventerprisek9-mz.152-4.M7.bin` (newer)

⚠ You are responsible for purchasing and downloading required Cisco software used in this book. This book does not provide any software used in this book, but points you to the sources to locate and download the correct software. At the end of the day, each reader is responsible for any software usages for their own learning needs.

Decompressing Cisco IOS for GNS3 Use

If you want to follow along with this book, you should have successfully located and downloaded `c3725-adventerprisek9-mz.124-15.T14.bin` in your `Downloads` folder. Then, you will decompress the `.bin` file into an `.image` file so the decompressed image file can be used in GNS3. There are different ways to decompress a Cisco IOS `.bin` file on different operating systems, but you will learn how to decompress an IOS file using the two most common Windows methods. The first method is to use `Unpack-0.1_win.zip`, and the second method is to decompress IOS by integrating GNS3 into Dynamips.

Decompressing Cisco IOS Using the Unpack.exe Method

Here, you will download `Unpack.exe` for Windows and decompress a Cisco IOS file for GNS3 use. Follow these simple instructions to decompress the original `.bin` file and save it as an `.image` file for GNS3 use. Please note that the file must be saved with the `.image` file extension and moved to your `Downloads` folder of your PC at the end of this task.

#	Task
1	First, download `Cisco image unpacker 0.1 binary for Windows` to your `Downloads` folder and extract it under the `Downloads` folder. The filename is `Unpack-0.1_win.zip`, and the download is available from SourceForge.net. URL: `https://sourceforge.net/projects/gns-3/files/Cisco%20Image%20Unpacker/v0.1/`
2	If you still have your IOS file in the `Downloads` folder, move it to the `Unpack` folder, as shown in Figure 10-14.

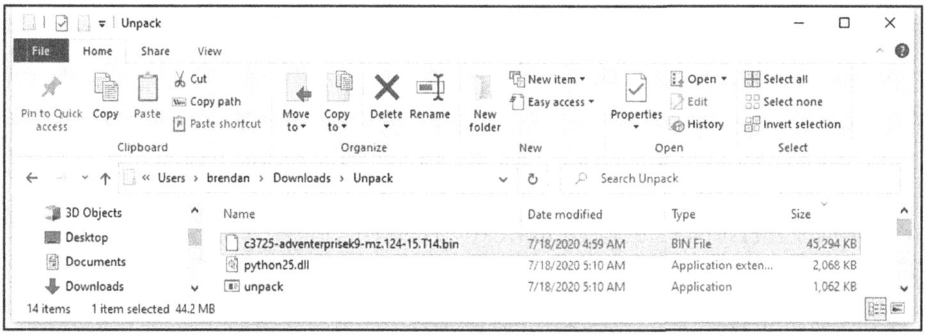

***Figure 10-14.** Decompressing IOS, moving the IOS file to the unpack folder*

3	From the Windows command-line prompt, run the following `unpack.exe` command to extract the file in the same folder. Once the file is decompressed, the decompressed filename will have `.bin.unpacked` as its file extension: `unpack.exe --format IOS [Your_IOS_Name]`. `C:\Users\your_name\Downloads\Unpack>unpack.exe --format IOS c3725-adventerprisek9-mz.124-15.T14.bin`

■ **Note** Replace `your_name` with your username.

#	Task
4	Now rename the `.bin.unpacked` file as a `.image` file. So, the filename changes from `c3725-adventerprisek9-mz.124-15.T14.bin.unpacked` to `c3725-adventerprisek9-mz.124-15.T14.image`. Also, notice that the decompressed IMAGE file is almost twice the size of the `.bin` file. See Figure 10-15.

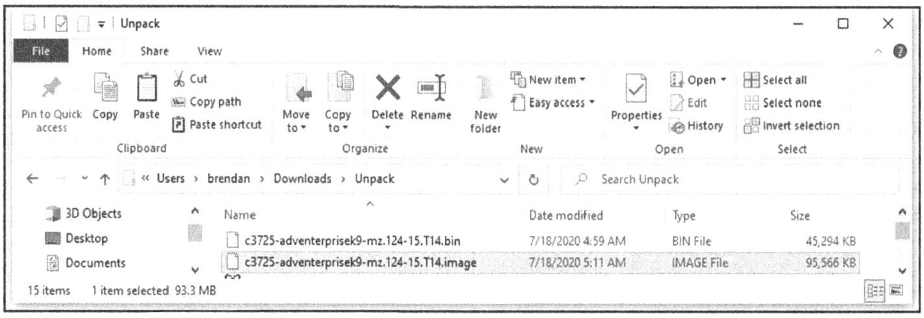

Figure 10-15. *Decompressing IOS, renaming the decompressed .bin.unpacked file to .image*

#	Task
6	Once the filename has been updated with the correct file extension, copy and paste the file into the `Downloads` folder again. This step is essential as GNS3 will be searching for a compatible `.image` file in the `Downloads` folder on your Windows. See Figure 10-16.

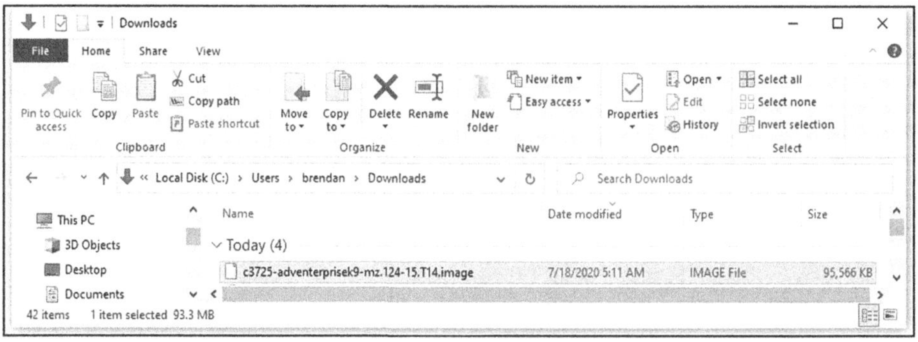

Figure 10-16. *Decompressing IOS, moving the .image file to the Downloads folder*

If you want to find out how to decompress the IOS file using the second method, the Dynamips method, please read 10.4.2.2, but if you immediately want to begin network lab building tasks, jump to 10.5.

Decompressing Cisco IOS Using Dynamips Method (Optional)

Follow these instructions to decompress your IOS `.bin` file into the `.image` file using the Dynamips server method. Once you have completed the task, make sure that a copy of the `.image` file has been placed under your host PC's `Downloads` folder. Some readers may find this process more manageable than the first decompression method.

#	Task
1	If you have not started your GNS3 and GNS3 VM, first launch it by double-clicking your desktop's GNS3 start icon. See Figure 10-17.

Figure 10-17. *GNS3, GNS3 desktop icon*

2 Give one to two minutes for the GNS3 VM to start up properly and settle down. Wait until both GNS3 VM and your local server's CPU and RAM levels settle down. See Figure 10-18.

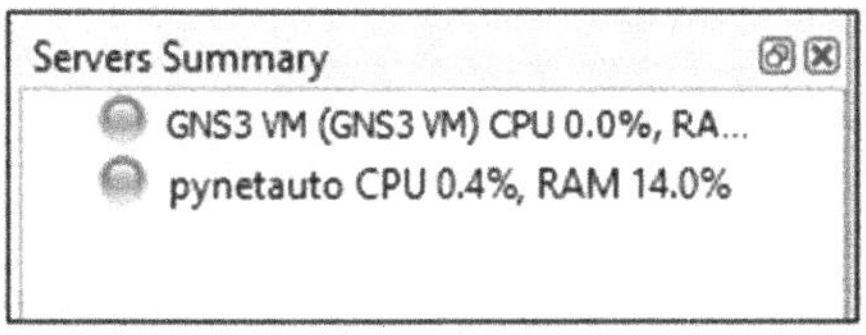

Figure 10-18. *GNS3, Servers Summary window*

3 GNS3 will prompt you with the Project window. Since we are interested only in decompressing the IOS, we will click the Cancel button. See Figure 10-19.

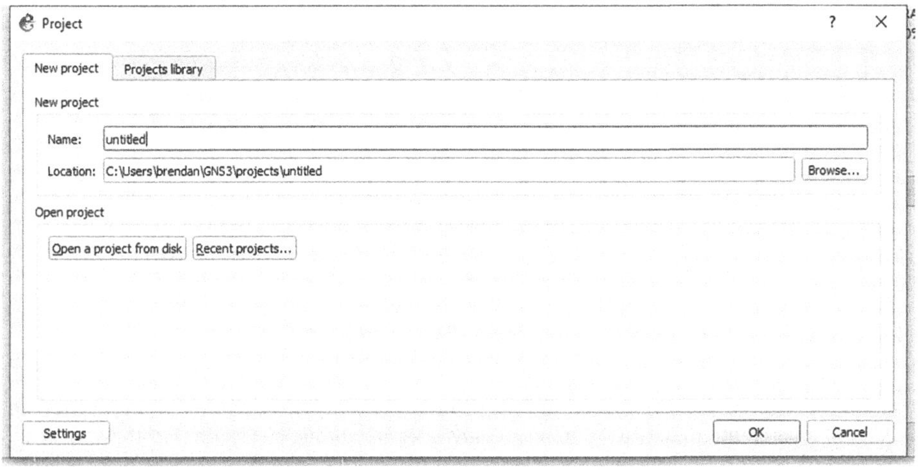

Figure 10-19. *GNS3, Project window cancel*

#	Task
4	To open the Preferences menu on GNS3, select Edit ➤ Preferences. See Figure 10-20.

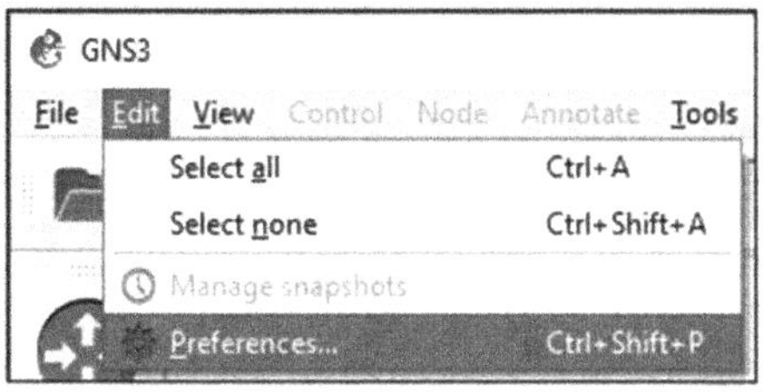

Figure 10-20. *GNS3, opening the Preferences menu*

5 Select the IOS routers under Dynamips, as shown in Figure 10-21.

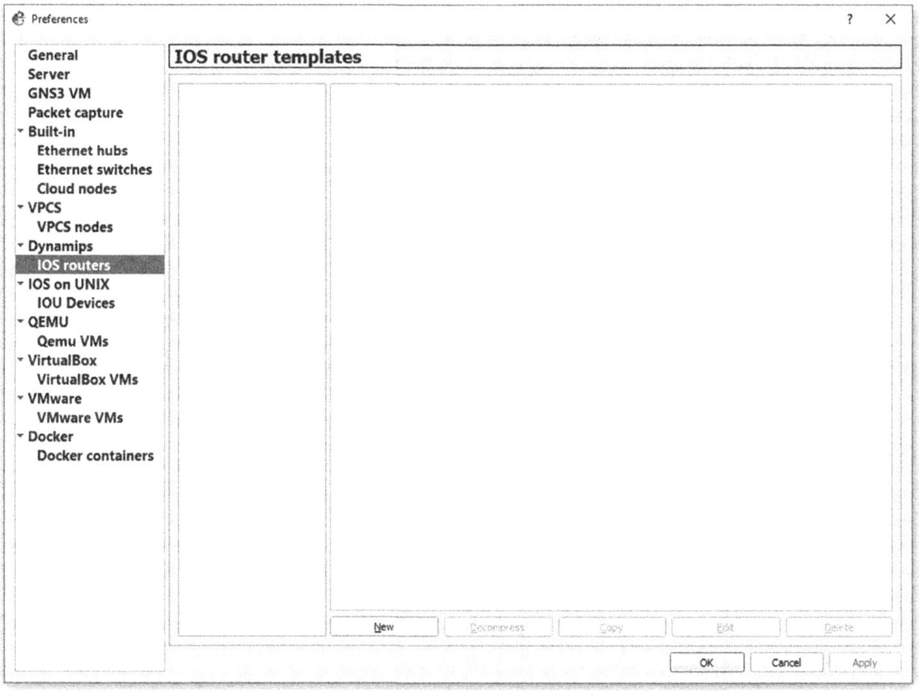

Figure 10-21. *GNS3, Dynamips, IOS routers*

(continued)

#	Task
6	Click the New button to open the New IOS router template window. In the Server screen, select "Run this IOS router on my local computer." You can also select the "Run this IOS router on the GNS3 VM" option, but we'll use the old method and remove the image after decompressing the file. See Figure 10-22.

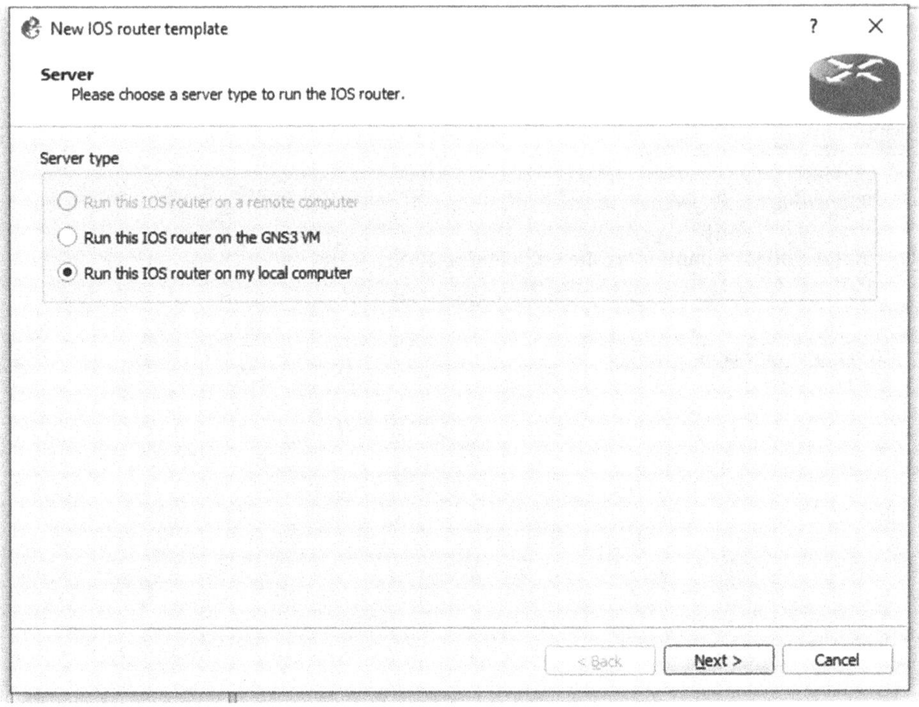

Figure 10-22. *GNS3, new IOS router template*

#	Task
7	In the IOS image window, click the Browse button on the right. See Figure 10-23.

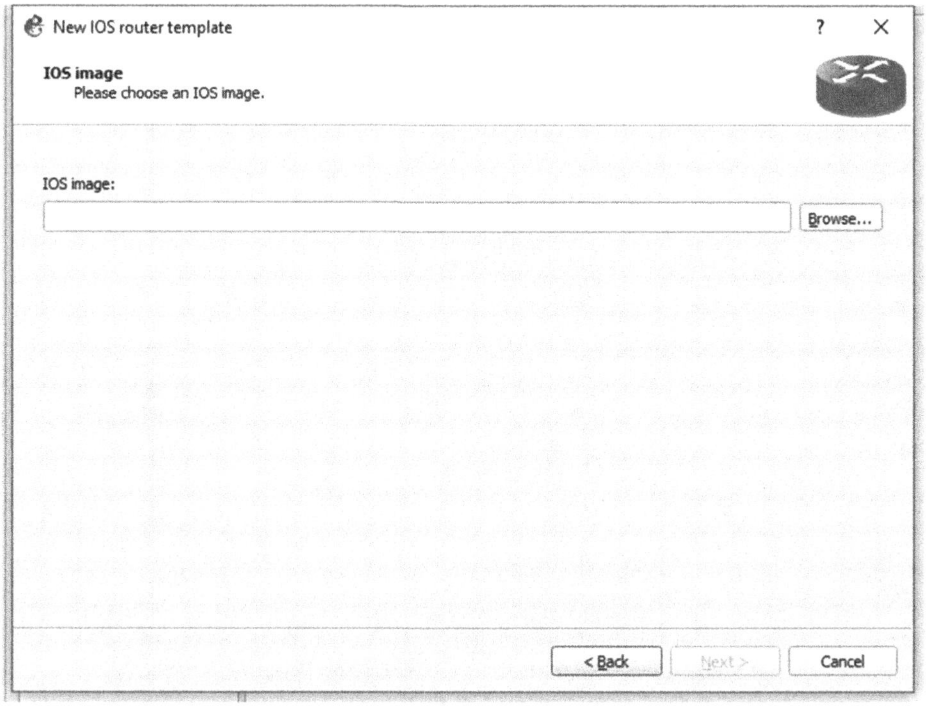

Figure 10-23. *GNS3, selecting the IOS image*

(*continued*)

#	Task
8	Select your IOS image in the `Downloads` folder and click the Open button. See Figure 10-24.

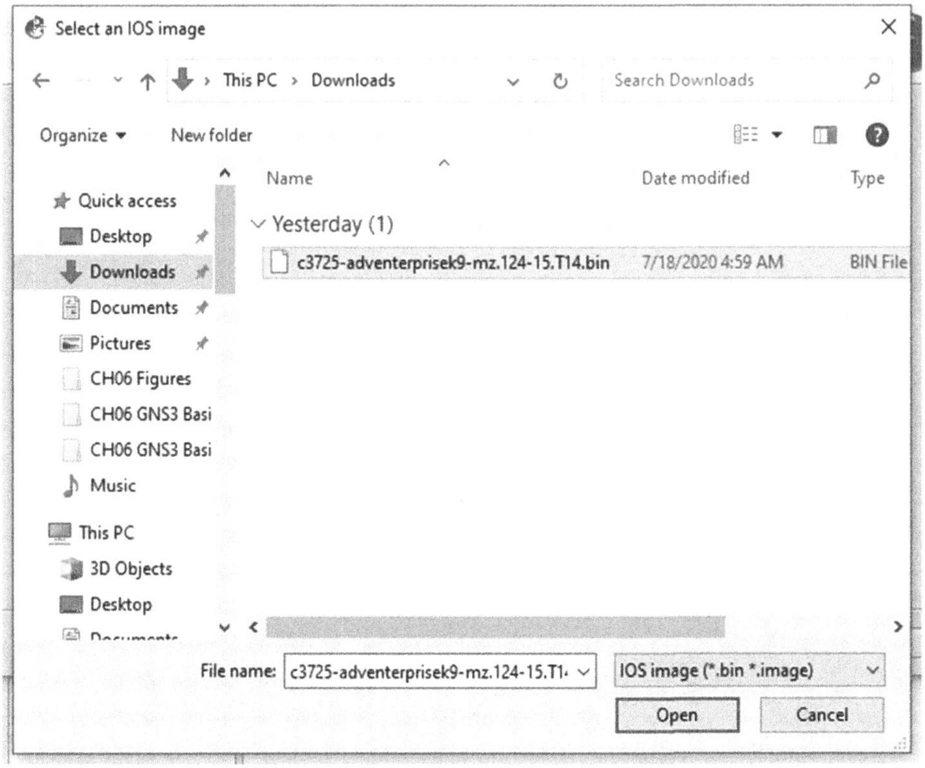

Figure 10-24. *GNS3, selecting IOS and opening*

9 Click Yes to decompress the IOS image. See Figure 10-25.

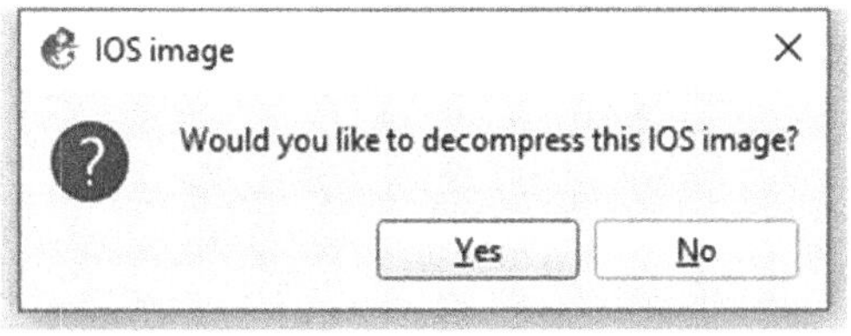

Figure 10-25. *GNS3, decompressing IOS image*

(continued)

#	Task
10	When you come back to the IOS image window, GNS3 will tell you where the `.image` file will be stored. For this demonstration, it is extracted to the user's `GNS3\images\IOS\` folder. See Figure 10-26. `C:\Users\your_name\GNS3\images\IOS\c3725-adventerprisek9-mz.124-15.T14.image`

■ **Note** Replace `your_name` with your name.

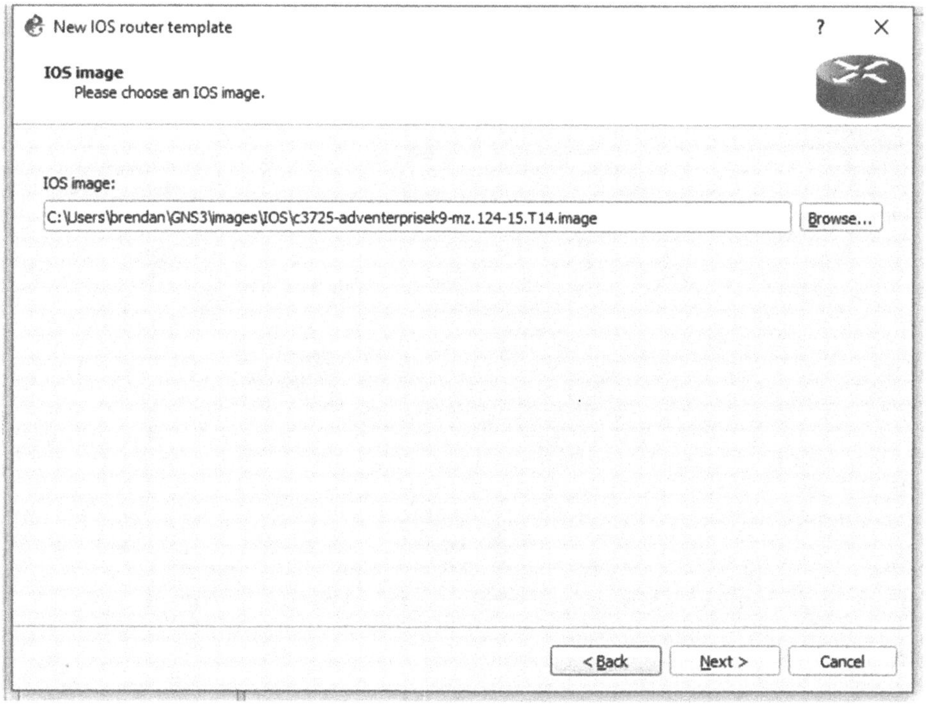

Figure 10-26. *GNS3, decompressed image location*

(continued)

#	Task
11	For the name and platform, leave all the settings as the defaults and click the Next button.
12	The recommended RAM size for 3725 is 256MB, but GNS3 will default the RAM to 128MB. This is only an example to demonstrate how to extract the `.bin` file into the `.image` file, so you can leave it as 128MB and click the OK button. See Figure 10-27.

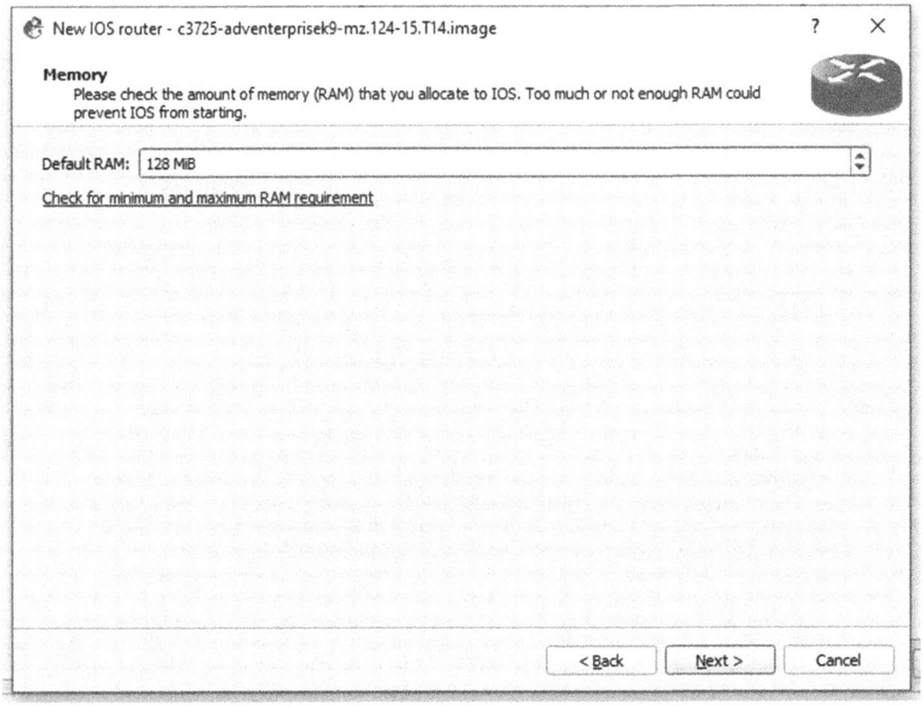

Figure 10-27. *GNS3, memory*

#	Task
13	In the "Network adapters" window, click the Next button.
14	In the "WIC module" window, click the Next button again.

#	Task
15	In Idle-PC window, click the Next button. See Figure 10-28.

Note If you choose to run the IOS router on the local machine and Dynamips, you can click the Idle-PC finder button to find a suitable Idle-PC, and it will automatically find an optimum value for your system. Since we will be configuring the IOS router to run from GNS3 VM, we can skip this process.

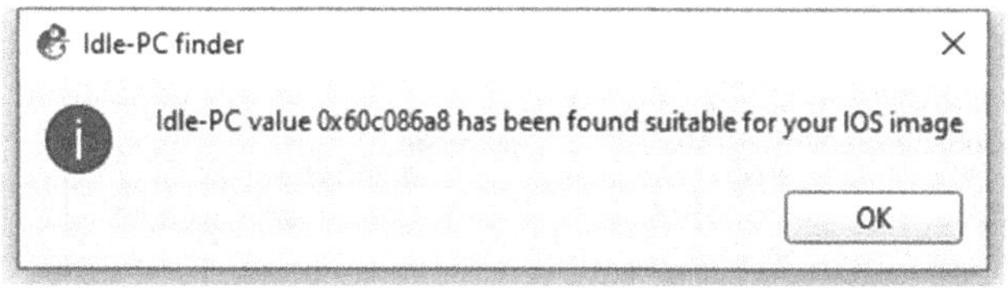

Figure 10-28. *GNS3, IOS idle-PC finder example only*

16 Now we extracted the `.image` file in a folder. We plan to run most of the devices on the GNS3 VM, so select the router and click the Delete button to remove the router from Dynamips ➤ IOS routers. Then, click OK to close the window. See Figure 10-29.

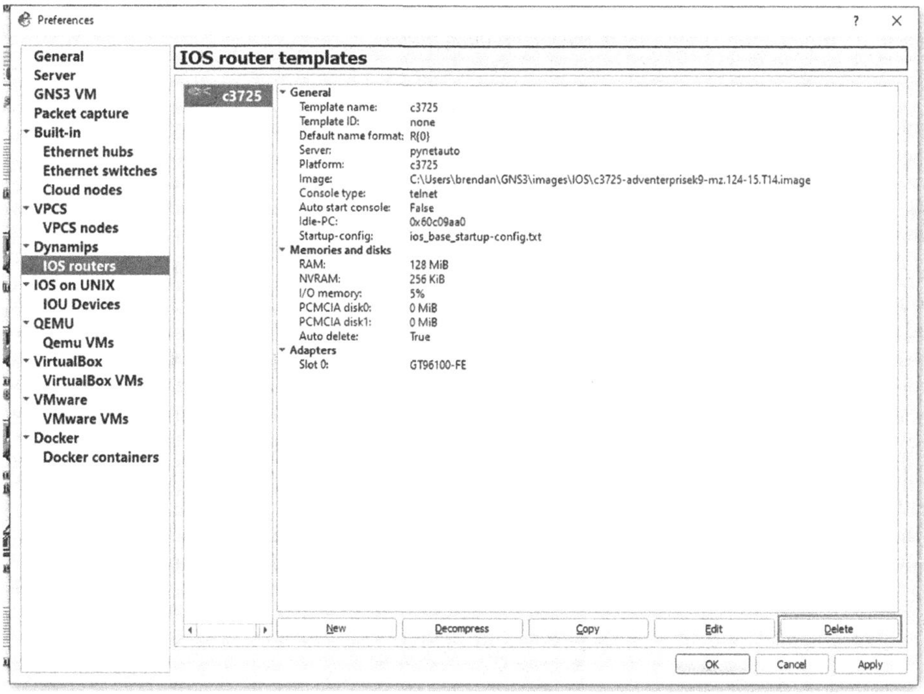

Figure 10-29. *GNS3, selecting and deleting the IOS router*

(continued)

#	Task
17	Now go to the following folder path: `C:\Users\your_name\GNS3\images\IOS`. You will find a copy of the decompressed IOS image file with the extension `.image`. Copy the file to the `Downloads` folder.

■ **Note** Replace `your_name` with your username. See Figure 10-30.

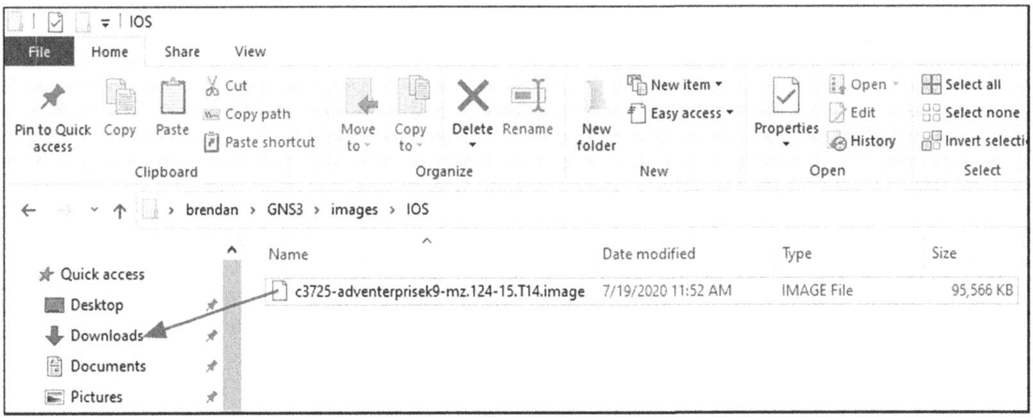

Figure 10-30. *Host PC, moving the .image file to the Downloads folder*

Now you are ready to install your Cisco IOS router on GNS3 VM. Let's follow through with this task.

Installing Cisco IOS on the GNS3 VM

You have successfully decompressed your IOS image and now are ready to create a GNS3 project using the `.image` file into either the local server (PC) or your GNS3 VM server. Since we are using the GNS3 VM as our GNS3 server and want to install most of the devices, this avoids high CPU utilization, idle PC, and memory contention issues associated with the local Dynamips server setup. We are going to install IOS on GNS3 VM instead of the local server. This is a recommended installation as the performance of the GNS3 VM will have less CPU and memory impact on your host PC's performance than when you run devices on the local server.

If your GNS3 is not already running, start the application and let it initialize the GNS3 VM on Workstation. Wait about one to two minutes for the GNS3 VM to boot up properly. Wait until your PC's CPU and memory settle down.

Assuming that both GNS3 and GNS3 VM on Workstation are correctly running on your PC, let's go ahead and complete the following set of tasks to create our first GNS3 project and install the `.image` file on the GNS3 VM server:

#	Task
1	After launching GNS3, when the GNS3 project window appears, create a new GNS3 project and give a name. Alternatively, you can use the New Project icon to open the Project menu and begin this task. You can give any meaningful name of your choice. Here, the project name given was `ios_lab`. You do not have to follow this naming convention strictly. See Figure 10-31.

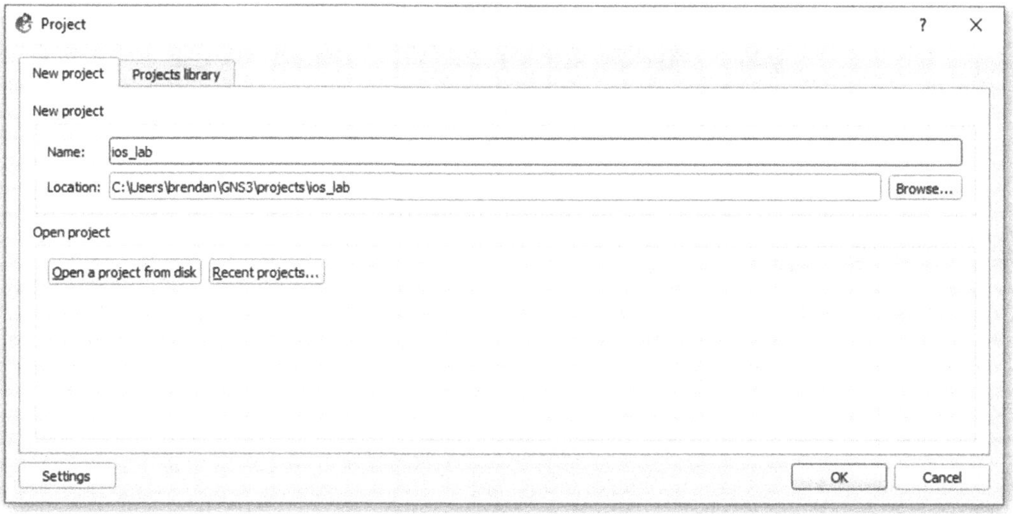

Figure 10-31. *GNS3, creating a new project*

(*continued*)

#	Task
2	From the GNS3 menu, select File ➤ + New template. Or, click the Router icon under Devices on the left and click + New template. See Figure 10-32.

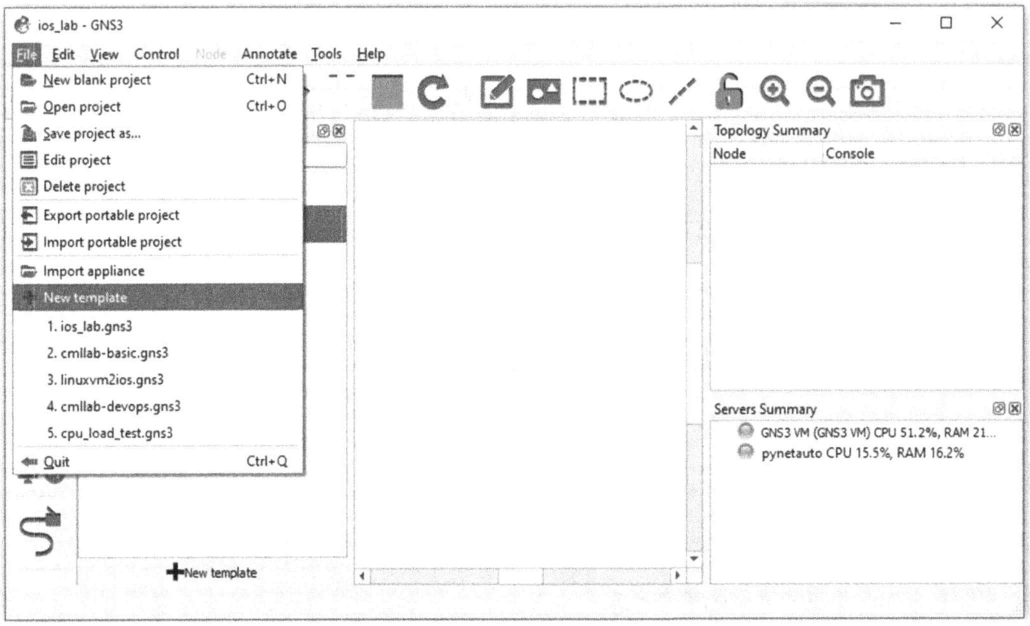

Figure 10-32. *GNS3, opening the "New template" menu*

#	Task
3	When the "New template" window appears, select the "Install an appliance from the GNS3 server (recommended)" option. Click the Next button. See Figure 10-33.

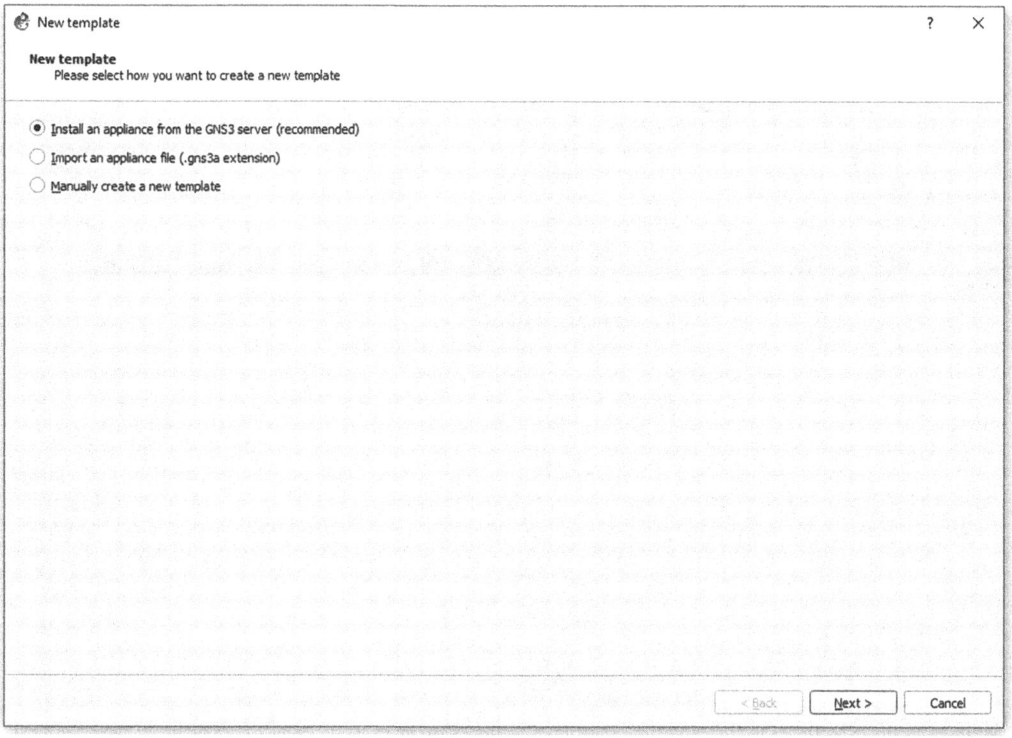

Figure 10-33. *GNS3, "New template" option*

(*continued*)

#	Task
4	Use the search field to locate your IOS device or use the drop-down device menu on the "Appliances from server" screen to select your device. Once you locate your IOS device, click it to select it and then click the Install button at the bottom. See Figure 10-34.

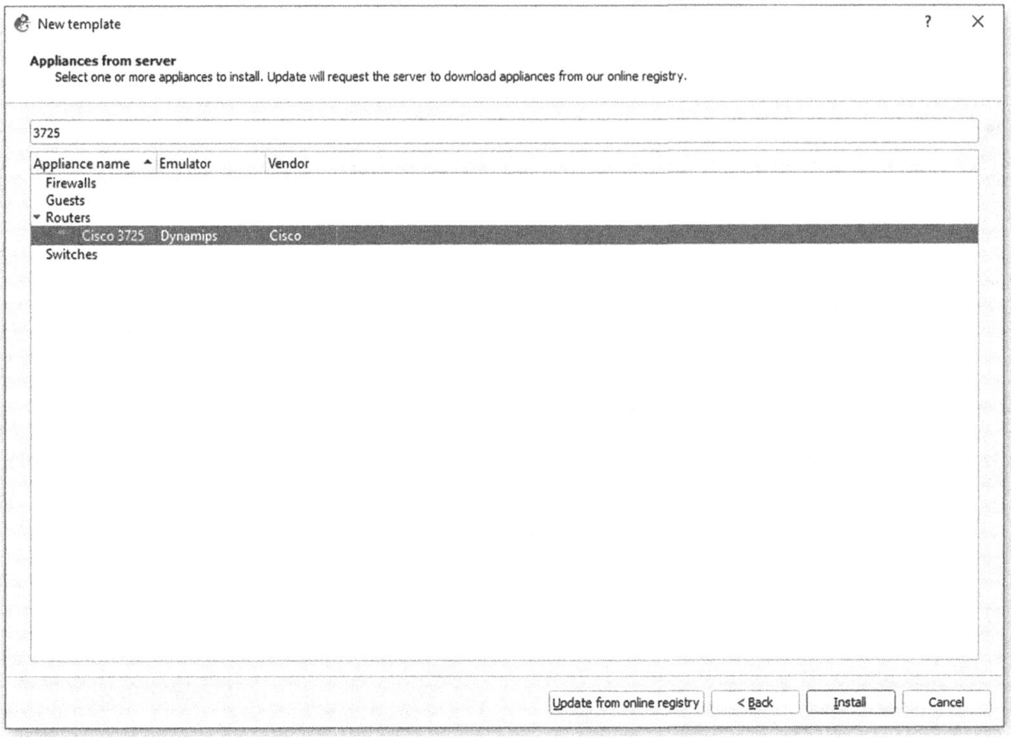

Figure 10-34. *GNS3, searching your IOS device*

#	Task
5	Next, leave the "Server type" selection as the default, "Install appliance on the GNS3 VM (recommended)," and click the Next button one more time. See Figure 10-35.

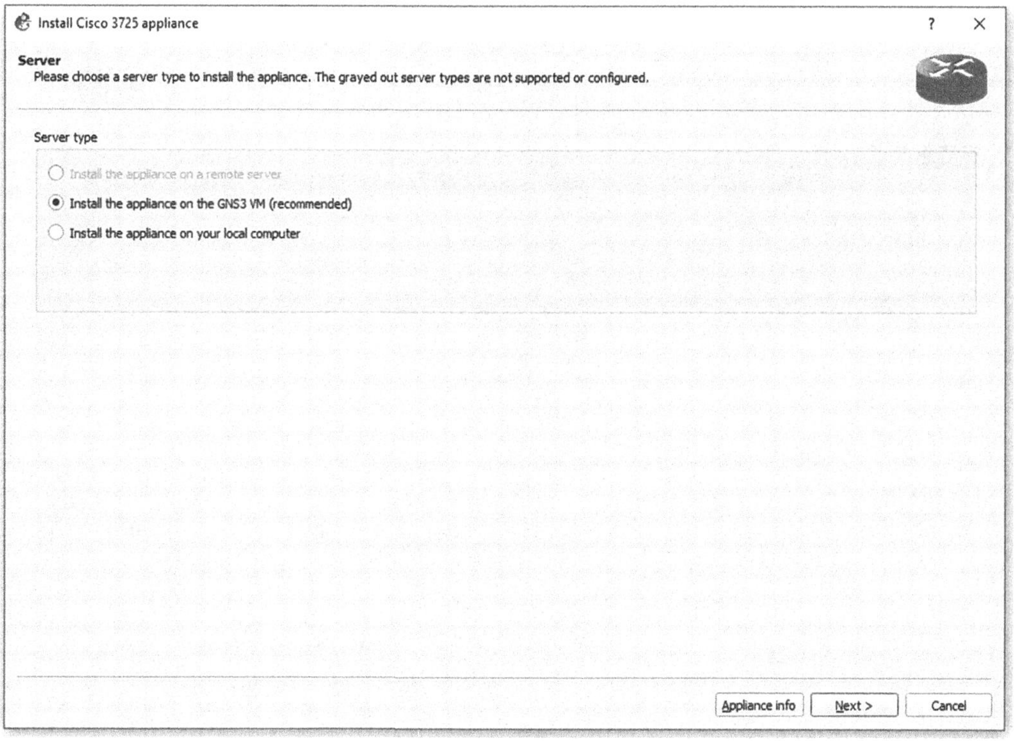

Figure 10-35. *GNS3, server type selection*

(*continued*)

#	Task
6	If you have successfully followed the previous steps, the "Required files" window will locate your `.image` file, and you will see the same or similar screen to Figure 10-36. Select the image file by highlighting the file and click the Next button again.

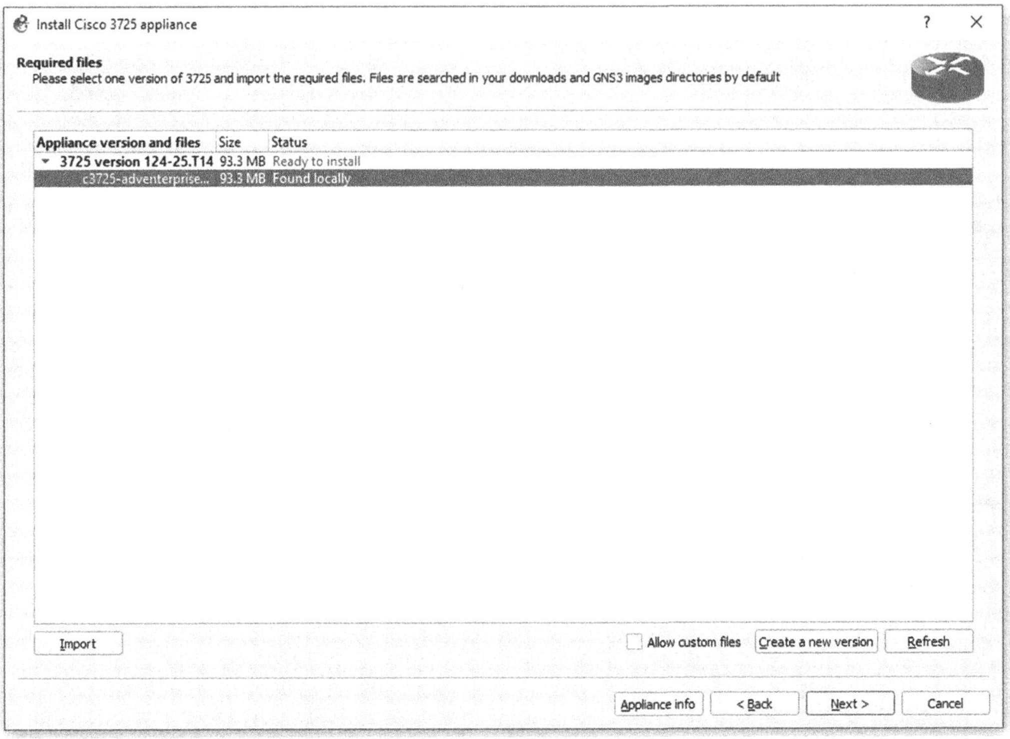

Figure 10-36. *GNS3, required files*

#	Task
7	Of course, you want to install the Cisco IOS on GNS3. Click the Yes button. See Figure 10-37.

Figure 10-37. GNS3, appliance installation confirmation message

8 You are almost there; click the Finish button to finish the installation. See Figure 10-38.

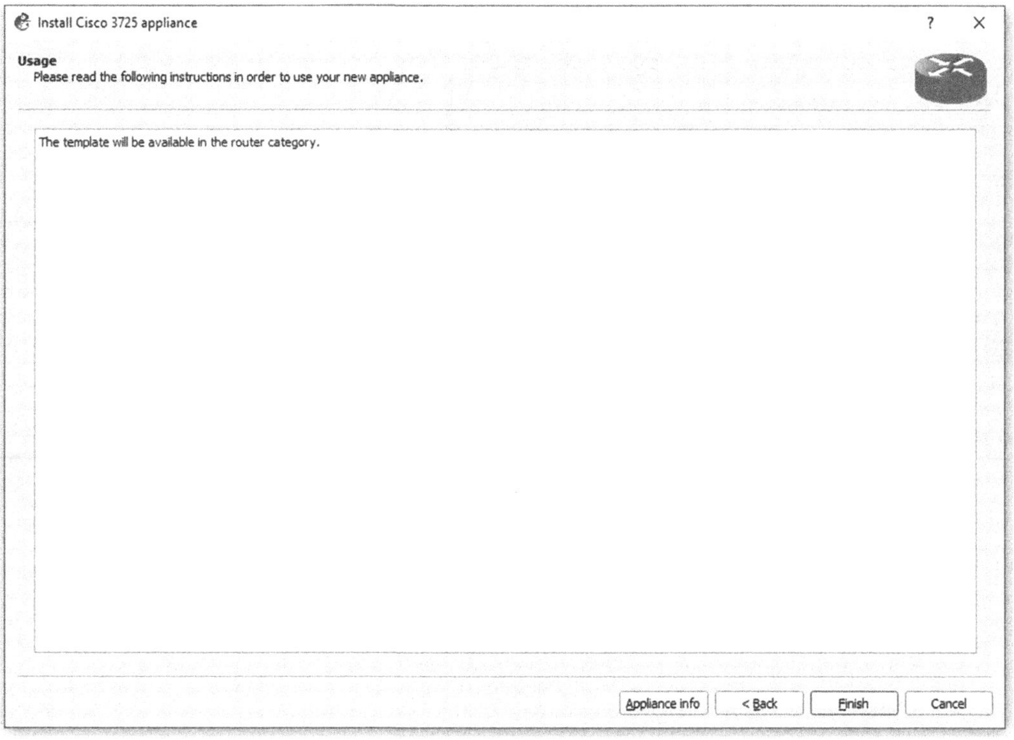

Figure 10-38. GNS3, usage prompt

(*continued*)

#	Task
9	If the installation is successful, you will be prompted with the message shown in Figure 10-39. Click the OK button.

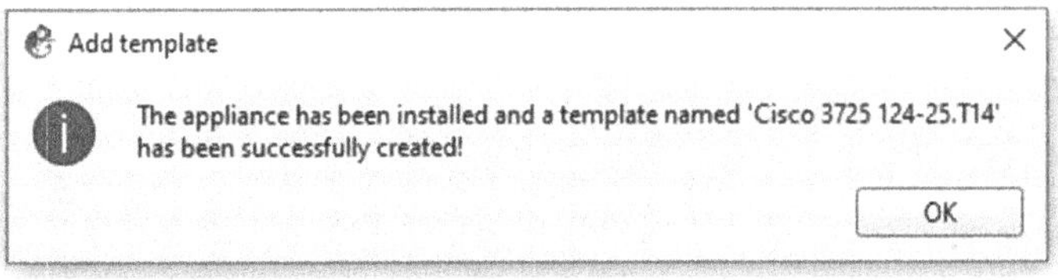

Figure 10-39. *GNS3, Adding the template success message*

#	Task
10	Now let's assign the correct RAM size for 3725 and add an extra FastEthernet interface for our lab. Finally, go back to the GNS3 main window and click the router icon. You will see the installed Cisco IOS router. Under the Routers icon, select the router icon and right-click and select "Configure template." See Figure 10-40.

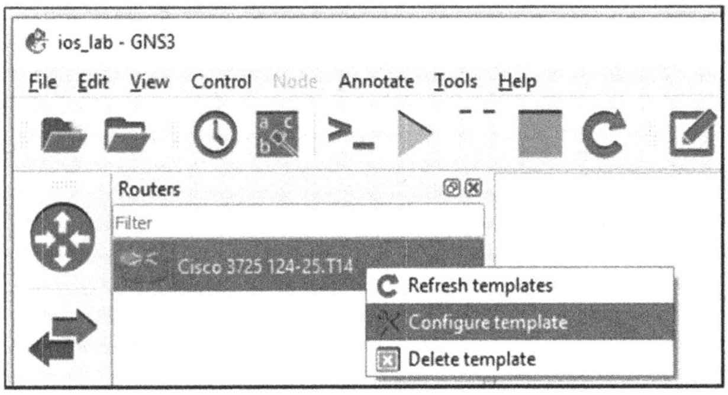

Figure 10-40. *GNS3, configuring the template*

#	Task
11	On the "Memories and disks" tab, change the default RAM size to 256MB and PCMCIA disk0 to the recommended 64MB and then click the OK button. You can go to the Cisco Feature Navigator page to check the RAM requirement for Cisco devices. You can go to `https://cfnng.cisco.com/archived-data` and search for your platform and IOS version for older IOS devices. You can download the requirement in Excel format. See Figure 10-41.

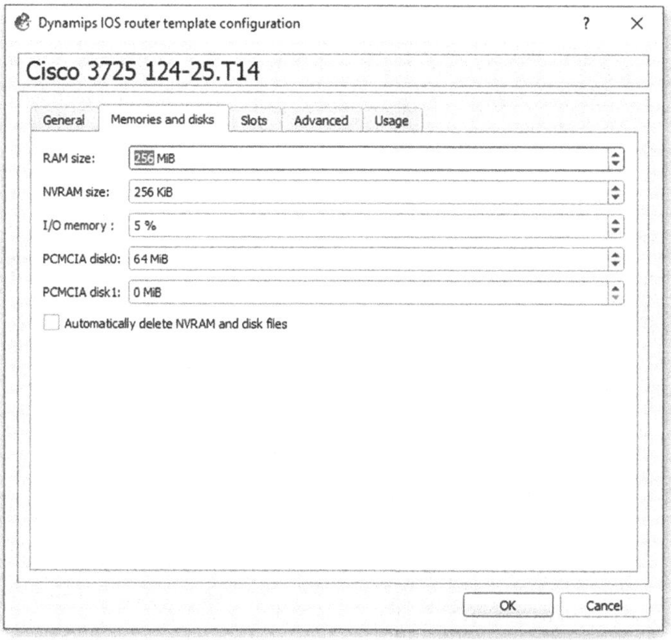

Figure 10-41. *GNS3, adding disk0 to IOS router*

(continued)

#	Task
12	On the Slots tab, add an NM-1FE-TX on slot 1. You can also add NM-4T for four more FastEthernet interfaces or NM-16ESW, which adds 16 L2 interfaces. If you want to use this router as an L2 switch, then NM-16ESW can be added, but this is an old GNS3 method with little relevance in the newer GNS3 labs. You can also add WIC-1T or WIC-2T under the WICs option on this tab. Since you are only going to connect through FastEthernet, you can leave the WIC slots blank. Click the OK button. See Figure 10-42.

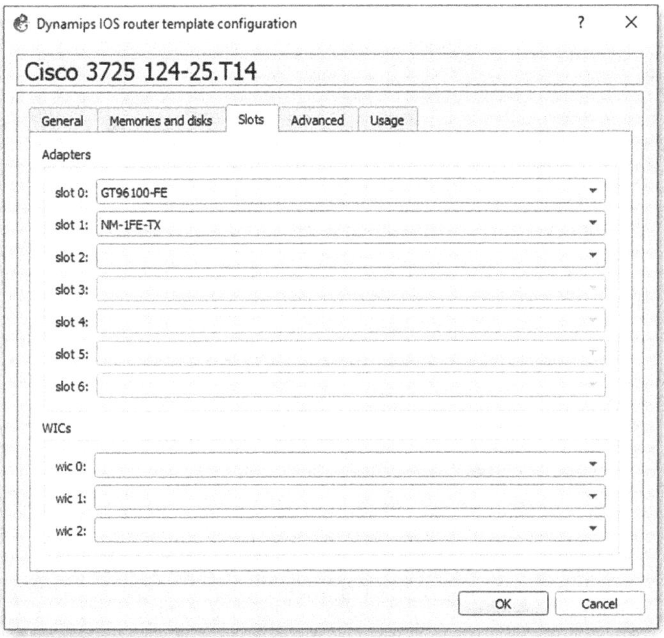

Figure 10-42. *GNS3, adding interfaces on IOS router*

#	Task
13	Now click the router icon and then drag and drop into the Topology canvas on the right. You have successfully installed an IOS image on the GNS3 VM. See Figure 10-43.

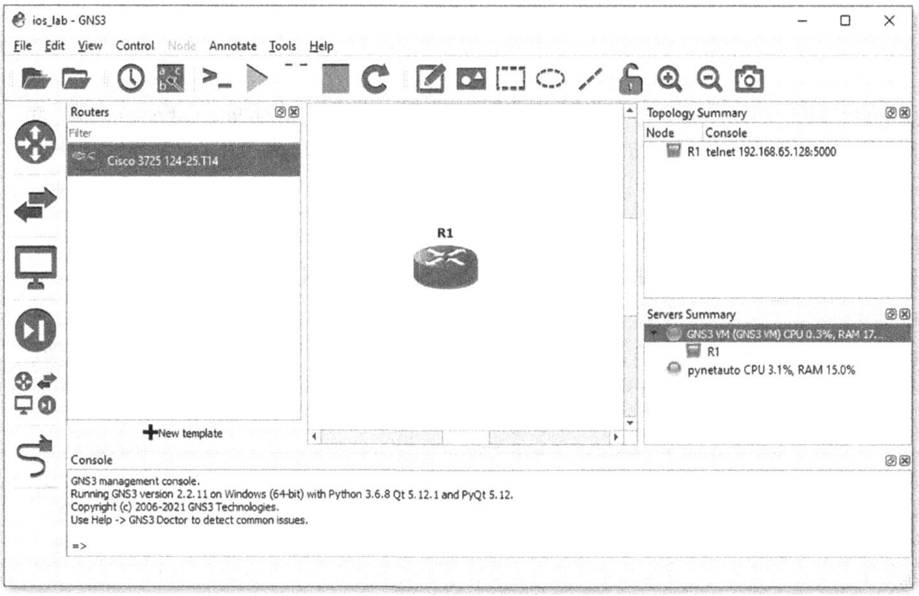

***Figure 10-43.** GNS3, checking the installation*

14	Now close GNS3 by clicking the top-right X button to close GNS3 and the GNS3 VM running on Workstation. Your GNS3 will be closed, followed by GNS3 VM shutdown. If you have another virtual machine running on VMware Workstation, the other VMs on Workstation will continue to run. See Figure 10-44.

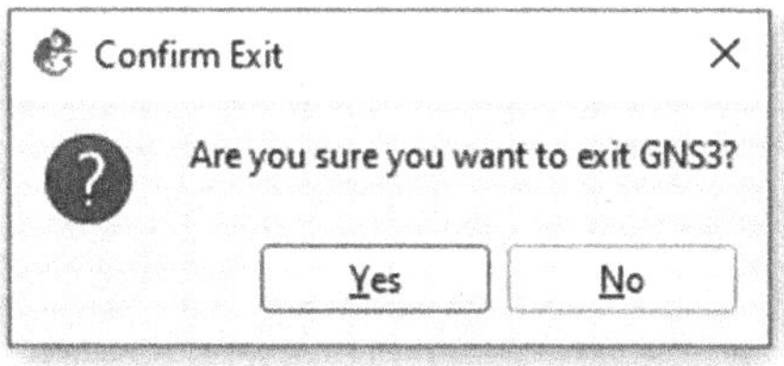

***Figure 10-44.** GNS3, closing GNS3 (and GNS3 VM)*

(continued)

Creating an IOS Lab Topology on GNS3 and Connecting to the Internet

For consistent and reliable lab results, the tasks involved in this section require an Internet connection, and it is recommended that your computer is connected by an Ethernet cable connection, not a wireless connection. Labs connecting through the wireless adapters may lead to different results than in the book. For the most part, the labs are carried out with the Ethernet cable connected to an Ethernet port on a home router. After this chapter, most of the labs will work fine on a wireless connection, but if you suspect that something is not working correctly, consider connecting your PC to a physical Ethernet port on your router or switch.

You have been asked to close both the GNS3 and GNS3 VMs in 10.5, and I have intentionally asked you to close the programs so you can properly reopen the previous lab. Now follow the steps to re-open the project to continue your IOS lab building.

#	Task
1	First, launch GNS3 using the GNS3 icon on your Windows desktop. When the GNS3 project window appears, wait for one to two minutes for the GNS3 VM to boot up. See Figure 10-45.

Figure 10-45. *GNS3, GNS3 desktop icon*

#	Task
2	Click the "Recent project" button under "Open project" to select the `ios_lab.gns3` project, and then click the OK button to re-open the first project. If the IOS installation and GNS3 integration were all OK, the project should normally open with a GNS3 VM kick-start on Workstation. See Figure 10-46.

 # Task

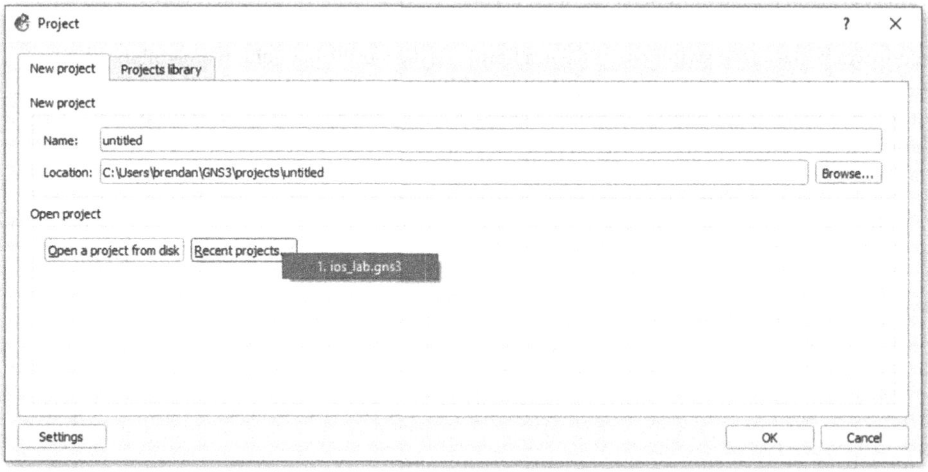

Figure 10-46. GNS3, opening recent project

3 As soon as the `ios_lab.gns3` project opens, click the "All devices" icon on the left and drop one NAT (NAT1), two routers (R1 and R2), and two VPCS (PC1 and PC2). When you drag and drop these devices, you will be prompted to select a server to run these devices. Pay close attention to which server you select here. See Figure 10-47.

Figure 10-47. GSN3, "All devices" icon

For NAT1, I select `pynetauto`, which is my PC name; your PC name will be different, so you should select your server name. This means that this device will run on the local server's NATted network, and the DHCP service will allocate an IP address from the VMnet8 (192.168.183.0/24) network.
You can also connect to the Internet via GNS3 VM's NATted network (192.168.122.0/24), but connecting to the outside network via GNS3 VM sometimes could be unreliable. Using the local server NAT address via VMnet8 provides a more reliable connection to the Internet and the Linux servers running on VMnet8. See Figure 10-48.

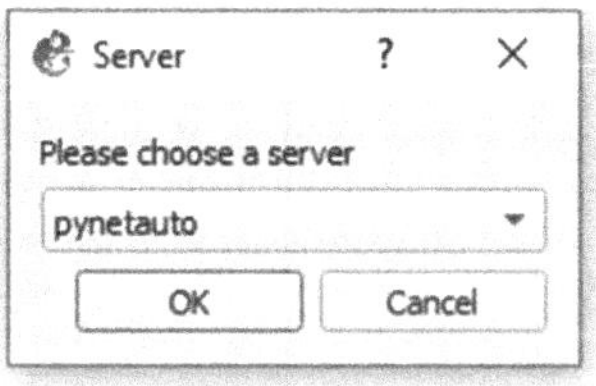

Figure 10-48. GSN3, NAT1 server selection

(*continued*)

#	Task
	For routers and VPCSs, select GNS3 VM as the server. These devices will run on the GNS3 VM server. The GNS3 built-in service is usually used to provide a seamless virtual connection to other devices; it is not a managed switch like Cisco switches. VPCS is a handy GNS3's built-in client, which allows the users to use them as end devices for simple ICMP tests. VPC saves a lot of computing power compared to running another virtual machine to run an end client. Using a VPC is like configuring a dummy loopback interface on a Cisco router or switch for end device reachability testing. Still, it is even better as you can still use ping and traceroute from VPCS, just like a real end device. See Figure 10-49.

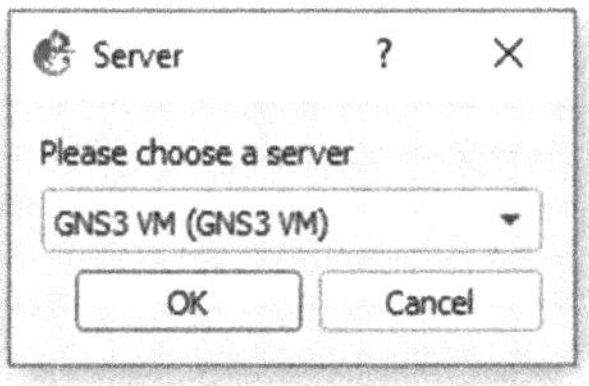

Figure 10-49. *GSN3, Switch1 and PC1 server selection*

4 Click the "Add a link" icon on the left bottom, and connect all devices as shown in Figure 10-50. Refer to the Topology and Servers summaries to connect your devices as shown.

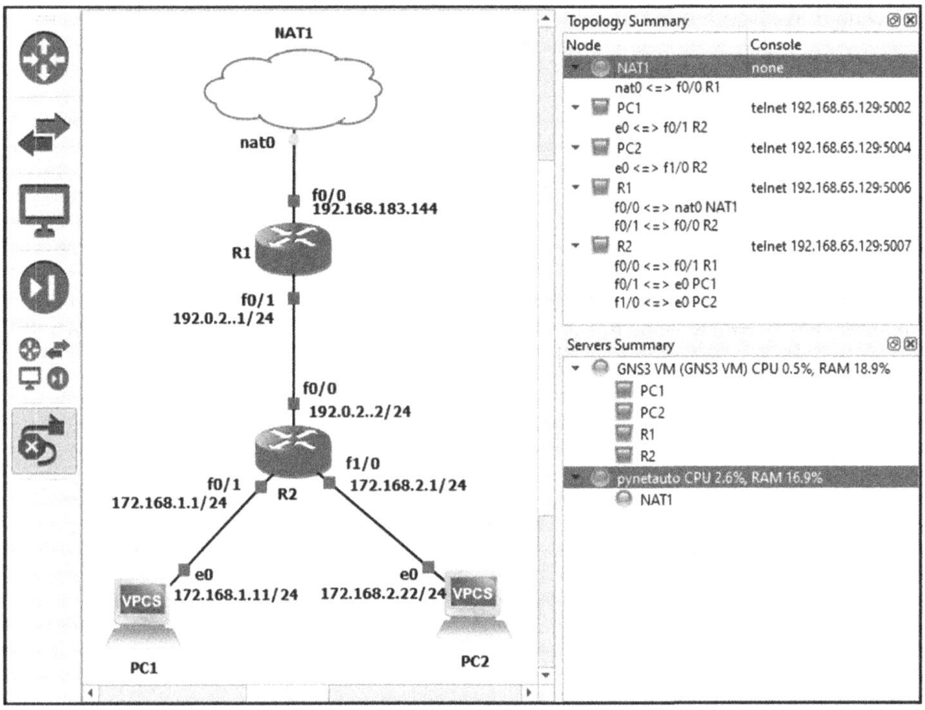

Figure 10-50. *GSN3, connecting devices*

#	Task
5	When you are happy with your topology, click the big green play icon to start all devices. Note that if there are more than five devices, it is a best practice to right-click each device and start one device at a time to avoid the CPU and memory hangs during the device bootup. Once all devices have started, the lights on the connections should turn all green, as shown in Figure 10-51.

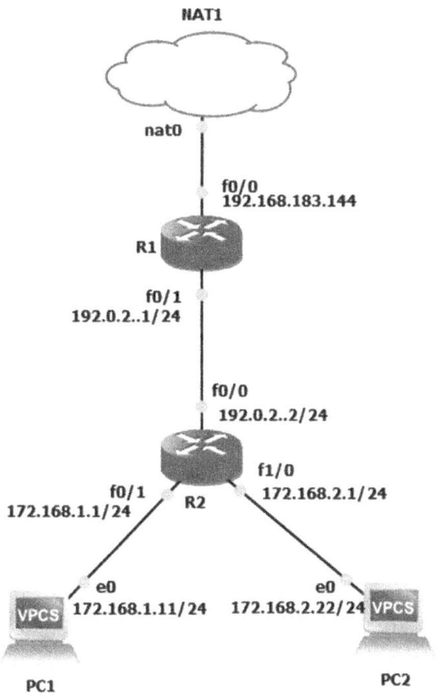

Figure 10-51. *GSN3, starting devices*

#	Task
6	Make sure that all lights under the Topology and Servers summaries are green and there are no errors. See Figure 10-52.

(continued)

#	Task

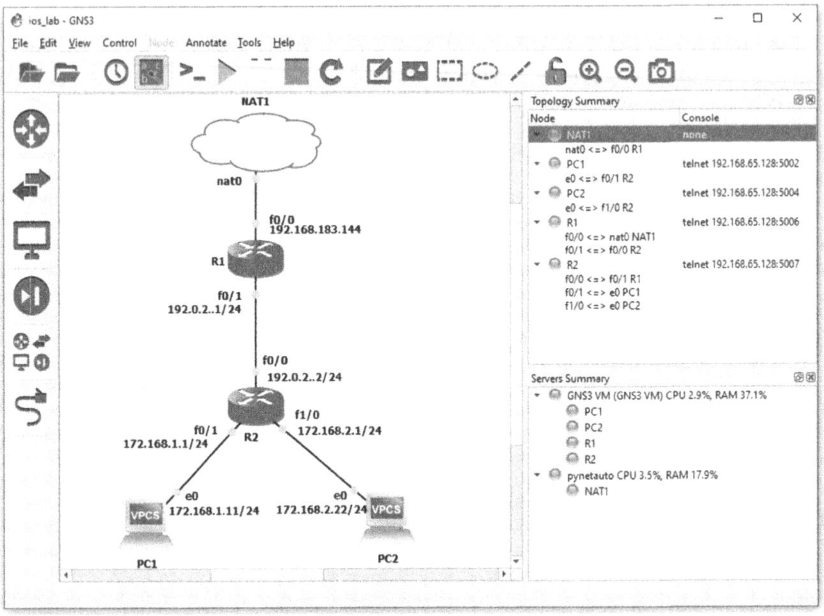

Figure 10-52. *GSN3, topology status*

7 To start a console of R1, simply double-click the R1 icon on the topology or right-click and select the console menu. At the console prompt, let's quickly configure R1 for our first lab.

hostname R1	Assigns R1 as the hostname
!	
ip name-server 8.8.8.8	Configures name server
!	
interface FastEthernet0/0	Fa0/0 gets the IP address from the DHCP server of
ip address dhcp	VMnet8 (NAT)
no shut	Brings up the interface
!	
interface FastEthernet0/1	Configures an IP address on f0/1
ip address 192.0.2.1 255.255.255.0	Connects to R2's f0/0
no shut	Brings up the interface
!	
router ospf 1	
network 192.0.2.0 0.0.0.255 area 0	OSPF 1 configuration to allow OSPF advertisement
network 192.168.183.0 0.0.0.255 area 0	
!	Saves R1's running configuration to startup
do write memory	configuration

#	Task	
8	Now let's configure R2. The configuration is similar to R1, but it has three interfaces on three different subnets.	
	hostname R2	Assigns R2 as hostname
	!	
	ip dhcp excluded-address 172.168.2.1 172.168.2.21	Excludes reserved IP addresses
	!	PC2 will get the next IP address, which is 172.168.2.22 via DHCP
	ip dhcp pool VPCS_2	
	network 172.168.2.0 255.255.255.0	
	default-router 172.168.2.1	PC2's DHCP pool configuration
	!	
	interface FastEthernet0/0	
	ip address 192.0.2.2 255.255.255.0	Configure an IP address on f0/0
	no shut	Connects to R1's f0/1
	!	Bring up the interface
	interface FastEthernet0/1	
	ip address 172.168.1.1 255.255.255.0	Configure an IP address on f0/1
	no shut	Connects to PC1
	!	Bring up the interface
	interface FastEthernet1/0	
	ip address 172.168.2.1 255.255.255.0	Configure an IP address on f1/0
	no shut	Connects to PC2
	!	Bring up the interface
	router ospf 1	
	network 172.168.0.0 0.0.0.255 area 0	
	network 172.168.1.0 0.0.0.255 area 0	Configure OSPF 1 for internal network advertisement
	network 172.168.2.0 0.0.0.255 area 0	
	network 192.0.2.0 0.0.0.255 area 0	
	!	
	ip route 0.0.0.0 0.0.0.0 192.0.2.1	Configure a static route for Gateway of last resort;
	!	static route to R1
	!	
	do write memory	Save R2's running configuration to startup configuration

(continued)

#	Task
9	Now open the PC1 (VPCS) console and practice configuring PC1's IP address manually. Type in the commands exactly shown below.

```
PC1> ip 172.168.1.11/24 172.168.1.1 <<< Assign IP address and Gateway
Checking for duplicate address...
PC1 : 172.168.1.11 255.255.255.0 gateway 172.168.1.1

PC1> ip dns 8.8.8.8 <<< Configure DNS IP address

PC1> show ip <<< Show ip address details

NAME                : PC1 1
IP/MASK             : 172.168.1.11/24
GATEWAY             : 172.168.1.1
DNS                 : 8.8.8.8
MAC                 : 00:50:79:66:68:00
LPORT               : 20000
RHOST:PORT          : 127.0.0.1:20001
MTU:                : 1500
```

Now validate your configuration by sending some ICMP messages from PC1 to R1, R2, and the Internet.

```
PC1> ping 172.168.1.1 -c 3 <<< To the Gateway f0/1
172.168.1.1 icmp_seq=1 timeout <<< first arp drop
84 bytes from 172.168.1.1 icmp_seq=2 ttl=255 time=3.098 ms
84 bytes from 172.168.1.1 icmp_seq=3 ttl=255 time=8.093 ms

PC1> ping 192.0.2.1 -c 3 <<< To R1's f0/1
84 bytes from 192.0.2.1 icmp_seq=1 ttl=254 time=25.297 ms
84 bytes from 192.0.2.1 icmp_seq=2 ttl=254 time=29.232 ms
84 bytes from 192.0.2.1 icmp_seq=3 ttl=254 time=31.170 ms

ping 8.8.8.8 -c 3 <<< To Google DNS server, Ethernet connection recommended
84 bytes from 8.8.8.8 icmp_seq=1 ttl=126 time=50.198 ms <<< On wireless you may get
timeouts
84 bytes from 8.8.8.8 icmp_seq=2 ttl=126 time=31.918 ms
84 bytes from 8.8.8.8 icmp_seq=3 ttl=126 time=58.199 ms
```

#	Task
10	This time, open the console of PC2 (VPCS) and configure the IP address using the `ip dhcp` command. Unlike the previous configuration, PC2 will get its IP from R2's DHCP services. If you have configured everything precisely the same, then PC2 should be assigned with an IP address of 172.168.2.22.

```
PC2> ip dhcp
DDORA IP 172.168.2.22/24 GW 172.168.2.1

PC2> show ip

NAME            : PC2 1
IP/MASK         : 172.168.2.22/24
GATEWAY         : 172.168.2.1
DNS             : 172.168.2.1
DHCP SERVER     : 172.168.2.1
DHCP LEASE      : 86391, 86400/43200/75600
MAC             : 00:50:79:66:68:01
LPORT           : 20002
RHOST:PORT      : 127.0.0.1:20003
MTU:            : 1500
```

Now validate your configuration by sending some ICMP messages from PC2 to R2, R1, PC1, and the Internet.

```
PC2> ping 172.168.1.1 -c 3 <<< To R2's f0/1 interface
84 bytes from 172.168.1.1 icmp_seq=1 ttl=255 time=4.515 ms
84 bytes from 172.168.1.1 icmp_seq=2 ttl=255 time=2.110 ms
84 bytes from 172.168.1.1 icmp_seq=3 ttl=255 time=5.558 ms
PC2> ping 172.168.1.11 -c 3 <<< To PC1, no entry in the ARP table.
172.168.1.11 icmp_seq=1 timeout <<< first arp drop
172.168.1.11 icmp_seq=2 timeout <<< second arp drop
84 bytes from 172.168.1.11 icmp_seq=3 ttl=63 time=12.709 ms
```

Note Whenever a router has to send a packet to the next hop (or directly attached destination) with no entry in the ARP table, the ARP request is sent out, but one to two original packets are dropped unconditionally.

```
PC2> ping 192.0.2.1 -c 3 <<< To R1's f0/1
84 bytes from 192.0.2.1 icmp_seq=1 ttl=126 time=33.306 ms
84 bytes from 192.0.2.1 icmp_seq=2 ttl=126 time=27.037 ms
84 bytes from 192.0.2.1 icmp_seq=3 ttl=126 time=23.962 ms

PC2> ping 8.8.8.8 -c 3 <<< To Google's DNS server
84 bytes from 8.8.8.8 icmp_seq=1 ttl=126 time=51.237 ms <<< On wireless you may get
timeouts
84 bytes from 8.8.8.8 icmp_seq=2 ttl=126 time=35.299 ms
84 bytes from 8.8.8.8 icmp_seq=3 ttl=126 time=24.883 ms
```

Once you have completed a lab, follow the standard procedure to save the configuration, shut down the devices, and close your project.

You have completed a GNS3 basic OSPF routing lab using two Cisco IOS routers and two VPCS. Although this is not a routing and switching book, you have built a topology, configured it, and completed the following tasks:

- Assigned IP addresses to routers' interface
- Configured a name server
- Configured DHCP services on R2
- Configured OSPF on R1 and R2 for internal routing
- Configured static router (gateway of last resort)
- Saved the running configuration to start up configuration

Also, you have learned how to configure and use GNS3's virtual PC (VPCS) feature using the manual and DHCP configuration method.

Next, let's learn how to install the Microsoft loopback adapter to manage GNS3 devices by communicating with the GNS3 topology from the host's Windows operating system. The Microsoft loopback adapter helps Windows hosts communicate with devices running on GNS3.

Installing the Microsoft Loopback Adapter

To communicate, control, and manage the Cisco devices running on GNS3 from the host PC, you can install the Microsoft loopback adapter and communicate to Cisco routers, switches, or other devices running on GNS3. The Microsoft loopback adapter is a virtual network adapter for testing purposes, which is provided by Windows. With Microsoft loopback, you can conveniently and reliably connect to the GNS3 devices from the host's operating system and communicate to virtual devices. Here's how to install the experimental Microsoft loopback on your host PC. Suppose you are a heavy Windows user and need some time to skill up on Linux administration. In that case, accessing and managing GNS3 devices from your Windows host will provide some more time for you to practice Linux while acquiring other skills.

If you are using your PC with a vanilla-flavored Windows 10 operating system, perform the following tasks. If you are using a company-provided standard operating environment (SOE) laptop or PC, adding a Microsoft loopback adapter may be slightly different. If you are using a personal computer, install the Microsoft loopback as described in the following steps. If you are using a company-provided SOE laptop or PC, menus may look different from the following example.

#	Task
1	Right-click the Microsoft icon at the bottom left of the host window. When the list appears, select Device Manager.
2	In the Device Manager window, first click Network Adapters to highlight it, then click Action located in the menu, and finally click Add Legacy Hardware. See Figure 10-53.

#	Task
	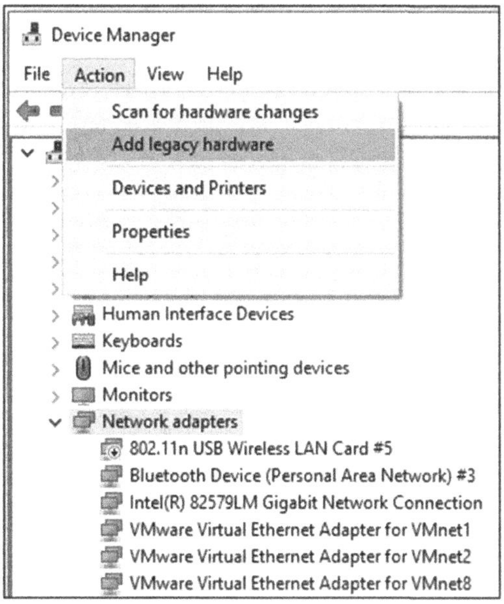 *Figure 10-53. Device Manager, network adapters, adding legacy hardware*
3	When the Add Hardware pop-up window appears, click the Next button.
4	In the next window, select "Install the hardware that I manually select from a list (Advanced)" and then click the Next button.
5	Scroll down to highlight Network Adapter and click the Next button. See Figure 10-54.

(*continued*)

#	Task
	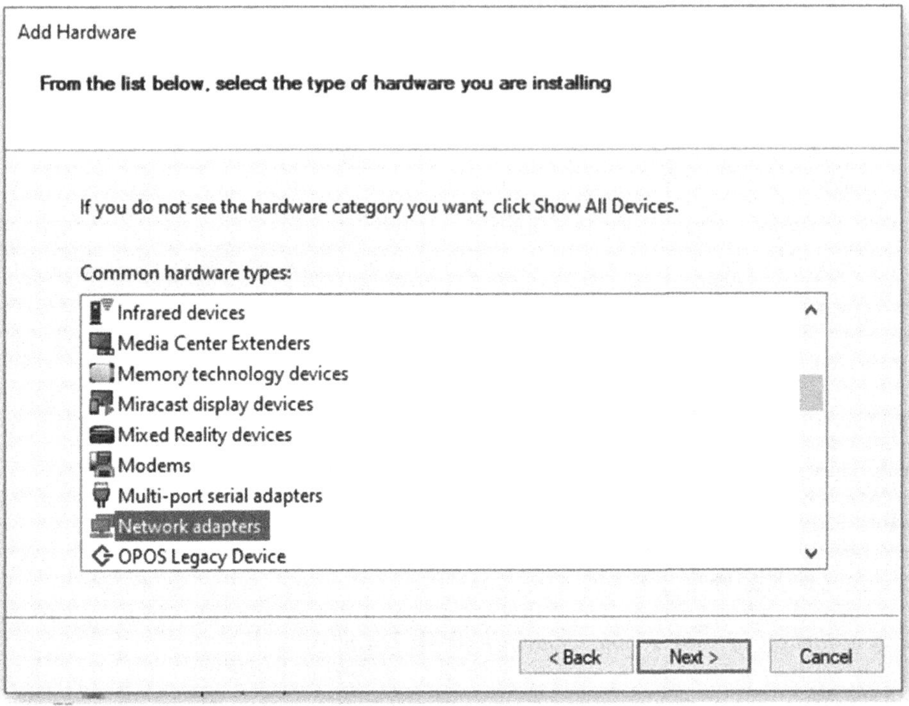 ***Figure 10-54.*** *Device Manager, adding network adapters*
6	When the hardware device driver window appears, first select Microsoft under Manufacturer, and then select Microsoft KM-TEST Loopback Adapter under Model on the right. Click the Next button one more time. See Figure 10-55.

#	Task

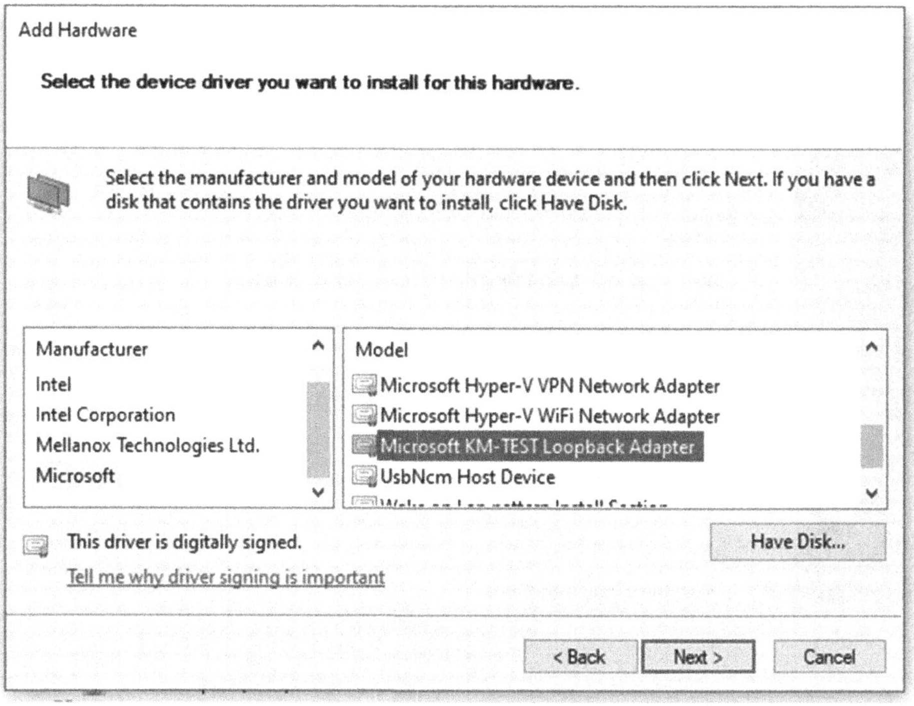

Figure 10-55. *Device Manager, adding the Microsoft loopback adapter*

7 On the next screen, click the Next button to install the hardware driver.

8 When the driver installation is completed and the "Complete Add Hardware Wizard" message appears, click the Finish button and also close the Device Manager. See Figure 10-56.

(continued)

#	Task

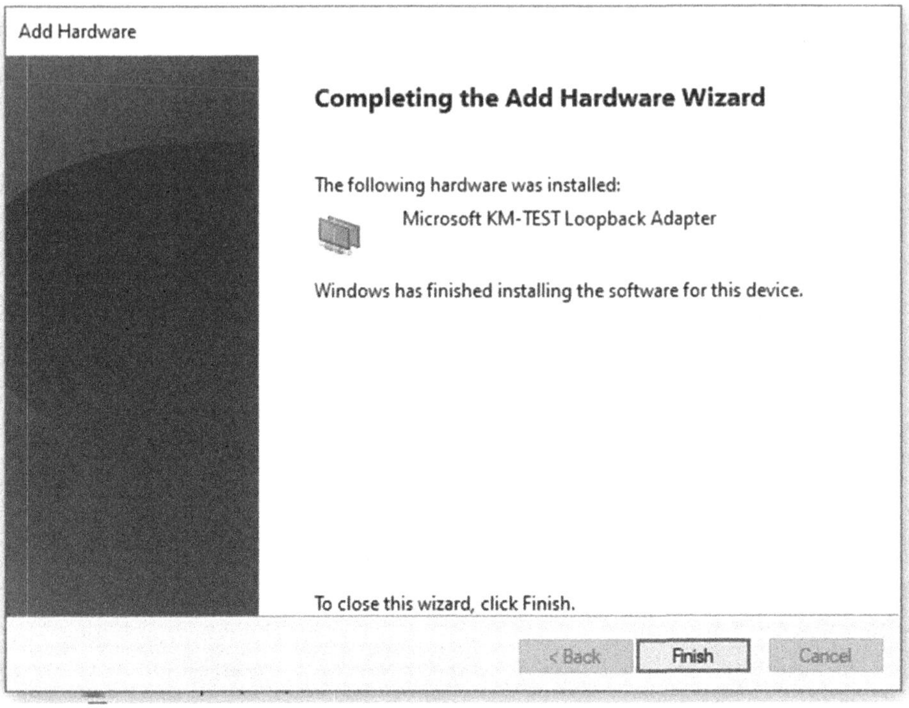

Figure 10-56. Device Manager, finishing the Microsoft loopback adapter installation

9 At the bottom-left corner, right-click the Windows icon and then select the Run menu. Next, type in **ncpa.cpl** in the Run window. This will open the Network Connections window with network adapters. See Figure 10-57.

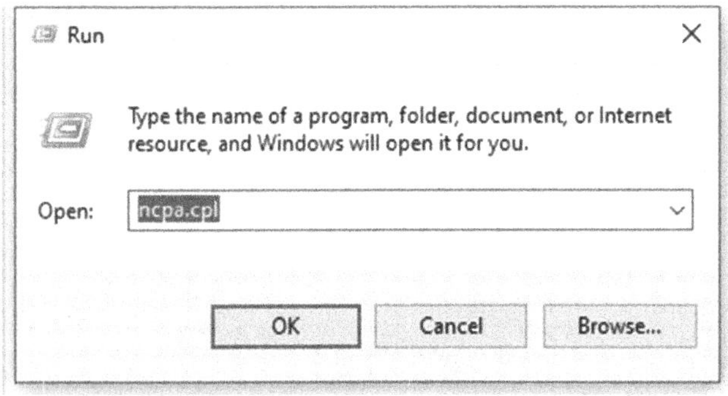

Figure 10-57. Windows 10, shortcut to running network connection

10 Locate and right-click the Microsoft KM-TEST loopback adapter icon, right-click the icon, and select the Rename option. Now change the name from Ethernet 2 to Loopback. See Figure 10-58.

Task

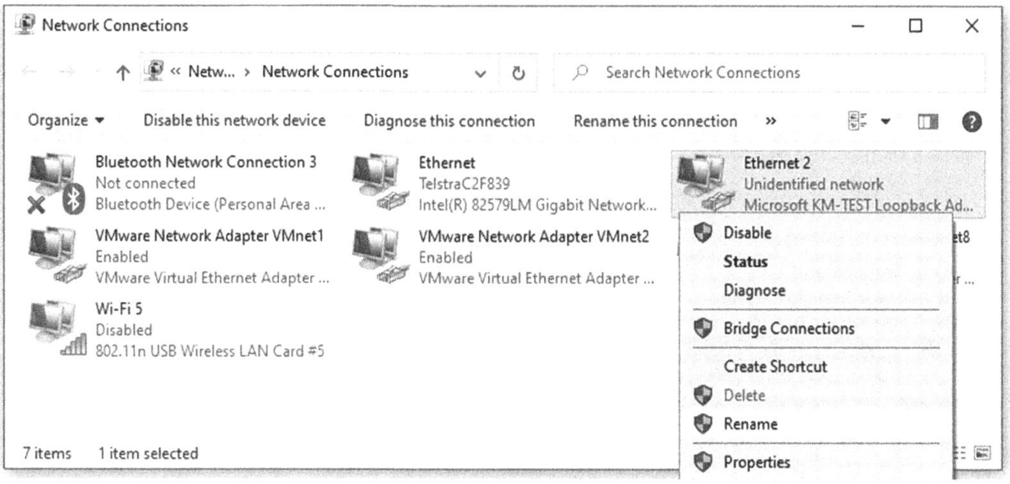

Figure 10-58. *Windows 10, renaming the Microsoft loopback adapter*

11 Once again, right-click the loopback adapter and select Properties. See Figure 10-59.

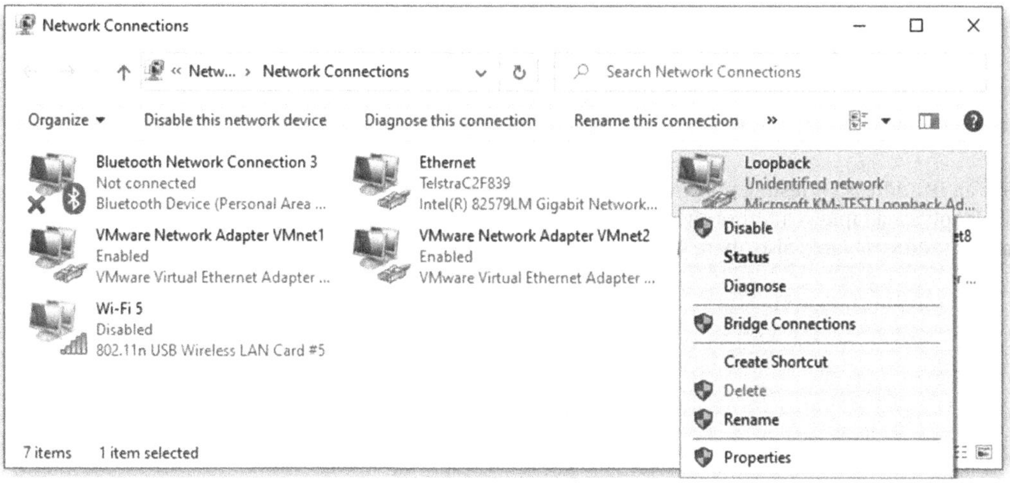

Figure 10-59. *Windows 10, changing the Microsoft loopback adapter properties*

12 Highlight Internet Protocol Version 4 (TCP/IP4) and then click the Properties button. See Figure 10-60.

(*continued*)

#	Task
	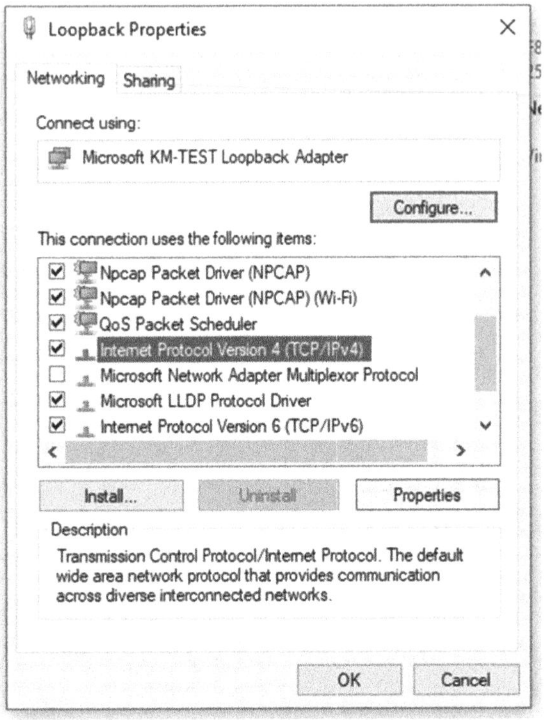 ***Figure 10-60.*** *Windows 10, selecting IPv4 properties*
13	Give an IP address for testing purposes; in this example, the IP address of the 7.7.7.0/24 subnet is used. The loopback adapter's address given is 7.7.7.1 with a subnet mask of 255.255.255.0. Leave the default gateway address blank; also, there's no need to fill in the DNS information. See Figure 10-61.

#	Task

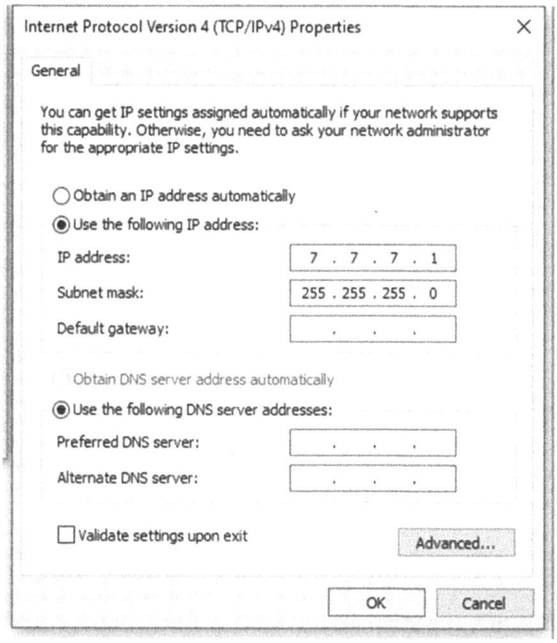

Figure 10-61. *Windows 10, hard-coding the IP address for loopback adapter*

14 Click the OK button, and close all the windows and running applications, including GNS3. To make GNS3 recognize the newly installed MS loopback interface, we need to restart the PC one more time.

When your PC restarts and boots up correctly, let's create a new GNS3 project using the Microsoft loopback adapter, set up a router, and connect the host machine with the virtual Cisco IOS router. Later, the same connection method can connect to other Cisco L2 and L3 devices and other types of GNS3 virtual devices.

Accessing GNS3 Network Devices Using MS Loopback

After creating a basic GNS3 project, you will test the communication between R1 and the host PC. Figure 10-62 shows the basic topology.

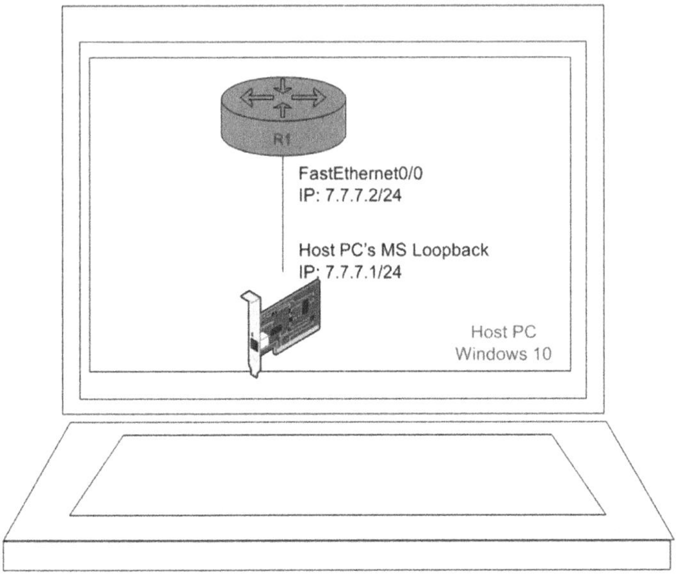

Figure 10-62. *Host PC to GNS3 router communication*

To configure a simple Microsoft loopback lab, follow these instructions:

#	Task
1	Use the GNS3 icon on the desktop to start GNS3. Wait until GNS3 VM starts and CPU settles down. See Figure 10-63.

Figure 10-63. *GNS3, GNS3 desktop icon*

#	Task
2	Now create a new project named `loopback_to_r1`. You do not have to follow this naming convention, so use your imagination to give a meaningful name. See Figure 10-64.

#	Task

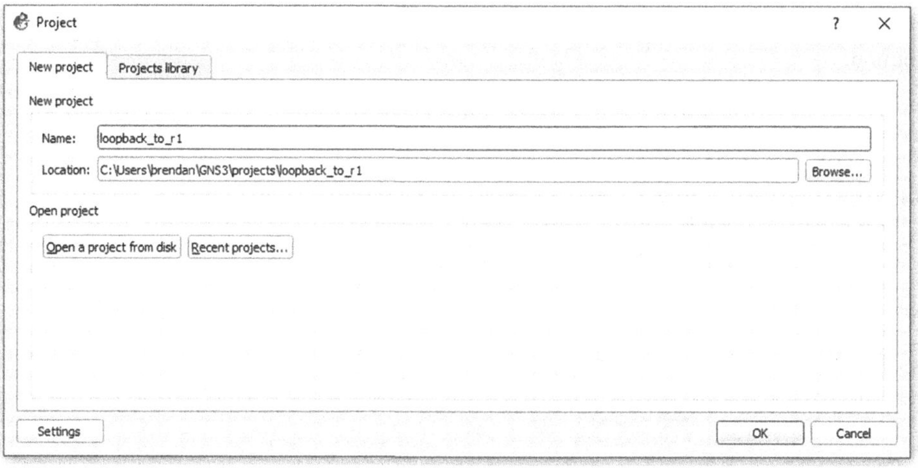

Figure 10-64. *GNS3, creating a new project, loopback_to_r1*

3 Now put together a simple lab topology. Open the "All devices" menu and drop one IOS router and one cloud onto the Topology canvas. R1 will run on GNS3 VM, and Cloud-1 will be running on the host PC. Look at the server's summary for your reference. See Figure 10-65.

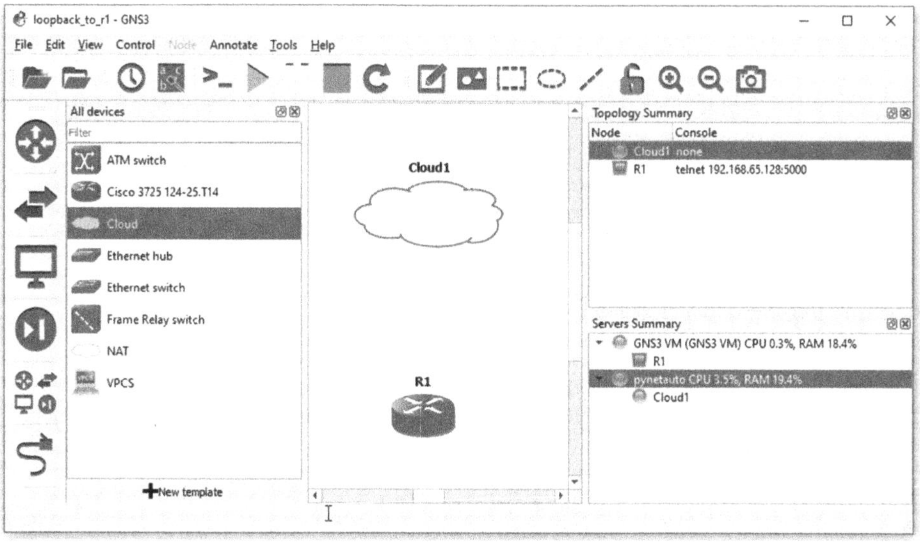

Figure 10-65. *GNS3, creating a topology*

(*continued*)

#	Task
4	Right-click Cloud-1, select Configure, and then select "Show special Ethernet interfaces." Add the loopback interface from the drop-down menu; delete the Ethernet and any other interfaces, and click the Close button. If you do not see the Microsoft loopback interface, you probably did not reboot your PC or incorrectly added the cloud to the GNS3 VM. Suppose the GNS3 does not recognize the Microsoft loopback even after rebooting. In that case, there may be a problem with the operating system you are using, or possibly, there was a problem during the interface installation. If you run into a problem at this point, go back to the previous steps and correct the issue. See Figure 10-66.

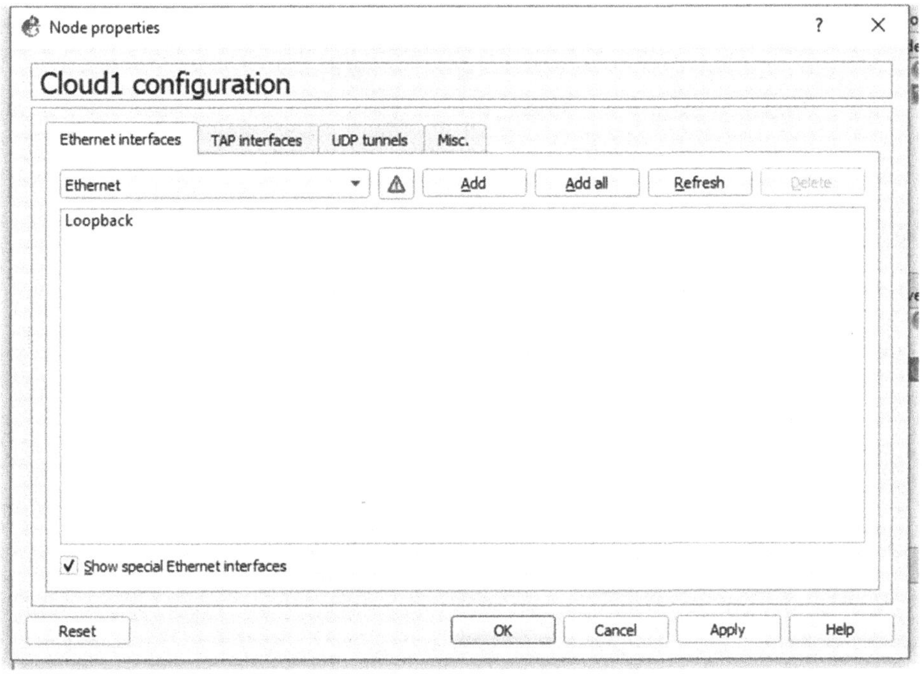

Figure 10-66. GNS3, adding the loopback interface to Cloud-1

#	Task
5	Right-click and rename Cloud-1 to Host-PC. Then connect the Loopback interface to R1s f0/0, as shown in Figure 10-67. Please note that if GNS3 throws an error and refuses to connect, you may need to change "User account control setting" on Windows 10.

#	Task

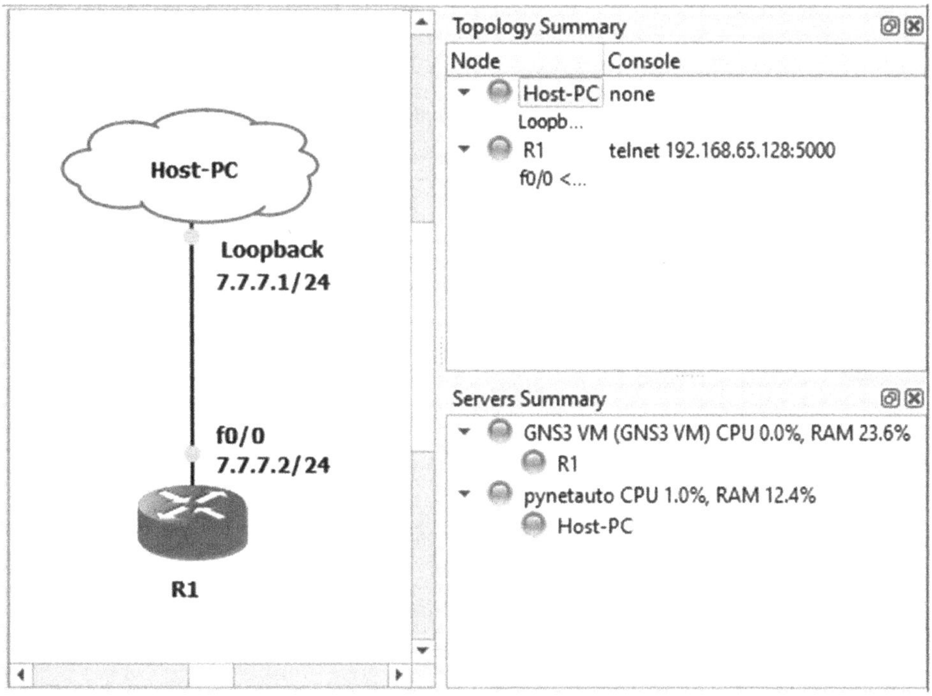

Figure 10-67. *GNS3, connecting the Microsoft loopback to R1's f0/0*

How do you change the User account control setting?

From Control Panel, open "User account control setting" and change the setting to "Never notify." This will allow you to connect the MS Loopback interface with GNS3 devices. After making this change, you must restart the PC one more time. See Figure 10-68 and Figure 10-69.

#	Task

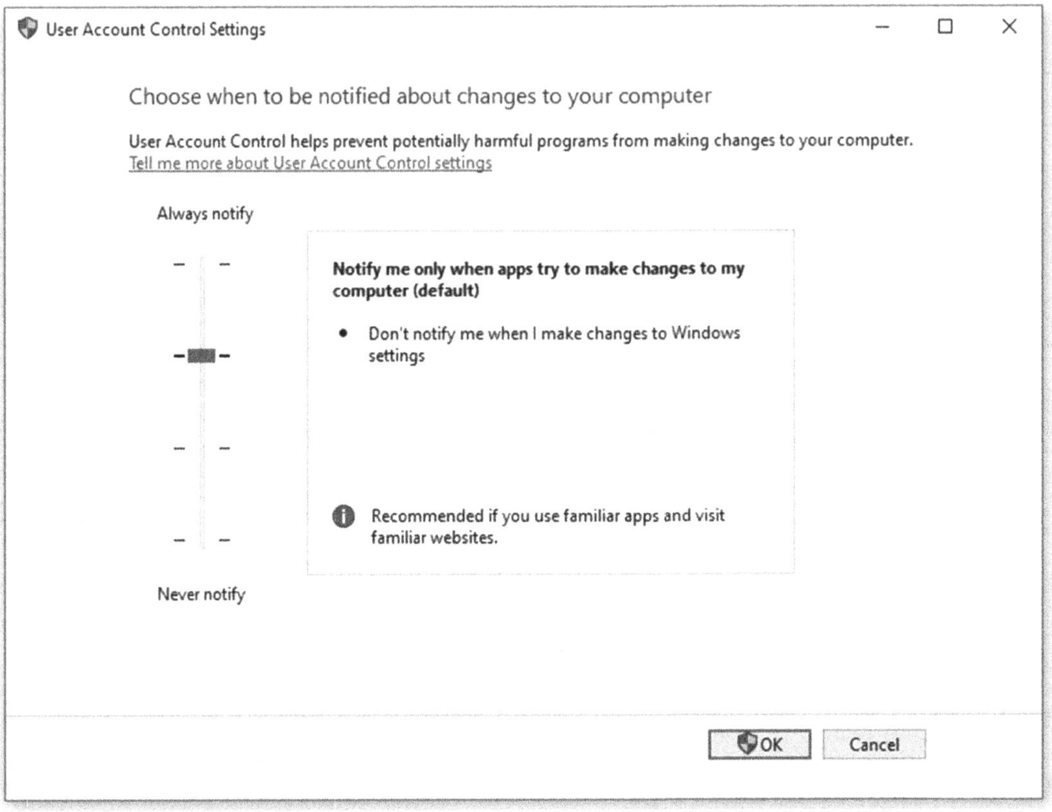

Figure 10-68. *User account control setting, default*

#	Task

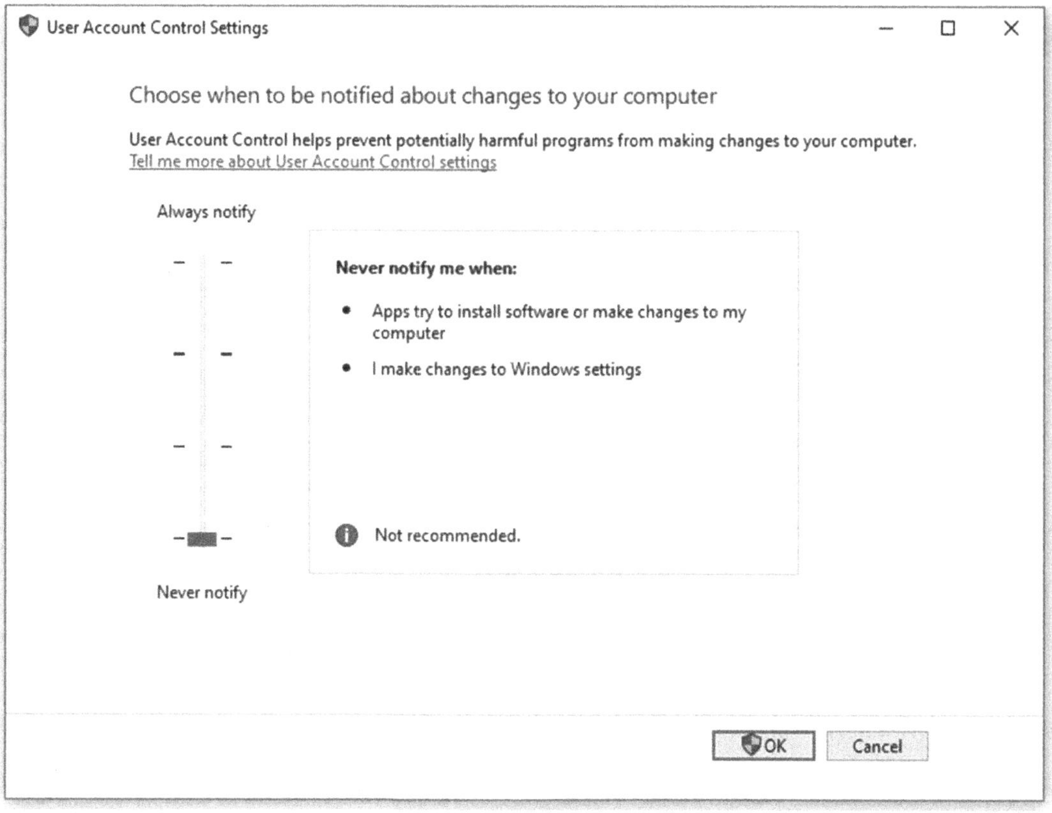

Figure 10-69. *User account control setting, changing to "Never notify"*

How to open Windows Defender Firewall to allow ICMP?

To allow GNS3's R1 to send ICMP (`ping`) packets to the host PC, you have to open Windows Defender Firewall with Advanced Security and enable the settings on the inbound rules shown in Figure 10-70.

#	Task

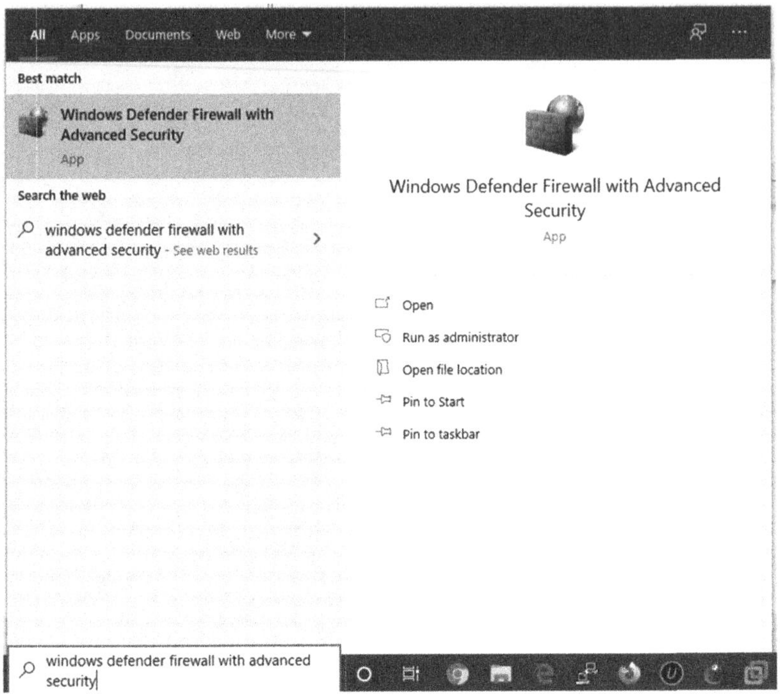

Figure 10-70. *Windows 10, opening Windows Defender Firewall with Advanced Security*

You can open Windows Defender Firewall in Figure 10-71.

- File and Printer Sharing (Echo Request – ICMPv4-In) Private
- File and Printer Sharing (Echo Request – ICMPv6-In) Private

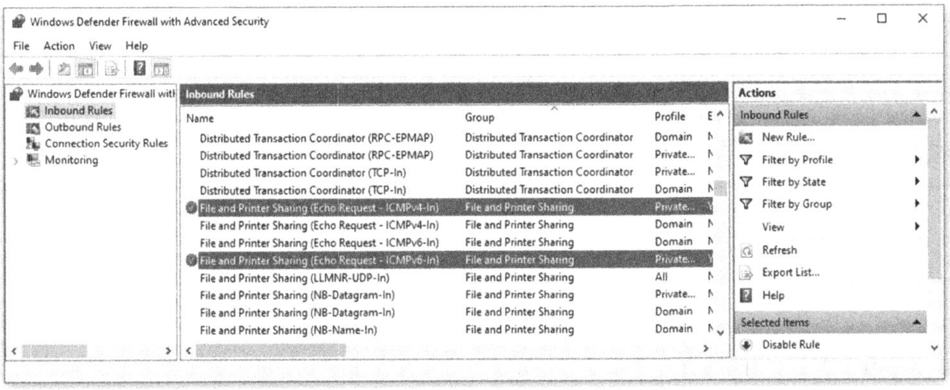

Figure 10-71. *Windows 10 Windows Defender Firewall with Advanced Security, enabling file and printer sharing to allow ICMP*

#	Task

6	Open R1's console and configure R1's f0/0 interface as follows:
	`R1(config)#interface FastEthernet 0/0`
	`R1(config-if)#ip address 7.7.7.2 255.255.255.0`
	`R1(config-if)#no shut`
	`R1(config-if)#end`
	`R1#ping 7.7.7.1`
	`Type escape sequence to abort.`
	`Sending 5, 100-byte ICMP Echos to 7.7.7.1, timeout is 2 seconds:`
	`.!!!!`
	`Success rate is 80 percent (4/5), round-trip min/avg/max = 8/11/12 ms`
	`R1#write memory`
	`Building configuration...`
	`OK`

7	On the host laptop/PC's command-line prompt, ping the R1's f0/0 interface IP address 7.7.7.2 to verify communication.
	`C:\Users\brendan>ping 7.7.7.2`
	
	`Pinging 7.7.7.2 with 32 bytes of data:`
	`Reply from 7.7.7.2: bytes=32 time=22ms TTL=255`
	`Reply from 7.7.7.2: bytes=32 time=6ms TTL=255`
	`Reply from 7.7.7.2: bytes=32 time=8ms TTL=255`
	`Reply from 7.7.7.2: bytes=32 time=11ms TTL=255`
	
	`Ping statistics for 7.7.7.2:`
	`Packets: Sent = 4, Received = 4, Lost = 0 (0% loss),`
	`Approximate round trip times in milli-seconds:`
	`Minimum = 6ms, Maximum = 22ms, Average = 11ms`

8	Configure the username and Telnet on R1. For testing purposes, Telnet is configured here: `R1#configure terminal` — Enter configuration mode `R1(config)#username pynetauto privilege 15 secret cisco123` — Add a local user named `pynetauto` with privilege 15 and password `cisco123` `R1(config)#line vty 0 15` — Enter vty line mode `R1(config-line)#transport input telnet` — Enable Telnet `R1(config-line)#login local` — Use local user credentials `R1(config-line)#logging synchronous` — Change lines when a log message is received `R1(config-line)#end` — Move back to exec-mode `R1#copy running-config startup-config` — Save the running configuration to the startup configuration
9	Using PuTTY, Telnet into R1 using port 23. See Figure 10-72.

(*continued*)

#	Task

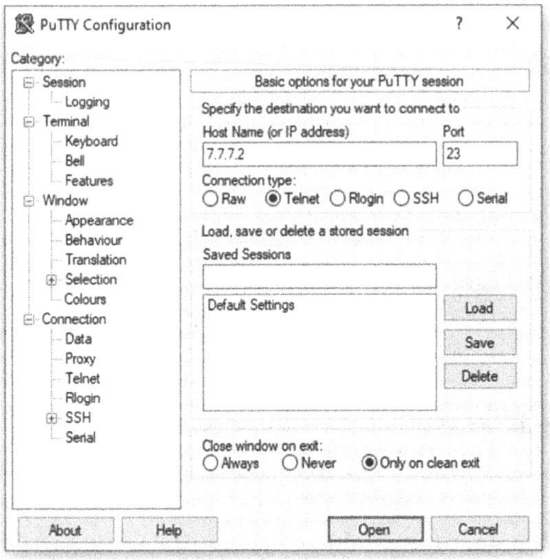

Figure 10-72. *PuTTY, Telnet into R1*

10 Enter the user ID and password to log into R1 (7.7.7.2) from the host PC (7.7.7.1).

```
User Access Verification
Username: pynetauto
Password: ********
R1#
```

You have successfully connected to the IOS device running on GNS3 from the host PC. Now you can configure the GNS3 router from the comfort of your Windows PC.

Configuring the GNS3 IOS Router Using a Python Script from the Windows Host PC

Here are some Python lab objectives:

- Locate Python resources and reuse the code for your learning
- Telnet into a single Cisco IOS device
- Configure a loopback interface and f0/1

Now let's create a simple Python Telnet script on the host PC's Windows and configure a loopback and FastEthernet 0/1 interfaces. Even if you have not written a working Python script before, just follow along and complete each task in this lab. Go to the URL mentioned in the task, scroll down to the bottom of the web page, and locate a Python Telnet example. Copying this example, you will create your first Cisco router interacting script via Telnet. This script uses Python built-in libraries to connect to your GNS3 R1 router using the `getpass` module to get the user input and password.

A Python library is a collection of useful modules. The Python modules can be considered small programs that are written and tested for other users, so you do not have to reinvent the wheel every time. The built-in or standard libraries are libraries installed when Python gets installed on your machine. The external or nonstandard libraries are the set of modules that get installed on your OS on-demand.

Do not try to understand everything in the sample code. I will provide explanations later. Try to focus on the given task and pay close attention to typing errors. When you write code, every comma, full stop, and space matters. Spacing really matters in Python scripting.

#	Task
1	First, go to the Python installation folder, `C:\Python38`, and create a new folder to store your scripts. Here I have created a folder named `myscripts`. See Figure 10-73.

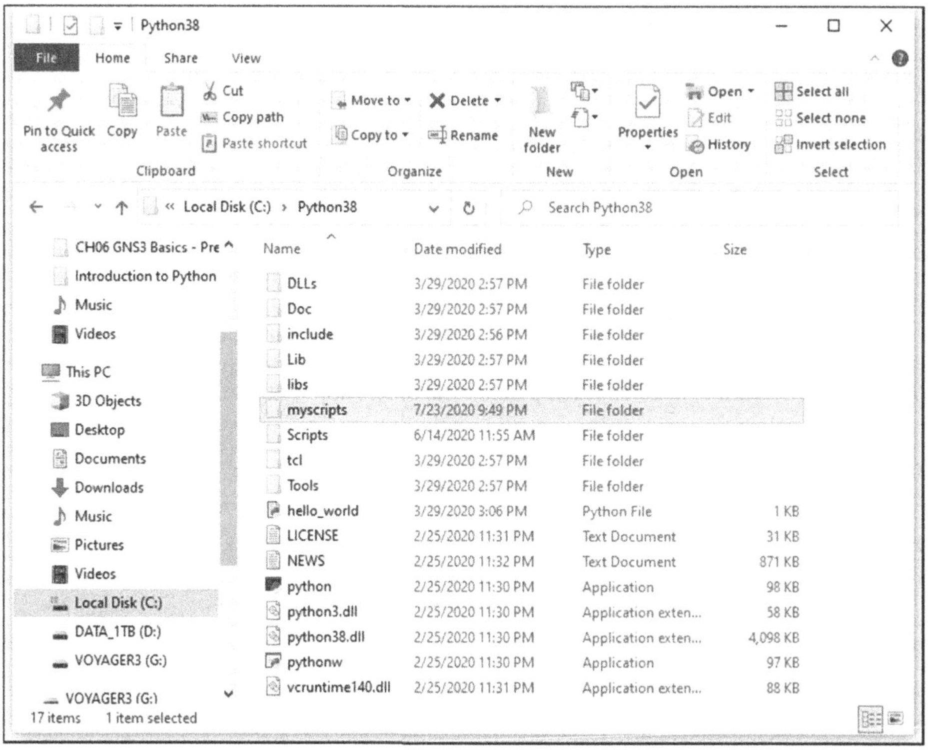

Figure 10-73. *Host PC, creating a new folder*

(continued)

#	Task
2	Both the getpass and telnet libraries used in this script are built-in (standard) Python libraries, so you do not need to install them separately. Just go to the following URL and follow along: https://docs.python.org/3/library/telnetlib.html.

Telnet Example

Here's a simple example illustrating the typical use:

```
import getpass
import telnetlib

HOST = "localhost"
user = input("Enter your remote account: ")
password = getpass.getpass()

tn = telnetlib.Telnet(HOST)

tn.read_until(b"login: ")
tn.write(user.encode('ascii') + b"\n")
if password:
    tn.read_until(b"Password: ")
    tn.write(password.encode('ascii') + b"\n")

tn.write(b"ls\n")
tn.write(b"exit\n")

print(tn.read_all().decode('ascii'))
```

#	Task
3	Copy and paste the previous content using Notepad++. Save the file as telnet_script1.py under the C:\python38\myscripts folder on your Windows PC. Modify the file as follows; the modified part of codes are in bold. Save the script as a .py file once completed. This script will be explained in detail in a later chapter, but for now, simply follow the lab word by word. When you start your Python coding journey, you will often learn the most from mimicking or copying other people's work; this is similar to how newborns learn to talk from their parents and others around them.

```
telnet_script1.py
import getpass
import telnetlib

HOST = "7.7.7.2" <<< Router ip
user = input("Enter your telnet username: ")
password = getpass.getpass()

tn = telnetlib.Telnet(HOST)

tn.read_until(b"Username: ") <<< Should be same as the router prompt, ensure to
update this line.
tn.write(user.encode('ascii') + b"\n")
if password:
    tn.read_until(b"Password: ")
    tn.write(password.encode('ascii') + b"\n")
```

#	Task
	``` tn.write(b"conf t\n") tn.write(b"int loop 0\n") tn.write(b"ip add 1.1.1.1 255.255.255.255\n") tn.write(b"int f0/1\n") tn.write(b"ip add 20.20.20.1 255.255.255.0\n") tn.write(b"no shut\n") tn.write(b"end\n") tn.write(b"show ip int bri\n") tn.write(b"exit\n") print(tn.read_all().decode('ascii')) ```
4	Open R1's console from GNS3, or use PuTTY to Telnet into R1 (7.7.7.2) and check the current interface status by running `show ip interface brief`. We confirmed that there is only one interface configured at this stage.

```
R1#show ip interface brief
Interface              IP-Address      OK? Method    Status
Protocol
FastEthernet0/0        7.7.7.2         YES NVRAM     up                        up
FastEthernet0/1        unassigned      YES NVRAM     administratively down     down
```

#	Task
5	On R1's console, enable debugging for Telnet authentication to confirm the authentication and activities. When you run the script and authenticate, keep R1's console window open and observe the logs.
	`R1# debug ip auth-proxy telnet` Enables debugging for telnet authentication
6	Now open Windows PowerShell, navigate to the `C:\Python38\myscripts\` folder, and run `python telnet_script1.py`. When prompted for a username and password, authenticate using the credentials created in the previous section. For a password, as you type in, you will not see any characters as the `getpass` module will hide this information automatically.

```
PS C:\Users\brendan> cd C:\Python38\myscripts\
PS C:\Python38\myscripts> python telnet_script1.py
Enter your telnet username: pynetauto
Password: ********

R1#conf t
Enter configuration commands, one per line.  End with CNTL/Z.
R1(config)#int loop 0
R1(config-if)#ip add 1.1.1.1 255.255.255.255
R1(config-if)#int f0/1
R1(config-if)#ip add 20.20.20.1 255.255.255.0
R1(config-if)#no shut
R1(config-if)#end
R1#show ip int bri
Interface                  IP-Address      OK? Method     Status
Protocol
FastEthernet0/0            7.7.7.2         YES NVRAM      up                   up
FastEthernet0/1            20.20.20.1      YES manual     up                   up
Loopback0                  1.1.1.1         YES manual     up                   up
R1#exit
```

(continued)

#	Task
7	Now go back to R1's console, check the Telnet logs, and run the `show ip interface brief` command again. The result will look similar to the following, with `Loopback0` and `FastEthernet0/1` configured with new IP addresses and showing as up/up.

```
Telnet session logs during remote configuration
R1#
AUTH-PROXY Telnet debugging is on
R1#
*Mar  1 00:59:51.655: %SYS-5-CONFIG_I: Configured from console by pynetauto on vty0
(7.7.7.1)
*Mar  1 00:59:51.687: %LINEPROTO-5-UPDOWN: Line protocol on Interface Loopback0,
changed state to up
R1#
*Mar  1 00:59:53.583: %LINK-3-UPDOWN: Interface FastEthernet0/1, changed state to up
*Mar  1 00:59:54.583: %LINEPROTO-5-UPDOWN: Line protocol on Interface
FastEthernet0/1, changed state to up
R1#show ip interface brief
Interface                  IP-Address      OK? Method    Status
Protocol
FastEthernet0/0            7.7.7.2         YES NVRAM     up                     up
FastEthernet0/1            20.20.20.1      YES manual    up                     up
Loopback0                  1.1.1.1         YES manual    up                     up
```

Cisco IOS and GNS3 Appliance Lab

GNS3 has many useful templates that you can use while studying networking, security, and systems concepts. You can add preconfigured templates and install them on the GNS3 VM as appliances and use them in your lab. You can even install Palo Alto firewalls with a full GUI interface and use them in your lab. For demonstration purposes, you will import a simple Linux Docker image and perform an interactive Telnet session from the Linux Docker image.

The objectives of this lab are as follows:

- Learn to install GNS3 appliance devices
- Learn to assign an IP address manually on a Linux server Ethernet interface
- Learn to run live interactive Telnet sessions to manage Cisco IOS devices

Importing and Installing the GNS3 Linux Appliance Server

This lab continues from the last loopback lab. First, let's add a Linux Docker appliance from the GNS3 template and then add it to the existing topology.

#	Task
1	In the GNS3 main window, go to File ➤ + New template (Figure 11-74). Introduce all the remaining figures. Alternatively, you can open "All devices" and click "+New template" as well.

#	Task

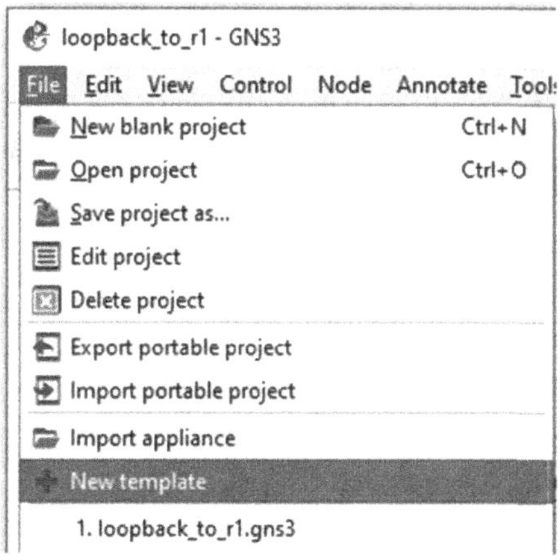

Figure 10-74. *GNS3, +New template*

#	Task
2	In the "New template" wizard window, leave the selection on "Install an appliance from the GNS3 server (recommended)" and click the Next button.
3	On the Appliances from the server screen, type in **Network Automation** or use the drop-down menu under Guests and select Network Automation Docker; then click the Install button. See Figure 10-75.

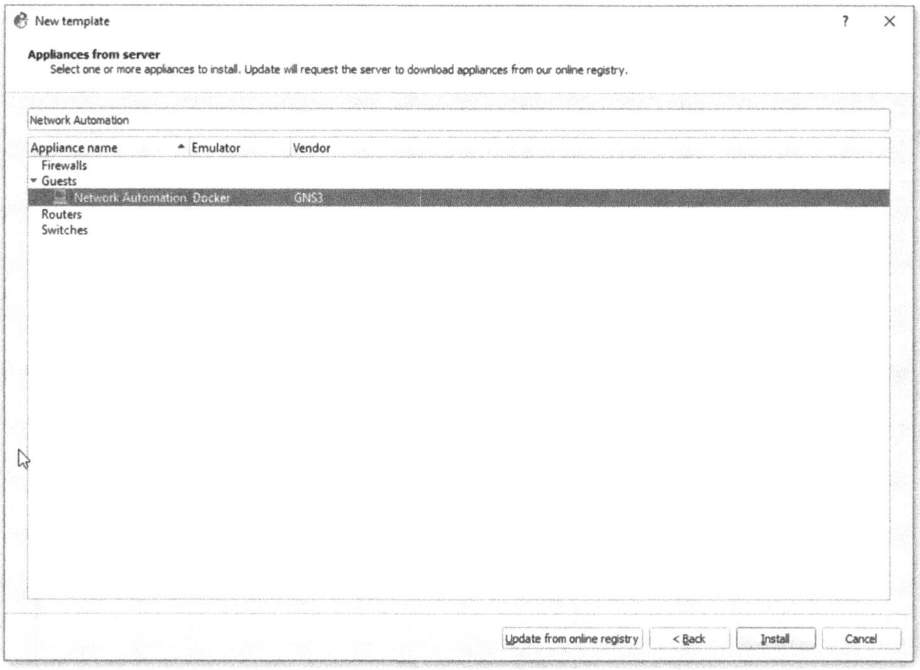

Figure 10-75. *GNS3 new template, selecting an appliance Linux server*

(continued)

#	Task

There are a lot of pre-installed appliance Dockerized and Qemu images for our convenience on GNS3. Network Automation Docker image is basically an Ubuntu 18 LTS server Dockerized image for running quick network labs. When Docker powers off, what gets installed will be defaulted to the original settings. Docker is not a fully blown virtual machine like your CentOS or Ubuntu VMs as it is a light-weight appliance and relies on hosting server's kernels for operation. You will learn more about Docker in the previous chapter.

4 On the Server screen, click the Next button to move to the next screen.

5 On the next screen, to finish and close the "New template" window, click the Finish button.

6 Click the OK button to add the Network Automation Server template. See Figure 10-76.

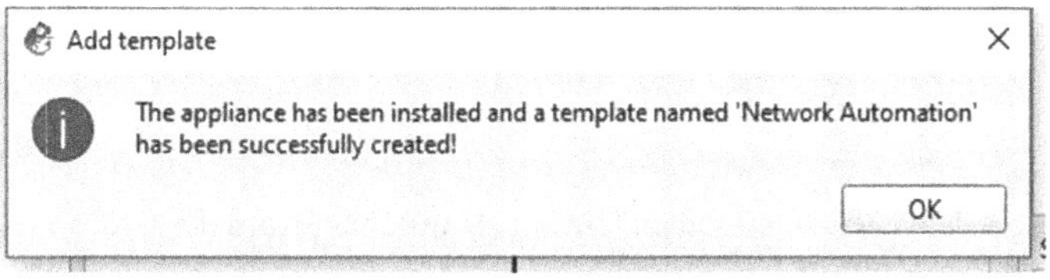

Figure 10-76. *GNS3 new template, "Add template" window*

7 Now go back to GNS3's main user interface and select the "End devices" icon on the left. The "End devices" icon is the one that looks like a computer screen. You will see your new appliance device, the Network Automation server, on the list. Make sure your computer is connected to the Internet and select the icon. Then drag and drop the icon onto the Topology canvas. This action will initiate the Docker pull action and start downloading the Docker image from the Internet (DockerHub). See Figure 10-77.

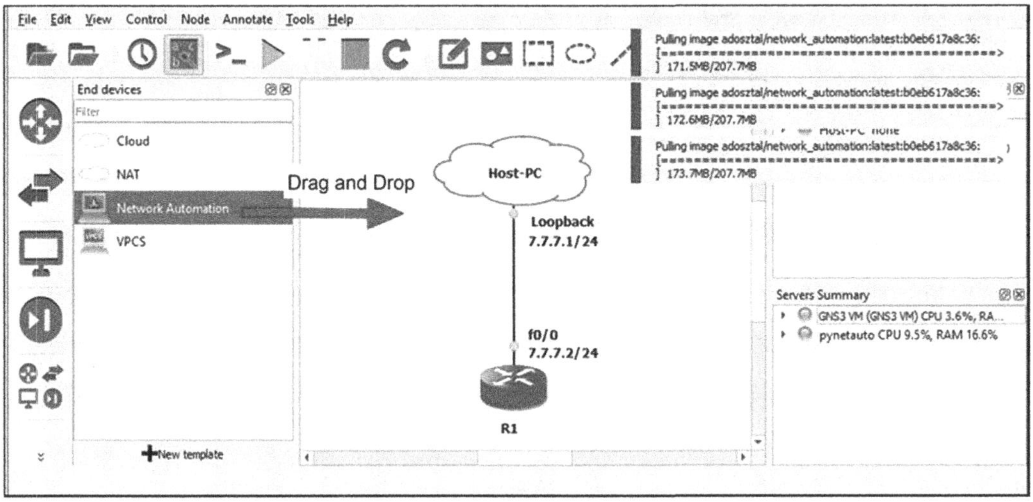

Figure 10-77. *GNS3, pulling the Network Automation appliance from the DockerHub*

#	Task
8	Now connect eth0 of NetworkAutomation-1 server to R1's f0/1 interface and power on the server. See Figure 10-78.

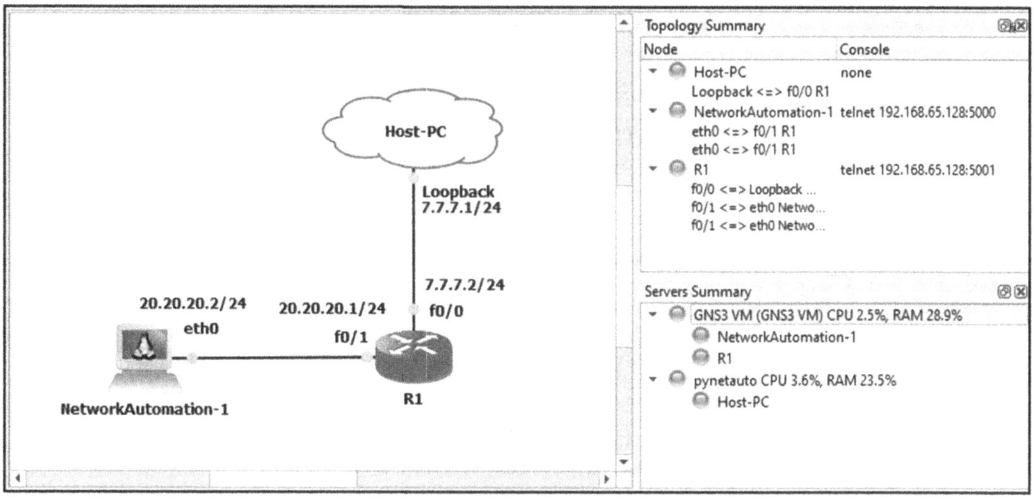

Figure 10-78. *GNS3, connecting NetworkAutomation-1 to R1*

9 Once the Docker server is booted up, check the OS version by running the `cat /etc/*release` Linux command. This server is a containerized (Docker) Ubuntu 18.04 LTS Server image.

```
root@NetworkAutomation-1:~# cat /etc/*release
DISTRIB_ID=Ubuntu
DISTRIB_RELEASE=18.04
DISTRIB_CODENAME=bionic
DISTRIB_DESCRIPTION="Ubuntu 18.04.4 LTS"
NAME="Ubuntu"
VERSION="18.04.4 LTS (Bionic Beaver)"
ID=ubuntu
ID_LIKE=debian
PRETTY_NAME="Ubuntu 18.04.4 LTS"
VERSION_ID="18.04"
HOME_URL="https://www.ubuntu.com/"
SUPPORT_URL="https://help.ubuntu.com/"
BUG_REPORT_URL="https://bugs.launchpad.net/ubuntu/"
PRIVACY_POLICY_URL="https://www.ubuntu.com/legal/terms-and-policies/privacy-policy"
VERSION_CODENAME=bionic
UBUNTU_CODENAME=bionic
```

Congratulations! Now you have another server where you can practice your Python scripts. You will be learning more about how to create a Docker image later. Remember, a Docker image is a kind of ad hoc server. When the Docker machine powers off, everything resets to the default, and you will lose your previous work. To save the work, you may have to save it to a mapped drive or capture another Docker image while it is in the running state. This is beyond our topic, but take time to research the Docker and Kubernetes concept as this is another hot topic in the systems automation space.

Manually Assigning IP Address to GNS3 Linux Appliance Server

Here, let's practice assigning an IP address, default gateway, and DNS server to the Linux appliance server you just installed in the previous steps. Make sure you send a ping to the default gateway to confirm the communication is OK. You will be connecting to the Internet in the next section, so you do not need to ping any Internet addresses.

#	Task
1	Run the following commands on your NetworkAutomation-1 Linux server to assign a new IP address and add a default gateway and Google's public name server. This same method can be used to assign IP addresses on a live Linux server too.

```
root@NetworkAutomation-1:~# ifconfig eth0 <<< Check eth0 interface
eth0: flags=4163<UP,BROADCAST,RUNNING,MULTICAST>  mtu 1500
    inet6 fe80::2cbb:cdff:fe4e:96fc  prefixlen 64  scopeid 0x20<link>
    ether 2e:bb:cd:4e:96:fc  txqueuelen 1000  (Ethernet)
    RX packets 105  bytes 10924 (10.9 KB)
    RX errors 0  dropped 91  overruns 0  frame 0
    TX packets 13  bytes 1006 (1.0 KB)
    TX errors 0  dropped 0 overruns 0  carrier 0  collisions 0

root@NetworkAutomation-1:~# ifconfig eth0 20.20.20.2 netmask 255.255.255.0 up <<<
manually configure IP address and bring up eth0
root@NetworkAutomation-1:~# route add default gw 20.20.20.1 <<< Configure Gateway
root@NetworkAutomation-1:~# echo "nameserver 8.8.8.8" > /etc/resolve.conf <<<
Configure DNS server
root@NetworkAutomation-1:~# ifconfig eth0 <<< Check configuration
eth0: flags=4163<UP,BROADCAST,RUNNING,MULTICAST>  mtu 1500
    inet 20.20.20.2  netmask 255.255.255.0  broadcast 20.20.20.255
    inet6 fe80::2cbb:cdff:fe4e:96fc  prefixlen 64  scopeid 0x20<link>
    ether 2e:bb:cd:4e:96:fc  txqueuelen 1000  (Ethernet)
    RX packets 109  bytes 11470 (11.4 KB)
    RX errors 0  dropped 94  overruns 0  frame 0
    TX packets 13  bytes 1006 (1.0 KB)
    TX errors 0  dropped 0 overruns 0  carrier 0  collisions 0

root@NetworkAutomation-1:~# ping 20.20.20.1 -c 3 <<< test IP connectivity
PING 20.20.20.1 (20.20.20.1) 56(84) bytes of data.
64 bytes from 20.20.20.1: icmp_seq=1 ttl=255 time=30.8 ms
64 bytes from 20.20.20.1: icmp_seq=2 ttl=255 time=11.0 ms
64 bytes from 20.20.20.1: icmp_seq=3 ttl=255 time=6.54 ms

--- 20.20.20.1 ping statistics ---
3 packets transmitted, 3 received, 0% packet loss, time 2002ms
rtt min/avg/max/mdev = 6.546/16.167/30.877/10.565 ms
```

You can also configure the network interface of an appliance machine by clicking the NetworkAutomation-1 icon with the right button and selecting the "Edit config" option. You can manually configure it from here or simply remove the # keys to get a valid IP address from a DHCP server. We have not set a DHCP service on the 20.20.20.0/24 network, so we chose to configure the IP address manually. See Figure 10-79.

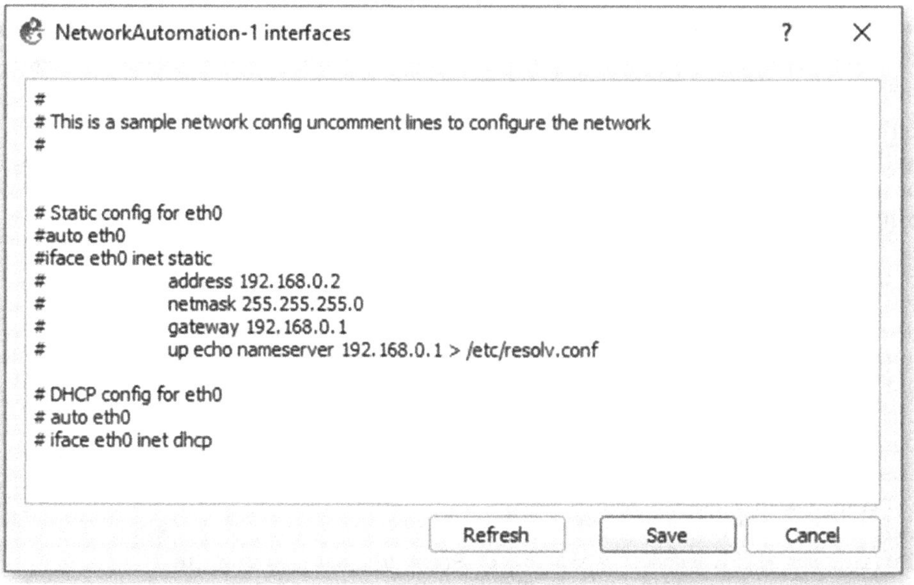

Figure 10-79. *NetworkAutomation-1, editing the config file*

Using the GNS3 Appliance Linux's Python to Manage R1

In this lab, you will use the Python installed on the GNS3 appliance Linux server to manage R1 from the live Telnet session. This lab continues from the previous section.

#	Task
1	First, check which Python versions are pre-installed on this server using the commands shown in Figure 10-79. If you have downloaded the same Dockerized Linux server as this book, it will be pre-installed with Python 2.7.17 and 3.8.3.

```
root@NetworkAutomation-1:~# which python
/usr/bin/python
root@NetworkAutomation-1:~# python --version
Python 2.7.17
root@NetworkAutomation-1:~# which python3
/usr/bin/python3
root@NetworkAutomation-1:~# python3 -V
Python 3.8.3
```

(continued)

 # Task

2 Now start the Python 3 interactive session by typing `python3`.

```
root@NetworkAutomation-1:~# python3
Python 3.8.3 (default, May 14 2020, 20:11:43)
GCC 7.5.0 on linux
Type "help", "copyright", "credits" or "license" for more information.
>>>
```

3 Now in the Python interpreter window of the GNS3 Appliance Linux server, type in the following Python commands word by word. Do not worry too much about these commands' deep meanings; for now, try to get familiar with the process within the environment.

Here, you add a loopback 5 to R1 via a Telnet session and then print out the session logs. After initiating the Telnet session, you send multiple `tn.write` commands for loopback 5 configurations. Then you must exit the session by sending the `tn.write(b"exit\n")` command to close the Telnet session; then, you can print them out of your Telnet session.

```
>>> import getpass <<< Import getpass module
>>> import telnetlib << Import telnetlib module
>>> tn = telnetlib.Telnet("20.20.20.1") <<< Create a telnet session to 20.20.20.1
>>> tn.write("pynetauto".encode('ascii') + b"\n") <<< Send username 'pynetauto' to R1
>>> tn.write("cisco123".encode('ascii') + b"\n") <<< Send password 'cisco123' to R1
>>> tn.write(b"configure terminal\n") <<< Enter config mode
>>> tn.write(b"interface loopback 5\n")
>>> tn.write(b"ip address 5.5.5.5 255.255.255.255\n")
>>> tn.write(b"end\n")
>>> tn.write(b"exit\n")
>>> print(tn.read_all().decode('ascii')) <<< Print all session logs in tn
```

On a successful interactive session, the output will look similar to the following. Watch out for every comma, full stop, and space and also avoid any typos. Python coding is not as glamorous as preached by some Python evangelists; your fingertips must touch the keyboard for every comma, full stop, space, and each character. Don't buy the snake oil.

```
User Access Verification

Username: pynetauto
Password:
R1#configure terminal
Enter configuration commands, one per line.  End with CNTL/Z.
R1(config)#interface loopback 5
R1(config-if)#ip address 5.5.5.5 255.255.255.255
R1(config-if)#end
R1#exit
```

#	Task
4	Now continue with the `show ip interface brief` command and print out the logs. Notice that you do not have to import the modules again as you have remained in the same session. The b before the router commands indicates that the commands in double quotation marks are sent as bytes, and \n represents a newline, which in this case means pressing down the Enter key once on your keyboard.

```
>>> tn = telnetlib.Telnet("20.20.20.1") <<< Create a telnet session to 20.20.20.1
>>> tn.write("pynetauto".encode('ascii') + b"\n") <<< Send username 'pynetauto' to R1
>>> tn.write("cisco123".encode('ascii') + b"\n") <<< Send password 'cisco123' to R1
>>> tn.write(b"show ip interface brief\n") <<< Send 'show ip int brief' command
>>> tn.write(b"exit\n") <<< Send 'exit' command
>>> print(tn.read_all().decode('ascii')) <<< Print all session logs in tn
```

Upon completing the lab task, you will see the result of the `show ip interface brief` command run on R1.

```
User Access Verification
Username: pynetauto
Password:
R1#show ip interface brief
Interface              IP-Address      OK? Method Status                Protocol
FastEthernet0/0        7.7.7.2         YES NVRAM  up                    up
FastEthernet0/1        20.20.20.1      YES manual up                    up
FastEthernet1/0        unassigned      YES NVRAM  administratively down down
Loopback0              1.1.1.1         YES manual up                    up
Loopback5              5.5.5.5         YES manual up                    up
R1#exit
```

You have completed an interactive Telnet session using Python 3. When you develop code to validate and verify the Python interpreter or interactive session with network devices, you can test parts of your Python code. Now, copy and paste the same commands into a text editor of your choice and give a filename a `.py` file extension. The Python scripts used in this chapter are saved as `chapter6_codes` and available for download at `https://github.com/pynetauto/apress_pynetauto`.

Summary

In this chapter, you learned many GNS3 techniques that will help you successfully run the rest of the labs in this book. You learned how to install GNS3, how to make simple GNS3 topologies, how to integrate a Cisco IOS router on GNS3, how to install a GNS3 appliance server to manage an IOS router running on GNS3, and how to install the Microsoft loopback interface for communication between a GNS3 device to the host PC. Also, you learned how to connect a GNS3 router to the GNS3's appliance Linux Python server. In Chapter 11, we will create a new GNS3 project to communicate with Ubuntu and CentOS virtual servers with the IOS router R1 via Telnet. We will expand on what we have learned in this chapter and get enough practice to step forward.

CHAPTER 11

Cisco IOS Labs

This will be one of the shortest chapters in this book. You will test-drive your Linux virtual machines (VMs) to interact with the IOS router, R1, via Telnet. You will learn to create a new GNS3 project, run a quick file transfer testing lab using simple Cisco configurations, and then finally make a clone of the GNS3 project. You are making progressive steps toward Python network automation.

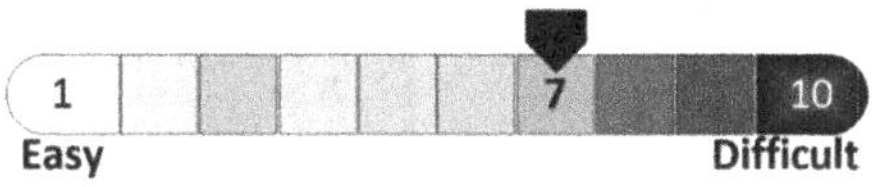

Cisco IOS and the Linux VM Lab

In this lab, you are going to connect your Linux virtual machines to GNS3 devices. In most production environments, running Python on Linux platforms is the norm to gain the numerous advantages of using Linux in an enterprise environment. So, merely understanding how to write Python code is insufficient to create a useful application to automate and streamline a network engineer's tasks. You need to have a deeper understanding of the whole IT ecosystem and know how different systems and technologies live harmoniously in an IT ecosystem. You have to be willing to step outside of your comfort zone and put personal effort into understanding other technologies in the IT ecosystem.

In this Cisco IOS and Linux VM example, we will configure a new topology to prepare for the next chapter. Figure 11-1 shows the topology that you are going to configure. Note that the CentOS 8.1 and Ubuntu 20 LTS Linux servers are already connected to VMnet8 on the VMware Workstation in the topology shown. In GNS3, we will use representational icons to mark that they are on the 192.168.130.0/24 subnet. If you are using a different IP subnet for VMnet8, your IP address will be different.

The topology uses NAT-1 running on the host PC, connected to VMnet8 of VMware Workstation; it also acts as a DHCP server and a gateway to connect to the Internet. The host PC with IP address 7.7.7.1 is the cloud with the Microsoft loopback interface connecting to R1's F0/1 on the 7.7.7.0/24 network.

B. Choi, *Introduction to Python Network Automation*, https://doi.org/10.1007/978-1-4842-6806-3_11

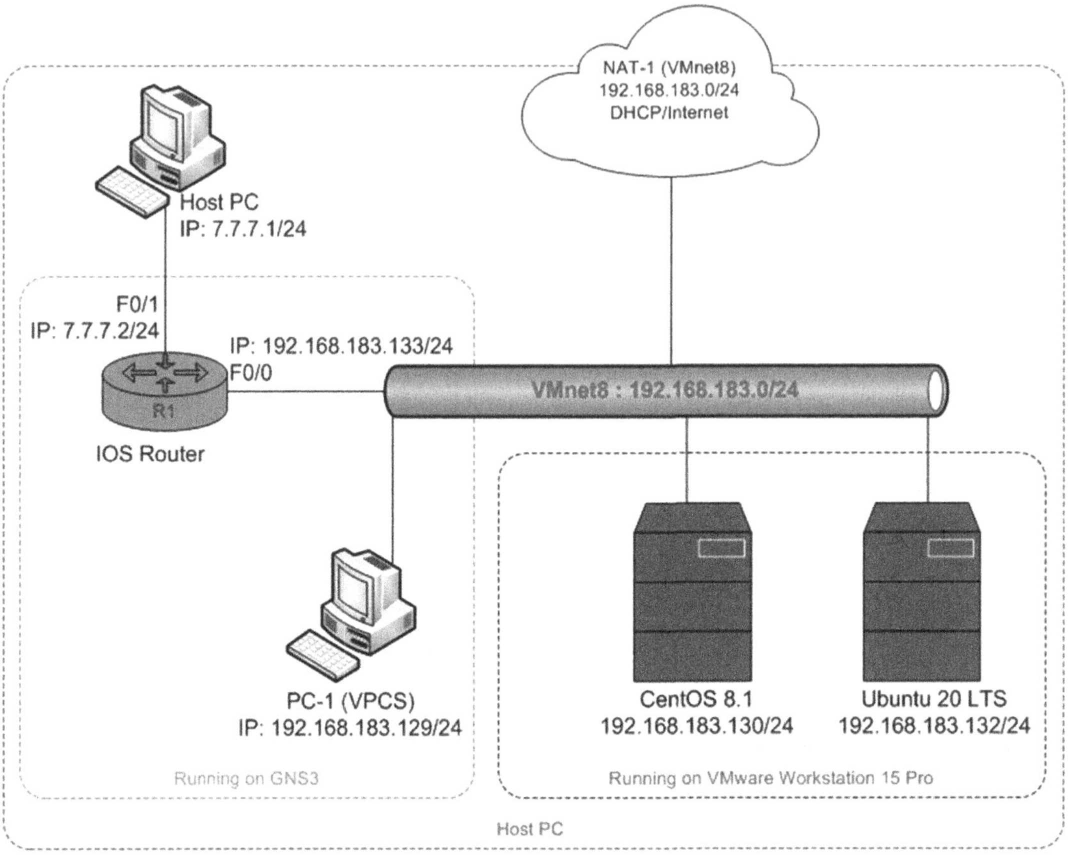

Figure 11-1. *linuxvm2ios lab topology*

Creating a New GNS3 Project for the Linux VM Lab

Let's create a new project to connect Linux VM servers to a new IOS router. The process of creating a new project is similar to the previous projects in Chapter 10. Let's create a new project to connect our Linux virtual machines to an IOS router.

#	Task
1	From the GNS3 main menu, select File ➤ New Blank Project to open a new project window.
2	Give your new project a new name. The new project name is `linuxvm2ios` for this lab. You do not have to follow the same naming convention. Feel free to give your project a unique and meaningful name. See Figure 11-2.

#	Task

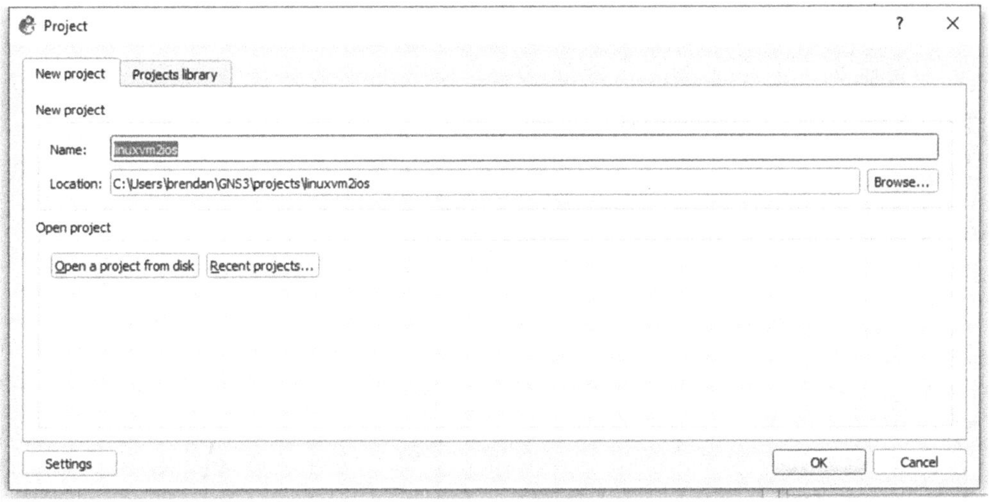

Figure 11-2. *linuxvm2ios project, creating a new GNS3 project*

3 Configure the GNS3 topology as shown in Figure 11-3. While building a new topology, refer to GNS3's topology and server summary window for more information. You will be able to see how each device is connected. When all devices are connected, start R1 and PC-1.

The following points are connection references while connecting and configuring the topology on the GNS3 canvas:

- Run NAT-1 on the host server. (Use NAT from VMnet8 of Workstation.)
- Ethernetswitch-1 is installed on the GNS3 VM server and only serves as a dummy switch to connect multiple devices.
- PC-1 is a VPCS installed on GNS3. VPCS makes it easy to test communication between devices. This is similar to configuring dummy loopback interfaces on the router.
- Host-PC marked with the Microsoft loopback is cloud-1, with a changed icon for aesthetics only.
- Lastly, the CentOS 8.1 and Ubuntu 20.4 LTS servers are directly connected to VMnet8 on VMware Workstation and will not show up on the GNS3 topology. These server icons are also for aesthetic representation.

(continued)

#	Task

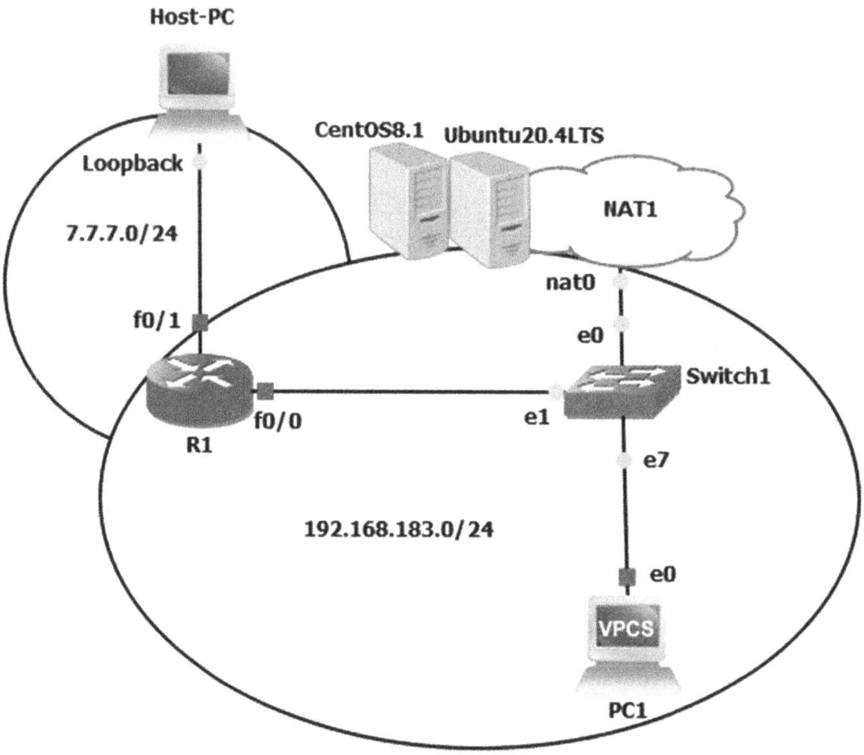

Figure 11-3. linuxvm2ios project, GNS3 topology connection

Note that in the topology in Figure 11-3, when you drag and drop NAT-1 and Host-PC (cloud-1), the network of VMnet8 should be used, so the host PC (pynetauto) should be selected. Your PC name will be different. See Figure 11-4.

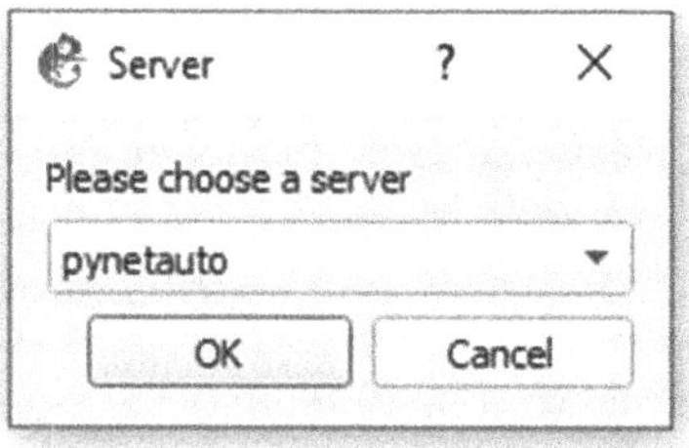

Figure 11-4. linuxvm2ios project, selecting the host server for NAT-1 and cloud-1

Use the Servers Summary window shown in Figure 11-5 as a reference point while configuring and running the GNS3 topology.

#	Task
	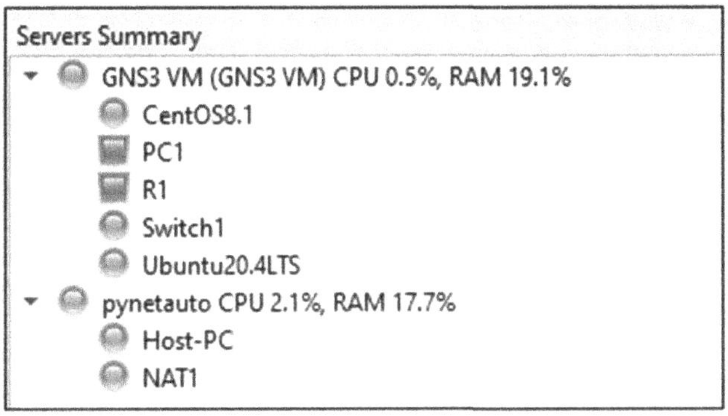 ***Figure 11-5.*** *linuxvm2ios project, Servers Summary window* When you connect Ethernetswitch-1, a VPCS (PC-1), and an IOS router (R1), select GNS3 VM as the server, as shown in Figure 11-6. 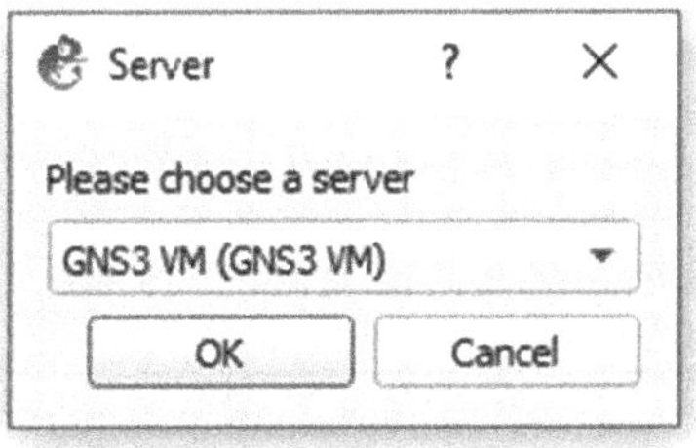 ***Figure 11-6.*** *linuxvm2ios project, selecting the GNS3 VM server for all other devices* Refer to the Topology Summary window shown in Figure 11-7 to connect each device.

(continued)

#	Task

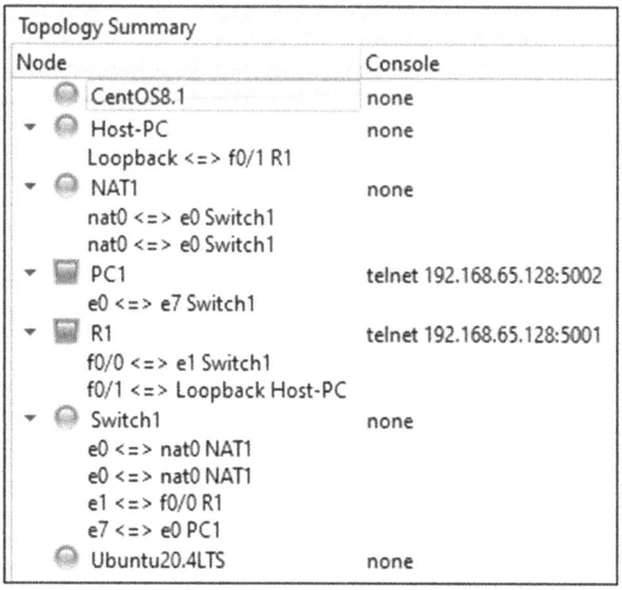

***Figure 11-7.** linuxvm2ios project, topology summary*

4	Next, go to VMware Workstation's main user window and start the CentOS 8.1 VM. When the server boots up, log in as the `pynetauto` user or your username. See Figure 11-8.

#	Task

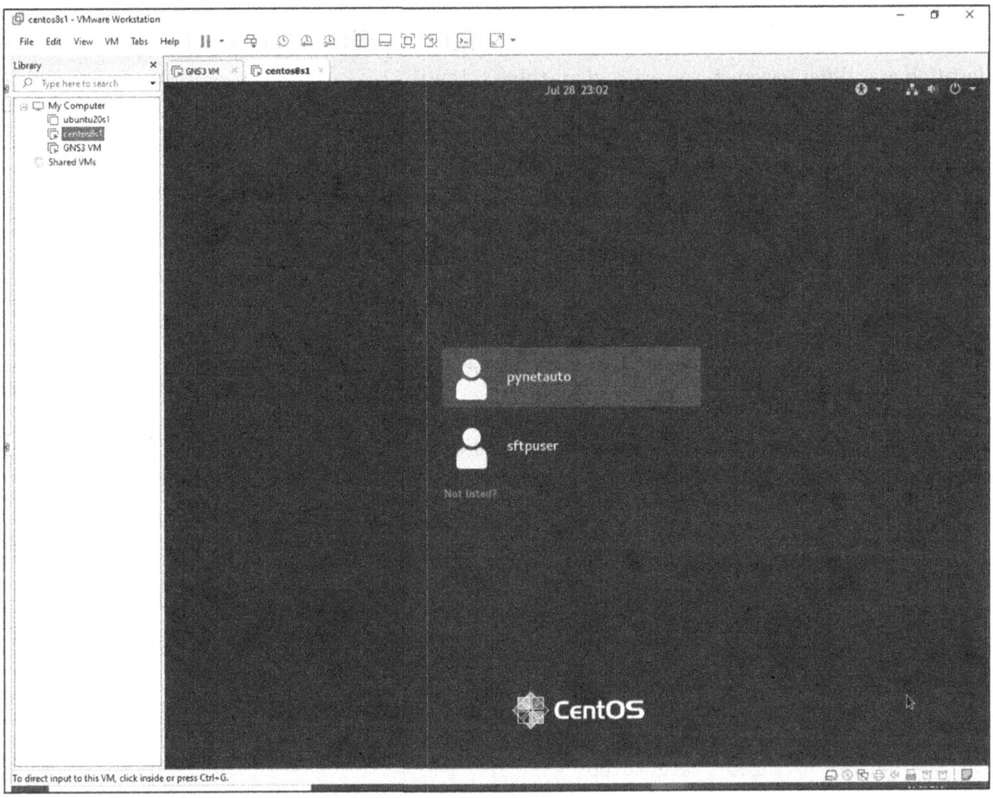

Figure 11-8. CentOS 8.1, login screen

5 Open a terminal on CentOS 8.1 and first check the IP address of this server. Use the `ifconfig ens160` command on the terminal to get or confirm the IP address of your server. You can alternatively SSH into your CentOS 8.1 server. An IP address from the 192.168.183.0/24 subnet should be assigned for this example, but if you are using a different subnet for VMnet8, you should receive a different IP address.

In this example, an IP address of 192.168.183.130 has been allocated to the Ethernet 160 interface. Your IP address allocation may differ based on your virtual machine subnet.

```
[pynetauto@centos8s1 ~]$ ifconfig ens160
ens160: flags=4163<UP,BROADCAST,RUNNING,MULTICAST>  mtu 1500
    inet 192.168.183.130  netmask 255.255.255.0  broadcast 192.168.183.255
    inet6 fe80::f49c:7ff4:fb3f:bf32  prefixlen 64  scopeid 0x20<link>
    ether 00:0c:29:85:a6:36  txqueuelen 1000  (Ethernet)
    RX packets 87  bytes 10302 (10.0 KiB)
    RX errors 0  dropped 0  overruns 0  frame 0
    TX packets 118  bytes 15005 (14.6 KiB)
    TX errors 0  dropped 0 overruns 0  carrier 0  collisions 0
```

(*continued*)

#	Task

6 Still on the VMware workstation, start the Ubuntu 20 LTS server and find out the IP address of this server in the same manner. Issue the `ifconfig ens33` or `ifconfig` or `ip address` command. An IP address of 192.168.183.132 has been assigned to the `ens33` interface. Your IP address allocation may differ based on your virtual machine subnet.

```
pynetauto@ubuntu20s1:~$ ifconfig ens33
ens33: flags=4163<UP,BROADCAST,RUNNING,MULTICAST>  mtu 1500
    inet 192.168.183.132  netmask 255.255.255.0  broadcast 192.168.183.255
    inet6 fe80::20c:29ff:fef3:877c  prefixlen 64  scopeid 0x20<link>
    ether 00:0c:29:f3:87:7c  txqueuelen 1000  (Ethernet)
    RX packets 222  bytes 18369 (18.3 KB)
    RX errors 0  dropped 0  overruns 0  frame 0
    TX packets 442  bytes 41326 (41.3 KB)
    TX errors 0  dropped 0 overruns 0  carrier 0  collisions 0
```

7 Now on GNS3, start R1 and wait for 1 minute. Open the console of R1 and configure the IP domain lookup and FastEthernet 0/0 interface to get an IP address from VMnet8's DHCP server. Also, configure interface FastEthernet 0/1 with an IP address of 7.7.7.2 255.255.255.0; this interface connects to the Microsoft loopback of the host PC.

```
R1(config)# ip domain lookup
R1(config)#interface FastEthernet0/0
R1(config-if)#ip address dhcp
R1(config-if)#no shut
R1(config-if)#
*Mar  1 00:01:15.543: %LINK-3-UPDOWN: Interface FastEthernet0/0, changed state to up
*Mar  1 00:01:16.543: %LINEPROTO-5-UPDOWN: Line protocol on Interface
FastEthernet0/0, changed state to up
*Mar  1 00:01:26.003: %DHCP-6-ADDRESS_ASSIGN: Interface FastEthernet0/0 assigned DHCP
address 192.168.183.133, mask 255.255.255.0, hostname R1

# Confirm the interface status by running "show ip interface brief"

R1#show ip interface brief
Interface                  IP-Address      OK? Method Status                Protocol
FastEthernet0/0            192.168.183.133 YES DHCP   up                    up
FastEthernet0/1            unassigned      YES unset  administratively down down
FastEthernet1/0            unassigned      YES unset  administratively down down
```

#	Task
	Now configure interface f0/1 to be connected to the Microsoft loopback and ping 7.7.7.1.

```
R1#configure terminal
Enter configuration commands, one per line.  End with CNTL/Z.
R1(config)#interface FastEthernet 0/1
R1(config-if)#ip address 7.7.7.2 255.255.255.0
R1(config-if)#no shut
R1(config-if)#exit
R1#
*Mar  1 00:47:12.911: %SYS-5-CONFIG_I: Configured from console by console
R1#ping 7.7.7.1

Type escape sequence to abort.
Sending 5, 100-byte ICMP Echos to 7.7.7.1, timeout is 2 seconds:
.!!!!
Success rate is 80 percent (4/5), round-trip min/avg/max = 8/12/20 ms
```

8 From R1's console, ping the NAT-1 gateway (192.168.183.2), Centos 8.1 server (192.168.183.130), and Ubuntu 20 LTS server (192.168.183.132). If all the ICMP responses are received, you are on the right track.

If you see the first packet dropped, that is the expected and normal ARP behavior, as explained earlier.

```
R1#ping 192.168.183.2

Type escape sequence to abort.
Sending 5, 100-byte ICMP Echos to 192.168.183.1, timeout is 2 seconds:
.!!!!
Success rate is 80 percent (4/5), round-trip min/avg/max = 8/13/24 ms
R1#ping 192.168.183.130

Type escape sequence to abort.
Sending 5, 100-byte ICMP Echos to 192.168.183.130, timeout is 2 seconds:
.!!!!
Success rate is 80 percent (4/5), round-trip min/avg/max = 8/13/20 ms
R1#ping 192.168.183.132

Type escape sequence to abort.
Sending 5, 100-byte ICMP Echos to 192.168.183.132, timeout is 2 seconds:
.!!!!
```

(*continued*)

#	Task
9	Similarly, start PC-1 (VPCS) on GNS3 and run the `ip dhcp` command to receive an IP address from the VMnet8 DHCP server. Use `show ip` to check the IP configuration.

```
PC1> ip dhcp
DDORA IP 192.168.183.129/24 GW 192.168.183.2

PC1> show ip

NAME        : PC1[1]
IP/MASK     : 192.168.183.129/24
GATEWAY     : 192.168.183.2
DNS         : 192.168.183.2
DHCP SERVER : 192.168.183.254
DHCP LEASE  : 1719, 1800/900/1575
DOMAIN NAME : localdomain
MAC         : 00:50:79:66:68:00
LPORT       : 20010
RHOST:PORT  : 127.0.0.1:20011
MTU:        : 1500
```

PC1's interface received an IP address of 192.168.183.129. DDORA is not the name of a kid's cartoon character (*Dora the Explorer*). Here, DORA stands for Discovery, Offer, Request, Acknowledge, which is a communication message used when assigning an IP address through DHCP services between a server and a client.

#	Task
10	Finally, from your host PC's Windows desktop, SSH into both Linux servers using PuTTY and perform similar ICMP tests. Enter the IP address of each server and save the sessions for easier access, as shown in Figure 11-9.

#	Task

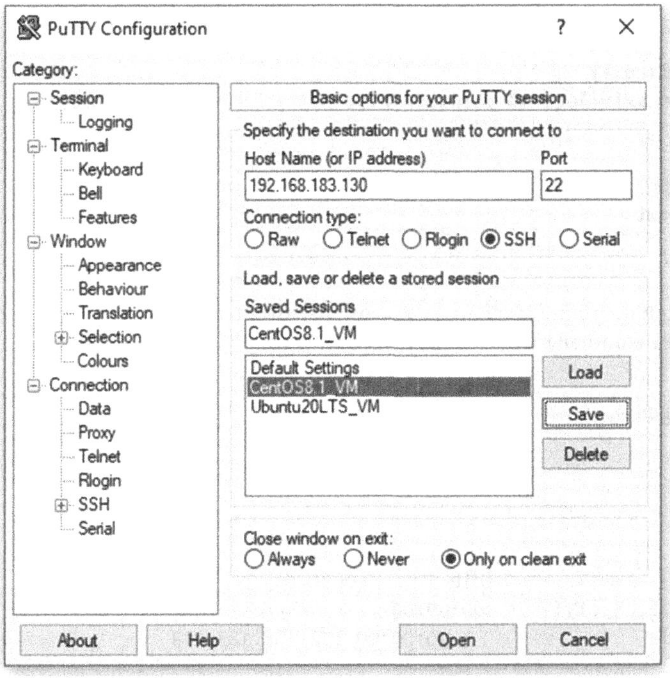

***Figure 11-9.** PuTTY, saving Linux sessions for convenience*

If there is no communication problem, you are now ready to write some Python scripts on Linux servers and communicate to the Cisco IOS router. From your Linux servers, send ICMP messages to R1's f0/0 interface for a quick verification.

```
[pynetauto@centos8s1 ~]$ ping 192.168.183.133 -c 3
PING 192.168.183.133 (192.168.183.133) 56(84) bytes of data.
64 bytes from 192.168.183.133: icmp_seq=1 ttl=64 time=0.547 ms
64 bytes from 192.168.183.133: icmp_seq=2 ttl=64 time=0.318 ms
64 bytes from 192.168.183.133: icmp_seq=3 ttl=64 time=0.372 ms

--- 192.168.183.133 ping statistics ---
3 packets transmitted, 3 received, 0% packet loss, time 44ms
rtt min/avg/max/mdev = 0.318/0.412/0.547/0.099 ms

pynetauto@ubuntu20s1:~$ ping 192.168.183.133 -c 3
PING 192.168.183.133 (192.168.183.133) 56(84) bytes of data.
64 bytes from 192.168.183.133: icmp_seq=1 ttl=255 time=5.92 ms
64 bytes from 192.168.183.133: icmp_seq=2 ttl=255 time=6.85 ms
64 bytes from 192.168.183.133: icmp_seq=3 ttl=255 time=5.70 ms

--- 192.168.183.133 ping statistics ---
3 packets transmitted, 3 received, 0% packet loss, time 2004ms
rtt min/avg/max/mdev = 5.699/6.158/6.851/0.498 ms
```

(*continued*)

#	Task
11	On R1, configure enable password, a username with level 15 privilege, and enable Telnet.

```
R1#configure terminal
R1(config)#enable password cisco123
R1(config)#username pynetauto privilege 15 password cisco123
R1(config)#line vty 0 15
R1(config-line)#login local
R1(config-line)#transport input telnet
R1(config-line)#no exec-timeout
R1(config-line)#end
R1#write memory
```

You can test the Telnet settings from the router itself, so on R1, run the `telnet 192.168.183.133` command. Also, use the `show user` command to check the logged-in user.

```
R1#telnet 192.168.183.133
Trying 192.168.183.133 ... Open

User Access Verification

Username: pynetauto
Password:
R1#show user
Line        User       Host(s)              Idle       Location
0 con 0                 192.168.183.133      00:00:00
* 98 vty 0     pynetauto  idle                   00:00:00 192.168.183.133

Interface    User               Mode           Idle      Peer Address
```

12 From your `ubuntu20s1` Linux server, Telnet to R1's `f0/0` interface (192.168.183.133) using PuTTY. Your allocated IP address may be different, so replace the IP address with your IP.

Run the `show user` command to check which users are logged in and the lines used for Telnet sessions. The asterisk (*) indicates access information from your active connection.

```
pynetauto@ubuntu20s1:~$ telnet 192.168.183.133
Trying 192.168.183.133...
Connected to 192.168.183.133.
Escape character is '^]'.

User Access Verification

Username: pynetauto
Password:
R1#show user
Line        User       Host(s)              Idle       Location
0 con 0                 192.168.183.133      00:05:07
98 vty 0     pynetauto  idle                 00:05:07 192.168.183.133
* 99 vty 1     pynetauto  idle                   00:00:00 192.168.183.132

Interface    User               Mode           Idle      Peer Address
```

Note, if you are using CentOS to Telnet into R1, then you many need to first install the Telnet client after connecting to the Internet.

```
[pynetauto@centos8s1 ~]$ sudo yum -y install telnet
```

or

```
[pynetauto@centos8s1 ~]$ sudo dnf -y install telnet
```

#	Task
13	Now, from your Windows host PC, open another PuTTY session, and this time log in to R1 via `f0/1` (7.7.7.2). The * indicates access information from the current connection. Let's run `write memory` to save the current configuration of R1.

```
R1#show user
Line       User       Host(s)              Idle       Location
0 con 0                idle                 00:05:43
98 vty 0     pynetauto  idle                 00:00:40 192.168.183.133
99 vty 1     pynetauto  idle                 00:01:10 192.168.183.132
*100 vty 2     pynetauto  idle                 00:00:00 7.7.7.1

Interface    User               Mode         Idle     Peer Address
R1#write memory
```

Now you have completed the communication and Telnet tests from all devices. Now you are ready to tackle another interesting IOS lab.

Uploading and Downloading Files to the GNS3 IOS Router from Linux VMs (File Transfer Testing Lab)

In this lab, you will add flash memory to GNS3's IOS router, R1, and upload and download files from a TFTP server (CentOS8.1). You will write and run the script from the Ubuntu 20 LTS server.

Write a Python script to achieve the following tasks:

- Check the TFTP service is running correctly on CentOS8.1.
- Make a backup of R1's running configuration to the TFTP server.
- Upload an IOS to the flash memory of R1 for a quick test.

#	Tasks
1	On GNS3, while creating the Cisco 3725 IOS router template, you have already added 64MB to Cisco 3725's PCMCIA disk0. If your router was not configured with a flash drive, first save the work and shut down the router. Then right-click, choose Configure, and move to the "Memories and disks" tab of R1. Add 64MB, click Apply, and then click the OK button. Once the flash memory has been configured, start R1 again. See Figure 11-10.

(continued)

#	Tasks

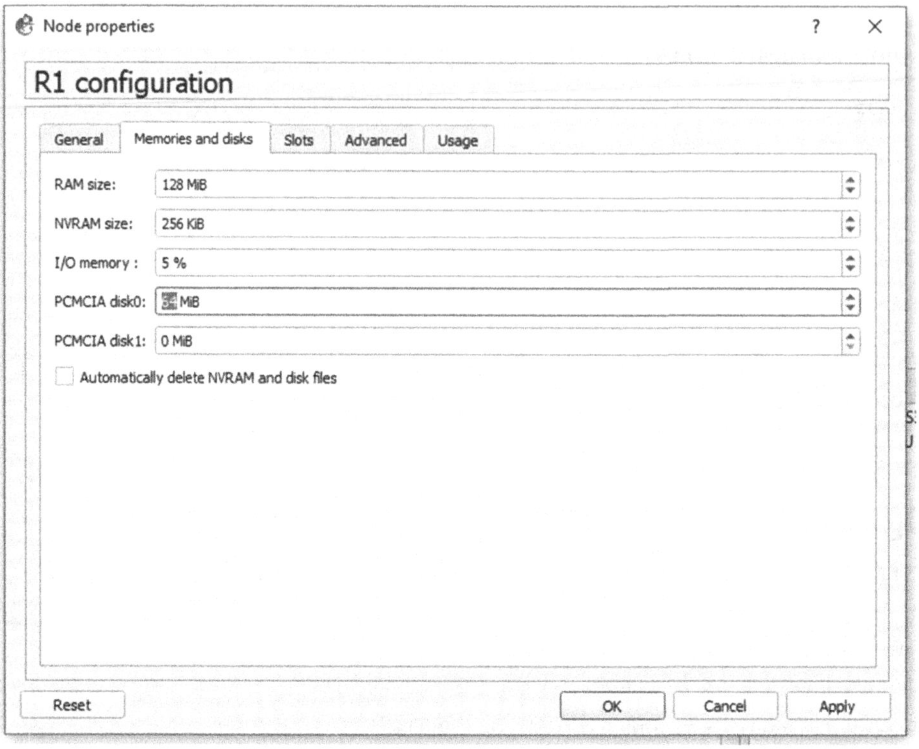

Figure 11-10. *R1, checking flash memory allocation*

2 Remember that in 8.3.3 we configured a TFTP server on CentOS8.1? Go to the PuTTY session of CentOS8.1 and now confirm the status of TFTP services. TFTP was configured during the IP Services installation on CentOS8.1 Linux.

Use the following commands to check for TFTP services running on CentOS8.1.

sudo systemctl status tftp	Checks TFTP service status
sudo systemctl enable tftp	Enables TFTP services on system startup
sudo systemctl start tftp	Starts TFTP services

If the TFTP service on CentOS 8.1 is running correctly, it should display active (running) in green. If you have issues with TFTP, use the `enable` and `start` commands shown earlier to start the service on this server. If CentOS asks for the `sudo` user password, enter your password. In 4.5.3, we have configured a default folder called `/var/tftpdir` for the TFTP service to share files from and to this folder.

```
[pynetauto@localhost ~]$ sudo systemctl enable tftp
[sudo] password for pynetauto: **********
[pynetauto@localhost ~]$ sudo systemctl start tftp
[pynetauto@localhost ~]$ sudo systemctl status tftp
● tftp.service - Tftp Server
```

#	Tasks

```
  Loaded: loaded (/usr/lib/systemd/system/tftp.service; indirect; vendor prese>
  Active: active (running) since Fri 2021-01-08 23:43:05 AEDT; 4s ago
    Docs: man:in.tftpd
Main PID: 4237 (in.tftpd)
   Tasks: 1 (limit: 11166)
  Memory: 328.0K
  CGroup: /system.slice/tftp.service
          └─4237 /usr/sbin/in.tftpd -s /var/lib/tftpboot

Jan 08 23:43:05 localhost systemd[1]: Started Tftp Server.
lines 1-11/11 (END)
```

3 On your Ubuntu server (primary Python server), reuse the Telnet sample code from telnet_script1 from Chapter 10, and let's rewrite the Telnet script to make a backup of R1's running configuration. I am going to rename the script as backup_config.py and modify the code. The sections of code that are modified are highlighted.

Go to Ubuntu 20 LTS Python server and create the following code using the nano text editor:

```
pynetauto@ubuntu20s1:~$ pwd
/home/pynetauto
pynetauto@ubuntu20s1:~$ mkdir ch11
pynetauto@ubuntu20s1:~$ cd ch11
pynetauto@ubuntu20s1:~/ch11$ nano backup_config.py
pynetauto@ubuntu20s1:~/ch11$ ls
backup_config.py
```

backup_config.py

```
import getpass
import telnetlib

HOST = "192.168.183.133"
user = input("Enter your telnet username: ")
password = getpass.getpass()

tn = telnetlib.Telnet(HOST)

tn.read_until(b"Username: ")
tn.write(user.encode('ascii') + b"\n")
if password:
    tn.read_until(b"Password: ")
    tn.write(password.encode('ascii') + b"\n")

tn.write(b"copy running-config tftp://192.168.183.130/running-config\n") #<<< Copy
command
tn.write(b"\n") #<<< Enter key action
tn.write(b"\n") #<<< Enter key action
tn.write(b"exit\n") #<<< end session

print(tn.read_all().decode('ascii'))
```

(continued)

#	Tasks

4 Before running the previous script, go to CentOS8s1 and confirm the files in the /var/tftpdir directory. You can see that there are only two transfer test files from 8.3.3.

```
[pynetauto@centos8s1 ~]$ pwd
/home/pynetauto
[pynetauto@centos8s1 ~]$ cd /var/tftpdir
[pynetauto@centos8s1 tftpdir]$ ls
transfer_file01                           transfer_file77
```

5 Now from Ubuntu 20 LTS Python server, run the python3 backup_config.py command. Follow the prompt and check the returned output.

Enter your network admin ID and password to run the script. As the running configuration gets copied to the TFTP server, you should see a similar message to the following:

```
pynetauto@ubuntu20s1:~/ch11$ python3 backup_config.py
Enter your telnet username: pynetauto
Password: *********

R1#copy running-config tftp://192.168.183.130/running-config
Address or name of remote host [192.168.183.130]?
Destination filename [running-config]?
!!
1155 bytes copied in 2.168 secs (533 bytes/sec)
R1#exit
```

6 Now go back to the CentOS8s1 server and recheck the directory (/var/tftpdir). You should now see that the running-config file was saved on the TFTP server.

```
[pynetauto@centos8s1 tftpdir]$ ls
running-config             transfer_file01                          transfer_file77
```

7 Now to upload an IOS image to GNS3's IOS router's flash, you first have to format the flash. Open R1's console and follow these instructions:

```
R1#show flash
No files on device

134211584 bytes available (2198889009152 bytes used)

R1#
*Mar  1 02:53:58.163: %PCMCIAFS-5-DIBERR: PCMCIA disk 0 is formatted from a different
router or PC. A format in this router is required before an image can be booted from
this device
R1#show file system
```

#	Tasks

```
File Systems:

Size(b)              Free(b)       Type      Flags  Prefixes
-                    -             opaque    rw     archive:
-                    -             opaque    rw     system:
-                    -             opaque    rw     tmpsys:
57336                54057         nvram     rw     nvram:
-                    -             opaque    rw     null:
-                    -             network   rw     tftp:
* 2199023220736      134211584     disk      rw     flash:
-                    -             flash     rw     slot0:
-                    -             opaque    wo     syslog:
-                    -             opaque    rw     xmodem:
-                    -             opaque    rw     ymodem:
-                    -             network   rw     rcp:
-                    -             network   rw     pram:
-                    -             network   rw     ftp:
-                    -             network   rw     http:
-                    -             network   rw     scp:
-                    -             opaque    ro     tar:
-                    -             network   rw     https:
-                    -             opaque    ro     cns:

R1#format flash:
Format operation may take a while. Continue? [confirm] <<< Press the [Enter] key
Format operation will destroy all data in "flash:".  Continue? [confirm] <<< Press
the [Enter] key
Writing Monlib sectors....
Monlib write complete

Format: All system sectors written. OK...

Format: Total sectors in formatted partition: 131040
Format: Total bytes in formatted partition: 67092480
Format: Operation completed successfully.

Format of flash: complete
R1#show flash:
No files on device

66936832 bytes available (0 bytes used)
```

(continued)

#	Tasks
8	You can use the FileZilla client for either Windows or WinSCP to upload any IOS file or any file for file transfer using the Python `telnetlib` module. If you do not have WinSCP on your Windows host PC, go to the following download site and install one: URL: `https://winscp.net/eng/download.php` (WinSCP download) URL: `https://filezilla-project.org/download.php?platform=win64` (FileZilla client for Windows) After installing WinSCP and launching the application, use the following settings to connect to the CentOS8.1 server via port 22 (SSH). See Figure 11-11. File protocol: **SCP** Host name: **192.168.183.130 (Your CentOS 8.1 IP address)** Username: **pynetauto (Your CentOS 8.1 username)** Password : ********* **(Your CentOS 8.1 password)**

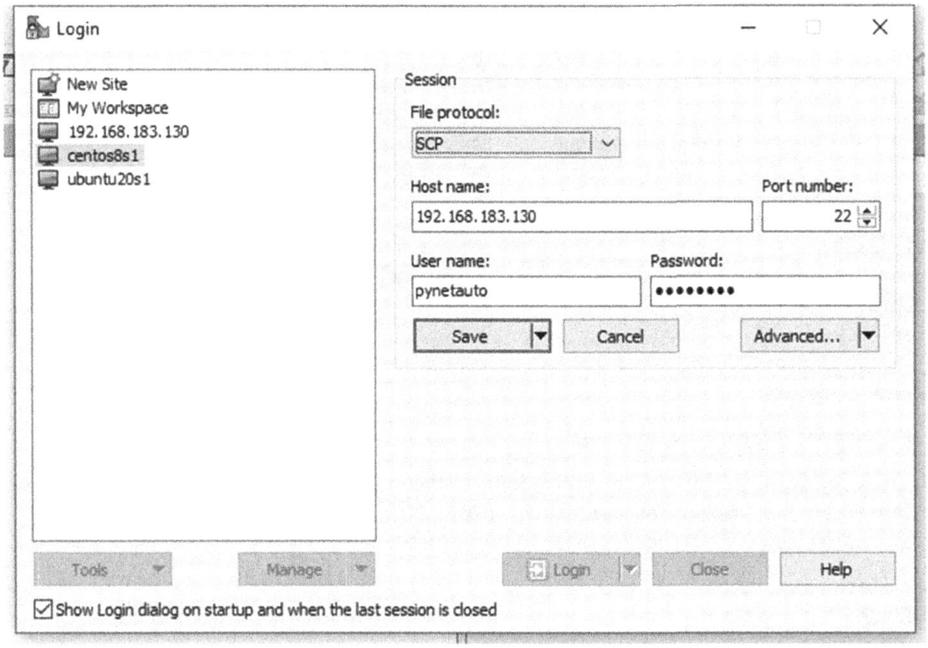

Figure 11-11. *WinSCP, connection to TFTP server (CentOS8.1)*

9	When you accept the SSH key and log in, drill down to the `/var/tftpdir/` directory of your TFTP (CentOS8.1) server and drag and drop an IOS file for file sharing. You can also use another file in place of the IOS file to save time as you will be testing the file transfer concept only using Python's `telnetlib` module. In this example, I am using the old IOS file named `c3725-adventerprisek9-mz.124-15.T14.bin`, but you can choose to use any file here for this test. See Figure 11-12.

#	Tasks

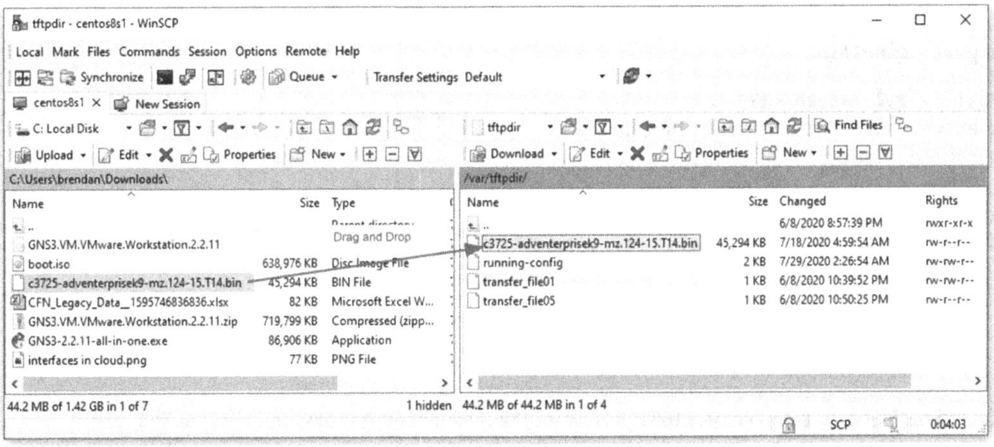

Figure 11-12. WinSCP, copying an IOS or any file transfer test file

10	On R1, the flash drive has been formatted in previous steps, and there is no need to check if any files exist on the flash.

11	Now on the Ubuntu 20 LTS server, copy `backup_config.py` and save it as `upload_ios.py`.
	`pynetauto@ubuntu20s1:~/ch11$ ls`
	`backup_config.py`
	`pynetauto@ubuntu20s1:~/ch11$ cp backup_config.py upload_ios.py`
	`pynetauto@ubuntu20s1:~/ch11$ nano upload_ios.py`
	Then modify the Python code so it looks like the following code. The updated parts are highlighted. You can type in the script from scratch, but it is easier to reuse the previous script and make the required modifications. Also, the script is available for download from the official download site.

(*continued*)

#	Tasks

upload_ios.py

```
import getpass
import telnetlib

HOST = "192.168.183.133"
user = input("Enter your telnet username: ")
password = getpass.getpass()

tn = telnetlib.Telnet(HOST)

tn.read_until(b"Username: ")
tn.write(user.encode('ascii') + b"\n")
if password:
    tn.read_until(b"Password: ")
    tn.write(password.encode('ascii') + b"\n")

tn.write(b" copy tftp://192.168.183.130/c3725-adventerprisek9-mz.124-15.T14.bin
flash:c3725-adventerprisek9-mz.124-15.T14.bin\n")  #<<< Run copy command
tn.write(b"\n") #<<< Enter key action
tn.write(b"exit\n") #<<< end session

print(tn.read_all().decode('ascii'))
```

12 Run the Python code. It looks like the application is hanging, but in fact, it is transferring the file from the TFTP server to R1's flash memory. TFTP is a slow protocol, and it takes a long time to transfer this 45MB file. In your practice, you can create any dummy `.txt` file that is small to save time.

```
pynetauto@ubuntu20s1:~/ch11$ python3 upload_ios.py
Enter your telnet username: pynetauto
Password: ********
|
```

13 After running the previous script, go back to R1's console and use the `show users` command for the vty session for Telnet and use the `dir` or `show flash:` command to check that the file transfer is taking place.

```
R1#show flash:
-#- --length-- -----date/time------ path
1      1470464 Mar 01 2002 01:02:28 c3725-adventerprisek9-mz.124-15.T14.bin

65466368 bytes available (1470464 bytes used)

R1#show flash:
-#- --length-- -----date/time------ path
1      2936832 Mar 01 2002 01:02:58 c3725-adventerprisek9-mz.124-15.T14.bin

64000000 bytes available (2936832 bytes used)
```

#	Tasks
14	If you are uploading an IOS file as shown in this example, it will take a while for the file transfer to complete via TFTP. The TFTP protocol uses the UDP port for file transfer but is a slow file transfer protocol in both lab and production. You are only uploading a file to learn the concept of TFTP file transfer using a Python 3 script. You cannot update the boot system configuration and reboot the GNS3 IOS router with the new IOS image; this is one of the downsides of using IOS on GNS3. However, using Cisco CSR1000v or Nexus 9000v on VMware Workstation, you can simulate the actual IOS XE upgrade process, including booting into the newly upgraded IOS. In the next chapter, we'll use Cisco CSR1000v on VMware Workstation and emulate the full IOS upgrade process. Once the file size reaches the expected file size, you know that the script and the file transfer have completed successfully.

```
R1#dir
Directory of flash:/

1  -rw-    46380064   Mar 1 2002 01:22:04 +00:00  c3725-adventerprisek9-mz.124-15.
T14.bin

66936832 bytes total (20553728 bytes free)
R1#show flash:
-#- --length-- -----date/time------ path
1      46380064 Mar 01 2002 01:22:04 c3725-adventerprisek9-mz.124-15.T14.bin

20553728 bytes available (46383104 bytes used)
```

#	Tasks
15	Because of the slow uploading time and issues with Python's `telnetlib` library, your Ubuntu Python server console may still look like it is uploading the IOS. Press Ctrl+Z to exit this state to complete this lab.

```
pynetauto@ubuntu20s1:~/ch11$ python3 upload_ios.py
Enter your telnet username: pynetauto
Password:
^Z
[1]+  Stopped                 python3 upload_ios.py
pynetauto@ubuntu20s1:~/ch11$
```

You have used the Telnet and TFTP services to upload files to R1's flash. A large part of the network engineer's work involves IOS patch management involving uploading IOS to many routers and switches. Imagine yourself writing a piece of code, which can upload multiple IOS files to hundreds of Cisco routers and switches during the night while you are safe and sound asleep. In reality, this was one of the very first tools I had to create for regular patching of my clients' network devices.

Copying (Cloning) a GNS3 Project

To prepare for the next chapter, let's copy and clone the current project. There are about three different ways you can make a carbon copy of a GNS3 project. The first method is using the "Save project as..." feature of the GNS3 menu, the second method is to export it as a portable project and re-import it on another host PC, and the last method is to use the "Export config" method to export your devices' configuration and manually clone your GNS3 project. These methods are mentioned in order of increasing difficulty. Also, note that if you use the first method, your existing lab's configuration will be moved to the newly saved `Project` folder.

You will lose the existing configurations of your devices' running configuration. The best way to clone a GNS3 project is by using the third method, which preserves your existing lab status and carries the same settings to the new project. Last, but most importantly, if you want to make a full backup of your GNS3 project at any time, you can copy the whole project folder under `C:\Users\[your_name]\GNS3\project`.

Since we will not be using the `linuxvm2ios` project beyond this point of the book, let's see how to clone the GNS3 project using a copy method. In the later chapter, another method will be demonstrated to give you another cloning option.

#	Task
1	Make sure all devices in the GNS3 project are powered off. To save the existing `linuxvm2ios` project to a new project name, first open GNS3's main user window, go to File, and select "Save project as." See Figure 11-13.

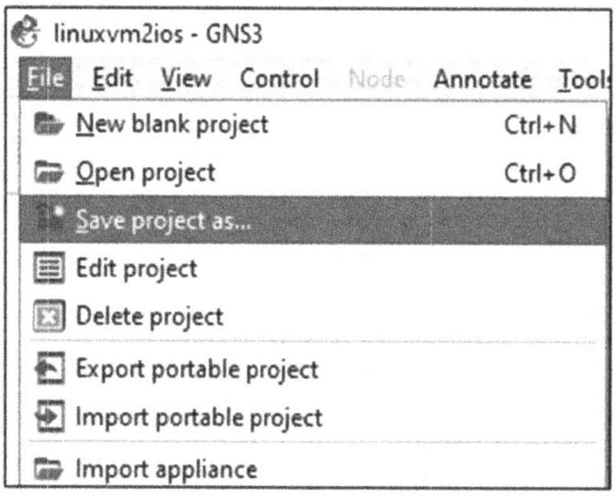

Figure 11-13. *GNS3, "Project as..." menu*

#	Task
2	The GNS3 projects are saved under the `C:\Users\[your_name]\GNS3\project` folder. Now, give a new name to your new project for Chapter 12. This lab will be used across subsequent labs. See Figure 11-14. GNS3 project folder location: `C:\Users\brendan\GNS3\projects`

#	Task

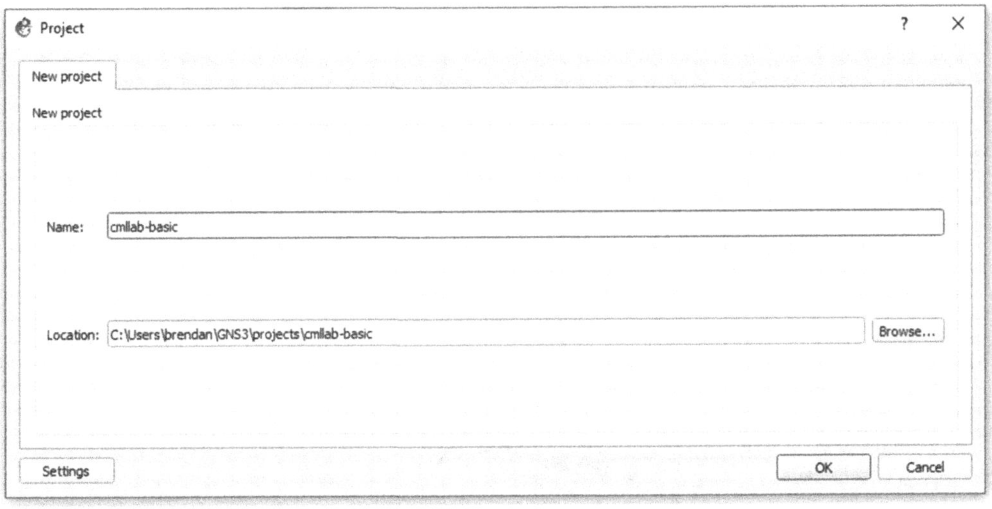

Figure 11-14. GNS3, cloning the existing linuxvm2ios project to cmllab-basic

3 After you saved the new project, go to the `Project` folder (`C:\Users\[your_name]\GNS3\projects`) and check the original and new project folders' file sizes. The original project folder size will be around 24KB in size, whereas the new project folder size will be over 2.1MB. Open the folder and check the folder and file contents. See Figure 11-15.

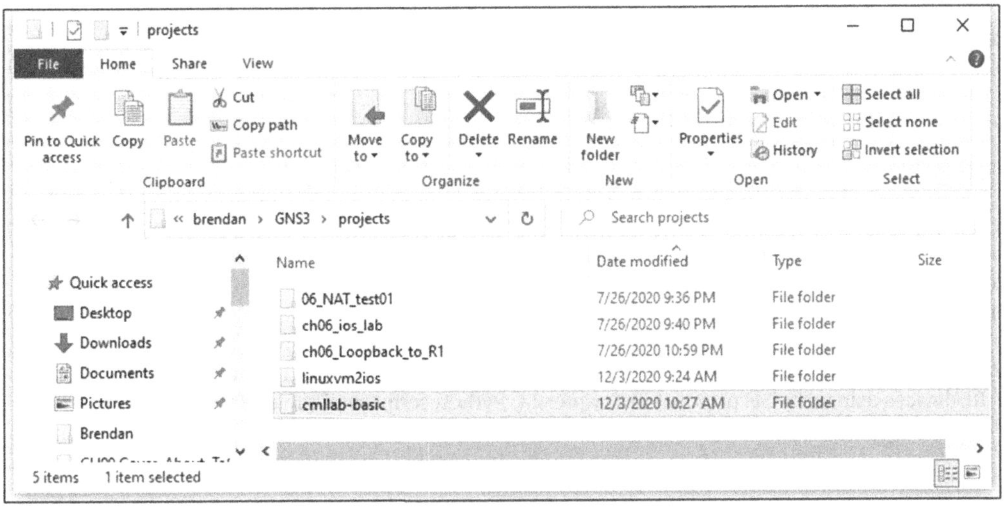

Figure 11-15. Host PC, confirming the new project folder

(*continued*)

#	Task
4	Now open the new project and run it. If you have saved the project correctly, it should run smoothly with no errors. Now you are ready for some CML-PE labs in Chapter 12. See Figure 11-16.

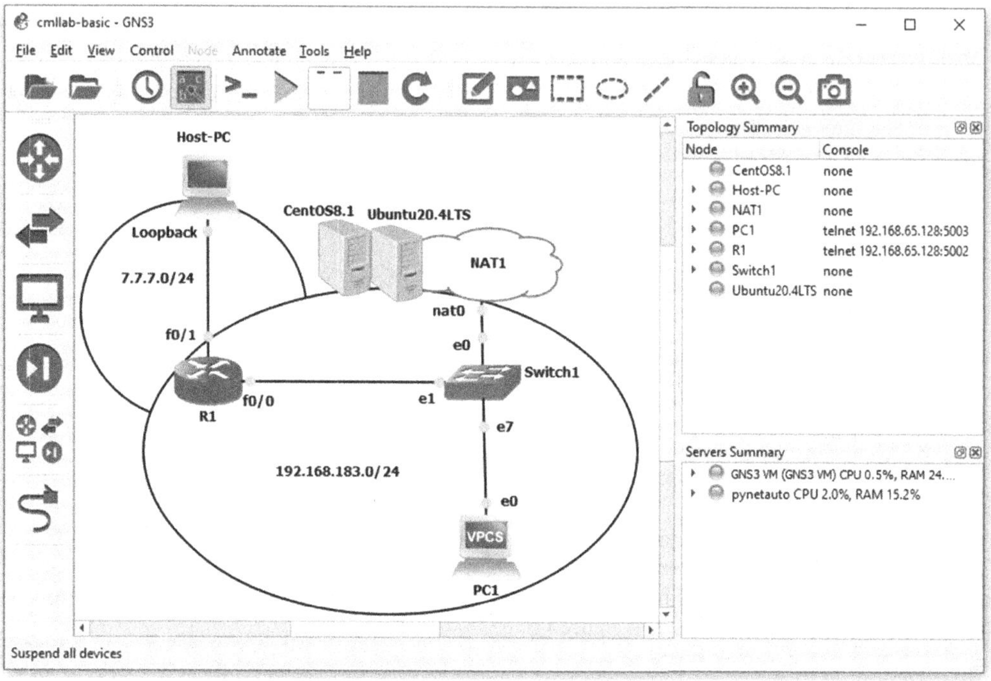

Figure 11-16. *GNS3, running the cmllab-basic project*

Summary

In this chapter, you tested Linux virtual machines' interaction with the IOS router, R1, via Telnet. You learned how to create a GNS3 project, ran a quick file transfer testing lab using simple Cisco configurations, and then finally learned to make a clone of the GNS3 project. You are now well positioned to tackle other labs in Chapters 12 to 18. In Chapter 12, we will use many of the skills acquired from previous chapters to build L3 routing and L2 switching labs using Cisco CML (VIRL) images integrated into GNS3. We will take some baby steps into Python network automation using the `telnetlib` module in Chapter 13 and then learn to control Cisco VIRL devices using the SSH protocol in Chapter 14. Python scripts will run on Linux VMs to control Cisco VIRL devices via the Telnet and SSH protocols using the `telnetlib`, `paramiko`, and `netmiko` libraries.

CHAPTER 12

Building a Python Automation Lab Environment

We have been test-driving an old Cisco device running an outdated IOS version (12.x) in our Telnet labs so far. To test newer features on newer IOS versions and equip our lab with the switching (L2) functionalities, we need to integrate Cisco CML-PE's L2 and L3 images into the GNS3 lab environment. This chapter will guide you through Cisco CML-PE L2 and L3 image integrations on GNS3. You will be guided through each step to download and integrate the L2 and L3 images in your GNS3 environment so you can conduct test with newer IOS feature sets in your network labs in the next chapter. You will learn about CML-PE as a product, download the required images for your lab use, integrate the downloaded images on GNS3, and then build a CML-PE basic lab topology to test various Python networking labs in the following chapters.

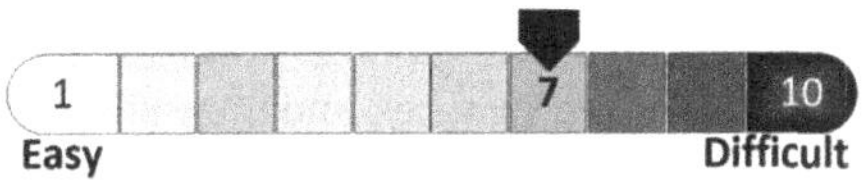

You have come a long way in this book on your first network automation journey. Thus far, I hope you have not lost your passion for learning Python network automation. To get the most from the second half of this book, this book assumes you have thoroughly read the previous 11 chapters. In your first half of Python network automation journey, you picked up various fundamental hands-on skills required to install, run, and configure an integrated virtual lab using a number of open source and proprietary software. You also started doing basic Python scripting using what you have learned so far. Of course, we could have covered many more exciting topics such as DevOps concepts, Ansible, ACI, REST API, HTML, Postman, YANG, NETCONF, and much more. However, this book's purpose is clear: we have been focusing on the quintessential tasks of getting you started with Python programming, which is the foundational skill of all Python application development engineers. You have probably heard the expression "Give a man a fish, and you feed him for a day; teach a man to fish, and you feed him for a lifetime." Borrowing this great idiom for Python network application development, "Teach a network engineer how to use Ansible, and you make him a driver; teach him how to write code in Python, and you turn him into a mechanic for a lifetime." Hence, it is your responsibility to expand on the skills you acquire from reading this book; only you can decide where you want to go next and how to apply the new skills to your work or study.

So far, you have learned various IT skills to prepare you for the following chapters that predominantly focus on Python network automation labs. If you followed along nicely without any technical hiccups up to now, you should be able to go through the remaining chapters with ease. If you have not fully set up your lab environment or if you only partially completed exercises in each chapter, I encourage you to go back and finish, as you will need all of those basics here and throughout the rest of the book.

B. Choi, *Introduction to Python Network Automation*, https://doi.org/10.1007/978-1-4842-6806-3_12

In this chapter, we will start from where we left off at the end of Chapter 11, completing the basic cmllab-basic lab topology built to start writing Python code and testing the code for network automation application development. Suppose you are an experienced network engineer with many years of experience on Cisco, Juniper, Arista, and HP network devices. In that case, you will have no issue following the contents of this lab. However, even if you are a new network engineer just starting your career, you will still be able to follow along with all the lab steps, as the labs are written with minimal networking concepts and come with enough explanations for training purposes. If you concentrate, you will be able to complete all the labs with little difficulty.

Cisco CML-PERSONAL Software License Information and Software Downloads

Cisco sells Cisco Modeling Labs - Personal (CML-PERSONAL) with a yearly subscription. If you are a network engineer or a networking student who wants to explore everything that Cisco CML-PERSONAL has to offer, purchasing the subscription is the way to go. In the first year of subscription, you are required to pay US $199, and you will continue to pay the same yearly subscription fee designated by the Cisco Learning Team. For a professional engineer who works on Cisco technologies for a living, the subscription fee is cheap compared to how much traditional network engineers had to spend on their old 3700 and 2600 series routers and 2950 series switches to break into this industry. Anyway, if you can get your hands on CML images, there are more cost-effective ways of setting up your lab, like integrating them into GNS3, which is the topic of this chapter.

As mentioned in the first chapter, CML-PERSONAL (renamed VIRL-PE, for Virtual Internet Routing Lab Personal Edition) is a virtual equipment emulator program for studying Cisco's technologies, so you can say it is vendor-specific. However, the networking concepts you will learn from this Cisco tool will be universal and replicable to other vendor technologies. Once you are subscribed to Cisco CML-PERSONAL, you can download and install Cisco's CML-PERSONAL software and use routers, switches, and firewall CML-PERSONAL images to emulate the various Cisco labs. With no surprise, this book does not use CML-PERSONAL PE but uses a hybrid lab setup using Cisco CML-PERSONAL's router (L3) and switch (L2) images on GNS3. The CML-PERSONAL images installation and integration procedures on GNS3 are almost identical to the Cisco router IOS image integration on GNS3. Once again, your Windows host PC needs a connection to the Internet. CML-PERSONAL is Cisco's proprietary software, and free distribution of CML-PERSONAL software and CML-PERSONAL images are prohibited by law. If you can afford the subscription, we recommend you subscribe to CML-PERSONAL at `https://learningnetworkstore.cisco.com/cisco-modeling-labs-personal/cisco-cml-personal`.

This book makes a disclaimer that any Cisco IOS, CML-PERSONAL, or any other proprietary software purchase and use are your responsibilities. No software is provided to you as part of this book. There are several ways to locate the software mentioned in this book. Please refer to `https://developer.cisco.com/modeling-labs/` for more information.

Downloading the Cisco CML-PERSONAL IOSvL2 (Switch) Image

Before we can integrate the Cisco CML-PERSONAL L2 switch image on GNS3, you will need to locate, download, and save it to your host PC's `Downloads` folder. You can get information on the CML-PERSONAL L2 switch from the official GNS3 website, which will take you to Cisco's CML-PERSONAL L2 site (`https://learningnetwork.cisco.com/s/article/iosvl2-more-info-updated-10-2-15-x`).

The name of the CML-PERSONAL switch image used in this book is `vios_l2-adventerprisek9-m.03.2017.qcow2`. You can use the same one or any newer images you can find and download. After downloading the switch image file, save it to the `Downloads` folder. Saving it to the `Downloads` folder is important to save time as GNS3 will first look for the image in the `Downloads` folder (see Figure 12-1).

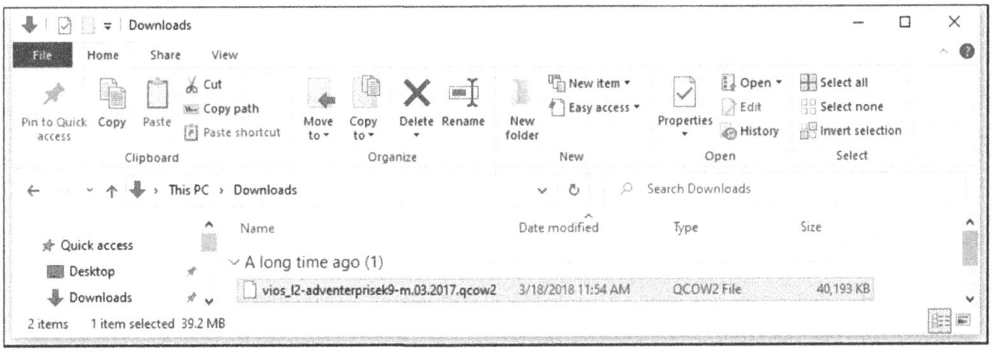

Figure 12-1. *CML-PERSONAL L2 switch image, saved to the Downloads folder*

Downloading the Cisco CML-PERSONAL IOSv (Router) Image and startup_config Files

To integrate a CML-PERSONAL L3 or router image, you have to download the working IOSv L3 Qemu (`qcow2`) and `IOSv_startup_config.img` image files. Unlike the L2 switch, the CML-PERSONAL router image integration with GNS3 also requires the `IOSv_startup_config.img` file for device startup, which can be downloaded from CML-PERSONAL's official site or `sourceforge.net`. Information on the GNS3 CML-PERSONAL L3 router and `IOSv_startup_config.img` can be obtained from Cisco's CML-PERSONAL site. Go to the following suggested sites to find out more about the Cisco CML-PERSONAL L3 software:

> *GNS3 CML-PERSONAL IOSv*: `https://learningnetwork.cisco.com/s/article/iosv-more-info-updated-4-20-15-x`
>
> *CML-PERSONAL IOSv_startup_config file download*: `https://sourceforge.net/projects/gns-3/files/Qemu%20Appliances/`

The CML-PERSONAL IOSv or L3 router image name used in this book is `IOSv-L3-15.6(2)T.qcow2`; this is an old image, but it still meets our needs. Since we are not exploring all the networking features, Cisco devices only serve our needs to learn the network automation concepts and Python application developments. We can use any version of CML L2 and L3 images as long as it can carry the traffic and saves us time and resources from running full-blown hardware-based labs. Although we are focusing on network automation, the routing and switching concepts are not the core of this book. So, Cisco CML-PERSONAL images provide us with the basic L2 and L3 connections to carry traffic and learn Python scripting skills using Telnet, SSH, RESTCONF, and other Python libraries. Download the two required files, as shown in Figure 12-2, and save them in the `Downloads` folder.

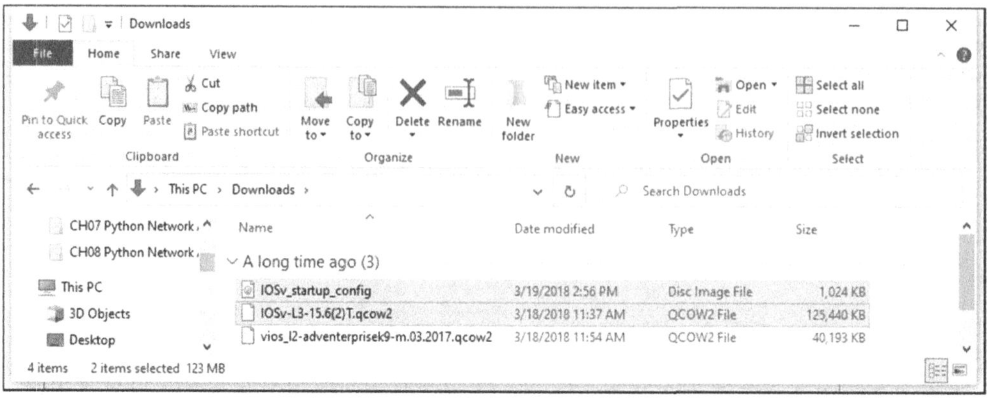

Figure 12-2. *CML-PERSONAL L3 router image, saved to the Downloads folder*

Once you have the vIOS L2 image, vIOS L3 image, and vIOS startup-config files, you are ready to install and integrate them to your GNS3.

Installing the Cisco CML-PERSONAL L2 Switch and CML-PERSONAL L3 on GNS3

At the end of Chapter 11, we copied and created a new project called `cmllab-basic`. Let's reopen that project as this is the starting point of our tasks in this chapter. If you are continuing your work from Chapter 11, continue working from GNS3, but if you have just powered on your PC, then first launch GNG3 using the GNS3 shortcut icon on your desktop. If the lab environment was set up correctly, GNS3 runs, and the GNS3 VM installed on VMware Workstation should start automatically after a few seconds.

Installation tip If the CML-PERSONAL installation does not work as described due to a software failure, you must delete the installed switch or router templates by right-clicking GNS3 and trying to install the images again. CML-PERSONAL images are not made for GNS3, so sometimes they will not integrate to GNS3 on the first try. If the CML-PERSONAL image does not get installed properly after the first attempt, do not give up; keep trying until it is installed properly.

Installing the Cisco CML-PERSONAL L2 Switch on GNS3

You will install the Cisco CML-PERSONAL L2 switch image on GNS3 first. For correct installation, the host PC must be connected to the Internet. After this installation, you will run the switching labs using the installed image, which was not possible on the older IOS image integration.

#	Task
1	In the GNS3 main window, go to File and click + New template. See Figure 12-3.

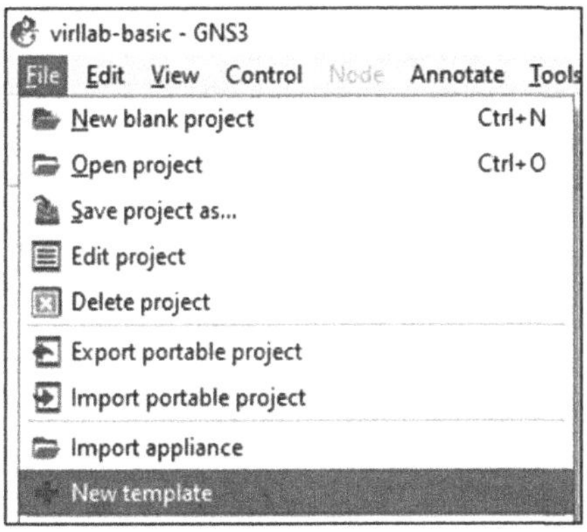

Figure 12-3. *CML L2 switch installation, adding a new template*

#	Task
2	When the "New template" wizard opens, leave the default selection of "Install an appliance from the GNS3 server (recommended)" and click Next. See Figure 12-4.

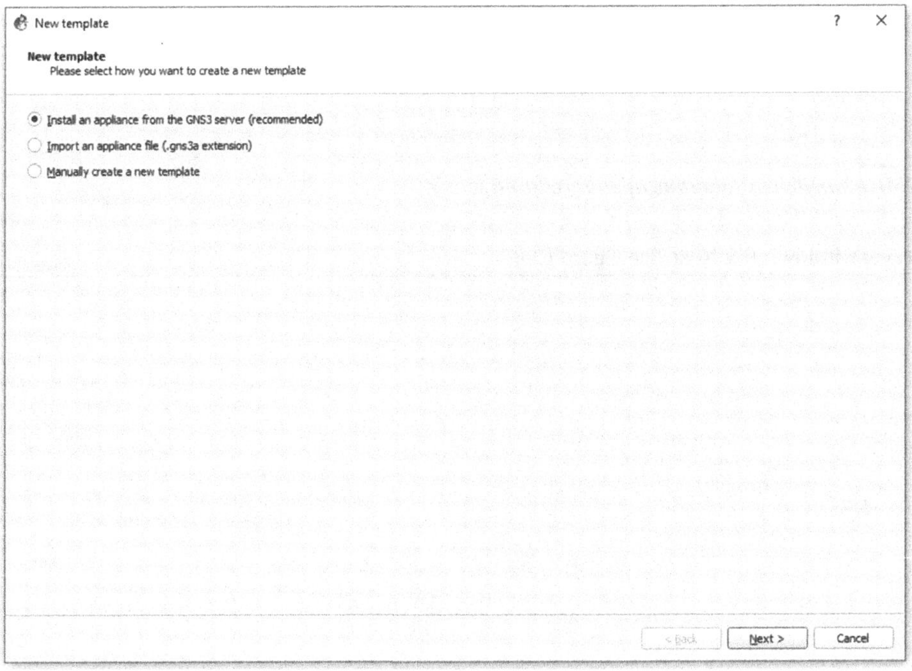

Figure 12-4. *CML L2 switch installation, new template selection*

(continued)

#	Task
3	In the "Appliances from server" window, in the search field, type in **IOSvL2** to locate Cisco IOSvL2 Qemu under Switches. Select the searched device and click Install; this is the template for the Cisco CML-PERSONAL L2 switch on GNS3. See Figure 12-5.

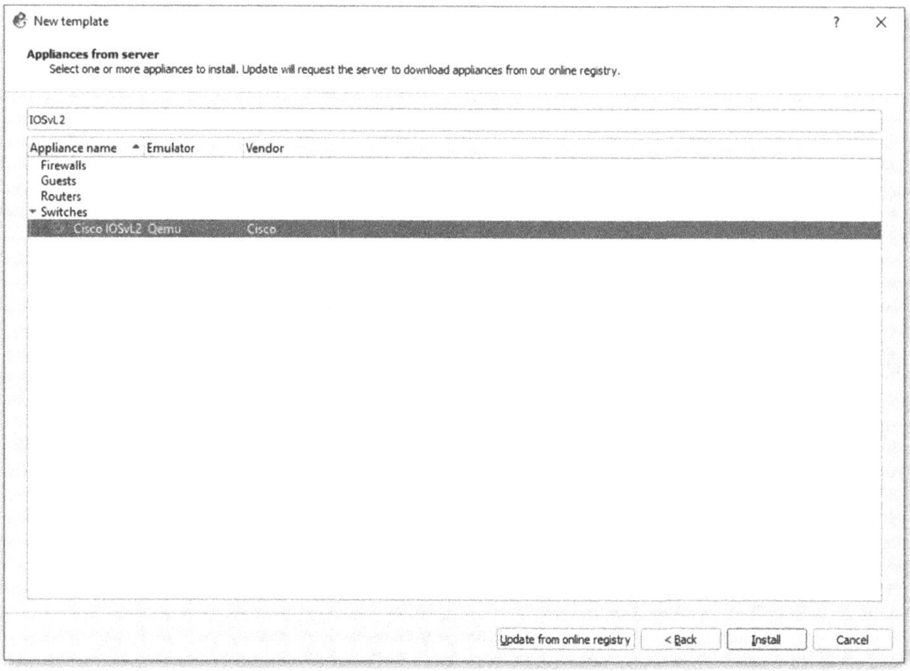

Figure 12-5. *CML L2 Switch installation, appliances from server*

4	In the Server window, click Next. See Figure 12-6.

#	Task

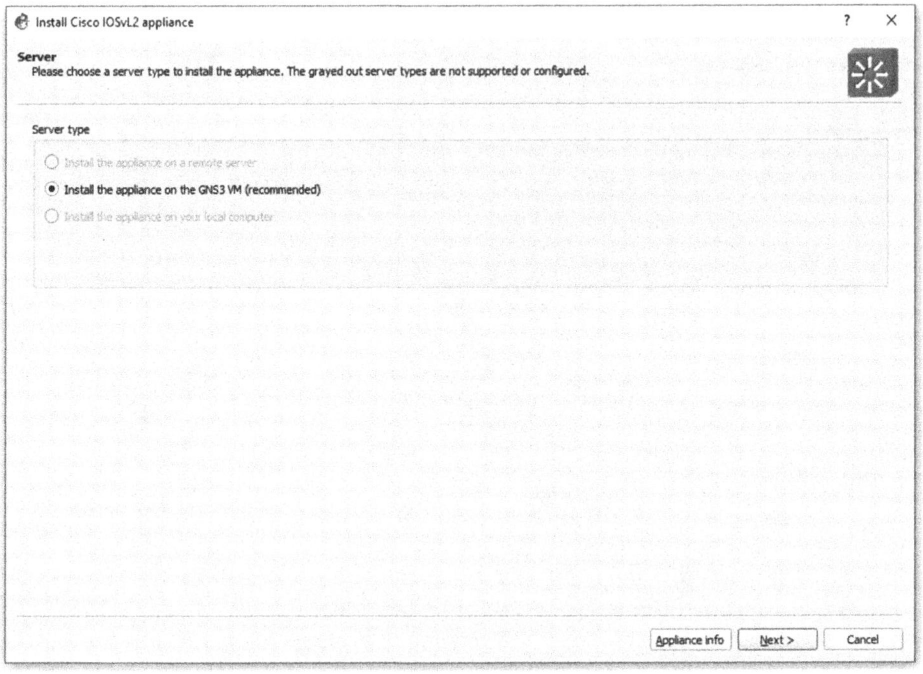

Figure 12-6. *CML L2 switch installation, server*

5	In the "Qemu settings" window, click Next. See Figure 12-7.

(*continued*)

#	Task
	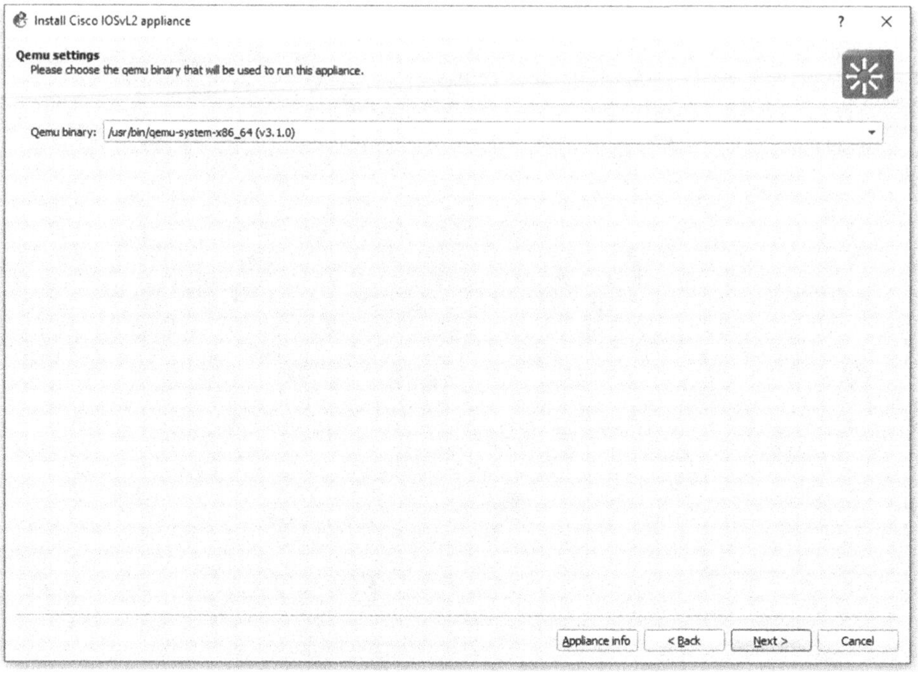 ***Figure 12-7.*** *CML L2 switch installation, Qemu settings*
6	Under "Required files," if you have placed the CML-PERSONAL L2 `.qcow2` file in the `Downloads` folder, the installation wizard will automatically detect the L2 image automatically and display it in green. You can also see the missing files in red. Highlight your image and click Next. See Figure 12-8.

#	Task

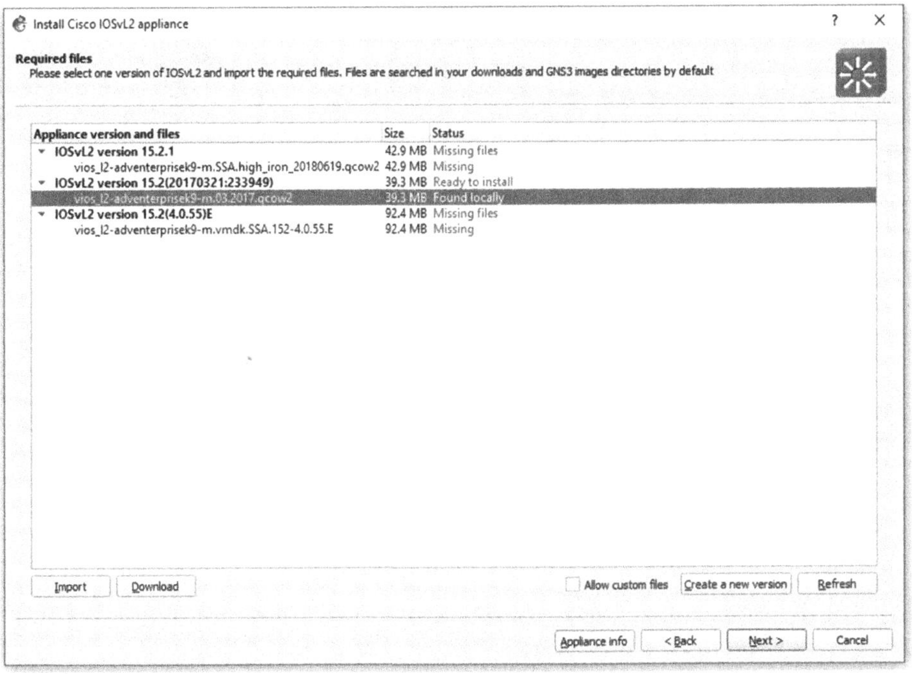

Figure 12-8. CML L2 switch installation, required files

7	When the Appliance window pops up, click Yes. See Figure 12-9.

Figure 12-9. CML L2 installation, appliance install pop-up

8	To complete the installation, click Finish. See Figure 12-10.

(continued)

#	Task

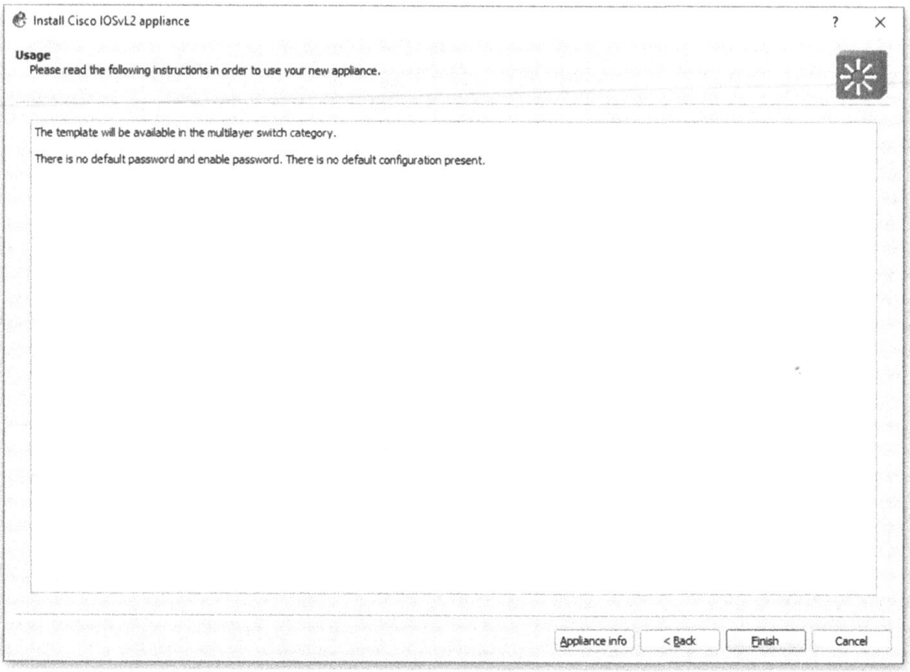

Figure 12-10. *CM L2 switch installation, usage*

9 The "Add template" window pops up; click OK to finish the installation. See Figure 12-11.

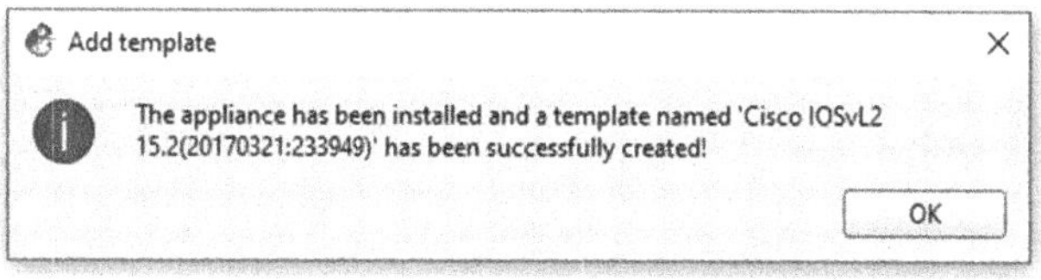

Figure 12-11. *CML L2 switch installation, "Add template" pop-up*

10 On GNS3, click the Switch button on the left, which looks like two opposite arrows, to open the switches. See Figure 12-12.

Figure 12-12. *CML L2 switch installation, select switch icon on GNS3*

#	Task
11	If Cisco CML-PERSONAL IOSvL2 was installed correctly, you would see your new switch devices installed under Switches. See Figure 12-13.

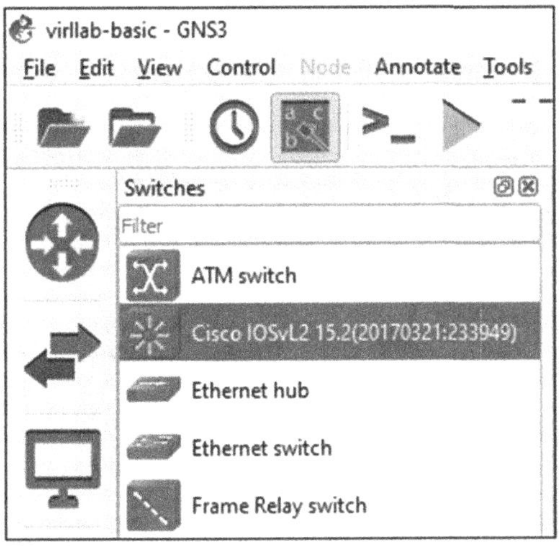

Figure 12-13. *CML L2 switch installation, selecting the Cisco IOSvL2 switch*

#	Task
12	Now, drag and drop the IOSvL2 switch to the cmllab-basic lab, as shown in Figure 12-14.

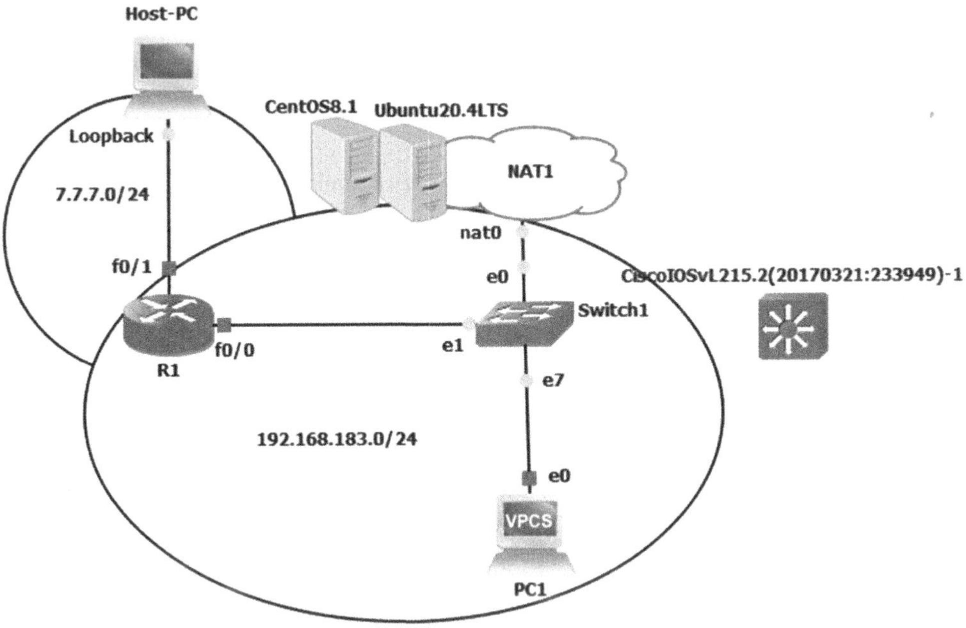

Figure 12-14. *CML L2 switch installation, dragging and dropping a CML switch*

(continued)

#	Task
13	Using the Add Link tool, connect Gi0/0 of the new switch to Switch1's e2 interface, as shown in Figure 12-15. Then power on all devices on the topology and also the CentOS8.1 and Ubuntu 20.04 LTS servers on VMware Workstation 15 Pro. Rename the switch to LAB-SW1 by right-clicking and clicking the Change Hostname menu.

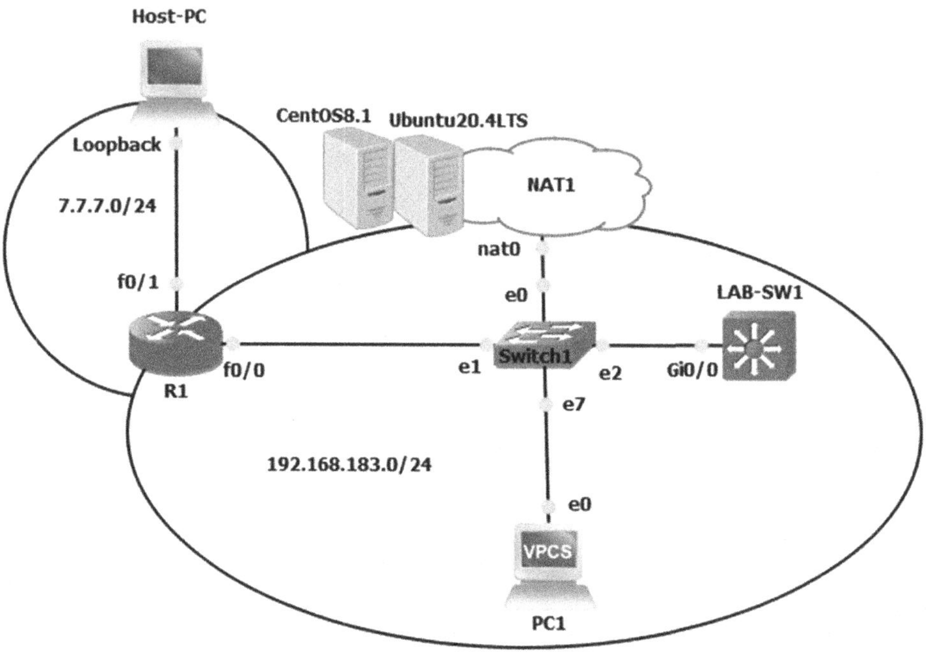

Figure 12-15. CML L2 switch installation, connecting the CML switch to the network

14	After powering on LAB-SW1, open its console, and you will see a similar power-on screen as shown in Figure 12-16.

#	Task

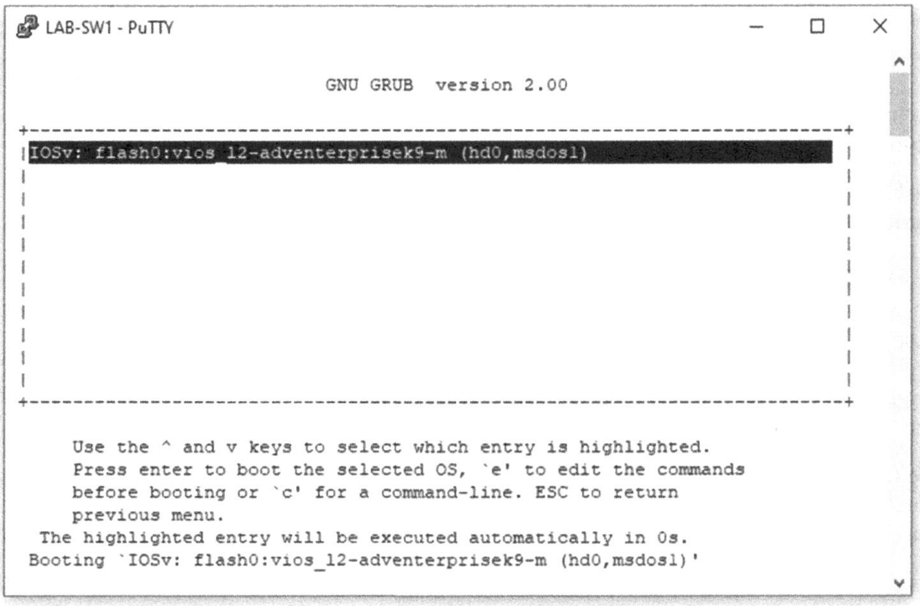

Figure 12-16. *CML L2 switch installation, powered-on CML switch screen*

15 Your new switch's console screen should look like the following if it successfully booted up. Now you have completed the CML-PERSONAL L2 switch installation on your GNS3. Get ready for some switching labs.

```
Cisco IOS Software, vios_l2 Software (vios_l2-ADVENTERPRISEK9-M), Experimental
Version 15.2(20170321:233949) [mmen 101]
Copyright (c) 1986-2017 by Cisco Systems, Inc.
Compiled Wed 22-Mar-17 08:38 by mmen
************************************************************************
* IOSv is strictly limited to use for evaluation, demonstration and IOS  *
* education. IOSv is provided as-is and is not supported by Cisco's      *
* Technical Advisory Center. Any use or disclosure, in whole or in part, *
* of the IOSv Software or Documentation to any third party for any       *
*
*Jan  9 10:36:48.512: %PLATFORM-5-SIGNATURE_VERIFIED: Image 'flash0:/vios_l2-
adventerprisek9-m' passed code signing verification purposes is expressly prohibited
except as otherwise authorized by      *
* Cisco in writing.                                                      *
************************************************************************
Switch>
```

Quick Communication Test on CML L2 Switch Integration on GNS3

At the end of the CML-PERSONAL L2 switch installation, quickly perform communication verification from the switch to other devices on the network. The recommended ICMP tests are described as follows:

#	Task

1	Quickly log in and configure the correct switch name and a VLAN 1 interface on the new switch with a valid IP address.
	`Switch>enable # Enter Privileged EXEC mode`
	`Switch#configure terminal # Enter Global Configuration mode`
	`LAB-SW1(config)#hostname LAB-SW1 # Rename hostname`
	`LAB-SW1(config)#spanning-tree vlan 1 root primary # Designate this switch as the root primary`
	`LAB-SW1(config)#interface vlan 1 # Enter interface vlan 1 config mode`
	`LAB-SW1(config-if)#ip add 192.168.183.101 255.255.255.0 # Configure an IP address`
	`LAB-SW1(config-if)#no shut # Bring up this interface`
	`LAB-SW1(config-if)#end # Go back to Privileged EXEC mode`

2	On LAB-SW1, as soon as you bring up Gi0/0, you may be prompted with duplex mismatch errors from R1's f0/0 interface. To stop this annoying CDP error message on LAB-SW1, you need to hard-code R1's f0/0 interface speed to 100 and duplex to full. If you do not get this error, you can continue to the next step.
	`LAB-SW1(config-if)#`
	`*Aug 2 11:16:38.977: %CDP-4-DUPLEX_MISMATCH: duplex mismatch discovered on GigabitEthernet0/0 (not half duplex), with R1 FastEthernet0/0 (half duplex).`
	Open console for R1 and change the interface speed and duplex as follows:
	`R1#configure terminal # Enter Global Configuration mode`
	`R1(config)#interface f0/0 # Enter interface configuration mode`
	`R1(config-if)#duplex full # Change interface duplex to full (default auto)`
	`R1(config-if)#speed 100 # Change interface speed to 100`
	`R1(config-if)# do write memory # save the configuration`

3	Go to PC1 and run the `ip dhcp` command to get an IP address, or if you are continuing your lab from the previous chapter, run the `show ip` command to check the IP address of PC1.
	`PC1> ip dhcp # Request an IP address from DHCP server`
	`DDORA IP 192.168.183.129/24 GW 192.168.183.2`
	`PC1> show ip # Display IP Settings of PC1 (VPCS)`
	`NAME : PC1[1]`
	`IP/MASK : 192.168.183.129/24`
	`GATEWAY : 192.168.183.2`
	`DNS : 192.168.183.2`
	`DHCP SERVER : 192.168.183.254`
	`DHCP LEASE : 1713, 1800/900/1575`
	`DOMAIN NAME : localdomain`
	`MAC : 00:50:79:66:68:00`
	`LPORT : 20012`
	`RHOST:PORT : 127.0.0.1:20013`
	`MTU: : 1500`

#	Task

4	From LAB-SW1 (192.168.183.101), send ICMP messages to PC1 (192.168.183.129) and R1's f0/0 (192.168.183.133).
	`LAB-SW1#ping 192.168.183.129`
	`Type escape sequence to abort.`
	`Sending 5, 100-byte ICMP Echos to 192.168.183.129, timeout is 2 seconds:`
	`.!!!!`
	`Success rate is 100 percent (5/5), round-trip min/avg/max = 2/3/5 ms`
	`LAB-SW1#ping 192.168.183.133`
	`Type escape sequence to abort.`
	`Sending 5, 100-byte ICMP Echos to 192.168.183.133, timeout is 2 seconds:`
	`.!!!!`
	`Success rate is 80 percent (4/5), round-trip min/avg/max = 2/4/6 ms`

5	Make sure that both Linux servers are up and running on VMware Workstation. From the previous chapter, we know the IP address of the `centos8s1` server is 192.168.183.130, and the `ubuntu20s1` server is 192.168.183.132.
	From LAB-SW1, send ICMP packets (ping) to both `centos8s1` and `ubuntu20s1`. Your server IP address may be different from the example shown here:
	`LAB-SW1#ping 192.168.183.130`
	`Type escape sequence to abort.`
	`Sending 5, 100-byte ICMP Echos to 192.168.183.130, timeout is 2 seconds:`
	`!!!!!`
	`Success rate is 100 percent (5/5), round-trip min/avg/max = 3/6/13 ms`
	`LAB-SW1#ping 192.168.183.132`
	`Type escape sequence to abort.`
	`Sending 5, 100-byte ICMP Echos to 192.168.183.132, timeout is 2 seconds:`
	`!!!!!`
	`Success rate is 100 percent (5/5), round-trip min/avg/max = 2/3/6 ms`

6	After successful communication testing, copy the running configuration to the startup configuration.
	`LAB-SW1#copy running-config startup-config # Save running configuration to startup configuration`
	`Destination filename [startup-config]?`
	`Building configuration...`
	`Compressed configuration from 3559 bytes to 1604 bytes[OK]`

You have now completed the integration and verification of the CML L2 switch image on GNS2. With this image, we can many switches to test multiple-device Python network automation labs. Next, go ahead and integrate the L3 router image.

Installing the Cisco CML-PERSONAL L3 Router on GNS3

Now you will follow the procedures shown in this section to install the CML-PERSONAL L3 router on GNS3; this will enable you to run the CML-PERSONAL router on GNS3. And as usual, you will require a connection to the Internet to complete this procedure. It is best to be connected to the home network than work during the installation process. Please note that if your host PC is connected to the internet via a company proxy, you may encounter some problems. See Figure 12-17.

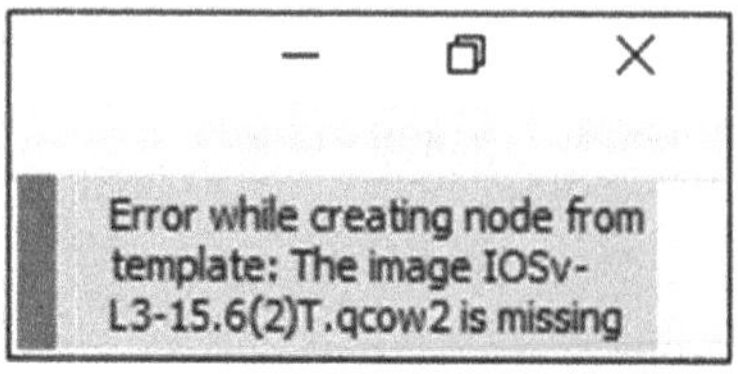

Figure 12-17. *GNS3, CML-PERSONAL L3 image error*

⚠ The integration of CML images looks normal until you drag and drop the icon onto the GNS3 Topology canvas. If GNS3 produces a qcow2 or other error and does not work, you may have to use the "Delete template" option as shown in Figure 12-18 and restart the integration process from scratch.

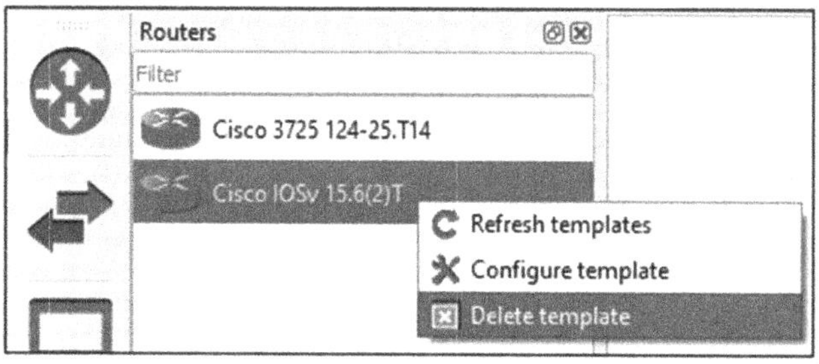

Figure 12-18. *GNS3, deleting the CML-PERSONAL L3 template*

Now add a new template for the CML L3 router image and complete the integration.

#	Task
1	In the GNS3 main window, go to File and click "+ New template." See Figure 12-19.

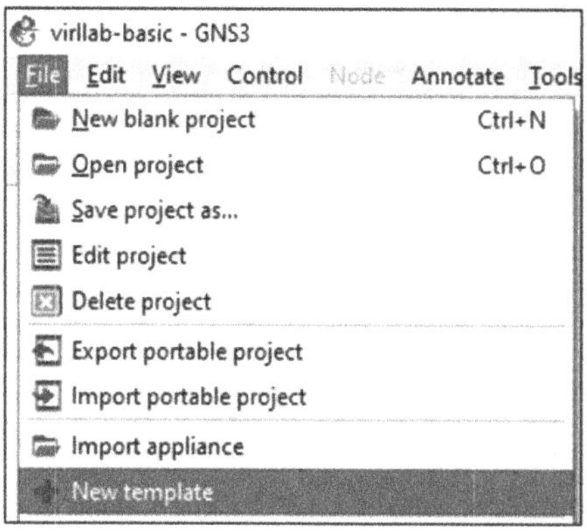

Figure 12-19. *CML L3 router installation, adding a new template*

#	Task
2	When the "New template" wizard opens, leave the default selection of "Install an appliance from the GNS3 server (recommended)" and click Next. See Figure 12-20.

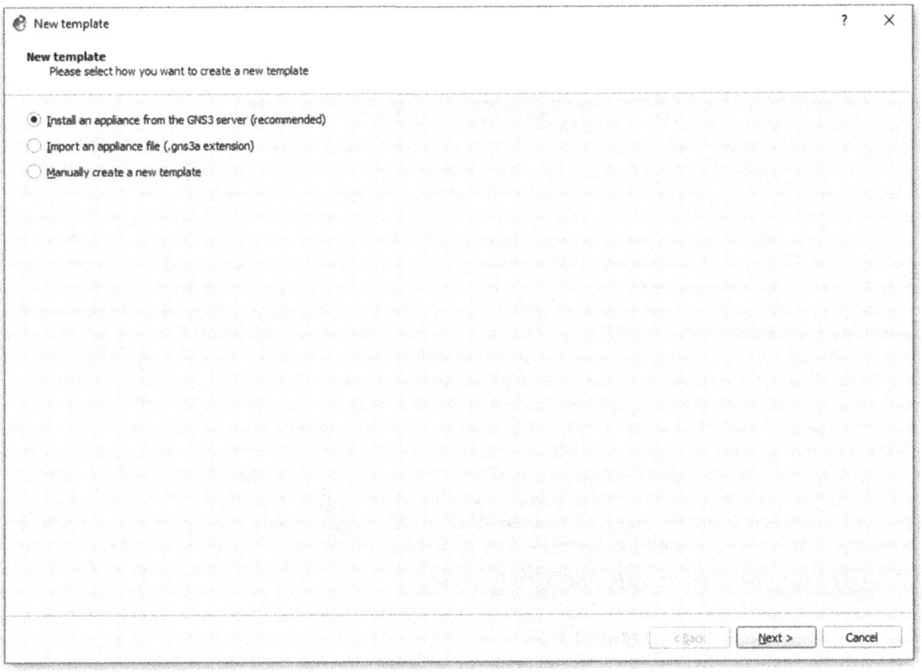

Figure 12-20. *CML L3 router installation, new template*

#	Task
3	In the "Appliances from server" window, type **IOSv** in the search field to locate Cisco IOSv Qemu under Switches. Select the searched device and click Install. This is the template for the Cisco CML-PERSONAL L3 router on GNS3. See Figure 12-21.

(*continued*)

#	Task

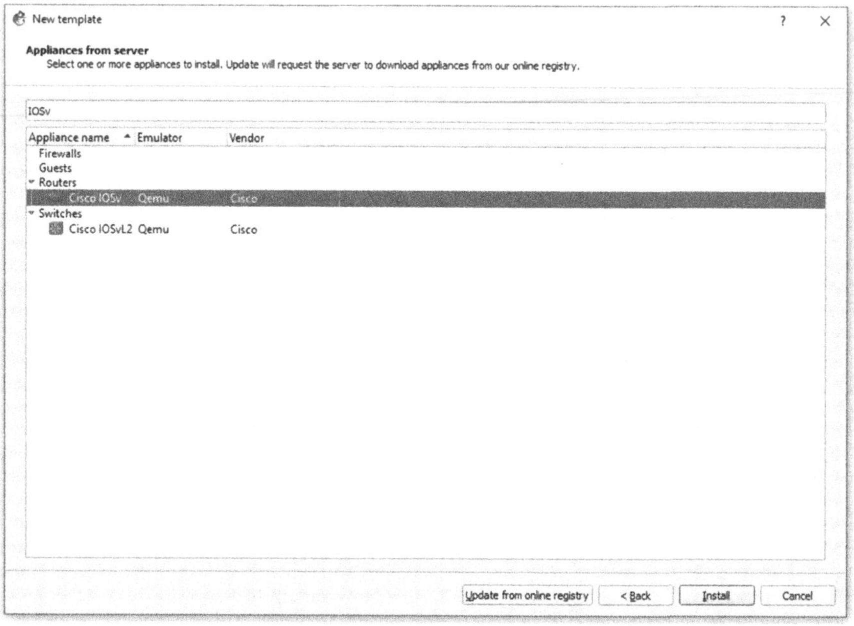

Figure 12-21. *CML L3 router installation, appliances from server*

4 In the next window, click Next. See Figure 12-22.

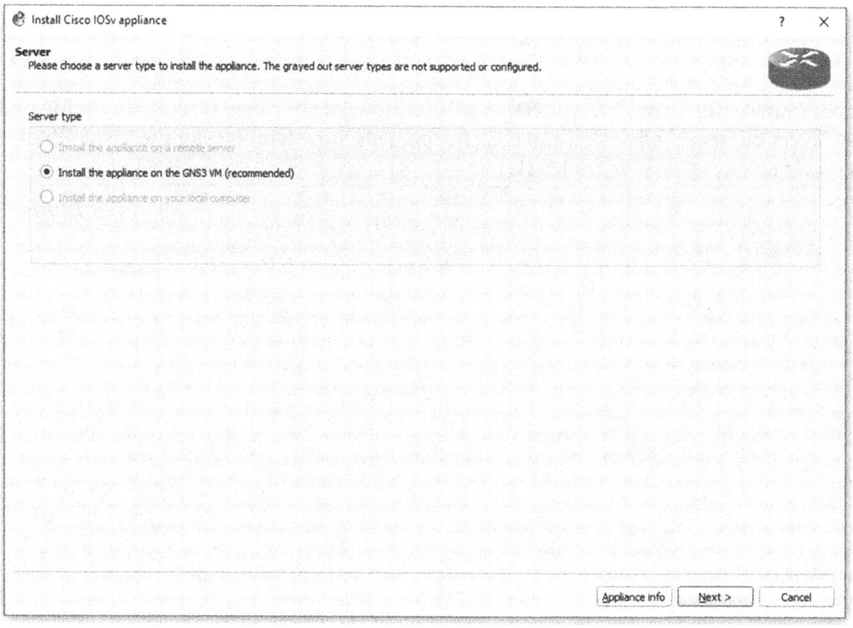

Figure 12-22. *CML L3 router installation, server selection*

#	Task
5	On the "Qemu settings" screen, click Next again. See Figure 12-23.

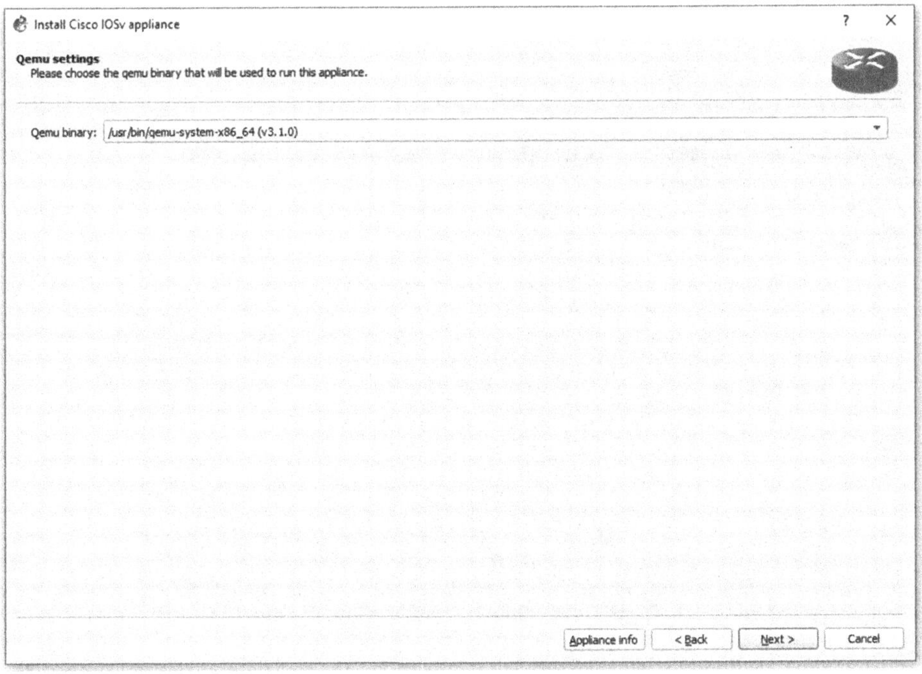

Figure 12-23. *CML L3 router installation, Qemu settings*

#	Task
6	It is recommended that you click the actual vIOS name under "Required files" and highlight it before clicking Next. Notice that the actual image name `vios-adventerprisek9-m.vmdk.SPA.156-2.T` is selected before clicking the Next button. See Figure 12-24.

(continued)

#	Task

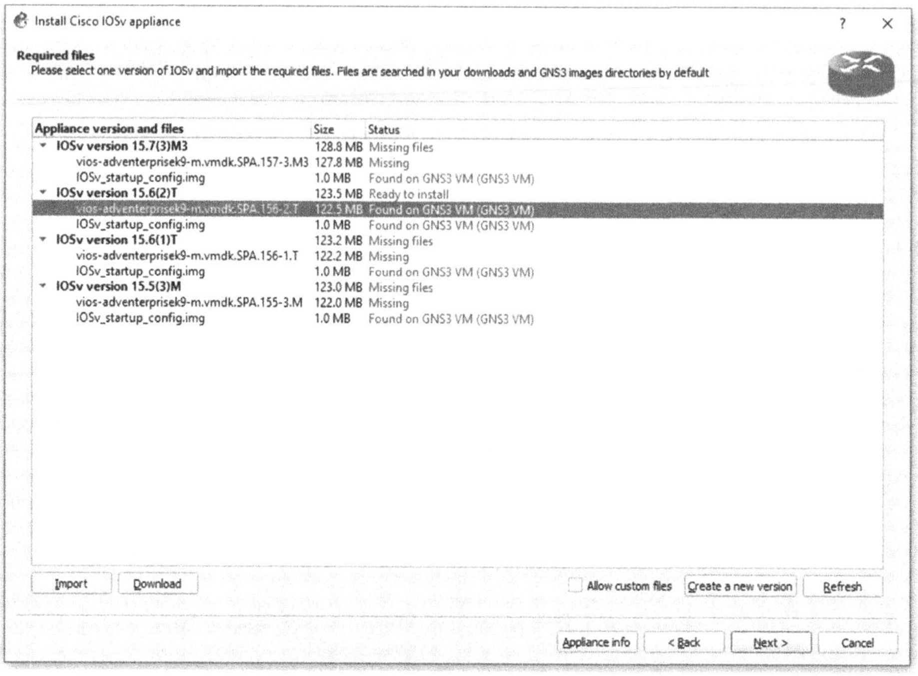

Figure 12-24. *CML L3 router installation, required files*

7 When the Appliance window pops up, click Yes. See Figure 12-25.

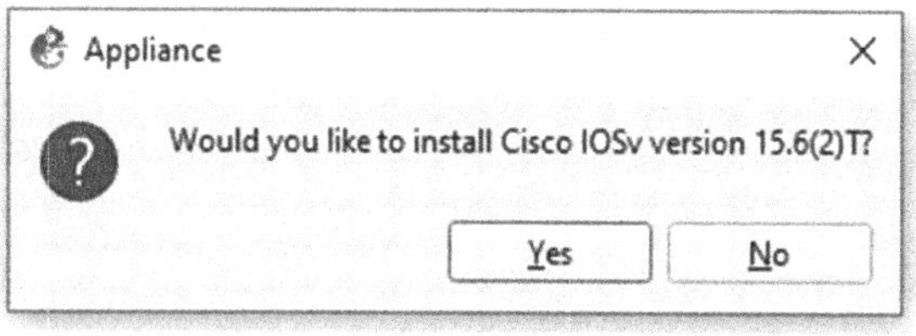

Figure 12-25. *CML L3 router installation, Appliance install pop-up*

8 In the Usage window, click Finish. See Figure 12-26.

#	Task

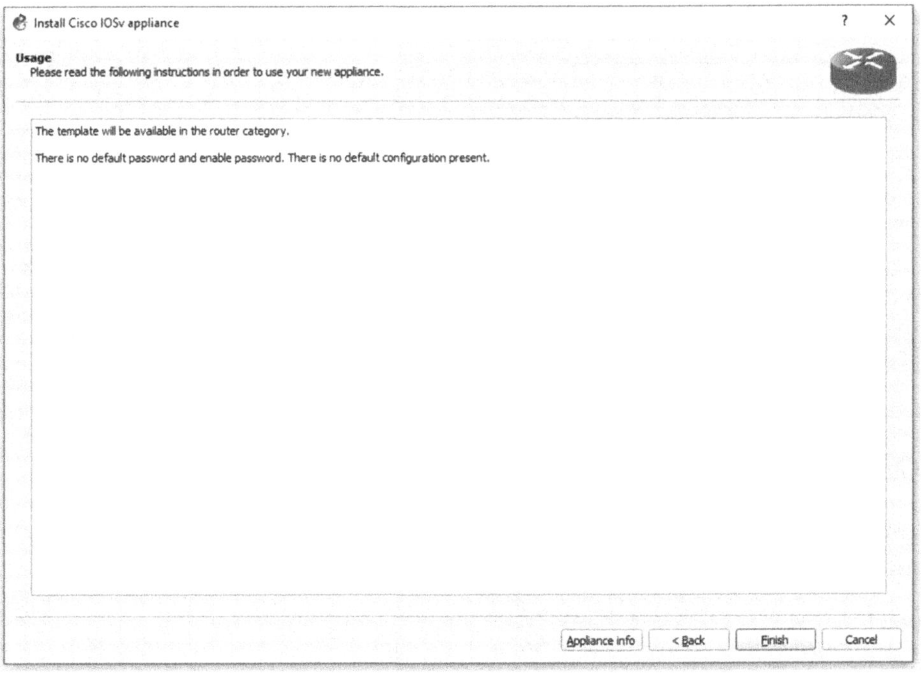

Figure 12-26. *CML L3 router installation, usage*

9 When the "Add template" message appears, click OK to complete the CML-PERSONAL L3 router image installation. See Figure 12-27.

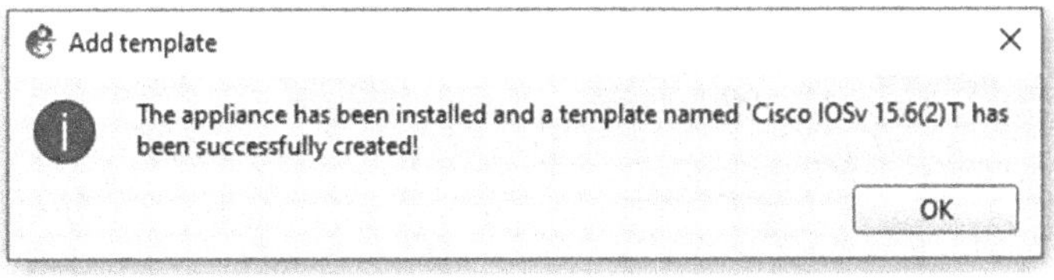

Figure 12-27. *CML L3 router installation, "Add template" pop-up*

10 Go back to the main user window, and this time click the Router icon that looks like a circle with four arrows. See Figure 12-28.

Figure 12-28. *CML L3 router installation, clicking the router icon on GNS3*

(continued)

#	Task
11	The Routers list appears as shown in Figure 12-29, and you will immediately notice that a new IOSv router has been added.

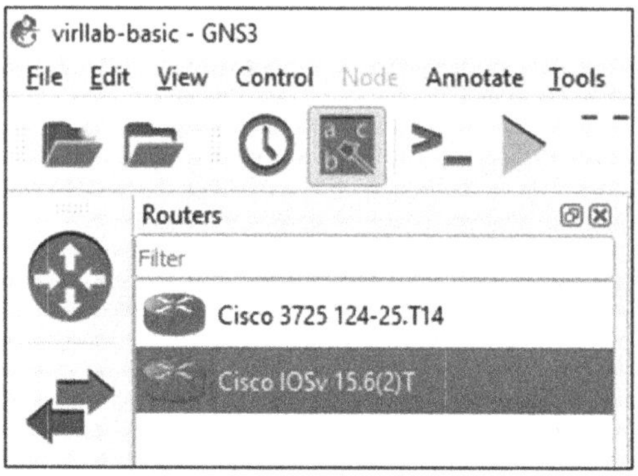

Figure 12-29. *CML L3 router installation, selecting the CML router*

12	Now drag and drop the new router onto the Topology canvas of the `cmllab-basic` project. Rename the router as LAB-R1. See Figure 12-30.

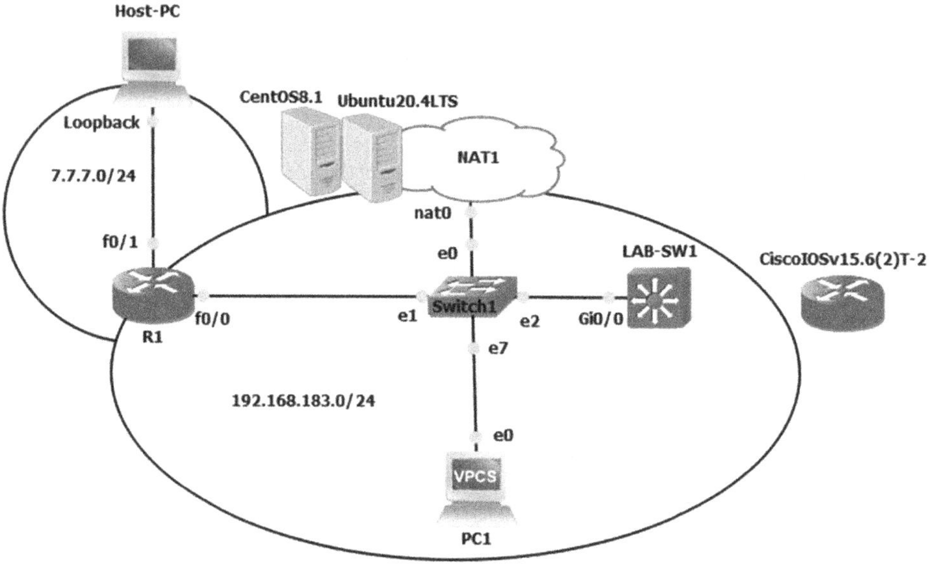

Figure 12-30. *CML L3 router installation, dragging and dropping the CML router*

13	Once the new router has been renamed, use the Add Link (connector) tool, and connect Lab-R1's Gi0/0 interface to LAB-SW1's Gi0/1 interface. You can make the connection while the other device is switched on. Now power on LAB-R1 and open the console window. See Figure 12-31. The Topology Summary window shows the virtual connection between devices (see Figure 12-32). The Servers Summary window shows where each device is hosted (see Figure 12-33).

#	Task

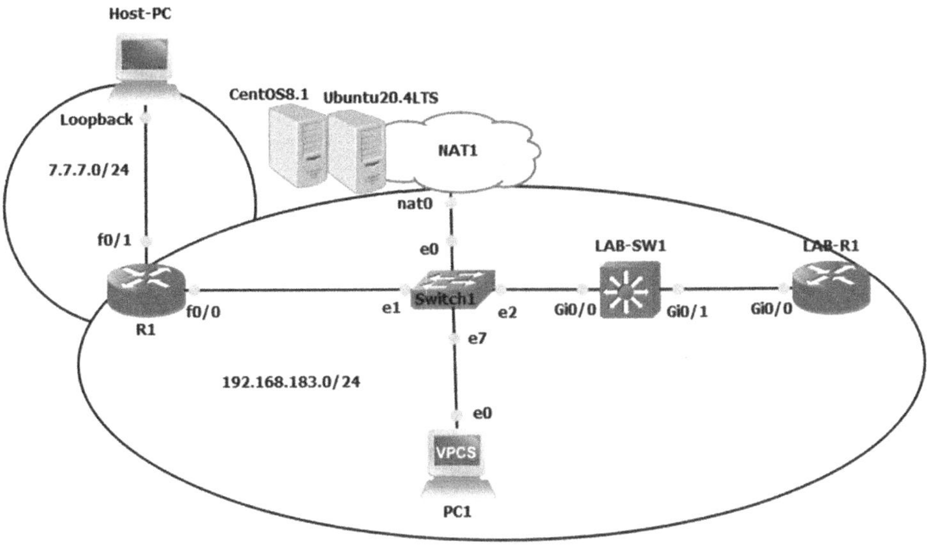

Figure 12-31. *CML L3 router installation, connecting and starting the CML router*

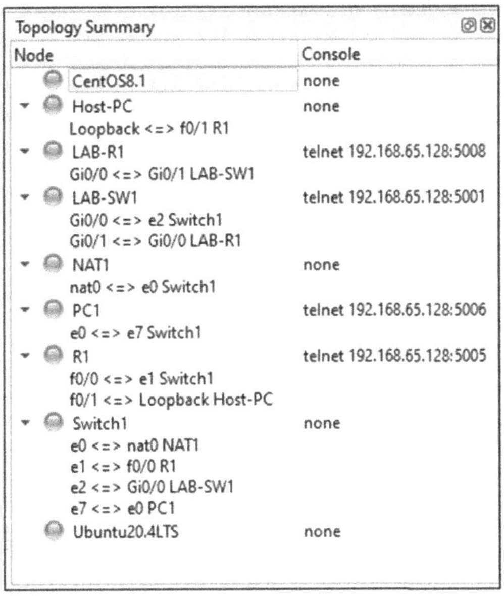

Figure 12-32. *Topology Summary window*

(*continued*)

#	Task

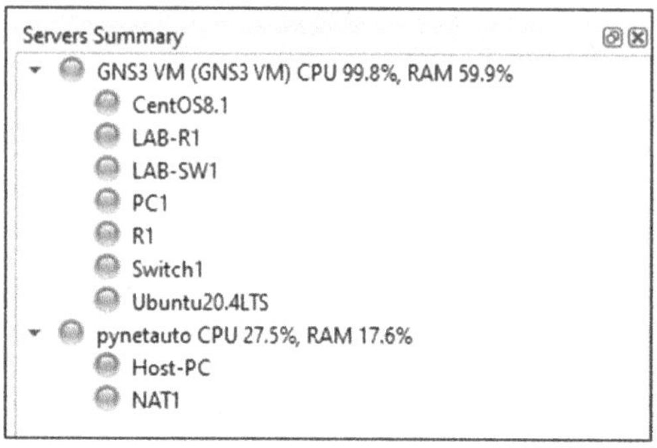

Figure 12-33. *Servers Summary window*

14 When the router boots up, it will display the vIOS version during the bootup. See Figure 12-34.

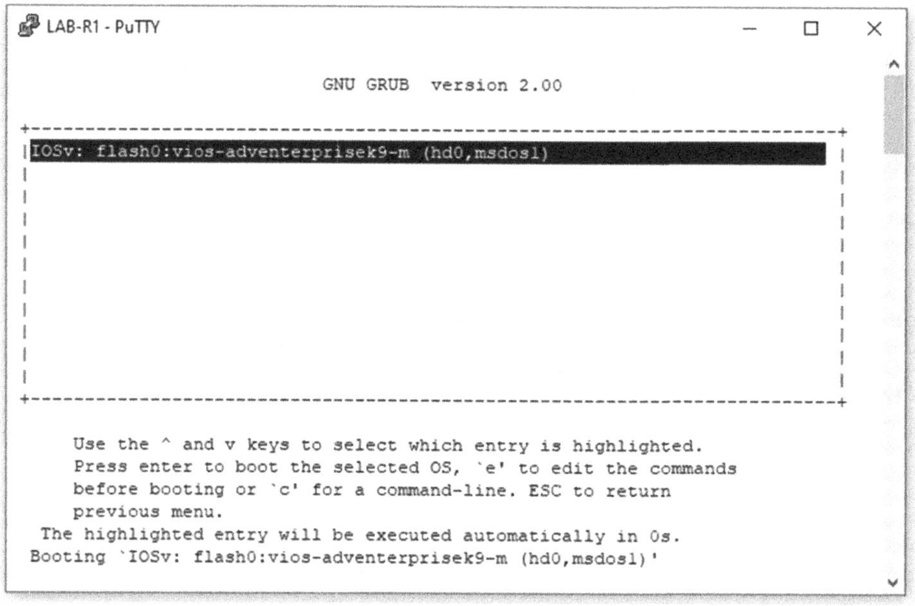

Figure 12-34. *CML L3 router installation, powered-on CML router screen*

#	Task
15	If you see a console screen similar to Figure 12-35, it means you have completed the CML-PERSONAL L3 router on GNS3. CML-PERSONAL is almost identical to Cisco IOS 15.x. Now you are ready for some routing labs using a newer IOS image.

```
Cisco IOS Software, IOSv Software (VIOS-ADVENTERPRISEK9-M), Version 15.6(2)T,
RELEASE SOFTWARE (fc2)
Technical Support: http://www.cisco.com/techsupport
Copyright (c) 1986-2016 by Cisco Systems, Inc.
Compiled Tue 22-Mar-16 16:19 by prod_rel_team
*Jan  9 11:12:35.500: %CRYPTO-6-ISAKMP_ON_OFF: ISAKMP is OFF
*Jan  9 11:12:35.501: %CRYPTO-6-GDOI_ON_OFF: GDOI is OFF
*Jan  9 11:12:37.708: %SYS-3-CPUHOG: Task is running for (1999)msecs, more than
(2000)msecs (0/0),process = Crypto CA.
**************************************************************************
* IOSv is strictly limited to use for evaluation, demonstration and IOS  *
* education. IOSv is provided as-is and is not supported by Cisco's      *
* Technical Advisory Center. Any use or disclosure, in whole or in part, *
* of the IOSv Software or Documentation to any third party for any       *
* purposes is expressly prohibited except as otherwise authorized by     *
* Cisco in writing.                                                      *
**************************************************************************
Router#
```

Quick Communication Test on CML L3 Router Integration on GNS3

Complete the following tasks to allow the newly installed router to communicate to the rest of the devices in your topology:

#	Task
1	Quickly log in to the new router and configure the correct router name. Also, configure a valid IP address from the same subnet as VMnet8 (192.168.183.0/24) to interface with GigabitEthernet 0/0. Please note that your subnet is maybe different. Make sure you issue the `no shut` command to bring up the interface.

```
Router#configure terminal # Enter Global Configuration mode
Router(config)#hostname LAB-R1 # Rename hostname
LAB-R1(config)#interface GigabitEthernet 0/0 # Enter interface Gi0/0 config mode
LAB-R1(config-if)#ip add 192.168.183.10 255.255.255.0 # Configure an IP address
LAB-R1(config-if)#no shut # Bring up this interface
LAB-R1(config-if)#end # Go back to Privileged EXEC mode
```

#	Task
2	On the Lab-R1 router, once the Gi0/0 interface comes up, start sending ICMP packets to the following IP addresses to ensure that LAB-R1 can communicate to all the other devices in our topology. VMnet8's default gateway IP (192.168.183.2), PC1's IP address (192.168.183.129), R1's f0/0 (192.168.183.133), the `centos8s1` server (192.168.183.130), and the `ubuntu20s1` server (192.168.183.132).

(continued)

#	Task

	`LAB-R1#`**`ping 192.168.183.2`**` # To Default Gateway`
	`Type escape sequence to abort.`
	`Sending 5, 100-byte ICMP Echos to 192.168.183.2, timeout is 2 seconds:`
	`.!!!!`
	`Success rate is 80 percent (4/5), round-trip min/avg/max = 8/10/11 ms`
	`LAB-R1#`**`ping 192.168.183.129`**` # To PC1`
	`Type escape sequence to abort.`
	`Sending 5, 100-byte ICMP Echos to 192.168.183.129, timeout is 2 seconds:`
	`.!!!!`
	`Success rate is 80 percent (4/5), round-trip min/avg/max = 7/9/12 ms`
	`LAB-R1#`**`ping 192.168.183.133`**` # To R1's f0/0 interface`
	`Type escape sequence to abort.`
	`Sending 5, 100-byte ICMP Echos to 192.168.183.133, timeout is 2 seconds:`
	`.!!!!`
	`Success rate is 80 percent (4/5), round-trip min/avg/max = 12/15/18 ms`
	`LAB-R1#`**`ping 192.168.183.130`**` # To centos8s1 server`
	`Type escape sequence to abort.`
	`Sending 5, 100-byte ICMP Echos to 192.168.183.130, timeout is 2 seconds:`
	`.!!!!`
	`Success rate is 80 percent (4/5), round-trip min/avg/max = 8/8/11 ms`
	`LAB-R1#`**`ping 192.168.183.132`**` # To ubuntu20s1 server`
	`Type escape sequence to abort.`
	`Sending 5, 100-byte ICMP Echos to 192.168.183.132, timeout is 2 seconds:`
	`.!!!!`
	`Success rate is 80 percent (4/5), round-trip min/avg/max = 8/9/10 ms`

3	For verification purposes only, we can also quickly test the SSH login to the CentOS8.1 server from LAB-R1 using the `ssh -l username server_IP` command.
	
	`LAB-R1#`**`ssh -l pynetauto 192.168.183.130`**` # SSH login to centos8s1 server`
	`Password:`
	`Activate the web console with: systemctl enable --now cockpit.socket`
	
	`Last login: Sat Jan  9 00:00:39 2021 from 192.168.183.1`
	`[pynetauto@centos8s1 ~]$ `**`exit`**
	`logout`
	
	`[Connection to 192.168.183.130 closed by foreign host]`
	`LAB-R1#`
	
	Please note that the SSH login to the `ubuntu20s1` server will not work due to a security algorithm mismatch. The SSH login sessions will be initiated from the server side to networking devices, and you do not have to worry about this at this stage.

4	Once you have completed the communication test, save the running configuration of LAB-R1 to the startup configuration.
	
	`LAB-R1#`**`copy running-config startup-config`**
	`Destination filename [startup-config]?`
	`Building configuration...`
	`[OK]`

Building a CML-PERSONAL Lab Topology

Before moving onto the actual lab task in the next chapter, let's add a few more devices to the `cmllab-basic` GNS3 project and complete our topology. This step assumes you are continuing the topology build from the last steps.

#	Task
1	Continuing from the previous section, add one more IOSvL2 switch and one more IOSv router to the topology as shown in Figure 12-35. Rename the switch to `lab-sw2` in lowercase and the router to `lab-r2` also in lowercase. The device names are not capitalized and standardized on purpose here, although it is a best practice to follow a strict naming convention for your network devices. In production, this convention is not followed by every engineer and becomes an annoyance. Hence, to emulate the imperfect production environment, we will not follow a strict device naming convention. Connect Gi0/0 of `lab-sw2` to Gi0/2 of LAB-SW1 and Gi0/1 of `lab-sw2` to Gi0/1 of lab-r2. Also, connect Gi0/0 of lab-r2 to Gi0/1 of LAB-R1.

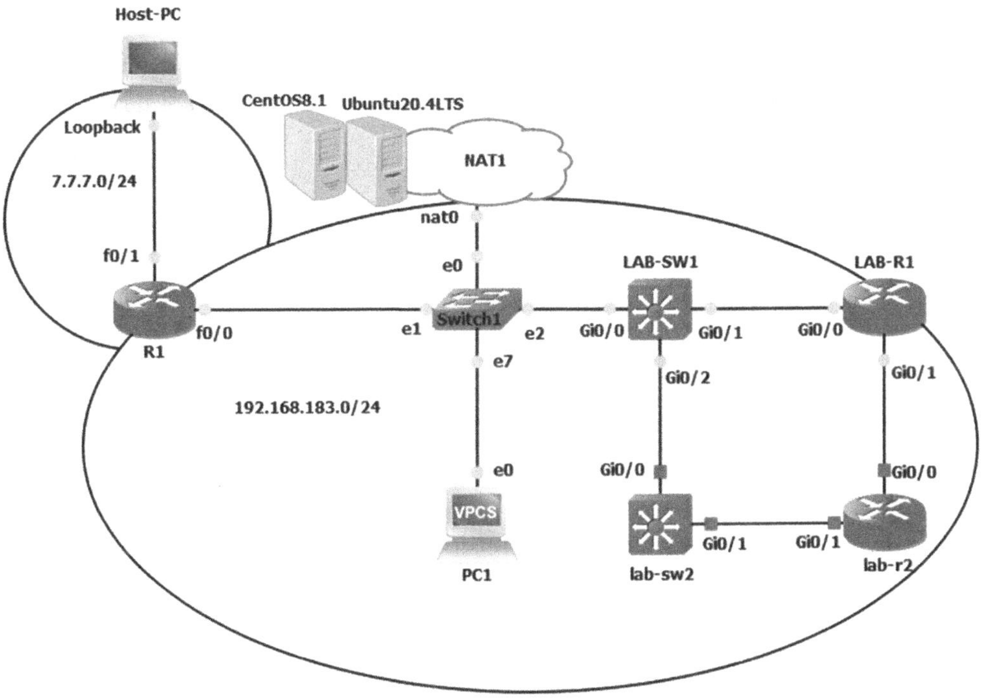

Figure 12-35. Configuring the CML lab topology, one of three

2	Now power on lab-sw2 and lab-r2 as shown in Figure 12-36.

(continued)

#	Task

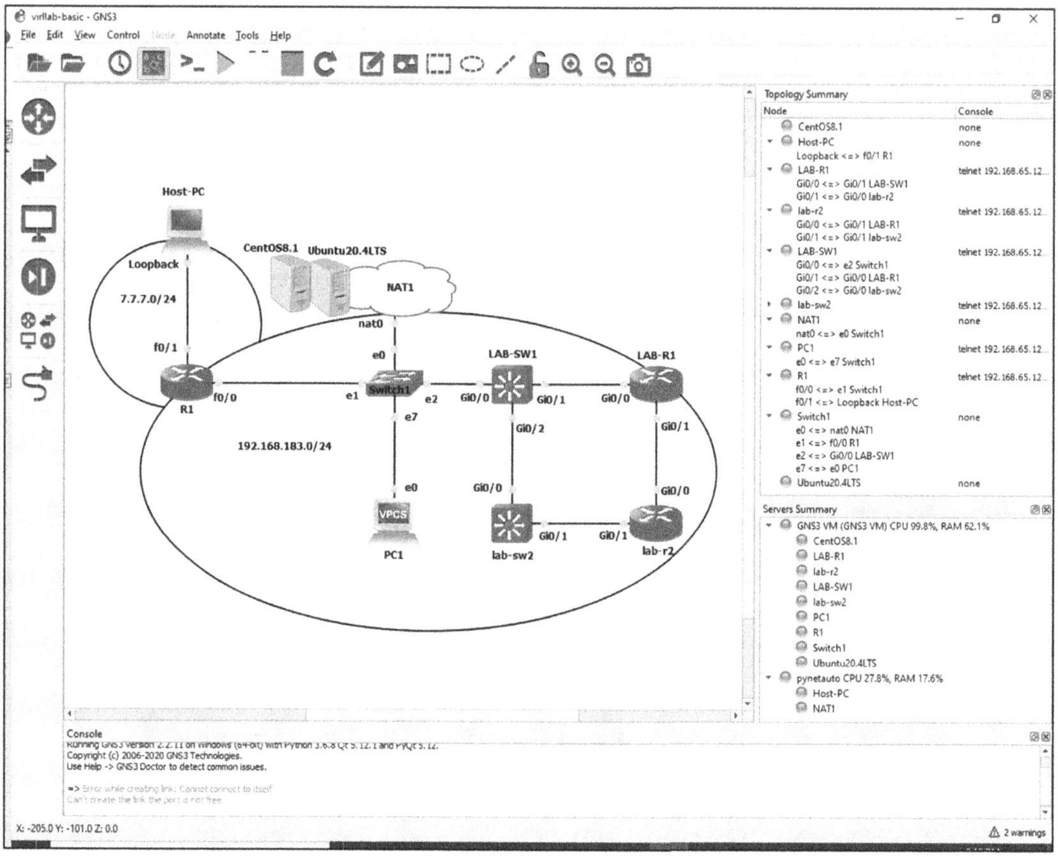

Figure 12-36. *Configuring CML lab topology, two of three*

3 At this stage, all devices, including the `centos8s1` IP Services server and `ubuntu20s1` Python server, should be powered on and running smoothly. Perform ping tests between the GNS3 network and the Linux servers to ensure that all devices can reach others on the VMnet8 network.

4 Here's the R1 IOS router configuration:

First, on R1 (IOS router), let's open the console to assign the IP address manually so its IP address does not change every time the DHCP lease time elapses.

```
R1#show ip interface brief # show interface configuration
Interface          IP-Address      OK? Method Status                Protocol
FastEthernet0/0    192.168.183.133 YES DHCP   up                    up
FastEthernet0/1    7.7.7.2         YES NVRAM  up                    up
FastEthernet1/0    unassigned      YES NVRAM  administratively down down

R1#configure terminal
Enter configuration commands, one per line.  End with CNTL/Z.
```

#	Task
	R1(config)#**interface FastEthernet0/0** # Enter interface configuration mode R1(config-if)#**no ip address dhcp** # Disable DHCP IP allocation from DHCP server R1(config-if)#**ip address 192.168.183.133 255.255.255.0** # Manually assign IP Address R1(config-if)#**speed 100** # Fix speed if you have not done so yet above R1(config-if)#**duplex full** # Fix duplex if you have not done so yet above R1(config-if)#**exit** # Move back to Global configuration mode R1(config)#**ip domain-lookup** # Enable DNS lookup R1(config)#**ip name-server 192.168.183.2** # Assign Default Gateway as the name-server R1(config)#**ip route** 0.0.0.0 0.0.0.0 192.168.183.2 # Add a default route R1(config)#**router ospf 1** # Configure basic ospf R1(config-router)#**network 0.0.0.0 255.255.255.255 area 0** # add all network to ospf area 0 R1(config-router)#**end** # Move back to Exec Privilege mode R1#**write memory** # Save current running configuration to startup configuration After saving the configuration, perform a quick ping test to the default gateway (192.168.183.2) and any other devices on the network. They should all be reachable from R1.
5	Here's the LAB-SW1 configuration: Now open the LAB-SW1 console and reconfigure the first CML-PERSONAL switch. This switch already has a VLAN 1 interface manually configured, so there's no need to reconfigure the IP address. Since the switches will be used as L2 devices, there is no need to configure DNS or static routes. LAB-SW1#**show ip interface brief | be Vlan1** Vlan1 192.168.183.101 YES NVRAM up up **Use the following configuration to complete the LAB-SW1 configuration.** LAB-SW1#**configure terminal** # Enter Global configuration mode LAB-SW1(config)#**enable password cisco123** # Configure enable password LAB-SW1(config)#**username pynetauto privilege 15 password cisco123** #configure L15 user with pwd LAB-SW1(config)#**line vty 0 15** # Enter Virtual Terminal Line configuration mode LAB-SW1(config-line)#**login local** # Allow locally configured account LAB-SW1(config-line)#**transport input all** # use both telnet and SSH connection LAB-SW1(config-line)#**logging synchronous** # Change line automatically during log message LAB-SW1(config-line)#**no exec-timeout** # No connection time-out, for Lab use only LAB-SW1(config-line)#**line console 0** # Enter Line Console 0 config mode LAB-SW1(config-line)#**logging synchronous** # Change line automatically during console message LAB-SW1(config-line)#**no exec-timeout** # No connection time-out, for Lab use only LAB-SW1(config-line)#**end** # Move back to Exec privilege mode LAB-SW1#copy running-config startup-config # Save running-config to startup-config Destination filename [startup-config]? Building configuration... [OK]

(continued)

#	Task
6	Here's the lab-sw2 configuration:

Let's apply a similar configuration to the newly added switch, `lab-sw2`. This switch will also be configured as a layer 2 switch, so there's no need to enable IP routing or to configure DNS. No explanation will be added to this configuration as it is almost identical to the previous LAB-SW2 configuration.

```
Switch>en
Switch#conf t
Switch(config)#hostname lab-sw2
lab-sw2(config)#interface vlan 1
lab-sw2(config-if)#ip add 196.168.183.102 255.255.255.0
lab-sw2(config-if)#no shut
lab-sw2(config-if)#enable password cisco123
lab-sw2(config)#username pynetauto pri 15 pass cisco123
lab-sw2(config)#line vty 0 15
lab-sw2(config-line)#login local
lab-sw2(config-line)#transport input all
lab-sw2(config-line)#logging synchronous
lab-sw2(config-line)#no exec-timeout
lab-sw2(config-line)#line console 0
lab-sw2(config-line)#logging synchronous
lab-sw2(config-line)#no exec-timeout
lab-sw2(config-line)#end
lab-sw2#copy running-config startup-config
Destination filename [startup-config]?
Building configuration...
[OK]
```

7 Here's the LAB-R1 configuration:

Next, open the console of LAB-R1, assign a DNS server, and then add a static route to allow smooth communication on our lab topology. LAB-R1's Gi0/0 has been manually configured with an IP address of 192.168.183.10/24, so there's no need to configure it. Configure the first CML-PERSONAL router, as shown here:

```
To configure LAB-R1, use the following configuration:
LAB-R1#configure terminal# Enter Global configuration mode
LAB-R1(config)#interface GigabitEthernet 0/1# Enter interface configuration mode
LAB-R1(config-if)#ip address 172.168.1.1 255.255.255.0# Assign IP address to Gi0/1
interfacing lab-r2
LAB-R1(config-if)#no shut# Bring up the interface
LAB-R1(config-if)#exit# Exit interface configuration mode
LAB-R1(config)#ip domain-lookup# Enable DNS lookup
LAB-R1(config)#ip name-server 192.168.183.2# Assign Default Gateway as DNS server
LAB-R1(config)#ip route 0.0.0.0 0.0.0.0 192.168.183.2# Add a static Gateway of last
resort
LAB-R1(config)#enable password cisco123# Configure enable password
LAB-R1(config)#username pynetauto privilege 15 password cisco123# configure level
15 user with pwd
```

#	Task

	`LAB-R1(config)#line vty 0 15# Enter Virtual Terminal Line configuration mode`
	`LAB-R1(config-line)#login local# Allow locally configured account`
	`LAB-R1(config-line)#transport input all# use both telnet and SSH connection`
	`LAB-R1(config-line)#logging synchronous#  Change line automatically during log message`
	`LAB-R1(config-line)#no exec-timeout# No connection time-out, for Lab use only`
	`LAB-R1(config-line)#line console 0# Enter Line Console 0 config mode`
	`LAB-R1(config-line)#logging synchronous# Change line automatically during console message`
	`LAB-R1(config-line)#no exec-timeout# No connection time-out, for Lab use only`
	`LAB-R1(config-line)#end# Move back to Exec privilege mode`
	`LAB-R1#copy running-config startup-config# Save running-config to startup-config`
	`Destination filename [startup-config]?`
	`Building configuration...`
	`[OK]`

8	Here's the lab-r2 configuration:
	
	Configure the second CML-PERSONAL L3 router using the following configuration suggestions. The basic configuration is almost identical to that of LAB-R1, so no line-by-line explanation is given.
	
	`Router#conf t`
	`Router(config)#hostname lab-r2`
	`lab-r2(config-if)#interface GigabitEthernet 0/0`
	`lab-r2(config-if)#ip address 172.168.1.2 255.255.255.0`
	`lab-r2(config)#interface GigabitEthernet 0/1`
	`lab-r2(config-if)#ip add 192.168.183.20 255.255.255.0`
	`lab-r2(config-if)#no shut`
	`lab-r2(config-if)#exit`
	`lab-r2(config)#ip domain-lookup`
	`lab-r2(config)#ip name-server 192.168.183.2`
	`lab-r2(config)#ip route 0.0.0.0 0.0.0.0 192.168.183.2`
	`lab-r2(config)#enable password cisco123`
	`lab-r2(config)#username pynetauto pri  15 password cisco123`
	`lab-r2(config)#line vty 0 15`
	`lab-r2(config-line)#login local`
	`lab-r2(config-line)#transport input all`
	`lab-r2(config-line)#logging synchronous`
	`lab-r2(config-line)#no exec-timeout`
	`lab-r2(config-line)#line console 0`
	`lab-r2(config-line)#logging synchronous`
	`lab-r2(config-line)#no exec-timeout`
	`lab-r2(config-line)#end`
	`lab-r2#copy running-config startup-config`
	`Destination filename [startup-config]?`
	`Building configuration...`
	`[OK]`

9	One of the background shapes has been changed from an oval to a rectangle to make the lab look better, and the topology has been decorated with IP addresses to make the lab steps clear. Take time to decorate your topology to help you with the IP addressing for the coming labs. See Figure 12-37, Figure 12-38, and Figure 12-39.

(*continued*)

#	Task

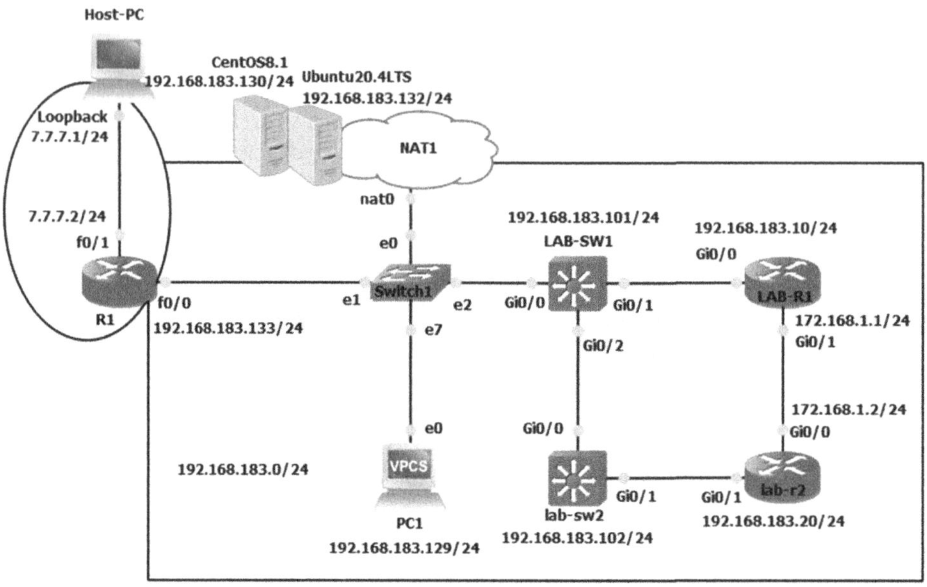

Figure 12-37. Configuring the CML lab topology, three out of three

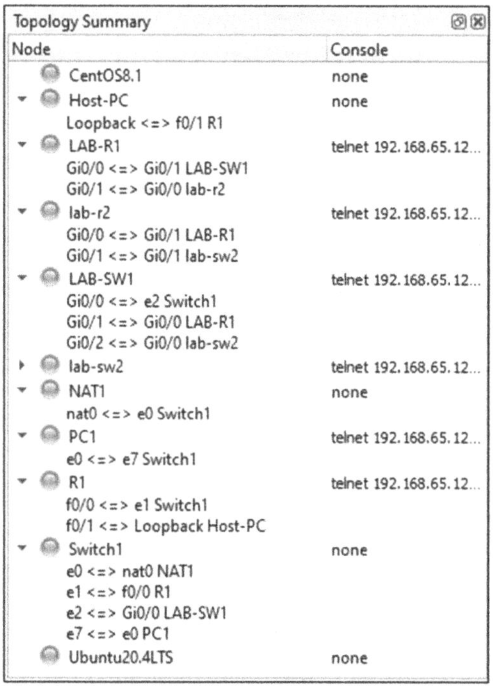

Figure 12-38. Topology Summary window

#	Task

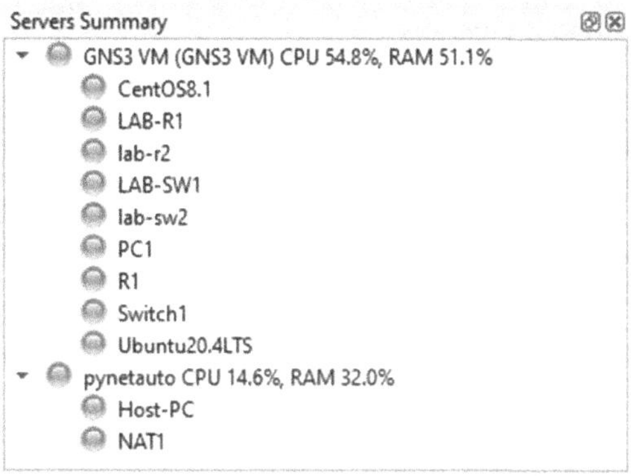

Figure 12-39. *Servers Summary window*

10 Now SSH into the `ubutun20s1` or `centos8s1` server and send some ICMP packets to each network device in our topology. Try to send some ICMP messages using the `ping` command. The IP addresses to ping and check connectivity are listed below. Your network IP addresses could be different if you are using a different subnet.

R1's f0/0	: 192.168.183.133
PC1	: 192.168.183.129
LAB-SW1 vlan 1	: 192.168.183.101
lab-sw2 vlan 1	: 192.168.183.102
LAB-R1 Gi0/0	: 192.168.183.10
lab-r2 Gi0/1	: 192.168.183.20

```
[pynetauto@centos8s1 ~]$ ping 192.168.183.133 -c 2

PING 192.168.183.133 (192.168.183.133) 56(84) bytes of data.
64 bytes from 192.168.183.133: icmp_seq=1 ttl=255 time=7.76 ms
64 bytes from 192.168.183.133: icmp_seq=2 ttl=255 time=4.56 ms

--- 192.168.183.133 ping statistics ---
2 packets transmitted, 2 received, 0% packet loss, time 3ms
rtt min/avg/max/mdev = 4.556/6.158/7.761/1.604 ms
[pynetauto@centos8s1 ~]$ ping 192.168.183.129 -c 2
PING 192.168.183.129 (192.168.183.129) 56(84) bytes of data.
64 bytes from 192.168.183.129: icmp_seq=1 ttl=255 time=31.8 ms
64 bytes from 192.168.183.129: icmp_seq=2 ttl=255 time=19.6 ms

--- 192.168.183.129 ping statistics ---
2 packets transmitted, 2 received, 0% packet loss, time 3ms
rtt min/avg/max/mdev = 19.562/25.669/31.776/6.107 ms
[pynetauto@centos8s1 ~]$ ping 192.168.183.101 -c 2
PING 192.168.183.101 (192.168.183.101) 56(84) bytes of data.
64 bytes from 192.168.183.101: icmp_seq=1 ttl=255 time=25.0 ms
64 bytes from 192.168.183.101: icmp_seq=2 ttl=255 time=24.1 ms
```

(continued)

#	Task

	`--- 192.168.183.101 ping statistics ---`
	`2 packets transmitted, 2 received, 0% packet loss, time 2ms`
	`rtt min/avg/max/mdev = 24.056/24.547/25.038/0.491 ms`
	`[pynetauto@centos8s1 ~]$` **`ping 192.168.183.102 -c 2`**
	`PING 192.168.183.102 (192.168.183.102) 56(84) bytes of data.`
	`64 bytes from 192.168.183.102: icmp_seq=1 ttl=255 time=35.5 ms`
	`64 bytes from 192.168.183.102: icmp_seq=2 ttl=255 time=33.0 ms`
	`64 bytes from 192.168.183.20: icmp_seq=1 ttl=255 time=184 ms`
	`64 bytes from 192.168.183.20: icmp_seq=2 ttl=255 time=46.10 ms`
	
	`--- 192.168.183.102 ping statistics ---`
	`2 packets transmitted, 2 received, 0% packet loss, time 3ms`
	`rtt min/avg/max/mdev = 33.049/34.295/35.542/1.260 ms`
	`[pynetauto@centos8s1 ~]$` **`ping 192.168.183.10 -c 2`**
	`PING 192.168.183.10 (192.168.183.10) 56(84) bytes of data.`
	`64 bytes from 192.168.183.10: icmp_seq=1 ttl=255 time=37.8 ms`
	`64 bytes from 192.168.183.10: icmp_seq=2 ttl=255 time=20.1 ms`
	
	`--- 192.168.183.10 ping statistics ---`
	`2 packets transmitted, 2 received, 0% packet loss, time 3ms`
	`rtt min/avg/max/mdev = 20.081/28.936/37.792/8.857 ms`
	`[pynetauto@centos8s1 ~]$` **`ping 192.168.183.20 -c 2`**
	`PING 192.168.183.20 (192.168.183.20) 56(84) bytes of data.`
	`64 bytes from 192.168.183.20: icmp_seq=1 ttl=255 time=184 ms`
	`64 bytes from 192.168.183.20: icmp_seq=2 ttl=255 time=46.10 ms`
	
	`--- 192.168.183.20 ping statistics ---`
	`2 packets transmitted, 2 received, 0% packet loss, time 3ms`
	`rtt min/avg/max/mdev = 46.992/115.296/183.601/68.305 ms`

Now you have completed the integration of the CML L3 router image and communication test between the Python server and other networking devices in your topology.

Summary

In this chapter, you were introduced to Cisco CML integration with GNS3. You downloaded and integrated the CML L2 and L3 images with GNS3; then you built a basic CML lab topology and took it for a quick test-drive. Then you confirmed the network connectivity between the Python automation server and all the routers and switches in a `cmllab-basic` topology. You have completed the CML lab preparation and now are ready to jump right in and start writing some Python code to Telnet or SSH and play with the Cisco virtual routers and switches on GNS3.

In Chapter 13, you will learn to control the network devices from the Python Linux server starting with the Python Telnet library.

CHAPTER 13

Python Network Automation Lab: Basic Telnet

This chapter is dedicated to Telnet labs using Python's `telnetlib` library. You will learn how to use a basic Telnet example to reiterate and convert your tasks performed on the keyboard into Python scripts. Although Telnet is an insecure protocol and the best practice is to use the SSH protocol for remote connections, it is still in use today in many production environments residing in a well-secured network where only a small number of engineers can access the environment. At the end of this lab, you will be able to do the following using the basic Telnet library: interact with network devices on Python interpreter session, configure a single and multiple-switch VLAN using a templated approach using loops, perform basic network engineer administration tasks such as adding users via an external file source, and make backup copies of `running-config` or `startup-configs` to the local Python server directory. In the next chapter, we will work with the Python SSH library to expand on the ideas learned in this chapter.

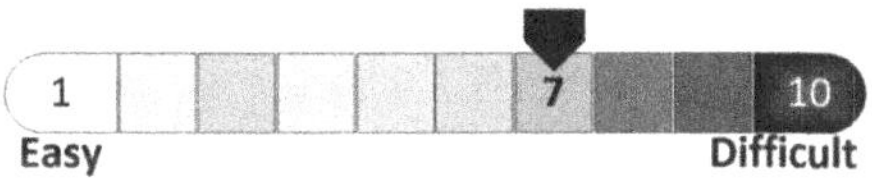

Python Network Automation: Telnet Labs

In this book, many hours were invested into making the lab experience close to a real physical equipment lab as possible so you can have a realistic lab experience without the hardware or worrying about different connector types. Under the current lab setup on your host PC, you can write code on three different operating systems: host PC on Windows 10, CentOS 8.1 Linux server, and Ubuntu 20.04 LTS Linux VM server. If you want to add more places to write code and test it, you can clone any of the Linux VMs. In Chapter 2, you were introduced to Python 3 on Windows OS, and then in Chapters 4, 5, and 6, you did most of the exercises on the Linux command-line interface (CLI). Companies almost never install Python on a Windows server and use it in a production environment. In other words, the vast majority of Python applications run on security-hardened Linux servers. Although Microsoft has introduced the concept of Windows Subsystem for Linux (WSL) and it can run Linux systems on Windows and is extremely easy to use, the actual virtual machine running on Windows is Linux OS.

The current craze of network automation is for fewer engineers who can do more work using an application programming interface (API) without opening a CLI console, Telnet, or SSH terminal windows. The introduction of API support across many newer networking platforms has also drastically reduced graphical user interface (GUI) use in the networking industry. However, industry insiders say the traditional

B. Choi, *Introduction to Python Network Automation*, https://doi.org/10.1007/978-1-4842-6806-3_13

way of logging into network devices and managing them will remain in place for many more years to come. We still use our keyboard to write our Python code and also call the API libraries used in our code, but unless we are API developers, we probably do not fully understand the inner workings of each API. At the end of the day, network automation is the act of mimicking how an experienced network engineer thinks. A good example of such a product is Red Hat's Ansible, which relies on the agentless SSH connection, instead of an API. In this sense, the API is the reinterpretation of this but for machine-to-machine interaction without the use of the keyboard and screen. In this chapter, you will start writing Python Telnet scripts to interact with the network devices in our basic lab topology. Even though using an API is becoming the new norm for administering enterprise networking devices, for now and the foreseeable future, there will still be many devices without API interfaces, and you still need to connect to these devices remotely using either a Telnet or SSH connection. This means we can still use Python in network automation, relying on Telnet and SSH libraries. Anyway, the necessary skills in writing Python code do not change; only the access methods and libraries change. See Figure 13-1.

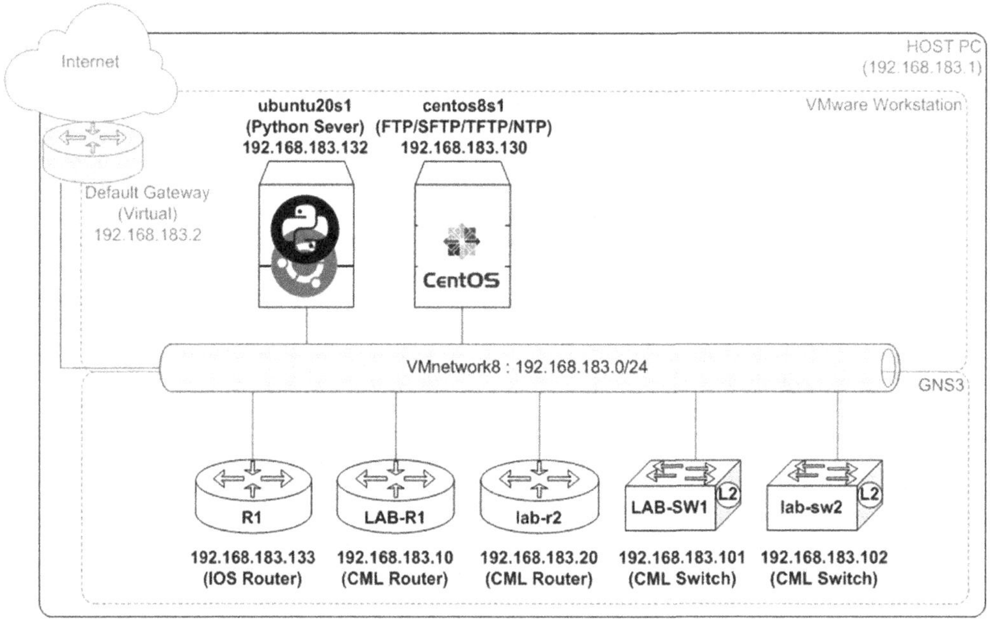

Figure 13-1. *cmllab-basic, logical topology*

In a highly secured client environment, you can only manage core network and system devices from designated servers called *jump hosts*. Jump hosts can be Windows or Linux OS based. The `cmllab-basic` GNS3 topology emulates this environment, and you have to use PuTTY on your host PC to SSH into the `ubuntu20s1` (Python and jump host) server to manage devices in the network. The `centos8s1` server provides IP services we will rely on for various lab scenarios. We will write Python scripts in Windows Notepad++ or enter the scripts directly on the `ubuntu20s1` server's text editor via an SSH session for the entire chapter. You can enter the Python script directly into the Ubuntu server for those who are fast and accurate typists. Still, if you prefer to work with the script from Windows Notepad or Notepad++ and cut and paste it to the Ubuntu server later, that is also an acceptable method. Let's fire up all devices in the `cmllab-basic` project, write some Python code, and see how Telnet Python scripts interact with Cisco routers and switches.

Telnet Lab 1: Interactive Telnet Session to Cisco Devices on a Python Interpreter

For this lab, you will need to power on the ubuntu20s1 Linux server (192.168.183.132), LAB-SW1 (192.168.183.101), and LAB-R1 (192.168.183.10). You will also power on the IOS router, R1 (192.168.183.133), to check the OSPF neighborship after running the first script. If you are using another subnet to connect to your NAT (VMnetwork8), your IP addresses will be different from this book, and you will have to replace the IP addresses. See Figure 13-2.

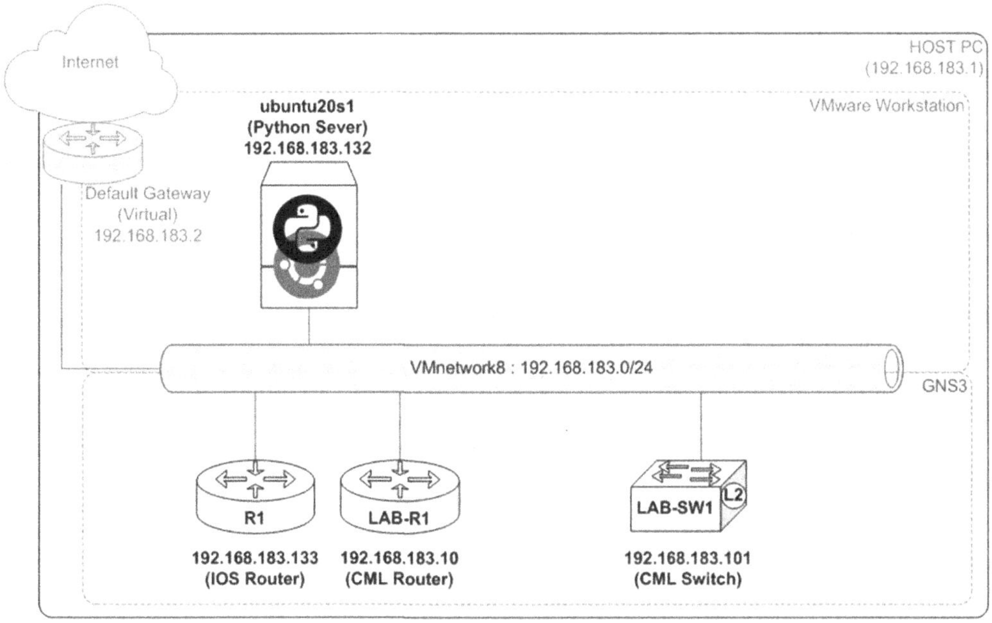

Figure 13-2. *Telnet lab 1, devices in use*

You will write a Telnet script and run it from the ubuntu20s1 Python server to Telnet into the LAB-R1 router to make configuration changes. At the end of this lab, LAB-R1 must have the following configurations in the running-config file:

- Loopback 0 with IP address of 2.2.2.2/32
- Loopback 1 with IP address of 4.4.4.4/32
- OSPF 1 with network 0.0.0.0 255.255.255.255 in area 0

#	Task

1	Open PuTTY on your host PC and SSH into the ubuntu20s1 (192.168.183.132) server. If you have assigned a different IP address, please use your server IP address. If you forgot about which IP address was assigned to the ubuntu20s1 server, open the Linux console from VMware Workstation and log in; then run the ip address command.
	
	Now log in with your username and password.
	
	`login as: pynetauto`
	`pynetauto@192.168.183.132's password: *********`
	`Welcome to Ubuntu 20.04.1 LTS (GNU/Linux 5.4.0-47-generic x86_64)`
	
	`* Documentation: https://help.ubuntu.com`
	`* Management:  https://landscape.canonical.com`
	`* Support:   https://ubuntu.com/advantage`
	
	`System information disabled due to load higher than 1.0`
	
	`327 updates can be installed immediately.`
	`142 of these updates are security updates.`
	`To see these additional updates run: apt list --upgradable`
	
	`Last login: Fri Jan  8 23:26:01 2021 from 192.168.183.1`
	`pynetauto@ubuntu20s1:~$`

2	Currently, to run Python from ubuntu20s1, we have to issue the python3 command. Since there is no Python 2.7 installed and Python 3 is the only version you are going to be using here, you can use an alias command to shorten python3 to python. Follow the instruction here to use the alias in Linux:
	
	`pynetauto@ubuntu20s1:~$ users`
	`pynetauto`
	`pynetauto@ubuntu20s1:~$ pwd`
	`/home/pynetauto`
	`pynetauto@ubuntu20s1:~$ nano /home/pynetauto/.bashrc`
	
	Once you open the .bashrc file in the /home/user/ directory, add a new line, alias python=python3, to the .bashrc file; this is similar to Figure 13-1. Once you finish adding a line, press Ctrl+X to save and exit the file.
	
	`GNU nano 4.8                    /home/pynetauto/.bashrc`
	
	`# alias ADDED by pynetauto`
	`alias python=python3`
	
	`^G Get Help  ^O Write Out  ^W Where Is  ^K Cut Text    ^J Justify   ^C Cur Pos`
	`^X Exit      ^R Read File  ^\ Replace   ^U Paste Text  ^T To Spell  ^_ Go To Line`

#	Task

3	After adding the alias line, run the `source ~/.bashrc` command to restart the user's `bashrc`. You can now use the python or `python3` command to run Python 3.8.2 on your `ubuntu20s1` server.
	`pynetauto@ubuntu20s1:~$ source ~/.bashrc`
	`pynetauto@ubuntu20s1:~$ python`
	`Python 3.8.2 (default, Jul 16 2020, 14:00:26)`
	`[GCC 9.3.0] on linux`
	`Type "help", "copyright", "credits" or "license" for more information.`
	`>>>`

4	As we have done in the IOS Telnet lab, go to `https://docs.python.org/3/library/telnetlib.html` and scroll down to the bottom of the page. Locate a sample Telnet code. You can alternatively reuse the old code from the `R1` IOS lab from Chapter 10.8. Let's copy this code to make our first Telnet script. This code will be used throughout the Telnet labs, so here are quick explanations of what each line does in the given Python script. Since we are using Cisco devices, more explanations are provided concerning Cisco Telnet sessions. **Telnet Example** A simple example illustrates the typical use:

`import getpass`	# import getpass module for password
`import telnetlib`	# import telnetlib module for telnet
`HOST = "localhost"`	# IP address or hostname of device to connect
`user = input("Enter your remote account: ")`	# User input for UserID
`password = getpass.getpass()`	# define a variable password as getpass.getpass function class
`tn = telnetlib.Telnet(HOST)`	# define a variable tn as telnetlib.Telnet type class
`tn.read_until(b"login: ")`	# "login: " appears on the telnet window, Python waits until "login: " binary information is returned to the login screen. On Cisco devices, the expected returned binary information is "Username: ", this needs to be updated in your script.
`tn.write(user.encode('ascii') + b"\n")`	# Encode userID in ASCII and sent to telnet virtual terminal
`if password:`	# if prompted for password
`  tn.read_until(b"Password: ")`	# Wait for password until entered
`  tn.write(password.encode('ascii') + b"\n")`	# Encode password in ASCII and send to telnet virtual terminal
`tn.write(b"ls\n")`	# 'ls' is a Linux command list. ls is not used in Cisco devices. Can be removed or modified.
`tn.write(b"exit\n")`	# Send 'exit' command to telnet virtual terminal
`print(tn.read_all().decode('ascii'))`	# Read all commands run in this session, decode in ASCII and print out on the user's screen.

(continued)

#	Task
5	Make a directory called telnet_labs, change the working directory, and then create the first CML Telnet script using the touch command. The script name is add_lo_ospf1.py. Follow these steps:

```
pynetauto@ubuntu20s1:~$ pwd
/home/pynetauto
pynetauto@ubuntu20s1:~$ mkdir telnet_labs
pynetauto@ubuntu20s1:~$ cd telnet_labs
pynetauto@ubuntu20s1:~/telnet_labs$ pwd
/home/pynetauto/telnet_labs
pynetauto@ubuntu20s1:~/telnet_labs$ touch add_lo_ospf1.py
pynetauto@ubuntu20s1:~/telnet_labs$ ls
7.2.1_add_lo_ospf1.py
```

#	Task
6	To speed up the lab, use the nano text editor on the Linux server. First, use nano add_lo_ospf1.py to open the blank Python script. Then, copy and paste the Telnet example by using the right-click menu. Finally, modify the sections highlighted in the following source code:

```
GNU nano 4.8                    add_lo_ospf1.py
import getpass
import telnetlib

HOST = "192.168.183.10"
user = input("Enter your username: ")
password = getpass.getpass()

tn = telnetlib.Telnet(HOST)

tn.read_until(b"Username: ")
tn.write(user.encode('ascii') + b"\n")
if password:
    tn.read_until(b"Password: ")
    tn.write(password.encode('ascii') + b"\n")

tn.write(b"enable\n")
tn.write(b"cisco123\n")
tn.write(b"conf t\n")
tn.write(b"int loopback 0\n")
tn.write(b"ip add 2.2.2.2 255.255.255.255\n")
tn.write(b"int loopback 1\n")
tn.write(b"ip add 4.4.4.4 255.255.255.255\n")
tn.write(b"router ospf 1\n")
tn.write(b"network 0.0.0.0 255.255.255.255 area 0\n")

tn.write(b"end\n")
tn.write(b"exit\n")

print(tn.read_all().decode('ascii'))
^G Get Help  ^O Write Out  ^W Where Is  ^K Cut Text    ^J Justify   ^C Cur Pos
^X Exit      ^R Read File  ^\ Replace   ^U Paste Text  ^T To Spell  ^_ Go To Line
```

#	Task
7	Before running the previous script from the ubuntu20s1 server, go to LAB-R1 and enable debug telnet to monitor the Telnet activities from LAB-R1. `LAB-R1#`**`debug telnet`** `Incoming Telnet debugging is on`
8	On ubuntu20s1, run the script using the python add_lo_ospf1.py command. When prompted for the username and password, enter your router username and password. Once the script runs successfully, your screen should look similar to this:

```
pynetauto@ubuntu20s1:~/telnet_labs$ python add_lo_ospf1.py
Enter your username: pynetauto
Password: **********

***************************************************************************
* IOSv is strictly limited to use for evaluation, demonstration and IOS  *
* education. IOSv is provided as-is and is not supported by Cisco's      *
* Technical Advisory Center. Any use or disclosure, in whole or in part, *
* of the IOSv Software or Documentation to any third party for any       *
* purposes is expressly prohibited except as otherwise authorized by     *
* Cisco in writing.                                                      *
***************************************************************************
LAB-R1#enable
LAB-R1#cisco123
Translating "cisco123"...domain server (192.168.183.2)
(192.168.183.2)
Translating "cisco123"...domain server (192.168.183.2)

% Bad IP address or host name
% Unknown command or computer name, or unable to find computer address
LAB-R1#conf t
Enter configuration commands, one per line.  End with CNTL/Z.
LAB-R1(config)#int loopback 0
LAB-R1(config-if)#ip add 2.2.2.2 255.255.255.255
LAB-R1(config-if)#int loopback 1
LAB-R1(config-if)#ip add 4.4.4.4 255.255.255.255
LAB-R1(config-if)#router ospf 1
LAB-R1(config-router)#network 0.0.0.0 255.255.255.255 area 0
LAB-R1(config-router)#end
LAB-R1#exit
```

(*continued*)

#	Task

9 Go to LAB-R1 and now check the console. You can see the Telnet activities that have just taken place.

```
LAB-R1#
*Jan 11 18:11:08.885: Telnet578: 1 1 251 1
*Jan 11 18:11:08.887: TCP578: Telnet sent WILL ECHO (1)
[...omitted for brevity]
*Jan 11 18:11:09.181: TCP578: Telnet received WONT TTY-TYPE (24)
*Jan 11 18:11:09.183: TCP578: Telnet received WONT WINDOW-SIZE (31)
LAB-R1#
*Jan 11 18:11:11.730: %LINEPROTO-5-UPDOWN: Line protocol on Interface Loopback0,
changed state to up
LAB-R1#
*Jan 11 18:11:12.972: %LINEPROTO-5-UPDOWN: Line protocol on Interface Loopback1,
changed state to up
*Jan 11 18:11:13.791: %SYS-5-CONFIG_I: Configured from console by pynetauto on vty0
(192.168.183.132)
LAB-R1#
```

10 From the LAB-R1 console, run the `show ip interface brief` command to check the newly configured `Loopback0` and `Loopback1` configurations.

```
LAB-R1#show ip interface brief
Interface              IP-Address      OK? Method Status                Protocol
GigabitEthernet0/0     192.168.183.10  YES manual up                    up
GigabitEthernet0/1     172.168.1.1     YES manual up                    up
GigabitEthernet0/2     unassigned      YES unset  administratively down down
GigabitEthernet0/3     unassigned      YES unset  administratively down down
Loopback0              2.2.2.2         YES manual up                    up
Loopback1              4.4.4.4         YES manual up                    up
```

11 On the IOS router, `R1`, let's power on `R1` and observe if the OSPF neighborship forms correctly between `R1` and `LAB-R1` routers. Once the OSPF status changes from `LOADING` to `FULL, Loading Done`, run the `show ip ospf neighbor` command to check the neighborship. At this stage, you should be able to ping `LAB-R1`'s `Loopback0` (2.2.2.2) and `Loopback1` (4.4.4.4) interfaces from `R1`.

```
R1#
*Mar  1 00:21:25.807: %OSPF-5-ADJCHG: Process 1, Nbr 4.4.4.4 on FastEthernet0/0 from
LOADING to FULL, Loading Done
R1#show ip ospf neighbor

Neighbor ID     Pri   State           Dead Time   Address         Interface
4.4.4.4           1   FULL/DR         00:00:39    192.168.183.10  FastEthernet0/0

R1#ping 2.2.2.2

Type escape sequence to abort.
Sending 5, 100-byte ICMP Echos to 2.2.2.2, timeout is 2 seconds:
!!!!!
Success rate is 100 percent (5/5), round-trip min/avg/max = 8/11/20 ms
R1#ping 4.4.4.4
```

#	Task

	`Type escape sequence to abort.`
	`Sending 5, 100-byte ICMP Echos to 4.4.4.4, timeout is 2 seconds:`
	`!!!!!`
	`Success rate is 100 percent (5/5), round-trip min/avg/max = 8/13/28 ms`

12	On LAB-R1, you will observe that the OSPF status changes from LOADING to FULL, Loading Done. Run the show ip ospf neighbor command to check the neighborship with R1. At this stage, you should be able to ping R1's f0/1 interface (7.7.7.2). Run the undebug all command to turn off Telnet debugging and complete your first CML-PERSONAL Telnet lab.

```
LAB-R1#
*Jan 11 18:11:21.417: %OSPF-5-ADJCHG: Process 1, Nbr 192.168.183.133 on
GigabitEthernet0/0 from LOADING to FULL, Loading Done
LAB-R1#show ip ospf neighbor

Neighbor ID     Pri   State           Dead Time   Address         Interface
192.168.183.133   1   FULL/BDR        00:00:39    192.168.183.133 GigabitEthernet0/0

LAB-R1#ping 7.7.7.2
Type escape sequence to abort.
Sending 5, 100-byte ICMP Echos to 7.7.7.2, timeout is 2 seconds:
!!!!!
Success rate is 100 percent (5/5), round-trip min/avg/max = 7/10/14 ms

LAB-R1#undebug all
All possible debugging has been turned off
```

All the Python code used can be downloaded from `https://github.com/pynetauto/apress_pynetauto`. If you enjoyed your first Telnet lab and want to try the second lab now, let's continue.

Telnet Lab 2: Configure a Single Switch with a Python Telnet Template

In this lab, you will be configuring some VLANs on LAB-SW1 via Telnet. You will need to power on the ubuntu20s1 Linux server (192.168.183.132) and LAB-SW1 (192.168.183.101) for this lab. To save time, we will be copying the first script, add_lo_ospf1.py, and renaming it as add_vlans_single.py. At the end of this lab, LAB-SW1 should be configured as shown in Figure 13-3.

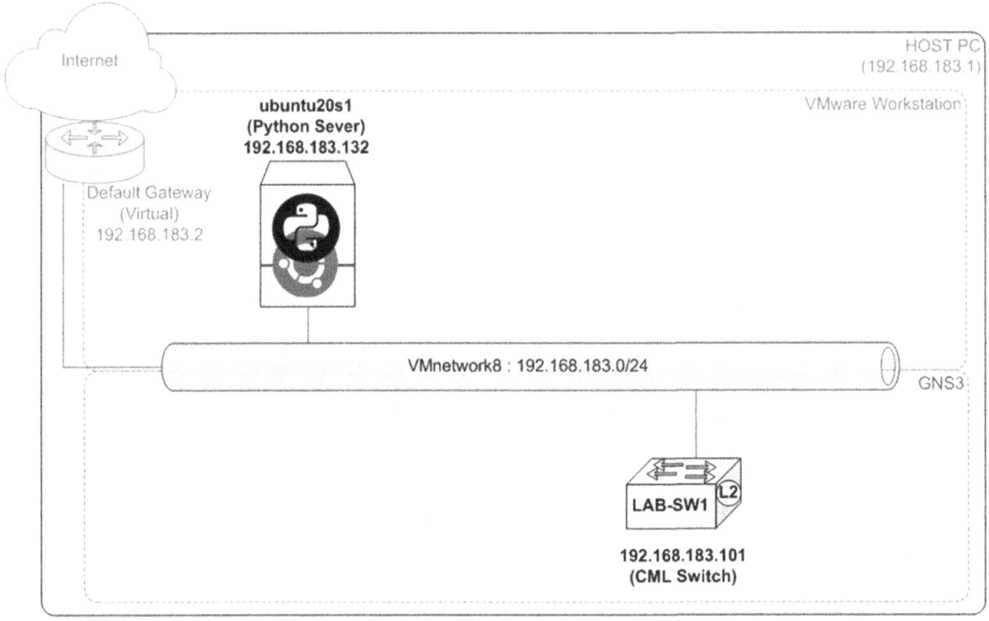

***Figure 13-3.** Telnet lab 2, devices in use*

- Configure VLANs 2 to 5 with the following VLAN descriptions:
  - VLAN 2, `Data_vlan_2`
  - VLAN 3, `Data_vlan_3`
  - VLAN 4, `Voice_vlan_4`
  - VLAN 5, `Wireless_vlan_5`
- Configure GigabitEthernet 1/0 to GigabitEthernet 1/3 range as access switch ports with `Wireless_vlan_5`.
- Configure GigabitEthernet 2/0 to GigabitEthernet 2/3 range as switch ports with `Data_vlan_2` (Data VLAN) and `voice_vlan_4` (Auxiliary VLAN).
- Bring up all configured interfaces with the `no shut` command.

#	Task

1	SSH into the `ubuntu20s1` server (192.168.183.132) and continue working in the same directory as the first lab. Follow the instructions here to copy the first Python script and rename it as `add_vlans_single.py`.
	`pynetauto@ubuntu20s1:~$ cd telnet_labs`
	`pynetauto@ubuntu20s1:~/telnet_labs$ ls`
	`7.2.1_add_lo_ospf1.py`
	`pynetauto@ubuntu20s1:~/telnet_labs$ cp add_lo_ospf1.py add_vlans_single.py`
	`pynetauto@ubuntu20s1:~/telnet_labs$ ls`
	`add_lo_ospf1.py   add_vlans_single.py`

#	Task
2	Open the newly created .py file with a nano text editor. Press Ctrl+K to copy/cut lines of codes and press Ctrl+U to paste information. Note that the IP address of LAB-SW1 is 192.168.183.101. Make sure you update the IP address next to HOST with this IP address.

Use the following information to modify your script. When writing code, every comma and full stop counts.

b = Byte literals; produces an instance of the `byte` type instead of the `str` type.

\n = Newline character to go to the next line. In other words, "[Enter] key"encode('ascii') means to use ASCII encoding for the switch/router.

```
GNU nano 4.8                    add_vlans_single.py
import getpass
import telnetlib

HOST = "192.168.183.101"
user = input("Enter your username: ")
password = getpass.getpass()

tn = telnetlib.Telnet(HOST)

tn.read_until(b"Username: ")
tn.write(user.encode('ascii') + b"\n")
if password:
   tn.read_until(b"Password: ")
   tn.write(password.encode('ascii') + b"\n")

# Get into config mode
tn.write(b"conf t\n")

# configure 4 VLANs with VLAN names
tn.write(b"vlan 2\n")
tn.write(b"name Data_vlan_2\n")
tn.write(b"vlan 3\n")
tn.write(b"name Data_vlan_3\n")
tn.write(b"vlan 4\n")
tn.write(b"name Voice_vlan_4\n")
tn.write(b"vlan 5\n")
tn.write(b"name Wireless_vlan_5\n")
tn.write(b"exit\n")

# configure Gi1/0 - Gi1/3 as access siwtchports and assign vlan 5 for wireless APs
tn.write(b"interface range gi1/0 - 3\n")
tn.write(b"switchport mode access\n")
tn.write(b"switchport access vlan 5\n")
tn.write(b"no shut\n")
```

(continued)

#	Task

```
#configure gi2/0 - gi2/3 as access switchports and assign vlan 2 for data and vlan 4
for voice
tn.write(b"interface range gi2/0 - 3\n")
tn.write(b"switchport mode access \n")
tn.write(b"switchport access vlan 2\n")
tn.write(b"switchport voice vlan 4\n")
tn.write(b"no shut\n")

tn.write(b"end\n")
tn.write(b"exit\n")

print(tn.read_all().decode('ascii'))
^G Get Help  ^O Write Out  ^W Where Is  ^K Cut Text    ^J Justify    ^C Cur Pos
^X Exit      ^R Read File  ^\ Replace   ^U Paste Text  ^T To Spell   ^_ Go To Line
```

3 From the ubuntu20s1 server, run the ping 192.168.183.101 -c 4 command to check the connectivity.

```
pynetauto@ubuntu20s1:~/telnet_labs$ ping 192.168.183.101 -c 3
PING 192.168.183.101 (192.168.183.101) 56(84) bytes of data.
64 bytes from 192.168.183.101: icmp_seq=1 ttl=255 time=20.3 ms
64 bytes from 192.168.183.101: icmp_seq=2 ttl=255 time=7.77 ms
64 bytes from 192.168.183.101: icmp_seq=3 ttl=255 time=17.5 ms

--- 192.168.183.101 ping statistics ---
4 packets transmitted, 4 received, 0% packet loss, time 3005ms
rtt min/avg/max/mdev = 7.773/14.035/20.312/5.067 ms
```

4 Optionally, on LAB-SW1, enable debug telnet to capture Telnet activities during the script run. After debugging has been switched on, leave the console window open.

```
LAB-SW1#debug telnet
```

5 Now we checked the connectivity. Let's run the python add_vlans_single.py command to run the script, add new VLANs, and configure the designated switch ports.

```
pynetauto@ubuntu20s1:~/telnet_labs$ python add_vlans_single.py

Enter your username: pynetauto
Password:********

**************************************************************************
* IOSv is strictly limited to use for evaluation, demonstration and IOS  *
* education. IOSv is provided as-is and is not supported by Cisco's      *
* Technical Advisory Center. Any use or disclosure, in whole or in part, *
* of the IOSv Software or Documentation to any third party for any       *
* purposes is expressly prohibited except as otherwise authorized by     *
* Cisco in writing.                                                      *
**************************************************************************
LAB-SW1#conf t
Enter configuration commands, one per line.  End with CNTL/Z.
LAB-SW1(config)#vlan 2
LAB-SW1(config-vlan)#name Data_vlan_2
LAB-SW1(config-vlan)#vlan 3
```

#	Task
	LAB-SW1(config-vlan)#name Data_vlan_3 LAB-SW1(config-vlan)#vlan 4 LAB-SW1(config-vlan)#name Voice_vlan_4 LAB-SW1(config-vlan)#vlan 5 LAB-SW1(config-vlan)#name Wireless_vlan_5 LAB-SW1(config-vlan)#exit LAB-SW1(config)#interface range gi1/0 - 3 LAB-SW1(config-if-range)#switchport mode access LAB-SW1(config-if-range)#switchport access vlan 5 LAB-SW1(config-if-range)#no shut LAB-SW1(config-if-range)#interface range gi2/0 - 3 LAB-SW1(config-if-range)#switchport mode access LAB-SW1(config-if-range)#switchport access vlan 2 LAB-SW1(config-if-range)#switchport voice vlan 4 LAB-SW1(config-if-range)#no shut LAB-SW1(config-if-range)#end LAB-SW1#exit
6	Check the LAB-SW1 console window for debugging information. LAB-SW1# *Jan 11 19:24:31.981: Telnet2: 1 1 251 1 *Jan 11 19:24:31.982: TCP2: Telnet sent WILL ECHO (1) *Jan 11 19:24:31.982: Telnet2: 2 2 251 3 *Jan 11 19:24:31.984: TCP2: Telnet sent WILL SUPPRESS-GA (3) *Jan 11 19:24:31.984: Telnet2: 80000 80000 253 24 *Jan 11 19:24:31.985: TCP2: Telnet sent DO TTY-TYPE (24) *Jan 11 19:24:31.985: Telnet2: 10000000 10000000 253 31 *Jan 11 19:24:31.986: TCP2: Telnet sent DO WINDOW-SIZE (31) *Jan 11 19:24:32.036: TCP2: Telnet received DONT ECHO (1) *Jan 11 19:24:32.037: TCP2: Telnet sent WONT ECHO (1) *Jan 11 19:24:32.042: TCP2: Telnet received DONT SUPPRESS-GA (3) *Jan 11 19:24:32.043: TCP2: Telnet sent WONT SUPPRESS-GA (3) LAB-SW1# *Jan 11 19:24:32.048: TCP2: Telnet received WONT TTY-TYPE (24) *Jan 11 19:24:32.050: TCP2: Telnet sent DONT TTY-TYPE (24) *Jan 11 19:24:32.054: TCP2: Telnet received WONT WINDOW-SIZE (31) *Jan 11 19:24:32.054: TCP2: Telnet sent DONT WINDOW-SIZE (31) *Jan 11 19:24:32.186: TCP2: Telnet received DONT ECHO (1) *Jan 11 19:24:32.187: TCP2: Telnet received DONT SUPPRESS-GA (3) *Jan 11 19:24:32.187: TCP2: Telnet received WONT TTY-TYPE (24) *Jan 11 19:24:32.189: TCP2: Telnet received WONT WINDOW-SIZE (31) LAB-SW1# *Jan 11 19:24:40.915: %SYS-5-CONFIG_I: Configured from console by pynetauto on vty0 (192.168.183.132)

(*continued*)

#	Task
7	Now check the VLANs configured and the switch ports on the `LAB-SW1` switch. Use `show vlan`, `show run`, and `show ip interface brief` to check the switch configuration changes. The `show vlan` example is shown here:

```
LAB-SW1#show vlan

VLAN Name                             Status    Ports
---- -------------------------------- --------- -------------------------------
1    default                          active    Gi0/0, Gi0/1, Gi0/2, Gi0/3
                                                Gi3/0, Gi3/1, Gi3/2, Gi3/3
2    Data_vlan_2                      active    Gi2/0, Gi2/1, Gi2/2, Gi2/3
3    Data_vlan_3                      active
4    Voice_vlan_4                     active    Gi2/0, Gi2/1, Gi2/2, Gi2/3
5    Wireless_vlan_5                  active    Gi1/0, Gi1/1, Gi1/2, Gi1/3
1002 fddi-default                     act/unsup
[...omitted for brevity]
------- --------- ----------------- ------------------------------------------
```

You have successfully added four VLANs and configured eight switch ports in their respective VLANs. Now let's check how we can use loops to add multiple random VLANs in labs 3 and 4.

Telnet Lab 3: Configure Random VLANs Using a for Loop

In the previous lab, we configured VLANs 2 to 5 with multiple lines of code; here, you are going to practice how to add VLANs with fewer lines of code using a `for` loop. For simplicity, we are only adding five random VLANs in this lab, but we are using a `for` loop, and you can save time and the number of code lines you have to write.

Follow the steps to configure random VLANs 101, 202, 303, 404, and 505 on `LAB-SW1` via Telnet. You can continue using the `ubuntu20s1` Linux server (192.168.183.132) and `LAB-SW1` (192.168.183.101) for this lab. Copy the `7.2.2_add_vlans_single.py` file and rename it as `7.2.3_add_vlans_for_loop.py` for this lab. At the end of this lab, `LAB-SW1` should be configured as shown in Figure 13-4.

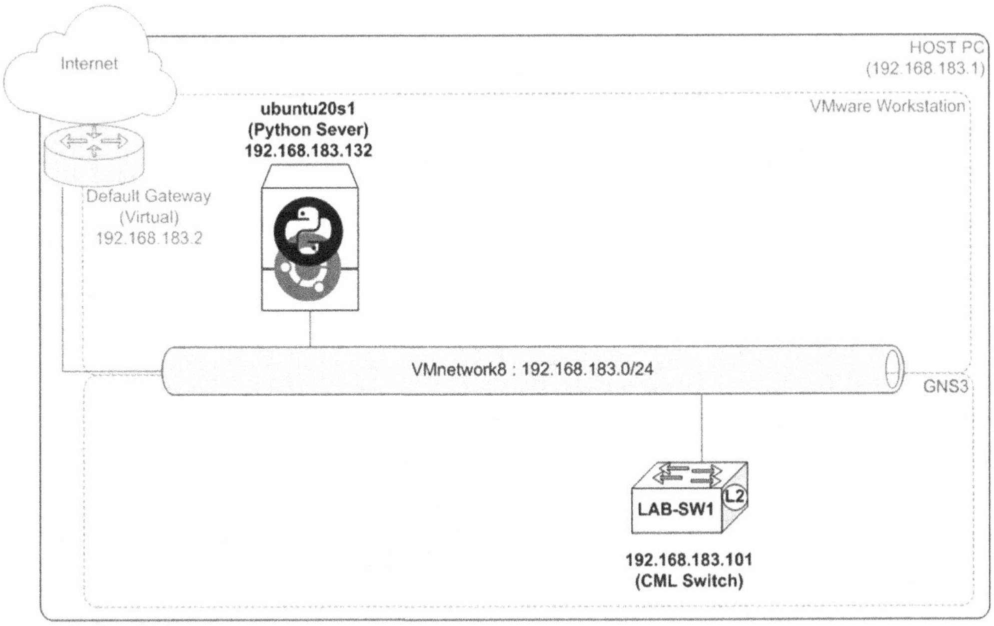

Figure 13-4. *Telnet lab 3: devices in use*

- Add VLANs 101, 202, 303, 404, and 505 with the following VLAN descriptions to `LAB-SW1`:
    - VLAN 101, `Data_vlan_101`
    - VLAN 202, `Data_vlan_202`
    - VLAN 303, `Voice_vlan_303`
    - VLAN 404, `Wireless_vlan_404`
    - VLAN 505, `Wireless_vlan_505`

In this lab, try to concentrate on how a `for` loop works and how it is used in this scenario. Loops are designed to carry out the same task repetitively, and now you are tapping into the true power of programming. Learning the Python concepts so you can apply them to your work is where you want to be. Good luck!

#	Task
1	First, move to the `telnet_labs` directory, use the `cp` command to copy `add_vlans_single.py`, and rename it `add_vlans_for_loop.py`. The commands are shown here:

```
pynetauto@ubuntu20s1:~$ cd telnet_labs
pynetauto@ubuntu20s1:~/telnet_labs$ ls
7.2.1_add_lo_ospf1.py  7.2.2_add_vlans_single.py
pynetauto@ubuntu20s1:~/telnet_labs$ cp add_vlans_single.py add_vlans_for_loop.py
pynetauto@ubuntu20s1:~/telnet_labs$ ls
add_lo_ospf1.py  add_vlans_single.py  add_vlans_for_loop.py
pynetauto@ubuntu20s1:~/telnet_labs$ nano add_vlans_for_loop.py
```

#	Task
2	Now, modify the script, so it looks like the following. Once again, press Ctrl+K to cut/copy the information, and press Ctrl+U to paste the copied information. Check your syntax and the whitespacing during this change. Every comma and space counts, especially the indentation or the four white spaces for code blocks.

```
GNU nano 4.8                    add_vlans_for_loop.py
#!/usr/bin/env python3 # This is called the shebang line; Python ignores this line, but the Linux Operating System can read this line and knows which application to run the .py file with.

import getpass
import telnetlib

HOST = "192.168.183.101"
user = input("Enter your username: ")
password = getpass.getpass()

tn = telnetlib.Telnet(HOST)

tn.read_until(b"Username: ")
tn.write(user.encode('ascii') + b"\n")
if password:
   tn.read_until(b"Password: ")
   tn.write(password.encode('ascii') + b"\n")

# Get into config mode
tn.write(b"conf t\n")

# Adds 5 vlans to the list with for loop
vlans = [101, 202, 303, 404, 505] # vlans to add in  a list
for i in vlans: # call (index) each item from list vlans
    command_1 = "vlan " + str(i) + "\n" # concatenate first command
    tn.write(command_1.encode('ascii')) # send command_1 with ASCII encoding
    command_2 = "name PYTHON_VLAN_" + str(i) + "\n" # concatenate second command
    tn.write(command_2.encode('ascii')) # send command_2 with ASCII encoding

tn.write(b"end\n")
tn.write(b"exit\n")
print("exiting")
print(tn.read_all().decode('ascii'))
^G Get Help  ^O Write Out  ^W Where Is  ^K Cut Text   ^J Justify   ^C Cur Pos
^X Exit      ^R Read File  ^\ Replace   ^U Paste Text ^T To Spell  ^_ Go To Line
```

#	Task
	As you can see, the encoding and decoding are rather messy with `telnetlib`; that is because `telnetlib` uses pyNUT to communicate with network devices, and the pyNUT code is using string literals to format strings internally. PyNUT was written for Python 2, and `telnetlib` expects most inputs to be in bytes. In Python 2, the `str` (string) type was a byte string, but in Python 3, it is all Unicode. Fortunately, the encoding and decoding are not as complicated in SSH Python applications.
3	Run the script using the following Python command. You can use either command. We have added an alias of the user's `/.bashrc` to use either Python3 or Python to run the script.

```
pynetauto@ubuntu20s1:~/telnet_labs$ python add_vlans_for_loop.py
OR
pynetauto@ubuntu20s1:~/telnet_labs$ python3 add_vlans_for_loop.py
pynetauto@ubuntu20s1:~/telnet_labs$ python add_vlans_for_loop.py
Enter your username: pynetauto
Password:********
exiting

**************************************************************************
* IOSv is strictly limited to use for evaluation, demonstration and IOS  *
* education. IOSv is provided as-is and is not supported by Cisco's      *
* Technical Advisory Center. Any use or disclosure, in whole or in part, *
* of the IOSv Software or Documentation to any third party for any       *
* purposes is expressly prohibited except as otherwise authorized by     *
* Cisco in writing.                                                      *
**************************************************************************
LAB-SW1#conf t
Enter configuration commands, one per line.  End with CNTL/Z.
LAB-SW1(config)#vlan 101
LAB-SW1(config-vlan)#name PYTHON_VLAN_101
LAB-SW1(config-vlan)#vlan 202
LAB-SW1(config-vlan)#name PYTHON_VLAN_202
LAB-SW1(config-vlan)#vlan 303
LAB-SW1(config-vlan)#name PYTHON_VLAN_303
LAB-SW1(config-vlan)#vlan 404
LAB-SW1(config-vlan)#name PYTHON_VLAN_404
LAB-SW1(config-vlan)#vlan 505
LAB-SW1(config-vlan)#name PYTHON_VLAN_505
LAB-SW1(config-vlan)#end
LAB-SW1#exit
```

(*continued*)

#	Task
4	Run the `show vlan` command on `LAB-SW1` to confirm newly configured VLANs. If you can see the new VLANs in the switch's vlan table, then your Python script used a for loop to add random VLANs to the switch.

```
LAB-SW1#show vlan

VLAN Name                             Status    Ports
---- -------------------------------- --------- -------------------------------
1    default                          active    Gi0/0, Gi0/1, Gi0/2, Gi0/3
                                                Gi3/0, Gi3/1, Gi3/2, Gi3/3
2    Data_vlan_2                      active    Gi2/0, Gi2/1, Gi2/2, Gi2/3
3    Data_vlan_3                      active
4    Voice_vlan_4                     active    Gi2/0, Gi2/1, Gi2/2, Gi2/3
5    Wireless_vlan_5                  active    Gi1/0, Gi1/1, Gi1/2, Gi1/3
101  PYTHON_VLAN_101                  active
202  PYTHON_VLAN_202                  active
303  PYTHON_VLAN_303                  active
404  PYTHON_VLAN_404                  active
505  PYTHON_VLAN_505                  active
[...omitted for brevity]
```

Telnet Lab 4: Configure Random VLANs Using a while Loop

As in the previous lab, this time we will create the same VLANs 101, 202, 303, 404, 505 on `lab-sw2` via Telnet. For this lab, you can continue working from the `ubuntu20s1` Linux server (192.168.183.132), but you also have to power on `lab-sw2` (192.168.183.102). Copy the `add_vlans_for_loop.py` file and create a new script called `add_vlans_while_loop.py`. At the end of this lab, `lab-sw2` should be configured with the same set of VLANs as `LAB-SW1`, as shown in Figure 13-5.

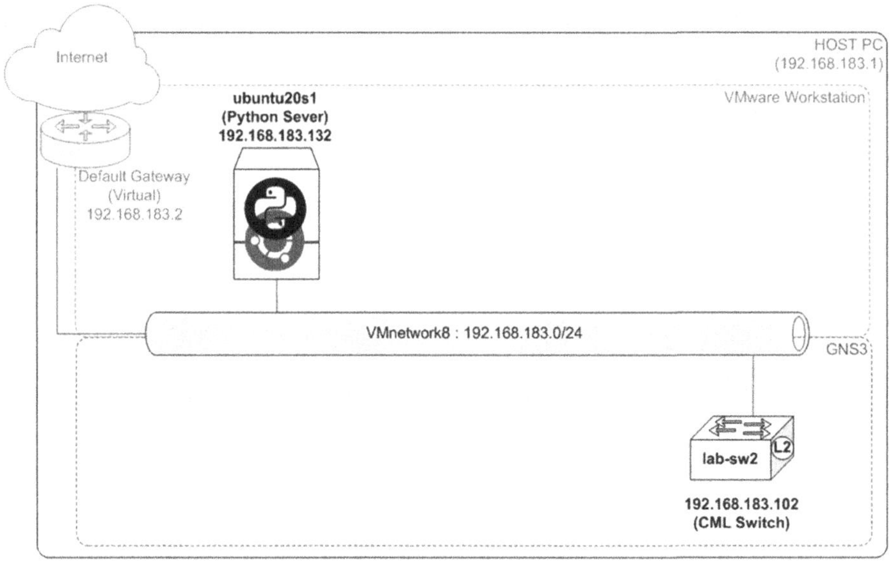

Figure 13-5. *Telnet lab 4, devices in use*

Add VLANs 101, 202, 303, 404 and 505 with the following VLAN descriptions to lab-sw2.

- VLAN 101, Data_vlan_101
- VLAN 202, Data_vlan_202
- VLAN 303, Voice_vlan_303
- VLAN 404, Wireless_vlan_404
- VLAN 505, Wireless_vlan_505

#	Task
1	Assuming that you are already working in the telnet_labs directory, use the cp command to copy add_vlans_for_loop.py and make add_vlans_while_loop.py. Follow the commands to create the new script, as shown here:

```
pynetauto@ubuntu20s1:~/telnet_labs$ ls
add_lo_ospf1.py       add_vlans_single.py        add_vlans_for_loop.py
pynetauto@ubuntu20s1:~/telnet_labs$ cp      add_vlans_for_loop.py   add_vlans_while_loop.py
pynetauto@ubuntu20s1:~/telnet_labs$ ls
add_lo_ospf1.py  add        vlans_single.py  add_      vlans_for_loop.py
add_vlans_while_loop.py
pynetauto@ubuntu20s1:~/telnet_labs$ nano add_vlans_while_loop.py
```

2 Now modify your new script so it looks like the following. This script uses a while loop example to add the same VLAN as the for loop example shown in Figure 13.3. Again, don't be so concerned about the actual login protocol you are using here. Try to understand the working logic of the while loop used in this example script. See the embedded explanation for more information.

```
GNU nano 4.8                         add_vlans_while_loop.py
#!/usr/bin/env python3

import getpass
import telnetlib

HOST = "192.168.183.102" # Update this to lab-sw2 switch IP
user = input("Enter your username: ")
password = getpass.getpass()

tn = telnetlib.Telnet(HOST)

tn.read_until(b"Username: ")
tn.write(user.encode('ascii') + b"\n")
if password:
    tn.read_until(b"Password: ")
    tn.write(password.encode('ascii') + b"\n")

# Get into to config mode
tn.write(b"conf t\n")

# Add 5 random vlans to vlans list and use  while loop to configure them to the switch
vlans = [101, 202, 303, 404, 505] # vlans to add in list
i = 0 # initial index value
while i < len(vlans): # while i is smaller than the length of vlans
    print(vlans[i]) # print vlans item
```

(continued)

#	Task

```
    command_1 = "vlan " + str(vlans[i]) + "\n"# concatenate first command
    tn.write(command_1.encode('ascii'))# send command_1 with ASCII encoding
    command_2 = "name PYTHON_VLAN_" + str(vlans[i]) + "\n"# concatenate second command
    tn.write(command_2.encode('ascii'))# send command_2 with ASCII encoding
    i +=1# Same as i = i + 1

tn.write(b"end\n")
tn.write(b"exit\n")
print("exiting")
print(tn.read_all().decode('ascii'))
^G Get Help  ^O Write Out   ^W Where Is   ^K Cut Text     ^J Justify     ^C Cur Pos
^X Exit      ^R Read File   ^\ Replace    ^U Paste Text   ^T To Spell    ^_ Go To Line
```

3 After you have finished the while loop script, check the connection to lab-sw2 (192.168.183.102) and run the command using either of the commands shown here:

```
pynetauto@ubuntu20s1:~/telnet_labs$ python add_vlans_while_loop.py
OR
pynetauto@ubuntu20s1:~/telnet_labs$ python3 add_vlans_while_loop.py

pynetauto@ubuntu20s1:~/telnet_labs$ ping 192.168.183.102 -c 3
PING 192.168.183.102 (192.168.183.102) 56(84) bytes of data.
64 bytes from 192.168.183.102: icmp_seq=1 ttl=255 time=41.1 ms
64 bytes from 192.168.183.102: icmp_seq=2 ttl=255 time=27.3 ms
64 bytes from 192.168.183.102: icmp_seq=3 ttl=255 time=22.5 ms

--- 192.168.183.102 ping statistics ---
3 packets transmitted, 3 received, 0% packet loss, time 2003ms
rtt min/avg/max/mdev = 22.537/30.294/41.086/7.870 ms
pynetauto@ubuntu20s1:~/telnet_labs$ python add_vlans_while_loop.py
Enter your username: pynetauto
Password:********
101
202
303
404
505
exiting

**************************************************************************
* IOSv is strictly limited to use for evaluation, demonstration and IOS  *
* education. IOSv is provided as-is and is not supported by Cisco's      *
* Technical Advisory Center. Any use or disclosure, in whole or in part, *
* of the IOSv Software or Documentation to any third party for any       *
* purposes is expressly prohibited except as otherwise authorized by     *
* Cisco in writing.                                                      *
**************************************************************************
lab-sw2#conf t
Enter configuration commands, one per line.  End with CNTL/Z.
lab-sw2(config)#vlan 101
lab-sw2(config-vlan)#name PYTHON_VLAN_101
lab-sw2(config-vlan)#vlan 202
```

#	Task
	``` lab-sw2(config-vlan)#name PYTHON_VLAN_202 lab-sw2(config-vlan)#vlan 303 lab-sw2(config-vlan)#name PYTHON_VLAN_303 lab-sw2(config-vlan)#vlan 404 lab-sw2(config-vlan)#name PYTHON_VLAN_404 lab-sw2(config-vlan)#vlan 505 lab-sw2(config-vlan)#name PYTHON_VLAN_505 lab-sw2(config-vlan)#end lab-sw2#exit ```
4	Run the `show vlan` command from `lab-sw2` to check the newly configured VLANs. If you see the VLANs added here, you have successfully configured random VLANs on a switch using a `while` loop.

```
lab-sw2#show vlan

VLAN Name                             Status    Ports
---- -------------------------------- --------- -------------------------------
1    default                          active    Gi0/0, Gi0/1, Gi0/2, Gi0/3
                                                Gi1/0, Gi1/1, Gi1/2, Gi1/3
                                                Gi2/0, Gi2/1, Gi2/2, Gi2/3
                                                Gi3/0, Gi3/1, Gi3/2, Gi3/3
101  PYTHON_VLAN_101                  active
202  PYTHON_VLAN_202                  active
303  PYTHON_VLAN_303                  active
404  PYTHON_VLAN_404                  active
505  PYTHON_VLAN_505                  active
[...omitted for brevity]
```

Telnet Lab 5: Configure 100 VLANs Using the for ~ in range Loop Method

In this lab, you will create 100 VLANs using the `for ~ in range` loop method on both the `LAB-SW1` (192.168.183.101) and `lab-sw2` (192.168.183.102) switches. You will create the script from the same Python server, the `ubuntu20s1` Linux server (192.168.183.132). Copy the `add_vlans_while_loop.py` file and create a new script called `add_vlans_for_range.py`. At the end of this lab, both `LAB-SW1` and `lab-sw2` should be configured with VLANs 700 to 799. See Figure 13-6.

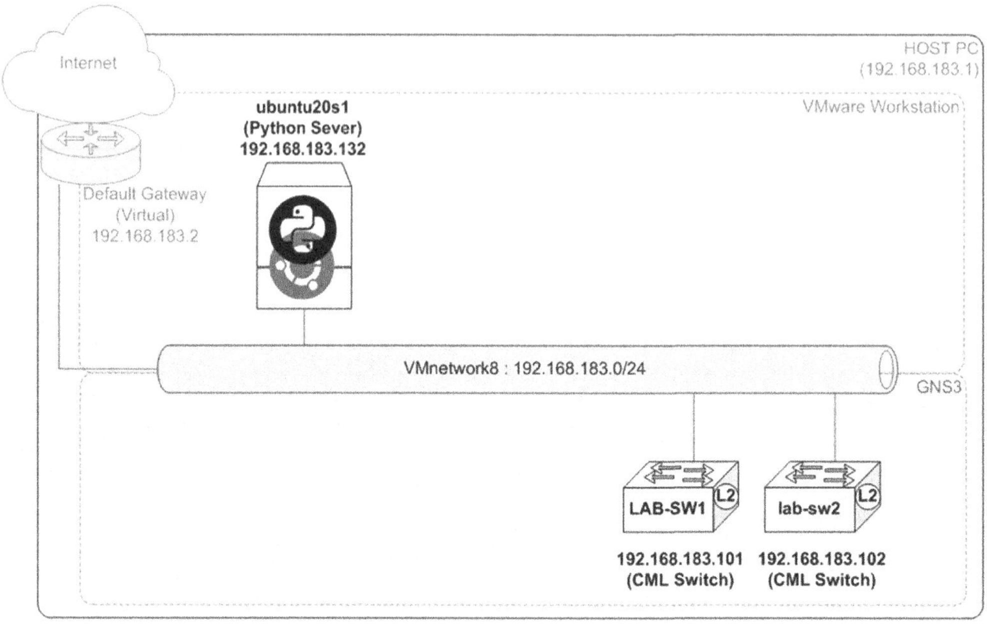

Figure 13-6. *Telnet lab 5, devices in use*

- Configure VLANs 700–799 with the following VLAN description:
    - VLANs 700–799 (i.e., PYTHON_VLAN_700 to PYTHON_VLAN_799)

#	Task

1	Use PuTTY to SSH into ubuntu20s1 (192.168.183.132) to copy the previous Telnet script and create the 7.2.5_add_100_vlans.py file.
	`pynetauto@ubuntu20s1:~$ cd telnet_labs`
	`pynetauto@ubuntu20s1:~/telnet_labs$ ls`
	`add_lo_ospf1.py    add_vlans_for_loop.py    add_vlans_single.py  add_vlans_while_loop.py`
	`pynetauto@ubuntu20s1:~/telnet_labs$ cp add_vlans_while_loop.py add_100_vlans.py`
	`pynetauto@ubuntu20s1:~/telnet_labs$ nano add_100_vlans.py`

2	This time you will be configuring 100 VLANs using a `for ~ range loop` on both switches using a single script. You have to be extremely careful with the leading whitespaces and the code blocks for this script. Be consistent with the whitespaces and the script's code blocks. Refer to the embedded explanation as you modify your script. Use # or """ """ to add as many comments as you want. At the end of the modification, your Python script should look similar to the following code.
	This script is available for download, but you should try to modify the script on Linux's nano text editor to get familiar with text editing on Linux.
	`GNU nano 4.8                    add_100_vlans.py`
	`#!/usr/bin/env python3.8`
	
	`import getpass`
	`import telnetlib`

#	Task
	(code continued below)

```
# HOSTS is a list with IP addresses of two switches
HOSTS = ["192.168.183.101", "192.168.183.102"] # Create a list called HOSTS with two IPs
user = input("Enter your username: ")
password = getpass.getpass()

# Use for loop to loop through the switch IPs
# The rest of the script have been indented  to run under this block
for HOST in HOSTS: # To loop through list, HOSTS
    print("SWITCH IP : " + HOST) # Marker to print out device IP
    tn = telnetlib.Telnet(HOST)

    tn.read_until(b"Username: ")
    tn.write(user.encode('ascii') + b"\n")
    if password:
       tn.read_until(b"Password: ")
       tn.write(password.encode('ascii') + b"\n")

    # Configure 100 VLANs with names using 'for ~ in range' loop # comment
    tn.write(b"conf t\n")
    # Use for n in range (starting vlan, ending vlan, (optional-stepping not used)) #
    comment
    for n in range (700, 800): # vlan range to add, 700 - 799, the last number is not
    counted
       tn.write(b"vlan " + str(n).encode('UTF-8') + b"\n") # Now part of vlan for loop
       tn.write(b"name PYTHON_VLAN_" + str(n).encode('UTF-8') + b"\n") # Now part of
       vlan for loop

    tn.write(b"end\n")
    tn.write(b"exit\n")
    print(tn.read_all().decode('ascii'))
^G Get Help   ^O Write Out   ^W Where Is   ^K Cut Text     ^J Justify     ^C Cur Pos
^X Exit       ^R Read File   ^\ Replace    ^U Paste Text   ^T To Spell    ^_ Go To Line
```

3 Your Python server needs good network connectivity to both switches from your Ubuntu Python server; check the switches' communication. Run the script only if your server can reach both IP addresses. If you have any communication issues, you will have to troubleshoot the issue before proceeding to the next step.

```
pynetauto@ubuntu20s1:~/telnet_labs$ ping 192.168.183.101 -c 3
PING 192.168.183.101 (192.168.183.101) 56(84) bytes of data.
64 bytes from 192.168.183.101: icmp_seq=1 ttl=255 time=5.15 ms
64 bytes from 192.168.183.101: icmp_seq=2 ttl=255 time=5.02 ms
64 bytes from 192.168.183.101: icmp_seq=3 ttl=255 time=5.42 ms

--- 192.168.183.101 ping statistics ---
4 packets transmitted, 4 received, 0% packet loss, time 3005ms
rtt min/avg/max/mdev = 5.019/5.208/5.419/0.145 ms

pynetauto@ubuntu20s1:~/telnet_labs$ ping 192.168.183.102 -c 3
PING 192.168.183.102 (192.168.183.102) 56(84) bytes of data.
64 bytes from 192.168.183.102: icmp_seq=1 ttl=255 time=9.91 ms
64 bytes from 192.168.183.102: icmp_seq=2 ttl=255 time=9.60 ms
64 bytes from 192.168.183.102: icmp_seq=3 ttl=255 time=9.55 ms
```

(continued)

#	Task

```
--- 192.168.183.102 ping statistics ---
4 packets transmitted, 4 received, 0% packet loss, time 3006ms
rtt min/avg/max/mdev = 9.549/9.726/9.909/0.154 ms
```

4 The network connection seems to be fine. Now, let's run the `add_100_vlans.py` script to add 100 VLANs on both switches. This script will Telnet into the first switch to add 100 VLANs and then Telnet into the second switch to add another 100 VLANs. This script may take a few minutes to complete, so be patient. Also, if your lab configuration is on an older computer like mine, consider reducing the number of range from 100 to 10 so you speed up the process.

```
pynetauto@ubuntu20s1:~/telnet_labs$ python add_100_vlans.py
Enter your username: pynetauto
Password:*******
SWITCH IP : 192.168.183.101

**************************************************************************
* IOSv is strictly limited to use for evaluation, demonstration and IOS  *
* education. IOSv is provided as-is and is not supported by Cisco's      *
* Technical Advisory Center. Any use or disclosure, in whole or in part, *
* of the IOSv Software or Documentation to any third party for any       *
* purposes is expressly prohibited except as otherwise authorized by     *
* Cisco in writing.                                                      *
**************************************************************************
LAB-SW1#conf t
Enter configuration commands, one per line.  End with CNTL/Z.
LAB-SW1(config)#vlan 700
LAB-SW1(config-vlan)#name PYTHON_VLAN_700
LAB-SW1(config-vlan)#vlan 701
[...omitted for brevity]
LAB-SW1(config-vlan)#vlan 799
LAB-SW1(config-vlan)#name PYTHON_VLAN_799
LAB-SW1(config-vlan)#end
LAB-SW1#exit

lab-sw2#
Enter configuration commands, one per line.  End with CNTL/Z.
[...omitted for brevity]
```

5 Give a brief moment for the script to complete its task and check both switches using `show vlan` to check the configuration changes. You should see newly configured VLANs, 700 to 799, on both switches.

```
Config message and check added vlans on LAB-SW1
LAB-SW1#
*Jan 11 21:38:00.558: %SYS-5-CONFIG_I: Configured from console by pynetauto on vty0
(192.168.183.132)
LAB-SW1#show vlan
[...omitted for brevity]
700  PYTHON_VLAN_700                    active
701  PYTHON_VLAN_701                    active
...
```

#	Task

	`798 PYTHON_VLAN_798 active`
	`799 PYTHON_VLAN_799 active`
	[...omitted for brevity]
	`Config message and check added vlans on lab-sw2`
	`lab-sw2#`
	`*Jan 11 21:47:09.432: %SYS-5-CONFIG_I: Configured from console by pynetauto on vty0 (192.168.183.132)`
	`lab-sw2#`**`show vlan`**
	[...omitted for brevity]
	`700 PYTHON_VLAN_700 active`
	`701 PYTHON_VLAN_701 active`
	`...`
	`798 PYTHON_VLAN_798 active`
	`799 PYTHON_VLAN_799 active`
	[...omitted for brevity]

6	(Optional task) To remove (reverse) the 100 VLANs from the switches, you only need to modify two lines of code in the original script. The following example will copy the original script and rename it to `reverse_100_vlans.py`. Open this new file and modify two lines of code, as shown here, before running the script.
	`pynetauto@ubuntu20s1:~/telnet_labs$` **`cp add_100_vlans.py reverse_100_vlans.py`**
	`pynetauto@ubuntu20s1:~/telnet_labs$` **`nano reverse_100_vlans.py`**
	`Original code to update:...`
	`for n in range (700, 800):`
	`tn.write(b"vlan " + str(n).encode('UTF-8') + b"\n")`
	`tn.write(b"name PYTHON_VLAN_" + str(n).encode('UTF-8') + b"\n")`
	Updated reverse code:
	`...`
	`for n in range (700, 800):`
	`tn.write(b"`**`no`**` vlan " + str(n).encode('UTF-8') + b"\n")`
	`#``tn.write(b"name PYTHON_VLAN_" + str(n).encode('UTF-8') + b"\n")`
	From your server, run **`python reverse_100_vlans.py`** to completely remove the vlans.
	`pynetauto@ubuntu20s1:~/telnet_labs$` **`python reverse_100_vlans.py`**
	`Enter your username:` **`pynetauto`**
	`Password: ********`

Telnet Lab 6: Add a Privilege 3 User on Multiple Devices Using IP Addresses from an External File

In this lab, you will configure a new user with limited privileges on all routers and switches in your network, so you will have to power on the devices shown in Figure 13-7. You have to create a separate file containing IP addresses so your script can read the IP addresses from the file and configure each device sequentially.

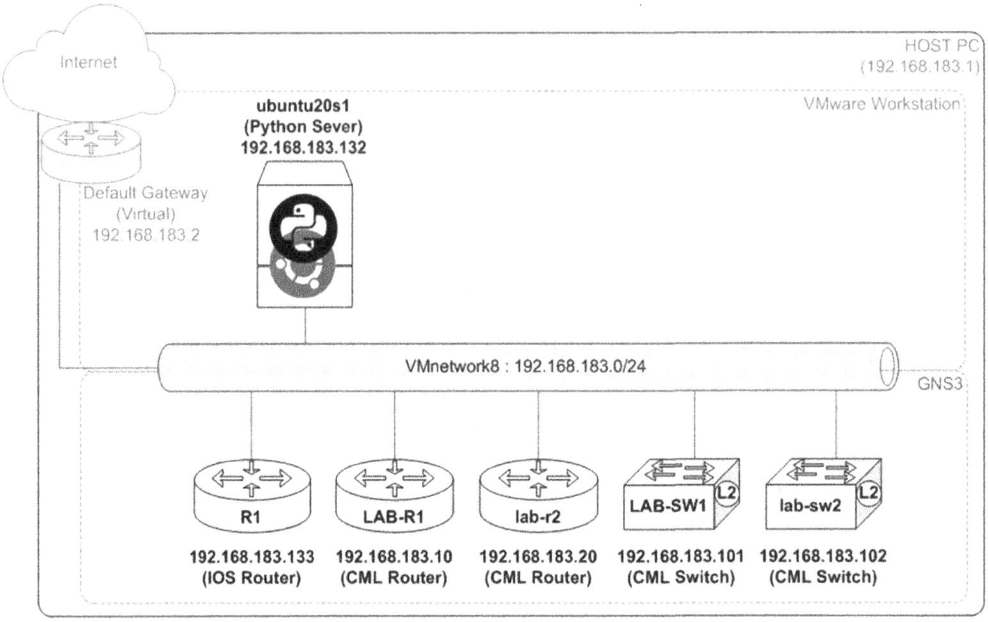

Figure 13-7. *Telnet lab 6, devices in use*

The new user should be given a junior network administrator privilege to run `show` commands. You will be assigning this new user a privilege 3 and allowing this user to view the network devices' running configuration and interface status. Also, change the file mode to the executable to run your script without typing `python` or `python3`.

At the end of this lab, you will have a local account created on each device, so the new user can run `show running-config view full`, `show ip interface brief`, and other `show` commands.

New username: `junioradmin`

- *Password*: `cisco321`
- *Privilege level*: 3
- *Command 1*: `privilege exec all level 3 show running-config`
- *Command 2*: `file privilege 3`

#	Task
1	On the `ubuntu20s1` Python server, create a text file containing all IP addresses of your network devices. Separate the IP addresses with a newline, so each line contains a single IP address of each device. To create and save this file, follow these instructions: `pynetauto@ubuntu20s1:~/telnet_labs$ ` **`touch ip_addresses.txt`** `pynetauto@ubuntu20s1:~/telnet_labs$ ` **`nano ip_addresses.txt`**

#	Task
	``` GNU nano 4.8 ip_addresses.txt 192.168.183.10 192.168.183.20 192.168.183.101 192.168.183.102 192.168.183.133 ^G Get Help ^O Write Out ^W Where Is ^K Cut Text ^J Justify ^C Cur Pos ^X Exit ^R Read File ^\ Replace ^U Paste Text ^T To Spell ^_ Go To Line ```
	* Note: The ip_addresses.txt file must be in the same directory as the add_junioradmin.py file.
2	As with the previous steps, let's reuse the old script to create a new one. Copy the script from lab 5 and create a new script called add_junioradmin.py.

```
pynetauto@ubuntu20s1:~/telnet_labs$ cp add_100_vlans.py add_junioradmin.py
```

```
GNU nano 4.8                    add_junioradmin.py

#!/usr/bin/env python3

import getpass
import telnetlib
import time  # imports time module

user = input("Enter your username: ")
password = getpass.getpass()

# Open ip_addresses.txt to read IP addresses
file = open("ip_addresses.txt") # Open and read an external file

for ip in file: # loop through read information
    print("Now configuring : " + ip) # Task beginning statement
    HOST = (ip.strip()) # Strips any white spaces
    tn = telnetlib.Telnet(HOST) # Use read IP to log into a single device

    tn.read_until(b"Username: ")
    tn.write(user.encode('ascii') + b"\n")
    if password:
       tn.read_until(b"Password: ")
       tn.write(password.encode('ascii') + b"\n")

    time.sleep(1) # Adds 1 second pause for device to respond
    # Configure a new user with privilege 3, allow show running-config # comment
    tn.write(b"conf t\n") # Enter configuration mode
    tn.write(b"username junioradmin privilege 3 password cisco321\n") # Configure new
    pri 3 user
    tn.write(b"privilege exec all level 3 show running-config\n") # Allow show
    running-config command
    print("Added a new privilege 3 user") # Task ending statement

    tn.write(b"end\n")
    tn.write(b"exit\n")
    print(tn.read_all().decode('ascii'))
^G Get Help  ^O Write Out   ^W Where Is   ^K Cut Text    ^J Justify   ^C Cur Pos
^X Exit      ^R Read File   ^\ Replace   ^U Paste Text  ^T To Spell  ^_ Go To Line
```

(continued)

#	Task

3	Before running the script, confirm that both the IP address and script files are in the same directory on your Linux server.
	`pynetauto@ubuntu20s1:~/telnet_labs$ ls`
	`add_lo_ospf1.py        add_vlans_while_loop.py   ip_addresses.txt     add_vlans_single.py    add_100_vlans.py       add_vlans_for_loop.py       add_junioradmin.py`

4	From the ubuntu20s1 server, check the connectivity to all the network devices in your network. We can install and ping multiple devices with a single command line using fping on Linux. Install it as shown here and ping all five devices in our topology.
	`pynetauto@ubuntu20s1:~/telnet_labs$ `**`sudo apt install fping`**
	`pynetauto@ubuntu20s1:~/telnet_labs$ `**`fping 192.168.183.10 192.168.183.20 192.168.183.101 192.168.183.102 192.168.183.133`**
	`192.168.183.10 is alive`
	`192.168.183.133 is alive`
	`192.168.183.20 is alive`
	`192.168.183.102 is alive`
	`192.168.183.101 is alive`
	To read about how to use fping, please visit the following URL.
	URL: https://www.2daygeek.com/how-to-use-ping-fping-gping-in-linux/

5	We have been adding `#!/usr/bin/env python3.8` at the beginning, and as explained, this line is used so the Linux system will recognize that this script or application needs to run from Python 3. To use this line, we first have to make our script executable. If you list the file we have just created and are about to run, you will see that the x (for executable) option is missing from the file.
	`pynetauto@ubuntu20s1:~/telnet_labs$ `**`ls -l add_junior*`**
	`-rw-rw-r-- 1 pynetauto pynetauto 1298 Jan 12 01:16 add_junioradmin.py`
	For us to be able to run this script without using the python command, we can change the mode of this file using the `chmod +x` command, as shown here:
	`pynetauto@ubuntu20s1:~/telnet_labs$ `**`chmod +x ./ add_junioradmin.py`**
	`pynetauto@ubuntu20s1:~/telnet_labs$ ls -l add_junior*`
	`-rwxrwxr-x 1 pynetauto pynetauto 1298 Jan 12 01:16 add_junioradmin.py`
	At this point, you can run your Python script using the `./add_junioradmin.py` command.
	If you want to go one step further and want to run the script only using the script filename, you can add the following PATH variable to your Linux server. This command is only temporary or sessional while you are logged into your session. There are ways to set this permanently, but this is not covered in this book. At this stage, you can run your Python script using the name of the script only.
	`pynetauto@ubuntu20s1:~/telnet_labs$ `**`PATH="$(pwd):$PATH"`**
	`pynetauto@ubuntu20s1:~/telnet_labs$ `**`add_junioradmin.py`**
	`Enter your username: ^Z`
	`[2]+  Stopped                 add_junioradmin.py`
	Press Ctrl+Z to exit if you want to run the script later; if not, continue to run the script as in step 6.

#	Task
6	Let's run the script using the name of the file. The script will add the junior admin to all five devices, as shown here:

```
pynetauto@ubuntu20s1:~/telnet_labs$ add_junioradmin.py
Enter your username: pynetauto
Password:********
Now configuring : 192.168.183.10

Added a new privilege 3 user

**************************************************************************
* IOSv is strictly limited to use for evaluation, demonstration and IOS  *
* education. IOSv is provided as-is and is not supported by Cisco's      *
* Technical Advisory Center. Any use or disclosure, in whole or in part, *
* of the IOSv Software or Documentation to any third party for any       *
* purposes is expressly prohibited except as otherwise authorized by     *
* Cisco in writing.                                                      *
**************************************************************************
LAB-R1#conf t
Enter configuration commands, one per line.  End with CNTL/Z.
LAB-R1(config)#username junioradmin privilege 3 password cisco321
LAB-R1(config)#privilege exec all level 3 show running-config
LAB-R1(config)#file privilege 3
LAB-R1(config)#end
LAB-R1#exit

Now configuring : 192.168.183.20

Added a new privilege 3 user
[...omitted for brevity]

lab-sw2#conf t
Enter configuration commands, one per line.  End with CNTL/Z.
lab-sw2(config)#username junioradmin privilege 3 password cisco321
lab-sw2(config)#privilege exec all level 3 show running-config
lab-sw2(config)#end
lab-sw2#exit

Now configuring : 192.168.183.133

Added a new privilege 3 user

R1#conf t
Enter configuration commands, one per line.  End with CNTL/Z.
R1(config)#username junioradmin privilege 3 password cisco321
R1(config)#privilege exec all level 3 show running-config
R1(config)#end
R1#exit
```

(continued)

#	Task
7	Log into each device and check the user configuration as well as the `privilege exec level 3` commands.

```
LAB-SW1#show run | in username junioradmin
username junioradmin privilege 3 password 0 cisco321
LAB-SW1#show run | in level 3
privilege exec all level 3 show running-config
privilege exec level 3 show
```

8 Now use PuTTY from your Windows host PC to log in with the `junioradmin` user and password `cisco321` and run the `show ip interface brief` or `show running-config view full` command. If you want to log into a device from the Ubuntu server, you can use Telnet 192.168.183.X, where X is the last octet of the device you want to log into.

The following example shows the login and commands run from the `LAB-SW1` switch and `lab-r2` router.

From your host PC, use PuTTY to log into `LAB-SW1` (192.168.183.101) via Telnet and log in as the `junioradmin` user with password `cisco321`.

```
LAB-SW1#
[...omitted for brevity]
User Access Verification

Username: junioradmin
Password:cisco321

[...omitted for brevity]

LAB-SW1#show ip interface brief
Interface              IP-Address      OK? Method Status                Protocol
GigabitEthernet0/0     unassigned      YES unset  up                    up
GigabitEthernet0/1     unassigned      YES unset  up                    up
GigabitEthernet0/2     unassigned      YES unset  up                    up
GigabitEthernet0/3     unassigned      YES unset  down                  down
[...omitted for brevity]
```

From your host PC, use PuTTY to log into `lab-r2` (192.168.183.20) via Telnet and log in as the `junioradmin` user with password `cisco321`.

```
lab-r2#
[...omitted for brevity]
User Access Verification

Username: junioradmin
Password:cisco321

[...omitted for brevity]

lab-r2#show running-config view full
Building configuration...

Current configuration : 3625 bytes
!
! Last configuration change at 23:21:58 UTC Mon Jan 11 2021
!
version 15.6
service timestamps debug datetime msec
[...omitted for brevity]
```

You have successfully created a junior admin user account on multiple devices using IP addresses read from an external file. Note that the IP addresses do not have to be contiguous; they can be random IP addresses if you use a list or external files. What you have been learning from these Telnet labs can also be used on SSH labs with some minor modifications.

Telnet Lab 7: Taking Backups of running-config (or startup-config) to Local Server Storage

In Telnet lab 7, you will copy and modify the previous Telnet script to capture the current running configuration of each device in your network. The backed-up `running-config` files will be saved on the local drive. In this lab, you will be using the `datetime` module to get the timestamp and add the name of the files with this timestamp so you know when the backups were taken. You will require all routers and switches to be powered on, as in lab 6. See Figure 13-8.

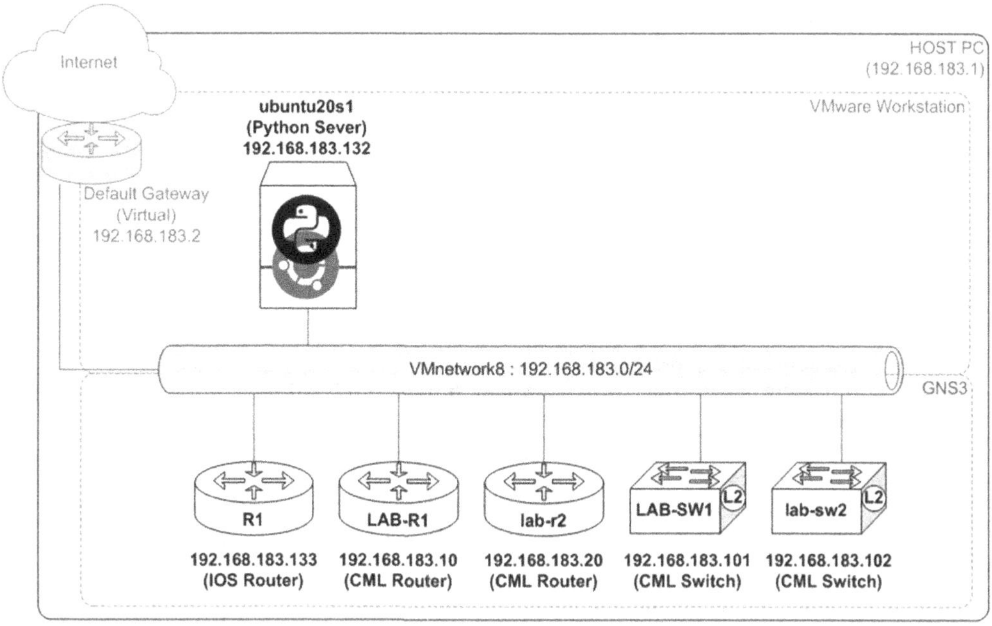

Figure 13-8. *Telnet lab 7, devices in use*

At the end of this lab, you will have the backups of each device's running configuration with the timestamp on your Python server's local storage.

#	Task
1	Once again, let's begin the lab by copying the script from the previous lab. The filename given here is `take_backups.py`, but you do not have to follow this naming convention; give a more meaningful name to this file so you can remember it easily. `pynetauto@ubuntu20s1:~/telnet_labs$` **`cp add_junior_user.py take_backups.py`** `pynetauto@ubuntu20s1:~/telnet_labs$` **`nano take_backups.py`**

(continued)

#	Task
2	Now, open the file in the nano (or vi) text editor and make the modifications highlighted in the following source code:

```
GNU nano 4.8                    take_backups.py
#!/usr/bin/env python3

import getpass
import telnetlib
from datetime import datetime # Import datetime module from datetime library

saved_time = datetime.now().strftime("%Y%m%d_%H%M%S") # Change the \
# format of current time into a string

user = input("Enter your username: ") # Ask for username and password
password = getpass.getpass()

file = open("ip_addresses.txt") # Open ip_addresses.txt to read IP addresses

# Telnets into Devices & runs show running-config and \
# save it to a file with a timestamp

for ip in file:
    print ("Getting running-config from " + (ip)) # First line print statement for admin
    HOST = ip.strip()
    tn = telnetlib.Telnet(HOST)
    tn.read_until(b"Username: ")
    tn.write(user.encode('ascii') + b"\n")

    if password:
       tn.read_until(b"Password: ")
       tn.write(password.encode('ascii') + b"\n")
    #Makes Term length to 0, run shows commands & reads all output, \
    # then saves files with time stamp # Comment
    tn.write(("terminal length 0\n").encode('ascii')) # Change terminal length to 0
    tn.write(("show clock\n").encode('ascii')) # Disply time
    tn.write(("show running-config\n").encode('ascii')) # Show running-configuration
    tn.write(("exit\n").encode('ascii')) # Exit session
    readoutput = tn.read_all() # Read output
    saveoutput = open(str(saved_time) + "_running_config_" + HOST, "wb") # saved_time
    is the time the file was saved, HOST is the IP address of the device.
    saveoutput.write(readoutput) # Write the output to the file
    saveoutput.close # Save and close the file
^G Get Help  ^O Write Out   ^W Where Is   ^K Cut Text    ^J Justify    ^C Cur Pos
^X Exit      ^R Read File   ^\ Replace    ^U Paste Text  ^T To Spell   ^_ Go To Line
```

#	Task
3	Use the Linux fping command again to check the network connectivity on your network. If you have any nodes (network devices) not reachable, you must troubleshoot the connectivity issue first.

```
pynetauto@ubuntu20s1:~/telnet_labs$ sudo apt install fping
pynetauto@ubuntu20s1:~/telnet_labs$ fping 192.168.183.10 192.168.183.20
192.168.183.101 192.168.183.102 192.168.183.133
192.168.183.10 is alive
192.168.183.133 is alive
192.168.183.20 is alive
```

#	Task
	192.168.183.102 is alive 192.168.183.101 is alive
4	Now, run the script using the `./take_backup.py` command from your `ubuntu20s1` server. If you copied the script from the previous lab, the file attributes should be carried over, and your new script should be an executable file already. It is time to run the code for one last time in this chapter.

	`pynetauto@ubuntu20s1:~/telnet_labs$ ls -l take*`
	`-rwxrwxr-x 1 pynetauto pynetauto 1574 Jan 12 10:50 take_backups.py`
	`pynetauto@ubuntu20s1:~/telnet_labs$ ./take_backups.py`
	`Enter your username: pynetauto`
	`Password:********`
	`Getting running-config from 192.168.183.10`
	`Getting running-config from 192.168.183.20`
	`Getting running-config from 192.168.183.101`
	`Getting running-config from 192.168.183.102`
	`Getting running-config from 192.168.183.133`

4	After the script runs successfully, you can run the `ls -lh` Linux command to check your local directory's backed-up `running-config` files of your devices. The files should begin with the year, month, and day, followed by the time the backup was taken.

	`pynetauto@ubuntu20s1:~/telnet_labs$ ls -lh 2021*`
	`-rw-rw-r-- 1 pynetauto pynetauto 4.3K Jan 12 10:53 20210112_105318_running_config_192.168.183.10`
	`-rw-rw-r-- 1 pynetauto pynetauto 5.4K Jan 12 10:53 20210112_105318_running_config_192.168.183.101`
	`-rw-rw-r-- 1 pynetauto pynetauto 4.8K Jan 12 10:54 20210112_105318_running_config_192.168.183.102`
	`-rw-rw-r-- 1 pynetauto pynetauto 1.7K Jan 12 10:54 20210112_105318_running_config_192.168.183.133`
	`-rw-rw-r-- 1 pynetauto pynetauto 4.5K Jan 12 10:53 20210112_105318_running_config_192.168.183.20`

5	Use the `cat` command to check if the correct information has been captured.

	`pynetauto@ubuntu20s1:~/telnet_labs$ cat 20210112_105318_running_config_192.168.183.10`
	`**************************************************************************`
	`* IOSv is strictly limited to use for evaluation, demonstration and IOS  *`
	`* education. IOSv is provided as-is and is not supported by Cisco's      *`
	`* Technical Advisory Center. Any use or disclosure, in whole or in part, *`
	`* of the IOSv Software or Documentation to any third party for any      *`
	`* purposes is expressly prohibited except as otherwise authorized by    *`
	`* Cisco in writing.                                                      *`
	`**************************************************************************`
	`LAB-R1#terminal length 0`
	`LAB-R1#show clock`
	`*08:01:50.307 UTC Tue Jan 12 2021`
	`LAB-R1#show running-config`
	`Building configuration...`

(continued)

#	Task
	Current configuration : 3418 bytes ! version 15.6 service timestamps debug datetime msec service timestamps log datetime msec no service password-encryption ! hostname LAB-R1 ! boot-start-marker boot-end-marker ! ! enable password cisco123 ! no aaa new-model *[...omitted for brevity]*

You have logged into each device and successfully backed up your routers' and switches' current running configurations to your local directory. Making the running configuration back up to an S/FTP server is even easier, but this lab has been reserved for SSH labs. At this point, try to modify your script and run `write memory` or `copy running-config startup-config` to save all the configuration changes. Next, you will be attempting to do some SSH labs using the `paramiko` and `netmiko` libraries.

Summary

In this chapter, we focused on seven simple Telnet labs to leverage the knowledge we have gained from earlier chapters. You learned how to use the `fping` and `datetime` modules along the way. You also performed simple configuration changes interactively first and then by using Python scripts made changes using the power of loops and `range` commands. Also, you learned to read IP addresses from an external file and use the information in your script. In the final labs, you made configuration backups of all five network devices using Python `telnetlib` with the timestamp on each filename. In Chapter 14, you will continue to explore Python network automation via SSH connections using the `paramiko` and `netmiko` SSH libraries.

CHAPTER 14

Python Network Automation Labs: SSH paramiko and netmiko

In this chapter, you will use Python's SSH libraries, `paramiko` and `netmiko`, to control your networking devices. `paramiko` is what Ansible relies on for SSH connection management to network devices, and `netmiko` is an engineer-friendly version of `paramiko` as `netmiko` also relies on `paramiko`. By studying how these network modules work, you can learn the inner workings of other applications relying on these network modules. In the first half of this chapter, you will learn to replace basic network engineer manual tasks using Python scripts and the `paramiko` library. In the second half of this chapter, you will learn to write Python scripts using the `netmiko` library. Once you master how to use these SSH modules, you can apply them to your work immediately. These SSH labs will serve as the cornerstones in developing the IOS XE upgrade application at the end of this book.

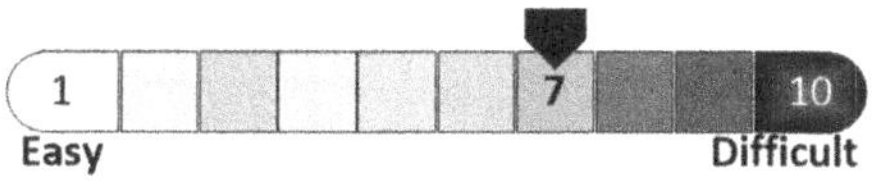

Python Network Automation Labs Using the paramiko and netmiko Libraries

In the previous chapter, we focused on the basic Python networking concepts using Telnet labs. Whether you are using Telnet or SSH, the same Python networking concepts can be applied. Of course, SSH is a more secure remote login protocol than Telnet, and it also uses a different library to log into networking devices. As you are aware already, Telnet is a plain-text network protocol that is insecure compared to SSH. In most secure networks, Telnet use is often prohibited, and only an encrypted SSH connection is allowed. To connect to Cisco devices that use SSH using Python, the Python `paramiko` library must be installed first, and the encrypted RSA keys must be configured on Cisco devices. To begin the chapter, let's first install the `paramiko` library to begin our SSH labs.

B. Choi, *Introduction to Python Network Automation*, https://doi.org/10.1007/978-1-4842-6806-3_14

Python SSH Labs: paramiko

On your Ubuntu Python automation server, you can install `paramiko` using the `pip` command shown here:

```
pynetauto@ubuntu20s1:~$ pip3 install paramiko
```

After you have finished the `paramiko` installation, quickly run the Python interpreter session, and run `import paramiko` to check that the library can be imported correctly. When you are ready, begin the first SSH lab.

```
pynetauto@ubuntu20s1:~$ python
Python 3.8.2 (default, Jul 16 2020, 14:00:26)
[GCC 9.3.0] on linux
Type "help", "copyright", "credits" or "license" for more information.
>>> import paramiko
>>>
```

paramiko Lab 1: Configure the Clock and Time Zone of All Devices Interactively in the Python Interpreter

In this lab, you will log into the Python interpreter on the `ubunsu20s1` Python automation server and write a real-time script to interact with all routers and switches to change their time and time zone settings. You have to power on all three routers and two switches. If your PC uses an older low-performance CPU or less memory, you are only required to power on one router and one switch; this will let you avoid high CPU utilization and memory contention issues in this lab. See Figure 14-1.

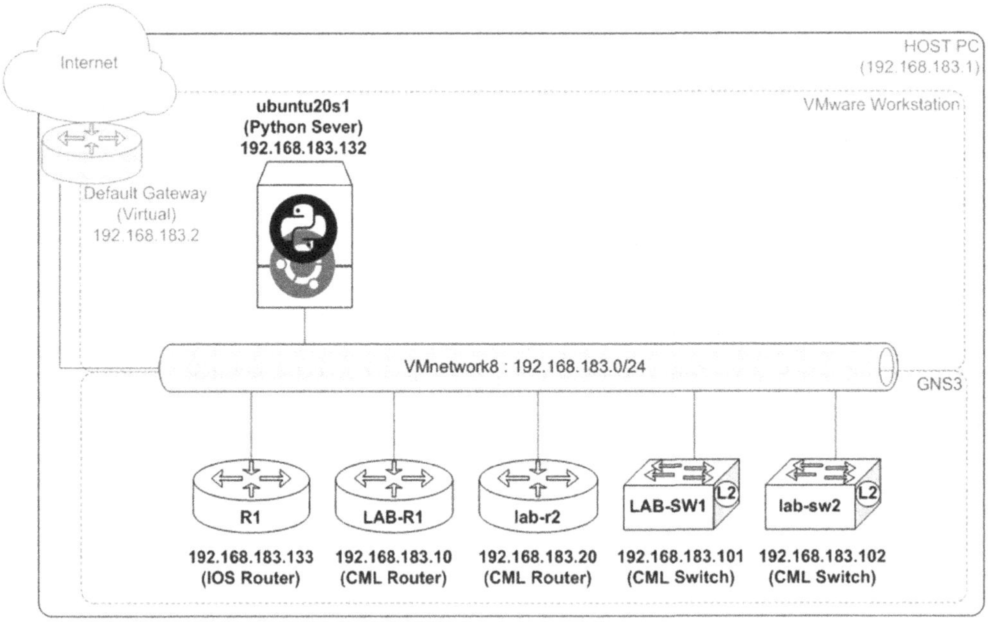

Figure 14-1. *SSH paramiko lab 1, devices in use*

You will be practicing an interactive SSH session to manage your network devices from the Python interpreter shell. Before connecting to the Cisco devices via SSH, we have to generate RSA keys for each device first. Since we are not using the AAA RADIUS server for authentication in our lab, we will create local certificates for each device. Follow these tasks to prepare for the first SSH lab:

#	Task

1	Use the following Cisco IOS commands to create 1,024-bit local RSA keys on each device and only enable SSH connections to manage each device. The following example shows the configuration on only the LAB-R1 router, but the same configuration must be applied to all other devices so that Telnet can be completely disabled on your network.
	`LAB-R1#configure terminal`
	`Enter configuration commands, one per line.  End with CNTL/Z.`
	`LAB-R1(config)#ip domain-name pynetauto.local`
	`LAB-R1(config)#crypto key generate rsa`
	`The name for the keys will be: LAB-R1.pynetauto.local`
	`Choose the size of the key modulus in the range of 360 to 4096 for your`
	`  General Purpose Keys. Choosing a key modulus greater than 512 may take`
	`  a few minutes.`
	
	`How many bits in the modulus [512]: 1024`
	`% Generating 1024 bit RSA keys, keys will be non-exportable...`
	`[OK] (elapsed time was 2 seconds)`
	
	`LAB-R1(config)#`
	`*Aug  9 13:04:41.381: %SSH-5-ENABLED: SSH 1.99 has been enabled`
	`LAB-R1(config)#line vty 0 15`
	`LAB-R1(config-line)#transport input all`
	`LAB-R1(config-line)#end`
	`LAB-R1#write memory`
	
	Now apply the previous configuration on lab-r2, LAB-SW1, lab-sw2, and R1. You can copy the following commands at once and paste them into each device's console:
	`configure terminal`
	`ip domain-name pynetauto.local`
	`crypto key generate rsa`
	`1024`
	`line vty 0 15`
	`transport input all`
	`do write memory`

(continued)

#	Task
2	You can use the `ssh -l user_name IP_address` command to SSH into the other device between any two Cisco devices. From R1, use the following commands to SSH into all the other routers and switches:

```
R1#ssh -l pynetauto 192.168.183.10

**************************************************************************
* IOSv is strictly limited to use for evaluation, demonstration and IOS  *
* education. IOSv is provided as-is and is not supported by Cisco's      *
* Technical Advisory Center. Any use or disclosure, in whole or in part, *
* of the IOSv Software or Documentation to any third party for any       *
* purposes is expressly prohibited except as otherwise authorized by     *
* Cisco in writing.                                                      *
**************************************************************************
Password:*******

[...omitted for brevity]

LAB-R1#exit

[Connection to 192.168.183.10 closed by foreign host]
R1#
```

Try to ssh into other devices and vise vesa.

```
R1#ssh -l pynetauto 192.168.183.20
R1#ssh -l pynetauto 192.168.183.101
R1#ssh -l pynetauto 192.168.183.102
```

#	Task
3	If you want to test the SSH connection from a Linux server, you can use the `ssh user_name IP_address` command. However, due to a legacy SSH key exchange issue, you may have to specify the encryption key type to SSH into Cisco devices from your Linux Python server.

Ubuntu SSH login to LAB-R1 (192.168.183.10) example:

```
pynetauto@ubuntu20s1:~$ ssh -oKexAlgorithms=+diffie-hellman-group1-sha1 -c 3des-cbc
pynetauto@192.168.183.10
The authenticity of host '192.168.183.10 (192.168.183.10)' can't be established.
RSA key fingerprint is SHA256:D9HqPuccjTD+WAGLMOYkyZ3KooHqYqe+5n7Hs2AI67I.
Are you sure you want to continue connecting (yes/no/[fingerprint])? yes
Warning: Permanently added '192.168.183.10' (RSA) to the list of known hosts.

[...omitted for brevity]

Password: *********

[...omitted for brevity]

LAB-R1#exit
Connection to 192.168.183.10 closed.
pynetauto@ubuntu20s1:~$
```

Ubuntu SSH login to LAB-SW1 (192.168.183.101) example:

```
pynetauto@ubuntu20s1:~$ ssh -l pynetauto 192.168.183.101 -c aes256-cbc
-oKexAlgorithms=+diffie-hellman-group1-sha1
The authenticity of host '192.168.183.101 (192.168.183.101)' can't be established.
RSA key fingerprint is SHA256:OsbazxGQ82A3KAC26l6msWR3BrklVXnWOsHChkij23g.
Are you sure you want to continue connecting (yes/no/[fingerprint])? yes
Warning: Permanently added '192.168.183.101' (RSA) to the list of known hosts.

[...omitted for brevity]

Password: *********

[...omitted for brevity]

LAB-SW1#exit
Connection to 192.168.183.101 closed.
pynetauto@ubuntu20s1:~$
```

(continued)

#	Task
4	Suppose you want to go one step further and simplify the SSH login from your Linux server. In that case, you first have to check the SSH version in use on your Linux server to avoid possible Diffie-Hellman key exchange issues between Linux server and Cisco devices. Use the `diffie-hellman-group1-sha1` key exchange method on your Linux server permanently by modifying the `.ssh/config` file on `ubuntu20s1`.

To check the SSH version on Python server, use this:

```
pynetauto@ubuntu20s1:~$ ssh -V
OpenSSH_8.2p1 Ubuntu-4, OpenSSL 1.1.1f  31 Mar 2020
```

To hard-code the key exchange method, open the `/home/user_name/.ssh/config` file and add the following information to the file. This will enable the old algorithms on the SSH client (`ubuntu20s1`), allowing it to connect to the older type of SSH servers (Cisco devices in this case).

```
pynetauto@ubuntu20s1:~$ nano /home/pynetauto/.ssh/config
```

```
GNU nano 4.8                    /home/pynetauto/.ssh/config
Host 192.168.183.10
    KexAlgorithms +diffie-hellman-group1-sha1
Host 192.168.183.20
    KexAlgorithms +diffie-hellman-group1-sha1
Host 192.168.183.101
    KexAlgorithms +diffie-hellman-group1-sha1
Host 192.168.183.102
    KexAlgorithms +diffie-hellman-group1-sha1
Host 192.168.183.133
    KexAlgorithms +diffie-hellman-group1-sha1
^G Get Help  ^O Write Out  ^W Where Is  ^K Cut Text   ^J Justify   ^C Cur Pos
^X Exit      ^R Read File  ^\ Replace   ^U Paste Text ^T To Spell  ^_ Go To Line
```

Also, if you run into known-hosts issues due to this problem, you can follow the instructions shown in the following forum to remove the records from your Linux server and try to re-establish the SSH connection to Cisco networking devices.

`https://superuser.com/questions/30087/remove-key-from-known-hosts`

Also, if you run into RSA key issues on your Cisco routers or switches, you can "zerorize" the RSA to re-create the RSA key. You can clear the previous key with the following command:

```
R1 (config)#crypto key zeroize rsa
Configure SSH Configuration again
R1(config)#hostname <name>
R1(config)#ip domain-name <domain>
R1(config)#crypto key generate rsa
R1(config)#ip ssh version 2
```

If your devices in GNS3 run into Diffie-Hellman key exchange issues and you cannot find a solution for them, then save the running configuration, remove the node from the topology, and then reconfigure your device; this could be related to the GNS3, VMware, and Cisco image file incompatibility issue.

#	Task
5	Now, let's open Python interpreter on the ubuntu20s1 server and type in the following to configure the correct time and time zone via an SSH real-time connection. Please update the time zone to your own local time. Yes, you are expected to type in the following word by word on the interactive session to practice writing code. Python development engineers are expected to write hundreds and thousands of lines of codes each day, and it is not a walk in the park.

Once again, if you are using a different IP address range, update the IP addresses. Also, be precise with the four leading whitespaces after each colon and look out for any capitalization in special methods. Make sure you change the time to your current time and time zone while running the Python Interpreter session's commands.

```
>>> import paramiko # import paramiko library
>>> import time # import time module
>>>
>>> ip_addresses = ["192.168.183.10", "192.168.183.20", "192.168.183.101",
"192.168.183.102", "192.168.183.133"] # a list of device ip addresses
>>>
>>> username = "pynetauto" # username variable
>>> password = "cisco123" # password variable
>>>
>>> ssh_client = paramiko.SSHClient() # create paramiko SSH Client object
>>> ssh_client.set_missing_host_key_policy(paramiko.AutoAddPolicy()) # Automatically
accept host key policy
>>> for ip in ip_addresses: # for loop to loop through ip_addresses list
...     ssh_client.connect(hostname=ip, username=username, password=password) # minimum
SSH connection objects
...     print("Connected to " + ip + "\n") # a print statement
...     remote_connection = ssh_client.invoke_shell() # Create a shell for the session
...     remote_connection.send("terminal length 0\n")
...     remote_connection.send("configure terminal\n") # Enter configuration mode
...     remote_connection.send("clock timezone AEST +10\n") # Set timezone to your
timezone
...     remote_connection.send("clock summer-time AEST recurring\n") # Set summertime
occurrence
...     remote_connection.send("exit\n") # Go back to exec privilege mode
...     time.sleep(1) # add 1 second pause
...     remote_connection.send("clock set 15:15:00 12 Jan 2021\n") # set clock to your
time
...     remote_connection.send("copy running-config startup-config\n") # Save
configuration
...     remote_connection.send("end\n") # end/exit session
...     output = remote_connection.recv(6000) # save remort_connection to variable
output
...     print((output).decode('ascii')) # print content of output using ASCII decoding
...     time.sleep(2) # add 1 second pause
...     ssh_client.close() # Clock SSH connection
```

(*continued*)

#	Task
6	If your interactive session went smoothly, it will print out the session as it logs into each device and configures the clock and time zone on each device. All your devices should be configured at the end of this lab with the correct time per your local time zone. To check the configuration, let's configure another quick script that runs the show command and displays it. Follow these tasks on Ubuntu Python automation server. You no longer have to log in to each device to run the same commands five times. Simply run them from your server.

```
pynetauto@ubuntu20s1:~$ mkdir ssh_labs
pynetauto@ubuntu20s1:~$ cd ssh_labs
pynetauto@ubuntu20s1:~/ssh_labs$ nano display_show.py
```

```
GNU nano 4.8                    /home/pynetauto/ssh_labs/ display_show.py
import time
import paramiko

ip_addresses = ["192.168.183.10", "192.168.183.20", "192.168.183.101",
"192.168.183.102", "192.168.183.133"]

username = "pynetauto"
password = "cisco123"

for ip in ip_addresses:
   ssh_client = paramiko.SSHClient()
   ssh_client.set_missing_host_key_policy(paramiko.AutoAddPolicy())
   ssh_client.connect(hostname=ip, username=username, password=password)
   print("Connected to " + ip + "\n")
   remote_connection = ssh_client.invoke_shell()
   output1 = remote_connection.recv(3000) # Catches and removes the login prompt output
   # print(output1.decode('ascii')) # remove hash to print the login prompt message
   # Now send the commands you want to run and display on the screen
   remote_connection.send("show clock detail\n")
   time.sleep(2)
   output2 = remote_connection.recv(6000)
   print((output2).decode('ascii'))
   print("-"*80)
^G Get Help  ^O Write Out  ^W Where Is   ^K Cut Text    ^J Justify    ^C Cur Pos
^X Exit      ^R Read File  ^\ Replace    ^U Paste Text  ^T To Spell   ^_ Go To Line
```

The previous Python script is like a show command tool for multiple network devices. Now run the script to check the clock and time zone changes on all devices.

```
pynetauto@ubuntu20s1:~/ssh_labs$ python3 display_show.py
Connected to 192.168.183.10

show clock detail
15:15:23.609 AEST Tue Jan 12 2021
Time source is user configuration
Summer time starts 02:00:00 AEST Sun Mar 14 2021
Summer time ends 02:00:00 AEST Sun Nov 7 2021
```

#	Task

```
LAB-R1#
--------------------------------------------------------------------------------
Connected to 192.168.183.20

show clock detail
15:15:23.615 AEST Tue Jan 12 2021
Time source is user configuration
Summer time starts 02:00:00 AEST Sun Mar 14 2021
Summer time ends 02:00:00 AEST Sun Nov 7 2021
lab-r2#
--------------------------------------------------------------------------------
[...omitted for brevity]
```

7 While you are in interactive mode, you can use `dir(library_name)` to display the modules available to each library after importing a library. You have used the `SSHClient` and `AutoAddPolicy` modules from the paramiko library in the previous example.

```
>>> import paramiko
>>> dir(paramiko)
['AUTH_FAILED', 'AUTH_PARTIALLY_SUCCESSFUL', 'AUTH_SUCCESSFUL', 'Agent', 'AgentKey',
'AuthHandler', 'AuthenticationException' , 'AutoAddPolicy', 'BadAuthenticationType',
[...omitted for brevity]
'SFTP_NO_CONNECTION', 'SFTP_NO_SUCH_FILE', 'SFTP_OK', 'SFTP_O P_UNSUPPORTED', 'SFTP_
PERMISSION_DENIED', 'SSHClient', 'SSHConfig', 'SSHException', 'SecurityOptions',
'ServerInterface', 'Su bsystemHandler', 'Transport', 'WarningPolicy', '__all__',
'__author__', '__builtins__', '__cached__',
[...omitted for brevity]
'sftp_client', 'sftp_file', 'sftp_handle', 'sftp_server', 'sftp_si', 'ssh_exception',
'ssh_gss', 'sys', 'transport',  'util']
```

8 To view each module's packages within `paramiko`, you can first import each module and again use `dir(module_name)` to view some details of this module.

```
>>> from paramiko import SSHClient
>>> dir(SSHClient)
['__class__', '__delattr__', '__dict__', '__dir__', '__doc__', '__enter__', '__eq__',
'__exit__', '__format__', '__ge__', '__ getattribute__', '__gt__', '__hash__', '__
init__', '__init_subclass__', '__le__', '__lt__', '__module__', '__ne__', '__new__'
, '__reduce__', '__reduce_ex__', '__repr__', '__setattr__', '__sizeof__', '__str__',
'__subclasshook__', '__weakref__', '_aut h', '_families_and_addresses', '_key_from_
filepath', '_log', 'close', 'connect', 'exec_command', 'get_host_keys', 'get_transp
ort', 'invoke_shell', 'load_host_keys', 'load_system_host_keys', 'open_sftp', 'save_
host_keys', 'set_log_channel', 'set_missi ng_host_key_policy']

>>> from paramiko import AutoAddPolicy
>>> dir(AutoAddPolicy)
['__class__', '__delattr__', '__dict__', '__dir__', '__doc__', '__eq__', '__
format__', '__ge__', '__getattribute__', '__gt__' , '__hash__', '__init__',
'__init_subclass__', '__le__', '__lt__', '__module__', '__ne__', '__new__', '__
reduce__', '__reduce _ex__', '__repr__', '__setattr__', '__sizeof__', '__str__',
'__subclasshook__', '__weakref__', 'missing_host_key']
```

paramiko Lab 2: Configuring an NTP Server on Cisco Devices Without User Interaction (NTP Lab)

In this lab, you will configure LAB-R1 and lab-r2, reading the information from two external files. The first file contains each router's IP address per line, and the other file contains the username and password. When you use external files, the network administrator does not have to be sitting in front of the device's remote console to type in the information interactively. In the next chapter, you will be learning how to use Linux cron as a scheduler to run your Python applications without your interaction so that your application becomes the bot. Using a Python script as an application and using Linux cron as the default scheduler may look rather humble (no cost to your company) and primitive (no prettified GUI) compared to the fancy features offered by Cisco ACI and Red Hat Ansible Tower. Still, you must understand how cron works and how to customize your environment as every client has a different network environment. No two networks are the same in size and complexity. After all, a scheduler is a scheduler. See Figure 14-2.

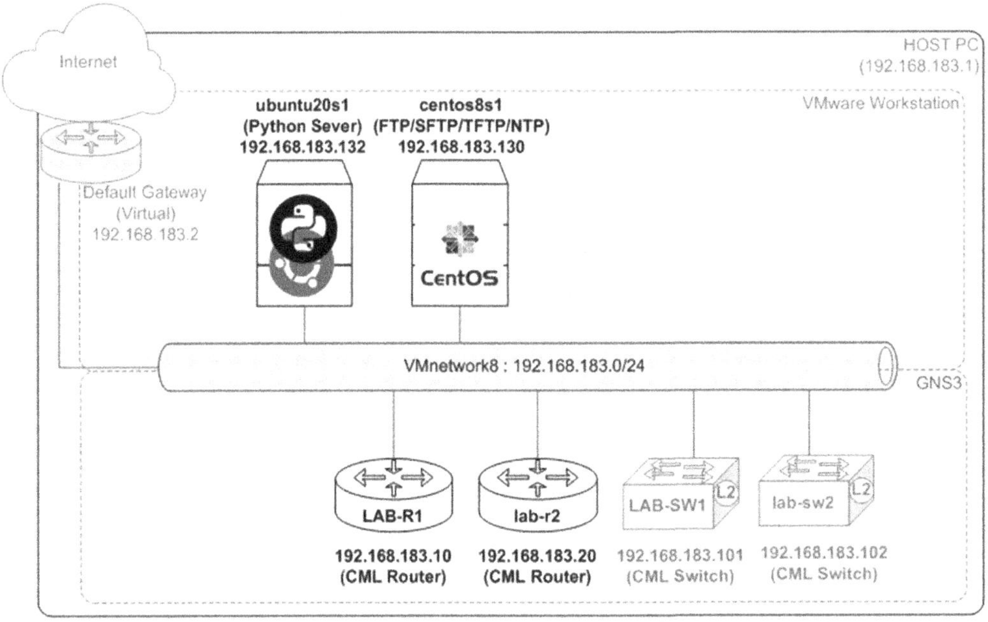

Figure 14-2. *SSH paramiko lab 2, devices in use*

You will need to power on the IP Services server, centos8s1, to provide NTP services to the routers. For this lab, you will need to power on ubuntu20s1, centos8s1, LAN-R1, and lab-r2 and power on LAB-SW1 and lab-sw2 to provide the connection to two routers. You have to complete many tasks in this lab, so let's write our script and run it in the lab.

#	Task

1	If you still have not created the `ssh_labs` directory, on the `ubuntu20s1` server, follow these steps to create a new directory for SSH labs and then create two external files in the same directory:
	
	`pynetauto@ubuntu20s1:~/telnet_labs$ cd ..`
	`pynetauto@ubuntu20s1:~$ mkdir ssh_labs`
	`pynetauto@ubuntu20s1:~$ cd ssh_labs`
	`pynetauto@ubuntu20s1:~/ssh_labs$ nano routerlist`
	`pynetauto@ubuntu20s1:~/ssh_labs$ cat routerlist`
	`192.168.183.10`
	`192.168.183.20`
	`pynetauto@ubuntu20s1:~/ssh_labs$ nano adminpass`
	`pynetauto@ubuntu20s1:~/ssh_labs$ cat adminpass`
	`pynetauto`
	`cisco123`

2	I have done a Google search, copied an example `ssh_client.py` script, and modified the content to suit my needs. You can go to the following site to grab the base template SSH script to begin your SSH scripting.
	
	URL: `https://gist.github.com/ghawkgu/944017`
	
	ssh_client.py
	
	`#!/usr/bin/env python`
	
	`import paramiko`
	
	`hostname = 'localhost'`
	`port = 22`
	`username = 'foo'`
	`password = 'xxxYYYxxx'`
	
	`if __name__ == "__main__":`
	`   paramiko.util.log_to_file('paramiko.log')`
	`   s = paramiko.SSHClient()`
	`   s.load_system_host_keys()`
	`   s.connect(hostname, port, username, password)`
	`   stdin, stdout, stderr = s.exec_command('ifconfig')`
	`   print stdout.read()`
	`   s.close()`
	
	The script will configure the NTP server on both routers and enable time synchronization on the network. NTP plays an important role in an enterprise network to keep all the devices' time in sync, so the timestamps on the syslog and reporting servers are accurate down to the second. As this is not a networking book, I will not go into too much detail on the stratum and NTP features, but note a couple of things here. First, Cisco and many vendor networking devices do not trust Microsoft W32tm services running on Windows machines. Second, certain Cisco networking and server devices' time must be set to a minimum stratum to be trusted as a reliable time source. Usually, this value is equal or less than stratum five, and the lower stratum is the more trustworthy time.

(continued)

#	Task
	Modify the base paramiko login configuration. Once you have finished, it should look similar to the following script:

```
pynetauto@ubuntu20s1:~/ssh_labs$ nano ssh_ntp_lab.py

GNU nano 4.8                                  /home/pynetauto/ssh_labs/ ssh_ntp_lab.py
#!/usr/bin/env python3

import paramiko # import paramiko library
import time # import time module
from datetime import datetime # import datetime module from datetime library
t_ref = datetime.now().strftime("%Y-%m-%d_%H-%M-%S") # Time reference in desired time format

file1 = open("routerlist") # open routerlist as file1

for line in file1: # for loop for router ip address
  print(t_ref) # print time reference
  print ("Now logging into " + (line)) # print statement
  ip_address = line.strip() # remove any white spaces

  file2= open("adminpass") # open adminpass as file2
  for line1 in file2: # read the first line(admin ID) in file 2
    username = line1.strip() # remove any white spaces
    for line2 in file2: # read the second line (password) in file2
      password = line2.strip() # remove any white spaces

      ssh_client = paramiko.SSHClient() # Create paramiko SSH client object
      ssh_client.set_missing_host_key_policy(paramiko.AutoAddPolicy()) # Automatically
accept host key policy
      ssh_client.connect(hostname=ip_address,username=username,password=password) # SSH
connection objects
      print ("Successful connection to " + (ip_address) +"\n") # print statement
      print ("Now completing following tasks : " + "\n") # print statement

      remote_connection = ssh_client.invoke_shell() # invoke shell session
      output1 = remote_connection.recv(3000) # Catches and removes the login prompt output
      # print(output1.decode('ascii')) # remove hash to print the login prompt message
      remote_connection.send("configure terminal\n") # Move to configuration mode

      print ("Configuring NTP Server") # print statement
      remote_connection.send("ntp server 192.168.183.130\n") # configure NTP server
      remote_connection.send("end\n") # go back to exec privilege mode
      remote_connection.send("copy running-config start-config\n") # send save command
      print ()# print remote_connections

      time.sleep(2) #
      output2 = remote_connection.recv(6000) # capture session in output variable
      print((output2).decode('ascii')) # print output using ASCII decoding

      print (("Successfully configured your device & Disconnecting from ") +
(ip_address)) # Print statement

      ssh_client.close # Close SSH connection
      time.sleep(2) # Pause for 2 seconds
```

#	Task

	file1.close() # Close file1
	file2.close() # Close file2
	`^G Get Help  ^O Write Out   ^W Where Is   ^K Cut Text    ^J Justify    ^C Cur Pos`
	`^X Exit      ^R Read File   ^\ Replace    ^U Paste Text  ^T To Spell   ^_ Go To Line`

3	Since we have only two devices to check, this time you can check the ports manually. Log into `LAB-R1` and `lab-r2` and then run the `show control-plane host open-ports` command to check that SSH port (22) is correctly working and in `LISTEN` status.

```
LAB-R1#show control-plane host open-ports
Active internet connections (servers and established)
Prot       Local Address      Foreign Address     Service                 State
tcp        *:22               *:0                 SSH-Server              LISTEN
tcp        *:23               *:0                 Telnet                  LISTEN
udp        *:56827            *:0                 udp_transport Server    LISTEN
```

```
lab-r2#show control-plane host open-ports
Active internet connections (servers and established)
Prot       Local Address      Foreign Address     Service                 State
tcp        *:22               *:0                 SSH-Server              LISTEN
tcp        *:23               *:0                 Telnet                  LISTEN
udp        *:18999            *:0                 udp_transport Server    LISTEN
```

Alternatively, you can modify the `display_show.py` file and get the information from the Python file. Download `display_show_control_plane.py` included in `chapter 14_codes.zip` and use it to get the same result.

Source code download URL: `https://github.com/pynetauto/apress_pynetauto`

4 Now, before running your script, check that the NTP service is running correctly on `centos8s1`. If you find that the NTP service is not running, you must troubleshoot the issue before running the script. On CentOS 8.1, we previously installed chronyd in Chapter 8, as an NTP server. Here are commands to troubleshoot common issues with chronyd. In the next step, we have to complete the server configuration by modifying the `chrony.conf` file to make it a functional server.

```
[pynetauto@centos8s1 ~]$ systemctl status chronyd
[pynetauto@centos8s1 ~]$ systemctl restart chronyd
[pynetauto@centos8s1 ~]$ systemctl enable chronyd
[pynetauto@centos8s1 ~]$ sudo firewall-cmd --add-port=123/udp --permanent
[pynetauto@centos8s1 ~]$ sudo firewall-cmd --reload
```

If you forgot to install chrony, use the `dnf install` command to install it.

```
[pynetauto@centos8s1 ~]$ dnf install chrony
```

Also, check the current time on your NTP server.

```
[pynetauto@centos8s1 ~]$ date
Tue Jan 12 17:13:16 AEDT 2021
```

(continued)

#	Task

For chronyd, you must obtain a list of NTP servers close to your home region from the URL specified here, and you have to update the NTP server pool as shown in Figure 14-1. Make sure you comment out the first default line with a hash (#). Ensure that you choose the public NTP server closest to your location from the following site:

URL: `https://www.pool.ntp.org/en/`

Open the file in sudo mode to modify the `chrony.conf` file under `/etc/`.

```
[pynetauto@centos8s1 ~]$ sudo nano /etc/chrony.conf
```

```
GNU nano 4.8                /etc/chrony.conf
# Use public servers from the pool.ntp.org project.
# Please consider joining the pool (http://www.pool.ntp.org/join.html).
# pool 2.centos.pool.ntp.org iburst
server 0.oceania.pool.ntp.org
server 1.oceania.pool.ntp.org
server 2.oceania.pool.ntp.org
server 3.oceania.pool.ntp.org

# Record the rate at which the system clock gains/losses time.
driftfile /var/lib/chrony/drift
[...omitted for brevity]
^G Get Help  ^O Write Out   ^W Where Is    ^K Cut Text    ^J Justify    ^C Cur Pos
^X Exit      ^R Read File   ^\ Replace     ^U Paste Text  ^T To Spell   ^_ Go To Line
```

While you are on the same config file, go to the end of the line and confirm that your network has been allowed to access this NTP server from the local network. If you have configured this in Chapter 8, it should be already there.

```
[... omitted for brevity]
# Allow NTP client access from the local network.
allow 192.168.183.0/24
```

5 If everything looks to be in good order, go back to the ubuntu8s1 Python server and run the `ssh_ntp_lab.py` script.

```
pynetauto@ubuntu20s1:~/ssh_labs$ python ssh_ntp_lab.py
2021-01-12_17-31-59
Now logging into 192.168.183.10

Successful connection to 192.168.183.10

Now completing following tasks :

Configuring NTP Server

configure terminal
Enter configuration commands, one per line.  End with CNTL/Z.
LAB-R1(config)#ntp server 192.168.183.130
LAB-R1(config)#end
LAB-R1#copy running-config start-config
Destination filename [start-config]?
Successfully configured your device & Disconnecting from 192.168.183.10
2021-01-12_17-31-59
Now logging into 192.168.183.20

Successful connection to 192.168.183.20
```

#	Task
	Now completing following tasks :

```
Configuring NTP Server
configure terminal
Enter configuration commands, one per line.  End with CNTL/Z.
lab-r2(config)#ntp server 192.168.183.130
lab-r2(config)#end
lab-r2#copy running-config start-config
Destination filename [start-config]?
Successfully configured your device & Disconnecting from 192.168.183.20
```

6 Once the NTP script successfully runs, modify the display_show.py script with the new show commands and run it. In this lab, I have named the new show command script display_show_ntp.py. To check the NTP status, include the show ntp status command in your script.

```
pynetauto@ubuntu20s1:~/ssh_labs$ cp display_show.py display_show_ntp.py
```

You can always check the status in the CLI for quick verification.

```
LAB-R1# show ntp status

lab-r2 # show ntp status
```

If you see a similar NTP status messages as shown here, your router's time has been synchronized with the Linux NTP server's time (192.168.183.130).

```
pynetauto@ubuntu20s1:~/ssh_labs$ python3 display_show_ntp.py
Connected to 192.168.183.10

show ntp status
Clock is synchronized, stratum 5, reference is 192.168.183.130
nominal freq is 1000.0003 Hz, actual freq is 1000.0003 Hz, precision is 2**15
ntp uptime is 191100 (1/100 of seconds), resolution is 1000
reference time is E3A7C697.1089E8E5 (06:56:23.064 UTC Tue Jan 12 2021)
clock offset is 9948.5451 msec, root delay is 7.75 msec
root dispersion is 16599.57 msec, peer dispersion is 2.51 msec
loopfilter state is 'SPIK' (Spike), drift is 0.000499999 s/s
system poll interval is 64, last update was 375 sec ago.
--------------------------------------------------------------------------------
Connected to 192.168.183.20

show ntp status
Clock is synchronized, stratum 5, reference is 192.168.183.130
nominal freq is 1000.0003 Hz, actual freq is 1000.0003 Hz, precision is 2**15
ntp uptime is 190000 (1/100 of seconds), resolution is 1000
reference time is E3A7C6A4.121D0A5D (06:56:36.070 UTC Tue Jan 12 2021)
clock offset is 2100.9149 msec, root delay is 12.98 msec
root dispersion is 7958.81 msec, peer dispersion is 4.38 msec
loopfilter state is 'CTRL' (Normal Controlled Loop), drift is 0.000499999 s/s
system poll interval is 64, last update was 736sec ago.
--------------------------------------------------------------------------------
```

You have successfully configured the NTP server on the LAB-R1 and lab-r2 routers and synchronized the time with the Linux NTP server within your network. Also, there was no need to enter the IP addresses and admin credentials one at a time; you preloaded them into two separate files before running your script. This will come in handy in the cron lab in Chapter 8. Password security and the password vault are important topics; however, they are beyond this book's scope. Now let's quickly move on to the next SSH lab and make backups of our devices to our TFTP server.

paramiko Lab 3: Create an Interactive paramiko SSH Script to Save Running Configurations to the TFTP Server

In this lab, you will make an interactive tool using Python's input function and getpass module to get the network administrator's ID and password. To keep this lab simple, the script will use a list with all IP addresses, and the backup files will be saved to the TFTP server running on centos8s1 (192.168.183.130). With simple modifications, you can customize and make operational tools to save time and resources. In this lab, you are making backups of only five devices, but imagine if this work has to be done on 500 devices as in some customers' networks. Also, if you want to run such scripts daily using an automated scheduler, engineers no longer need to sit in front of their computers taking backups. Of course, there are enterprise-level network device backup solutions, but we want to get to the bottom of this subject and understand how these tools work by re-creating such tools and running them in our lab. See Figure 14-3.

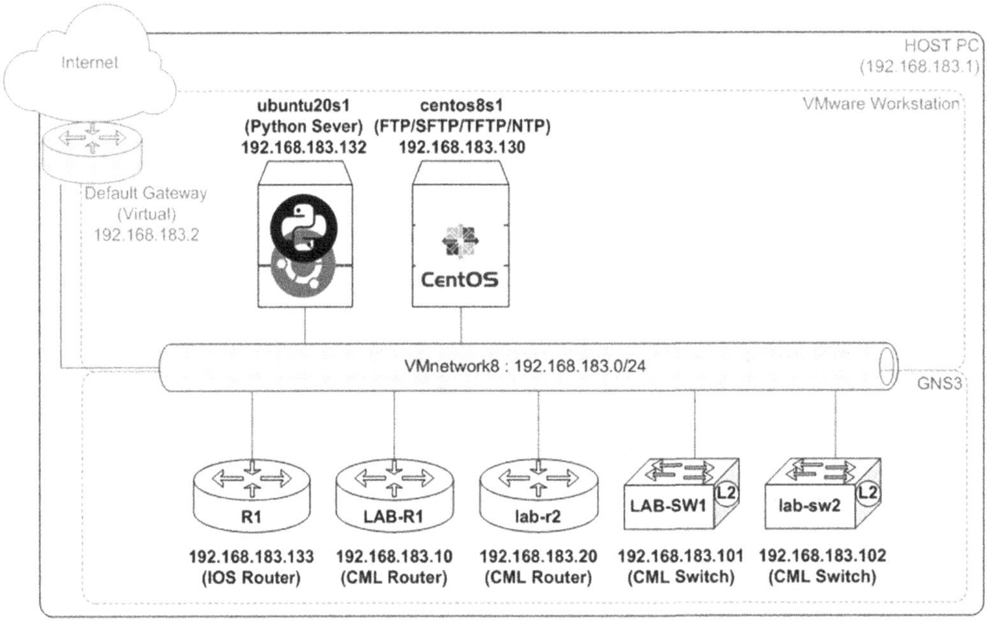

***Figure 14-3.** SSH paramiko lab 3, devices in use*

Out of the box, vendor solutions have exceptional features and fit most of the sizable standardized customer environments. Still, you almost always need some customization to make the solution even more versatile and useful in a real production environment. Without further discussion, let's write an interactive tool to SSH into our routers and switches and take some backups.

#	Task

1	As the first step, check if you can ping all network devices from your Python automation server. This time you are going to use `fping` again and check the connectivity from a single command. If you still have not installed `fping`, use the following command to do so now:
	`pynetauto@ubuntu20s1:~/ssh_labs$ sudo apt-get install fping`
	After `fping` has been installed successfully, run the command like this to confirm your server's network connectivity:
	`pynetauto@ubuntu20s1:~/ssh_labs$ fping 192.168.183.10 192.168.183.20 192.168.183.101 192.168.183.102 192.168.183.133`
	`192.168.183.10 is alive`
	`192.168.183.20 is alive`
	`192.168.183.133 is alive`
	`192.168.183.102 is alive`
	`192.168.183.101 is alive`

2	You have confirmed network connectivity, and this time let's confirm whether our previously installed TFTP service is working correctly on the `centos8s1` multi-IP Services server. Use the following commands to check the operational status of TFTP services on your Linux server.
	The TFTP (`xinetd`) is active and working correctly with port 69 in listening mode.
	`[pynetauto@centos8s1 ~]$ systemctl is-active xinetd.service`
	`active`
	`[pynetauto@centos8s1 ~]$ sudo netstat -anp | grep 69`
	`[sudo] password for pynetauto:`
	`udp        0      0 0.0.0.0:69          0.0.0.0:*          1241/xinetd`
	`udp6       0      0 :::69               :::*`
	`[... omitted for brevity]`

If your server's port 69 is not listed, you will have to use the `ufw` command to allow the ports on your server with the following command:

```
[pynetauto@centos8s1 ~]$ sudo ufw allow 69/udp
```

#	Task
3	Now, to make this lab even more interesting, we want to measure how long the end-to-end task takes from start to finish, so we can measure the speed of our script and adjust sleep timers as required. As you have already observed in both the `paramiko` and `telnet` scripts, `time.sleep(s)` code has been added to allow enough response time for the virtual routers and switches, and with `netmiko` scripts, many timers are built into the library. However, it is not always 100 percent accurate, so sometimes, you still have to use the sleep timers to customize for different devices. As you create applications, you have to develop small ideas and small tools to make your Python script more valuable. The timer toll script shown next is a suggestion, and this tool measures the time it takes to count from 1 to 10 million. You can adjust the numbers and see how fast your computer is at counting numbers. You can also put your function or tasks in the middle of the script to measure how quickly your script runs.

(continued)

#	Task
	In Python, one function processes data much quicker than another, and it is worth spending time to test the speed of your scripts. After all, Python is not well known for its speed, but often, it is the Python coder making the wrong module or tools selection and adding the lag to a script. Also, in the world of network automation, speed is important but not the most critical part of a Python application. Often the precision takes higher priority over the speed. If you genuinely need the speed, there is always a C programming language closest to the machine language. Anyway, write the following code on your server and check how this simple script works. Although this is a simple script, many simple scripts form the basis of your application.

```
pynetauto@ubuntu20s1:~/ssh_labs$ nano timer_tool.py
```

```
GNU nano 4.8                                    /home/pynetauto/ssh_labs/timer_tool.py
import time # Import time module

start_timer = time.mktime(time.localtime()) # Start time

########## REPLACE ME! #########
big_number = range(10000000)      # Put some function or task to run here

for i in big_number:
    print(i,end=" ")
# print(" ".join(str(i) for i in big_number)) # This is a join method to print the
number, can replace above two lines of code
##############################
total_time = time.mktime(time.localtime()) - start_timer # End time minus start time
print("Total time : ", total_time, "seconds") # Total time format
^G Get Help  ^O Write Out   ^W Where Is   ^K Cut Text    ^J Justify   ^C Cur Pos
^X Exit      ^R Read File   ^\ Replace    ^U Paste Text  ^T To Spell  ^_ Go To Line
```

4 Guess how long your computer will take to count 1 to 10 million? From your ubuntu20s1 Python server, run the timer tool by typing `python timer_tool.py`. For the testing computer, it took a full 22 seconds to count from 1 to 10 million.

```
pynetauto@ubuntu20s1:~/ssh_labs$ python timer_tool.py
[...omitted for brevity]
9999974 9999975 9999976 9999977 9999978 9999979 9999980 9999981 9999982 9999983
9999984 9999985 9999986 9999987 9999988 9999989 9999990 9999991 9999992 9999993
9999994 9999995 9999996 9999997 9999998 9999999
Total time :  22.0 seconds
```

#	Task
5	To make our script interactive to talk back to the network administrator, let's make a username and password collector tool using the getpass module of the getpass library. Using the getpass module, we can hide the passwords typed, and also, by making some modifications, we can make the user enter the password for the second time for verification of the first password. Often the passwords are mistyped, and we can solve this problem by incorporating if statements into our password script.

```
pynetauto@ubuntu20s1:~/ssh_labs$ nano password_tool.py

GNU nano 4.8                  /home/pynetauto/ssh_labs/password_tool.py
from getpass import getpass # Import getpass module from getpass library

def get_credentials():# Create get_credentials function
   #Prompts for and returns a username and password # Comment
   username = input("*Enter Network Admin ID : ") # Prompt user for username
   password = None # Set original password to None
   while not password: # Keep prompting til password is entered
      password = getpass("*Enter Network Admin PWD : ") # Prompt for password
      password_verify = getpass("**Confirm Network Admin PWD : ") # Verify password
      again
      if password != password_verify: # If password fails to verify, run the following
      script
         print("! Network Admin Passwords do not match. Please try again.")
# Inform the user of mismatch
         password = None # Reset password to None and ask for the password again
   print(username, password) # For testing purpose only, remove this when applied to
   the script
   return username, password #returns username and password

get_credentials() # Run get_credentials() function
^G Get Help  ^O Write Out   ^W Where Is   ^K Cut Text   ^J Justify   ^C Cur Pos
^X Exit      ^R Read File   ^\ Replace    ^U Paste Text ^T To Spell  ^_ Go To Line
```

#	Task
6	Please create a password tool script and run it from your ubuntu20s1 server. We will print the username and password here for testing purposes, but you have to remove the print *(username, password)* command from the function and go silent after you press the Enter key. Go ahead and comment out the print statement as required.

```
pynetauto@ubuntu20s1:~/ssh_labs$ python password_tool.py
*Enter Network Admin ID : pynetauto
*Enter Network Admin PWD :********
**Confirm Network Admin PWD : ********
pynetauto cisco123
pynetauto@ubuntu20s1:~/ssh_labs$
```

(continued)

#	Task
7	Now that you have two mini tools developed, let's write out our interactive code to make backups of our devices' lab network. After completing the paramiko script, your script should look similar to the following. Detailed explanations are embedded in the code, so study the code before writing the script in full. If you run into issues, refer to the source code, but only if you have to. Typically most code is typed in on the keyboard by you, not cut and pasted!

```
pynetauto@ubuntu20s1:~/ssh_labs$ nano interactive_backup.py
GNU nano 4.8                    /home/pynetauto/ssh_labs/interactive_backup.py
#!/usr/bin/env python3 # for Linux system to run this script as python3 file
import re # import regular expression module
import time # import time module
import paramiko # import paramiko library
from datetime import datetime # import datetime module from datetime library
from getpass import getpass # Import getpass module from getpass library

t_ref = datetime.now().strftime("%Y-%m-%d_%H-%M-%S") # Time reference to be used for
file name

device_list = ["192.168.183.10", "192.168.183.20", "192.168.183.101",
"192.168.183.102", "192.168.183.133"] # Device list

start_timer = time.mktime(time.localtime()) # Start time

def get_credentials():# Define a function called get_credentials
    #Prompts for, and returns a username and password # comment
    global username # Make username global, so it can be used throughout this script
    global password # Make password global, so it can be used throughout this script
    username = input("*Enter Network Admin ID : ") # Enter username
    password = None # set password default value to None
    while not password: # Until password is entered
        password = getpass("*Enter Network Admin PWD : ") # Enter the password first time
        password_verify = getpass("**Confirm Network Admin PWD : ") # Get password for
        verification, second time
        if password != password_verify: # Password verification
            print("! Network Admin Passwords do not match. Please try again.")
            # Informational
            password = None # Set password to None
    return username, password # Optional, returns username and password

get_credentials()# Run get_credentials function, to save username and password

for ip in device_list: # for loop to grab device IP addresses
    print(t_ref) # Comment for user information
    print("Now logging into " + (ip)) # Informational
    ssh_client = paramiko.SSHClient()# Initiate paramiko SSH client session as ssh_client
    ssh_client.set_missing_host_key_policy(paramiko.AutoAddPolicy()) # Accept missing
    host key policy
    ssh_client.connect(hostname=ip,username=username,password=password) # SSH
    connection with credentials

    print("Successful connection to " + (ip) +"\n") # Informational
    print("Now making running-config backup of " + (ip) + "\n") # Comment for user
    information
    remote_connection = ssh_client.invoke_shell() # Invoke shell
    time.sleep(3) # Pause 3 seconds to invoke shell
```

#	Task

```
    remote_connection.send("copy running-config tftp\n") # Send copy command
    remote_connection.send("192.168.183.130\n") # Respond to TFTP server IP request, TFTP IP
    remote_connection.send((ip)+ ".bak@" + (t_ref)+ "\n") # Respond to backup file name request
    time.sleep(3) ## Pause for 3 seconds, give device to respond
    print() # Print screen
    time.sleep(3) # Pause for 3 seconds, give time to process data
    output = remote_connection.recv(65535) # Receive output up to 65535 lines
    print((output).decode('ascii')) #Print output using ASCII decoding method

    print(("Successfully backed-up running-config to TFTP & Disconnecting from ") +
    (ip) + "\n") # Print statement to provide an update to the user
    print("-"*80) # Print ~ 80 times
    ssh_client.close # Close SSH session
    time.sleep(1) # Pause for 1 second
    total_time = time.mktime(time.localtime()) - start_timer # Start time minus current time
    print("Total time : ", total_time, "seconds") # Print the total time to run the
    script in seconds
^G Get Help   ^O Write Out    ^W Where Is    ^K Cut Text     ^J Justify    ^C Cur Pos
^X Exit       ^R Read File    ^\ Replace     ^U Paste Text   ^T To Spell   ^_ Go To Line
```

8 In Chapter 8, you created a `tftpdir` directory for TFTP file sharing and storage on the `centos8s1` server. As a pre-check to running the previous script, check the files in the `/var/tftpdir` directory. Files that change in size usually go under the var (variable) directory in Linux.

```
[pynetauto@centos8s1 ~]$ cd /var/tftpdir
[pynetauto@centos8s1 tftpdir]$ pwd
/var/tftpdir
[pynetauto@centos8s1 tftpdir]$ ls -lh
total 45M
-rw-r--r--. 1 pynetauto pynetauto  45M Jul 18 04:59 c3725-adventerprisek9-mz.124-15.
T14.bin
-rw-rw-r--. 1 tftpuser  tftpuser  1.2K Jan  9 00:07 running-config
-rw-rw-r--. 1 tftpuser  tftpuser   100 Jun  8  2020 transfer_file01
-rw-r--r--. 1 root      root       100 Jun  8  2020 transfer_file77
```

9 Go back to the Python automation server (`ubuntu20s1`). OK, now let's run the interactive backup script to SSH into each device and make backups of each device's running configuration on the TFTP server. Run the python `interactive_backup.py` command, enter the network administrator credentials, and sit back and observe.

```
pynetauto@ubuntu20s1:~/ssh_labs$ python interactive_backup.py
*Enter Network Admin ID : pynetauto
*Enter Network Admin PWD : ********
**Confirm Network Admin PWD : ********
2021-01-12_18-42-23
Now logging into 192.168.183.10
Successful connection to 192.168.183.10

Now making running-config backup of 192.168.183.10
[...omitted for brevity]
Destination filename [lab-r1-confg]? 192.168.183.10.bak@2021-01-12_18-42-23
!!
```

(continued)

#	Task

```
3953 bytes copied in 2.972 secs (1330 bytes/sec)
LAB-R1#
Successfully backed-up running-config to TFTP & Disconnecting from 192.168.183.10
--------------------------------------------------------------------------------
2021-01-12_18-42-23
Now logging into 192.168.183.20
Successful connection to 192.168.183.20
[...omitted for brevity]
lab-r2#
Successfully backed-up running-config to TFTP & Disconnecting from 192.168.183.20
--------------------------------------------------------------------------------
2021-01-12_18-42-23
Now logging into 192.168.183.101
Successful connection to 192.168.183.101
[...omitted for brevity]
LAB-SW1#
Successfully backed-up running-config to TFTP & Disconnecting from 192.168.183.101
--------------------------------------------------------------------------------
2021-01-12_18-42-23
Now logging into 192.168.183.102
Successful connection to 192.168.183.102
[...omitted for brevity]
lab-sw2#
Successfully backed-up running-config to TFTP & Disconnecting from 192.168.183.102
--------------------------------------------------------------------------------
2021-01-12_18-42-23
Now logging into 192.168.183.133
Successful connection to 192.168.183.133
[...omitted for brevity]
R1#
Successfully backed-up running-config to TFTP & Disconnecting from 192.168.183.133
--------------------------------------------------------------------------------
Total time :  78.0 seconds
```

It took 78 seconds to make backups of five lab devices to the TFTP server. We'll also look at file management to FTP during the following netmiko labs, but the concepts we have learned so far can be reused in FTP or SFTP scenarios.

10 Now log back into your centos8s1 server; then change your directory to /var/tftpdir and run the ls -lh command. You should find all your device backups with the date and time stamp specified in our code. Now you have completed the SSH interactive script to capture the running configuration of all devices. We are only using five devices here, but the number of devices will multiply by tens and hundreds, and you do not even have to sweat it in production. Sweet!

```
[pynetauto@centos8s1 tftpdir]$ls -lh 192.*
-rw-rw-r--. 1 tftpuser tftpuser 4.5K Jan 12 18:43 192.168.183.101.bak@2021-01-12_18-42-23
-rw-rw-r--. 1 tftpuser tftpuser 3.8K Jan 12 18:43 192.168.183.102.bak@2021-01-12_18-42-23
-rw-rw-r--. 1 tftpuser tftpuser 3.5K Jan 12 18:43 192.168.183.10.bak@2021-01-12_18-42-23
-rw-rw-r--. 1 tftpuser tftpuser 1.4K Jan 12 18:43 192.168.183.133.bak@2021-01-12_18-42-23
-rw-rw-r--. 1 tftpuser tftpuser 3.7K Jan 12 18:43 192.168.183.20.bak@2021-01-12_18-42-23
```

Now you have completed the paramiko labs by completing the running configuration backups via an SSH connection and TFTP file transfer. You can easily tweak the configuration to use either FTP or SFTP file transfer for further testing and development. In the second half of this chapter, you will be working with the versatile netmiko library in different scenarios.

Python SSH Labs: netmiko

paramiko is an excellent SSH library to manage network devices via an SSH connection. Still, you have to work hard to fine-tune parts of your script to make it run smoothly. For example, the timing of the connection and the running of different commands via SSH requires special care with the timing and prompts. Luckily, a CCIE emeritus engineer has already worked hard and thought about many of the problems we may run into while using paramiko. He has developed an incredible Python library called netmiko. netmiko is a multivendor library to simplify paramiko SSH connections to network devices; Kirk Byers developed it to support various vendor networking devices. In Python, many hidden technology masters in the world are not afraid of sharing their knowledge and wisdom. After using netmiko for about two years, I cannot thank Kirk Byers enough for saving me from many pitfalls of paramiko. He already has thought of paramiko's SSH connection problems. We have to enjoy the fruits of one engineer's artistry and sweat, pioneering Python network automation. Here are Kirk's official netmiko link and GitHub sites for further reading. Also, the nornir project is an extension of netmiko; it has the same features of Ansible but is written in Python. nornir is beyond the scope of this book, but when you have time, please look it up on the Internet.

URL: https://pynet.twb-tech.com/ (Kirk Byers' Python for Network Engineers)

URL: https://ktbyers.github.io/netmiko/#tutorialsexamplesgetting-started (getting started with Netmiko)

URL: https://github.com/ktbyers/netmiko/blob/master/netmiko/ssh_dispatcher.py (supported device list)

Now, before writing your first netmiko Python script, make sure that you have netmiko libraries installed using sudo pip3 install netmiko, as shown here:

```
pynetauto@ubuntu20s1:~$ sudo pip3 install netmiko
[sudo] password for pynetauto:
Collecting netmiko
  Downloading netmiko-3.2.0-py2.py3-none-any.whl (157 kB)
     |████████████████████████████████| 157 kB 4.8 MB/s
Requirement already satisfied: pyserial in /usr/lib/python3/dist-packages (from netmiko)
(3.4)
[... omitted for brevity]
Successfully installed netmiko-3.2.0 scp-0.13.2 textfsm-1.1.0
```

After netmiko installation, start your Python interpreter and import the netmiko module. You can use the pip3 freeze command to check the installed libraries, but sometimes even if it is listed, you will not be able to use the module in an environment where more than one version of Python is running on your system. If no error was returned on the interpreter, it has been installed successfully, and you are ready to write the following code:

```
pynetauto@ubuntu20s1:~/ssh_labs$ pip3 freeze
...
netmiko==3.3.2
...
```

```
pynetauto@ubuntu20s1:~$ python3
Python 3.8.2 (default, Jul 16 2020, 14:00:26)
[GCC 9.3.0] on linux
Type "help", "copyright", "credits" or "license" for more information.
>>> import netmiko
>>>
```

After verification, press Ctrl+Z or type in `exit()` or `quit()` to close your Python 3 interpreter.

netmiko Lab 1: netmiko Uses a Dictionary for Device Information, Not a JSON Object

Using netmiko, you have to provide the device information in a dictionary format with basic SSH login information such as the device type, IP (hostname), administrator ID, and password as the bare minimum. You can also provide other optional information, such as the secret password, port number, and logging status. At a glance, this dictionary format looks similar to a data set in JavaScript Object Notation (JSON) format. The `netmiko` device information is a built-in Python dictionary, not a JSON data set used by a browser and a server to send data. A typical `netmiko` dictionary usually looks like this:

```
cisco_3850 = {
    'device_type': 'cisco_ios',
    'host':   '10.20.30.40',
    'username': 'cisco',
    'password': 'password123',
    'port' : 8022,          # optional, if not used defaults to 22
    'secret': 'secret123',     # optional, if not used defaults to ''
}
```

If you want to flatten out the previous dictionary as in the earlier `paramiko` examples, you can write the dictionary like this. Still, the previous structured information looks nicer on the eyes.

```
cisco_csr1k = {"device_type":"cisco_xe", "ip":"192.168.183.1", "username":"pynetauto",
"password":"cisco123"}
```

We can also enhance the `netmiko` dictionary by mixing it with some input statements and `getpass` functions to request user inputs, which looks similar to this:

```
from netmiko import ConnectHandler
from getpass import getpass

device1 = {
'device_type': 'cisco_ios',
'ip': input('IP Address : '),
'username': input('Enter username : '),
'password': getpass('SSH password : '),
}
```

Before moving onto `netmiko` lab 1, we will confirm that the `netmiko` dictionary is not a JSON object. Let's quickly type this code into the Python interpreter to confirm this fact.

Open your Python interpreter and type the following into the interpreter window. Make sure that you use the double quotation marks when creating the dictionary, `device1`. Python will automatically convert them to single quotation marks, and you will find out why. First, check the attributes of a `netmiko` dictionary.

```
>>> device1 = {"device_type":"cisco_ios", "ip":"192.168.183.10", "username":"pynetauto",
"password":"cisco123"}
>>> print(device1)
{'device_type': 'cisco_ios', 'ip': '192.168.183.10', 'username': 'pynetauto', 'password':
'cisco123'}
>>> print(type(device1))
<class 'dict'>
>>> dir(device1)
['__class__', '__contains__', '__delattr__', '__delitem__', '__dir__', '__doc__', '__eq__',
(omitted for brevity)
  'update', 'values']
```

Convert the `device1` dictionary into the JSON format using the `dumps` method. When we print the converted JSON objects, they look like a Python dictionary, but the key difference is that all key and value sets are enclosed in double quotation marks.

```
>>> import json
>>> device2 = json.dumps(device1)
>>> print(device2)
{"device_type": "cisco_ios", "ip": "192.168.183.10", "username": "pynetauto", "password":
"cisco123"}
>>> print(type(device2))
<class 'str'>
```

At first glance, you would think that the JSON object is the same as the `netmiko` dictionary object, but it is a string object, as revealed by the `dir()` method. The JSON object belongs to Python's built-in `str` class, and of course, the `netmiko` dictionary belongs to the built-in `dict` class.

```
>>> dir(device2)
['__add__', '__class__', '__contains__', '__delattr__', '__dir__', '__doc__', '__eq__',
'__format__', (omitted for brevity)
, 'rsplit', 'rstrip', 'split', 'splitlines', 'startswith', 'strip', 'swapcase', 'title',
'translate', 'upper', 'zfill']

# Quickly check if device1 is the same as device2
```

```
>>> if device1 == device2:
...     print(True)
... else:
...     print(False)
...
False
```

In netmiko lab 1, you will learn how to make a directory and create a file using the TCL shell commands on a Cisco router so that you can create dummy files to practice deleting files from the router's flash:. You will be using an IOSv router, LAB-R1, to keep it simple because the actual script you will be writing is starting to become complicated, especially if you come from a non-Cisco networking background. Try to focus on the concepts rather than how old the IOSv image is. As I explained in the first chapter, the latest and greatest tools are good, but they are not required to learn the basic concepts of networking or Python network automation. See Figure 14-4.

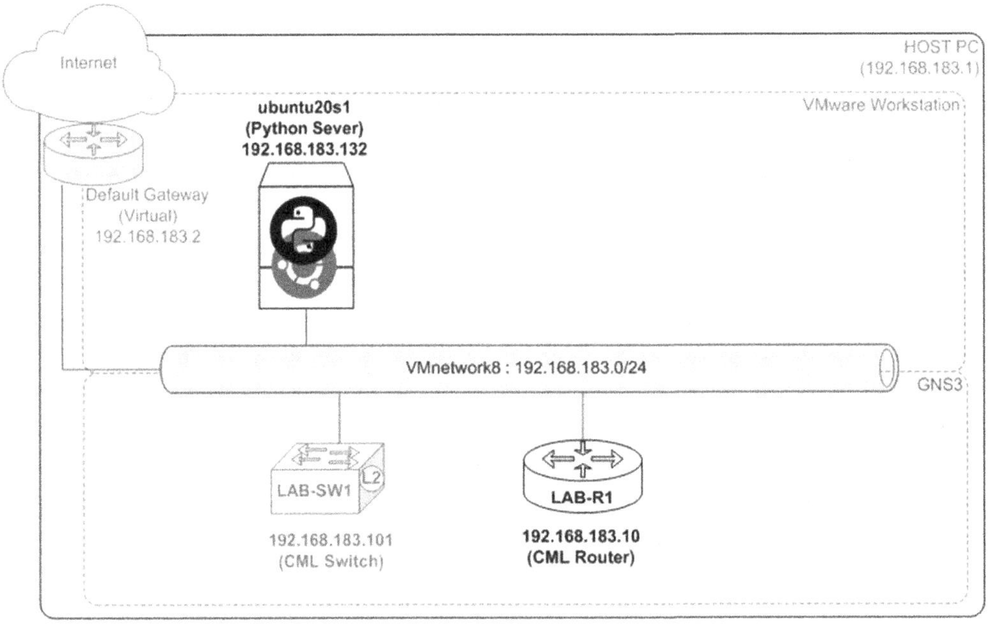

Figure 14-4. *SSH netmiko lab 1, devices in use*

The purpose of this lab is to get you some practice in deleting files from the Cisco device's flash: using your Python script instead of directly consoling into a Cisco device. You will first format the flash memory of LAB-R1, make a directory using the mkdir command, and use good old TCL shell commands to create some files to be deleted. We should be able to write Python code that allows us to remove old files and also allows us to navigate to a folder to locate the file we are looking for so the Python application can remove the files as required. Although you may not see any relation to your work, this feature comes in handy in IOS upgrade application development.

#	Task

1	Open the console window of LAB-R1 and format disk 0 so there are no files.
	`LAB-R1#format flash:`
	`Format operation may take a while. Continue? [confirm]`
	`Format operation will destroy all data in "flash:".  Continue? [confirm]`
	`Format: All system sectors written. OK...`
	`Format: Total sectors in formatted partition: 4193217`
	`Format: Total bytes in formatted partition: 2146927104`
	`Format: Operation completed successfully.`
	`Format of flash0: complete`
	`LAB-R1#show flash:`
	`-#- --length-- -----date/time------ path`
	`2142711808 bytes available (8192 bytes used)`

2	Use `mkdir flash:/directory_name` to create a directory under `flash:`.
	`LAB-R1#mkdir flash:/old_files`
	`Create directory filename [old_files]?`
	`Created dir flash0:/old_files`
	`LAB-R1#dir`
	`Directory of flash0:/`
	`4  drw-           0  Jan 12 2021 08:09:26 +00:00  old_files`
	`2142720000 bytes total (2142707712 bytes free)`

3	Now use the good old TCL shell to create four files, as shown here. Two files will be created under `flash:`, and the other two files will be created under `flash:old_files/`.
	`LAB-R1#tclsh`
	`LAB-R1(tcl)#puts [open "flash:Delete_me_1.bin" w+]`
	`file0`
	`LAB-R1(tcl)#puts [open "flash:Don't_delete_me_1.txt" w+]`
	`file1`
	`LAB-R1(tcl)#puts [open "flash:old_files/Delete_me_2.bin" w+]`
	`file2`
	`LAB-R1(tcl)#puts [open "flash:old_files/Don't_delete_me_2.txt" w+]`
	`file3`
	`LAB-R1(tcl)#dir`
	`Directory of flash0:/`
	`4  drw-           0  Jan 12 2021 08:09:26 +00:00  old_files`
	`5  -rw-           0  Jan 12 2021 08:11:16 +00:00  Delete_me_1.bin`
	`6  -rw-           0  Jan 12 2021 08:11:24 +00:00  Don't_delete_me_1.txt`
	`2142720000 bytes total (2142707712 bytes free)`

(*continued*)

#	Task

```
LAB-R1#dir flash:/old_files/
Directory of flash0:/old_files/

7  -rw-           0  Jan 12 2021 08:11:32 +00:00  Delete_me_2.bin
8  -rw-           0  Jan 12 2021 08:11:40 +00:00  Don't_delete_me_2.txt

2142720000 bytes total (2142707712 bytes free)
```

4 We have completed creating a dummy directory and dummy IOS (`.bin`) files on `LAB-R1`'s `flash:`. Let's write a cool SSH script to log into `LAB-R1` using the `netmiko` library and then delete some `.bin` files using a Python script. Yes, you can log into the CLI of the router and delete the file, but you may be asking why bother with such trouble to create this in a Python script? First, as a reader who wants to write code for network automation, you have to do the hard work to enjoy the fruits of your labor. Second, this script can talk back to you and work together as a team. Lastly, imagine if you were dealing with 100 routers or switches, not a single device. Also, imagine you have to do this kind of drill regularly as part of your job. Python network automation's real power is in its loops (`for` loops and `while` loops), and in the next lab, let's revise this script to a newer version and use it on multiple devices.

Review the script referencing the embedded descriptions. Once you have finished writing the code, move to step 5 to run the script.

```
GNU nano 4.8                    /home/pynetauto/ssh_labs/netmiko_delete_me.py
#!/usr/bin/env python3
import re
from netmiko import ConnectHandler
from getpass import getpass
import time

device1 = {             #Netmiko dictionary for device1
'device_type': 'cisco_ios',
'ip': input('IP Address : '),
'username': input('Enter username : '),
'password': getpass('SSH password : '),
}

net_connect = ConnectHandler(**device1) # Netmiko ConnectHandler object
net_connect.send_command("terminal length 0\n") # Make terminal length to 0 to display all
time.sleep(1) # Pause for 1 second
dir_flash = net_connect.send_command("dir flash:\n") # Send "dir flash:" command
print(dir_flash) # Display content of dir flash output

p30 = re.compile(r'D[0-9a-zA-Z]{4}.*.bin') # Regular Expression to capture any file
starting with "D", ends with "bin"
m30 = p30.search(dir_flash) # Search for first match of p30
time.sleep(1) # Pause for 1 second

# net_connect1.enable() (Optional, not required with privilege 15 access)
print("!!! WARNING - You cannot reverse this step.") # Message to user
# If dir_flash contains a string which satisfies p30 (True),
# then run this script to delete a file.
if bool(m30) == True: # If m30 is true
    print("If you can see 'Delete_me.bin' file, select it and press Enter.") #
    Informational
    del_cmd = "del flash:/" # Partial command 1
```

#	Task

```
        old_ios = input("*Old IOS (bin) file to delete : ") # Partial command 2, select a
    file under flash:
        while not p30.match(old_ios) or old_ios not in dir_flash: # User input request
        until correct file name is given
            old_ios = input("**Old IOS (bin) file to delete : ")
        command = del_cmd + old_ios # Complete command (1 + 2)
        output = net_connect.send_command_timing( # Special netmiko send_command_timing
        command with timer
            command_string=command,
            strip_prompt=False,
            strip_command=False
        )
        if "Delete filename" in output: # if the returned output contains "Delete
        filename", send "Enter" (change line)
            output += net_connect.send_command_timing(
                command_string="\n",
                strip_prompt=False,
                strip_command=False
            )
        if "confirm" in output: # if the returned output contains "confirm", send "y"
            output += net_connect.send_command_timing(
                command_string="y",
                strip_prompt=False,
                strip_command=False
            )
        net_connect.disconnect # Disconnect from SSH session
        print(output) # Informational

    # If None (False), then run this script to search directory for .bin file to delete
    elif bool(m30) == False: # If no .bin file starting with D is found under "flash:",
    run this script
        print("No IOS file under 'flash:/', select the directory to view.") # Informational
        open_dir = input("*Enter Directory name : ") # Partial command 1
        while not open_dir in dir_flash: # Ask until correct response is received
            open_dir = input("** Enter Directory name : ") # If file does not exist,
            request user input again
        open_dir_cmd = (r"dir flash:/" + open_dir) # Completed command
        send_open_dir = net_connect.send_command(open_dir_cmd) # Send the command
        print(send_open_dir) # Informational
        p31 = re.compile(r'D[0-9a-zA-Z]{4}.*.bin') # Regular Expression to capture any
        file starting with "D", ends with "bin"
        m31 = p31.search(send_open_dir) # Send completed command
        if bool(m31) == True: # If there is a file with the string satisfy p31 expression
            print("If you see old IOS (bin) in the directory. Select it and press
            Enter.") # Informational
            del_cmd = "del flash:/" + open_dir + "/" # Completed command
            old_ios = input("*Old IOS (bin) file to delete : ") # Enter the .bin file to delete
            while not p30.match(old_ios) or old_ios not in send_open_dir: # User input
            request until correct file name is given
```

(*continued*)

#	Task

```
            old_ios = input("**Old IOS (bin) file to delete : ")
        command = del_cmd + old_ios # Complete command
        output = net_connect.send_command_timing( # Special netmiko send_command_
        timing command with timer
            command_string=command,
            strip_prompt=False,
            strip_command=False
        )
        if "Delete filename" in output: # if the returned output contains "Delete
        filename", send "Enter" (change line)
            output += net_connect.send_command_timing(
                command_string="\n",
                strip_prompt=False,
                strip_command=False
            )
        if "confirm" in output: # if the returned output contains "confirm", send "y"
            output += net_connect.send_command_timing(
                command_string="y",
                strip_prompt=False,
                strip_command=False
            )
        net_connect.disconnect # Disconnect from SSH session
        print(output) # Print content of output
    else: # Both conditions failed to satisfy, exit the script
        ("No IOS found.")
        exit()
    net_connect.disconnect # Disconnect from SSH session
^G Get Help  ^O Write Out   ^W Where Is   ^K Cut Text    ^J Justify    ^C Cur Pos
^X Exit      ^R Read File   ^\ Replace    ^U Paste Text  ^T To Spell   ^_ Go To Line
```

5 Now, navigate back to your ubuntu20s1 (192.168.183.132) Python server and ping LAB-R1 (192.168.183.10) to confirm the device's connectivity. You are still working with the SSH protocol, and the netmiko lab is still part of SSH labs, so you should be working within the /home/pynetauto/ssh_labs directory.

```
pynetauto@ubuntu20s1:~/ssh_labs$ ping 192.168.183.10 -c 3
PING 192.168.183.10 (192.168.183.10) 56(84) bytes of data.
64 bytes from 192.168.183.10: icmp_seq=1 ttl=255 time=7.37 ms
64 bytes from 192.168.183.10: icmp_seq=2 ttl=255 time=6.73 ms
64 bytes from 192.168.183.10: icmp_seq=3 ttl=255 time=12.9 ms

--- 192.168.183.10 ping statistics ---
3 packets transmitted, 3 received, 0% packet loss, time 2004ms
rtt min/avg/max/mdev = 6.734/9.016/12.948/2.791 ms
pynetauto@ubuntu20s1:~/ssh_labs$ ls netmiko*
netmiko_delete_me.py
```

#	Task
6	Now run the script using python netmiko_delete_me.py. When the script returns the output, select the .bin file, and press the Enter key to remove it from LAB-R1's flash.

```
pynetauto@ubuntu20s1:~/ssh_labs$ python netmiko_delete_me.py
IP Address : 192.168.183.10
Enter username : pynetauto
SSH password :

Directory of flash0:/

    4  drw-           0  Jan 12 2021 08:09:26 +00:00  old_files
    5  -rw-           0  Jan 12 2021 08:11:16 +00:00  Delete_me_1.bin
    6  -rw-           0  Jan 12 2021 08:11:24 +00:00  Don't_delete_me_1.txt

2142720000 bytes total (2142707712 bytes free)
!!! WARNING - You cannot reverse this step.
If you can see 'Delete_me.bin' file, select it and press Enter.
*Old IOS (bin) file to delete : Delete_me_1.bin
del flash:/Delete_me_1.bin
Delete filename [Delete_me_1.bin]?
Delete flash0:/Delete_me_1.bin? [confirm]y
LAB-R1#
```

7 Now open LAB-R1's console and check whether the file Delete_me_1.bin has been deleted from flash:. If you see only one file and one folder here, you have completed the first task. Move to step 9 to rerun the same script.

```
LAB-R1#dir
Directory of flash0:/

    4  drw-           0  Jan 12 2021 08:09:26 +00:00  old_files
    6  -rw-           0  Jan 12 2021 08:11:24 +00:00  Don't_delete_me_1.txt

2142720000 bytes total (2142707712 bytes free)
```

8 Run the same script for the second time; this time, since there is no .bin file under flash:, a different message will be prompted, and you will be asked to select a directory to search for the .bin file. When you cut and paste the directory name, it will run the script to look for the elusive .bin file and display the result. When the script finds the .bin file, go ahead and remove the Delete_me_2.bin file.

```
pynetauto@ubuntu20s1:~/ssh_labs$ python netmiko_delete_me.py
IP Address : 192.168.183.10
Enter username : pynetauto
SSH password : ********

Directory of flash0:/

    4  drw-           0  Jan 12 2021 08:09:26 +00:00  old_files
    6  -rw-           0  Jan 12 2021 08:11:24 +00:00  Don't_delete_me_1.txt

2142720000 bytes total (2142707712 bytes free)
!!! WARNING - You cannot reverse this step.
No IOS file under 'flash:/', select the directory to view.
*Enter Directory name : old_files # Enter the directory name
```

(continued)

#	Task

	`Directory of flash0:/old_files/`
	
	`  7  -rw-          0  Jan 12 2021 08:11:32 +00:00  Delete_me_2.bin`
	`  8  -rw-          0  Jan 12 2021 08:11:40 +00:00  Don't_delete_me_2.txt`
	
	`2142720000 bytes total (2142707712 bytes free)`
	`If you see old IOS (bin) in the directory. Select it and press Enter.`
	`*Old IOS (bin) file to delete :` **`Delete_me_2.bin`** `# Cut and paste the .bin file`
	`del flash:/old_files/Delete_me_2.bin`
	`Delete filename [/old_files/Delete_me_2.bin]?`
	`Delete flash0:/old_files/Delete_me_2.bin? [confirm]y`
	`LAB-R1#`

9	Go back to LAB-R1 and run the `dir flash:old_files/` command to view the directory content. If you see only a single file under the directory, you have completed this lab's second task.
	
	`LAB-R1#`**`dir flash:/old_files/`**
	`Directory of flash0:/old_files/`
	
	`  8  -rw-          0  Jan 12 2021 08:11:40 +00:00  Don't_delete_me_2.txt`
	
	`2142720000 bytes total (2142707712 bytes free)`

10	Now delete the working directory and file as we have completed this lab.
	
	`LAB-R1#`**`delete /recursive /force flash:old_files`**
	`LAB-R1#delete flash:`**`Don't_delete_me_1.txt`**
	`Delete filename [Don't_delete_me_1.txt]?`
	`Delete flash0:/Don't_delete_me_1.txt? [confirm]`
	`LAB-R1#`**`dir`**
	`Directory of flash0:/`
	
	`No files in directory`
	
	`2142720000 bytes total (2142711808 bytes free)`

You have now learned how to write Python code to delete and search for a router's flash file. You can turn your task into a Python script, which is the beginning of Python network automation. Next, we will develop a port scanning tool to check an open port and apply it to our work.

netmiko Lab 2: Develop a Simple Port Scanner Using a Socket Module and Then Develop a nemiko Disable Telnet Script

In this lab, you will learn how to develop a simple port scanner tool using a socket module and then use this scanning tool in your `netmiko` lab 2 scripts (`netmiko_disable_telnet.py`) to check for opened port 23 and disable the ports using the `netmiko` library. Earlier, we configured `transport input all` under `line vty 0 15` to allow both Telnet and SSH connections for all device management. To disable Telnet, you have to reconfigure the Virtual Teletype (`vty`) lines with `transport input ssh` command. You are going to need all the routers and switches powered on for this lab.

At the end of this lab, you will be able to scan network devices for any open ports; you will check whether port 23 (or 22 or any other ports of interest) is in use. Secure your devices by disabling Telnet port 23 on all devices and only allow SSH connections for device management. Once again, try to concentrate on the concepts and develop the tools required to achieve your goal in this lab. See Figure 14-5.

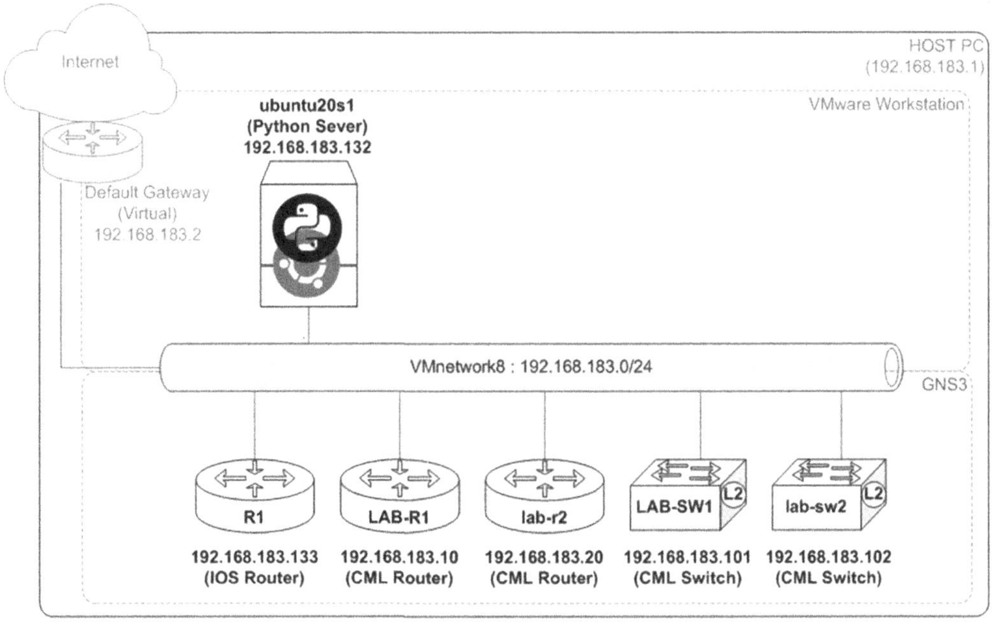

Figure 14-5. *SSH netmiko lab 2, devices in use*

Let's first develop a mini scanning tool and verify the open ports on our routers and switches. Then incorporate the scanning tool into our script, `netmiko_disable_telnet.py`.

#	Task

1	First, you have to create a socket object using `socket.socket(family, type)` with the family set to `socket.AF_INET` and type set to `socket.SOCK_STREAM`. According to Python socket programming, `socket.AF_INET` specifies the IP address family for IPv4, and `socket.SOCK_STREAM` specifies the socket type for TCP. To check a port status, use `socket.connect_ex(dest)` with the socket as the socket object and `dest` as a tuple containing the IP address and desired port number. If the port is open, `socket.connect_ex()` returns 0, but if the port is closed, it will return different digits based on the port being scanned. At the end of the port scan, you have to close the socket using `socket.close()`.
	A simple port scanner template we are going to use looks like this, and it allows us to scan only a single device of a single port. If you put this onto your Linux server, create a new file called `scan_open_port.py`, and run the code, you will be able to check the port status on a single destination.
	
	`pynetauto@ubuntu20s1:~/ssh_labs$ nano scan_open_port.py`
	
	`GNU nano 4.8 /home/pynetauto/ssh_labs/scan_open_port.py`
	`import socket # Import socket module`
	
	`sock = socket.socket(socket.AF_INET, socket.SOCK_STREAM) # Create a socket object`

(continued)

#	Task
	(continued)

```
dest = ("192.168.183.10", 22) # IP and Port to scan
port_open = sock.connect_ex(dest) # Create socket connect object
# open returns int 0, closed returns an integer based on port number
if port_open == 0: # If port is opened, it returns 0
    print(port_open) # print result = 0
    print("On ", {dest[0]}, "port is open.") # Informational
else:
    print(port_open) # print result, an integer other than 0
    print("On ", {dest[0]}, "port is closed.") # Informational
sock.close() # close socket object
^G Get Help  ^O Write Out  ^W Where Is  ^K Cut Text    ^J Justify   ^C Cur Pos
^X Exit      ^R Read File  ^\ Replace   ^U Paste Text  ^T To Spell  ^_ Go To Line
```

When you run the script in your lab on the LAB-R1 (192.168.183.10) router, the result will look like this:

```
pynetauto@ubuntu20s1:~/ssh_labs$ python3 scan_open_port.py
0
On  {'192.168.183.10'} port is open.
```

When you change port 22 (SSH) to 80 (HTTP) and scan the port again, it returns 111 and the "port is closed" message.

```
pynetauto@ubuntu20s1:~/ssh_labs$ python3 scan_open_port.py
111
On  {'192.168.183.10'} port is closed.
```

2 The previous script works well but does not scale well with our use cases, and we have to modify the script to make it more scalable and versatile in our environment. Using the previous script as our template, let's rewrite the script to scan ports of multiple devices at once. My script looks like the following, but there is no right or wrong way of coding, so you can also add your flair by making modifications as you like. Since this script scans multiple ports, I have named it scan_open_ports.py (with the plural "s" at the end).

```
pynetauto@ubuntu20s1:~/ssh_labs$ nano scan_open_ports.py

GNU nano 4.8                  /home/pynetauto/ssh_labs/scan_open_ports.py
import  socket # Import socket module

ip_addresses = ["192.168.183.10", "192.168.183.20", "192.168.183.101",
"192.168.183.102", "192.168.183.133"] # IP address list

for ip in ip_addresses: # get ip from the list, ip_addresses
    for port in range (22, 24): # port range, ports 22-23, always n-1 for the last digit
        dest = (ip, port) # combine both ip and port number into one object as socket
        method takes 1 attribute
        try: # Use try except method
            with socket.socket(socket.AF_INET, socket.SOCK_STREAM) as sock: # s as a
            socket object
                sock.settimeout(3) #
                connection = sock.connect(dest) # connect to destination on specified port
                print(f"On {ip}, port {port} is open!") # Informational
```

#	Task

	``
	        except:
	            print(f"On {ip}, port {port} is closed.") # Informational
	^G Get Help ^O Write Out ^W Where Is ^K Cut Text ^J Justify ^C Cur Pos
	^X Exit ^R Read File ^\ Replace ^U Paste Text ^T To Spell ^_ Go To Line
	``

	Once you have completed the script as shown, run the script, and the result should be similar to the following if you have both Telnet (22) and SSH (23) opened on your network devices. You can also specify a different range of ports for another port scanning task.
	``` pynetauto@ubuntu20s1:~/ssh_labs$ python3 scan_open_ports.py On 192.168.183.10, port 22 is open! On 192.168.183.10, port 23 is open! On 192.168.183.20, port 22 is open! On 192.168.183.20, port 23 is open! On 192.168.183.101, port 22 is open! On 192.168.183.101, port 23 is open! On 192.168.183.102, port 22 is open! On 192.168.183.102, port 23 is open! On 192.168.183.133, port 22 is open! On 192.168.183.133, port 23 is open! ```
3	In two steps, you have developed a Python port scanner you can use for your work.

Warning! Be careful where and how you use this sort of tool; you do not want to breach company security policies at work or your clients' sites. Do not run port scanners if your work does not recommend performing port scanning tasks without proper change control and approval.

OK, now you have another tool under your belt; based on the previous script, let's go ahead and write some code to check the port, and if Telnet is enabled on our devices, let the Python application SSH in and modify the settings; then save the changed configuration.

```
pynetauto@ubuntu20s1:~/ssh_labs$ nano netmiko_disable_telnet.py

GNU nano 4.8                    /home/pynetauto/ssh_labs/netmiko_disable_telnet.py
#!/usr/bin/env python3
import re
from netmiko import ConnectHandler
from getpass import getpass
import time
import  socket

def get_credentials():# Enhanced User ID and password collection tool
    #Prompts for, and returns a username and password
    global username # Make username as a global variable to be used throughout this script
    global password # Make password as a global variable to be used throughout this script
    username = input("Enter your username : ")
    password = None
    while not password:
        password = getpass()
```

(continued)

#	Task

```
        password_verify = getpass("Retype your password : ")# Verify the password is
        correctly typed
        if password != password_verify:
            print("Passwords do not match. Please try again.")
            password = None
    return username, password

get_credentials() # Run this function first to collect the username and password

device1 = {             # Netmiko dictionary for device1
'device_type': 'cisco_ios',
'ip': '192.168.183.10',
'username': username,
'password': password,
}
device2 = {             # Netmiko dictionary for device2
'device_type': 'cisco_ios',
'ip': '192.168.183.20',
'username': username,
'password': password,
}
device3 = {             # Netmiko dictionary for device3
'device_type': 'cisco_ios',
'ip': '192.168.183.101',
'username': username,
'password': password,
}
device4 = {             # Netmiko dictionary for device4
'device_type': 'cisco_ios',
'ip': '192.168.183.102',
'username': username,
'password': password,
}
device5 = {             # Netmiko dictionary for device5
'device_type': 'cisco_ios',
'ip': '192.168.183.133',
'username': username,
'password': password,
}

devices = [device1, device2, device3, device4, device5] # List of netmiko devices

for device in devices: # Loop through   devices
    ip = device.get("ip", "") # get value of the key "ip"
    for port in range (23, 24): # only port 23
        dest = (ip, port) # Combine ip and port number to form dest object
        try:
            with socket.socket(socket.AF_INET, socket.SOCK_STREAM) as sock: # port
            scanner tool
                sock.settimeout(3) # add 3 seconds pause to socket application
                connection = sock.connect(dest) #
                print(f"On {ip}, port {port} is open!") # Informational
                net_connect = ConnectHandler(**device) # create a netmiko
                ConnectHandler object
                show_clock = net_connect.send_command("show clock\n") # Send "show
                clock" command
```

#	Task

```
                print(show_clock) # Display time
                config_commands = ['line vty 0 15', 'transport input ssh'] # netmiko
                config_commands
                net_connect.send_config_set(config_commands) # send netmiko send_
                config_set
                output = net_connect.send_command("show run | b line vty")# send a
                show command to check vty 0 15
                print()# Informational
                print('-' * 80) # Displayed information separator line
                print(output) # Informational
                print('-' * 80) # Displayed information separator line
                print()# Informational
                net_connect.disconnect() # close netmiko connection
        except:
            print(f"On {ip}, port {port} is closed.")
            # # This is for saving the configuration after a successful configuration change.
            # net_connect = ConnectHandler(**device) # Commented out for third run
            # write_mem = net_connect.send_command("write mem\n") # Commented out for
            third run
            # print()
            # print('-' * 80)
            # print(write_mem) # Commented out for third run
            # print('-' * 80)
            # print()
            # net_connect.disconnect()
^G Get Help  ^O Write Out   ^W Where Is   ^K Cut Text   ^J Justify   ^C Cur Pos
^X Exit      ^R Read File   ^\ Replace    ^U Paste Text ^T To Spell  ^_ Go To Line
```

4 Run the netmiko_disable_telnet.py script and update the configuration to disable Telnet logins.

⚠ Warning! If you are using a similar script in the production, make sure that your primary remote console management protocol is SSH. You have followed the company policy to remove Telnet services using an automated script.

```
pynetauto@ubuntu20s1:~/ssh_labs$ python netmiko_disable_telnet.py
Enter your username : pynetauto
Password: ********
Retype your password : ********
On 192.168.183.10, port 23 is open!

*09:48:17.800 UTC Tue Jan 12 2021

--------------------------------------------------------------------------------
line vty 0 4
logging synchronous
login local
transport input ssh
line vty 5 15
logging synchronous
login local
transport input ssh
!
```

(continued)

#	Task

```
no scheduler allocate
ntp server 192.168.183.130
!
end
---------------------------------------------------------------------------
[... omitted for brevity]
---------------------------------------------------------------------------
On 192.168.183.133, port 23 is open!

*01:40:37.823 UTC Fri Mar 1 2002
---------------------------------------------------------------------------
line vty 0 4
exec-timeout 0 0
logging synchronous
login local
transport input ssh
line vty 5 15
exec-timeout 0 0
logging synchronous
login local
transport input ssh
!
!
end
---------------------------------------------------------------------------
```

5 Run the script for the second time for verification. Now Telnet is disallowed to the devices, and we should get a closed message as follows:

```
pynetauto@ubuntu20s1:~/ssh_labs$ python3 netmiko_disable_telnet.py
Enter your username : pynetauto
Password:********
Retype your password : ********
On 192.168.183.10, port 23 is closed.
On 192.168.183.20, port 23 is closed.
On 192.168.183.101, port 23 is closed.
On 192.168.183.102, port 23 is closed.
On 192.168.183.133, port 23 is closed.
```

6 Once the previous task is completed successfully, remove the # (uncomment) from the same code under the `except:` line. Then rerun the Python code to save all five devices' configurations. Here, I am making a copy of the original script and uncommenting the lines at the end of the script:

```
pynetauto@ubuntu20s1:~/ssh_labs$ cp netmiko_disable_telnet.py netmiko_disable_telnet_uncommented.py
pynetauto@ubuntu20s1:~/ssh_labs$ nano netmiko_disable_telnet_uncommented.py
pynetauto@ubuntu20s1:~/ssh_labs$ python netmiko_disable_telnet_uncommented.py
```

After uncommenting, the last lines of code should look like this:

```
except:
print(f"On {ip}, port {port} is closed.")
# This is for saving the configuration after a successful configuration change.
net_connect = ConnectHandler(**device)
```

#	Task

	`write_mem = net_connect.send_command("write mem\n")`
	`print()`
	`print('-' * 80)`
	`print(write_mem)`
	`print('-' * 80)`
	`print()`
	`net_connect.disconnect()`

7	Run the script one more time to save the currently running configuration.

```
pynetauto@ubuntu20s1:~/ssh_labs$ python netmiko_disable_telnet_uncommented.py
Enter your username : pynetauto
Password:
Retype your password :
On 192.168.183.10, port 23 is closed.
--------------------------------------------------------------------------------
Building configuration...
[OK]
--------------------------------------------------------------------------------
[... omitted for brevity]
--------------------------------------------------------------------------------
On 192.168.183.133, port 23 is closed.
--------------------------------------------------------------------------------
Building configuration...
[OK]
--------------------------------------------------------------------------------
```

You just developed a mini port scanning tool and then used it as the template for developing your SSH (netmiko) tool to shut down the Telnet ports on all your lab devices. Your lab topology is more secure now, and you can only access routers and switches using SSH connections for device management.

netmiko Lab 3: config compare

In this netmiko lab, you will be developing a quick device configuration comparison tool using difflib libraries. The script will borrow parts of the script from the previous lab and use the port scanner as the precheck communication verification tool by checking the open port status of port 22 for SSH connection. The running configurations of two similar devices will be compared side by side in this lab. If you have been a network engineer for some time, you should be familiar with the compare module in Notepad++ and similar tools. You have to manually log in to each device and run the show command to scrap the configuration as two separate logs or two text files and then open them on Notepad++ and run the compare tool. Once they are compared, you have to manually fish out the difference to apply the missing configuration to the second device. Here we are developing a tool for legacy devices accessible via an SSH connection; however, with the REST API-capable network devices, the same comparison can be used to collect the running configuration via API calls. The same script can be applied to the set of collected data. Also, suppose you want to take this script further. In that case, we can utilize the powerful data modules such as pandas and xlsxwriter to read the lines as data frames and extract only the differences between two configurations, so many manual tasks can be automated.

For this lab, you will require access to Lab-R1 (192.168.183.10) and lab-r2 (192.168.183.20). Also, both switches as well as transit devices for the routers need to be powered on. You will be using WinSCP to access data collected on the ubuntu20s1 Python server. So if you can download and install WinSCP or FileZilla in advance for the file retrieval, you are well prepared. See Figure 14-6.

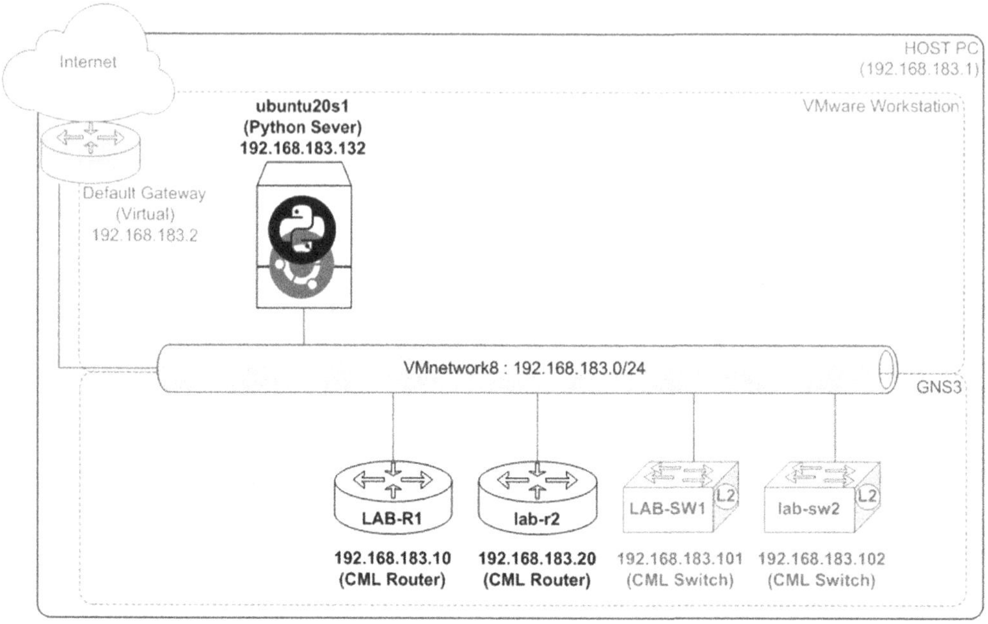

Figure 14-6. *SSH netmiko lab 3, devices in use*

After you have successfully completed the lab, you will have three files created in your script's running directory: two text files with the running configuration and one XML file with the comparison result. Follow these steps to complete this lab:

#	Task
1	First, copy the port scanner tool from the previous lab and make the necessary modifications so that SSH port 22's open status is probed by this tool. After you have made changes, the script should look similar to the following:

```
for device in devices: # Loop through netmiko devices list
    ip = device.get("ip", "") # Get value of the key "ip" from device dictionary
    for port in range (22, 23): # For only port 22
        dest = (ip, port) # Combine ip and port number to form dest object
        try:
            with socket.socket(socket.AF_INET, socket.SOCK_STREAM) as sock:
                sock.settimeout(3)
                connection = sock.connect(dest) # Send socket request
                print (f"on {ip}, port {port} is open!") # Informational, pass object
                using format string {}
        except:
            print (f"On {ip}, port {port} is closed. Check the connectivity to {ip}
            again.")
            exit()
```

#	Task
2	Now here is the full source code of the netmiko_compare_config.py script. This application uses the getpass module to get the password, time module to add a pause, socket module to probe for an open port, difflib to compare the configuration files, and, of course, netmiko's ConnectHandler to connect to two devices via the SSH protocol. Try to type the code on the keyboard to get a feel for writing Python code. It is inevitable that while you are coding, you have to spend hours in front of your screen and keyboard. For further explanation, refer to the explanation embedded in the code.

```
GNU nano 4.8                    /home/pynetauto/ssh_labs/netmiko_compare_config.py
#!/usr/bin/env python3
#---------------------------------------------------# Import required modules

import time
import socket
import difflib
from getpass import getpass
from netmiko import ConnectHandler

#---------------------------------------------------# Borrowed from previous labs
# Functions to collect credentials and IP addresses of devices
def get_input(prompt=''):
    try:
        line = input(prompt)
    except NameError:
        line = input(prompt)
    return line

def get_credentials():
    #Prompts for, and returns a username and password
    username= get_input("Enter Network Admin ID     : ")
    password = None
    while not password:
        password = getpass("Enter Network Admin PWD    : ")
        password_verify = getpass("Confirm Network Admin PWD   : ")
        if password != password_verify:
            print("Passwords do not match. Please try again.")
            password = None
    return username, password
# For IP addresses of comparing devices
def get_device_ip():
    #Prompts for, and returns a first_ip and second_ip
    first_ip = get_input("Enter primary device IP      : ")
    while not first_ip:
        first_ip = get_input("* Enter primary device IP     : ")
    second_ip = get_input("Enter secondary device IP    : ")
    while not second_ip:
        second_ip = get_input("* Enter secondary device IP : ")
    return first_ip, second_ip

#-----------------------------------------------------------------------------
# Run the functions to collect credentials and ip addresses
print("-"*40)
username, password = get_credentials()
```

(*continued*)

#	Task

```
first_ip, second_ip = get_device_ip()
print("-"*40)
#-----------------------------------------------------------------------------
# Netmiko device dictionaries
device1 = {          # Netmiko dictionary for device1
'device_type': 'cisco_ios',
'ip': first_ip,
'username': username,
'password': password,
}
device2 = {          # Netmiko dictionary for device2
'device_type': 'cisco_ios',
'ip': second_ip,
'username': username,
'password': password,
}
devices = [device1, device2]
#-----------------------------------------------------------------------------
# Re-use port scanner as a pre-check tool for reachability verification tools.
# If an IP is not reachable, the application will exit due to a communication problem.
for device in devices: # Loop through   devices
    ip = device.get("ip", "") # get value of the key "ip"
    for port in range (22, 23): # only port 22
        dest = (ip, port) # Combine ip and port number to form dest object
        try:
            with socket.socket(socket.AF_INET, socket.SOCK_STREAM) as sock:
                sock.settimeout(3)
                connection = sock.connect(dest)
                print(f"on {ip}, port {port} is open!")
        except:
            print(f"On {ip}, port {port} is closed. Check the connectivity to {ip}
            again.")
            exit()
# Prompt the user to make a decision to run the tool
response = input(f"Make a comparison of {first_ip} and {second_ip} now? [Yes/No]")
response = response.lower()
if response == 'yes':
    print(f"* Now making a comparison : {first_ip} vs {second_ip}") # Informational
    for device in devices: # Loop through   devices
        ip = device.get("ip", "") # Get value of the key "ip"
        try:
            net_connect = ConnectHandler(**device) # Create netmiko connection object
            net_connect.send_command("terminal length 0\n")
            output = net_connect.send_command("show running-config\n") # Run show
            running config
            show_run_file = open(f"{ip}_show_run.txt", "w+") # Create a file
            show_run_file.write(output) # Write output to file
            show_run_file.close() # Close-out the file
            time.sleep(1)
            net_connect.disconnect() # Disconnect SSH connection
```

#	Task
	(code continued below)

```
        except KeyboardInterrupt: # Keyboard Interrupt
            print("-"*80)
else:
    print("You have selected No. Exiting the application.") # Informational
    exit()

#-----------------------------------------------------------------------------
# Compare the two show running config files and display it in html file format.
# Informational
# Prepare for comparison of the text files
device1_run = f"./{first_ip}_show_run.txt" # Create device1_run object, ./ is present
working folder
device2_run = f"./{second_ip}_show_run.txt" # Create device2_run object
device1_run_lines = open(device1_run).readlines() # Convert into strings first for comparison
time.sleep(1)
device2_run_lines = open(device2_run).readlines() # Convert into strings first for comparison
time.sleep(1)
# Four arguments required in HtmlDiff function
difference = difflib.HtmlDiff(wrapcolumn=60).make_file(device1_run_lines, device2_run_
lines, device1_run, device2_run)
difference_report = open(first_ip + "_vs_" + second_ip + "_compared.html", "w") #
Create html file to write the difference
difference_report.write(difference) # Writes the differences to the difference_report
difference_report.close()
print("** Device configuration comparison completed. Please Check the html file to
check the differences.")
print("-"*80)
time.sleep(1)
^G Get Help  ^O Write Out  ^W Where Is  ^K Cut Text   ^J Justify  ^C Cur Pos
^X Exit      ^R Read File  ^\ Replace   ^U Paste Text ^T To Spell ^_ Go To Line
```

3 After completing writing the previous script, use the Python command to run it under the ssh_labs directory. After running this interactive application, you should have three files automatically created in your Linux Python server's present working directory (pwd).

```
pynetauto@ubuntu20s1:~/ssh_labs$ python netmiko_compare_config.py
---------------------------------------
Enter Network Admin ID       : pynetauto
Enter Network Admin PWD      :********
Confirm Network Admin PWD     : ********
Enter primary device IP        : 192.168.183.10
Enter secondary device IP     : 192.168.183.20
---------------------------------------
on 192.168.183.10, port 22 is open!
on 192.168.183.20, port 22 is open!
Make a comparison of 192.168.183.10 and 192.168.183.20 now? [Yes/No]yes
* Now making a comparison : 192.168.183.10 vs 192.168.183.20
** Device configuration comparison completed. Please Check the html file to check
the differences.
--------------------------------------------------------------------------------
```

(continued)

#	Task
	If you are running into errors or issues, download the source code from my GitHub repository and carefully re-examine your code and settings.

Source code downloads URL: `https://github.com/pynetauto/apress_pynetauto`

Run the `ls` command on the Python network automation server, and you should find the three files under the current working directory.

```
pynetauto@ubuntu20s1:~/ssh_labs$ ls -lh 192.168*
-rw-rw-r-- 1 pynetauto pynetauto 3.6K Jan 12 21:45 192.168.183.10_show_run.txt
-rw-rw-r-- 1 pynetauto pynetauto  56K Jan 12 21:46 192.168.183.10_vs_192.168.183.20_
compared.html
-rw-rw-r-- 1 pynetauto pynetauto 3.7K Jan 12 21:46 192.168.183.20_show_run.txt
```

4 Now, using WinSCP or FileZilla, log into the Ubuntu Python automation server with your credentials and move the files to your Windows host. If you have not installed the software, please install it here before logging in. I am using the SCP protocol with port 22.

URL: `https://winscp.net/eng/download.php`

Figure 14-7 shows a WinSCP example with an SCP connection (port 22) to the server. Locate the three files under `/home/pynetauto/ssh_labs/` and drag and drop them to your Windows host PC folder.

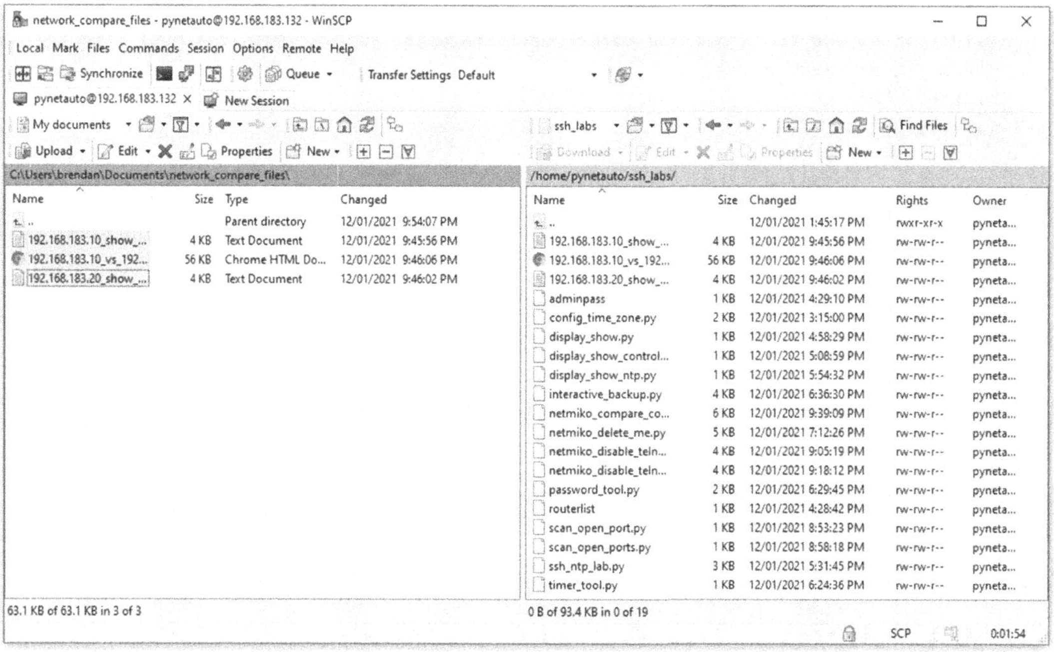

Figure 14-7. *Win-SCP, copying compared and running-config backups to Windows host*

#	Task
12	Now, go to the downloaded folder and open the `.html` file to review the script's result. Now you can compare any similar devices using this interactive tool. This tool can be modified slightly to compare the difference between firewall rules and configuration, and one practical example is to use such a tool to compare Palo Alto firewalls. Using its simple XML API call feature, you can compare the primary to standby configurations. The same script can also be used to compare the configuration before and after a change has been performed on a device. How you want to use the tool is totally up to your imagination. See Figure 14-8.

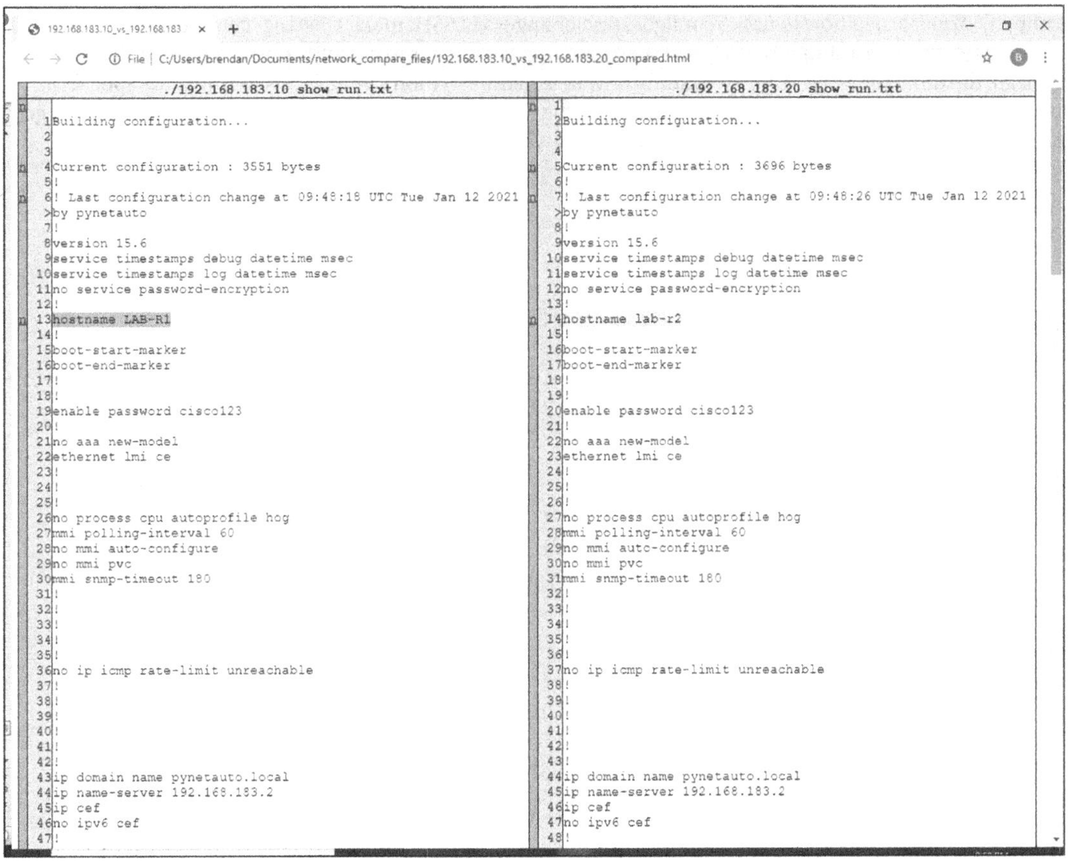

***Figure 14-8.** Web browser, opening an HTML file for a review*

Most new networking devices support REST/XML APIs. However, companies invested millions in enterprise network devices that only support Telnet, SSH, and SNMP, which are still under active technical support for more years. Network engineers usually start their life in front of a black command-line console connected via SSH or Telnet. Now expand your knowledge into network programmability. You first have to study different network engineers' behaviors and understand their decision-making processes sitting in front of the dark CLI screen, staring into it. Network automation is not about making robots or bots or software to work hard. It is about understanding our behavior as network engineers and seeing where automation matters and can help others as technicians. Almost all enterprise networking devices support SSH, so being able to automate engineers' mundane tasks using the power of Python, Python modules, and SSH are still a potent tool during this transition period. What is more critical in this new software-defined network (SDN) and "cloud for anything" era is understanding the real foundation of what adds more resilience and stability to our managed network and how software programming such as Python can take us to the next level.

Summary

This chapter has focused on the Python network automation of routers and switches using two SSH libraries, `paramiko` and `netmiko`. You have been introduced to developing smaller tools and then incorporating them into a more significant tool to create tools that can empower your work and your team and, in the end, your company. You learned how to make configuration changes via SSH, make `running-config` backups to the TFTP server, develop a simple socket port scan tool, apply it to your work, and compare two similar devices to locate the differences. Next, you will study how to schedule Python applications to run at the specified time and dip your toes in Python SNMPv3. You will be introduced to `cron` and SNMP exploration labs to get you more exposure to how Python can be used in network automation at work.

CHAPTER 15

Python Network Automation Labs: cron and SNMPv3

Eventually, you want to learn Python so you can write code to automate mundane tasks at work. After writing your code and developing your scripted application, you will want to run the scripts without you being in attendance. There is the Windows Task Scheduler on Windows systems, and on Linux, you have `cron` to help you schedule your script to run at 2 a.m. or to run periodically until you tell your Linux system to stop. You can write and schedule scripts to run automatically once you get comfortable with Python and Linux. You will also want to explore more about how Python works with SNMP so your company can consider SNMP monitoring using an in-house script; you may want to find out how Python interacts with SNMP in general. By the end of this chapter, you will be able to clone the GNS3 project, use `cron` to schedule tasks on Linux, and interact with routers and switches using SNMPv3. Along the way, we will borrow a Python community member's publicly shared code to explore SNMPv3 with Python and learn what it can do for us. This chapter aims to give you more exposure to different scenarios while practically applying Python to network automation scenarios.

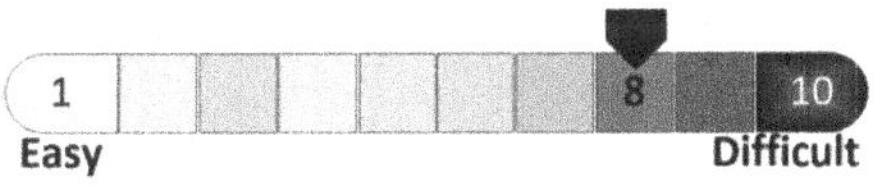

Cron and SNMPv3 Labs

You have done well following the first 14 chapters of this book. You can write simple and functioning Python scripts for specific networking tasks. You will quickly realize that you need to find a way to run your scripted applications without actual user interaction or user intervention, possibly using a task scheduler. You probably realize that you might be able to tap into the power of Python automation and apply it to more traditional network concepts such as SNMP monitoring; the possibilities are endless. First, in preparation for the next chapter, you will learn how to make a real clone of the GNS3 project.

B. Choi, *Introduction to Python Network Automation*, https://doi.org/10.1007/978-1-4842-6806-3_15

Cloning a GNS3 Project for the Next Lab

To prepare for our lab, you will make a true clone of the GNS3 project from Chapter 14. The GNS3 project export cloning method helped us to make a new project, but it compromised the original lab's configuration files, so in this sense, it is not a true clone of a GNS3 project. Sometimes this may not be the result you want for your labs. You might want to keep the original files intact and create a true clone of an old GNS3 project. With project export method of cloning, the original lab becomes unusable as the Dynamips files also get exported as the new project is created. A better way to create a new project without compromising the original project is to make a real duplicate of the original project folder and then reimport it with another name. You want to keep the `cmllab-basic` project as a fully working project, but at the same time, you do not want to create a new GNS3 project from the ground up. Let's learn how we can achieve this.

#	Task
1	If you are still using the `cmllab-basic` project, first save all the Cisco devices' running configurations using the `copy running-config startup-config` command. Once the configurations of three routers and two switches have been saved, power off all devices normally.
2	Once all routers and switches are powered off, exit GNS3 so both GNS3 and GNS3 VM are closed completely. See Figure 15-1.

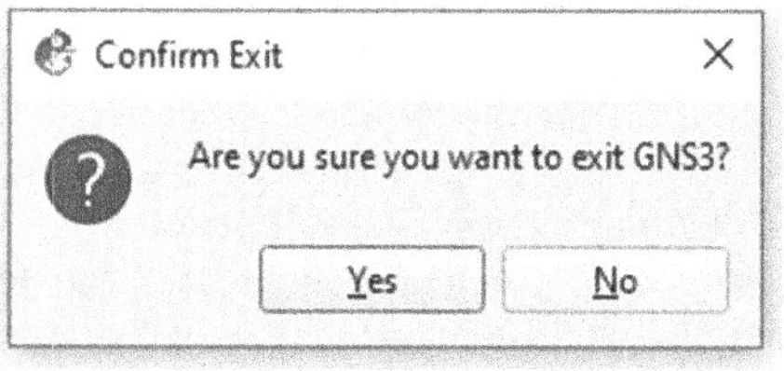

Figure 15-1. *cmllab-basic GNS3 project, exiting GNS3 and GNS3 VM*

#	Task
3	Go to the `C:\Users\brendan\GNS3\projects` folder and make a copy of the `cmllab-basic` folder so it looks like Figure 15-2.

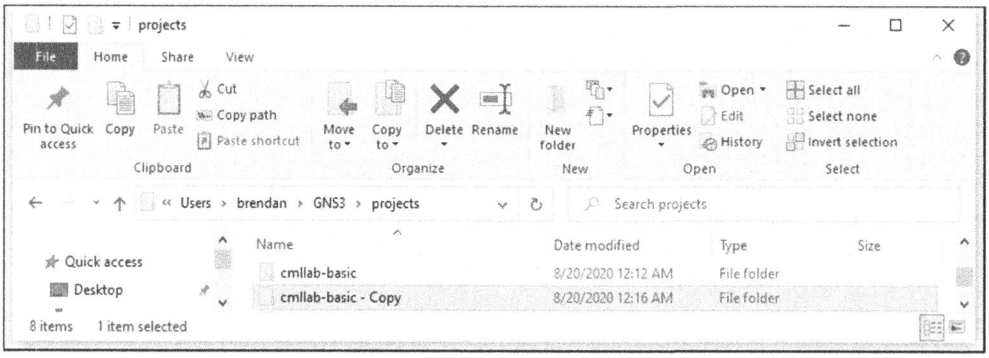

Figure 15-2. *GNS3 project, making a copy of an existing project folder*

#	Task
4	Go to the desktop of your Windows host PC and double-click the GNS3 icon on the desktop. Wait until both GNS3 and GNS3 VM become fully operational. See Figure 15-3.

Figure 15-3. *GNS3 start desktop icon*

5	When the project window opens, select "Open a project from disk," open the `C:\Users\brendan\GNS3\projects\cmllab-basic - Copy` folder, select the `cmllab-basic` GNS3 project file, and then click the Open button. See Figure 15-4.

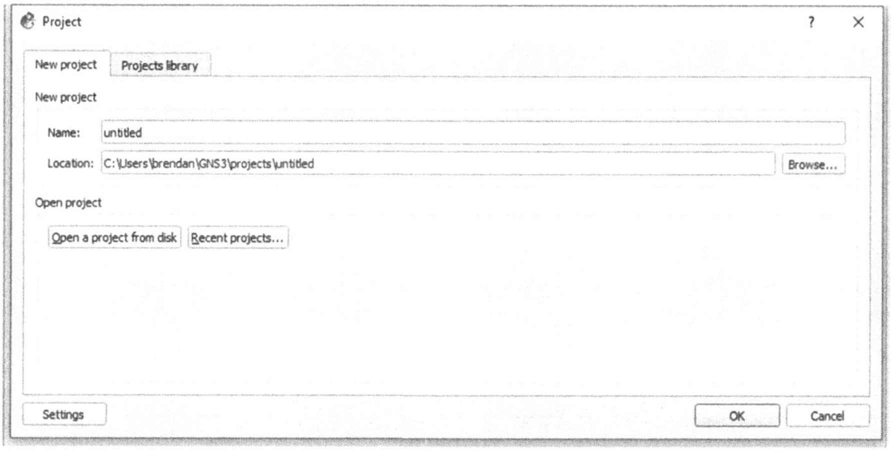

Figure 15-4. *GNS3, selecting "Open a project from disk"*

6	Once the copy of the `cmllab-basic` project is fully launched, wait for the lab to open correctly and then select GNS3's File ➤ Save project as. See Figure 15-5.

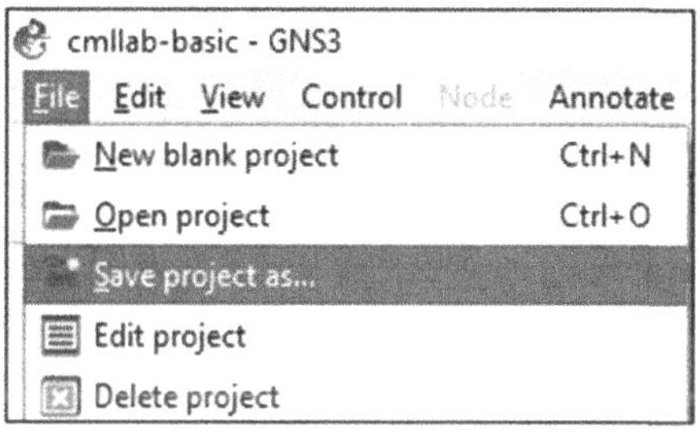

Figure 15-5. *GNS3, "Save project as" menu item*

(continued)

#	Task
7	Name your project and save the new project as `cmllab-devops`. See Figure 15-6.

Figure 15-6. *GNS3, saving as a new project*

#	Task
8	Now, go back to the `C:\Users\brendan\GNS3\projects` folder, and you will find a new project folder called `cmllab-devops`. The temporary folder has served its purpose and has now become redundant; you can go ahead and delete the `cmllab-basic - Copy` folder permanently. See Figure 15-7.

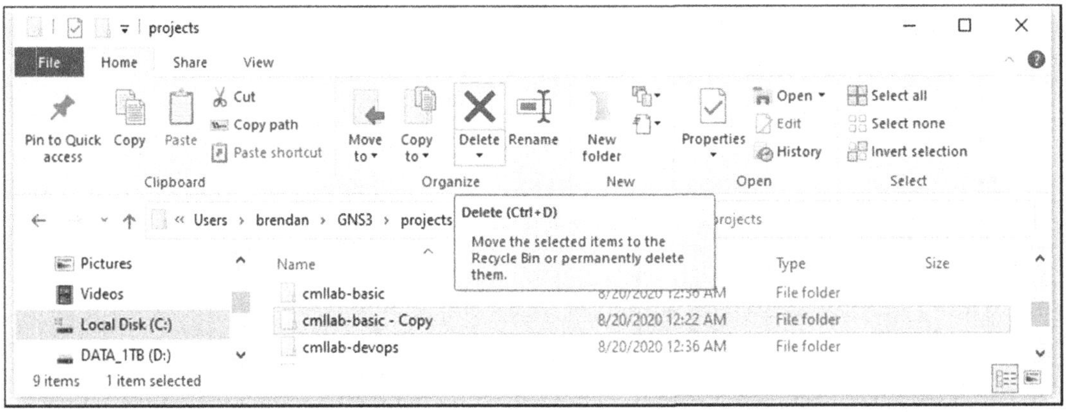

Figure 15-7. *GNS3, deleting the redundant copy*

#	Task
9	Open the `cmllab-devops` folder, and you will find your new GNS3 project file with the correct name. Now power up all devices and check their running configurations. You have successfully made a true clone of the last GNS3 project. See Figure 15-8.

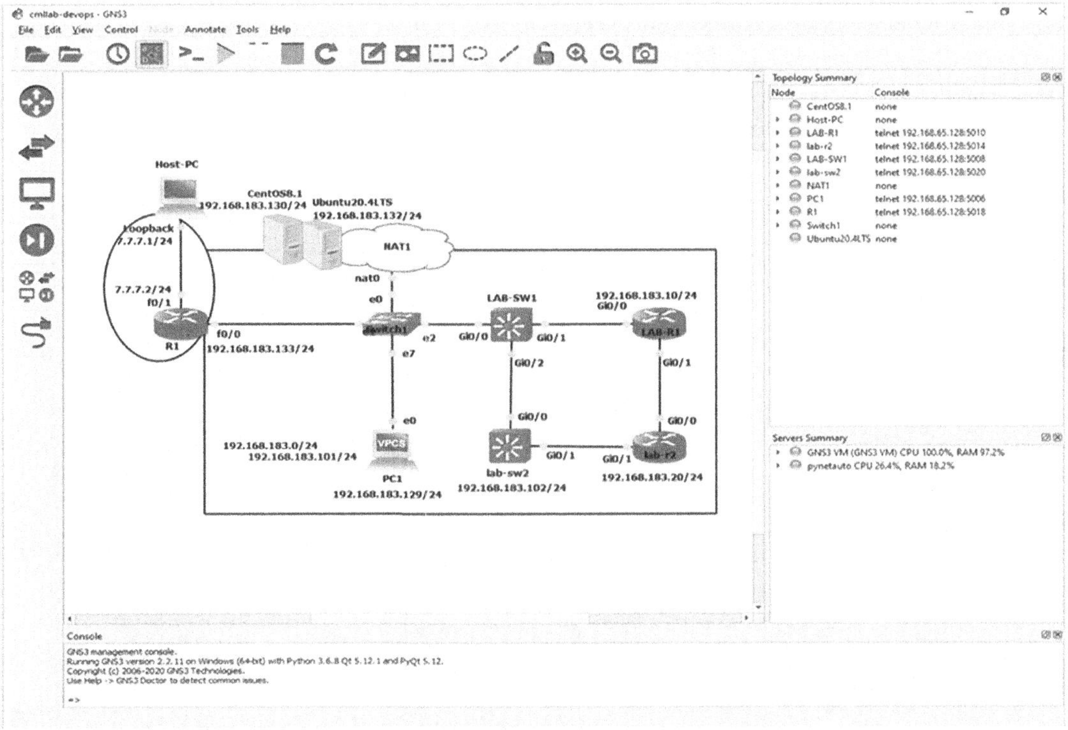

Figure 15-8. GNS3, fully cloned cmllab-devops project

(*continued*)

#	Task

10 To prepare you for the next part of our exploration, you will now add two more switches, as shown in Figure 15-9. First, delete `PC1` (VPCS) and replace it with `Lab-sw3` with a random IP address of 192.168.183.153/24 and with `Lab-SW4` with a random IP address 192.168.183.244/24. Power on new switches and let the CPU and memory settle down. Also shown is a Cisco CSR 1000v router to be installed on VMware for a later IOS upgrade lab; this icon is only a placeholder, so you do not have to worry about the `csr1000v` router until the next chapter.

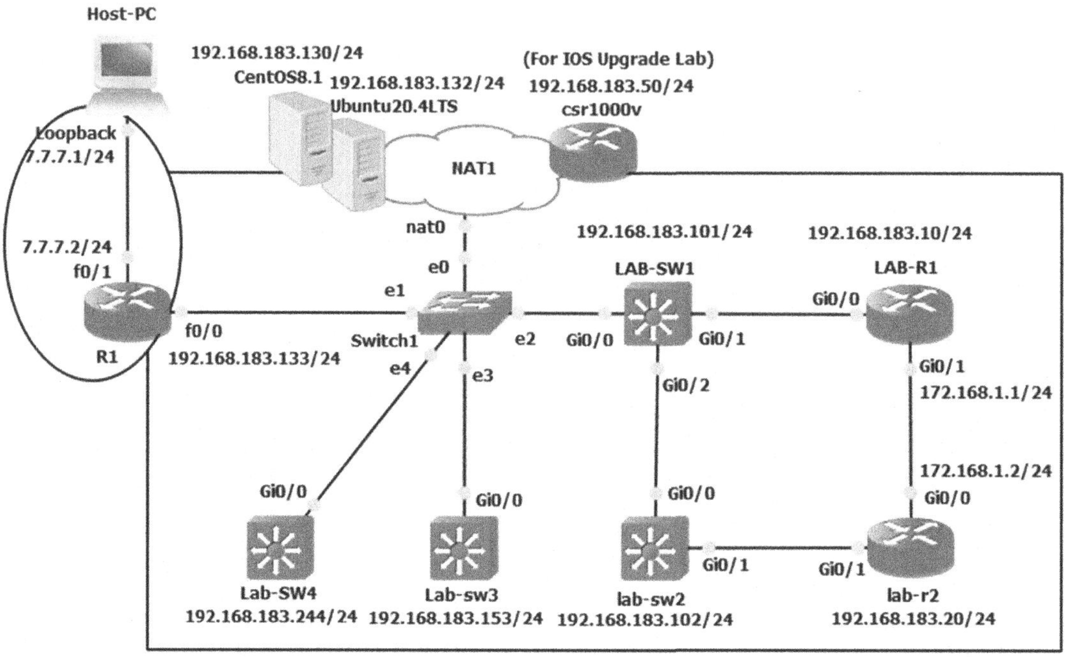

***Figure 15-9.** GNS3, adding two new switches*

11 While you are configuring the new switches, run an extended ping from `LAB-R1` and `lab-r2`: `ping ip 192.168.183.153 repeat counter 10000" and "ping ip 192.168.183.244 repeat counter 10000`. Let the ping run continuously in the background.

```
LAB-R1#ping ip 192.168.183.153 repeat 10000
Type escape sequence to abort.
Sending 10000, 100-byte ICMP Echos to 192.168.183.153, timeout is 2 seconds:
..............................................................................
lab-r2#ping ip 192.168.183.244 repeat 10000
Type escape sequence to abort.
Sending 10000, 100-byte ICMP Echos to 192.168.183.244, timeout is 2 seconds:
.....................................
```

#	Task
12	Once the switches are powered on, configure both switches using the following configurations. Make sure you disable IP routing on both switches and configure the gateway of the last resort. For `LAB-sw3`, the outbound traffic will go through `LAB-R1`, and for `Lab-SW4`, the unknown traffic will go through `R1` first.

Lab-sw3 configuration:

```
Switch>en
Switch#configure terminal
Switch(config)#hostname Lab-sw3
Lab- sw3 (config)#no ip routing
Lab-sw3(config)#ip default-gateway 192.168.183.10 !Route unknown destination to
LAB-R1
Lab- sw3 (config)#enable password cisco123
Lab-sw3(config)# username pynetauto privilege 15 secret cisco123
Lab-sw3(config)#line vty 0 15
Lab-sw3(config-line)#login local
Lab-sw3(config-line)#transport input all
Lab-sw3(config-line)#exit
Lab-sw3(config)#ip domain name pynetauto. local
Lab-sw3(config)#crypto key generate rsa !use 1024 bits
Lab-sw3(config)#interface vlan 1
Lab-sw3(config-if)#description "Native interface" !For later SNMP lab
Lab-sw3(config-if)#ip address 192.168.183.153 255.255.255.0
Lab-sw3(config-if)#no shut
Lab-sw3(config-if)#interface GigabitEthernet0/0
Lab-sw3(config-line)#description "1GB Main Connection" !For later SNMP lab
Lab-sw3(config-if)#end
Lab-sw3#copy running-config startup-config
```

Lab-SW4 configuration:

```
Switch>en
Switch#configure terminal
Switch(config)#hostname Lab-SW4
Lab-SW4(config)#no ip routing
Lab-SW4(config)#ip default-gateway 192.168.183.133 !Route unknown destination to R1
Lab-SW4(config)#enable password cisco123
Lab-SW4(config)#username pynetauto privilege 15 secret cisco123
Lab-SW4(config)#line vty 0 15
Lab-SW4(config-line)#login local
Lab-SW4(config-line)#transport input all
Lab-SW4(config-line)#exit
Lab-SW4(config)#ip domain name pynetauto. local
Lab-SW4(config)#crypto key generate rsa !use 1024 bits
Lab-SW4(config)#interface vlan 1
Lab-SW4(config-if)#ip address 192.168.183.244 255.255.255.0
Lab-SW4(config-if)#no shut
Lab-SW4(config-if)#end
Lab-SW4# copy running-config startup-config
```

(continued)

#	Task
13	After the configuration has been completed, you will get the new switches' ping responses. To stop and escape the continuous (extended) ping (or traceroute) request, use the Ctrl+^ or Ctrl+Shift+6 key.

```
LAB-R1#ping ip 192.168.183.153 repeat 10000

Type escape sequence to abort.
Sending 10000, 100-byte ICMP Echos to 192.168.183.153, timeout is 2 seconds:
......................................................................
..........................................!!!!!!!!!!!!!!!!!!!!!
Success rate is 85 percent (102/115), round-trip min/avg/max = 17/25/55 ms

lab-r1#ping ip 192.168.183.244 repeat 10000

Type escape sequence to abort.
Sending 10000, 100-byte ICMP Echos to 192.168.183.244, timeout is 2 seconds:
......................................................................
.... !!!!!!!!!!!!!!!!!!!!!!!!!!!!!!!!!!!!!!!!
Success rate is 88 percent (102/115), round-trip min/avg/max = 12/21/44 ms
```

Remember the Ctrl+Shift+6 keys. If your router or switch hangs or you want to interrupt an operation, you can use this key combination to exit from the operation.

#	Task
14	To confirm that all unknown outbound destinations from the new switches are routing through `LAB-R1` and `R1` routers, respectively, try to use `clear arp` and `traceroute` on Google's public DNS, 8.8.8.8 or 8.8.4.4.

If you have issues pinging the Google DNS, there might be an issue with your Internet's DNS or you have not configured your devices correctly. Another possibility is Windows' latest update causing GNS3 to malfunction and breaking the loopback interface used by GNS3. Even if you cannot ping the DNS IP address, leave it for now and move onto the next section.

```
Lab-sw3#clear arp
Lab-sw3#traceroute 8.8.8.8
Type escape sequence to abort.
Tracing the route to 8.8.8.8
VRF info: (vrf in name/id, vrf out name/id)
  1 192.168.183.10 36 msec 22 msec 16 msec
  2 192.168.183.2 43 msec *  *
  3  *  *  *
[omitted for brevity]
30  *  *  *

Lab-SW4#clear arp
Lab-SW4#traceroute 8.8.4.4
Type escape sequence to abort.
Tracing the route to 8.8.4.4
```

#	Task

	``
	VRF info: (vrf in name/id, vrf out name/id)
	  1 192.168.183.133 1020 msec 41 msec 6 msec
	  2 192.168.183.2 38 msec * *
	  3 * * *
	[omitted for brevity]
	30 * * *
	``

If you have completed the previous tasks, then you are ready to do more labs. At the end of the previous task, you should have two more IOSvL2 switches in your topology. Let's log into your Linux servers and master how to use Linux task scheduler, `cron`.

Quick-Start to the Linux Scheduler, cron

Earlier in this book, you were introduced to some Linux basics, and you also got familiar with building a Linux server to function as a server for multiple IP services. As you discover Linux, you will quickly realize that many of the things you could not or were not allowed to do on Windows operating systems suddenly become possible with Linux systems. It allows you to install features and services quickly, and your IP services can be up and running in no time. If you are a Windows person, you will remember the good old Windows Task Scheduler; as the name suggests, Windows also has a task scheduler tool.

Linux has the equivalent task scheduler, but it is called `cron` (without a GUI). `cron` is the equivalent of the Windows Task Scheduler, but its operation is much simpler, reliable, and incredibly agile as it carries no burden of a GUI. Linux's `cron` tool is Linux's default tool for task scheduling. It can perform Linux's native command executions and set applications such as Python scripts to run at set intervals. Skilled Linux system administrators do a lot of work using automated shell-based scripting or other programming languages when working with system monitoring and backup tasks. To help with this task, the most commonly used tool in Linux is the `cron` tool, which serves the same purpose as Windows Task Scheduler for Windows systems. As you finish writing Python applications (scripts), you have to learn how to schedule your scripts to run at specific times and in a specific cycle for repetitive tasks, so it is essential that you master how to use `cron` and correctly run the scheduled tasks. Of course, if the company you work for has a bottomless IT budget, there is always an easy way out by purchasing an out-of-the-box task scheduler, but when they have hired smart people like you, why should your company pay for these free and open source tools?

In this section, you will be learning how to schedule tasks using `cron` in both Ubuntu and CentOS systems. The basic syntax is almost identical, but there are enough variations to treat them differently.

Ubuntu 20.04 LTS Task Scheduler: crontab

On a Ubuntu 20.04 server, `cron` is called `crontab`. You will write a greeting Python application and use it to learn task scheduling with Ubuntu's `crontab`. You will be required to follow the tasks on your Ubuntu virtual server. What you have learned here to schedule a simple script can also be used to schedule more complicated scripts. The script's difficulty does not matter while scheduling a task; creating a script schedule is relatively straightforward.

#	Task
1	First, make a new directory to place your script in, write the three-line Python code for `crontab` testing, and save it as `print_hello_friend.py`. You can change the greeting in your script. Here we will import the `datatime` module from the `datetime` library and put the `print (datetime.now())` statement before printing `hello`. Since I am from Australia, my favorite greeting is "G'day mate."

```
pynetauto@ubuntu20s1:~$ mkdir my_cron
pynetauto@ubuntu20s1:~$ cd my_cron
pynetauto@ubuntu20s1:~/my_cron$ nano print_hello_friend.py
pynetauto@ubuntu20s1:~/my_cron$ cat print_hello_friend.py
from datetime import datetime
print(datetime.now())
print("G'day Mate!")
```

2 Next, run the code once to check that it prints out the time and your "hello" statement.

```
pynetauto@ubuntu20s1:~/my_cron$ python3 print_hello_friend.py
2021-01-13 14:01:40.770547
G'day Mate!
```

3 Now you are going to use `crontab` to schedule this Python code to run. Before you can create a schedule, you are going to learn how to use `crontab` quickly. First, you have to choose whether you want to run the script as a standard user or a root user. Second, decide whether you want to run your Python code in a nonexecutable file mode or change it to executable and then run it. You have already learned how to turn a nonexecutable file into an executable on a Linux server. If you have decided to run `crontab` as a nonroot Linux user, you must execute the `crontab -e` command with the leading `sudo` command so that you can type in `sudo crontab -e`. On the other hand, if you have decided to run `crontab` as the root user, you do not need to affix the `sudo` command.

a. non-root user crontab scheduler execution

```
pynetauto@ubuntu20s1:~/my_cron$ sudo crontab -e
```

b. root user crontab scheduler execution

```
pynetauto@ubuntu20s1:~/my_cron$ crontab -e
```

4 To make `cron` to execute your script correctly, you need to check the Python executable file location and run the `which python3` or `which python3.8` command to confirm the directory. Also, run the `pwd` command to check your working directory for your Python script.

```
pynetauto@ubuntu20s1:~/my_cron$ which python3.8
/usr/bin/python3.8
pynetauto@ubuntu20s1:~/my_cron$ pwd
/home/pynetauto/my_cron
```

#	Task
5	Next, run crontab using the crontab -e command to open the crontab scheduler. The pynetauto user is a sudoer to run the command without the sudo command. When you use the crontab -e command for the first time, a message will pop up to select the text editor of your choice. Choose the easiest or the recommended one, which is a nano text editor, 1.

```
pynetauto@ubuntu20s1:~/my_cron$ crontab -e
no crontab for pynetauto - using an empty one

Select an editor.  To change later, run 'select-editor'.
  1. /bin/nano        <---- easiest
  2. /usr/bin/vim.basic
  3. /usr/bin/vim.tiny
  4. /bin/ed

Choose 1-4 [1]: 1
```

6 After selecting nano as your text editor for the crontab scheduler, press the Enter key to open the crontab scheduler file, as shown next. Quickly browse the information and move your cursor to the bottom line of the file. Type in exactly what is shown here and save the file. You will learn more about cron time formats later, so you do not know what each line or each character means. For now, you must try it first with your own hands.

```
[...omitted for brevity]
# For more information see the manual pages of crontab(5) and cron(8)
#
# m h  dom mon dow   command
* * * * * /usr/bin/python3.8 /home/pynetauto/my_cron/print_hello_friend.py >>
/home/pynetauto/my_cron/cron.log
```

7 Next, wait for one to two minutes. You should see that a logging file called cron.log is automatically created under your /home/pynetauto/my_cron directory.

```
pynetauto@ubuntu20s1:~/my_cron$ ls -lh
total 8.0K
-rw-rw-r-- 1 pynetauto pynetauto 39 Jan 13 14:09 cron.log
-rw-rw-r-- 1 pynetauto pynetauto 73 Aug 27 22:48 print_hello_friend.py
```

Check the cron.log file with the cat command to check if the crontab is running normally. You will see that the cron job is running every minute, and the greeting is recorded in the cron.log file. So, now you have learned that the five stars (* * * * *) in the crontab -e meant every minute.

```
pynetauto@ubuntu20s1:~/my_cron$ cat cron.log
2021-01-13 14:09:01.393031
G'day Mate!
2021-01-13 14:10:01.423129
G'day Mate!
```

8 To check your cron job, use the crontab -l command. Specify the user is an option if you are already logged in as the user. There is no cron job under the root user, so use it to check another user's cron schedule.

```
pynetauto@ubuntu20s1:~/my_cron$ crontab -l
* * * * * /usr/bin/python3.8 /home/pynetauto/my_cron/print_hello_friend.py >>
/home/pynetauto/my_cron/cron.log
```

(continued)

#	Task

	`pynetauto@ubuntu20s1:~/my_cron$ sudo crontab -u root -l`
	`[sudo] password for pynetauto:**********`
	`no crontab for root`

9	To manage another user's cron job, you can run sudo `crontab -u user_name -l`. To modify time intervals or cancel another user's cron job, use sudo `crontab -u user_name -e` and make the required time changes. If the user does not have any cron job, it will return the no `crontab for user_name` message.
	`pynetauto@ubuntu20s1:~$ sudo crontab -u pythonadmin -e`
	`pynetauto@ubuntu20s1:~$ sudo crontab -u pythonadmin -l`
	`no crontab for pythonadmin`

10	Finally, to cancel (deactivate) the currently running `crontab` schedule, open the scheduler file with `crontab -e`, add # in front of a specific `cron` task line, delete the line in question, and save the file. Another way to control `crontab`'s `cron` job is to stop/start/restart the `crontab` service by using the `service cron stop`, `service cron start`, and `service cron restart` commands. **`#* * * * * /usr/bin/python3.8 /home/pynetauto/my_cron/print_hello_friend.py >> /home/pynetauto/my_cron/cron.log`**

In step 6, each time `cron` job runs and executes the script, the activity is logged to the `cron.log` file. But, what do the two right arrows or greater-sign symbols (>>) mean here? What if a single arrow was used? Let's check the difference.

```
* * * * * /usr/bin/python3.8 /home/pynetauto/my_cron/print_hello_friend.py >>
/home/pynetauto/my_cron/cron.log
```

Using two right arrows appends the logs in the next line. So, the previous content is not overwritten.

```
pynetauto@ubuntu20s1:~/my_cron$ cat cron.log

...
2021-01-13 14:39:01.318529
G'day Mate!
2021-01-13 14:40:01.348718
G'day Mate!
...
```

If only one right arrow was used as shown here, the previous content would be overwritten entirely, and only the last executed content would be recorded to the file. Try it for yourself and check it out with your own eyes.

```
* * * * * /usr/bin/python3.8 /home/pynetauto/my_cron/print_hello_friend.py >
/home/pynetauto/my_cron/cron.log
```

```
pynetauto@ubuntu20s1:~/my_cron$ cat cron.log
2021-01-13 14:44:01.467980
G'day Mate!
```

CentOS8.1 Task Scheduler: crond

There are some minor differences between the CentOS and Ubuntu `cron` versions. You have to become familiar with both Red Hat and Debian-derived Linux OSs in production as they are most commonly found Linux OS in the enterprise IT ecosystems. Similar to Ubuntu's `crontab`, CentOS offers a `cron` called `crond`. Follow the instructions here in your CentOS 8.1 server to learn how to use `crond`. To complete the following tasks, log into `centos8s1` via an SSH connection. You will need some or all routers and switches running in your lab topology. See Figure 15-10.

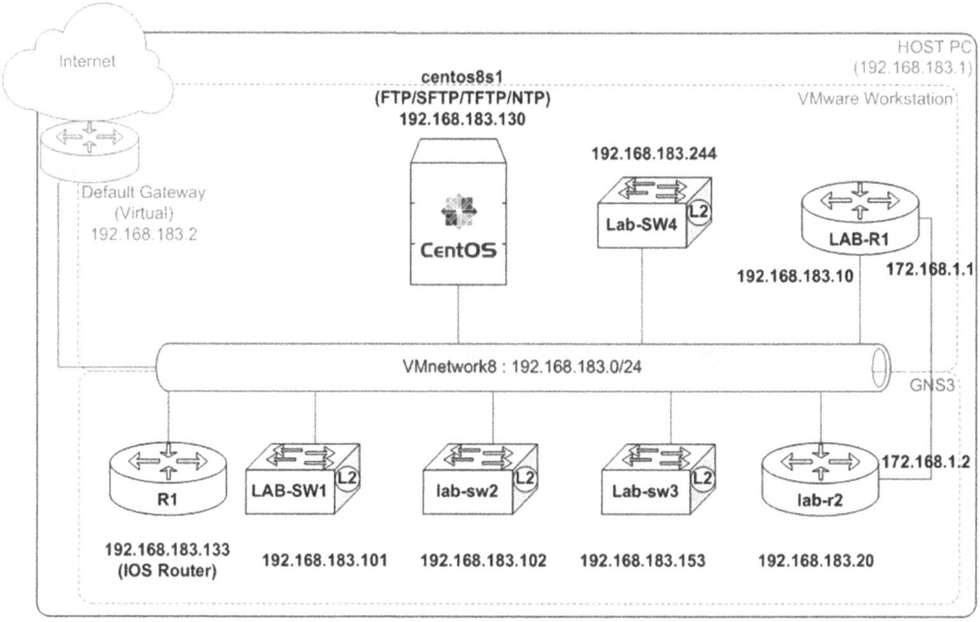

Figure 15-10. *centos8s1, crond lab required equipment*

#	Task

1	In the earlier chapter, you were introduced to probing a specific port (port 22); here, you will learn how to ping an IP address from your Linux server using a Python script. Let's create a simple ICMP pinging script and make it ping all IP addresses in our network and log it to the `cron.log` file. This time, we will create an external text file called `ip_addresses.txt` to read each device's IP addresses and then ping three times and record the activity to the `cron.log` file.
	First, create two files, `ip_addresses.txt` and `ping_sweep1.py`, following these instructions:
	
	`[pynetauto@centos8s1 ~]$ mkdir icmp_sweeper`
	`[pynetauto@centos8s1 ~]$ cd icmp_ sweeper`
	`[pynetauto@centos8s1 icmp_ sweeper]$ touch ip_addresses.txt`
	`[pynetauto@centos8s1 icmp_ sweeper]$ nano ip_addresses.txt`

(continued)

#	Task

ip_addresses.txt

```
192.168.183.10
192.168.183.20
192.168.183.101
192.168.183.102
192.168.183.133
192.168.183.153
192.168.183.244
```

Create a ping_ip_add.py file and start writing your code. It is important that you type this code yourself to get enough practice.

```
[pynetauto@centos8s1 icmp_ sweeper]$ nano ping_sweep1.py
```

ping_sweep1.py

```
#!/usr/bin/python3 # shebang line to tell Linux to run this file as Python3
application

import os # import os module
import datetime # import datetime module

with open("/home/pynetauto/icmp_sweeper/ip_addresses.txt", "r") as ip_addresses:
#with open closes file automatically, read the file from specified directory
    print("-"*80) # Divider
    print(datetime.datetime.now()) # Print current time
    for ip_add in ip_addresses: # Use a simple for loop through each line in a file
    to get ip
        ip = ip_add.strip() # Remove any white spaces
        rep = os.system('ping -c 3 ' + ip) # Use Linux OS to send 3 ping (ICMP)
        messages
        if rep == 0: # response 0 means up
            print(f"{ip} is reachable.") # Informational
        else: # response is not 0, then there maybe network connectivity issue
            print(f"{ip} is either offline or icmp is filtered.") # Informational

print("-"*80) # Divider
print("All tasks completed.")
```

The previous script will print the current time and then ping each IP address three times. Then if it is on the network, it will print "IP is reachable." Otherwise, it will print "IP is either offline or icmp is filtered."

#	Task
2	This time, make the Python script an executable file so the code is simplified when scheduling in crond. First, check the user permissions for the script. Use the chmod +x command to make the file executable and check the permission again. The file's color should turn green after running the chmod command and x's added to the file attributes.

```
[pynetauto@centos8s1 icmp_sweeper]$ls -l
total 8
-rw-rw-r--. 1 pynetauto pynetauto 110 Jan 13 15:03 ip_addresses.txt
-rw-rw-r--. 1 pynetauto pynetauto 954 Jan 13 15:02 ping_sweep1.py
[pynetauto@centos8s1 icmp_sweeper]$chmod +x ping_sweep1.py
[pynetauto@centos8s1 icmp_sweeper]$ls -l
total 8
-rw-rw-r--. 1 pynetauto pynetauto 110 Jan 13 15:03 ip_addresses.txt
-rwxrwxr-x. 1 pynetauto pynetauto 954 Jan 13 15:02 ping_sweep1.py
```

#	Task
3.	CentOS's crond has two noticeable differences from Ubuntu's crontab. The first obvious difference is the name, and also, when you have to reinstall cron on CentOS, you have to use the name sudo yum install cronie to install crond. You can use the rpm -q cronie command to check the crond version on CentOS.

```
[pynetauto@centos8s1 icmp_pinger]$ rpm -q cronie
cronie-1.5.2-4.el8.x86_64
```

The second difference is where the cron job is scheduled. Unlike Ubuntu, CentOS's crond schedules tasks directly in the /etc/crontab file, as shown here:

```
[pynetauto@centos8s1 icmp_sweeper]$cat /etc/crontab
HELL=/bin/bash
PATH=/sbin:/bin:/usr/sbin:/usr/bin
MAILTO=root

# For details see man 4 crontabs

# Example of job definition:
# .---------------- minute (0 - 59)
# |  .------------- hour (0 - 23)
# |  |  .---------- day of month (1 - 31)
# |  |  |  .------- month (1 - 12) OR jan,feb,mar,apr ...
# |  |  |  |  .---- day of week (0 - 6) (Sunday=0 or 7) OR
sun,mon,tue,wed,thu,fri,sat
# |  |  |  |  |
# *  *  *  *  * user-name  command to be executed
```

(continued)

#	Task

4	Next, use the `systemctl status crond` command to check whether the crond service is operational.
	`[pynetauto@centos8s1 icmp_sweeper]$ systemctl status crond`
	`● crond.service - Command Scheduler`
	`  Loaded: loaded (/usr/lib/systemd/system/crond.service; enabled; vendor prese>`
	`  Active: active (running) since Wed 2021-01-13 14:55:14 AEDT; 19min ago`
	`Main PID: 1405 (crond)`
	`  Tasks: 6 (limit: 11166)`
	`  Memory: 4.4M`
	`  CGroup: /system.slice/crond.service`
	`      ├─1405 /usr/sbin/crond -n`
	`[...omitted for brevity]`

5	When scheduling a shell command or Python script to run on CentOS crond, you can configure and schedule cron commands in different formats. For example, just as in the Ubuntu example earlier, you could use a full path method to schedule a cron job. In CentOS 8.1, the same method will work, as shown here:
	`[pynetauto@centos8s1 icmp_sweeper]$ which python3.6`
	`/usr/bin/python3.6`
	`[pynetauto@centos8s1 icmp_ sweeper]$ pwd`
	`/home/pynetauto/icmp_pinger`
	`[pynetauto@centos8s1 icmp_ sweeper]$ sudo nano /etc/crontab`
	`[... omitted for brevity]`
	`*/5 * * * * root /usr/bin/python3.6 /home/pynetauto/icmp_sweeper/ping_sweep1.py >> /home/pynetauto/icmp_sweeper/cron.log 2>&1`
	Here we are making the Python script an executable file and running it without specifying the application location. Your Python script must have the first shebang line (`#!/usr/bin/python3`) included in the script. Also, note that you have to specify a user to run the script; since `/etc/crontab` is a root user file, it is easiest to run the script as the root user, so when you schedule the task, make sure that the `root` user is specified for the cron job to run successfully. Now, open `etc/crontab` and schedule your ICMP script to send pings to all routers and switches in your lab every five minutes. `*/5 * * * *` denotes every fifth minute. The script will run at 0, 5, 10, 15, 20, 25, 30, 35, 40, 45, 50, 55, and again 0 or 60th minutes until you pause or remove the cron job.
	`[pynetauto@centos8s1 icmp_pinger]$ sudo nano /etc/crontab`
	`[... omitted for brevity]`
	`*/5 * * * * root /home/pynetauto/icmp_sweeper/ping_sweep1.py >> /home/pynetauto/icmp_sweeper/cron.log 2>&1`

#	Task
6	Finally, open the `cron.log` file under the current working directory and check that the communication check task is taking place every five minutes. You may have to wait for five minutes for the `cron.log` file to appear in your working directory, and when you view the file, it would look similar to this:

```
[pynetauto@centos8s1 icmp_sweeper]$ ls -lh
total 12K
-rw-r--r--. 1 root       root       3.2K Jan 13 15:35 cron.log
-rw-rw-r--. 1 pynetauto pynetauto  110 Jan 13 15:03 ip_addresses.txt
-rwxrwxr-x. 1 pynetauto pynetauto  886 Jan 13 15:35 ping_sweep1.py
[pynetauto@centos8s1 icmp_pinger]$ cat cron.log
PING 192.168.183.10 (192.168.183.10) 56(84) bytes of data.
64 bytes from 192.168.183.10: icmp_seq=1 ttl=255 time=15.8 ms
64 bytes from 192.168.183.10: icmp_seq=2 ttl=255 time=15.8 ms
64 bytes from 192.168.183.10: icmp_seq=3 ttl=255 time=21.9 ms

--- 192.168.183.10 ping statistics ---
3 packets transmitted, 3 received, 0% packet loss, time 6ms
rtt min/avg/max/mdev = 15.768/17.798/21.850/2.865 ms

[... omitted for brevity]

PING 192.168.183.244 (192.168.183.244) 56(84) bytes of data.
64 bytes from 192.168.183.244: icmp_seq=2 ttl=255 time=8.33 ms
64 bytes from 192.168.183.244: icmp_seq=3 ttl=255 time=7.81 ms

--- 192.168.183.244 ping statistics ---
3 packets transmitted, 2 received, 33.3333% packet loss, time 7ms
rtt min/avg/max/mdev = 7.808/8.070/8.333/0.277 ms
-----------------------------------------------------------------------------
2021-01-13 15:35:01.973235
192.168.183.10 is reachable.
192.168.183.20 is reachable.
192.168.183.101 is reachable.
192.168.183.102 is reachable.
192.168.183.133 is reachable.
192.168.183.153 is reachable.
192.168.183.244 is reachable.
-----------------------------------------------------------------------------

All tasks are completed.
```

#	Task
7	At the end of this lab, make sure you go back to the `/etc/crontab` file and add # to the beginning of each line to deactivate it. You can optionally delete the line and then save the changes.

Out of the box, crontab is much easier to use than crond. Also, it has the flexibility of scheduling cron jobs under different user accounts, so many users will find crontab more intuitive to use. If you are like me, you can choose to install crontab on the CentOS8.1 server using the following Linux commands. But note that, in the production environment, some old Linux servers are not connected to the Internet, and you may have to use crond to schedule the tasks, so it is always good to know the difference between different cron tools on different Linux operating systems. Anyway, to install crontab on your CentOS8 VM, follow these commands:

```
[pynetauto@centos8s1 ~]$ sudo dnf update
[pynetauto@centos8s1 ~]$ sudo dnf install crontabs
[pynetauto@centos8s1 ~]$ sudo systemctl enable crond.service
[pynetauto@centos8s1 ~]$ sudo systemctl start crond.service
```

Note dnf (aka the next-generation package management utility for RPM-based distributions) will be replacing old YUM package management utilities in the Fedora, CentOS, and Red Hat distributions.

Next, let's review the cron job definitions or the five asterisks.

Learn cron Job Definitions with Examples

To use Linux cron effectively, you must understand the meaning of the five stars (asterisks) at the beginning of each cron job line. If you are an existing cron user and understand what five asterisks denote and how they are used, that is great; then you can move to the next section. If you are new to cron, please read the rest of this section to grasp the meaning of the five asterisks. The following snippet is straight from the /etc/crontab file from CentOS; this is all you need to know to understand how a command, script, or task is scheduled on cron:

```
# Example of job definition:
# .---------------- minute (0 - 59)
# |  .------------- hour (0 - 23)
# |  |  .---------- day of month (1 - 31)
# |  |  |  .------- month (1 - 12) OR jan,feb,mar,apr ...
# |  |  |  |  .---- day of week (0 - 6) (Sunday=0 or 7) OR sun,mon,tue,wed,thu,fri,sat
# |  |  |  |  |
# *  *  *  *  * user-name  command to be executed
```

For ease of explanation, all exercises will be based on crontab rather than crond, so open your crond in Ubuntu 20 LTS.

Generally, a default cron job begins with five stars (asterisks). These five stars relate to the frequency of task run, or, in other words, the time and date interval of a certain task. After the five values is the command (CMD) required to run a specific task. Here's an example:

Minute	Hour	Day of month	Month	Day of week	CMD
0	1	31	12	*	`/home/pynetauto/ny_eve.py >> ~/cron_time.log`

Table 15-1 is the tabulated version of the example of a job definition shown earlier.

Table 15-1. *Linux crontab: Time Unit*

Unit	Available Values	Conversion
Min of an hour	0–59 minutes	1 hour = 60 minutes
Hour of a day	0–23 hours	1 day = 24 hours
Day of month	1–31 days	1 month = 28–31 days
Month	1–12 or Jan, Feb, Mar, Apr...Dec	Jan, Feb, Mar, Apr...
Day of week	0–6	1 week = 7 days
CMD	Command to run	N/A

Depending on your Linux OS type, each command also has slightly different variations, but they are almost identical for the most part. If these values use another format, you should refer to the OS distributor's documentation for different time unit variations. Let's study some more examples to get an understanding of the `cron` schedule's job definitions. The following examples cover the most common job definitions. If you have a different requirement, you can make variations to the following examples and use them in your `cron` job scheduling.

#	Examples (Alternatives in Brackets)	Explanation
1	`* * * * *`	The five asterisks are the default value, which tells the Linux system to execute a task every minute. You have used the five asterisks to run a Python script already.
2	`15 03 25 03 *`	At 3:15 on the 25th day of March.
3	`15 1,13 * * *`	At 1:15 a.m. and 1:15 p.m.
4	`00 07-11 * * *`	On the hour between 7 a.m. to 11 a.m. (every day)
5	`00 07-11 * * 1-5`	Same as example 4, but only run on the weekdays (1 = Mon, to 5 = Fri)
6	`0 2 * * 6,0`	At 2 a.m. on Saturdays and Sundays only
7	`00 23 * * 1` (`00 23 * * Mon`)	At 11 p.m. on Mondays
8	`0/5 * * * *`	At every 5th minute, every 5 minutes
9	`0/15 * * * *`	At every 15th minute, every quarter of an hour
10	`0/30 * * * *`	At every 30th minute, every half an hour
11	`0 0 * 1/1 *`	At midnight on the first day of each month
12	`0/10 * * * 0` (`0,10,20,30,40,50 * * * 0`)	At every 10th minute; supported on newer `cron` versions At every 10th minute; supported on older `cron` versions

(continued)

13	`@reboot`	After rebooting
14	`@hourly` `(0 * * * *)`	At minute 0

15	`@daily`
	`(@midnight)`
	`(0 0 * * *)`
		At 00:00 (midnight)

16	`@weekly` `(0 0 * * 0)`	At midnight every Sunday
17	`@monthly` `(0 0 1 * *)`	At midnight, first day of the month

18	`@yearly`
	`(@annually)`
	`(0 0 1 1 *)`
		At midnight on January 1st every year

A more detailed description of `cron` can also be found on Wikipedia. You can learn more about `cron` and how to use `cron` by visiting the following Wikipedia site.

URL: `https://en.wikipedia.org/wiki/Cron`

And, you can learn more about how to use `cron` practically by using one of the `cron` maker sites listed here:

URL: `http://www.cronmaker.com/`

URL: `https://crontab.guru/`

URL: `http://corntab.com/`

In this section, you configured and completed scheduling for simple Python scripts using Linux `cron`, and then you learned the meanings behind the five stars using examples. For now, you do not have to comprehend the `cron` definitions by heart; you can always come back to this page as a reference. Next, you will be revisiting SNMP basics to get you ready for Python interaction with SNMPv3 on network devices and discuss how Python can be used for system monitoring using SNMPv3.

Using Python to Run an SNMPv3 Query

Although SNMP is used everywhere for enterprise network monitoring, it is an under-appreciated technology that keeps checking our network all the time. Not many network engineers pay much attention to how SNMP works in depth or what it does because it works seamlessly. We really cannot blame engineers for being ignorant about SNMP as network monitoring is considered an entry-level engineer job. When you move up the ladder, you focus more on the client services as the number-one priority and then the design, implementation, and consulting parts of network administration. But, should you know how Python interacts with SNMP? The answer is yes!

In this section, you will quickly review SNMP concepts to get you up to speed and then borrow some Python SNMPv2c code to rewrite the code to interact with the network devices using SNMPv3. A full Python tools development using SNMP may take weeks or months, so here you will simply dip in your toes to learn how Python interacts with network devices using SNMP.

Quick-Start Guide to SNMP

To help you refresh your SNMP knowledge, we will be going through some basic SNMP facts. If you have been working with SNMP technology every day, you can skip this part and jump to the SNMP lab. If you are not familiar with SNMP, this will be a quick-start guide to SNMP to learn how Python interacts with SNMP.

Quick SNMP History

To get a bigger picture of a particular technology, it is always good to know a technology's history. SNMP began its life as ICMP and evolved until it became the monitoring tool of choice.

- *1981*: The Internet Engineering Task Force (IETF) defined the Internet Control Management Protocol (ICMP), which is a protocol used to probe the network communication status of devices on the network.
- *1987*: ICMP was redefined as the Simple Gateway Monitoring Protocol (SGMP) as part of RFC 1028.
- *1989 to 1990*: SGMP was redefined as the Simple Network Monitoring Protocol (SNMP), which was introduced as part of RFC 1155, 1156, and 1157.
- *1990 to present*: Most IT and networking vendors accepted SNMP as the standard protocol to monitor IP devices.

Source: `https://tools.ietf.org/html/` (RFC: 777, 1028, 1155, 1156, 1157)

SNMP Standard Operation

As in many server and client model, SNMP also uses server and client model. The SNMP server is known as the *manager*, and it works with clients (nodes), known as *agents*. Even if you have completed your CCNA studies, you may not be familiar with the ins and outs of standard SNMP operations. If this is your first time using SNMP, don't skip this section.

- SNMP works as the server (manager) and client (agent).
- Generally, the SNMP agent is installed on monitored devices as agents.
- SNMP follows the preset rules to monitor network devices and collect and store information to monitor devices.
- An agent can send its status to the manager using either polling or event reporting methods.
- Management Information Base (MIB) is the information standard used by the agent to collect data.
- Object identification (OID) is the primary key of MIB's management object.

SNMP Polling vs. Trap (Event Reporting) Method

To collect data, the SNMP manager sends the Get request message to the agent, and then the agent sends back a response message with its status. The SNMP server requests specific information, and then the SNMP client responds. In an environment where the SNMP server can change the SNMP client's status, the server can use the SNMP Set request to change the SNMP client's status. In other words, you can use SNMP to control the client, but usually, SNMP's function is limited to monitoring the network. The polling method is talkative on the network, so it generates more traffic than the Trap method. In the Trap method, the SNMP client sends information to the SNMP server's Trap receiver, only if there was any monitored information in its system. This is the most common network monitoring in the industry today. Also, it generates a relatively small amount of network traffic in a stable network.

SNMP Versions

Table 15-2 shows all the SNMP versions in action. Many legacy systems do not support the more secure SNMPv3, so in most networks, SNMPv2c commonly known as SNMPv2 is used the most, but due to security issues, more and more enterprises are moving toward SNMPv3. As the old devices get refreshed, more devices can support SNMPv3, and it is slowly getting deployed as the legacy devices are decommissioned. Another significant catalyst to move away from SNMPv2 is the introduction of virtualized and cloud-based infrastructures that are now the norm of enterprise network and server networking. In a virtualized cloud world, besides the actual server farm and physical connections, almost everything exists as files or software, meaning that technologies are not anchored down to their hardware limitations. Review Table 15-2 to check the features of each version.

Table 15-2. *SNMP Versions*

Version	Features
SNMPv1	Uses a community string (key); no built-in security; only supports 32-bit systems
SNMPv2c	Most commonly used; supports 32/64-bit systems; improved performance for 64-bit systems; almost identical features to v1; low security; cross-platform support
SNMPv3	Manager and agent system changed to objects; increased 64-bit system security; guarantees authentication and privacy; detects each SNMP entities as unique EngineID names

Understanding the SNMP Protocol in the TCP/IP Stack

SNMP is an application protocol in the TCP/IP protocol stack and is sitting on the transport layer in the OSI model; it uses UDP to communicate between the server and the client. Here is a quick summary of SNMP communication port information and how the manager and agents communicate:

- The SNMP Get message communicates via UDP port 161.
- The SNMP Set message also communicates via UDP port 161.
- When SNMP Trap is used, SNMP Trap communicates via UDP port 162, and the agent that sends the message does not have to check if the trap was sent correctly.
- When SNMP Inform is used, it behaves the same way except it confirms that the Inform message has been received correctly via UDP port 162.

About SNMP Message Types

There are six types of messages sent and received between the SNMP manager and SNMP agent; these message types are summarized in Table 15-3.

Table 15-3. *SNMP Message Types*

Message Type	PDU Type	Explanation
`get-request`	0	Gets the value of the object specified in the agent management MIB.
`get-next-request`	1	Gets the next object value of the object specified in the agent management MIB. It is used when the MIB item has a table.
`get-bulk-request`	1	It works like `get-next-request` and gets the object's value specified in the agent management MIB as many times as specified.
`set-request`	2	Sets (changes) the value of the object specified in the agent management MIB.
`get-response`	3	Returns the result of the manager's request.
`traps`	4	This message is sent to the manager to inform the manager when a particular event occurs in the agent management MIB.

**PDU type values range between 0 and 4 only.*

Understanding SNMP's SMI, MIB, and OID

Next, after briefly explaining the definition of SMI, MIB, and OID of SNMP, you will take a look at security methods, access policies, synchronization, and asynchronization of traps. Let's quickly cover SNMP terminologies and what purpose they serve in SNMP monitored networks.

- *Structured Management Information (SMI)*: SMI is a tool for defining and configuring MIBs and creating and managing MIB standards.
- *Management Information Base (MIB)*: The MIB is a set of objects managed from the SNMP server's perspective. The MIB is a database of objects that can be viewed or set by an administrator. Each object has a tree-like structure, and you can check the status or change the value of an agent with specific MIB values. ASN.1 (Abstract Notation One), all organized in a tree structure, is a scripting language for describing objects, including SNMP objects.
- *Object-Identifier (OID)*: OID must be assigned to generate the MIB. OIDs are represented as a sequence of unique, specific numbers, using a notation similar to IP addresses. OID is an identifier (primary key) that designates the administered object of the MIB. You can run OID lookup tools to gain an understanding of OID in detail.

SNMP Access Policy

To ensure SNMP security, SNMP community strings are used between manager and agent communication. The manager requires the appropriate community string to access key device information across your network. Most network vendors configure the default public community string as public when the network equipment leaves the factory; many network administrators change the community string to keep intruders from getting information about the network setup. SNMP can offer different access levels to information based on different community strings. There are Read-Only, Read-Write, and Trap community strings.

- *SNMP Read-only community string*: The agent's information can be read from other SNMP managers. `InterMapper` maps devices using read-only information.

- *SNMP Read-Write community string*: This is used for communication using requests and can read and change other devices' status or settings. Note that the `InterMapper` is read-only, so it does not use the read-write string mode.
- *SNMP Trap community string*: This is the community string used by the agent to send SNMP traps to the `InterMapper`, which receives and stores information no matter which SNMP Trap community string is used.

Synchronous vs. Asynchronous Communication While Using SNMP Traps

The following is a brief description of two SNMP Trap methods used by SNMP. In general, if the trap message is communicated between the SNMP manager (server) and the agent (client) using SNMP, the SNMP must use either synchronous or asynchronous mode. The differences between these two modes are explained here:

- *Synchronous mode*: While using synchronous mode, the sending and receiving sides use one reference clock separately from the data. The manager and the agent must operate together according to the synchronization signal. To perform continuous data transmission, it is a mode in which one data transmission/reception must be completed between the sending side and the receiving side to transmit the next data.
- *Asynchronous mode*: In the case of using the asynchronous mode, the time difference is identified with the received signal clock and transmitted one character at a time regardless of the sender's clock. The start bit and stop bit are added to the front of the packet to be sent. In other words, in the case of the SNMP agent operating in the asynchronous mode, various data is exchanged when communicating with Get requests, and irregular transmission may be possible regardless of time and order.

When using SNMP Trap, the message is generated as a general trap or inform trap message. The trap uses an asynchronous communication method. The SNMP agent unilaterally sends information that does not require confirmation of the receiver, the SNMP manager. On the contrary, the SNMP agent works in the synchronous mode because the information sent must be acknowledged by the receiver, which is the SNMP manager.

SNMP-Related Python Libraries

For Python to use SNMP to communicate with other network devices, you must first install the correct SNMP library to help you achieve your goal. In this book, the `pysnmp` module will be installed to interact with routers and switches using Python. But there are several SNMP Python modules you can utilize based on what you want to achieve with Python and SNMP. Table 15-4 describes the Python SNMP-related modules for your future reference.

Table 15-4. *Python SNMP Libraries*

SNMP Package Name	Features and Download Link
pysnmp	Python-based SNMP module Program execution speed is slow https://pypi.org/project/pysnmp/
python-netsnmp	Use default Python bindings for net-snmp Supports non-Pythonic interface http://net-snmp.sourceforge.net/wiki/index.php/Python_Bindings
snimpy	Python tool developed for SNMP query Developed based on PySNMP Program execution speed is slow https://snimpy.readthedocs.io/en/latest/
easy-snmp	Library developed based on net-snmp Python-style interface support and operation Program execution speed is fast https://easysnmp.readthedocs.io/en/latest/
fastsnmpy	Using an asynchronous wrapper based on net-snmp Developed for SNMPwalk https://github.com/ajaysdesk/fastsnmpy

Understanding MIBs and OIDs and Browsing OIDs Directly

The SNMP agent shares a lot of information with the SNMP manager. Let's get familiar with MIBs and OIDs. As discussed earlier, OID is an identifier that designates an administered object in the MIB. This means that OID is part of MIB, and it uses a unique ID to represent each MIB. An example of OID is 1.3.6.1.2.1.1.3.0; this OID is an identifier that contains information about the uptime after a system has booted up. These unique numbers for each SNMP can be found through the MIB library, and equipment manufacturers share this information through their official websites. If the device is connected to the network, both the systems and network devices can communicate their system status via SNMP using MIBs and unique OIDs. Here, you will use an interactive Linux session to perform `snmpwalk` on Cisco CML routers and switches in our GNS3 lab. Later, you will find working SNMPv2c Python code from the Internet and change it to support SNMPv3 and probe device information within our lab topology.

Learn to Use SNMPwalk on a Linux Server

First, you need to install SNMP software to make your Linux server an SNMP manager. Then, set a password to authenticate with the manager depending on which agents use the SNMP version. In general, the SNMP manager is installed as an independent server on a Linux or Windows server, and a program that supports the SNMP API is installed and used. The most commonly used SNMP server programs are SolarWinds Network Performance Monitor, Paessler PRTG Network Monitor, and SysAid Monitoring. Most of this software provides a free distribution version for testing use. For more detailed information on these programs, please refer to each vendor's website and resources.

Here, we will install the SNMP server software on a Linux server, configure SNMPv3 on all network devices, and then execute the OID of the virtual network devices' MIB at the command line. First, install the SNMP manager software on the Linux server as described in the following section. If you want to monitor from another SNMP server, you can choose to install the SNMP agent (client) software. The Linux server used is a CentOS 8.1 server, so you will have to be log into the `centos8s1` server to follow the tasks step by step. The lab topology is the same as before; you will need a CentOS server and all routers and switches powered on.

Installing and Configuring SNMP Server on CentOS8

Follow these steps to install SNMP services on your CentOS 8 server and configure the user and user's authentication and authorization settings. You have to type in the commands in your `centos8s1` server that are marked in bold.

#	Task
1	First, install the `net-snmp-utils` and `net-snmp-devel` packages on the CentOS server using the commands shown here. `net-snmp-utils` is a tool used for `snmpwalk`. `[pynetauto@centos8s1 ~]$ sudo yum install -y net-snmp net-snmp-utils net-snmp-devel`

2	Configure an SNMPv3 user and an authentication password. The information configured here will be used to configure SNMP agents, network devices in this case. First, enable and start `snmpd` on the CentOS server; then check the running status. After that, stop the service before configuring the new SNMP user and password.
	
	`[pynetauto@centos8s1 ~]$ sudo systemctl enable snmpd`
	`[pynetauto@centos8s1 ~]$ sudo systemctl start snmpd`
	`[pynetauto@centos8s1 ~]$ sudo  systemctl status snmpd`
	`[pynetauto@centos8s1 ~]$ sudo systemctl stop snmpd`
	
	There are three methods to configure an SNMPv3 user with a password on a Linux system, and all three methods will be discussed here. If authentication and encryption methods are not specified during the user configuration step, MD5 and AES will be used automatically, and the access level will be set to read-only (`-ro`).
	
	Use the one of the methods to add an SNMP user and passphrase.
	
	A. *Command-line method*: If you set up a user via a command, you can simultaneously set the username, authentication password, and encryption-only key in one command line. Typical command options look like this:
	
	`net-snmp-config --create-snmpv3-user [-ro] [-A authpass] [-X privpass] [-a MD5|SHA] [-x DES|AES] [username]`
	
	Example 1: SNMP user creation without specifying a private password using default MD5 and DES:
	
	`[pynetauto@centos8s1 ~]$ sudo net-snmp-config --create-snmpv3-user -A AUTHPass1 SNMPUser2`
	`adding the following line to /var/lib/net-snmp/snmpd.conf:`
	`  createUser SNMPUser1 MD5 "AUTHPass1" DES ""`
	`adding the following line to /etc/snmp/snmpd.conf:`
	`  rwuser SNMPUser1`

#	Task

Example 2: SNMP user creation specifying authentication and encryption and a private password method. The following example configures MD5 authentication with DES encryption:

```
[pynetauto@centos8s1 ~]$ sudo net-snmp-config --create-snmpv3-user -ro -A AUTHPass1
-X PRIVPass1 -a MD5 -x DES SNMPUser3
adding the following line to /var/lib/net-snmp/snmpd.conf:
  createUser SNMPUser2 MD5 "AUTHPass1" DES "PRIVPass1"
adding the following line to /etc/snmp/snmpd.conf:
  rouser SNMPUser2
```

Example 3: This is SNMP user creation using SHA authentication and AES encryption:

```
[pynetauto@centos8s1 ~]$ sudo net-snmp-config --create-snmpv3-user -ro -A AUTHPass1
-X PRIVPass1 -a SHA -x AES SNMPUser1
adding the following line to /var/lib/net-snmp/snmpd.conf:
  createUser SNMPUser3 SHA "AUTHPass1" AES "PRIVPass1"
adding the following line to /etc/snmp/snmpd.conf:
  rouser SNMPUser3
```

B. *Manual configuration*: You can also set up SNMP users by opening the SNMP configuration file yourself and appending the new user information at the end of the file. Just open the two files and add the user information.

Example 4: This is a user account called `SNMPUser1` using MD5, and DES is created. Add the last line and username, as shown here:

```
[pynetauto@centos8s1 ~]$ sudo nano /var/lib/net-snmp/snmpd.conf
[...omitted for brevity]
###########################################################################
#
# snmpNotifyFilterTable persistent data
#
###########################################################################

engineBoots 18
oldEngineID 0x80001f8880acfa8434b71f4a5f00000000
createUser SNMPUser4 MD5 "AUTHPass1" DES "PRIVPass1" <<< Add this to the last line

[pynetauto@centos8s1 ~]$ sudo nano /etc/snmp/snmpd.conf
[...omitted for brevity]
###############################################################################
# Further Information
#
# See the snmpd.conf manual page, and the output of "snmpd -H".
rwuser SNMPUser2
rouser SNMPUser3
rouser SNMPUser1
rwuser SNMPUser4 <<< Add this to the last line
```

(*continued*)

#	Task

Interactive mode: This interactive command is useful when creating SNMP users using MD5 and DES.

```
[pynetauto@centos8s1 ~]$ sudo net-snmp-create-v3-user
[sudo] password for pynetauto:
Enter a SNMPv3 user name to create:
SNMPUser5
Enter authentication pass-phrase:
AUTHPass1
Enter encryption pass-phrase:
[press return to reuse the authentication pass-phrase]
PRIVPass1
adding the following line to /var/lib/net-snmp/snmpd.conf:
  createUser SNMPUser MD5 "AUTHPass1" DES "PRIVPass1"
adding the following line to /etc/snmp/snmpd.conf:
  rwuser SNMPUser5
```

3 Enter the following command to start the SNMP service again and check the status of the snmpd service. The status must be "Active: active (running)."

```
[pynetauto@centos8s1 ~]$ sudo systemctl start snmpd
[pynetauto@centos8s1 ~]$ sudo systemctl status snmpd
● snmpd.service - Simple Network Management Protocol (SNMP) Daemon.
Loaded: loaded (/usr/lib/systemd/system/snmpd.service; enabled; vendor preset:
disabled)
Active: active (running) since Wed 2021-01-13 16:23:03 AEDT; 5s ago
Main PID: 43244 (snmpd)
  Tasks: 1 (limit: 11166)
  Memory: 4.9M
  CGroup: /system.slice/snmpd.service
   └─43244 /usr/sbin/snmpd -LS0-6d -f
```

4 Use the SNMPwalk command to check if SNMP is working correctly on the local server. Run snmpwalk of the CentOS server using SNMPUser created in method C.

```
[pynetauto@centos8s1 icmp_sweeper]$ snmpwalk -v3 -u SNMPUser5 -l authPriv -a MD5 -A
AUTHPass1 -X PRIVPass1 localhost
SNMPv2-MIB::sysDescr.0 = STRING: Linux centos8s1 4.18.0-193.14.2.el8_2.x86_64 #1 SMP
Sun Jul 26 03:54:29 UTC 2020 x86_64
SNMPv2-MIB::sysObjectID.0 = OID: NET-SNMP-MIB::netSnmpAgentOIDs.10
DISMAN-EVENT-MIB::sysUpTimeInstance = Timeticks: (15885) 0:02:38.85
SNMPv2-MIB::sysContact.0 = STRING: Root <root@localhost> (configure /etc/snmp/snmp.
local.conf)
SNMPv2-MIB::sysName.0 = STRING: centos8s1
SNMPv2-MIB::sysLocation.0 = STRING: Unknown (edit /etc/snmp/snmpd.conf)
SNMPv2-MIB::sysORLastChange.0 = Timeticks: (0) 0:00:00.00
SNMPv2-MIB::sysORID.1 = OID: SNMP-FRAMEWORK-MIB::snmpFrameworkMIBCompliance
SNMPv2-MIB::sysORID.2 = OID: SNMP-MPD-MIB::snmpMPDCompliance
SNMPv2-MIB::sysORID.3 = OID: SNMP-USER-BASED-SM-MIB::usmMIBCompliance
SNMPv2-MIB::sysORID.4 = OID: SNMPv2-MIB::snmpMIB
```

#	Task

	`SNMPv2-MIB::sysORID.5 = OID: SNMP-VIEW-BASED-ACM-MIB::vacmBasicGroup`
	`SNMPv2-MIB::sysORID.6 = OID: TCP-MIB::tcpMIB`
	`SNMPv2-MIB::sysORID.7 = OID: IP-MIB::ip`
	`SNMPv2-MIB::sysORID.8 = OID: UDP-MIB::udpMIB`
	[... omitted for brevity]

The following is a brief description of the option handles used in the Linux `snmpwalk` command:

snmpwalk -v3 -u SNMPUser2 -l authPriv -a MD5 -A AUTHPass1 -X PRIVPass1 127.0.0.1

-v3 (version)

-u (SNMP username)

-l (security level)

-a (authentication method)

-A (pass-phrase)

Configuring Cisco Routers and Switches to Support SNMPv3 Using a Python Script

The following are the SNMP-related settings for Cisco devices. To implement SNMPv3 instead of SNMPv2c, you have to understand more about SNMP authentication than SNMPv2c. SNMP v2c still is the most popular SNMP version in use today due to the legacy compatibility issues of SNMPv3. Older devices do not have the software code to support the SNMP version3, so unless your network consists of old devices, SNMPv2c will be the way to go. In the future, almost all devices will support more secure SNMPv3. In this book, you are going to use SNMPv3 instead. You are going to write a quick Python script to add SNMP configurations on all Cisco devices.

#	Task
1	All SNMP agents manage their own (system) information separately, which can be used in SNMPv3 messages. For SNMP agent devices such as Cisco routers and switches, Cisco recommends setting unique SNMP engine IDs before configuring and using SNMPv3. If the SNMP engine ID is not specified during configuration, then a combination of the enterprise number and the default MAC address will generate a unique engine ID. To correctly add an SNMPv3 configuration to Cisco devices, you have to use three `snmp-server` commands as suggested here. A. The engine ID configuration command example looks like this: `LAB-R1(config)#`**`snmp-server engineID local 19216818310`** B. The SNMP group name configuration command is shown next. `GROUP1` is the SNMP group name in this case. This command will create an SNMPv3 group called `GROUP1` with a private password. `LAB-R1(config)#`**`snmp-server group GROUP1 v3 priv`**

(*continued*)

#	Task

	C. Use the same information as the manager-side SNMP user credentials, and you can configure the SNMP user on a Cisco device using the following command:
	`LAB-R1(config)#` **`snmp-server user SNMPUser1 GROUP1 v3 auth sha AUTHPass1 priv aes 128 PRIVPass1`**
	You can use `show snmp user` to check the SNMP user information on Cisco devices. In the next step, based on the previous commands, let's write a Python script to add this configuration to all devices at once.
	`LAB-R1#`**`show snmp user`**
	`*Jan 13 05:22:55.217: %SYS-5-CONFIG_I: Configured from console by console`
	`User name: SNMPUser1`
	`Engine ID: 192168183100`
	`storage-type: nonvolatile        active`
	`Authentication Protocol: SHA`
	`Privacy Protocol: AES128`
	`Group-name: GROUP1`

2	To make this lab more enjoyable, we will copy the ICMP sweeper tool we created earlier and use it as the precommunication check tool in our script before SSHing into devices and configuring SNMP. So, use these commands to copy the files and then rename the `ping_sweep1.py` script as `precheck_tool.py`:
	`[pynetauto@centos8s1 ~]$` **`pwd`**
	`/home/pynetauto`
	`[pynetauto@centos8s1 ~]$` **`mkdir snmp_test`**
	`[pynetauto@centos8s1 ~]$` **`ls icmp_sweeper`**
	`cron.log  ip_addresses.txt  ping_sweep1.py`
	`[pynetauto@centos8s1 ~]$` **`mkdir snmp_test`**
	`[pynetauto@centos8s1 ~]$` **`cp ./icmp_sweeper/ping_sweep1.py ./snmp_test/precheck_tool.py`**
	`[pynetauto@centos8s1 ~]$` **`cp ./icmp_sweeper/ip_addresses.txt ./snmp_test/ip_addresses.txt`**
	`[pynetauto@centos8s1 ~]$` **`cd snmp_test`**
	`[pynetauto@centos8s1 snmp_test]$` **`ls`**
	`ip_addresses.txt  precheck_tool.py`
	You should have two files under the `/home/pynetauto/snmp_test` directory at the end of this task. The `ip_addresses.txt` file should already contain the IP addresses of all routers and switches in our topology.

#	Task
3	You will open and modify `precheck_tool.py` in the nano text editor so that the main part of the script becomes a function. This way, we can call upon this function from another Python script as a module. Modify the file as follows:

```
[pynetauto@centos8s1 snmp_test]$ nano precheck_tool.py

GNU nano 4.8                  /home/pynetauto/snmp_test/precheck_tool.py
#!/usr/bin/python3

import os

def icmp_pinger(ip):
    rep = os.system('ping -c 3 ' + ip)
    if rep == 0:
        print(f"{ip} is reachable.") # Print ip is reachable if the device is on the network
    else:
        print(f"{ip} is either offline or icmp is filtered. Exiting.")
        exit() # Exit application if any ip address is unreachable.
    print("-"*80)
^G Get Help   ^O Write Out   ^W Where Is   ^K Cut Text    ^J Justify    ^C Cur Pos
^X Exit       ^R Read File   ^\ Replace    ^U Paste Text  ^T To Spell   ^_ Go To Line
```

When the else condition is met, for example, 192.168.183.10 is unreachable, it will exit the program as shown here:

```
[pynetauto@centos8s1 snmp_test]$ python3 snmp_config.py
PING 192.168.183.10 (192.168.183.10) 56(84) bytes of data.

--- 192.168.183.10 ping statistics ---
3 packets transmitted, 0 received, 100% packet loss, time 62ms

192.168.183.10 is either offline or icmp is filtered. Exiting.
```

#	Task
4	Now, it is time for you to create the configuration script `snmp_config.py`. As a best practice, we will specify the SNMP engine ID using each device's IP address. The dots in IP addresses will be removed, and the whole number will be reused as the device's SNMP engine ID.

```
[pynetauto@centos8s1 snmp_test]$ nano snmp_config.py

GNU nano 4.8                  /home/pynetauto/snmp_test/snmp_config.py
#!/usr/bin/python3

import time
import paramiko
from getpass import getpass
# Custom tools
from precheck_tool import icmp_pinger

with open("/home/pynetauto/snmp_test/ip_addresses.txt", "r") as ip_addresses:
    for ip in ip_addresses:
        ip = ip.strip()
        icmp_pinger(ip)

username = input("Enter username : ") # Ask for username
password = getpass("Enter password : " ) # Ask for password
```

(continued)

#	Task

```
with open("/home/pynetauto/snmp_test/ip_addresses.txt", "r") as ip_addresses:
    for ip in ip_addresses:
        ip = ip.strip()
        eng_id = ip.replace(".", "") # Remove dot in ip address and use it as SNMP
        Engine ID
        print ("Now logging into " + (ip))
        ssh_client = paramiko.SSHClient()
        ssh_client.set_missing_host_key_policy(paramiko.AutoAddPolicy())
        ssh_client.connect(hostname=ip,username=username,password=password)
        print (f"Successful connection to {ip}\n")
        print ("Now completing following tasks : " + "\n")
        remote_connection = ssh_client.invoke_shell()
        print (f"Adding SNMP configuration to {ip}")
        remote_connection.send("show clock\n")
        remote_connection.send("configure terminal\n") # Add SNMP configurations
        remote_connection.send(f"snmp-server engineID local {eng_id}\n")
        remote_connection.send("snmp-server group GROUP1 v3 priv\n")
        remote_connection.send("snmp-server user SNMPUser1 GROUP1 v3 auth sha
        AUTHPass1 priv aes 128 PRIVPass1\n")
        remote_connection.send("do wri\n")
        remote_connection.send("exit\n")
        time.sleep(2)
        print ()
        time.sleep(2)
        output = remote_connection.recv(65535)
        print((output).decode('ascii'))
        print(f"Successfully configured {ip} & Disconnecting.")
        print("-"*80)
        ssh_client.close
        time.sleep(2)

print("All tasks were completed successfully. Bye!")
^G Get Help  ^O Write Out  ^W Where Is  ^K Cut Text   ^J Justify   ^C Cur Pos
^X Exit      ^R Read File  ^\ Replace   ^U Paste Text ^T To Spell  ^_ Go To Line
```

5 Before running the script, you will need to install the paramiko library by running the following pip3 command. Install paramiko on the centos8s1 server.

```
[pynetauto@centos8s1 snmp_test]$ sudo pip3 install paramiko
```

6 You should see the last line of code as a successful configuration script, which is outside of the for loop in the main script. Run snmp_config.py and configure SNMP group settings on all devices. The script will check the network connection using ICMP initially. If any device is unreachable, the application will exit. If all devices are on the network, the script will run and complete the SNMP configuration on all devices.

```
[pynetauto@centos8s1 snmp_test]$ python3 snmp_config.py
PING 192.168.183.10 (192.168.183.10) 56(84) bytes of data.
64 bytes from 192.168.183.10: icmp_seq=1 ttl=255 time=14.7 ms
64 bytes from 192.168.183.10: icmp_seq=2 ttl=255 time=11.5 ms
64 bytes from 192.168.183.10: icmp_seq=3 ttl=255 time=6.22 ms
```

#	Task
	(output continued, see code below)

```
--- 192.168.183.10 ping statistics ---
3 packets transmitted, 3 received, 0% packet loss, time 6ms
rtt min/avg/max/mdev = 6.215/10.819/14.749/3.516 ms
192.168.183.10 is reachable.
-----------------------------------------------------------------------------
PING 192.168.183.20 (192.168.183.20) 56(84) bytes of data.
64 bytes from 192.168.183.20: icmp_seq=1 ttl=255 time=22.4 ms
64 bytes from 192.168.183.20: icmp_seq=2 ttl=255 time=25.0 ms
64 bytes from 192.168.183.20: icmp_seq=3 ttl=255 time=22.5 ms

[...omitted for brevity]

Successfully configured 192.168.183.153 & Disconnecting.
-----------------------------------------------------------------------------
Now logging into 192.168.183.244
Successful connection to 192.168.183.244

Now completing following tasks :

Adding SNMP configuration to 192.168.183.244

**************************************************************************
* IOSv is strictly limited to use for evaluation, demonstration and IOS  *
* education. IOSv is provided as-is and is not supported by Cisco's      *
* Technical Advisory Center. Any use or disclosure, in whole or in part, *
* of the IOSv Software or Documentation to any third party for any       *
* purposes is expressly prohibited except as otherwise authorized by     *
* Cisco in writing.                                                      *
**************************************************************************
Lab-SW4#show clock
*12:33:19.576 UTC Wed Jan 13 2021
Lab-SW4#configure terminal
Enter configuration commands, one per line.  End with CNTL/Z.
Lab-SW4(config)#snmp-server engineID local 192168183244
Lab-SW4(config)#snmp-server group GROUP1 v3 priv
Lab-SW4(config)#$User1 GROUP1 v3 auth sha AUTHPass1 priv aes 128 PRIVPass1
Lab-SW4(config)#do wri
Building configuration...

Successfully configured 192.168.183.244 & Disconnecting.
-----------------------------------------------------------------------------
All tasks were completed successfully. Bye!
```

#	Task
7	At the end of the successful SNMP configuration run, log in to each device to confirm SNMP-related configurations on each device. An example of the Lab-SW4 configuration is shown, but all other devices should have the SNMP user and group configurations.

(continued)

#	Task
	Lab-SW4#show snmp user User name: **SNMPUser1** Engine ID: 192168183244 storage-type: nonvolatile active Authentication Protocol: SHA Privacy Protocol: AES128 Group-name: GROUP1 Lab-SW4#show run | in snmp snmp-server engineID local 192168183244 snmp-server group GROUP1 v3 priv

Your Cisco devices are now ready for SNMP communication with your SNMP server.

SNMPwalk from Linux Server

From your centos8s1 server, let's continue to perform snmpwalk using SNMPv3 commands; there is a lot to be learned here.

#	Task
1	The CentOS 8.1 server uses the following snmpwalk command to retrieve the OID information used by LAB-R1's vIOS MIB via SNMP. If you use this command, all OID information is loaded, as shown here: [pynetauto@centos8s1 snmp_test]$ **snmpwalk -v3 -l authPriv -u SNMPUser1 -a SHA -A "AUTHPass1" -x AES -X "PRIVPass1" 192.168.183.10** SNMPv2-MIB::sysDescr.0 = STRING: Cisco IOS Software, IOSv Software (VIOS-ADVENTERPRISEK9-M), Version 15.6(2)T, RELEASE SOFTWARE (fc2) Technical Support: http://www.cisco.com/techsupport Copyright (c) 1986-2016 by Cisco Systems, Inc. Compiled Tue 22-Mar-16 16:19 by prod_rel_team SNMPv2-MIB::sysObjectID.0 = OID: SNMPv2-SMI::enterprises.9.1.1041 DISMAN-EVENT-MIB::sysUpTimeInstance = Timeticks: (157667) 0:26:16.67 SNMPv2-MIB::sysContact.0 = STRING: SNMPv2-MIB::sysName.0 = STRING: LAB-R1.pynetauto.local SNMPv2-MIB::sysLocation.0 = STRING: SNMPv2-MIB::sysServices.0 = INTEGER: 78 SNMPv2-MIB::sysORLastChange.0 = Timeticks: (0) 0:00:00.00 SNMPv2-MIB::sysORID.1 = OID: SNMPv2-SMI::enterprises.9.7.129 SNMPv2-MIB::sysORID.2 = OID: SNMPv2-SMI::enterprises.9.7.115 SNMPv2-MIB::sysORID.3 = OID: SNMPv2-SMI::enterprises.9.7.265 SNMPv2-MIB::sysORID.4 = OID: SNMPv2-SMI::enterprises.9.7.112 SNMPv2-MIB::sysORID.5 = OID: SNMPv2-SMI::enterprises.9.7.106 SNMPv2-MIB::sysORID.6 = OID: SNMPv2-SMI::enterprises.9.7.47 SNMPv2-MIB::sysORID.7 = OID: SNMPv2-SMI::enterprises.9.7.122 *[... omitted for brevity]*

#	Task

2	If you run the same command on other devices, you should also see all MIB information for each device.
	
	`[pynetauto@centos8s1 snmp_test]$ snmpwalk -v3  -l authPriv -u SNMPUser1 -a SHA -A "AUTHPass1"  -x AES -X "PRIVPass1" 192.168.183.20`
	`[pynetauto@centos8s1 snmp_test]$ snmpwalk -v3  -l authPriv -u SNMPUser1 -a SHA -A "AUTHPass1"  -x AES -X "PRIVPass1" 192.168.183.101`
	`[pynetauto@centos8s1 snmp_test]$ snmpwalk -v3  -l authPriv -u SNMPUser1 -a SHA -A "AUTHPass1"  -x AES -X "PRIVPass1" 192.168.183.102`
	`[pynetauto@centos8s1 snmp_test]$ snmpwalk -v3  -l authPriv -u SNMPUser1 -a SHA -A "AUTHPass1"  -x AES -X "PRIVPass1" 192.168.183.133`
	`[pynetauto@centos8s1 snmp_test]$ snmpwalk -v3  -l authPriv -u SNMPUser1 -a SHA -A "AUTHPass1"  -x AES -X "PRIVPass1" 192.168.183.153`
	`[pynetauto@centos8s1 snmp_test]$ snmpwalk -v3  -l authPriv -u SNMPUser1 -a SHA -A "AUTHPass1"  -x AES -X "PRIVPass1" 192.168.183.244`

3	Practice retrieving `LAB-SW1`'s system information using the `snmpwalk` or `snmpget` command. 1.3.6.1.2.1.1.3.0 (`sysUpTime.0`) is an OID indicating the time the system was started. You can use the `snmpget` command to retrieve and check information from the SNMP manager to the SNMP agent.
	
	`[pynetauto@centos8s1 snmp_test]$ snmpwalk -v3  -l authPriv -u SNMPUser1 -a SHA -A "AUTHPass1"  -x AES -X "PRIVPass1" 192.168.183.10 sysUpTime.0`
	`DISMAN-EVENT-MIB::sysUpTimeInstance = Timeticks: (1606783) 4:27:47.83`
	
	The SNMP agent `LAB-SW1` tells us the uptime since system restart is 4 hours 27 minutes and 47 seconds.

4	Check a router or switch's name using 1.3.6.1.2.1.1.5.0 (`sysName.0` or `sysName`).
	
	`[pynetauto@centos8s1 snmp_test]$ snmpwalk -v3  -l authPriv -u SNMPUser1 -a SHA -A "AUTHPass1"  -x AES -X "PRIVPass1" 192.168.183.10 sysName.0`
	`SNMPv2-MIB::sysName.0 = STRING: LAB-R1.pynetauto.local`
	
	`[pynetauto@centos8s1 snmp_test]$ snmpwalk -v3  -l authPriv -u SNMPUser1 -a SHA -A "AUTHPass1"  -x AES -X "PRIVPass1" 192.168.183.10 sysName`
	`SNMPv2-MIB::sysName.0 = STRING: LAB-R1.pynetauto.local`
	
	`[pynetauto@centos8s1 snmp_test]$ snmpwalk -v3  -l authPriv -u SNMPUser1 -a SHA -A "AUTHPass1"  -x AES -X "PRIVPass1" 192.168.183.10 1.3.6.1.2.1.1.5.0`
	`SNMPv2-MIB::sysName.0 = STRING: LAB-R1.pynetauto.local`

5	If you use 1.3.6.1.2.1.2.2.1.7(`ifAdminStatus.1`), you can check the interface's setting status. This information confirms that the administrator has activated the interface.
	
	`[pynetauto@centos8s1 snmp_test]$ snmpwalk -v3  -l authPriv -u SNMPUser1 -a SHA -A "AUTHPass1"  -x AES -X "PRIVPass1" 192.168.183.10 ifAdminStatus`
	`IF-MIB::ifAdminStatus.1 = INTEGER: up(1)`
	`IF-MIB::ifAdminStatus.2 = INTEGER: up(1)`
	`IF-MIB::ifAdminStatus.3 = INTEGER: down(2)`
	`IF-MIB::ifAdminStatus.4 = INTEGER: down(2)`
	`IF-MIB::ifAdminStatus.5 = INTEGER: up(1)`
	`IF-MIB::ifAdminStatus.6 = INTEGER: up(1)`
	`IF-MIB::ifAdminStatus.7 = INTEGER: up(1)`

(continued)

#	Task

	`[pynetauto@centos8s1 snmp_test]$ **snmpwalk -v3 -l authPriv -u SNMPUser1 -a SHA -A "AUTHPass1" -x AES -X "PRIVPass1" 192.168.183.10 1.3.6.1.2.1.2.2.1.7**`
	`IF-MIB::ifAdminStatus.1 = INTEGER: up(1)`
	`IF-MIB::ifAdminStatus.2 = INTEGER: up(1)`
	`IF-MIB::ifAdminStatus.3 = INTEGER: down(2)`
	`IF-MIB::ifAdminStatus.4 = INTEGER: down(2)`
	`IF-MIB::ifAdminStatus.5 = INTEGER: up(1)`
	`IF-MIB::ifAdminStatus.6 = INTEGER: up(1)`
	`IF-MIB::ifAdminStatus.7 = INTEGER: up(1)`

6	As you may have noticed previously, the OID of the first interface is the ID with .1 appended after 1.3.6.1.2.1.2.2.1.7. If .1 is added and executed, as shown next, the status of the GigabitEthernet0/0 port is displayed as up(1).
	`[pynetauto@centos8s1 snmp_test]$ **snmpwalk -v3 -l authPriv -u SNMPUser1 -a SHA -A "AUTHPass1" -x AES -X "PRIVPass1" 192.168.183.10 1.3.6.1.2.1.2.2.1.7.1**`
	`IF-MIB::ifAdminStatus.1 = INTEGER: up(1)`

7	Likewise, adding .3 at the end means GigabitEthernet0/1. This port is currently disabled, so it is displayed as down(2).
	`[pynetauto@centos8s1 snmp_test]$ **snmpwalk -v3 -l authPriv -u SNMPUser1 -a SHA -A "AUTHPass1" -x AES -X "PRIVPass1" 192.168.183.10 1.3.6.1.2.1.2.2.1.7.3**`
	`IF-MIB::ifAdminStatus.3 = INTEGER: down(2)`

8	If you use OID 1.3.6.1.2.1.2.2.1.8 (`ifOperStatus`), you can query all the interfaces' operational status. Quickly run a `snmpwalk` command from your server for confirmation.
	`[pynetauto@centos8s1 snmp_test]$ **snmpwalk -v3 -l authPriv -u SNMPUser1 -a SHA -A "AUTHPass1" -x AES -X "PRIVPass1" 192.168.183.10 ifOperStatus**`
	`IF-MIB::ifOperStatus.1 = INTEGER: up(1)`
	`IF-MIB::ifOperStatus.2 = INTEGER: up(1)`
	`IF-MIB::ifOperStatus.3 = INTEGER: down(2)`
	`IF-MIB::ifOperStatus.4 = INTEGER: down(2)`
	`IF-MIB::ifOperStatus.5 = INTEGER: up(1)`
	`IF-MIB::ifOperStatus.6 = INTEGER: up(1)`
	`IF-MIB::ifOperStatus.7 = INTEGER: up(1)`

9	Use the `snmpget` command to query information about an interface, in this case, GigabitEthernet0/0. `IfDescr.1` queries the interface's description, and `ifOperStatus.1` queries the interface's operational status. You can replace the number 1 with 2 to query the next GigabitEthernet2 interface.
	`[pynetauto@centos8s1 snmp_test]$ **snmpget -v3 -l authPriv -u SNMPUser1 -a SHA -A "AUTHPass1" -x AES -X "PRIVPass1" 192.168.183.10 ifDescr.1 ifOperStatus.1**`
	`IF-MIB::ifDescr.1 = STRING: GigabitEthernet0/0`
	`IF-MIB::ifOperStatus.1 = INTEGER: up(1)`

10	The following `snmpget` command queries for the interface status of GigabitEthernet0/3; since it is not in use, it is marked as `down(2)`.
	`[pynetauto@centos8s1 snmp_test]$ **snmpget -v3 -l authPriv -u SNMPUser1 -a SHA -A "AUTHPass1" -x AES -X "PRIVPass1" 192.168.183.10 ifDescr.4 ifOperStatus.4**`
	`IF-MIB::ifDescr.4 = STRING: GigabitEthernet0/3`
	`IF-MIB::ifOperStatus.4 = INTEGER: down(2)`

#	Task
11	Many OIDs can reveal each component and configuration's current status. Another fact worth noting is the RMON OID; it can reveal the software version number and the booting information. The example shows the router RMON OID.

```
[pynetauto@centos8s1 snmp_test]$ snmpwalk -v3  -l authPriv -u SNMPUser1 -a SHA -A
"AUTHPass1"  -x AES -X "PRIVPass1" 192.168.183.10 rmon
RMON-MIB::rmon.19.1.0 = Hex-STRING: FF C0 00 40
RMON-MIB::rmon.19.2.0 = STRING: "15.6(2)T"
RMON-MIB::rmon.19.3.0 = ""
RMON-MIB::rmon.19.4.0 = Hex-STRING: 07 E4 08 1E 02 15 16 07
RMON-MIB::rmon.19.5.0 = INTEGER: 1
RMON-MIB::rmon.19.6.0 = STRING: "flash0:/vios-adventerprisek9-m"
RMON-MIB::rmon.19.7.0 = IpAddress: 0.0.0.0
RMON-MIB::rmon.19.8.0 = INTEGER: 1
RMON-MIB::rmon.19.9.0 = INTEGER: 1
RMON-MIB::rmon.19.12.0 = IpAddress: 0.0.0.0
RMON-MIB::rmon.19.15.0 = Hex-STRING: 00
RMON-MIB::rmon.19.16.0 = Hex-STRING: 7E 00
```

The OID information used in vIOS is almost identical to real IOS equipment. There is a lot you can study from this lab and gain useful information from the previous examples. Once again, you must type the commands yourself on the keyboard and learn the previous concept. See Figure 15-11.

For Cisco networking devices, you can find the required OID information using the Cisco Feature Navigator.

URL: `https://cfnng.cisco.com/mibs`

For some Q&A on Cisco MIBs, refer to the following:

URL: `https://www.cisco.com/c/en/us/support/docs/ip/simple-network-management-protocol-snmp/9226-mibs-9226.html`

For your information, the following MIBs are among the most useful for Cisco devices:

- IF-MIB: Interface counter

URL: `https://www.cisco.com/c/en/us/td/docs/ios-xml/ios/interface/configuration/15-s/ir-15-s-book/ir-if-mibs.html`

- IP-MIB: Contains IP address
- IP-FORWARD-MIB: Contains a routing table
- ENTITY-MIB: Contains inventory information
- LLDP-MIB: Contains neighbor information

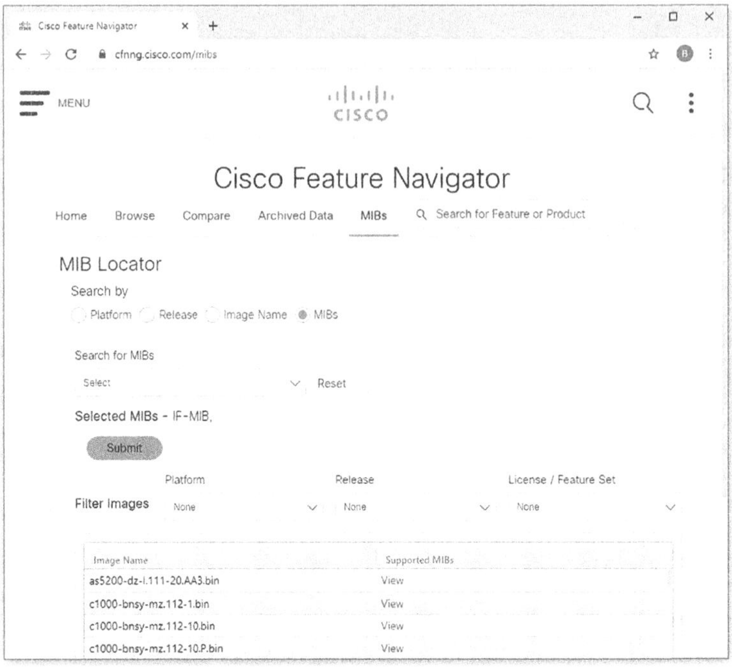

Figure 15-11. *Cisco Feature Navigator, MIBs*

Borrowing Some Example Python SNMP Code

As discussed throughout this book, learning a single programming language such as Python, JavaScript, or Perl does not turn you into a network engineer who is immediately ready to develop applications. Based on your strong foundational network knowledge, you have to try your best to broaden your supported technologies. Your journey might become a long haul, perhaps painfully too slow for some people. Luckily, you can often find the right code on the Internet for your use and borrow it. Why bother reinventing the wheel? If you are not the first person to come across a specific problem, then somebody else has solved the problem ahead of you. You just have to know how and where to look for the specific information you are looking for. (Of course, I believe that some knowledge is more dependable and better transferred in other forms.)

On the web, I was looking for some Python use cases with SNMP and came across a good article and bookmarked the site for my future reference. When the time came to write this book, I was asked to include SNMP and Python as part of this book. But I did not want to spend weeks trying to write new code; I wanted to find an existing SNMP Python script to show an example of how Python is used in SNMP. The SNMP Python code that will be introduced in this section is sourced from Alessandro Maggio's home page. Thanks to Alessandro, I have included the script as part of this book with his consent. To get the full explanation of the code, please visit Alex's blog.

Find Alessandro Maggio's blog and code tutorial here:

URL: `https://www.ictshore.com/`

URL: `https://www.ictshore.com/sdn/python-snmp-tutorial/`

SNMP Lab Source Code

The following code is the Python code for SNMPv2c. SNMPv2c uses read-only community strings, simplifying SNMP configuration on both the server and agent sides. Still, as we all know, SNMPv2c is less secure than SNMPv3, so you will quickly review the code and make minor modifications to convert it into SNMPv3 code. Later, based on a scenario, we will write a simple Python integration script to work in harmony with this script. First, let's take a closer look at the original SNMP Python code. The explanations always begin with # or """ """.

```
[pynetauto@centos8s1 snmp_test]$ nano quicksnmp.py
```

```
GNU nano 4.8                                /home/pynetauto/snmp_test/quicksnmp.py
# This code uses the High-Level API module included in the pysnmp library.
from pysnmp import hlapi

"""
The first function or get () function defines pre-requisite information to initiate and
make device information requests. Generally, for such a function to work, you specifically
have to provide the target IP (or DNS name), Object ID(OID), Credentials, SNMP port number
(161), EngineID, or SNMP context.  There is no strict requirement to parse the EngineID
and SNMP context in simpler Python code, so in this example, the EngineID or SNMP context
is not parsed to communicate with the Agent. All this information forms a handler, which
this script enables the Server to communicate with the Agent so that the Agent can send the
requested information about itself.
"""

def get(target, oids, credentials, port=161, engine=hlapi.SnmpEngine(), context=hlapi.
ContextData()):
    handler = hlapi.getCmd(
        engine,
        credentials,
        hlapi.UdpTransportTarget((target, port)),
        context,
        *construct_object_types(oids)
    )
    return fetch(handler, 1)[0]
```

```
# Second function needs a single argument list_of_oids, a blank list is used to collect and
return object types
# information.
def construct_object_types(list_of_oids):
    object_types = []
    for oid in list_of_oids:
        object_types.append(hlapi.ObjectType(hlapi.ObjectIdentity(oid)))
    return object_types

# Third function requires two arguments and uses the result list to handle any errors in the
script.
def fetch(handler, count):
    result = []
    for i in range(count):
        try:
            error_indication, error_status, error_index, var_binds = next(handler)
            if not error_indication and not error_status:
                items = {}
                for var_bind in var_binds:
                    items[str(var_bind[0])] = cast(var_bind[1])
                result.append(items)
            else:
                raise RuntimeError('Got SNMP error: {0}'.format(error_indication))
        except StopIteration:
            break
    return result

# The fourth function, cast() uses the information received from PySNMP to pass the values,
this function
# plays the role of changing the value into int or float or string type.
def cast(value):
    try:
        return int(value)
    except (ValueError, TypeError):
        try:
            return float(value)
        except (ValueError, TypeError):
            try:
                return str(value)
            except (ValueError, TypeError):
                pass
    return value

# This code is written for SNMPv2c and uses a community string named 'ICTSHORE'.
hlapi.CommunityData('ICTSHORE')

# If SNMPv3 is used, a user ID and two authentication keys should be used. The script (or
the Server) uses
# this information to communicate with the desired SNMP Agent to get device information.
hlapi.UsmUserData('testuser', authKey='authenticationkey', privKey='encryptionkey',
authProtocol=hlapi.usmHMACSHAAuthProtocol, privProtocol=hlapi.usmAesCfb128Protocol)
```

```
# Specifies the specific OID to obtain specified information from the SNMP Agent.
'1.3.6.1.2.1.1.5.0' denotes the dot IOD for a hostname.
print(get('192.168.47.10', ['1.3.6.1.2.1.1.5.0'], hlapi.CommunityData('ICTSHORE')))

^G Get Help  ^O Write Out   ^W Where Is   ^K Cut Text    ^J Justify    ^C Cur Pos
^X Exit      ^R Read File   ^\ Replace    ^U Paste Text  ^T To Spell   ^_ Go To Line
```

Source code: https://www.ictshore.com/sdn/python-snmp-tutorial/

SNMPv3 Python Code to Query Cisco Device Information

Now you are going to reiterate the previous SNMPv2c Python code to support SNMPv3. By studying someone else's code and testing the script in a lab environment, you can gain more insight into how Python interacts with different applications and behaves. This is also a perfect opportunity to watch and learn the real difference between SNMPv2c and SNMPv3 in action.

#	Task
1	For the server (centos8s1) to communicate with network devices over SNMP, you will first install the server's pysnmp library. Complete the installation using the sudo pip3 install pysnmp command. `[pynetauto@centos8s1 ~]$ sudo pip3 install pysnmp`

2	After creating an SNMP Python code called quicksnmp_v3.py, open the file with the nano editor and copy and paste all lines of code from quicksnmp.py into quicksnmp_v3.py.
	
	`[pynetauto@centos8s1 ~]$cd snmp_test`
	`[pynetauto@centos8s1 snmp_test]$ nano quicksnmp_v3.py`

3	The following modifications are required to turn quicksnmp.py into the SNMP version 3 script. First, when you read the documentation on pysnmplabs.com, you will see that you need to import and use from pysnmp.hlapi import UsmUserData. http://snmplabs.com/pysnmp/docs/api-reference.html#pysnmp.hlapi.UsmUserData A. Add from pysnmp.hlapi import UsmUserData at the top of your code, as shown here:

```
GNU nano 4.8                 /home/pynetauto/snmp_test/quicksnmp_v3.py
from pysnmp import hlapi
from pysnmp.hlapi import UsmUserData

def get(target, oids, credentials, port=161, engine=hlapi.SnmpEngine(),
context=hlapi.ContextData()):
        handler = hlapi.getCmd(
        engine,
        credentials,
        hlapi.UdpTransportTarget((target, port)),
        context,
        *construct_object_types(oids)
    )
    return fetch(handler, 1)[0]
```

(*continued*)

#	Task

```
def construct_object_types(list_of_oids):
    object_types = []
    for oid in list_of_oids:
        object_types.append(hlapi.ObjectType(hlapi.ObjectIdentity(oid)))
    return object_types

def fetch(handler, count):
    result = []
    for i in range(count):
        try:
            error_indication, error_status, error_index, var_binds = next(handler)
            if not error_indication and not error_status:
                items = {}
                for var_bind in var_binds:
                    items[str(var_bind[0])] = cast(var_bind[1])
                result.append(items)
            else:
                raise RuntimeError('Got SNMP error: {0}'.format(error_indication))
        except StopIteration:
            break
    return result

def cast(value):
    try:
        return int(value)
    except (ValueError, TypeError):
        try:
            return float(value)
        except (ValueError, TypeError):
            try:
                return str(value)
            except (ValueError, TypeError):
                pass
    return value
^G Get Help  ^O Write Out  ^W Where Is  ^K Cut Text   ^J Justify  ^C Cur Pos
^X Exit      ^R Read File  ^\ Replace   ^U Paste Text ^T To Spell ^_ Go To Line
```

B. Next, you need to enter your user information, authentication key, and privacy key. As shown in the earlier SNMP user configuration, the SNMPv3 user, `SNMPUser1`, was configured with SHA authentication keys and the AES128 privacy key. So, add the following line exactly as shown here:

```
hlapi.UsmUserData('SNMPUser1', authKey='AUTHPass1', privKey='PRIVPass1', authProtocol=hlapi.usmHMACSHAAuthProtocol, privProtocol=hlapi.usmAesCfb128Protocol)
```

C. Enter the `print` statement so that the `get()` function can pass the correct agent IP information and other credential variables to print the information on the screen.

```
print(get('192.168.183.10', ['1.3.6.1.2.1.1.5.0'], hlapi.UsmUserData('SNMPUser1', authKey='AUTHPass1', privKey='PRIVPass1', authProtocol=hlapi.usmHMACSHAAuthProtocol, privProtocol=hlapi.usmAesCfb128Protocol)))
```

#	Task

4	Use dot OID '1.3.6.1.2.1.1.5.0' in the last line of code and execute the previous Python code to retrieve and print the device name of 192.168.183.10.
	`[pynetauto@centos8s1 snmp_test]$ python3 quicksnmp_v3.py`
	`{'1.3.6.1.2.1.1.5.0': 'LAB-R1.pynetauto.local'}`

5	If you want to retrieve the operational status of GigabitEthernet0/0, you can add another dot OID line with an OID value of '1.3.6.1.2.1.2.2.1.7.1' in the last line. When you run the changed script, the interface state will be returned as a number: 1 for On and 2 for Off.
	D. Add the following line to the end of quicksnmp_v3.py:
	`print(get('192.168.183.10', ['1.3.6.1.2.1.2.2.1.7.1'], hlapi.`
	`UsmUserData('SNMPUser1', authKey='AUTHPass1', privKey='PRIVP$`
	`52`
	`[pynetauto@centos8s1 snmp_test]$ python3 quicksnmp_v3.py`
	`{'1.3.6.1.2.1.1.5.0': 'LAB-R1.pynetauto.local'}`
	`{'1.3.6.1.2.1.2.2.1.7.1': 1}`

6	When you increase the last digit and run the script for the GigabitEthernet 0/3 interface status, it returns 2. It is not connected to anything. 4 is the interface reference number, and 2 denotes the Off status.
	`[pynetauto@centos8s1 snmp_test]$ python3 quicksnmp_v3.py`
	`{'1.3.6.1.2.1.1.5.0': 'LAB-R1.pynetauto.local'}`
	`{'1.3.6.1.2.1.2.2.1.7.4': 2}`

Using Python SNMP Code to Run a Query for an Interface Description

This lab is a continuation of the previous one, and you first have to make a copy of the quicksnmp_v3.py script and create another script to complete it. The following script will let you run SNMP queries on interfaces and their descriptions using the SNMPv3 Python code. Since this book is an introductory book that tries to introduce as much Python and network automation as possible, we will not go too deep into SNMP in-depth knowledge, leaving that task for the Cisco documentation. What is important here is to learn how Python is used to interact with Cisco devices using basic SNMP MIB and OID information.

#	Task

1	Now, using the Linux cp command, copy quicksnmp_v3.py and create another file named quicksnmp_v3_get_bulk_auto.py.
	`[pynetauto@centos8s1 snmp_test]$ cp quicksnmp_v3.py quicksnmp_v3_get_bulk_auto.py`
	`[pynetauto@centos8s1 snmp_test]$ nano quicksnmp_v3_get_bulk_auto.py`

(continued)

#	Task
2	At the end of the line, add the following code, and run it. You are appending the next line of code at the bottom. Also, make sure you use the SW3 IP address of 192.168.183.153. What this code will do is run the SNMP query on the interface's name and descriptions.

```
GNU nano 4.8      /home/pynetauto/snmp_test/quicksnmp_v3_get_bulk_auto.py
[... omitted for brevity]
def cast(value):
    try:
        return int(value)
    except (ValueError, TypeError):
        try:
            return float(value)
        except (ValueError, TypeError):
            try:
                return str(value)
            except (ValueError, TypeError):
                pass
    return value # existing quicksnmp_v3.py

#Append the following to the end of the code
def get_bulk(target, oids, credentials, count, start_from=0, port=161,
            engine=hlapi.SnmpEngine(), context=hlapi.ContextData()):
    handler = hlapi.bulkCmd(
        engine,
        credentials,
        hlapi.UdpTransportTarget((target, port)),
        context,
        start_from, count,
        *construct_object_types(oids)
    )
    return fetch(handler, count)
def get_bulk_auto(target, oids, credentials, count_oid, start_from=0, port=161,
            engine=hlapi.SnmpEngine(), context=hlapi.ContextData()):
    count = get(target, [count_oid], credentials, port, engine, context)[count_oid]
    return get_bulk(target, oids, credentials, count, start_from, port, engine,
    context)

its = get_bulk_auto('192.168.183.153', ['1.3.6.1.2.1.2.2.1.2 ',
'1.3.6.1.2.1.31.1.1.1.18'], hlapi.UsmUserData('SNMPUser1', authKey='AUTHPass1',
privKey='PRIVPass1', authProtocol=hlapi.usmHMACSHAAuthProtocol, privProtocol=hlapi.
usmAesCfb128Protocol), '1.3.6.1.2.1.2.1.0')
for it in its:
    for k, v in it.items():
        print("{0}={1}".format(k, v))
    print('')
^G Get Help  ^O Write Out  ^W Where Is  ^K Cut Text   ^J Justify  ^C Cur Pos
^X Exit      ^R Read File  ^\ Replace   ^U Paste Text ^T To Spell ^_ Go To Line
```

#	Task
3	Finally, run the `quicksnmp_v3_get_bulk_auto.py` code, and you should get the interface names and their descriptions; since we only configured the description for `Gi0/0` and `vlan1`, you will see the names of these interfaces.

```
[pynetauto@centos8s1 snmp_test]$ python3 quicksnmp_v3_get_bulk_auto.py
{'1.3.6.1.2.1.1.5.0': 'Lab-sw3.pynetauto.com'}
1.3.6.1.2.1.2.2.1.2.1=GigabitEthernet0/0
1.3.6.1.2.1.31.1.1.1.18.1="1GB Main Connection"

1.3.6.1.2.1.2.2.1.2.2=GigabitEthernet0/1
1.3.6.1.2.1.31.1.1.1.18.2=

[... omitted for brevity]

1.3.6.1.2.1.2.2.1.2.16=GigabitEthernet3/3
1.3.6.1.2.1.31.1.1.1.18.16=

1.3.6.1.2.1.2.2.1.2.17=Null0
1.3.6.1.2.1.31.1.1.1.18.17=

1.3.6.1.2.1.2.2.1.2.18=Vlan1
1.3.6.1.2.1.31.1.1.1.18.18="Native interface"
```

There are hundreds of SNMP OID objects you can query and learn about. If you have a little bit of spare time, you can explore more about Cisco Device MIBs, especially the CPU and processes related to MIB information. Here is a Cisco link that shows you how to query CPUs using SNMP:

URL: `https://www.cisco.com/c/en/us/support/docs/ip/simple-network-management-protocol-snmp/15215-collect-cpu-util-snmp.html`

Summary

In this chapter, you learned how to use the Linux scheduler `cron` on Ubuntu and CentOS. You can now schedule your Python applications to run at a specified time or at specified intervals. Once you finish developing an application, you can use `cron` to run the tasks even at odd hours of the day, and you will not lose any beauty sleep. The tool `cron` is a powerful, free, and open source task scheduler, and whenever we can, we should rely on open source tools. You also learned the SNMP foundations and looked at the `SNMPwalk` examples using the `pysnmp` module; in the process, we borrowed another developer's work so that we did not have to reinvent the wheel. This can save you a lot of time.

With SNMP and Python, there is a lot we can do, but that would be another entire book. In Chapter 16, you will be exploring even more network automation scenarios. Also, you will learn to use `virtualenv`, the virtual environment used for Python testing as well as Ansible, pyATS and Docker, sendmail, and Twilio SMS Python network automation application development.

CHAPTER 16

Python Network Automation Labs: Ansible, pyATS, Docker, and the Twilio API

This chapter is designed to introduce you to Python `virtualenv` and to Docker concepts and expose you to other ways of exploring Python external modules and features. Thus far in this book, we have focused on using Python's basic Telnet and SSH remote access methods to probe, configure, and manage network devices in the lab topology. In a production environment, often we do not always get a dedicated Linux server for testing and implementation; often you will be given a limited resource on a Linux server with shared access with other engineers. We have to learn how to get around these obstacles and still implement our solutions (or applications) in such a production environment. At the end of this chapter, you will be able to work in a Python virtual environment for testing without affecting the existing Python setup. You will have made a quick start on Ansible and pyATS (Genie) and learned how sending an email works on Linux and Python using Sendmail. Finally, you will learn to monitor your network device's CPU utilization with your Python application and then use a free Twilio SMS account to send an SMS to your smartphone using the Twilio API. You will explore how to adapt to other open source tools and write Python programs accordingly.

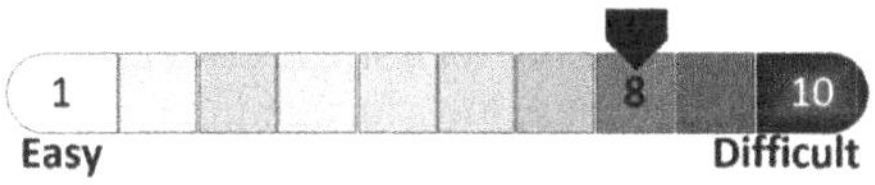

Python Network Automation Development Labs

We are nearing the end of this book, and in this chapter you will explore some Python network automation labs. This chapter will introduce you to different network automation tools that will help you on your network automation journey. There are dedicated websites and documentation about Ansible, pyATS, and Docker. Hence, it is technically impossible to gain an in-depth understanding of these tools merely by reading a single chapter from this book. Still, it is worth installing and learning about these tools so you can decide for yourself if these tools can help your network automation dreams come true. Not every network engineer wants to write lines of Python code for a living but still wants to experiment with network automation's real power. In this case, these out-of-the-box tools will serve the most common network automation scenarios, and you do not have to write real Python code.

B. Choi, *Introduction to Python Network Automation*, https://doi.org/10.1007/978-1-4842-6806-3_16

However, note that no two client network environments are the same, and no two organizations' IP traffic have the same priorities or characteristics. If you have read thus far and still think that network automation only involves automating a network engineer's general tasks and their thinking process, you are incorrect. Half of the job is all about handling data, namely, how you extract and use that data to your organization's advantage to replace repeatable tasks with lines of code. Therefore, it is inevitable that some customization and writing code are involved in every scenario. In short, this chapter will serve as a quick-start guide for Ansible, pyATS, and Docker.

Red Hat's Ansible is gaining popularity for network configuration management; it is an open source tool initially developed as a configuration management tool for operating systems. Lately, the same tools are used to manage network devices. The big plus of Ansible is that the Ansible users do not have to write real code such as Python or JavaScript; they write code in pseudocode called YAML. Yes, writing YAML code is between writing real code and using the GUI-based Jelly Bean code. Ansible is nothing more than a simplified YAML application based on Python's `paramiko`, `netmiko`, and `nornir` libraries, but it is a lot more user friendly than just coding in Python. It uses YAML files for endpoint automation using an agentless push method over pull method like other competitors. Ansible could be the first network automation tool many network engineers will interface with even before getting into Python. Or, you could be a seasoned Python programmer and fall in love with Ansible and Ansible Tower for its friendly user interface and easy-to-follow and understand YAML workflow design. Ansible uses YAML, which has a closer resemblance to an application than a scripted programming language; with Ansible, the users are not expected to know any programming language. Not all network engineers want to become proficient at Python programming; they want a premade tool, so Ansible might be the answer. I firmly believe that Ansible's biggest attraction for many organizations is its low entry barrier (even lower than Python). But at the same time, this is a disappointment from an engineer's perspective, which may lead many engineers to abandon their programming language journey too prematurely.

In this chapter, you will see some quick installation and startup labs. pyATS, along with Nornir, are Cisco-endorsed and developed tools; here you will be introduced to pyATS as a quick startup guide. pyATS is not a programming language; instead, it is a network probing and information gathering tool rather than a configuration tool. For configuration, Nornir can be used, but it is simply a rewritten version of `netmiko` with more user-friendly features, where `netmiko` is an improved version of `paramiko`, which focuses explicitly on multivendor network automation. These are great tools and are worth spending time exploring them. This chapter will also touch on Docker as a resource-saving tool in production. Docker is a containerized solution to run on your Linux or Windows systems. Docker has many use cases in enterprise network automation. Still, Docker is mainly used as an instance on a Linux server to run and execute tasks or applications. Their small footprint can run where a full virtual-machine cannot be justified to run for a single task such as running a nightly system check on a dedicated VM. We will discuss each of these tools further in their respective sections. In the second half of this chapter, you will be guided through setting up two labs on Docker images and learn how Docker can be used. Also, as part of the lab, you will look at how the REST API can be used in Python.

First, you will install Python's `virtualenv` and learn how to work in a Python virtual environment; then you will get introduced to Ansible and pyATS using `virtualenv`. In the third lab, you will install Docker and download my purpose-built Python network automation server from Docker Hub and learn to use a Docker container in place of an actual virtual machine. In some scenarios, Docker might be the best alternative environment to run your stand-alone Python applications without wasting a lot of computing power.

Quick-Start Guide to Ansible: virtualenv Lab 1

While you are developing your Python applications, there are many instances where you want to try to test a new Python module without impacting a production Python server. As discussed in the earlier chapters, Python servers, in general, are implemented on Linux operating systems. As you learn more about Linux operating systems, Linux systems are a joy to operate when everything is working as designed. Still, while introducing new software or, in this case, different Python libraries into a working Python environment, things can and will go horribly wrong. You may have to spend hours troubleshooting incorrectly installed programs and try to remove the software and restore your operating system to good system health. `virutalenv` is a Python tool for creating isolated environments containing their copy of Python, `pip`, and dedicated storage space to keep testing libraries installed from PyPl. It allows the users to work on multiple projects with varying dependencies on the same machine simultaneously. You can think of `virtualenv` as a quick sandbox for Python library testing.

In this lab, you will quickly learn how to set up Python `virtualenv` on your Ubuntu server, create `virtualenv` for Ansible and test-drive Ansible to probe information, and make quick configuration changes on Cisco devices in your lab. Note that Ansible is not a programming language like Python, Perl, or JavaScript; it is a framework that uses YAML to orchestrate IP devices. Underneath Ansible, it is written in Python, and also, for the SSH connection, it relies on `paramiko` as we have learned in Chapter 7.

Many people ask me if they should learn Ansible first or Python first. I think the answer depends on how much each individual wants to know about network automation using Python. Since you have reached this far in this book, you probably know your answer already: learn Python first and then dip your toes into Ansible. Because Ansible from Red Hat (and pyATS [Genie] from Cisco to some extent) is so powerful without the need for engineers to write the real code, it can misguide Python learners to think that there is no need for you to learn Python; this is the biggest drawback of learning Ansible first and Python second.

The following content is a quick startup guide for installing the `virtenv` module on Ubuntu 20.04 LTS server environment. Follow these simple steps to set up your environment to complete the following Ansible startup lab. If you are using CentOS (or any Red Hat) OS, this process changes slightly, but the fundamental features are the same. Figure 16-1 displays the logical connection and the devices used in this lab.

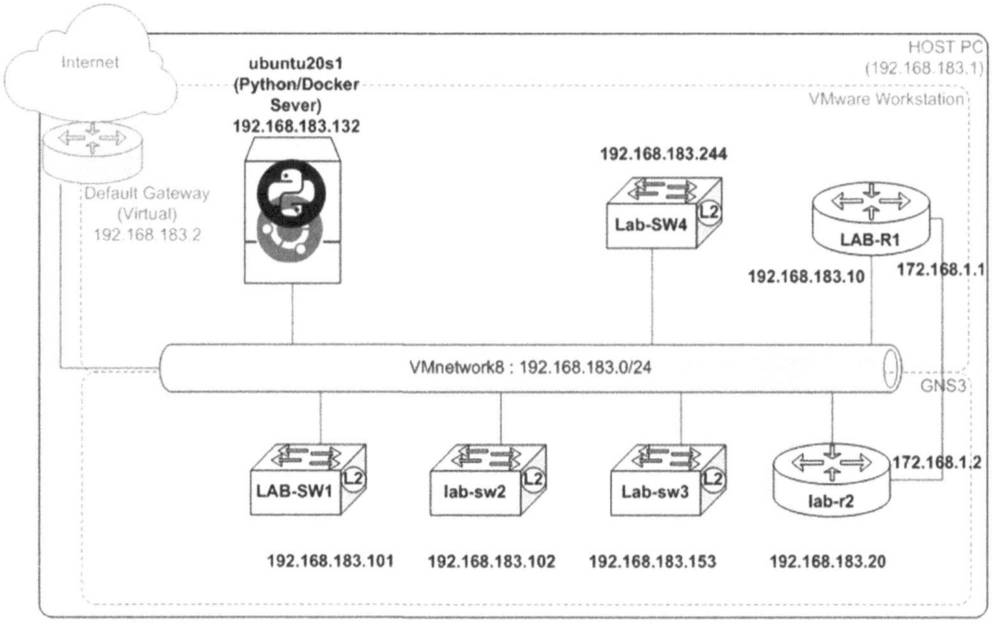

Figure 16-1. *Ansible virtualenv lab used devices*

Installing virtualenv and Getting Started with Ansible

Let's install the `virtualenv` module on your Ubuntu 20 LTS server and set you up for the first lab in this chapter. Follow each step to complete the `virtualenv` installation.

#	Task

1	SSH into your Ubuntu server and perform the following steps to get you up and running for the next lab.
	
	Update and upgrade Ubuntu 20.04 LTS to the latest version using Ubuntu's Advanced Packaging Tool.
	
	`pynetauto@ubuntu20s1:~$ sudo apt update`
	`pynetauto@ubuntu20s1:~$ sudo apt -y upgrade`

2	To make your Python environment more robust, install some extra packages and development tools to ensure that the Linux server is set up for a programming environment. It is best to install these packages as a root user.
	
	`pynetauto@ubuntu20s1:~$ su -`
	`Password: ********`
	`root@ubuntu20s1:~# apt update`
	`root@ubuntu20s1:~# apt-get install -y`
	`root@ubuntu20s1:~# apt install -y build-essential python3-dev libssl-dev libffi-dev`
	`root@ubuntu20s1:~# apt install -y python3-pip`
	`root@ubuntu20s1:~# apt install -y python3-pip`

3	You will be using the venv Python module to configure the `python3` virtual environment, which is part of the standard Python 3 library.
	
	`root@ubuntu20s1:~# apt install -y python3-venv`
	`root@ubuntu20s1:~# apt install sshpass # For ansible ssh login`
	`root@ubuntu20s1:~# su - pynetauto`

4	Use `mkdir` to create a directory (environment) where your virtual environments will live. Use the `cd` command to change into the new directory.
	
	`pynetauto@ubuntu20s1:~$ mkdir venv1`
	`pynetauto@ubuntu20s1:~$ cd venv1`
	`pynetauto@ubuntu20s1:~/venv1$`

5	Once you are in the directory, create your testing environment. Use the `ls` Linux command to view items in your environment directory, in this case, `ansible_venv`.
	
	`pynetauto@ubuntu20s1:~/venv1$ python3 -m venv ansible_venv`
	`pynetauto@ubuntu20s1:~/venv1$ ls ansible_venv`
	`bin  include  lib  lib64  pyvenv.cfg  share`

6	Activate and start your new virtual environment. `./` means the currently working directory or the directory you are working within. Once you have activated your virtual environment, you will see `(ansible_venv)` at the beginning of the CLI.
	
	`pynetauto@ubuntu20s1:~/venv1$ source ./ansible_venv/bin/activate`
	`(ansible_venv) pynetauto@ubuntu20s1:~/venv1$`

#	Task

7	If you have (ansible_venv) in front of your Linux command line, it means you are in the virtual environment. Run Python -V or python3 -V to confirm the Python version. If you only have Python version 3, you can use either Python or Python3 to run your script in this environment.
	`(ansible_venv) pynetauto@ubuntu20s1:~/venv1$ Python -V`
	`Python 3.8.2`
	`(ansible_venv) pynetauto@ubuntu20s1:~/venv1$ python3 -V`
	`Python 3.8.2`

8	To exit or deactivate the environment, use the deactivate command to exit your virtualenv.
	`(ansible_venv) pynetauto@ubuntu20s1:~/venv1$ deactivate`
	`pynetauto@ubuntu20s1:~/venv1$`

9	To reactivate the same environment, if you are already in the netautovenv directory, use the same ./ansible_venv/bin/activate command.
	`pynetauto@ubuntu20s1:~/venv1$ source ./ansible_venv/bin/activate`
	`(ansible_venv) pynetauto@ubuntu20s1:~/venv1$`

10	To start our Ansible lab, install paramiko first and then Ansible using the pip3 install commands. Ansible uses paramiko for its SSH connection into network devices, so it is a prerequisite.
	`pynetauto@ubuntu20s1:~/venv1$ source ./ansible_venv/bin/activate`
	`(ansible_venv) pynetauto@ubuntu20s1:~/venv1$ pip3 install paramiko`
	`(ansible_venv) pynetauto@ubuntu20s1:~/venv1$ pip3 install ansible # install ansible on your virtualenv`
	`(ansible_venv) pynetauto@ubuntu20s1:~/venv1$ ansible --version`
	`ansible 2.9.12`

11	Generate the SSH key on the ubuntu20s1 server again after the Ansible installation.
	`(ansible_venv) pynetauto@ubuntu20s1:~/venv1$ ssh-keygen`
	`Generating public/private rsa key pair.`
	`Enter file in which to save the key (/home/pynetauto/.ssh/id_rsa):`
	`Created directory '/home/pynetauto/.ssh'.`
	`Enter passphrase (empty for no passphrase): **********`
	`Enter same passphrase again: **********`
	`Your identification has been saved in /home/pynetauto/.ssh/id_rsa`
	`[... omitted for brevity]`
	`+----[SHA256]-----+`
	`(ansible_venv) pynetauto@ubuntu20s1:~/venv1$`

12	Use ls ansible_venv/bin/ansible* to check the available commands from Ansible.
	`(ansible_venv) pynetauto@ubuntu20s1:~/netautovenv$ ls ansible_venv/bin/ansible*`
	`ansible_venv/bin/ansible ansible_venv/bin/ansible-console ansible_venv/bin/ansible-inventory ansible_venv/bin/ansible-test ansible_venv/bin/ansible-config ansible_venv/bin/ansible-doc ansible_venv/bin/ansible-playbook ansible_venv/bin/ansible-vault ansible_venv/bin/ansible-connection ansible_venv/bin/ansible-galaxy ansible_venv/bin/ansible-pull`

(continued)

#	Task
13	Next, use the sudo `/home/pynetauto/.ssh/config` command to open the SSH configuration file and add the security key exchange supported by Cisco devices. After the update, your file should look like this:

```
(ansible_venv) pynetauto@ubuntu20s1:~/venv1$ nano /home/pynetauto/.ssh/config
```

Update the ~/.ssh/config file for the correct security key exchange.

```
GNU nano 4.8                  /home/pynetauto/.ssh/config
Host 192.168.183.10
  KexAlgorithms +diffie-hellman-group1-sha1
Host 192.168.183.20
  KexAlgorithms +diffie-hellman-group1-sha1
Host 192.168.183.101
  KexAlgorithms +diffie-hellman-group1-sha1
Host 192.168.183.102
  KexAlgorithms +diffie-hellman-group1-sha1
Host 192.168.183.153
  KexAlgorithms +diffie-hellman-group1-sha1
Host 192.168.183.244
  KexAlgorithms +diffie-hellman-group1-sha1
^G Get Help  ^O Write Out   ^W Where Is   ^K Cut Text    ^J Justify   ^C Cur Pos
^X Exit      ^R Read File   ^\ Replace    ^U Paste Text  ^T To Spell  ^_ Go To Line
```

Now, try to SSH into each device using the following commands. Make sure you can successfully log into each device. Also, R1 uses an old AES type key exchange and has an issue with Ubuntu servers, so it was excluded from this lab. For CML or newer Cisco devices, you can also force the server to use `diffie-hellman-group1-sha1` for the key exchange.

```
(ansible_venv) pynetauto@ubuntu20s1:~/netautovenv$ ssh pynetauto@192.168.183.10
(ansible_venv) pynetauto@ubuntu20s1:~/netautovenv$ ssh pynetauto@192.168.183.20
(ansible_venv) pynetauto@ubuntu20s1:~/netautovenv$ ssh pynetauto@192.168.183.101
(ansible_venv) pynetauto@ubuntu20s1:~/netautovenv$ ssh pynetauto@192.168.183.102
(ansible_venv) pynetauto@ubuntu20s1:~/netautovenv$ ssh -oKexAlgorithms=+diffie-hellman-group1-sha1 pynetauto@192.168.183.153 <<< Force your server to use diffie-hellman-group1-sha1 (Newer IOS)
(ansible_venv) pynetauto@ubuntu20s1:~/netautovenv$ ssh -oKexAlgorithms=+diffie-hellman-group1-sha1 pynetauto@192.168.183.244
```

⚠ It is important that you SSH into each router and switch. On the first prompt, accept the new RSA key fingerprints to allow the SSH connection into each device from your Python server.

```
(ansible_venv) pynetauto@ubuntu20s1:~/venv1/ansible$ ssh pynetauto@192.168.183.244
```

The authenticity of host '192.168.183.244 (192.168.183.244)' can't be established.
RSA key fingerprint is SHA256:1yPe2xGthhAnA9EE+nVBqEmNnW6eHa5i/Xygj8Zu1p4.
Are you sure you want to continue connecting (yes/no/[fingerprint])? **yes**
Warning: Permanently added '192.168.183.244' (RSA) to the list of known hosts.

If you have issues logging in via SSH, open the known_hosts file and clear the entries and attempt the SSH login again.

```
(ansible_venv) pynetauto@ubuntu20s1:~/venv1$ sudo nano /home/pynetauto/.ssh/known_hosts
```

#	Task
14	Now use the Ansible command to log into one of your network devices interactively for the first time. Run the following command for each device in your network. The following example is an SSH login to LAB-R1 (192.168.183.10) using the Ansible ad hoc command.

```
(ansible_venv) pynetauto@ubuntu20s1:~/netautovenv$ ansible all -i 192.168.183.10,
-c network_cli -u pynetauto -k -m ios_facts -e ansible_network_os=ios
SSH password:********
[WARNING]: default value for `gather_subset` will be changed to `min` from `!config`
v2.11 onwards
192.168.183.10 | SUCCESS => {
    "ansible_facts": {
        "ansible_net_all_ipv4_addresses": [
            "192.168.183.10",
            "172.168.1.1"
        ],
        "ansible_net_all_ipv6_addresses": [],
        "ansible_net_api": "cliconf",
        "ansible_net_filesystems": [
            "flash0:"
[...omitted for brevity]
        "ansible_net_iostype": "IOS",
        "ansible_net_memfree_mb": 246866.65625,
        "ansible_net_memtotal_mb": 314934.875,
        "ansible_net_model": "IOSv",
        "ansible_net_neighbors": {},
        "ansible_net_python_version": "3.8.2",
        "ansible_net_serialnum": "9M39W7I30DBU6XCMNZ5GB",
        "ansible_net_system": "ios",
        "ansible_net_version": "15.6(2)T",
        "ansible_network_resources": {},
        "discovered_interpreter_python": "/usr/bin/python3"
    },
    "changed": false
}
(ansible_venv) pynetauto@ubuntu20s1:~/venv1$
```

(continued)

#	Task
15	We can go to Ansible's official site for helpful information and technical documentation. Red Hat offers extensive documentation on how to get started with Ansible and how to use Ansible for network automation.

URL: `https://docs.ansible.com/ansible/latest/network/getting_started/first_playbook.html`

URL: `https://docs.ansible.com/ansible/latest/modules/ios_facts_module.html`

Let's go to the first playbook HTML URL and quickly test what Ansible can do for you. Once you are on the website, go to `first_playbook.yml`, and in your `virtualenv`, create a new YAML file with the same name. Modify it to replace Vyatta with Cisco, and the first playbook will look similar to this. This playbook will fetch the hostname and OS of your device.

```
(ansible_venv) pynetauto@ubuntu20s1:~/venv1$ pwd
/home/pynetauto/venv1
(ansible_venv) pynetauto@ubuntu20s1:~/venv1$ nano first_playbook.yml
```

```
GNU nano 4.8                    first_playbook.yml
--- # indicates that this is a YAML file

- name: Network Getting Started First Playbook
  connection: network_cli
  gather_facts: false
  hosts: all
  tasks:

    - name: Get config for Cisco devices
      ios_facts:
        gather_subset: all

    - name: Display the config
      debug:
        msg: "The hostname is {{ ansible_net_hostname }} and the OS is {{ ansible_
        net_version }}"

^G Get Help  ^O Write Out   ^W Where Is   ^K Cut Text    ^J Justify    ^C Cur Pos
^X Exit      ^R Read File   ^\ Replace    ^U Paste Text  ^T To Spell   ^_ Go To Line
```

source: `https://docs.ansible.com/ansible/latest/network/getting_started/first_playbook.html`

#	Task
16	Follow the documentation to run `first_playbook.yml`. The following example uses `LAB-R1`, but you can use another device's IP address to run the `ansible-playbook` command. You have now run your first `ansible-playbook`

```
(ansible_venv) pynetauto@ubuntu20s1:~/netautovenv$ ansible-playbook -i
192.168.183.10, -u pynetauto -k -e ansible_network_os=ios first_playbook.yml
SSH password: ********

PLAY [Network Getting Started First Playbook] **************************************

TASK [Get config for Cisco IOS devices] *******************************************
[WARNING]: default value for `gather_subset` will be changed to `min` from `!config`
v2.11 onwards
ok: [192.168.183.10]
```

#	Task

```
TASK [Display the config] ********************************************************
ok: [192.168.183.10] => {
    "msg": "The hostname is LAB-R1 and the OS is 15.6(2)T"
}

PLAY RECAP ***********************************************************************
192.168.183.10             : ok=2    changed=0    unreachable=0    failed=0
skipped=0    rescued=0    ignored=0
```

17 Now create a simple show_clock.yml to get the time on a device. Since we do not want to reinvent the wheel, we will be borrowing an old Ansible playbook to perform the show clock on your device. The source code location is referenced after the code.

```
(ansible_venv) pynetauto@ubuntu20s1:~/venv1$ nano show_clock.yml

GNU nano 4.8                show_clock.yml
---
- hosts: all
  gather_facts: no
  connection: local

  vars_prompt:
  - name: "mgmt_username"
    prompt: "Username"
    private: no
  - name: "mgmt_password"
    prompt: "Password"

  tasks:

  - name: SYS | Define provider
    set_fact:
      provider:
        host: "{{ inventory_hostname }}"
        username: "{{ mgmt_username }}"
        password: "{{ mgmt_password }}"

  - name: IOS | Show clock
    ios_command:
      provider: "{{ provider }}"
      commands:
        - show clock
    register: clock

  - debug: msg="{{ clock.stdout }}"

^G Get Help  ^O Write Out   ^W Where Is   ^K Cut Text    ^J Justify   ^C Cur Pos
^X Exit      ^R Read File   ^\ Replace    ^U Paste Text  ^T To Spell  ^_ Go To Line
```

source: https://github.com/brona/ansible-cisco-ios-example/blob/master/show_clock.yml

(continued)

#	Task

18 Now to check the time on your devices, run the following `ansible-playbook` command. Note that this virtual environment does not affect the actual host Linux OS or other software installed on your virtual machine. Ansible will work only within this virtual environment, and once `ansible_venv` gets deactivated, you no longer will have access to Ansible until you reactivate `ansible_venv`.

The following is an example of playbook run on `lab-sw2` (192.168.183.102).

```
(ansible_venv) pynetauto@ubuntu20s1:~/netautovenv$ ansible-playbook -i
192.168.183.102, -u pynetauto -k -e ansible_network_os=ios show_clock.yml
SSH password:********
Username: pynetauto
Password: ********

PLAY [show clock] ******************************************************************

TASK [SYS | Define provider] *******************************************************
ok: [192.168.183.102]

TASK [IOS | Show clock] ************************************************************
[WARNING]: provider is unnecessary when using network_cli and will be ignored
ok: [192.168.183.102]

TASK [debug] ***********************************************************************
ok: [192.168.183.102] => {
    "msg": [
        "*19:17:03.351 UTC Wed Jan 13 2021"
    ]
}
PLAY RECAP *************************************************************************
192.168.183.102            : ok=3    changed=0    unreachable=0    failed=0
skipped=0    rescued=0    ignored=0
```

19 Now, deactivate the testing Python virtual environment and check if you have Ansible installed on your local server.

```
(ansible_venv) pynetauto@ubuntu20s1:~/venv1/ansible$ deactivate
pynetauto@ubuntu20s1:~/venv1/ansible$ python3
Python 3.8.2 (default, Jul 16 2020, 14:00:26)
[GCC 9.3.0] on linux
Type "help", "copyright", "credits" or "license" for more information.
>>> import ansible
Traceback (most recent call last):
File "<stdin>", line 1, in <module>
ModuleNotFoundError: No module named 'ansible'
```

You have just learned how to use `virtualenv`. You installed Ansible on your Python virtual environment and got a brief introduction to Ansible as a network tool. Ansible is a great configuration management tool and a must-have a toolset. But, this is not a book about Ansible or network automation using Ansible. This is where the Ansible discussion ends in this book. If you want to learn more about Ansible, you should visit Red Hat's official Ansible site or purchase a separate Ansible book to extend your knowledge.

Next, let's install pyATS within Python `virtualenv` and find out how pyATS differs from other tools.

Quick-Start Guide to pyATS (Genie): VirtualEnv Lab 2

pyATS is the core framework supported within Cisco Systems, and it was initially developed for the internal Cisco engineering team's use. It uses the Genie library as the pyATS standard library and XPRESSO for the pyATS web dashboard. At the moment, pyATS is at the core of Cisco's test automation solution. This tool is relatively new to the networking community as a networking automation tool. It is more of an information gathering and network system monitoring tool than a real configuration management tool like Red Hat's Ansible.

pyATS is more of a supplementary tool than the primary automation tool. Some of the supported features include the following:

- Cisco's default test framework for internal Cisco engineers across different platform/functions, running millions of CI/CD, sanity, regression, scale, HA, solution
- Used by millions of engineers and developers
- A standard open source, platform/vendor-agnostic library system (Genie)
- A web dashboard to manage your test suites, testbeds, test results, and their insights (XPRESSO)
- Integration support for other integration tools in the form of libraries, extensions, plugins, and APIs
- Support for building customers' business logic and solutions on top of the infrastructure stack
- Primarily focuses on Cisco devices

The following are links to Cisco's official pyATS documentation and getting-started guide. If you plan to remain within the Cisco networking space, it is worth reading about pyATS and Nonir. But if you have bigger plans for your network automation use cases, stick to network automation tools, which are more vendor-neutral. See Figure 16-2.

URL: `https://developer.cisco.com/docs/pyats/` (pyATS introduction)

URL: `https://developer.cisco.com/docs/pyats-getting-started/` (pyATS getting started)

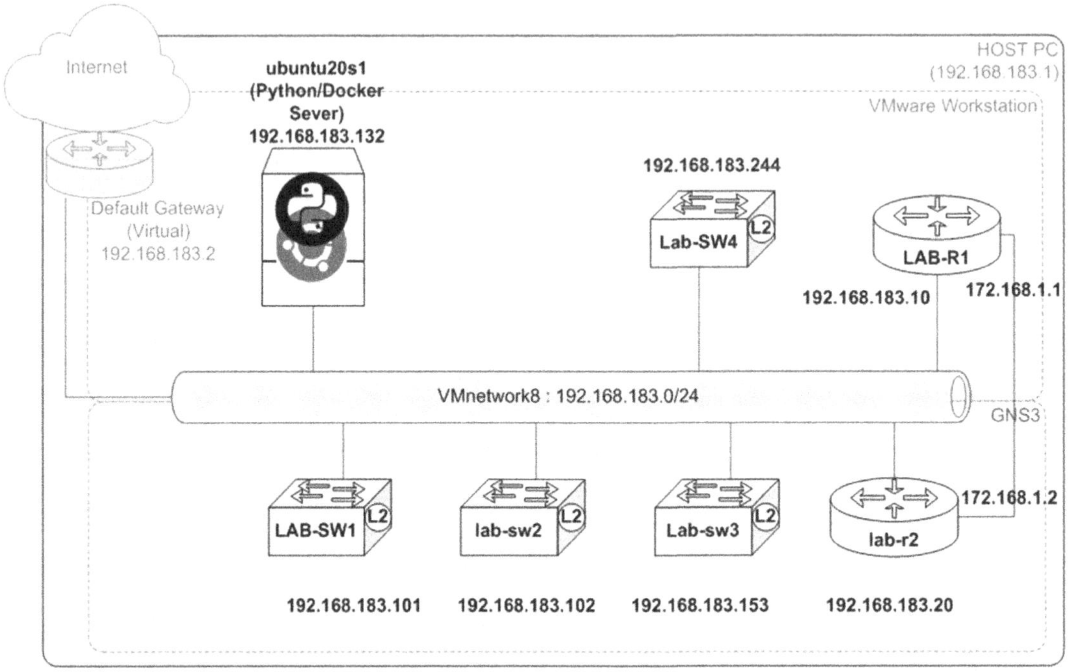

Figure 16-2. *pyATS virtualenv lab used devices*

As in the previous `virtualenv` lab, you will be creating a new directory and running `virtualenv` in the new directory. Follow these steps to start your new `virtualenv` for pyATS.

#	Task
1	Create a new directory called `mygenie` and `cd` into the new directory. Once you are inside the directory, create a new virtual environment to test pyATS. To create and activate the pyATS test environment, type in the following commands:
2	Install pyATS with the library. You may get some `bdist_wheel`-related messages, but you can ignore the messages and continue.

Step 1 commands:

```
pynetauto@ubuntu20s1:~/venv1$ mkdir mygenie
pynetauto@ubuntu20s1:~/venv1$ cd mygenie
pynetauto@ubuntu20s1:~/venv1/mygenie$ python3 -m venv genie_venv
pynetauto@ubuntu20s1:~/venv1/mygenie$ ls genie_venv
bin  include  lib  lib64  pyvenv.cfg  share
pynetauto@ubuntu20s1:~/venv1/mygenie$ source ./genie_venv/bin/activate
(genie_venv) pynetauto@ubuntu20s1:~/venv1/mygenie$
```

Step 2 command:

```
(genie_venv) pynetauto@ubuntu20s1:~/venv1/mygenie$ pip3 install pyATS[library]
```

#	Task

3	Run the `git clone` command to download the examples from GitHub.com.
	`(genie_venv) pynetauto@ubuntu20s1:~/venv1/mygenie$ `**`git clone`**` https://github.com/CiscoTestAutomation/examples`
	`Cloning into 'examples'...`
	`remote: Enumerating objects: 142, done.`
	`remote: Counting objects: 100% (142/142), done.`
	`remote: Compressing objects: 100% (103/103), done.`
	`remote: Total 765 (delta 58), reused 94 (delta 32), pack-reused 623`
	`Receiving objects: 100% (765/765), 1.03 MiB | 1.05 MiB/s, done.`
	`Resolving deltas: 100% (385/385), done.`

4	Then run the `pyats run job` command to check the operational status of pyATS. If `basic_example_job.py` runs successfully, then your installation is good, and you are ready to go. `(genie_venv) pynetauto@ubuntu20s1:~/venv1/mygenie$ `**`cd examples`** `(genie_venv) pynetauto@ubuntu20s1:~/venv1/mygenie/examples$ `**`pyats run job basic/basic_example_job.py`**
5	Before moving further, you must install extra libraries for Excel, a prerequisite for pyATS to work correctly later. `(genie_venv) pynetauto@ubuntu20s1:~/venv1/mygenie/examples$ `**`cd ..`** `(genie_venv) pynetauto@ubuntu20s1:~/venv1/mygenie$ `**`pip3 install xlrd xlwt xlsxwriter`**
6	Genie uses a YAML testbed JSON file for device connection and authentication. Install `pyats.contrib`, which is a requirement. `(genie) pynetauto@ubuntu20s:~/genie$ `**`pip3 install pyats.contrib`**

7	Next, create a `testbed.yml` file to be used for authentication. Use the same `pyats create` command to help you create a `testbed.yml` file. The following example is creating a `testbed.yml` file for switch 3 and switch 4:
	`(genie_venv) pynetauto@ubuntu20s1:~/venv1/mygenie$ `**`genie create testbed interactive --output testbed.yml --encode-password`**
	`Start creating Testbed yaml file ...`
	`Do all of the devices have the same username? [y/n] y`
	`Common Username: `**`pynetauto`**
	
	`Do all of the devices have the same default password? [y/n] y`
	`Common Default Password (leave blank if you want to enter on demand):`
	
	`Do all of the devices have the same enable password? [y/n] y`
	`Common Enable Password (leave blank if you want to enter on demand):`
	
	`Device hostname: `**`Lab-sw3`**
	`   IP (ip, or ip:port): `**`192.168.183.153`**
	`   Protocol (ssh, Telnet, ...): ssh`
	`   OS (iosxr, iosxe, ios, nxos, linux, ...): `**`iosxe`**
	`More devices to add ? [y/n] `**`y`**

(continued)

#	Task

	`Device hostname:` **`Lab-SW4`**
	`IP (ip, or ip:port):` **`192.168.183.244`**
	Protocol (ssh, telnet, ...): ssh
	`OS (iosxr, iosxe, ios, nxos, linux, ...):` **`iosxe`**
	`More devices to add ? [y/n]` **`n`**
	`Testbed file generated:`
	`testbed.yml`

■ **Note** Depending on the version of pyATS installed, the previous command `genie create testbed interactive --output testbed.yml --encode-password` needs to be replaced with the `pyats create testbed interactive --output testbed.yml --encode-password` command.

#	Task
8	Quickly review the newly created `testbed.yml` file.

```
(genie_venv) pynetauto@ubuntu20s1:~/venv1/mygenie$ cat testbed.yml
devices:
  Lab-SW4:
    connections:
      cli:
        ip: 192.168.183.244
        protocol: ssh
    credentials:
      default:
        password: '%ENC{w5PDosOUw5fDosKQwpbCmA==}'
        username: pynetauto
      enable:
        password: '%ENC{w5PDosOUw5fDosKQwpbCmA==}'
    os: iosxe
    type: iosxe
  Lab-sw3:
    connections:
    cli:
      ip: 192.168.183.153
      protocol: ssh
    credentials:
      default:
        password: '%ENC{w5PDosOUw5fDosKQwpbCmA==}'
        username: pynetauto
      enable:
        password: '%ENC{w5PDosOUw5fDosKQwpbCmA==}'
    os: iosxe
    type: iosxe
```

#	Task
9	First, use the genie parse command, followed by the show version commands on both switches. You can use the device name to run the command as follows. The following example displays the result from switch 4.

For Lab-sw3:

```
(genie_venv) pynetauto@ubuntu20s1:~/venv1/mygenie$ genie parse "show version"
--testbed-file testbed.yml --devices Lab-sw3
  0%|                                                         | 0/1 [00:00<?, ?it/s]{
  "version": {
    "chassis_sn": "93RJPGR4I08",
    "compiled_by": "mmen",
    "compiled_date": "Wed 22-Mar-17 08:38",
    "curr_config_register": "0x101",
    "hostname": "Lab-sw3",
    "image_id": "vios_l2-ADVENTERPRISEK9-M",
    "image_type": "developer image",
    "last_reload_reason": "Unknown reason",
    "mem_size": {
      "non-volatile configuration": "256"
    },
    "number_of_intfs": {
    "Gigabit Ethernet": "16",
    "Virtual Ethernet": "1"
    },
    "os": "IOS",
    "platform": "vios_l2",
    "processor_board_flash": "OK",
    "returned_to_rom_by": "reload",
    "rom": "Bootstrap program is IOSv",
    "system_image": "flash0:/vios_l2-adventerprisek9-m",
    "uptime": "1 hour, 47 minutes",
    "version": "15.2(20170321:233949)",
    "version_short": "15.2"
  }
}
100%|██████████████████████████████████████████████████| 1/1 [00:01<00:00,  1.17s/it]
```

For Lab-SW4:

```
(genie_venv) pynetauto@ubuntu20s1:~/venv1/mygenie$ genie parse "show version"
--testbed-file testbed.yml --devices Lab-SW4
  0%|                                                         | 0/1 [00:00<?, ?it/s]{
  "version": {
    "chassis_sn": "9B66XQMVHID",
    "compiled_by": "mmen",
    "compiled_date": "Wed 22-Mar-17 08:38",
    "curr_config_register": "0x101",
    "hostname": "Lab-SW4",
    "image_id": "vios_l2-ADVENTERPRISEK9-M",
```

(*continued*)

#	Task

```
    "image_type": "developer image",
    "last_reload_reason": "Unknown reason",
    "mem_size": {
      "non-volatile configuration": "256"
    },
    "number_of_intfs": {
      "Gigabit Ethernet": "16",
      "Virtual Ethernet": "1"
    },
    "os": "IOS",
    "platform": "vios_l2",
    "processor_board_flash": "OK",
    "returned_to_rom_by": "reload",
    "rom": "Bootstrap program is IOSv",
    "system_image": "flash0:/vios_l2-adventerprisek9-m",
    "uptime": "1 hour, 51 minutes",
    "version": "15.2(20170321:233949)",
    "version_short": "15.2"
  }
}
100%|
                                                     | 1/1 [00:00<00:00,  1.38it/s]
```

10 Use the following genie parse command to retrieve your device information:

```
(genie_venv) pynetauto@ubuntu20s1:~/venv1/mygenie$ genie parse "show ip int brief"
--testbed-file testbed.yml --devices Lab-sw3
  0%|                                                  | 0/1 [00:00<?, ?it/s]{
  "interface": {
    "GigabitEthernet0/0": {
      "interface_is_ok": "YES",
      "ip_address": "unassigned",
      "method": "unset",
      "protocol": "up",
      "status": "up"
    },
[...omitted for brevity]
    "Vlan1": {
      "interface_is_ok": "YES",
      "ip_address": "192.168.183.153",
      "method": "NVRAM",
      "protocol": "up",
      "status": "up"
    }
  }
}
100%|
                                                     | 1/1 [00:00<00:00,  1.08it/s]
```

#	Task
11	Modify `testbed.yml` in the nano text editor to include all CML routers and switches. Leave `SW3` and `SW4` to use Telnet and configure others to use SSH for testing purposes. Optionally, you can rerun the `pyats create testbed interactive --output testbed.yml --encode-password` command to re-create this file. You can find the `testbed.yml` file from the download page for this chapter. Because of the page restrictions, parts of the content have been omitted.

```
(genie_venv) pynetauto@ubuntu20s1:~/venv1/mygenie$ pyats create testbed interactive
--output testbed.yml --encode-password
(genie_venv) pynetauto@ubuntu20s1:~/venv1/mygenie$ cat testbed.yml
devices:
  LAB-R1:
    connections:
      cli:
        ip: 192.168.183.10
        protocol: ssh
    credentials:
      default:
        password: '%ENC{w5PDosOUw5fDosKQwpbCmA==}'
        username: pynetauto
      enable:
        password: '%ENC{w5PDosOUw5fDosKQwpbCmA==}'
    os: iosxe
    type: iosxe
[... omitted for brevity]
  lab-sw2:
    connections:
      cli:
        ip: 192.168.183.102
        protocol: ssh
    credentials:
      default:
        password: '%ENC{w5PDosOUw5fDosKQwpbCmA==}'
        username: pynetauto
      enable:
        password: '%ENC{w5PDosOUw5fDosKQwpbCmA==}'
    os: iosxe
    type: iosxe
```

(continued)

#	Task
12	Use the following commands to test-drive Genie:

```
(genie_venv) pynetauto@ubuntu20s1:~/venv1/mygenie$ genie parse "show clock"
--testbed-file testbed.yml --devices[hostname]
  0%|                                                     | 0/1 [00:00<?, ?it/s]{
  "day": "13",
  "day_of_week": "Wed",
  "month": "Jan",
  "time": "20:02:59.396",
  "timezone": "UTC",
  "year": "2021"
}
100%|[redacted]| 1/1 [00:00<00:00,  1.50it/s]
[...omitted for brevity]
  0%|                                                     | 0/1 [00:00<?, ?it/s]{
  "day": "13",
  "day_of_week": "Wed",
  "month": "Jan",
  "time": "19:59:35.229",
  "timezone": "UTC",
  "year": "2021"
}
```

Now change the show command and run the show cdp neigh command on multiple devices.

```
(genie_venv) pynetauto@ubuntu20s1:~/venv1/mygenie$ genie parse "show cdp neigh"
--testbed-file testbed.yml --devices[hostname]
  0%|                                                   | 0/1 [00:00<?, ?it/s]
Parsed command 'show cdp neigh' but it returned empty
100%|[redacted]| 1/1 [00:00<00:00,  1.28it/s]
  0%|                                                   | 0/1 [00:00<?, ?it/s]{
  "cdp": {
    "index": {
      "1": {
        "capability": "S I",
        "device_id": "Lab-sw3.pynetauto.local",
        "hold_time": 141,
        "local_interface": "GigabitEthernet0/0",
        "platform": "Gig",
        "port_id": "0/0"
      },
```

#	Task

```
    "2": {
      "capability": "S I",
      "device_id": "Lab-SW4.pynetauto.local",
      "hold_time": 146,
      "local_interface": "GigabitEthernet0/0",
      "platform": "Gig",
      "port_id": "0/0"
    },
[...omitted for brevity]
```

If the connected interface has CDP disabled, the result will come back as an error: `Parsed command 'show cdp neigh' but it returned empty`. You may have to enable the `cdp enable` command on the affected interface.

13 Let's quickly install the pandas library to be used in this lab. If you already have pandas installed, you can skip this step. Let's install the pandas module for data analytics and store the data to Excel.

```
(genie_venv) pynetauto@ubuntu20s1:~/venv1/mygenie$ pip3 install pandas
```

14 pyATS is an excellent tool endorsed by Cisco and its internal engineering team, but where is its real power? If the data collection power of pyATS is combined with the power of Python's data handling, this will allow us to collect and store data with minor effort.

Here is an example of pyATS combined with Python re (the regular expression module) in an interactive session. You can combine pyATS with a Python regular expression and use any of the values as variables or store them into Excel files. This is an interactive example that you can follow along with, but what you have typed can also be saved as a script file with a `.py` extension.

```
(genie_venv) pynetauto@ubuntu20s1:~/venv1/mygenie$ python3
Python 3.8.2 (default, Jul 16 2020, 14:00:26)
[GCC 9.3.0] on linux
Type "help", "copyright", "credits" or "license" for more information.
>>> import os
>>> show_ver = os.popen('genie parse "show version" --testbed-file testbed.yml
--devices[hostname]')
100%|████████████████████████████████████████| 1/1 [00:00<00:00,  1.54it/s]
100%|████████████████████████████████████████| 1/1 [00:00<00:00,  2.84it/s]
100%|████████████████████████████████████████| 1/1 [00:00<00:00,  2.80it/s]
100%|████████████████████████████████████████| 1/1 [00:00<00:00,  2.07it/s]
100%|████████████████████████████████████████| 1/1 [00:00<00:00,  3.48it/s]
100%|████████████████████████████████████████| 1/1 [00:00<00:00,  2.41it/s]
```

(continued)

#	Task

```
# Press [Enter] key once.

>>> output = show_ver.read()
>>> print(output)
{
  "version": {
    "chassis": "IOSv",
    "chassis_sn": "9M39W7I3ODBU6XCMNZ5GB",
    "compiled_by": "prod_rel_team",
    "compiled_date": "Tue 22-Mar-16 16:19",
    "curr_config_register": "0x0",
    "hostname": "LAB-R1",
    "image_id": "VIOS-ADVENTERPRISEK9-M",
    "image_type": "production image",
    "last_reload_reason": "Unknown reason",
    "main_mem": "460017",
    "mem_size": {
      "non-volatile configuration": "256"
    },
[...omitted for brevity]
{
  "version": {
    "chassis_sn": "93GM5TOAAL2",
    "compiled_by": "mmen",
    "compiled_date": "Wed 22-Mar-17 08:38",
    "curr_config_register": "0x101",
    "hostname": "lab-sw2",
    "image_id": "vios_l2-ADVENTERPRISEK9-M",
    "image_type": "developer image",
    "last_reload_reason": "Unknown reason",
    "mem_size": {
      "non-volatile configuration": "256"
    },
    "number_of_intfs": {
      "Gigabit Ethernet": "16",
      "Virtual Ethernet": "1"
    },
    "os": "IOS",
    "platform": "vios_l2",
    "processor_board_flash": "OK",
    "returned_to_rom_by": "reload",
    "rom": "Bootstrap program is IOSv",
    "system_image": "flash0:/vios_l2-adventerprisek9-m",
    "uptime": "2 hours, 25 minutes",
    "version": "15.2(20170321:233949)",
    "version_short": "15.2"
  }
}
```

#	Task
15	As confirmed in the interactive session, the output data type is a string type that is saved to the variable output.

```
>>> type(output)
<class 'str'>
```

Import the re module and use one of the cool regular expressions you learned in Chapter 5 to capture the specific information you are after. Here, the example uses lookahead (?=) and lookbehind (?<=) regular expression examples.

In the following code, a positive lookbehind and positive lookahead are used to get the hostnames of each device from the output in the previous step:

```
>>> import re
>>> p1 = re.compile(r'(?<=\"hostname\": \").+(?=\")')
>>> m1 = p1.findall(output)
>>> m1
['LAB-R1', 'LAB-SW1', 'Lab-SW4', 'Lab-sw3', 'lab-r2', 'lab-sw2']
```

In the following lines, once again, lookbehind and lookahead are used to get each device's uptime from the output:

```
>>> p2 = re.compile(r'(?<=\"uptime\": \").+(?=\")')
>>> m2 = p2.findall(output)
>>> m2
['6 hours, 52 minutes', '6 hours, 52 minutes', '12 hours, 14 minutes', '10 hours, 13
minutes', '12 hours, 12 minutes', '10 hours, 39 minutes']
```

We want to convert the uptime information into a bar graph using Python, so you must first convert the hours and minutes into the correct decimal format. Take a look at the following conversion to convert the time into two decimal places. The following Python code will work only if all of your devices have been up and running for more than an hour, so the output of the uptime is "x hours y minutes."

```
>>> uptime = [] # create empty list called uptime
>>> for x in m2: # for loop to call out each item in list m2
...     y = [int(s) for s in x.split() if s.isdigit()] # If string is a digit, then
save it as y
...     z = (y[1]/60) # y[1] or the second number from y is minute value, divide it by
60 minutes and convert it into a decimal points
...     a = round(y[0] + z, 2) # y[0] or the first number from y is hour value, combine
it with z, then roud it to 2 decimal places
...     uptime.append(a) # append the value a to uptime list
...
>>> print(uptime) # print the result of uptime list
[6.87, 6.87, 12.23, 10.22, 12.2, 10.65]
```

(*continued*)

#	Task

If your devices' uptime is less than 60 minutes, use the following Python code instead:

```
>>> uptime = []
>>> for x in m2:
...     y = [int(s) for s in x.split() if s.isdigit()]
...     z = (y[0]/60)
...     a = round(z, 2)
...     uptime.append(a)
...
>>> print(uptime)
[0.25, 0.22, 0.24, 0.19, 0.18, 0.21]
```

Now, use the dictionary zip feature to turn the two lists into a Python dictionary. We need to combine the device name list and uptime list in decimal using the dict(zip(m1, uptime)) function. The outcome should look as follows:

```
>>> device_uptime = dict(zip(m1,uptime)) # Combine m1 and uptime lists and make them into a dictionary
>>> print(device_uptime) # display device_uptime dictionary
{'LAB-R1': 6.87, 'LAB-SW1': 6.87, 'Lab-SW4': 12.23, 'Lab-sw3': 10.22, 'lab-r2': 12.2, 'lab-sw2': 10.65}
```

Let's use the pandas module to turn the dictionary into a pandas dataframe and save it as an Excel spreadsheet for reporting purposes. While converting the dictionary into a pandas dataframe, you will add the headers: host for device names and uptime for running time. The key success factor in Python network automation is how you can process and handle this crucial data to suit you and your company's needs.

```
>>> type(device_uptime) # Check type
<class 'dict'>
>>> import pandas as pd # import pandas
>>> df = pd.DataFrame(list(device_uptime.items()),columns = ['host','uptime'])
# convert to dataframe
>>> df # Check dataframe
host  uptime
0    LAB-R1    6.87
1   LAB-SW1    6.87
2   Lab-SW4   12.23
3   Lab-sw3   10.22
4    lab-r2   12.20
5   lab-sw2   10.65
>>> df.to_excel('device_uptime.xlsx') # Write data frame to excel using panda's to_
excel feature.
```

16 Check if the file exists in the mygenie directory. Use WinSCP to log into the ubuntu20s1 server via SCP, download a copy of the device_uptime.xlsx file to your Windows host PC, and open it in Excel to confirm the data has been correctly saved in Excel format. See Figure 16-3 and Figure 16-4.

```
pynetauto@ubuntu20s1:~$ cd venv1
pynetauto@ubuntu20s1:~/venv1$ cd mygenie
pynetauto@ubuntu20s1:~/venv1/mygenie$ ls
device_uptime.xlsx  examples  genie_venv  testbed.yml
```

#	Task

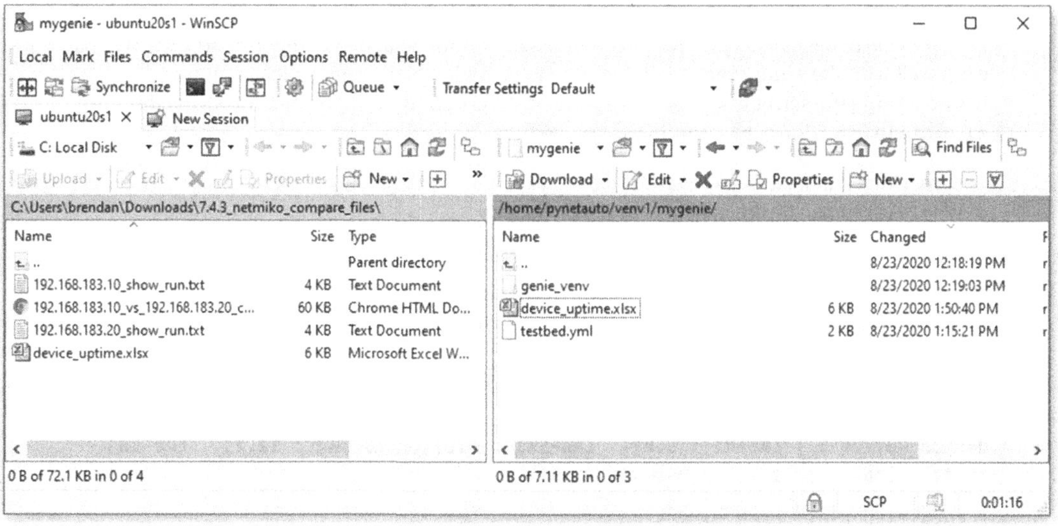

Figure 16-3. WinSCP, retrieving device_uptime.xlsx from ubuntu20s1 server

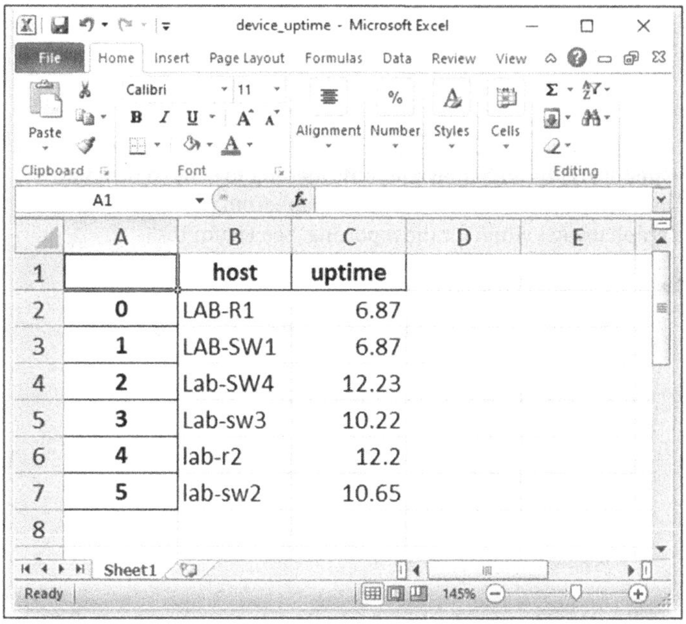

Figure 16-4. Host PC, opening device_uptime.xlsx in Excel

#	Task
17	Now, on your Windows host PC (or desktop of your Ubuntu server), you can write some simple Python code to convert the dictionary from step 15 and convert it into a graph. You also can read the Excel file using pandas and convert it into a dataframe to achieve the same result. (This will not work well with the Linux command line as it does not have direct graphical support.) Before writing the script from your Windows host PC's command prompt, install pandas and matplotlib using the pip3 commands shown here:

```
C:\Users\brendan>cd Desktop
C:\Users\brendan\Desktop>pip3 install pandas
C:\Users\brendan\Desktop>pip3 install matplotlib
```

Write the following code and save the script on your Windows desktop. Create a Python file on your Windows desktop and save it as device_uptime_graph.py.

```
import matplotlib.pyplot as plt # import matplotlib library
import pandas as pd # import pandas library

device_uptime = {'LAB-R1': 6.87, 'LAB-SW1': 6.87, 'Lab-SW4': 12.23, 'Lab-sw3':
10.22, 'lab-r2': 12.2, 'lab-sw2': 10.65}

# Resulting dictionary from step 15
df = pd.DataFrame(list(device_uptime.items()),columns = ['host','uptime']) # Convert
dictionary into pandas dataframe with column titles 'host' & 'uptime'

#print(df)
df.plot(kind='bar',x='host',y='uptime') # Plot a bar graph with host as x-axis and
uptime(float) as y-axis
plt.show() # Display graph
```

Now, run the script from PowerShell or Windows command prompt or double-click the script. If everything works correctly, your data will come out as a bar graph, as shown here. Alternatively, you can turn them into different types of graphs and apply the same method to convert data into dataframes and create graphs as you want. You can create the same graph from Excel, but you now know another method to create a graph using Python for the reporting. See Figure 16-5.

```
C:\Users\brendan\Desktop>python device_uptime_graph.py
```

#	Task
	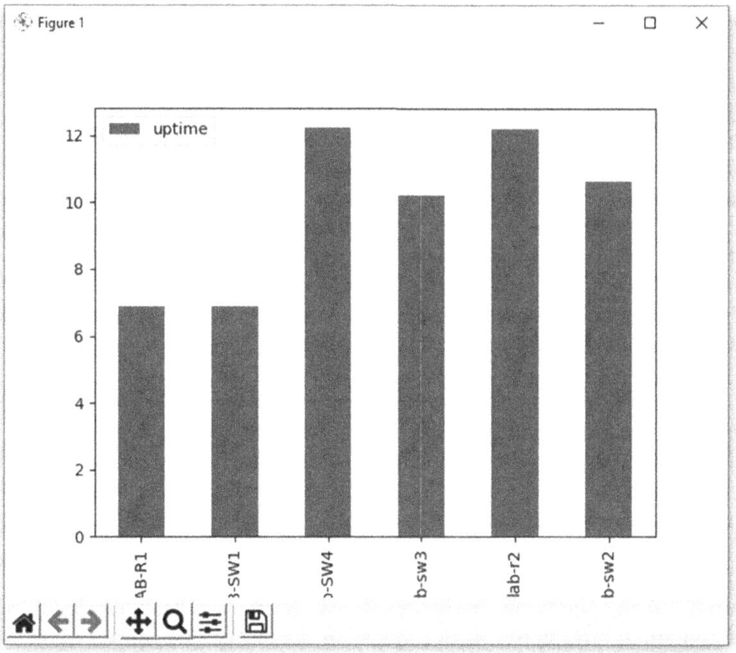 ***Figure 16-5.*** *matplotlib graph of device uptime example*
18	At the end of this lab, make sure you use the `deactivate` command and stop the virtual environment. `(genie_venv) pynetauto@ubuntu20s1:~/venv1/mygenie$` **`deactivate`** `pynetauto@ubuntu20s1:~/venv1/mygenie$`

You have been introduced to Cisco's own pyATS to help you with your network automation journey. You have used Python's re module to collect devices' system uptime data, then used `pandas` module to convert the data into a pandas data frame. As the last step, you have converted the data into a simple bar graph using the `matplotlib` libraries. The task of converting data to a graph is referred to as data visualization.

If you want to run the previous lab from Ubuntu Server's desktop, try to install the VMware Workstation tool first to make copying and pasting easier between your Windows host PC and your Linux VM. Follow the instructions at the following URL and use "Method 2: Install from VMware Host."

URL: `https://websiteforstudents.com/how-to-install-vmware-guest-tools-on-ubuntu-20-04-18-04/`

Sendmail Lab Using an Imported Docker Image

Docker is an open platform for distributed applications for developers and system administrators, and its motto is "Build, ship, run." It is a scalable container management service. It is another virtual technology that can help you succeed with the deployment of a Linux network automation server into production and only utilize a minor portion of the server resources. Docker was first introduced in March 2013, and it is a container based on the platform as a service software application. Docker uses virtualization technology to provide isolated containers for software and tools. These containers use well-defined channels to communicate between the host and Docker containers. It also provides a framework to isolate an application and its dependencies on a self-contained unit called *containers*. The Docker containers are similar to virtual machines, but Docker is a virtual machine without its kernels and operating system, and the containers have to rely on the hosting server's kernel for operation. Containerization has become the buzzword in the IT world because companies can do more with fewer server resources, especially in Agile and DevOps-based projects. In other words, Docker solutions orchestrated through Kubernetes can save hundreds and thousands of dollars for companies by improving the utilization of IT resources and reducing the cost of operation per node.

The famous slogan of Docker is "develop, ship, and run anywhere." Docker is a developer's tool that helps them develop applications quickly and ship them into containers that can then be deployed anywhere in the network. Docker has a tiny footprint as it relies on the host server's local resources, and it is not a virtual machine in a true sense as it does not have its own operating system. Docker container images are simply runnable instances or processes of a snapshot image. You can create, start, stop, move, or delete a container. Although a container does not have its operating system, it runs with its file system, own networking, and own isolated process tree separate from the host. It becomes easier for teams across different units, such as development, QA, and operations, to work seamlessly across applications with containers. You can deploy Docker containers anywhere, on any physical or virtual machine, and even on the cloud.

If we have to cover Docker in less than 20 pages, it would be best to get your hands dirty with a real image. You can learn about Docker at your own pace, outside of this book. Here, to fast-forward your progress, you will be downloading a prestaged Python network automation Docker image from Docker Hub and using the downloaded image to test-drive a Python lab as you have been doing with the `ubuntu20s1` and `centos8s1` servers. See Figure 16-6.

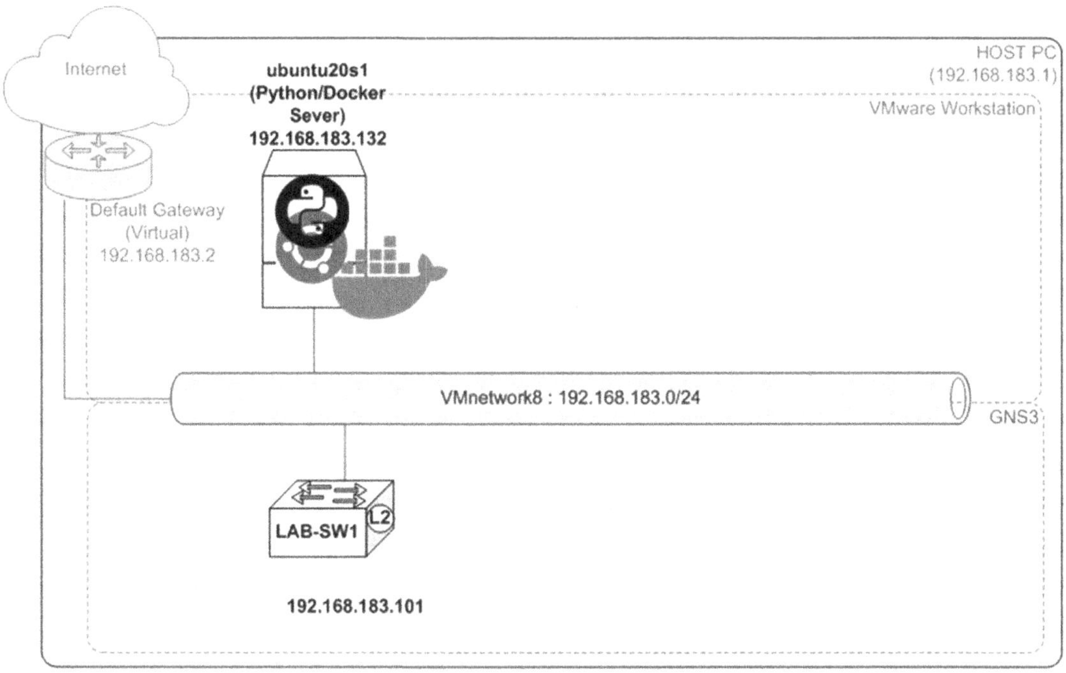

Figure 16-6. *Sendmail Docker lab, used devices*

Docker Components and Account Registration

Docker is like a purpose-built virtual machine without the burden of carrying a full operating system as it relies on the host's Linux kernels to run on a tiny footprint. You can spin up many Docker containers on a single platform without the system resource contention issues. Let's quickly go over what components make up a Docker solution; we will not go into too much detail as we want to focus on the practical side of Docker.

Docker has the following components:

- Docker has cross-platform support; it can be installed on Linux, macOS, and Windows as a service.
- Docker Engine is used for building Docker images and creating Docker containers.
- Docker Hub is the registry that is used to host various Docker images.
- Docker Compose is used to define applications using multiple Docker containers.

Docker account registration is required to use the full Docker features online. After the registration, we can tap into hundreds of purpose-built Docker images without a sweat and have our applications up and running in no time. To log in and download a Docker image from Docker Hub, you will need a Docker Hub account. To get you ready for this lab, please go to the following URL and register your Docker Hub account. This is an important step as you will need your account to follow this section.

URL: `https://hub.docker.com/`

Once you have completed your registration and have some spare time to read, go to the Docker Hub page and get familiar with how Docker works.

URL: `https://www.docker.com/get-started`

Docker Installation

For this lab, all tasks will be performed from Ubuntu Server. Follow these steps to install Docker on your `ubuntu20s1` server. Luckily, Docker's installation on Ubuntu is pretty painless, and you will be up and running in less than 15 minutes.

#	Task

1	As always, let's begin with an `apt update` command and upgrade your Ubuntu 20 LTS server. This will take a few minutes if you have not updated your server package for some time.
	`pynetauto@ubuntu20s1:~$ sudo apt update`
	`[sudo] password for pynetauto: ***********`
	`pynetauto@ubuntu20s1:~$ sudo apt upgrade -y`

2	Enter the following command to download and install the Docker package: `pynetauto@ubuntus20s1:~$ sudo apt install docker.io -y`

3	To enable Docker, enter the `enable` command and also use the `docker -version` command to check the version installed.
	`pynetauto@ubuntus20s1:~$ sudo systemctl enable --now Docker`
	`pynetauto@ubuntu20s1:~$ sudo systemctl status docker`
	`pynetauto@ubuntu20s1:~$ sudo docker --version`
	`Docker version 19.03.8, build afacb8b7f0`

4	Add yourself to the Docker group to run `sudo` commands. Replace `pynetauto` with your user ID. Run the last command for the change to take effect.
	`pynetauto@ubuntus20s1:~$ sudo usermod -aG docker pynetauto`
	`pynetauto@ubuntu20s1:~$ sudo gpasswd -a $USER docker`
	`pynetauto@ubuntu20s1:~$ newgrp docker`

5	Test Docker by running the `hello-world` command, which will open a container to run the `hello-world` command.
	`pynetauto@ubuntu20s1:~$ docker run hello-world`
	`Unable to find image 'hello-world:latest' locally`
	`latest: Pulling from library/hello-world`
	`0e03bdcc26d7: Pull complete`
	`Digest: sha256:4cf9c47f86df71d48364001ede3a4fcd85ae80ce02ebad74156906caff5378bc`
	`Status: Downloaded newer image for hello-world:latest`
	
	`Hello from Docker!`
	`This message shows that your installation appears to be working correctly.`
	`[... omitted for brevity]`
	`For more examples and ideas, visit:`
	`https://docs.docker.com/get-started/`

#	Task
6	Run docker ps -a to check if the hello-world command ran successfully. Also, run the docker images command to check downloaded Docker images.

```
pynetauto@ubuntu20s1:~$ docker ps -a
CONTAINER ID        IMAGE               COMMAND             CREATED
STATUS                     PORTS               NAMES
ef48902f0801        hello-world         "/hello"            2 minutes ago
Exited (0) 2 minutes ago                       modest_goldberg
pynetauto@ubuntu20s1:~$ docker images
REPOSITORY          TAG                 IMAGE ID            CREATED        SIZE
hello-world         latest              bf756fb1ae65        8 months ago   13.3kB
```

Test-Driving Docker

A Python network automation Docker image has already been created for this book's readers using the Dockerfile method to save time. The image you are about to download to your Ubuntu20s1 server is also a Ubuntu 20.04 LTS server with many IP services and network automation libraries pre-installed on the Docker image. There are several steps involved with creating a template Docker image from a Dockerfile, but we will not go into the details in this book as it is another topic that could require its own chapter. Please go to YouTube to locate and watch the basic Docker training. In this lab, you will download the pre-installed Python network automation Docker image and run it from your Ubuntu server.

#	Task
1	After you have created a Docker Hub ID, go to the following Docker Hub site to review the image you will download.

URL: https://hub.docker.com/u/pynetauto

#	Task
2	From your Linux command line, use docker login to log into Docker Hub. Replace the username with yours and enter your password to log in. You need to get a "Login Succeeded" message at the bottom. When you create an account and log into Docker Hub, you can push the Docker image to Docker Hub, save the image as a template, and share it with others in the community.

```
pynetauto@ubuntu20s1:~$ docker login
```

Log in with your Docker ID to push and pull images from Docker Hub. If you don't have a Docker ID, head over to https://hub.docker.com to create one.

```
Username: pynetauto
Password: ***********
WARNING! Your password will be stored unencrypted in /home/pynetauto/.docker/
config.json.
Configure a csredential helper to remove this warning. See
https://docs.docker.com/engine/reference/commandline/login/#credentials-store
Login Succeeded
```

(continued)

#	Task
3	Use the following docker pull command to download this image onto your virtual machine's Docker image repository. It is recommended that you connect to the Internet through your home network, not on a 4G or 5G network, as it will use up your mobile data.

```
pynetauto@ubuntu20s1:~$ docker pull pynetauto/pynetauto_ubuntu20:latest

latest: Pulling from pynetauto/pynetauto_ubuntu20
d51af753c3d3: Pull complete
[... omitted for brevity]
f92a9a96eae3: Pull complete
Digest: sha256:86f2178825cf09a1b7f7c370a460b34b109f62ce4471d944ef108d0a29162ed4
Status: Downloaded newer image for pynetauto/pynetauto_ubuntu20:latest
docker.io/pynetauto/pynetauto_ubuntu20:latest
```

4 Using the docker images command, check the new image with the correct details, as shown here:

```
pynetauto@ubuntu20s1:~$ docker images
REPOSITORY                      TAG      IMAGE ID       CREATED         SIZE
pynetauto/pynetauto_ubuntu20    latest   39ea52cc1e39   12 days ago     1.69GB
hello-world                     latest   bf756fb1ae65   8 months ago    13.3kB
```

5 To initiate a Docker container instance in a bash shell with a local server directory mounting point with the container, use the exact command shown here. Refer to Table 16-1 for the command explanation.

```
pynetauto@ubuntu20s1:~$ docker run -it --entrypoint=/bin/bash -v /home/pynetauto/
mnt/:/home --name pynetauto_ubuntu20 pynetauto/pynetauto_ubuntu20

root@2f81da41426b:/#
```

Table 16-1. *Breakdown and Explanation of the Previous Commands*

Command Breakdown	Explanation
`docker run -it --entrypoint=/bin/bash`	Run Docker with the `-i` and `-t` options where the entry point is the bash shell. `-i` denotes interactive mode, whereas `-t` denotes allocation of a `pseudo-tty`.
`-v /home/pynetauto/mnt/:/home`	`-v` is related to a volume (shared filesystem); in this case, `unbuntu20s1`'s `/home/pynetauto/mnt` directory is linked to the `/home` directory of the new Docker container.
`--name pynetauto_ubuntu20`	The `--name` option allows you to give a more meaningful name to this instance of the container. If `-name` is not used, then Docker will assign a random name automatically.
`pynetauto/pynetauto_ubuntu20`	This is the actual Docker image name in the local image pool.

For full Docker run references, visit the following site.
URL: `https://docs.docker.com/engine/reference/run/`

#	Task

6	Check the Docker image and the Python version installed on the pynetauto_ubuntu20 Docker container. Most of the commands are the same as the Linux standard commands and should behave like another Linux machine. However, the basic services or systemctl or any Linux standard software are not available from the Docker container instance; in other words, you must precisely specify which Linux software you want to install during the Docker image build process. If you want to install more software on an existing Docker image, you can make the modifications. However, the Docker base image modification topic is outside of this book's scope.
	
	`root@2f81da41426b:/# cat /etc/*release`
	`DISTRIB_ID=Ubuntu`
	`DISTRIB_RELEASE=20.04`
	`DISTRIB_CODENAME=focal`
	`DISTRIB_DESCRIPTION="Ubuntu 20.04 LTS"`
	`NAME="Ubuntu"`
	`VERSION="20.04 LTS (Focal Fossa)"`
	`ID=ubuntu`
	`ID_LIKE=debian`
	`PRETTY_NAME="Ubuntu 20.04 LTS"`
	`VERSION_ID="20.04"`
	`HOME_URL="https://www.ubuntu.com/"`
	`SUPPORT_URL="https://help.ubuntu.com/"`
	`BUG_REPORT_URL="https://bugs.launchpad.net/ubuntu/"`
	`PRIVACY_POLICY_URL="https://www.ubuntu.com/legal/terms-and-policies/privacy-policy"`
	`VERSION_CODENAME=focal`
	`UBUNTU_CODENAME=focal`
	`root@2f81da41426b:/# python3 --version`
	`Python 3.8.2`

7	Create a testfile999.txt file on the Docker bash shell. `root@2f81da41426b:/# touch home/testfile999.txt`

8	Detach and check the newly created file on the host PC. Use Ctrl+P followed by Ctrl+Q to detach from the Docker container. This will move you back into your Linux host OS. Check the /home/pynetauto/mnt folder. You should find the testfile999.txt file in the Linux server's directory.
	
	`pynetauto@ubuntu20s1:~$ pwd`
	`/home/pynetauto`
	`pynetauto@ubuntu20s1:~$ ls /home/pynetauto/mnt`
	`testfil999.txt`

(continued)

#	Task

9	Now from your Linux host, create a new file under the shared directory. Then, reattach to the Docker instance to check the file from the Docker container instance. When you reattach to the running Docker instance, you can use either the container ID or names.
	`pynetauto@ubuntu20s1:~$ touch /home/pynetauto/mnt/testfile123.txt`
	`pynetauto@ubuntu20s1:~$ docker ps`
	`CONTAINER ID   IMAGE   COMMAND   CREATED   STATUS`
	`PORTS   NAMES`
	`2f81da41426b   pynetauto/pynetauto_ubuntu20   "/bin/bash"   6 minutes ago   Up 6 minutes`
	`20-22/tcp, 25/tcp, 12020-12025/tcp   pynetauto_ubuntu20`
	`pynetauto@ubuntu20s1:~$ docker attach pynetauto_ubuntu20`
	`root@2f81da41426b:/# ls`
	`bin  boot  dev  etc  ftp  home  lib  lib32  lib64  libx32  media  mnt  opt  proc`
	`pynetauto  root  run  sbin  srv  sys  tmp  usr  var`
	`root@2f81da41426b:/# ls /home/`
	`testfile999.txt  testfile123.txt`

10	To stop and exit Docker, press Ctrl+D or type in `exit`. This will stop and exit the currently logged in Docker container.
	`root@2f81da41426b:/# exit`
	`pynetauto@ubuntu20s1:~$ docker ps -a`
	`CONTAINER ID   IMAGE   COMMAND   CREATED   STATUS`
	`PORTS   NAMES`
	`2f81da41426b   pynetauto/pynetauto_ubuntu20 "/bin/bash"   9 minutes ago   Exited (130) 11`
	`seconds ago   pynetauto_ubuntu20`
	`ef48902f0801   hello-world   "/hello"   42 minutes ago Exited (0)   42 minutes ago`
	`modest_goldberg`

11	To restart a stopped Docker instance, use the `docker start instance_name` command.
	`pynetauto@ubuntu20s1:~$ docker start pynetauto_ubuntu20`
	`pynetauto_ubuntu20`
	`pynetauto@ubuntu20s1:~$ docker ps -a`
	`CONTAINER ID   IMAGE   COMMAND   CREATED   STATUS`
	`PORTS   NAMES`
	`2f81da41426b   pynetauto/pynetauto_ubuntu20   "/bin/bash"   11 minutes ago Up 4 seconds`
	`20-22/tcp, 25/tcp, 12020-12025/tcp   pynetauto_ubuntu20`
	`ef48902f0801   hello-world   "/hello"   44 minutes ago   Exited (0) 44 minutes ago`
	`modest_goldberg`

#	Task
12	To prune nonrunning Docker instances and keep your environment clean, run the docker system prune command.

```
pynetauto@ubuntu20s1:~$ docker system prune
WARNING! This will remove:
- all stopped containers
- all networks not used by at least one container
- all dangling images
- all dangling build cache

Are you sure you want to continue? [y/N] Y
Deleted Containers:
ef48902f0801b692e963c317873075d0152a3c09fd992f8b2f5e3f8d55b71f01

Total reclaimed space: 0B

pynetauto@ubuntu20s1:~$ docker ps -a
CONTAINER ID        IMAGE         COMMAND                  CREATED          STATUS
PORTS                               NAMES
2f81da41426b  pynetauto/pynetauto_ubuntu20   "/bin/bash"  13 minutes ago  Up 2 minutes
20-22/tcp, 25/tcp, 12020-12025/tcp    pynetauto_ubuntu20
```

#	Task
13	To delete Docker images, use docker rmi image_name:version.

```
pynetauto@ubuntu20s1:~$ docker images
REPOSITORY                     TAG        IMAGE ID         CREATED         SIZE
pynetauto/pynetauto_ubuntu20   latest     39ea52cc1e39     12 days ago     1.69GB
hello-world                    latest     bf756fb1ae65     8 months ago    13.3kB
pynetauto@ubuntu20s1:~$ docker rmi hello-world:latest
Untagged: hello-world:latest
Untagged: hello-world@sha256:4cf9c47f86df71d48364001ede3a4fcd85ae80ce02ebad74156906
caff5378bc
Deleted: sha256:bf756fb1ae65adf866bd8c456593cd24beb6a0a061dedf42b26a993176745f6b
Deleted: sha256:9c27e219663c25e0f28493790cc0b88bc973ba3b1686355f221c38a36978ac63
pynetauto@ubuntu20s1:~$ docker images
REPOSITORY                     TAG        IMAGE ID         CREATED         SIZE
pynetauto/pynetauto_ubuntu20   latest     39ea52cc1e39     12 days ago     1.69GB
```

Docker Sendmail Python Lab

Now we are getting familiar with Docker, let's quickly learn how to benefit from Docker and run our Python scripts. In this lab, you will use the pre-installed Sendmail on your pynetauto/pynetauto_ubuntu20:latest Docker container and send a test email from your Python script. Then you will be guided through writing a Python script to monitor the CPU utilization of one of the devices in the topology. When the utilization goes above the yellow watermark, then your Python script will trigger an email alert to your email inbox. First, let's get you set up for Sendmail on your Docker image. For Sendmail to work on your Docker container, Sendmail needs to be pre-installed and configured, and port 25 must be opened up for SMTP. Also, to receive the test email, your email account security has to be lowered. In this example, a Gmail account is used for demonstration purposes, and you can do the same with your testing Gmail account.

#	Task

1 If you have followed the Docker installation processes in the previous steps, you should have the Docker image named `pynetauto_ubuntu20`.

```
pynetauto@ubuntu20s1:~$ docker images
REPOSITORY                      TAG       IMAGE ID        CREATED         SIZE
pynetauto/pynetauto_ubuntu20    latest    39ea52cc1e39    2 weeks ago     1.69GB
```

2 Now, let's start a new Docker instance by rerunning the following command. If you already have an existing instance, you can start the instance and attach it to the Docker instance. In this example, we will start a new instance. If your Docker instance starts, you will be logged into the bash shell of your new Docker instance and should be ready to go.

```
pynetauto@ubuntu20s1:~$ docker run -it --entrypoint=/bin/bash -v  /home/pynetauto/
mnt/:/home --name pynetauto_ubuntu20sendmail pynetauto/pynetauto_ubuntu20
root@062fc2a30243:/#
```

3 First, let's check if port 25 is in listening mode. Check for open ports using the `netstat -tuna` command. No result was returned, so it looks like you will have to configure Sendmail and allow port 25 on this Docker instance or machine. Also, check the Sendmail installation status by quickly running `apt install Sendmail`; it should be installed already.

```
root@062fc2a30243:/# netstat -tuna
Active Internet connections (servers and established)
Proto Recv-Q Send-Q Local Address           Foreign Address         State
root@062fc2a30243:/# apt install sendmail
Reading package lists... Done
Building dependency tree
Reading state information... Done
sendmail is already the newest version (8.15.2-18).
0 upgraded, 0 newly installed, 0 to remove and 2 not upgraded.
```

4 Let's quickly configure Sendmail on our Docker container instance now. Run the `sendmailconfig` command. When prompted for Y, press Y and then the Enter keys three times. After the second Y, it may take a little while for the files to be updated, so be patient and complete and reload the Sendmail service.

```
root@062fc2a30243:/# sendmailconfig
Configure sendmail with the existing /etc/mail/sendmail.conf? [Y] Y
Reading configuration from /etc/mail/sendmail.conf.
Validating configuration.
Writing configuration to /etc/mail/sendmail.conf.
Writing /etc/cron.d/sendmail.
Configure sendmail with the existing /etc/mail/sendmail.mc? [Y] Y <<< may take a
few minutes
Updating sendmail environment ...
Reading configuration from /etc/mail/sendmail.conf.
```

#	Task

	`[... omitted for brevity]`
	`Updating /etc/mail/aliases...`
	`WARNING: local host name (062fc2a30243) is not qualified; see cf/README: WHO AM I?`
	`/etc/mail/aliases: 0 aliases, longest 0 bytes, 0 bytes total`
	`Reload the running sendmail now with the new configuration? [Y] Y`
	`Reloading sendmail ...`

5	Use the following command to check that Sendmail-related directories have been created successfully on Docker:
	
	`root@062fc2a30243:/# ls /usr/sbin/send*`
	`/usr/sbin/sendmail  /usr/sbin/sendmail-msp  /usr/sbin/sendmail-mta  /usr/sbin/sendmailconfig`

6	Run the `netstat -tuna` command again to confirm port 25 is in LISTENing mode.
	
	`root@062fc2a30243:/# netstat -tuna`
	`Active Internet connections (servers and established)`
	`Proto Recv-Q Send-Q Local Address   Foreign Address   State`
	`tcp   0   0 127.0.0.1:587   0.0.0.0:*   LISTEN`
	`tcp   0   0 127.0.0.1:25   0.0.0.0:*   LISTEN`

7	Connect to the Internet from your Windows host PC. Next, go to your test Gmail account and turn on the "Less secure apps" settings as a mailbox user. It should be off by default, and you have to switch this to On to allow emails through. Try to create a test account for such testing; do not use your private Gmail account for this testing. See Figure 16-7. 1. Go to the Google Account Security section. 2. In the left navigation panel, click Security. 3. At the bottom of the page, in the "Less secure app access" panel, click "Turn on" access.

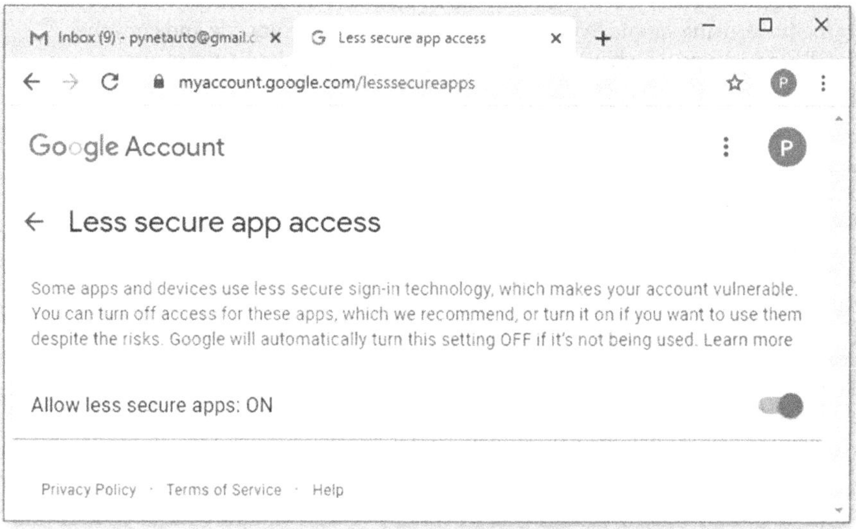

Figure 16-7. *Gmail, switching less secure app access to On*

(*continued*)

#	Task
	After you have turned on this feature, your security setting should look like Figure 16-8.

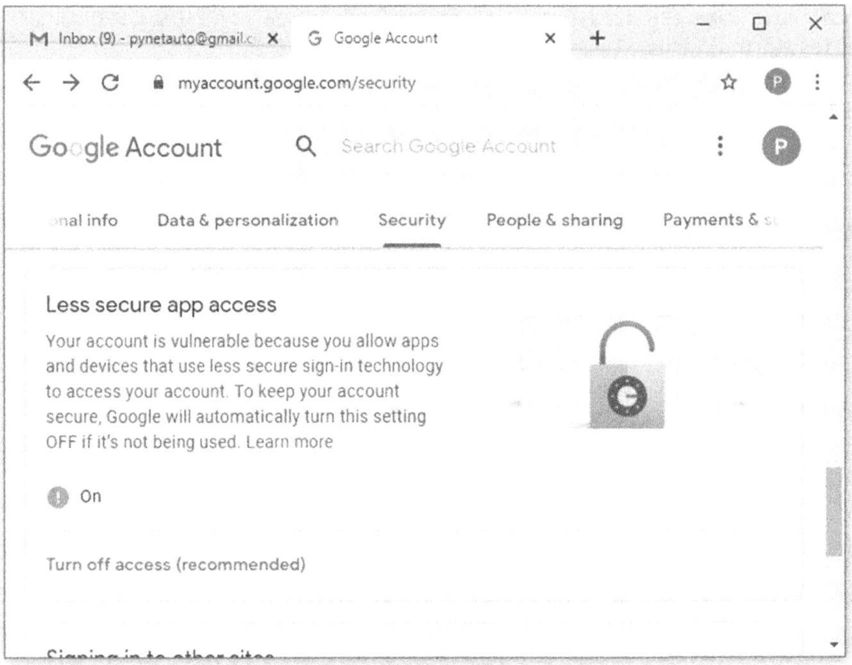

Figure 16-8. *Gmail, allowing less secure app access On - Security*

8 Go back to your Docker instance; you will send two test emails to yourself using two different email sending methods, using simple Python scripts. First, create a Python file and copy the content of the following script, which uses `email.mime.text` and the Linux subprocess.

```
root@062fc2a30243:/#nano sendmail_test01.py
```

```
GNU nano 4.8                                         sendmail_test01.py
from email.mime.text import MIMEText
from subprocess import Popen, PIPE
msg = MIMEText("Python & sendmail email test 01.")
msg["From"] = "brendanchoi@italchemy.com" # Update to your test email address
msg["To"] = "pynetauto@gmail.com" # Update to your test email address
msg["Subject"] = "Python & sendmail email test 01"
p = Popen(["/usr/sbin/sendmail", "-t", "-oi"], stdin=PIPE, universal_newlines=True)
p.communicate(msg.as_string())
print("Email sent!")
^G Get Help   ^O Write Out   ^W Where Is   ^K Cut Text    ^J Justify    ^C Cur Pos
^X Exit       ^R Read File   ^\ Replace    ^U Paste Text  ^T To Spell   ^_ Go To Line
```

Update the testing email addresses to your email addresses.

9 After you completed the script, run it from your Docker instance. There will be a little delay in sending the email. Give it about two to five minutes for the email to be sent.

```
root@062fc2a30243:/# cat sendmail_test01.py
```

#	Task
10	Another method to send email is to use Python's standard `smtplib`. Let's create the second script and send another test email, this time using `smtplib`.

```
root@062fc2a30243:/# nano sendmail_test02.py

GNU nano 4.8                    sendmail_test02.py
import smtplib

sender = 'no_reply@italchemy.com'
receivers = ['pynetauto@gmail.com']

message = """
From: No Reply <no_reply@italchemy.com>
To: Python Network Automation <pynetauto@gmail.com>
Subject: Sendmail SMTP Email test 01
This is a Sendmail SMTP Email test 01
"""

try:
   smtpObj = smtplib.SMTP('localhost')
   smtpObj.sendmail(sender, receivers, message)
   print("Successfully sent email")
except SMTPException:
   print("Error: unable to send email")
^G Get Help  ^O Write Out  ^W Where Is   ^K Cut Text    ^J Justify   ^C Cur Pos
^X Exit      ^R Read File  ^\ Replace    ^U Paste Text  ^T To Spell  ^_ Go To Line
```

11 Use the following command to send the second test email:

```
root@062fc2a30243:/# python3 sendmail_test02.py
Successfully sent email
```

12 Wait for a couple of minutes and check your email's Spam folder. If both scripts worked correctly, you should receive your first and second test emails in your Gmail Spam folder. See Figure 16-9.

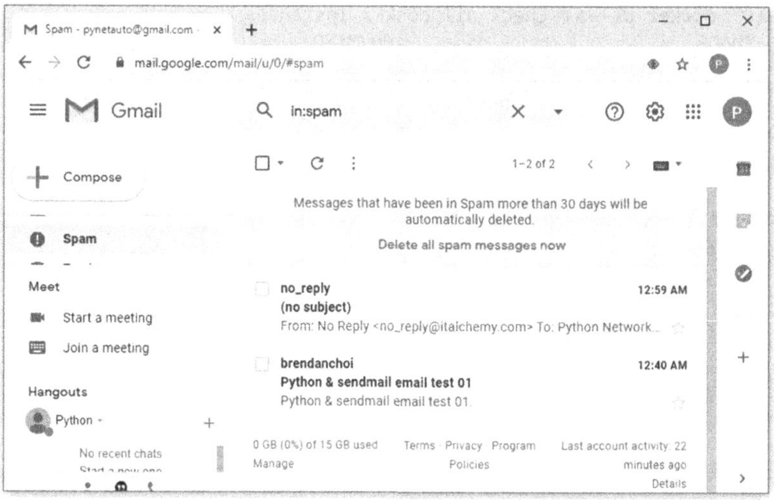

Figure 16-9. *Python Sendmail test email, checking the Spam folder*

Lab: Sendmail Email Notification script Development

In this lab, let's create a simple Python monitoring script that monitors a socket of LAN-SW1 (on port 22 for convenience) and triggers an email notification if the switch becomes unreachable on the network. In the real world, such email notifications will be directed to the 24/7 service desk team or SNMP server, and these actions will trigger automatic case logging on an IT enterprise ticketing system such as ITSM, ServiceNow, and Remedy. The beauty of building a lab is that you have the freedom to test anything and everything you want to study and validate various concepts. What is demonstrated in this book is only the tip of the iceberg of what you can automate in your network using Python and other Python-based automated tools. As individuals, everyone comes from different backgrounds. We have different backgrounds and upbringing, so we think and act differently, which is where your creativity is required while writing your code. You will be more creative in some areas than the person next to you, and she will be more creative in other areas. While you are coding, there are no right or wrong answers, only recommendations. Open your mind and keep your imagination open; think about what you want to achieve with Python at work or in study. We know that better tools are available, and they are made explicitly for SNMP monitoring, email notification tools, and case logging tools. Still, by writing code to simulate such tools, we will gain a deeper understanding of how such tools work within IT ecosystems at work.All the tasks in this lab will be completed in the Docker environment, so you can also get some exposure to Docker's power at work. Borrowing from the previous labs, let's create a socket monitoring tool that checks the socket's availability every three seconds. If the socket is unavailable for ten times straight, it is offline for 30 seconds, and the script will trigger an email notification to your test email inbox using Sendmail. The script will monitor the socket continuously until you stop the application. Imagine you have a device with link flap that you have to monitor, and you have been asked to monitor the link every number of minutes. You do not want to be sitting in front of your computer all day or night and keep staring at the console messages. You will create a simple script, save the logs to a file, and make your script notify the right staff to be notified, in this case by email. Let's see how this can be achieved with ease.

#	Task
1	You will continue working within the Docker instance from the previous section. If you have stopped or detached from the Docker instance, please reattach it to the Docker instance. The following example shows an example of starting and reattaching to the Docker instance:

```
pynetauto@ubuntu20s1:~$ docker ps -a # Check all docker instances
CONTAINER ID        IMAGE                             COMMAND             CREATED
STATUS                      PORTS                     NAMES
062fc2a30243        pynetauto/pynetauto_ubuntu20   "/bin/bash"         45 hours ago
Exited (130) 43 hours ago                             pynetauto_ubuntu20sendmail
pynetauto@ubuntu20s1:~$ docker start pynetauto_ubuntu20sendmail # Start with instance
NAME
pynetauto_ubuntu20sendmail
pynetauto@ubuntu20s1:~$ docker ps # Check running docker instances
CONTAINER ID        IMAGE                             COMMAND             CREATED
STATUS              PORTS                                     NAMES
062fc2a30243        pynetauto/pynetauto_ubuntu20   "/bin/bash"         45 hours ago
Up 5 seconds        20-22/tcp, 25/tcp, 12020-12025/tcp   pynetauto_ubuntu20sendmail
pynetauto@ubuntu20s1:~$ docker attach pynetauto_ubuntu20sendmail # Reattach to docker
instance
root@062fc2a30243:/#
```

#	Task

2	Go to the /home directory mapped to the host and create a new directory; for simplicity purposes, the directory was named monitoring. Change the working directory to the new directory.
	`root@062fc2a30243:/# ls /home`
	`testfil999.txt  testfile123.txt`
	`root@062fc2a30243:/# cd /home`
	`root@062fc2a30243:/home# mkdir monitoring`
	`root@062fc2a30243:/home# cd monitoring`
	`root@062fc2a30243:/home/monitoring#`

3	Now, create two empty Python files, one for the script and another for the email message.
	`root@062fc2a30243:/home/monitoring# touch monitor_sw1.py send_email.py`
	`root@062fc2a30243:/home/monitoring# ls`
	`monitor_sw1.py send_email.py`

4	The following script is a socket-checking script that I often use to check the SSH port, port 22. If you have another port opened on your devices, such as port 23 (Telnet), 69 (TFTP), or 80 (HTTP), they can also be replaced in this example, but you already know that port 22 is an open port on all of your Cisco devices in your topology; hence, this script will check port 22. Using this basic port checking script and what we have learned from the previous exercises, you will be rewriting the code and apply it to solving our problem.

```
GNU nano 4.8                          check_port_22.py
import socket

ip = '192.168.183.101'

def check_port_22(): # Define a function
   for port in range (22, 23): # port 22
      dest = (ip, port) # new tuple variable
      try: # using try & except, we can avoid check process being stuck in a loop
         with socket.socket(socket.AF_INET, socket.SOCK_STREAM) as s:
            s.settimeout(3)
            connection = s.connect(dest) # Connect to socket
            print(f"On {ip}, port {port} is open!") # Informational
            print("OK - This device is on the network.") # Informational
      except:
         print(f"On {ip}, port {port} is closed. Exiting!") # Informational
         print("! FAILED - to reach the device. Check the connectivity to this
         device") # Informational
         exit() # Exit application
check_port_22() # Run the function

^G Get Help  ^O Write Out  ^W Where Is  ^K Cut Text   ^J Justify  ^C Cur Pos
^X Exit      ^R Read File  ^\ Replace   ^U Paste Text ^T To Spell ^_ Go To Line
```

(continued)

#	Task
5	Now open monitor_sw1.py in the nano text editor and start typing in the following script. Yes, the script is available for your download, and it would be time-saving to cut and paste the code. But, in the real world, it is never as simple as cutting and pasting. Most of the time, you have to type in all the code, unless your company has paid someone to write a complete and working application. So, try to follow the script and write each line of code.

```
root@062fc2a30243:/home/monitoring# nano monitor_sw1.py
GNU nano 4.8                     monitor_sw1.py
import socket
import time
from datetime import datetime

# Custom module
from send_email import send_email # import send_email module from email_send.py

starttime = time.time()

# Variables
ip = "192.168.183.101"
port = 22
dest = (ip, port)

def check_sw1(): # Define check_sw1 function
    counter = 0 # Set counter's original value to 0
    while (counter < 10): # Run the script until counter 10 is reached
        f = open('./monitoring_logs.txt', 'a') # Open monitoring logs file for record
            in appending mode
        try: # This is basically the same code as check_port_22.py
          with socket.socket(socket.AF_INET, socket.SOCK_STREAM) as s:
              s.settimeout(3)
              connection = s.connect(dest)
              counter = 0 # Reset the counter to 0 on successful check
              counter1 = str(counter) # convert counter to string
              f.write(datetime.now().strftime('%Y-%m-%d %H:%M:%S')) # Write time to file
              print(f" {counter1} port {port} is open") # Informations for console user
              f.write(f" {counter1} port {port} is open\n") # Write to log file for
              task completion
              f.close() # close file
              time.sleep(3) # Wait for 3 seconds before another check

          except: # If port 22 is closed
              counter += 1 # Adds 1 to counter every loop
              counter2 = str(counter) # convert counter to string
              f.write(datetime.now().strftime('%Y-%m-%d %H:%M:%S')) # Write time to file
              print(f" {counter2} port {port} is closed") # Informations for console user
              f.write(f" {counter2} port {port} is closed\n") # Write to log file for
              task completion
              time.sleep(3) # Wait for 3 seconds before another check
              if counter == 10: # Check if counter is 10
                  counter=0 # Only resets the counter to 0 on 10th time
                  print("send failed email here") # Informations for console user
                  send_email() # Send an email notification, calling send_email() from
                  send_email.py script
              f.close()# close file
```

#	Task
	check_sw1() # Run check_sw1 function ^G Get Help ^O Write Out ^W Where Is ^K Cut Text ^J Justify ^C Cur Pos ^X Exit ^R Read File ^\ Replace ^U Paste Text ^T To Spell ^_ Go To Line
6	Now let's write a smtplib Python file so the previous main script can import it and send an email. This is the email part of the script. By breaking up scripts into multiple functional parts, you can keep you code clean.

```
root@062fc2a30243:/home/monitoring# nano send_email.py
GNU nano 4.8                    send_email.py
import smtplib

sender = 'no_reply@italchemy.com' # A variable, sender
receivers = ['pynetauto@gmail.com'] # A variable, receivers. Add more emails using
comma separator

# This is the main message which will be sent to the email recipient(s). Anything
between the triple quotes
message = """
From: No Reply <no_reply@italchemy.com>
To: Python Network Automation <pynetauto@gmail.com>
Subject: SW1 not reachable for more than 30 seconds

SW1 is not reachable. Please investigate.

"""

def send_email(): # Define send_email function
   try:
      smtpObj = smtplib.SMTP('localhost') # Define smtpObj
      smtpObj.sendmail(sender, receivers, message) # Send an email using smtpObj and
      variables
      print("Successfully sent email") # Informational
   except SMTPException: # SMTP Exception
      print("Error: unable to send email") # Informational

^G Get Help  ^O Write Out  ^W Where Is  ^K Cut Text   ^J Justify  ^C Cur Pos
^X Exit      ^R Read File  ^\ Replace   ^U Paste Text ^T To Spell ^_ Go To Line
```

#	Task

7	Once both the main and supplementary scripts have been created, run the code in your Docker environment using the following command. Once you see the message on the screen, you can let the script run continuously.
	`root@062fc2a30243:/home/monitoring# python3 monitor_sw1.py`
	Log in to LAN-SW1 (192.168.183.101) and shut down port Gi0/0, wait for approximately 30 seconds, and send no shut command. Then wait for another 30 seconds; this will emulate the link flap scenario and will trigger the script to change its state.
	`LAB-SW1(config)#interface Gi0/0`
	`LAB-SW1(config-if)#shut # wait for 30 seconds`
	`LAB-SW1(config-if)#no shut # wait for 30 seconds`

(*continued*)

#	Task
	If you let the port shut down (unreachable) for more than 30 seconds, then the script will trigger an email, and you will receive an email in your inbox. Until you bring up the interface, the script should send notification emails every 30 seconds and continue.

```
root@062fc2a30243:/home/monitoring# python3 monitor_sw1.py
...
0 port 22 is open
0 port 22 is open
0 port 22 is open
1 port 22 is closed
2 port 22 is closed
3 port 22 is closed
4 port 22 is closed
5 port 22 is closed
6 port 22 is closed
7 port 22 is closed
8 port 22 is closed
9 port 22 is closed
10 port 22 is closed
send failed email here
Successfully sent email
...
```

#	Task
8	Check the Spam folder of your email account. If you keep the interface shut down for three minutes, you should receive six email notifications, as shown in Figure 16-10.

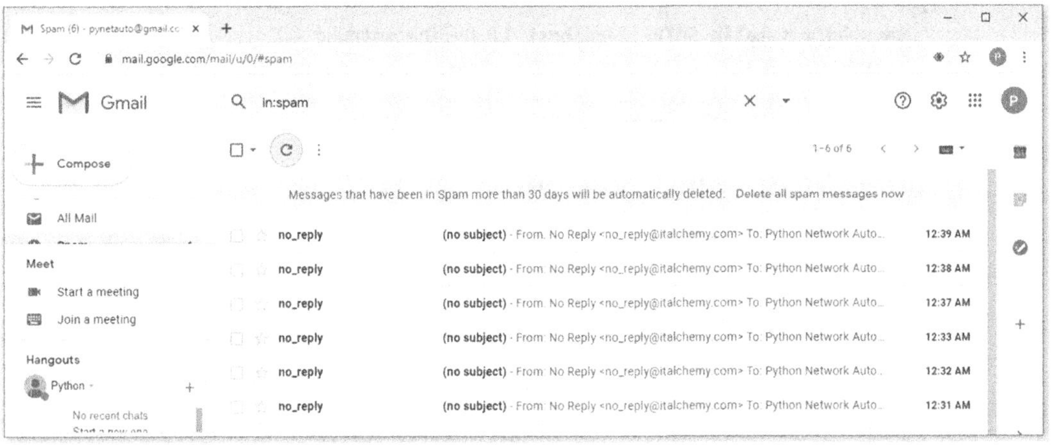

Figure 16-10. *Checking the test email received in SPAM folder*

#	Task
	The following content of the testing email will look similar to this: **From: No Reply** <no_reply@italchemy.com> **To: Python Network Automation** <pynetauto@gmail.com> **Subject: SW1 not reachable for more than 30 seconds** **SW1 is not reachable. Please investigate.**
9	Press Ctrl+P and then the Ctrl+Q keys to detach from the Docker instance. This will keep the script running continuously. To stop the script and the Docker instance as well, press Ctrl+Z. You can also use `docker stop <container>` to shut down the container instance gracefully.

Say it is 5 p.m. on Friday, and your boss asks you to monitor a device (router, switch, or firewall) with an unreliable connection. If the device loses the connection, immediately notify all stakeholders. The script running on a Docker instance can check the communication to the network for you, and when an incident occurs, it will send you email notifications. You can check the email from your smartphone at any time you want, even on the way home or after dinner. At 5 p.m., when you leave your office, use `cron` to schedule to run the script and let your Python application go to work for you.

CPU Utilization Monitoring Lab: Send an SMS Message Using Twilio

In this lab, you will develop a REST API SMS message tool quickly; then, you will write the Python code to monitor your router's CPU utilization. When a certain threshold is reached, the script will trigger an SMS message to your smartphone using REST API calls. As the newer network device platforms and most of the virtual and cloud networking platforms start to support REST API, understanding the REST API and applying the theory to practical use cases will be one of the must-have skill sets in network automation. This book will not discuss how to start on your REST API studies or attempt to cover the topic extensively; this is one simple example to give you a taste. However, you can start learning about the REST API from YouTube or LinkedIn video tutorials; most of the tutorials will have you install one of the REST clients such as POSTMAN or REST for Visual Studio. If you have some time, you are recommended to go to the following sites and do some preliminary reading before completing this lab. See Figure 16-11.

URL: `https://www.postman.com/` (POSTMAN REST client)

URL: `https://marketplace.visualstudio.com/items?itemName=humao.rest-client` (REST client for Microsoft Visual Studio)

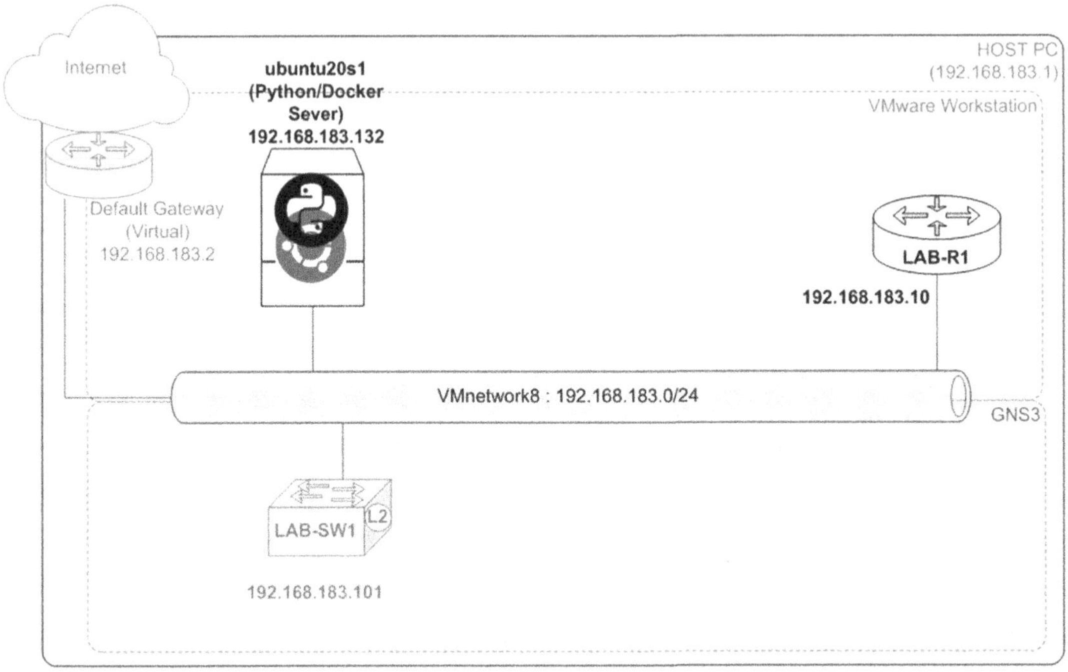

Figure 16-11. *CPU utilization monitoring lab, used devices*

TWILIO Account Creation, Install Twilio Python Module and SMS Message Setup

In this section, you will set up a Twilio testing account to send SMS messages for free. According to Wikipedia, Twilio is a cloud communications platform as a service company, allowing software developers to programmatically make and receive phone calls, send and receive text messages, and perform other communication functions using Twilio's web service APIs. For our use, we need to send SMS notification messages when a particular condition is met during our system monitoring of the network devices in the topology. First, create an account to receive a U.S. testing number, account SID, and authorization code; then install the Twilio module on Python and write a simple SMS message to send to your smartphone number. After this, you will be writing a CPU utilization monitoring script, emulating a high CPU utilization scenario under security attack, and triggering an SMS notification. First, let's quickly set up the account and get the first testing message out to your smartphone number.

#	Task
1	Go to Twilio and create a trial account. See Figure 16-12. URL: `https://www.twilio.com/try-twilio`

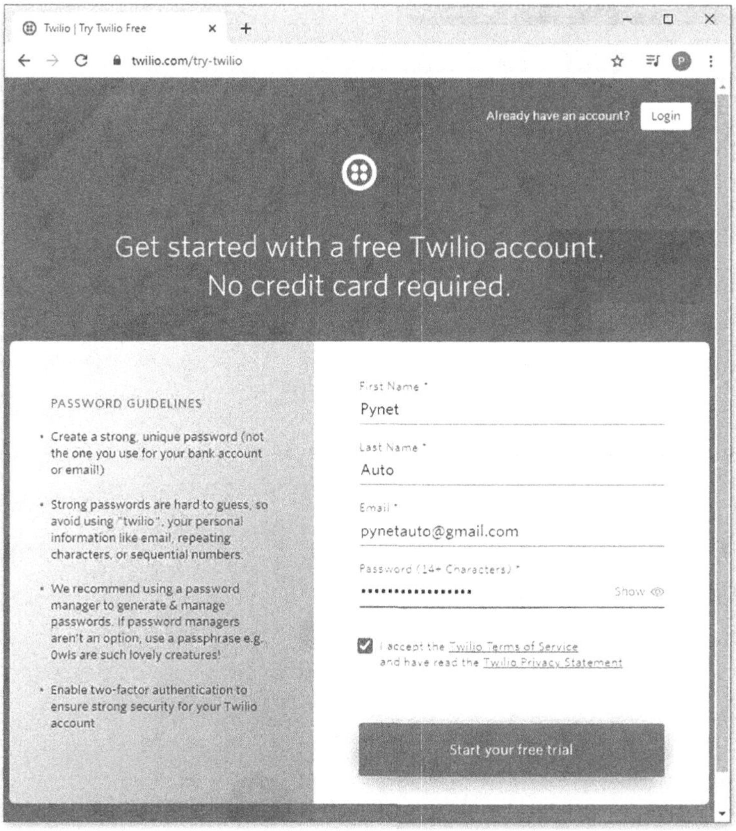

Figure 16-12. *Twilio account registration*

#	Task
2	After registration, you have to log into your email account and confirm your email. Enter your smartphone number, and once the verification code is sent to your smartphone, enter the code into the Twilio code verification site. Follow the prompts to complete the account registration. See Figure 16-13.

(continued)

#	Task

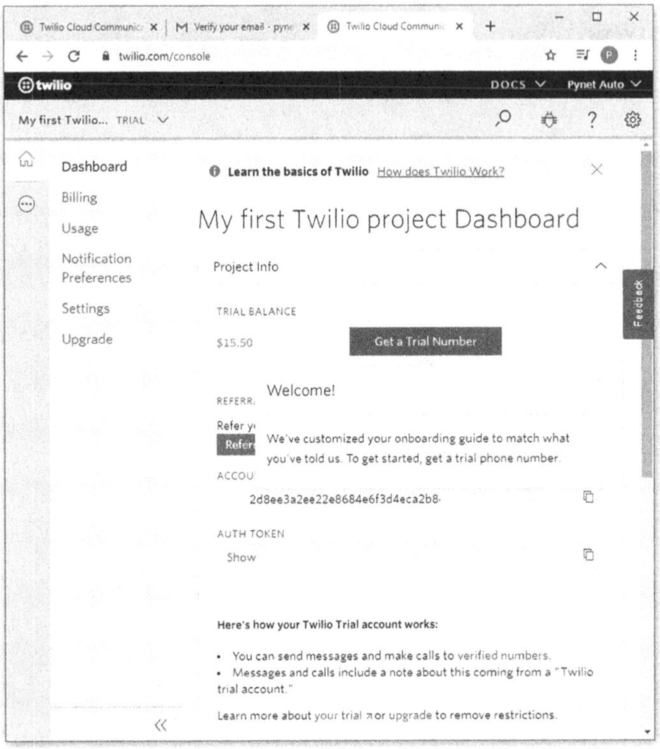

Figure 16-13. *Twilio project dashboard*

3 A trial number will be offered from an available number range. Choose the first number. See Figure 16-14.

Figure 16-14. *Twilio trial U.S. phone number*

#	Task
4	You will get the free trial balance and account SID and authorization token along with your new phone number. An account SID and authorization token will be used in the code to send an SMS message. See Figure 16-15.

Figure 16-15. *Project dashboard with a trial number*

#	Task
5	To read more about how to get started with Twilio, go to the following website and read the official documentation. URL: `https://www.twilio.com/docs/sms/quickstart/python`
6	In this lab, we will be working within the Docker instance to isolate the instance so it does not directly impact your lab setup. With Docker, you can delete the instance and re-create as many instances as required on demand. Let's go ahead and create another Docker instance to run the Twilio lab. `pynetauto@ubuntu20s1:~$`

(continued)

#	Task

7	To get ready for Twilio SMS messaging, use the pip3 command to install Twilio on your Docker instance. Since you are testing this in a Docker environment, you do not have to worry about breaking the software compatibility issues with the real Linux host.
	`pynetauto@ubuntu20s1:~/monitor_cpu$ pip3 install Twilio`
	`[...omitted for brevity]`
	`Successfully installed twilio-6.45.3`
	If you are getting a `bash: snmpwalk: command not found` error message, install snmp on your Linux server.
	`pynetauto@ubuntu20s1:~$ apt-get install snmp -y`

8	You are going to create two files to send the testing SMS message from the Python script. Create a credential feeder script called `credentials.py` and then the SMS script to send an SMS called `twilio_sms.py`. Please update and replace the credentials and numbers with yours.
	`pynetauto@ubuntu20s1:~$ mkdir monitor_cpu`
	`pynetauto@ubuntu20s1:~$ cd monitor_cpu`
	`pynetauto@ubuntu20s1:~/monitor_cpu$ nano credentials.py`
	`GNU nano 4.8 /home/pynetauto/monitor_cpu/credentials.py`
	`account_sid = " AC42d8ee3a2ee22e8684e6f3d4eca2b8c7"`
	`auth_token = "5233e8502a3dd3a2d006913c937a6f26"`
	`my_smartphone = "+61498765432"`
	`twilio_trial = "+16076003338"`
	`^G Get Help ^O Write Out ^W Where Is ^K Cut Text ^J Justify ^C Cur Pos`
	`^X Exit ^R Read File ^\ Replace ^U Paste Text ^T To Spell ^_ Go To Line`
	This is the SMS script that will send out `my_message` to your smartphone.
	`pynetauto@ubuntu20s1:~/monitor_cpu$ nano twilio_sms.py`
	`GNU nano 4.8 /home/pynetauto/monitor_cpu/twilio_sms.py`
	`from twilio.rest import Client`
	`from credentials import account_sid, auth_token, my_smartphone, twilio_trial`
	`client = Client(account_sid, auth_token)`
	`my_message = f"High CPU utilization notice, LAB-R1 has reached 99% CPU utilization."`
	`message = client.messages.create(body=my_message, from_=twilio_trial, to=my_smartphone)`
	`print(message.sid)`
	`^G Get Help ^O Write Out ^W Where Is ^K Cut Text ^J Justify ^C Cur Pos`
	`^X Exit ^R Read File ^\ Replace ^U Paste Text ^T To Spell ^_ Go To Line`

9	From the Docker container command line, run the python3 command to run the SMS script to send your first Twilio SMS. If everything has been set up correctly, it will send an SMS to your smartphone.
	`pynetauto@ubuntu20s1:~/monitor_cpu$ python3 twilio_sms.py`
	`SMf1c0d46e60b245b08e56a58563a434aa`

10	On your smartphone, check the SMS message, and you should receive an SMS message similar to Figure 16-16.

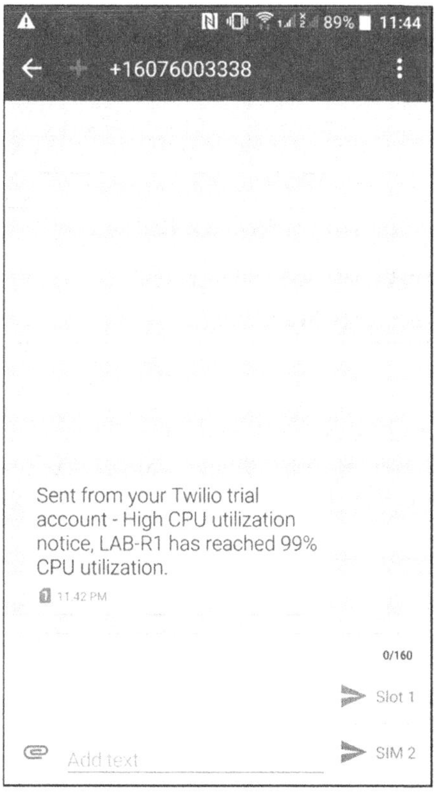

Figure 16-16. *Test SMS message received example*

If you have received an SMS message successfully on your smartphone, you are ready for the next lab.

CPU Utilization Monitoring Lab with an SMS Message

Now that you know how to send an SMS message to your smartphone, it is time to write some code and integrate the previous code snippet for use in a real-world simulation. Let's write a simple CPU monitoring application for network devices using SNMP v3, and this application can monitor the 5-minute interval CPU utilization levels of LAB-R1. We could use a third-party traffic generator to make our router very busy and push the CPU utilization up above 90 percent, but that means you have to learn another tool to complete this lab. To keep it simple, we will use the `debug all` command and multiple `ping` packets to push up the CPU utilization of `LAB-R1`. Yes, you will enable the `debug all` commands on `LAB-R1`, which will increase the CPU utilization to around 50 percent. You will be sending large ping packets to push the CPU utilization above 90 percent from other routers and switches. Be careful with using the `debug all` command in the production environment and leaving it running on your Cisco devices in the production environment; you may bring down your network and cause an outage.

First, let's write a simple CPU monitoring script and integrate the SMS script into it, so when the CPU utilization is more than 90 percent for more than 5 minutes, our script will send out an SMS alert message to your smartphone stating that the CPU utilization has exceeded 90 percent for more than five minutes.

For this, we need to find out exact OID reference number, as shown in Table 16-2. Go to `https://oidref.com/1.3.6.1.4.1.9.9.109.1.1.1.1` and check out the various Cisco IOS device CPU-related OID values.

Table 16-2. *Cisco Device CPU Utilization OID IDs*

OID ID	Description
1.3.6.1.4.1.9.9.109.1.1.1.1.3	The overall CPU busy percentage in the last five-second period
1.3.6.1.4.1.9.9.109.1.1.1.1.4	The overall CPU busy percentage in the last one-minute period
1.3.6.1.4.1.9.9.109.1.1.1.1.5	The overall CPU busy percentage in the last five-minute period

Source: `https://oidref.com/`

You are going to be using an OID ID of 1.3.6.1.4.1.9.9.109.1.1.1.1.5 for CPU utilization and check every five minutes. You will use `crontab` on the Ubuntu server to run the script every five minutes. When the CPU utilization for the last five minutes is more than 90 percent, the script will send an SMS alert using the Twilio API account from the previous lab+.

#	Task
1	Let's first write a simple `snmpwalk` script that sends a `snmpwalk` command to `LAB-R1` and retrieves the CPU utilization information. The following command should return the CPU utilization of the router in the last five minutes. Under regular operation, the CPU utilization of a router should be less than 80 percent, but while some change or update is done, it is normal to see high CPU utilization during the change window.

```
pynetauto@ubuntu20s1:~/monitor_cpu$ python3 cpu_util_5min.py
iso.3.6.1.4.1.9.9.109.1.1.1.1.5.1 = Gauge32: 3
```

This is the original script. Create the following file and check if it still works. If you have not yet read the SNMP section, go back to the previous chapter for further reading.

cpu_util_5min.py

```
import os

stream = os.popen('snmpwalk -v3  -l authPriv -u SNMPUser1 -a SHA -A "AUTHPass1"  -x
AES -X "PRIVPass1" 192.168.183.10 1.3.6.1.4.1.9.9.109.1.1.1.1.5')
output = stream.read()
print(output)
```

#	Task

2	Now let's use the Twilio SMS scripts from the previous exercises and update the information.
	
	`pynetauto@ubuntu20s1:~/monitor_cpu$ nano credentials.py`
	
	credentials.py
	
	`account_sid = "2d8ee3a2ee22e8684e6f3d4eca2b8" # Twilio Account SID`
	`auth_token = "3e8502a3dd3a2d006913c937a6" # Twilio Authorization Token`
	`my_smartphone = "+61498765432" # Your country code and smartphone number`
	`twilio_trial = "+16076003338" # Your Twilio trial number`
	
	Create another python file called, 'twilio_sms.py'.
	
	`pynetauto@ubuntu20s1:~/monitor_cpu$ nano twilio_sms.py`
	
	twilio_sms1.py
	
	`from twilio.rest import Client # Import required twilio module`
	`from credentials import account_sid, auth_token, my_smartphone, twilio_trial # import information from credentials.py file`
	
	`client = Client(account_sid, auth_token) # Create a variable`
	`my_message = f" High CPU utilization notice, LAB-R1 has reached 90% CPU utilization. # Write a SMS message to send`
	
	`message = client.messages.create \`
	`(body=my_message, from=twilio_trial, to=my_smartphone) # Send SMS message`
	`print(message.sid) # Print sent message SID`

3	Now let's see how we can get the exact value we want from the output and extract the CPU utilization value using the power of good old regular expressions again. Create the new code and run it against LAB-R1.
	
	cpu_util_5min1.py
	
	`import os # Import os and re modules`
	`import re`
	
	`stream = os.popen('snmpwalk -v3  -l authPriv -u SNMPUser1 -a SHA -A "AUTHPass1"  -x AES -X "PRIVPass1" 192.168.183.10 1.3.6.1.4.1.9.9.109.1.1.1.1.5') # SNMPwalk from previous chapter modified`
	`output = stream.read() # Read output`
	`print(output)`
	
	`p1 = re.compile(r"(?:Gauge32: )(\d+)") # Use re positive lookbehind and match the digit`
	`m1 = p1.findall(output) # Match the CPU utilization value (digit) in output`
	
	`cpu_util_value = int(m1[0]) # Index item 0 in the list and convert to an integer`
	`print(pu_util_value) # print the integer`

4	When you run the code from your server, you should get the CPU utilization value between 1 and 100. In the following example, 5 or 5 percent utilization has been returned.
	
	`pynetauto@ubuntu20s1:~/monitor_cpu$ python3 cpu_util_5min.py`
	`iso.3.6.1.4.1.9.9.109.1.1.1.1.5.1 = Gauge32: 5`
	`5`

(*continued*)

#	Task
5	Combining the scripts shown earlier, it is time to complete our script. For the simplicity of the lab, all three scripts, `credentials.py`, `twilio_sms1.py`, and `cpu_util_5min1.py`, will be rewritten into `cpu_util_5min_monitor.py`. Reiterations and integration are the keys to developing a working application like this, and this approach will be extended into the final IOS upgrade lab.

```
pynetauto@ubuntu20s1:~/monitor_cpu$ nano cpu_util_5min_monitor.py
```

At the end of combining all three scripts, your working script should look similar to this:

```
GNU nano 4.8              /home/pynetauto/monitor_cpu/cpu_util_5min_monitor.py
from twilio.rest import Client # import required libraries and modules
import os
import re
import time
from time import strftime

current_time = strftime("%a, %d %b %Y %H:%M:%S") # Create your own time string format

account_sid = "AC42d8ee3a2ee22e8684e6f3d4eca2b8c7" # Replace this with your own
Twilio SID
auth_token = "5233e8502a3dd3a2d006913c937a6f26" # Replace this with your own Twilio
token
my_smartphone = "+61490417510" # Replace this your own country code and Smartphone
number
twilio_trial = "+16076003338" # Twilio trial number

def send_sms(): # Define send_sms function
   client = Client(account_sid, auth_token)
   my_message = f"High CPU utilization notice, LAB-R1 has reached 90% CPU
   utilization."
   message = client.messages.create (body=my_message, from_=twilio_trial, to=my_
   smartphone)
   print(message.sid)

stream = os.popen('snmpwalk -v3 -l authPriv -u SNMPUser1 -a SHA -A "AUTHPass1"  -x
AES -X "PRIVPass1" 192.168.183.10 1.3.6.1.4.1.9.9.109.1.1.1.1.5') # SNMPwalk command
output = stream.read() # Read and capture output
time.sleep(3) # Pause script for 3 seconds
print("-"*80)
print(current_time, output) # Informational

with open('./cpu_oid_log.txt', 'a+') as f: # When manually run, writes to this file
   if "Gauge32:" in output: # Check if 'Gauge32' is in the output
      p1 = re.compile(r"(?:Gauge32: )(\d+)") # Positive look behind to locate CPU
      digit value
      m1 = p1.findall(output) # Find and match the digit
      cpu_util_value = m1[0] # Re findall returns value as a list, so index it to get
      it as an item
```

#	Task

```
            if int(cpu_util_value) < 90: # If CPU utilization value is less than 90 ( 90%)
                f.write(f"{current_time} {cpu_util_value}%, OK\n'") # Write to file
                print("OK") # Write to cron.log
            elif int(cpu_util_value)>= 90: # If CPU utilization value is more than 90 ( 90%)
                f.write(f"{current_time} {cpu_util_value}%, High CPU\n'")
                print("High CPU") # Write to cron.log
                send_sms()

        elif "Timeout:" in output: # if 'Timeout' is in output, send an SMS
            f.write(f"{current_time} High CPU, Timeout: No Response\n'")
            print("Timeout: No Response") # Write to cron.log
            send_sms()
        elif "snmpwalk:" in output: # if 'snmpwalk' is in output, send an SMS
            f.write(f"{current_time} High CPU, snmpwalk: Timeout\n'")
            print("No Response") # Write to cron.log
            send_sms()
        else: # Everything else
            f.write(f"{current_time} High CPU utilization, IndexError\n")
            print("IndexError occured due to High CPU Utilization") # Write to cron.log
            send_sms()

print("Finished") # This should print when the script runs successfully.
^G Get Help  ^O Write Out  ^W Where Is  ^K Cut Text   ^J Justify  ^C Cur Pos
^X Exit      ^R Read File  ^\ Replace   ^U Paste Text ^T To Spell ^_ Go To Line
```

6 To induce high CPU utilization on LAB-R1, do the following. Here we want to increase the CPU utilization on this router so our script can go to work and send an SMS when a certain condition is met.

Here is how to turn on all debugging on LAB-R1:

```
LAB-R1#debug all # Enable all debugging on LAB-R1. Do not do this on a production device!
```

This may severely impact network performance. Continue? (yes/[no]): **yes** # Lab environment, a big yes

Persistent variable debugs All enabled

From other switches and routers, send a large-size datagram continuously. What we want is the CPU utilization of 90 percent or more on LAB-R1.

```
LAB-SW1#ping # initialize ping configuration
Protocol [ip]:
Target IP address: 192.168.183.10 # LAB-R1 IP address
Repeat count [5]: 100000 # number of continuous pings
Datagram size [100]: 1500 # datagram, also try 3000 to overload the router's CPU more
Timeout in seconds [2]:
Extended commands [n]:
Sweep range of sizes [n]:
```

Repeat and enable the same ping commands from lab-sw2 and lab-r2. Wait about two to five minutes for LAB-R1 to reach 90 percent or above CPU utilization.

(continued)

#	Task

7	Under normal load, the CPU utilization will remain relatively low and steady. When debugging significant changes or odd problems, the CPU utilization can spike above 90 percent. Suppose the CPU utilization continues to operate at or above 90 percent for a prolonged period, this can have a sinificant impact on the performance of the services running on this device, and the issue becomes critical if the device is a core or edge router.
	Here is an example of logs under normal load condition:
	`pynetauto@ubuntu20s1:~/monitor_cpu$ cat cpu_oid_log.txt`
	`'Thu, 24 Sep 2020 12:22:44 16% OK`
	`'Thu, 24 Sep 2020 12:22:47 16% OK`
	`'Thu, 24 Sep 2020 12:23:56 24% OK`
	`'Thu, 24 Sep 2020 12:24:13 26% OK`
	`'Thu, 24 Sep 2020 12:24:39 31% OK`
	Here is an example of logs under high CPU utilization:
	`pynetauto@ubuntu20s1:~/monitor_cpu$ cat cpu_oid_log.txt`
	`'Thu, 24 Sep 2020 13:06:25 96%, High CPU`
	`'Thu, 24 Sep 2020 13:10:53 97%, High CPU`
	`'Thu, 24 Sep 2020 13:29:56 High CPU utilization, IndexError`
	`Thu, 24 Sep 2020 13:31:12 98%, High CPU`
	`Thu, 24 Sep 2020 13:50:24 High CPU utilization, IndexError`

8	The script will send an SMS message to your phone if the CPU utilization in the last five minutes has been above 90 percent. Run the completed application using the Python command shown here. This lab could be a little bit tricky to emulate and time correctly, but if you followed the steps exactly, your application will trigger the Twilio server (somewhere in the cloud) to send the SMS message to your smartphone.
	`pynetauto@ubuntu20s1:~/monitor_cpu$ python3 cpu_util_5min_monitor2.py`
	`iso.3.6.1.4.1.9.9.109.1.1.1.1.5.1 = Gauge32: 97`
	`97`
	`SM9bc812d18dd74a6d95cb8c4cc4c8d758`
	`Finished`

9	The script will also send an SMS if the `snmpwalk timeout` or `Timeout: No Response` message is received from the router.
	`Example of "snmpwalk: Timeout"`
	`pynetauto@ubuntu20s1:~/monitor_cpu$ python3 cpu_util_5min_monitor2.py`
	`snmpwalk: Timeout`
	`SMfe169235c757467cb16fd621ee58e457`
	`Finished`
	`Example of "Timeout: No Response"`
	`pynetauto@ubuntu20s1:~/monitor_cpu$ python3 cpu_util_5min_monitor2.py`
	`Timeout: No Response from 192.168.183.10`
	`SMbd36cc1b70ec4e61a988b8a51b524ee6`
	`Finished`

10	If you followed the steps correctly, then when the router meets the high CPU utilization conditions we have set, it should send an SMS message similar to Figure 16-17. Now that everything is working as tested, let's use `cron` to run the script every five minutes to check the CPU utilization of `LAB-R1`. Remember, if this was in a real production environment, the ultimate goal would be to make you spend less time in front of your computer physically monitoring the high CPU utilization in use.

#	Task
	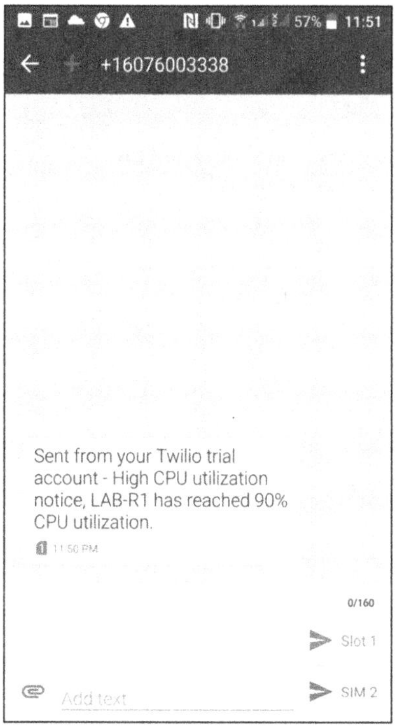 *Figure 16-17. SMS message received from Python script*
11	From your ubuntu20s1 server, open cron using the crontab -e command and schedule the script to run every five minutes to check the router's CPU utilization.

```
pynetauto@ubuntu20s1:~/monitor_cpu$ pwd
/home/pynetauto/monitor_cpu
pynetauto@ubuntu20s1:~/monitor_cpu$ ls
cpu_util_5min_monitor.py  cpu_oid_log.txt  credentials.py  nano.save  __pycache__
twilio_sms.py
```

The last line added to the crontab is shown next. As soon as the following task is scheduled in crontab, it will start to run every five minutes.

```
pynetauto@ubuntu20s1:~/monitor_cpu$ crontab -e
GNU nano 4.8                    /tmp/crontab.DbnMHK/crontab
[...omitted for brevity]
# For more information see the manual pages of crontab(5) and cron(8)
#
# m h  dom mon dow   command
*/5 * * * * /usr/bin/python3.8 /home/pynetauto/monitor_cpu/cpu_util_5min_monitor.py
>> /home/pynetauto/monitor_cpu/cron.log
^G Get Help  ^O Write Out  ^W Where Is  ^K Cut Text  ^J Justify  ^C Cur Pos
^X Exit      ^R Read File  ^\ Replace   ^U Paste Text ^T To Spell ^_ Go To Line
```

(*continued*)

#	Task

12	Let the script run and use the `ls` command to check whether `cron.log` has been created.
	`pynetauto@ubuntu20s1:~/monitor_cpu$ ls`
	`cpu_util_5min_monitor.py  credentials.py  nano.save  twilio_sms.py`
	`cpu_oid_log.txt  cron.log  __pycache__`

13	Check the logs logged to the `cron.log` file under the working directory. You should find the timestamped CPU utilization logs as the script runs and writes records to the log file. (see output below)
14	Check SMS alerts on your smartphone. If the `cron` job properly runs every five minutes, it should check for high CPU utilization, and if high CPU utilization has been detected, then send an SMS message. If the CPU for the last five minutes is less than 90 percent, it just writes the `cron` logs and should not send the SMS utilization. See Figure 16-18.

```
pynetauto@ubuntu20s1:~/monitor_cpu$ cat cron.log
---------------------------------------------------------------------------
Thu, 24 Sep 2020 14:25:01 iso.3.6.1.4.1.9.9.109.1.1.1.1.5.1 = Gauge32: 97

97
High CPU
SM5d062edec4e844bda63ab372a568c883
Finished
---------------------------------------------------------------------------
Thu, 24 Sep 2020 14:30:02 iso.3.6.1.4.1.9.9.109.1.1.1.1.5.1 = Gauge32: 98

High CPU
SMde58b1ebfc554ea1b94637ab26db256e
Finished
---------------------------------------------------------------------------
Thu, 24 Sep 2020 14:35:02 iso.3.6.1.4.1.9.9.109.1.1.1.1.5.1 = Gauge32: 97

High CPU
SMb5365d20960848459d87e0b14570596d
Finished
```

#	Task

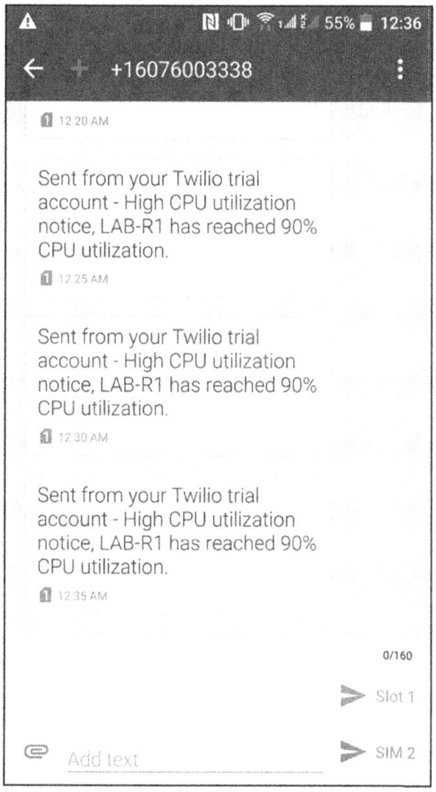

Figure 16-18. *SMS messages received at 90 percent or above CPU utilization*

15 At the end of your lab, use the Ctrl+^ keys on all pinging devices to stop ICMP pings to `LAB-R1`.

16 Finally, stop the debugging on `LAB-R1` by issuing the `u all`, `un all`, or `undebug all` command.

```
LAB-R1#un all
All possible debugging has been turned off
```

You have completed CPU monitoring lab and sent SMS alerts to your smartphone for notification of the events. This has been a simple integration on a personal laptop/PC; however, the ideas extend to the production infrastructure at a much larger scale.

Summary

Well done for completing all the tasks in this chapter! This chapter was designed to make you think outside of the box and explore various Python use cases in managing network infrastructure. At this stage, you should start thinking about what automation challenges you have at work and start researching how you are going to solve your company's problems. In this chapter, you have installed `virtualenv` on your Python and briefly tested Ansible and pyATS. Then, you started on the Docker concept and completed the email-sending application running on a Docker environment. Lastly, you registered a free account on Twilio. You wrote a Python application to check a router's CPU utilization, and when a specific condition was met, you sent an SMS warning message to your smartphone. I hope you can start thinking about other Python application use cases at work and try to solve the problem by putting together various open source and proprietary source tools available to you. In Chapter 17, we will discuss Cisco IOS XE upgrades in detail as the first phase of developing our application. Only if tasks are documented can they be automated using a programming language in the correct order.

CHAPTER 17

Upgrading Multiple Cisco IOS XE Routers

This chapter explains object-oriented programming (OOP) by using a real production example. Then the chapter will discuss Python application flow controls using a username and password application example. Finally, we will discuss the logical thinking processes involved in planning an IOS upgrade.

IOS upgrades on Cisco devices are a critical part of network operations to add reliability and security to all Cisco devices. Regular IOS patch management is also part of the network team's key performance indicators, so it is a critical part of the business. You will be guided through installing two Cisco CRS1000v IOS XE routers to prepare you for the next two chapters. Finally, we will discuss the manual Cisco IOS upgrade processes and tasks performed by a network engineer and translate the manual tasks and engineer's thinking into Python scripts. All tasks and processes must be documented in a process flowchart before writing the Python code. If you want to automate something, you must write it, documenting each step.

Difficulty level will be relative to reader's previous experience with Cisco Networking Technology.

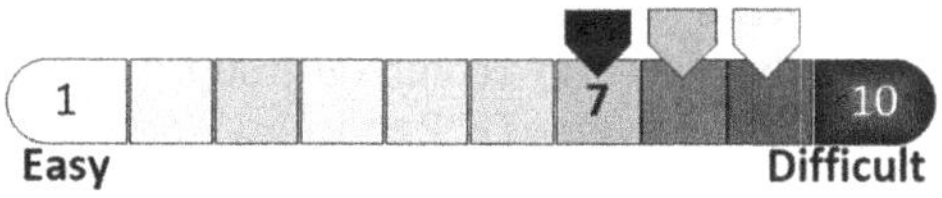

Practical Python Network Automation Lab: IOS XE Upgrade Lab

I hope your initial enthusiasm for your Python network automation journey has not worn off too much along the way. If you enjoyed every chapter leading up to this one, that is fantastic. However, you probably encountered a few obstacles and need to work on those areas more. Every chapter was designed to teach you some new IT skills to empower you. Get ready for the most exciting three chapters in this book!

Throughout this book, you have learned various IT system management skills, and finally you are here. Like many other popular programming languages, Python is classified as an object-oriented programming language. I have left the OOP discussion until now because a discussion of OOP could easily scare away novice Python learners. In this chapter, I will give a working example of how OOP can be applied to a real work scenario so you can relate OOP immediately to your work. Next, you will review how we can use the basic flow controls using the user ID and password inputs in our scripts. In many environments, you may not have a secure password vault; often you will write interactive code, requiring the users to provide the user

B. Choi, *Introduction to Python Network Automation*, https://doi.org/10.1007/978-1-4842-6806-3_17

ID and password to the application you have developed. In the last labs, you will build two Cisco CSR 1000v virtual routers on VMware Workstation 15 Pro to set you up for mini tools development in Chapter 18. We will discuss the Cisco IOS upgrade process in detail at the end of this chapter.

Applying OOP Concepts to Your Network

Until this point, we have not discussed object-oriented programming in Python. Even without knowing a lot about OOP, our Python scripts were working fine. But when intermediate to advanced Python users start talking about optimizing Python scripts, they always emphasize that Python is an OOP language. So, we have to take full advantage of the OOP concepts. Just like with another popular OOP language, Java, we need to know four fundamental concepts: encapsulation, abstraction, inheritance, and polymorphism. The ultimate aim of OOP is to bind the data better so a lot of duplication is removed and the same code can be reused throughout the same program or application.

Let's quickly cover the basics, and then we will look at OOP in action by writing an OOP example using routers and switches. We'll keep the theory to the minimum and get into the practical example to help you better understand the OOP concepts.

- *Object-oriented programming*: From an OOP perspective, everything is considered an object. The C language is called a *procedure-oriented programming* language because it runs based on the processes running in a functional order. On the other hand, in OOP, the objects are related to each other and connected to run the program. OOP treats anything and everything as an object, and it is viewed that they are linked to each other by some relationship.

- *Object*: As the word suggests, an *object* in OOP is a thing or an object. For example, a human or a robot can be considered an object, and also, a book or a router is an object. Since the same router (or switches) models look the same, every router can be called an object because if you make a dent on one of the routers, it does not necessarily make dents on other routers. Objects with similar characteristics or features are in the same group of objects, meaning that they can be grouped. Certain characteristics are the same or similar between the same objects in a common group. Even we humans can be considered as objects based on the Python OOP concept.

- *Class*: People generally have almost identical attributes such as two eyes, a nose, a mouth, hands, feet, and other physical body parts. Books also have the same attributes, such as book title, author, publisher, and publication dates. Switches from different vendors will still have the same switch model, serial number, rack unit size, and Ethernet ports. Classes are defined by a collection of common properties of objects such as people, books, and switches have in common.

- *Abstraction*: This refers to showing only essential attributes and hide unnecessary objects from the user. For example, a complex function in a class hides (abstracts) detailed information from the user, so s/he can implement logic on top of abstraction without understanding the actual function or even thinking about all the hidden complexities of the class.

- *Encapsulation*: This refers to the idea of binding the data and methods which manipulate the data into a unit. Again, a class is an excellent example of encapsulation as the objects inside a class keep their state private and not directly accessible; instead, the state of the objects are accessed through methods by calling a list of public functions.

- *Polymorphism*: This is the process of making one operator and using it in many ways; it has one form but with many use cases. A good analogy is that different kinds of pens are all classified as pens, but their uses are vastly different. For example, there are pens for taking notes, and there are pens for drawing and creating artwork.
- *Inheritance*: This is the process of making a class from an existing class. Consider parents to children and children to parents; if you are born in a family and your parents are your birth parents, you and your siblings as children take or inherit both parents' characteristics. If you create a new class that derives from and is associated with an existing class, then the new class inherits the old class's characteristics.

Now that we have the basic OOP theory out of the way, let's use our routers and switches example to write classes to understand the OOP style of coding better. As your applications become more complex, the power of OOP truly shines as it binds the data. Let's take a look at a real example. Read and follow along in your Python interpreter.

#	Task
1	Let's write a class for routers and switches. For the most part, the routers and switches will have identical attributes; the difference is in the functions or the features. In this example, using inheritance, we can collapse or move the `def __init__` to the parent class. Let's quickly write our first classes. As you can see, both the router and switch classes have `serialnumber`, `hostname`, `ipaddress` (management), `modelnumber`, and `devicetype` attributes. The `__init__` is a reserved method in classes known as a *constructor* in OOP. The programmers read `__init__` as "dunder init dunder" and it allows the class to initialize a class's attributes. The word `self` in the class is used to represent the class's instance; with the `self` keyword, you can access the class's attributes and methods. `self` is used to bind the attributes with the given arguments to the `@` syntax used in Java. It adds a special attribute to the class, method, and variable.

```
class Router:
   def __init__(self, serialnumber, hostname, ipaddress, modelnumber, devicetype):
      self.serialnumber = serialnumber # 12 Hexadecimal numbers
      self.hostname = hostname
      self.ipaddress = ipaddress # format 1.0.0.X - 254.254.254.XXX
      self.modelnumber = modelnumber
      self.devicetype = devicetype
   def process(self):
      print("Packet routing")

class Switch:
   def __init__(self, serialnumber, hostname, ipaddress, modelnumber, devicetype):
      self.serialnumber = serialnumber # 12 Hexadecimal numbers
      self.hostname = hostname
      self.ipaddress = ipaddress # format 1.0.0.X - 254.254.254.XXX
      self.modelnumber = modelnumber
      self.devicetype = devicetype
   def process(self):
      print("Packet switching")
```

The router and switch both process packets; one does packet routing and the other packet switching, so a process was created to describe their functions. You have successfully created your first set of classes for your network devices.

(*continued*)

#	Task
2	Create a parent class called Devices, as shown next. The Devices class also takes the same attributes as the Router and Switch classes you created in task 1. So, create the Devices class in the same manner. You also want to add another function called show to let the function display the information when it is invoked.

```
>>> class Devices:
...   def __init__(self, serialnumber, hostname, ipaddress, modelnumber, devicetype):
...           self.serialnumber = serialnumber # 12 Hexadecimal numbers
...     self.hostname = hostname
...     self.ipaddress = ipaddress # format 1.0.0.X - 254.254.254.XXX
...     self.modelnumber = modelnumber
...     self.devicetype = devicetype
...   def show(self): # show all the attributes
...     print(f"{self.serialnumber},{self.hostname},{self.ipaddress},
{self.modelnumber},{self.devicetype}")
...
>>>
```

Now, create three classes called Router, Switch, and Firewall, respectively, and pass the class Devices to each device type class. Now all three classes will inherit the characteristics of the parent class, Devices. You can already see how classes and OOP simplify your code, because you did not have to create the same attributes three separate times. We have just created one for the parent class and applied it to all three child classes.

```
>>> class Router(Devices):
...      def process(self):
...          print("Packet routing")
...
>>> class Switch(Devices):
...      def process(self):
...          print("Packet switching")
...
>>> class Firewall(Devices):
...      def process(self):
...          print("Packet filtering")
...
```

Now create three variables, one for each child class as shown here:

```
>>> rt1 = Switch("001122AABBCC", "RT01", "1.1.1.1", "C4431-K9", "RT")
>>> sw1 = Router("001122DDEEFF", "SW02", "2.2.2.2", "WS-3850-48T", "SW")
>>> fw1 = Firewall("003344ABCDEF", "FW02", "3.3.3.3", "PA-5280", "FW")
```

From your Python interpreter, run the following commands to retrieve your device information. The show() method was automatically inherited from the parent class, Devices. This example was shown on the interpreter, but you can also write it into the code or download oop1.py and run it as a script. You have just finished studying the inheritance of OOP classes.

```
>>> rt1.show()
001122AABBCC,RT01,1.1.1.1,C4431-K9,RT
>>> sw1.show()
001122DDEEFF,SW02,2.2.2.2,WS-3850-48T,SW
>>> fw1.show()
003344ABCDEF,FW02,3.3.3.3,PA-5280,FW
```

#	Task
3	Next, let's build hierarchical classes so our comprehension of OOP solidifies, and we can use this in our real-life scenarios. The following example has the top-tier class called `Pynetauto_co`, which represents your company. The following is the child class called `Cisco`, representing the vendor of your company's networking devices. This is followed by the child class, `Devices`, and then under `Devices`, there are two child classes called `Router` and `Switch`. The inheritance is like a waterfall, so it is top-down. You can write this in Notepad or directly in the nano text editor.

oop_task1.py

```
class Pynetauto_co: # parent class of Cisco class
   "Parent class of Cisco, HP, Juniper, Arista"
   def __init__(self, companyname):
      self.companyname = companyname
   def PrintInfo_P1(self):
      print("Pynetauto Company")
      #print("www.xyzptyltd.com")

class Cisco(Pynetauto_co): # parent class of Devices class
   "Parent class of Switch, Router and Firewall"
   def __init__(self, vendor):
      self.Vendor = vendor
   def PrintInfo_P2(self):
      print("Cisco")
      #print("www.cisco.com")

class Devices (Cisco): # parent class of Router and Switch classes
   "Parent class of Switch, Router and Firewall"
   def __init__(self, serialnumber, hostname, ipaddress, modelnumber, devicetype):
      self.serialnumber = serialnumber # 12 Hexadecimal numbers
      self.hostname = hostname
      self.ipaddress = ipaddress # format 1.0.0.X - 254.254.254.XXX
      self.modelnumber = modelnumber
      self.devicetype = devicetype
   def show(self): # show all the attributes
      print(f"{self.serialnumber},{self.hostname},{self.ipaddress},\
            {self.modelnumber},{self.devicetype}")
class Router(Devices):
   def process(self):
      print("Packet switching")
class Switch(Devices):
   def process(self):
      print("Packet routing")

rt3 = Router("000111222222", "RT03", "2.2.2.2", "C4351/K9", "RT")
sw3 = Switch("000111222111", "SW03", "1.1.1.1", "WS-3850-48T", "SW")

rt3.PrintInfo_P1()
rt3.PrintInfo_P2()
rt3.show()

sw3.PrintInfo_P1()
sw3.PrintInfo_P2()
sw3.show()
```

(continued)

#	Task

	When you save the previous OOP task script and run it from Python, it will return the following output:
	`Pynetauto Company`
	`Cisco`
	`000111222222,RT03,2.2.2.2,C4351/K9,RT`
	`Pynetauto Company`
	`Cisco`
	`000111222111,SW03,1.1.1.1,WS-3850-48T,SW`

OOP will bind the data together and empower you to write clean code. When you have to deal with many objects with similar attributes and cannot create each object's attributes, OOP will come to your rescue. Also, when we have to manage data in a dataframe or any SQL type, the OOP structure can help us better manage and handle data within our Python scripts. Now let's quickly move onto the next topic.

Flow Control and Controlling User Input: UID, PWD, and Information Collector

In this section, you will learn something fun and practical. While developing an interactive or noninteractive Python application, you often want to control an interactive user's data input. You want to make sure that the user input is precisely what is defined in your script. This, in turn, can be used to change the flow of your Python script. A straightforward example would be asking the user to enter yes or no. There could be four possible user input scenarios. In this case, first, type in yes or y; second, type in no or n; third, type something other than yes or no; and fourth, stare at the screen and type nothing in. Also, by introducing regular expressions into user input, you can home in to accept the information you want and reject any other variable values. You will see this in action in the next example, but first, let's have some fun with the yes/no user input scenario; then we'll reiterate the script to make it more useful, and study how it can change the flow of your Python script and how the reiteration can enhance your simple script.The first script you will develop is a username and password input application using a yes/no script.

#	Task
1	The following is a simple yes/no user input example using the `if ~ else` statement. Create a new Python script called `yes_or_no1.py`, and run the script. There are a few flaws with this script, but we will enhance this first input script to make it useful in our real Python applications.

Create a separate directory on your server and create your first script as shown here:

```
pynetauto@ubuntu20s1:~$ mkdir user_input
pynetauto@ubuntu20s1:~$ cd user_input
pynetauto@ubuntu20s1:~/user_input$ nano yes_or_no1.py
```

```
GNU nano 4.8                              /home/pynetauto/user_input/yes_or_no1.py
def yes_or_no(): # Create function called yes_or_no
   yes_or_no = input("Enter yes or no : ") # Ask for user input
   yes_or_no = yes_or_no.lower()# change all input casing to lower casing
   if yes_or_no == "yes": # if answer is 'yes' take the following action
      print("Oh Yes!")
   else: # if answer is 'no' or other input, take the following action
      print("Oh No!")
yes_or_no() # Run the function
```

#	Task

	`^G Get Help  ^O Write Out  ^W Where Is  ^K Cut Text  ^J Justify  ^C Cur Pos`
	`^X Exit  ^R Read File  ^\ Replace  ^U Paste Text  ^T To Spell  ^_ Go To Line`
	
	When you run the previous script and give input, the output should look like this for each response.
	
	This Python code is pretty basic. Think about where we can improve on this script.
	
	`pynetauto@ubuntu20s1:~/user_input$ python3 yes_or_no1.py`
	`Enter yes or no : Yes`
	`Oh Yes!`
	`pynetauto@ubuntu20s1:~/user_input$ python3 yes_or_no1.py`
	`Enter yes or no : no`
	`Oh No!`
	`pynetauto@ubuntu20s1:~/user_input$ python3 yes_or_no1.py`
	`Enter yes or no : maybe`
	`Oh No!`

2	The first example had the following flaws:
	
	a. Not considering the abbreviated response from the user, y for yes and n for no.
	
	b. No response and the incorrect response were treated as the same response.
	
	Let's quickly correct the previous and see if we can reiterate this simple code and make it better.
	
	Name your code file yes_or_no2.py.
	
	`pynetauto@ubuntu20s1:~/user_input$ nano yes_or_no2.py`
	
	`GNU nano 4.8  /home/pynetauto/user_input/yes_or_no2.py`
	`def yes_or_no():`
	`    yes_or_no = input("Enter yes or no : ")`
	`    yes_or_no = yes_or_no.lower()`
	`    if yes_or_no == "yes" or yes_or_no == "y": # Takes abbreviated response`
	`        print("Oh Yes!")`
	`    elif yes_or_no == "no" or yes_or_no == "n": # Takes abbreviated response`
	`        print("Oh No!")`
	`    else: # Any other responses, print the following statement`
	`        print("You have not entered the correct response.")`
	`yes_or_no()`
	`^G Get Help  ^O Write Out  ^W Where Is  ^K Cut Text  ^J Justify  ^C Cur Pos`
	`^X Exit  ^R Read File  ^\ Replace  ^U Paste Text  ^T To Spell  ^_ Go To Line`
	
	The expected output examples are as shown here, but we can still improve this further:
	
	`pynetauto@ubuntu20s1:~/user_input$ python3 yes_or_no2.py`
	`Enter yes or no : y`
	`Oh Yes!`
	`pynetauto@ubuntu20s1:~/user_input$ python3 yes_or_no2.py`
	`Enter yes or no : no`
	`Oh No!`
	`pynetauto@ubuntu20s1:~/user_input$ python3 yes_or_no2.py`
	`Enter yes or no : maybe`
	`You have not entered the correct response.`

(continued)

#	Task
3	You only want to allow yes or no as a response and want to prompt the user until a yes, y, no, or n response is provided. By restricting the users response, you are now dictating and controlling the flow of your script. How would you achieve this goal? What part of the script do you have to change to get a yes or a no from the respondent? There are a few possible ways to achieve this, and as always, there are no right or wrong answers with Python coding, only the best recommendations. Let's look at the next example to achieve our goal.

In the following example, you will use a simple list with the expected answers, and you will only allow your script to run when those values are received as a response. Until you get the correct response, you will prompt the user that you expect a yes or no response.

```
pynetauto@ubuntu20s1:~/user_input$ nano yes_or_no3.py
```

```
GNU nano 4.8                          /home/pynetauto/user_input/yes_or_no3.py
def yes_or_no():
   yes_or_no = input("Enter yes or no : ")
   yes_or_no = yes_or_no.lower()
   expected_response = ['yes', 'y', 'no', 'n'] # Expected responses
   while yes_or_no not in expected_response: # Prompt until 'yes' or 'no' response is
   given
      yes_or_no = input("Expecting yes or no : ")
   if yes_or_no == "yes" or yes_or_no == "y": # 'yes' or 'y' action
      print("Oh Yes!")
   else: # 'no' or 'n' action
      print("Oh No!")

yes_or_no()
^G Get Help  ^O Write Out  ^W Where Is  ^K Cut Text   ^J Justify   ^C Cur Pos
^X Exit      ^R Read File  ^\ Replace   ^U Paste Text ^T To Spell  ^_ Go To Line
```

The expected output should look as follows, and the response must meet the criteria to pass the while loop. Otherwise, the user is asked over and over again for the correct response. Now, this looks quite promising, but where can you use this piece of code? In the next example, let's look at the real example and how it is used.

```
pynetauto@ubuntu20s1:~/user_input$ python3 yes_or_no3.py
Enter yes or no : Y
Oh Yes!
pynetauto@ubuntu20s1:~/user_input$ python3 yes_or_no3.py
Enter yes or no : NO
Oh No!
pynetauto@ubuntu20s1:~/user_input$ python3 yes_or_no3.py
Enter yes or no : maybe
Expecting yes or no : maybe
Expecting yes or no : yes
Oh Yes!
```

#	Task
4	The following script collects two sets of network administrator ID and password. To start, get the first administrator's credentials, and then ask if the second administrator's credentials are the same. If the response is yes or y, the user ID and passwords are the same. If the response is no or n, then collect the second set of user ID and password.

```
pynetauto@ubuntu20s1:~/user_input$ nano yes_or_no4.py
```

```
GNU nano 4.8                          /home/pynetauto/user_input/ yes_or_no4.py
from getpass import getpass

def get_credentials():
   #Prompts for, and returns a username1 and password1
   username1 = input("Enter Network Admin1 ID: ") # Request for username 1
   password1 = getpass("Enter Network Admin1 PWD: ") #  Request for password 1
   print("Username1 :", username1, "Password1 :", password1) # Print username and password

   #Prompts for  username2 and password2
   yes_or_no = input("Network Admin2 credentials same as Network Admin1 credentials?
   (Yes/No): ").lower() # Ask if Network Admin 2 has the same credentials as Admin 1
   expected_response = ['yes', 'y', 'no', 'n'] # Expect any of these four responses
   while yes_or_no not in expected_response: # Prompt until 'yes' or 'no' response is given
      yes_or_no = input("Expecting yes or no : ")
   if yes_or_no == "yes" or yes_or_no == "y": # If 'yes' or 'y', credentials ate the
      same as Admin1
      username2 = username1
      password2 = password1
      print("Username2 :", username2, "Password2: ", password2) # Print username and password
   else: # If 'no' or 'n', request for Admin2 username and password
      username2 = input("Enter Network Admin2 ID : ")
      password2 = getpass("Enter Network Admin2 Password : ")
      print("Username2 :", username2, "Password2 :", password2) # Print username and password
get_credentials()
^G Get Help  ^O Write Out   ^W Where Is  ^K Cut Text   ^J Justify   ^C Cur Pos
^X Exit      ^R Read File   ^\ Replace   ^U Paste Text ^T To Spell  ^_ Go To Line
```

Run the script to test the user ID and password collector script. The expected output should be similar to the following output. Do you think you can reiterate this script and improve this script? Let's see the final example.

```
pynetauto@ubuntu20s1:~/user_input$ python3 yes_or_no4.py
Enter Network Admin1 ID: hugh
Enter Network Admin1 PWD:*********
Username1 : john Password1 : password1
Network Admin2 credentials same as Network Admin1 credentials? (Yes/No): yes
Username2 : john Password2:  password1
pynetauto@ubuntu20s1:~/user_input$ python3 yes_or_no4.py
Enter Network Admin1 ID: hugh
Enter Network Admin1 PWD: *********
Username1 : hugh Password1 : password1
Network Admin2 credentials same as Network Admin1 credentials? (Yes/No): no
```

(*continued*)

#	Task

```
Enter Network Admin2 ID : john
Enter Network Admin2 Password : ***********
Username2 : john Password2 : password777
```

5 In this final reiteration of the yes or no example, you will add a password verification feature to make sure that the user's first password is verified with the second password. Both passwords must match; the getpass module from the getpass library hides the password while the user is typing the password. By adding the password verification feature, you are minimizing the likelihood of an incorrect password.

```
pynetauto@ubuntu20s1:~/user_input$ nano yes_or_no5.py
```

```
GNU nano 4.8                              /home/pynetauto/user_input/yes_or_no5.py
from getpass import getpass

def get_credentials():
    #Prompts for, and returns a username1 and password1
    username1 = input("Enter Network Admin1 ID: ") # Request for username 1
    password1 = None # Set password1 to None (initial value to None)
    while not password1: # Until password1 is given
        password1 = getpass("Enter Network Admin1 PWD : ") # Get password1
        password1_verify = getpass("Confirm Network Admin1 PWD : ") # Request for
        validation
        if password1 != password1_verify: # If the password1 and verification password
        does not match
            print("Passwords do not match. Please try again.") # Print this information
            password1 = None # Set the password to None and ask for password1 again
    print("Username1 :", username1, "Password1 :", password1) # Print username and
    password

    #Prompts for  username2 and password2
    yes_or_no = input("Network Admin2 credentials same as Network Admin1 credentials?
    (Yes/No): ").lower() # Ask if Network Admin 2 has the same credentials as Admin 1
    expected_response = ['yes', 'y', 'no', 'n'] # Expect any of these four responses
    while yes_or_no not in expected_response: # Prompt until 'yes' or 'no' response is given
        yes_or_no = input("Expecting yes or no : ")
    if yes_or_no == "yes" or yes_or_no == "y": # If 'yes' or 'y', credentials ate the
    same as Admin1
        username2 = username1
        password2 = password1
        print("Username2 :", username2, "Password2 :", password2) # Print username and
        password
    else: # If 'no' or 'n', request for Admin2 username and password
        username2 = input("Enter Network Admin2 ID: ") # Request for username 2
        password2 = None # Explanation same as above
        while not password2: # Explanation same as above
            password2 = getpass("Enter Network Admin2 PWD : ") # Explanation same as above
            password2_verify = getpass("Confirm Network Admin2 PWD : ")
            if password2 != password2_verify: # Explanation same as above
                print("Passwords do not match. Please try again.")
                password2 = None # Explanation same as above
```

#	Task

```
        print("Username2 :", username2, "Password2 :", password2) # Print username and
        password

    get_credentials()
    ^G Get Help  ^O Write Out   ^W Where Is  ^K Cut Text    ^J Justify    ^C Cur Pos
    ^X Exit      ^R Read File   ^\ Replace   ^U Paste Text  ^T To Spell   ^_ Go To Line
```

You can learn the process of reiterating code to improve the original code. Once you are happy with your code's quality, you can save it to your code repository and document it, or you can also choose to share it with others on your team or on the online community. In reality, Python coding is not always fun as you have to get anal about everything you code. You frequently have to adjust the reiteration of your code and other code. Learn to start with an elementary script and then make improvements through reiterations.

Here is the expected output:

```
pynetauto@ubuntu20s1:~/user_input$ python3 yes_or_no5.py
Enter Network Admin1 ID: hugh
Enter Network Admin1 PWD :***********
Confirm Network Admin1 PWD : ********* # incorrect password typed
Passwords do not match. Please try again.
Enter Network Admin1 PWD : ***********
Confirm Network Admin1 PWD : *********** # correct password typed
Username1 : hugh Password1 : password123
Network Admin2 credentials same as Network Admin1 credentials? (Yes/No): yes
Username2 : hugh Password2 : password123
pynetauto@ubuntu20s1:~/user_input$ python3 yes_or_no5.py
Enter Network Admin1 ID: john
Enter Network Admin1 PWD : ***********
Confirm Network Admin1 PWD : ***********
Username1 : john Password1 : password777
Network Admin2 credentials same as Network Admin1 credentials? (Yes/No): no
Enter Network Admin2 ID: bill
Enter Network Admin2 PWD : ***********
Confirm Network Admin2 PWD : ***********
Username2 : bill Password2 : password888
```

You have completed an exercise to write a basic Python application and then improve the code by adding new features and ideas through reiterations. Your first code is never perfect; it takes time and imagination to make even the most straightforward Python programs for your work. Next, let's prepare for the final lab and plan for IOS upgrade application development by discussing the actual IOS upgrade tasks and processes.

Lab Preparation

One problem with IOS upgrade tests on GNS3 is that it does not fully support the reloading feature within GNS3. This is one of the downfalls of emulation software compared to real IOS software. There are two possible ways we can start developing and testing IOS upgrade scenarios. The first way is to purchase the real hardware and test, and the second way is to find an alternative or virtual IOS image that supports upgrading IOS in a virtual environment. From the first chapter of this book, I have promised you that everything we do in this book can be emulated and practiced without expensive Cisco devices. Also, all learning will be completed from a single PC or laptop. However, in developing an application to upgrade a Cisco IOS, I have to admit there is no replacement for the actual hardware equipment. A virtualized Cisco router or a switch is not the same as a physical router or a switch. The virtual routers and switches have logical parts as in files but without the real motherboard, pluggable ports, power-consuming power supply, and noisy cooling fans. Also, some parts of switching can be emulated, as you have seen in the use of IOSvL2 switches. These switches are not 100 percent like production equipment as they miss the real ASCII support for LAN switching. We can use the closest Cisco IOS device on a single laptop to emulate the IOS upgrade using the virtual cloud router, Cisco CSR 1000v. As long as you can get your hands on a copy of Cisco CSR 1000v, you can still practice the IOS upgrading scenario using Python scripts. Unfortunately, I cannot share this software with every reader, if you can get your own copy, you will be able to follow the whole lab from beginning to end. If you cannot get ahold of the CSR 1000v IOS XE images or similar images used here, you may have to purchase a couple of very outdated Cisco 2621XM/2651XM routers for $10 each on eBay and emulate the reloading section of the code.

CSR 1000v IOS XE Software and Download

To prepare for this lab, we have to download a set of Cisco CSR 1000v IOS XE images. Pay close attention and take notes on the different file extensions of the set of files we are about to download for our final lab. For virtual machine (router) creation, we first need to download the file ending with the `.ova` file extension. The VMware ESXi6.5 virtual machine template file and the IOS upgrading practice need the latest IOS XE file with the file extension `.bin`. You can find more details on each of these files in Table 17-1.

Table 17-1. *CSR 1000v IOS XE Files Used in This Chapter*

Item	From IOS XE Detail	To IOS XE Detail
Release Date	30-Nov-2018	04-Sep-2020
Release	Fuji-16.7.3	Fuji-16.9.6
FileName	csr1000v-universalk9.16.07.03.ova	csr1000v-universalk9.16.09.06.SPA.bin
Release Date	30-Nov-2018	04-Sep-2020
Min Memory	DRAM 4096 Flash 8192	DRAM 4096 Flash 8192
Size	397.99 MB	416.35 MB
MD5	aa6cba7ff85afb3e7ca29831a28aefb4	77878ae6db8e34de90e2e3e83741bf39

As you have noticed, the minimum memory and flash size requirements are quite demanding to run on GNS3, and the GNS3 will struggle to run Cisco CRS 1000v routers in GNS3 environment. Since network automation's power is realized only when the same application can run on more than a single device, you will be creating two virtual CSR 1000v routers on your computer. That means the memory consumption from these two virtual routers alone will be 8 GB combined. Also, as mentioned, on the basic GNS3 configuration, the rebooting emulation does not have the expected behaviors as you would expect from a real production environment, so rather than building the IOS XE routers on GNS3, you will be importing the `.ova` file and creating two Cisco IOS XE routers on VMware Workstation 15 Pro. Then, you can follow the IOS upgrade by uploading the latest `.bin` file of the same IOS XE train. Since you will not be testing any serious routing concepts but only required to emulate IOS upgrade, this lab setup is sufficient and helpful to develop a real working Python application for end-to-end IOS upgrade scenarios.

If you have an active Cisco service contract and have access to CCO, please log in and download the following or similar sets of files for your lab practice. It does not have to be Fuji. If you prefer another IOS XE flavor for CSR 1000v, you should download a set of files for this lab. See Figure 17-1.

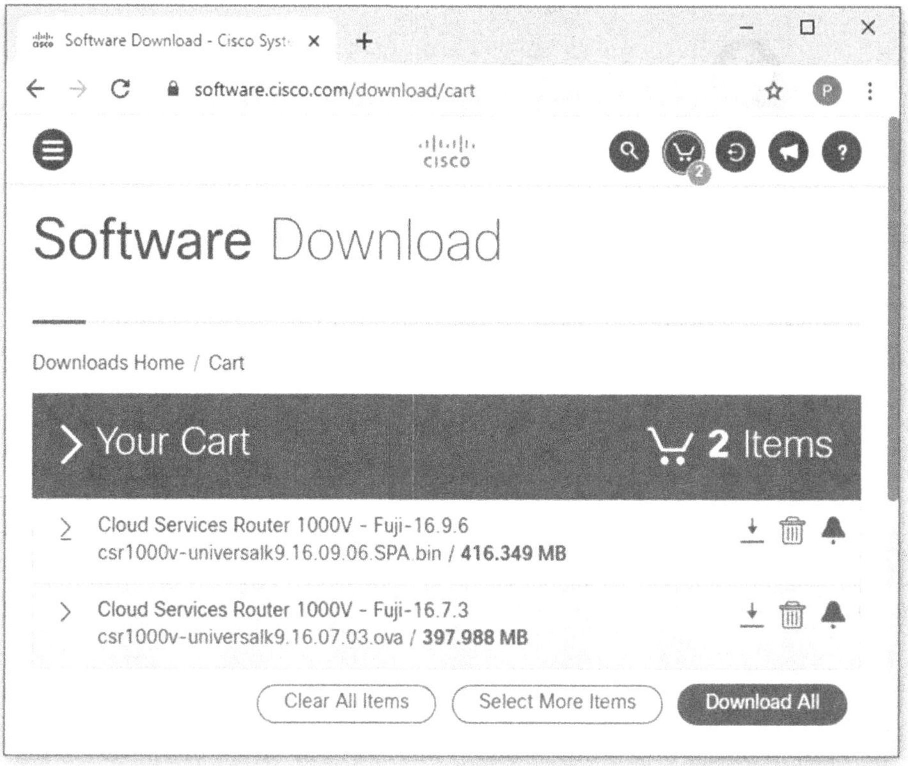

Figure 17-1. *CSR 1000v IOS XE downloads from Cisco software download site*

Cisco CSR 1000v Installation on VMware Workstation

Installing CSR 1000v on VMware Workstation 15 is no different from installing the GNS3 VM `.ova` file you previously installed. But this time, you are going to create two virtual machines instead of one. Also, for this lab, you can keep the GNS3 completely powered off, but you will still need the Python server, `ubuntu20s1`, powered on. As soon as we build the virtual routers, we will configure both routers with the minimal configuration and get on with the IOS upgrade application development. See Figure 17-2.

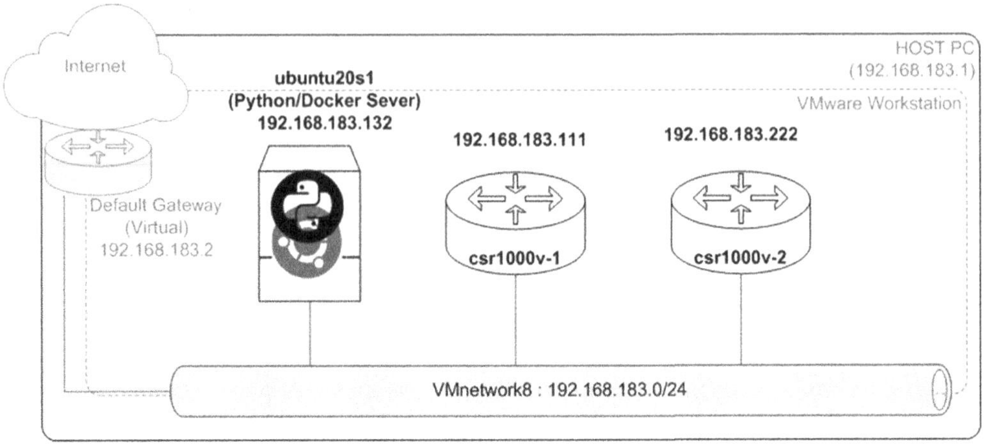

Figure 17-2. *Chapter 10 lab equipment*

Now follow these tasks to install both `csr1000v-1` and `csr1000v-2` virtual routers. The installation of csr100-v is straightforward.

#	Task
1	To create the virtual machine, first open the VMware Workstation main window and go to File ➤ Open. Then go to the Downloads folder and select the `csr1000v-universalk9.16.07.03.ova` file. See Figure 17-3.

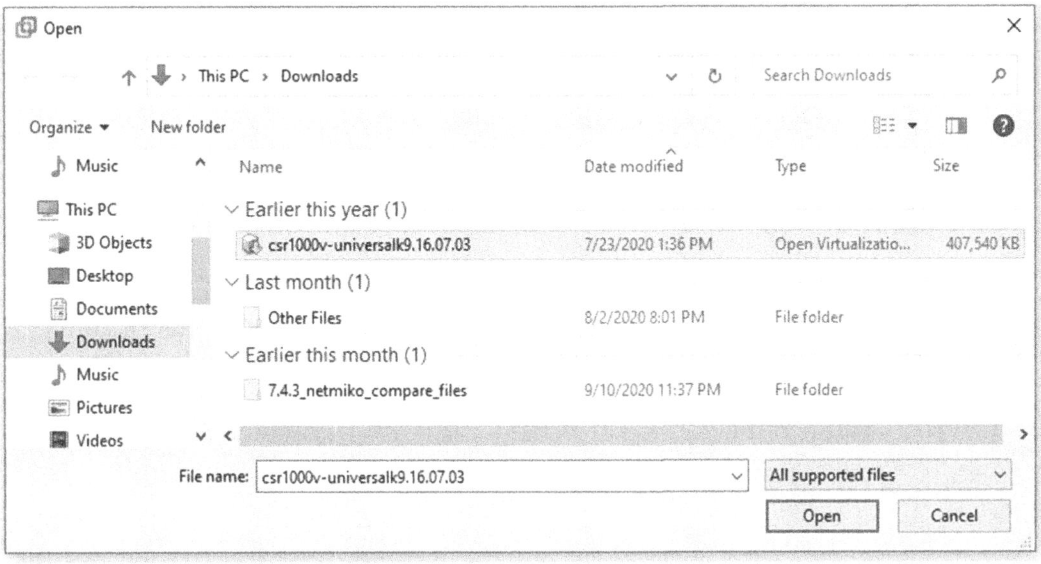

Figure 17-3. *VMware Workstation, selecting the csr1000v .ova file*

#	Task
2	For the first virtual router, give `csr1000v-1` as the name of this device. When you create the second virtual router, you just need to change the last digit of the router name to 2, so it would be `csr1000v-2`. See Figure 17-4.

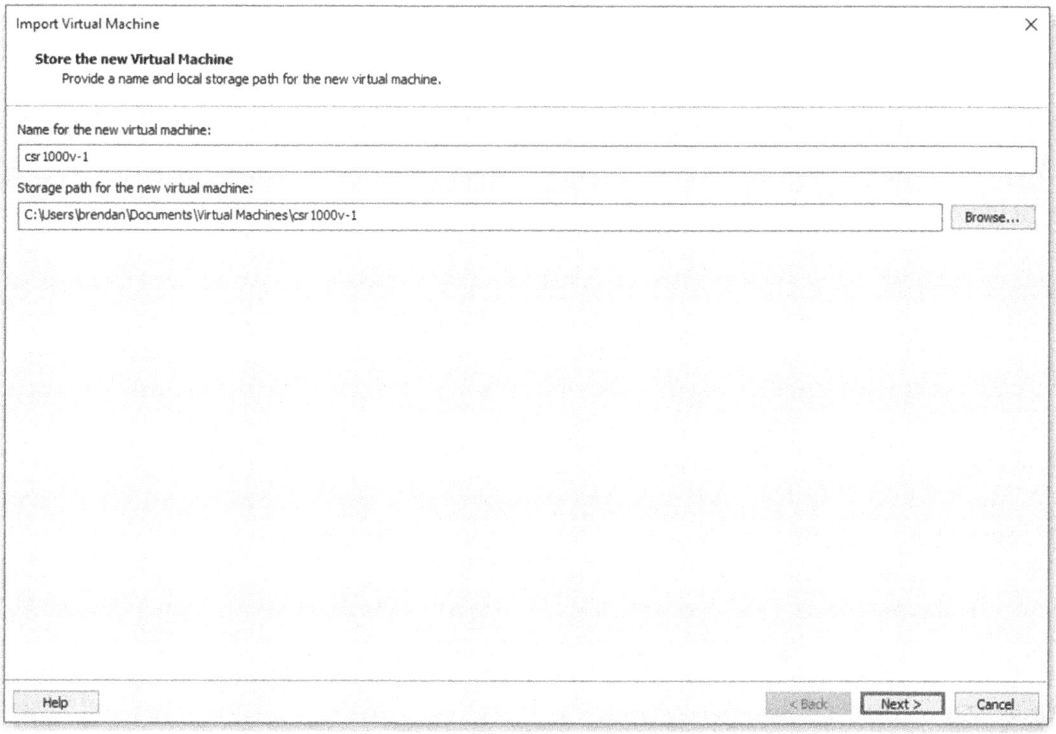

Figure 17-4. *csr1000v-1, giving the new router name*

(*continued*)

#	Task
3	Leave the Deployment Options setting as Small and click the Next button. See Figure 17-5.

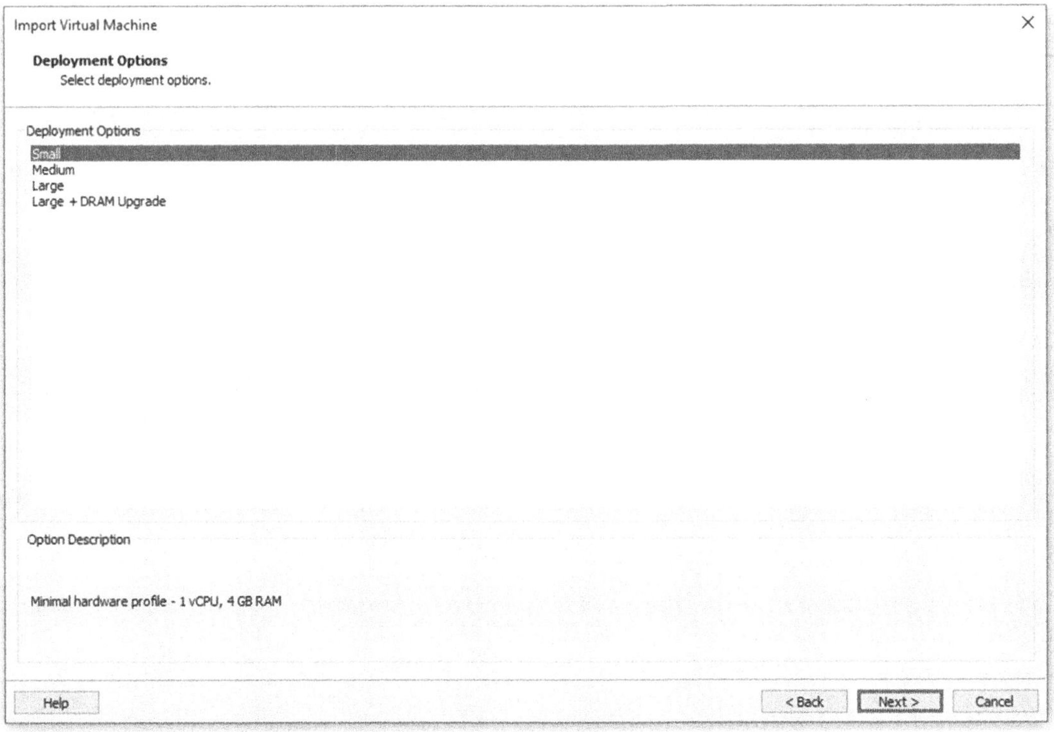

Figure 17-5. *csr1000v-1, deployment options*

#	Task
4	Now to import the virtual router, you are going to fill out the following properties. Configuring the properties on the GUI is the same as configuring these settings through the CLI. For 1. Bootstrap Properties, fill in the Router Name, Login Username, and Login Password fields. See Figure 17-6.

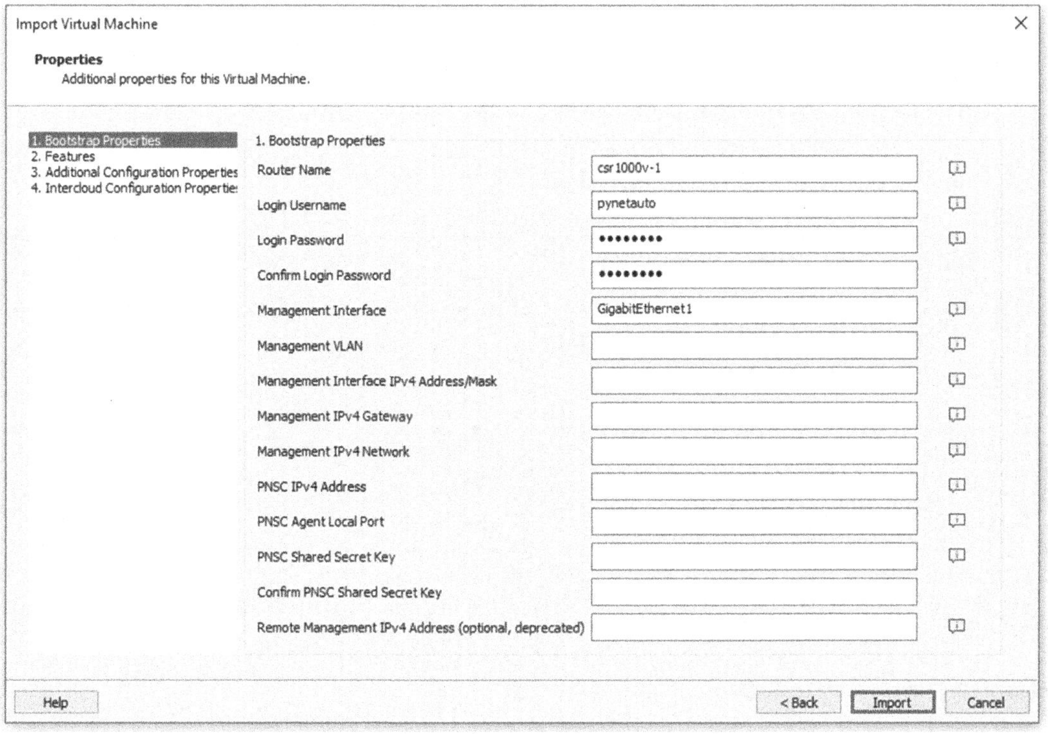

Figure 17-6. *csr1000v-1, 1. Bootstrap Properties*

(*continued*)

#	Task
	For 2. Features, change False to True for both Enable SCP Server and Enable SSH and Disable Telnet Login. See Figure 17-7.

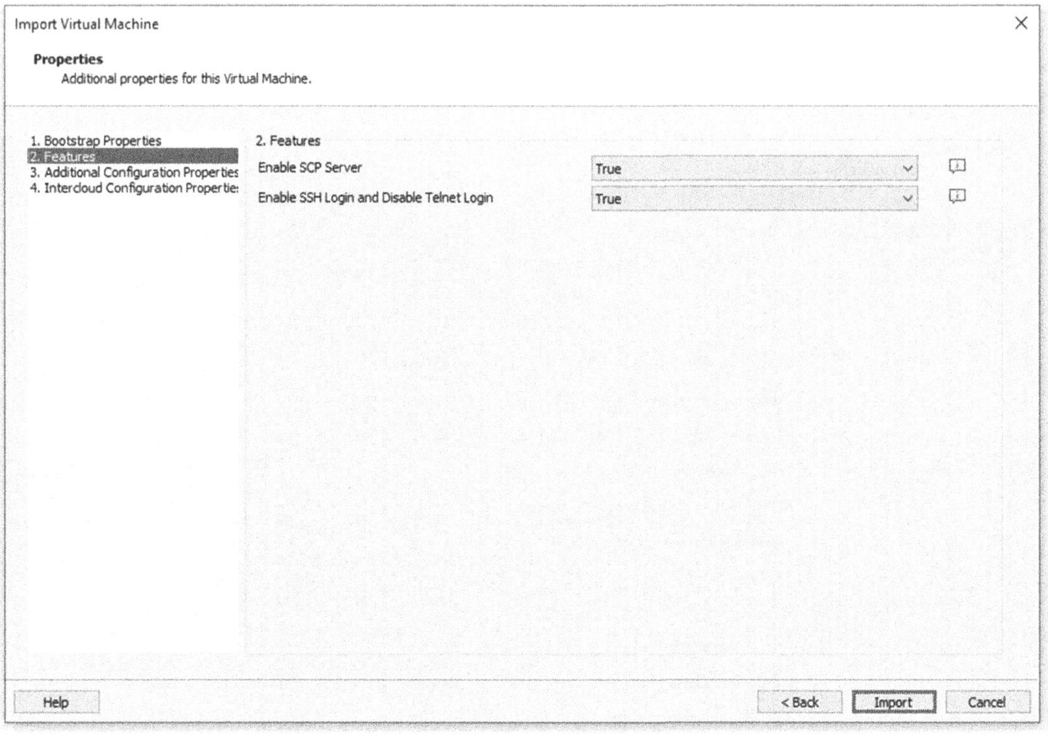

Figure 17-7. *csr1000v-1, 2. Features*

For 3. Additional Configuration Properties, fill in Enable Password and a testing domain name. See Figure 17-8.

No configuration is required for 4. Intercloud Configuration Properties; leave the settings at the defaults.

#	Task

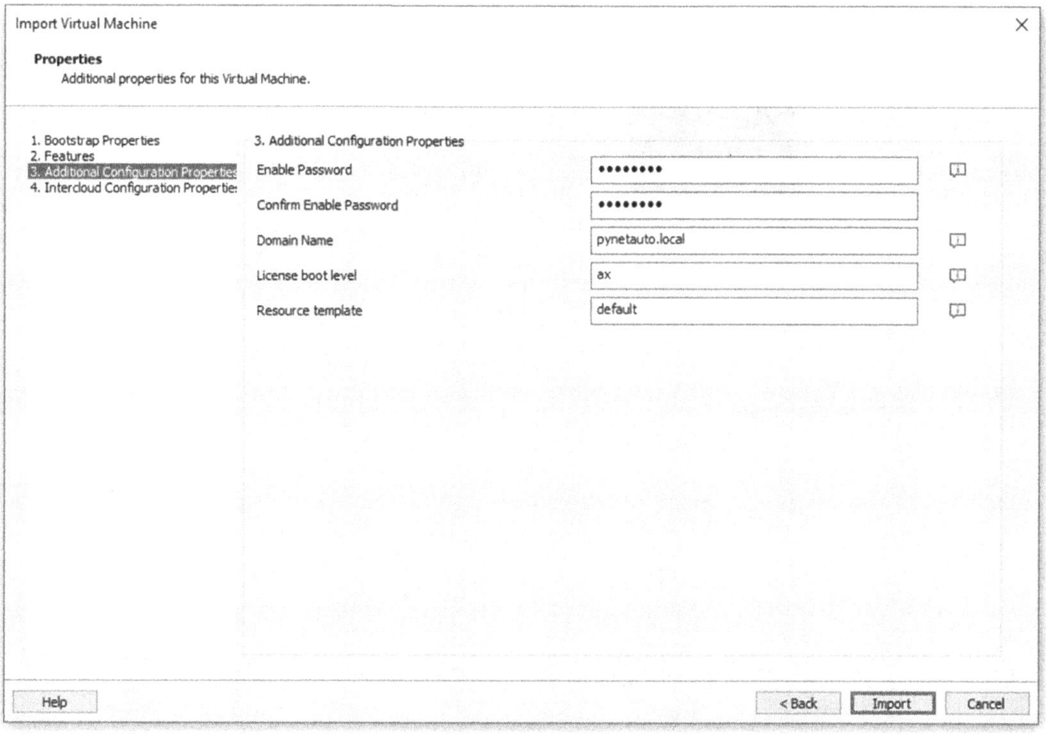

Figure 17-8. *csr1000v-1, 3. Additional Configuration Properties*

5 Double-click the screen (pr press Ctrl+G) and hit any key to continue the router import. Press Ctrl+Alt to move back to the host Windows machine. Press any key to continue when you see the following message on the screen:

```
LoLoading stage2 ......
Press any key to continue
ading stage2 ......
```

6 You may have to wait for three to five minutes for the virtual machine to be imported to the workstation. Given enough time, the router import will be completed as shown next. As soon as the importing completes, log in and check the interface status.

```
Ecsr1000v-1>enable
Password :
csr1000v-1#show ip interface brief
Interface          IP-Address  OK?  Method  Status            Protocol
GigabitEthernet1   unassigned  YES  unset   administratively  down down
GigabitEthernet2   unassigned  YES  unset   administratively  down down
GigabitEthernet3   unassigned  YES  unset   administratively  down down
                                 S  unset   administratively  down down
```

(*continued*)

#	Task
7	Right-click the new virtual router, `csr1000v-1`, and select Settings. The network adapter type needs to be changed. See Figure 17-9.

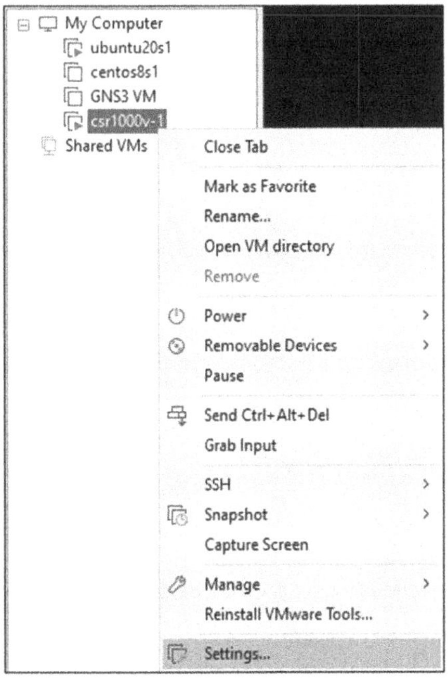

Figure 17-9. *csr1000v-1, opening Settings...*

#	Task
8	Under Hardware, change the Network Adapter configuration from Bridged (Automatic) to "NAT: Used to share the host's IP address." See Figure 17-10.

#	Task

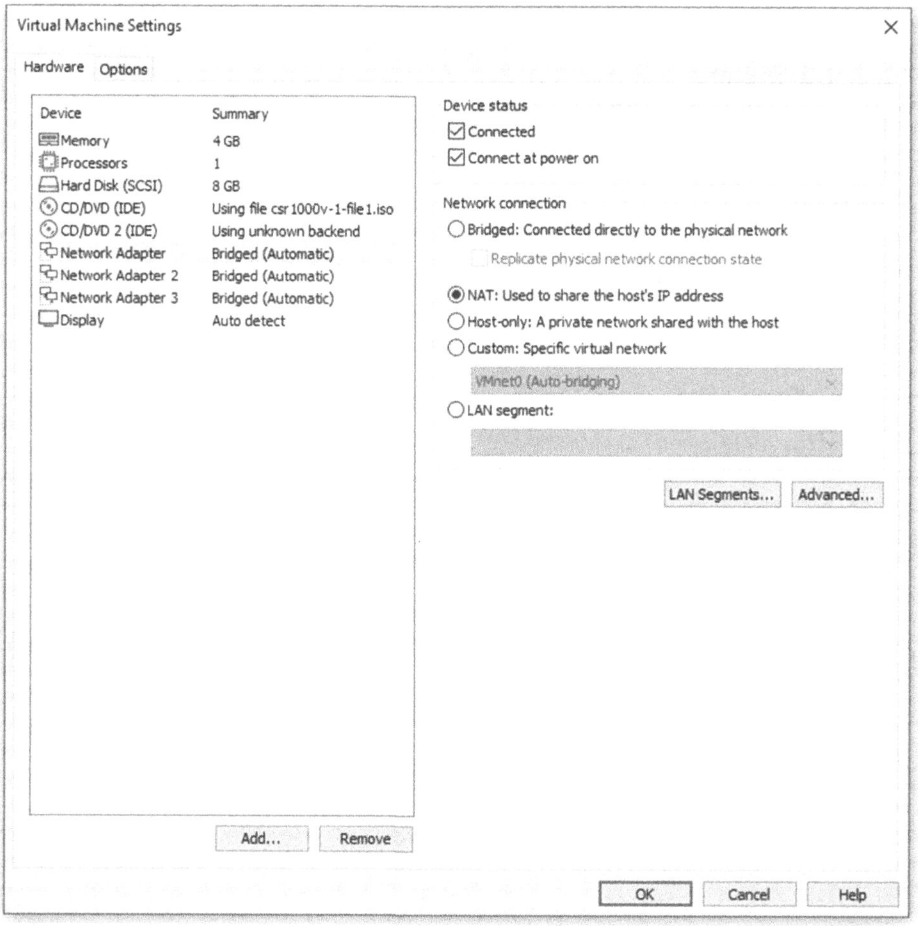

Figure 17-10. *csr1000v-1, changing Network Adapter (GigabitEthernet1) to NAT*

9 When the virtual router build completes, the interfaces will be in an administrative down/down state like all other Cisco routers. Before bringing up the interface, let's quickly assign the correct IP address for the GigabitEthernet1 interface with 192.168.183.111/24. Since we need only one interface for our IOS upgrade tool development, you do not have to configure the other interfaces.

```
csr1000v-1#config terminal
csr1000v-1(config)#interface GigabitEthernet1
csr1000v-1(config-if)#ip address 192.168.183.111 255.255.255.0
csr1000v-1(config-if)#no shut
csr1000v-1(config-if)#end
```

(continued)

#	Task

Note that once you create the second virtual router, you should configure the GigabitEthernet1 interface with 192.168.183.222/24.

```
csr1000v-2#config terminal
csr1000v-2(config)#interface GigabitEthernet1
csr1000v-2(config-if)#ip address 192.168.183.222 255.255.255.0
csr1000v-2(config-if)#no shut
csr1000v-2(config-if)#end
```

10 On your Windows host, open the PuTTY SSH client and log into csr1000v-1 (192.168.183.111). When you are prompted with PuTTY security alert, make sure you click the Yes button to accept the device's host key. Also, don't forget to send some ICMP commands to the ubuntu20s1 server to test the connectivity. See Figure 17-11.

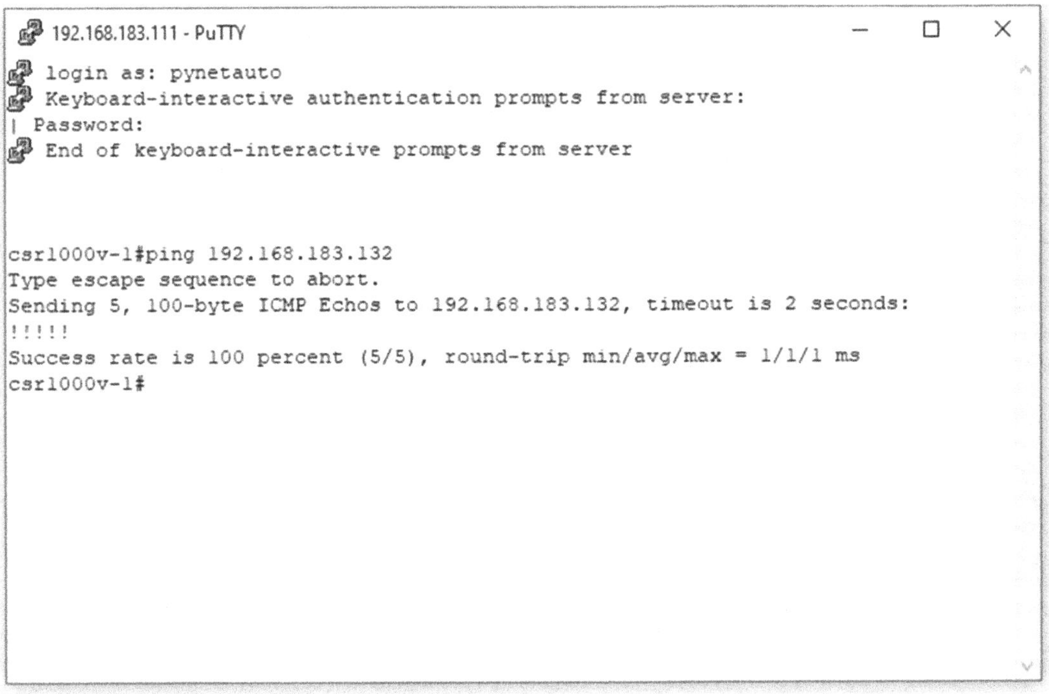

Figure 17-11. *csr1000v-1, PuTTY login for the first time*

#	Task
11	To complete the basic configuration, let's check the domain and create the RSA key for secure key exchange. Also, disable the timeout for VTY lines to stop the SSH session timeouts; only use this feature for the lab environment. Save the configuration by running `write memory`.

```
csr1000v-1#show run | in ip domain
ip domain name pynetauto.local
csr1000v-1#conf terminal
Enter configuration commands, one per line.  End with CNTL/Z.
csr1000v-1(config)#crypto key generate rsa
The name for the keys will be: csr1000v-1.pynetauto.local
Choose the size of the key modulus in the range of 360 to 4096 for your
   General Purpose Keys. Choosing a key modulus greater than 512 may take
   a few minutes.

How many bits in the modulus [512]: 1024
% Generating 1024 bit RSA keys, keys will be non-exportable...
[OK] (elapsed time was 0 seconds)

csr1000v-1(config)#line vty 0 15
csr1000v-1(config-line)#exec-timeout 0
csr1000v-1(config-line)#end
csr1000v-1#write memory
Building configuration...
[OK]
```

12 Once you are happy with the basic configuration, take a snapshot of the virtual router, as shown in Figure 17-12.

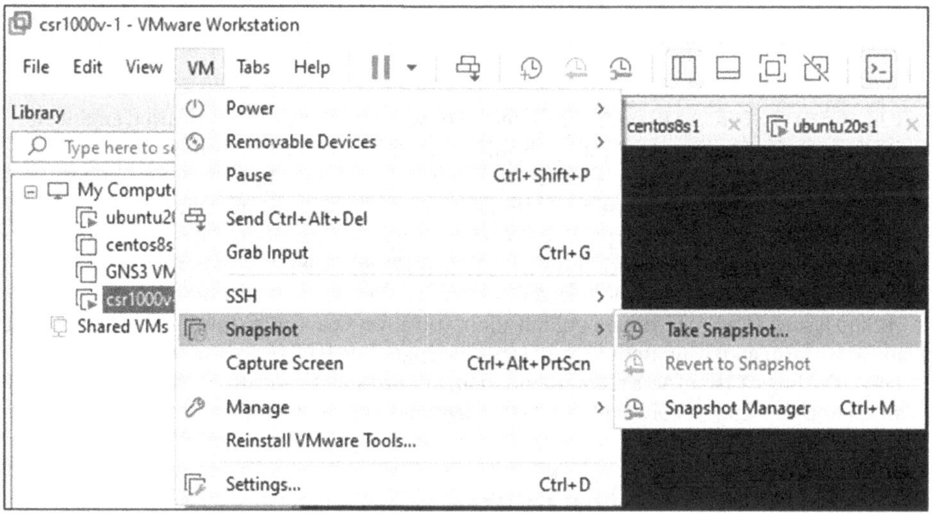

Figure 17-12. *csr1000v-1, taking a snapshot*

(*continued*)

#	Task
13	Now, repeat steps 1 through 12 to create the second virtual router (`csr1000v-2`) with the following details: `Second router name:` **`csr1000v-2`** `Second router IP:` **`192.168.183.222 255.255.255.0`**
14	Once you have two `csr1000v` routers (`csr1000v-1` and `csr1000v-2`) installed, then you are ready to move on to the Cisco IOS upgrade processes. See Figure 17-13.

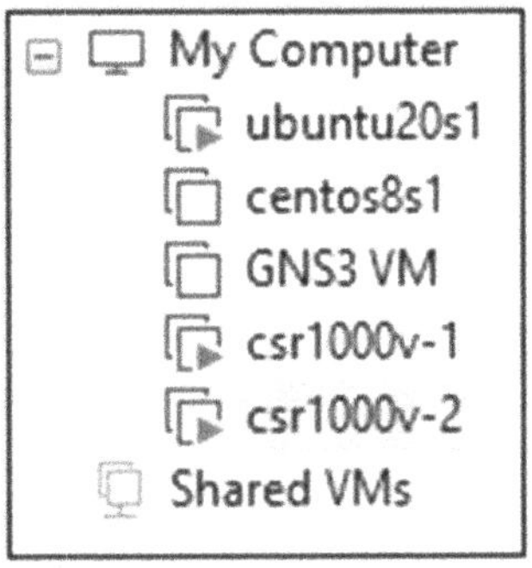

Figure 17-13. *csr1000v-1 and csr1000v-2 up and running*

You have now completed installing two Cisco CSR 1000v routers for IOS upgrade application development. Let's quickly go over the process of upgrading the Cisco IOS devices.

Discussion of How an IOS (IOS-XE/XR) Is Upgraded on Cisco Devices

Upgrading Cisco IOS (IOS/IOS-XE/IOS-XR) on Cisco routers and switches is not for faint-hearted engineers when hundreds and thousands of business-critical applications are operating during business hours as well as out of business hours. Even when the system and DevOps engineers go home, the enterprise routers and switches must provide IP connectivity to end users and IP services to other systems, allowing the backup services to run in the middle of the night. Enterprise networking devices are operational almost 24/7/365, and this is why you have to buy reputable vendor products (such as Cisco) for enterprise networking. If any services fail, then the first finger pointing goes to IP gateway (routers) devices, even for company email, cloud, or system backup issues. In an ITIL-driven organization, you always have to go through change control with a lot of red tape to perform an IOS upgrade. The reasons for upgrading IOS devices are many. The most common are outdated IOS, bugs, Cisco TAC's recommendation, or third-party agreements. The IOS upgrade commitment is written into the support contract, and IOS is upgraded as part of network patch management.

Tasks Involved in a Cisco IOS Upgrade

Let's quickly look at how a seasoned network engineer would upgrade an outdated IOS to the latest IOS version. The IOS upgrade process involves a predefined set of tasks, but there will be varying differences in the pre- and post-checks from one engineer to another. However, most of the time, the IOS upgrade process is relatively standardized but requires a lot of attention and takes place outside of business hours to avoid major outages. You are only allowed to perform IOS upgrades after midnight with a small change window in extreme cases. This type of change usually occurs at odd hours, which contributes to insomnia among long-time network engineers and puts a lot of pressure on marriages in the long term. Anyway, network automation is good news for both network engineers and their families.

Let's study a general IOS upgrade workflow that an engineer needs to follow to complete an IOS upgrade on Cisco routers or switches. Figure 17-14 illustrates a general Cisco IOS upgrade workflow for many of its common platforms.

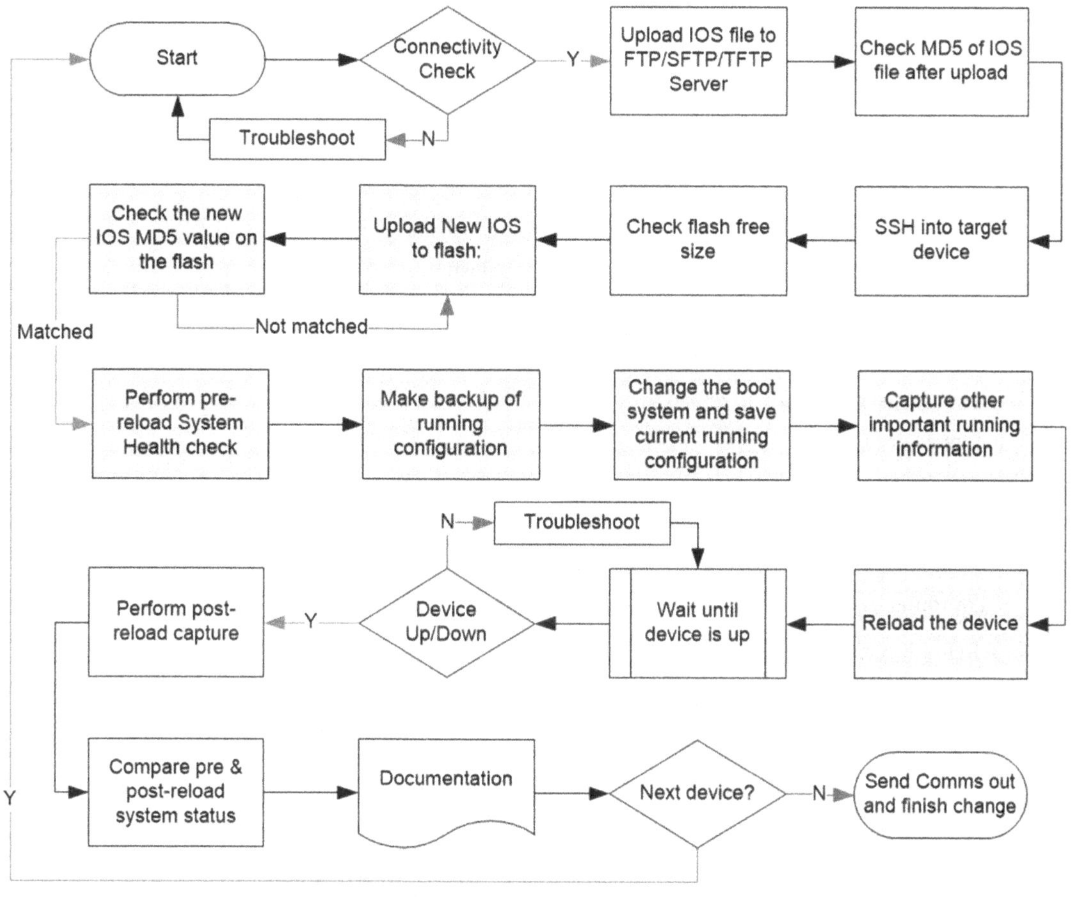

Figure 17-14. General Cisco IOS upgrade workflow

As depicted in Figure 17-14, the Cisco IOS upgrade process is quite involved; in other words, it's labor-intensive. If there is more than one device to upgrade, then the whole process immediately becomes repetitive. So, why not automate an engineer's tasks? In the final lab in the final two chapters, you will be guided to develop small Python modules to replace most of the tasks depicted in Figure 17-14.

Let's break down Figure 17-14 into three significant stages and many linear steps to better understand what tasks must be translated and written into the Python code. Here you really must wear an application developer/programmer's hat while keeping your network engineer's hat on. Table 17-2 provides the manual task-driven Cisco IOS upgrade breakdown; this process may be slightly different from one generation to another and from one platform to another. In general, the principles are almost identical.

Table 17-2. IOS Upgrade Task Breakdown

Phase 1: Pre-check

1 Check the network connectivity between the server and network devices.

2 Collect the user's login credentials and also user input as variables.

3 Check the MD5 value of new IOS as a variable.

- Compare the user's MD5 value versus the server's checked MD5 value.

4 Check the flash size on the Cisco device as a variable.

- Give the user an option to delete an old IOS file on `flash:/`.
- Give an option to look inside a directory on a Cisco switch and delete an old IOS file.

5 Make backups of `running-config`.

Phase 2: IOS Uploading and Pre-uploading Check

6 Upload the new IOS file from a file server to the router's flash.

7 Check the new IOS MD5 value on the Cisco device's flash.

- Compare the server's MD5 value versus the switch MD5 value.

8 Give the user a review of the result.

- Give the user an option to reload the device at a deferred time if required.

9 Before device reload:

- Change the boot system and save the current `running-config` to `start-up` config.
- Take backups of the running configuration on local/TFTP/FTP storage (as required).
- Optionally capture any other important information.
- For switches, run `show ip interface brief`.
- For routers, run `show ip routing`, which is the routing table.

Phase 3: Reloading and Post-upgrade Check

10 During device reload (reloading state):

- Check if the device is on the network.

11 After the reload (the device is back on the network):

- Log back into the device and perform a post-upgrade verification using before and after configurations.
- Optionally, send an email notification to the engineer at the end of the upgrade completion.

We have reviewed the manual IOS upgrade processes shown previously, but how can we translate each item into Python code? Where do we begin, and is it even possible to create such sophisticated IOS upgrading applications in production? Compared to what other tools offer us in the current market, there are many tasks (and an engineer's logical thinking) that must be translated into code lines (a program). Next, let's study Figure 17-15, which is my translation of Table 17-2 and Figure 17-14 into automatable tasks.

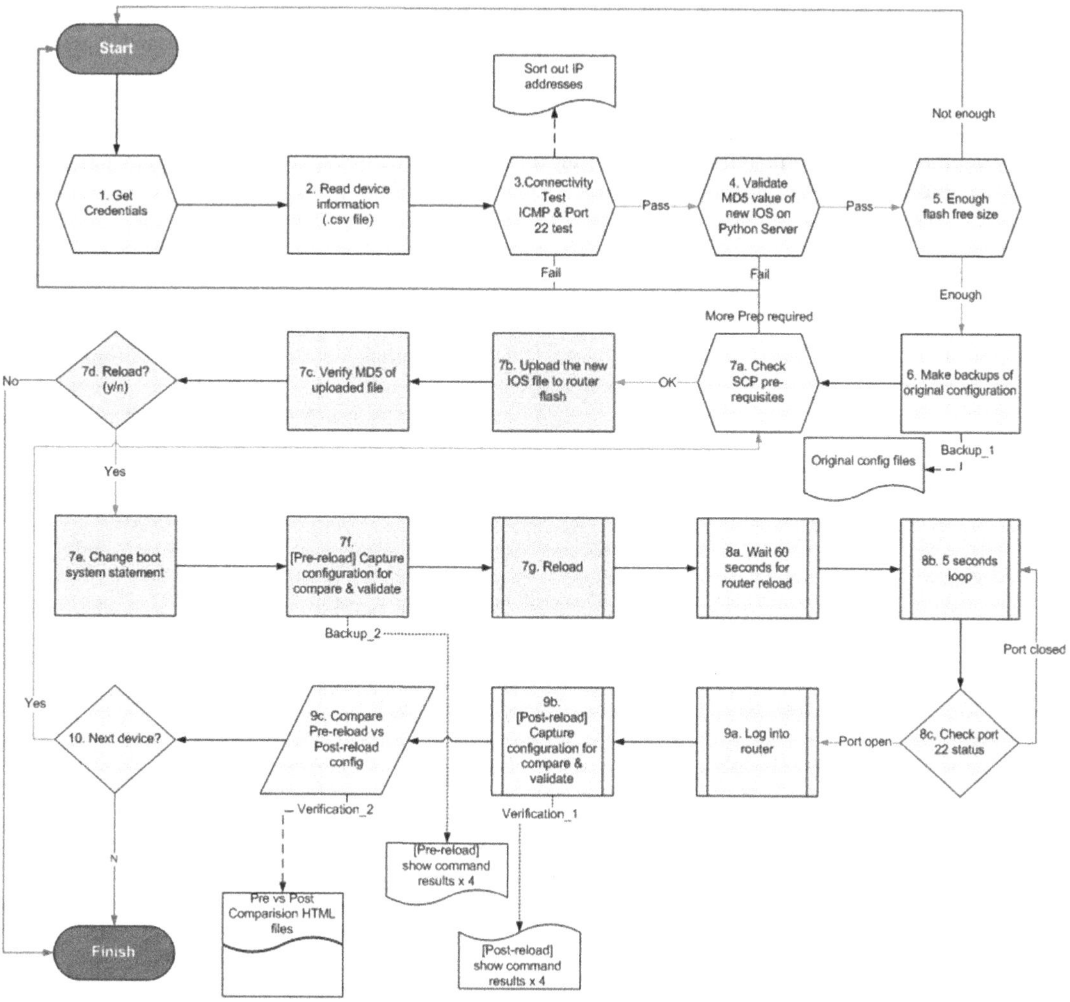

Figure 17-15. *Cisco IOS/IOS XE automated upgrade, suggested workflow example*

Figure 17-15 is almost a direct translation of the tasks discussed in Table 17-2, and the numbers correspond to that of Table 17-2. You should carefully study it before moving on to the next chapter. In Chapter 18, we will turn each step in the upgrade process into smaller snippets of Python code. In Chapter 18, tools developed for each process will become individual tools themselves. Then, in Chapter 19, you will combine them into a single tool (application) to replace the Cisco IOS upgrade tasks from end to end, that is, the pre-check, IOS upgrade, and post-check processes.

Summary

The processes discussed in this chapter are still somewhat generalized, but if you want to be more detailed, you can break down each task into even smaller tasks. A programmer without essential networking background will have little or no idea of the processes typically performed by experienced network engineers. Only network engineers who can write code will string together each task into sequenced tasks and cover all the essential tasks required to turn their actions into actionable code lines. So, in this vein, the foreseeable future for network (including security) engineers is bright as they cannot be replaced by pure application developers or untrained artificial intelligence (AI). Still, organizations will prefer engineers with coding skills over traditional engineers with no coding skills. Perhaps most network engineers will agree that, soon, AI will be replacing much of the work we perform today. At least this is true for the initial design and development of these AI platforms, because they must be initiated by experienced and intelligent network engineers, not the application developers.

CHAPTER 18

Python Network Automation Lab: Cisco IOS Upgrade Mini Tools Development

This chapter is the second-to-last chapter of this book, and you will be completing ten applications. You will turn them into a single, functional IOS upgrade application in the next chapter. The tools developed in this chapter include the following: connectivity validation tool, username and password interactive collection tool, file information read tool, MD5 check tool for file integrity on a Linux server, configuration backup tool for network devices, IOS file uploading tool, router flash IOS MD5 check tool, user input tool to change the application flow, and router reload tool with a post-check tool. In this chapter, you will also test the tools and validate their functionalities.

**Difficulty level will be relative to reader's previous experience with Cisco Networking Technology.*

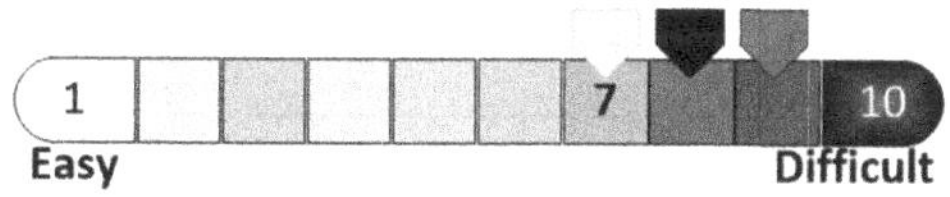

Cisco IOS Upgrade Application Development

Now it is time to develop a series of small Python tools (applications) to use like small Lego blocks to, in the next chapter, create a more sophisticated and complete network automation application.

To begin developing the first application (tool), let's talk about how you can feed information into a script to be converted into Python variables and arguments. There are three ways we can feed the user and device information into our Cisco IOS XE upgrade application. First, we can create an interactive information collector tool and collect both user and device information interactively from the user. Second, we can interactively collect user login information but read the device information from a file such as a text file, Excel file, CSV file, or a database. Third, we can get all information from files (text, Excel, or CSV) or a database. The biggest issue with a reading a username and password from insecure text files is that it could be a significant security threat in the production environment. You have to consider using an encrypted password vault, which will protect your credentials on the network. This topic is beyond this book's topics and will be left for you to research; we will replace this with a more straightforward user interaction tool.

B. Choi, *Introduction to Python Network Automation*, https://doi.org/10.1007/978-1-4842-6806-3_18

To draw on everything we have learned through Chapters 1 to 17, let's use the second method of feeding information to the application. In this example, we will be getting the user credentials from an interactive user session and getting the device information from a CSV file using the `pandas` module.

Part A: Pre-check Tools Development Connectivity Validation Tool

Network Engineers continuously strive to keep various IP devices, applications, and users connected to their network, with no or minor network interruptions possible. Even before the word network programmability, infrastructure as code or *network automation* was on everyone's lips; every organization wants their managed networks secure and stable. When we write a scripted network automation application, we have to put network stability and security as the first priority. We always have to reference the best practices in networking and security. You can write sound network automation applications when you are across the best practices in networking and programming.

The very first mini tool we are going to develop here is the network connectivity tool. A similar tool was introduced to you in an earlier chapter, but we will refactor the codes and make it better. After writing a stand-alone network connectivity checking tool, you will be able to test the communication between the server (`ubuntu20s1`) and two routers (`csr1000v-1` and `csr1000v-2`). Every Network Engineer uses ICMP (ping) and socket (port) scanning at work, and your application will replace the manual tasks on the terminal console with the lines of Python code. Here, we will develop the ICMP application by reiterating (code refactoring) the same codes over and over. All applications developed in this chapter will be incorporated directly into the final Cisco IOS upgrade application in the final chapter.

> Please note that no one will write this code for you in the real world, so you must get used to writing each line of code yourself accurately and swiftly. As in other code in this book, the explanations for important code lines appear next to each line following the # mark.

#	Task
1	SSH into your Python automation server (`ubuntu20s1`) server using PuTTY and write the following code. You will write one ICMP script and then one socket script to test the network connectivity between the server and the routers. Then run and validate the scripts and modify them to change the flow of the scripts. Here we will only use the native `os` and `socket` modules; although the `scapy` module is an excellent external tool, the native tools can achieve what we want, so you will use what comes out of the box.

```
pynetauto@ubuntu20s1:~$ mkdir my_tools
pynetauto@ubuntu20s1:~$ cd my_tools
pynetauto@ubuntu20s1:~/my_tools$ mkdir tool1_ping
pynetauto@ubuntu20s1:~/my_tools$ cd tool1_ping
pynetauto@ubuntu20s1:~/my_tools/tool1_ping$ nano ping_tool1.py
```

#	Task
	ping_tool1.py

```
import os

device_list = ['192.168.183.111', '192.168.183.222']

for ip in device_list: # for loop for IP address
    if len(ip) != 0: # Only run this part of script if the list is not empty
        print(f'Sending icmp packets to {ip}') # Informational
        resp = os.system(f'ping -c 3 {ip}') # send ICMP packets 4 times
        if resp == 0: # If on the network (pingable), run this script
            print(f'{ip} is on the network.') # Informational
            print('-'*80) # Line divider
        else:
            print(f'{ip} is unreachable.') # Informational
            print('-'*80) # Line divider
    else:
        exit() # If not on the network, exit application
```

2 If your server can communicate to both routers and run the previous script, you should see a similar result on your SSH console. Run python3 ping_tool1.py, and the result will look like this:

```
pynetauto@ubuntu20s1:~/my_tools/tool1_ping$ python3 ping_tool1.py
Sending icmp packets to 192.168.183.111
PING 192.168.183.111 (192.168.183.111) 56(84) bytes of data.
64 bytes from 192.168.183.111: icmp_seq=2 ttl=255 time=1.63 ms
64 bytes from 192.168.183.111: icmp_seq=3 ttl=255 time=1.60 ms
64 bytes from 192.168.183.111: icmp_seq=4 ttl=255 time=1.58 ms

--- 192.168.183.111 ping statistics ---
4 packets transmitted, 3 received, 25% packet loss, time 3032ms
rtt min/avg/max/mdev = 1.581/1.603/1.628/0.019 ms
192.168.183.111 is on the network.
--------------------------------------------------------------------------------
[...omitted for brevity]
```

(*continued*)

#	Task
3	Now, let's modify `device_list = ['192.168.183.111', '192.168.183.222']` to `device_list = ['10.10.10.1', '192.168.183.111', '192.172.1.33', '192.168.183.222']`. The two dummy IP addresses added to the list do not exist, and you are going to use this new list to iterate and develop your script. We will add a feature, so if the devices are reachable (pingable), the script will append the IP address to a new `reachable_ips` list. If the IP addresses are unreachable, then append the IP addresses to a new list called `unreachable_ips`. Many things are going on in the production network, and we have to counter these situations. Suppose you are working on a single device at a time. In that case, you are concerned with only one device, so if the device is not reachable remotely, you cannot upgrade that device to a newer IOS version until you troubleshoot the connectivity issue. However, when you are working with many devices at once, if one or two devices are offline, you want to know which devices are not reachable, but at the same time, you would want to continue the IOS upgrade with the rest of the devices. We will use the ICMP tool to separate the IP addresses between the reachable IP addresses and the unreachable IP addresses and save them to two separate lists.

```
pynetauto@ubuntu20s1:~/my_tools/tool1_ping$ cp ping_tool1.py ping_tool2.py
pynetauto@ubuntu20s1:~/my_tools/tool1_ping$ nano ping_tool2.py
```

Modified code:

```
ping_tool2.py
import os

device_list = ['10.10.10.1',  '192.168.183.111', '192.172.1.33',  '192.168.183.222']

reachable_ips = [] # Define a blank list for on the network ips
unreachable_ips = []# Define a blank list for off the network ips

for ip in device_list:
    if len(ip) != 0:
        print(f'Sending icmp packets to {ip}')
        resp = os.system(f'ping -c 3 {ip}')
        if resp == 0:
            reachable_ips.append(ip) # Append ip to reachable_ips list
            print('-'*80)
        else:
            unreachable_ips.append(ip) # Append ip to unreachable_ips list
            print('-'*80)
    else:
        exit()

print("Reachable IPs: ", reachable_ips) # Print result 1
print("Unreachable IPs: ", unreachable_ips) # Print result 2
```

#	Task
4	Now run the python3 ping_tool2.py command, and you should get a similar result to this:

```
pynetauto@ubuntu20s1:~/my_tools/tool1_ping$ python3 ping_tool2.py
Sending icmp packets to 10.10.10.1
PING 10.10.10.1 (10.10.10.1) 56(84) bytes of data.

--- 10.10.10.1 ping statistics ---
3 packets transmitted, 0 received, 100% packet loss, time 2035ms

--------------------------------------------------------------------------------
Sending icmp packets to 192.168.183.111
PING 192.168.183.111 (192.168.183.111) 56(84) bytes of data.
64 bytes from 192.168.183.111: icmp_seq=1 ttl=255 time=1.85 ms
64 bytes from 192.168.183.111: icmp_seq=2 ttl=255 time=1.58 ms
64 bytes from 192.168.183.111: icmp_seq=3 ttl=255 time=1.66 ms

--- 192.168.183.111 ping statistics ---
3 packets transmitted, 3 received, 0% packet loss, time 2004ms
rtt min/avg/max/mdev = 1.583/1.694/1.845/0.110 ms
--------------------------------------------------------------------------------
[...omitted for brevity]
--------------------------------------------------------------------------------
Reachable IPs:  ['192.168.183.111', '192.168.183.222']
Unreachable IPs:  ['10.10.10.1', '192.172.1.33']
```

So, as expected, the reachable IP addresses are 192.168.183.111 and 192.168.183.222. This list can be used to continue to run the rest of the script. Also, the unreachable IP addresses are 10.10.10.1 and 192.172.1.33. This is an expected result. Still, in production, if these devices are meant to be on the network, then you will need to troubleshoot the connectivity issue and perform the changes after the connectivity issue has been resolved.

5 The lists as variables are useful, but this information is only displayed while the script is running and you are sitting in front of the console to watch this information. Note that the server's random access memory is only temporary, and Python's `print` statement is only used for the user's convenience. The actual Python script does not use what's printed on the screen. If we want to access this information when the script runs successfully by a job scheduler such as `cron`, you have to write and save the information to a file. Let's write two lists into two separate files for later use.

```
pynetauto@ubuntu20s1:~/my_tools/tool1_ping$ cp ping_tool2.py ping_tool3.py
pynetauto@ubuntu20s1:~/my_tools/tool1_ping$ nano ping_tool3.py

ping_tool3.py
import os

device_list = ['10.10.10.1',  '192.168.183.111', '192.172.1.33',  '192.168.183.222']

# reachable_ips = [] # Add '#' to make this line inactive
f1 = open('reachable_ips.txt',  'w+') # Create and open reachable_ips.txt file to
write on
```

(continued)

#	Task

```
# unreachable_ips = []# Add '#' to make this line inactive
f2 = open('unreachable_ips.txt', 'w+') # Create and open unreachable_ips.txt file to
write on

for ip in device_list:
    if len(ip) != 0:
        print(f'Sending icmp packets to {ip}')
        resp = os.system('ping -c 3 ' + ip)
        if resp == 0:
            #reachable_ips.append(ip) # Add '#' to make this line inactive
            f1.write(f'{ip}\n') # write ip address to each line of reachable_ips.txt
            file
            print('-'*80)
        else:
            #unreachable_ips.append(ip) # Add '#' to make this line inactive
            f2.write(f'{ip}\n') # write ip address to each line of unreachable_ips.
            txt file
            print('-'*80)
    else:
        exit()

f1.close() # Close f1 file
f2.close() # Close f2 file
```

6 Run the third iteration of your original code, and it should produce two text files, one containing the reachable IP addresses and one containing the unreachable IP addresses. Note, the output has been omitted to save space.

```
pynetauto@ubuntu20s1:~/my_tools/tool1_ping$ ls
ping_tool1.py  ping_tool2.py  ping_tool3.py
pynetauto@ubuntu20s1:~/my_tools/tool1_ping$ python3 _ping_tool3.py
[... output omitted for brevity]
pynetauto@ubuntu20s1:~/my_tools/tool1_ping$ ls
ping_tool1.py  ping_tool2.py  ping_tool3.py  reachable_ips.txt  unreachable_ips.txt
pynetauto@ubuntu20s1:~/my_tools/tool1_ping$ more reachable_ips.txt
192.168.183.111
192.168.183.222
pynetauto@ubuntu20s1:~/my_tools/tool1_ping$ more unreachable_ips.txt
10.10.10.1
192.172.1.33
```

So, your tool can test network connectivity and sort the IP addresses between online and offline devices at this stage. Also, the IP addresses can be saved (documented) in their respective files.

7 We will now convert the IP address list used in the previous scripts into a file, `ip_addresses.txt`. This will allow you to add and manage a large number of IP addresses more efficiently, rather than reading and entering each IP address in a list. We are reading the IP addresses from a text file, but we also can read the IP addresses directly from an Excel or CSV file. When we read the information from either Excel or CSV, we can turn the data into two-dimensional data. The information becomes more meaningful and powerful at the same time.

Note the last IP address of 192.168.183.133 that is the IP address of GNS3 R1's router IP address, so you will need to start R1 from GNS3's `cmllab-devops` project.

#	Task
8	Power on GNS3 and start the IOS router, R1. Create an access list to stop any inbound SSH traffic to this device. Create an access list and apply it to FastEthernet 0/0 of R1. Also, you can enable both Telnet and SSH on line vty 0 15.
9	Now create and write a socket tool, as shown here, and run the script. The result should be similar to what's shown here.

Task 8 commands:

```
R1#ping 192.168.183.132
R1#configure terminal
R1(config)#access-list 100 deny tcp any any eq 22
R1(config)#access-list 100 permit ip any any
R1(config)#interface f0/0
R1(config-if)#ip access-group 100 in
R1(config)#line vty 0 15
R1(config-line)#transport input telnet ssh
R1(config-line)#do write memory
```

Task 9 commands:

```
pynetauto@ubuntu20s1:~/my_tools/tool1_ping$ nano socket_tool.py
```

```
socket_tool.py
import socket

device_list = ['10.10.10.1', '192.168.183.111', '192.172.1.33', '192.168.183.222',
'192.168.183.133']

for ip in device_list:
    print("-"*80)
    for port in range (22, 24):
        destination = (ip, port)
        try:
            with socket.socket(socket.AF_INET, socket.SOCK_STREAM) as s:
                s.settimeout(3)
                connection = s.connect(destination)
                print(f"On {ip}, SSH port {port} is open!")
        except:
            print(f"On {ip}, SSH port {port} is closed.")
```

When you run the previous script, you should expect to get similar responses to what's shown here. If you did, then it is time to integrate this script into the ping_tool3.py script.

```
pynetauto@ubuntu20s1:~/my_tools/tool1_ping$ python3 socket_tool.py
--------------------------------------------------------------------------------
On 10.10.10.1, SSH port 22 is closed.
On 10.10.10.1, SSH port 23 is closed.
--------------------------------------------------------------------------------
On 192.168.183.111, SSH port 22 is open!
On 192.168.183.111, SSH port 23 is closed.
--------------------------------------------------------------------------------
On 192.172.1.33, SSH port 22 is closed.
On 192.172.1.33, SSH port 23 is closed.
```

(continued)

#	Task

```
--------------------------------------------------------------------------------
On 192.168.183.222, SSH port 22 is open!
On 192.168.183.222, SSH port 23 is closed.
--------------------------------------------------------------------------------
On 192.168.183.133, SSH port 22 is closed.
On 192.168.183.133, SSH port 23 is open!
```

10 Now let's combine the two tools and enhance the ping tool to send ICMP messages and then check the open ports for Telnet or SSH connections. After you complete this tool, you can use it as a stand-alone tool to check the connectivity and port status.

Our preferred connection method is an SSH connection. When the script runs, it will create three files, first containing the IP addresses with an SSH connection, second containing the IP addresses with a Telnet connection, and third containing the unreachable IP addresses and logs of closed ports.

We will replace device_list with the information read from the ip_addresses.txt file, so go ahead and create the file with the IP addresses.

```
pynetauto@ubuntu20s1:~/my_tools/tool1_ping$ nano ip_addresses.txt

ip_addresses.txt
10.10.10.1
192.168.183.111
192.172.1.33
192.168.183.222
192.168.183.133
```

Copy ping_tool3.py, save it as ping_tool4.py, and then merge socket_tool.py from the previous step into ping_tool4.py. Once you have combined the two scripts into one file, it should look like ping_tool4.py. Here, we are breaking the rules of writing more Pythonic code because our code uses multiple for loops and the indentation consists of eight spaces. For code readability, the recommended indentation is four; we'll look at this soon. Note that if port 22 is opened in this script, it will not check port 23 because our interest is only whether port 22 is opened. Also note that we have added the time module to check the time to run the application; the time module was covered in Chapters 2 and 14.

```
pynetauto@ubuntu20s1:~/my_tools/tool1_ping$ cp ping_tool3.py ping_tool4.py
pynetauto@ubuntu20s1:~/my_tools/tool1_ping$ nano ping_tool4.py

ping_tool4.py
import os
import socket
import time

t = time.mktime(time.localtime()) # Timer start to measure script running time

# device_list = ['10.10.10.1',  '192.168.183.111', '192.172.1.33',
'192.168.183.222'] # Hashed out line
ip_add_file = './ip_addresses.txt' # IP address location variable, "./" denotes pwd
# reachable_ips = []
f1 = open('reachable_ips_ssh.txt',  'w+') # Open f1 file
f2 = open('reachable_ips_telnet.txt', 'w+') # Open f2 file
```

#	Task

```
# unreachable_ips = []
f3 = open('unreachable_ips.txt', 'w+') # Open f3 file

with open(ip_add_file, 'r') as ip_addresses: # Use with file open method
    for ip in ip_addresses: # Loop through and read IP address from each line
        ip = ip.strip() # Remove any white spaces
        resp = os.system('ping -c 3 ' + ip) # Send four ICMP packets
        if resp == 0: # If 0, in other words, the device is on the network
            for port in range (22, 23): # Check port 22 (SSH)
                destination = (ip, port) # Create arrayed tuple variable with ip and
                port as items
                try: # First try
                    with socket.socket(socket.AF_INET, socket.SOCK_STREAM) as s: #
                    socket command
                        s.settimeout(3) # Set socket timeout to 3 seconds
                        connection = s.connect(destination) # Send socket connection
                        using destination variable
                        print(f"{ip} {port} opened") #Informational, all print
                        statements are informational
                        f1.write(f"{ip}\n") # write the IP to reachable_ips_ssh.txt
                except:
                    print(f"{ip} {port} closed")
                    f3.write(f"{ip} {port} closed\n") # write the IP to unreachable_
                    ips.txt
                    for port in range (23, 24): # Check port 23 (telnet)
                        destination = (ip, port)
                        try:
                            with socket.socket(socket.AF_INET, socket.SOCK_STREAM) as s:
                                s.settimeout(3)
                                connection = s.connect(destination)
                                print(f"{ip} {port} opened")
                                f2.write(f"{ip}\n") # write the IP to reachable_ips_
                                telnet.txt
                        except:
                            print(f"{ip} {port} closed")
                            f3.write(f"{ip} {port} closed\n") # write the IP to
                            unreachable_ips.txt
        else:
        print(f"{ip} unreachable")
        f3.write(f"{ip} unreachable\n") # write the IP to unreachable_ips.txt

f1.close() # Close f1 file
f2.close() # Close f2 file
f3.close() # Close f3 file
tt = time.mktime(time.localtime()) - t # Timer finish to measure script running time
print("Total wait time : {0} seconds".format(tt)) #Informational
```

(*continued*)

#	Task
11	Run the combined script, and it should create three files with sorted IP addresses based on the ICMP and port verification. Imagine running such connectivity checks on hundreds or thousands of devices for troubleshooting or making changes; this type of tool can save you a lot of time, and the files created here can be read from another application to carry out further programming tasks.

```
pynetauto@ubuntu20s1:~/my_tools/tool1_ping$ python3 ping_tool4.py
[... output omitted for brevity]
--- 192.168.183.133 ping statistics ---
3 packets transmitted, 3 received, 0% packet loss, time 2004ms
rtt min/avg/max/mdev = 4.046/7.700/12.147/3.354 ms
192.168.183.133 22 closed
192.168.183.133 23 opened
Total wait time : 31.0 seconds
pynetauto@ubuntu20s1:~/my_tools/tool1_ping$ ls
ip_addresses.txt  ping_tool4.py             socket_tool.py
ping_tool1.py     reachable_ips_ssh.txt     unreachable_ips.txt
ping_tool2.py     reachable_ips_telnet.txt
ping_tool3.py     reachable_ips.txt
pynetauto@ubuntu20s1:~/my_tools/tool1_ping$ more reachable_ips_ssh.txt
192.168.183.111
192.168.183.222
pynetauto@ubuntu20s1:~/my_tools/tool1_ping$ more reachable_ips_telnet.txt
192.168.183.133
pynetauto@ubuntu20s1:~/my_tools/tool1_ping$ more unreachable_ips.txt
10.10.10.1 unreachable
192.172.1.33 unreachable
192.168.183.133 22 closed
```

12 Now create a check_port() function and make this job function a separate function. When you run the following code, it will produce the same result in a more Pythonic way. Best practice is to separate the function, save it under another filename as a module, and then import it as a tool so the main script is less crowded and easier to digest. But for now, this should be acceptable. Rewrite the code in ping_tool4.py so that it will look like ping_tool5.py.

```
pynetauto@ubuntu20s1:~/my_tools/tool1_ping$ cp ping_tool4.py ping_tool5.py
pynetauto@ubuntu20s1:~/my_tools/tool1_ping$ nano ping_tool5.py
```

```
ping_tool5.py
import os
import socket
import time

t = time.mktime(time.localtime())

def check_port(ip):
    for port in range (22, 23):
        destination = (ip, port)
```

#	Task

```
        try:
            with socket.socket(socket.AF_INET, socket.SOCK_STREAM) as s:
                s.settimeout(3)
                connection = s.connect(destination)
                print(f"{ip} {port} opened")
                f1.write(f"{ip}\n")
        except:
            print(f"{ip} {port} closed")
            f3.write(f"{ip} {port} closed\n")
            for port in range (23, 24):
                destination = (ip, port)
                try:
                    with socket.socket(socket.AF_INET, socket.SOCK_STREAM) as s:
                        s.settimeout(3)
                        connection = s.connect(destination)
                        print(f"{ip} {port} opened")
                        f2.write(f"{ip}\n")
                except:
                    print(f"{ip} {port} closed")
                    f3.write(f"{ip} {port} closed\n")

ip_add_file = './ip_addresses.txt'
f1 = open('reachable_ips_ssh.txt',  'w+')
f2 = open('reachable_ips_telnet.txt', 'w+')
f3 = open('unreachable_ips.txt', 'w+')

with open(ip_add_file, 'r') as ip_addresses:
    for ip in ip_addresses:
        ip = ip.strip()
        resp = os.system('ping -c 3 ' + ip) # there is a whitespace after the digit
        3, be careful.
        if resp == 0:
            check_port(ip)
        else:
            print(f"{ip} unreachable")
            f3.write(f"{ip} unreachable\n")

f1.close()
f2.close()
f3.close()
tt = time.mktime(time.localtime()) - t
print("Total wait time : {0} seconds".format(tt))
```

Now run the application and check the result. We expect to see the same result as in `ping_tool4.py`.

```
pynetauto@ubuntu20s1:~/my_tools/tool1_ping$ python3 ping_tool5.py
[... output omitted for brevity]
64 bytes from 192.168.183.133: icmp_seq=2 ttl=255 time=2.43 ms
64 bytes from 192.168.183.133: icmp_seq=3 ttl=255 time=12.7 ms
```

(continued)

#	Task

	`--- 192.168.183.133 ping statistics ---`
	`3 packets transmitted, 3 received, 0% packet loss, time 2002ms`
	`rtt min/avg/max/mdev = 2.429/6.314/12.670/4.531 ms`
	`192.168.183.133 22 closed`
	`192.168.183.133 23 opened`
	`Total wait time : 30.0 seconds`

13	Let's simplify the main script by separating the port checking tool into a separate module (a separate file). When you run ping_tool6.py, you will get the same result, but we can say our code is a little more Pythonic.

Separate the check_port function as a separate tool, so create and save it as ping_tool6_tools.py.

```
pynetauto@ubuntu20s1:~/my_tools/tool1_ping$ nano ping_tool6_tools.py
```

```
ping_tool6_tools.py
# ping_tool6_tools.py for ping_tool6.py
import socket

def check_port(ip, f1, f2, f3):
    for port in range (22, 23):
        destination = (ip, port)
        try:
            with socket.socket(socket.AF_INET, socket.SOCK_STREAM) as s:
                s.settimeout(3)
                connection = s.connect(destination)
                print(f"{ip} {port} open")
                f1.write(f"{ip}\n")
        except:
            print(f"{ip} {port} closed")
            f3.write(f"{ip} {port} closed\n")
            for port in range (23, 24):
                destination = (ip, port)
                try:
                    with socket.socket(socket.AF_INET, socket.SOCK_STREAM) as s:
                        s.settimeout(3)
                        connection = s.connect(destination)
                        print(f"{ip} {port} open")
                        f2.write(f"{ip}\n")
                except:
                    print(f"{ip} {port} closed")
                    f3.write(f"{ip} {port} closed\n")
```

Copy ping_tool5.py and create ping_tool6.py; then create the main script as shown here:

```
pynetauto@ubuntu20s1:~/my_tools/tool1_ping$ cp ping_tool5.py ping_tool6.py
pynetauto@ubuntu20s1:~/my_tools/tool1_ping$ nano ping_tool6.py
```

#	Task

Make sure you remove the check_port() function and modify the file as shown here:

```
ping_tool6.py
import os
import time
from ping_tool6_tools import check_port # importing check_port tool from ping_tool6_
tools.py

t = time.mktime(time.localtime())

ip_add_file = './ip_addresses.txt'
f1 = open('reachable_ips_ssh.txt',  'w+')
f2 = open('reachable_ips_telnet.txt', 'w+')
f3 = open('unreachable_ips.txt', 'w+')

with open(ip_add_file, 'r') as ip_addresses:
    for ip in ip_addresses:
        ip = ip.strip()
        resp = os.system('ping -c 3 ' + ip)
        if resp == 0:
            check_port(ip, f1, f2, f3) # parsing arguments ip, f1, f2, f3
        else:
            print(f"{ip} unreachable")
            f3.write(f"{ip} unreachable\n")

f1.close()
f2.close()
f3.close()
tt = time.mktime(time.localtime()) - t
print("Total wait time : {0} seconds".format(tt))
```

Now, run the final tool, ping_tool6.py, and you should expect to see the same result as the ping_tool5.py and ping_tool4.py reiterations.

```
pynetauto@ubuntu20s1:~/my_tools/tool1_ping$ python3 ping_tool6.py
[... output omitted for brevity]
64 bytes from 192.168.183.133: icmp_seq=3 ttl=255 time=13.8 ms

--- 192.168.183.133 ping statistics ---
3 packets transmitted, 3 received, 0% packet loss, time 2004ms
rtt min/avg/max/mdev = 5.775/9.237/13.752/3.340 ms
192.168.183.133 22 closed
192.168.183.133 23 open
Total wait time : 30.0 seconds
```

Our ping tool's last iteration is ready for immediate use in production and is good enough to integrate into our Cisco IOS upgrade application. This is the end of the first tool development; let's look at the second tool now.

Collect User's Login Credentials and User Input

When a network engineer performs an IOS upgrade on Cisco routers and switches, the engineer has to type in their network administrator credentials with the correct user privileges: the level 15 administrator user ID and password. The device access level and security could be using locally configured user credentials or they could be on the TACACS server. In this book, we are using the local logins to keep things simple. After successful authentication and login, the network administrator must manually run some commands to check the device's upgradability. That is, the device needs to have enough flash memory (storage) to hold the new IOS image. Then, the network administrator has to run a command with the new IOS image filename along with the FTP/TFTP server information. In the case of TFTP, no administrator username or password is required. Still, in most cases, you have to provide another username and password combination for further authentication for the FTP server. Some information is fed through one piece at a time, line by line. But with scripting, we can simplify and collect the administrator's data right at the beginning of the script run using one of the data collection methods. The easiest way is to use a single file to collect all the required information at once. The most cumbersome way would be to make the user manually enter the information one piece at a time. For demonstration purposes, we can write some code that uses both to get the user ID, password, and secret password. We'll use an interactive data collection tool for the IOS name and MD5 value. The information will be read from a CSV file.

#	Task
1	To develop a get credentials tool, you will begin with the `input` function and `getpass` module; the `getpass` module hides the password entered into the console. As we are developing the tool, we'll print the password using the `print` statement for our convenience.

```
pynetauto@ubuntu20s1:~/my_tools$ mkdir tool2_login
pynetauto@ubuntu20s1:~/my_tools$ cd tool2_login
pynetauto@ubuntu20s1:~/my_tools/tool2_login$ nano get_cred1.py
```

To collect the user ID and network password and enable the secret password, the most basic tool will look similar to this:

```
get_cred1.py
from getpass import getpass
uid = input("Enter Network Admin ID : ")
pwd = getpass("Enter Network Admin PWD : ")
secret = getpass("Enter secret password : ")
print(uid, pwd, secret)
```

Run the initial script for a quick test.

```
pynetauto@ubuntu20s1:~/my_tools/tool2_login$ python3 get_cred1.py
Enter Network Admin ID : pynetauto
Enter Network Admin PWD : ********
Enter secret password : *********
pynetauto cisco123 secret123
```

With a simple user ID and password collection tool as shown earlier, there are two problems. First, you can enter any information or nothing and still move to the next step, so the script at least needs to get a valid entry from the user before proceeding to the next step. Second, with the `getpass` module, it does not display the password entered, so you cannot tell if you have entered the correct password until the script runs and errors out during the SSH or Telnet authentication process. So, we have to improve this script by adding a validation step.

#	Task
2	Let's make some improvements to this tool to bring it up to acceptable standards. In this iteration, we will take care of the second problem, the getpass module, by adding the validation script for the password and secret. You have to enter the password and secret twice to make sure that the entered passwords match and are correct. We will also prompt the user if the password and secret are the same as in the production environment. Both the password and secrets are the same, and hence by answering y or yes, the user does not have to type the secret again. After the first reiteration, your code will look similar to the code written next. Notice that I have moved the secret collection into a separate function to make this script more concise, and also, if the user answers other than y, yes, n, or no, the user will be prompted to provide the correct response. This function makes the user provide only the expected responses: any one of the y, yes, n, or no responses. Referencing get_cred1.py, let's start putting it together.

```
pynetauto@ubuntu20s1:~/my_tools/tool2_login$ nano get_cred2.py
```

```
get_cred2.py
from getpass import getpass
def get_secret():
    global secret
    resp = input("Is secret the same as password? (y/n) : ")
    resp = resp.lower()
    if resp == "yes" or resp == "y":
        secret = pwd
    elif resp == "no" or resp == "n":
        secret = None
        while not secret:
            secret = getpass("Enter the secret : ")
            secret_verify = getpass("Confirm the secret : ")
            if secret != secret_verify:
                print("! Secrets do not match. Please try again.")
                secret = None
    else:
        get_secret()

def get_credentials():
    global uid
    uid = input("Enter Network Admin ID : ")
    global pwd
    pwd = None
    while not pwd:
        pwd = getpass("Enter Network Admin PWD : ")
        pwd_verify = getpass("Confirm Network Admin PWD : ")
        if pwd != pwd_verify:
            print("! Network Admin Passwords do not match. Please try again.")
            pwd = None
    get_secret()
    return uid, pwd, secret
get_credentials()
print(uid, pwd,secret)
```

(*continued*)

#	Task

Once you have completed writing the previous script, test your application.

```
pynetauto@ubuntu20s1:~/my_tools/tool2_login$ python3 get_cred2.py
Enter Network Admin ID : pynetauto
Enter Network Admin PWD : ********
Confirm Network Admin PWD : ******* # Enter mismatched password
! Network Admin Passwords do not match. Please try again.
Enter Network Admin PWD : ********
Confirm Network Admin PWD : ********
Is secret the same as password? (y/n) : n
Enter the secret : ********
Confirm the secret : ******** # Enter mismatched password
! secret do not match. Please try again.
Enter the secret : ********
Confirm the secret : ********
pynetauto cisco123 secret123
```

The previous user ID, password, and secret collection tool looks a lot better than the original in task 1. Still, as mentioned, it has another flaw where the user can input a username, password, or secret of any length, so this is another problem we have to solve to make the tool more realistic. Look at the following example to see what this means:

```
pynetauto@ubuntu20s1:~/my_tools/tool2_login$ python3 get_cred_b_test.py
Enter Network Admin ID : a
Enter Network Admin PWD : *
Confirm Network Admin PWD : *
Is secret the same as password? (y/n) : n
Enter the secret : *
Confirm the secret : *
```

3 We can use a couple of regular expressions to control the user inputs, which will fix the previous problem. In a well-managed IT environment, administrators always enforce conventions for usernames and passwords. Hence, for our script, we will follow the same practice and only allow acceptable inputs to our standards. For the username, the convention is that it needs to be 5 to 30 characters long and must begin with a letter and use no special characters anywhere in the username except _ and -. For the password conventions, the password must begin with a lowercase or uppercase letter, and the password must be longer than eight characters but equal or less than 50 characters. The characters between the 2nd and 50th can include special characters. Let's see how we can enforce these conventions on usernames and passwords. While writing the Python code, you have to be flexible and creative with your regular expressions to make your code do what you want, and this is one of those instances.

Referencing `get_cred2.py`, start putting the code together.

```
pynetauto@ubuntu20s1:~/my_tools/tool2_login$ nano get_cred3.py
```

get_cred3.py

```
import re
from getpass import getpass

p1 = re.compile(r'^[a-zA-Z0-9][a-zA-Z0-9_-]{3,28}[a-zA-Z0-9]$') # You must
comprehend Chapter 9!
p2 = re.compile(r'^[a-zA-Z].{7,49}') # You must read through and complete all
exercise in Chapter 9.
```

#	Task

```
def get_secret():
    global secret
    resp = input("Is secret the same as password? (y/n) : ")
    resp = resp.lower()
    if resp == "yes" or resp == "y":
        secret = pwd
    elif resp == "no" or resp == "n":
        secret = None
        while not secret:
            secret = getpass("Enter the secret : ")
            while not p2.match(secret): # apply the re pattern 2 secret
                secret = getpass(r"*Enter the secret : ")
            secret_verify = getpass("Confirm the secret : ")
            if secret != secret_verify:
                print("!!! secret do not match. Please try again.")
                secret = None
    else:
        get_secret()

def get_credentials():
    global uid
    uid = input("Enter Network Admin ID : ")
    while not p1.match(uid): # apply the re pattern 1 to uid
        uid = input(r"*Enter Network Admin ID : ")
    global pwd
    pwd = None
    while not pwd:
        pwd = getpass("Enter Network Admin PWD : ")
        while not p2.match(pwd): # apply the re pattern 2 password
            pwd = getpass(r"*Enter Network Admin PWD : ")
        pwd_verify = getpass("Confirm Network Admin PWD : ")
        if pwd != pwd_verify:
            print("!!! Network Admin Passwords do not match. Please try again.")
            pwd = None
    get_secret()
    return uid, pwd, secret
get_credentials()
print(uid, pwd,secret)
```

Run the final application and validate the functions; your test run should look similar to the below result.

```
pynetauto@ubuntu20s1:~/my_tools/tool2_login$ python3 get_cred3.py
Enter Network Admin ID : jdoe # Entered only four characters. Minimum of five
characters required
*Enter Network Admin ID : pynetauto
Enter Network Admin PWD : ******* # Entered only seven characters. Minimum eight
characters long
*Enter Network Admin PWD : ********
Confirm Network Admin PWD : ********
```

(continued)

#	Task

	```Is secret the same as password? (y/n) : n```
	```Enter the secret : ******* # Entered only seven characters, minimum of 8 characters long```
	```*Enter the secret : *********```
	```Confirm the secret : *********```
	```pynetauto cisco123 secret123```
	After three reiterations of the original code, it looks almost complete and ready for use in the upgrade script. Next, let's see how we can read the IOS name and MD5 values from a CSV file and convert them to Python variables.

Now that you have collected the user ID and password from the application user, let's see how you can collect the new IOS filename and MD5 values by reading a file. If you have multiple devices and multiple values, entering this information through a command line will be too cumbersome. It is also prone to mistakes, so ideally these values are entered into a two-dimensional array form such as Excel or CSV files, letting your Python script read the information. We want to save time and reduce human errors during the cut-and-paste operation in the command-line console.

Collect a New IOS Filename and MD5 Value from a CSV File

After the user ID and password are collected, we want to collect even more information required for the Cisco IOS upgrade, but this time by reading the contents from a CSV file. The extra information includes new IOS names and their respective MD5 values. We can also include the hostname, device type, IP address, and other information to feed our script with two-dimensional data.

IOS can be downloaded from the Cisco download site to upgrade to the latest IOS version if you have an active service contract or work for Cisco Partners. The engineer who will perform the IOS upgrade usually downloads the file and obtains the MD5 value from the vendor's download site. After the IOS has been downloaded to the engineer's computer, the engineer confirms the MD5 values of that copy of IOS so they know that all the software is all intact and not corrupted during the download process. This is one of the first verification steps during an IOS upgrade preparation process. Imagine not checking the MD5 values and using this file to upgrade the Cisco devices' IOS software! It could turn into a nasty situation instead of a straightforward IOS upgrade.

When we upgrade IOS or any operating system on any vendor product, you have to make sure that the vendor's downloaded software version is correct. You need to make sure the download process has not corrupted the IOS due to a lousy Internet connection or other issues. There are two places in the IOS upgrade tool where new IOS MD5 values will be validated. First, the user-provided MD5 value of the new IOS is validated against the server-checked MD5 value. Second, validate the server-checked MD5 value against the MD5 value checked by the Cisco router. Before the router can check the MD5 of a new IOS file, the new IOS must be transferred to the router's flash memory using TFTP/FTP/SFTP/SCP protocol. To be sure, we want to check all MD5 tests every time to avoid the unthinkable. Before we can compare the MD5 value found on Cisco's website against the server-side MD5 value, we must feed our script the correct MD5 value. An excellent way to feed this information is through an Excel or CSV file. Unlike when using a text file, we can use two-dimensional values (with a header) in Python scripts, and they can be handled by the pandas module.

Let's see how we can import the new IOS name and MD5 value from a file such as an `.xlsx` or `.csv` file. Although it is more convenient to create two-dimensional files from Windows-based computers, it is more advantageous to save the file as a `.csv` file. It gives you more flexibility in the Linux server's command-line text editors to modify the content. Here in this example, you will work on the file using Excel and then save it as a CSV file. Once the pandas module reads the two-dimensional values into our script, you can access and turn them into any variable forms that you want.

#	Task
1	Let's open a new Excel file and enter the following details, with the header on the first row and the router information on the second and third rows. At this stage, you must have a copy of the new IOS `.bin` file and the correct MD5 value from the Cisco download site. While we are at it, we can enter more information about each device such as the `devicename` (router name), `device` (type), `devicetype` (for `netmiko` dictionary), `host` (IP address or DNS hostname), `newios`, and `newiosmd5` values, as shown in Figure 18-1. If you are using another IOS version, then you will have to update the information accordingly.

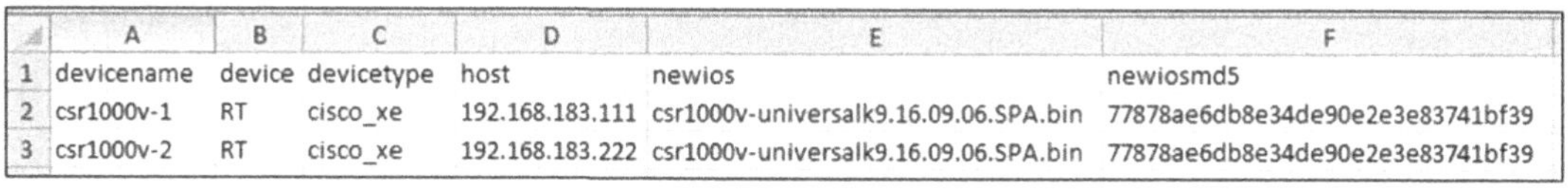

	A	B	C	D	E	F
1	devicename	device	devicetype	host	newios	newiosmd5
2	csr1000v-1	RT	cisco_xe	192.168.183.111	csr1000v-universalk9.16.09.06.SPA.bin	77878ae6db8e34de90e2e3e83741bf39
3	csr1000v-2	RT	cisco_xe	192.168.183.222	csr1000v-universalk9.16.09.06.SPA.bin	77878ae6db8e34de90e2e3e83741bf39

Figure 18-1. *Creating a CSV file in Microsoft Excel*

If you don't have Microsoft Excel on your host computer, then you can work in any text editor using commas as separators, as shown in Figure 18-2. Alternatively, if you have a couple of devices like our example, you can directly enter this information in the Linux server's vi or nano text editor. If you have hundreds of devices, use a spreadsheet program such as Microsoft Excel or Google Sheets.

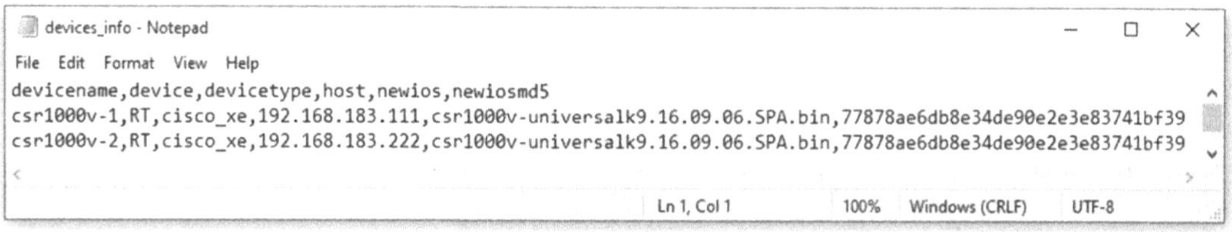

Figure 18-2. *Creating a CSV file using a text editor*

#	Task
2	Once you have finished entering the information in Microsoft Excel, save the file as `device_info.csv`. Make sure you select "Save as type" and select "CSV (Comma delimited)." See Figure 18-3.

(continued)

#	Task

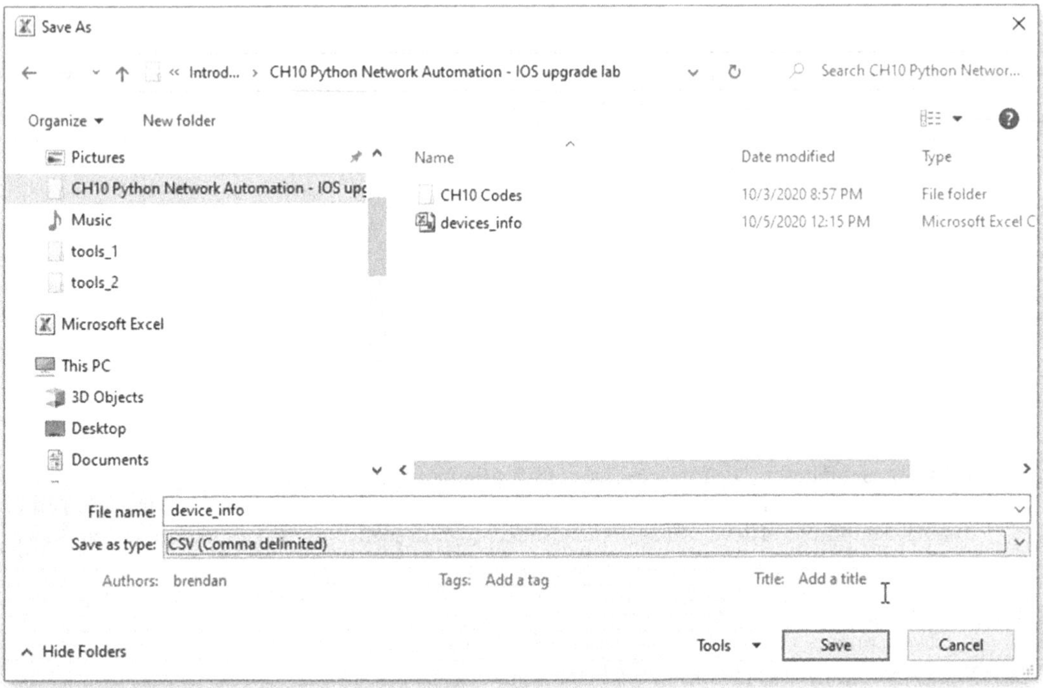

Figure 18-3. *Saving a file as a CSV file in Microsoft Excel*

3 In the earlier chapters, you used WinSCP to upload files to your Python automation server. If you want to upload the file to your Linux server's working directory, you can do so now. Since the CSV file you are trying to upload here is a text (`.txt`) file with a different file extension (`.csv`), it is possible to copy and paste the information into a new file in Linux's vi or nano text editor and then save the file as a `.csv` file.

```
pynetauto@ubuntu20s1:~/my_tools$ mkdir tool3_read_csv
pynetauto@ubuntu20s1:~/my_tools$ cd tool3_read_csv
pynetauto@ubuntu20s1:~/my_tools/tool3_read_csv$ pwd
/home/pynetauto/my_tools/tool3_read_csv
pynetauto@ubuntu20s1:~/my_tools/tool3_read_csv$ nano devices_info.csv
```

devices_info.csv

```
devices_info.csv
devicename,device,devicetype,host,newios,newiosmd5
csr1000v-1,RT,cisco_xe,192.168.183.111,csr1000v-universalk9.16.09.06.SPA.bin,77878a
e6db8e34de90e2e3e83741bf39
csr1000v-2,RT,cisco_xe,192.168.183.222,csr1000v-universalk9.16.09.06.SPA.bin,77878a
e6db8e34de90e2e3e83741bf39
```

#	Task
	Write the base script to read your CSV file. If you are using an `.xlsx` file, replace the file extension type with `.xlsx`, and pandas will read the file in the same way as a `.csv` file.

```
pynetauto@ubuntu20s1:~/my_tools/tool3_read_csv$ nano read_info1.py

read_info1.py
import pandas as pd

df = pd.read_csv(r'./devices_info.csv')
print(df)
```

Run the script and print out the dataframe (`df`).

```
pynetauto@ubuntu20s1:~/my_tools/tool3_read_csv$ python3 read_info1.py
devicename device  ...                newios                        newiosmd5
0  csr1000v-1     RT  ...  csr1000v-universalk9.16.09.06.SPA.bin
77878ae6db8e34de90e2e3e83741bf39
1  csr1000v-2     RT  ...  csr1000v-universalk9.16.09.06.SPA.bin
77878ae6db8e34de90e2e3e83741bf39

[2 rows x 6 columns]
```

Now reiterate the script and add two lines of code to read the number of rows; the number of rows can also be used as a variable to control the flow of our application.

```
pynetauto@ubuntu20s1:~/my_tools/tool3_read_csv$ cp read_info1.py read_info2.py
ynetauto@ubuntu20s1:~/my_tools/tool3_read_csv$ nano read_info2.py

read_info2.py
import pandas as pd

df = pd.read_csv(r'./devices_info.csv')
print(df)
number_of_rows = len(df.index)
print(number_of_rows)
```

Run the previous script to get the number of rows; we are expecting 2 as pandas by default reads the first row as the header row.

```
pynetauto@ubuntu20s1:~/my_tools/tool3_read_csv$ python3 read_info2.py
devicename device  ...                newios                        newiosmd5
0  csr1000v-1     RT  ...  csr1000v-universalk9.16.09.06.SPA.bin
77878ae6db8e34de90e2e3e83741bf39
1  csr1000v-2     RT  ...  csr1000v-universalk9.16.09.06.SPA.bin
77878ae6db8e34de90e2e3e83741bf39

[2 rows x 6 columns]
2
```

(continued)

#	Task
4	We are trying to read each value and use them as variables, so we use the specific information in our script. We want to read each row and convert it into a type of array such as a list or tuple.

```
pynetauto@ubuntu20s1:~/my_tools/tool3_read_csv$ nano read_info3.py

read_info3.py
import pandas as pd

df = pd.read_csv(r'./devices_info.csv')
number_of_rows = len(df.index)

# Read the values and save as a list, read column as df and save it as a list
devicename = list(df['devicename'])
device = list(df['device'])
devicetype = list(df['devicetype'])
ip = list(df['host'])
newios = list(df['newios'])
newiosmd5 = list(df['newiosmd5'])

print(devicename)
print(device)
print(devicetype)
print(ip)
print(newios)
print(newiosmd5)
```

When you run the previous script, the data is easily accessible now, and it is retrieved as Python lists.

```
pynetauto@ubuntu20s1:~/my_tools/tool3_read_csv$ python3 read_info3.py
['csr1000v-1', 'csr1000v-2']
['RT', 'RT']
['cisco_xe', 'cisco_xe']
['192.168.183.111', '192.168.183.222']
['csr1000v-universalk9.16.09.06.SPA.bin', 'csr1000v-universalk9.16.09.06.SPA.bin']
['77878ae6db8e34de90e2e3e83741bf39', '77878ae6db8e34de90e2e3e83741bf39']
```

5 Let's massage the data a little bit and put it into a single list containing list items.

```
pynetauto@ubuntu20s1:~/my_tools/tool3_read_csv$ nano read_info4.py

read_info4.py
import pandas as pd

df = pd.read_csv(r'./devices_info.csv')
number_of_rows = len(df.index)
```

#	Task
	(continued)

```
# Read the values and save as a list, read column as df and save it as a list
devicename = list(df['devicename'])
device = list(df['device'])
devicetype = list(df['devicetype'])
ip = list(df['host'])
newios = list(df['newios'])
newiosmd5 = list(df['newiosmd5'])

# Convert the list into a device_list
device_list = []
for index, rows in df.iterrows():
    device_append = [rows.devicename, rows.device, \
    rows.devicetype, rows.host, rows.newios, rows.newiosmd5]
    device_list.append(device_append)
print(device_list)
```

Run the script, and you will notice that the device information read has now turned into a list of lists.

```
pynetauto@ubuntu20s1:~/my_tools/tool3_read_csv$ python3 read_info4.py
[['csr1000v-1', 'RT', 'cisco_xe', '192.168.183.111', 'csr1000v-
universalk9.16.09.06.SPA.bin', '77878ae6db8e34de90e2e3e83741bf39'], ['csr1000v-2',
'RT', 'cisco_xe', '192.168.183.222', 'csr1000v-universalk9.16.09.06.SPA.bin',
'77878ae6db8e34de90e2e3e83741bf39']]
```

6 If we need only specific information from device_list created by reading the CSV file, such as newios and newiosmd5, we can use a simple loop to recall these numbers.

```
pynetauto@ubuntu20s1:~/my_tools/tool3_read_csv$ cp read_info4.py read_info5.py
pynetauto@ubuntu20s1:~/my_tools/tool3_read_csv$ nano read_info5.py

read_info5.py
import pandas as pd

df = pd.read_csv(r'./devices_info.csv')
number_of_rows = len(df.index)

# Read the values and save as a list, read column as df and save it as a list
devicename = list(df['devicename'])
device = list(df['device'])
devicetype = list(df['devicetype'])
ip = list(df['host'])
newios = list(df['newios'])
newiosmd5 = list(df['newiosmd5'])
```

(continued)

#	Task

```
# Convert the list into a device_list
device_list = []
for index, rows in df.iterrows():
    device_append = [rows.devicename, rows.device, \
    rows.devicetype, rows.host, rows.newios, rows.newiosmd5]
    device_list.append(device_append)

for x in device_list:
    newios, newiosmd5 = x[4], x[5].lower()
    print(newios, newiosmd5)
```

Run the script now, and you will get each device's new IOS filename and MD5 value. Since we have the same device types, the new IOS name and MD5 values will be the same.

```
pynetauto@ubuntu20s1:~/my_tools/tool3_read_csv$ python3 read_info5.py
csr1000v-universalk9.16.09.06.SPA.bin 77878ae6db8e34de90e2e3e83741bf39
csr1000v-universalk9.16.09.06.SPA.bin 77878ae6db8e34de90e2e3e83741bf39
```

7 Initially, when we created the CSV file, we used more information than required, and there is a reason behind this. Using the pandas file read method, we also want to create a list containing the `netmiko` dictionary format. We can pass the values of a dictionary to `netmiko ConnectHandler` for SSH connections while logging into the routers. Let's study the simple `netmiko` dictionary format and use IP address, and `devicetype` information from `device_list` to make another dictionary for SSH logins. A device dictionary looks like the following example. You can also add the `logging` and `delay factors` options, but we'll keep it simple for our lab use.

```
device1 = {
    'device_type': 'cisco_ios',
    'host': '10.10.10.1',
    'username': 'username',
    'password': 'password',
    'secret': 'secret',
}
```

So, from 10.5.2, we can already collect the username, password, and secret from the user via an interactive input session. Now we have read the `device_type` and `host` (IP address) values from a CSV file. We can use the collected information to turn it into a `netmiko` compatible dictionary format for the SSH connection. Please note that we added the username and password collection tool to teach you how they can be collected interactively. If you are running Python scripts in an extremely secure environment, you can feed all information through the file read method, including the username, password, and secret.

```
pynetauto@ubuntu20s1:~/my_tools/tool3_read_csv$ cp read_info5.py read_info6.py
pynetauto@ubuntu20s1:~/my_tools/tool3_read_csv$ nano read_info6.py
```

read_info6.py

```
import pandas as pd
```

#	Task

```
df = pd.read_csv(r'./devices_info.csv')
number_of_rows = len(df.index)

# Read the values and save as a list, read column as df and save it as a list
devicename = list(df['devicename'])
device = list(df['device'])
devicetype = list(df['devicetype'])
ip = list(df['host'])
newios = list(df['newios'])
newiosmd5 = list(df['newiosmd5'])

# Convert the list into a device_list
device_list = []
for index, rows in df.iterrows():
    device_append = [rows.devicename, rows.device, \
    rows.devicetype, rows.host, rows.newios, rows.newiosmd5]
    device_list.append(device_append)
i = 0
for x in device_list:
    if len(x) !=0:
        i += 1
        name = f'device{str(i)}'
        devicetype, host = x[2], x[3]
        device = {
        'device_type': devicetype,
        'host': host,
        'username': 'username',
        'password': 'password',
        'secret': 'secret',
        }
        print(name, "=" ,device)
```

Now when you run the script, you will see that the information is formatted into a dictionary, and we can assign the dictionary to variables, in this case, device1 and device2. Imagine you have 20 or 200 devices to turn the read information into netmiko-friendly dictionaries. Some people say that automation is all in the loop commands. If a task is repetitive, that is a potential target for automation.

```
pynetauto@ubuntu20s1:~/my_tools/tool3_read_csv$ python3 read_info6.py
device1 = {'device_type': 'cisco_xe', 'host': '192.168.183.111', 'username':
'username', 'password': 'password', 'secret': 'secret'}
device2 = {'device_type': 'cisco_xe', 'host': '192.168.183.222', 'username':
'username', 'password': 'password', 'secret': 'secret'}
```

(continued)

#	Task
8	Copy the previous script and create a new script called `read_info7.py`. You are going to modify it, so the dictionaries are now stored in a list. In other words, you will create a list with multiple dictionaries as its items. This way, we can call them out and the dictionary during the SSH connection to your devices.

```
pynetauto@ubuntu20s1:~/my_tools/tool3_read_csv$ cp read_info6.py read_info7.py
pynetauto@ubuntu20s1:~/my_tools/tool3_read_csv$ nano read_info7.py
```

Notice that I have manually added the username, password, and secret to this script for testing purposes. However, when we integrate the user ID and password collection tool developed earlier, the variables will be replaced. When you work in a production environment, it is highly recommended that you remove usernames and password information or completely delete the file if they contain sensitive information.

read_info7.py

```
import pandas as pd

df = pd.read_csv(r'./devices_info.csv')
number_of_rows = len(df.index)

# Read the values and save as a list, read column as df and save it as a list
devicename = list(df['devicename'])
device = list(df['device'])
devicetype = list(df['devicetype'])
ip = list(df['host'])
newios = list(df['newios'])
newiosmd5 = list(df['newiosmd5'])
# Convert the list into a device_list
device_list = []
for index, rows in df.iterrows():
    device_append = [rows.devicename, rows.device, \
    rows.devicetype, rows.host, rows.newios, rows.newiosmd5]
    device_list.append(device_append)

device_list_netmiko = []
i = 0
for x in device_list:
    if len(x) !=0:
        i += 1
        name = f'device{str(i)}'
        devicetype, host = x[2], x[3]
        device = {
        'device_type': devicetype,
        'host': host,
        'username': 'pynetauto',
        'password': 'cisco123',
        'secret': 'cisco123',
        }
        device_list_netmiko.append(device)

print(device_list_netmiko)
```

#	Task
	When you run the script, you should get a list with two dictionaries as items. You must get familiar with massaging the data if you want to parse it to Python scripts to access any information from any network device.

```
pynetauto@ubuntu20s1:~/my_tools/tool3_read_csv$ python3 read_info7.py
[{'device_type': 'cisco_xe', 'host': '192.168.183.111', 'username': 'pynetauto',
'password': 'cisco123', 'secret': 'cisco123'}, {'device_type': 'cisco_xe', 'host':
'192.168.183.222', 'username': 'pynetauto', 'password': 'cisco123', 'secret':
'cisco123'}]
```

9 To test that this script will be working as expected, add a `netmiko ConnectHandler`, and run the Cisco `router` command. Note that only one `import` statement (`from netmiko import ConnectHandler`) and the last four lines of code are added to the previous script. This Python script is available for download from my GitHub site.

Download URL: `https://github.com/pynetauto/apress_pynetauto`

Create the final script to use the read data and then perform a simple task; in this case, run the `show clock` command to display the time of the CSR routers.

```
pynetauto@ubuntu20s1:~/my_tools/tool3_read_csv$ cp read_info7.py read_info8.py
pynetauto@ubuntu20s1:~/my_tools/tool3_read_csv$ nano read_info8.py
```

```
read_info8.py
import pandas as pd
from netmiko import ConnectHandler

[... omitted for brevity. Same as read_info7.py]
[... See the source code for full details.]

for device in device_list_netmiko:
    net_connect = ConnectHandler(**device)
    show_clock = net_connect.send_command("show clock")
    print(show_clock)
```

When you run the script, you should see each router's time. The `show clock` command is one of the simplest commands that you can run from your script to check if your SSH connection is working. Checking port 22 does not test your credentials, so it is worth writing such code that runs a simple `show clock` command.

```
pynetauto@ubuntu20s1:~/my_tools/tool3_read_csv$ python3 read_info8.py
*13:37:19.262 UTC Fri Jan 15 2021
*13:37:20.403 UTC Fri Jan 15 2021
```

Check the MD5 Value of the New IOS on the Server

As discussed earlier, authenticating the new IOS file is the key to a successful IOS upgrade. The MD5 value is available from Cisco's website, or you can use a tool such as `WinMD5.exe` or even a command line to check the MD5 value of the file after the new IOS download. Before uploading the file, we want to check if this MD5 value is correct to double-check the file's integrity you are about to upload. When you upload a new IOS file manually to a TFTP or FTP server, you will verify this manually, but in our IOS upgrade tool, we are replacing the TFTP/FTP file transfer method with Secure Copy Protocol (SCP) file transfer. Before the file transfer occurs, we want to check the MD5 value of the IOS file in the SCP folder against the good MD5 value, so the file integrity is guaranteed to avoid unexpected results.

#	Task
1	First, create a directory to place your new IOS file in using WinSCP or FileZilla. See Figure 18-4.

```
pynetauto@ubuntu20s1:~/my_tools$ mkdir new_ios
pynetauto@ubuntu20s1:~/my_tools$ cd new_ios
pynetauto@ubuntu20s1:~/my_tools/new_ios$ pwd
/home/pynetauto/my_tools/new_ios
pynetauto@ubuntu20s1:~/my_tools/new_ios$ ls
csr1000v-universalk9.16.09.06.SPA.bin
```

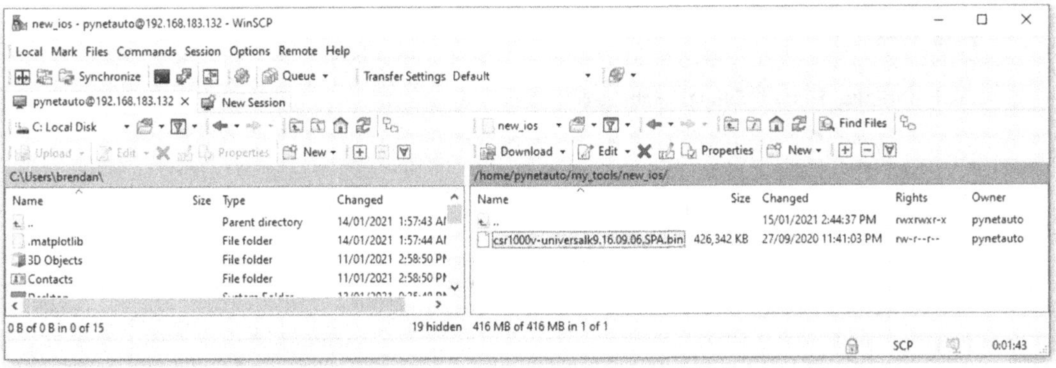

Figure 18-4. *ubuntu20s1, copying new IOS to the new_ios directory*

#	Task
2	Create the tool4_md5_linux directory; then copy the read_info5.py file as the basis of the md5_validate1.py script. Also, to help our development, copy the devices_info.csv file. Both the read_info5.py and devices_info.csv files are from the tool3 development.

```
pynetauto@ubuntu20s1:~/my_tools/new_ios$ cd ..
pynetauto@ubuntu20s1:~/my_tools$ pwd
/home/pynetauto/my_tools
pynetauto@ubuntu20s1:~/my_tools$ mkdir tool4_md5_linux
pynetauto@ubuntu20s1:~/my_tools$ cd tool4_md5_linux
pynetauto@ubuntu20s1:~/my_tools/tool4_md5_linux$ cp /home/pynetauto/my_tools/tool3_
read_csv/read_info5.py ./md5_validate1.py
pynetauto@ubuntu20s1:~/my_tools/tool4_md5_linux$ cp /home/pynetauto/my_tools/tool3_
read_csv/devices_info.csv ./devices_info.csv
```

We want to modify the last for loop of the code from read_info5.py, so our task is to modify this for loop and add a function to check the MD5 value of the just copied IOS file and also check the file size to be used during the flash size check later.

md5_validate1.py

```
import pandas as pd

df = pd.read_csv(r'./devices_info.csv')
number_of_rows = len(df.index)

# Read the values and save as a list, read column as df and save it as a list
devicename = list(df['devicename'])
device = list(df['device'])
devicetype = list(df['devicetype'])
ip = list(df['host'])
newios = list(df['newios'])
newiosmd5 = list(df['newiosmd5'])

# Convert the list into a device_list
device_list = []
for index, rows in df.iterrows():
    device_append = [rows.devicename, rows.device, \
    rows.devicetype, rows.host, rows.newios, rows.newiosmd5]
    device_list.append(device_append)

for x in device_list:
    newios, newiosmd5 = x[4], x[5].lower()
    print(newios, newiosmd5)
```

(*continued*)

#	Task
3	Now add the import code for the built-in `os.path` and `hashlib` modules. `hashlib` will be used to check the MD5 of the file on the Linux server, and `os.path` will be used to calculate the actual file size. The middle part of the script is the same as the copied script. Still, you will change the `for x in device_list:` so the script returns the MD5 value calculated on the server side and the `newios` size, which will be used later to check if the free size on the router's flash can accommodate the new IOS size. After the change, `md5_validate1.py` should look similar to this:

```
pynetauto@ubuntu20s1:~/my_tools/tool4_md5_linux$ nano md5_validate2.py

md5_validate2.py
import pandas as pd
import os.path
import hashlib

[... omitted for brevity, same as read_info5.py]

for x in device_list:
    print(x[0])
    newios = x[4]
    newiosmd5 = x[5].lower()
    newiosmd5hash = hashlib.md5()
    file = open(f'/home/pynetauto/my_tools/new_ios/{newios}', 'rb') # change path to
    your own path
    content = file.read()
    newiosmd5hash.update(content)
    newiosmd5server = newiosmd5hash.hexdigest()
    print(newiosmd5server)
    newiossize = round(os.path.getsize(f'/home/pynetauto/my_tools/new_ios/
    {newios}')/1000000, 2)
    print(newiossize, "MB")
```

Run the script, and it should return the server-side IOS MD5 value and the actual IOS size in megabytes. You will also learn how to check the router's used, free, and total size to make sure that the flash has enough free space to accommodate the new IOS.

```
pynetauto@ubuntu20s1:~/my_tools/tool4_md5_linux$ python3 md5_validate2.py
csr1000v-1
77878ae6db8e34de90e2e3e83741bf39
436.57 MB
csr1000v-2
77878ae6db8e34de90e2e3e83741bf39
436.57 MB
```

#	Task
4	Once you are happy with the result in step 3, add an `if-else` statement to the end of the last print line and see how you can control the script flow by testing the two MD5 values.

md5_validate3.py

```
import pandas as pd
import os.path
import hashlib

df = pd.read_csv(r'./devices_info.csv')
number_of_rows = len(df.index)

# Read the values and save as a list, read column as df and save it as a list
devicename = list(df['devicename'])
device = list(df['device'])
devicetype = list(df['devicetype'])
ip = list(df['host'])
newios = list(df['newios'])
newiosmd5 = list(df['newiosmd5'])

# Convert the list into a device_list
device_list = []
for index, rows in df.iterrows():
    device_append = [rows.devicename, rows.device, \
    rows.devicetype, rows.host, rows.newios, rows.newiosmd5]
    device_list.append(device_append)

for x in device_list:
    print(x[0])
    newios = x[4]
    newiosmd5 = str(x[5].lower()).strip()
    print(newiosmd5)
    newiosmd5hash = hashlib.md5()
    file = open(f'/home/pynetauto/my_tools/new_ios/{newios}', 'rb')
    content = file.read()
    newiosmd5hash.update(content)
    newiosmd5server = newiosmd5hash.hexdigest()
    print(newiosmd5server.strip())
    newiossize = round(os.path.getsize(f'/home/pynetauto/my_tools/new_ios/
    {newios}')/1000000, 2)
    print(newiossize, "MB")

    if newiosmd5server == newiosmd5:
        print("MD5 values matched!")
    else:
        print("Mismatched MD5 values. Exit")
        exit()
```

(continued)

#	Task
	When you run the script, you will see a result similar to the following output. You have now confirmed that the information read has been turned into a Python variable for use in our script. ``` pynetauto@ubuntu20s1:~/my_tools/tool4_md5_linux$ python3 md5_validate3.py csr1000v-1 77878ae6db8e34de90e2e3e83741bf39 77878ae6db8e34de90e2e3e83741bf39 436.57 MB MD5 values matched! csr1000v-2 77878ae6db8e34de90e2e3e83741bf39 77878ae6db8e34de90e2e3e83741bf39 436.57 MB MD5 values matched! ```

Check the Flash Size on Cisco Routers

You learned how to get the IOS size on the server in the previous script, and the new IOS file size was 436.57 MB. Before you can upload this new IOS file to the router's flash memory, you have to check if there is enough free space in the flash memory. If the flash memory has enough free space, uploading can occur immediately. Still, if the flash size is not big enough, you will have to delete old or redundant files, or for older IOS devices, you will need to delete the currently running IOS file from the flash. During the boot process, the IOS is copied and decompressed in random access memory (RAM) from flash. On some of the latest Cisco platforms, the files are already decompressed to save time during the Power On Self-Test (POST) process. Either way, you need to make enough room for a new IOS file. To get the free flash size on a Cisco device, you can use a `show flash:` or `dir` command and then dissect the information using a regular expression. If you know what command to run and which information you need, it's easy to get it. Still, many vendor network devices do not provide API support. Also, SNMP has its limitations while trying to work out this type of information. Although this is not the smartest or the most sophisticated way to collect the data we want, this could be the only option for some devices.

After working out the free flash size, if the IOS size exceeds the flash-free size, we want to give the user (or the script) an option to locate the old IOS file and remove it. Sometimes, there might a large sized file on the router's flash memory, so in this case, we also have to give the user (or the script) an option to search the file and delete a large file. Let's see how this can be achieved.

#	Task
1	Create another working directory called `tool5_fsize_cisco`, and then create a new script to run and capture either the `dir` or `show flash:` command. ``` pynetauto@ubuntu20s1:~/my_tools/tool4_md5_linux$ cd .. pynetauto@ubuntu20s1:~/my_tools$ mkdir tool5_fsize_cisco pynetauto@ubuntu20s1:~/my_tools$ cd tool5_fsize_cisco pynetauto@ubuntu20s1:~/my_tools/tool5_fsize_cisco$ nano check_flash1.py ``` Write the following script to capture the output of the `dir` command on the Cisco router. On IOS XE routers, it is easier to capture the information using the `dir` command, but on other devices, the `show flash:` command works on most devices. For this practice, we'll use the `dir` command because the output is shorter.

#	Task

check_flash1.py

```
import time
from netmiko import ConnectHandler

# Borrowed from read_info7.py result.
devices_list =[
{
    'device_type': 'cisco_xe',
    'host': '192.168.183.111',
    'username': 'pynetauto',
    'password': 'cisco123',
    'secret': 'cisco123'
},
{
    'device_type': 'cisco_xe',
    'host': '192.168.183.222',
    'username': 'pynetauto',
    'password': 'cisco123',
    'secret': 'cisco123'
}]

for device in devices_list:
    net_connect = ConnectHandler(**device)
    net_connect.send_command("terminal length 0")
    showdir = net_connect.send_command("dir")
    #showflash = net_connect.send_command("show flash:") # Alternatively use 'show
    flash:'
    print(showdir)
    print("-"*80)
    time.sleep(2)
```

When you run the check_flash1.py script one more time, the output displays the file details and flash memory use. We are interested in the free size in the router's flash memory. Here, we are interested in "7897796608 bytes total (5230376448 bytes free) in the last line of the output.

```
pynetauto@ubuntu20s1:~/my_tools/tool5_fsize_cisco$ python3 check_flash1.py
Directory of bootflash:/

   11  drwx            16384  Sep 28 2020 22:15:16 +00:00  lost+found
32513  drwx             4096  Jan 15 2021 08:38:08 +00:00  .installer
   12  -rw-        377500632  Sep 28 2020 22:15:59 +00:00  csr1000v-mono-
universalk9.16.07.03.SPA.pkg
   13  -rw-      38978681  Sep 28 2020 22:15:59 +00:00  csr1000v-rpboot.16.07.03.SPA.pkg
[...omitted for brevity]
430785  drwx            4096  Dec 3 2020 10:21:10 +00:00  iox
65025  drwx            4096  Dec 3 2020 10:21:25 +00:00  .dbpersist
89409  drwx            4096  Dec 3 2020 10:22:16 +00:00  onep

7897796608 bytes total (6230376448 bytes free)
--------------------------------------------------------------------------------
```

(continued)

#	Task
2	So, this is the dir output from the first router. Let's see how we can use a regular expression to get the "bytes free."

```
Directory of bootflash:/

   11  drwx            16384  Sep 28 2020 22:15:16 +00:00  lost+found
32513  drwx             4096   Oct 5 2020 11:50:08 +00:00  .installer
   12  -rw-        377500632  Sep 28 2020 22:15:59 +00:00  csr1000v-mono-
universalk9.16.07.03.SPA.pkg
   13  -rw-         38978681  Sep 28 2020 22:15:59 +00:00  csr1000v-rpboot.16.07.03.
SPA.pkg
   14  -rw-             1941  Sep 28 2020 22:15:59 +00:00  packages.conf
365761  drwx            4096  Sep 28 2020 22:16:36 +00:00  core
390145  drwx            4096  Sep 28 2020 22:16:29 +00:00  .prst_sync
81281  drwx             4096  Sep 28 2020 22:16:36 +00:00  .rollback_timer
455169  drwx           12288   Oct 5 2020 12:00:45 +00:00  tracelogs
48769  drwx             4096  Sep 28 2020 22:16:55 +00:00  virtual-instance
   15  -rw-               30   Oct 5 2020 11:51:27 +00:00  throughput_monitor_params
   16  -rw-              848   Oct 5 2020 11:51:35 +00:00  cvac.log
447041  drwx            4096  Sep 28 2020 22:17:39 +00:00  CRDU
   17  -rw-               16  Sep 28 2020 22:17:43 +00:00  ovf-env.xml.md5
   18  -rw-              157   Oct 5 2020 11:51:35 +00:00  csrlxc-cfg.log
   19  -rw-               35  Sep 28 2020 22:22:44 +00:00  pnp-tech-time
   20  -rw-            51746  Sep 28 2020 22:22:45 +00:00  pnp-tech-discovery-summary

7897796608 bytes total (7060598784 bytes free)
```

Since there are many digits, we have to locate the number with pinpoint accuracy, which can be achieved by using a positive lookahead method. Since the digits are in front of `bytes free`, we can use this as the search handle and simply find the string of digits ahead of this specific string. So the regular expression required is as shown here:

`\d+(?=\sbytes\sfree\))`

Regular Expression	Explanation
`\d+`	This means any digits more than a single number.
`(?=)`	This is the positive lookahead regular expression.
`\sbytes\sfree\)`	We are looking for an actual string, but we only use it to search, and we match the string in front of this string. `\s` means a whitespace.

So, the previous regular expression should match any digits occurring in front of `bytes free`, which is 7060598784 in our example.

#	Task
3	Make a copy of the first script and create the following script to apply our regular expression:

```
pynetauto@ubuntu20s1:~/my_tools/tool5_fsize_cisco$ cp check_flash1.py check_flash2.py
pynetauto@ubuntu20s1:~/my_tools/tool5_fsize_cisco$ nano check_flash2.py
nano check_flash2.py
import time

from netmiko import ConnectHandler
import re # Import re module
# This is borrowed from read_info7.py result
devices_list =[
{
    'device_type': 'cisco_xe',
    'host': '192.168.183.111',
    'username': 'pynetauto',
    'password': 'cisco123',
    'secret': 'cisco123'
},
{
    'device_type': 'cisco_xe',
    'host': '192.168.183.222',
    'username': 'pynetauto',
    'password': 'cisco123',
    'secret': 'cisco123'
}]

for device in devices_list:
    net_connect = ConnectHandler(**device)
    net_connect.send_command("terminal length 0")
    showdir = net_connect.send_command("dir")
    #showflash = net_connect.send_command("show flash:")
    #print(showdir) # Hash out the line
    print("-"*80)
    time.sleep(2)

    p1 = re.compile("\d+(?=\sbytes\sfree\))") # Compiled Regular expression
    m1 = p1.findall(showdir) # Match regular expression
    flashfree =  ((int(m1[0])/1000000)) # convert bytes into MB
    print(flashfree)
```

Run the previous script, and now you have the free bytes in megabytes. The first value is from csr1000v-1, and the second value is from csr1000v-2.

```
pynetauto@ubuntu20s1:~/my_tools/tool5_fsize_cisco$ python3 check_flash2.py
--------------------------------------------------------------------------------
7060.598784
--------------------------------------------------------------------------------
7060.578304
```

(*continued*)

#	Task
	When we combine the previous script with `md5_validate2.py` from previous exercises, we can check if the flash's free size is bigger than the new IOS file size. The application flow can be altered using the result of the comparison. There is almost 7 GB of free flash memory on the routers, and our IOS size is 436.57 MB, so there is no need to remove any files before uploading the file to the flash. However, as mentioned, on older Cisco devices, the flash memory size is often tight, and as part of your script, you may have to offer the user an option to delete some files from the flash memory to make room for a new IOS upload. Usually, we are upgrading IOS on a mission-critical device such as a router or switch. Engineers invest more than 80 percent of their time preparing for this type of change, meaning that a lack of space in the flash memory will be detected at the beginning of the preparations. Most of the time, the problem needs to be taken care of before the actual upgrade takes place. But sometimes an engineer will try to cut corners during the change preparation process. These days, most reputable IT-driven companies have taken up the ITIL process, and ITIL guides the change management. The owners of such change cases perform end-to-end checks even before a change is approved by stakeholders, and only then can the change begin. For this reason, to save pages in this chapter, I am excluding the script that would give the user an option to remove a file or look for a file in a directory. I will leave this as your homework to figure out how you can add this feature to your script.

Make Backups of running-config, the Interface Status, and the Routing Table

Assuming that our routers have enough flash memory to accommodate the new IOS for the router, you now want to make backups of the running configuration. In most production environments, the routers' configurations will be backed up daily or weekly on a configuration backup server. In this case, you have to make sure that the last backed-up configuration of the device you are upgrading is not older than a couple of hours old. In other words, the most up-to-date `running-config` backup of your router is the one you captured just before the router goes into a reload. With the Python script in use, there are two ways that you can make backups of your routers' `running-config`. The first is to save the configuration on your Python server's local disk, and the second method is to run the `copy running-config tftp/ftp:` command. The second method will be the preferred `running-config` backup method if the backup will be stored for a while. Still, if this backup is for a recovery process, if the system loses the configuration for some unseen reason, making a backup on your server will be more than enough. For this reason, you will learn how to save the running configurations using the `show` command via an SSH connection.

Before making any changes, make backups of the running configuration before reloading the routers.

#	Task
1	Once again, make a separate directory to work on a new tool. Since this section's content has been covered in the earlier chapters, you should be quite familiar with file handling. You will write this tool in a single attempt without reiteration, so follow along here by typing in each word and refer to the explanation noted in the lines of code.

```
pynetauto@ubuntu20s1:~/my_tools/tool5_fsize_cisco$ cd ..
pynetauto@ubuntu20s1:~/my_tools$ mkdir tool6_make_backup
pynetauto@ubuntu20s1:~/my_tools$ cd tool6_make_backup
pynetauto@ubuntu20s1:~/my_tools/tool6_make_backup$ nano make_backup1.py
```

This script will make each device's dictionaries with their variables to make it more straightforward. You will call out each device's IP address to form the names of each file. This way, each device will have its own unique backup filename, and when troubleshooting issues later, you will not have a single file containing multiple devices' configurations. You can run any `show` command and make backups of your router's running configurations. However, some of the basic `show` commands worth capturing for Cisco routers are `show running-config`, `show ip route`, and `show ip interface brief`. If you are working with Cisco switches, the `show running-config`, `show ip interface brief`, and `show switch` commands could be helpful. Now, let's write this code and run it.

make_backup1.py

```
import time
from netmiko import ConnectHandler
# Converted the list of dictionaries back to each variables
device1 = {
    'device_type': 'cisco_xe',
    'host': '192.168.183.111',
    'username': 'pynetauto',
    'password': 'cisco123',
    'secret': 'cisco123'
}
device2 = {
    'device_type': 'cisco_xe',
    'host': '192.168.183.222',
    'username': 'pynetauto',
    'password': 'cisco123',
    'secret': 'cisco123'
}
devices_list = [device1, device2] # Make a list of devices

for device in devices_list: # Read each device from device_list
    print(device) # Print out each device information during development
    ip = str(device['host']) # To make unique file names, assign IP address of device
    as variable, ip.
    f1 = open(ip + '_showrun_1.txt', 'w+') # Create and open f1
    net_connect = ConnectHandler(**device) #Connect to device, ** denotes parsing of a
    dictionary
    net_connect.send_command("terminal length 0") # Change terminal length to 0
    showrun = net_connect.send_command("show running-config") # Run show run and save
    to showrun variable
```

(continued)

#	Task

	``
	        f1.write(showrun) # Write showrun to f1. showrun is in the memory.
	        time.sleep(1) # Pause for 1 second
	        f1.close() # Close f1
	# The remaining codes are same as above except the file name and actual command
	        f2 = open(ip + '_show_ip_route_1.txt', 'w') # Crate and open f2
	        #net_connect.enable()
	        showiproute = net_connect.send_command("show ip route")
	        #net_connect.exit_enable_mode()
	        f2.write(showiproute)
	        time.sleep(1)
	        f2.close()
	
	        f3 = open(ip + '_show_ip_int_bri_1.txt', 'w')
	        showiproute = net_connect.send_command("show ip interface brief")
	        f3.write(showiproute)
	        time.sleep(1)
	        f3.close()
	
	print("All tasks completed successfully") # Information to let you know that all tasks completed
	``

2	Now run the script. It will make backups by running the show commands of your choice. Here we are capturing three show command outputs to separate files. Later, the post-upgrade check will rerun the same commands and create post-reload files. Then, the script will perform the post-upgrade check to ensure that the before and after configurations remain the same and the IOS upgrade did not cause any failures. Once you have completed writing the make_backup1.py Python code, run it to make backups of the show commands. pynetauto@ubuntu20s1:~/my_tools/tool6_make_backup$ **python3 make_backup1.py** {'device_type': 'cisco_xe', 'host': '192.168.183.111', 'username': 'pynetauto', 'password': 'cisco123', 'secret': 'cisco123'} {'device_type': 'cisco_xe', 'host': '192.168.183.222', 'username': 'pynetauto', 'password': 'cisco123', 'secret': 'cisco123'} All tasks completed successfully Use the ls -lh Linux command to check the backups of the show commands and running configuration. pynetauto@ubuntu20s1:~/my_tools/tool6_make_backup$ **ls -lh** total 28K -rw-rw-r-- 1 pynetauto pynetauto 323 Jan 15 15:33 192.168.183.111_show_ip_int_bri_1.txt -rw-rw-r-- 1 pynetauto pynetauto 842 Jan 15 15:33 192.168.183.111_show_ip_route_1.txt -rw-rw-r-- 1 pynetauto pynetauto 4.0K Jan 15 15:33 192.168.183.111_showrun_1.txt -rw-rw-r-- 1 pynetauto pynetauto 323 Jan 15 15:33 192.168.183.222_show_ip_int_bri_1.txt -rw-rw-r-- 1 pynetauto pynetauto 842 Jan 15 15:33 192.168.183.222_show_ip_route_1.txt -rw-rw-r-- 1 pynetauto pynetauto 1.8K Jan 15 15:33 192.168.183.222_showrun_1.txt -rw-rw-r-- 1 pynetauto pynetauto 1.8K Jan 15 15:33 make_backup1.py

You have successfully created a handy tool to make your device backups before making any configuration changes. Now we are going to complete the initial pre-check tools before we can upload the new IOS to the Cisco routers. Let's see how we can upload the new IOS to the router's flash.

Part B: IOS Uploading and More Pre-check Tools Development

Let's move on to the next topic.

IOS Uploading Tool

After the entire pre-check has passed and the current running configurations of each device have been backed up, we need to upload the new IOS from a server to the router's flash. As discussed earlier, the file upload process uses SCP because the netmiko library has a built-in module that supports the timing of different file sizes. As a netmiko library user, we do not have to worry about how big the file is to upload the file; netmiko already has a built-in module taking care of this. Thanks again to Kirk Byers for writing and sharing such a handy library. I have tested file transfers using both the FTP and TFTP methods, and although they worked OK, they were not as reliable as netmiko's SCPConn file transfer method.

We already know that the actual IOS file we are trying to upload is 436.57 MB in size, and uploading such a file to a networking device's flash memory will take around 8 to 15 minutes on the production network. Even within your lab topology on your computer, it will take several minutes. So, while you are developing a testing tool, you should be using a smaller file, saving you time. In this example, I am using the full 436.57 MB file for demonstration purposes. In production, one network's speed will differ from another network; hence, the file transfer time will also vary significantly from one network to another.

#	Task
1	Create another working directory for the IOS uploading tool. This time, you will copy the script created in the last section and rewrite the code to test the file uploading.

```
pynetauto@ubuntu20s1:~/my_tools/tool6_make_backup$ cd ..
pynetauto@ubuntu20s1:~/my_tools$ mkdir tool7_upload_ios
pynetauto@ubuntu20s1:~/my_tools$ cd tool7_upload_ios
pynetauto@ubuntu20s1:~/my_tools/tool7_upload_ios$ pwd
/home/pynetauto/my_tools/tool7_upload_ios
pynetauto@ubuntu20s1:~/my_tools/tool7_upload_ios$ cp /home/pynetauto/my_tools/tool6_
make_backup/make_backup1.py ./upload_ios1.py
pynetauto@ubuntu20s1:~/my_tools/tool7_upload_ios$ ls
upload_ios1.py
```

(*continued*)

#	Task
2	In the IOS uploading section, we copied the new IOS file to the /home/pynetauto/my_tools/new_ios/ directory. For the SCP file uploading test, we can point the file location to this folder or copy the current working directory. So, s_newios (source file location) points to the new IOS file: /home/pynetauto/my_tools/new_ios/csr1000v-universalk9.16.09.06.SPA.bin. For d_newios (for the destination filename, use the new IOS filename, ending with .bin). The file will be saved to the router's flash:/ directory.

Three configuration items are required on Cisco routers (or switches) for the SCP file transfer to initiate and successfully copy files across to the routers. First, the user must have level 15 privilege, second, aaa authentication login must be configured, and third, an authorization exec must be preconfigured. If device access is controlled by the TACACS server in the production environment, you should make a slight change to the following script. The login will work in the same way except that the authentication is via the server. Also, in many environments, the TACACS server is not used. In this case, we can take advantage of local aaa authorization and authentication, and this is what you are going to use in this example. The script will check if your username has level 15 privileges first and then check if aaa authentication and authorization are configured.

One last requirement for SCP file transfer is that the router must play the role of SCP server, so we will check if the ip scp server command has been configured, and if it has not been configured, the script will enable the SCP service on the router and then start the IOS file transfer process. At the end of file transfer, this SCP service will be disabled.

Now modify the content of your Python file, and when you complete your SCP IOS upload application, it should look similar to the following. If you want to add some other features, you can do so and explore other options. The beauty of free Python scripting is that there are no shackles around your ankles like with YAML code in Ansible. With Python scripting, you are the designer, mechanic, and driver in your car, where with Ansible, you are only a driver. You are free to go ahead and write your tools with Python scripting. As before, you will find explanations next to the important lines of code.

upload_ios1.py

```
import time
from netmiko import ConnectHandler, SCPConn # Import SCPConn

# From section 10.5.3
s_newios = "/home/pynetauto/my_tools/new_ios/csr1000v-universalk9.16.09.06.SPA.bin" #
Source file, ensure you have specified the correct directory path
d_newios = "csr1000v-universalk9.16.09.06.SPA.bin" # Destination file name
# newiosmd5 = "77878ae6db8e34de90e2e3e83741bf39" # MD5 value of new IOS file

device1 = {
    'device_type': 'cisco_xe',
    'host': '192.168.183.111',
    'username': 'pynetauto',
    'password': 'cisco123',
    'secret': 'cisco123'
}
device2 = {
    'device_type': 'cisco_xe',
    'host': '192.168.183.222',
    'username': 'pynetauto',
    'password': 'cisco123',
    'secret': 'cisco123'
}
```

#	Task

```
devices_list = [device1, device2]

for device in devices_list:
    print(device) # Print dictionary item for confirmation only
    ip = str(device['host']) # Assign a variable, ip to IP Address of device
    username = str(device['username']) # Assign a variable, username to username of device
    net_connect = ConnectHandler(**device) # Parse netmiko dictionary to ConnectHandler
    net_connect.send_command("terminal length 0") # Set terminal to display without any
    breaks
    showrun = net_connect.send_command("show running-config") # Run show running-config
    check_priv15 = (f'username {username} privilege 15') # Assign a variable to
    username config
    aaa_authenication = "aaa authentication login default local enable" # Assign a
    variable to authentication config
    aaa_authorization = "aaa authorization exec default local" # Assign a variable to
    authorization config

    if check_priv15 in showrun: # Check if showrun contains (meets) basic
    configuration requirements
        print(f"{username} has level 15 privilege - OK")
        if aaa_authenication in showrun:
            print("check_aaa_authentication - OK")
            if aaa_authorization in showrun:
                print("check_aaa_authorization - OK") # All three conditions are met,
                then continue
            else:
                print("aaa_authorization - FAILED ")
                exit() # exit application for a review
        else:
            print("aaa_authentication - FAILED ")
            exit() # exit application for a review
    else:
        print(f"{username} has not enough privilege - FAILED")
        exit() # exit application for a review

    net_connect.enable(cmd='enable 15') # Enable level 15 privilage
    net_connect.config_mode() # Enter configuration mode
    net_connect.send_command('ip scp server enable') # Enable SCP service on the router
    net_connect.exit_config_mode() # Exit configuration mode
    time.sleep(1) # Pause for  1 second
    print("New IOS uploading in progress! Please wait...")
    scp_conn = SCPConn(net_connect) # Create object for netmiko SCPConn
    scp_conn.scp_transfer_file(s_newios, d_newios) # Start file transfer from source to
    destination
    scp_conn.close() # close scp_conn session
    time.sleep(1) # Pause for 1 second
    net_connect.config_mode() # Enter configuration mode
    net_connect.send_command('no ip scp server enable') # Disable SCP service on the router
    net_connect.exit_config_mode() # Exit configurator mode
    print("-"*80) # Line divider
```

(*continued*)

#	Task

3	We know that the user pynetauto is correctly configured with level 15 admin privileges, but the aaa new model is not enabled on the csr1000v-1 router. Let's run the previous script to test which error message is returned.
	`pynetauto@ubuntu20s1:~/my_tools/tool7_upload_ios$ python3 upload_ios1.py`
	`{'device_type': 'cisco_xe', 'host': '192.168.183.111', 'username': 'pynetauto', 'password': 'cisco123', 'secret': 'cisco123'}`
	`pynetauto has level 15 privilege - OK`
	`aaa_authentication - FAILED`
	Now, go ahead and add the following aaa configurations to the first router:
	`csr1000v-1(config)#aaa new-model`
	`csr1000v-1(config)#aaa authentication login default local enable`

4	Let's run the IOS upload application one more time and observe where the script stops. Although the admin user has a level 15 privilege, the script complains that the user does not have the right privilege because it has now moved to aaa local authentication.
	`pynetauto@ubuntu20s1:~/my_tools/tool7_upload_ios$ python3 upload_ios1.py`
	`{'device_type': 'cisco_xe', 'host': '192.168.183.111', 'username': 'pynetauto', 'password': 'cisco123', 'secret': 'cisco123'}`
	`pynetauto has not enough privilege - FAILED`
	To counter this problem, add the last aaa configuration to the first router.
	`csr1000v-1(config)#aaa authorization exec default local`

5	Stop! Do not run the script yet. If you run the application one more time, you should see the following messages on your console, and the application will move to the next phase to check for SCP configuration on the router.
	To keep things simple, we can check this before initiating the new IOS upload to the first device. This check can be performed on all devices at the beginning of the script so we can detect any configuration issues on all devices before uploading begins. In the final script, we will try to slightly change this part so that this becomes part of the pre-check script.
	`pynetauto@ubuntu20s1:~/my_tools/tool7_upload_ios$ python3 upload_ios1.py`
	`{'device_type': 'cisco_xe', 'host': '192.168.183.111', 'username': 'pynetauto', 'password': 'cisco123', 'secret': 'cisco123'}`
	`pynetauto has level 15 privilege - OK`
	`check_aaa_authentication - OK`
	`check_aaa_authorization - OK`

6	Go ahead and enable aaa configurations on the second router, csr1000v-2, as well.
	`csr1000v-2(config)#aaa new-model`
	`csr1000v-2(config)#aaa authentication login default local enable`
	`csr1000v-2(config)#aaa authorization exec default local`

#	Task
7	Then, enable the following debugging command on both routers:

```
csr1000v-2#debug ip scp
Incoming SCP debugging is on
csr1000v-2#terminal monitor

csr1000v-1# debug ip scp
Incoming SCP debugging is on
csr1000v-1#ter mon
```

8 Now rerun the Python script. If all the configuration verifications have passed, the new IOS file transfer will begin for the first router. When the file transfer completes on `csr1000v-1`, the same script will run against the second router, `csr1000v-2`. Here, I am only demonstrating IOS uploading on two routers, but imagine if we had 20 or 200 routers to upload IOS images to. Also, note that now we can schedule this script to run outside of business hours, so you no longer have to stare at the screen for hours before you are excused to go home. This probably is the best part of automating boring and repetitive tasks such as this.

```
pynetauto@ubuntu20s1:~/my_tools/tool7_upload_ios$ python3 upload_ios1.py
{'device_type': 'cisco_xe', 'host': '192.168.183.111', 'username': 'pynetauto',
'password': 'cisco123', 'secret': 'cisco123'}
pynetauto has level 15 privilege - OK
check_aaa_authentication - OK
check_aaa_authorization - OK
New IOS uploading in progress! Please wait...
--------------------------------------------------------------------------------
{'device_type': 'cisco_xe', 'host': '192.168.183.222', 'username': 'pynetauto',
'password': 'cisco123', 'secret': 'cisco123'}
pynetauto has level 15 privilege - OK
check_aaa_authentication - OK
check_aaa_authorization - OK
New IOS uploading in progress! Please wait...
--------------------------------------------------------------------------------
```

The username, password, and secret are printed on the screen during development to check that the developing applications are working as they were designed, but in the production implementations, you must disable any redundant `print()` statements. As mentioned at the beginning of this book, the `print()` function is for us; the computer does not have to output the information to the screen.

9 While the script is running, check the terminal screens of both routers. If you observe the following on-screen logs, you know that the new IOS file transfer has been completed successfully.

```
csr1000v-1#
*Jan 15 03:21:00.687: %SYS-5-CONFIG_I: Configured from console by pynetauto on vty1
(192.168.183.132)
*Jan 15 03:21:02.228: SCP: [22 -> 192.168.183.132:46546] send <OK>
*Jan 15 03:21:02.229: SCP: [22 <- 192.168.183.132:46546] recv C0644 436573677
csr1000v-universalk9.16.09.06.SPA.bin
*Jan 15 03:21:02.230: SCP: [22 -> 192.168.183.132:46546] send <OK>
*Jan 15 03:25:34.917: SCP: [22 <- 192.168.183.132:46546] recv 436573677 bytes
```

(continued)

#	Task

```
*Jan 15 03:25:34.918: SCP: [22 <- 192.168.183.132:46546] recv <OK>
*Jan 15 03:25:34.918: SCP: [22 -> 192.168.183.132:46546] send <OK>
*Jan 15 03:25:34.922: SCP: [22 <- 192.168.183.132:46546] recv <EOF>
*Jan 15 03:25:36.192: %SYS-5-CONFIG_I: Configured from console by pynetauto on vty1
(192.168.183.132)

csr1000v-2#
*Jan 15 03:25:37.522: %SYS-5-CONFIG_I: Configured from console by pynetauto on vty1
(192.168.183.132)
*Jan 15 03:25:39.072: SCP: [22 -> 192.168.183.132:36148] send <OK>
*Jan 15 03:25:39.073: SCP: [22 <- 192.168.183.132:36148] recv C0644 436573677
csr1000v-universalk9.16.09.06.SPA.bin
*Jan 15 03:25:39.074: SCP: [22 -> 192.168.183.132:36148] send <OK>
*Jan 15 03:30:10.935: SCP: [22 <- 192.168.183.132:36148] recv 436573677 bytes
*Jan 15 03:30:10.935: SCP: [22 <- 192.168.183.132:36148] recv <OK>
*Jan 15 03:30:10.935: SCP: [22 -> 192.168.183.132:36148] send <OK>
*Jan 15 03:30:10.937: SCP: [22 <- 192.168.183.132:36148] recv <EOF>
*Jan 15 03:30:12.230: %SYS-5-CONFIG_I: Configured from console by pynetauto on vty1
(192.168.183.132)
```

10 Check the uploaded file on both routers and save the configuration to complete the task.

```
csr1000v-1#show flash: | in csr1000v-universalk9.16.09.06.SPA.bin
215  436573677 Oct 07 2020 03:25:34.0000000000 +00:00 /bootflash/csr1000v-
universalk9.16.09.06.SPA.bin
csr1000v-1#write memory
Building configuration...
[OK]

csr1000v-2#show flash: | in csr1000v-universalk9.16.09.06.SPA.bin
215  436573677 Oct 07 2020 03:30:10.0000000000 +00:00 /bootflash/csr1000v-
universalk9.16.09.06.SPA.bin
csr1000v-2#write memory
Building configuration...
[OK]
```

Check the New IOS MD5 Value on the Cisco Device's Flash

In the previous IOS uploading tool development, you have successfully uploaded the new IOS version to both the `csr1000v-1` and `csr1000v-2` routers. We need to write a script to validate the verify IOS command and validate the MD5 value of the IOS copy on the router's flash. This time we will only allow the script to run if the actual IOS file is found in the `flash:/` root. Then run the `verify` command and check that after a successful IOS verification command, the script will expect "Verified" in the output, so a regular expression will be used to verify the IOS verification result. If it is successful, the script will print out the MD5 value of the original value and the MD5 value of the new IOS file on the flash. We also want to continue to run this application even if the first router is not reachable on the network, so we have to include a `netmiko` timeout exception to counter this problem. Often, even if your script encounters an exception, you want to continue to run the script until the last device in your list.

Let's quickly write this application and test-drive it in our lab.

#	Task

1	As always, let's begin with creating a new directory and then create a new Python script.
	`pynetauto@ubuntu20s1:~/my_tools/tool7_upload_ios$ cd ..`
	`pynetauto@ubuntu20s1:~/my_tools$ mkdir tool8_md5_cisco`
	`pynetauto@ubuntu20s1:~/my_tools$ cd tool8_md5_cisco`
	`pynetauto@ubuntu20s1:~/my_tools/tool8_md5_cisco$ nano md5_verify1.py`

2	Most of this script is the same as the previous script. Let's quickly rewrite the code to verify the command and compare the MD5 provided by the user and the MD5 calculated on the router. The application flow will be based on the result of the two MD5 value comparisons. Your script will look similar to the following after completing the IOS MD5 checker application for Cisco IOS routers. As always, your script does not have to look the same as this one as long as it is optimized and works well. Try to write the code one line at a time as this is good practice to get a feel for what it is like to write code for a living. If you like to do everything yourself, then you will enjoy writing lines of code.

```
md5_verify1.py
from netmiko import ConnectHandler
from netmiko.ssh_exception import  NetMikoTimeoutException # To handle Timeout/
Network exception
import re # For match specific characters from the verified output

d_newios = "csr1000v-universalk9.16.09.06.SPA.bin"
newiosmd5 = "77878ae6db8e34de90e2e3e83741bf39"

device1 = {
    'device_type': 'cisco_xe',
    'host': '192.168.183.111',
    'username': 'pynetauto',
    'password': 'cisco123',
    'secret': 'cisco123',
    'global_delay_factor': 2 # Run netmiko commands twice slower. If you are getting
    errors due to slow router/switch response, use these attributes to slow down the
    script
}
device2 = {
    'device_type': 'cisco_xe',
    'host': '192.168.183.222',
    'username': 'pynetauto',
    'password': 'cisco123',
    'secret': 'cisco123',
    'global_delay_factor': 2
}
```

(continued)

#	Task

```
devices_list = [device1, device2]

for device in devices_list:
    print(device)
    ip = str(device['host'])
    try:
        net_connect = ConnectHandler(**device)
        net_connect.send_command("terminal length 0")
        locate_newios = net_connect.send_command(f"show flash: | in {d_newios}") #
        Check router's flash for new IOS image file

        if d_newios in locate_newios: # If new IOS is found on the router's flash, run
        this script
            result = net_connect.send_command("verify /md5 flash:{} {}".format(d_
            newios,newiosmd5)) # Cisco IOS/IOS XE verify command, run and assign
            variable result to the output
            print(result) # Print the result, informational for user
            net_connect.disconnect() # Disconnect session
            p1 = re.compile(r'Verified') # Regular Expression (re) compiler for word
            'Verified'
            p2 = re.compile(r'[a-fA-F0-9]{31}[a-fA-F0-9]') # re compiler for MD5 value
            verified = p1.findall(result) # Find 'Verified' in result
            newiosmd5flash = p2.findall(result) # Find the MD5 value from result
            if verified: # If 'Verified' was found in result, run this part of the script
                result = True
                print("-"*80)
                print("MD5 values MATCH! Continue")
                print("MD5 of new IOS on Server : ",newiosmd5)
                print("MD5 of new IOS on flash  : ",newiosmd5flash[0])
                print("-"*80)
            else: # If 'Verified' was not found in result, print and exit the application
                result = False
                print("-"*80)
                print("MD5 values DO NOT MATCH! Exiting.")
                print("-"*80)
                exit()
        else: # If no new IOS file was found on the router's flash:/. Print the statement
            print("No new IOS found on router's flash. Continue to next device...")
            print("-"*80)
    except (NetMikoTimeoutException): # Handle Timeout error due to network issue
        print (f'Timeout error to : {ip}')
        print("-"*80)
        continue # Continue to next device
    except unknown_error: # Handle other errors as exception
        print ('Unknown error occured : ' + str(unknown_error))
        print("-"*80)
        continue # Continue to next device

print("Completed new IOS verification.") # Informational
```

#	Task
3	Make sure that both routers are powered on and in normal operational mode. Run the application to check the MD5 value of the newly uploaded IOS image file. If everything worked correctly, you should get the same output as shown here. Some of the output has been omitted to save space.

```
pynetauto@ubuntu20s1:~/my_tools/tool8_md5_cisco$ python3 md5_verify1.py
{'device_type': 'cisco_xe', 'host': '192.168.183.111', 'username': 'pynetauto',
'password': 'cisco123', 'secret': 'cisco123', 'global_delay_factor': 2}
.........................................................[omitted for brevity]
...........................................................................Done!
Verified (bootflash:csr1000v-universalk9.16.09.06.SPA.bin) =
77878ae6db8e34de90e2e3e83741bf39

------------------------------------------------------------------------------
MD5 values MATCH! Continue
MD5 of new IOS on Server :  77878ae6db8e34de90e2e3e83741bf39
MD5 of new IOS on flash  :  77878ae6db8e34de90e2e3e83741bf39
------------------------------------------------------------------------------
{'device_type': 'cisco_xe', 'host': '192.168.183.222', 'username': 'pynetauto',
'password': 'cisco123', 'secret': 'cisco123', 'global_delay_factor': 2}
........................................................[...omitted for brevity]
...........................................................................Done!
Verified (bootflash:csr1000v-universalk9.16.09.06.SPA.bin) =
77878ae6db8e34de90e2e3e83741bf39

------------------------------------------------------------------------------
MD5 values MATCH! Continue
MD5 of new IOS on Server :  77878ae6db8e34de90e2e3e83741bf39
MD5 of new IOS on flash  :  77878ae6db8e34de90e2e3e83741bf39
------------------------------------------------------------------------------
Completed new verification.
```

#	Task
4	To simulate a scenario where csr1000v-1 is not on the network (unreachable), disable GigabitEthernet1. You have to disable the port via VMware Workstation's main console.

```
csr1000v-1#config terminal
csr1000v-1(config)#interface GigabitEthernet1
csr1000v-1(config-if)#shutdown
```

Now rerun the Python script to check the result. Because we have already added an exception to counter this problem, the script will continue to run until the end. If the exception handler was not added, then you will see the following errors:

```
pynetauto@ubuntu20s1:~/my_tools/tool8_md5_cisco$ python3 md5_verify1.py
{'device_type': 'cisco_xe', 'host': '192.168.183.111', 'username': 'pynetauto',
'password': 'cisco123', 'secret': 'cisco123', 'global_delay_factor': 2}
Traceback (most recent call last):
  File "/usr/local/lib/python3.8/dist-packages/netmiko/base_connection.py", line 920,
  in establish_connection
```

(*continued*)

#	Task

```
    self.remote_conn_pre.connect(**ssh_connect_params)
  File "/usr/lib/python3/dist-packages/paramiko/client.py", line 368, in connect
    raise NoValidConnectionsError(errors)
paramiko.ssh_exception.NoValidConnectionsError: [Errno None] Unable to connect to
port 22 on 192.168.183.111
```

During handling of the previous exception, another exception occurred:

```
Traceback (most recent call last):
  File " md5_verify1.py", line 29, in <module>
    net_connect = ConnectHandler(**device)
  File "/usr/local/lib/python3.8/dist-packages/netmiko/ssh_dispatcher.py", line 312,
  in ConnectHandler
    return ConnectionClass(*args, **kwargs)
  File "/usr/local/lib/python3.8/dist-packages/netmiko/cisco/cisco_ios.py", line 17,
  in __init__
    return super().__init__(*args, **kwargs)
  File "/usr/local/lib/python3.8/dist-packages/netmiko/base_connection.py", line
  346, in __init__
    self._open()
  File "/usr/local/lib/python3.8/dist-packages/netmiko/base_connection.py", line
  351, in _open
    self.establish_connection()
  File "/usr/local/lib/python3.8/dist-packages/netmiko/base_connection.py", line
  942, in establish_connection
    raise NetmikoTimeoutException(msg)
netmiko.ssh_exception.NetmikoTimeoutException: TCP connection to device failed.

Common causes of this problem are:
1. Incorrect hostname or IP address.
2. Wrong TCP port.
3. Intermediate firewall blocking access.

Device settings: cisco_xe 192.168.183.111:22
```

#	Task
5	Now delete the new IOS version from the first router and check if your script runs successfully. You will have to enable csr1000v-1's GigabitEthernet1 port from the VMware Workstation console as you will lose the connection to this device via SSH.

```
csr1000v-1#delete flash:/csr1000v-universalk9.16.09.06.SPA.bin
Delete filename [csr1000v-universalk9.16.09.06.SPA.bin]?
Delete bootflash:/csr1000v-universalk9.16.09.06.SPA.bin? [confirm]
```

The script should run successfully and continue to run till the end, this also should not be a show stopper in our script.

```
pynetauto@ubuntu20s1:~/my_tools/tool8_md5_cisco$ python3 md5_verify2.py
{'device_type': 'cisco_xe', 'host': '192.168.183.111', 'username': 'pynetauto',
'password': 'cisco123', 'secret': 'cisco123', 'global_delay_factor': 2}
No new IOS found on router's flash. Continue to the next device...
------------------------------------------------------------------------------
{'device_type': 'cisco_xe', 'host': '192.168.183.222', 'username': 'pynetauto',
'password': 'cisco123', 'secret': 'cisco123', 'global_delay_factor': 2}
.........................................................[omitted for brevity]
..........................................................................Done!
Verified (bootflash:csr1000v-universalk9.16.09.06.SPA.bin) =
77878ae6db8e34de90e2e3e83741bf39

------------------------------------------------------------------------------
MD5 values MATCH! Continue
MD5 of new IOS on Server :  77878ae6db8e34de90e2e3e83741bf39
MD5 of new IOS on flash  :  77878ae6db8e34de90e2e3e83741bf39
------------------------------------------------------------------------------
Completed new IOS verification.
```

#	Task
6	You have deleted the new IOS version from csr1000v-1's flash to validate our script. To prepare for the next lab, we have to run the IOS upload tool one more time. Run the new IOS uploading script one more time so you have the new IOS on csr1000v-1's flash.

If you want to upload the file on the first router only, delete or comment out the device2 or csr1000v-2 information shown here; this will save you about five minutes.

```
# device2 = {
    # 'device_type': 'cisco_xe',
    # 'host': '192.168.183.222',
    # 'username': 'pynetauto',
    # 'password': 'cisco123',
    # 'secret': 'cisco123',
    # 'global_delay_factor': 2
# }
```

While developing your Python tools, you have to test your scripts multiple times to ensure the automated tasks are repeatable with the same expected results.

(continued)

Options to Stop or Reload the Routers

Here, you will write a script to give the user two options: an option to change the boot system's backup running configuration and reload and an option to exit the application for a reload later. For the first option, you will have to write the code to change the boot system, save the change, and then optionally make a backup of the `running-config` for change validation later.

#	Task
1	Change the directory, create a new directory for this section, and create a new base script to work on.

```
pynetauto@ubuntu20s1:~/my_tools/tool8_md5_cisco$ cd ..
pynetauto@ubuntu20s1:~/my_tools$ mkdir tool9_yes_no
pynetauto@ubuntu20s1:~/my_tools$ cd tool9_yes_no
pynetauto@ubuntu20s1:~/my_tools/tool9_yes_no$ nano yesno.py
```

#	Task
2	This time you will write a quick yes/no function, so the expected input is either yes/y or no/n. If the user input is anything else, then the yes_or_no function will run again until the correct input is entered. This way, you control the input, and based on the input, the script flow will change. If the response is yes, we can change the configuration of routers and reload. If the response is no, exit the application to reload the routers later.

```
yesno.py
yes = ['yes', 'y']
no = ['no', 'n']

def yes_or_no():
    resp = input("Would you like to reload your devices? (y/n)? ").lower()
    if resp in yes:
        print("YES")
    elif resp in no:
        print("NO")
    else:
        yes_or_no()

yes_or_no()

print("All tasks completed.")
```

After completing the previous script, run the script and test it as shown here:

```
pynetauto@ubuntu20s1:~/my_tools/tool9_yes_no$ python3 yesno.py
Would you like to reload your devices? (y/n)? y
YES
All tasks completed.
pynetauto@ubuntu20s1:~/my_tools/tool9_yes_no$ python3 yesno.py
Would you like to reload your devices? (y/n)? yes
YES
All tasks completed.
pynetauto@ubuntu20s1:~/my_tools/tool9_yes_no$ python3 yesno.py
```

#	Task

```
Would you like to reload your devices? (y/n)? N
NO
All tasks completed.
pynetauto@ubuntu20s1:~/my_tools/tool9_yes_no$ python3 yesno.py
Would you like to reload your devices? (y/n)? NO
NO
All tasks completed.
pynetauto@ubuntu20s1:~/my_tools/tool9_yes_no$ python3 yesno.py
Would you like to reload your devices? (y/n)? sure
Would you like to reload your devices? (y/n)? Why not?
Would you like to reload your devices? (y/n)? 12345
Would you like to reload your devices? (y/n)? OK
Would you like to reload your devices? (y/n)? YES
YES
All tasks completed.
```

3 Now it is time to use this base script and expand it to our scenario. Make a copy and modify the script, as shown in reload_yesno1.py.

```
pynetauto@ubuntu20s1:~/my_tools/tool9_yes_no$ cp yesno.py reload_yesno1.py
pynetauto@ubuntu20s1:~/my_tools/tool9_yes_no$ nano reload_yesno1.py
```

The following script will change the boot system statement on the device, save the configuration, and perform some show commands to capture the pre-reload operational status. Finally, it will reload the router.

reload_yesno1.py

```
from netmiko import ConnectHandler
import time

d_newios = "csr1000v-universalk9.16.09.06.SPA.bin"
newiosmd5 = "77878ae6db8e34de90e2e3e83741bf39"

device1 = {
    'device_type': 'cisco_xe',
    'host': '192.168.183.111',
    'username': 'pynetauto',
    'password': 'cisco123',
    'secret': 'cisco123',
    'global_delay_factor': 2 # Used to slow down the script
}
device2 = {
    'device_type': 'cisco_xe',
    'host': '192.168.183.222',
    'username': 'pynetauto',
    'password': 'cisco123',
    'secret': 'cisco123',
    'global_delay_factor': 2
}
```

(continued)

#	Task

```
devices_list = [device1, device2]
yes_list = ['yes', 'y']
no_list = ['no', 'n']

def yes_or_no():
    resp = input("Would you like to reload your devices? (y/n)? ").lower()
    if resp in yes_list:
        print("Reloading devices")
        for device in devices_list:
            ip = str(device['host'])
            net_connect = ConnectHandler(**device)
            net_connect.enable(cmd='enable 15')
            config_commands1 = ['no boot system', 'boot system flash:/' + d_newios,
            'do write memory']
            output = net_connect.send_config_set(config_commands1)
            print (output)
            net_connect.send_command('terminal length 0\n')
            show_boot = net_connect.send_command('show boot\n')
            show_dir = net_connect.send_command('dir\n')
            if d_newios not in show_dir:
                print('Unable to locate new IOS on the flash:/. Exiting.')
                print("-"*80)
                exit()
            elif d_newios not in show_boot:
                print('Boot system was not correctly configured. Exiting.')
                print("-"*80)
                exit()
            elif d_newios in show_boot and d_newios in show_dir:
                print(f'Found {d_newios} in show boot')
                print("-"*80)
                net_connect.send_command("terminal length 0")
                time.sleep(1)
                with open(f'{ip}_showver_pre.txt', 'w+') as f1:
                    print("Capturing pre-reload 'show version'")
                    showver_pre = net_connect.send_command("show version")
                    f1.write(showver_pre)
                time.sleep(1)
                with open(f'{ip}_showrun_pre.txt', 'w+') as f2:
                    print("Capturing pre-reload 'show running-config'")
                    showrun_pre = net_connect.send_command("show running-config")
                    f2.write(showrun_pre)
                time.sleep(1)
                with open(f'{ip}_showint_pre.txt', 'w+') as f3:
                    print("Capturing pre-reload 'show ip interface brief'")
                    showint_pre = net_connect.send_command("show ip interface brief")
                    f3.write(showint_pre)
                time.sleep(1)
                with open(f'{ip}_showroute_pre.txt', 'w+') as f4:
```

#	Task

```
                    print("Capturing pre-reload 'show ip route'")
                    showroute_pre = net_connect.send_command("show ip route")
                    f4.write(showroute_pre)
                time.sleep(1)
                print("-"*80)
                # Trigger the device reload
                print("Your device is now reloading.")
                net_connect.send_command('reload', expect_string='[confirm]')
                net_connect.send_command('yes\n')
                net_connect.send_command('\n')
                net_connect.disconnect()
                print("-"*80)
    elif resp in no_list:
        print("You have chosen to reload the devices later. Exiting the application.")
    else:
        yes_or_no()

yes_or_no()
print("All tasks completed.")
```

4 When you run the previous script, it will hang in the middle of the script, time out, and continue to run until the end of the script. But the script does not initiate the routers to reload.

When you try to reload the router manually, it will complain about the end-user license agreement and reveal the actual problem. We forgot to accept the end-user license agreement and have not set the router platform's correct feature set.

```
csr1000v-1#reload
% Unfortunately EULA is not detected for following feature/features:
% ax
% Please configure 'license accept end user agreement' and
% use 'write' command to ensure license configurations take effect
% Continue reload will cause functionality loss for above feature/features.

Continue to reload? (yes/[no]):
```

We will follow the instructions, add the ax (Enterprise) license level, and then accept the EULA and save the configuration. After you have accepted the license on csr1000v-1, repeat the process on csr1000v-2.

```
csr1000v-1#configure terminal
csr1000v-1(config)#license boot level ax
% use 'write' command to make license boot config take effect on next boot
csr1000v-1(config)#license accept end user agreement
[omitted for brevity]
Activation  of the  software command line interface will be evidence of
your acceptance of this agreement.
ACCEPT? (yes/[no]): yes
csr1000v-1(config)#exit
csr1000v-1#write memory
Building configuration...
[OK]
```

(continued)

#	Task

When you issue a reload command, we expect to see [confirm] from the router.

```
csr1000v-1#reload
Proceed with reload? [confirm]
```

You have to accept the end-user license agreement on the second router, csr1000v-2, as well. Repeat the process shown earlier.

5 After accepting the end-user license agreement (EULA) and saving the configuration, this is the right time to take a snapshot of your routers. You will be running your script against these devices multiple times and do not want to reverse the change every time you want to test this feature. So, on VMware Workstation, go to the Snapshot Manager feature and take another snapshot of both routers. See Figure 18-5.

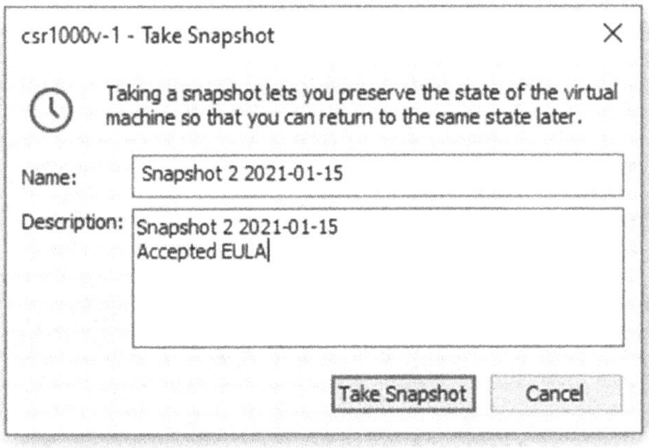

Figure 18-5. *Snapshot Manager, taking a snapshot of csr1000v-1*

Take a snapshot of the csr1000v-2 router as well. VMware Workstation Pro allows you to take a snapshot of Cisco routers, and if you want to come back to re-run the same test, you can always come back to this snapshot. Take a special note, in the production environment, and Cisco usually does not allow administrators to take snapshots of Cisco virtual machines due to timestamp and database-related issues.

6 Now run the script one more time, and this time the first router reloads OK but returns the "OSError: Socket is closed" error and disconnects our netmiko ConnectHandler connection. This is good if we are working with only a single device upgrade and want to finish the task. We want the script to continue to run the set of commands on the second router as well. Network automation's real power is realized only if we can apply the solution on multiple devices with a consistent result. It looks like we have to make an exception for this error so that it runs and reloads the second router. This can be achieved by using the try ~ except method.

```
pynetauto@ubuntu20s1:~/my_tools/tool9_yes_no$ python3 reload_yesno1.py
Would you like to reload your devices? (y/n)? y
Reloading devices
configure terminal
Enter configuration commands, one per line.  End with CNTL/Z.
csr1000v-1(config)#no boot system
csr1000v-1(config)#boot system flash:/csr1000v-universalk9.16.09.06.SPA.bin
```

#	Task

```
csr1000v-1(config)#do write memory
Building configuration...
[OK]
csr1000v-1(config)#end
csr1000v-1#
Found csr1000v-universalk9.16.09.06.SPA.bin in show boot
--------------------------------------------------------------------------------
Capturing pre-reload 'show version'
Capturing pre-reload 'show running-config'
Capturing pre-reload 'show ip interface brief'
Capturing pre-reload 'show ip route'
--------------------------------------------------------------------------------
Your device is now reloading.
Traceback (most recent call last):
  File "reload_yesno1.py", line 88, in <module>
    yes_or_no()
  File "reload_yesno1.py", line 79, in yes_or_no
[...omitted for brevity]
  File "/usr/lib/python3/dist-packages/paramiko/channel.py", line 1198, in _send
    raise socket.error("Socket is closed")
OSError: Socket is closed
```

7 Let's copy and refactor our script so it includes the `try ~ except` statement to catch the `OSError` so, the script continues to run.

```
pynetauto@ubuntu20s1:~/my_tools/tool9_yes_no$ cp reload_yesno1.py reload_yesno2.py
pynetauto@ubuntu20s1:~/my_tools/tool9_yes_no$ nano reload_yesno2.py
```

reload_yesno2.py

```
from netmiko import ConnectHandler
import time

d_newios = "csr1000v-universalk9.16.09.06.SPA.bin"
newiosmd5 = "77878ae6db8e34de90e2e3e83741bf39"

device1 = {
    'device_type': 'cisco_xe',
    'host': '192.168.183.111',
    'username': 'pynetauto',
    'password': 'cisco123',
    'secret': 'cisco123',
    'global_delay_factor': 2
}
device2 = {
    'device_type': 'cisco_xe',
    'host': '192.168.183.222',
    'username': 'pynetauto',
    'password': 'cisco123',
    'secret': 'cisco123',
    'global_delay_factor': 2
}
```

(continued)

#	Task

```
devices_list = [device1, device2]
yes_list = ['yes', 'y']
no_list = ['no', 'n']

def yes_or_no():
    resp = input("Would you like to reload your devices? (y/n)? ").lower()
    if resp in yes_list:
        print("Reloading devices")
        for device in devices_list:
            ip = str(device['host'])
            net_connect = ConnectHandler(**device)
            net_connect.enable(cmd='enable 15')
            config_commands1 = ['no boot system', 'boot system flash:/' + d_newios,
            'do write memory']
            output = net_connect.send_config_set(config_commands1)
            print (output)
            net_connect.send_command('terminal length 0\n')
            show_boot = net_connect.send_command('show boot\n')
            show_dir = net_connect.send_command('dir\n')
            if d_newios not in show_dir:
                print('Unable to locate new IOS on the flash:/. Exiting.')
                print("-"*80)
                exit()
            elif d_newios not in show_boot:
                print('Boot system was not correctly configured. Exiting.')
                print("-"*80)
                exit()
            elif d_newios in show_boot and d_newios in show_dir:
                try:
                    print(f'Found {d_newios} in show boot')
                    print("-"*80)
                    net_connect.send_command("terminal length 0")
                    time.sleep(1)
                    with open(f'{ip}_showver_pre.txt', 'w+') as f1:
                        print("Capturing pre-reload 'show version'")
                        showver_pre = net_connect.send_command("show version")
                        f1.write(showver_pre)
                    time.sleep(1)
                    with open(f'{ip}_showrun_pre.txt', 'w+') as f2:
                        print("Capturing pre-reload 'show running-config'")
                        showrun_pre = net_connect.send_command("show running-
                        config")
                        f2.write(showrun_pre)
                    time.sleep(1)
                    with open(f'{ip}_showint_pre.txt', 'w+') as f3:
                        print("Capturing pre-reload 'show ip interface brief'")
                        showint_pre = net_connect.send_command("show ip interface
                        brief")
                        f3.write(showint_pre)
```

#	Task

```
                        time.sleep(1)
                        with open(f'{ip}_showroute_pre.txt', 'w+') as f4:
                            print("Capturing pre-reload 'show ip route'")
                            showroute_pre = net_connect.send_command("show ip route")
                            f4.write(showroute_pre)
                        time.sleep(1)
                        print("-"*80)
                        # Trigger the device reload
                        print("Your device is now reloading.")
                        net_connect.send_command('reload', expect_string='[confirm]')
                        net_connect.send_command('yes')
                        net_connect.send_command('\n')
                        net_connect.disconnect()
                        print("-"*80)
                    except OSError:
                        print("Device is now reloading. This may take 2-5 minutes.")
                        time.sleep(10)
                        print("-"*80)
        elif resp in no_list:
            print("You have chosen to reload the devices later. Exiting the application.")
        else:
            yes_or_no()

yes_or_no()
print("All tasks completed.")
```

Now, rerun the script, and you will see that the script reaches the last line of code successfully. Also, both csr1000v-1 and csr1000v-2 should be reloaded and POST into the new IOS XE image, csr1000v-universalk9.16.09.06.SPA.bin.

```
pynetauto@ubuntu20s1:~/my_tools/tool9_yes_no$ python3 reload_yesno2.py
Would you like to reload your devices? (y/n)? yes
Reloading devices
configure terminal
Enter configuration commands, one per line.  End with CNTL/Z.
csr1000v-1(config)#no boot system
csr1000v-1(config)#boot system flash:/csr1000v-universalk9.16.09.06.SPA.bin
csr1000v-1(config)#do write memory
Building configuration...
[OK]
[...omitted for brevity]
Your device is now reloading.
Device is now reloading. This may take 2-5 minutes.
--------------------------------------------------------------------------------
All tasks completed.
```

(continued)

#	Task
8	While the script runs, keep an eye on the first router's console, and you will see that the system is booting into the `.bin` file of the new IOS XE image. See Figure 18-6.

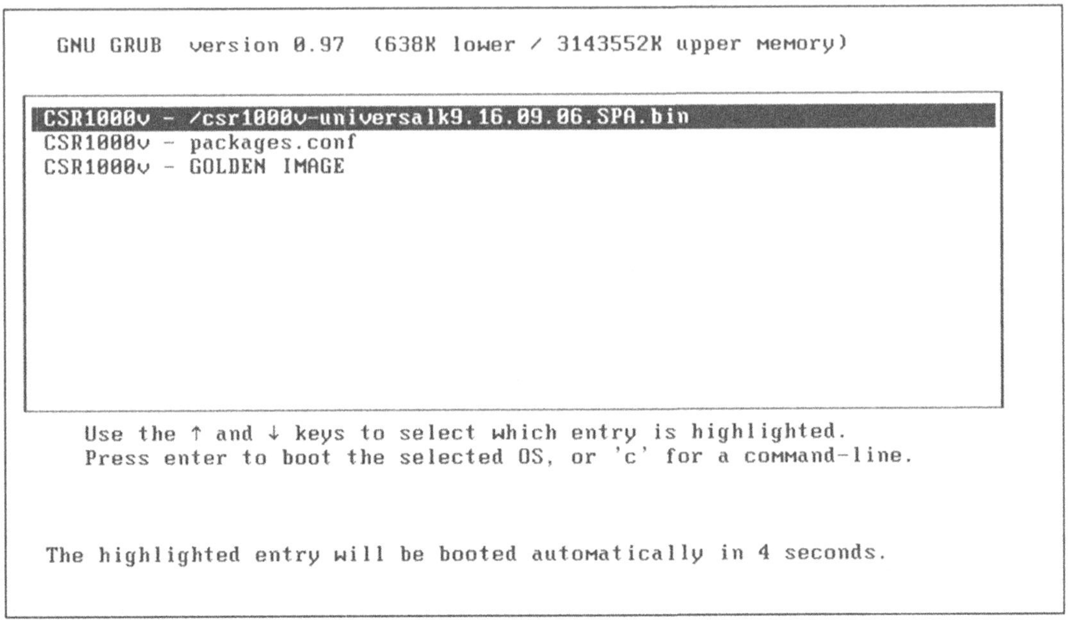
GNU GRUB version 0.97 (638K lower / 3143552K upper memory)
CSR1000v - /csr1000v-universalk9.16.09.06.SPA.bin
CSR1000v - packages.conf
CSR1000v - GOLDEN IMAGE
Use the ↑ and ↓ keys to select which entry is highlighted.
Press enter to boot the selected OS, or 'c' for a command-line.
The highlighted entry will be booted automatically in 4 seconds.

Figure 18-6. *csr1000v-1, booting into new IOS XE image*

After the router goes through the POST process, check the IOS version by running the `show version` command, and now the router is running on the new IOS image. The script continues to run on the second router, and the same result will be observed on the `csr1000v-2` router.

```
csr1000v-1#show version
Cisco IOS XE Software, Version 16.09.06
Cisco IOS Software [Fuji], Virtual XE Software (X86_64_LINUX_IOSD-UNIVERSALK9-M),
Version 16.9.6, RELEASE SOFTWARE (fc2)
Technical Support: http://www.cisco.com/techsupport
Copyright (c) 1986-2020 by Cisco Systems, Inc.
Compiled Thu 27-Aug-20 02:35 by mcpre

Cisco IOS-XE software, Copyright (c) 2005-2020 by cisco Systems, Inc.
All rights reserved.  Certain components of Cisco IOS-XE software are
licensed under the GNU General Public License ("GPL") Version 2.0.  The
software code licensed under GPL Version 2.0 is free software that comes
with ABSOLUTELY NO WARRANTY.  You can redistribute and/or modify such
GPL code under the terms of GPL Version 2.0.  For more details, see the
documentation or "License Notice" file accompanying the IOS-XE software,
or the applicable URL provided on the flyer accompanying the IOS-XE
software.
```

#	Task

	`ROM: IOS-XE ROMMON`
	
	`csr1000v-1 uptime is 1 minute`
	`Uptime for this control processor is 2 minutes`
	`System returned to ROM by reload`
	`System image file is "bootflash:/csr1000v-universalk9.16.09.06.SPA.bin"`
	`Last reload reason: Reload Command`

9	You will also get copies of four show commands for each router on the previous application's successful run. These files will be compared to the same set of show command results after the IOS upgrade. This gives a full validation that the IOS upgrade ran successfully without causing any outages to the network serviced via these devices. This is only a development lab, but if you run the script in a production environment, the file may contain hundreds of lines.
	
	`pynetauto@ubuntu20s1:~/my_tools/tool9_yes_no$ ls -lh`
	`total 44K`
	`-rw-rw-r-- 1 pynetauto pynetauto  323 Jan 15 16:57 192.168.183.111_showint_pre.txt`
	`-rw-rw-r-- 1 pynetauto pynetauto  842 Jan 15 16:57 192.168.183.111_showroute_pre.txt`
	`-rw-rw-r-- 1 pynetauto pynetauto 4.0K Jan 15 16:57 192.168.183.111_showrun_pre.txt`
	`-rw-rw-r-- 1 pynetauto pynetauto 2.3K Jan 15 16:57 192.168.183.111_showver_pre.txt`
	`-rw-rw-r-- 1 pynetauto pynetauto  323 Jan 15 16:57 192.168.183.222_showint_pre.txt`
	`-rw-rw-r-- 1 pynetauto pynetauto  842 Jan 15 16:57 192.168.183.222_showroute_pre.txt`
	`-rw-rw-r-- 1 pynetauto pynetauto 1.8K Jan 15 16:57 192.168.183.222_showrun_pre.txt`
	`-rw-rw-r-- 1 pynetauto pynetauto 2.3K Jan 15 16:57 192.168.183.222_showver_pre.txt`
	`-rw-rw-r-- 1 pynetauto pynetauto 3.6K Jan 15 16:31 reload_yesno1.py`
	`-rw-rw-r-- 1 pynetauto pynetauto 3.9K Jan 15 16:56 reload_yesno2.py`
	`-rw-rw-r-- 1 pynetauto pynetauto  285 Jan 15 16:30 yesno.py`

Now that we have reloaded both routers and they are running the newest IOS XE images, we have to put the icing on the cake by logging back into the device and performing the post-upgrade check using the captured information. Continue to the next section.

Check the Reloading Device and Perform a Post-Reload Configuration Verification

You have reached the final tool we will develop. You will learn how to create a tool to scan and check that port 22 is in open status after a router reload was initiated by our script. When the script detects an open port 22, the application will SSH into the device and then perform the post-reload capture of running configurations. The pre-reload capture can be compared to using Python's `difflib` library. Let's follow the step-by-step process to develop the final tool.

#	Task
1	To keep things simple, you can copy the previous script and modify it to create the last mini script for this chapter. `pynetauto@ubuntu20s1:~/my_tools/tool9_yes_no$` **`cd ..`** `pynetauto@ubuntu20s1:~/my_tools$` **`mkdir tool10_post_check`** `pynetauto@ubuntu20s1:~/my_tools$` **`cd tool10_post_check`** `pynetauto@ubuntu20s1:~/my_tools/ tool10_post_check $` **`touch post_check1.py`** `pynetauto@ubuntu20s1:~/my_tools/tool10_post_check$` **`nano post_check1.py`**

(*continued*)

#	Task
2	Here, we are going to create a socket application that checks port 22. When it detects that port 22 is open, it will log into that device and run the `show clock` command. Otherwise, it will go to sleep for 10 seconds and recheck port 22. This check will repeat 60 times, which means that the check will run for 10 minutes, and this is when we are having the router reboot and boot into the new IOS XE image. In production, this value will have to be different based on the network speed and actual hardware CPU processor speed, and you have to work out the estimate of the wait time. This lab assumes that if the device's port 22 is not back in service after the `reload` command, it may require troubleshooting.

post_check1.py

```
import socket
import time
from netmiko import ConnectHandler

t1 = time.mktime(time.localtime()) # Timer start to measure script running time

device1 = {
    'device_type': 'cisco_xe',
    'host': '192.168.183.111',
    'username': 'pynetauto',
    'password': 'cisco123',
    'secret': 'cisco123',
    'global_delay_factor': 2
}
device2 = {
    'device_type': 'cisco_xe',
    'host': '192.168.183.222',
    'username': 'pynetauto',
    'password': 'cisco123',
    'secret': 'cisco123',
    'global_delay_factor': 2
}

devices_list = [device1, device2]

for device in devices_list:
    ip = str(device['host'])
    port = 22
    retry = 60
    delay = 10
    def isOpen(ip, port):
        s = socket.socket(socket.AF_INET, socket.SOCK_STREAM)
        s.settimeout(3)
        try:
            s.connect((ip, int(port)))
            s.shutdown(socket.SHUT_RDWR)
            return True
```

#	Task

```
        except:
            return False
        finally:
            s.close()
    t1 = time.mktime(time.localtime())
    ipup = False
    for i in range(retry):
        if isOpen(ip, port):
            ipup = True
            print(f"{ip} is online. Logging into device to perform post reload check")
            net_connect = ConnectHandler(**device)
            print(net_connect.send_command("show clock"))
            break
        else:
            print("Device is still reloading. Please wait...")
            time.sleep(delay)

t2 = time.mktime(time.localtime()) - t1
print("Total wait time : {0} seconds".format(t2))
```

When you run the previous script, it will check for port 22, and if port 22 is opened on the target device, it should SSH into the router and run the `show clock` command. Then it will break out of the `for` loop and move to the next device, so your result should look similar to this output. Now you know that the port 22 post-checkers are working fine, and we are ready to write our full post-check application.

```
pynetauto@ubuntu20s1:~/my_tools/tool10_post_check$ python3 post_check1.py
192.168.183.111 is online. Logging into device to perform post reload check
*16:13:37.425 UTC Fri Jan 15 2021
192.168.183.222 is online. Logging into device to perform post reload check
*16:13:42.200 UTC Fri Jan 15 2021
Total wait time : 4.0 seconds
```

3 Now from the VMware Workstation user interface, go to `csr1000v-1`'s console and enable an access list to block port 22 to test the application. Enable `access-list 100` to block traffic on port 22 on `csr1000v-1`. See Figure 18-7.

```
Username: pynetauto
Password: ********
csr1000v-1> enable
csr1000v-1#conf terminal
csr1000v-1(config)#access-list 100 deny tcp any any eq 22
csr1000v-1(config)#access-list 100 permit ip any any
csr1000v-1(config)#interface Gi1
csr1000v-1(config-if)#ip access-group 100 in
csr1000v-1(config-if)#
```

(continued)

#	Task

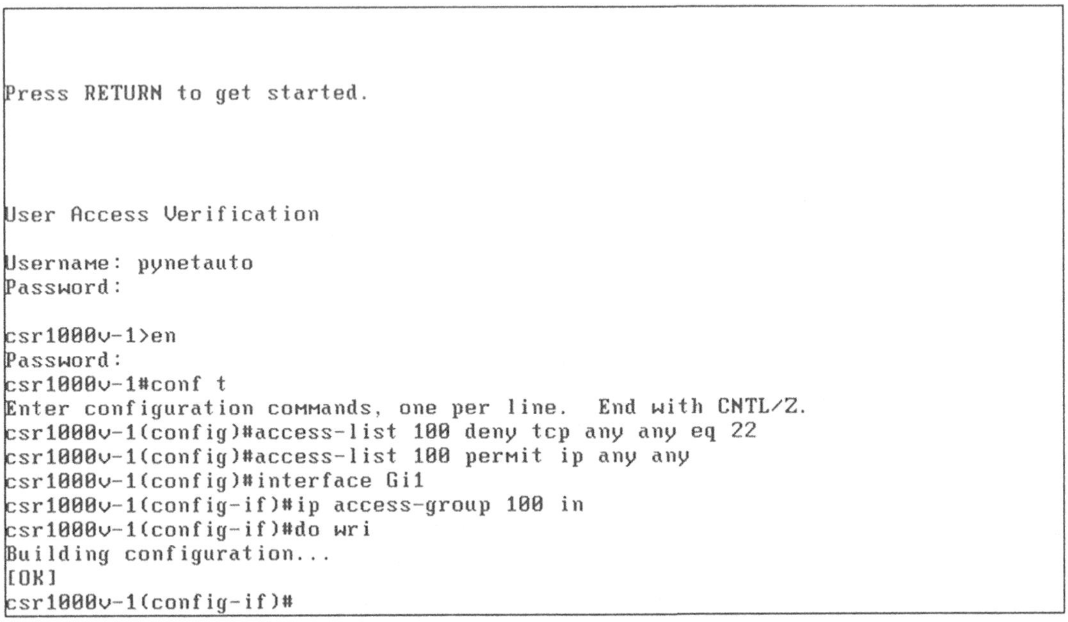
Press RETURN to get started.
User Access Verification
Username: pynetauto
Password:
csr1000v-1>en
Password:
csr1000v-1#conf t
Enter configuration commands, one per line. End with CNTL/Z.
csr1000v-1(config)#access-list 100 deny tcp any any eq 22
csr1000v-1(config)#access-list 100 permit ip any any
csr1000v-1(config)#interface Gi1
csr1000v-1(config-if)#ip access-group 100 in
csr1000v-1(config-if)#do wri
Building configuration...
[OK]
csr1000v-1(config-if)#

Figure 18-7. *VMware console, csr1000v-1, enabling access-list 100 to block traffic on port 22*

4 Use the following Python command to run the base post-check script. Since we blocked port 22 to simulate an unreachable device, it will return the "Device is still reloading. Please wait..." message every 10 seconds.

```
pynetauto@ubuntu20s1:~/my_tools/tool10_post_check$ python3 post_check1.py
Device is still reloading. Please wait...
Device is still reloading. Please wait...
```

On VMware Workstation's main console, log into `csr1000v-1` and remove access group 100 from the GigabitEthernet1 interface; this will allow the script to detect when port 22 is open for SSH.

```
csr1000v-1(config-if)#no ip access-group 100 in
```

As soon as the access list is removed from interface GigabitEthernet1, your script will detect an open port 22, log into the router, and run the `show clock` command. Then continues to the second router and completes the loop.

```
pynetauto@ubuntu20s1:~/my_tools/tool10_post_check$ python3 post_check1.py
Device is still reloading. Please wait...
Device is still reloading. Please wait...
Device is still reloading. Please wait...
Device is still reloading. Please wait...
```

#	Task

```
192.168.183.111 is online. Logging into device to perform post reload check
*16:19:26.299 UTC Fri Jan 15 2021
192.168.183.222 is online. Logging into device to perform post reload check
*16:19:29.063 UTC Fri Jan 15 2021
Total wait time : 2.0 seconds
```

5 To test the previous application, you are going to need the files created from the previous development. Let's copy all of the pre-reload show files from the tool9 development.

```
pynetauto@ubuntu20s1:~/my_tools/tool10_post_check$ pwd
/home/pynetauto/my_tools/tool10_post_check
pynetauto@ubuntu20s1:~/my_tools/tool10_post_check$ ls
post_check1.py
pynetauto@ubuntu20s1:~/my_tools/tool10_post_check$ ls /home/pynetauto/my_tools/
tool9_yes_no/
reload_yesno1.py  192.168.183.111_showroute_pre.txt  192.168.183.222_showroute_pre.
txt
reload_yesno2.py  192.168.183.111_showrun_pre.txt    192.168.183.222_showrun_pre.txt
yesno.py          192.168.183.111_showver_pre.txt    192.168.183.222_showver_pre.txt
192.168.183.111_showint_pre.txt  192.168.183.222_showint_pre.txt
pynetauto@ubuntu20s1:~/my_tools/tool10_post_check$ cp /home/pynetauto/my_tools/tool9_
yes_no/192.* ./
pynetauto@ubuntu20s1:~/my_tools/tool10_post_check$ ls
192.168.183.111_showint_pre.txt    192.168.183.111_showver_pre.txt
192.168.183.222_showrun_pre.txt
192.168.183.111_showroute_pre.txt  192.168.183.222_showint_pre.txt
192.168.183.222_showver_pre.txt
192.168.183.111_showrun_pre.txt    192.168.183.222_showroute_pre.txt  post_check1.py
```

6 Make a copy of the first file and name it `post_check2.py`. Use this as the base for our final script.

```
pynetauto@ubuntu20s1:~/my_tools/tool10_post_check$ cp post_check1.py post_check2.py
```

Write the following code and complete the application. This application will check port 22 and then log into each router and capture the four `show` commands from each router. Then, using Python's `difflib` library, we compare the pre- and post-capture configurations line by line. Next, we save each comparison set in HTML format for easy viewing for a review. Read and study each line of code carefully; the explanations are embedded in the following code for your reference:

post_check2.py

```
from netmiko import ConnectHandler
import socket
import time
import difflib
```

(continued)

#	Task

```
d_newios = "csr1000v-universalk9.16.09.06.SPA.bin"

device1 = {
    'device_type': 'cisco_xe',
    'host': '192.168.183.111',
    'username': 'pynetauto',
    'password': 'cisco123',
    'secret': 'cisco123',
    'global_delay_factor': 2
}
device2 = {
    'device_type': 'cisco_xe',
    'host': '192.168.183.222',
    'username': 'pynetauto',
    'password': 'cisco123',
    'secret': 'cisco123',
    'global_delay_factor': 2
}

devices_list = [device1, device2]

# Checks SSH port and then logs back in to complete the post-upgrade check.
def post_check():
    for device in devices_list:
        ip = str(device['host'])
        port = 22
        retry = 120
        delay = 10
        def isOpen(ip, port):
            s = socket.socket(socket.AF_INET, socket.SOCK_STREAM)
            s.settimeout(3)
            try:
                s.connect((ip, int(port)))
                s.shutdown(socket.SHUT_RDWR)
                return True
            except:
                return False
                finally:
                s.close()

        t1 = time.mktime(time.localtime())
        ipup = False
        for i in range(retry):
            if isOpen(ip, port):
                ipup = True
                print(f"{ip} is online. Logging into device to perform post reload
                check")
```

#	Task

```
# Capture four show commands result from each router
print("Performing post upgrade check.")
net_connect = ConnectHandler(**device)
net_connect.enable(cmd='enable 15')
config_commands1 = ['no boot system', 'boot system flash:/' + d_
newios, 'do write memory']
output = net_connect.send_config_set(config_commands1)
print (output)
net_connect.send_command('terminal length 0\n')
with open(f'{ip}_showver_post.txt', 'w+') as f1:
    print("Capturing post-reload 'show version'")
    showver_post = net_connect.send_command("show version")
    f1.write(showver_post)
time.sleep(1)
with open(f'{ip}_showrun_post.txt', 'w+') as f2:
    print("Capturing post-reload 'show running-config'")
    showrun_post = net_connect.send_command("show running-config")
    f2.write(showrun_post)
time.sleep(1)
with open(f'{ip}_showint_post.txt', 'w+') as f3:
    print("Capturing post-reload 'show ip interface brief'")
    showint_post = net_connect.send_command("show ip interface brief")
    f3.write(showint_post)
time.sleep(1)
with open(f'{ip}_showroute_post.txt', 'w+') as f4:
    print("Capturing post-reload 'show ip route'")
    showroute_post = net_connect.send_command("show ip route")
    f4.write(showroute_post)
time.sleep(1)

# Compare pre vs post configurations
showver_pre = "showver_pre"
showver_post = "showver_post"
showver_pre_lines = open(f"{ip}_showver_pre.txt").readlines()
#converts into strings first for comparison
#time.sleep(1)
showver_post_lines = open(f"{ip}_showver_post.txt").readlines()
#converts into strings first for comparison
#time.sleep(1)
# Four arguments required in HtmlDiff function
difference = difflib.HtmlDiff(wrapcolumn=70).make_file(showver_pre_
lines, showver_post_lines, showver_pre, showver_post)
difference_report = open(f"{ip}_show_ver_compared.html", "w+")
difference_report.write(difference) # Writes the differences to html
file
difference_report.close()
time.sleep(1)
print("-"*80)
```

(continued)

#	Task

```
                showrun_pre = "showrun_pre"
                showrun_post = "showrun_post"
                showrun_pre_lines = open(f"{ip}_showrun_pre.txt").readlines()
                showrun_post_lines = open(f"{ip}_showrun_post.txt").readlines()
                difference = difflib.HtmlDiff(wrapcolumn=70).make_file(showrun_pre_
                lines, showrun_post_lines, showrun_pre, showrun_post)
                difference_report = open(f"{ip}_show_run_compared.html", "w+")
                difference_report.write(difference)
                difference_report.close()
                time.sleep(1)

                showint_pre = "showint_pre"
                showint_post = "showint_post"
                showint_pre_lines = open(f"{ip}_showint_pre.txt").readlines()
                showint_post_lines = open(f"{ip}_showint_post.txt").readlines()
                difference = difflib.HtmlDiff(wrapcolumn=70).make_file(showint_pre_
                lines, showint_post_lines, showint_pre, showint_post)
                difference_report = open(f"{ip}_show_int_compared.html", "w+")
                difference_report.write(difference)
                difference_report.close()
                time.sleep(1)

                showroute_pre = "showroute_pre"
                showroute_post = "showroute_post"
                showroute_pre_lines = open(f"{ip}_showroute_pre.txt").readlines()
                showroute_post_lines = open(f"{ip}_showroute_post.txt").readlines()
                difference = difflib.HtmlDiff(wrapcolumn=70).make_file(showroute_
                pre_lines, showroute_post_lines, showroute_pre, showroute_post)
                difference_report = open(f"{ip}_show_route_compared.html", "w+")
                difference_report.write(difference)
                difference_report.close()
                time.sleep(1)
                print("-"*80)
                break
            else:
                print("Device is still reloading. Please wait...")
                time.sleep(delay)
        t2 = time.mktime(time.localtime()) - t1
        print("Total wait time : {0} seconds".format(t2))
        print("="*80)
        time.sleep(1)

post_check()
print("All tasks completed. Check pre and post configuration comparison html
files.")
```

#	Task
5	Run the script; it should create backup files post-reload and then create the HTML files after comparing each line. This script will not trigger the routers to reload as part of the previous script. Here we are interested in creating the files, and then pre- and post-file contents are compared. In the final script, we will need to add this script to `reload_yesno2.py` and turn it into a fully working application. So, don't be alarmed if the HTML is different from what you have expected.

```
pynetauto@ubuntu20s1:~/my_tools/tool10_post_check$ python3 post_check2.py
192.168.183.111 is online. Logging into device to perform post reload check
Performing post upgrade check.
configure terminal
Enter configuration commands, one per line.  End with CNTL/Z.
csr1000v-1(config)#no boot system
csr1000v-1(config)#boot system flash:/csr1000v-universalk9.16.09.06.SPA.bin
csr1000v-1(config)#do write memory
Building configuration...
[OK]
csr1000v-1(config)#end
csr1000v-1#
Capturing post-reload 'show version'
Capturing post-reload 'show running-config'
Capturing post-reload 'show ip interface brief'
Capturing post-reload 'show ip route'
--------------------------------------------------------------------------------
--------------------------------------------------------------------------------
Total wait time : 19.0 seconds
================================================================================
192.168.183.222 is online. Logging into device to perform post reload check
Performing post upgrade check.
configure terminal
Enter configuration commands, one per line.  End with CNTL/Z.
csr1000v-2(config)#no boot system
csr1000v-2(config)#boot system flash:/csr1000v-universalk9.16.09.06.SPA.bin
csr1000v-2(config)#do write memory
Building configuration...
[OK]
csr1000v-2(config)#end
csr1000v-2#
Capturing post-reload 'show version'
Capturing post-reload 'show running-config'
Capturing post-reload 'show ip interface brief'
Capturing post-reload 'show ip route'
--------------------------------------------------------------------------------
--------------------------------------------------------------------------------
Total wait time : 18.0 seconds
================================================================================
All tasks completed. Check pre and post configuration comparison html files.
```

(continued)

#	Task
	Connect to the ubuntu20s1 server using WinSCP or FileZilla and locate the backup and comparison files in the /home/yourname/my_tools/tool10_post_check/ directory. You can copy the HTML files and open them in a web browser. See Figure 18-8.

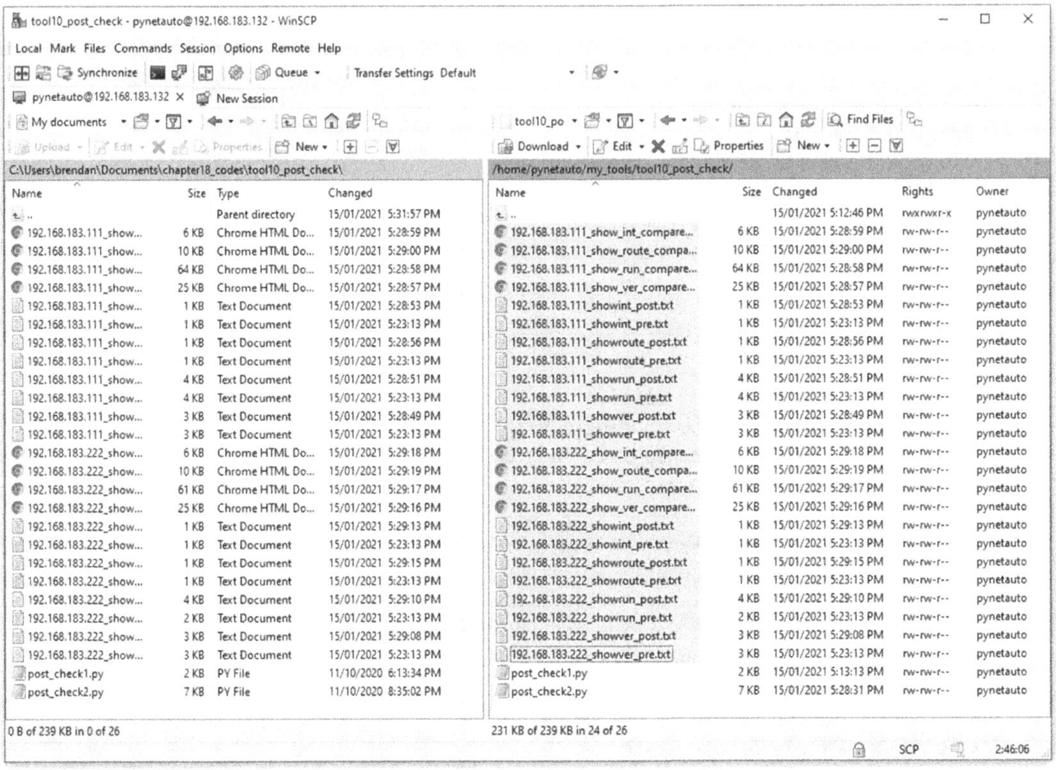

Figure 18-8. *WinSCP, checking and copying HTML compared files*

#	Task
6	Copy the files from the automation server onto your Windows host PC and open the HTML files in a web browser. If everything worked, you will see the headings with `_pre` and `_post` for each respective `show` command. Since we have not integrated this script with the `reload_yesno2.py` script, it will still display the currently running configurations. We will integrate all ten applications we have developed so far in the next chapter and turn them into an end-to-end working application. See Figure 18-9.

#	Task

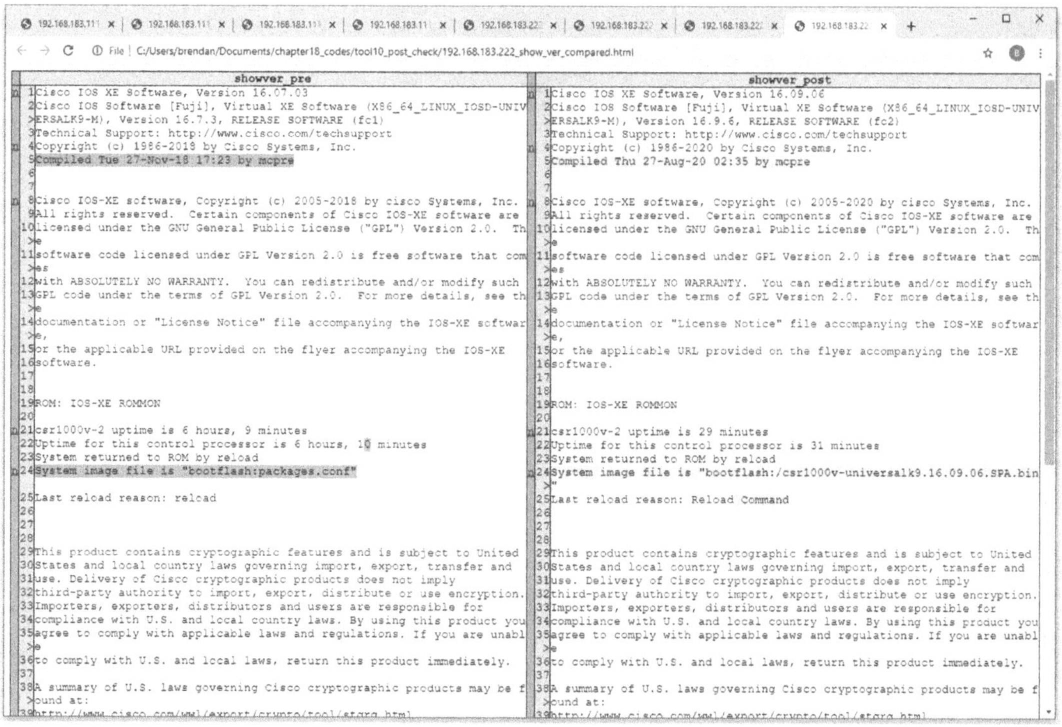

***Figure 18-9.** Copying and opening an HTML file check example*

Summary

You developed ten mini tools in this chapter, which has prepared you for the final Cisco IOS upgrade application in the next chapter. Each tool developed in this chapter has its use cases and can also be used as a stand-alone tool with minor or no modifications for production use. As you have seen, we have used various Python modules to develop our own Python applications that fulfill our requirements. These tools can be combined into one application; we can come up with various workflows and develop different Python network applications (tools). The general process of writing a Python program is much the same across all vendor networking devices. As long as Python modules support specific vendor products, you can apply similar automation application development strategies for any vendor product. Now let's combine all ten applications and create a fully functioning Cisco IOS XE upgrade tool.

CHAPTER 19

Python Network Automation Labs: Combining and Completing the Cisco IOS Upgrade Application

In this final chapter, you will put together the ten Python stand-alone applications we developed in Chapter 18. The application will be a fully functional Cisco IOS/IOS-XE upgrade application consisting of pre-check, IOS upload, pre-reload check, pre-reload configuration backup, reload, and post-upgrade verification check. We have been upgrading IOS on Cisco network devices manually for years, but now you can develop and combine various Python tools to let your Python code do to work for you.

Once you have reached the end of this chapter, you will have learned how to put together smaller applications to make a sophisticated and production-ready application. Python allows programmers the freedom to write almost any code they like, and the only limitation is the programmer's imagination. On the other hand, configuration and orchestration tools such as Ansible and Puppet provide nonprogramming engineers with idempotent features to configure and manage network devices with a lot of flexibility. However, you still have to work within the framework set by production. After completing this chapter, and hence this book, you will have reached the first milestone in your Python network programming journey.

Difficulty level will be relative to reader's previous experience with Cisco Networking Technology.

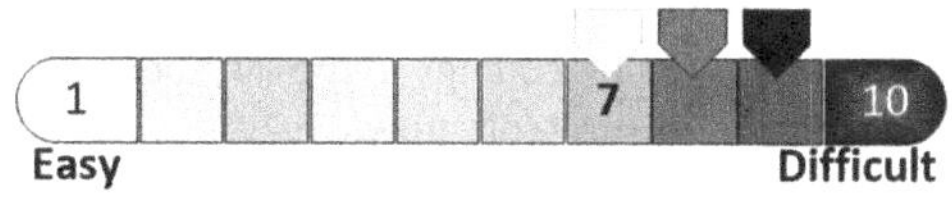

In the previous chapter, you developed ten applications related to the Cisco IOS upgrade. Now it is time to combine those tools and make a fully functioning Cisco IOS XE upgrade tool. As you work on more Python projects, you will always find something new that you have not encountered before. One of the best ways to learn is through project work with lots of unknowns and challenges. However, if you are starting your Python network automation journey, then try to find a smaller task to focus your efforts and document what tasks you can. Start to automate more straightforward tasks and then spend the time researching and studying books, taking online courses, searching the information on Google, or seeking advice from others who have already done something similar.

I briefly introduced you to object-oriented programming (OOP) at the beginning of the previous chapter. We will not use it here in our final IOS XE upgrade application as it adds more complexity. Even though OOP is a must-understand concept, we can still write code without creating custom OOP classes.

B. Choi, *Introduction to Python Network Automation*, https://doi.org/10.1007/978-1-4842-6806-3_19

In Python, almost everything can be considered an object, and even if you are not aware of OOP, you are still using it. Please note that I have purposefully removed the OOP portion of the final script, and it will not be part of our final Python application.

You have made it to the final exercise, which is the book's real climax. I want to congratulate you on a mammoth effort for following along with all the chapters of the book. A few years back, when I began my first journey in network automation with Python, it was still considered a relatively new technology trend and felt like a distant dream to automate tasks such as a Cisco IOS upgrade on enterprise routers and switches. Network automation has recently gained momentum, and now network automation and Python coding are on every IT/network team's mind. So without further ado, let's get on with completing the final application: a working IOS upgrade tool.

Before starting your final tasks in this section, please review Figure 17-14 and Figure 17-15 in Chapter 17. You may need a quick refresher to gauge what we are about to achieve in this final lab. The final script's workflow will be almost identical to the automation tasks described in Figure 17-15.

Creating a Single Python File

For simplicity, we will create only a single Python file (`upgrade_crs1000v.py`). In a real-world production environment, the best practice is to create and save tools into smaller files (modules) to reduce the number of lines written to the main script. However, here we are still exploring and learning, so it is more important to see the whole picture of how each application works. After you have finished the book, you can move some parts of the code into separate modules, which was discussed in the previous chapter. As discussed earlier, we will make this application an interactive tool, getting the user credentials and user inputs while the script runs. The device information will be written to a `.csv` file and read from the file using the `pandas` module as `df` (dataframe); this is a more convenient way to read a large text-based data than to make the user enter the data.

#	Task

1	You will be continuing the tasks from the `/home/pynetauto/my_tools/` directory; this directory contains all the mini Python applications we developed in Chapter 18. Change to the `my_tools` directory and then create the `upgrade_crs1000v.py` file inside this directory now.
	`pynetauto@ubuntu20s1:~$ pwd`
	`/home/pynetauto`
	`pynetauto@ubuntu20s1:~$ cd my_tools`
	`pynetauto@ubuntu20s1:~/my_tools$ touch upgrade_crs1000v.py`
	`pynetauto@ubuntu20s1:~/my_tools$ ls`
	`upgrade_crs1000v.py`
	We will start filling in the final `upgrade_crs1000v.py` script soon; leave it there as a placeholder for the time being.

#	Task
2	Let's quickly discuss which files will be referenced for our application development. If you followed Chapter 18 in detail and completed all of the development tasks, you will remember the ten applications we have developed and each corresponding tool's directory names. The names of the files you will reference are listed next. If you prefer to work in the Windows text editor or an IDE, you can save the listed files to your Windows folder. I have copied the files to the `/home/pynetauto/my_tools/` directory for reference, but for the completed IOS applications to work, you will require the `upgrade_crs1000v.py` and `devices_info.csv` files in the `/home/pynetauto/my_tools/` directory and also a new IOS file in the `/home/pynetauto/my_tools/new_ios/` directory. If you have completed the development task in the IOS uploading section, you will have the new IOS file already in this directory. If you have not uploaded the new IOS file (`csr1000v-universalk9.16.09.06.SPA.bin`) yet, refer to the IOS uploading section and complete that task now.

```
pynetauto@ubuntu20s1:~/my_tools$ ls -lh
total 52K
# Main script and files
-rw-rw-r-- 1 pynetauto pynetauto    0 Jan 15 22:03 upgrade_crs1000v.py
-rw-rw-r-- 1 pynetauto pynetauto  271 Jan 15 23:13 devices_info.csv
# Python application scripts referenced:
-rw-rw-r-- 1 pynetauto pynetauto  955 Jan 15 23:14 check_flash2.py
-rw-rw-r-- 1 pynetauto pynetauto 1.5K Jan 15 23:13 get_cred2.py
-rw-rw-r-- 1 pynetauto pynetauto 1.8K Jan 15 23:18 make_backup1.py
-rw-rw-r-- 1 pynetauto pynetauto 1.3K Jan 15 23:14 md5_validate3.py
-rw-rw-r-- 1 pynetauto pynetauto 2.4K Jan 15 23:18 md5_verify2.py
-rw-rw-r-- 1 pynetauto pynetauto  681 Jan 15 23:14 ping_tool6.py
-rw-rw-r-- 1 pynetauto pynetauto 1009 Jan 15 23:14 ping_tool6_tools.py
-rw-rw-r-- 1 pynetauto pynetauto 6.1K Jan 15 23:18 post_check2.py
-rw-rw-r-- 1 pynetauto pynetauto 1.3K Jan 15 23:13 read_info8.py
-rw-rw-r-- 1 pynetauto pynetauto 3.9K Jan 15 23:18 reload_yesno2.py
-rw-rw-r-- 1 pynetauto pynetauto 3.2K Jan 15 23:14 upload_ios1.py
# new IOS .bin file location
pynetauto@ubuntu20s1:~/my_tools$ ls /home/pynetauto/my_tools/new_ios
csr1000v-universalk9.16.09.06.SPA.bin
```

#	Task
3	If you do not have the `devices_info.csv` file from the previous chapter, you can create it now. You can create this file using Microsoft Excel or directly in a text editor using comma-separated values (separate values with a comma and no spaces). After creating your file, it should look the same as the following:

```
pynetauto@ubuntu20s1:~/my_tools$ nano devices_info.csv
```

devices_info.csv

```
devicename,device,devicetype,host,newios,newiosmd5
csr1000v-1,RT,cisco_xe,192.168.183.111,csr1000v-universalk9.16.09.06.SPA.bin,77878ae
6db8e34de90e2e3e83741bf39
csr1000v-2,RT,cisco_xe,192.168.183.222,csr1000v-universalk9.16.09.06.SPA.bin,77878ae
6db8e34de90e2e3e83741bf39
```

(*continued*)

#	Task

4 Now that the standard procedures are out of the way, let's begin the final application development. You will now add the series of scripts to the `upgrade_crs1000v.py` script in a linear fashion, and once everything has been strung together, it will work as an application that can be directly used in most production environments.

First, you will add all the Python modules that will be used in our application and then add and modify the scripts one at a time. Follow these instructions to initially create and test a single file application, which will run from end to end.

```
pynetauto@ubuntu20s1:~/my_tools$ nano upgrade_crs1000v.py
```

Add all the modules used, as shown here:

```
upgrade_crs1000v.py
import socket # For socket networking
import os # For Python Server OS
import time # Python time module
import pandas as pd # Pandas to read data into a data frame
import re # Python regular expression module
from getpass import getpass # For password collection
import os.path # For Python Server OS directory
import hashlib # For MD5 checks
from netmiko import ConnectHandler, SCPConn # For netmiko's SSH connection and SCP
file transfer
from netmiko.ssh_exception import  NetMikoTimeoutException # To accept netmiko
timeout exceptions
import difflib # For analyzing two files and differences

t = time.mktime(time.localtime()) # Timer start to measure script running time
```

In the next step, you will append and modify sections of code from each tool and slowly build up the main application script.

5 A. Use `get_cred2.py` (`tool2_login`) and turn it into a function. This script will interactively get the network administrator ID and password, prompt to enable the secret, and give the user the option to select yes or no. We are also using a regular expression to control the user's input for the username and password. For `p1`, the expected characters are from 5 to 30 characters long, starting with a letter and finishing with a letter or a number. For `p2`, the expected characters are from 8 to 50 characters long, starting with a letter and finishing with any character. Regular expression can be a difficult topic for some people; you should review Chapter 9 if you need help.

```
"""
Step 1. From get_cred2.py (tool2_login) application:
Get network administrator ID and password, also prompt for enable secret and give
the user option to select yes or no.
p1: Between 5-30 characters long, starting with an alphabet & finishes with an
alphabet or a number
p2: Between 8 to 50 characters long, starting with an alphabet & finishes with any
characters
"""

def get_secret(p2):
    global secret
    resp = input("Is secret same as password? (y/n) : ")
```

#	Task
	(code below)

```
    print("-"*80)
    resp = resp.lower()
    if resp == "yes" or resp == "y":
        secret = pwd

    elif resp == "no" or resp == "n":
        secret = None
        while not secret:
            secret = getpass("Enter the secret : ")
            while not p2.match(secret):
                secret = getpass(r"*Enter the secret : ")
            secret_verify = getpass("Confirm the secret : ")
            if secret != secret_verify:
                print("!!! the secret does not match. Please try again.")
                print("-"*80)
                secret = None
    else:
        get_secret(p2)

def get_credentials():
    p1 = re.compile(r'^[a-zA-Z][a-zA-Z0-9_-]{3,28}[a-zA-Z0-9]$')
    p2 = re.compile(r'^[a-zA-Z].{7,49}')
    global uid
    uid = input("Enter Network Admin ID : ")
    while not p1.match(uid):
        uid = input(r"*Enter Network Admin ID : ")
    global pwd
    pwd = None
    while not pwd:
        pwd = getpass("Enter Network Admin PWD : ")
        while not p2.match(pwd):
            pwd = getpass(r"*Enter Network Admin PWD : ")
        pwd_verify = getpass("Confirm Network Admin PWD : ")
        if pwd != pwd_verify:
            print("!!! Network Passwords do not match. Please try again.")
            print("-"*80)
            pwd = None
    # Trigger get_secret function to run
    get_secret(p2)
    return uid, pwd, secret
# Trigger get_Credential function to run
get_credentials()
```

Now you have completed the above task A, continue with the task B.

(continued)

#	Task
6	B. Copy and paste read_info8.py (tool3_read_csv); this is the script that reads the devices_info.csv file to feed our script and convert the read items into variables to be used throughout our script. Turn this into a function for portability and readability. Ensure that you pass the three arguments received from task A, so that the script runs without argument error. Remember, this application expects three arguments from the previous workflow: uid, pwd, and secret.

```
"""
Step 2. From read_info8.py (tool3_read_csv) application:
Read the content of the devices_info.csv file and convert the values into two lists.
device_list to be used as an information feeder to the script device_list_netmiko to
be used as netmiko friendly dictionary items for SSH connection
"""

def read_info(uid, pwd, secret):
    df = pd.read_csv(r'./devices_info.csv') # ensure the correct file location
    number_of_rows = len(df.index)
    # Read the values and save as a list, read column as df and save it as a list
    devicename = list(df['devicename'])
    device = list(df['device'])
    devicetype = list(df['devicetype'])
    ip = list(df['host'])
    newios = list(df['newios'])
    newiosmd5 = list(df['newiosmd5'])
    # Append the items and convert to a list, device_list
    global device_list # For md5_validate3.py
    device_list = []
    for index, rows in df.iterrows():
        device_append = [rows.devicename, rows.device, \
        rows.devicetype, rows.host, rows.newios, rows.newiosmd5]
        device_list.append(device_append)
    # Using device_list, create a netmiko friendly list device_list_netmiko
    global device_list_netmiko
    device_list_netmiko = []
    i = 0
    for x in device_list:
        if len(x) != 0: # As long as number of items in device_list is not 0 (empty)
            i += 1
            name = f'device{str(i)}' # Each for loop, the name is updated to device1,
            device2, device3, ...
            devicetype, host = x[2], x[3]
            device = {
            'device_type': devicetype,
            'host': host,
            'username': uid,
            'password': pwd,
            'secret': secret,
            }
            device_list_netmiko.append(device)
# Trigger read_info function to run
read_info(uid, pwd, secret)
```

#	Task
7	C. This module is almost straight out of `ping_tool6.py` and `ping_tool6_tools.py` (`tool1_ping`). Copy the script and modify it; then use it to test the connectivity to all devices in our device list. This script uses both Linux's OS `ping` command and socket networking to check for an open socket 22 status. If an IP address is unreachable, the script will exit the application, and you must troubleshoot why the particular device is unreachable on the network. This script should produce three separate files containing reachability status. If port 22 is open, then the device's IP address gets written to `f1`; if port 22 is closed, the script will test port 23's status and write the IP address to `f2`. If the device is unreachable, then the IP address will be written to `f3`.

```
"""
Step 3. From ping_tool6.py and ping_tool6_tools.py (tool1_ping) application:
Perform connectivity tests, first using ICMP ping, Second, check port 22. Also,
separate the ips with open port 22. If port 22 is closed, then test port 23 create
three files containing the result of the reachability tests
"""
def test_connectivity(device_list_netmiko):
    f1 = open('reachable_ips_ssh.txt',  'w+')
    f2 = open('reachable_ips_telnet.txt', 'w+')
    f3 = open('unreachable_ips.txt', 'w+')
    for device in device_list_netmiko:
    ip = device['host'].strip()
    print(ip)
    resp = os.system('ping -c 4 ' + ip)
    if resp == 0:
        for port in range (22, 23):
            destination = (ip, port)
            try:
                with socket.socket(socket.AF_INET, socket.SOCK_STREAM) as s:
                    s.settimeout(3)
                    connection = s.connect(destination)
                    print(f"{ip} {port} open")
                    print("-"*80)
                    f1.write(f"{ip}\n")
            except:
                print(f"{ip} {port} closed")
                f3.write(f"{ip} {port} closed\n")
                for port in range (23, 24):
                    destination = (ip, port)
                    try:
                        with socket.socket(socket.AF_INET, socket.SOCK_STREAM) as s:
                            s.settimeout(3)
                            connection = s.connect(destination)
                            print(f"{ip} {port} open")
                            print("-"*80)
                            f2.write(f"{ip}\n")
                    except:
                        print(f"{ip} {port} closed")
                        print("-"*80)
                        f3.write(f"{ip} {port} closed\n")
```

(continued)

#	Task

	``
	        else:
	            print(f"{ip} unreachable")
	            print("-"*80)
	            f3.write(f"{ip} unreachable\n")
	    f1.close()
	    f2.close()
	    f3.close()
	# Trigger test_connectivity function to run
	test_connectivity(device_list_netmiko)
	``

8	D. This part is from md5_validate3.py (tool4_md5_linux), and as explained earlier, this will validate the MD5 value of the new IOS file on the server. Since the file and script runs from a single Python automation server, we can use Python's hashilib to test the IOS's MD5 value in a directory. Testing the MD5 values rigorously throughout our workflow will guarantee a successful IOS upgrade to a newer IOS XE version. Also, you have to ensure that your new IOS is in the correct directory.

```
"""
Step 4. From md5_validate3.py (tool4_md5_linux) application:
Validate the MD5 value of the new IOS file on the Python Server against the value
you have provided on the csv file. Must be validated before moving on.
"""

def validate_md5(device_list):
    for x in device_list:
        print(x[3], x[0], x[1], x[2])
        newios = x[4]
        newiosmd5 = str(x[5].lower()).strip()
        print(newiosmd5)
        newiosmd5hash = hashlib.md5()
        file = open(f'/home/pynetauto/my_tools/new_ios/{newios}', 'rb') # New IOS
        directory here
        content = file.read()
        newiosmd5hash.update(content)
        newiosmd5server = newiosmd5hash.hexdigest()
        print(newiosmd5server.strip())
        global newiossize
        newiossize = round(os.path.getsize(f'/home/pynetauto/my_tools/new_ios/
        {newios}')/1000000, 2)
        print(newiossize, "MB")
        if newiosmd5server == newiosmd5:
            print("MD5 values matched!")
            print("-"*80)
        else:
            print("Mismatched MD5 values. Exit")
            print("-"*80)
            exit()
    return newiossize
# Trigger validate_md5 function to run
validate_md5(device_list)
```

#	Task
9	E. In this task, the script is almost a carbon copy of `check_flash2.py` (`tool5_fsize_cisco`). As you create the function, make sure you parse the correct variables from the previous workflow. In this case, we are parsing in the `device_list_netmiko` list for the SSH connection and in the variable `newiossize` to confirm that the router has enough free space in the flash memory to accommodate the new IOS file size. If the free space is less than one-and-a-half times the new IOS file size, the script will exit. On newer Cisco devices, the flash free size is not much of a challenge as they can accommodate multiple larger IOS and IOS XE files, but on older devices, you will have to remove the old IOS from the flash to make room. You could write something funky here and automatically locate the largest or oldest file if you want. Anyway, always check the free size during your change planning process.

```
"""
Step 5. From check_flash2.py (tool5_fsize_cisco) application:
Checks available flash size on the router
"""

def check_flash(device_list_netmiko, newiossize):
    for device in device_list_netmiko:
        ip = str(device['host'])
        net_connect = ConnectHandler(**device)
        net_connect.send_command("terminal length 0")
        showdir = net_connect.send_command("dir")
        #showflash = net_connect.send_command("show flash:") # For switches
        time.sleep(2)
        p1 = re.compile("\d+(?=\sbytes\sfree\))")
        m1 = p1.findall(showdir)
        flashfree = ((int(m1[0])/1000000))
        print(f"{ip} Free flash size : ", flashfree, "MB")
        print("-"*80)
        if flashfree < (newiossize * 1.5):
            print(f"Not enough space on {ip}'s flash! Exiting")
            print("!"*80)
            exit()
        else:
            print(f"{ip} has enough space for new IOS.")
            print("-"*80)
# Trigger check_flash function to run
check_flash(device_list_netmiko, newiossize)
```

(*continued*)

#	Task
10	F. This script is from `upload_ios1.py` (`tool7_upload_ios`), and it forms a big part of the main script. As the name suggests, after the previous task, the application is ready to upload the new IOS to the first router's flash, but before uploading the file, some housekeeping needs to take place. First, the logged-in user has a level 15 privilege to perform IOS uploading tasks via SCP. Second, the router has the right configuration allowing aaa authentication and authorization for this user. If the first and second requirements are not met, you have overlooked your change preparation, so you must go back and fix the access issue first before attempting to run this application. But if everything is correctly configured with the right access to this device, then the application checks for `ip scp server enable` to turn on the SCP server service on the Cisco device. If this feature is disabled, the script will automatically enable it before the new IOS file upload and then disable it after the upload finishes. Note that the next task will continue at the end of this task.

```
"""
Step 6. From upload_ios1.py (tool7_upload_ios) application:
First, check the aaa configuration requirements. If not met, exit for correct configuration.
Second, check if 'ip scp enable' is enabled for SCP file transfer. Enable ip scp.
Third, upload the IOS file to the router, then disable ip scp.
"""

def ios_upload(device_list_netmiko, device_list):
    i = 0
    for device in device_list_netmiko:
        device_x = device_list[i]
        newios = device_x[4] # Call out newios value
        newiosmd5 = device_x[5] # Call out newiosmd5 value
        i += 1

        s_newios = f'/home/pynetauto/my_tools/new_ios/{newios}'
        print("*"*80)
        #print(device)
        ip = str(device['host'])
        print(f'{ip} beginning IOS XE upgrade.')
        username = str(device['username'])
        net_connect = ConnectHandler(**device)
        net_connect.send_command("terminal length 0")
        showrun = net_connect.send_command("show running-config")
        check_priv15 = (f'username {username} privilege 15')
        aaa_authenication = "aaa authentication login default local enable"
        aaa_authorization = "aaa authorization exec default local"
        if check_priv15 in showrun:
            print(f"{username} has level 15 privilege - OK")
            if aaa_authenication in showrun:
                print("check_aaa_authentication - OK")
                if aaa_authorization in showrun:
                    print("check_aaa_authorization - OK")
                else:
                    print("aaa_authorization - FAILED ")
                    exit()
            else:
                print("aaa_authentication - FAILED ")
                exit()
```

#	Task
	(code continued below)

```
        else:
            print(f"{username} has not enough privilege - FAILED")
            exit()
        net_connect.enable(cmd='enable 15')
        net_connect.config_mode()
        net_connect.send_command('ip scp server enable')
        net_connect.exit_config_mode()
        time.sleep(1)
        print("New IOS uploading in progress! Please wait...")
        scp_conn = SCPConn(net_connect)
        scp_conn.scp_transfer_file(s_newios, newios)
        scp_conn.close()
        time.sleep(1)
        net_connect.config_mode()
        net_connect.send_command('no ip scp server enable')
        net_connect.exit_config_mode()
```

11 G. In this task, you can borrow the script from `md5_verify2.py` (in `tool8_md5_cisco`) to perform the MD5 verification of the newly uploaded IOS on the router's flash and compare it to the MD5 value calculated on the server. Once again, we are utilizing the power of regular expressions to test if Cisco IOS XE's `verify` command has run successfully by examining the "Verified" characters in the command's output. Then we find the 32-character MD5 value using the `re` (regular expression) compiler and use it as a variable to test the validity of the MD5 value. If any errors occur, `try` and `except` will catch most of them.

```
"""
Step 7. From md5_verify2.py (in tool8_md5_cisco) application:
Fourth, verify the MD5 value of the new IOS on the router flash, then
compare it with the server-side MD5 value.
"""

try:
    locate_newios = net_connect.send_command(f"show flash: | in {newios}")
    if newios in locate_newios:
        result = net_connect.send_command("verify /md5 flash:{} {}".format(newios,newiosmd5))
        print(result)
        p1 = re.compile(r'Verified')
        p2 = re.compile(r'[a-fA-F0-9]{31}[a-fA-F0-9]')
        verified = p1.findall(result)
        newiosmd5flash = p2.findall(result)
        if verified:
            result = True
            print("MD5 values MATCH! Continue")
            print("MD5 of new IOS on Server : ",newiosmd5)
            print("MD5 of new IOS on flash  : ",newiosmd5flash[0])
            print("-"*80)
        else:
            result = False
            print("MD5 values DO NOT MATCH! Exiting.")
            print("-"*80)
            exit()
```

(*continued*)

#	Task

```
        else:
            print("No new IOS found on router's flash. Continue to next device...")
            print("-"*80)
    except (NetMikoTimeoutException):
        print (f'Timeout error to : {ip}')
        print("-"*80)
        continue
    except unknown_error:
        print ('Unknown error occurred : ' + str(unknown_error))
        print("-"*80)
        continue
```

12 H. Under normal circumstances, this may not be required, but to make the application a little more real, I have decided to make this application more interactive where on completion of a new IOS upload, it gives the user an option to reload the router by answering yes or no. This is a large portion of the script. As soon as you respond with y or yes and press the Enter key, the script will reconfigure the router's boot system configuration and then save the running configuration to the startup configuration. This is followed by pre-reload configuration captures of the four `show` commands. It issues a `reload` command to initiate the reloading of the device. As soon as the router goes into reloading mode, you will lose the SSH connection, and also, the Python automation server will return `EoFError`. To continue running our script on the server, we use the `try` and `except` methods to catch this error and wait for the first 60 seconds; then we run the `check_port_22_post` function to scan port 22 for its status every 5 seconds. The `check_port_22_post` application is smart, so it will automatically detect that the router is up and follow through with the post-reload configuration check; then it will produce multiple HTML comparison files for IOS upgrade validation.

```
"""
Step 8. From reload_yesno2.py (in tool9_yes_no) application:
Fifth, give the user a chance to review the result and let
him/her decide if he wants to reload the device. This can be removed to automate
this process fully, but this is included to demonstrate how interactive session
works. If 'Y", reload now, if "n", reload later.      Sixth, change the boot system
command to boot into new IOS on the flash:/ Save configuration.
"""

yes_list = ['yes', 'y']
no_list = ['no', 'n']
print("!"*80)
print("Note: Devices will be reloaded one at a time.")
resp = input(f"Do you want to reload {ip} now? (y/n)? ").lower()
if resp in yes_list:
    print("Reloading devices")
    #net_connect = ConnectHandler(**device)
    net_connect.enable(cmd='enable 15')
    config_commands1 = ['no boot system', 'boot system flash:/' + newios, 'do write
    memory']
    output = net_connect.send_config_set(config_commands1)
    print (output)
    net_connect.send_command('terminal length 0\n')
    show_boot = net_connect.send_command('show boot\n')
    show_dir = net_connect.send_command('dir\n')
```

#	Task

```
    if newios not in show_dir:
        print('Unable to locate new IOS on the flash:/. Exiting.')
        print("-"*80)
        exit()
    elif newios not in show_boot:
        print('Boot system was not correctly configured. Exiting.')
        print("-"*80)
        exit()
    # Seventh, if boot commands are correct, capture another running backup of the
    device for comparison.
    elif newios in show_boot and newios in show_dir:
        try:
            print(f'Found {newios} in show boot')
            print("-"*80)
            print(f"{ip} [Pre-reload] Capture configuration")
            net_connect.send_command("terminal length 0")
            time.sleep(1)
            with open(f'{ip}_showver_pre.txt', 'w+') as f1:
                print("* [Pre-reload] Capturing 'show version'")
                showver_pre = net_connect.send_command("show version")
                f1.write(showver_pre)
            time.sleep(1)
            with open(f'{ip}_showrun_pre.txt', 'w+') as f2:
                print("* [Pre-reload] Capturing 'show running-config'")
                showrun_pre = net_connect.send_command("show running-config")
                f2.write(showrun_pre)
            time.sleep(1)
            with open(f'{ip}_showint_pre.txt', 'w+') as f3:
                print("* [Pre-reload] Capturing 'show ip interface brief'")
                showint_pre = net_connect.send_command("show ip interface brief")
                f3.write(showint_pre)
            time.sleep(1)
            with open(f'{ip}_showroute_pre.txt', 'w+') as f4:
                print("* [Pre-reload] Capturing 'show ip route'")
                showroute_pre = net_connect.send_command("show ip route")
                f4.write(showroute_pre)
            time.sleep(1)
            print("-"*80)

            t1 = time.mktime(time.localtime()) # To measure time elapsed for reload

            # Eighth, initiate the device reload
            print(f"{ip} is now reloading.")
            net_connect.send_command('reload', expect_string='[confirm]')
            net_connect.send_command('yes')
            net_connect.send_command('\n')
            print("-"*80)
            # If you remove the "y" or "n" prompt when reloading is initiated, the
            server will generate
            # OSError, use this code to catch the OSError to run the code continuously.
```

(continued)

#	Task

```
                    # If using the interactive as in this example, then it will produce
                    EoFError, so leave this
                    # code as is
                # except OSError:
                    # print("***Device is now reloading. This may take 2-5 minutes.")
                    # time.sleep(45)
                    # print("-"*80)
                    # port = 22
                    # check_port_22_post(ip, port, device, t1)
                    # print("-"*80)
                except EOFError:
                    print("***Device is now reloading. This may take 2-5 minutes.")
                    time.sleep(60)
                    print("-"*80)
                    port = 22
                    # Trigger check_port_22_post function for check port 22 and post check
                    check_port_22_post(ip, port, device, t1)
                    print("-"*80)
            # If chosen 'n', break out of the operation
            elif resp in no_list:
                print("You have chosen to reload the devices later. Exiting the application.")
                break
            print("*"*80)
        # Trigger ios_upload main function
        ios_upload(device_list_netmiko, device_list)
```

13 I. This script needs to go before the main script, which needs to be called within the same file. Place this script just before task A, so this function is predefined before the main script runs. This script will run as the final script within the main script, so Python must be aware of this script. Previously, we briefly discussed how this script works, but this is the same script as `post_check2.py` (`tool10_post_check`). This part of the application will check that port 22 is open or closed with the `delay` (wait) timer of 5 seconds and `retry` value of 90 (times). The IOS-XE router under a typical operation and a virtual router such as CSR 1000v will complete the reloading in approximately three to five minutes. Still, it may take longer if multiple routing protocols are enabled and heavy IP traffic traverses the production network.

Once the router interface comes back up and port 22 is detected as open for connection, this application will SSH back into the router, perform the post-reload tasks, and capture the four `show` configurations post-reload. The two sets of files, pre and post, are compared using the `difflib` library. The library creates four sets of HTML files for IOS upgrade success verification and validation. This basically means reusing a `make_backup1.py` (`tool6_make_backup`) application. In this task, two applications are combined into one. If there is another device, in this case, yes, the script will go back to task G and start uploading IOS on the second router and follow the same workflow as before. If there are no other devices left for the IOS upgrade, the application will finish and output the success message, and also time is taken to run the whole script from end to end.

```
"""
Step 9. From post_check2.py (tool10_post_check) and make_backup1.py (tool6_make_backup).
Check SSH port 22 and then log back in. Then complete the post-upgrade verification
check. This script compares before and after running configurations to validate the
IOS XE upgrade's success for your devices.
"""
```

#	Task

```
def check_port_22_post(ip, port, device, t1):
    retry = 90 # Try 90 times
    delay = 5 # 5 seconds wait
    def isOpen(ip, port):
        s = socket.socket(socket.AF_INET, socket.SOCK_STREAM)
        s.settimeout(3)
        try:
            s.connect((ip, int(port)))
            s.shutdown(socket.SHUT_RDWR)
            return True # The statements after the return statements are not executed.
        except:
            return False
        finally:
            s.close()
    # Retry 90 times until the port is in open state.
    for i in range(retry):
        if isOpen(ip, port):
            print(ip + " is back online.")
            t2 = time.mktime(time.localtime()) - t1
            print(f"{ip}'s reload time : {0} seconds".format(t2))
            print(f"Logging back into {ip} to perform post-reload tasks.")
            print("Please wait...")
            # When port 22 is open, start postreload_check here.
            print(ip)
            net_connect = ConnectHandler(**device)
            print(f'*** {ip} is back online.')
            print("-"*80)
            # [Post-reload] Capture configuration
            print(f"{ip} [Post-reload] Capture configuration")
            file14 = open(ip + '_showver_post.txt', 'w+')
            net_connect.send_command("terminal length 0")
            showver_postreload = net_connect.send_command("show version")
            print("* [Post-reload] Capturing 'show version'")
            file14.write(showver_postreload)
            file14.close()
            # Successful upgrade will print IP and correct system boot image name.
            p99= re.compile(r'System image file is ".+[?=\"]')
            m99 = p99.findall(showver_postreload)
            print(f"! {ip}'s {m99}.")
            time.sleep(2)
            file15 = open(ip + '_showrun_post.txt', 'w+')
            showrun_postreload = net_connect.send_command("show running-config")
            print("* [Post-reload] Capturing 'show running-config'")
            file15.write(showrun_postreload)
            file15.close()
            time.sleep(2)
            file16 = open(ip + '_showint_post.txt', 'w+')
            showint_postreload = net_connect.send_command("show ip interface brief")
            print("* [Post-reload] Capturing 'show ip interface brief'")
```

(continued)

#	Task

```
file16.write(showint_postreload)
file16.close()
time.sleep(2)
file17= open(ip + '_showroute_post.txt', 'w+')
showroute_postreload = net_connect.send_command("show ip route")
print("* [Post-reload] Capturing 'show ip route'")
file17.write(showroute_postreload)
file17.close()
time.sleep(2)
# Compare pre and post configurations to create four html files
showver_pre = "showver_pre"
showver_post = "showver_post"
showver_pre_lines = open(ip+ '_showver_pre.txt').readlines() # Convert to
strings first for
comparison
time.sleep(1)
showver_post_lines = open(ip+ '_showver_post.txt').readlines() #Convert
to strings first for
comparison
time.sleep(1)
# Note, four arguments required in HtmlDiff function
difference = difflib.HtmlDiff(wrapcolumn=70).make_file(showver_pre_lines,
showver_post_lines, showver_pre, showver_post)
difference_report = open(ip + "_show_ver_comparison.html", "w+")
difference_report.write(difference) # Write the differences to the
difference_report
difference_report.close()
time.sleep(1)
showrun_pre = "showrun_pre"
showrun_post = "showrun_post"
showrun_pre_lines = open(ip+ '_showrun_pre.txt').readlines() # Convert to
strings first for
comparison
time.sleep(1)
showrun_post_lines = open(ip+ '_showrun_post.txt').readlines() # Convert
to strings first for
comparison
time.sleep(1)
difference = difflib.HtmlDiff(wrapcolumn=70).make_file(showrun_pre_lines,
showrun_post_lines, showrun_pre, showrun_post)
difference_report = open(ip + "_show_run_comparison.html", "w+")
difference_report.write(difference) # Write the differences to the
difference_report
difference_report.close()
time.sleep(1)
showint_pre = "showint_pre"
showint_post = "showint_post"
showint_pre_lines = open(ip+ '_showint_pre.txt').readlines()
time.sleep(1)
```

#	Task

```
                showint_post_lines = open(ip+ '_showint_post.txt').readlines()
                time.sleep(1)
                difference = difflib.HtmlDiff(wrapcolumn=70).make_file(showint_pre_lines,
                showint_post_lines, showint_pre, showint_post)
                difference_report = open(ip + "_show_int_comparison.html", "w+")
                difference_report.write(difference)
                difference_report.close()
                time.sleep(1)
                showroute_pre = "showroute_pre"
                showroute_post = "showroute_post"
                showroute_pre_lines = open(ip+ '_showroute_pre.txt').readlines()
                time.sleep(1)
                showroute_post_lines = open(ip+ '_showroute_post.txt').readlines()
                time.sleep(1)
                difference = difflib.HtmlDiff(wrapcolumn=70).make_file(showroute_pre_lines,
                showroute_post_lines, showroute_pre, showroute_post)
                difference_report1 = open(ip + "_show_route_comparison.html", "w+")
                difference_report1.write(difference)
                difference_report1.close()
                time.sleep(1)
                print("-"*80)
                break
            else:
                print(f'{ip} is still reloading. Please wait...')
                time.sleep(delay)
```

14 J. Append the following script at the end of task H script. When the final application runs successfully, the statements in the print functions will be printed on the user screen, including the time taken for the whole IOS upgrade process. These are the last lines of code in the IOS upgrade application.

```
print("Completed new IOS verification.")
print("All tasks completed successfully!")

tt = time.mktime(time.localtime()) - t # Timer finish to measure script running time
print("Total time taken : {0} seconds".format(tt)) # Informational
```

15 Remember Lego blocks? Like with Lego bricks, we have converted small pieces of scripts and converted them into a large script. Now we have a working application written in Python. You will find the completed script on my GitHub download page for full reference.

URL: `https://github.com/pynetauto/apress_pynetauto`

Once you have completed building the Cisco IOS XE upgrade application, run it as shown here, and you should get a result similar to what's shown. Before running the completed application, ensure that the new IOS files uploaded in Chapter 18 on `csr1000v-1` and `csr1000v-2` have been deleted from the flash. If the file exists in the flash memory, the script will overwrite it anyway, but it is recommended that you delete the testing files from the router's flash for greater success with the IOS upgrade testing. We could also write some code to check whether the same IOS file exists and skip the IOS uploading process, but in a production network, you should only trust the files you have prepared and uploaded yourself. Hence, leave this script to overwrite any pre-existing files.

(*continued*)

#	Task
	K. Now, let's run the final script. Remember, after the IOS uploads to the flash, you will be prompted to select Yes or No to reload the router. Select y for yes.

```
pynetauto@ubuntu20s1:~/my tools/ios_upgrade_tool$ python3 upgrade_crs1000v.py
Enter Network Admin ID : pynetauto
Enter Network Admin PWD : ********
Confirm Network Admin PWD : ********
Is the secret same as the password? (y/n) : y # Type in 'y' for same secret password
--------------------------------------------------------------------------------
192.168.183.111
PING 192.168.183.111 (192.168.183.111) 56(84) bytes of data.
64 bytes from 192.168.183.111: icmp_seq=2 ttl=255 time=1.57 ms
64 bytes from 192.168.183.111: icmp_seq=3 ttl=255 time=1.61 ms
64 bytes from 192.168.183.111: icmp_seq=4 ttl=255 time=1.62 ms

--- 192.168.183.111 ping statistics ---
4 packets transmitted, 3 received, 25% packet loss, time 3019ms
rtt min/avg/max/mdev = 1.573/1.599/1.617/0.019 ms
192.168.183.111 22 open
--------------------------------------------------------------------------------
192.168.183.222
PING 192.168.183.222 (192.168.183.222) 56(84) bytes of data.
64 bytes from 192.168.183.222: icmp_seq=1 ttl=255 time=1.44 ms
64 bytes from 192.168.183.222: icmp_seq=2 ttl=255 time=1.61 ms
64 bytes from 192.168.183.222: icmp_seq=3 ttl=255 time=1.58 ms
64 bytes from 192.168.183.222: icmp_seq=4 ttl=255 time=1.56 ms

--- 192.168.183.222 ping statistics ---
4 packets transmitted, 4 received, 0% packet loss, time 3006ms
rtt min/avg/max/mdev = 1.438/1.545/1.607/0.064 ms
192.168.183.222 22 open
--------------------------------------------------------------------------------
192.168.183.111 csr1000v-1 RT cisco_xe
77878ae6db8e34de90e2e3e83741bf39
77878ae6db8e34de90e2e3e83741bf39436.57 MB
MD5 values matched!
--------------------------------------------------------------------------------
192.168.183.222 csr1000v-2 RT cisco_xe
77878ae6db8e34de90e2e3e83741bf39
77878ae6db8e34de90e2e3e83741bf39
436.57 MB
MD5 values matched!
--------------------------------------------------------------------------------
192.168.183.111 Free flash size :  6623.248384 MB
--------------------------------------------------------------------------------
192.168.183.111 has enough space for a new IOS.
--------------------------------------------------------------------------------
192.168.183.222 Free flash size :  6623.55968 MB
--------------------------------------------------------------------------------
192.168.183.222 has enough space for a new IOS.
```

#	Task

```
--------------------------------------------------------------------------------
192.168.183.111 original config backup completed.
--------------------------------------------------------------------------------
192.168.183.222 original config backup completed.
--------------------------------------------------------------------------------
********************************************************************************
192.168.183.111 beginning IOS XE upgrade.
pynetauto has level 15 privilege - OK
check_aaa_authentication - OK
check_aaa_authorization - OK
New IOS uploading in progress! Please wait...
........................................................................
........................................................................
.......................
[omitted for brevity]
..................................................................................
..................................................................................
..................Done!
Verified (bootflash:csr1000v-universalk9.16.09.06.SPA.bin) =
77878ae6db8e34de90e2e3e83741bf39
MD5 values MATCH! Continue
MD5 of new IOS on Server :  77878ae6db8e34de90e2e3e83741bf39
MD5 of new IOS on flash  :  77878ae6db8e34de90e2e3e83741bf39
--------------------------------------------------------------------------------
!!!!!!!!!!!!!!!!!!!!!!!!!!!!!!!!!!!!!!!!!!!!!!!!!!!!!!!!!!!!!!!!!!!!!!!!!!!!!!!!
Note: Devices will be reloaded one at a time.
Do you want to reload 192.168.183.111 now? (y/n)? y # Type in 'y' to reload
csr1000v-1
Reloading devices
configure terminal
Enter configuration commands, one per line.  End with CNTL/Z.
csr1000v-1(config)#no boot system
csr1000v-1(config)#boot system flash:/csr1000v-universalk9.16.09.06.SPA.bin
csr1000v-1(config)#do write memory
Building configuration...
[OK]
csr1000v-1(config)#end
csr1000v-1#
Found csr1000v-universalk9.16.09.06.SPA.bin in show boot
--------------------------------------------------------------------------------
192.168.183.111 [Pre-reload] Capture configuration
* [Pre-reload] Capturing 'show version'
* [Pre-reload] Capturing 'show running-config'
* [Pre-reload] Capturing 'show ip interface brief'
* [Pre-reload] Capturing 'show ip route'
--------------------------------------------------------------------------------
```

(*continued*)

#	Task

```
192.168.183.111 is now reloading.
***Device is now reloading. This may take 2-5 minutes.
--------------------------------------------------------------------------------
192.168.183.111 is still reloading. Please wait...
192.168.183.111 is still reloading. Please wait...
192.168.183.111 is still reloading. Please wait...
192.168.183.111 is still reloading. Please wait...
192.168.183.111 is still reloading. Please wait...
192.168.183.111 is still reloading. Please wait...
192.168.183.111 is still reloading. Please wait...
192.168.183.111 is still reloading. Please wait...
192.168.183.111 is still reloading. Please wait...
192.168.183.111 is still reloading. Please wait...
192.168.183.111 is back online.
192.168.183.111's reload time : 0 seconds
Logging back into 192.168.183.111 to perform post-reload tasks.
Please wait...
192.168.183.111
*** 192.168.183.111 is back online.
--------------------------------------------------------------------------------
192.168.183.111 [Post-reload] Capture configuration
* [Post-reload] Capturing 'show version'
! 192.168.183.111's ['System image file is "bootflash:/csr1000v-universalk9.16.09.06.
SPA.bin"'].
* [Post-reload] Capturing 'show running-config'
* [Post-reload] Capturing 'show ip interface brief'
* [Post-reload] Capturing 'show ip route'
--------------------------------------------------------------------------------
--------------------------------------------------------------------------------
********************************************************************************
********************************************************************************
192.168.183.222 beginning IOS XE upgrade.
pynetauto has level 15 privilege - OK
check_aaa_authentication - OK
check_aaa_authorization - OK
New IOS uploading in progress! Please wait...
................................................................................
[omitted for brevity]
............................................................................Done!
Verified (bootflash:csr1000v-universalk9.16.09.06.SPA.bin) =
77878ae6db8e34de90e2e3e83741bf39
MD5 values MATCH! Continue
MD5 of new IOS on Server :  77878ae6db8e34de90e2e3e83741bf39
MD5 of new IOS on flash  :  77878ae6db8e34de90e2e3e83741bf39
--------------------------------------------------------------------------------
!!!!!!!!!!!!!!!!!!!!!!!!!!!!!!!!!!!!!!!!!!!!!!!!!!!!!!!!!!!!!!!!!!!!!!!!!!!!!!!!
Note: Devices will be reloaded one at a time.
Do you want to reload 192.168.183.222 now? (y/n)? y # Type in 'y' to reload csr1000v-2
Reloading devices
```

#	Task

```
configure terminal
Enter configuration commands, one per line.  End with CNTL/Z.
csr1000v-2(config)#no boot system
csr1000v-2(config)#boot system flash:/csr1000v-universalk9.16.09.06.SPA.bin
csr1000v-2(config)#do write memory
Building configuration...
[OK]
csr1000v-2(config)#end
csr1000v-2#
Found csr1000v-universalk9.16.09.06.SPA.bin in show boot
--------------------------------------------------------------------------------
192.168.183.222 [Pre-reload] Capture configuration
* [Pre-reload] Capturing 'show version'
* [Pre-reload] Capturing 'show running-config'
* [Pre-reload] Capturing 'show ip interface brief'
* [Pre-reload] Capturing 'show ip route'
--------------------------------------------------------------------------------
192.168.183.222 is now reloading.
***Device is now reloading. This may take 2-5 minutes.
--------------------------------------------------------------------------------
192.168.183.222 is still reloading. Please wait...
192.168.183.222 is still reloading. Please wait...
192.168.183.222 is still reloading. Please wait...
192.168.183.222 is still reloading. Please wait...
192.168.183.222 is still reloading. Please wait...
192.168.183.222 is still reloading. Please wait...
192.168.183.222 is still reloading. Please wait...
192.168.183.222 is still reloading. Please wait...
192.168.183.222 is still reloading. Please wait...
192.168.183.222 is still reloading. Please wait...
192.168.183.222 is back online.
192.168.183.222's reload time : 0 seconds
Logging back into 192.168.183.222 to perform post-reload tasks.
Please wait...
192.168.183.222
*** 192.168.183.222 is back online.
--------------------------------------------------------------------------------
192.168.183.222 [Post-reload] Capture configuration
* [Post-reload] Capturing 'show version'
! 192.168.183.222's ['System image file is "bootflash:/csr1000v-universalk9.16.09.06.
SPA.bin"'].
* [Post-reload] Capturing 'show running-config'
* [Post-reload] Capturing 'show ip interface brief'
* [Post-reload] Capturing 'show ip route'
--------------------------------------------------------------------------------
--------------------------------------------------------------------------------
********************************************************************************
Completed new IOS verification.
All tasks completed successfully!
Total time taken : 976.0 seconds # = 16.27 minutes in total
```

After the IOS XE upgrades complete successfully on both `csr1000v-1` and `csr1000v-2`, you will find all files under `/home/pynetauto/my_tools/` directory (see Figure 19-1). Copy and open the files to check the success of your IOS upgrade. You have now upgraded two IOS-XE routers using a handwritten Python network automation code. I hope you have enjoyed this experience.

To watch a demo video of the Cisco IOS-XE upgrade, visit `https://www.youtube.com/watch?v=tnNEeXAGdoM`.

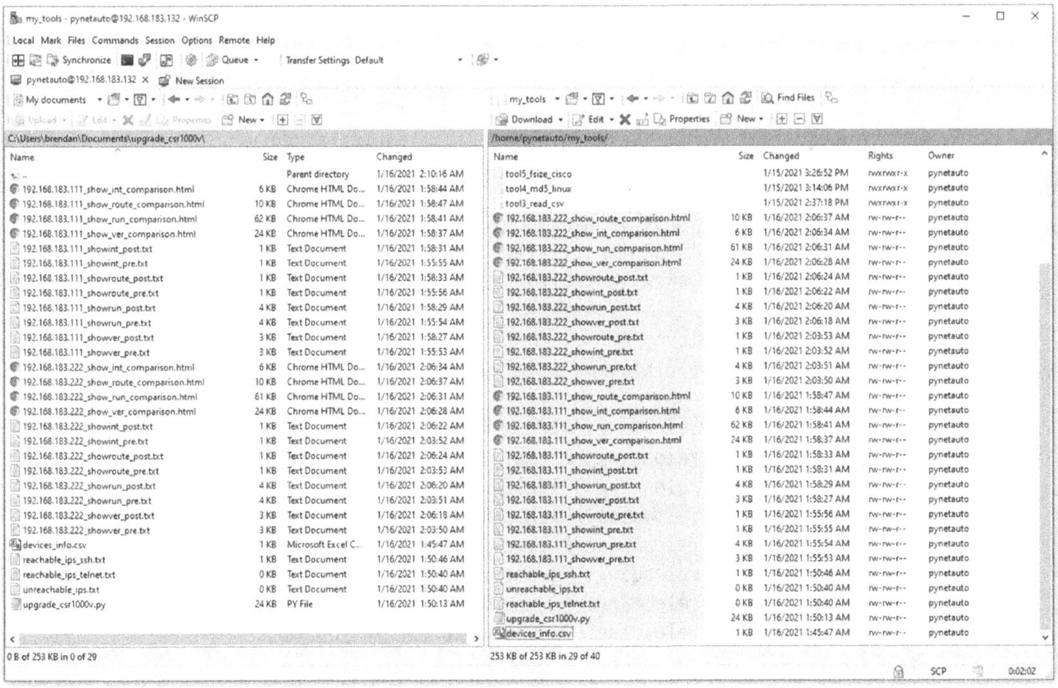

***Figure 19-1.** WinSCP, copying files to validate successful Cisco router IOS-XE upgrades*

Summary

In a real production environment, the scripts are separated into various functioning scripts, called *modules*. Another way to keep the main script lightweight is to save each application as a different module in another file. I have chosen to create this whole application in a single Python script to help you understand how it works, but you probably have already noticed how inefficient it is to work with a lengthy scripted code. Although I can continue writing this code in several separate modules or files and re-import the functions as a module into the main script, I will leave this challenge for you.

I hope your first Python network automation journey was a pleasant surprise and that you are looking forward to the next part of your journey. Together, we have covered a lot of ground in this book, but possibly we have also left many holes open for improvement. You cannot become good at something overnight; writing Python code is not like winning the lottery or becoming an overnight YouTube sensation. It will take many months and years to reach a certain level of confidence in Python programming. Remember Joseph M. Marshall's quote, "Life is a circle. The end of a journey means the start of another one."

Final Words

Taking on a new programming language to take one's career to the next level may feel like a daunting task for many of us. It is like embarking on a new journey into the unknown. Many Technology evangelists encourage people to learn a programming language and start writing code today. Some evangelists preach that Python is for everyone. Here, I disagree politely. Programming or writing code is not for everyone. However, if you spend hours working in front of a computer, learning a high-level programming language like Python can do many wonders at work. If your job involves supporting IT services or infrastructure, I cannot find a single excuse not to learn Python coding. Although Python is one of the easiest programming languages to learn, not many people talk about what happens after reaching a certain level. Python is the same as all other programming languages, and Python or another programming language is only as bright as the person writing the code. Learning a programming language cannot be a means to an end. Instead, it is another beginning or a new journey with no finish line. So, you always have to keep at school and seek opportunities to apply the concepts and skills you have learned along the journey.

In this book, I tried to write a hands-on Python network automation book for new and existing network engineers, covering various essential IT administration skills required to build an infrastructure from the ground up and write a working application that can help them better manage their network infrastructure. I hope you have enjoyed a broad exposure to various technologies, and you have built a strong foundation towards better enterprise network administration. Lastly, thank you for purchasing my book to start your Python network automation journey. I want to congratulate everyone who has reached this page after running the final lab successfully. Even if you are still working toward completing the final lab, you still have plenty of time to go over the contents of this book as you now own it.

Index

A

B

C

B. Choi, *Introduction to Python Network Automation*, https://doi.org/10.1007/978-1-4842-6806-3

D

E

F

G

H

M

N

O

P, Q

R

S

T

U

V

W, X, Y, Z

'nited States
Publisher Services